Nelson MindTap + **You** = Learning amplified

"*I love that everything is interconnected, relevant and that there is a clear learning sequence. I have the tools to create a learning experience that meets the needs of all my students and can easily see how they're progressing.*"

— **Sarah,** Secondary School Teacher

nelson maths.

10

Advanced

Rachel Theunissen
Rashmi Bhagwati
Klaas Bootsma
David Badger
Sarah Hamper
Series editor
Robert Yen

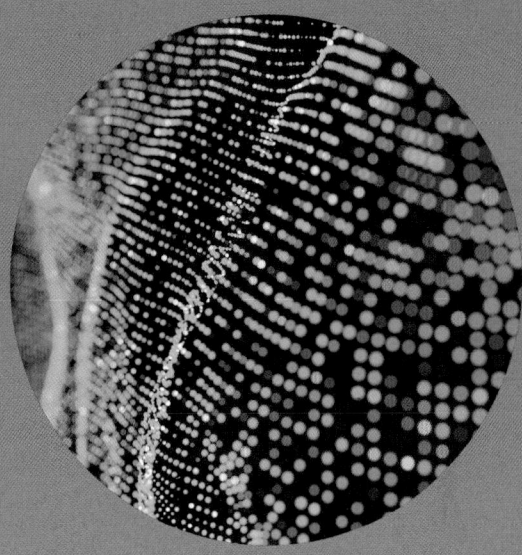

Mathematics is key to creating accurate terrain or topographical (3D) maps, like the one you see on this cover and on Google Earth. Surveyors measure the land's topography and use mathematical models to make precise representations. But since they can't measure every single point, they use maths to interpolate the missing spaces and fill in gaps.

Interpolation uses functions to estimate missing elevations based on nearby data points. Terrain maps are used in everything from urban planning to creating recreational hiking trails.

WA
Australian Curriculum

Nelson Maths 10 Advanced for the Australian Curriculum WA
1st Edition
Rachel Theunissen
Rashmi Bhagwati
Klaas Bootsma
David Badger
Sarah Hamper
ISBN 9780170465595

Publisher: Robert Yen
Project editor: Alan Stewart
Series cover design: Leigh Ashforth (Watershed Art & Design) and Cengage
    Creative Studio
Cover image: iStock.com/piranka
Series text design: Leigh Ashforth (Watershed Art & Design)
Series designer: Danielle Maccarone
Permissions researcher: Catherine Kerstjens
Production controller: Karen Young
Typeset by: KGL

Any URLs contained in this publication were checked for currency during the
production process. Note, however, that the publisher cannot vouch for the
ongoing currency of URLs.

For product information and technology assistance,
        in Australia call **1300 790 853**;
        in New Zealand call **0800 449 725**

For permission to use material from this text or product, please email
aust.permissions@cengage.com

National Library of Australia Cataloguing-in-Publication Data
A catalogue record for this book is available from the National Library of
Australia.

Cengage Learning Australia
Level 5, 80 Dorcas Street
Southbank VIC 3006 Australia

For learning solutions, visit **cengage.com.au**

Printed in China by 1010 Printing International Limited.
1 2 3 4 5 6 7 27 26 25 24 23

Table of contents

Preface   xi
About the authors   xi
Curriculum grids   xii
About this book   xv
Mathematical verbs   xix
Symbols and abbreviations   xxi

* = EXTENSION

1 GRAPHING LINES   2

SkillCheck   5
9A03   1.01 Length, midpoint and
        gradient of an interval   5
        Investigation: Parallel and
        perpendicular lines   13
10A05   1.02 Parallel and
        perpendicular lines   13
        Technology: Parallel and
        perpendicular lines   17
9A03   1.03 Graphing linear functions   18
9A03   1.04 The gradient-intercept
        equation $y = mx + c$ 22
        Mental skills 1: Percentage
        of a quantity   26
        1.05 Extension: The general
        equation $ax + by + c = 0$*   27
        Investigation: A line, its
        gradient and a point   29
        1.06 Extension: The
        point-gradient equation
        $y - y_1 = m(x - x_1)$*   30
9A03   1.07 Finding the equation
        of a line   32
        Investigation: Sausage sizzle   34
10A05   1.08 Equations of parallel
        and perpendicular lines   35
        Investigation: Regions on the
        number plane   38
10A02, 5 1.09 Graphing linear
        inequalities   39
        Power plus   44
        Chapter 1 review   45

2 SURFACE AREA AND VOLUME   48

SkillCheck   51
9M04   2.01 Absolute error and
        percentage error   51
10N01, 2.02 Rounding error   56
10M04
8M01   2.03 Areas of composite
        shapes   61
9M01   2.04 Surface area of a prism   66
        Investigation: A surface
        area shortcut   70
9M01   2.05 Surface area of a
        cylinder   71
        2.06 Extension: Surface
        area of a pyramid*   74
        Investigation: The surface
        area of a cone   78
        2.07 Extension: Surface
        areas of cones and
        spheres*   79
10M01   2.08 Surface areas of
        composite solids   83
        Mental skills 2: Time
        differences   89
9M01, 10M01 2.09 Volumes of prisms
        and cylinders   90
        Investigation: How many
        pyramids are needed to
        fill the prism?   94
        Technology: Approximating
        the volume of a pyramid   95
        2.10 Extension: Volumes of
        pyramids, cones and spheres*   96
        2.11 Extension: Volumes of
        composite solids*   103
        Power plus   106
        Chapter 2 review   107

3 INTEREST AND DEPRECIATION   112

SkillCheck   114
        3.01 Earning an income   115
        Investigation: Workers'
        entitlements   120
        3.02 Income tax   121
        Technology: Online
        income tax calculators   124
8N05   3.03 Simple interest   125
10A04   3.04 Compound interest   129
        Mental skills 3: Finding
        15%, $2\frac{1}{2}$%, 25% and $12\frac{1}{2}$%   131
10A04   3.05 The compound
        interest formula   133

	Technology: Comparing simple interest with compound interest	137
10A04	**3.06** Depreciation	138
	Power plus	142
	Chapter 3 review	143
Practice set 1		**146**

4 PRODUCTS, FACTORS AND SURDS 150

	SkillCheck	153
10A01	**4.01** The index laws	154
	4.02 Extension: Fractional indices*	156
10A01	**4.03** Expanding and factorising expressions	160
10A01	**4.04** Expanding binomial products	162
	Investigation: Squaring a number ending in 5	166
	4.05 Extension: Factorising special binomial products*	166
10A01	**4.06** Factorising quadratic expressions $x^2 + bx + c$	168
	Mental skills 4: Estimating answers	171
	4.07 Extension: Factorising quadratic expressions of the form $ax^2 + bx + c$*	172
	4.08 Extension: Mixed factorisations*	175
	4.09 Extension: Surds and irrational numbers*	177
	Investigation: Proof that $\sqrt{2}$ is irrational	181
	4.10 Extension: Simplifying surds*	182
	4.11 Extension: Adding and subtracting surds*	185
	4.12 Extension: Multiplying and dividing surds*	186
	4.13 Extension: Binomial products involving surds*	189
	Investigation: Making the denominator rational	192
	4.14 Extension: Rationalising the denominator*	192
	Power plus	194
	Chapter 4 review	195

5 COMPARING DATA 198

	SkillCheck	201
10ST02	**5.01** Quartiles and interquartile range	202
10ST02	**5.02** Boxplots	206
	Technology: Boxplots	211
10ST02	**5.03** Parallel boxplots	211
10ST02	**5.04** Cumulative frequency and quartiles	216
10ST02	**5.05** Cumulative frequency histograms and polygons	221
	5.06 Extension: Deciles and percentiles*	226
	5.07 Extension: Standard deviation*	232
	5.08 Extension: Comparing means and standard deviations*	236
10ST02	**5.09** Comparing data sets	239
	Mental skills 5: Multiplying hy 9, 11, 99 and 101	246
10ST01	**5.10** Statistics in the media	247
	Investigation: Australian Bureau of Statistics	250
10ST01	**5.11** Statistical investigations	251
10ST03, 5	**5.12** Scatterplots	254
	Technology: Scatterplot patterns	258
10ST03, 5	**5.13** Line of best fit	258
	Technology: Lines of best fit	263
10ST04, 5	**5.14** Association and two-way tables	264
	Investigation: What is the association?	267
	Power plus	267
	Chapter 5 review	268

6 EQUATIONS AND LOGARITHMS 272

	SkillCheck	274
10A01	**6.01** Linear equations	275
	6.02 Extension: Algebraic fractions*	277
	6.03 Extension: Equations with algebraic fractions*	279
10A01	**6.04** Quadratic equations $x^2 + bx + c = 0$	281

6.05 Extension: Simple cubic equations $ax^3 = c$*   285

10A01 **6.06** Equation problems   287

Mental skills 6: Multiplying and dividing by 5, 15, 25 and 50   289

10A01 **6.07** Equations and formulas   290

6.08 Extension: Changing the subject of a formula*   293

10A02 **6.09** Graphing inequalities on a number line   294

10A02 **6.10** Solving inequalities   296

Investigation: Power tables   298

6.11 Extension: Logarithms*   298

6.12 Extension: Logarithm laws*   301

6.13 Extension: Exponential and logarithmic equations*   304

Power plus   307

Chapter 6 review   308

Practice set 2   311

7

GRAPHING CURVES   **314**

SkillCheck   317

9A04, 6 **7.01** Graphing quadratic functions $y = ax^2 + bx + c$ 317

10A04 **7.02** Applying quadratic functions   323

9M05 **7.03** Direct proportion   327

7.04 Extension: Inverse proportion*   330

Investigation: Graphing $y = \dfrac{1}{x}$ 335

Technology: Graphing $y = \dfrac{k}{x}$ 336

7.05 Extension: Graphing hyperbolas $y = \dfrac{k}{x}$*   336

Mental skills 7: Multiplying decimals   340

Investigation: Graphing $y = 2^x$ 341

Technology: Exponential curves   342

10A03, 4 **7.06** Graphing exponential functions $y = a^x$ 342

10A03, 4 **7.07** Exponential equations   345

10A03, 4 **7.08** Exponential growth and decay   348

10M02 **7.09** Logarithmic scales   351

10A02 **7.10** Solving equations graphically   358

10A05 **7.11** Graphing circles $x^2 + y^2 = r^2$ 360

10A03, 5 **7.12** Identifying graphs   362

Technology: Identifying graphs   366

Power plus   366

Chapter 7 review   367

8

TRIGONOMETRY   **370**

SkillCheck   373

9M03, 10M03 **8.01** Right-angled trigonometry   373

10M03 **8.02** Bearings   378

Mental skills 8: Divisibility tests   383

10M03 **8.03** Pythagoras' theorem and trigonometry in 3D   384

8.04 Extension: Complementary relations and exact ratios*   388

8.05 Extension: The trigonometric functions*   391

8.06 Extension: Trigonometric equations*   398

Investigation: Sides and opposite angles   400

8.07 Extension: The sine rule*   400

8.08 Extension: The sine rule for angles*   403

8.09 Extension: The cosine rule*   406

8.10 Extension: The cosine rule for angles*   408

8.11 Extension: The area of a triangle*   410

8.12 Extension: Problems involving the sine and cosine rules*   413

Power plus   415

Chapter 8 review   416

9	**NETWORKS**	**420**
SkillCheck	422
10SP02	**9.01** Networks	423
10SP02	**9.02** Polyhedra	426
Investigation: Tracing over a network	431
10SP02, 3	**9.03** Traversable networks	432
Mental skills 9: The unitary method with percentages	436
10SP02, 3	**9.04** Spanning trees	437
10SP02, 3	**9.05** Shortest paths	443
Power plus	448
Chapter 9 review	449
Practice set 3	**452**

10	**SIMULTANEOUS EQUATIONS**	**458**
SkillCheck	460
Investigation: When 2 lines meet	461
10A02	**10.01** Solving simultaneous equations graphically	462
Technology: Solving simultaneous equations graphically	464
10A02	**10.02** The elimination method	464
10A02	**10.03** The substitution method	467
Investigation: Elimination or substitution method?	469
10A02	**10.04** Problems involving simultaneous equations	471
Mental skills 10: Simplifying fractions and ratios	474
Power plus	476
Chapter 10 review	477

11	**PROBABILITY**	**480**
SkillCheck	483
9P02, 3	**11.01** Relative frequency	483
9P02	**11.02** Venn diagrams	488
9P02	**11.03** Two-way tables	493
9P01, 3	**11.04** Tree diagrams	497
Mental skills 11: Percentage increase and decrease	501
Investigation: The birth month paradox	502

9P01, 3	**11.05** Selecting with and without replacement	503
10P01	**11.06** Conditional probability	508
Investigation: Dependent or independent?	512
10P02	**11.07** Dependent and independent events	513
10P02	**11.08** Probability simulations	517
11.09 Extension: The multiplication principle of counting*	518
Investigation: Subsets of a set	523
11.10 Extension: Permutations*	523
11.11 Extension: Combinations*	526
Power plus	530
Chapter 11 review	531

12	**CONGRUENT AND SIMILAR FIGURES**	**536**
SkillCheck	539
10SP01	**12.01** Congruent triangle proofs	540
10SP01	**12.02** Tests for quadrilaterals	544
Investigation: Is a square a rhombus?	549
10SP01	**12.03** Proving properties of triangles and quadrilaterals	550
Mental skills 12: Dividing a quantity in a given ratio	553
10SP01	**12.04** Extension: Formal geometrical proofs*	554
Technology: Properties of similar figures	557
9SP02	**12.05** Similar figures	558
10M05	**12.06** Scale diagrams, maps and plans	562
10M05	**12.07** Finding sides in similar figures	567
10SP01	**12.08** Similar triangle proofs	570
10M05	**12.09** Areas of similar figures	576

	Investigation: Surface areas and volumes of similar solids	578
10M05	**12.10** Surface areas and volumes of similar solids	579
	Power plus	581
	Chapter 12 review	582
Practice set 4		**586**
General practice		**592**
Answers		**598**
Glossary and index		**666**

OPTIONAL EXTENSION CHAPTERS (online)

13 **QUADRATIC EQUATIONS AND THE PARABOLA** **Q2**

13.01 Quadratic equations $ax^2 + bx + c = 0$		Q4
13.02 Completing the square		Q7
13.03 The quadratic formula		Q10
13.04 Which method is best?		Q12
13.05 Applying quadratic equations		Q13
13.06 Graphing quadratic functions $y = ax^2 + bx + c$		Q15
13.07 The axis of symmetry and vertex		Q19
13.08 Graphing quadratic functions $y = a(x - b)^2 + c$		Q21
13.09 Non-linear simultaneous equations		Q24

14 **POLYNOMIALS** **P2**

14.01 Polynomials	P4
14.02 Adding and subtracting polynomials	P7
14.03 Multiplying polynomials	P8
14.04 Dividing polynomials	P8

14.05 The remainder theorem	P10
14.06 The factor theorem	P11
14.07 Graphing cubic functions $y = ax^3 + c$	P14
14.08 Graphing cubic functions $y = a(x - b)(x - c)(x - d)$	P17
14.09 Graphing polynomials	P20
14.10 Transforming graphs of polynomials	P22

15 **FUNCTIONS** **F2**

15.01 Functions	F4
15.02 Function notation	F7
15.03 Inverse functions	F11
15.04 Graphing logarithmic functions $y = \log_a x$	F14
15.05 Graphing translations of functions	F16
15.06 Average rate of change on a graph	F18

16 **CIRCLE GEOMETRY** **C2**

16.01 Parts of a circle	C4
16.02 Chord properties of circles	C6
16.03 Angle properties of circles	C12
16.04 Tangent and secant properties of circles	C19
16.05 Proofs using circle theorems	C24
Answers to Chapters 13–16	**A2**

Preface

Nelson Maths 7–10 has been designed for the 2020s classroom, focusing on core skills with explicit grading of exercise questions, 'flipped classroom' video tutorials, online interactivity, more applications and problem-solving questions, and worked solutions to every question.

This new series is carefully mapped to the Australian Curriculum and built on solid pedagogical foundations that integrate into every chapter practical classroom activities, engaging investigations, problem solving, reasoning, communicating, reflecting, summarising, extension, revision, mental calculation, technology, numeracy and literacy.

This book, *Nelson Maths 10 Advanced*, has been designed for Year 10 students, but covers the course at a faster pace, with less revision and more content suitable for students who will be studying Mathematical Methods and Specialist Mathematics in Years 11 and 12.

The *Nelson MindTap* online learning platform contains print and multimedia content: worksheets, videos, quizzes, interactives, topic tests, worked solutions and much more. We have provided an abundance of resources for teachers to plan and teach for a variety of pathways. *Nelson Maths* is clear, concise, fresh and smart. We have designed this series to be user-friendly and uncomplicated so that teachers and students everywhere can pick it up and use it straight away. So, let's get started.

About the authors

Rashmi Bhagwati teaches at a high school in southeast Brisbane and has been a mathematics educator for over 20 years. She has been involved in external exam marking and was a QCAA Panellist for Mathematics A (senior General Mathematics). Rashmi wrote topic tests for the *Nelson Senior Maths Essential Mathematics* series for Queensland and WA.

Rachel Theunissen is the Head of Mathematics at Lesmurdie Senior High School in Perth, where she also leads the Literacy and Numeracy team. She is a Curriculum Support Teacher with the Department of Education and a volunteer of MAWA and the Australian Mathematics Trust (AMT). Rachel has been teaching for over 25 years and presents regularly at conferences on mathematics and problem solving.

Klaas Bootsma was the Head of Mathematics at Ambarvale High School in Sydney and has been a mathematics author for over 25 years.

David Badger was principal of Toongabbie Christian School in Sydney and currently teaches at Wollondilly Anglican College.

Sarah Hamper is the Head of Mathematics at Cheltenham Girls High School in Sydney. She has an interest in gifted and talented students, technology and girls' education.

Series editor **Robert Yen** taught at Hurlstone Agricultural High School in Sydney and works for Cengage as a mathematics publisher.

Contributing authors

Kahlia Dreyer, Lachlan Grierson, Brook Johns, Teresa Grimm, Megan Boltze, Robert Yen and **Deborah Smith** wrote many of the worksheets and topic tests.

Rashmi Bhagwati, Jade Lori, Deborah Da Cruz, Monique Ellement, John Drake, Katie Jackson, Joanne Magner, Scott Smith and **Robert Yen** created the video tutorials.

Curriculum grids

Australian Curriculum

Strand		Nelson Maths 9 Advanced chapter		Nelson Maths 10 Advanced chapter
NUMBER AND ALGEBRA				
NUMBER	2	Surds and Pythagoras' theorem	3	Interest and depreciation
	3	Numeracy and calculation	4	Products, factors and surds
	7	Equations and inequalities		
	8	Earning money		
ALGEBRA	1	Products and factors	1	Graphing lines
	5	Indices	3	Interest and depreciation
	7	Equations and inequalities	4	Products, factors and surds
	11	Coordinate geometry and graphs	6	Equations and logarithms
			7	Graphing curves
			10	Simultaneous equations
			13	Quadratic equations and the parabola
			14	Polynomials
			15	Functions
MEASUREMENT	2	Surds and Pythagoras' theorem	2	Surface area and volume
	3	Numeracy and calculation	8	Further trigonometry
	4	Trigonometry	12	Congruent and similar figures
	5	Indices		
	10	Surface area and volume		
	13	Congruent and similar figures		
SPACE	2	Surds and Pythagoras' theorem	9	Networks
	4	Trigonometry	12	Congruent and similar figures
	6	Geometry	16	Circle geometry
	13	Congruent and similar figures		
STATISTICS	9	Analysing data	5	Comparing data
PROBABILITY	12	Probability	11	Probability

Year 10 content descriptions

Australian Curriculum descriptions (© ACARA 2022)

Content description		*Nelson Maths 10* **Advanced** chapter
NUMBER (N)		
AC9M10N01: recognise the effect of using approximations of real numbers in repeated calculations and compare the results when using exact representations	2	Surface area and volume
	5	Comparing data
OPTIONAL CONTENT: operations on numbers involving fractional exponents and surds	4	Products, factors and surds
ALGEBRA (A)		
AC9M10A01: expand, factorise and simplify expressions and solve equations algebraically, applying exponent laws involving products, quotients and powers of variables, and the distributive property	4	Products, factors and surds
	6	Equations and logarithms
	7	Graphing curves
AC9M10A02: solve linear inequalities and simultaneous linear equations in 2 variables; interpret solutions graphically and communicate solutions in terms of the situation	6	Equations and logarithms
	10	Simultaneous equations
AC9M10A03: recognise the connection between algebraic and graphical representations of exponential relations and solve related exponential equations, using digital tools where appropriate	7	Graphing curves
AC9M10A04: use mathematical modelling to solve applied problems involving growth and decay, including financial contexts; formulate problems, choosing to apply linear, quadratic or exponential models; interpret solutions in terms of the situation; evaluate and modify models as necessary and report assumptions, methods and findings	7	Graphing curves
	11	Probability
AC9M10A05: experiment with functions and relations using digital tools, making and testing conjectures and generalising emerging patterns	7	Graphing curves
	11	Probability
OPTIONAL CONTENT: algebraic representations of quadratic functions of the form $f(x) = ax^2 + bx + c$ where a, b and c are non-zero integers, and their transformation to the form $f(x) = a(x + h)^2 + k$ where h and k are non-zero rational-numbers, and the solution of related questions	7	Graphing curves
	13	Quadratic equations and the parabola
OPTIONAL CONTENT: the graphs of $y = \sin(x)$ and $y = \cos(x)$ as functions of a real variable and the solution of related equations	8	Further trigonometry
OPTIONAL CONTENT: the inverse relationship between exponential and logarithmic functions and the solution of related equations	15	Functions
MEASUREMENT (M)		
AC9M10M01: solve problems involving the surface area and volume of composite objects using appropriate units	2	Surface area and volume
AC9M10M02: interpret and use logarithmic scales in applied contexts involving small and large quantities and change	7	Graphing curves
AC9M10M03: solve practical problems applying Pythagoras' theorem and trigonometry of right-angled triangles, including problems involving direction and angles of elevation and depression	8	Trigonometry

Content description		*Nelson Maths 10* Advanced chapter
AC9M10M04: identify the impact of measurement errors on the accuracy of results in practical contexts	2	Surface area and volume
AC9M10M05: use mathematical modelling to solve practical problems involving proportion and scaling of objects; formulate problems and interpret solutions in terms of the situation; evaluate and modify models as necessary, and report assumptions, methods and findings	12	Congruent and similar figures
OPTIONAL CONTENT: the effect of increasingly small changes in the values of variables on the average rate of change and in relation to limiting values	15	Functions

SPACE (SP)

AC9M10SP01: apply deductive reasoning to proofs involving shapes in the plane and use theorems to solve spatial problems	12	Congruent and similar figures
AC9M10SP02: interpret networks and network diagrams used to represent relationships in practical situations and describe connectedness	9	Networks
AC9M10SP03: design, test and refine solutions to spatial problems using algorithms and digital tools; communicate and justify solutions	12	Congruent and similar figures
OPTIONAL CONTENT: relationships between angles and various lines associated with circles (radii, diameters, chords, tangents)	16	Circle geometry

STATISTICS (ST)

AC9M10ST01: analyse claims, inferences and conclusions of statistical reports in the media, including ethical considerations and identification of potential sources of bias	5	Comparing data
AC9M10ST02: compare data distributions for continuous numerical variables using appropriate data displays including boxplots; discuss the shapes of these distributions in terms of centre, spread, shape and outliers in the context of the data	5	Comparing data
AC9M10ST03: construct scatterplots and comment on the association between the 2 numerical variables in terms of strength, direction and linearity	5	Comparing data
AC9M10ST04: construct two-way tables and discuss possible relationship between categorical variables	5	Comparing data
AC9M10ST05: plan and conduct statistical investigations of situations that involve bivariate data; evaluate and report findings with consideration of limitations of any inferences	5	Comparing data
OPTIONAL CONTENT: measures of spread, their interpretation and usefulness with respect to different data distributions	5	Comparing data

PROBABILITY (P)

AC9M10P01: use the language of "if .... then", "given", "of", "knowing that" to describe and interpret situations involving conditional probability	11	Probability
AC9M10P02: design and conduct repeated chance experiments and simulations using digital tools to model conditional probability and interpret results	11	Probability
OPTIONAL CONTENT: counting principles, and factorial notation as a representation that provides efficient counting in multiplicative contexts, including calculations of probabilities	11	Probability

9780170465595

About this book

Coverage of the Australian Curriculum

- *Nelson Maths 10 Advanced* covers the Australian Curriculum, as shown by the table of contents and curriculum grid on the previous pages.
- This book contains Year 10 content. It also contains revision of some Year 9 content, and some extension work marked in **red** and by *.
- Each chapter begins with a **chapter outline** that includes the curriculum proficiencies covered in each section.

U = UNDERSTANDING

Understanding is 'knowing and relating' maths. It is more than just learning facts. It's deep understanding, seeing how mathematical content is interconnected, knowing 'why' as well as 'how'.

F = FLUENCY

Fluency is 'applying' maths. It is being able to use mathematics competently and effectively. When you are fluent in a language, you have mastered it so that you can improvise and confidently use the correct word or phrase. Fluency in maths is choosing an appropriate skill, method or formula to use at the right place and time.

PS = PROBLEM SOLVING

Problem solving is 'modelling and investigating' with maths. It involves interpreting a rich, elaborate problem, selecting an appropriate strategy or model, solving the problem, then evaluating, communicating and justifying the solution.

R = REASONING

Reasoning is 'generalising and proving' with maths, using higher-order thinking to connect specific facts to general principles, using algebra, logic, proof and justification.

To these proficiencies, we have added **C = COMMUNICATING**

Communicating is 'describing and explaining' maths, representing mathematical theory and solutions in words, algebraic symbols, special notations, diagrams, graphs and tables.

Understanding and **Fluency** can be found in every exercise and activity, whereas **Problem solving**, **Reasoning** and **Communicating** are found in the **Investigations**, **Technology**, **Mental skills**, **Language of maths** and **Topic summary** activities, and explicitly labelled in every exercise (see below).

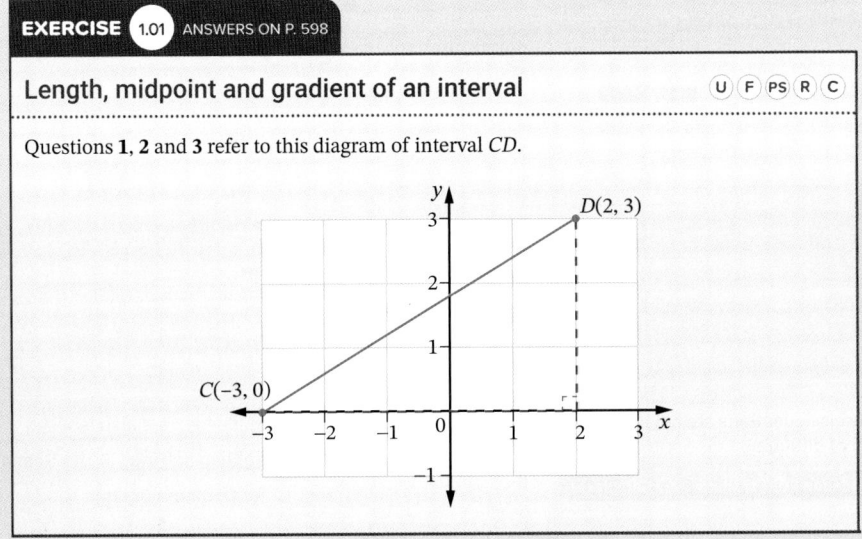

EXERCISE 1.01 ANSWERS ON P. 598

Length, midpoint and gradient of an interval U F PS R C

Questions **1**, **2** and **3** refer to this diagram of interval *CD*.

At the beginning of each chapter

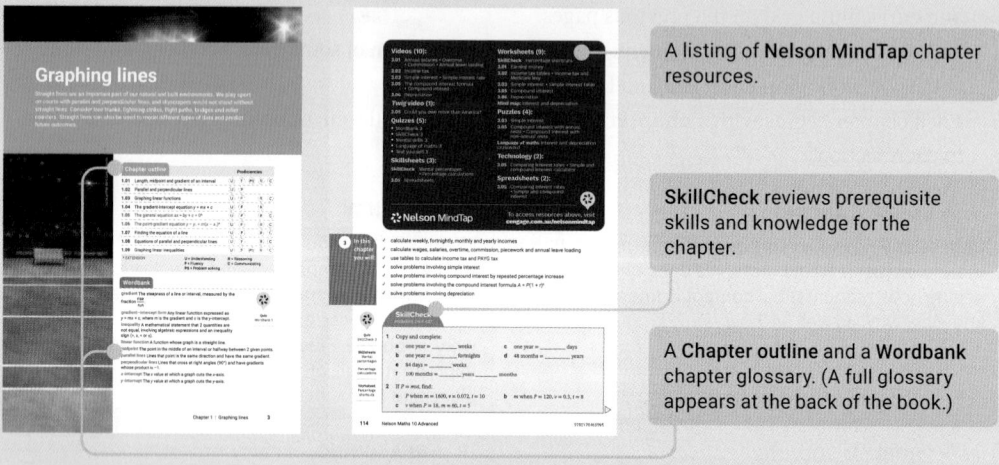

A listing of **Nelson MindTap** chapter resources.

SkillCheck reviews prerequisite skills and knowledge for the chapter.

A **Chapter outline** and a **Wordbank** chapter glossary. (A full glossary appears at the back of the book.)

In each chapter

Important facts and formulas are highlighted in a shaded box.

Glossary terms are printed in **blue.**

Graded exercises are linked to worked examples and include multiple-choice questions, exam-style problems and realistic applications.

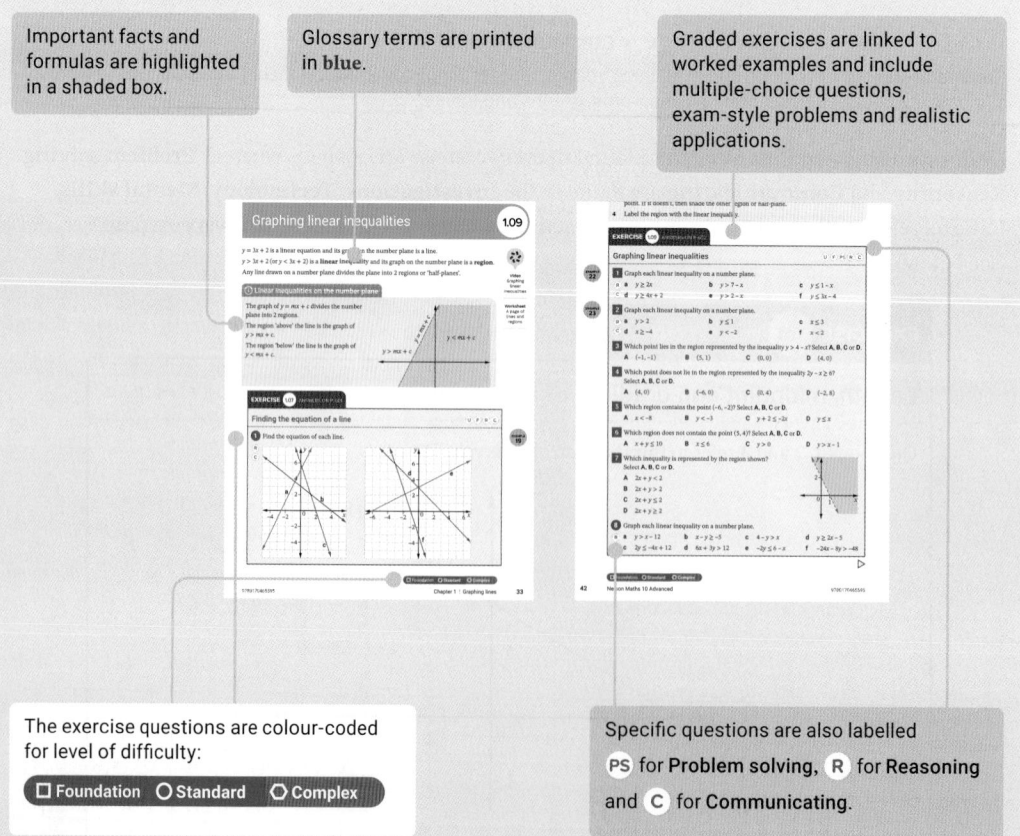

The exercise questions are colour-coded for level of difficulty:

□ Foundation ○ Standard ○ Complex

Specific questions are also labelled **PS** for **Problem solving, R** for **Reasoning** and **C** for **Communicating**.

TECHNOLOGY

INVESTIGATION

DID YOU KNOW?

☆ MENTAL SKILLS

Mental skills reinforce mental calculation strategies ('calculator-free maths').

Technology includes spreadsheets, dynamic geometry software and the internet.

Investigations explore the curriculum in more detail, through group work, discovery and modelling activities.

Did you know? contains interesting facts and applications of the mathematics learned in the chapter.

At the end of each chapter

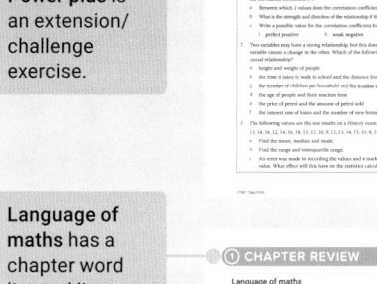

Power plus is an extension/ challenge exercise.

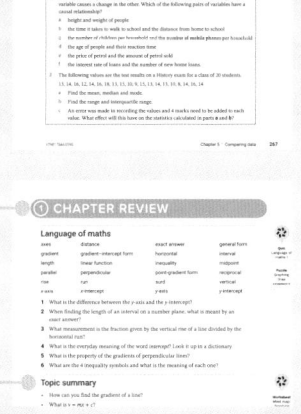

Language of maths has a chapter word list and literacy questions.

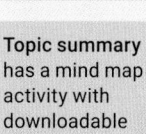

Topic summary has a mind map activity with downloadable solutions.

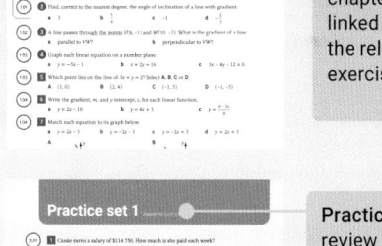

Test yourself contains chapter revision linked to the relevant exercise set.

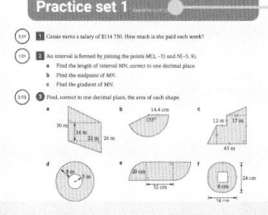

Practice sets review concepts after every 3 chapters.

At the end of the book

General practice exercise

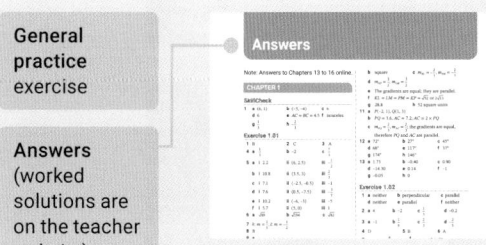

Answers (worked solutions are on the teacher website).

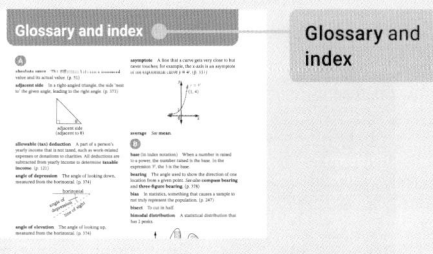

Glossary and index

✦ Nelson MindTap

An online learning space that provides students with tailored learning experiences.

- Access tools and content that make learning simpler yet smarter to help you achieve maths mastery.
- Includes an eText with integrated interactives and online assessment.
- Margin links in the student book signpost multimedia student resources found on *MindTap*.

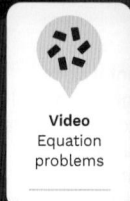

Video
Equation
problems

For students:

- **Watch** video tutorials featuring expert teacher advice to unpack new concepts and develop your understanding.
- **Revise** using quizzes, worksheets and skillsheets to practise your skills and build your confidence.
- **Navigate** your own path, accessing the content, analytics and support as you need it.
- *Twig* **mini-documentaries** showing the background or context of mathematics.
- *PhET* **interactives**: maths simulations.

For teachers*:

- Tailor content to different learning needs – assign directly to the student, or the whole class.
- Monitor progress using assessment tools like Gradebook and Reports.
- Integrate content and assessment directly within your school's LMS for ease of access.
- Access topic tests, teaching plans and worked solutions to each exercise set.

* Complimentary access to these resources is only available to teachers who use this book as part of a class set, book hire or booklist. Contact your Cengage Education Consultant for information about access and conditions.

Nelson Maths 7–10 series

Mathematical verbs

A glossary of 'doing words' commonly found in mathematics problems

analyse: study in detail the parts of a situation.

bisect: cut in half.

calculate: *see* **evaluate**.

classify, identify: state the type, category or feature of an item or situation.

comment: express an observation or opinion about a result.

compare: show how 2 or more things are similar or different.

complete: fill in detail to make a statement, diagram or table correct or finished.

construct: draw an accurate diagram.

convert: change from one form to another, for example, from a fraction to a decimal, or from kilograms to grams.

decrease: make smaller.

describe: state the features of a situation.

estimate: make an educated guess for a number, measurement or solution, to find roughly or approximately.

evaluate, calculate: find the value of a numerical expression; for example, 3×8^2 or $4x + 1$ when $x = 5$.

expand: remove brackets in an algebraic expression by multiplying; for example, expanding $3(2y + 1)$ gives $6y + 3$.

explain: describe why or how.

factorise: take out the highest common factor (HCF) of an expression and insert brackets; for example, factorising $5x - 20$ gives $5(x - 4)$. The opposite of **expand**.

give reasons: show the rules or thinking used when solving a problem. *See also* **justify**.

graph: display on a number line, number plane or statistical graph.

hence find/prove: find an answer or prove a result using previous answers or information supplied.

identify: *see* **classify**.

increase: make larger.

interpret: find meaning in an answer or result.

justify: give reasons or evidence to support your argument or conclusion. *See also* **give reasons**.

measure: determine the size of something, for example, use a ruler to determine the length of a pen.

prove that: *see* **show that**.

recall: remember and state.

reduce (a fraction) to its lowest terms: *see* **simplify (a fraction)**.

round (a number): find the nearest approximation of a number. For example, 4.3 rounded to the nearest whole number is 4, \$12.9598 rounded to the nearest cent is \$12.96, 0.166 66 rounded to 3 decimal places is 0.167.

show that, prove that: (in questions where the answer is given) use calculation, procedure or reasoning to prove that an answer or result is true.

show working: show the steps you used to find the answer.

simplify: give a result in its most basic, shortest, neatest form; for example, simplifying a ratio or algebraic expression.

simplify (a fraction): reduce the numerator and denominator of a fraction by dividing by their highest common factor (HCF); for example, $\frac{16}{20}$ simplified is $\frac{4}{5}$.

simplify (a ratio or rate): reduce the terms or units of a ratio or rate by dividing by their highest common factor (HCF); for example, 10 : 4 simplified is 5 : 2.

sketch: draw a rough diagram that shows the general shape or idea (less accurate than **construct**).

solve: find the value(s) of an unknown variable in an equation or inequality.

state: *see* **write**.

substitute: replace a variable by a number and evaluate; replace part of an expression with an equivalent expression.

verify: check that a solution or result is correct, usually by substituting back into the equation or referring back to the problem.

write correct to: *see* **round (a number)**.

write, state: give an answer, formula or result without showing any working or explanation. (This usually means that the answer can be found mentally, or in one step.)

Symbols and abbreviations

$=$	is equal to	x^2	x squared, $x \times x$
$\neq$	is not equal to	x^3	x cubed, $x \times x \times x$
$\approx$	is approximately equal to	$\sqrt{}$	square root, radical sign
$<$	is less than	$\sqrt[3]{}$	cube root
$>$	is greater than	$P(E)$	the probability of event E
$\leq$	is less than or equal to	$P(\bar{E})$	the probability of event 'not E'
$\geq$	is greater than or equal to	$P(B\|A)$	the probability of B given A
$(\ )$	parentheses, round brackets	LHS	left-hand side
$[\ ]$	(square) brackets	RHS	right-hand side
$\{\ \}$	braces	sin	sine ratio
$\pm$	plus or minus	cos	cosine ratio
-3	negative 3	tan	tangent ratio
π	pi = 3.14159 …	$\bar{x}$	the mean (average)
$0.\dot{1}5\dot{2}$	the recurring decimal 0.152152 …	σ	the standard deviation
$^\circ$	degree	Σ	the sum of
$42°17'54''$	42 degrees, 17 minutes, 54 seconds	Q_1	first quartile or lower quartile
$\angle A$	angle A	Q_2	median (second quartile)
$\triangle ABC$	triangle ABC	Q_3	third quartile or upper quartile
$\|\|$	is parallel to	IQR	interquartile range
$\perp$	is perpendicular to	α	alpha
$\equiv$	is congruent (identical) to	θ	theta
$\|\|\|$	is similar to	φ	phi
$\therefore$	therefore	m	gradient
$\%$	percentage		
p.a.	per annum (per year)		

1

ALGEBRA

Graphing lines

Straight lines are an important part of our natural and built environments. We play sport on courts with parallel and perpendicular lines, and skyscrapers would not stand without straight lines. Consider tree trunks, lightning strikes, flight paths, bridges and roller coasters. Straight lines can also be used to model different types of data and predict future outcomes.

stock.adobe.com/LeArchitecto

Chapter outline

		Proficiencies				
1.01	Length, midpoint and gradient of an interval	U	F	PS	R	C
1.02	Parallel and perpendicular lines	U	F			
1.03	Graphing linear functions	U	F		R	C
1.04	The gradient-intercept equation $y = mx + c$	U	F		R	
1.05	The general equation $ax + by + c = 0$*	U	F		R	C
1.06	The point-gradient equation $y - y_1 = m(x - x_1)$*	U	F		R	C
1.07	Finding the equation of a line	U	F		R	C
1.08	Equations of parallel and perpendicular lines	U	F		R	C
1.09	Graphing linear inequalities	U	F	PS	R	C

* EXTENSION

U = Understanding
F = Fluency
PS = Problem solving

R = Reasoning
C = Communicating

Wordbank

gradient The steepness of a line or interval, measured by the fraction $\dfrac{\text{rise}}{\text{run}}$.

gradient–intercept form Any linear function expressed as $y = mx + c$, where m is the gradient and c is the y-intercept.

inequality A mathematical statement that 2 quantities are not equal, involving algebraic expressions and an inequality sign ($>$, $\geq$, $<$ or $\leq$).

linear function A function whose graph is a straight line.

midpoint The point in the middle of an interval or halfway between 2 given points.

parallel lines Lines that point in the same direction and have the same gradient.

perpendicular lines Lines that cross at right angles (90°) and have gradients whose product is −1.

x-intercept The x value at which a graph cuts the x-axis.

y-intercept The y value at which a graph cuts the y-axis.

Quiz
Wordbank 1

Videos (16):

1.01 The gradient of a line • Coordinate geometry • Distance, midpoint and gradient formulas

1.02 Gradients of perpendicular lines

1.03 Graphing linear equations • Testing if a point lies on a line • Horizontal and vertical lines

1.04 Gradient and y-intercept of a line • The gradient-intercept formula • Graphing $y = mx + c$

1.05 The general equation $ax + by + c = 0$

1.06 The point-gradient formula

1.07 Finding the equation of a line

1.08 Equations of parallel lines • Equations of perpendicular lines

1.09 Graphing linear inequalities

PhET interactives (4):

1.03 Graphing lines • Function builder: Basics • Function builder

1.04 Graphing slope-intercept

Quizzes (5):

- Wordbank 1
- SkillCheck 1
- Mental skills 1
- Language of maths 1
- Test yourself 1

Skillsheets (2):

SkillCheck Pythagoras' theorem

1.03 Graphing linear equations

Worksheets (11):

1.01 Gradient, midpoint, distance • Gradient between 2 points

1.03 A page of lines • A page of number planes • Graphing linear equations • Straight-line equations

1.05 Parallel and perpendicular lines

1.07 Finding the equation of a line • A page of lines

1.08 Writing equations of lines

1.09 A page of lines and regions

Mind map: Graphing lines

Puzzles (10):

1.01 Intervals match-up • Finding coordinates for given segment lengths

1.02 Gradients of parallel and perpendicular lines

1.04 Equation of a line • Equations in gradient form

1.05 Linear equations code puzzle

1.07 Straight-line equations

1.08 Linear equations match-up • Equations of parallel lines

Language of maths Graphing lines crossword

Technology (1):

1.01 Midpoint and distance between 2 points

Spreadsheets (2):

1.01 Midpoint and distance between 2 points

1.04 Drawing straight lines: $y = mx + c$

Nelson MindTap

To access resources above, visit
cengage.com.au/nelsonmindtap

---

1 In this chapter you will:

✓ find the length, midpoint and gradient of an interval on a number plane

✓ (EXTENSION) find the angle of inclination θ of a line using the formula $m = \tan \theta$

✓ find the properties of the gradients of parallel and perpendicular lines

✓ graph a linear function on a number plane

✓ test whether a point lies on a line

✓ use the gradient–intercept equation of a straight line $y = mx + c$

✓ (EXTENSION) convert between gradient–intercept form and general form $ax + by + c = 0$

✓ (EXTENSION) use the point-gradient form of a linear equation $y - y_1 = m(x - x_1)$

✓ find the equation of a line from its graph

✓ find the equation of a line that is parallel or perpendicular to a given line

✓ graph a linear inequality as a region on a number plane

SkillCheck
ANSWERS ON P. 598

1.01

Quiz
SkillCheck 1

Skillsheet
Pythagoras'
theorem

1 For this number plane, find:

a the midpoint of interval *BC*

b the midpoint of interval *HE*

c the length of interval *GC*

d the length of interval *GH*

e the lengths of *AC* and *BC*, correct to one decimal place

f the type of triangle △*ABC* is

g the gradient of *GE*

h the gradient of *EH*

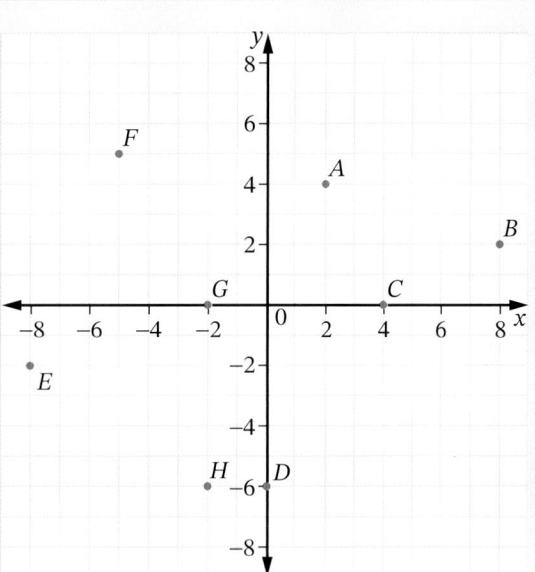

Length, midpoint and gradient of an interval

1.01

The **midpoint** of an interval *AB* is the point in the middle of *AB* or halfway between *A* and *B*.

- Its *x*-coordinate is the average of the *x*-coordinates of *A* and *B*.

- Its *y*-coordinate is the average of the *y*-coordinates of *A* and *B*.

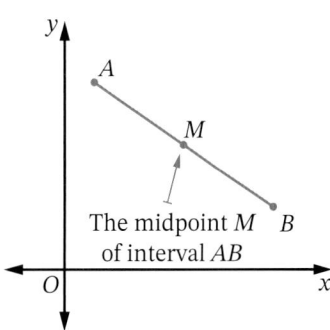

The midpoint *M* of interval *AB*

Video
The gradient
of a line

Worksheets
Gradient,
midpoint,
distance

Gradient
between
2 points

Puzzle
Intervals
match-up

Technology
Midpoint
and distance
between
2 points

Spreadsheet
Midpoint
and distance
between
2 points

The **gradient** of an interval measures its steepness. It is given by the formula:

$$m = \frac{\text{vertical rise}}{\text{horizontal run}} = \frac{\text{rise}}{\text{run}}$$

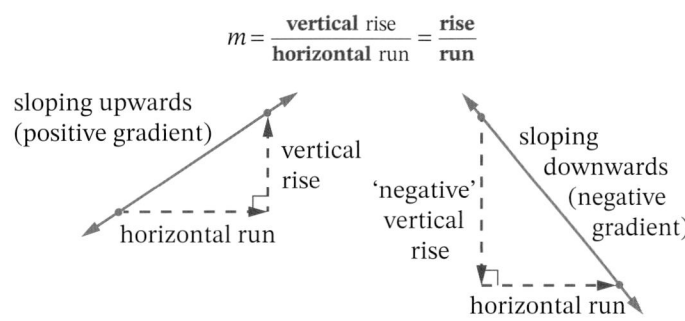

sloping upwards (positive gradient) — vertical rise — horizontal run

'negative' vertical rise — sloping downwards (negative gradient) — horizontal run

- A line **sloping upwards** has a **positive rise** and a **positive gradient**.
- A line **sloping downwards** has a **negative rise** and a **negative gradient**.
- The **run** is always **positive**.

Example 1

For the interval joining $P(-5, 8)$ and $Q(3, 6)$, find:

a   the length of the interval, correct to one decimal place

b   the midpoint of the interval

c   the gradient of the interval.

SOLUTION

a   Draw a right-angled triangle on a number plane with PQ as the hypotenuse.

The height of the triangle is 2 units.

The base of the triangle is 8 units.

$$PQ^2 = 2^2 + 8^2$$
$$= 68$$
$$PQ = \sqrt{68}$$
$$= 8.2462...$$
$$\approx 8.2 \text{ units}$$

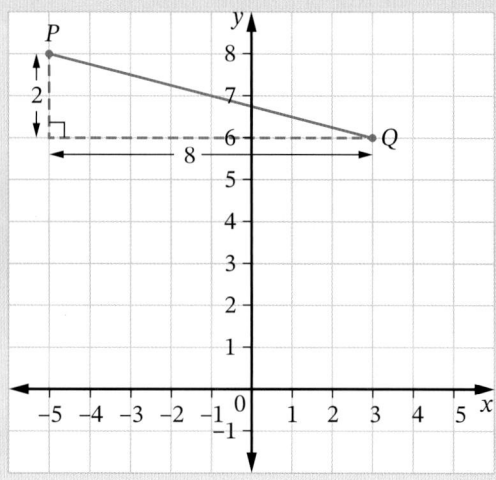

b   For $P(-5, 8)$ and $Q(3, 6)$, the average of the x-coordinates is $\frac{-5+3}{2} = -1$.

The average of the y-coordinates is $\frac{8+6}{2} = 7$.

$\therefore$ the midpoint of PQ is $(-1, 7)$.   From the diagram above, a midpoint at $(-1, 7)$ looks reasonable.

c   The rise is -2 units.   line slopes downwards

The run is 8 units.

$$m = \frac{\text{rise}}{\text{run}}$$
$$= \frac{-2}{8}$$
$$= -\frac{1}{4}$$

The gradient is negative, the line slopes downward.

The distance, midpoint and gradient formulas

ⓘ The distance, midpoint and gradient formulas

For an interval joining $P(x_1, y_1)$ and $Q(x_2, y_2)$:

Distance $d = \sqrt{(x_2 - x_1)^2 + (y_2 - y_1)^2}$

Midpoint $M(x, y) \equiv \left(\dfrac{x_1 + x_2}{2}, \dfrac{y_1 + y_2}{2} \right)$

> We've used '≡' ('is identical to') rather than '=' because we are referring to the point (x, y), not a number.

Gradient, $m = \dfrac{\text{difference in } y}{\text{difference in } x} = \dfrac{y_2 - y_1}{x_2 - x_1}$

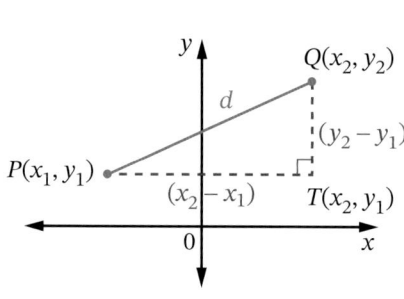

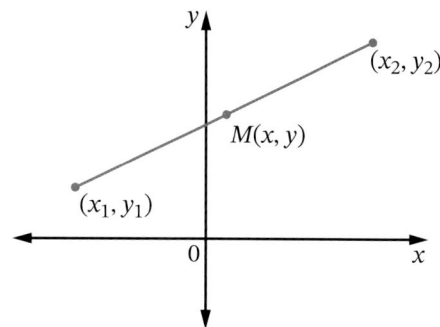

Example 2

For the interval joining $P(-5, 8)$ and $Q(3, 6)$ from Example **1**, use a formula to find:

a   the length of the interval, correct to one decimal place

b   the midpoint of the interval

c   the gradient of the interval.

Video
Distance,
midpoint
and gradient
formulas

Puzzle
Finding
coordinates
for given
segment
lengths

SOLUTION

For $P(-5, 8)$ and $Q(3, 6)$: $x_1 = -5, y_1 = 8, x_2 = 3, y_2 = 6.$

(x_1, y_1) (x_2, y_2)

a $d = \sqrt{(x_2 - x_1)^2 + (y_2 - y_1)^2}$

$= \sqrt{(3 - (-5))^2 + (6 - 8)^2}$

$= \sqrt{68}$

$= 8.2462\ldots$

≈ 8.2 units

b $M(x, y) \equiv \left(\dfrac{x_1 + x_2}{2}, \dfrac{y_1 + y_2}{2} \right)$

$\equiv \left(\dfrac{-5 + 3}{2}, \dfrac{8 + 6}{2} \right)$

$\equiv (-1, 7)$

c $m = \dfrac{\text{difference in } y}{\text{difference in } x}$

$\quad = \dfrac{y_2 - y_1}{x_2 - x_1}$

$\quad = \dfrac{6 - 8}{3 - (-5)}$

$\quad = \dfrac{-2}{8}$

$\quad = -\dfrac{1}{4}$

Example 3

a   Plot the points $A(0, 6)$, $B(5, 6)$, $C(5, 2)$ and $D(-4, 2)$ on a number plane and join them to make the quadrilateral $ABCD$.

b   What type of quadrilateral is $ABCD$?

c   Find the exact length of AD.

d   Hence find the perimeter of $ABCD$, correct to 2 decimal places.

SOLUTION

a

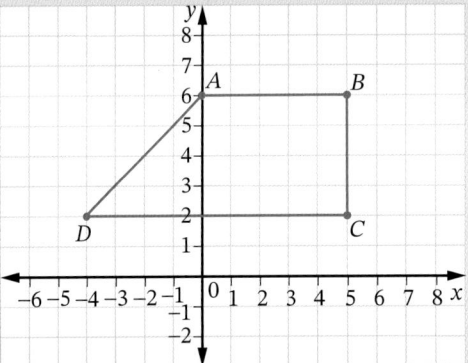

join the points in the correct order

b   Since $AB \parallel CD$, the quadrilateral is a trapezium.

c $AD^2 = 4^2 + 4^2$

$\qquad = 32$

$AD = \sqrt{32}$ units   in exact surd form

d   By counting grid squares, $AB = 5$, $BC = 4$, $CD = 9$.

Perimeter of $ABCD = 5 + 4 + 9 + \sqrt{32}$

$\qquad\qquad\qquad\quad = 23.656...$

$\qquad\qquad\qquad\quad \approx 23.66$ units

The angle of inclination of a line

The **angle of inclination**, θ, of a line is the angle it makes with the x-axis in the positive direction.

acute angle = positive gradient   obtuse angle = negative gradient

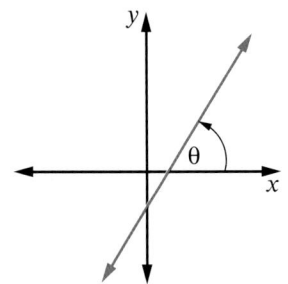 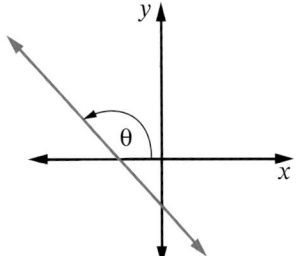

Note from the above diagrams that θ is **acute** when the line has a **positive gradient**, and **obtuse** when the line has a **negative gradient**.

We can use trigonometry to calculate the angle of inclination of a line using its gradient, m.

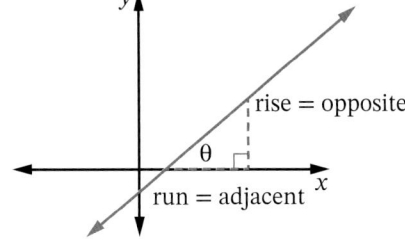

The diagram shows that $m = \dfrac{\text{rise}}{\text{run}}$, but in trigonometry,

$$\tan \theta = \frac{\text{opposite}}{\text{adjacent}} = \frac{\text{rise}}{\text{run}}$$

∴ $m = \tan \theta$.

ⓘ The angle of inclination of a line

The angle of inclination, θ, of a line is related to the gradient, m, of the line by the formula:

$$m = \tan \theta.$$

Example 4

Find, correct to the nearest degree, the angle of inclination of a line with gradient:

a $\dfrac{1}{3}$

b −4

SOLUTION

a $m = \tan \theta$

   $\dfrac{1}{3} = \tan \theta$

   $\tan \theta = \dfrac{1}{3}$

   $\theta = 18.4349...$ On a calculator: SHIFT tan 1 aᵇ/c 3 =

   $\approx 18°$

> The positive gradient means it is an acute angle.

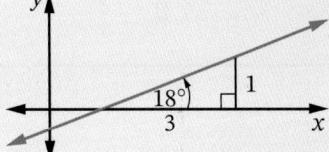

b

$$m = \tan \theta$$

$$-4 = \tan \theta$$

$$\tan \theta = -4$$

$$\theta = -75.9637...$$

$$\approx -76°$$

On calculator: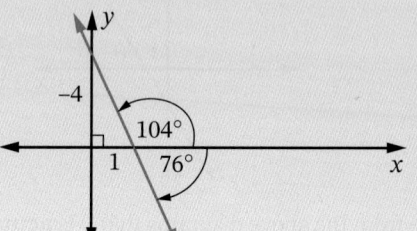

But this negative angle is the angle below the *x*-axis.

To find the angle of inclination,

$$\theta \approx 180° - 76°$$

$$\approx 104°$$

> Negative gradient means it is an obtuse angle.

EXERCISE **1.01** ANSWERS ON P. 598

Length, midpoint and gradient of an interval (U)(F)(PS)(R)(C)

Questions **1**, **2** and **3** refer to this diagram of interval *CD*.

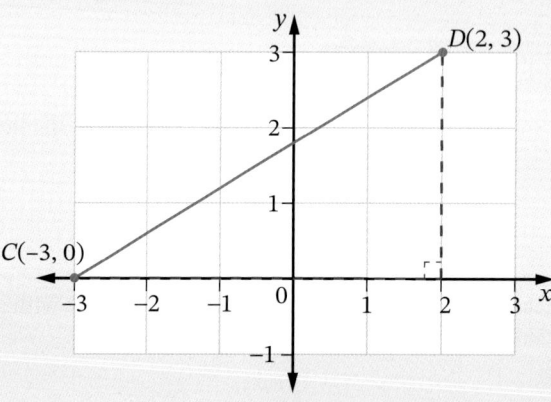

1 What is the length of interval *CD*? Select **A**, **B**, **C** or **D**.

   A 2 units   **B** 5.8 units   **C** 3.2 units   **D** 8 units

2 What is the midpoint of *CD*? Select **A**, **B**, **C** or **D**.

   A $(-1, 3)$ **B** $(-5, 3)$ **C** $(-0.5, 1.5)$ **D** $(-2.5, 1.5)$

3 What is the gradient of *CD*? Select **A**, **B**, **C** or **D**.

   A $\dfrac{3}{5}$ **B** $-\dfrac{3}{5}$ **C** $-\dfrac{5}{3}$ **D** $\dfrac{5}{3}$

☐ Foundation   ◯ Standard   ◯ Complex

4 Calculate the gradient of each line.

a

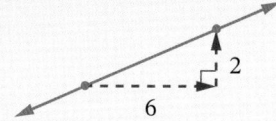

b

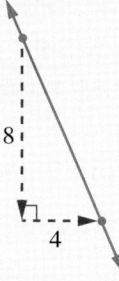

c

5 For the interval joining each pair of points given, find:

  i the length of the interval, correct to one decimal place

  ii the midpoint of the interval

  iii the gradient of the interval.

a $A(5, 3)$ and $B(7, 2)$ **b** $J(-1, 0)$ and $K(8, 6)$ **c** $M(0, -3)$ and $N(-5, 2)$

d $R(-3, -6)$ and $S(4, -9)$ **e** $A(-7, 2)$ and $B(-5, -8)$ **f** $U(3, -2)$ and $V(7, 2)$

6 Calculate, in exact (surd) form, the distance between each pair of points.

a $(-8, -1)$ and $(0, 4)$ **b** $(12, -6)$ and $(-1, -1)$ **c** $(7, -2)$ and $(-2, -3)$

7 Find the gradient of the lines labelled k and l.

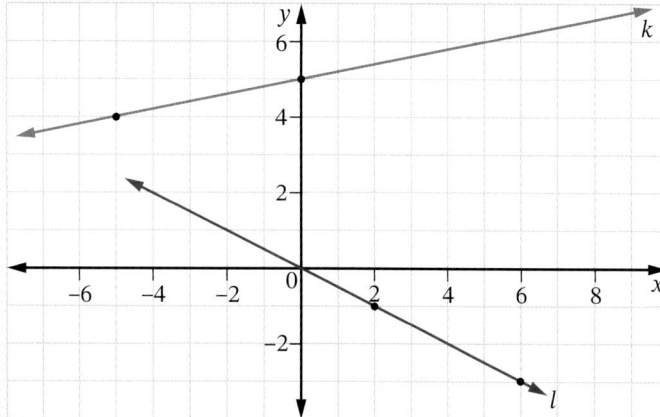

8 Which expression gives the y-coordinate of the midpoint of the interval joining points $(3, 8)$ and $(-1, 5)$? Select **A**, **B**, **C** or **D**.

A $\dfrac{-1+5}{2}$ **B** $\dfrac{8+5}{2}$ **C** $\dfrac{8-5}{2}$ **D** $\dfrac{5-8}{2}$

☐ Foundation   ○ Standard   ◇ Complex

9 The vertices of triangle *ABC* are *A*(−1, −1), *B*(1, 3) and *C*(3, 1).

(PS) **a** Draw △*ABC* on a number plane.

(R) **b** Find the exact length of each side of the triangle.

(C) **c** Are any sides of the triangle equal in length?

d What type of triangle is *ABC*?

e Find the perimeter of △*ABC*, correct to one decimal place.

10 The vertices of quadrilateral *KLMP* are *K*(1, 6), *L*(7, 2), *M*(3, −4) and *P*(−3, 0).

(PS) **a** Draw the quadrilateral on a number plane.

(R) **b** What type of quadrilateral is *KLMP*?

(C) **c** Find the gradients of sides *KL* and *PM*.

d Find the gradients of sides *KP* and *LM*.

e What do you notice about the gradients of the opposite sides of this quadrilateral? What does that mean about those sides?

f Find the exact length of each side of *KLMP*.

g Find the perimeter of *KLMP*, correct to one decimal place.

h Find the area of *KLMP*.

11 The diagram shows a right-angled triangle

(R) with vertices *A*(−2, −1), *B*(−2, 3) and

(C) *C*(4, 3).

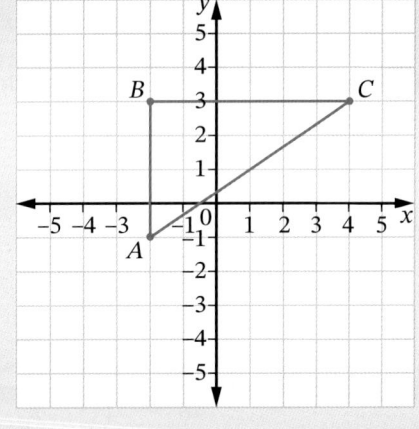

a Copy the diagram and find the coordinates of *P* and *Q*, the midpoints of *BA* and *BC*, respectively. Mark *P* and *Q* on your diagram.

b Calculate, correct to one decimal place, the lengths of *PQ* and *AC*. What do you notice about your answers?

c Find the gradients of *PQ* and *AC*. What do you notice about your answers?

EXTENSION

EXAMPLE
4

12 Find, correct to the nearest degree, the angle of inclination of a line with gradient:

a 3   **b** $\frac{1}{2}$ **c** 1   **d** 2.5

e −2   **f** $\frac{3}{4}$ **g** $-\frac{1}{10}$ **h** $-\frac{2}{3}$

13 Find, correct to 2 decimal places, the gradient of the line with angle of inclination:

a 60°   **b** 158°   **c** 42°   **d** 94°

e 8°   **f** 135°   **g** 177°   **h** 0°

INVESTIGATION

Parallel and perpendicular lines

1 These 3 lines are parallel. Calculate the gradient of:

   a AB

   b PQ

   c ZV

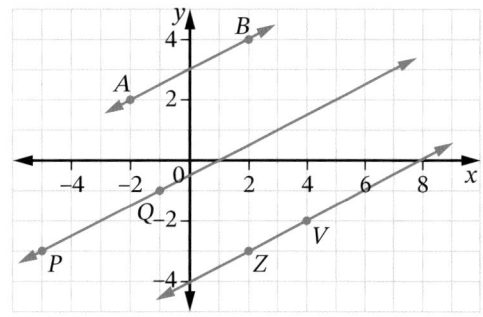

2 What can you conclude about the gradients of parallel lines?

3 This diagram shows 2 pairs of perpendicular lines. $AB \perp CD$ and $PQ \perp ST$. Calculate the gradient of:

   a AB b CD

   c PQ d ST

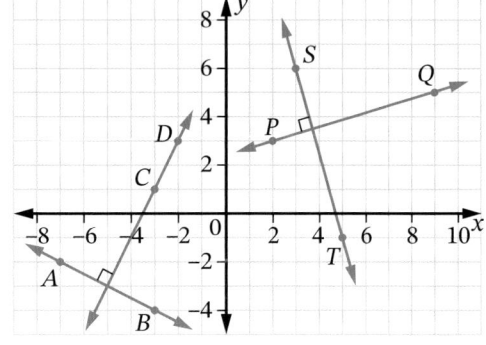

4 Is there a relationship between:

   a the gradients of AB and CD?   b the gradients of PQ and ST?

5 Calculate the product of:

   a the gradients of AB and CD b the gradients of PQ and ST

6 What can you conclude about the gradients of perpendicular lines?

Parallel and perpendicular lines   1.02

(i) Parallel and perpendicular lines

Parallel lines have the same gradient.

If 2 lines with gradients m_1 and m_2 are parallel, then $m_1 = m_2$.

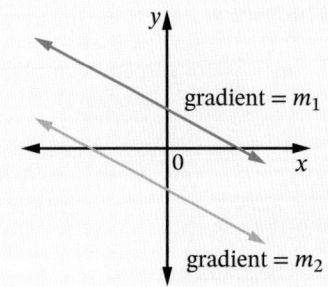

Puzzle
Gradients of parallel and perpendicular lines

Perpendicular lines have gradients with a **product** of -1.

If 2 lines with gradients m_1 and m_2 are perpendicular, then

$$m_1 \times m_2 = -1 \text{ or } m_2 = -\frac{1}{m_1}$$

Note that m_2 is the **negative reciprocal** of m_1.

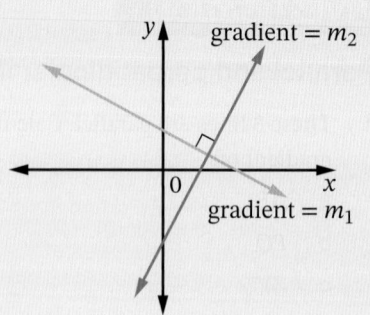
gradient = m_2
gradient = m_1

Example 5

State whether each pair of gradients represent parallel lines, perpendicular lines or neither.

a $m_1 = \frac{1}{2}, m_2 = 2$ **b** $m_1 = 0.4, m_2 = \frac{2}{5}$ **c** $m_1 = 1\frac{3}{5}, m_2 = -\frac{5}{8}$

SOLUTION

a $m_1 \neq m_2$ so the lines are not parallel.

$m_1 \times m_2 = \frac{1}{2} \times 2$

$\qquad\qquad = 1$

$\qquad\qquad \neq -1$

so the lines are not perpendicular.

∴ the lines are neither parallel nor perpendicular.

b $m_2 = \frac{2}{5} = 0.4$

$m_1 = m_2$

∴ the lines are parallel.

c $m_1 = 1\frac{3}{5} = \frac{8}{5}$

$m_1 \times m_2 = \frac{8}{5} \times \left(-\frac{5}{8}\right)$

$\qquad\qquad = -1$

∴ the lines are perpendicular.

Example 6

Video
Gradients of perpendicular lines

Find the gradient of a line that is perpendicular to a line with gradient:

a 2   **b** -3 **c** $\frac{3}{4}$ **d** -0.6

SOLUTION

a $m_1 = 2$

$m_2 = \frac{-1}{m_1}$ for perpendicular lines

$\quad = \frac{-1}{2}$

$\quad = -\frac{1}{2}$ The negative reciprocal of m_1.

The gradient is $-\frac{1}{2}$.

b $m_1 = -3$

$m_2 = \frac{-1}{m_1}$

$\quad = \frac{-1}{-3}$

$\quad = \frac{1}{3}$

The gradient is $\frac{1}{3}$.

c $m_1 = \dfrac{3}{4}$

$m_2 = \dfrac{-1}{m_1}$

$\quad = \dfrac{-1}{\left(\dfrac{3}{4}\right)}$

$\quad = -\dfrac{4}{3}$

The gradient is $-\dfrac{4}{3}$.

d $m_1 = -0.6 = -\dfrac{3}{5}$

$m_2 = \dfrac{-1}{\left(-\dfrac{3}{5}\right)} = \dfrac{5}{3}$

The gradient is $\dfrac{5}{3}$.

Example 7

A line passes through the points $A(-2, 5)$ and $B(4, 1)$. What is the gradient of a line:

a parallel to AB?   **b** perpendicular to AB?

SOLUTION

Find the gradient of AB by calculating the rise and run.

Sometimes drawing a diagram helps you to understand the problem.

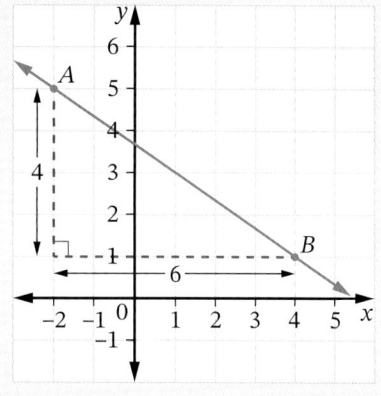

rise $= 1 - 5 = -4$ difference between
                          y-coordinates

run $= 4 - (-2) = 6$ difference between
                          x-coordinates

gradient $AB = \dfrac{-4}{6} = -\dfrac{2}{3}$ $\dfrac{\text{rise}}{\text{run}}$

a Any line parallel to AB will have the same gradient as AB.

$\therefore m = -\dfrac{2}{3}$

b The gradient of a line perpendicular to AB will be given by:

$m = \dfrac{-1}{\left(-\dfrac{2}{3}\right)} = \dfrac{3}{2}$

Parallel and perpendicular lines   (U) (F)

EXAMPLE
5

1 State whether each pair of gradients represent parallel lines, perpendicular lines or neither.

a $m_1 = \frac{1}{4}, m_2 = 4$ **b** $m_1 = 3, m_2 = -\frac{1}{3}$ **c** $m_1 = 0.5, m_2 = \frac{1}{2}$

d $m_1 = \frac{2}{7}, m_2 = \frac{7}{2}$ **e** $m_1 = \frac{3}{10}, m_2 = 0.3$ **f** $m_1 = 1\frac{1}{5}, m_2 = -\frac{6}{5}$

2 Find the gradient of a line that is parallel to a line with gradient:

a 4   **b** −2   **c** $\frac{1}{3}$ **d** −0.2

EXAMPLE
6

3 Find the gradient of a line that is perpendicular to a line with gradient:

a 1   **b** −6   **c** −1.5   **d** $\frac{5}{2}$

4 What is the gradient of a line that is perpendicular to a line with a gradient of 0.8? Select **A**, **B**, **C** or **D**.

A 0.2   **B** −0.2   **C** 1.25   **D** −1.25

5 What is the gradient of a line that is parallel to a line that goes through $P(0, 3)$ and $Q(5, -2)$? Select **A**, **B**, **C** or **D**.

A 1   **B** −1   **C** $\frac{1}{5}$ **D** $-\frac{1}{5}$

EXAMPLE
7

6 What is the gradient of a line perpendicular to the line shown? Select **A**, **B**, **C** or **D**.

A $\frac{5}{3}$ **B** −5

C $\frac{3}{5}$ **D** $\frac{1}{5}$

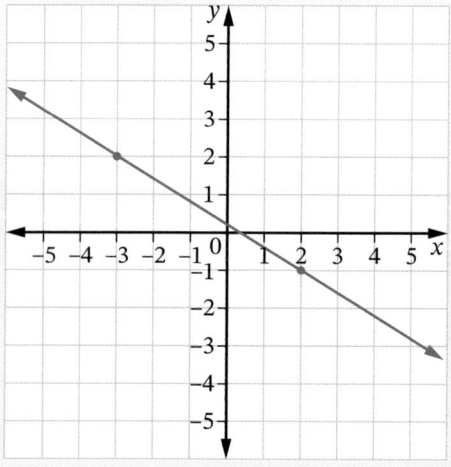

☐ Foundation   ○ Standard   ○ Complex

7 Calculate the gradient of each line shown and test whether:

a $AB \parallel CD$

b $PQ \perp CD$.

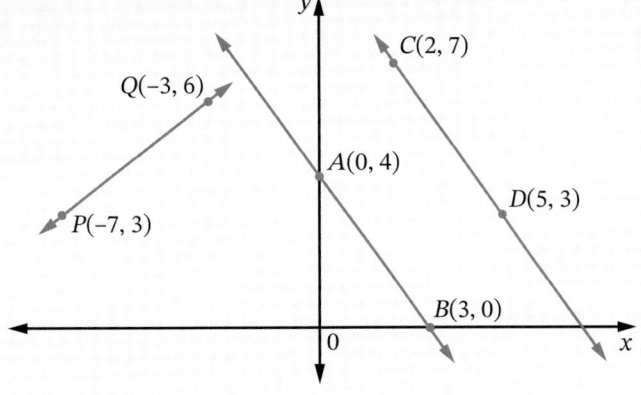

8 A line passes through the points $R(-5, 2)$ and $S(1, 4)$. What is the gradient of a line:

a parallel to RS?

b perpendicular to RS?

TECHNOLOGY

Parallel and perpendicular lines

Use dynamic geometry software to find out if sets of linear functions represent parallel or perpendicular lines.

1 **Parallel lines**

Graph the following lines and use the **Slope/Gradient** function to find their gradients and check whether they are parallel using $m_1 = m_2$.

a $5x - 3y = 0$ and $y = \dfrac{5x}{3}$

b $x + y + 4 = 0$ and $x + y - 6 = 0$

c $x - 2y = 0$ and $y = 0.5x$

d $y = 5x - 9$ and $5x - y - 1 = 0$

2 **Perpendicular lines**

Graph the following lines and use the **Slope/Gradient** function to find their gradients and check whether they are perpendicular using $m_1 \times m_2 = -1$.

a $y = 0.6x + 2$ and $y = \dfrac{5}{3}x$

b $x - 4y + 1 = 0$ and $y = -4x - 3$

c $3x - 2y = 0$ and $y = -\dfrac{2x}{3}$

d $y = 2x + 4$ and $x - 2y - 1 = 0$

☐ Foundation ○ Standard ○ Complex

1.03 Graphing linear functions

Video
Graphing linear equations

Interactives
Graphing lines

Function builder: Basics

Function builder

Skillsheet
Graphing linear equations

Worksheets
A page of lines

A page of number planes

Graphing linear equations

A relationship between 2 variables, x and y, whose graph is a straight line is called a **linear relationship**. The expression of that relationship as an algebraic formula, such as $y = 3x + 2$, is called a **linear function** or **linear equation**.

Example 8

Graph $y = 3x + 2$ on a number plane and find its x- and y-intercepts.

SOLUTION

Complete a table of values. Choose x values close to 0 for easy calculation and graphing.

x	−1	0	1
y	−1	2	5

Graph $(-1, -1)$, $(0, 2)$ and $(1, 5)$ on a number plane. Rule a straight line through the points, place arrows at each end, and label the line with its **equation**.

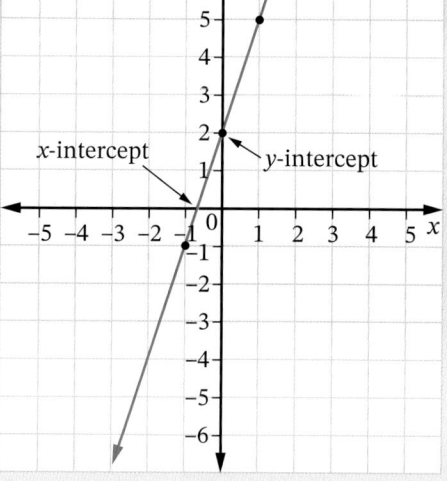

The **x-intercept** is found by substituting $y = 0$ into the equation $y = 3x + 2$:

$0 = 3x + 2$

$3x = -2$

$x = -\dfrac{2}{3}$ which agrees with what is shown on the graph

The x-intercept is $-\dfrac{2}{3}$.

The **y-intercept** is found by looking at the graph, or looking at the **constant term** in the equation $y = 3x + 2$, or substituting $x = 0$ into the equation $y = 3x + 2$ (which has already been done for the table of values).

The y-intercept is 2.

9780170465595

Example 9

Find the x- and y-intercepts of the line $2x - 3y = 6$ to draw its graph.

SOLUTION

For x-intercept, $y = 0$:

$2x - 3 \times 0 = 6$

$\qquad 2x = 6$

$\qquad x = 3$

The x-intercept is 3.

For y-intercept, $x = 0$:

$2 \times 0 - 3y = 6$

$\qquad -3y = 6$

$\qquad y = -2$

The y-intercept is -2.

Plot both intercepts on the axes, draw a line through the 2 points and label the line with its equation.

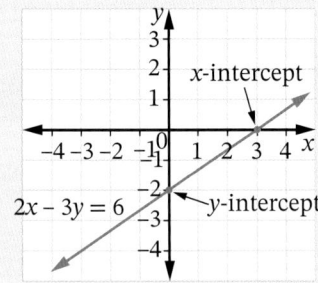

ⓘ Testing if a point lies on a line

A point lies on a line if its (x, y) coordinates satisfy the equation of the line.

Video
Testing if a point lies on a line

Example 10

Test whether each point lies on the line $x - 2y = 5$.

a $(17, 6)$

b $(8, -4)$

Worksheet
Straight-line equations

SOLUTION

a Substitute $x = 17$, $y = 6$ into $x - 2y = 5$.

$\text{LHS} = x - 2y$

$\qquad = 17 - 2 \times 6$

$\qquad = 5$

$\text{RHS} = 5$

$\text{LHS} = \text{RHS}$, so $(17, 6)$ lies on the line.

b Substitute $x = 8$, $y = -4$ into $x - 2y = 5$.

$\text{LHS} = x - 2y$

$\qquad = 8 - 2 \times (-4)$

$\qquad = 16$

$\text{RHS} = 5$

$\text{LHS} \neq \text{RHS}$, so $(8, -4)$ does not lie on the line.

Video
Horizontal
and vertical
lines

ⓘ Horizontal and vertical lines

The equation of a horizontal line is of the form $y = c$ (where c is a constant number).

The equation of a vertical line is of the form $x = c$ (where c is a constant number).

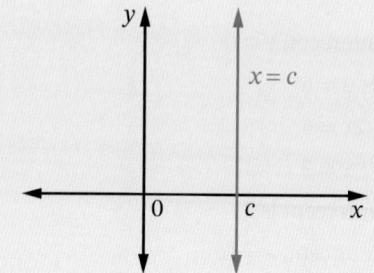

Note: The x-axis has equation $y = 0$.

Note: The y-axis has equation $x = 0$.

Example 11

Find the equation of the line that is:

a parallel to the x-axis and passes through the point $(1, -6)$

b always 3 units to the left of the y-axis.

SOLUTION

a The equation of the line is $y = -6$.

b The equation of the line is $x = -3$.

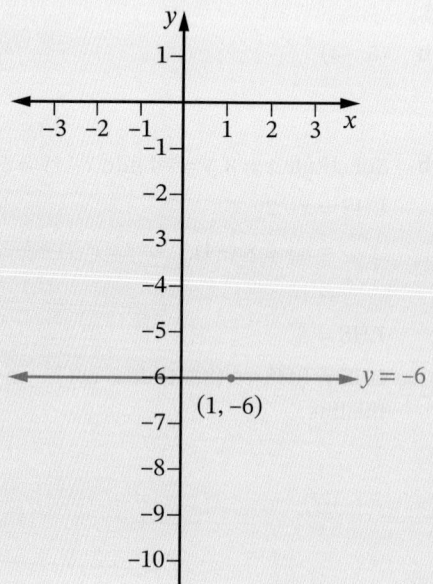

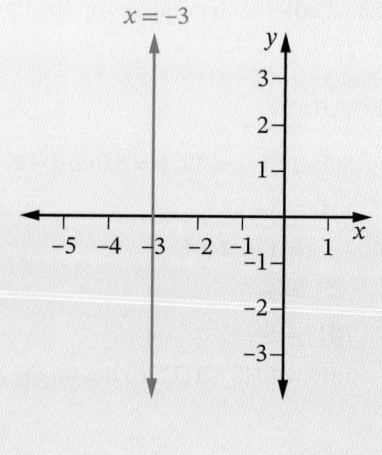

Graphing linear functions Ⓤ Ⓕ Ⓡ Ⓒ

1 Graph each linear function on a number plane, and find:

    i   its x-intercept   **ii**   its y-intercept.

  a $y = 3x - 1$ **b** $y = 2x + 5$ **c** $y = -x + 4$

  d $y = -2x - 2$ **e** $y = 4x$ **f** $y = \dfrac{x}{2} + 3$

EXAMPLE 8

2 Graph each linear equation after finding its x- and y-intercepts.

  a $y = 4 - 2x$ **b** $2x = 4y - 8$ **c** $y - x = 6$

  d $3x - 2y = 12$ **e** $2x + 2y = 5$ **f** $6 - x = 2y$

  g $y = 4 + 2x$ **h** $5x + 3y - 15 = 0$ **i** $3x - y = 6$

  j $2x - 5y - 20 = 0$ **k** $4x + 2y - 8 = 0$ **l** $x - 4y - 2 = 0$

EXAMPLE 9

3 Test whether the point $(3, -1)$ lies on each line.

  a $y = 2x - 5$ **b** $x - y = 4$ **c** $y + 2x = 5$

  d $y = x - 4$ **e** $x + y = 5$ **f** $3x + y + 8 = 0$

EXAMPLE 10

4 Which point lies on the line $y = 6x - 5$? Select **A**, **B**, **C** or **D**.

  A $(-1, 11)$ **B** $(3, -13)$ **C** $(-2, -17)$ **D** $(-5, 25)$

5 Find the equation of each line shown.

EXAMPLE 11

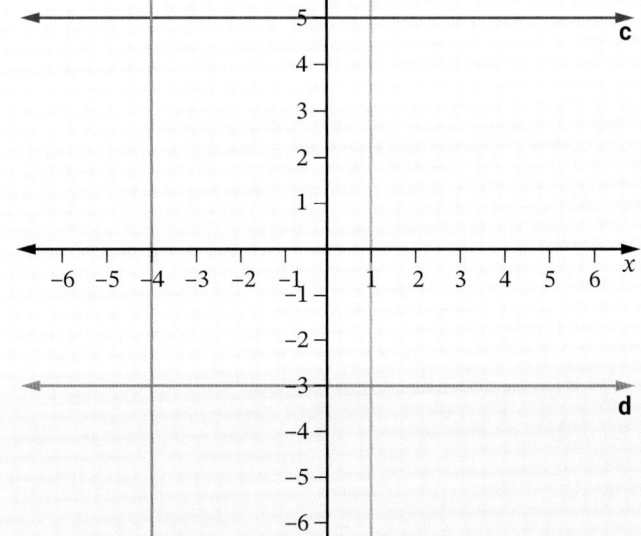

6 Graph each set of lines on a number plane.

   a $x = 2\frac{1}{2}, y = -3, y = 1$ **b** $x = 6, y = -2, x = -\frac{1}{2}$

EXAMPLE 10

7 Find the equation of the line that is:

   (R) **a** horizontal and passes through the y-axis at 2

   (C) **b** vertical with an x-intercept of 4

       c parallel to the y-axis and passes through the point $(-1, 4)$

       d parallel to the x-axis and passes through the point $(0, -2)$

       e 3 units above the x-axis

       f 1 unit to the left of the y-axis

       g drawn through the points $(-1, 6)$ and $(2, 6)$

       h drawn through the points $(-1, 8)$ and $(-1, 2)$.

8 Which point lies on the line $4x + y = 1$? Select **A**, **B**, **C** or **D**.

   A $(-1, 5)$ **B** $(-2, 7)$ **C** $(6, 9)$ **D** $\left(-\frac{1}{2}, 1\right)$

9 Which line is horizontal and passes through the point $(8, -2)$? Select **A**, **B**, **C** or **D**.

   A $y = 8$ **B** $x = 8$ **C** $y = -2$ **D** $x = -2$

10 **a** What is another name for the line $y = 0$?

  (C) **b** What is another name for the line $x = 0$?

1.04   The gradient–intercept equation $y = mx + c$

Videos
Gradient and
y-intercept
of a line

The gradient-
intercept
formula

Interactive
Graphing
slope-
intercept

Puzzles
Equation
of a line

Equations
in gradient
form

ⓘ The gradient–intercept form of a linear equation

The equation of a line is $y = mx + c$, where m is the **gradient** and c is the **y-intercept**.

$y = mx + c$ is called the **gradient–intercept form** of a linear equation.

Example 12

Find the gradient and y-intercept of the line with equation:

  a $y = -4x + 9$ **b** $y = 10 - 6x$ **c** $y = \frac{5x + 4}{2}$ **d** $3x + 2y - 6 = 0$

  SOLUTION

  a $y = -4x + 9$ is in the form $y = mx + c$.

      ∴ gradient $m = -4$ and y-intercept $c = 9$.

□ Foundation ○ Standard ○ Complex

1.04

b $y = 10 - 6x$ can be rewritten as $y = -6x + 10$.

∴ gradient $m = -6$ and y-intercept $c = 10$.

Spreadsheet
Drawing
straight
lines:
$y = mx + c$

c $y = \dfrac{5x + 4}{2}$ can be rewritten as $y = \dfrac{5x}{2} + \dfrac{4}{2} = \dfrac{5x}{2} + 2$.

∴ gradient $m = \dfrac{5}{2}$ and y-intercept $c = 2$.

d $3x + 2y - 6 = 0$ can be rearranged in the form $y = mx + c$.

$$3x + 2y - 6 - 3x = 0 - 3x$$

$$2y - 6 = -3x$$

$$2y = -3x + 6$$

$$\frac{2y}{2} = \frac{-3x + 6}{2}$$

$$y = \frac{-3x}{2} + 3$$

∴ gradient $m = -\dfrac{3}{2}$ and y-intercept $c = 3$.

Example 13

Graph each linear function by finding the gradient and y-intercept first.

a $y = -2x + 5$

b $y = \dfrac{3}{4}x - 2$

Video
Graphing
$y = mx + c$

SOLUTION

a $y = -2x + 5$ has a gradient of -2 and a y-intercept of 5.

- Plot the y-intercept 5 on the y-axis.

- Make a gradient of $-2 = \dfrac{-2}{1}$ by moving

  across 1 unit (**run**) and **down** 2 units
  (**'negative' rise**) and marking the point
  at $(1, 3)$.

- Rule a line through this point and
  the y-intercept.

Don't forget to label the line
with its equation '$y = -2x + 5$'

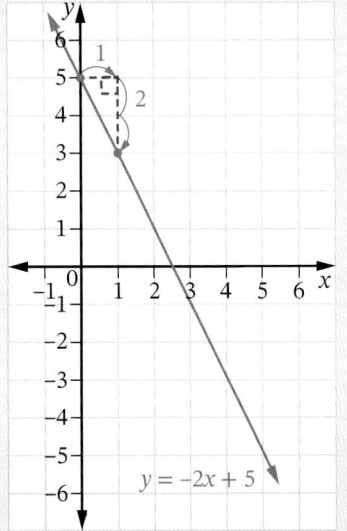

b $y = \frac{3}{4}x - 2$ has gradient $\frac{3}{4}$ and y-intercept -2.

- Plot the y-intercept -2 on the y-axis.

- Make a gradient of $\frac{3}{4}$ by moving **across** 4 units (**run**) and **up** 3 units (**rise**) and marking the point at $(4, 1)$.

- Rule a line through this point and the y-intercept.

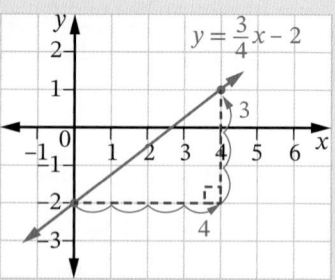

Example 14

Test whether each line is parallel to $y = -2x + 3$.

a $y = 2x + 3$ **b** $y = -2x + 1$ **c** $y = -2x$ **d** $y = 5x + 3$

SOLUTION

Parallel lines have the **same gradient**. The line $y = -2x + 3$ has the gradient $m = -2$.

a $y = 2x + 3$ has a different gradient, 2, so it is not parallel to $y = -2x + 3$.

b $y = -2x + 1$ has the same gradient, -2, so it is parallel to $y = -2x + 3$.

c $y = -2x$ has the same gradient, -2, so it is parallel to $y = -2x + 3$.

d $y = 5x + 3$ has a different gradient, 5, so it is not parallel to $y = -2x + 3$.

EXERCISE (1.04) ANSWERS ON P. 600

The gradient–intercept equation $y = mx + c$ Ⓤ Ⓕ Ⓡ

EXAMPLE
12

1 Find the gradient and y-intercept of each line.

  a $y = 3x - 2$ **b** $y = -2x + 7$ **c** $y = x + 4$ **d** $y = 9 - x$

  e $y = \frac{3x}{4} + 6$ **f** $y = x$ **g** $y = \frac{x}{2} - 11$ **h** $y = \frac{2x + 18}{3}$

  i $y = \frac{-24 - x}{3}$ **j** $y = 2(x - 3)$ **k** $11 - 3x = y$ **l** $\frac{2x - 7}{2} = y$

2 Find the equation of a line with:

  a a gradient of 2 and a y-intercept of 1 **b** a gradient of $\frac{3}{4}$ and a y-intercept of 2

  c a gradient of -7 and a y-intercept of 5 **d** a gradient of $-\frac{2}{5}$ and a y-intercept of 3

  e $m = -2, c = -3$ **f** $m = -3, c = \frac{1}{2}$

□ Foundation ○ Standard ○ Complex

EXAMPLE **13**   1.04

3 Graph each linear function by finding the gradient and y-intercept first.

    a $y = 2x + 1$ **b** $y = 3x - 2$ **c** $y = 2x$ **d** $y = \dfrac{x}{2} - 1$

    e $y = -2x + 3$ **f** $y = -\dfrac{3x}{4}$ **g** $y = \dfrac{-5x + 2}{2}$ **h** $y = \dfrac{3x - 20}{5}$

4 Write the equation of a line with a gradient of 2 that passes through the origin.

  Ⓡ

5 Match each equation to its graph below.

  Ⓡ   **a** $y = 4x + 1$ **b** $y = -4x + 1$ **c** $y = -4x - 1$ **d** $y = 4x - 1$

A

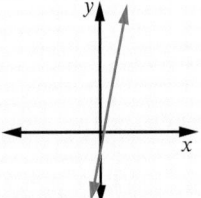

B

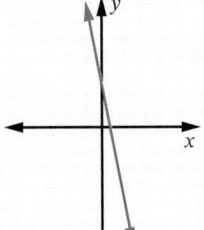

C

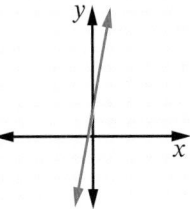

D

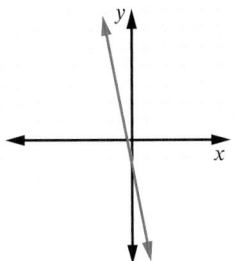

6 For each given line, select the lines that are parallel. There may be more than

  Ⓡ   one answer.

EXAMPLE **14**

    a $y = x + 6$

        A $y = 6x$ **B** $y = 6 - x$ **C** $y = x + 1$ **D** $y = 2x$

    b $y = 3x + 10$

        A $y = 10x + 3$ **B** $y = 3x - 1$ **C** $y = 1 - 3x$ **D** $y = 4 + 3x$

    c $y = \dfrac{x}{2} + 5$

        A $y = 2x - 1$ **B** $y = \dfrac{x + 6}{2}$ **C** $y = 1 - \dfrac{x}{2}$ **D** $y = x + 2$

    d $y = 6$

        A $y = 2x + 6$ **B** $y = 6x$ **C** $y = -1$ **D** $y = 10$

□ Foundation   ○ Standard   ◇ Complex

e $y = 4x$

    A $y = 4x - 2$ **B** $y = 4x + 3$ **C** $y = 4$ **D** $y = 1 - 4x$

f $x = 10$

    A $y = 10$ **B** $y = 10x$ **C** $x = 2y$ **D** $x = -6$

7 For each set of linear functions, find a pair of equations whose graphs are parallel lines.

  (R) **a** $y = 4x + 3$ $y = x + 2$ $y = 4x - 6$ $y = 2x$

     b $y = 5x + 1$ $3x - y + 7 = 0$ $y = 3x - 2$ $y = -5x + 2$

Quiz
Mental
skills 1

☆ **MENTAL SKILLS** ① ANSWERS ON P. 601   **Maths without calculators**

Percentage of a quantity

Learn these commonly-used percentages and their fraction equivalents.

Percentage	50%	25%	12.5%	75%	20%	10%	$33\frac{1}{3}\%$	$66\frac{2}{3}\%$
Fraction	$\frac{1}{2}$	$\frac{1}{4}$	$\frac{1}{8}$	$\frac{3}{4}$	$\frac{1}{5}$	$\frac{1}{10}$	$\frac{1}{3}$	$\frac{2}{3}$

Now we will use them to find a percentage of a quantity.

1 Study each example.

  a $\begin{aligned} 20\% \times 25 &= \frac{1}{5} \times 25 \\ &= 5 \end{aligned}$ **b** $\begin{aligned} 50\% \times 120 &= \frac{1}{2} \times 120 \\ &= 60 \end{aligned}$ **c** $\begin{aligned} 12.5\% \times 32 &= \frac{1}{8} \times 32 \\ &= 4 \end{aligned}$

  d $\begin{aligned} 75\% \times 56 &= \frac{3}{4} \times 60 \\ &= \left(\frac{1}{4} \times 60\right) \times 3 \\ &= 15 \times 3 \\ &= 45 \end{aligned}$ **e** $\begin{aligned} 33\frac{1}{3}\% \times 27 &= \frac{1}{3} \times 27 \\ &= 9 \end{aligned}$ **f** $\begin{aligned} 66\frac{2}{3}\% \times 60 &= \frac{2}{3} \times 60 \\ &= \left(\frac{1}{3} \times 60\right) \times 2 \\ &= 20 \times 2 \\ &= 40 \end{aligned}$

2 Now simplify each expression.

  a $25\% \times 44$ **b** $33\frac{1}{3}\% \times 120$ **c** $20\% \times 35$ **d** $66\frac{2}{3}\% \times 36$

  e $10\% \times 230$ **f** $12\frac{1}{2}\% \times 48$ **g** $50\% \times 86$ **h** $20\% \times 400$

  i $75\% \times 24$ **j** $33\frac{1}{3}\% \times 45$ **k** $25\% \times 160$ **l** $10\% \times 650$

  m $12.5\% \times 88$ **n** $66\frac{2}{3}\% \times 21$ **o** $20\% \times 60$ **p** $75\% \times 180$

□ Foundation ○ Standard ○ Complex

Extension: The general equation $ax + by + c = 0$

A linear equation written in **gradient–intercept form**, such as $y = -\frac{3}{4}x + 2$, can also be written in **general form** ($3x + 4y - 8 = 0$). Note that, for the general form, all the **terms** on the left-hand side of the equation are written with no fractions, and only 0 is on the right-hand side. Sometimes the general form is neater and more convenient.

EXTENSION

Video
The general equation $ax + by + c = 0$

ⓘ The general form of a linear equation

The **general form of a linear equation** is written as $ax + by + c = 0$, where a, b and c are integers and a is positive.

Worksheet
Parallel and perpendicular lines

Example 15

Write each linear equation in general form.

a $y = 6x + 2$
b $y = -\frac{2}{3}x + 2$
c $y = 2x - \frac{3}{5}$

Puzzle
Linear equations code puzzle

SOLUTION

a
$$y = 6x + 2$$
$$0 = 6x - y + 2 \qquad \text{subtracting } y \text{ from both sides}$$
$$6x - y + 2 = 0 \qquad \text{swapping sides so that 0 appears on the RHS}$$

b
$$y = -\frac{2}{3}x + 2$$
$$3y = 3\left(-\frac{2}{3}x + 2\right) \qquad \text{multiplying both sides by 3 to remove the fraction}$$
$$3y = -2x + 6$$
$$2x + 3y = 6 \qquad \text{adding } 2x \text{ to both sides}$$
$$2x + 3y - 6 = 0 \qquad \text{subtracting 6 from both sides}$$

c $y = 2x - \frac{3}{5}$
$$5y = 5\left(2x - \frac{3}{5}\right) \qquad \text{multiplying both sides by 5}$$
$$5y = 10x - 3$$
$$0 = 10x - 5y - 3 \qquad \text{subtracting } 5y \text{ from both sides}$$
$$10x - 5y - 3 = 0 \qquad \text{swapping sides so that 0 appears on the RHS}$$

Example 16

Find the gradient and y-intercept of the line whose equation is $5x + 2y - 10 = 0$.

SOLUTION

Rewrite $5x + 2y - 10$ in the form $y = mx + c$.

Make y the subject, solve for y.

$5x + 2y - 10 = 0$

$\qquad 2y - 10 = -5x$ subtracting $5x$ from both sides

$\qquad\quad 2y = -5x + 10$ adding 10 to both sides

$\qquad\quad\ y = \dfrac{-5x + 10}{2}$ dividing both sides by 2

$\qquad\qquad = \dfrac{-5x}{2} + 5$ Aim to have y on its own on the LHS of the equation.

∴ gradient, $m = -\dfrac{5}{2}$ and y-intercept, $c = 5$.

EXERCISE 1.05   ANSWERS ON P. 601

The general equation $ax + by + c = 0$ U F R C

 1 Write each linear equation in general form.

R   **a** $y = x + 2$ **b** $y = 3x - 1$ **c** $y = 8 + 5x$

C   **d** $x + 2y = 3$ **e** $x - 2y = 6$ **f** $y = 8x + 2$

    g $y + 3 = 6x$ **h** $2y = x - 6$ **i** $y = \dfrac{3}{5}x + 2$

 2 Find the gradient and y-intercept of the line with equation:

R   **a** $2x + y = 6$ **b** $8x - 2y = 10$ **c** $3x - 2y + 4 = 0$

C   **d** $y + 2x - 1 = 0$ **e** $2x + y + 5 = 0$ **f** $4x + 3y - 12 = 0$

3 Find the gradient, m, and the y-intercept, c, of the line with equation $x - 3y + 5 = 0$.
Select **A**, **B**, **C** or **D**.

   A $m = -1, c = 5$ **B** $m = \dfrac{1}{3}, c = \dfrac{5}{3}$ **C** $m = 1, c = -5$ **D** $m = \dfrac{1}{3}, c = -\dfrac{5}{3}$

4 Which statement is FALSE about the line whose equation is $3x + y - 6 = 0$?
R   Select **A**, **B**, **C** or **D**.

C   **A**   Its gradient is –3.   **B**   Its y-intercept is –6.

    C   Its x-intercept is 2.   **D**   It is parallel to the line $y = -3x$.

▷

□ Foundation   ○ Standard   ○ Complex

5 Express each linear equation in general form.

R **C**

a $y = \dfrac{x}{3} + \dfrac{1}{4}$ **b** $y = -\dfrac{5x}{8} + \dfrac{3}{2}$ **c** $y = \dfrac{3x}{4} - \dfrac{2}{5}$

d $y = -\dfrac{x}{2} - \dfrac{3}{4}$ **e** $y = \dfrac{3x}{2} + \dfrac{2}{5}$ **f** $y = -\dfrac{9x}{10} - \dfrac{7}{15}$

INVESTIGATION

A line, its gradient and a point

1 The graph shows the line $y = 3x - 2$.

   a What is its gradient?

   b If (x, y) is any other point on the line, show that $m = \dfrac{y-1}{x-1}$.

   c Explain why $\dfrac{y-1}{x-1} = 3$

   d Hence show that this equation simplifies to $y = 3x - 2$.

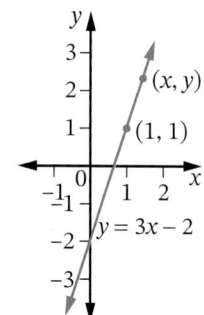

2 The graph shows the line $y = -\dfrac{5}{2}x + 3$.

   a What is its gradient?

   b If (x, y) is any other point on the line, show that $m = \dfrac{y+2}{x-2}$.

   c Explain why $\dfrac{y+2}{x-2} = -\dfrac{5}{2}$

   d Hence show that this equation simplifies to $y = -\dfrac{5}{2}x + 3$.

3 The equation of a line is given by $\dfrac{y-2}{x-7} = \dfrac{3}{4}$.

   a What is the gradient of the line?

   b Can you give the coordinates of a point on this line by looking at its equation? Why?

4 Write the equation of a line that passes through the point $(-3, 5)$ and has a gradient equal to 2. Compare your result with other groups.

5 A line with gradient m passes through the point (x_1, y_1).

   a Show that $m = \dfrac{y - y_1}{x - x_1}$, where (x, y) is any other point on the line.

   b Explain why $y - y_1 = m(x - x_1)$.

□ Foundation   ○ Standard   ◇ Complex

Extension: The point–gradient equation $y - y_1 = m(x - x_1)$

There is a formula for finding the equation of a line if we know its gradient m and a point on the line (x_1, y_1).

Let (x, y) be any other point on the line.

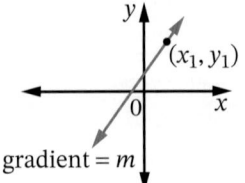

Then $m = \dfrac{y - y_1}{x - x_1}$

or $y - y_1 = m(x - x_1)$.

This is called the **point–gradient form** of a linear equation.

> ### ⓘ The point–gradient form of a linear equation
>
> The equation of a line with gradient m and which passes through the point (x_1, y_1) is:
>
> $$y - y_1 = m(x - x_1)$$

Example 17

Video
The point–gradient formula

Find the equation of the line with a gradient of $\dfrac{2}{3}$ that passes through the point $(-2, 1)$.

SOLUTION

$m = \dfrac{2}{3}, x_1 = -2, y_1 = 1.$

$y - y_1 = m(x - x_1)$

$y - 1 = \dfrac{2}{3}[x - (-2)]$

$3(y - 1) = 2(x + 2)$

$3y - 3 = 2x + 4$

$0 = 2x - 3y + 7$

$2x - 3y + 7 = 0$

In general form

Example 18

Video
The point–gradient formula

Find the equation of the line passing through the points $(1, 3)$ and $(4, -3)$.

SOLUTION

First find the gradient of the line by using the points $(1, 3)$ and $(4, -3)$.

$m = \dfrac{-3 - 3}{4 - 1}$ (x_1, y_1) (x_2, y_2)

$\quad = \dfrac{-6}{3}$

$\quad = -2$

Now use $y - y_1 = m(x - x_1)$ with $m = -2$ and $(1, 3)$.

$y - 3 = -2(x - 1)$

$\quad\;\; = -2x + 2$

$y = -2x + 5$ or $2x + y - 5 = 0$ in general form

> Either point $(1, 3)$ or $(4, -3)$ can be used to find the equation of the line.

OR: using the other point (4, –3) instead:

$$y - (-3) = -2(x - 4)$$
$$y + 3 = -2x + 8$$
$$y = -2x + 5 \qquad \text{or} \qquad 2x + y - 5 = 0 \text{ in general form}$$

EXERCISE 1.06 ANSWERS ON P. 601

The point–gradient equation $y - y_1 = m(x - x_1)$ (U)(F)(R)(C)

In this exercise, express all equations of lines in general form.

1 Find the equation of each line, given a point on the line and the gradient.

   a (2, 5), gradient 2

   b (–6, 4), gradient –1

   c (3, –8), gradient 4

   d (–1, –2), gradient $\frac{2}{3}$

   e (2, –8), gradient $-\frac{1}{5}$

   f (–1, 7), gradient –3

   g $\left(\frac{1}{2}, -3\right)$, gradient –4

   h $\left(-4, -\frac{1}{2}\right)$, gradient $\frac{3}{4}$

   i (–2, –6), gradient –2

EXAMPLE
17

2 4 lines a, b, c and d intersect at $P(3, -2)$.

(R)(C) The gradients of a, b, c and d are 1, $-\frac{1}{3}$, –4 and $\frac{1}{5}$, respectively.

   a Copy the diagram and correctly label the lines a, b, c and d.

   b Find the equation of each line.

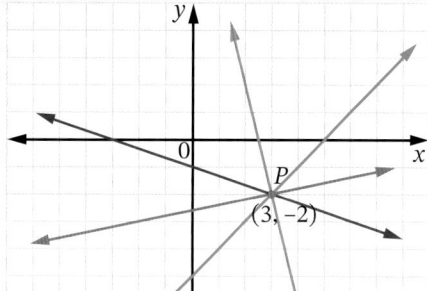

3 Find the equation of the line passing through each pair of points.

   a (7, 3) and (10, 6)

   b (8, 10) and (–2, 2)

   c (–1, 3) and (5, 8)

   d (2, –2) and (–1, 6)

   e (4, –3) and (6, –6)

   f (–1, –2) and (2, 3)

   g (–10, 2) and (1, –4)

   h (–3, 6) and (1, 2)

   i (–4, –9) and (–1, –5)

EXAMPLE
18

4 2 lines k and l intersect at (–1, 4). Line k has a gradient of $-\frac{1}{2}$, while line l has a gradient of 3. Find the equations of lines k and l.

(R)(C)

5 Find the equation of a line with a gradient of –4 and an x-intercept of 5.

(R)(C)

6 A line passes through the y-axis at (0, 6) and has a gradient of $\frac{5}{7}$. What is its equation?

(R)(C)

☐ Foundation   ○ Standard   ○ Complex

▷

7 A line with a gradient of $\frac{2}{3}$ passes through the midpoint of (5, 6) and (1, 10).

(R) Find the equation of the line.

(C)

8 A line with a gradient of $-\frac{3}{5}$ passes through the midpoint of (−8, −2) and (−2, 20).

(R) Find its equation.

(C)

9 The gradient–intercept form of a line, $y = mx + c$, can also be used to find the equation

(R) of a line, given its gradient and a point on the line.

(C) **a** Use $y = mx + c$ to find the equation of the line with gradient 2 that passes through the point (2, 5).

b Compare your equation with your answer to question **1a**.

10 The point–gradient formula can be converted to a formula for finding the equation of a

(R) line passing through 2 points (x_1, y_1) and (x_2, y_2).

(C) **a** Prove that the 'two-point formula' is $\frac{y - y_1}{x - x_1} = \frac{y_2 - y_1}{x_2 - x_1}$.

b Use the two-point form to find the equation of a line passing through the points (7, 3) and (10, 6).

c Compare your equation with your answer to question **3a**.

1.07 Finding the equation of a line

Example 19

Find the equation of each line.

a

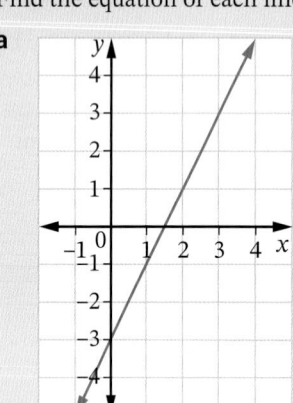

b

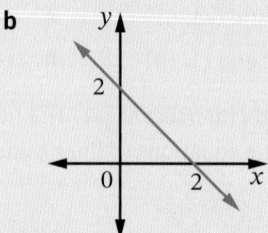

□ Foundation   ○ Standard   ○ Complex

SOLUTION

a Select 2 points on the line to find the gradient, say (0, –3) and (2, 1).

gradient: $m = \dfrac{\text{rise}}{\text{run}} = \dfrac{4}{2} = 2$ from the graph

y-intercept: $c = -3$

∴ the equation of the line is $y = 2x - 3$. $y = mx + c$

We can check that this equation is correct for any point on the line, say (3, 3).

When $x = 3$, $y = 2 \times 3 - 3 = 3$.

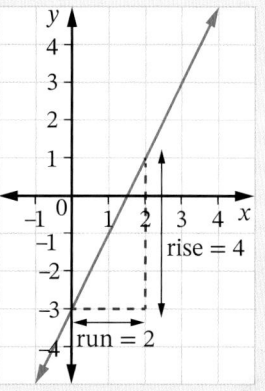

b Find the gradient of the line passing through (0, 2) and (2, 0).

gradient: $m = \dfrac{\text{rise}}{\text{run}} = \dfrac{-2}{2} = -1$ from the graph

y-intercept: $c = 2$

∴ the equation of the line is $y = -x + 2$. $y = mx + c$

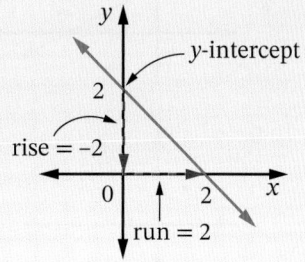

EXERCISE **1.07** ANSWERS ON P. 601

Finding the equation of a line   U F R C

1 Find the equation of each line.

EXAMPLE
19

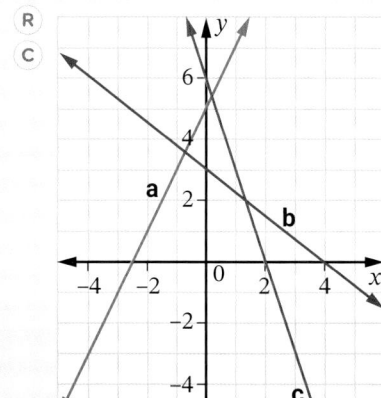

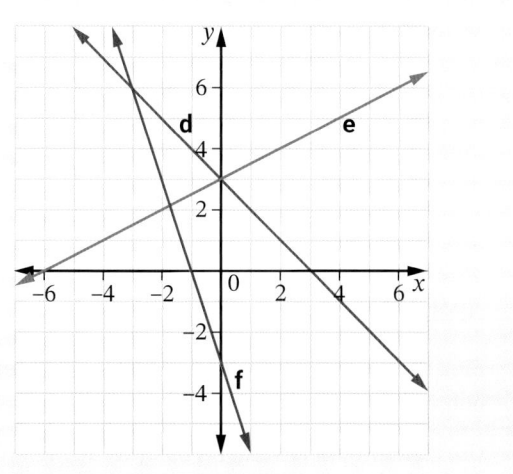

☐ Foundation   ⬡ Standard   ⬡ Complex

2 Find the equation of each line.

R **C**

a

(4, 4)
2
0
y
x

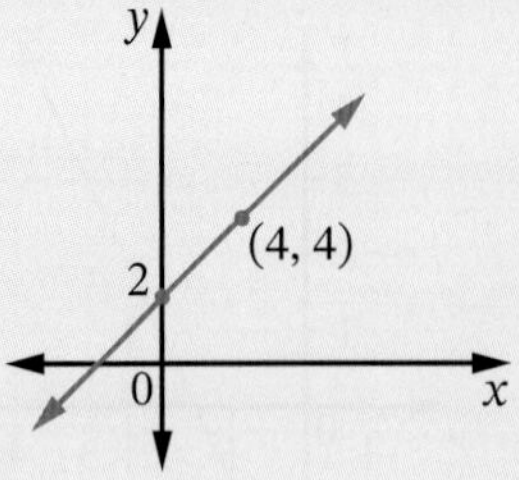

b
(3, 3)
0
y
x

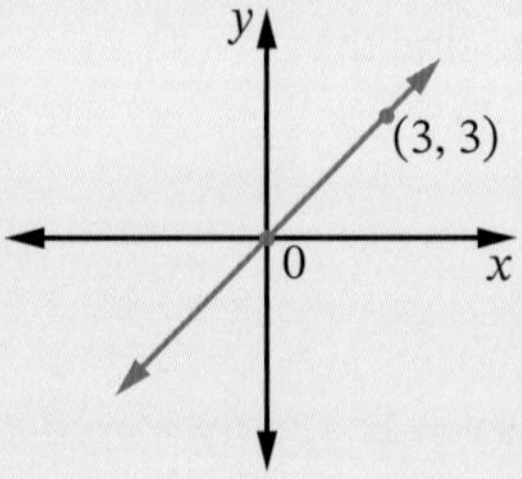

c
(−8, 9)
5
0
y
x

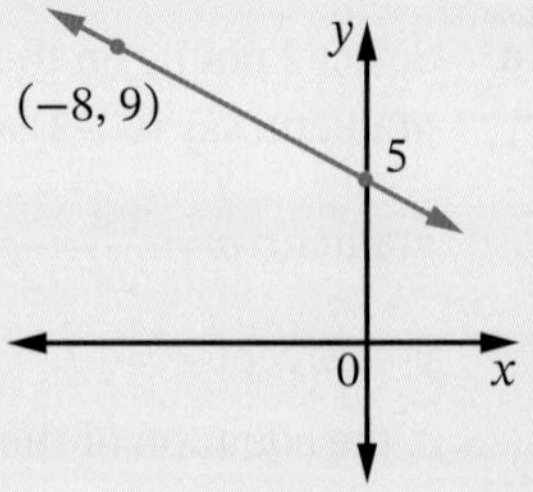

d
3
6
0
y
x

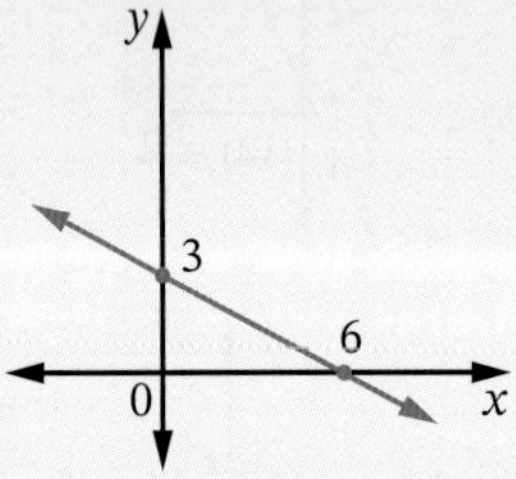

e
−1
0
−3
y
x

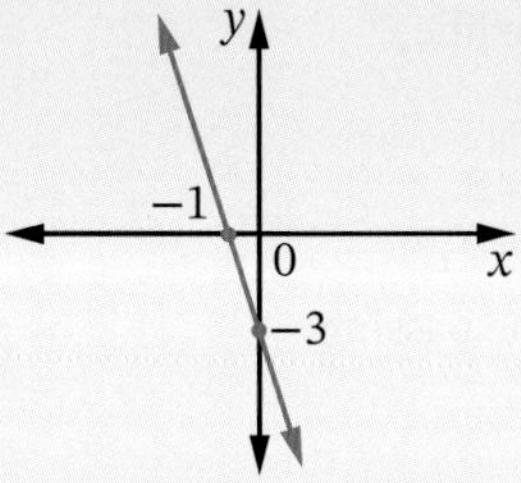

f
(−4, 2)
0
−2
y
x

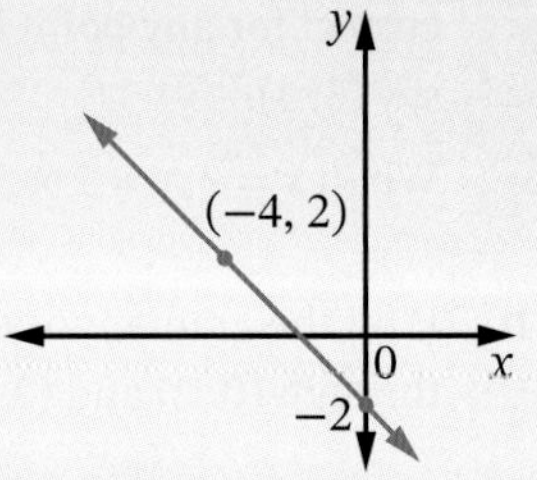

g
(5, 5)
0
−10
y
x

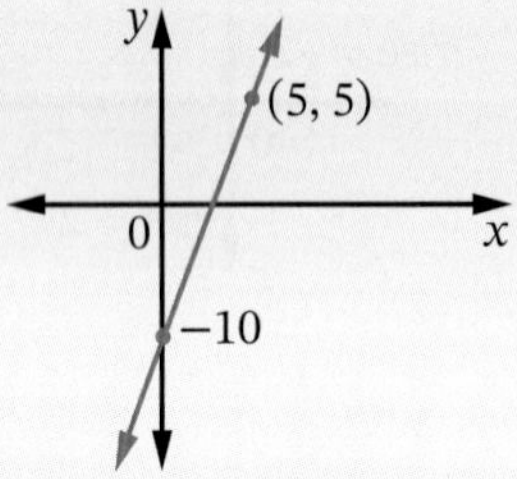

h
2
−5
0
y
x

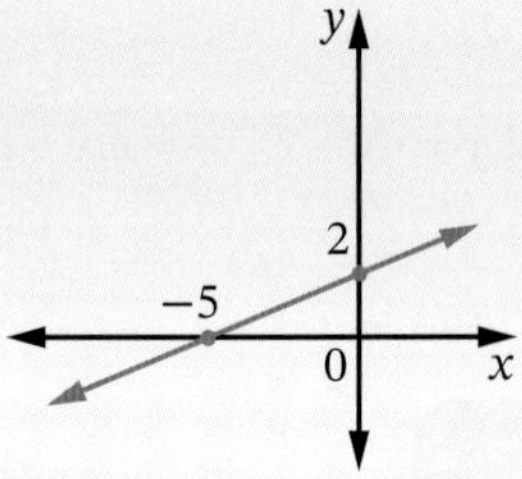

i
1.5
0
−3
y
x

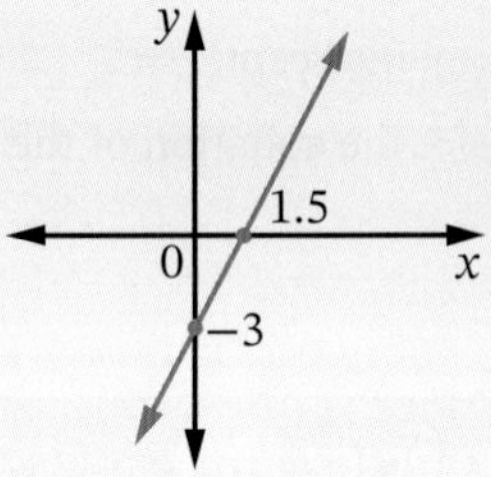

INVESTIGATION

Sausage sizzle

A local football club is organising a sausage sizzle on Saturday to raise money to buy new equipment. It costs $50 to hire a gas bottle to run the barbecue and each sausage in bread costs $1 to make. They hope to sell 100 sausages in bread.

1   Copy and complete this table to show the cost of making sausages in bread. Include the cost of hiring the gas bottle.

No. of sausages in bread (x)	0	10	20	30	40	50	60	70	80	90	100
Cost ($y)	50	60									

2   Find the linear equation (formula) for *y* that represents the cost of making *x* sausages in bread.

3   Use an appropriate scale to construct a graph that shows the cost of making from *x* = 0 to 100 sausages in bread. Label your axes and give your graph an appropriate title.

4   How much will it cost to make 35 sausages in bread?

5   How many sausages in bread can be made for $132?

6   How much would it cost to make 120 sausages in bread?

7   a   If the club sold all 100 sausages in bread for $5 each, how much money would they take?

   b   How much profit would the club make?

Equations of parallel and perpendicular lines

Example 20

Find the equation of the line parallel to $y = 8 - 3x$ that passes through the point $(-1, 6)$.

SOLUTION

Worksheet
Writing equations of lines

For $y = 8 - 3x$ (or $y = -3x + 8$), the gradient is $m = -3$.

A line parallel to $y = 8 - 3x$, will also have $m = -3$.

Using the point–gradient formula $y - y_1 = m(x - x_1)$ with $m = -3$ and point $(-1, 6)$:

$y - 6 = -3[x - (-1)]$

$\quad\;\; = -3(x + 1)$

$\quad\;\; = -3x - 3$

$\quad y = -3x + 3$

EXTENSION

OR: Using the gradient-intercept equation $y = mx + c = -3x + c$, where c is a constant.

To find the value of c, substitute the point $(-1, 6)$ into the equation:

$y = -3x + c$

$6 = -3 \times (-1) + c \qquad\qquad x = -1, y = 6$

$6 = 3 + c$

$c = 3$

$\therefore$ the equation is $y = -3x + 3$.

Video
Equations of parallel lines

Puzzles
Linear equations match-up

Equations of parallel lines

Example 21

Find the equation of the line perpendicular to $3x - 4y + 6 = 0$ that passes through the point $(5, 4)$.

Video
Equations of perpendicular lines

SOLUTION

To find the gradient of $3x - 4y + 6 = 0$, first convert it to the form $y = mx + c$:

$3x - 4y + 6 = 0$

$\qquad 3x + 6 = 4y$

$\qquad\quad 4y = 3x + 6$

$\qquad\qquad y = \dfrac{3x + 6}{4}$

$\qquad\qquad y = \dfrac{3}{4}x + \dfrac{3}{2}$ $\qquad\qquad\qquad y = mx + c$

$\therefore$ gradient $= \dfrac{3}{4}$

$\therefore$ gradient of perpendicular line $= \dfrac{-1}{\left(\dfrac{3}{4}\right)}$ $\qquad$ the negative reciprocal of $\dfrac{3}{4}$

$\qquad\qquad\qquad\qquad\qquad = -\dfrac{4}{3}$

EXTENSION

Using the point–gradient formula $y - y_1 = m(x - x_1)$

$\qquad\qquad y - 4 = -\dfrac{4}{3}(x - 5)$ $\qquad\qquad x_1 = 5, y_1 = 4$

$\qquad 3(y - 4) = -4(x - 5)$

$\qquad 3y - 12 = -4x + 20$

$4x + 3y - 32 = 0$ $\qquad\qquad\qquad\qquad$ In general form.

OR: Using $y = mx + c$, the equation of this line is $y = -\dfrac{4x}{3} + c$

To find the value of c, substitute the point $(5, 4)$ into the equation.

$4 = \left(-\dfrac{4}{3}\right) \times 5 + c$

$\quad = -\dfrac{20}{3} + c$

$c = \dfrac{32}{3}$

$\therefore$ the equation is $y = -\dfrac{4x}{3} + \dfrac{32}{3}$ or $y = \dfrac{-4x + 32}{3}$.

Converting to general form: $4x + 3y - 32 = 0$

Equations of parallel and perpendicular lines (U)(F)(R)(C)

1 Find the equation of the line that is parallel to:

EXAMPLE
20

(R) **a** $y = 2x + 9$ and has a y-intercept of 4

(C) **b** $y = 3x$ and has an x-intercept of –2

c $y = 5 - \dfrac{x}{2}$. and passes through $(-1, 6)$

d $2x - y = 6$ and passes through $(5, -2)$

e $y = -5x - 8$ and passes through the midpoint of $(3, -10)$ and $(-5, -6)$

f $2y = x - 3$ and passes through $(6, -7)$

2 Find the equation of a line that is perpendicular to:

EXAMPLE
21

(R) **a** $y = \dfrac{x}{2}$ and has a y-intercept of –2

(C)

b $y = -5x$ and has an x-intercept of 1

c $y = 3x - 1$ and passes through the x-axis at 4

d $y = \dfrac{x-6}{3}$ and passes through $(1, -6)$

e $x + y - 6 = 0$ and passes through $(-4, 2)$

f $3x - y - 9 = 0$ and passes through $(-10, -7)$

3 a Find the gradient of interval ST in the diagram.

b Find the midpoint of ST.

c The dotted line is perpendicular to ST and passes through its midpoint. What is its gradient?

d Find the equation of the dotted line, in the form $y = mx + c$.

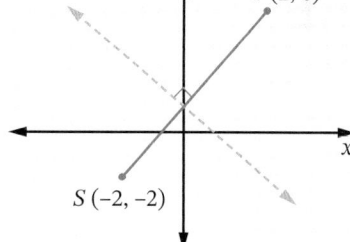

4 a Find the equation of line h in the diagram.

(R) **b** Find the gradient of line j (which is

(C) perpendicular to line h).

c Find the equation of line j.

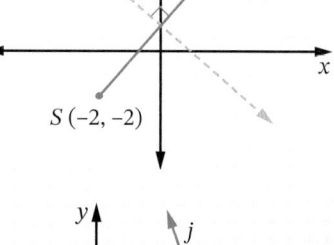

5 a Find the equation of line k.

(R) **b** Find the coordinates of point A.

(C) **c** Find the gradient of line w.

d Find the equation of line w.

e Find the coordinates of point B.

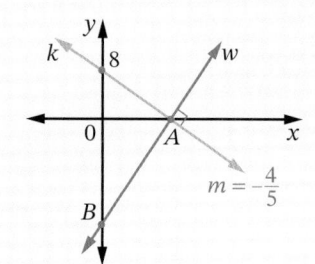

Constants

Expressions like 'k is a constant' are often used in mathematics, but constants are also used in areas such as physics, chemistry, biology and astronomy. A constant may be:

- a numerical part of an algebraic expression. For example, in the expression $3x^2 + 5$, the 3 and 5 are constants and 5 is usually called the constant term.

- a quantity that has a fixed value for an expression or calculation. For example, in the equation of a line, $ax + by + c = 0$, the a, b and c are constants (while x and y are variables).

- a number or quantity that does not change in any circumstances. Examples are c (the speed of light) in the formula $E = mc^2$ and π.

Other constants that do not change include Faraday's constant, Planck's constant, Boltzmann's constant, Avogadro's number, 1 astronomical unit, and the gravitational constant.

1   **Find the symbol and value of each of the constants listed above.**

2   **Explain the meaning of the word 'constants' in this saying:**
    'There are only 2 constants in life—death and taxes'.

Regions on the number plane

This is the graph of $y = 3x + 2$ from page 18.

Every point on the line, such as $(-1, -1)$, $(0, 2)$ and $(1, 5)$, satisfies the equation $y = 3x + 2$.

It then follows that any point *not* on the line does *not* satisfy the equation $y = 3x + 2$.

So for any point *not* on the line, it either satisfies the inequality $y > 3x + 2$ or $y < 3x + 2$.

For example, $(5, 1)$ does not lie on the line.

Substitute $x = 5$, $y = 1$ into $y = 3x + 2$.

LHS $= y$ RHS $= 3 \times 5 + 2$

     $= 1$ $= 17$

LHS $<$ RHS, so $(5, 1)$ satisfies the inequality $y < 3x + 2$.

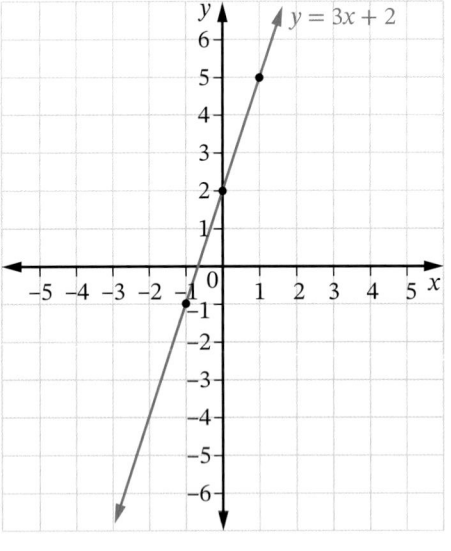

1 Copy this table.

Point	$y > 3x + 2$	$y < 3x + 2$
(5, 1)		✓
(3, 3)		
(−4, 2)		
(−2, −6)		
(0, −3)		
(2, −2)		

2 Test each point in the table for $y = 3x + 2$ and tick whether it satisfies the inequality $y > 3x + 2$ or $y < 3x + 2$. The last 4 rows have been left blank for you to choose points that are not on the line.

3 Do you notice a pattern between the points that satisfy $y > 3x + 2$? Can you describe it in words?

Graphing linear inequalities

$y = 3x + 2$ is a linear equation and its graph on the number plane is a line.

$y > 3x + 2$ (or $y < 3x + 2$) is a **linear inequality** and its graph on the number plane is a **region**.

Any line drawn on a number plane divides the plane into 2 regions or 'half-planes'.

Video
Graphing linear inequalities

ⓘ Linear inequalities on the number plane

The graph of $y = mx + c$ divides the number plane into 2 regions.

The region 'above' the line is the graph of $y > mx + c$.

The region 'below' the line is the graph of $y < mx + c$.

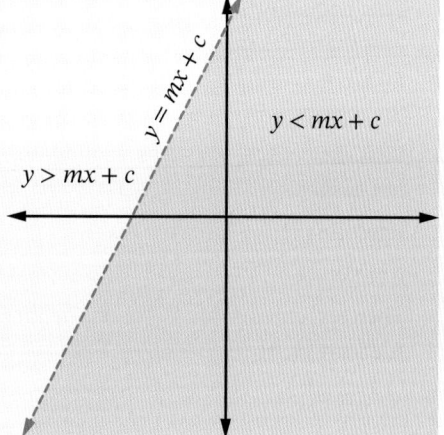

Worksheet
A page of lines and regions

Example 22

Graph the linear inequality $y > 2x - 1$ on a number plane.

SOLUTION

First sketch $y = 2x - 1$ as a dashed (broken) line, because it is not part of the region of the inequality.

Then test a point that is not on the line, an 'easy' point such as $(0, 0)$.

$y = 2x - 1$

$\text{LHS} = 0$

$\text{RHS} = 2 \times 0 - 1$

$\quad\;\; = -1$

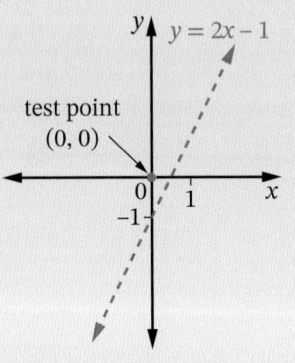

$\text{LHS} > \text{RHS}$, so $(0, 0)$ lies in the region or half-plane where $y > 2x - 1$, so shade and label that region.

Note that the shaded region is 'above' the line $y = 2x - 1$.

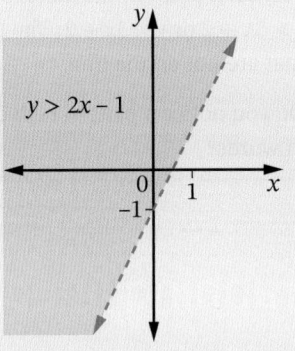

Example 23

Graph each linear inequality on a number plane.

a $3x + y \leq -2$ **b** $x < 2$ **c** $y \geq 3$

SOLUTION

a   The inequality $3x + y \leq -2$ involves '$\leq$', 'less than or equal to', so the line $3x + y = -2$ will be included with the region.

First sketch $3x + y = -2$ as a solid line, not dashed.

Rewriting in the form $y = mx + c$.

$y = -3x - 2$

Then test a point that is not on the line, such as $(-3, 0)$.

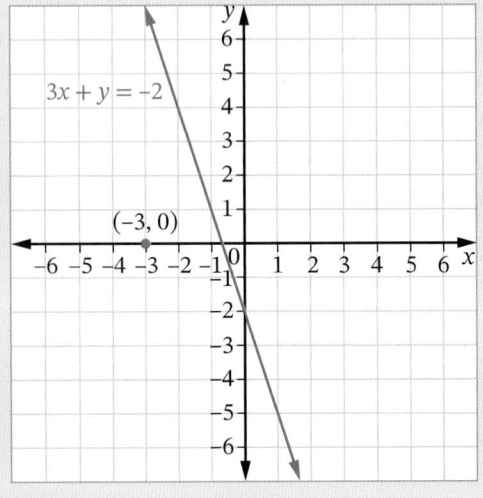

$3x + y = -2$

$LHS = 3 \times (-3) + 0$

$\qquad = -9$

$RHS = -2$

LHS < RHS, so $(-3, 0)$ lies in the region or half-plane where $3x + y < -2$, so shade and label that region.

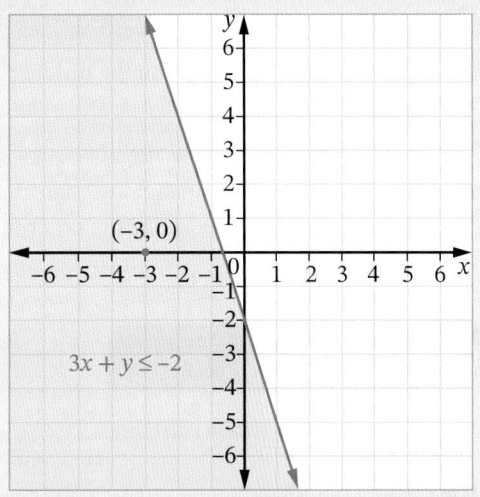

b First, sketch $x = 2$ as a dashed vertical line.

To graph $x < 2$, we want the half of the plane where the points have x-coordinates that are less than 2.

This would be the region on the left side of the line.

For example, for $(0, 0)$, $0 < 2$.

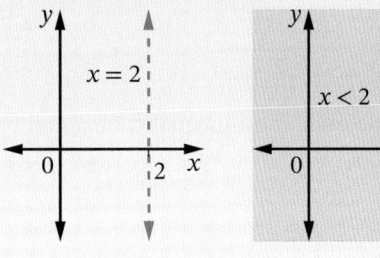

c First, sketch $y = -3$ as a solid horizontal line, as it is included in the region $y \geq -3$.

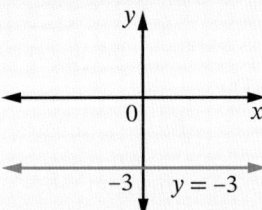

To graph $y \geq -3$, we want the half of the plane where the points have y-coordinates that are greater than -3. This would be the region above the line.

For example, for $(0, 0)$, $0 \geq -3$.

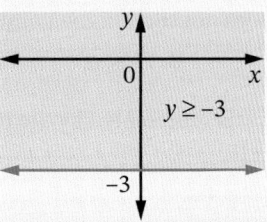

ⓘ Graphing linear inequalities on the number plane

1   Graph the linear equation on the number plane first. If the inequality involves > or <, then graph a dashed line.

2   Test a point on one side of the line.

3   If it satisfies the linear inequality, then shade the region or half-plane that contains that point. If it doesn't, then shade the other region or half-plane.

4   Label the region with the linear inequality.

EXERCISE 1.09   ANSWERS ON P. 602

Graphing linear inequalities   U F PS R C

EXAMPLE 22

1   Graph each linear inequality on a number plane.

R **a** $y \geq 2x$ **b** $y > 7 - x$ **c** $y \leq 1 - x$

C **d** $y \geq 4x + 2$ **e** $y > 2 - x$ **f** $y \leq 3x - 4$

EXAMPLE 23

2   Graph each linear inequality on a number plane.

R **a** $y > 2$ **b** $y \leq 1$ **c** $x \leq 3$

C **d** $x \geq -4$ **e** $y < -2$ **f** $x < 2$

3   Which point lies in the region represented by the inequality $y > 4 - x$? Select **A**, **B**, **C** or **D**.

   A $(-1, -1)$ **B** $(5, 1)$ **C** $(0, 0)$ **D** $(4, 0)$

4   Which point does not lie in the region represented by the inequality $2y - x \geq 6$? Select **A**, **B**, **C** or **D**.

   A $(4, 0)$ **B** $(-6, 0)$ **C** $(0, 4)$ **D** $(-2, 8)$

5   Which region contains the point $(-6, -2)$? Select **A**, **B**, **C** or **D**.

   A $x < -8$ **B** $y < -3$ **C** $y + 2 \leq -2x$ **D** $y \leq x$

6   Which region does not contain the point $(5, 4)$? Select **A**, **B**, **C** or **D**.

   A $x + y \leq 10$ **B** $x \leq 6$ **C** $y > 0$ **D** $y > x - 1$

7   Which inequality is represented by the region shown? Select **A**, **B**, **C** or **D**.

   A $2x + y < 2$

   B $2x + y > 2$

   C $2x + y \leq 2$

   D $2x + y \geq 2$

8   Graph each linear inequality on a number plane.

R **a** $y > x - 12$ **b** $x - y \geq -5$ **c** $4 - y > x$ **d** $y \geq 2x - 5$

C **c** $2y \leq -4x + 12$ **d** $6x + 3y > 12$ **e** $-2y \leq 6 - x$ **f** $-24x - 8y > -48$

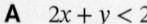

☐ Foundation   ○ Standard   ○ Complex

9 Find the linear inequality represented by each region shown.

a
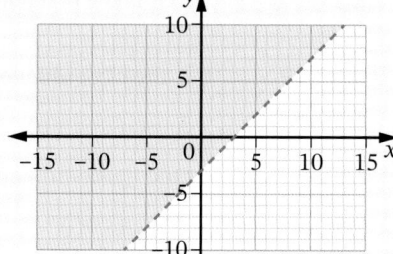

b
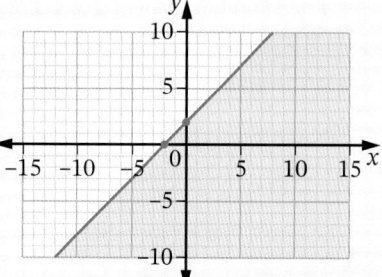

c
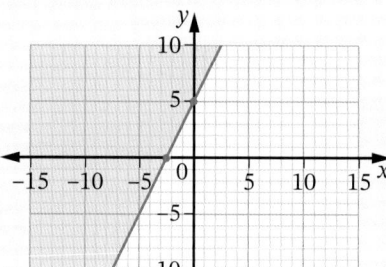

d
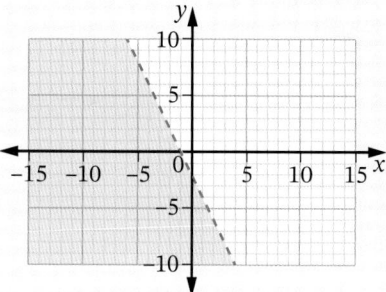

e
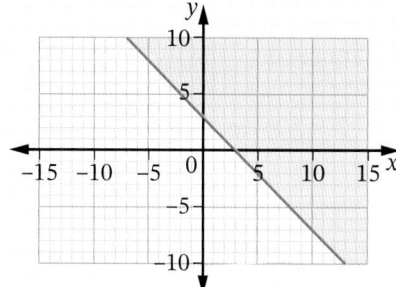

f
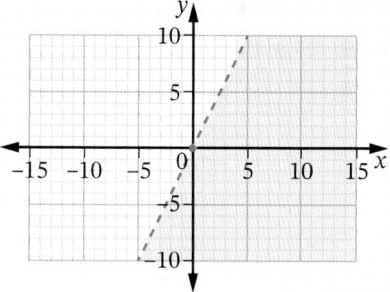

10 The local soccer club is having a fete to raise funds for upgrades to their fields. They will get to keep the money from the sale of entry tickets. The upgrade will cost the club $6000. The club will sell adult tickets for $30 each and children's tickets for $15 each.

a Let x be the number of adult tickets sold and y be the number of children's tickets sold. The club needs to raise at least $6000. Write an inequality to represent this situation.

b Simplify the inequality.

c Graph the inequality on a number plane and determine 5 combinations of ticket sales that will generate the $6000 required for the upgrade.

11 A scooter hire business has weekly expenses of $1600. They hire out electric scooters for $25 a day, or regular scooters for $10 a day. Use an inequality to suggest combinations for the number of regular and electric scooters the business must hire out every week in order to cover the costs of $1600.

□ Foundation   ○ Standard   ◇ Complex

1   A line is drawn through the points $A(0, -2)$ and $B(3, 0)$. The x-coordinate of a point C on AB is 9. Find:

   a   the gradient of AB b   the equation of AB c   the y-coordinate of C.

2   The point $(-1, 6)$ lies on the line $kx + 3y - 13 = 0$, where k is a constant number. Find k.

3   $Z(-1, 3)$ is the midpoint of the interval joining $A(-4, 7)$ and B. Find the coordinates of B.

4   The circle has XY as a diameter and centre Z. What are the coordinates of X?

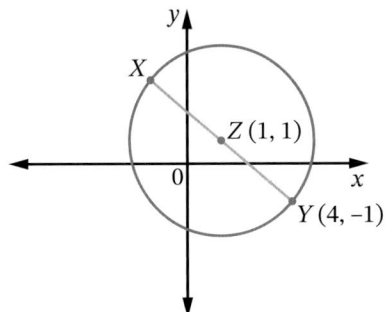

5   Show that the points $(4, 2)$, $(10, -4)$ and $(1, 5)$ are collinear.

6   a   Find the gradient of any line parallel to $3x + 2y = 4$.

   b   Find the equation of the line that passes through the point $(0, -1)$ and is parallel to $3x + 2y = 4$.

7   $A(-1, 4)$, $B(4, 6)$, $C(2, 7)$ and D are the vertices of a parallelogram. Find the coordinates of D.

Language of maths

axes	distance	exact answer	general form
gradient	gradient–intercept form	horizontal	interval
length	linear function	inequality	midpoint
parallel	perpendicular	point-gradient form	reciprocal
rise	run	surd	vertical
x-axis	*x*-intercept	*y*-axis	*y*-intercept

Quiz
Language of maths 1

Puzzle
Graphing lines crossword

1 What is the difference between the *y*-axis and the *y*-intercept?

2 When finding the length of an interval on a number plane, what is meant by an *exact* answer?

3 What measurement is the fraction given by the vertical rise of a line divided by the horizontal run?

4 What is the everyday meaning of the word *intercept*? Look it up in a dictionary.

5 What is the property of the gradients of perpendicular lines?

6 What are the 4 inequality symbols and what is the meaning of each one?

Topic summary

Worksheet
Mind map: Graphing lines

- How can you find the gradient of a line?
- What is $y = mx + c$?
- How can you test whether a pair of lines are parallel?
- What parts of this topic did you find difficult?

Print (or copy) and complete this mind map of the topic, adding detail to its branches and using pictures, symbols and colour where needed. Ask your teacher to check your work.

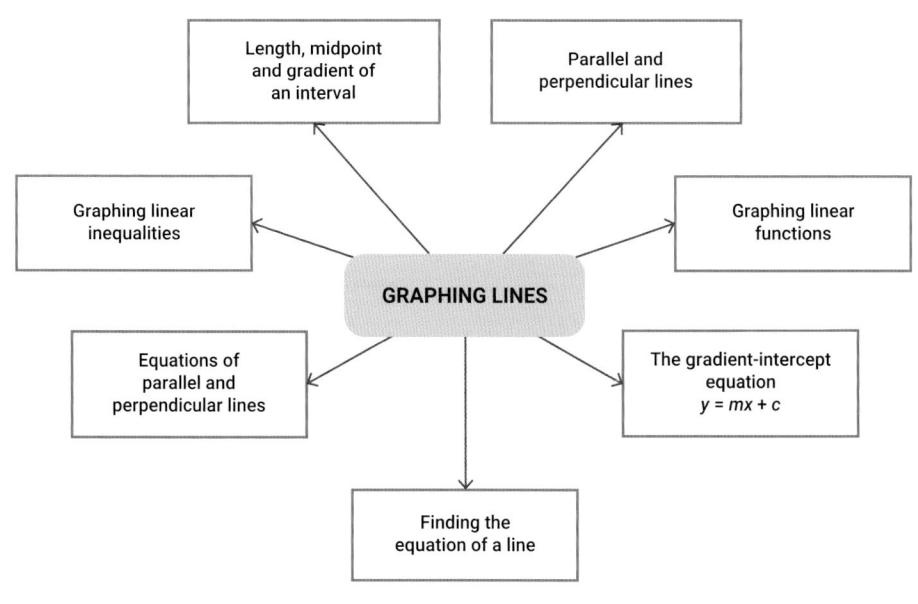

1 TEST YOURSELF
ANSWERS ON P. 604

1.01

EXTENSION

1 The vertices of a quadrilateral *HJKL* are *H*(−8, −5), *J*(−1, −2), *K*(2, 5) and *L*(−5, 2).

    a Find the exact length of the sides of the quadrilateral.

    b Find the gradient of each side of *HJKL*.

    c Find the exact length of the diagonals *HK* and *JL*.

    d What type of quadrilateral is *HJKL*?

1.01

2 Find, correct to the nearest degree, the angle of inclination of a line with gradient:

    a 3   **b** $\dfrac{5}{4}$ **c** −1   **d** $-\dfrac{2}{3}$

1.02

3 A line passes through the points *V*(8, −1) and *W*(10, −2). What is the gradient of a line:

    a parallel to *VW*?   **b** perpendicular to *VW*?

1.03

4 Graph each linear equation on a number plane.

    a $y = -5x - 1$ **b** $x + 2y = 16$ **c** $3x - 4y - 12 = 0$

1.03

5 Which point lies on the line of $3x + y = 2$? Select **A**, **B**, **C** or **D**.

    A (1, 0)   **B** (2, 4)   **C** (−1, 5)   **D** (−1, −5)

1.04

6 Write the gradient, *m*, and *y*-intercept, *c*, for each linear function.

    a $y = 2x - 10$ **b** $y = 4x + 3$ **c** $y = \dfrac{4 - 3x}{8}$

1.04

7 Match each equation to its graph below.

    a $y = 2x - 3$ **b** $y = -2x - 3$ **c** $y = -2x + 3$ **d** $y = 2x + 3$

A

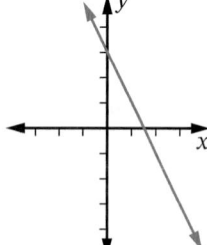

B

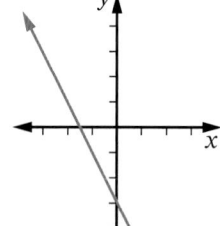

C

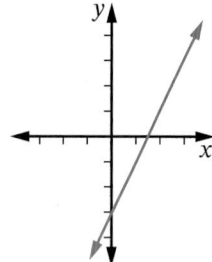

D

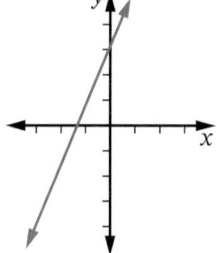

☐ Foundation   ○ Standard   ○ Complex

8 Convert each equation to the form $y = mx + c$, then state the gradient, m, and the y-intercept, c of its graph.

 1.04

EXTENSION

a $x - y + 2 = 0$ **b** $2x - 8y + 8 = 0$ **c** $3x + y - 9 = 0$

9 Convert each equation to general form $ax + by + c = 0$.

1.05

a $y = 3x + 5$ **b** $y = \dfrac{2x}{5} - 10$ **c** $x = 3y + 6$

10 Find in general form the equation of a line that passes through the point:

1.06

a $(5, 5)$ and has a gradient of -3 **b** $(-1, 8)$ and has a gradient of $\dfrac{2}{3}$

11 Find in general form the equation of a line that passes through the points:

1.06

a $(10, 2)$ and $(5, -1)$ **b** $(-6, 3)$ and $(-2, -1)$

12 Find the equation of each line and show that they are perpendicular.

1.07

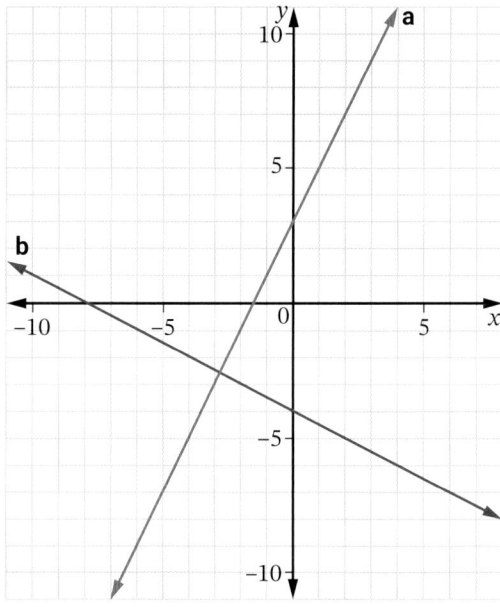

13 Find the equation of a line that is:

1.08

a parallel to $y = 3x + 1$ and passes through the x-axis at 2

b perpendicular to $y = \dfrac{x}{2}$ and passes through the origin.

EXTENSION

14 The line $3x - 8y + 10 = 0$ and another line intersect at right angles at the point $(10, 5)$. Find the equation of the other line.

1.08

15 Graph each linear inequality on a number plane.

1.09

a $y > 2x - 8$ **b** $-2y \geq 6x + 14$

☐ Foundation ○ Standard ◇ Complex

2

Surface area and volume

Some theme parks have wave pools, large swimming pools that simulate the movement of the water at a beach. A large volume of water is quickly released into one end of the pool, which produces a large wave that moves from one end of the pool to the other. The excess water from each wave recycles back to produce more waves.

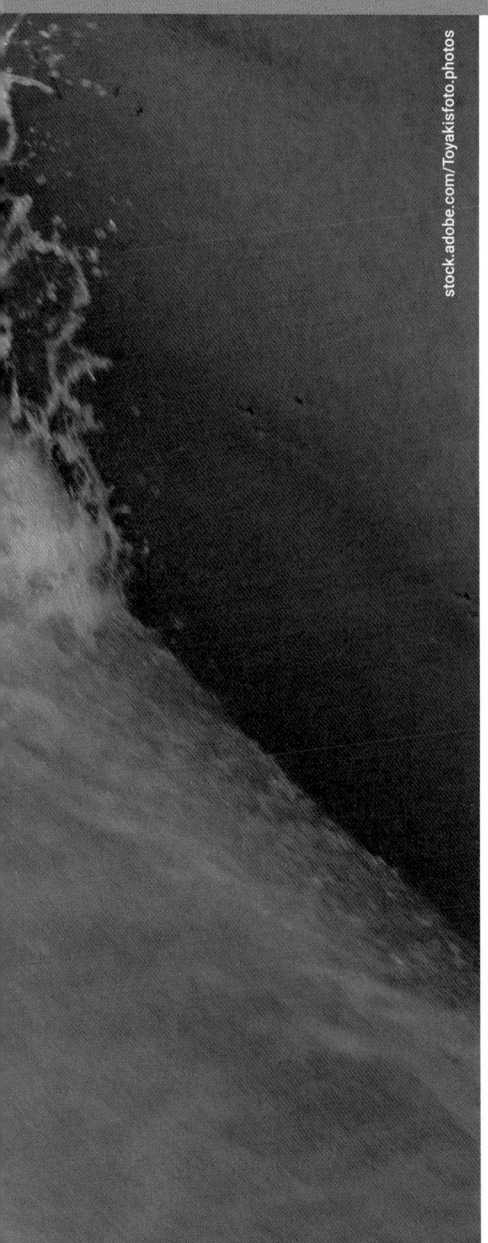

stock.adobe.com/Toyakisfoto.photos

Chapter outline

		Proficiencies				
2.01	Absolute error and percentage error	U	F		R	C
2.02	Rounding error	U	F		R	C
2.03	Areas of composite shapes	U	F	PS	R	
2.04	Surface area of a prism	U	F	PS	R	C
2.05	Surface area of a cylinder	U	F	PS	R	
2.06	Surface area of a pyramid*	U	F	PS	R	
2.07	Surface areas of cones and spheres	U	F	PS	R	C
2.08	Surface areas of composite solids	U	F	PS	R	
2.09	Volumes of prisms and cylinders	U	F		R	
2.10	Volumes of pyramids, cones and spheres*	U	F	PS	R	C
2.11	Volumes of composite solids	U	F	PS	R	

* EXTENSION

U = Understanding
F = Fluency
PS = Problem solving
R = Reasoning
C = Communicating

Wordbank

absolute error The difference between the actual value and the measured value of a quantity.

capacity The amount of fluid (liquid or gas) in a container.

composite shape A shape made up of 2 or more basic shapes.

cross-section A 'slice' of a solid, taken across the solid rather than along it.

curved surface area The area of the curved surface of a solid such as a cylinder or sphere. For example, the curved surface of a cylinder is a rectangle when flattened.

cylinder A can-shaped solid with identical cross-sections that are circles.

rounding error The difference between a calculated answer and an exact answer due to rounding in measurement or calculation.

surface area The total area of all faces of a solid shape.

Quiz
Wordbank 2

Videos (11):

2.04 Surface area of a prism
• Surface area of prisms

2.05 Surface area of a cylinder

2.06 Surface area of a pyramid

2.07 Surface area of a cone and sphere •
Surface area and volume of a cone

2.09 Volumes of prisms and cylinders
• Capacity of a cylinder

2.10 Volume of a pyramid • Surface area
and volume of a cone • Volume of a
sphere

Twig videos (6):

2.01 Decimal places: Photo finish

2.08 The power of the Sun

2.09 Bees and their hives • The incredible
strength of ants • The Menger sponge

2.10 The Pacific Flyer

Quizzes (5):

• Wordbank 2
• SkillCheck 2
• Mental skills 2
• Language of maths 2
• Test yourself 2

Skillsheets (2):

SkillCheck Solid shapes • What is volume?

Worksheets (13):

2.01 Accuracy in measurement

2.03 A page of circular shapes

2.04 Surface area 2 • Nets of solids

2.08 A page of prisms and cylinders

2.09 A page of prisms and cylinders
• Back-to-front problems • Volumes
of solids • Volume and capacity
• Biggest volume

2.10 Volume and capacity • Back-to-front
problems (Advanced)

Mind map: Surface area and volume

Puzzles (4):

2.04 Area

2.05 Surface area

2.09 Formula matching game

Language of maths Surface area and
volume crossword (Advanced)

Technology (2):

2.09 Measuring pyramids • Approximating
the volume of a cone

Presentation (1):

2.09 Volumes of shapes

Nelson MindTap

To access resources above, visit
cengage.com.au/nelsonmindtap

2 **In this chapter you will:**

✓ calculate the absolute error and percentage error of a measurement

✓ investigate rounding errors and their effect on the result of measurement calculations

✓ calculate the areas of triangles, quadrilaterals, circles, sectors and composite shapes

✓ calculate the surface areas of rectangular and triangular prisms

✓ calculate the surface areas of right prisms and cylinders

✓ calculate the volumes and capacities of right prisms and cylinders

✓ calculate the surface areas and volumes of composite solids

✓ (EXTENSION) calculate the surface areas, volumes and capacities of pyramids, cones, spheres and composite solids

9780170465595

SkillCheck
ANSWERS ON P. 605

Skillsheets
Solid
shapes

What is
volume?

1 Calculate the area of each shape. All measurements are in centimetres.

a

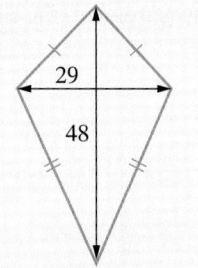

29
48

b

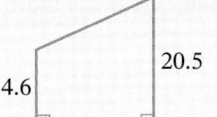

14.6
20.5
19.2

c

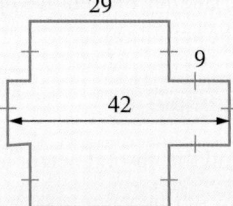

29
42
9

d

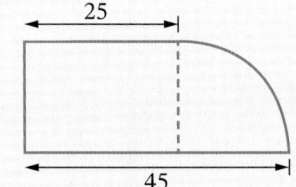

25
45

e

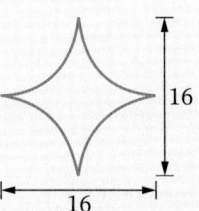

16
16

f

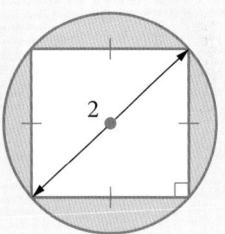

2

2 Find, correct to one decimal place, the area of each sector.

a

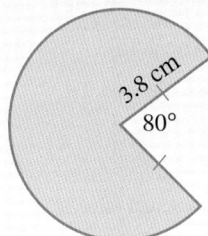

3.8 cm
80°

b

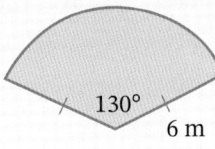

130°
6 m

c

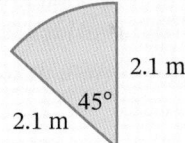

2.1 m
45°
2.1 m

Absolute error and percentage error

Absolute error is the difference between a **measured value** (or approximate value) and the **actual value** (or exact value), expressed as a **positive value**.

Video
Decimal
places:
Photo finish

ⓘ Absolute error

Absolute error = measured value – actual value   (if measured value > actual value)

Absolute error = actual value – measured value   (if measured value < actual value)

To understand how big the errors are when something is measured and be able to compare errors in measurement, we can calculate **relative error** and **percentage error**.

Relative error is the absolute error as a fraction of the actual value.

Percentage error is the absolute error as a percentage of the actual value, or the relative error expressed as a percentage.

ⓘ Relative error and percentage error

$$\text{relative error} = \frac{\text{absolute error}}{\text{actual value}}$$

$$\text{percentage error} = \frac{\text{absolute error}}{\text{actual value}} \times 100\%$$

The smaller the relative or percentage error, the more accurate the measurement, the closer it is to the actual value.

Example 1

Find the absolute error and relative error (correct to 3 decimal places) for each measurement.

a Actual value = 413, measured value = 394

b

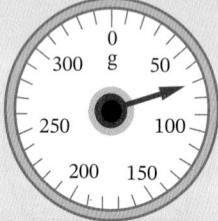

Actual mass = 68.9 g

SOLUTION

a The measured value (394) is lower than the actual value (413).

absolute error = 413 – 394

$$= 19$$

$$\text{relative error} = \frac{\text{absolute error}}{\text{actual value}}$$

$$= \frac{19}{413}$$

$$= 0.046\ 00...$$

$$\approx 0.046$$

b The measured mass from the scale is 70 g. It is larger than the actual mass (68.9 g).

absolute error = 70 g – 68.9 g

$$= 1.1\ g$$

$$\text{relative error} = \frac{\text{absolute error}}{\text{actual value}}$$

$$= \frac{1.1}{68.9}$$

$$= 0.015\ 96...$$

$$\approx 0.016$$

Example 2

Mohammad estimates the length of an essay to be 1270 words. If there are exactly 1405 words in the essay, calculate the percentage error of his estimation, correct to two decimal places.

SOLUTION

measured value = 1270 words

actual value = 1405 words

absolute error = 1405 – 1270

$$= 135\ \text{words}$$

$$\text{percentage error} = \frac{\text{absolute error}}{\text{actual value}} \times 100\%$$

$$= \frac{135}{1405} \times 100\%$$

$$= 9.608\ 54\ ...\%$$

$$\approx 9.61\%$$

Absolute error of a measuring instrument

This ruler is marked in centimetres, so any length measured with it can only be given to the nearest centimetre.

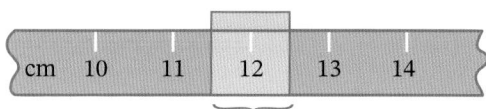

Any measurement in the shaded region should be recorded as 12 cm. The measured length is 12 cm, but the actual length is 12 ± 0.5 cm, or '11.5 to 12.5 cm'.

The **limits of accuracy** of this measurement are **11.5 to 12.5 cm**.

The **absolute error** of this ruler is **0.5 cm**.

> ⓘ **Absolute error of measuring instruments**
>
> The absolute error of a measuring instrument is 0.5 of the unit shown on the instrument's scale.

Example 3

Find the absolute error for each measuring scale.

a

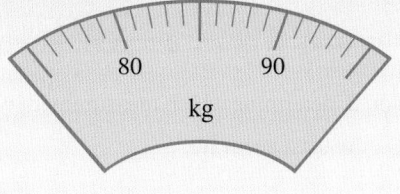

b

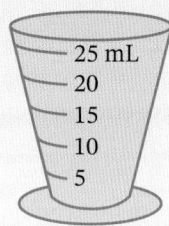

SOLUTION

a The size of one unit on the scale is 1 kg.
The absolute error is 0.5×1 kg $= 0.5$ kg.

b The size of one unit on the scale is 5 mL.
The absolute error is 0.5×5 mL $= 2.5$ mL.

EXERCISE 2.01 ANSWERS ON P. 605

Absolute error and percentage error

1 Calculate the absolute error for each pair of values.

EXAMPLE
1

   a actual value = 210 cm, measured value = 215 cm

   b actual value = 2.72 kg, measured value = 2.68 kg

   c actual value = 362 mL, measured value = 370 mL

   d actual value = 150 minutes, measured value = 155 minutes

☐ Foundation   ○ Standard   ○ Complex

2 Write the measured value on each scale shown.

a

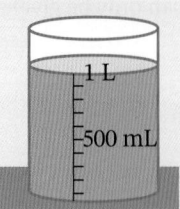

b

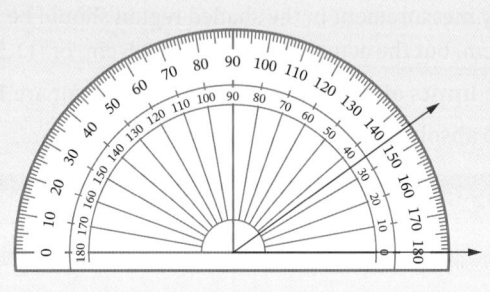

c

d

3 Use your measured values from question **2** and the actual values listed below to calculate the absolute error and relative error (correct to 3 decimal places) for each measurement.

a 987 mL   **b** 9.2 cm   **c** 1.07 kg   **d** 35.7°

4 By comparing the relative error answers in question **3**, determine which measurement was:

a the most accurate   **b** the least accurate.

5 A soccer club estimates there to be approximately 2500 members of their club. If the actual number of members is 2473, calculate the percentage error of this estimation.

6 Kavya estimates that there are 70 lollypops in a giant bag. If the actual number of lollypops is 77, calculate the percentage error of Kavya's estimation.

7 The actual weight of a bag of pasta is 0.6 kg. Lachlan measures the weight of the

(R)

(C) pasta to be 0.62 kg, whereas Aaria measures the weight to be 588 g. Calculate the percentage error of each measurement, correct to 2 decimal places, to determine whose measurement is more accurate.

8 At an auction, Kartik valued the price of a painting to be $18 000 and Nandini valued

(R)

(C) the price to be $25 000. The painting sold for $22 180. Calculate the percentage error of each valuation, correct to 2 decimal places, to determine whose valuation was more accurate.

9 For each measuring instrument, state:

EXAMPLE 3
2.01

(R) (C)

   i   the size of one unit on the scale   **ii**   the absolute error.

a   **b**

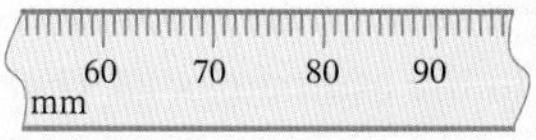

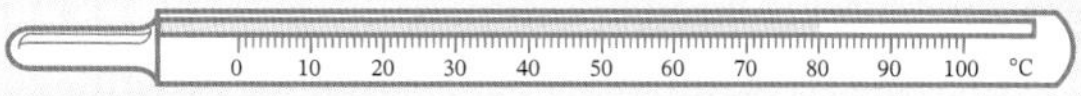

c 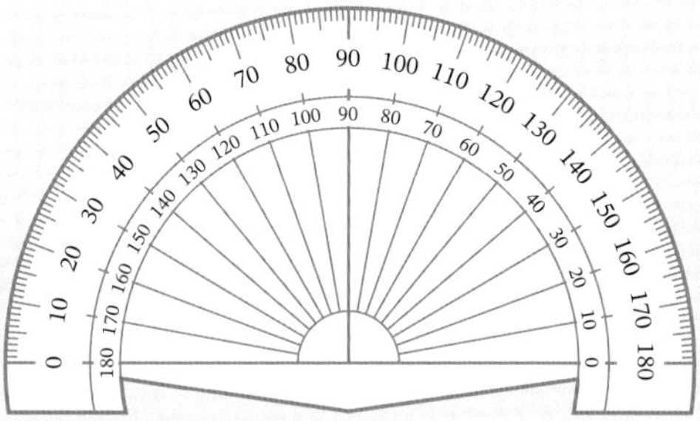   **d**

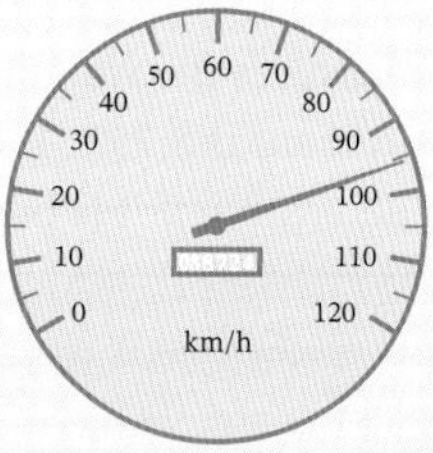

e 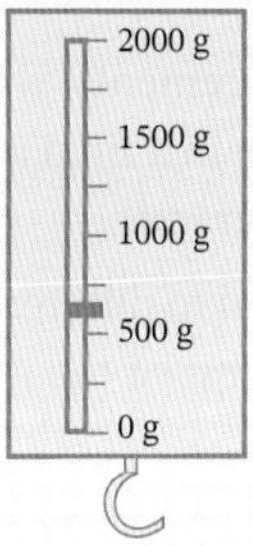   **f**

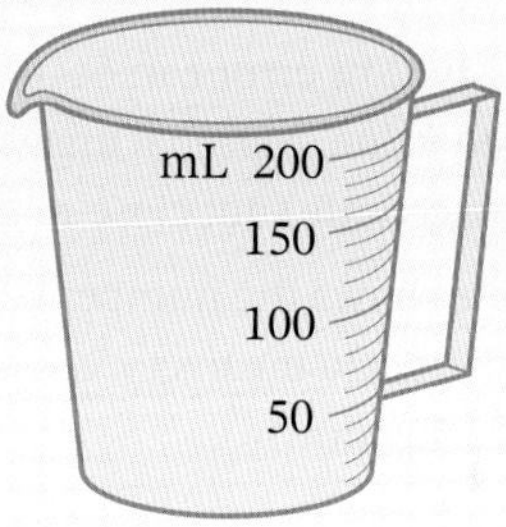

g 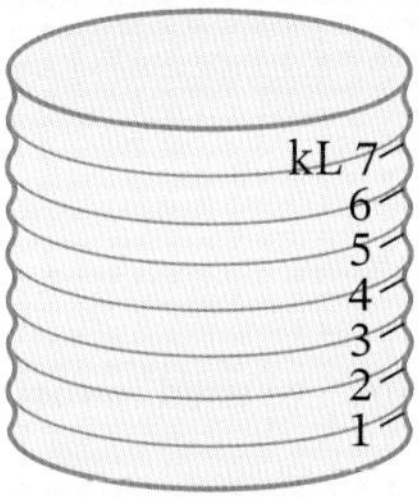   **h**

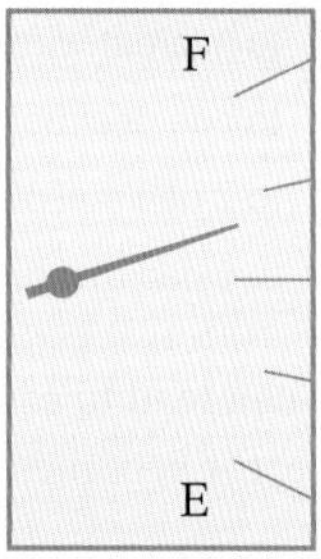

10 Measuring with a ruler, Gemma correctly gives a measurement as 26.5 to 27.5 cm.

(R)   **a**   What is the size of a unit on the ruler?

(C)   **b**   What is the absolute error of this measurement?

     c   Using a ruler marked in millimetres, Emily gives the same measurement as 26.8 cm. What is the absolute error of this measurement?

     d   What are the limits of accuracy between which this measurement must lie?

11 The weight of a box of chocolates is 800 g, correct to the nearest 20 g.
Calculate the percentage error for a box of chocolates.

12 The height of a building is approximately 20 m, correct to the nearest 0.3 m. Calculate the percentage error for this height.

13 An expert is hired to estimate the price of an antique necklace. If the absolute error in
  Ⓡ the expert's estimate is $2750 and the percentage error in the estimate is 12.97%, can the
  Ⓒ actual value of the painting be greater than $20 000? Explain your answer.

14 Beth measures the weight of 2000 pencils to be 16 kg. The percentage error of this measurement is 8.75%. If the actual weight of one pencil is x g, find the possible range of x and determine if it is possible for one of the pencils in this batch to weigh 6.5 g.

2.02 Rounding error

Another type of error can occur when performing calculations with measurements, where the measured value or partial answer is rounded too early or severely, resulting in a final answer that is inaccurate (not close to the exact answer). This is called **rounding error**.

This table shows the number 6.863 791 654 835 62 ... rounded and truncated to different decimal places. Truncate means to 'cut off' the number at the decimal place regardless of the next digit (or 'rounding down').

6.863 791 654 835 62...	Rounded	Truncated
to nearest whole number	7	6
to one decimal place	6.9	6.8
to 2 decimal places	6.86	6.86
to 6 decimal places	6.863 792	6.863 791

Rounding values can lead to errors in solutions. If approximate values are used in further calculations, the error becomes more significant.

Example 4

A rectangle has length 8.25 cm and width 6.09 cm.

a Calculate its perimeter and area.

b Truncate the rectangle's length and width to one decimal place, then calculate its perimeter and area with these values, then find correct to one decimal place the percentage error of the calculated perimeter and area.

c Round the rectangle's length and width to the nearest whole number, then calculate its perimeter and area with these values, then find correct to one decimal place the percentage error of the perimeter and area.

☐ Foundation   ○ Standard   ○ Complex

   9780170465595

SOLUTION

a perimeter $= 2 \times 8.25 + 2 \times 6.09$

$= 28.68$ cm

area $= 8.25 \times 6.09$

$= 50.2425$ cm^2

b length $= 8.2$ cm, width $= 6.0$ cm

perimeter $= 2 \times 8.2 + 2 \times 6.0$

$= 28.4$ cm

absolute error $= 28.68 - 28.4 = 0.28$

percentage error $= \dfrac{0.28}{28.68} \times 100\%$

$= 0.9762...\%$

$\approx 1.0\%$

area $= 8.2 \times 6.0$

$= 49.2$ cm^2

absolute error $= 50.2425 - 49.2 = 1.0425$

percentage error $= \dfrac{1.0425}{50.2425} \times 100\%$

$= 2.0749...\%$

$\approx 2.1\%$

c length $= 8$ cm, width $= 6$ cm

perimeter $= 2 \times 8 + 2 \times 6$

$= 28$ cm

absolute error $= 28.68 - 28 = 0.68$

percentage error $= \dfrac{0.68}{28.68} \times 100\%$

$= 2.3709...\%$

$\approx 2.4\%$

area $= 8 \times 6$

$= 48$ cm^2

absolute error $= 50.2425 - 48 = 2.2425$

percentage error $= \dfrac{2.2425}{50.2425} \times 100\%$

$= 4.4633...\%$

$\approx 4.5\%$

- Notice that the percentage error is higher for area than perimeter: this is because when calculating perimeter, we are adding the errors in the measurements but when calculating area, we are multiplying the errors
- Notice also that the percentage error is higher the more we round or truncate the measurements. When calculating, it is always best to use exact or the most accurate values to minimise the rounding error

Example 5

Kane earns $22.46 per hour working at a supermarket. This week, he worked for 44 hours.

a Calculate his weekly pay.

b Round his hourly wage to the nearest 10 cents, then find, correct to one decimal place, the percentage error of his weekly pay using this value.

c Round his hourly wage to the nearest dollar, then find, correct to one decimal place, the percentage error of his weekly pay using this value.

SOLUTION

a weekly pay $= 44 \times \$22.46$

$= \$988.24$

b rounded wage = $22.50

weekly pay = 44 × $22.50

= $990

absolute error = $990 – $988.24 = $1.76

percentage error = $\dfrac{1.76}{988.24} \times 100\%$

= 0.1780... %

≈ 0.2%

c rounded wage = $22

weekly pay = 44 × $22

= $968

absolute error = $988.24 – $968 = $20.24

percentage error = $\dfrac{20.24}{988.24} \times 100\%$

= 2.0480... %

≈ 2.0%

> The more you round, the more rounding error in your final answer.

Example 6

The radius of a circle is given as 15 cm, correct to the nearest cm.

a Calculate the area of the circle, correct to 4 decimal places.

b Write the limits of accuracy of the radius.

c Hence, calculate, correct to 4 decimal places, the minimum possible area of the circle, and its percentage error, correct to one decimal place.

d Hence, calculate, correct to 4 decimal places, the maximum possible area of the circle, and its percentage error, correct to one decimal place.

SOLUTION

a area = $\pi \times 15^2$

= 706.858 347...

≈ 706.8583 cm^2

b limits of accuracy = 14.5 to 15.5 cm

c minimum possible area = $\pi \times 14.5^2$

= 660.519 8554...

≈ 660.5199 cm^2

absolute error = 706.8583 – 660.5199

= 46.3384

percentage error = $\dfrac{46.3384}{706.8583} \times 100\%$

= 6.5555... %

≈ 6.6%

d maximum possible area = $\pi \times 15.5^2$

= 754.767 635...

≈ 754.7676 cm^2

absolute error = 754.7676 – 706.8583

= 47.9093

percentage error = $\dfrac{47.0903}{706.8583} \times 100\%$

= 6.7777... %

≈ 6.8%

9780170465595

Rounding error

(U) (F) (R) (C)

1 Truncate 7.456 923 5643... to:

  a   the nearest whole number   **b**   one decimal place

  c   2 decimal places   **d**   4 decimal places

2 Truncate 175.956 987 258... to:

  a   the nearest whole number   **b**   one decimal place

  c   2 decimal places   **d**   5 decimal places

3 Round 7.456 923 5643... to:

  a   the nearest whole number   **b**   one decimal place

  c   2 decimal places   **d**   4 decimal places

4 A square has length 10.37 metres.

  a   Calculate its perimeter and area.

  b   Truncate the square's length to one decimal place and use this value to calculate its perimeter and area, then find, correct to one decimal place, the percentage error of the calculated perimeter and area.

  c   Round the square's length to the nearest whole number and use this value to calculate its perimeter and area, then find, correct to one decimal place, the percentage error of the perimeter and area.

EXAMPLE
4

5 A right-angled triangle has a base length 7.59 cm and perpendicular height 13.21 cm.

  a   Calculate its area.

  b   Calculate the length of its hypotenuse, correct to 4 decimal places.

  c   Round the triangle's base and height to one decimal place and use these values to calculate its area and hypotenuse, then find, correct to one decimal place, the percentage error of the calculated area and hypotenuse.

  d   Truncate the triangle's base and height to the nearest whole number and use these values to calculate its area and hypotenuse, then find, correct to one decimal place, the percentage error of the calculated area and hypotenuse.

6 A circle has radius 382 mm.

  a   Calculate its circumference correct to 4 decimal places.

  b   Use $\pi = 3.14$ to calculate its circumference, correct to 4 decimal places, then find, correct to one decimal place, the percentage error of the calculated circumference.

  c   Round the circle's radius to the nearest 10 and use this value to calculate its circumference, correct to 4 decimal places, then find, correct to one decimal place, the percentage error of the calculated circumference.

☐ Foundation   ○ Standard   ○ Complex

EXAMPLE 5

7 Rakhi earns an annual salary of $104 258. Based on an average year having 365.25 days, there are approximately 52.18 weeks in a year.

    a Calculate to the nearest cent her weekly pay by dividing her salary by 52.18.

    b Calculate to the nearest cent Rakhi's weekly pay by dividing her salary by 52.2, then find, correct to one decimal place, the percentage error from using this value.

    c Calculate to the nearest cent Rakhi's weekly pay by dividing her salary by 52, then find, correct to one decimal place, the percentage error from using this value.

8 Sam invested $20 488 into a bank account earning simple interest at 3.71% p.a. for 5 years.

    a Calculate the total interest earned.

    b Round his investment to the nearest $100, then find, correct to one decimal place, the percentage error of his total interest using this value.

    c Round the interest rate to 2 decimal places, then find, correct to one decimal place, the percentage error of his total interest using this value.

EXAMPLE 6

9 Write the limits of accuracy of each measurement.

    a 12 cm to the nearest cm   **b** 360 mL to the nearest mL

    c 8 kg to the nearest kg   **d** 750 mm to the nearest mm

    e 6 L to the nearest L   **f** 1250 g to the nearest g

    g 73 m to the nearest m   **h** 5 kL to the nearest kL

    i 87 km to the nearest km   **j** 60 mg to the nearest mg

10 A square has length 12 cm, measured correct to the nearest centimetre.

  (R) **a** Calculate the area of the square.

  (C) **b** Write the limits of accuracy of the square's length.

       c Hence, calculate the minimum possible area of the square, and its percentage error, correct to 2 decimal places.

       d Hence, calculate the maximum possible area of the square, and its percentage error, correct to 2 decimal places.

11 A circle has radius 3 m, measured correct to the nearest metre.

  (R) **a** Calculate the circumference of the circle, correct to 4 decimal places.

  (C) **b** Write the limits of accuracy of the radius.

       c Hence calculate, correct to 4 decimal places, the minimum possible circumference of the circle, and its percentage error correct to 2 decimal places.

       d Hence calculate, correct to 4 decimal places, the maximum possible circumference of the circle, and its percentage error, correct to 2 decimal places.

12 A rectangular prism has length 12 cm, width 5 cm and height 2 cm, all measured correct to the nearest centimetre. What is the maximum possible percentage error when calculating the volume of this prism?

13 The radius of a cylinder is 3 m and its height is 2 m, measured to the nearest metre.

    a Calculate its volume, correct to 4 decimal places.

    b Use $\pi = 3.14$ to calculate its volume correct to 4 decimal places, then find, correct to one decimal place, the percentage error of the calculated circumference.

    c Calculate the minimum possible volume of the cylinder, and its percentage error, correct to 2 decimal places.

    d Calculate the maximum possible volume of the cylinder, and its percentage error, correct to 2 decimal places.

14 A rectangular swimming pool has side lengths of 4 m and 11 m, correct to the nearest metre. A fence needs to be placed 1 m out from the edge of the pool enclosing the entire pool. If the fencing costs \$123.50/m to install, calculate the maximum and minimum possible cost of fencing the pool.

15 The exact formula to convert a temperature measured in degrees Fahrenheit (F) to degrees Celsius (C) is $C = \dfrac{5(F-32)}{9}$. An approximate formula that can be used as a 'rule-of-thumb' is $C = \dfrac{1}{2}(F-30)$. Hayley is baking a cake for her mum's birthday at a temperature of 356°F.

    a Use the exact formula to convert 356°F to Celsius.

    b Use the approximate formula to convert 356°F to Celsius.

    c Calculate, correct to one decimal place, the percentage error when using the approximate formula.

Areas of composite shapes

2.03

Example 7

Find the area of each **composite shape**, correct to one decimal place where appropriate.

a 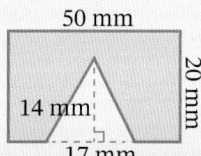   **b** 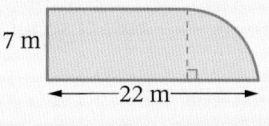   **c**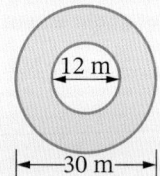

Worksheet
A page of circular shapes

Puzzle
Area

SOLUTION

a   area $= 50 \times 20 - \dfrac{1}{2} \times 17 \times 14$ area of rectangle – area of triangle

       $= 881 \text{ mm}^2$

□ Foundation   ○ Standard   ○ Complex

b   radius of **quadrant** = 7 m

length of rectangle = 22 − 7

$$= 15 \text{ m}$$

area of shape = area of rectangle + quadrant

$$= 15 \times 7 + \frac{1}{4} \times \pi \times 7^2$$

$$= 143.4845...$$

$$\approx 143.5 \text{ m}^2$$

c   radius of large circle = $\frac{1}{2} \times 30$ m

$$= 15 \text{ m}$$

radius of small circle = $\frac{1}{2} \times 12$ m

$$= 6 \text{ m}$$

area of **annulus** = $\pi \times 15^2 - \pi \times 6^2$

$$= 593.7610...$$

$$= 593.8 \text{ m}^2$$

ⓘ Area of a sector

Area of a sector $= \dfrac{\theta}{360} \times \pi r^2$

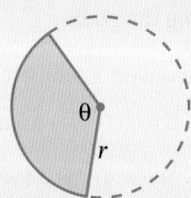

Example 8

Calculate, correct to 2 decimal places, the area of each sector.

a   2.6 m   145°

b   9 m   115°

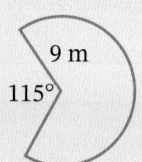

> A **sector** is a fraction of a circle 'cut' along 2 radii, like a pizza slice.

SOLUTION

a   area $= \dfrac{145}{360} \times \pi \times 2.6^2$ $\dfrac{145}{360} \times$ area of circle

$$= 8.55385...$$

$$\approx 8.55 \text{ m}^2$$

> There are 360° in a circle, but a sector is a fraction of a circle.

b   sector angle = 360° − 115°

$$= 245°$$

area of sector $= \dfrac{245}{360} \times \pi \times 9^2$

$$= 173.18029...$$

$$\approx 173.18 \text{ m}^2$$

EXERCISE 2.03 ANSWERS ON P. 605

Area of composite shapes

U F PS R

EXAMPLE 7

1 Find the area of each composite shape.

PS R

a

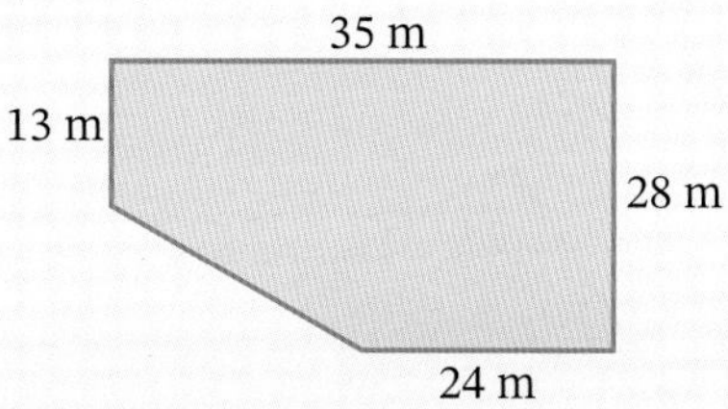
35 m
13 m
28 m
24 m

b

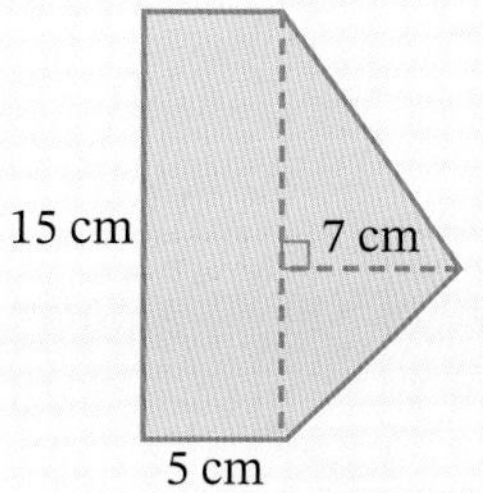
15 cm
7 cm
5 cm

c

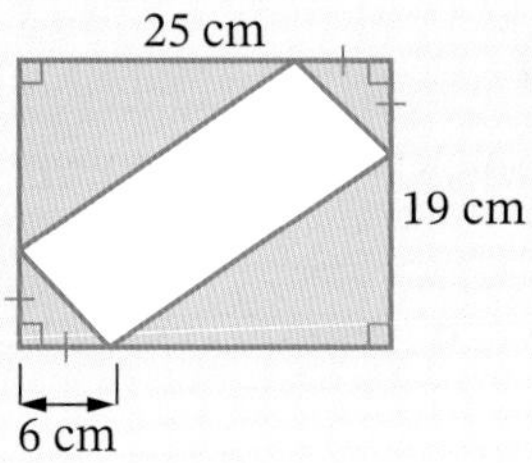
25 cm
19 cm
6 cm

d

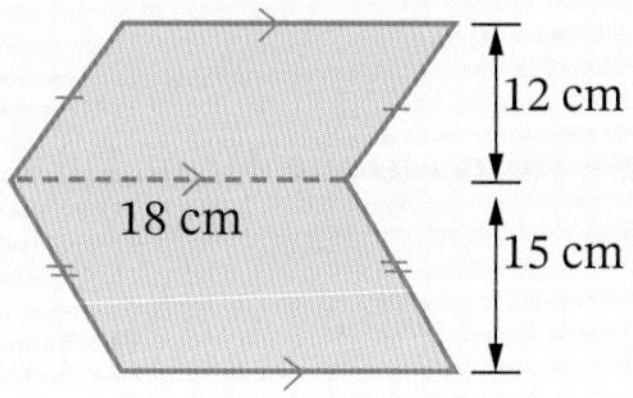
12 cm
18 cm
15 cm

e

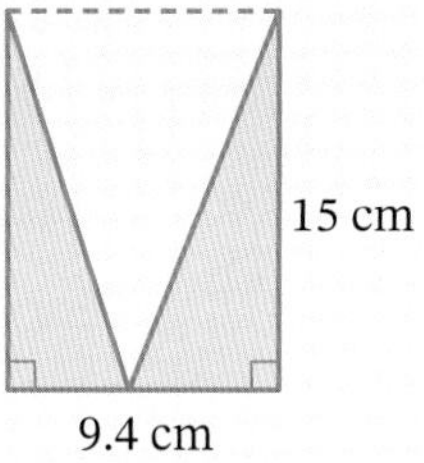
15 cm
9.4 cm

f

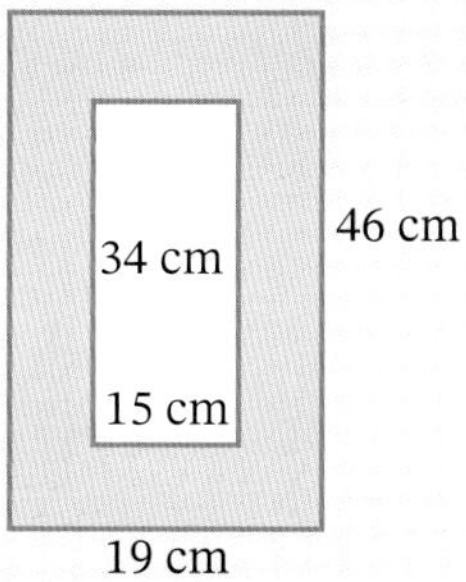
34 cm
46 cm
15 cm
19 cm

g

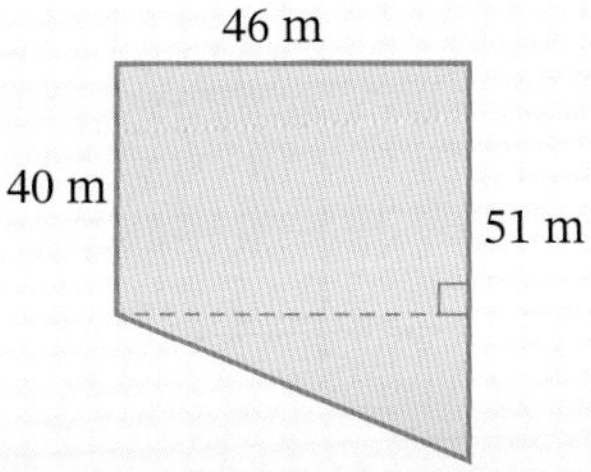
46 m
40 m
51 m

h

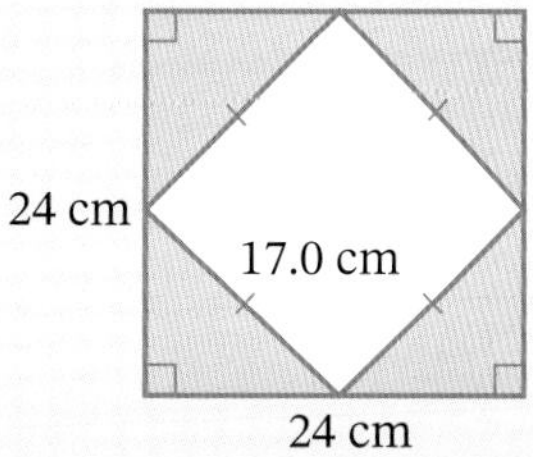
24 cm
17.0 cm
24 cm

▷

□ Foundation ○ Standard ⬡ Complex

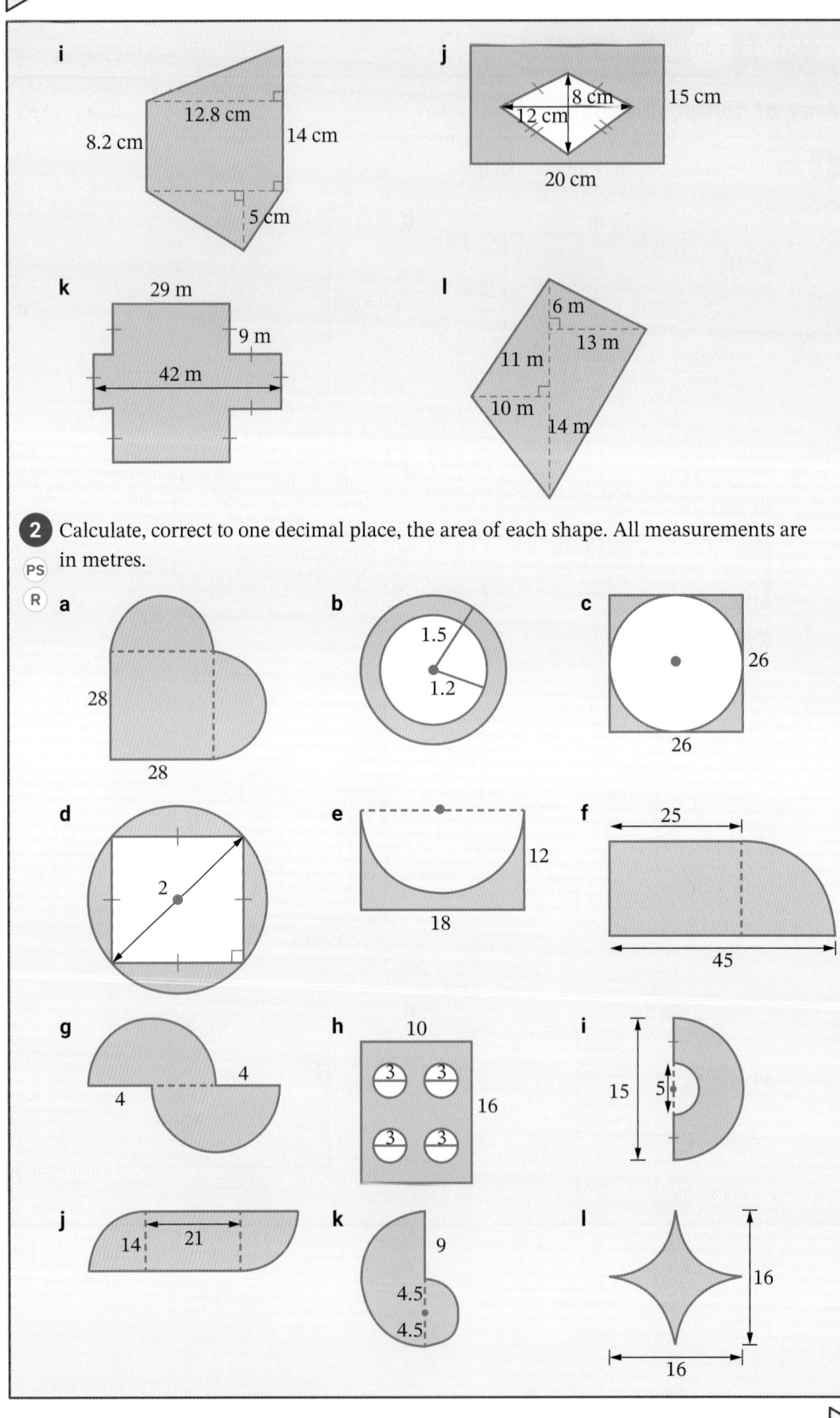

i

12.8 cm

8.2 cm   14 cm

5 cm

j

8 cm   15 cm

12 cm

20 cm

k

29 m

9 m

42 m

l

6 m

13 m

11 m

10 m

14 m

2 Calculate, correct to one decimal place, the area of each shape. All measurements are in metres.

PS

R

a

28

28

b

1.5

1.2

c

26

26

d

2

e

12

18

f

25

45

g

4

4

h

10

3   3

16

3   3

i

15   5

j

14   21

k

9

4.5

4.5

l

16

16

3 Find, correct to one decimal place, the area of each sector.

EXAMPLE 8   2.03

a

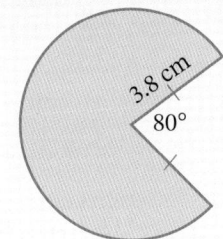

3.8 cm
80°

b

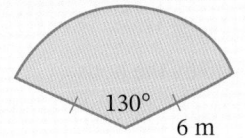

130°
6 m

c

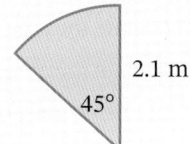

2.1 m
45°

4 A bike tyre has a diameter of 715 mm.

   a How far will the bike travel in one revolution of the tyre? Give your answer in metres, correct to 2 decimal places.

   b How many revolutions of the tyre are required to travel a distance of 5 km?

5 Calculate the area of the shaded region.

R Select the correct answer **A**, **B**, **C** or **D**.

   A 362.7 cm²   **B** 452.4 cm²

   C 188.5 cm²   **D** 263.9 cm²

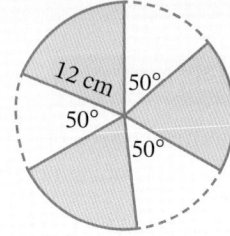

12 cm 50°
50°
50°

6 A rectangular metal plate with dimensions 2.5 m × 2.2 m has 9 circular holes of diameter 46 cm drilled in it.

   a Find the total area of the holes that have been drilled. Give your answer in m², correct to 2 decimal places.

   b What percentage of the metal plate remains?

7 A rectangular courtyard 15 m long and 8 m wide is to be covered with square pavers of side length 400 mm,

PS costing $79.29/m².

R

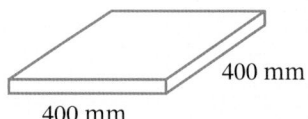

400 mm
400 mm

   a What is the area of one paver, in m²?

   b How many pavers will be required to pave the courtyard?

   c Calculate the cost of paving the courtyard.

8 A circular sports ground of diameter 140 m has a rectangular soccer pitch measuring 110 m by 70 m inside it. The area outside the soccer pitch is to be painted in the team colour of red.

   a Calculate the area that is to be painted red, correct to the nearest m².

   b If the cost of paint is $29.50 per 50 m², calculate the cost of painting this area.

□ Foundation ○ Standard ○ Complex

9
PS
R
The diagram shows the floor plan of a house on a block of land.

a   Calculate the area of the block.

b   Calculate the area taken up by the house.

c   What percentage of the area of the block is taken up by the house?

d   The area not covered by the house and is to be turfed. Find the cost of turfing the yard at a cost of $11.75 per m².

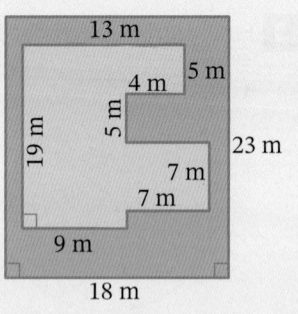

2.04 Surface area of a prism

Videos
Surface area
of a prism

Surface area
of prisms

Worksheets
Surface
area 2

Nets of
solids

ⓘ Surface area

The **surface area** of a solid is the total area of all the faces of the solid. To calculate the surface area of a solid, find the area of each face and add the areas together.

Example 9

Find the surface area of each **prism**.

a
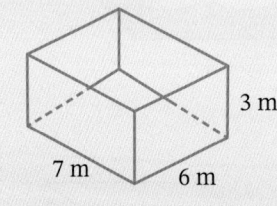
open rectangular prism

b
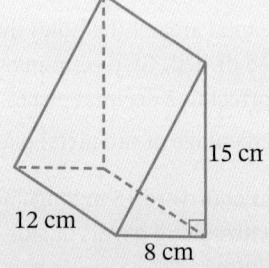
closed triangular prism

SOLUTION

a   This open prism has 5 faces (see net diagram).

surface area = 2 ends + 2 sides + base

$$= 2 \times (3 \times 6) + 2 \times (3 \times 7) + (6 \times 7)$$

$$= 120 \text{ m}^2$$

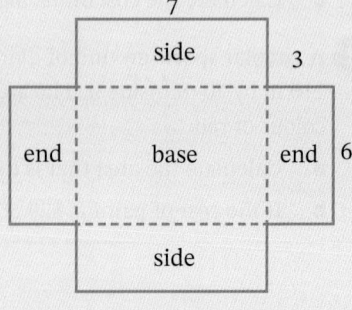

☐ Foundation   ○ Standard   ○ Complex

b This closed prism has 5 faces: 2 identical triangles (front and back) and 3 different rectangles.

Using Pythagoras' theorem to find m, the hypotenuse of the triangle:

$m^2 = 8^2 + 15^2$ 　　　$m = \sqrt{289}$

　$= 289$ 　　　　　　$= 17$

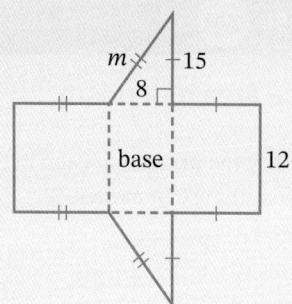

surface area = 2 triangles + 3 rectangles

$$= 2 \times \left(\frac{1}{2} \times 8 \times 15 \right) + (17 \times 12) + (8 \times 12) + (15 \times 12)$$

$$= 600 \text{ cm}^2$$

Example 10

Calculate the surface area of this trapezoidal prism.

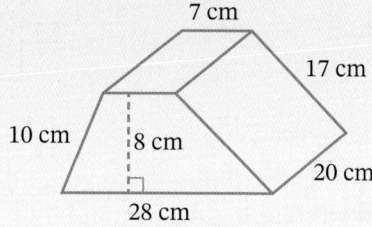

SOLUTION

This trapezoidal prism has 6 faces:

2 identical trapeziums (front and back) and 4 different rectangles.

Area of each trapezium $= \frac{1}{2} \times (7 + 28) \times 8$

$$= 140 \text{ cm}^2$$

surface area $= (2 \times 140) + (20 \times 7) + (20 \times 10)$

$$+ (20 \times 28) + (20 \times 17)$$

$$= 1520 \text{ cm}^2$$

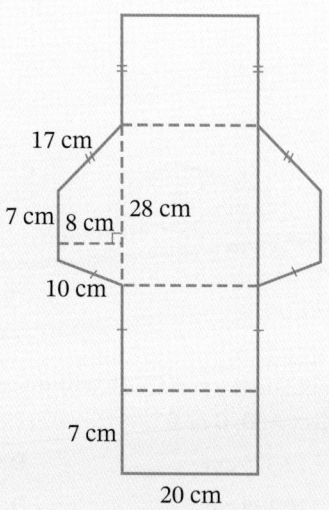

Surface area of a prism

(U) (F) (PS) (R) (C)

1 Identify the prism that each net represents, then calculate the surface area of the prism. All lengths are in metres.

(R)

(C)

a
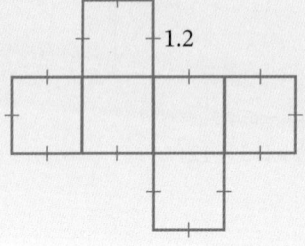
1.2

b
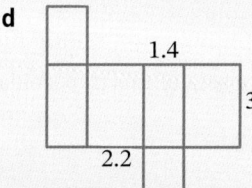
5.8
4
4.2

c
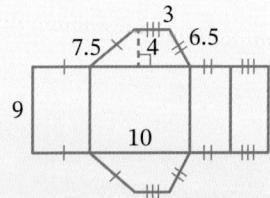
3
7.5 4 6.5
9
10

d
1.4
3
2.2

EXAMPLE 9

2 Find the surface area of each prism.

a
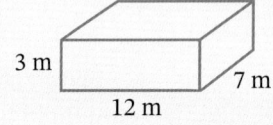
3 m
12 m
7 m

b
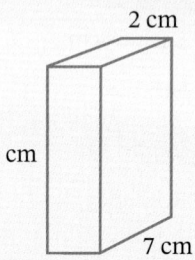
2 cm
15 cm
7 cm

c
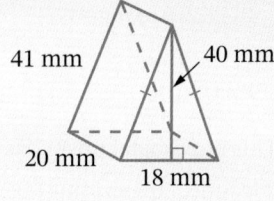
41 mm
40 mm
20 mm
18 mm

d
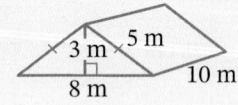
3 m 5 m
8 m 10 m

e
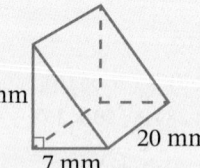
24 mm
20 mm
7 mm

f
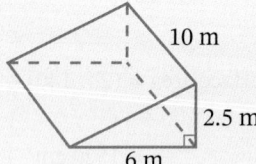
10 m
2.5 m
6 m

3 Calculate the surface area of this triangular prism.
Select **A**, **B**, **C** or **D**.

A 12 375 cm²

B 11 250 cm²

C 10 125 cm²

D 12 431.25 cm²

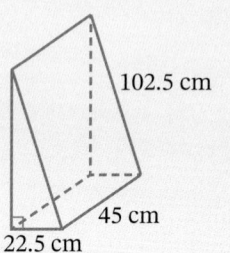
102.5 cm
45 cm
22.5 cm

▷

□ **Foundation** ○ **Standard** ○ **Complex**

4 This classroom is being renovated. Find:

(PS) **a** the area of the floor to be carpeted and the total cost, at $55 per square metre.

b the ceiling and wall area to be painted, if the room contains 4 windows, each 2.5 m by 1.5 m, and a doorway 2 m by 0.8 m.

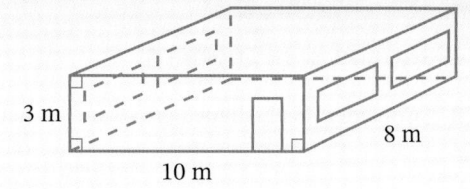

5 Calculate the surface area of each prism.

EXAMPLE
10

a
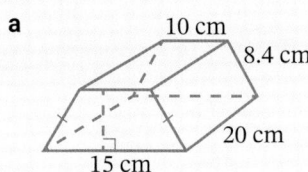

b
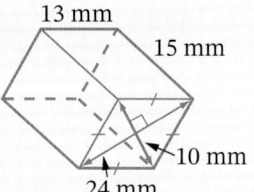

c
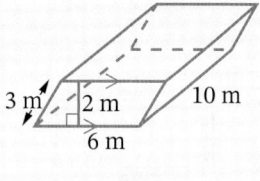

d
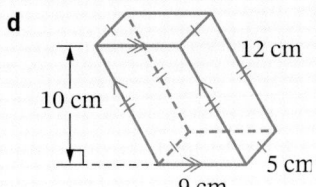

e
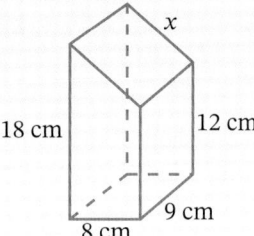

f
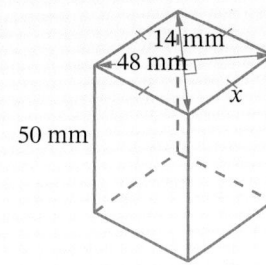

6 Calculate the surface area of the trapezoidal prism. Select **A**, **B**, **C** or **D**.

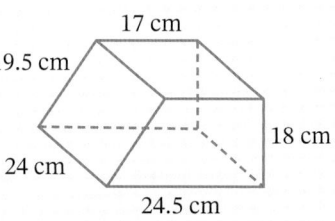

A 10 584 cm²

B 2643 cm²

C 2082.75 cm²

D 8964 cm²

7 The wooden toy box is in the shape of a trapezoidal prism.

a Calculate how much timber is required to make the toy box, correct to the nearest cm².

b If the price of the timber is $25 per m², what is the cost of making the box?

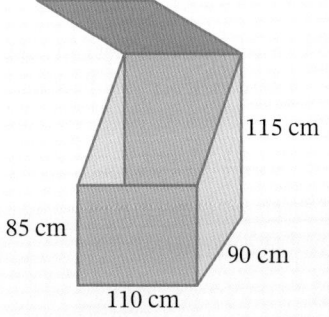

Foundation   ○ Standard   ◇ Complex

A surface area shortcut

1 Consider this L-shaped prism and its net. We will find its surface area.

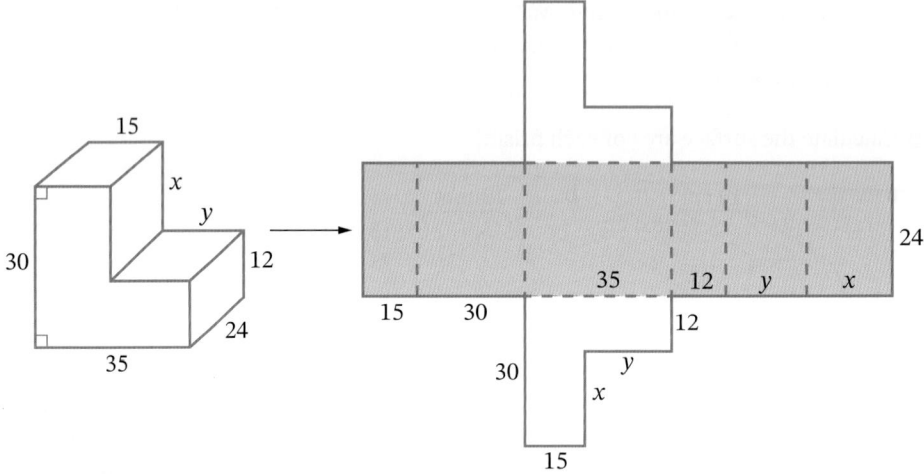

a Find x and y.

b This prism has 8 faces: 2 'L-shaped' ends and 6 rectangles. Instead of calculating the areas of the 6 rectangles separately, we can combine them into one long rectangle, as shaded in the net above. The length of the rectangle is the same as the perimeter of the L-shape. What is the length of this long rectangle?

c What is the area of this long rectangle?

d Copy and complete:

Length of shaded rectangle = p _____ of the L-shape.

e Find the surface area of the prism by copying and completing the following:

Surface area = 2 'L-shaped' ends + shaded rectangle

$$= 2 \times (15 \times 30 + 20 \times 12) + \text{_____}$$

$$= \text{_____}$$

2 From question **1**, it can be seen that the surface area of any prism with end faces of area A and perpendicular height (distance between end faces) h can be calculated using the formula:

$$SA = 2A + Ph$$

where P = perimeter of the end face.

Use this method to calculate the surface area of each prism. All measurements are in centimetres.

a

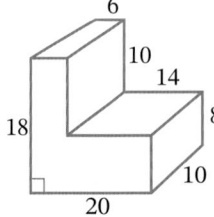

b

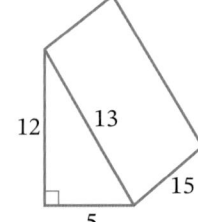

c

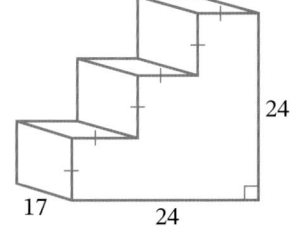

Surface area of a cylinder

ⓘ Surface area of a closed cylinder

$$SA = 2\pi r^2 + 2\pi rh$$

where r = radius of circular base

h = perpendicular height

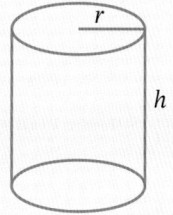

Video
Surface area
of a cylinder

Puzzle
Surface area

The area of the 2 circular ends = $2\pi r^2$ and the area of the curved surface = $2\pi rh$.

Example 11

Find, correct to the nearest mm², the surface area of this cylinder.

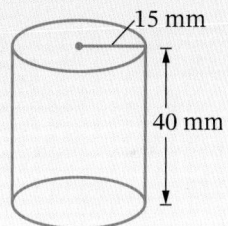

SOLUTION

surface area = area of 2 ends + area of the $r = 15, h = 40$
                      curved surface

$= 2\pi r^2 + 2\pi rh$

$= 2 \times \pi \times 15^2 + 2 \times \pi \times 15 \times 40$

$= 5183.627...$

≈ 5184 mm²

Example 12

Calculate in exact form (in terms of π) the surface area of a cylinder open at one end with radius 12 cm and height 15 cm.

SOLUTION

Surface area = circular end + curved surface

$= \pi \times 12^2 + 2 \times \pi \times 12 \times 15$

$= 144\pi + 360\pi$

$= 504\pi$ cm²

Example 13

Find, correct to one decimal place, the surface area of:

a a cylindrical tube, open at both ends, with radius 3 cm and height 55 cm

b an open half-cylinder with radius 0.65 m and length 2.4 m.

SOLUTION

a

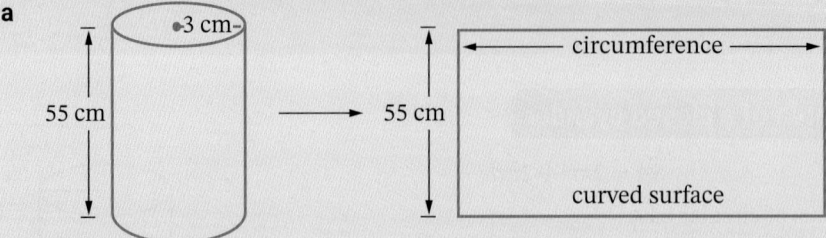

surface area = curved surface

$= 2\pi rh$ $r = 3$ and $h = 55$

$= 2 \times \pi \times 3 \times 55$

$= 1036.725...$

$\approx 1036.7 \text{ cm}^2$

b

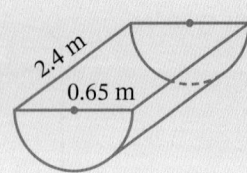

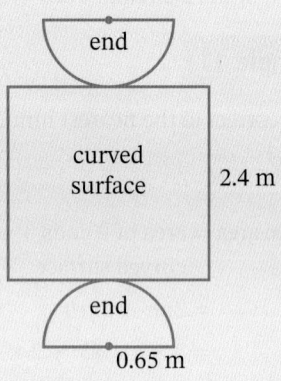

surface area $= 2$ semicircle ends $+ \frac{1}{2} \times$ curved surface

$$= 2 \times \left(\frac{1}{2} \times \pi \times 0.65^2\right) + \frac{1}{2} \times (2 \times \pi \times 0.65 \times 2.4)$$

$= 6.2282...$

$\approx 6.2 \text{ m}^2$

EXERCISE 2.05 ANSWERS ON P. 605

Surface area of a cylinder   U F PS R

EXAMPLE **11**

1 Calculate, correct to one decimal place, the surface area of a cylinder with:

  a radius 1.4 m, height 2.2 m   **b** diameter 45 cm, height 65 cm

  c diameter 9 cm, height 24 cm   **d** radius 1.3 m, height 3.8 m

2 Find, correct to the nearest whole number, the curved surface area of a cylinder with:

  a radius 1.5 m, height 3.75 m   **b** diameter 27 cm, height 41 cm

EXAMPLE **12**

3 A container of potato crisps is a cylinder with diameter 8 cm and height 24 cm. Calculate its surface area in terms of π.

▷

□ Foundation   ○ Standard   ◇ Complex

4 Find the surface area of a cylinder in exact form, open at one end with diameter 12 mm
and length 15 cm. Select the closest answer **A**, **B**, **C** or **D**.

A 226π cm² **B** 2844π cm² **C** 1944π mm² **D** 1836π mm²

2.05

5 Calculate, in exact form, the surface area of:

a a closed cylinder, radius 6 cm, height 2.5 cm

b a cylinder open at one end with radius 1.25 m and height 3.5 m

c a piece of cylindrical tubing, open at both ends, with radius 1.5 cm and length 6.5 m

6 Calculate, correct to the nearest whole number, the surface area of each solid.

EXAMPLE
13

a closed cylinder **b** closed cylinder **c** cylinder with one open end

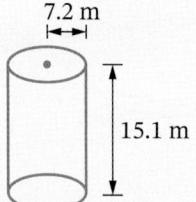
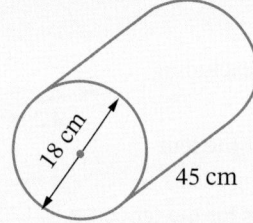
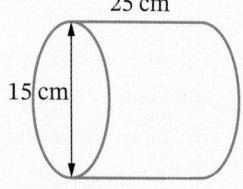

d half cylinder with open top **e** cylinder open both ends

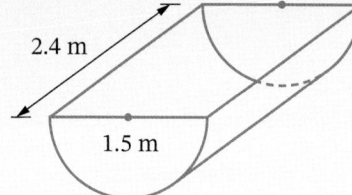
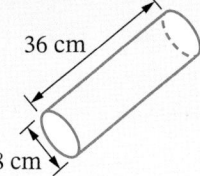

f closed half cylinder **g** half cylinder with open top, one end open

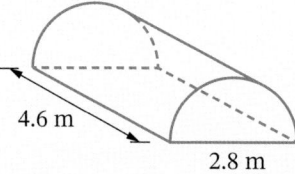
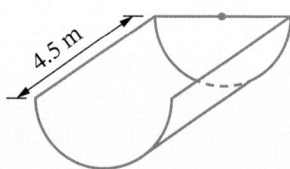

h closed cylinder **i** half cylinder, open both ends

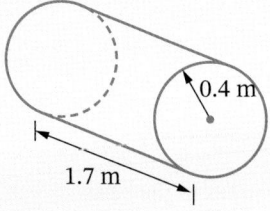
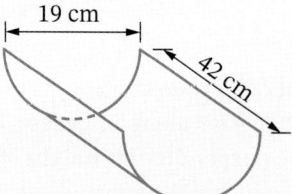

Foundation ○ Standard ○ Complex

7 The inside of the swimming pool, including the floor, is to be repainted. Find:

(PS)
(R)

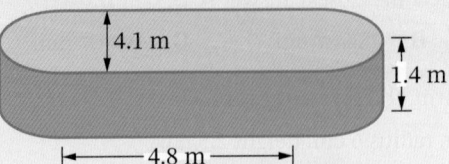

4.1 m

1.4 m

|←——— 4.8 m ———→|

a the area to be repainted, correct to one decimal place

b the number of whole litres of paint needed if coverage is 9 m² per litre.

8 The diagram shows a tent to be made in the shape of half a cylinder. Find:

(PS)
(R) **a** the area of the floor of the tent.

b the surface area of the tent, excluding the floor.

c the total cost of materials for the tent if the material for the flooring costs $18.50 per m² and the canvas for the tent costs $21.75 per m².

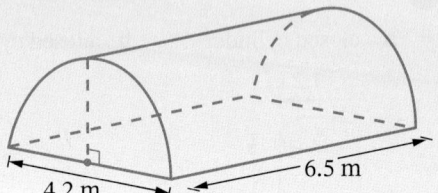

6.5 m

4.2 m

2.06 Extension: Surface area of a pyramid

EXTENSION

A **pyramid** is a solid shape with a polygon for its base and triangular faces that meet at a point or vertex called its **apex**. Like a prism, a pyramid is named by the shape of its base.

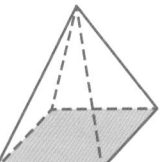
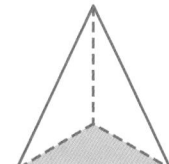
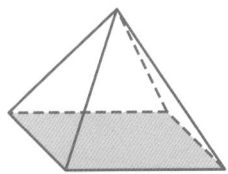

Square pyramid   Triangular pyramid   Rectangular pyramid

A **cone** is a solid shape with a circular base and a curved surface that also has an **apex**. However, a cone is not a pyramid because its base is not a polygon (a circle does not have straight sides).

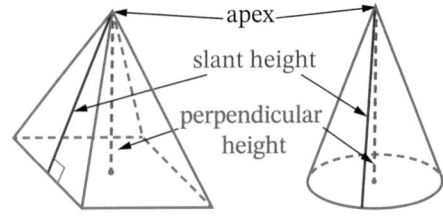

apex

slant height

perpendicular height

The **slant height** of a pyramid or cone is the height from the apex to the base, along a side face. It is different from the **perpendicular height** of a pyramid or cone, which is the perpendicular distance from the apex to the base.

The surface area of a pyramid is calculated by adding the areas of its base and its triangular faces.

Example 14

Find the surface area of each square pyramid.

a

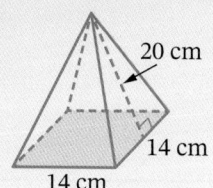

20 cm

This pyramid has a slant height of 20 cm.

14 cm

14 cm

b

This pyramid has a perpendicular height of 20 cm.

20 cm

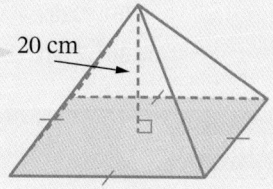

30 cm

EXTENSION 2.06

Video
Surface area of a pyramid

SOLUTION

a   Surface area = area of square base + area of 4 triangular faces

$$= 14 \times 14 + 4 \times \frac{1}{2} \times 14 \times 20$$

$$= 756 \text{ cm}^2$$

b   First find the slant height, s, using Pythagoras' theorem.

In $\triangle ABC$, $s^2 = 20^2 + 15^2$

$$= 625$$

$$s = \sqrt{625}$$

$$= 25 \text{ cm}$$

Surface area $= 30 \times 30 + 4 \times \frac{1}{2} \times 30 \times 25$

$$= 2400 \text{ cm}^2$$

$BC = \frac{1}{2} \times 30$

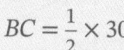

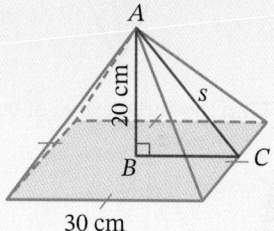

30 cm

Example 15

A rectangular pyramid with base 10 cm by 8 cm has a perpendicular height of 15 cm. Find its surface area, correct to one decimal place.

SOLUTION

First find the slant heights AP and AQ.

$AP^2 = AX^2 + XP^2$

$$= 15^2 + 4^2$$

$$= 241$$

$AP = \sqrt{241}$ cm

$AQ^2 = AX^2 + XQ^2$

$$= 15^2 + 5^2$$

$$= 250$$

$AQ = \sqrt{250}$ cm

$XP = \frac{1}{2} \times 8$

$XQ = \frac{1}{2} \times 10$

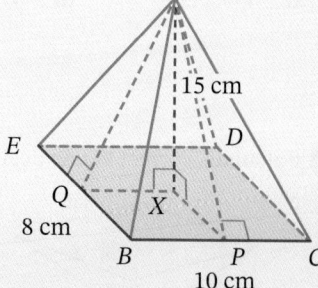

It is better to leave the lengths of AP and AQ in surd form rather than round them to decimals so that the final answer is accurate.

Surface area = area of rectangle base + 2 × Area △ABC + 2 × Area △ADC

$$= 10 \times 8 + 2 \times \frac{1}{2} \times 10 \times \sqrt{241} + 2 \times \frac{1}{2} \times 8 \times \sqrt{250}$$

$$= 361.7328...$$

$$\approx 361.7 \text{ cm}^2$$

EXERCISE 2.06 ANSWERS ON P. 606

Surface area of a pyramid

U F PS R

1 Find the area of each net and hence the surface area of the corresponding pyramid. All measurements are in centimetres.

a

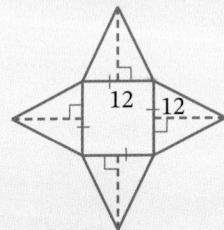

b

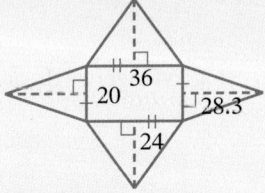

c

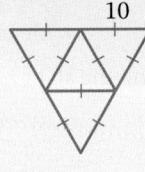

2 Find the surface area of each pyramid.

a

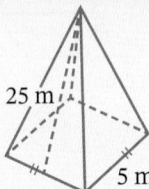

b

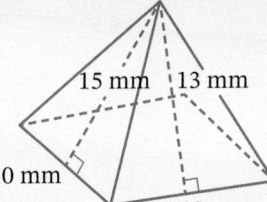

c

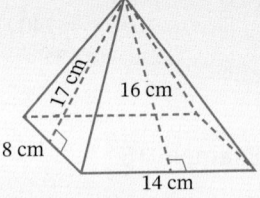

3 Find the surface area of this pyramid. Select the closest answer **A**, **B**, **C** or **D**.

A 288.0 cm²   **B** 453.9 cm²

C 459.8 cm²   **D** 471.0 cm²

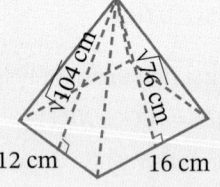

4 Calculate, correct to one decimal place, the surface area of each pyramid.

R **a**

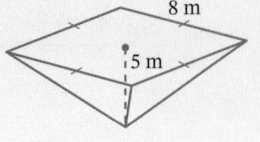

b

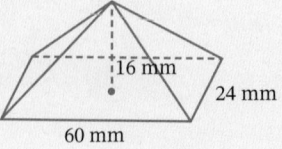

c

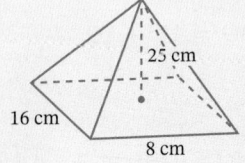

□ Foundation   ○ Standard   ◇ Complex

5 Calculate, correct to the nearest square centimetre, the surface area of each pyramid.
(PS) All measurements are in centimetres.

(R)

a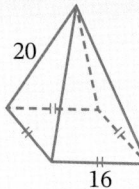
20
16

b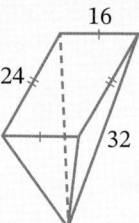
16
24
32

c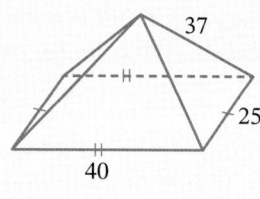
37
25
40

6 The great pyramid of Khufu (or Cheops) in Egypt has a height of 147 m, and each side of
(PS) its square base measures 230 m. Find its surface area (excluding the base), correct to the
(R) nearest square metre.

7 The Louvre Art Museum in Paris, France, has a large pyramid at its entrance (built
(PS) in 1989). It reaches a height of 21.6, has a square base of length 34 m and its sides are
(R) covered in rhombus and triangular glass pieces. Calculate the surface area of the glass
pyramid (to the nearest m²).

8 Calculate, correct to one decimal place, the surface area of each pyramid.

(PS)
(R)

a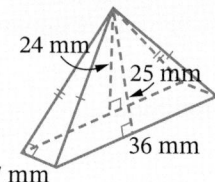
24 mm
25 mm
36 mm
7 mm

b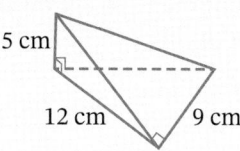
5 cm
12 cm
9 cm
All faces are right-angled
triangles

c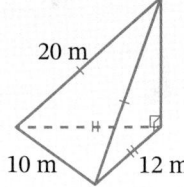
20 m
10 m
12 m

9 A square pyramid has a surface area of 4704 m² and a base area of 1764 m². Find:
(R) **a** the length of its base

b the area of each triangular face

c the slant height of each triangular face

d the perpendicular height of the pyramid

□ Foundation ○ Standard ○ Complex

INVESTIGATION

The surface area of a cone

The net of a cone is made up of a circle (for the base) and a sector of a circle (for the curved surface). The second diagram below shows the curved surface of a cone.

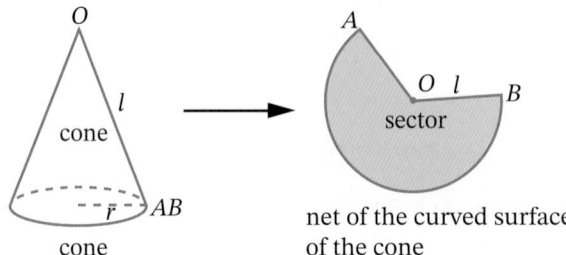

net of the curved surface
of the cone

We can use this fact to find a formula for the curved surface area of a cone. Suppose the cone has base radius r and slant height l. Then the sector must have radius l.

Looking at the sector, the major arc length AB is a fraction of the circumference of the circle and the area of the sector is a fraction of the area of the circle. They should be the same fraction, so:

$$\frac{\text{Area of sector}}{\text{Area of circle}} = \frac{\text{Arc length}}{\text{Circumference}}$$

1   The major arc length AB is the same as the circumference AB of the base of the cone in the first diagram. Write an algebraic expression for the circumference of the circle in the first diagram.

2   Write an algebraic expression for the circumference of the complete circle in the second diagram.

3   Write an algebraic expression for the *area* of the complete circle in the second diagram.

4   $\dfrac{\text{Area of sector}}{\text{Area of circle}} = \dfrac{\text{Arc length}}{\text{Circumference}}$ becomes $\dfrac{\text{Area of sector}}{\pi l^2} = \dfrac{2\pi r}{2\pi l}$

   Copy and complete: $\therefore$ Area of sector $= \dfrac{2\pi r}{2\pi l} \times \pi l^2 = \underline{\hspace{1cm}}$

5   But the area of the sector is equal to the curved surface area of the cone.

   Copy and complete:

   Surface area of cone = area of circular base + area of curved surface

   $= \underline{\hspace{1cm}} + \underline{\hspace{1cm}}$

Extension: Surface areas of cones and spheres

ⓘ Surface area of a cone

$SA = \pi r^2 + \pi r l$

where r = radius of circular base

l = slant height

The area of the circular base $= \pi r^2$

and the area of the curved surface $= \pi r l$

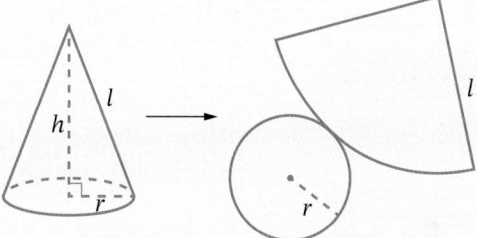

Example 16

For this cone, find correct to one decimal place:

a   the curved surface area

b   the total surface area

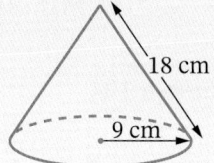

18 cm

9 cm

SOLUTION

$r = 9$ cm and $l = 18$ cm

a   Curved surface area $= \pi r l$

$= \pi \times 9 \times 18$

$= 508.9380 \ldots$

$\approx 508.9 \text{ cm}^2$

b   Total surface area $= \pi r^2 + \pi r l$

$= \pi \times 9^2 + \pi \times 9 \times 18$

$= 763.4070\ldots$

$\approx 763.4 \text{ cm}^2$

Example 17

Find, correct to 2 decimal places, the surface area of this cone.

Videos
Surface area of a cone and sphere

Surface area and volume of a cone

SOLUTION

First calculate the slant height:

$l^2 = 7.8^2 + 10.4^2$

$= 169$

$l = \sqrt{169}$

$= 13$

Surface area $= \pi r^2 + \pi r l$

$= \pi \times 7.8^2 + \pi \times 7.8 \times 13$

$= 509.6919\ldots$

$\approx 509.69 \text{ cm}^2$

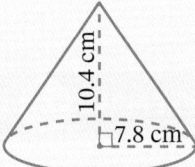

10.4 cm

7.8 cm

A **sphere** is a ball shape, completely round. A **hemisphere** is half a sphere.

ⓘ Surface area of a sphere

$$SA = 4\pi r^2$$

where r = radius of the sphere

Note that the surface area of a sphere is 4 times the area of a circle that shares its centre.

video
Surface area
of a cone
and sphere

Example 18

Find, correct to 2 decimal places, the surface area of this sphere.

SOLUTION

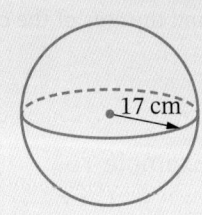

Surface area $= 4\pi r^2$

$\quad\quad\quad\quad = 4 \times \pi \times 17^2$

$\quad\quad\quad\quad = 3631.6811...$

$\quad\quad\quad\quad = 3631.68 \text{ cm}^2$

Example 19

Find the surface area of this hemisphere in exact form, in terms of π.

SOLUTION

5 m

Surface area $=$ Area of circular base $+$ Curved surface area

$\quad\quad\quad\quad = \pi r^2 + \dfrac{1}{2} \times 4\pi r^2$

$\quad\quad\quad\quad = \pi r^2 + 2\pi r^2$

$\quad\quad\quad\quad = 3\pi r^2$

$\quad\quad\quad\quad = 3 \times \pi \times 5^2$

$\quad\quad\quad\quad = 75\pi \text{ m}^2$

Answers written as surds or in terms of π are exact because they are not decimal approximations.

EXERCISE (2.07) ANSWERS ON P. 606

Surface areas of cones and spheres

Ⓤ Ⓕ Ⓟ Ⓢ Ⓡ Ⓒ

EXAMPLE
16

1 Calculate, correct to the nearest cm², the curved surface area of each cone. All measurements are in centimetres.

a

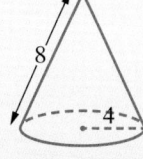

8

4

b

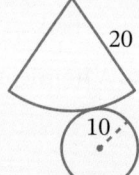

20

10

c

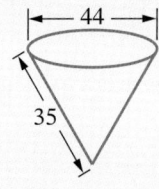

44

35

☐ **Foundation** ◯ **Standard** ◯ **Complex** ▷

2 Find, correct to one decimal place, the total surface area of each cone.

a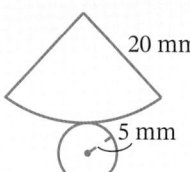
20 mm
5 mm

b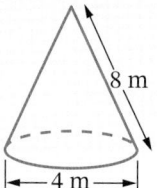
8 m
←—4 m—→

c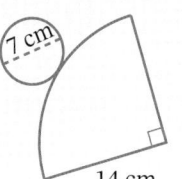
7 cm
14 cm

3 Calculate, correct to one decimal place, the surface area of each cone.

EXAMPLE 17

(R) **a**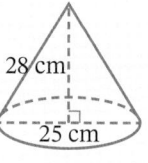
28 cm
25 cm

b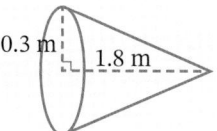
0.3 m 1.8 m

c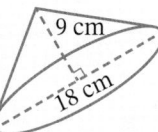
9 cm
18 cm

4 Find in exact form (in terms of π) the total surface area of each cone.

(R)(C) **a**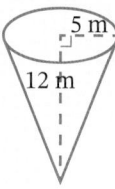
5 m
12 m

b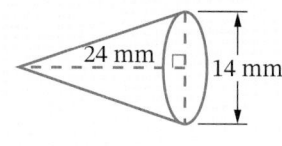
24 mm 14 mm

c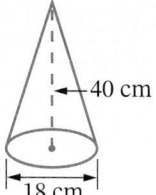
40 cm
18 cm

5 Calculate, correct to one decimal place, the surface area of each sphere.

EXAMPLE 18

a
15 mm

b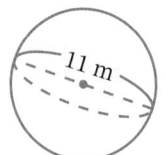
11 m

c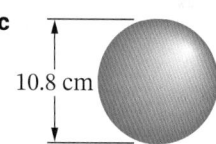
10.8 cm

6 Find in exact form the surface area of each closed hemisphere.

(R)(C) **a**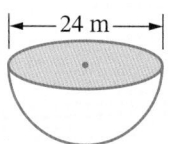
|←—24 m—→|

b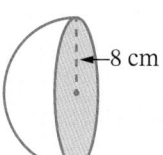
8 cm

c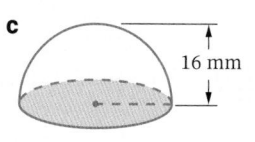
16 mm

EXAMPLE 19

7 Calculate the surface area of a closed hemisphere with radius 1.4 m. Select the closest

(R) answer **A**, **B**, **C** or **D**.

   A 12.32 m²   **B** 18.47 m²   **C** 24.63 m²   **D** 49.26 m²

8 Find, correct to the nearest square metre, the surface area of:

(PS) **a** a sphere with diameter 10 m

(R) **b** an open cone with base radius 10 m, slant height 20 m

c an open hemisphere with radius 10 m

d a cone with base diameter 10 m, perpendicular height 20 m

9 The Earth has a radius of approximately 6378 km.

(PS) **a** Calculate the surface area of the Earth in scientific notation, correct to 3 significant
(R) figures.

(C) **b** If 70.9% of the Earth's surface is covered by water, calculate the land area of the
Earth's surface, correct to 3 significant figures.

c The land area of Australia is 7 692 000 km². Calculate Australia's land area as a
percentage of the Earth's land area (correct to 2 decimal places).

10 Find the amount of sheet metal needed to form a conical funnel of base radius 30 cm
and vertical height 50 cm, allowing for a 0.5 cm overlap at the join.

(PS)

(R)

(C)

11 A cone is made from a sector of a circle with radius 8 cm and
central angle 216°. Find:

(PS)

(R) **a** the length of the arc of the circle which forms the
(C) circumference of the cone's base

b the radius of the cone's base

c the slant height of the cone

d the total surface area of the cone, including the base

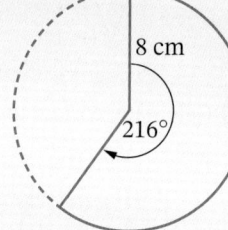

12 Find the radius of each solid if it has a surface area of 6000 mm². Give your answer
(R) correct to 3 significant figures.

a a sphere   **b** a closed hemisphere   **c** an open hemisphere

13 A cone has a surface area of 2000 cm². If the area of its base is 150 cm², find:

(R) **a** the radius of its base   **b** its slant height   **c** its perpendicular height

□ Foundation   ○ Standard   ○ Complex

Surface areas of composite solids

When calculating surface areas of composite solids, remember to not include the areas common to both solids.

Video
The power of the Sun

Example 20

Find, correct to one decimal place, the surface area of each solid. All measurements are in centimetres.

a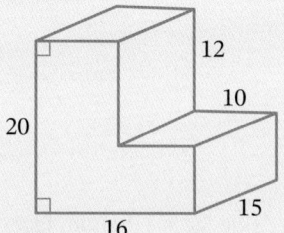

b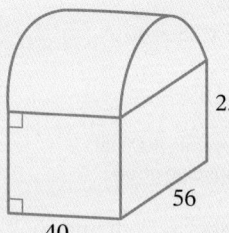

c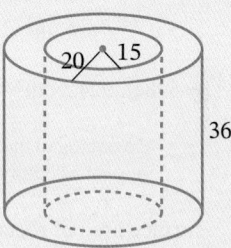

Worksheet
A page of prisms and cylinders

SOLUTION

a This prism has 8 faces: 2 identical L-shapes (front and back) and 6 different rectangles.

area of L-shape $= 16 \times 20 - 10 \times 12$

$\qquad = 200 \text{ cm}^2$

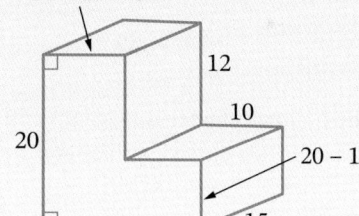

surface area = front and back L-faces + 1st top + 1st right + 2nd top + 2nd right
$\qquad$ + bottom + left

$\qquad = (2 \times 200) + (6 \times 15) + (12 \times 15) + (10 \times 15) + (8 \times 15) + (16 \times 15) + (20 \times 15)$

$\qquad = 1480 \text{ cm}^2$

Note that the 6 rectangles can also be thought of as one long rectangle of width 15 cm.

length of long rectangle = perimeter of L-shape

$\qquad = 6 + 12 + 10 + 8 + 16 + 20$

$\qquad = 72$

surface area $= (2 \times 200) + (72 \times 15)$

$\qquad = 1480 \text{ cm}^2$

b The solid is made up of a half-cylinder (3 faces) and a rectangular prism (5 faces).

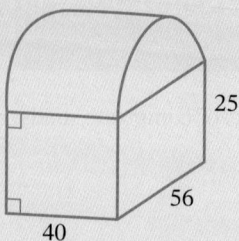

surface area of half-cylinder

= 2 semi-circular ends + curved surface area   radius of a semi-circle = $\frac{1}{2} \times 56$

$= 2 \times \frac{1}{2} \times \pi \times 28^2 + \frac{1}{2} \times 2 \times \pi \times 28 \times 40$ = 28

= 5981.5924... cm²

> Do not round this partial answer as the final answer will be inaccurate (rounding error).

surface area of rectangular prism = front and back faces + 2 side faces + bottom face

$= (2 \times 40 \times 25) + (2 \times 56 \times 25) + (40 \times 56)$

= 7040 cm²

total surface area = 5981.5924... + 7040

= 13 021.5924...

≈ 13 021.6 cm²

c The hollow cylinder is made up of 2 annulus (ring) faces, an outside curved surface area and an inside curved surface area.

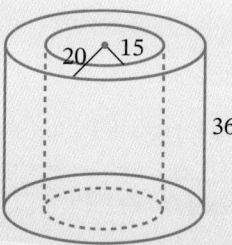

surface area of annulus faces = $2 \times (\pi \times 20^2 - \pi \times 15^2)$ 2 × area between 2 circles

= 1099.5574... cm²

outside curved surface area = $2 \times \pi \times 20 \times 36$

= 4523.8934... cm²

inside curved surface area = $2 \times \pi \times 15 \times 36$

= 3392.9200... cm²

total surface area = 1099.5574... + 4523.8934... + 3392.9200...

= 9016.3709...

= 9016.4 cm²

Example 21

Find, correct to the nearest square centimetre, the surface area of each solid.
All measurements are in centimetres.

a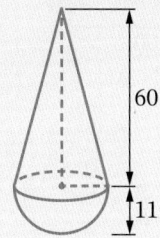

60

11

b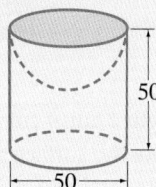

50

50

SOLUTION

a Surface area = curved surface area of cone + curved surface area of hemisphere

$$= \pi r l + \frac{1}{2} \times 4\pi r^2$$

$r = 11, h = 60$ and $l = ?$

$$l^2 = 11^2 + 60^2$$

$$= 3721$$

$$l = \sqrt{3721}$$

$$= 61 \text{ cm}$$

Surface area $= \pi \times 11 \times 61 + \frac{1}{2} \times 4 \times \pi \times 11^2$

$$= 2868.2740 \ldots$$

$$\approx 2868 \text{ cm}^2$$

b Surface area = curved surface of cylinder + circular base + curved surface of hemisphere

$$= 2\pi r h + \pi r^2 + \frac{1}{2} \times 4\pi r^2$$

$$= 2\pi r h + 3\pi r^2 \qquad\qquad \pi r^2 + 2\pi r^2 = 3\pi r^2$$

$$= 2 \times \pi \times 25 \times 50 + 3 \times \pi \times 25^2 \qquad r = \frac{1}{2} \times 50 = 25$$

$$= 13\,744.4678\ldots$$

$$\approx 13\,744 \text{ cm}^2$$

EXERCISE 2.08 ANSWERS ON P. 606

Surface areas of composite solids

U F PS R

1 Find the surface area of each prism. All measurements are in centimetres.

EXAMPLE 20

PS R **a**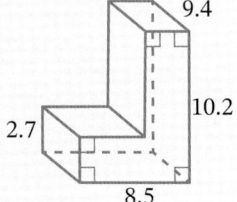

3.3

9.4

10.2

2.7

8.5

b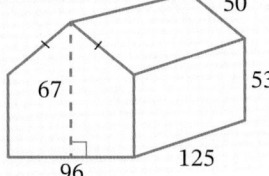

50

67

53

96

125

c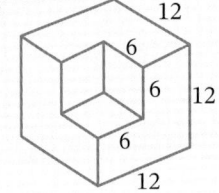

12

6

6

12

6

12

□ Foundation   ○ Standard   ◊ Complex

d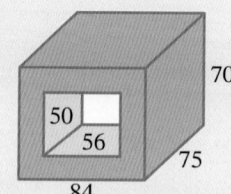
18

18 13 13
60 40

e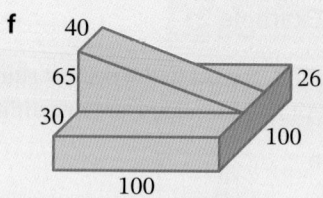
70
50
56
75
84

f
40
65 26
30 100
100

2 Three cubes of length 2 cm, 4 cm and 8 cm are glued on top of
each other. Calculate the surface area of the new solid.

PS

R

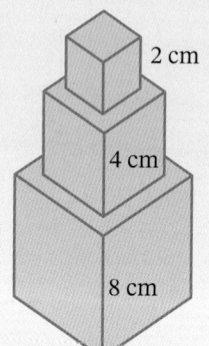
2 cm
4 cm
8 cm

3 Circular cracker biscuits of diameter 4 cm are packed in a
cardboard box of length 20 cm.

   a Calculate the surface area of the box.

   b How much cardboard would be saved if the biscuits
   were packed into a cylindrical box?

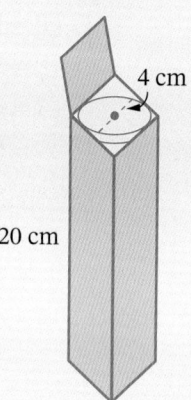
4 cm
20 cm

4 Find, correct to one decimal place, the surface area of each solid. All measurements are
in centimetres.

PS

R **a**
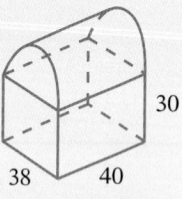
30
38 40

b
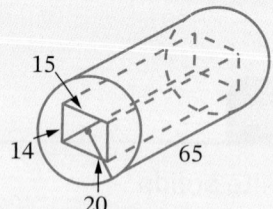
15
14
65
20

c 25 17
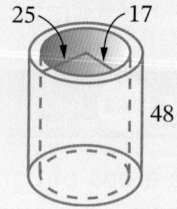
48

d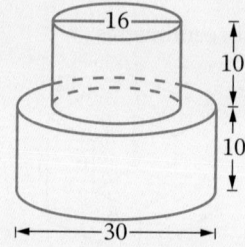
16
10
10
30

e
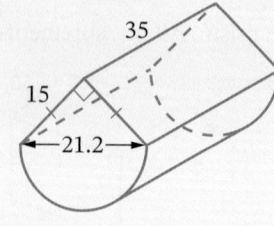
35
15
21.2

f
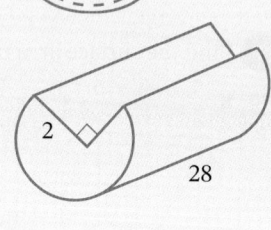
2
28

☐ Foundation ○ Standard ○ Complex

9780170465595

5 Calculate the surface area of the solid, correct to one decimal place. All measurements are in centimetres.

Select the correct answer **A**, **B**, **C** or **D**.

A 86.0 cm²   **B** 103.2 cm²

C 108.3 cm²   **D** 113.4 cm²

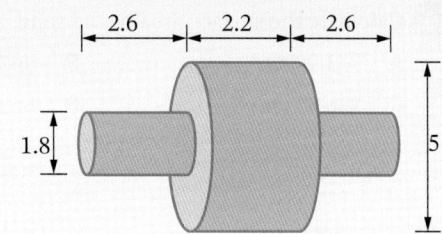

6 A wedding cake with 3 tiers rests on a table. Each tier is 6 cm high. The layers have radii of 20 cm, 15 cm and 10 cm respectively.

Find the total visible surface area, correct to the nearest cm².

7 a Find, correct to 2 decimal places, the total external area of the wall of this above-ground swimming pool.

b Calculate the area of the water surface, correct to the nearest m².

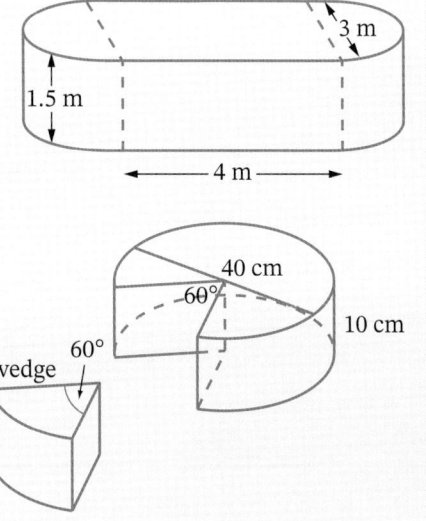

8 A wedge of cheese is cut from a cylindrical block of height 10 cm and diameter 40 cm. Find the total surface area of the wedge, correct to 2 decimal places.

9780170465595

□ Foundation   ○ Standard   ○ Complex

2.08

EXTENSION

EXAMPLE 21

9 Calculate the surface area of the solid. Select **A**, **B**, **C** or **D**.

(PS) **A** 923.98 cm²   **B** 962.46 cm²

(R) **C** 736.62 cm²   **D** 669.51 cm²

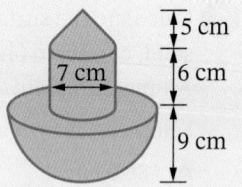

10 Calculate the total surface of a hemispherical bird bath that is 1 cm thick and has an outer radius of 40 cm.

(PS)

(R)

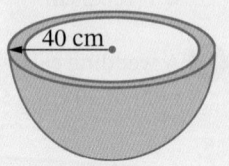

11 Find, correct to one decimal place, the surface area of each solid. All measurements are in centimetres.

(PS)

(R) **a**

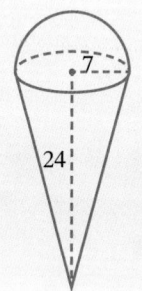

b

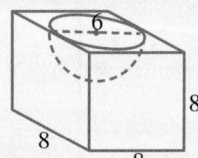

c

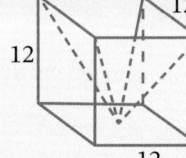

d

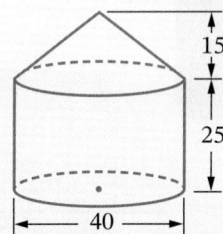

e

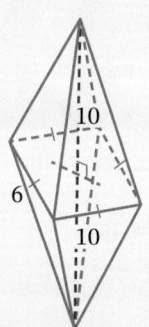

f

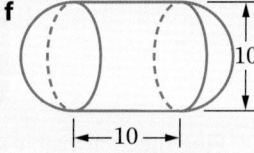

g

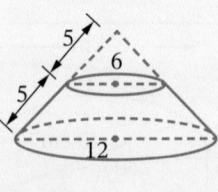

h

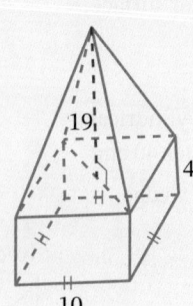

i

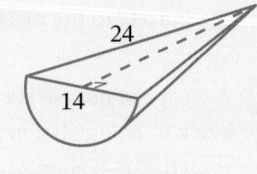

▷

☐ Foundation   ○ Standard   ○ Complex

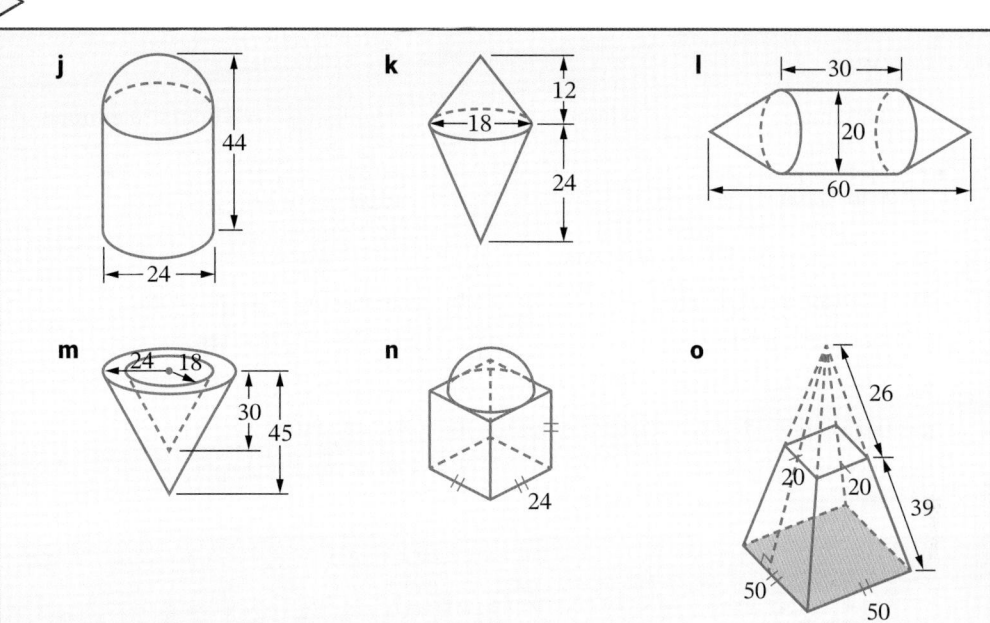

☆ **MENTAL SKILLS** (2) ANSWERS ON P. 606 **Maths without calculators**

Quiz
Mental
skills 2

Time differences

1 Study each example.

a What is the time difference between 11:40 am and 6:15 pm?

From 11:40 am to 5:40 pm = 6 hours

Count: '11:40, 12:40, 1:40, 2:40, 3:40, 4:40, 5:40'

From 5:40 am to 6:00 pm = 20 min

From 6:00 pm to 6:15 pm = 15 min

5 hours + 20 min + 15 min = 6 hours 35 min

OR:

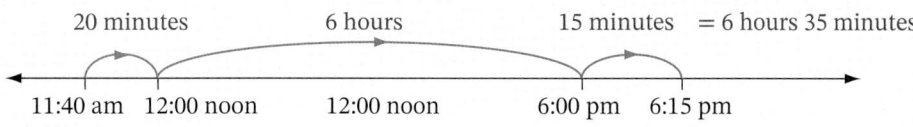

b In 24-hour time, what is the time difference between 2030 and 0120?

From 2030 to 0030 = 4 hours (24 − 20 = 4)

From 0030 to 0100 = 30 min

From 0100 to 0120 = 20 min

4 hours + 30 minutes + 20 minutes = 4 hours 50 minutes

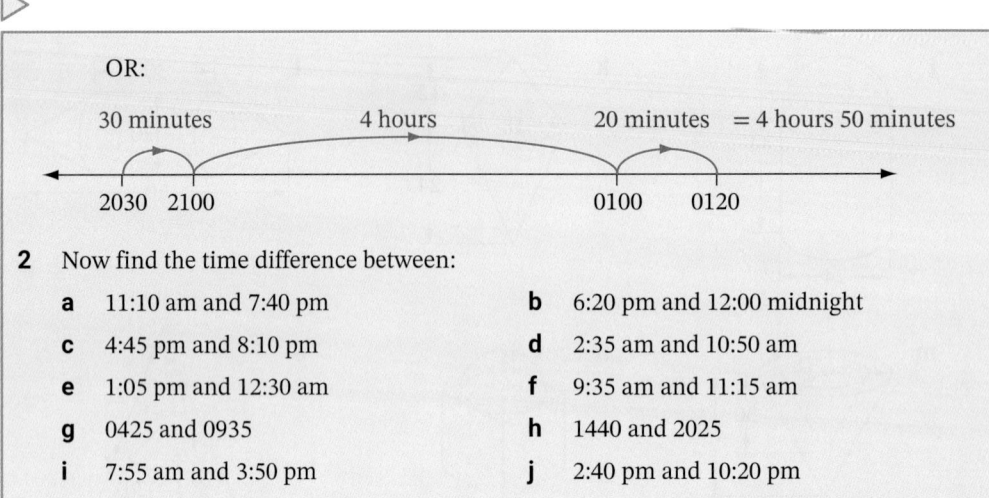

OR:

30 minutes   4 hours   20 minutes   = 4 hours 50 minutes

2030 2100   0100   0120

2 Now find the time difference between:

a 11:10 am and 7:40 pm   **b** 6:20 pm and 12:00 midnight

c 4:45 pm and 8:10 pm   **d** 2:35 am and 10:50 am

e 1:05 pm and 12:30 am   **f** 9:35 am and 11:15 am

g 0425 and 0935   **h** 1440 and 2025

i 7:55 am and 3:50 pm   **j** 2:40 pm and 10:20 pm

2.09 Volumes of prisms and cylinders

Videos
Volumes of prisms and cylinders

Bees and their hives

The incredible strength of ants

The Menger sponge

Worksheets
A page of prisms and cylinders

Back-to-front problems

Volumes of solids

Volume and capacity

Puzzle
Formula matching game

Presentation
Volumes of shapes

ⓘ Volume of a prism

$$V = Ah$$

where A = area of base

h = perpendicular height

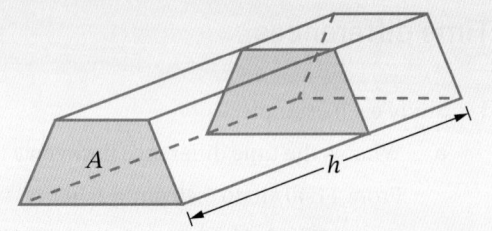

ⓘ Volume of a cylinder

$$V = \pi r^2 h$$

where r = radius of circular base

h = perpendicular height

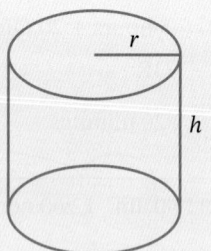

ⓘ Volume and capacity

1 cm³ contains 1 mL

1 m³ contains 1000 L or 1 kL

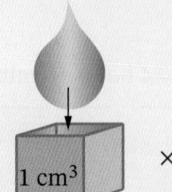

1 cm³

× 1 000 000 =

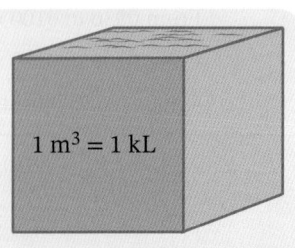

1 m³ = 1 kL

Example 22

For this cylinder, calculate:

a its volume, correct to the nearest cm³

b its capacity in kL, correct to one decimal place.

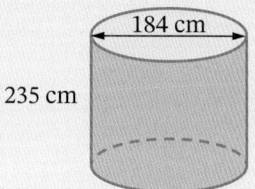

Video
Capacity of a cylinder

SOLUTION

a   radius $= \dfrac{1}{2} \times 184$ $V = \pi \times 92^2 \times 235$

$= 92$ cm $= 6\,248\,753.452...$

$\approx 6\,248\,753$ cm³

b   capacity $= 6\,248\,753$ mL 1 cm³ $= 1$ mL

$= 6\,248\,753 \div 1000 \div 1000$ kL

$= 6.248\,753$ kL

≈ 6.2 kL

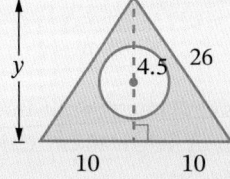

kL $\div 1000$ L $\div 1000$ mL

Example 23

Find, correct to the nearest whole number, the volume of each solid.

a
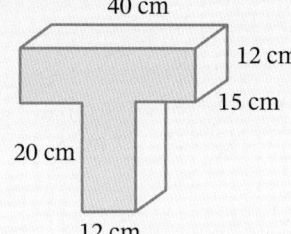

b
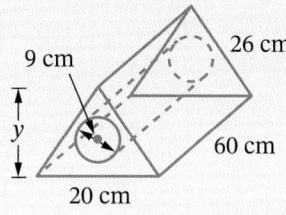

c
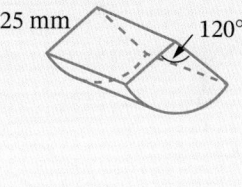

SOLUTION

a $A = 40 \times 12 + 20 \times 12$ $V = Ah$

$= 720$ cm² $= 720 \times 15$

$= 10\,800$ cm³

b   Cross-section is the triangle minus the circle.

Use Pythagoras' theorem to find y.

$26^2 = y^2 + 10^2$

$y^2 = 26^2 - 10^2$

$= 576$

$y = \sqrt{576}$

$= 24$ cm

radius of circle $= \dfrac{1}{2} \times 9 = 4.5$

$$A = \frac{1}{2} \times 20 \times 24 - \pi \times 4.5^2$$
$$= 176.3827... \text{ cm}^2$$

$$V = Ah$$
$$= 176.3827... \times 60$$
$$= 10\,582.9649...$$
$$\approx 10\,583 \text{ cm}^3$$

c $\quad A = \frac{120}{360} \times \pi \times 25^2$
$$= 654.498... \text{ mm}^2$$

$$V = Ah$$
$$= 654.498... \times 40$$
$$= 26\,179.938...$$
$$\approx 26\,180 \text{ mm}^2$$

EXERCISE 2.09 ANSWERS ON P. 606

Volumes of prisms and cylinders

(U) (F) (R)

EXAMPLE 22

1 Calculate, correct to one decimal place, the volume of each solid.

a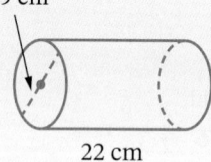
9 cm
22 cm

b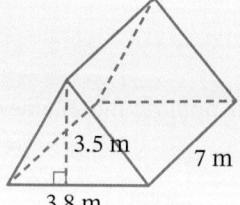
3.5 m
7 m
3.8 m

c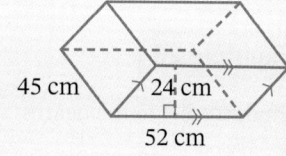
45 cm 24 cm
52 cm

d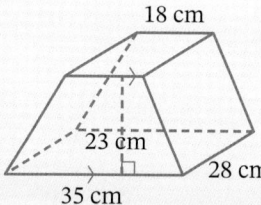
18 cm
23 cm
28 cm
35 cm

e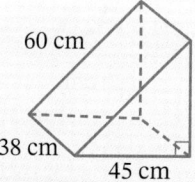
60 cm
38 cm
45 cm

f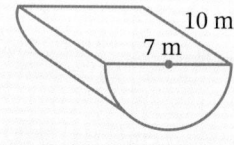
10 m
7 m

g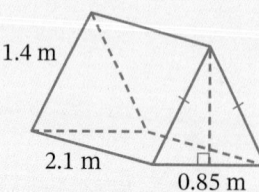
1.4 m
2.1 m
0.85 m

h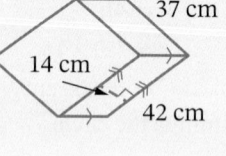
37 cm
14 cm
42 cm

i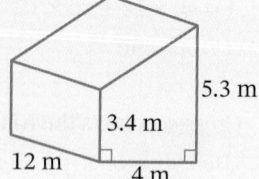
5.3 m
3.4 m
12 m
4 m

2 Rice crackers of diameter 4 cm are packed in a cardboard box of height 20 cm. Calculate, correct to one decimal place:

a the volume of the crackers in the box

b the volume of the box

c the percentage of the box that is empty space.

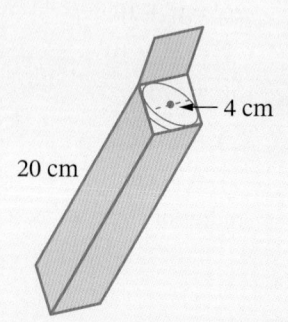
4 cm
20 cm

□ Foundation ○ Standard ○ Complex

9780170465595

3 Calculate, correct to one decimal place, the volume of the shed.

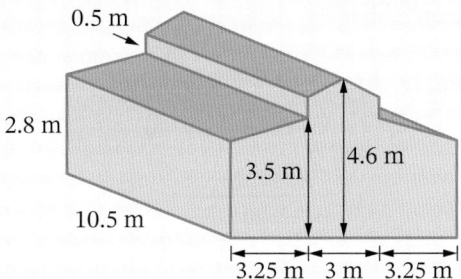

4 This swimming pool is 12 m long and 6 m wide. The depth of the pool ranges from 1.2 m to 2.1 m.

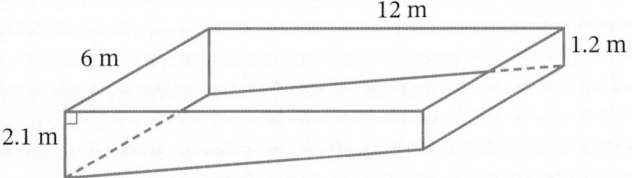

    a Calculate the capacity of this pool in litres.

    b If the pool is filled so that the water is 8 cm from the top of the pool, calculate the amount of water in the pool (to the nearest litre).

5 An Olympic sized swimming pool is 50 m long, 25 m wide and 2 m deep. What is the capacity of an Olympic pool in litres?

6 **a** Find, correct to 2 decimal places, the volume of this greenhouse.

    b If this greenhouse costs 0.5c per m³ per hour to heat, how much is this per day (correct to the nearest cent)?

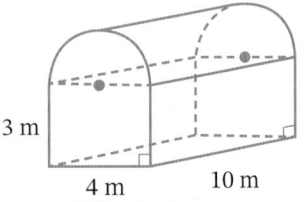

7 A child's toy involves placing 5 coloured cylinders on a wooden stick (diameter 1 cm) on a base (diameter 18 cm). The cylinders are of varying diameters, each with a height of 2 cm. Find the volume of the toy, including the base and peg, correct to one decimal place.

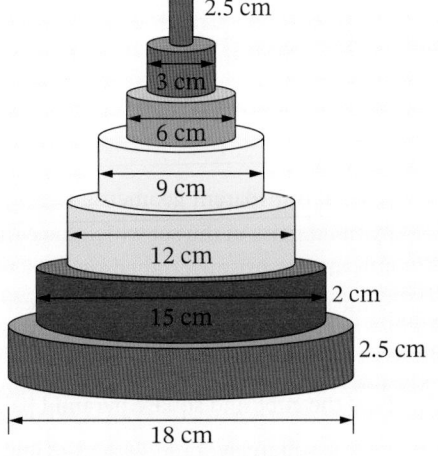

□ Foundation   ○ Standard   ○ Complex

EXAMPLE 23

8 Find, correct to 2 decimal places where appropriate, the volume of each solid. All lengths shown are in centimetres.

a

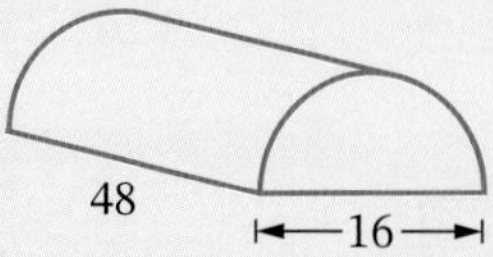

48

|← 16 →|

b

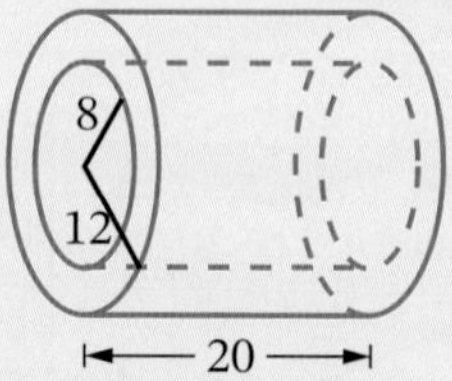

8

12

|← 20 →|

c

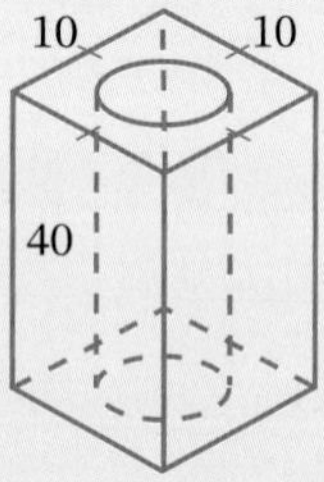

10   10

40

radius of circle = 4 cm

d

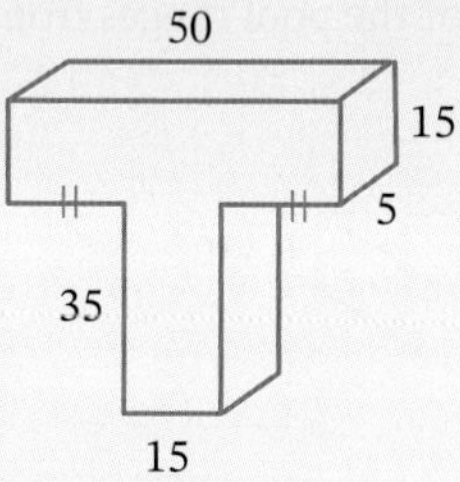

50

15

5

35

15

e

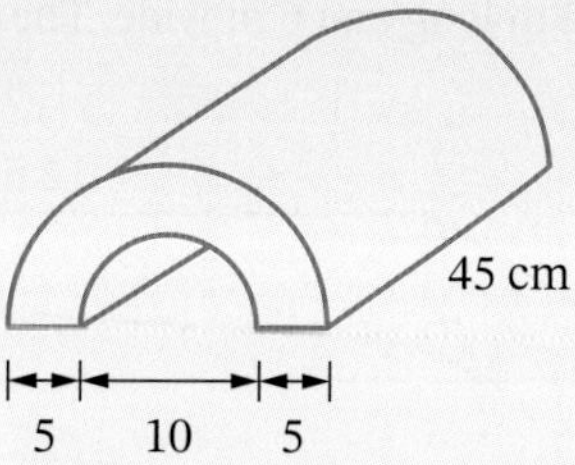

45 cm

|←→|←   →|←→|
5   10   5

f

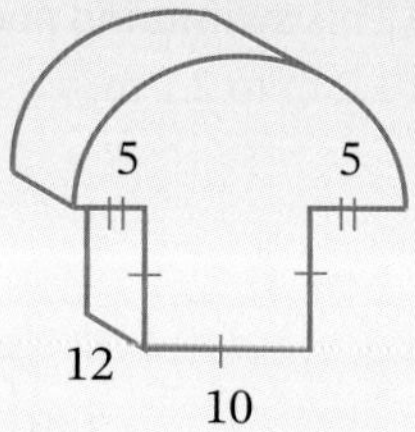

5   5

12

10

g

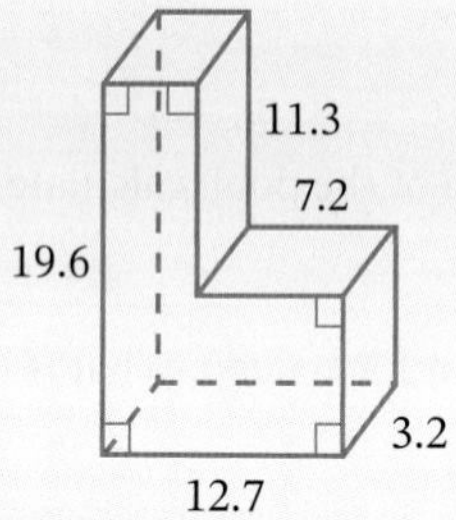

11.3

7.2

19.6

3.2

12.7

h

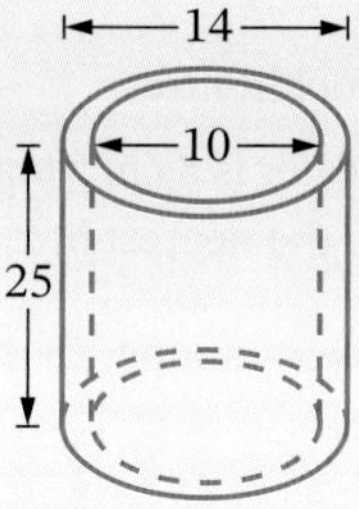

|← 14 →|

|← 10 →|

25

i

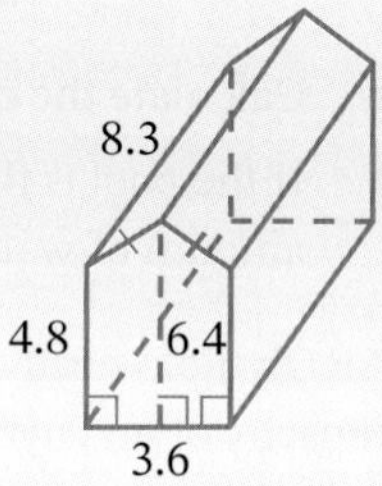

8.3

4.8   6.4

3.6

j

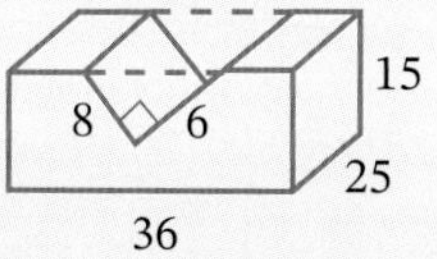

15

8   6

25

36

k

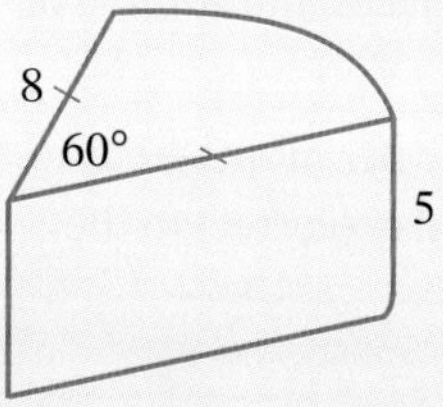

8

60°

5

l

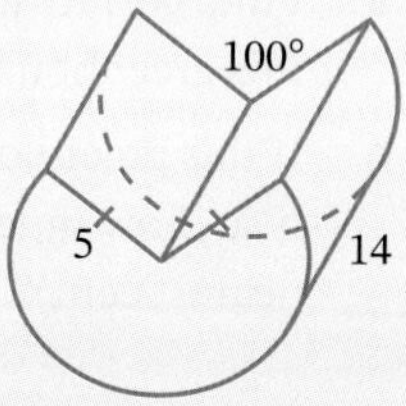

100°

5   14

EXTENSION

INVESTIGATION

How many pyramids are needed to fill the prism?

You will need:

- A set of transparent geometric solids that can be opened and filled. Find the prism and pyramid pairs in the set which have the same size base: a cube/square pyramid pair, a triangular prism/tetrahedron pair, and cylinder/cone pair.
- Some packing material that flows (can be sand, rice grains, lentils or water).

Instructions

1   Find the cube and square pyramid pair.

2   Fill the square pyramid with sand and transfer the contents into the corresponding cube.

3   How much of the cube has been filled?

☐ Foundation ○ Standard ○ Complex

4 How many times would you need to transfer the contents of a filled square pyramid into the cube in order to fill it?

5 Repeat steps **1** to **4** above using the triangular prism and tetrahedron pair.

6 Repeat steps **1** to **4** above using the cylinder and cone pair.

7 What do you notice about your answers to the question in step **4** for all 3 prism/pyramid pairs?

8 Write a general rule that can be used to find the volume of any pyramid by relating it to a prism that has the same base.

EXTENSION

2.09

TECHNOLOGY

Approximating the volume of a pyramid

We can approximate the volume of a pyramid by dividing it into of layers of prisms as shown below.

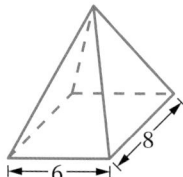 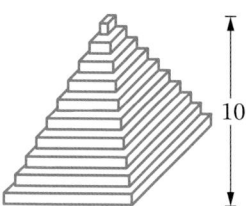

Technology
Measuring
pyramids

Approximating
the volume
of a cone

We will create a spreadsheet that approximates the volume of a rectangular pyramid with a base of length 8 units and width 6 units, and a perpendicular height of 10 units.

The volume of each layer can be easily calculated using $V = lwh$. Finding the sum of the layers will then give an approximation of the volume of the pyramid.

Let n be the number of layers. Then the height of each layer is $\frac{10}{n}$.

The length and width of each layer decreases from 8 units and 6 units by a constant amount of $\frac{8}{n}$ and $\frac{6}{n}$ respectively from layer to layer.

1 Create this spreadsheet for calculating the volume if each layer and the sum of the volumes.

	A	B	C	D	E	F
1				Number of layers		
2						
3	Height	Length	Width	Thickness of layer	Volume of layer	Sum of volumes
4	10	8	6	=$A$4/$D$2	=B4*C4*D4	=E4
5		=B4-$B$4/$D$2	=C4-$C$4/$D$2			=E5+F4
6						
13						

▷

2 a To divide the volume of the pyramid into 10 layers, enter **10** in cell D2.

 b Copy each formula down to row 13.

 c Explain the results in cells E13 and F13.

 d How accurate was your result in F13? Explain.

 e Print out your spreadsheet.

3 a To divide the pyramid into 40 layers to calculate a better approximation, enter **40** in cell D2 and copy each formula down to row 43.

 b In 1–2 sentences, compare your volume approximation in F43 with the previous approximation in F13.

4 a Enter each of these values in cell D2, copy the formulas down to the appropriate row and write down the approximation for the volume of the pyramid.

 i 100 (copy down to row 104)

 ii 200 (copy down to row 204)

 iii 400 (copy down to row 404)

 b Use the formula $V = \frac{1}{3}Ah$ to calculate the exact volume of the pyramid.

 c Write a brief report about your results in parts **a** and **b**.

2.10 Extension: Volumes of pyramids, cones and spheres

Worksheets
Volume and capacity

Back-to-front problems (Advanced)

Video
The Pacific Flyer

ⓘ Volume of a pyramid

$$V = \frac{1}{3}Ah$$

where A = area of base

h = perpendicular height

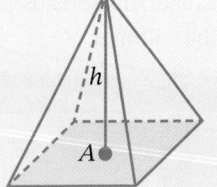

The volume of a pyramid is $\frac{1}{3}$ of the volume of a prism with the same base and height.

This fact is difficult to prove mathematically, but here's a diagram that might help. This is a square pyramid with dimensions s, s and $\frac{s}{2}$, with an identical pyramid balancing on top of it upside-down.

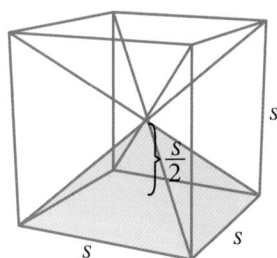

Now look at the big cube that surrounds these 2 square pyramids.

- Can you see how many such pyramids fit into this big cube exactly?
- What is the volume of the big cube?
- So, what is the volume of one pyramid?
- Is this the same as $V = \dfrac{1}{3}Ah$?

EXTENSION

2.10

Example 24

Find the volume of each pyramid.

a

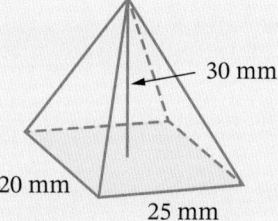

30 mm

20 mm

25 mm

b

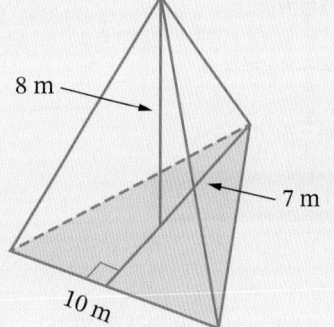

8 m

7 m

10 m

Video
Volume of
a pyramid

SOLUTION

a $A = 25 \times 20$

  $= 500 \text{ mm}^2$

  $V = \dfrac{1}{3} \times 500 \times 30$

  $= 5000 \text{ mm}^3$

b $A = \dfrac{1}{2} \times 10 \times 7$

  $= 35 \text{ mm}^2$

  $V = \dfrac{1}{3} \times 35 \times 8$

  $= 93\dfrac{1}{3} \text{ m}^3$

Example 25

Find the capacity (to the nearest mL) of a square
pyramid with base edge 64 mm and slant
height 40 mm.

SOLUTION

First find h, the perpendicular height of the pyramid.

$h^2 = 40^2 - 32^2$ using Pythagoras' theorem

  $= 576$

$h = \sqrt{576}$

  $= 24 \text{ mm}$

$A = 64^2$ area of square base

  $= 4096 \text{ mm}^2$

h

40 mm

64 mm

$$V = \frac{1}{3} \times 4096 \times 24 \qquad\qquad V = \frac{1}{3}Ah, \text{ where height } h = 24$$

$$= 32\,768 \text{ mm}^3$$

$$= 32.768 \text{ cm}^3 \qquad\qquad 1 \text{ cm}^3 = 1000 \text{ mm}^3$$

$$\text{capacity} = 32.768 \text{ mL} \qquad\qquad 1 \text{ cm}^3 = 1 \text{ mL}$$

$$\approx 33 \text{ mL}$$

A cone is like a 'circular pyramid' so:

$$\text{Volume} = \frac{1}{3}Ah$$

$$= \frac{1}{3} \times \pi r^2 \times h$$

$$= \frac{1}{3}\pi r^2 h$$

ⓘ Volume of a cone

Video
Surface area
and volume
of a cone

$$V = \frac{1}{3}\pi r^2 h$$

where r = radius of circular base

$\quad h$ = perpendicular height

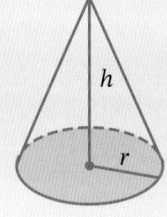

Example 26

Calculate the volume of the cone, correct to the nearest cm³.

SOLUTION

$$V = \frac{1}{3} \times \pi \times 10.5^2 \times 30 \qquad V = \frac{1}{3}\pi r^2 h, \text{ where } r = \frac{1}{2} \times 21 = 10.5$$

$$= 3463.6059...$$

$$\approx 3464 \text{ cm}^3$$

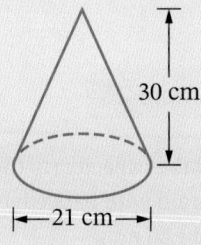

30 cm

⟵ 21 cm ⟶

Example 27

A cone has a slant edge of 61 mm and a base radius of 11 mm.
Find its volume, correct to one decimal place.

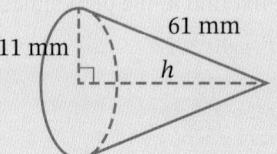

11 mm   61 mm h

SOLUTION

First, find the height, h.

$$h^2 = 61^2 - 11^2 \qquad\qquad V = \frac{1}{3} \times \pi \times 11^2 \times 60$$

$$= 3600 \qquad\qquad\qquad = 7602.6542...$$

$$h = \sqrt{3600} \qquad\qquad\quad \approx 7602.7 \text{ mm}^2$$

$$= 60$$

ⓘ Volume of a sphere

$$V = \frac{4}{3}\pi r^3$$

where r = radius of the sphere

Video
Volume of
a sphere

Example 28

Find, correct to one decimal place, the volume of each solid.

a

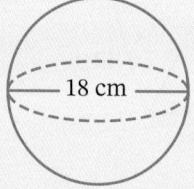

18 cm

b

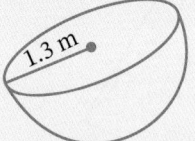

1.3 m

SOLUTION

a $V = \frac{4}{3}\pi r^3$

$= \frac{4}{3} \times \pi \times 9^3 \qquad r = \frac{1}{2} \times 18 = 9$

$= 3053.6280...$

$\approx 3053.6 \text{ cm}^3$

b $V = \frac{1}{2} \times \frac{4}{3}\pi r^3 = \frac{2}{3}\pi r^3$

$= \frac{2}{3} \times \pi \times 1.3^3$

$= 4.6013...$

$\approx 4.6 \text{ m}^3$

EXERCISE 2.10 ANSWERS ON P. 606

Volumes of pyramids, cones and spheres Ⓤ Ⓕ ⓅⓈ Ⓡ Ⓒ

EXAMPLE
24

1 Calculate the volume of each pyramid (correct to one decimal place where necessary).

a

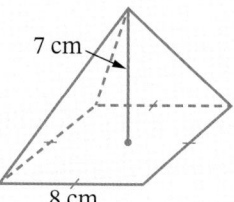

7 cm

8 cm

b

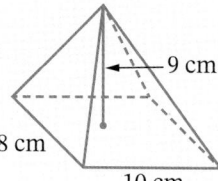

9 cm

8 cm

10 cm

c

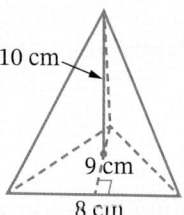

10 cm

9 cm

8 cm

d

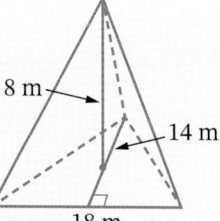

8 m

14 m

18 m

e

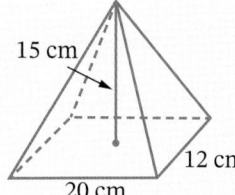

15 cm

12 cm

20 cm

f

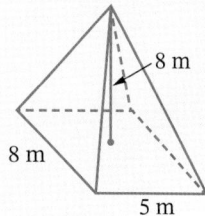

8 m

8 m

5 m

☐ Foundation ○ Standard ○ Complex

▷

2 A grain hopper is in the shape of a square pyramid.

(PS) **a** Find the volume of grain it holds when full.

(R) **b** If there are 750 kg of wheat per m³, find the mass of
(C) grain in the hopper when it is filled to three-quarters of
   its capacity. Give your answer correct to the nearest tonne.

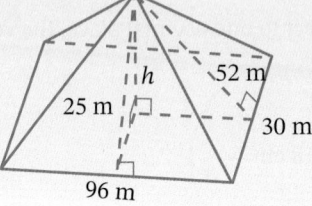

4.5 m   4.5 m

5 m

EXAMPLE
25

3 For each pyramid, find correct to 2 decimal places:

(R) **i** its perpendicular height, *h*   **ii** its volume   **iii** its capacity.

a

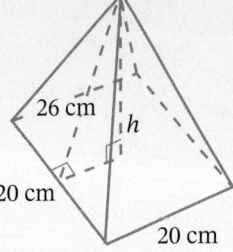

26 cm   *h*

20 cm

20 cm

b

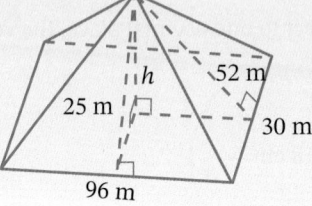

h   52 m

25 m   30 m

96 m

c

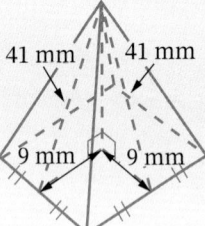

41 mm   41 mm

9 mm   9 mm

d

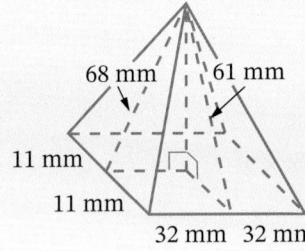

68 mm   61 mm

11 mm

11 mm

32 mm   32 mm

e

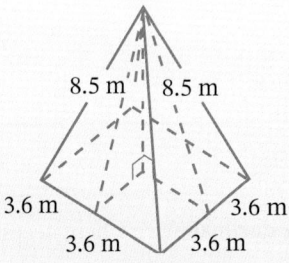

8.5 m   8.5 m

3.6 m   3.6 m

3.6 m   3.6 m

f

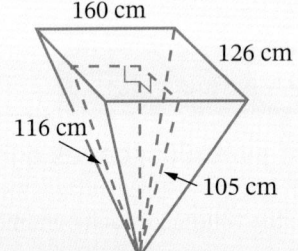

160 cm

126 cm

116 cm

105 cm

4 The Great Pyramid of Khufu (or Cheops) in Egypt was built on a square base with side
(PS) lengths approximately 230 m.

(R) **a** Find the volume in cubic metres if the original height of the pyramid was 147 m.

(C) **b** There are an estimated 2.3 million stone blocks in the pyramid. Calculate the
   average volume of each block.

▷

□ Foundation ○ Standard ◇ Complex

147 m

230 m

5 The area of the base of a pyramid is 40 m². If its volume is 360 m³, calculate its perpendicular height.

Ⓡ

6 The volume of a square pyramid toy is 1620 mm³. If the length of its base is 8 mm, calculate, correct to the nearest millimetre, the height of the pyramid.

Ⓡ

7 A square pyramid has a volume of 80 cm³ and a height of 10 cm. Calculate, correct to one decimal place, the length of the base of the pyramid.

Ⓡ

8 Calculate the volume of each cone, correct to one decimal place.

EXAMPLE
26

a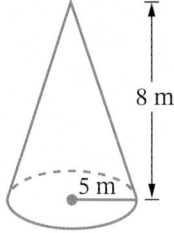
8 m
5 m

b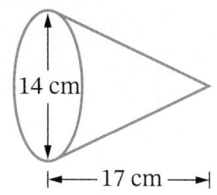
14 cm
17 cm

c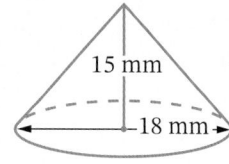
15 mm
18 mm

d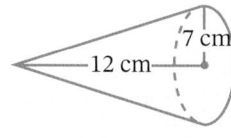
7 cm
12 cm

e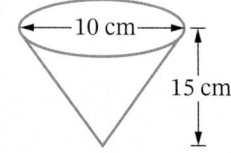
10 cm
15 cm

f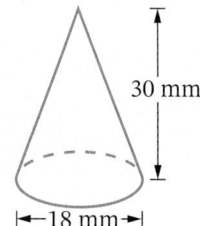
30 mm
18 mm

9 For each cone, find correct to 2 decimal places:

Ⓡ

   i its perpendicular height, h **ii** its volume   **iii** its capacity.

EXAMPLE
27

a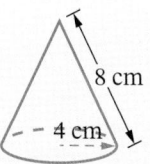
8 cm
4 cm

b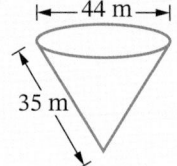
44 m
35 m

c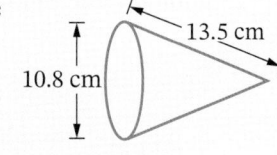
13.5 cm
10.8 cm

□ Foundation   ○ Standard   ◇ Complex

d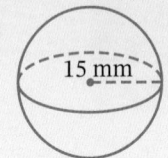
0.8 m
3.6 m

e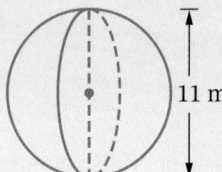
68 m
247 m

f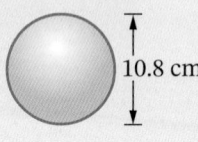
83 cm
83 cm

EXAMPLE
28

10 Find the volume of each sphere or hemisphere, correct to one decimal place.

a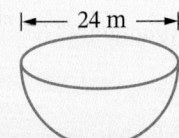
15 mm

b
11 m

c
10.8 cm

d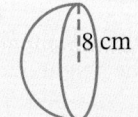
24 m

e
8 cm

f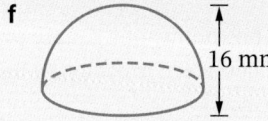
16 mm

11 The Earth has a radius of approximately 6378 km. Calculate its volume in scientific
Ⓒ notation, correct to the nearest cubic kilometre.

12 A cone has a volume of 1468 cm³ and a base radius of 12 cm. Find its height, correct to
Ⓡ one decimal place.

13 A cone has a volume of 820 m³ and a perpendicular height of 10 m. Find its radius,
Ⓡ correct to one decimal place.

14 A cone has a volume of 150 m³. If the height and radius of the cone are equal in length,
Ⓡ calculate the radius of the cone. Give your answer to 2 decimal places.

15 The volume of a spherical light is 2664 cm³. What is its diameter, correct to one decimal
Ⓡ place? Select **A**, **B**, **C** or **D**.
  A 17.2 cm   **B** 8.6 cm   **C** 17.0 cm   **D** 8.5 cm

16 A cone has a base radius of 20 cm and a perpendicular height of 48 cm.
Ⓡ **a** Find the volume of the cone.
  b The top of the cone is removed at half its height. What percentage
  of the cone remains?

Extension: Volumes of composite solids   2.11

ⓘ Volume formulas

Prism

$V = Ah$

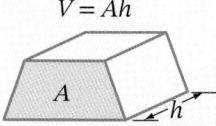

Cylinder

$V = \pi r^2 h$

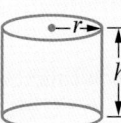

Pyramid

$V = \dfrac{1}{3} Ah$

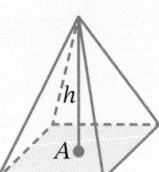

Cone

$V = \dfrac{1}{3} \pi r^2 h$

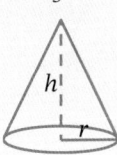

Sphere

$V = \dfrac{4}{3} \pi r^3$

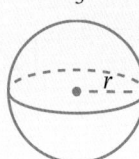

Note that the formulas for **surface area** involve **2 dimensions,** for example, r^2 or rh, while the formulas for **volume** involve **3 dimensions,** for example, $r^2 h$ or r^3 or Ah.

Example 29

For this packing capsule, find correct to the nearest whole number:

a its volume

b its capacity in litres

20 cm

35 cm

SOLUTION

a Volume $= \pi r^2 h + \dfrac{1}{2} \times \dfrac{4}{3} \pi r^3$

$= \pi \times 10^2 \times 35 + \dfrac{2}{3} \times \pi \times 10^3$

$= 13\,089.9693...$

$\approx 13\,090 \text{ cm}^3$

b Capacity $\approx 13\,090$ mL

$= 13.09$ L

≈ 13 L

EXERCISE **2.11** ANSWERS ON P. 606

Volumes of composite solids

U F PS R

EXAMPLE
29

1 This storage tank shown is completely filled with water.

a Calculate to the nearest cubic metre the volume of the tank.

b Find the capacity of the tank, correct to the nearest kilolitre.

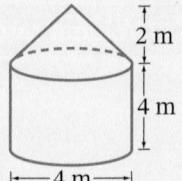

2 m

4 m

4 m

2 Find the volume of each solid. All measurements are centimetres.

R **a**

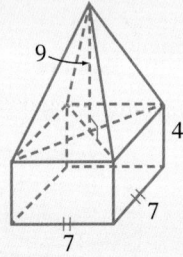

9

4

7

7

b

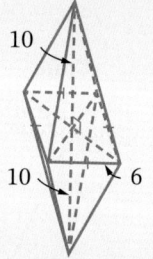

10

10 6

c

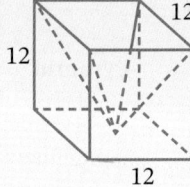

12

12

12

d

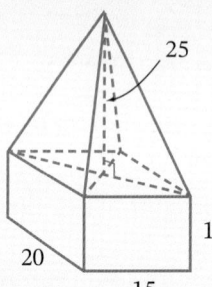

25

12

20

15

e

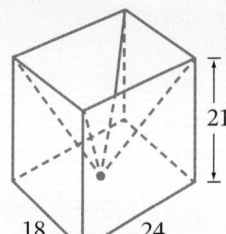

21

18 24

f

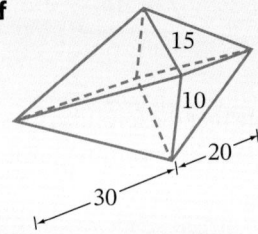

15

10

20

30

3 For each solid, find:

i the volume (to the nearest cm³)

ii the capacity (in litres, correct to 3 decimal places).

All measurements are in centimetres.

a

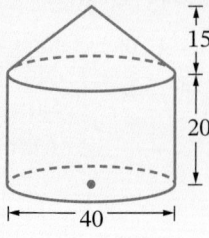

15

20

40

b

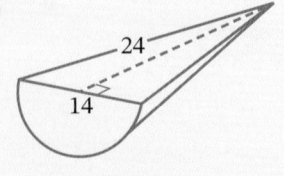

24

14

c

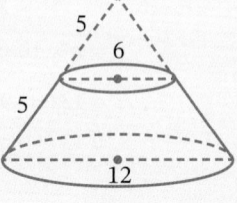

5

6

5

12

□ Foundation ○ Standard ◇ Complex

4 A conical tank (A) and a hemispherical tank (B) have measurements as shown. How much more does tank B hold compared to tank A? Answer correct to 2 decimal places.

A
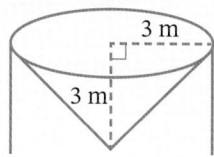
3 m
3 m

B
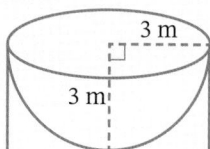
3 m
3 m

5 Spherical balls of diameter 10 cm are stacked inside a box as shown.

PS

R **a** How many balls will fit in the bottom layer?

b If the balls are stacked in the same manner as the bottom layer until the box is full, how many balls will fit in the box?

c Calculate the volume of the space occupied by the balls when the box is full.

d What percentage of the box is empty space? Give your answer to the nearest whole percentage.

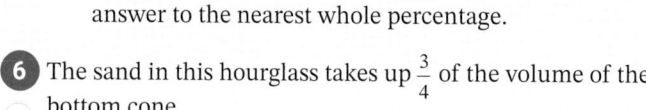
50 cm
30 cm
40 cm

6 The sand in this hourglass takes up $\frac{3}{4}$ of the volume of the bottom cone.

PS

R **a** Calculate, correct to the nearest cubic centimetre, the volume of sand in the hourglass.

b If the sand takes one hour to fall from the top cone to the bottom cone, at what rate is it falling? Give your answer in cm³/s, correct to 2 significant figures.

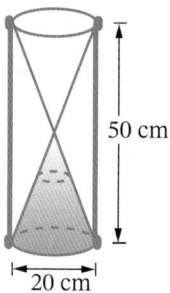
50 cm
20 cm

7 **a** Calculate the volume of this swimming pool.

PS

R **b** Calculate the capacity of the pool if it is filled to a depth 20 cm from the top.

c If water costs $1.98/kL, find the cost of filling the pool.

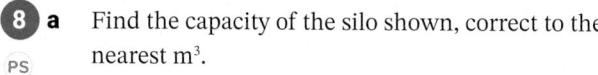
20 m
1 m
10 m
2 m
10 m

8 **a** Find the capacity of the silo shown, correct to the nearest m³.

PS

R **b** How many tonnes of barley grain will the silo hold if the density of barley grain is 600 kg/m³?

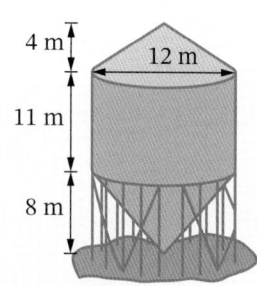
4 m
12 m
11 m
8 m

1   A square prism and square pyramid have the same base and the same surface area. Show that the slant height, l, of the pyramid is $l = \frac{5}{2}s$, where s is the length of the base.

2   A cylinder with diameter and height $2r$ has the same surface area as a sphere of radius R.

Show that $R = \sqrt{\frac{3}{2}}r$.

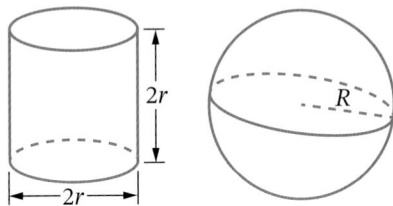

3   A sphere and a cone have the same radius and volume. Show that the cone's height, h, is 4 times the radius, r.

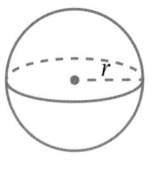
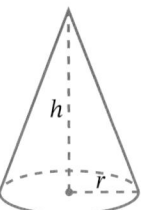

4   A sphere and a cone fit inside identical cylinders with the same base diameter and height.

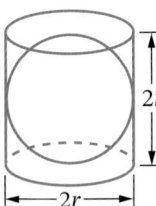
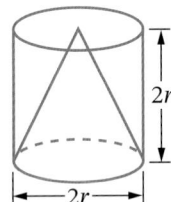

   a   Find the ratio Volume of cone: Volume of sphere : Volume of cylinder.

   b   Show that Volume of cone + Volume of sphere = Volume of cylinder.

② CHAPTER REVIEW

Language of maths

absolute error	base	capacity	cone
cross-section	cubic	curved surface	cylinder
diameter	kilolitre	net	open
percentage error	perpendicular height	prism	pyramid
quadrant	radius	rounding error	sector
sphere	surface area	truncate	volume

Quiz
Language of
maths 2

Puzzle
Surface area
and volume
crossword

1   Which word means a 'slice' of a prism or cylinder?

2   What is the formula for the curved surface area of a cylinder?

3   What is the formula $V = \pi r^2 h$ used for?

4   What causes **rounding error**?

5   How is the volume of a pyramid related to the volume of a prism?

6   What type of measurement has units of **cubic metres**?

Topic summary

Print (or copy) and complete this mind map of the topic, adding detail to its branches and using pictures, symbols and colour where needed. Ask your teacher to check your work.

Worksheet
Mind map:
Surface area
and volume

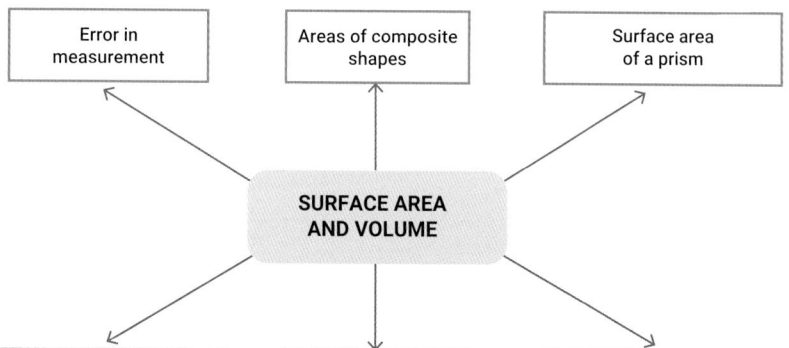

Quiz
Test yourself 2

② TEST YOURSELF ANSWERS ON P. 607

1 Liam estimates there to be approximately 1800 students at his school. If the actual number of students is 1693, calculate correct to 2 decimal places the percentage error of Liam's estimation.

2.01

2 The radius of a circle is measured as 20 cm.

2.02

    a Calculate its area correct to 4 decimal places.

    b Use π = 3.14 to calculate its area, then find, correct to one decimal place, the percentage error of the calculated area.

2.03

3 Find the area of each shape. Give your answers correct to one decimal place where necessary.

    a

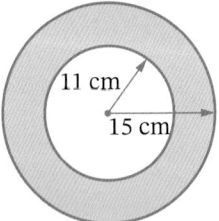

    11 cm, 15 cm

    b

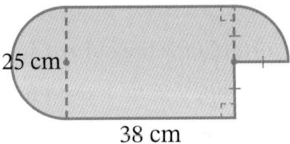

    25 cm, 38 cm

    c

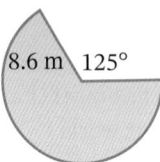

    8.6 m 125°

    d

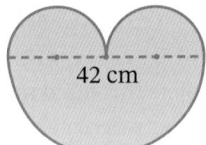

    42 cm

2.04

4 Find the surface area of each prism.

    a

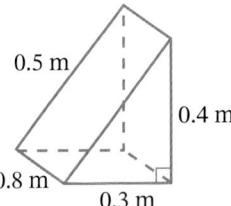

    0.5 m, 0.4 m, 0.8 m, 0.3 m

    b

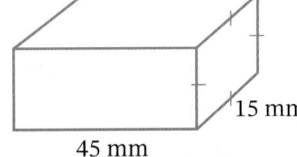

    15 mm, 45 mm

    c

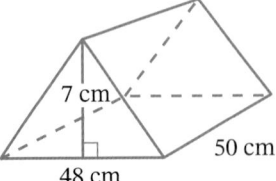

    7 cm, 50 cm, 48 cm

    d

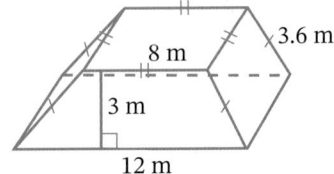

    3.6 m, 8 m, 3 m, 12 m

□ Foundation ○ Standard ◇ Complex

5 Calculate, correct to one decimal place, the surface area of each solid.

2.05

a

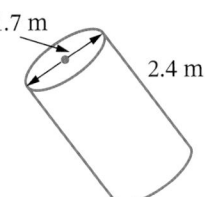

1.7 m

2.4 m

b

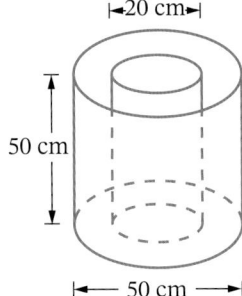

|◄20 cm►|

50 cm

|◄ 50 cm ►|

c

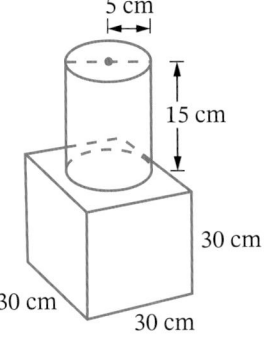

5 cm

15 cm

30 cm

30 cm

30 cm

d

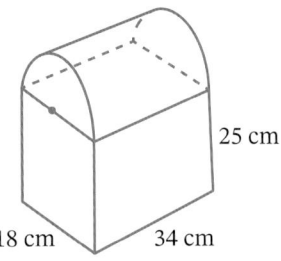

25 cm

18 cm   34 cm

6 Find the surface area of each pyramid.

2.06

a

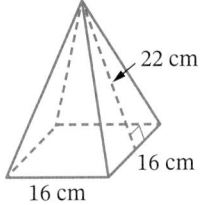

22 cm

16 cm

16 cm

b

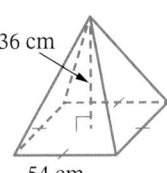

36 cm

54 cm

c

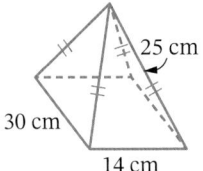

25 cm

30 cm

14 cm

7 Find the surface area of each solid. All measurements are in metres.

2.07

a

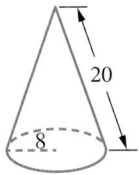

20

8

b

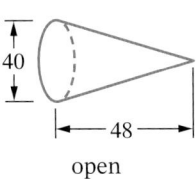

40

◄— 48 —►

open

c

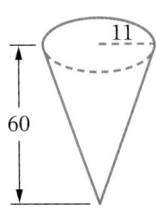

11

60

d

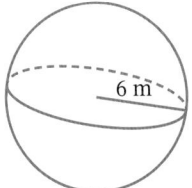

6 m

e

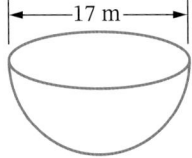

|◄—17 m—►|

f

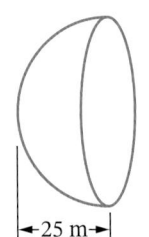

◄25 m►|

□ Foundation   ○ Standard   ○ Complex

8 Find, correct to the nearest square centimetre, the surface area of each solid. All measurements are in centimetres.

a

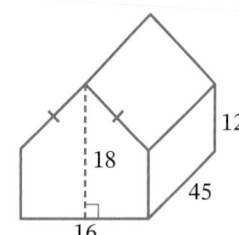

12
18
45
16

b

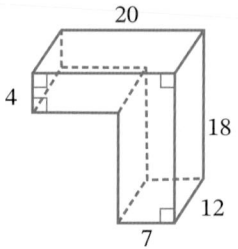

20
4
18
12
7

c

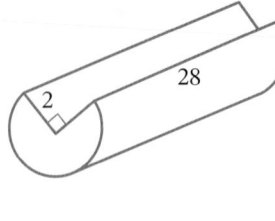

28
2

EXTENSION

d

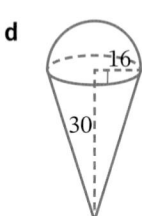

16
30

e

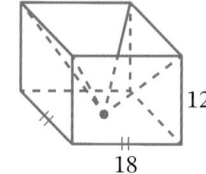

12
18

f

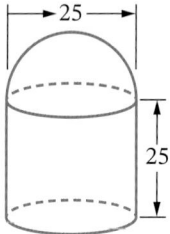

25
25

9 Calculate, correct to the nearest cubic metre, the volume of each solid. All lengths shown are in metres.

a

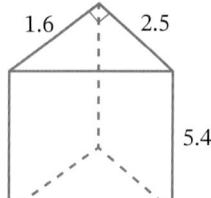

1.6   2.5
5.4

b

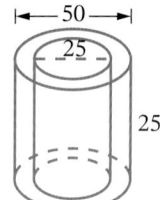

50
25
25

c

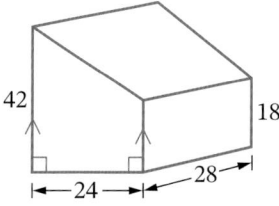

42
18
24
28

d

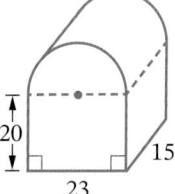

20
15
23

10 A rectangular fish tank measures 75 cm long by 55 cm wide by 35 cm deep. Find the capacity of the tank in litres if it is filled to 4 cm from the top.

11 A cylindrical rainwater tank has a radius of 2.8 m and a height of 2.4 m.

    a Calculate, correct to 2 decimal places, the capacity of the tank in kilolitres.

    b If the tank is 60% full, what is the height of the water in the tank? Answer correct to 2 decimal places.

□ Foundation   ○ Standard   ○ Complex

12 Find, correct to 2 decimal places (where necessary), the volume of each solid.

EXTENSION
2.10

a

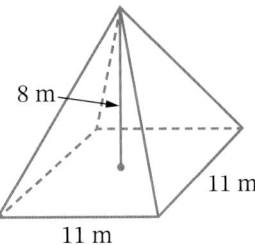

8 m
11 m
11 m

b

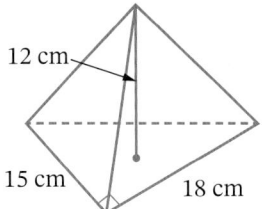

12 cm
15 cm
18 cm

c

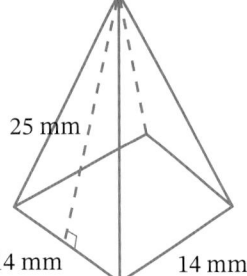

25 mm
14 mm
14 mm

d

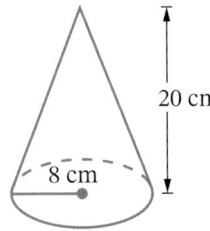

20 cm
8 cm

e

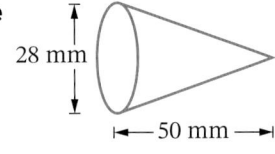

28 mm
50 mm

f

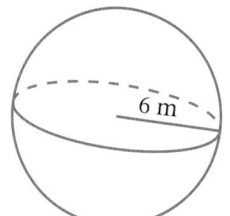

6 m

13 Find, correct to the nearest whole number, the volume of each solid.

2.11

a

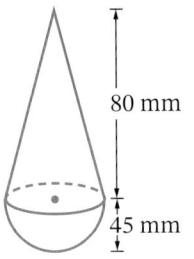

80 mm
45 mm

b

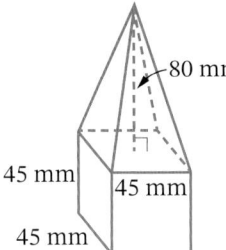

80 mm
45 mm
45 mm
45 mm
45 mm

c

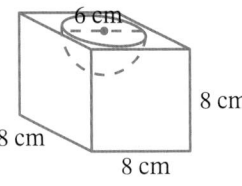

6 cm
8 cm
8 cm
8 cm

d

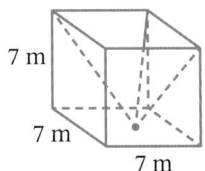

7 m
7 m
7 m

e

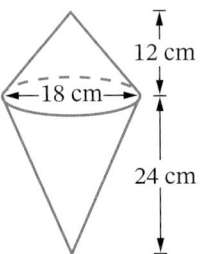

12 cm
18 cm
24 cm

f

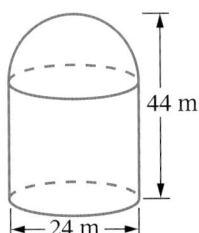

44 m
24 m

☐ Foundation ○ Standard ○ Complex

3

Interest and depreciation

The value of an investment increases over time as a result of interest being added to it, whether it be simple or compound interest. On the other hand, the value of assets and items such as cars and office equipment decrease over time due to age and wear-and-tear. Compound interest and depreciation use formulas that involve repeated percentage increase and decrease respectively.

stock.adobe.com/czchampz

Chapter outline

		Proficiencies
3.01	Earning an income	U F PS R
3.02	Income tax	U F PS C
3.03	Simple interest	U F PS R
3.04	Compound interest	U F
3.05	The compound interest formula	U F PS R
3.06	Depreciation	U F PS R C

U = Understanding R = Reasoning
F = Fluency C = Communicating
PS = Problem solving

Note: 3.01, 3.02, 3.06 are not strictly part of the Australian Curriculum but can be taught within Financial Mathematics as an application of number. Compound interest and depreciation are applications of exponential growth and decay.

Wordbank

Quiz
Wordbank 3

allowable deduction A part of a person's yearly income that is not taxed, such as work-related expenses and donations to charities.

compound interest Interest calculated on the principal invested as well as on any accumulated interest.

depreciation The decrease in the value of items over time due to ageing.

net pay Pay received after deductions from gross pay; 'take-home' pay.

per annum (p.a.) Per year.

principal The original amount of money invested or borrowed, for the purpose of calculating interest.

simple interest Interest calculated on the original principal invested only.

Videos (10):

3.01 Annual salaries • Overtime • Commission • Annual leave loading

3.02 Income tax

3.03 Simple interest • Simple interest rate

3.05 The compound interest formula • Compound interest

3.06 Depreciation

Twig **video (1):**

3.05 Could you owe more than America?

Quizzes (5):

• Wordbank 3
• SkillCheck 3
• Mental skills 3
• Language of maths 3
• Test yourself 3

Skillsheets (3):

SkillCheck Mental percentages • Percentage calculations

3.05 Spreadsheets

Worksheets (9):

SkillCheck Percentage shortcuts

3.01 Earning money

3.02 Income tax tables • Income tax and Medicare levy

3.03 Simple interest • Simple interest table

3.05 Compound interest

3.06 Depreciation

Mind map: Interest and depreciation

Puzzles (4):

3.03 Simple interest

3.05 Compound interest with annual rests • Compound interest with non-annual rests

Language of maths Interest and depreciation crossword

Technology (2):

3.05 Comparing interest rates • Simple and compound interest calculator

Spreadsheets (2):

3.05 Comparing interest rates • Simple and compound interest

Nelson MindTap

To access resources above, visit
cengage.com.au/nelsonmindtap

---

3 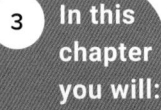 **In this chapter you will:**

✓ calculate weekly, fortnightly, monthly and yearly incomes

✓ calculate wages, salaries, overtime, commission, piecework and annual leave loading

✓ use tables to calculate income tax and PAYG tax

✓ solve problems involving simple interest

✓ solve problems involving compound interest by repeated percentage increase

✓ solve problems involving the compound interest formula $A = P(1 + r)^n$

✓ solve problems involving depreciation

Quiz
SkillCheck 3

Skillsheets
Mental
percentages

Percentage
calculations

Worksheet
Percentage
shortcuts

SkillCheck

ANSWERS ON P. 607

1 Copy and complete:

   a one year = _____ weeks   **c** one year = _____ days

   b one year = _____ fortnights   **d** 48 months = _____ years

   e 84 days = _____ weeks

   f 100 months = _____ years _____ months

2 If $P = mvt$, find:

   a P when $m = 1600$, $v = 0.072$, $t = 10$ **b** m when $P = 120$, $v = 0.3$, $t = 8$

   c v when $P = 18$, $m = 60$, $t = 5$

3   Evaluate, correct to the nearest cent:

   a $\$5000 \times (1.045)^4$

   b $\$28\,000 \times (1.03)^6$

   c $\$15\,300 \times (1.065)^3$

   d $\$32\,400 \times (1.072)^{10}$

Earning an income

3.01

Wages, salaries and overtime

Videos
Annual salaries

Overtime

Commission

Worksheet
Earning money

A **wage** is calculated from the number of hours worked and is usually paid weekly. Wage earners can make more income by working extra hours (**overtime**).

A **salary** is a fixed annual amount, paid weekly, fortnightly or monthly. Salary earners do not earn overtime pay but can receive benefits such as a computer, company car, expense account or shares in the company.

ⓘ Units of time for wages and salaries

1 year = 12 months

1 fortnight = 2 weeks

1 year = 52 weeks for wage earners

1 year = 52.18 weeks for salary earners

The 2 most common rates of overtime pay are:

- **time-and-a-half**: 1.5 × normal hourly rate
- **double time**: 2 × normal hourly rate

Example 1

Tyrone earns a salary of $70 400 p.a.   *p.a. = per annum = per year*

How much does he earn:

a   each week?   **b**   each fortnight?   **c**   each month?

   SOLUTION

a   Weekly income = $70 400 ÷ 52.18

              = $1349.1759...

              ≈ $1349.18   rounded to the nearest cent

b   Fortnightly income = 2 × $1349.18   1 fortnight = 2 weeks

              = $2698.36

c   Monthly income = $70 400 ÷ 12   1 year = 12 months

              = $5866.6666...

              ≈ $5866.67   rounded to the nearest cent

Example 2

Noor earns $22.65 per hour at normal rates. Last week, she worked 38 hours at normal rates, 6 hours at time-and-a-half and 3 hours at double time. Calculate Noor's total earnings for the week.

SOLUTION

normal pay = $22.65 × 38

$\qquad$ = $860.70

time-and-a-half pay = 6 × $22.65 × 1.5

$\qquad$ = $203.85

double time pay = 3 × $22.65 × 2

$\qquad$ = $135.90

total earnings = $860.70 + $203.85 + $135.90

$\qquad$ = $1200.45

Commission, piecework and annual leave loading

Commission is earned by salespeople and agents, and is a percentage of the value of items sold or income made.

Piecework is earned according to the number of items made or tasks completed.

Annual leave loading or holiday loading is extra pay given during annual leave (holidays) and is 17.5% of 4 weeks' normal pay.

Example 3

Sarah is a real estate agent and is paid a commission of 2.5% on the value of apartments she sells. She also receives a weekly retainer of $750. How much will Sarah earn if she sells an apartment for $590 000?

A **retainer** is a fixed amount paid regardless of how many items are sold.

SOLUTION

commission = 2.5% of $590 000

$\qquad$ = $14 750

total earnings = commission + retainer

$\qquad$ = $14 750 + $750

$\qquad$ = $15 500

∴ Sarah earns $15 500.

Example 4

Emad is a jewellery designer. He makes handmade jewellery and is paid at the following rates:

$278 per necklace $72 per pair of earrings $105 per bracelet

This month, Emad made 23 necklaces, 7 pairs of earrings and 19 bracelets. How much did he earn?

SOLUTION

monthly earnings = 23 × $278 + 7 × $72 + 19 × $105

$\qquad\qquad$ = $8893

Example 5

Kham's annual salary is $70 590. For his Christmas holidays, he received 4 weeks' normal pay plus 17.5% annual leave loading for the 4 weeks. Calculate Kham's:

a normal weekly pay

b annual leave loading

c total pay for the Christmas holiday.

Video
Annual leave loading

SOLUTION

a weekly pay = $70 590 ÷ 52.18

$\qquad\qquad$ = $1352.8171...

$\qquad\qquad$ ≈ $1352.82

b annual leave loading = 17.5% × $1352.82 × 4   17.5% of 4 weeks' pay

$\qquad\qquad\qquad$ = $946.974

$\qquad\qquad\qquad$ ≈ $946.97

c total holiday pay = (4 × $1352.82) + $946.97   4 weeks' pay + leave loading

$\qquad\qquad\qquad$ = $6358.25

Earning an income (U) (F) (PS) (R)

Express all answers correct to the nearest cent where necessary.

EXAMPLE 1

1 Find the weekly wage for each person.
  a Eva earns $21.85 per hour and works for 40 hours.
  b Robert works 8 hours a day, Monday to Friday, and is paid $23.47 per hour.
  c Jasmine works on Monday and Tuesday from 8:30 am until 4:00 pm and Thursday from midday until 9:00 pm, and earns $30.60 per hour.

2 Juanita earns $19.56 an hour and works for 31 hours each week. Vivek earns $21.44 per hour for his 27 hours of work. Who earns more per week and by how much?

EXAMPLE 1

3 Mike earns a salary of $180 640 p.a. How much does he earn:
  a each week?   **b** each fortnight?   **c** each month?

4 Rakitu considers 2 jobs, one locally with an annual salary of $57 640 p.a. and the other (R) one in the city with a fortnightly pay of $2320. Calculate the weekly income for each job, determine which one pays more per week, and by how much.

EXAMPLE 2

5 Anan works 38 hours at normal rates, 7 hours at time-and-a-half and 4 hours at double time. Calculate Anan's total earnings if he earns $19.60 per hour at normal rates.

6 Rhianna works 8.5 hours per day from Tuesday to Friday. She is paid $21.78 per hour. She also works on Saturday for 4.5 hours at a special rate of $24.59 per hour. How much did Rhianna earn for the week?

7 Idra works the following hours in a week at the clothing chain Shop til U Drop.

(PS)
(R)

Day	Hours worked
Monday	9 am – 5 pm
Tuesday	9 am – 4 pm
Thursday	10 am – 7:30 pm
Friday	10 am – 5 pm
Saturday	10:30 am – 5 pm

She is paid at the following rates.

Day	Rate of pay
Monday to Friday	$19.62 per hour
Saturday	$23.15 per hour
Thursday after 4:00 pm	

What is Idra's total income for the week?

□ Foundation ○ Standard ○ Complex

8 Fatimah is paid a commission of 2.5% on the value of goods she sells. She also receives a weekly retainer of $875. How much will Fatimah earn if she sells goods to the value of $41 600 in one week? Select the correct answer **A**, **B**, **C** or **D**.

EXAMPLE 3 3.01

   A $1915.00   **B** $1061.88   **C** $2187.50   **D** $1018.13

9 Nathan is a real estate agent whose commission is calculated on the value of the properties he sells:

- 3% paid on first $300 000
- 1.5% paid on next $250 000
- 0.75% paid on any value thereafter

How much commission did Nathan earn for selling a house for $625 000?

10 Briana designed an app, KeyFinder, that sells for $2.49. If she makes 70% profit on the sale price of each app sold, how much would she make from selling 800 units of this app?

11 Matt charges $60 for each lawn he mows and $45 for trimming hedges in each yard. In a week, he mows 24 lawns and trims 15 hedges. How much does he earn for the week?

EXAMPLE 4

Shutterstock.com/welcomia

12 Clean2Swim charges $86 to clean backyard pools. If this business earned $4644 in the first week of summer, how many pools were cleaned?

▷

☐ Foundation ○ Standard ○ Complex

13 Jade makes homemade eco-friendly soaps, shampoos and cleaning products. A customer purchases 3 homemade soaps, 2 bottles of shampoo and 3 of the cleaning sprays. How much does Jade receive for these purchases?

  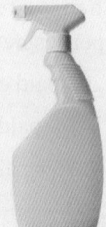

Homemade soaps	Eco-friendly shampoo	Natural cleaning spray
$5.60	$12.70	$7.25

14 Calculate the annual leave loading for each person if it is 17.5% of 4 weeks' pay.

    a   Peter earns $1220 per week   **b**   Jamilla earns $2000 per fortnight

    c   Samir earns $5944 per month   **d**   Ellie earns $46 630 p.a.

EXAMPLE 5

15 For his annual holidays, Jake received 4 weeks' normal pay plus 17.5% annual leave loading for the 4 weeks. If Jake's annual salary is $50 725, find his:

    a   normal weekly pay   **b**   annual leave loading

    c   total pay for the 4-week holiday.

INVESTIGATION

Workers' entitlements

The Australian Government sets the minimum standards for pay and conditions for all Australian workers. Different industries can have different needs from employees in terms of:

- normal and overtime hours worked; breaks allowed
- allowances
- dress codes, such as uniforms
- working conditions

1   Visit the Fair Work Ombudsman website **www.fairwork.gov.au** and select **Awards and agreements**.

2   Select 2 industries and identify any similarities and differences in the requirements of those industries.

3   Write a summary of your findings.

4   Give a report in class.

Income tax

Not all of a person's income is taxed. If we use some of our income for work-related expenses or to donate money to charities, these amounts are called **allowable deductions** (or tax deductions) and are not taxed. Examples of allowable deductions are tools of trade, uniforms, car/travel expenses, subscriptions to professional organisations and journals.

Video
Income tax

ⓘ Income tax

Income tax is calculated on a person's **taxable income**, which is the gross income (total earnings) less all allowable deductions, *rounded down to the nearest dollar.*

taxable income = gross income – allowable deductions

Worksheets
Income tax tables

Income tax and Medicare levy

The more a person earns, the higher the rate of tax to be paid.

Tax rates for Australian residents	
Taxable income	**Tax on this income**
0 – $18 200	Nil
$18 201 – $45 000	19c for each $1 over $18 200
$45 001 – $120 000	$5092 plus 32.5c for each $1 over $45 000
$120 001 – $180 000	$29 467 plus 37c for each $1 over $120 000
$180 001 and over	$51 667 plus 45c for each $1 over $180 000

Source: © Australian Taxation Office for the Commonwealth of Australia

Example 6

Sophia earned $62 348 last financial year and collected bank interest of $440.81. She had allowable deductions of $427.52 in work expenses and $110 in donations to charities.

a Calculate her taxable income.

b Use the tax table to calculate the income tax that Sophie must pay.

SOLUTION

a Taxable income = $62 348 + $440.81 – $427.52 – $110

$\qquad$ = $62 251.29

$\qquad$ ≈ $62 251 $\qquad\qquad$ rounded down to the nearest dollar

b According to the table, a taxable income of $62 251 is in the $45 001 – $120 000 tax bracket.

'32.5c for each $1' means 32.5% or 0.325.

Income tax = $5092 + 0.325 × ($62 251 – $45 000)

$\qquad$ = $10 698.575

$\qquad$ ≈ $10 698.58

PAYG tax and net pay

Income tax deducted from your pay by your employer every payday is called **PAYG (Pay As You Go) tax**. The total amount of PAYG tax paid over the year is usually more than the actual income tax payable, so at the end of the financial year you will receive the difference as a tax refund.

Gross pay is the total amount a person earns or receives, but most workers have a variety of deductions taken from their pay before they receive it, including PAYG tax, superannuation contributions, union fees and health fund payments. The amount of income left after the deductions is called **net pay**.

 **Net pay**

net pay = gross pay – tax – other deductions

Example 7

Jayden earns a gross pay of $2290.33 per fortnight. His deductions are for PAYG tax, $44.10 for private health insurance and $55.82 for superannuation.

Fortnightly earnings ($)	PAYG tax withheld ($)
2270–2275	460
2276–2281	462
2282–2287	464
2288–2293	466
2294–2299	468
2300–2305	470

a Use the PAYG tax table to find Jayden's PAYG tax per fortnight.

b Calculate Jayden's net pay.

c Calculate Jayden's total deductions as a percentage of his gross income (correct to one decimal place).

SOLUTION

a In the table, $2290.33 falls in the $2288 – $2293 range.

fortnightly PAYG tax = $466

b net pay = $2290.33 – ($466 + $44.10 + $55.82)   net pay = gross pay – total deductions

= $2290.33 – $565.92

= $1724.41

c total deductions = $565.92

deductions percentage = $\frac{\$565.92}{\$2290.33} \times 100\%$ $\frac{\text{total deductions}}{\text{gross pay}} \times 100\%$

= 24.7091...%

≈ 24.7%

9780170465595

Income tax

U F PS C

Express all answers correct to the nearest cent where necessary.

1 Shilpa earns $47 628 in a year and has allowable deductions of $1930.46.

   a Calculate her taxable income, rounded down to the nearest dollar.

   b Use the tax table on page 113 to calculate the income tax that Shilpa must pay.

EXAMPLE 6

2 Aiden is an environmental engineer who had a gross income of $148 742 this year and work-related expenses totalling $4022.80, which are tax-deductible. Calculate Aiden's:

   a taxable income, rounded down to the nearest dollar

   b income tax.

3 Ellie is a graphic designer who earns an annual salary of $90 541 and has collected $1029.45 in bank interest. She has allowable deductions of $379 for tools related to her work and $287 in donations to charity. Calculate:

PS

   a Ellie's taxable income
         b the amount of tax payable.

4 Riley the builder had a gross income of $56 922 this year. He is entitled to these tax deductions: tools $1538, training courses $445 and outdoor protective clothing $506. How much should Riley pay in tax? Select the correct answer **A**, **B**, **C** or **D**.

PS

   A $13 046.65   **B** $10 855.58   **C** $8157.73   **D** $6884.27

5 Nicola is a nurse earning $87 996 per year. Her allowable deductions are the cost of non-slip footwear $225, the cost of laundering uniforms $1046, and union fees $297.60. How much should Nicola pay in tax?

PS

6 Will owns a photography business and earned $216 000 last year. His allowable deductions were Internet costs for his website $968, photographic equipment $23 672, and travel to photo shoots $15 930. Calculate the amount that Will should pay in tax.

PS

7 Jackson earns a gross weekly income of $1075.26. His weekly deductions are $309.11 PAYG tax, $44.55 for private health insurance and $25.18 for superannuation. Calculate Jackson's net weekly pay.

C

8 Isha earns a gross income of $788.20 per week. Her deductions are $132.44 tax and $32.24 for private health insurance. Calculate Isha's net income.

C

Use the PAYG table from Example 7 on page 114 to answer questions **9** to **12**.

9 Every fortnight, Mr Bhagwati earns $2278 and pays $22.80 in union fees and $94.10 in superannuation.

EXAMPLE 7

   a Find how much PAYG tax he pays per fortnight.

   b Calculate Mr Bhagwati's fortnightly net pay.

   c What percentage (correct to one decimal place) of his gross pay do the deductions make up?

☐ Foundation ○ Standard ○ Complex

10 Holly earns a gross pay of $2295 per fortnight. Her deductions are PAYG tax, $64.35 for superannuation and $30 for life insurance. Find Holly's:

    a PAYG tax   **b** net pay

    c total deductions as a percentage of her gross income (correct to one decimal place).

11 Stefan earns $1148 per week.

    a If he is paid fortnightly, what is his fortnightly gross pay?

    b Find the PAYG tax that is taken out of his gross pay.

    c Stefan's deductions are $141.94 for his health fund and $51.33 for superannuation. Calculate Stefan's net fortnightly pay.

12 Agata earns a salary of $60 135 p.a. Each fortnight she has deductions of $256.20 for family health insurance and $35 for superannuation taken from her gross income.

    a Calculate Agata's fortnightly gross income.

    b How much PAYG tax does she pay per fortnight?

    c Calculate Agata's fortnightly net income.

13 Copy and complete this pay slip.

(PS) (C)

Employee: Ziad Chaker		Hourly pay rate: $19.65	
Hours worked		**Deductions**	
Normal	39	Tax: $205.72	Other: $168.38
Time-and-a-half	2	Gross weekly income	
Double time	0	Total deductions	
		Net weekly income	

TECHNOLOGY

Online income tax calculators

The Australian Taxation Office (ATO) website **www.ato.gov.au** has online calculators for income tax and PAYG tax. Visit the website and search **Simple Tax Calculator** to find the income tax calculator for individuals.

1 Enter the taxable income $63 000 as **63000** (no spaces).

2 Select the current financial year.

3 Select **Resident for full year** and click **Next**.

4 The estimated tax payable will be shown on a new screen.

5 Repeat for at least 2 more taxable incomes.

6 Find the PAYG tax calculator and use it to find the PAYG tax payable and net pay for a gross pay of:

    a $1408 weekly   **b** $2870 fortnightly   **c** $5610 monthly

□ Foundation   ○ Standard   ○ Complex

Simple interest

- When you invest money, you receive interest from your investment.
- When you borrow money, you pay interest on your loan.
- The original amount of money invested or borrowed is called the **principal**.
- This interest rate is a percentage of the principal, usually written as a rate **per annum** ('per year'), abbreviated 'p.a.'
- **Simple interest** (or **flat rate interest**) is interest calculated simply on the original principal.

Video
Simple
interest

Worksheets
Simple
interest

Simple
interest
table

Puzzle
Simple
interest

(i) The simple interest formula

$$I = Prn$$

where I is the simple interest

P is the principal

r is the interest rate per time period, expressed as a decimal

n is the number of time periods

This formula can also be written as $I = Pin$ (where i is the interest rate) or $I = Prt$ (where t is the number of time periods).

Example 8

Find the simple interest on:

a $4000 at 3.5% p.a. for 6 years

b $13 500 at 5.5% p.a. for 7 months

c $75 640 at 0.42% per month for 2 years.

SOLUTION

a $P = \$4000$, $r = 3.5\% = 0.035$, $n = 6$ years

$I = Prn$ $r = 0.035$ per year, $n = 6$ years, so the time

$= \$4000 \times 0.035 \times 6$ period is years.

$= \$840$

b $P = \$13\,500$, $r = 5.5\% = 0.055$, $n = \dfrac{7}{12}$ years $r = 0.055$ per year, $n = 7$ months, so we

$I = Prn$ must change 7 months to years so that

$= \$13\,500 \times 0.055 \times \dfrac{7}{12}$ the time period is years.

$= \$433.125$

$\approx \$433.13$ rounded to the nearest cent

c $P = \$75\,640, r = 0.42\% = 0.0042,$
$n = 2 \times 12 = 24$ months

$I = Prn$

    $= \$75\,640 \times 0.0042 \times 24$

    $= \$7624.512$

    $\approx \$7624.51$

$r = 0.0042$ per month, $n = 2$ years, so we must change 2 years to months so that the time period is months.

rounded to the nearest cent

Example 9

Petra invests $17 400 for 2 years at 3.75% p.a. flat rate interest. To what final value will her investment grow?

SOLUTION

$P = \$17\,400, r = 3.75\% = 0.0375, n = 2$ years n and r are in years.

$I = Prn$

    $= \$17\,400 \times 0.0375 \times 2$

    $= \$1305$

Value of investment $= \$17\,400 + \$1305$ principal + interest

                  $= \$18\,705$

Example 10

Video
Simple interest rate

After 4 years, an investment of $13 000 has earned $1092 in simple interest.

What is the annual interest rate?

SOLUTION

$I = \$1092, P = \$13\,000, n = 4$ years

    $I = Prn$

$\$1092 = \$13\,000 \times r \times 4$

$\$1092 = \$52\,000r$

$r = \dfrac{\$1092}{\$52000}$

    $= 0.021$

    $= 2.1\%$

$\therefore$ annual interest rate is 2.1%.

Example 11

Video
Simple interest rate

For how many months will $10 000 need to be invested to earn $250 in simple interest at 3.25% p.a.?

SOLUTION

$I = \$250, P = \$10\,000, r = 3.25\% = 0.0325$

    $I = Prn$

$\$250 = \$10\,000 \times 0.0325 \times n$

$\$250 = \$325n$

  $n = \dfrac{\$250}{\$325}$

= 0.7692... years n is in years, so convert to months

= 0.7692... × 12 months

= 9.230... months

≈ 10 months   rounded up to the nearest month

EXERCISE (3.03) ANSWERS ON P. 607

Simple interest   U F PS R

In this exercise, round all money answers to the nearest cent.

1 Calculate the simple interest earned on each investment.

  a $35 000 for 4 years at 3.6% p.a.

  b $26 850 at 1.95% p.a. for 2 years

  c $8200 invested for 5 months at 3% p.a.

  d $6590 invested for 16 months at 0.25% per month

  e $5250 invested for 250 days at 3.04% p.a.

  f $18 400 invested for 3 years at 0.18% per month

EXAMPLE 8

2 Calculate the flat rate interest charged on each loan.

  a $1250 for 2 years at 3.5% p.a.

  b $18 900 for $5\frac{1}{2}$ years at 5.7% p.a.

  c $1.15 million at 4.5% p.a. for 48 months

  d $12 000 for 10 months at 0.575% per month

  e $9750 for 2.5 years at 0.48% per month

  f $24 720 for 136 days at 7.85% p.a.

3 Harry owed $783.26 on his credit card. The credit card company charged him one month's simple interest at 21% p.a. How much interest was he charged? Select the correct answer **A**, **B**, **C** or **D**.

  A $13.71   **B** $16.45   **C** $25.38   **D** $37.30

4 Find the final value of each investment using simple interest.

  a $10 000 invested for 3 years at 4% p.a.

  b $1500 invested for 18 months at 0.19% per month

  c $8500 invested for 3.5 years at 0.25% per month

  d $9250 invested for 50 months at 3.75% p.a.

EXAMPLE 9

5 Liong borrowed $6000 to go on an overseas holiday, at 12% p.a. flat rate interest for 2 years. Calculate:

a the total interest

b the total amount Liong must repay.

EXAMPLE 10

6 The interest on a loan of $2500 over 4 years is $450. Calculate the flat rate of interest p.a.

R

7 Katy took out a loan for $22 000 over 5 years. If her total loan repayments amounted to $28 400, calculate:

PS

R a the interest charged

b the flat rate of interest p.a., correct to 2 decimal places.

8 After 5 years, the interest on a loan of $8000 amounts to $2340. Calculate the annual simple interest rate.

EXAMPLE 11

9 For how many years will $4200 need to be invested to earn $200 interest, if the interest rate is 2.5% p.a.?

R

10 How many weeks will it take for $50 000 to earn $750 in interest if the rate is 2.6% p.a.?

R

11 How many days will it take for $20 000 to earn $300 in interest if the rate is 4% p.a.?

R

12 An online bank offered the following investment to its customers.

PS • A rate of 2.35% p.a. simple interest for the first 4 months only

R • Then the principal and interest reinvested at 0.45% p.a. simple interest

What will Shweta's investment of $3480 be worth after 7 months? Select **A**, **B**, **C** or **D**.

A $31.21   **B** $374.10   **C** $3511.21   **D** $3854.10

13 For how many months will $20 000 need to be invested to amount to $22 000, if interest is paid at the rate of 0.33% per month?

PS

R

14 What is the flat rate of interest (as a percentage p.a., correct to one decimal place) when $1650 earns $85 in interest over 2 years?

R

15 Toula used a credit card to buy a netbook computer for $799 and some extra accessories for $246. She pays off this debt in 30 days. The credit card charges 22% p.a. simple interest.

PS

R a Calculate the simple interest charged.

b How much will Toula pay after 30 days?

16 Bhashine earned $185 interest each year for 4 years on an investment account. At the end of the 4 years, she closed her account and withdrew $6000 in total. What was the annual flat rate of interest paid into Bhashine's account? Select **A**, **B**, **C** or **D**.

PS

R

A 3.1%   **B** 3.5%   **C** 12.3%   **D** 14.1%

□ Foundation   ○ Standard   ○ Complex

Compound interest

Most investments earn **compound interest** rather than simple interest. With compound interest, the interest earned is **added** to the principal so that next time, the interest is calculated on a larger principal. This means that more interest is earned, because we are also earning interest on the interest we have already earned. The word **compound** means 'combined'.

Example 12

A principal of $23 000 is invested at 4% p.a. interest, compounded yearly for 2 years.

a   What is the total value of the investment after 2 years?

b   What is the amount of compound interest earned?

SOLUTION

a   The interest for each year is calculated separately.

After the first year:

interest = $23 000 × 0.04

= $920

investment = $23 000 + $920   principal + interest

= $23 920

After the second year:

interest = $23 920 × 0.04

= $956.80

investment = $23 920 + $956.80   new principal + interest

= $24 876.80

b   compound interest earned = final investment − principal

= $24 876.80 − $23 000

= $1876.80

Notice that compound interest involves repeated percentage increase. In the above example, to calculate compound interest on a principal of $23 000 over 2 years at 4% p.a., we are actually increasing $23 000 by 4% twice. Adding 4% to the principal is the same as increasing the principal by 4%, which is the same as multiplying the principal by 104% or 3.04.

Investment after 1st year = $23 000 × 3.04 = $23 920

Investment after 2nd year = $23 920 × 3.04 = $24 876.80

We can even combine these 2 steps into one step by repeated percentage increases:

Investment after 2nd year = $23 000 × 3.04 × 3.04 = $24 876.80

Using repeated percentage increases can simplify our compound interest calculations.

Example 13

A principal of $9000 is invested at 3.7% p.a. compounded yearly over 3 years. What is:

a the value of the investment after 3 years?

b the compound interest earned?

SOLUTION

a Adding 3.7% interest to the principal is the same as multiplying the principal by 3.037.

∴ investment after 3 years = $9000 × 3.037 × 3.037 × 3.037

$$= \$9000 \times (3.037)^3$$
$$= \$10\,036.4188...$$
$$\approx \$10\,036.42 \qquad \text{rounded to the nearest cent}$$

b compound interest earned = final investment – original principal

$$= \$10\,036.42 - \$9000$$
$$= \$1036.42$$

EXERCISE **3.04** ANSWERS ON P. 607

Compound interest

In this exercise, round all money answers to the nearest cent.

1 A principal of $23 000 is invested at 5% p.a. interest, compounded yearly over 2 years.

a Copy and complete the following working to calculate the value of the investment after 2 years.

After the first year: Investment = $23 000 + $_____

$I = \$23\,000 \times 0.05$ = $_____

  = $_____

After the second year: Investment = $_____ + _____

$I = \$\text{_____} \times 0.05$ = $_____

  = $_____

b Copy and complete the following working to calculate the amount of compound interest earned.

Compound interest earned = final investment – principal

$$= \$\text{_____} - \$23\,000$$
$$= \$\text{_____}$$

▷

☐ Foundation ○ Standard ○ Complex

2 Finn invests \$15 000 at 2.5% p.a. compounded yearly over 3 years. Show all working (as in question **1**) to find:

  a the value of the investment after 3 years

  b the total amount of compound interest earned.

3 Selina invests \$34 100 at 6.2% p.a. interest compounded yearly over 2 years. Calculate:

  a the final value of the investment   **b** the compound interest earned.

4 Use repeated percentage increases to calculate the final value of each investment compounded annually, then calculate the compound interest earned.

  a \$5000 for 2 years at 4% p.a.

  b \$27 800 for 3 years at 2.85% p.a.

  c \$9600 for 3 years at 5% p.a.

  d \$39 500 for 2 years at 3% p.a.

  e \$18 400 for 4 years at 1.25% p.a.

5 For each investment, calculate the compound interest earned.

  a \$30 400 at 5% p.a. interest for 3 years.

  b \$19 150 at 4.2% p.a. interest for 2 years.

  c \$8750 at 1.75% p.a. interest for 2 years.

  d \$36 000 at 3.5% p.a. interest for 3 years.

  e \$18 960 at 6.35% p.a. interest for 5 years.

EXAMPLE
13

☆ **MENTAL SKILLS** ③ ANSWERS ON P. 607   **Maths without calculators**

Quiz
Mental
skills 3

Finding 15%, $2\frac{1}{2}$%, 25% and $12\frac{1}{2}$%

- To find 10% or $\frac{1}{10}$ of a number, divide by 10.

- To find 5% of a number, find 10% first, then halve it (since 5% is half of 10%).

- So, to find 15% of a number, find 10% and 5% of the number separately, then add the answers together.

1 Study each example.

  a $15\% \times 80 = (10\% \times 80) + (5\% \times 80) = 8 + 4 = 12$

  b $15\% \times \$170 = (10\% \times \$170) + (5\% \times \$170) = \$17 + \$8.50 = \$25.50$

  c $15\% \times 3600 = (10\% \times 3600) + (5\% \times 3600) = 360 + 180 = 540$

  d $15\% \times \$28 = (10\% \times \$28) + (5\% \times \$28) = \$2.80 + \$1.40 = \$4.20$

□ Foundation ○ Standard ○ Complex

2 Now find 15% of each amount.

a	120	**b**	$840	**c**	260	**d**	$202
e	$50	**f**	72	**g**	$180	**h**	400
i	$1600	**j**	$22	**k**	6000	**l**	$350

To find $2\frac{1}{2}\%$ of a number, first find 5%, then halve it.

3 Study each example.

a $2\frac{1}{2}\% \times 600$

$10\% \times 600 = 60$

$5\% \times 600 = \frac{1}{2} \times 60 = 30$

$2\frac{1}{2}\% \times 600 = \frac{1}{2} \times 30 = 15$

b $2\frac{1}{2}\% \times \$820$

$10\% \times \$820 = \$82$

$5\% \times \$820 = \frac{1}{2} \times 82 = \$41$

$2\frac{1}{2}\% \times \$820 = \frac{1}{2} \times \$41 = \$20.50$

4 Now find $2\frac{1}{2}\%$ of each amount.

a	400	**b**	6640	**c**	$2000	**d**	$880
e	1500	**f**	$232	**g**	5400	**h**	$904

To find 25% of a number, halve the number twice as $25\% = \frac{1}{4}$.

5 Study each example.

a $25\% \times 700$

$50\% \times 700 = \frac{1}{2} \times 700 = 350$

$\therefore 25\% \times 700 = \frac{1}{2} \times 350 = 175$

b $25\% \times \$86$

$50\% \times \$86 = \frac{1}{2} \times \$86 = \$43$

$\therefore 25\% \times \$86 = \frac{1}{2} \times \$43 = \$21.50$

6 Now find 25% of each amount.

a	2000	**b**	$80	**c**	18	**d**	$25
e	$324	**f**	$140	**g**	66	**h**	298
i	$780	**j**	$1700	**k**	$126	**l**	1160

To find $12\frac{1}{2}\%$ of a number, find 25% first, then halve it. In other words, halve 3 times because $12\frac{1}{2}\% = \frac{1}{8}$.

7 Study each example.

a $12\frac{1}{2}\% \times 400$

$50\% \times 400 = \frac{1}{2} \times 400 = 200$

$25\% \times 400 = \frac{1}{2} \times 200 = 100$

$12\frac{1}{2}\% \times 400 = \frac{1}{2} \times 100 = 50$

b $12\frac{1}{2}\% \times \$144$

$50\% \times \$144 = \frac{1}{2} \times \$144 = \$72$

$25\% \times \$144 = \frac{1}{2} \times \$72 = \$36$

$12\frac{1}{2}\% \times \$144 = \frac{1}{2} \times \$36 = \$18$

8 Now find $12\frac{1}{2}\%$ of each amount.

a	1280	**b**	$12	**c**	60	**d**	$260
e	$540	**f**	$250	**g**	304	**h**	1360

9780170465595

The compound interest formula

There is a formula for calculating the final amount of an investment earning compound interest. Note the following pattern:

- final amount of $23 000 at 4% p.a. interest for 2 years = $23 000 × (3.04)²
- final amount of $9000 at 3.7% p.a. interest for 3 years = $9000 × (3.037)³
- final amount of $18 960 at 6.35% p.a. interest for 5 years = $18 960 × (3.0635)⁵

Worksheet
Compound interest

Puzzles
Compound interest with annual rests

Compound interest with non-annual rests

Technologies
Comparing interest rates

Simple and compound interest calculator

Spreadsheets
Comparing interest rates

Simple and compound interest

ⓘ Compound interest formula

$$A = P(1 + r)^n$$

where A is the total (final) amount of the investment

P is the principal

r is the interest rate per compounding period, expressed as a decimal

n is the number of compounding periods

The compound interest is then calculated using this formula:

compound interest = total amount – principal

$$I = A - P$$

The formula $A = P(1 + r)^n$ can also be written as $A = P(1 + i)^n$ or $A = P(1 + r)^t$.

Example 14

For each investment, calculate:

i the total amount of the investment

ii the compound interest earned if interest is compounded annually

a $26 750 is invested at 4% p.a. for 3 years

b $52 000 is invested at 3.8% p.a. for 5 years

Videos
The compound interest formula

Could you owe more than America?

SOLUTION

a i $P = \$26\ 750, r = 4\% = 0.04, n = 3$

$A = P(1 + r)^n$

$= \$26\ 750(1 + 0.04)^3$

$= \$26\ 750(1.04)^3$

$= \$30\ 090.112...$

$\approx \$30\ 090.11$

The total amount of the investment is $30 090.11.

ii compound interest = $30 090.11 – $26 750 $I = A - P$

$= \$3340.11$

b **i** $P = \$52\,000, r = 3.8\% = 0.038, n = 5$

$A = P(1 + r)^n$

$= \$52\,000(1 + 0.038)^5$

$= \$52\,000(1.038)^5$

$= \$62\,659.9597...$

$\approx \$62\,659.96$

ii compound interest $= \$62\,659.96 - \$52\,000$

$= \$10\,659.96$

Example 15

Video
Compound
interest

Calculate the compound interest when \$24 500 is invested at 6.3% p.a. for 5 years:

a compounded annually   **b** compounded monthly.

SOLUTION

a $P = \$24\,500, r = 0.063, n = 5$

$A = \$24\,500(1 + 0.063)^5$

$= \$24\,500(1.063)^5$

$= \$33\,253.1205...$

$\approx \$33\,253.12$

$I = \$33\,253.12 - \$24\,500$

$= \$8753.12$

b Because interest is compounded monthly, r and n must be expressed in months, not years.

$P = \$24\,500, r = \dfrac{0.063}{12} = 0.00525$ per month, $n = 5 \times 12 = 60$ months

$A = \$24\,500(1 + 0.005\,25)^{60}$

$= \$24\,500(1.005\,25)^{60}$

$= \$33\,543.701\,98$

$\approx \$33\,543.70$

$I = \$33\,543.70 - \$24\,500$

$= \$9043.70$

Note: More interest is earned when it is compounded monthly rather than yearly.

Why do you think this is so?

The compound interest formula (U) (F) (PS) (R)

In this exercise, round all money answers to the nearest cent.

1 An amount of $13 000 is invested at 5% p.a. interest, compounded annually over 2 years. Which expression represents the total value of the investment? Select **A**, **B**, **C** or **D**.

A $13\,000 \times 0.05 \times 2$ **B** $13\,000 (1 + 0.05)^2$

C $13\,000 \times (0.05)^2$ **D** $13\,000 (1 - 0.05)^2$

EXAMPLE **14**

2 For each investment, where interest is compounded yearly, calculate:

    i the total amount of the investment, A

    ii the compound interest, I, earned.

  a $6500 invested at 7% p.a. for 6 years   **b** $10 000 invested at 8.5% p.a. for 4 years

  c $12 240 invested at 1.6% p.a. for 2 years   **d** $34 600 invested at 4.9% p.a. for 5 years

  e $8000 invested at 1.75% p.a. for 3 years

3 Calculate the amount of interest earned on an investment of $6500 if it is invested at 2.5% p.a. compounded annually for 8 years. Select **A**, **B**, **C** or **D**.

  A $131.14   **B** $832.81   **C** $1300   **D** $1419.62

4 Find the amount of interest earned on one million dollars invested at 14.9% p.a. compounded annually for 6 years.

5 Find the amount of interest charged on a loan of $25 000 if it is borrowed over 10 years at 8% p.a. compounded annually. Select **A**, **B**, **C** or **D**.

  A $31 250   **B** $28 973.12   **C** $28 589.72   **D** $20 000

6 Yasmin was given $2000 when she turned 3 years old. Her parents invested it at a 2% p.a. compounded annually. No deposits or withdrawals were made. Which expression can be used to determine how much money Yasmin had in the account when she turned 16? Select **A**, **B**, **C** or **D**.

  A $2000(1 + 0.02)^{13}$ **B** $2000(1 + 0.2)^{13}$

  C $2000(1 + 0.02)^{16}$ **D** $2000(1 + 0.2)^{16}$

7 For each investment, calculate:

EXAMPLE **15**

    i the total amount   **ii** the interest earned.

  a $10 000 for 5 years at 2.4% p.a., compounded monthly

  b $35 500 for 10 years at 2% per half-year, compounded half-yearly

> Half-yearly means 'twice a year' or 'every 6 months'.

  c $8900 for 2 years at 3% p.a., compounded quarterly

> Quarterly means '4 times per year' or 'every 3 months'.

  d $42 000 for 5 years at 0.225% per month, compounded monthly

  e $16 500 for 3 years at 2.6% p.a., compounded half-yearly

  f $4900 for 1 year at 0.005% per day, compounded daily

☐ Foundation ◯ Standard ◇ Complex

8 Find the total value of an investment of $4300 over 5 years at 4.6% p.a. interest, compounded every 6 months. Select the correct answer **A**, **B**, **C** or **D**.

   A $4817.78   **B** $5384.27   **C** $5397.90   **D** $8506.24

9   **a**   Reese invested $6000 for 2 years at a flat rate of 5% p.a. Calculate the amount of interest earned.

   b   Tamsin invested $6000 for 2 years at an interest rate of 5% p.a. compounded annually. Calculate the amount of interest earned.

   c   Whose investment earned more interest? How much more?

10 A principal of $5000 is invested at 3.5% p.a. for 3 years. Match each compounding period for this investment to its correct expression for the final value of the expression.

   a   compounded yearly   **A** $5000\left(1+\dfrac{0.035}{2}\right)^{3\times2}$

   b   compounded half-yearly   **B** $5000\left(1+\dfrac{0.035}{12}\right)^{3\times12}$

   c   compounded quarterly   **C** $5000\left(1+\dfrac{0.035}{4}\right)^{3\times4}$

   d   compounded monthly   **D** $5000(1+0.035)^3$

11 Tania is setting up a trust account for her new granddaughter, Alice. In 18 years' time, she wants the investment to be worth $30 000, to help with the cost of university fees or the purchase of a car. Suppose the interest rate for the account is 2.94% p.a. compounding yearly.

(PS)
(R)

   a   How much should Tania invest now to achieve the $30 000 target?

   b   If Tania opened a trust account that earns 2.94% p.a. compounding monthly instead, how much less would she need to invest?

12 Yumi is 5 years old and about to start school. Her parents want to invest $25 000, for her high school education expenses, in an account that earns 3% p.a. over 7 years.

   a   Calculate the total interest earned if interest is compounded:

      i   yearly   **ii**   half-yearly   **iii**   quarterly   **iv**   monthly

   b   Which compounding period should Yumi's parents choose? Why?

13 A principal of $10 000 is invested for 4 years, earning interest at the rate of 3% p.a., compounded monthly. Which expression represents the total value of the investment? Select **A**, **B**, **C** or **D**.

   A $10\,000\left(1+\dfrac{3}{100}\right)^{4}$ **B** $10\,000\left(1+\dfrac{3}{100}\right)^{48}$

   C $10\,000\times\left(1+\dfrac{3}{1200}\right)^{4}$ **D** $10\,000\left(1+\dfrac{3}{1200}\right)^{48}$

□ Foundation   ○ Standard   ○ Complex

Comparing simple interest with compound interest

In this activity, you will compare the interest earned on an investment of $1000 for 10 years at 8% p.a. simple interest and 8% p.a. compound interest, compounded annually.

1   Create this spreadsheet. The principal (P) is entered in cell A1 and the annual interest rates (in decimal form) in cells B1 and C1.

	A	B	C
1	$1000.00	0.08	0.08
2			
3	**Years**	**Simple interest**	**Compound interest**
4	1		
5	2		
6	3		
7	4		
8	5		
9	6		
10	7		
11	8		
12	9		
13	10		

2   To calculate the simple interest in column B, in cell B4 enter the formula **=$A$1*$B$1*A4**. Now **Fill Down** from cell B4 to B13.

3   To calculate the compound interest in column C, in cell C4 enter the formula **=$A$1*(1+$C$1)^A4-$A$1**. Now **Fill Down** from cell C4 to C13.

4   Highlight cells A3 to C13. Insert **Scatter with Smooth lines and markers**.

5   When the interest rate is the same, which account pays better interest: simple or compound interest? (Type your answer in cell A15)

6   Now compare the interest earned on an investment of $1000 for 10 years at 9% p.a. simple interest and 7% p.a. compound interest, compounded annually. Change the interest rates in cells B1 (0.09) and C1 (0.07) respectively.

Answer the following questions in the spreadsheet cells indicated in brackets.

7   After how many years did the compound interest rate pay more than the simple interest rate? (A16)

8   How much extra interest did the compound interest rate pay at the end of the 10 years? (A17)

9   Change the interest rate in B1 to 10% (0.1) and C1 to 9% (0.09). How does the change in interest rate affect the amount of interest paid? Include calculations to justify your answer. (A18)

10 Change the interest rate in B1 to 12% (0.12) and C1 to 8.5% (0.085). After how many years did the amount of compound interest earned overtake the amount of simple interest earned? (A19)

11 What is the difference in the amount of compound interest earned for the 10-year period compared to the simple interest investment? Is it a significant amount? Justify your answer. (A20)

3.06 Depreciation

Worksheet
Depreciation

Depreciation is the decrease in value of an item over time. When items lose value because of age or frequency of use, they are said to depreciate.

The compound interest formula can be adapted to find the depreciated value of an item. While compound interest involves repeated percentage increases, depreciation involves repeated percentage decreases, so its formula has a minus sign.

ⓘ Depreciation formula

$$A = P(1 - r)^n$$

where A is the final value of the item

P is the original value of the item

r is the rate of depreciation per period, expressed as a decimal

n is the number of periods of depreciation

The amount of depreciation is then calculated using this formula:

depreciation = original value – final value

Example 16

Video
Depreciation

An accountant's computer system depreciates by 15% each year.

a   If the computer system is currently valued at $2600, what will its value be in 5 years?

b   What is the depreciation over this time?

SOLUTION

a $P = \$2600, r = 15\% = 0.15, n = 5$

$A = P(1 - r)^n$
$\quad = \$2600 (1 - 0.15)^5$
$\quad = \$2600 (0.85)^5$
$\quad = \$1153.6338...$
$\quad \approx \$1153.63$

The value of the computer system in 5 years will be $1153.63.

b   depreciation = $2600 – $1153.63   original value – final value
$\qquad\qquad\quad = \$1446.37$

9780170465595

Example 17

An industrial oven in a restaurant originally costs \$19 800, then depreciates at a rate of 12% p.a.

a Find the value of the oven after 6 years, correct to the nearest dollar.

b Express the depreciated value as a percentage of the cost price, correct to one decimal place.

SOLUTION

a $P = \$19\,800$, $r = 0.12$, $n = 6$

$A = P(1 - r)^n$

$= \$19\,800 (1 - 0.12)^6$

$= \$19\,800 (0.88)^6$

$= \$9195.2009...$

$\approx \$9195$

b percentage of cost price $= \dfrac{\$9195}{\$19800} \times 100\%$

$= 46.4393...\,\%$

$\approx 46.4\%$

This means that after 6 years, the oven is worth approximately 46% of its original price (or has lost 54% of its original value).

EXERCISE 3.06 ANSWERS ON P. 608

Depreciation

 U F PS R C

In this exercise, round all money answers to the nearest cent.

1 Find the value of a photocopier after 5 years if its purchase price was \$2850 and the annual depreciation rate is 20%.

EXAMPLE
16

2 **a** Find the value of a car after 7 years if it is purchased new for \$49 990 and it depreciates at 12% p.a.

b Find the amount of depreciation over this time.

3 For each item shown in the table, calculate:

   i   its value after 4 years of depreciation

   ii   its value after 4 years as a percentage of its original value, correct to one decimal place.

	Item	Original value	Depreciation rate (p.a.)
a	Stove	\$1100	12%
b	Fishing boat	\$38 500	18%
c	Library	\$8460	12%
d	Computer	\$2500	20%
e	Furniture	\$27 500	15.5%
f	Bike	\$2900	22%
g	Electrical tools	\$870	17.5%
h	Air conditioner	\$2600	9%

□ Foundation ○ Standard ○ Complex

EXAMPLE 17

4 A smartphone originally valued at $1729 depreciates at 37% p.a.

(R) **a** What percentage (to 2 decimal places where necessary) of the original value remains after:

i 1 year? **ii** 3 years? **iii** 6 years?

b Approximately, how long would it take the smartphone to halve its original value?

5 A security system costs a company $12 500 to buy new. It depreciates at a yearly rate of 20%.

a Find the value of the system after:

i 1 year **ii** 2 years **iii** 5 years

b Find the value of the system after 5 years as a percentage of its original value. Answer correct to one decimal place.

6 Nicole pays $25 490 for a new car. The car will depreciate in value by an average of 11% p.a.

a Find, correct to the nearest dollar, the market value of the car in 3 years.

b Calculate the amount of depreciation in the car after 3 years.

7 Hover has spent $175 000 on equipment to set up his hairdressing salon. The equipment depreciates at 20% per year.

(R) **a** Find the value of the equipment after 4 years.

b Find the amount of depreciation in the equipment after 4 years.

c Find, by trial and error, how long it will take for the value to be over $50 000. Answer in years and months.

d Find the value of Hover's equipment after 9 years as a percentage of its original value, correct to one decimal place.

8 Kamal says that, at 10% p.a. depreciation, a car will lose half its value after 7 years.

(PS) Is he correct? Show all working to justify your answer.

(R)

(C)

9 Office equipment that is worth $12 000 when new, depreciates at 15% p.a. as shown in the table.

PS
R
C

Year	Depreciated value
0	$12 000
1	$10 200
2	$8670
3	$7369.50
4	$6264.08
5	$5324.46
6	$4525.79
7	$3846.93
8	$3269.89
9	$2779.40
10	$2362.49
11	$2008.12
12	$1706.90
13	$1450.87
14	$1233.24

a How much did the office equipment lose in value in the first year?

b After how many years did the office equipment fall below half its original value?

c By how much did the office equipment depreciate between the 5th and 6th years?

d Will the value of the office equipment ever fall below $100?

e Will the value of the office equipment ever be zero?

1. How long, in years and days, will it take an investment of $3000 to earn $500 in simple interest at 4% p.a.?

2. How much money should Owen invest to earn $100 in simple interest if the investment will last for 9 months and the interest rate is 3% p.a.?

3. A principal of $10 000 is invested for 5 years at an interest rate of 5% p.a., with interest compounded weekly. Calculate the final value of the investment.

4. Meghan needs $80 000 in 4 years' time. What amount should she invest now at an interest rate of 6% p.a., with interest compounded annually, to reach her target?

5. A painting appreciates in value at a rate of 3% p.a., whereas a computer depreciates in value at a rate of 10% p.a. If I bought the painting for $1200 and the computer for $1500 new, what would be their combined value in 5 years' time?

6. A bacteria colony is growing at a rate of 20% per hour. If there are 10 000 bacteria now, use the compound interest formula to calculate how many there will be after 1 day. (Give your answer correct to the nearest 10 000.)

7. a You invest $2000 in a bank account at an interest rate of 4% p.a. with interest compounded annually. How long will it take for your investment to double in value?

   b If you invested $4000 instead of $2000 at the same interest rate, how long will it take to double in value?

   c Does the size of the principal make any difference to the time taken for it to double?

③ CHAPTER REVIEW

Language of maths

allowable deductions	annual leave loading	commission	compound interest
deposit	depreciation	double time	flat rate
fortnightly	gross pay	income tax	interest
net pay	overtime	PAYG tax	per annum (p.a.)
piecework	principal	quarterly	salary
simple interest	taxable income	time-and-a-half	wage

1 When investing, why is **compound interest** better than **simple interest**?

2 What do the P and r stand for in the formulas $I = Prn$ and $A = P(1 + r)^n$?

3 What is another name for **flat-rate interest**?

4 What word means a decrease in the value of an item over time?

5 Why is **gross pay** higher than **net pay**?

6 Use a dictionary to find 2 different meanings of **principal**.

Quiz
Language of maths 3

Puzzle
Interest and depreciation crossword

Topic summary

- Which parts of this chapter were revision of Year 9 knowledge and skills?
- Which parts of this chapter were new to you?
- Do you know how to use the simple interest and compound interest formulas?
- How is income tax calculated?
- How is the depreciation formula similar to the compound interest formula?

Print (or copy) and complete this mind map of the topic, adding detail to its branches and using pictures, symbols and colour where needed. Ask your teacher to check your work.

Worksheet
Mind map: Interest and depreciation

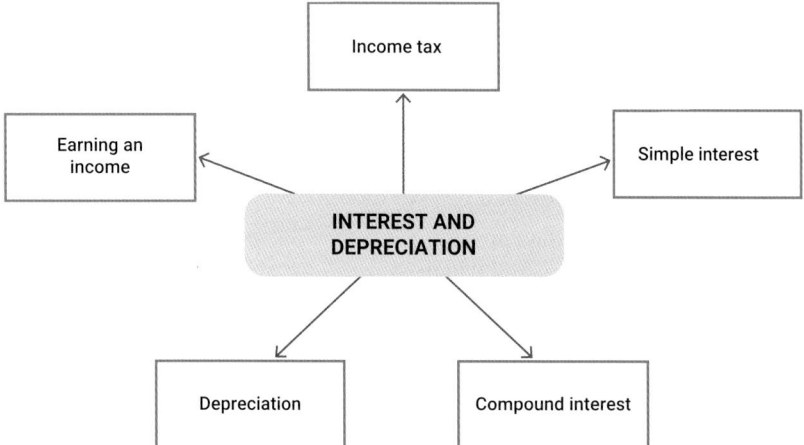

(3) TEST YOURSELF ANSWERS ON P. 608

In this exercise, round all money answers to the nearest cent.

3.01 **1** Hayley is paid a commission of 2.5% on the value of the properties she sells. She also receives a weekly retainer of $1150. How much will Hayley earn if she sells a house for $475 830?

3.01 **2** Caleb earns a salary of $70 400 p.a. How much is he paid each week?

3.01 **3** A supermarket cashier is employed under the following award.

Normal rate: $21.45 per hour	
Normal rate	For 0 to 38 hours worked
Time-and-a-half	For the next 4 hours worked
Double time	For each hour worked after that

Calculate the wage for working:

a 40 hours

b 46 hours.

3.01 **4** For his Christmas holidays, Nirmal received 4 weeks normal pay plus 17.5% annual leave loading for the 4 weeks. If Nirmal's annual salary is $54 920, find:

a his normal weekly pay

b his leave loading

c his total pay for the 4-week holiday.

3.02 **5** Alia earns a salary of $68 650 p.a. Her allowable deductions are donations to charities of $540 and work-related expenses of $385.

a Calculate Alia's taxable income.

b Use the tax table on page 113 to calculate the income tax Alia should pay.

3.03 **6** Calculate the simple interest earned on each investment.

a $20 000 invested for 3 years at 4% p.a.

b $7850 invested at 2.5% p.a for 15 months

c $4500 invested for 6 months at 0.17% per month

d $25 200 invested for 100 days at 3.45% p.a.

3.04 **7** An amount of $5000 is invested at 2.35% p.a. interest, compounded annually over 3 years.

a What is the total value of the investment after 3 years?

b What is the amount of compound interest earned?

3.05 **8** Calculate the value of the investment when $34 200 is invested at 3% p.a. for 2 years, with interest compounded annually.

☐ Foundation ○ Standard ○ Complex

9 Find the final value if $11 000 is invested for 4 years at 2.4% p.a., with interest compounded monthly. 3.05

10 Find the interest earned when $4895 is invested at 1.95% p.a. for 3 years, with interest compounded annually. 3.05

11 Calculate the interest earned when $46 230 is invested for 9 years at 2.8% p.a., with interest compounded half-yearly. 3.05

12 Bindi bought a new car for $24 990, which depreciates by 10% p.a. 3.06

    a Find correct to the nearest dollar the depreciated value of the car after 5 years.

    b What is the depreciation over this time?

    c Express the depreciated value as a percentage of the original price (correct to one decimal place).

□ Foundation ○ Standard ○ Complex

3.01

1 Cassie earns a salary of $114 750. How much is she paid each week?

1.01

2 An interval is formed by joining the points $M(2, -3)$ and $N(-5, 9)$.
   a Find the length of interval MN, correct to one decimal place.
   b Find the midpoint of MN.
   c Find the gradient of MN.

2.03

3 Find, correct to one decimal place, the area of each shape.

a
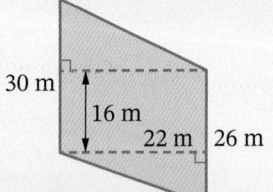

b
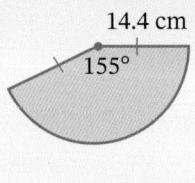

c
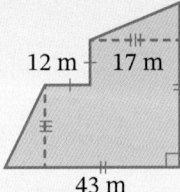

d
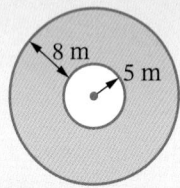

e
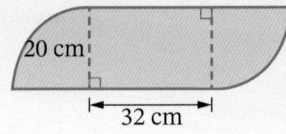

f
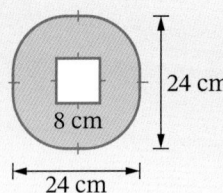

3.01

4 Naved is paid 4 weeks' normal pay plus 17.5% annual leave loading for his 4-week holiday. If Naved's salary is $78 580, find his:
   a normal weekly pay
   b leave loading
   c total pay for the 4-week holiday.

2.04

5 Find the surface area of each prism.

a
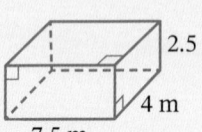

b
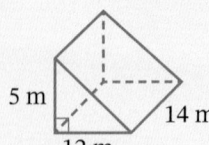

c
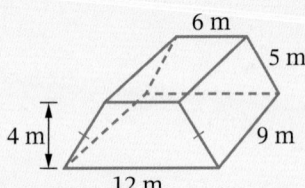

6 A call centre operator is employed under the following award.

3.01

Normal rate: $28.75 per hour	
Normal rate	For 0 to 36 hours worked
Time-and-a-half	For the next 4 hours worked
Double time	For each hour worked after that

Calculate the wage for working:

a   20 hours **b**   39 hours **c**   45 hours

7 A line passes through the points $H(5, -3)$ and $K(8, -7)$. Calculate the gradient of the line:

1.02

a   parallel to HK **b**   perpendicular to HK

8 Nikita earns a weekly wage of $1485. She has annual deductions of $1756 for a health fund and $3560 for work expenses.

3.02

a   Calculate Nikita's taxable income.

b   Use the tax table on page 123 to calculate the income tax that Nikita should pay.

9 Graph the linear equations $y = 3x - 2$ and $y = -2x + 3$ on a number plane. Where do the lines intersect?

1.03

10 Find to the nearest degree the angle of inclination of a line with gradient $-\frac{3}{4}$.

EXTENSION

1.01

11 Calculate, correct to one decimal place, the external surface area of each cylinder. All lengths shown are in centimetres.

2.05

a
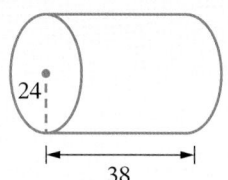

b
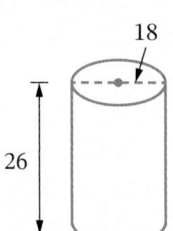

c
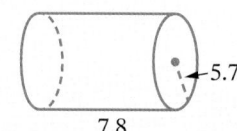
Cylinder, open at both ends

EXTENSION

12 Find, in general form, the equation of the line passing through the point $(-8, 3)$ with gradient $-\frac{2}{3}$.

1.06

13 Which of the following points lie on the line of $2x + y = 3$? Select the correct answer **A**, **B**, **C** or **D**.

1.03

A $(1, 0)$ **B** $(2, -1)$ **C** $(-1, -1)$ **D** $(-1, -5)$

EXTENSION

14 Find the equation of a line passing through points $(3, -2)$ and $(-1, 3)$.

1.06

15 Graph each linear inequality on a number plane.

1.09

a $y \le 2x - 6$ **b** $3y > -9x + 12$

☐ Foundation   ○ Standard   ◇ Complex

2.06 **16** Calculate, correct to nearest square metre, the surface area of each solid. All lengths shown are in metres.

a
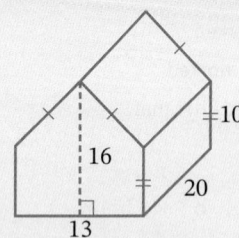

b
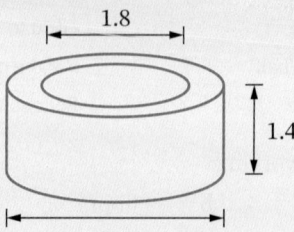

c
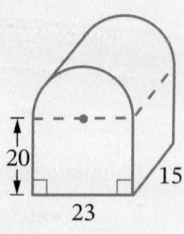

3.05 **17** Calculate the value of an investment if \$46 000 is invested at 4.2% p.a. for 3 years with interest compounded:

    a   annually   **b**   quarterly   **c**   monthly.

3.05 **18** Find the compound interest earned when \$50 000 is invested for 10 years at 6.5% p.a., with interest compounded half-yearly.

1.04 **19** Find the gradient, m, and y-intercept, c, for each linear equation.

    a $y = -3x + 8$ **b** $y = 7 + x$ **c** $y = \dfrac{3 - 2x}{3}$

EXTENSION

1.05 **20** Convert each equation to general form $ax + by + c = 0$.

    a $y = 2x - 3$ **b** $2x = y + 5$ **c** $y = \dfrac{3x}{4} + 6$

21 Find the surface area of each pyramid.

2.06

a
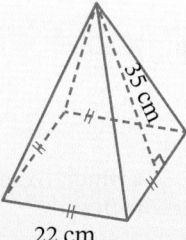

b
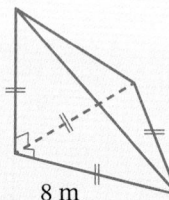

c
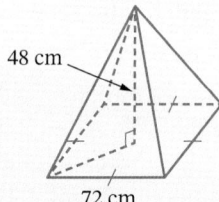

2.07 **22** Find, correct to the nearest square metre, the surface area of each solid. All measurements are in metres.

a
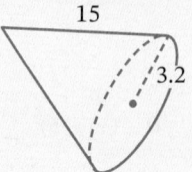

b
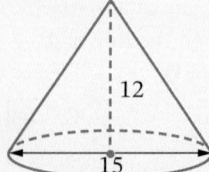

c
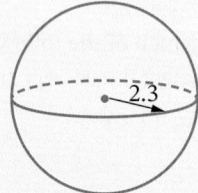

1.08 **23** Find the equation of a line that is:

    a   parallel to $y = 4x - 3$ and has an x-intercept of -8

    b   perpendicular to $y = -\dfrac{x}{5} + 3$ and passes through $(0, 0)$.

☐ Foundation   ○ Standard   ○ Complex

24 Annieke purchases a new car for \$39 990, which depreciates by 10% p.a.

3.06

a   Find the depreciated value of the car after 4 years.

b   What is the depreciation over this time?

c   Express the depreciated value as a percentage of the cost price (correct to one decimal place).

25 Find the gradient, m, and the y-intercept, c, of the line with equation $2x + 5y - 3 = 0$. Select **A**, **B**, **C** or **D**.

1.05

A $m = -2, c = 3$

B $m = \dfrac{3}{5}, c = \dfrac{2}{5}$

C $m = -\dfrac{2}{5}, c = \dfrac{3}{5}$

D $m = 2, c = -3$

26 The line $2x + 5y + 7 = 0$ and another line intersect at right angles at the point $(4, -5)$.

Find the equation of the other line.

EXTENSION

1.08

27 Find correct to one decimal place the volume of each solid.

2.11

a
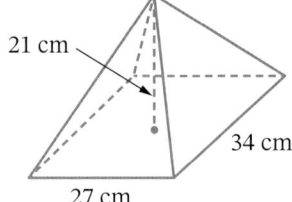
21 cm
34 cm
27 cm

b
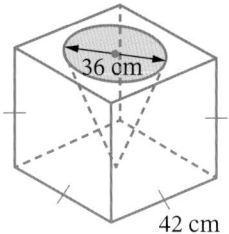
36 cm
42 cm

c
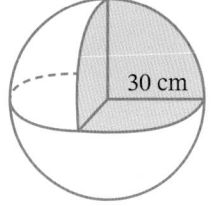
30 cm

28 Max's weekly wage is \$1249.20.

3.01

a   If he works 36 hours per week, find his hourly rate of pay.

b   How much does Max earn per month?

29 A circular swimming pool has a radius of 3.5 metres and a depth of 2 metres. The pool is to be filled to within 30 centimetres from the top.

2.09

a   Calculate the volume of water in the pool to the nearest m³.

b   If water costs \$2.11 per kilolitre, find the cost of filling the pool.

30 What is the flat rate of interest per annum when \$5600 earns \$470 in interest over 3 years? Select **A**, **B**, **C** or **D**.

3.03

A   2.8%   **B**   2.7%   **C**   3.0%   **D**   27.9%

31 The diameter of a circle is given as 8 metres, correct to the nearest metre.

2.02

a   Calculate the area of this circle, correct to 4 decimal places.

b   Calculate the maximum possible area of this circle, correct to 4 decimal places, and its percentage error, correct to 2 decimal places.

□ Foundation   ○ Standard   ◇ Complex

PRACTICE SET 1

9780170465595

Practice set 1   **149**

4

ALGEBRA

Products, factors and surds

Rubik's Cube is a puzzle that was invented by Hungarian Professor of Architecture Erno Rubik in 1974. In Hungary, it was originally called the Magic Cube.

The cube has 210 × 37 × 8! × 12! ≈ 43 252 003 274 489 856 000 different possible arrangements (8! or '8 factorial' means 8 × 7 × 6 × 5 × 4 × 3 × 2 × 1). In 2018, Chinese 'speedcuber' Yusheng Du solved a Rubik's cube puzzle in 27 moves in 3.47 seconds!

iStock.com/Inchendio

Chapter outline

		Proficiencies			
4.01	The index laws	U	F	R	C
4.02	Fractional indices*	U	F	R	C
4.03	Expanding and factorising expressions	U	F		
4.04	Expanding binomial products	U	F	R	C
4.05	Factorising special binomial products*	U	F		
4.06	Factorising quadratic expressions $x^2 + bx + c$	U	F	R	
4.07	Factorising quadratic expressions $ax^2 + bx + c$*	U	F	R	
4.08	Mixed factorisations*	U	F	R	
4.09	Surds and irrational numbers*	U	F	R	C
4.10	Simplifying surds*	U	F	R	
4.11	Adding and subtracting surds*	U	F		
4.12	Multiplying and dividing surds*	U	F		
4.13	Binomial products involving surds*	U	F		
4.14	Rationalising the denominator*	U	F		

* EXTENSION

U = Understanding
F = Fluency
PS = Problem solving

R = Reasoning
C = Communicating

Wordbank

binomial product An algebraic expression showing 2 or more binomials multiplied together, for example, $(x + 9)(3x - 4)$.

index laws Rules for simplifying algebraic expressions involving powers of the same base, for example, $a^m \div a^n = a^{m-n}$.

irrational number A number such as π or $\sqrt{2}$ that cannot be expressed as a fraction $\dfrac{a}{b}$

perfect square A square number or an algebraic expression that represents one, for example, 64, $(x + 9)^2$

quadratic trinomial An algebraic expression that consists of 3 terms, for example, $x^2 + 2x + 6$

Quiz
Wordbank 4

(More next page)

rational number Any number that can be written in the form $\frac{a}{b}$, where a and b are integers and $b \neq 0$

rationalise the denominator To simplify a fraction involving a surd by making its denominator rational (that is, not a surd)

simplify a surd To write a surd $\sqrt{x}$ in its simplest form so that x has no factors that are perfect squares

Videos (19):

4.01 Numbers and powers • Simplifying with the index laws • Negative indices • Index laws

4.02 Fractional indices

4.03 Factorising expressions

4.04 Expanding binomial products 1 • Expanding binomial products 2

4.05 Difference of 2 squares

4.06 Factorising quadratic expressions 1 • Special binomial products • Difference of 2 squares

4.07 Factorising quadratic expressions 2 • Factorising quadratic expressions (Advanced) • Advanced algebra

4.10 Simplifying surds 2 • Simplifying surds 1

4.13 Binomial products involving surds

4.14 Rationalising the denomoinator

Quizzes (5):

- Wordbank 4
- SkillCheck 4
- Mental skills 4
- Language of maths 4
- Test yourself 4

Skillsheets (3):

4.03 Algebra using diagrams • HCF by factor trees • Factorising using diagrams

Worksheets (13):

4.01 Index laws review

4.03 Expanding and factorising • Algebra 4

4.04 Mixed expansions • Algebra 2 • Binomial products • Area diagrams

4.06 Simplifying algebraic fractions • Special products

4.09 Surds on the number line

4.12 Multiplying and dividing surds

Language of maths Algebra 6

Mind map: Products, factors and surds

Puzzles (21):

4.01 Indices puzzle • Indices squaresaw

4.02 Indices squaresaw (Advanced) • Exponential equations

4.03 Factorising puzzle • The distributive law

4.04 Expanding brackets • Factorominoes • Trinominoes • Products and factors squaresaw • Enough time

4.05 Grouping • Difference of 2 perfect squares

4.06 Factorominoes • Trinominoes

4.07 Factorising puzzle (Advanced) • Products and factors squaresaw • Perfect squares

4.08 Factorominoes • Mixed factorisations

4.10 Simplifying surds

4.11 Surds code puzzle

4.12 Surds

Language of maths Algebra crossword • Surds crossword

Technology (3):

4.04 Expanding binomials

4.07 Factorising trinomials

4.10 Simplifying surds quiz

Spreadsheets (3):

4.04 Expanding binomials

4.07 Factorising trinomials

4.10 Simplifying surds quiz

Presentation (1):

4.01 Index laws

Nelson MindTap

To access resources above, visit
cengage.com.au/nelsonmindtap

✓ apply index laws to algebraic expressions with integer indices

✓ (EXTENSION) apply index laws to algebraic expressions with fractional indices

✓ expand and factorise algebraic expressions involving terms with indices

✓ expand binomial products and factorise (monic) quadratic expressions of the form $x^2 + bx + c$

✓ (EXTENSION) expand and factorise special binomial products that are perfect squares or the difference of 2 squares

✓ (EXTENSION) factorise an expression with 4 terms by grouping in pairs

✓ (EXTENSION) factorise (non-monic) quadratic expressions of the form $ax^2 + bx + c$, including those that are perfect squares or the difference of 2 squares

✓ (EXTENSION) describe real, rational and irrational numbers and surds

✓ (EXTENSION) simplify, add, subtract, multiply and divide surds

✓ (EXTENSION) expand and simplify binomial products involving surds

✓ (EXTENSION) rationalise the denominator of expressions of the form $\dfrac{a\sqrt{b}}{c\sqrt{d}}$

4 In this chapter, you will:

SkillCheck
ANSWERS ON P. 609

1 Simplify each expression.

a	$g^4 \times g^5$	**b**	$r^8 \div r^2$	**c**	$(d^5)^3$	**d**	$(-k)^2$
e	$h \times h^9$	**f**	$m^5 \div m$	**g**	a^1	**h**	c^0
i	$3e^2 \times 2e^5$	**j**	$18n^6 \div 6n^2$	**k**	$(10w^3)^3$	**l**	$25q^0$
m	$(vw)^5$	**n**	$\left(\dfrac{m}{n}\right)^3$	**o**	y^{-1}	**p**	p^{-2}

2 Select the square numbers from the following list of numbers.

44   81   25   100   75   72   16   50   64   32

3 Expand and simplify each expression.

a $(m + 3)(m + 7)$

b $(y + 1)(y - 4)$

c $(n - 2)(n - 3)$

d $(2d + 3)(1 + 3d)$

e $(1 - 5p)(4 + 3p)$

f $(3a + 2f)(a + 5f)$

g $(x + 4)^2$

h $(y - 3)^2$

i $(2k + 1)^2$

j $(a - 5)(a + 5)$

k $(t + 7)(t - 7)$

l $(3m + 4)(3m - 4)$

Quiz
SkillCheck 4

Videos
Numbers and powers

Simplifying with the index laws

Negative indices

Index laws

Worksheet
Index laws review

Presentation
Index laws

Puzzles
Indices puzzle

Indices squaresaw

ⓘ The index laws

$$a^m \times a^n = a^{m+n} \qquad a^m \div a^n = \frac{a^m}{a^n} = a^{m-n} \qquad (a^m)^n = a^{m \times n}$$

$$(ab)^n = a^n b^n \qquad \left(\frac{a}{b}\right)^n = \frac{a^n}{b^n} \qquad a^0 = 1$$

$$a^{-n} = \frac{1}{a^n} \qquad a^{-1} = \frac{1}{a} \quad \left(\frac{a}{b}\right)^{-1} = \frac{b}{a} \qquad \left(\frac{a}{b}\right)^{-n} = \left(\frac{b}{a}\right)^n = \frac{b^n}{a^n}$$

Example 1

Simplify each expression.

a $\dfrac{24e^6 n^{12}}{8en^4}$ **b** $(4d^4 q^2 r)^3$ **c** $\left(\dfrac{2c^2}{d}\right)^4$

d $31x^0 - (31x)^0$ **e** $9x^{-1}$ **f** $(4q)^{-3}$

SOLUTION

a $\dfrac{24e^6 n^{12}}{8en^4} = \dfrac{^3 \cancel{24} e^6 n^{12}}{_1 \cancel{8} en^4}$

     $= 3e^5 n^8$

b $(4d^4 q^2 r)^3 = 4^3 d^{4 \times 3} q^{2 \times 3} r^3$

           $= 64 d^{12} q^6 r^3$

c $\left(\dfrac{2c^2}{d}\right)^4 = \dfrac{\left(2c^2\right)^4}{d^4}$

         $= \dfrac{2^4 c^{2 \times 4}}{d^4}$

         $= \dfrac{16 c^8}{d^4}$

d $31x^0 - (31x)^0 = 31 \times 1 - 1$

             $= 30$

e $9x^{-1} = 9 \times \dfrac{1}{x}$

      $= \dfrac{9}{x}$

f $(4q)^{-3} = \dfrac{1}{(4q)^3}$

       $= \dfrac{1}{64q^3}$

Example 2

Simplify:

a $\left(-1\dfrac{2}{3}\right)^{-5}$ **b** $\left(\dfrac{2}{3r}\right)^{-3}$

SOLUTION

a $\left(-1\dfrac{2}{3}\right)^{-5} = \left(-\dfrac{5}{3}\right)^{-5}$

          $= \left(-\dfrac{3}{5}\right)^5$

          $= -\dfrac{243}{3125}$

b $\left(\dfrac{2}{3r}\right)^{-3} = \left(\dfrac{3r}{2}\right)^3$

          $= \dfrac{27r^3}{8}$

The index laws

(U) (F) (R) (C)

EXAMPLE
1

1 Simplify each expression.

(R) **a** $8m^5 \times 3m^9$ **b** $30k^{10} \div 25k^2$ **c** $(-y^2)^5$

(C) **d** $(3q^3)^2$ **e** $32a^7d^4 \div 8ad^3$ **f** $3x^6y^8 \times 7xy^4$

g $5e^4g^3 \times (-e^6g)$ **h** $\dfrac{27w^3y^8}{-9w^2y}$ **i** $(4c^7)^3$

j $(-2p)^5$ **k** $\dfrac{45hk^5m^3}{30hk^3m^2}$ **l** $9u^3vw^2 \times 6uv^2w^8$

2 Simplify each expression.

(R)(C) **a** $(l^3m^5)^6$ **b** $\left(\dfrac{n}{2}\right)^3$ **c** $\left(\dfrac{w^4}{m^3}\right)^5$ **d** $\left(\dfrac{5}{2}\right)^0$

e $(-8ky^5)^2$ **f** $(3p^2q^3r^4)^4$ **g** $5x^0 - (7x)^0$ **h** $(-5d^3y^5)^3$

i $\left(\dfrac{2b}{3d}\right)^4$ **j** $-9(a^2b^3)^0$ **k** $12h^0$ **l** $\left(-\dfrac{3k^4}{10}\right)^3$

3 Evaluate each expression.

(R)(C) **a** 7^0 **b** 5×4^0 **c** $(-4)^3$ **d** $(2^3)^2$

e $6^5 \div 6^3$ **f** $(-3^2)^0$ **g** $8^2 \div 8^3$ **h** $5^4 \times 5^{-3}$

i $\left(\dfrac{3}{5}\right)^0$ **j** $7^5 \div 7^3$ **k** $12^2 \div 12^2$ **l** $3^5 \times 3^{-5}$

m $15^0 \div 15^1$ **n** $(4^{-1})^2$ **o** $(2^3)^0 + (2^0)^3$ **p** $(5^0)^3 \times 5^2$

4 Find the value of $(3x)^0 + 3 \times 2^0$. Select the correct answer **A**, **B**, **C** or **D**.

     A 6   **B** 1   **C** 7   **D** 4

5 Express each term as a fraction.

(R)(C) **a** 2^{-3} **b** 10^{-6} **c** 8^{-1} **d** 6^{-2} **e** 3^{-4}

6 Simplify each expression using a positive index.

(R)(C) **a** 5^{-4} **b** 8^{-2} **c** w^{-6} **d** m^{-5}

e $4y^{-3}$ **f** $(ad)^{-2}$ **g** $(2x)^{-5}$ **h** $3mp^{-2}$

i $10g^{-2}h^{-3}$ **j** $(4u)^{-4}$ **k** $2a^5q^{-2}$ **l** $4p^2x^{-3}$

m $10a^{-5}c^3$ **n** $(-3r^6)^{-3}$ **o** $\dfrac{3}{4}q^{-2}p^{-1}$ **p** $4(5k^3)^{-3}$

7 Simplify $2c^{-3}$. Select **A**, **B**, **C** or **D**.

     A $-6c$ **B** $\dfrac{1}{2c^3}$ **C** $\dfrac{2}{c^3}$ **D** $\dfrac{1}{8c^3}$

□ Foundation   ○ Standard   ○ Complex

8 Simplify each expression using positive indices.

R **a** $\left(\dfrac{5}{2d}\right)^{-2}$ **C**
b $5y^{-2}$
c $(5m)^{-3}$
d $x^2y^3w^{-2}$

e $\left(\dfrac{4y^3}{3}\right)^{-2}$
f $\left(\dfrac{a}{7k}\right)^{-1}$
g $8(3ab^2)^{-2}$
h $\left(\dfrac{6c}{5k^2}\right)^{-1}$

EXAMPLE 2

9 Simplify each expression.

R **a** $\left(\dfrac{1}{4}\right)^{-2}$ **C**
b $\left(\dfrac{5}{3}\right)^{-3}$
c $\left(-1\dfrac{2}{3}\right)^{-4}$
d $\left(2\dfrac{3}{5}\right)^{-2}$

e $\left(\dfrac{4}{m}\right)^{-3}$
f $\left(\dfrac{3a}{7}\right)^{-2}$
g $\left(-\dfrac{2}{y}\right)^{-5}$
h $\left(\dfrac{8q^2}{5}\right)^{-2}$

i $\left(-\dfrac{4}{w^3}\right)^{-3}$
j $\left(\dfrac{k^2}{d^5}\right)^{-2}$
k $\left(-\dfrac{10g^4}{3d^3}\right)^{-5}$
l $\left(\dfrac{7h^6}{5}\right)^{-4}$

10 Simplify each expression.

R **a** $(10x^{10}y)^3 \times 5x^{-2}y^3$
b $(20k^7m^2 \div 5k^{-4}m)^4$

C **c** $(2q^{-3}r^3)^4 \div 8(qr^2)^2$
d $8w^{-5}m^3 \div (6wm^2)^2$

e $\left(\dfrac{4a^5x^6}{a^6x^2}\right)^4$
f $\left(\dfrac{3g^7n^6}{2g^5n^2}\right)^{-2}$

g $(4p^{-3}h^4)^3 \times (-2p^6h^9)$
h $(8d^7n^5)^2 \div (-2d^3n^2)^3$

i $(-2c^3e \times 5c^4e^5)^3$

4.02 Extension: Fractional indices

EXTENSION

Puzzles
Indices
squaresaw
(Advanced)

Exponential
equations

ⓘ Fractional indices

$a^{\frac{1}{2}} = \sqrt{a}$ — Any number raised to the power of $\dfrac{1}{2}$ is the square root of that number.

$a^{\frac{1}{3}} = \sqrt[3]{a}$ — Any number raised to the power of $\dfrac{1}{3}$ is the cube root of that number.

$a^{\frac{1}{n}} = \sqrt[n]{a}$ — Any number raised to the power of $\dfrac{1}{n}$ is the nth root of that number.

$a^{\frac{m}{n}} = \left(\sqrt[n]{a}\right)^m$ or $\sqrt[n]{a^m}$ — Any number raised to the power of $\dfrac{m}{n}$ is the nth root of that number raised to the power of m.

Note: Taking the root first $\left(\sqrt[n]{a}\right)^m$ often makes the calculation simpler.

On a calculator, the nth root key is ▢ or ▢ found by pressing the **SHIFT** or **2nd F** key before pressing ▢ or ▢ respectively.

▢ Foundation   ○ Standard   ◇ Complex

Example 3

Evaluate each expression.

a $961^{\frac{1}{2}}$ **b** $1331^{\frac{1}{3}}$ **c** $6561^{\frac{1}{8}}$

SOLUTION

a $961^{\frac{1}{2}} = \sqrt{961}$
$= 31$

b $1331^{\frac{1}{3}} = \sqrt[3]{1331}$
$= 11$

c $6561^{\frac{1}{8}} = \sqrt[8]{6561}$
$= 3$

On a calculator: 8 6561 =
because $3^8 = 6561$

Example 4

Evaluate each expression.

a $32^{\frac{3}{5}}$ **b** $27^{-\frac{1}{3}}$ **c** $25^{-\frac{5}{2}}$

SOLUTION

A $32^{\frac{3}{5}} = \left(\sqrt[5]{32}\right)^3$
$= 2^3$
$= 8$

B $27^{-\frac{1}{3}} = \dfrac{1}{27^{\frac{1}{3}}}$
$= \dfrac{1}{\sqrt[3]{27}}$
$= \dfrac{1}{3}$

C $25^{-\frac{5}{2}} = \dfrac{1}{25^{\frac{5}{2}}}$
$= \dfrac{1}{\left(\sqrt{25}\right)^5}$
$= \dfrac{1}{5^5}$
$= \dfrac{1}{3125}$

Video
Fractional indices

Example 5

Write each expression using a fractional index.

a $\sqrt{w^9}$ **b** $\sqrt[4]{m^5}$ **c** $\dfrac{1}{\sqrt[3]{y^8}}$

SOLUTION

a $\sqrt{w^9} = \left(w^9\right)^{\frac{1}{2}}$
$= w^{\frac{9}{2}}$

b $\sqrt[4]{m^5} = \left(m^5\right)^{\frac{1}{4}}$
$= m^{\frac{5}{4}}$

c $\dfrac{1}{\sqrt[3]{y^8}} = \dfrac{1}{\left(y^8\right)^{\frac{1}{3}}}$
$= \dfrac{1}{y^{\frac{8}{3}}}$ or $y^{-\frac{8}{3}}$

Example 6

Simplify each expression.

a $\sqrt[4]{\left(81a^2\right)^5}$ **b** $\left(64k^6\right)^{-\frac{5}{3}}$ **c** $4m^{\frac{3}{4}}n^2 \times \sqrt[3]{8m^2n}$

SOLUTION

a $\sqrt[4]{\left(81a^2\right)^5} = \left(81a^2\right)^{\frac{5}{4}}$

$\qquad = 81^{\frac{5}{4}}a^{2\times\frac{5}{4}}$

$\qquad = 243a^{\frac{5}{2}}$

b $\left(64k^6\right)^{-\frac{5}{3}} = \dfrac{1}{\left(64k^6\right)^{\frac{5}{3}}}$

$\qquad = \dfrac{1}{64^{\frac{5}{3}}k^{6\times\frac{5}{3}}}$

$\qquad = \dfrac{1}{1024k^{10}}$

c $4m^{\frac{3}{4}}n^2 \times \sqrt[3]{8m^2n} = 4m^{\frac{3}{4}}n^2 \times \left(8m^2n\right)^{\frac{1}{3}}$

$\qquad = 4m^{\frac{3}{4}}n^2 \times 8^{\frac{1}{3}}m^{2\times\frac{1}{3}}n^{\frac{1}{3}}$

$\qquad = 4m^{\frac{3}{4}}n^2 \times 2m^{\frac{2}{3}}n^{\frac{1}{3}}$

$\qquad = 8m^{\frac{3}{4}+\frac{2}{3}}n^{2+\frac{1}{3}}$

$\qquad = 8m^{\frac{17}{12}}n^{\frac{7}{3}}$

EXERCISE (4.02) ANSWERS ON P. 610

Fractional indices
    U F R C

EXAMPLE 3

1 Evaluate each expression.

(R) **a** $64^{\frac{1}{2}}$ **b** $-27^{\frac{1}{3}}$ **c** $625^{\frac{1}{2}}$ **d** $1000^{\frac{1}{3}}$

   e $16^{\frac{1}{4}}$ **f** $(-0.00032)^{\frac{1}{5}}$ **g** $(0.01)^{\frac{1}{2}}$ **h** $(-512)^{\frac{1}{9}}$

   i $(-8)^{\frac{1}{3}}$ **j** $(-729)^{\frac{1}{3}}$ **k** $256^{\frac{1}{8}}$ **l** $3125^{\frac{1}{5}}$

2 Write each expression using a radical (root) sign.

(R)(C) **a** $7^{\frac{1}{3}}$ **b** $15^{\frac{1}{2}}$ **c** $d^{\frac{1}{4}}$ **d** $y^{\frac{1}{2}}$

   e $(4x)^{\frac{1}{6}}$ **f** $\left(10m^3\right)^{\frac{1}{2}}$ **g** $\left(2a^7\right)^{\frac{1}{10}}$ **h** $(12m)^{\frac{1}{3}}$

3 Write $\sqrt[4]{100k}$ using a fractional index. Select the correct answer **A**, **B**, **C** or **D**.

(R)(C) **A** $25k^{\frac{1}{4}}$ **B** $100k^{\frac{1}{4}}$ **C** $(100k)^{\frac{1}{4}}$ **D** $5k^{\frac{1}{4}}$

▷

□ Foundation ○ Standard ◇ Complex

4 Write each expression using a fractional index.

Ⓡ Ⓒ

a $\sqrt[3]{80}$ b $\sqrt[6]{40}$ c $\sqrt{20}$ d $\sqrt[4]{c}$

e $\sqrt{b}$ f $\sqrt[3]{xy}$ g $\sqrt[5]{25w}$ h $\sqrt[8]{4y}$

EXAMPLE
4

5 Evaluate each expression.

Ⓡ Ⓒ

a $16^{\frac{3}{4}}$ b $25^{\frac{5}{2}}$ c $(-27)^{-\frac{5}{3}}$ d $8^{\frac{2}{3}}$

e $(-128)^{-\frac{3}{7}}$ f $32^{-\frac{1}{5}}$ g $1000^{\frac{5}{3}}$ h $900^{-\frac{1}{2}}$

i $64^{\frac{5}{6}}$ j $9^{-\frac{7}{2}}$ k $(-216)^{-\frac{4}{3}}$ l $(-243)^{-\frac{2}{5}}$

6 Evaluate the expression $100000^{-\frac{7}{5}}$. Select **A**, **B**, **C** or **D**.

Ⓡ Ⓒ

A $\dfrac{1}{1000000}$ B $\dfrac{1}{10000000}$ C $\dfrac{1}{1000}$ D $\dfrac{1}{100000}$

7 Evaluate each expression correct to 2 decimal places.

a $\sqrt[3]{-250}$ b $37^{\frac{1}{2}}$ c $14^{-\frac{3}{4}}$ d $\sqrt[7]{-138}$

e $4^{-\frac{5}{3}}$ f $200^{\frac{3}{10}}$ g $(-50)^{-\frac{6}{5}}$ h $\sqrt[4]{82}$

EXAMPLE
5

8 Write each expression using a fractional index.

Ⓡ Ⓒ

a $\sqrt[4]{k^3}$ b $\dfrac{1}{\sqrt{m}}$ c $\sqrt[3]{x^7}$ d $\sqrt{y^3}$

e $\dfrac{1}{\sqrt[5]{d^2}}$ f $\sqrt{2a^3}$ g $\dfrac{1}{\sqrt[5]{4p}}$ h $\dfrac{1}{\sqrt[4]{vw}}$

EXAMPLE
6

9 Simplify $\sqrt[3]{\left(8d^2\right)^5}$. Select **A**, **B**, **C** or **D**.

Ⓡ Ⓒ

A $32d^{30}$ B $4d^{\frac{5}{3}}$ C $16d^{\frac{10}{3}}$ D $32d^{\frac{10}{3}}$

10 Simplify each expression.

Ⓡ Ⓒ

a $\left(25m^8\right)^{\frac{5}{2}}$ b $\sqrt[3]{\left(8y^6\right)^2}$ c $\sqrt[4]{\left(16x^2w^6\right)^6}$

d $\left(27c^6\right)^{-\frac{5}{3}}$ e $\left(8k^9\right)^{-\frac{4}{3}}$ f $\left(\dfrac{1}{\sqrt[5]{32p^{15}}}\right)^2$

g $\left(10\,000n^4w^6\right)^{-\frac{1}{2}}$ h $\sqrt[5]{\left(243x^{10}y^5\right)^4}$ i $6p^{\frac{2}{3}}n^{\frac{1}{2}} \times \sqrt{36p^4n^5}$

j $\dfrac{1}{\left(\sqrt[4]{625y^8d^4}\right)^3}$ k $\left(64m^6\right)^{-\frac{1}{3}} \times \left(4m\right)^2$ l $\sqrt[3]{\left(216a^6b^9\right)^2}$

☐ Foundation   ◯ Standard   ◯ Complex

4.03 Expanding and factorising expressions

Skillsheets
Algebra using diagrams

HCF by factor trees

Factorising using diagrams

Worksheets
Expanding and factorising

Algebra 4

Puzzles
Factorising puzzle

The distributive law

Video
Factorising expressions

Example 7

Expand and simplify by collecting like terms.

a $-3r^2(4r + 2) - 5r^3$

b $9(m - 3) + m(m - 10)$

SOLUTION

a $-3r^2(4r + 2) - 5r^2 = -12r^3 + (-6r^2) - 5r^3$ expanding

$\qquad\qquad\qquad = -17r^3 - 6r^2$ collecting like terms to simplify

b $9(m - 3) + m(m - 10) = 9m - 27 + m^2 - 10m$

$\qquad\qquad\qquad = m^2 - m - 27$ It's neater to place m^2 at the front.

Example 8

Factorise each expression.

a $18xy^2 - 24xy$ **b** $3m(5 + 2d) + 7(5 + 2d)$ **c** $-5k^2 + 15k$

SOLUTION

a $18xy^2 - 24xy = 6xy \times 3y - 6xy \times 4$ rewrite the expression using the HCF $6xy$

$\qquad\qquad = 6xy(3y - 4)$ write the HCF at the front of the brackets

b $3m(5 + 2d) + 7(5 + 2d) = (5 + 2d) \times 3m + (5 + 2d) \times 7$

$\qquad\qquad\qquad = (5 + 2d)(3m + 7)$

c $-5k^2 + 15k = (-5k) \times k + (-5k) \times (-3)$ $(-5k) \times (-3) = +15k$

$\qquad\qquad = (-5k)[k + (-3)]$

$\qquad\qquad = -5k(k - 3)$

Example 9

Factorise each expression.

a $8a^3 + 4a^2$ **b** $20h^3k + 25h^4k - 10h^2k$

SOLUTION

a $8a^3 + 4a^2 = 4a^2(2a + 1)$ rewrite the expression using the HCF $4a^2$

b $20h^3k + 25h^4k - 10h^2k = 5h^2k(4h + 5h^2 - 2)$

Expanding and factorising expressions (U) (F)

1 Expand each expression.

a $5(d + 11)$ **b** $-3(r + 10)$ **c** $7(x - 9y)$ **d** $-4(a - 5w)$

e $-(2 - p^2)$ **f** $-10e(2e^2 + 3)$ **g** $6y(1 + 7y)$ **h** $4xy(3xy - 1)$

i $8rq(2q - r)$ **j** $3ab(4b - 7a)$ **k** $-6h^2(1 - 3h)$ **l** $-5x(5x^2 + 4y)$

m $-(3 + 8a)$ **n** $-2m^2(3m - 4n)$ **o** $5g(3 + 7g^2)$ **p** $-(5e - 12)$

2 Expand $-2y(5 + 7y)$. Select the correct answer **A**, **B**, **C** or **D**.

A $3y - 5y^2$ **B** $-10y + 14y^2$ **C** $-10y - 14y^2$ **D** $-10y - 5y^2$

3 Use the substitution $x = 2$ to test whether each equation is correct or incorrect.

a $4(x + 10) = 4x + 40$ **b** $5(x - 1) = 5x - 6$ **c** $x(3 - x) = 3x - x^2$

4 Expand and simplify by collecting like terms.

a $4k(3k - 5) - 9k^2$ **b** $5h - 7h(4 - h)$ **c** $9w^3 - 3w(5 + 2w^2)$

d $24x^3 - 5x^2(2x^2 - 5x)$ **e** $8 - 3(2 - 7d)$ **f** $4n(3 - 5n) - 6n^2$

g $4y(y - 4) + 5(2y + 1)$ **h** $5(1 - 2a) - a(3 + 4a)$ **i** $7(3 + 6w) - (5 - 8w)$

j $4y^2(5y + 5) + 4(2 - 7y^2)$ **k** $-v(2v + 7) + 6(v - 1)$ **l** $2(4 - 3a) - a(3 - a)$

m $2c(5c - 1) - 4(7c - 5)$ **n** $3m(m + 5m^2) - m^2(1 - 3m)$ **o** $4x(2y + 5) - 6y(10 - 3x)$

EXAMPLE 7

5 Factorise each expression.

a $15y - 20$ **b** $21 + 35w$ **c** $2p + p^2$

d $30y - 20y^2$ **e** $36d^2 + 24d$ **f** $28k^2 - 21k$

g $8(c - 5) - c(c - 5)$ **h** $m(3 + 2m) + 7(3 + 2m)$ **i** $-q^2 - 36q$

j $-8x + 12x^2$ **k** $b(3b + 5) - 2(3b + 5)$ **l** $-12cd^2 + 8cd$

m $-hn^2 + h^2n$ **n** $-15g^2 - 18g$ **o** $48q^2 - 54q$

EXAMPLE 8

6 Factorise $-16pw + 10xw$. Select **A**, **B**, **C** or **D**.

A $-2w(8p - 10x)$ **B** $-2w(8p - 5x)$

C $-8w(2p - x)$ **D** $-4w(5p + 2x)$

7 Factorise each expression.

EXAMPLE 9

a $8m^2y^2 - 12my$ **b** $36ab^2c + 27bc$ **c** $24m^2n - 108mn^2$

d $20dg^2 - 35ag$ **e** $40wy^3 + 24w^2y^2$ **f** $75g^3h^2 - 125gh$

g $-4p^3 - 8p^2 + p$ **h** $6mn^2 + 3mn + 48m^2n$ **i** $32p^3g + 8pg^2 - 8pg$

j $18a^5 - 12a^2 + 15a^4$ **k** $28m^3h^2 - 21mh^2$ **l** $15kwp - 24wp^2 - 9kw$

☐ Foundation   ◯ Standard   ◇ Complex

Expanding binomial products

Videos
Expanding
binomial
products 1

Expanding
binomial
products 2

Worksheets
Mixed
expansions

Algebra 2

Binomial
products

Area
diagrams

Puzzles
Expanding
brackets

Trinominoes

Technology
Expanding
binomials

Example 10

Expand each binomial product.

a $(m + 8)(m - 3)$

b $(4y - 5)(3y - 2)$

SOLUTION

a $(m + 8)(m - 3) = m(m - 3) + 8(m - 3)$ Each term in $(m + 8)$ is multiplied by $(m - 3)$.

$\quad = m^2 - 3m + 8m - 24$ expanding

$\quad = m^2 + 5m - 24$ simplifying

One way of remembering which pairs of terms to multiply together in a binomial product is called the **FOIL method** (First-Outer-Inner-Last), as shown.

$(m + 8)(m - 3) = m^2 - 3m + 8m - 24$
$ = m^2 + 5m - 24$

b $(4y - 5)(3y - 2) = 12y^2 - 8y - 15y + 10$ using FOIL

$\quad = 12y^2 - 23y + 10$ simplifying

EXTENSION

Spreadsheet
Expanding
binomials

Video
Special
binomial
products

(i) Perfect squares

The formulas for expanding the **perfect square** of a binomial are:

$$(a + b)^2 = a^2 + 2ab + b^2$$
$$(a - b)^2 = a^2 - 2ab + b^2$$

Example 11

Expand each perfect square.

a $(n - 5)^2$ **b** $(k + 4)^2$ **c** $(3y - 8)^2$

SOLUTION

a $(n - 5)^2 = n^2 - 2 \times n \times 5 + 5^2$ 1st term squared – double product + 2nd term squared

$\quad = n^2 - 10n + 25$

b $(k + 4)^2 = k^2 + 2 \times k \times 4 + 4^2$ **c** $(3y - 8)^2 = (3y)^2 - 2 \times 3y \times 8 + 8^2$

$\quad = k^2 + 8k + 16$ $\quad = 9y^2 - 48y + 64$

Videos
Difference
of 2 squares

Special
binomial
products

(i) Difference of 2 squares

$$(a + b)(a - b) = a^2 - b^2$$

The answer is called the **difference of 2 squares**.

Example 12

Expand each expression.

a $(m + 6)(m - 6)$

b $(10 - e)(10 + e)$

c $(8g - 3)(8g + 3)$

d $(2x + 7w)(2x - 7w)$

SOLUTION

a $(m + 6)(m - 6) = m^2 - 6^2$
$$= m^2 - 36$$

b $(10 - e)(10 + e) = 10^2 - e^2$
$$= 100 - e^2$$

c $(8g - 3)(8g + 3) = (8g)^2 - 3^2$
$$= 64g^2 - 9$$

d $(2x + 7w)(2x - 7w) = (2x)^2 - (7w)^2$
$$= 4x^2 - 49w^2$$

Worksheet
Special products

Puzzles
Products and factors squaresaw

Factoro-minoes

Trinominoes

Enough time

Example 13

Expand and simplify each expression.

a $x(5y - x)^2$

b $(2a - 3)(2a + 3) - (a + 3)^2$

SOLUTION

a $x(5y - x)^2 = x(25y^2 - 10xy + x^2)$
$$= 25xy^2 - 10x^2y + x^3$$

b $(2a - 3)(2a + 3) - (a + 3)^2 = 4a^2 - 9 - (a^2 + 6a + 9)$
$$= 4a^2 - 9 - a^2 - 6a - 9$$
$$= 3a^2 - 6a - 18$$

EXERCISE (4.04) ANSWERS ON P. 610

Expanding binomial products

U F R C

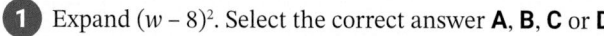

1 Expand $(w - 8)^2$. Select the correct answer **A, B, C** or **D**.

EXAMPLE
10

A $w^2 - 64$ **B** $w^2 + 64w$ **C** $w^2 + 16w - 64$ **D** $w^2 - 16w + 64$

2 Expand $(12 - a)^2$. Select **A, B, C** or **D**.

A $144 - a^2$ **B** $144 - 24a + a^2$ **C** $a^2 + 24a + 144$ **D** $a^2 + 144$

3 Expand each binomial product.

a $(3b - 4)(3b - 4)$ **b** $(5a + 6)(5a + 6)$ **c** $(2q - 7)(5q + 7)$

d $(6 + 5p)(p - 3)$ **e** $(4d - 11)(1 + 3d)$ **f** $(2r - 5)(9 - 4r)$

g $(7y + 3)(3 - 2y)$ **h** $(8h - 3)(8h + 3)$ **i** $(9 - 7w)(7w - 9)$

j $(4d - 1)(4d + 1)$ **k** $(f - 1)(1 + 3f)$ **l** $(6u - 5)(5 - 6u)$

4 Expand $(5 - 3k)(5 + 3k)$. Select **A, B, C** or **D**.

A $25 - 30k - 9k^2$ **B** $25 - 9k^2$ **C** $9k^2 - 30k - 25$ **D** $9k^2 - 25$

▷

☐ Foundation ○ Standard ◇ Complex

5 Copy and complete the expansion of each perfect square.

a $(y + 8)^2 = y^2 + $ _____ $+ 64$

b $(h - 2)^2 = $ _____ $- 4h + 4$

c $(g - m)^2 = g^2 - 2gm + $ _____

d $(u + 11)^2 = u^2$ _____ $+ 121$

e $(3k + 5)^2 = 9k^2$ _____ $+ 25$

f $(8x - 3w)^2 = 64x^2$_____ $+$ _____

6 Expand each perfect square.

a $(h + 7)^2$ b $(p - 5)^2$ c $(w - 6)^2$ d $(4 - c)^2$

e $(11 + y)^2$ f $(d - w)^2$ g $(10 - x)^2$ h $(d + q)^2$

i $(5u + 1)^2$ j $(3b + 7)^2$ k $(7e - 11)^2$ l $(2 - 5h)^2$

m $(8x - 3y)^2$ n $(6m + 5c)^2$ o $(g + 12w)^2$ p $\left(2 + \dfrac{2}{a}\right)^2$

q $\left(\dfrac{6}{m} - m\right)^2$ r $\left(\dfrac{3}{x} + 3x\right)^2$

7 Expand $(4a - 5w)^2$. Select **A**, **B**, **C** or **D**.

A $16a^2 + 25w^2$

B $16a^2 - 9aw - 25w^2$

C $16a^2 + 18aw - 25w^2$

D $16a^2 - 40aw + 25w^2$

EXAMPLE
12

8 Expand each expression.

a $(k + 7)(k - 7)$ b $(x + 8)(x - 8)$ c $(g - 1)(g + 1)$

d $(12 + w)(12 - w)$ e $(4 + d)(4 - d)$ f $(7b - 5)(7b + 5)$

g $(3h + 7)(3h - 7)$ h $(10e - 1)(10e + 1)$ i $(11 + 4y)(11 - 4y)$

j $(1 - 5p)(1 + 5p)$ k $(3a - 7c)(3a + 7c)$ l $(9h - 5m)(9h + 5m)$

m $\left(\dfrac{4}{m} - m\right)\left(\dfrac{4}{m} + m\right)$ n $\left(3g + \dfrac{1}{g}\right)\left(3g - \dfrac{1}{g}\right)$ o $\left(\dfrac{4a}{3} + 2\right)\left(\dfrac{4a}{3} - 2\right)$

9 Expand $(8g - 3y)(8g + 3y)$. Select **A**, **B**, **C** or **D**.

A $16g^2 - 9y^2$ **B** $64g^2 - 9y^2$ **C** $16g^2 - 6w^2$ **D** $64g^2 - 48gy + 25w^2$

10 Expand each expression.

a $(3t - d)^2$ b $(7k + 3)(3 + 7k)$ c $(9 - 4g)(4g + 9)$

d $(5 + 2a)(2a - 5)$ e $(ab - 8)(ab + 8)$ f $(4n + 5p)(5n - 4p)$

g $(10x - 7y)^2$ h $(2 - 11hm)(2 + 11hm)$ i $\left(xy - \dfrac{1}{y}\right)\left(xy + \dfrac{1}{y}\right)$

EXAMPLE
13

11 Expand and simplify each expression.

a $8y - (4y - 1)(1 - 2y)$

b $5(3w + 7) - (2w - 7)(w + 5)$

c $(a - b)^2 - (b - 2a)^2$

d $4(p - 5)^2 - 5(p - 3)(p + 8)$

e $(3 - y)^2 - (3 + y)^2$

f $8x^2 - (2x - 5)(2x + 5)$

g $(m + 2)^2 - (m + 2)(m - 2) - (m - 2)^2$

h $2(6 - d)^2 - (d + 5)^2 - (6 - d)(d + 5)$

12 Expand and simplify $(4d - m)^2 - (4d - m)(4d + m)$. Select **A**, **B**, **C** or **D**.

A $8dm$ **B** $32d^2 - 8dm$ **C** $2m^2 - 8dm$ **D** $32d^2 - 2m^2$

13 This diagram shows a house $(3x - 10)$ m long and $(2x + 15)$ wide on a block of land with dimensions 30 m × 20 m.

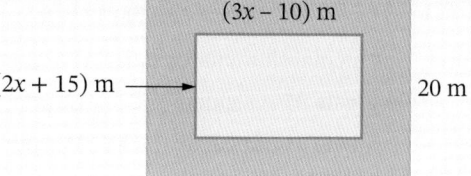

30 m

$(3x - 10)$ m

$(2x + 15)$ m →

20 m

a Write down a binomial expression for the area of the house in square metres.

b Expand and simplify your expression for the area.

c The blue area of the block of land not covered by the house is to be turfed. Write a simplified expression for this area in square metres.

14 A photograph frame is $(k + 5)$ cm wide and $3k$ cm long. The gap between the photo and frame is 4 cm at the top and bottom and 2 cm on each side.

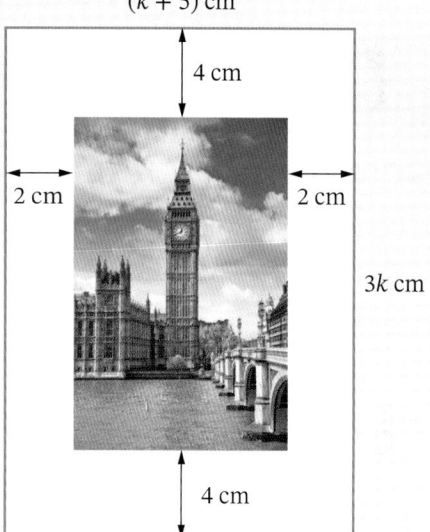

$(k + 5)$ cm

4 cm

2 cm   2 cm

$3k$ cm

4 cm

a What is the area of the photo frame?

b Write down expressions for the length and width of the photo.

c Write down a binomial expression for the area of the photo.

d Expand and simplify your expression for the area of the photo.

e Find an expression for the area of the frame not taken up by the photo.

15 A family room in a house is to be extended. The room is a metres long and b metres wide. The length is to be increased by 3 metres and the width by 1 metre.

a Write down expressions for the new length and width in metres.

b Write down a binomial expression for the new area of the room in square metres.

c Expand and simplify your expression for the area.

d By how much has the area of the room increased in square metres?

16 Find an expression for the area of each shape in simplest form.

a
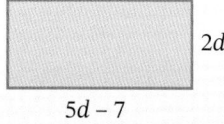
$2d + 3$
$5d - 7$

b
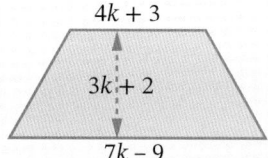
$4k + 3$
$3k + 2$
$7k - 9$

c
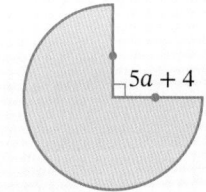
$5a + 4$

17 Prove that:

a $(a - b)^2 = (b - a)^2$ **b** $(a + b)(a - b) = a^2 - b^2$ **c** $(a - b)^2 = a^2 - 2ab + b^2$

□ Foundation   ○ Standard   ○ Complex

Shutterstock.com/S.Borisov

INVESTIGATION

Squaring a number ending in 5

Study this mental shortcut for squaring a number ending in 5:

- To evaluate 35^2, calculate $3 \times 4 = 12$, add '25' to the end: $35^2 = 1225$.
- To evaluate 75^2, calculate $7 \times 8 = 56$, add '25' to the end: $75^2 = 5625$.
- To evaluate 105^2, calculate $10 \times 11 = 110$, add '25' to the end: $105^2 = 11\,025$.

Let n stand for the tens digit of the number ending in 5 being squared.

Expand $(10n + 5)^2$ and investigate why the above method works.

Extension: Factorising special binomial products

Factorising by grouping in pairs

An **algebraic expression with 4 terms** can often be factorised in pairs, that is, 2 terms at a time, to make a binomial product.

Puzzle
Grouping

Example 14

Factorise each expression.

a $6ae + 4cd + 8ad + 3ce$ **b** $3xy - 4px - 6y^2 + 8py$ **c** $12aw + 20cx - 8cw - 30ax$

SOLUTION

a $6ae + 4cd + 8ad + 3ce = 6ae + 8ad + 4cd + 3ce$ Grouping into pairs

$\qquad\qquad\qquad\qquad = 2a(3e + 4d) + c(4d + 3e)$ Factorising each pair

$\qquad\qquad\qquad\qquad = (3e + 4d)(2a + c)$ Factorising again

b $3xy - 4px - 6y^2 + 8py = x(3y - 4p) - 2y(3y - 4p)$ Factorising each pair

$\qquad\qquad\qquad\qquad = (3y - 4p)(x - 2y)$ Factorising again

c $12aw + 20cx - 8cw - 30ax = 2(6aw + 10cx - 4cw - 15ax)$ Factorising all terms first

$\qquad\qquad\qquad\qquad = 2(6aw - 15ax - 4cw + 10cx)$ Grouping into pairs

$\qquad\qquad\qquad\qquad = 2[3a(2w - 5x) - 2c(2w - 5x)]$ Factorising each pair

$\qquad\qquad\qquad\qquad = 2(2w - 5x)(3a - 2c)$ Factorising again

Factorising the difference of 2 squares

EXTENSION

ⓘ The difference of 2 squares

$$a^2 - b^2 = (a + b)(a - b)$$

Example 15

Factorise each expression.

a $m^2 - 25$ **b** $36 - 49y^2$ **c** $48k^2 - 3x^2$ **d** $w^4 - 4w^2$

SOLUTION

a $m^2 - 25 = m^2 - 5^2$

         $= (m + 5)(m - 5)$

b $36 - 49y^2 = 6^2 - (7y)^2$

            $= (6 + 7y)(6 - 7y)$

c $48k^2 - 3x^2 = 3(16k^2 - x^2)$

            $= 3[(4k)^2 - x^2]$

            $= 3(4k + x)(4k - x)$

d $w^4 - 4w^2 = w^2(w^2 - 4)$

            $= w^2(w^2 - 2^2)$

            $= w^2(w + 2)(w - 2)$

Puzzle
Difference of 2 perfect squares

Video
Difference of 2 squares

EXERCISE 4.05   ANSWERS ON P. 611

Factorising special binomial products   ⓊⒻ

1 Factorise each expression.

a $3px + 2qx + 3py + 2qy$

b $2wh + 2wk - 3uh - 3uk$

c $15mk + 20mg + 6nk + 8ng$

d $4yx - 8ay + 7ax - 14a^2$

e $14ak - 35af + 8k - 20f$

f $cd + cy - hd - hy$

g $4am + 4at + 4em + 4et$

h $3yk - 6by + 12k - 24b$

i $12ac - 21mc - 35mw + 20aw$

j $21hk - 28he + 6pk - 8pe$

k $30y^2 - 6yq - 15y + 3q$

l $32gh + 24gk - 4mh - 3mk$

m $6ng - 10ch - 4cg + 15nh$

n $p^2w - p^3 - w + p$

o $m(d - 3) - mx + a(d - 3) - ax$

p $ek + k(x + y) + d(x + y) + ed$

EXAMPLE **14**

2 Factorise each expression.

a $d^2 - 16$ **b** $x^2 - 25$ **c** $y^2 - 169$ **d** $p^2 - 81$

e $25 - h^2$ **f** $121 - a^2$ **g** $4r^2 - 9d^2$ **h** $25g^2 - 4e^2$

i $144 - 49m^2$ **j** $81y^2 - 16k^2$ **k** $1 - 4d^2$ **l** $m^2 - 25n^2$

m $25q^2 - 9b^2$ **n** $64b^2 - u^2$ **o** $144x^2 - 1$ **p** $36k^2 - w^2$

q $g^2 - 16p^2$ **r** $4e^2 - 121d^2$ **s** $m^2p^2 - 25$ **t** $a^2 - q^2w^2$

u $x^2 - \dfrac{1}{16}$ **v** $\dfrac{25}{9} - h^2$ **w** $6\dfrac{1}{4} - 9c^2$ **x** $16v^2 - \dfrac{9}{4}$

EXAMPLE **15**

□ Foundation   ○ Standard   ◇ Complex

3 Factorise each expression.

a	$4m^2 - 16p^2$	**b**	$3y^2 - 27$	**c**	$w^3 - 36w$
d	$q - 64q^3$	**e**	$12 - 48u^2$	**f**	$rh^2 - r^3$
g	$125a^2b^2 - 20v^2$	**h**	$3x^4 - 27p^2$	**i**	$54g^3p - 6gp^3$
j	$28c - 63cw^2$	**k**	$144e^5 - 36e^3$	**l**	$9d^2 - 2\frac{1}{4}$
m	$100k^2 - 6\frac{1}{4}$	**n**	$98a^2 - 2w^2$	**o**	$c^2 - 1\frac{7}{9}$
p	$108m^3n^2 - 27m$				

4 Factorise each expression.

a	$\frac{1}{25} - x^2$	**b**	$\frac{d^2}{9} - \frac{w^2}{49}$	**c**	$3p^2 - \frac{48}{p^2}$
d	$\frac{64b^2}{25} - \frac{4y^2}{81}$	**e**	$u^4 - 16$	**f**	$(m + 3)^2 - 25$
g	$(x - y)^2 - y^2$	**h**	$2a^5 - 162a$	**i**	$(p + x)^2 - (p - x)^2$
j	$\frac{4c^2}{9} - \frac{e^2}{36}$	**k**	$4g^2 - (g - 2k)^2$	**l**	$5w^5 - 80w$

4.06 Factorising quadratic expressions $x^2 + bx + c$

Worksheet
Simplifying algebraic fractions

Puzzles
Factorominoes

Trinominoes

A **quadratic expression** is an algebraic expression in which the highest power of the **variable** is 2, such as $x^2 - 5x + 7$, $x^2 - 15$, $2x^2 - 3x + 9$ and $-4x^2 + 7x$.

A quadratic expression such as $x^2 - 5x + 7$ is called a **trinomial** because it has 3 terms.

The expansion of $(x + 2)(x + 4)$ is $x^2 + 6x + 8$, a quadratic trinomial.

∴ the factorisation of $x^2 + 6x + 8$ is $(x + 2)(x + 4)$.

ⓘ Factorising quadratic trinomials

In the factorisation of a quadratic trinomial such as $x^2 + 6x + 8$:

- each **factor** must have an x term to give x^2

  $x^2 + 6x + 8 = (x + 2)(x + 4)$

- $2 + 4 = 6$, which is the **coefficient** of x, the number in front of the x

  $x^2 + 6x + 8 = (x + 2)(x + 4)$

- $2 \times 4 = 8$, which is the **constant term** with no x

  $x^2 + 6x + 8 = (x + 2)(x + 4)$

☐ Foundation ○ Standard ◇ Complex

Example 16

Factorise each quadratic trinomial.

a $a^2 + 7a + 12$

b $x^2 + 9x + 8$

Video
Factorising
quadratic
expressions 1

4.06

 **SOLUTION**

a Find the 2 numbers that have a sum of 7 and a product of 12.

It is best to test numbers that have a **product of 12** and then check if their sums equal 7.

Pair of numbers	Product	Sum
6, 2	6 × 2 = 12	6 + 2 = 8
3, 4	3 × 4 = 12	3 + 4 = 7

The correct numbers are 3 and 4.

$\therefore a^2 + 7a + 12 = (a + 3)(a + 4)$

b Find 2 numbers with a sum of 9 and a product of 8.

Test numbers that have a **product of 8** and check if their sums equal 9.

Pair of numbers	Product	Sum
2, 4	2 × 4 = 8	4 + 2 = 6
8, 1	8 × 1 = 8	1 + 8 = 9

The correct numbers are 8 and 1.

$\therefore x^2 + 9x + 8 = (x + 8)(x + 1)$

ⓘ Factorising quadratic expressions of the form $x^2 + bx + c$

- Find 2 numbers that have a sum of b and a product of c.
- Use these 2 numbers to write a binomial product of the form $(x \underline{\quad})(x \underline{\quad})$.

Example 17

Factorise each quadratic expression.

a $x^2 + x - 6$

b $a^2 - 2a - 15$

c $y^2 - 6y + 8$

Video
Factorising
quadratic
expressions 1

SOLUTION

a $x^2 + x - 6$

Find 2 numbers that have a product of −6 and a sum of 1.

Since the product is negative, one number must be negative.

They are +3 and −2.

$\therefore x^2 + x - 6 = (x + 3)(x - 2)$

b $a^2 - 2a - 15$

product = −15, sum = −2.

Since the product is negative, one number must be negative.

They are −5 and +3.

$\therefore a^2 - 2a - 15 = (a - 5)(a + 3)$

c $y^2 - 6y + 8$

product = 8, sum = −6.

Since the sum is negative, one number must be negative.

Since the product is positive, both numbers must be negative.

They are −2 and −4.

$\therefore y^2 - 6y + 8 = (y - 2)(y - 4)$

Factorising quadratic expressions $x^2 + bx + c$ ⓤ ⓕ ⓡ

EXAMPLE
16

1 Find 2 numbers whose:

ⓡ **a** product is −15 and sum is 2   **b** product is 40 and sum is −14

c product is 42 and sum is 13   **d** product is −6 and sum is −1

e product is 45 and sum is 14   **f** product is −24 and sum is 2

g product is 54 and sum is 15   **h** product is −16 and sum is 0

i product is −10 and sum is 3   **j** product is 35 and sum is −12

EXAMPLE
17

2 Factorise each quadratic expression.

ⓡ **a** $q^2 - 8q - 20$ **b** $h^2 - 5h - 36$ **c** $y^2 + 7y - 44$

d $x^2 - 2x - 63$ **e** $u^2 + 9u - 10$ **f** $e^2 + 7e - 30$

g $a^2 - a - 110$ **h** $y^2 + 6y - 27$ **i** $m^2 - 6m - 7$

j $c^2 + 7c - 18$ **k** $k^2 + 3k - 54$ **l** $r^2 - 9r - 22$

m $p^2 - 4p - 32$ **n** $u^2 + 12u - 45$ **o** $b^2 - 6b - 16$

3 Factorise each quadratic trinomial.

ⓡ **a** $h^2 - 2h + 1$ **b** $x^2 + 15x + 50$ **c** $r^2 + 20r + 96$

d $a^2 - 3a - 28$ **e** $u^2 - 7u - 60$ **f** $y^2 - 18y + 81$

g $v^2 - v - 56$ **h** $w^2 - 11w - 60$ **i** $g^2 + 3g - 18$

j $p^2 + 14p + 48$ **k** $e^2 + 7e - 8$ **l** $x^2 - 19x + 84$

☐ Foundation ○ Standard ○ Complex

Estimating answers

Quiz
Mental
skills 4

A quick way of estimating an answer is to round each number in the calculation.

1 Study each example.

    a $55 + 132 - 34 + 17 - 78 \approx 60 + 130 - 30 + 20 - 80$

$$= (60 + 20 - 80) + (130 - 30)$$

$$= 0 + 100$$

$$= 100 \text{ (actual answer = 92)}$$

    b $78 \times 7 \approx 80 \times 7$ **c** $510 \div 24 \approx 500 \div 20$

$$= 560 \text{ (actual answer = 546)} \qquad\qquad = 50 \div 2$$

$$= 25 \text{ (actual answer = 21.25)}$$

2 Now estimate each answer.

    a $27 + 11 + 87 + 142 + 64$ **b** $55 + 34 - 22 - 46 + 136$ **c** $684 + 903$

    d $35 + 81 + 110 + 22 + 7$ **e** $517 - 96$ **f** $210 - 38 - 71 + 151 - 49$

    g $766 - 353$ **h** 367×2 **i** 83×81

    j 984×16 **k** $828 \div 3$ **l** $507 \div 7$

3 Study each example involving decimals.

    a $20.91 - 11.3 + 2.5 \approx 21 - 11 + 3$ **c** $\dfrac{37.6 + 9.3}{41.2 - 12.7} \approx \dfrac{38 + 9}{40 - 13}$

$$= 13 \text{ (exact answer = 12.11)} \qquad\qquad = \dfrac{47}{27}$$

    b $4.78 \times 19.2 \approx 5 \times 20$ $= \dfrac{50}{30}$

$$= 100 \text{ (exact answer = 91.776)} \qquad\qquad = 1.6$$

$$\text{(exact answer = 1.6456...)}$$

4 Now estimate each answer.

    a $3.75 + 9.381 + 4.6 + 10.5$ **b** $14.807 + 6.6 - 7.22$ **c** 18.47×9.61

    d 4.27×97.6 **e** $\dfrac{11.07 + 18.4}{12.2}$ **f** $\dfrac{38.18}{17.2 - 9.6}$

    g $\dfrac{18.46 \times 4.9}{39.72 - 15.2}$ **h** $62.13 \div 10.7$ **i** $(4.89)^2$

4.07 Extension: Factorising quadratic expressions of the form $ax^2 + bx + c$

EXTENSION

Puzzles
Factorising puzzle (Advanced)

Product and factors squaresaw

Perfect squares

Technology
Factorising trinomials

Spreadsheet
Factorising trinomials

Video
Factorising quadratic expressions 2

We have factorised quadratic trinomials of the type $x^2 + bx + c$. For example, the factorisation of $x^2 + 6x + 8$ is $(x + 2)(x + 4)$. These are called **monic** quadratic expressions because x^2 does not have a **coefficient** (or its coefficient is 1).

We will now factorise quadratic trinomials of the type $ax^2 + bx + c$, such as $8x^2 + 14x - 15$, where x^2 has a coefficient. These are called **non-monic** quadratic expressions.

Example 18

Factorise each quadratic expression.

a $4y^2 + 8y - 140$

b $60 + 7d - d^2$

SOLUTION

a $4y^2 + 8y - 140 = 4(y^2 + 2y - 35)$
$\qquad\qquad\qquad\quad = 4(y + 7)(y - 5)$

b $60 + 7d - d^2 = -d^2 + 7d + 60$
$\qquad\qquad\qquad = -1(d^2 - 7d - 60)$
$\qquad\qquad\qquad = -(d - 12)(d + 5)$

Example 19

Factorise $5k^2 - 12k + 4$.

SOLUTION

There is no HCF, so we need to split up the middle term $-12k$.

Find 2 numbers that have a product of 20 and a sum of -12.

$$5k^2 - 12k + 4 = 5k^2 - 12k + 4$$

sum of -12

product of $5 \times 4 = 20$

Since the sum is negative, at least one of the numbers must be negative.

Since the product is positive, **both** of the numbers must be negative.

The 2 numbers are -10 and -2, so we will split $-12k$ into $-10k$ and $-2k$.

$\therefore 5k^2 - 12k + 4 = 5k^2 - 10k - 2k + 4$
$\qquad\qquad\qquad\quad = 5k(k - 2) - 2(k - 2)$ Factorising by grouping in pairs
$\qquad\qquad\qquad\quad = (k - 2)(5k - 2)$ Factorising again

- Find 2 numbers that have a sum of b and a product of ac
- Use these 2 numbers to split the middle term bx into 2 terms
- Factorise by grouping in pairs

Example 20

Factorise each quadratic expression.

a $3x^2 + 8x + 4$　　　　　**b** $3x^2 - 11x + 10$　　　　　**c** $4x^2 - 3x - 7$

Videos
Factorising quadratic expressions (Advanced)

Advanced algebra

SOLUTION

a $3x^2 + 8x + 4$

$3 \times 4 = 12$.

Find 2 numbers that have a product of 12 and a sum of 8. They are 6 and 2.

Split $8x$ into $6x$ and $2x$.

$3x^2 + 8x + 4 = 3x^2 + 6x + 2x + 4$

$\qquad = 3x(x + 2) + 2(x + 2)$　　　　　Factorising by grouping in pairs

$\qquad = (x + 2)(3x + 2)$

b $3x^2 - 11x + 10$

$3 \times 10 = 30$.

Find 2 numbers that have a product of 30 and a sum of -11.

Since the sum is negative and the product is positive, both numbers must be negative.

They are -6 and -5.

$3x^2 - 11x + 10 = 3x^2 - 6x - 5x + 10$

$\qquad = 3x(x - 2) - 5(x - 2)$

$\qquad = (x - 2)(3x - 5)$

c $4x^2 - 3x - 7$

$4 \times (-7) = -28$.

Find 2 numbers with a product of -28 and a sum of -3.

Since the product is negative, one of the numbers must be negative. They are -7 and 4.

$4x^2 - 3x - 7 = 4x^2 - 7x + 4x - 7$

$\qquad = x(4x - 7) + 1(4x - 7)$

$\qquad = (4x - 7)(x + 1)$

Example 21

Factorise each quadratic expression.

a $24k^2 - 54k - 15$ **b** $14 + 29a - 15a^2$

SOLUTION

a $24k^2 - 54k - 15 = 3(8k^2 - 18k - 5)$ Taking out the HCF of 3 first

$\qquad\qquad\qquad = 3(8k^2 - 20k + 2k - 5)$ Product $= -40$, sum $= -18$

$\qquad\qquad\qquad = 3[4k(2k - 5) + 1(2k - 5)]$

$\qquad\qquad\qquad = 3(2k - 5)(4k + 1)$

b $14 + 29a - 15a^2 = -15a^2 + 29a + 14$ Rearranging to make the a^2 term first

$\qquad\qquad\qquad = -(15a^2 - 29a - 14)$ Taking out a common factor of -1

$\qquad\qquad\qquad = -(15a^2 + 6a - 35a - 14)$ Product $= -210$, sum $= -29$

$\qquad\qquad\qquad = -[3a(5a + 2) - 7(5a + 2)]$

$\qquad\qquad\qquad = -(5a + 2)(3a - 7)$

EXERCISE 4.07 ANSWERS ON P. 611

Factorising quadratic expressions $ax^2 + bx + c$ Ⓤ Ⓕ Ⓡ

EXAMPLE
18

1 Factorise each quadratic expression. Look for the highest common factor first.

Ⓡ **a** $2k^2 + 16k + 30$ **b** $3q^2 - 3q - 90$ **c** $5x^2 - 55x + 140$

d $6y^2 + 12y - 18$ **e** $n^3 - 16n^2 + 63n$ **f** $24 + 2a - a^2$

g $4p + 32 - p^2$ **h** $-x^4 - 4x^3 + 21x^2$ **i** $-20 + 24h - 4h^2$

EXAMPLE
19

2 Factorise each quadratic expression.

Ⓡ **a** $6d^2 + 19d + 15$ **b** $8m^2 + 10m + 3$ **c** $2y^2 + 7y + 5$

d $2w^2 + 31w + 15$ **e** $6k^2 + 23k + 20$ **f** $3u^2 + 22u + 35$

g $4x^2 + 21x + 27$ **h** $5e^2 + 39e + 28$ **i** $12h^2 + 13h + 3$

EXAMPLE
20

3 Factorise each quadratic expression.

Ⓡ **a** $4k^2 - 11k + 6$ **b** $6w^2 - 17w + 5$ **c** $5p^2 - 23p + 12$

d $6g^2 - 35g + 49$ **e** $3x^2 - 32x + 20$ **f** $21m^2 - 26m + 8$

g $20r^2 - 23r + 6$ **h** $10a^2 - 7a - 6$ **i** $20u^2 - 23u - 21$

j $2p^2 - 17p - 9$ **k** $6y^2 - y - 40$ **l** $12b^2 - 17b - 5$

m $12q^2 - 8q - 15$ **n** $4h^2 + 13h - 12$ **o** $10n^2 + 31n - 14$

▷

☐ Foundation ○ Standard ○ Complex

4 Factorise each expression given it is a perfect square. EXTENSION

(R) **a** $16w^2 - 56w + 49$ **b** $121h^2 + 176h + 64$ **c** $9p^2 - 90p + 225$

5 Factorise each quadratic expression by first taking out a common factor.

(R) **a** $6m^2 - 9m - 60$ **b** $8x^3 - 18x^2 + 4x$ **c** $6 - 5e^2 - 29e$

d $-18w^2 - 51w + 42$ **e** $4 - 4k - 48k^2$ **f** $8 + 2n - 15n^2$

g $48d^2 + 156d + 90$ **h** $30h - 24h^2 + 9$ **i** $3 + 5p - 28p^2$

6 Factorise the quadratic expression $8a^2 + 14ax - 15x^2$. Select **A**, **B**, **C** or **D**.

(R) **A** $(4a - 3x)(2a + 5x)$ **B** $(2a - 5x)(4a + 3x)$

C $(5a + 4x)(3a - 2x)$ **D** $(4a - 5x)(2a + 3x)$

7 Factorise each quadratic expression.

(R) **a** $28d^2 - 11d + 1$ **b** $6 - 2y - 20y^2$ **c** $30w^2 + 41w - 15$

d $4p^2 + 23p + 15$ **e** $23a - 12 - 10a^2$ **f** $9r^2 + 29r + 20$

g $28k^2 + 19ky + 3y^2$ **h** $72p - 6p^2 - 3p^3$ **i** $4 - 21m - 18m^2$

j $10g - 54g^2 - 36g^3$ **k** $44u^2 - u - 3$ **l** $32h^2 + 28hm - 15m^2$

Extension: Mixed factorisations

4.08

ⓘ Factorisation strategies

EXTENSION

- Look for any common factors and factorise first
- If there are 2 terms, try factorising using the difference of two squares
- If there are 3 terms, try factorising as a quadratic trinomial
- If there are 4 terms, try factorising by grouping in pairs

Puzzles
Factorominoes

Mixed
factorisations

```
Algebraic expression
        ↓
Take out any common factors
   ↓         ↓         ↓
2 terms    3 terms    4 terms
   ↓         ↓         ↓
Factorise if difference   If quadratic trinomial,   Try to factorise by
   of 2 squares            try to factorise          grouping in pairs
```

Example 22

Factorise each quadratic expression.

a $5k^2 - 80$

b $4y^2 + 60d^2$

c $24u^2 - 68u + 20$

d $9m^3 - 18m^2 - 4m + 8$

SOLUTION

a $\begin{aligned} 5k^2 - 80 &= 5(k^2 - 16) \\ &= 5(k + 4)(k - 4) \end{aligned}$

Taking out the HCF of 5 first.

Difference of 2 squares

b $4y^2 + 60d^2 = 4(y^2 + 15d^2)$

2 terms but not a difference of 2 squares.

c $\begin{aligned} 24u^2 - 68u + 20 &= 4(6u^2 - 17u + 5) \\ &= 4(6u^2 - 15u - 2u + 5) \\ &= 4[3u(2u - 5) - 1(2u - 5)] \\ &= 4(2u - 5)(3u - 1) \end{aligned}$

Taking out the HCF of 4 first.

Product = 30, sum = −17

Factorising each pair.

Factorising again.

d $\begin{aligned} 9m^3 - 18m^2 - 4m + 8 &= 9m^2(m - 2) - 4(m - 2) \\ &= (m - 2)(9m^2 - 4) \\ &= (m - 2)(3m + 2)(3m - 2) \end{aligned}$

Factorising by grouping in pairs

Difference of 2 squares

EXERCISE 4.08 ANSWERS ON P. 612

Mixed factorisations

EXAMPLE 22

1 Factorise each expression.

a $60y^2 - 15$

b $15m^2 - 41m + 14$

c $k^2 - 14k + 49$

d $11a - 12 - 2a^2$

e $6gy + 12cp + 8cy + 9gp$

f $15 - 17x - 4x^2$

g $64q^2 - 16q + 1$

h $81r^2 - 36w^2$

i $3bn^2 - 3np + 2bnd - 2dp$

j $6k^2 + 23k + 20$

k $42a^2 + 73a + 28$

l $4 - 100h^2$

m $36c^2 + 53c - 63$

n $16 - 46d - 35d^2$

o $25u^2 + 10u + 4$

p $3xy - 8w + 4x - 6wy$

q $1 - b^2 + b^3 - b$

r $28c^2 - 9ch - 4h^2$

s $15n^2 - 19n - 56$

t $a^3p - ap$

u $16r^2 - 146rk + 18k^2$

2 Factorise each expression.

a $48c^2 - 75$

b $8q^2 + 22q - 40$

c $15x^2 + x^3 - 2x^4$

d $27p^2 - 24pr - 16r^2$

e $9w^2 + 24w - 105$

f $n^4 - 4n^2$

g $y - y^2 - y^3 + y^4$

h $36u^2 + 105u + 49$

i $121k^2 - 198k + 81$

j $4(c - d)^2 - (c + d)^2$

k $20y^2 + 18d + 12y + 30dy$

l $ah^2 - 6ah - ah^3$

m $18b^2 - 54b + 27b - 81$

n $32g - 8g^3y^2$

o $8 - 42e - 36e^2$

p $27q^2p - 3p$

q $30h - 15h^2 - 15h^3$

r $w^4 - w^3 - w^2 + 1$

s $a^5 - 256a^3$

t $m^2 - k^2 + 9m - 9k$

u $30a^2 + 65a - 25$

□ Foundation ○ Standard ◌ Complex

3 Factorise the expression $w^6 - w^4 - w^2 + 1$. Select the correct answer **A, B, C** or **D**.

(R)   **A** $w^4(w-1)(w+1)$ **B** $(w^2+1)^2(w+1)(w-1)$

     C $(w^2+1)^2(w+1)^2(w-1)^2$ **D** $(w^2+1)(w+1)^2(w-1)^2$

Extension: Surds and irrational numbers   4.09

A **surd** is a square root ($\sqrt{\ }$), cube root ($\sqrt[3]{\ }$), or any type of root whose exact decimal or fraction value cannot be found. As a decimal, its digits run endlessly *without repeating* (like π), so they are neither terminating nor recurring decimals.

$\sqrt{7}$ is called the **exact value**, $\sqrt{7} \approx 2.64575$ is the **approximate value**.

Rational numbers such as fractions, decimals and percentages, can be expressed in the form $\frac{a}{b}$, where a and b are integers ($b \neq 0$), but surds are **irrational numbers** because they cannot be expressed in this form.

Rational numbers

can be expressed in the form $\frac{a}{b}$

> **Integers**
>
> $\frac{4}{1} = 4, \frac{26}{1} = 26, \frac{-3}{1} = -3$

> **Recurring decimals**
>
> $\frac{2}{3} = 0.666\ldots$
>
> $\frac{5}{6} = 0.833\ldots$
>
> $\frac{4}{11} = 0.3636\ldots$

> **Terminating decimals**
>
> $0.5, 7\frac{1}{8} = 7.125,$
>
> $16\% = 0.16, 1.32$

Irrational numbers

cannot be expressed in the form $\frac{a}{b}$

> **Surds**
>
> $\sqrt{5}, -\sqrt{2}, \frac{\sqrt{11}}{3}, 8\sqrt{6}$

> **Transcendental numbers**
>
> Have no pattern and are non-recurring
>
> e.g. $\pi = 3.14159\ldots,$
>
> $\cos 38° = 0.78801\ldots, e = 2.71828\ldots$

□ Foundation   ○ Standard   ◇ Complex

Example 23

Is each number rational or irrational?

a $4\frac{2}{5}$ **b** $\sqrt[3]{-8}$ **c** $-\sqrt{7}$ **d** $0.\dot{6}$ **e** 5π

SOLUTION

a $4\frac{2}{5} = \frac{22}{5}$ which is in the form of a fraction $\frac{a}{b}$

    $\therefore 4\frac{2}{5}$ is a rational number.

b $\sqrt[3]{-8} = -2$ which can be written as $\frac{-2}{1}$

    $\therefore \sqrt[3]{-8}$ is a rational number.

c $-\sqrt{7} = -2.645751311\ldots$ The digits run endlessly without repeating.

    $\therefore -\sqrt{7}$ is an irrational number.

d $0.\dot{6} = 0.666\ldots$ which is a recurring decimal

       $= \frac{2}{3}$ which is a fraction

    $\therefore 0.\dot{6}$ is a rational number.

e $5\pi = 15.707\,963\,27\ldots$ The digits run endlessly without repeating.

    $\therefore 5\pi$ is an irrational number.

Surds on a number line

The rational and irrational numbers together make up the **real numbers**. Any real number can be represented by a point on the number line.

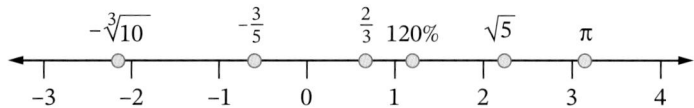

$-\sqrt[3]{10} \approx -2.1544\ldots$ irrational (surd) $120\% = 1.2$ rational (percentage)

    $-\frac{3}{5} = -0.6$ rational (fraction) $\sqrt{5} \approx 2.2360\ldots$ irrational (surd)

     $\frac{2}{3} \approx 0.6666\ldots$ rational (fraction) $\pi \approx 3.1415\ldots$ irrational (pi)

Example 24

Use a pair of compasses and Pythagoras' theorem to estimate the value of $\sqrt{2}$ on a number line.

SOLUTION

Worksheet
Surds on the number line

Step 1: Using a scale of 1 unit to 2 cm, draw a number line as shown.

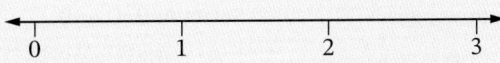

Step 2: Construct a right-angled triangle on the number line with base length and height 1 unit as shown. By Pythagoras' theorem, show that $XZ = \sqrt{2}$ units.

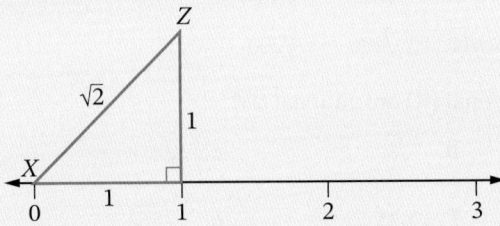

Step 3: With 0 as the centre, use compasses with radius $XZ\left(\sqrt{2}\right)$ to draw an arc to meet the number line at A as shown. The point A represents the value of $\sqrt{2}$ and should be approximately 1.4142 ...

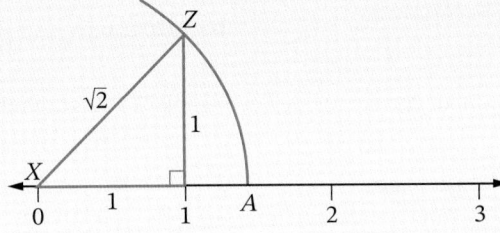

EXERCISE (4.09) ANSWERS ON P. 612

Surds and irrational numbers   (U) (F) (R) (C)

1 Which one of the following is a surd? Select the correct answer **A, B, C** or **D**.

(C) **A** $\sqrt{9}$ **B** $\sqrt{225}$ **C** $\sqrt{160}$ **D** $\sqrt{81}$

2 Which one of the following is NOT a surd? Select **A, B, C** or **D**.

(C) **A** $\sqrt{77}$ **B** $\sqrt{144}$ **C** $\sqrt{18}$ **D** $\sqrt{200}$

3 Select the surds from the following list of square roots.

(C) $\sqrt{32}$ $\sqrt{33}$ $\sqrt{289}$ $\sqrt{81}$ $\sqrt{4.9}$

$\sqrt{52}$ $\sqrt{121}$ $\sqrt{144}$ $\sqrt{196}$ $\sqrt{200}$

EXAMPLE 23

4 Is each number rational (R) or irrational (I)?

(R) **a** $5.\dot{6}$ **b** $\sqrt{8}$ **c** $\sqrt{4}$ **d** $3\frac{1}{7}$
(C)

e $\sqrt[3]{27}$ **f** $1.3\dot{5}$ **g** $\sqrt[3]{-64}$ **h** $27\frac{1}{2}\%$

i $\sqrt{5 \times 10^3}$ **j** $\frac{3}{11}$ **k** $\frac{\sqrt{50}}{3}$ **l** $\sqrt{\sqrt{4}}$

5 Arrange each set of numbers in descending order.

a $1\frac{4}{7}, \sqrt{2}, \frac{\pi}{2}$ **b** $\sqrt[3]{20}, 2.\dot{6}, 2\frac{7}{9}$

6 Express each real number correct to one decimal place and graph them on a number line.

a $-1\frac{4}{5}$ **b** 74% **c** $\frac{4}{11}$ **d** $-\sqrt{12}$

e $-\sqrt[3]{15}$ **f** $2\frac{5}{9}$ **g** $\frac{\pi}{2}$ **h** 187%

EXAMPLE 24

7 Use the method from Example **24** to estimate the value of $\sqrt{2}$ on a number line.

8 a Use the method from Example **24** to estimate the value of $\sqrt{5}$ on a number line by constructing a right-angled triangle with base length 2 units and height 1 unit.

b Use a similar method to estimate the following surds on a number line:

i $\sqrt{10}$ **ii** $\sqrt{17}$

□ Foundation ○ Standard ○ Complex

Proof that $\sqrt{2}$ is irrational

A method of proof sometimes used in mathematics is to assume the **opposite** of what is being proved, and show that it is **impossible**. This is called a **proof by contradiction**, and we will use it to prove that $\sqrt{2}$ is irrational.

First, we assume that $\sqrt{2}$ is rational. So, assume that $\sqrt{2}$ can be written as a simplified fraction $\dfrac{a}{b}$, where a and b are integers ($b \neq 0$) with no common factor.

$$\sqrt{2} = \frac{a}{b}$$

$$2 = \frac{a^2}{b^2} \qquad \text{Squaring both sides}$$

$$a^2 = 2b^2$$

$2b^2$ is an even number because it is divisible by 2, $\therefore a^2$ is even.

$\therefore a$ is even, because an even integer multiplied by itself is always even and an odd integer multiplied by itself is always odd.

$\therefore a = 2m$, where m is another integer.

$\therefore a^2 = (2m)^2 = 2b^2$

$4m^2 = 2b^2$

$2m^2 = b^2$

$b^2 = 2m^2$

$\therefore b^2$ is even

$\therefore b$ is even.

But a and b can't **both** be even because this contradicts the assumption that a and b have no common factors. Therefore, the assumption that $\sqrt{2}$ is rational is false, so $\sqrt{2}$ must be irrational.

Use proof by contradiction to show that these surds are irrational:

a $\sqrt{3}$

b $\sqrt{5}$

EXTENSION

Puzzle
Simplifying
surds

Technology
Simplifying
surds quiz

Spreadsheet
Simplifying
surds quiz

ⓘ The square root of x

For $x < 0$ (negative), $\sqrt{x}$ is undefined.

For $x = 0$, $\sqrt{x} = 0$.

For $x > 0$ (positive), $\sqrt{x}$ is the positive square root of x.

For $x \geq 0$, $\left(\sqrt{x}\right)^2 = \sqrt{x} \times \sqrt{x} = x$ and $\sqrt{x^2} = x$.

Example 25

Simplify each expression.

a $\left(\sqrt{7}\right)^2$ b $\left(3\sqrt{5}\right)^2$ c $\left(-2\sqrt{3}\right)^2$

SOLUTION

a $\left(\sqrt{7}\right)^2 = 7$

b $\left(3\sqrt{5}\right)^2 = 3\sqrt{5} \times 3\sqrt{5}$

$\phantom{\left(3\sqrt{5}\right)^2} = 3^2 \times \left(\sqrt{5}\right)^2$

$\phantom{\left(3\sqrt{5}\right)^2} = 9 \times 5$

$\phantom{\left(3\sqrt{5}\right)^2} = 45$

c $\left(-2\sqrt{3}\right)^2 = (-2)^2 \times \left(\sqrt{3}\right)^2$

$\phantom{\left(-2\sqrt{3}\right)^2} = 4 \times 3$

$\phantom{\left(-2\sqrt{3}\right)^2} = 12$

ⓘ The square root of a product

For $x > 0$ and $y > 0$:

$$\sqrt{xy} = \sqrt{x} \times \sqrt{y}$$

A surd $\sqrt{n}$ can be simplified if n can be divided into 2 factors, where one of them is a square number such as 4, 9, 16, 25, 36, 49, ...

Example 26

Simplify each surd.

a $\sqrt{8}$ **b** $\sqrt{108}$ **c** $4\sqrt{45}$ **d** $\dfrac{\sqrt{288}}{3}$

Videos
Simplifying surds 2

Simplifying surds 1

SOLUTION

a $\sqrt{8} = \sqrt{4} \times \sqrt{2}$ 4 is a square number

$\phantom{\sqrt{8}} = 2 \times \sqrt{2}$

$\phantom{\sqrt{8}} = 2\sqrt{2}$

b *Method 1:*

$\sqrt{108} = \sqrt{36} \times \sqrt{3}$

$\phantom{\sqrt{108}} = 6 \times \sqrt{3}$

$\phantom{\sqrt{108}} = 6\sqrt{3}$

Method 2:

$\sqrt{108} = \sqrt{4} \times \sqrt{27}$

$\phantom{\sqrt{108}} = 2 \times \sqrt{9} \times \sqrt{3}$

$\phantom{\sqrt{108}} = 2 \times 3 \times \sqrt{3}$

$\phantom{\sqrt{108}} = 6\sqrt{3}$

Method 2 involves simplifying surds *twice* ($\sqrt{108}$ and $\sqrt{27}$). Method 1 shows that when simplifying surds, look for the highest square factor possible.

c $4\sqrt{45} = 4 \times \sqrt{9} \times \sqrt{5}$

$\phantom{4\sqrt{45}} = 4 \times 3 \times \sqrt{5}$

$\phantom{4\sqrt{45}} = 12\sqrt{5}$

d $\dfrac{\sqrt{288}}{3} = \dfrac{\sqrt{144} \times \sqrt{2}}{3}$

$\phantom{\dfrac{\sqrt{288}}{3}} = \dfrac{12\sqrt{2}}{3}$

$\phantom{\dfrac{\sqrt{288}}{3}} = \dfrac{12^{4}\sqrt{2}}{3^{1}}$

$\phantom{\dfrac{\sqrt{288}}{3}} = 4\sqrt{2}$

EXERCISE 4.10   ANSWERS ON P. 612

Simplifying surds   U F R

1 Simplify each expression.

a $\left(\sqrt{2}\right)^2$ **b** $\left(\sqrt{5}\right)^2$ **c** $\left(3\sqrt{3}\right)^2$ **d** $\left(5\sqrt{10}\right)^2$

e $\left(\sqrt{0.09}\right)^2$ **f** $\left(-2\sqrt{7}\right)^2$ **g** $\left(-3\sqrt{5}\right)^2$ **h** $\left(-5\sqrt{2}\right)^2$

EXAMPLE 25

2 Simplify each surd.

a $\sqrt{50}$ **b** $\sqrt{27}$ **c** $\sqrt{24}$ **d** $\sqrt{54}$

e $\sqrt{243}$ **f** $\sqrt{45}$ **g** $\sqrt{48}$ **h** $\sqrt{200}$

i $\sqrt{96}$ **j** $\sqrt{63}$ **k** $\sqrt{288}$ **l** $\sqrt{108}$

m $\sqrt{75}$ **n** $\sqrt{147}$ **o** $\sqrt{32}$ **p** $\sqrt{242}$

q $\sqrt{162}$ **r** $\sqrt{245}$ **s** $\sqrt{125}$ **t** $\sqrt{512}$

EXAMPLE 26

□ Foundation   ○ Standard   ◇ Complex

▷

3 Simplify each expression.

a $5\sqrt{50}$

b $3\sqrt{8}$

c $4\sqrt{27}$

d $8\sqrt{98}$

e $\dfrac{\sqrt{40}}{2}$

f $\dfrac{\sqrt{243}}{9}$

g $\dfrac{\sqrt{28}}{6}$

h $3\sqrt{24}$

i $9\sqrt{68}$

j $\dfrac{\sqrt{3125}}{10}$

k $\dfrac{1}{2}\sqrt{72}$

l $\dfrac{3}{4}\sqrt{48}$

m $10\sqrt{160}$

n $3\sqrt{75}$

o $7\sqrt{68}$

p $\dfrac{\sqrt{52}}{6}$

4 Which surd below is equivalent to $4\sqrt{50}$? Select **A**, **B**, **C** or **D**.

A $8\sqrt{5}$

B $20\sqrt{2}$

C $8\sqrt{2}$

D $20\sqrt{5}$

5 Which surd below is equivalent to $\dfrac{\sqrt{250}}{10}$? Select **A**, **B**, **C** or **D**.

A $\dfrac{\sqrt{5}}{10}$

B $\dfrac{\sqrt{10}}{2}$

C $2\sqrt{10}$

D $5\sqrt{10}$

6 Decide whether each statement is true (T) or false (F).

(R) a $3\sqrt{7} = \sqrt{21}$

b $\sqrt{12} = 6$

c $\left(\sqrt{9.4}\right)^2 = 9.4$

d $\sqrt{75} = 5\sqrt{3}$

e $\sqrt{3} \approx 1.7$

f The exact value of $\sqrt{10}$ is 3.162 277 8

DID YOU KNOW?

Unreal numbers are imaginary!

$\sqrt{-2}$ is not a real number, because there is no real number which, if squared, equals –2. Numbers such as $\sqrt{-2}$, $\sqrt{-10}$, $\sqrt[4]{-17}$ are called **unreal** or **imaginary numbers** and cannot be graphed on a number line (that is, their values cannot be ordered).

Imaginary numbers were first noticed by the Greek mathematician Hero of Alexandria in the 1st century CE. Imaginary numbers were largely ignored until the 18th century when they were studied by Swiss mathematician Leonhard Euler and the German mathematician Carl Friedrich Gauss.

$\sqrt{-1}$ is defined to be the imaginary number i, so $\sqrt{-1} = i$ and $i^2 = -1$.

$\therefore \sqrt{-36} = \sqrt{36 \times (-1)} = \sqrt{36} \times \sqrt{-1} = 6i$.

Imaginary numbers are useful for solving physics and engineering problems involving heat conduction, elasticity, hydrodynamics and the flow of electric current.

Simplify each imaginary number:

a $\sqrt{-100}$

b $\sqrt{-25}$

c $\sqrt[6]{-64}$

d $\sqrt[10]{-243}$

□ Foundation ○ Standard ○ Complex

Extension: Adding and subtracting surds **4.11**

Just as you can only add or subtract 'like terms' in algebra, you can only add or subtract 'like surds'. You may first need to express all the surds in their simplest forms.

Example 27

Simplify each expression.

a $4\sqrt{2} + 5\sqrt{2}$ **b** $7\sqrt{3} - 2\sqrt{3}$ **c** $5\sqrt{2} - 3\sqrt{3} + \sqrt{2}$

d $\sqrt{50} + \sqrt{32}$ **e** $\sqrt{8} - \sqrt{27} + \sqrt{18}$ **f** $5\sqrt{20} - 3\sqrt{125}$

SOLUTION

a $4\sqrt{2} + 5\sqrt{2} = 9\sqrt{2}$ **b** $7\sqrt{3} - 2\sqrt{3} = 5\sqrt{3}$

c $5\sqrt{2} - 3\sqrt{3} + \sqrt{2} = 6\sqrt{2} - 3\sqrt{3}$ **d** $\sqrt{50} + \sqrt{32} = \sqrt{25}\sqrt{2} + \sqrt{16}\sqrt{2}$
$$= 5\sqrt{2} + 4\sqrt{2}$$
$$= 9\sqrt{2}$$

e $\sqrt{8} - \sqrt{27} + \sqrt{18} = \sqrt{4}\sqrt{2} - \sqrt{9}\sqrt{3} + \sqrt{9}\sqrt{2}$ **f** $5\sqrt{20} - 3\sqrt{125} = 5\sqrt{4}\sqrt{5} - 3\sqrt{25}\sqrt{5}$
$$= 2\sqrt{2} - 3\sqrt{3} + 3\sqrt{2} \qquad = 5 \times 2\sqrt{5} - 3 \times 5\sqrt{5}$$
$$= 5\sqrt{2} - 3\sqrt{3} \qquad\qquad = 10\sqrt{5} - 15\sqrt{5}$$
$$= -5\sqrt{5}$$

EXERCISE **4.11** ANSWERS ON P. 612

Adding and subtracting surds U F

EXAMPLE
27

1 Simplify each expression.

a $5\sqrt{7} + 2\sqrt{7}$ **b** $3\sqrt{2} - 8\sqrt{2}$ **c** $7\sqrt{5} - \sqrt{5}$

d $\sqrt{5} + 3\sqrt{5}$ **e** $5\sqrt{17} - 5\sqrt{17}$ **f** $3\sqrt{10} - 2\sqrt{10}$

g $4\sqrt{15} - 3\sqrt{15} + 7\sqrt{15}$ **h** $5\sqrt{6} - 2\sqrt{6} - 4\sqrt{6}$ **i** $3\sqrt{3} + 4\sqrt{3} - 5\sqrt{3}$

j $4\sqrt{5} + 7\sqrt{5} - \sqrt{5}$ **k** $8\sqrt{10} - 5\sqrt{10} + 3\sqrt{10}$ **l** $10\sqrt{3} - 3\sqrt{3} - 12\sqrt{3}$

2 Simplify each expression.

a $3\sqrt{5} - 8 + 2\sqrt{5}$ **b** $11\sqrt{10} + 3\sqrt{2} + 2\sqrt{10}$

c $-4\sqrt{3} + 5\sqrt{2} - 5\sqrt{3}$ **d** $3\sqrt{15} + 3\sqrt{2} + 4\sqrt{15} + 5\sqrt{2}$

e $\sqrt{7} - 3\sqrt{5} - 4\sqrt{7} + \sqrt{5}$ **f** $4\sqrt{6} - 3\sqrt{3} - 2\sqrt{6} - 5\sqrt{3}$

g $10\sqrt{11} - 5\sqrt{3} + 3\sqrt{11} + 4\sqrt{3}$ **h** $\sqrt{13} + 8\sqrt{7} - 7\sqrt{13} + 3\sqrt{7}$

i $2\sqrt{5} - 3\sqrt{7} - 2\sqrt{5} - 3\sqrt{7}$ **j** $4\sqrt{10} - 3\sqrt{5} - 4\sqrt{10}$

$\triangleright$

☐ Foundation ○ Standard ○ Complex

3 For each expression, select the correct simplified answer **A, B, C** or **D**.

a $\sqrt{3} + \sqrt{12}$

    A $5\sqrt{3}$ **B** $\sqrt{15}$ **C** $2\sqrt{6}$ **D** $3\sqrt{3}$

b $4\sqrt{5} - 2\sqrt{125}$

    A $-6\sqrt{5}$ **B** $\sqrt{5}$ **C** $-\sqrt{45}$ **D** $-46\sqrt{5}$

4 Simplify each expression.

a $\sqrt{8} + \sqrt{32}$ **b** $\sqrt{108} - \sqrt{27}$ **c** $\sqrt{20} - \sqrt{80}$ **d** $\sqrt{28} - \sqrt{63}$

e $3\sqrt{6} + \sqrt{24}$ **f** $2\sqrt{5} + \sqrt{125}$ **g** $\sqrt{40} - \sqrt{90}$ **h** $5\sqrt{11} + \sqrt{99}$

i $3\sqrt{2} + \sqrt{18}$ **j** $\sqrt{27} + 5\sqrt{3}$ **k** $\sqrt{200} - 7\sqrt{2}$ **l** $\sqrt{50} + \sqrt{32}$

m $5\sqrt{3} + 2\sqrt{27}$ **n** $3\sqrt{20} - \sqrt{245}$ **o** $7\sqrt{12} - 5\sqrt{48}$ **p** $4\sqrt{27} + 2\sqrt{243}$

q $3\sqrt{63} - 2\sqrt{28}$ **r** $2\sqrt{98} + 3\sqrt{162}$ **s** $-5\sqrt{6} + 2\sqrt{150}$ **t** $4\sqrt{50} + 3\sqrt{18}$

u $5\sqrt{27} - 6\sqrt{75}$ **v** $3\sqrt{112} - 2\sqrt{252}$ **w** $\sqrt{32} + \sqrt{8} + \sqrt{12}$ **x** $\sqrt{27} + \sqrt{54} + \sqrt{243}$

y $\sqrt{98} - 3\sqrt{20} - 2\sqrt{8}$ **z** $3\sqrt{96} - 2\sqrt{150} + \sqrt{24}$

4.12   Extension: Multiplying and dividing surds

Puzzle
Surds

Worksheet
Multiplying
and dividing
surds

ⓘ The square root of products and quotients

For $x > 0$ and $y > 0$:

$$\sqrt{xy} = \sqrt{x} \times \sqrt{y}$$

$$\sqrt{\frac{x}{y}} = \frac{\sqrt{x}}{\sqrt{y}}$$

Example 28

Simplify each expression.

a $\sqrt{3} \times \sqrt{5}$ **b** $\sqrt{10} \times \sqrt{6}$ **c** $3\sqrt{7} \times 5\sqrt{7}$

d $5\sqrt{27} \times 3\sqrt{6}$ **e** $\sqrt{54} \div \left(-\sqrt{2}\right)$ **f** $\frac{15\sqrt{32}}{5\sqrt{8}}$

SOLUTION

a $\sqrt{3} \times \sqrt{5} = \sqrt{15}$

b $\sqrt{10} \times \sqrt{6} = \sqrt{60}$
$= \sqrt{4} \times \sqrt{15}$
$= 2\sqrt{15}$

□ Foundation   ○ Standard   ◇ Complex

c $3\sqrt{7} \times 5\sqrt{7} = 3 \times 5 \times \sqrt{7} \times \sqrt{7}$
$\qquad = 15 \times 7$
$\qquad = 105$

d $5\sqrt{27} \times 3\sqrt{6} = 5 \times 3 \times \sqrt{27} \times \sqrt{6}$
$\qquad = 15\sqrt{162}$
$\qquad = 15 \times \sqrt{81} \times \sqrt{2}$
$\qquad = 15 \times 9\sqrt{2}$
$\qquad = 135\sqrt{2}$

e $\sqrt{54} \div \left(-\sqrt{2}\right) = -\dfrac{\sqrt{54}}{\sqrt{2}}$
$\qquad = -\sqrt{27}$
$\qquad = -\sqrt{9} \times \sqrt{3}$
$\qquad = -3\sqrt{3}$

f $\dfrac{15\sqrt{32}}{5\sqrt{8}} = 3\sqrt{4}$
$\qquad = 3 \times 2$
$\qquad = 6$

Example 29

Simplify $\dfrac{5\sqrt{2} \times 4\sqrt{12}}{10\sqrt{8}}$.

SOLUTION

$\dfrac{5\sqrt{2} \times 4\sqrt{12}}{10\sqrt{8}} = \dfrac{20\sqrt{24}}{10\sqrt{8}}$
$\qquad\qquad = 2\sqrt{3}$

EXERCISE 4.12 ANSWERS ON P. 612

Multiplying and dividing surds

EXAMPLE
28

1 Simplify each expression.

a $\sqrt{7} \times \sqrt{2}$

b $-\sqrt{5} \times \sqrt{7}$

c $\sqrt{6} \times \sqrt{8}$

d $\sqrt{12} \times \sqrt{3}$

e $\sqrt{10} \times \left(-\sqrt{5}\right)$

f $3\sqrt{3} \times 5\sqrt{3}$

g $5\sqrt{10} \times 3\sqrt{3}$

h $-2\sqrt{7} \times 5\sqrt{3}$

i $7\sqrt{5} \times 4\sqrt{5}$

j $2\sqrt{3} \times \left(-5\sqrt{6}\right)$

k $4\sqrt{3} \times \sqrt{27}$

l $-3\sqrt{5} \times 4\sqrt{10}$

m $-7\sqrt{2} \times 4\sqrt{8}$

n $\sqrt{18} \times 8\sqrt{3}$

o $10\sqrt{2} \times 2\sqrt{8}$

p $3\sqrt{18} \times 5\sqrt{12}$

q $3\sqrt{44} \times \left(-2\sqrt{99}\right)$

r $5\sqrt{8} \times 4\sqrt{40}$

s $8\sqrt{3} \times 3\sqrt{54}$

t $-8\sqrt{32} \times \sqrt{27}$

u $\sqrt{90} \times \sqrt{72}$

v $-5\sqrt{20} \times 3\sqrt{8}$

w $7\sqrt{18} \times 3\sqrt{24}$

x $3\sqrt{48} \times 2\sqrt{12}$

☐ Foundation   ○ Standard   ○ Complex

2 Simplify each expression.

a $\sqrt{15} \div \sqrt{3}$

b $\sqrt{18} \div \left(-\sqrt{6}\right)$

c $\dfrac{6\sqrt{48}}{2\sqrt{8}}$

d $10\sqrt{54} \div 5\sqrt{27}$

e $-3\sqrt{98} \div 6\sqrt{14}$

f $\dfrac{7\sqrt{18}}{\sqrt{2}}$

g $2\sqrt{24} \div 4\sqrt{6}$

h $\dfrac{\sqrt{128}}{\sqrt{2}}$

i $15\sqrt{18} \div 3\sqrt{6}$

j $\dfrac{-20\sqrt{10}}{-4\sqrt{5}}$

k $36\sqrt{24} \div 9\sqrt{8}$

l $16\sqrt{30} \div 8\sqrt{5}$

m $12\sqrt{14} \div 6$

n $\dfrac{3\sqrt{2}}{-12}$

o $\sqrt{80} \div 4\sqrt{5}$

p $5\sqrt{60} \div \sqrt{15}$

q $6\sqrt{8} \div 3\sqrt{2}$

r $\dfrac{-42\sqrt{54}}{6\sqrt{3}}$

s $12\sqrt{63} \div 3\sqrt{7}$

t $\dfrac{8\sqrt{50}}{2\sqrt{200}}$

u $6\sqrt{3} \div \sqrt{243}$

3 Simplify:

a $\sqrt{6} \times \sqrt{6}$

b $\sqrt{7} \times \sqrt{7}$

c $2\sqrt{3} \times \sqrt{3}$

d $5\sqrt{y} \times 3\sqrt{y}$

e $\sqrt{x} \times \sqrt{x}$

f $\sqrt{a^2} \times \sqrt{a}$

4 Simplify $3\sqrt{2} \times \sqrt{6}$. Select the correct answer **A, B, C** or **D**.

A 6

B $6\sqrt{2}$

C $6\sqrt{3}$

D $12\sqrt{2}$

5 Simplify $20\sqrt{10} \div 5\sqrt{2}$. Select **A, B, C** or **D**.

A $4\sqrt{5}$

B $15\sqrt{5}$

C 10

D 20

EXAMPLE
29

6 Simplify each expression.

a $\dfrac{3\sqrt{5} \times 4\sqrt{2}}{3\sqrt{40}}$

b $\dfrac{3\sqrt{12} \times 8\sqrt{6}}{4\sqrt{27}}$

c $\dfrac{5\sqrt{8} \times 2\sqrt{90}}{10\sqrt{24}}$

d $\dfrac{4\sqrt{5}}{2\sqrt{15} \times 5\sqrt{27}}$

e $\dfrac{10\sqrt{686} \times 3\sqrt{12}}{5\sqrt{28} \times \sqrt{18}}$

f $\dfrac{8\sqrt{80} \times 3\sqrt{2}}{4\sqrt{5} \times 6\sqrt{8}}$

□ Foundation ○ Standard ○ Complex

Example 30

Expand and simplify each expression.

a $\sqrt{3}\left(\sqrt{5}+\sqrt{7}\right)$

b $2\sqrt{11}\left(3\sqrt{11}-5\sqrt{2}\right)$

SOLUTION

a $\sqrt{3}\left(\sqrt{5}+\sqrt{7}\right)=\sqrt{3}\times\sqrt{5}+\sqrt{3}\times\sqrt{7}$

$=\sqrt{15}+\sqrt{21}$

b $2\sqrt{11}\left(3\sqrt{11}-5\sqrt{2}\right)=2\sqrt{11}\times3\sqrt{11}-2\sqrt{11}\times5\sqrt{2}$

$=6\times11-10\times\sqrt{22}$

$=66-10\sqrt{22}$

Example 31

Expand and simplify each binomial product.

a $\left(\sqrt{7}+\sqrt{5}\right)\left(3\sqrt{2}-\sqrt{3}\right)$

b $\left(3-2\sqrt{10}\right)\left(\sqrt{5}-3\sqrt{2}\right)$

SOLUTION

a $\left(\sqrt{7}+\sqrt{5}\right)\left(3\sqrt{2}-\sqrt{3}\right)=\sqrt{7}\left(3\sqrt{2}-\sqrt{3}\right)+\sqrt{5}\left(3\sqrt{2}-\sqrt{3}\right)$

$=\sqrt{7}\times3\sqrt{2}-\sqrt{7}\times\sqrt{3}+\sqrt{5}\times3\sqrt{2}-\sqrt{5}\times\sqrt{3}$

$=3\sqrt{14}-\sqrt{21}+3\sqrt{10}-\sqrt{15}$

b $\left(3-2\sqrt{10}\right)\left(\sqrt{5}-3\sqrt{2}\right)=3\left(\sqrt{5}-3\sqrt{2}\right)-2\sqrt{10}\left(\sqrt{5}-3\sqrt{2}\right)$

$=3\sqrt{5}-9\sqrt{2}-2\sqrt{50}+6\sqrt{20}$

$=3\sqrt{5}-9\sqrt{2}-2\left(5\sqrt{2}\right)+6\left(2\sqrt{5}\right)$

$=3\sqrt{5}-9\sqrt{2}-10\sqrt{2}+12\sqrt{5}$

$=15\sqrt{5}-19\sqrt{2}$

(i) Special binomial products

Perfect squares

$(a+b)^2 = a^2 + 2ab + b^2$

$(a-b)^2 = a^2 - 2ab + b^2$

Difference of 2 squares

$(a+b)(a-b) = a^2 - b^2$

Example 32

Expand and simplify each expression.

a $\left(\sqrt{7}-\sqrt{5}\right)^2$

b $\left(2\sqrt{3}+3\sqrt{5}\right)^2$

c $\left(\sqrt{5}-\sqrt{2}\right)\left(\sqrt{5}+\sqrt{2}\right)$

d $\left(3\sqrt{11}+4\right)\left(3\sqrt{11}-4\right)$

SOLUTION

a $\left(\sqrt{7}-\sqrt{5}\right)^2 = \left(\sqrt{7}\right)^2 - 2 \times \sqrt{7} \times \sqrt{5} + \left(\sqrt{5}\right)^2$ using $(a - b)^2 = a^2 - 2ab + b^2$

$$= 7 - 2\sqrt{35} + 5$$
$$= 12 - 2\sqrt{35}$$

b $\left(2\sqrt{3}+3\sqrt{5}\right)^2 = \left(2\sqrt{3}\right)^2 + 2 \times 2\sqrt{3} \times 3\sqrt{5} + \left(3\sqrt{5}\right)^2$ using $(a + b)^2 = a^2 + 2ab + b^2$

$$= \left(4 \times 3\right) + 12\sqrt{15} + \left(9 \times 5\right)$$
$$= 12 + 12\sqrt{15} + 45$$
$$= 57 + 12\sqrt{15}$$

c $\left(\sqrt{5}-\sqrt{2}\right)\left(\sqrt{5}+\sqrt{2}\right) = \left(\sqrt{5}\right)^2 - \left(\sqrt{2}\right)^2$ using $(a + b)(a - b) = a^2 - b^2$

$$= 5 - 2$$
$$= 3$$

> Note that because of the 'difference of 2 squares', the answer is not a surd but a rational number.

d $\left(3\sqrt{11}+4\right)\left(3\sqrt{11}-4\right) = \left(3\sqrt{11}\right)^2 - 4^2$ using $(a + b)(a - b) = a^2 - b^2$

$$= \left(9 \times 11\right) - 16$$
$$= 83$$

EXERCISE (4.13) ANSWERS ON P. 613

Binomial products involving surds   U F

EXAMPLE
30

1 Expand and simplify each expression.

a $\sqrt{5}\left(\sqrt{3}+\sqrt{2}\right)$

b $\sqrt{6}\left(\sqrt{2}-1\right)$

c $\sqrt{2}\left(\sqrt{3}+\sqrt{7}\right)$

d $\sqrt{5}\left(3\sqrt{2}-\sqrt{5}\right)$

e $3\sqrt{2}\left(\sqrt{2}+2\sqrt{3}\right)$

f $-\sqrt{11}\left(4-\sqrt{5}\right)$

g $2\sqrt{7}\left(3\sqrt{7}-4\right)$

h $5\sqrt{5}\left(1+3\sqrt{5}\right)$

i $3\sqrt{2}\left(4\sqrt{2}+\sqrt{3}\right)$

☐ Foundation   ○ Standard   ◇ Complex

2 Expand and simplify $(\sqrt{3}+2\sqrt{5})(5\sqrt{2}+\sqrt{3})$. Select the correct answer **A**, **B**, **C** or **D**.

EXAMPLE
31

A $20\sqrt{10}$

B $2\sqrt{15}+5\sqrt{6}$

C $5\sqrt{6}+3+10\sqrt{10}+2\sqrt{15}$

D $5\sqrt{5}+\sqrt{3}+7\sqrt{7}+4\sqrt{2}$

3 Expand and simplify each expression.

a $(\sqrt{5}-3)(2\sqrt{5}+\sqrt{2})$

b $(\sqrt{7}-\sqrt{3})(\sqrt{7}+2)$

c $(7\sqrt{3}+2)(4\sqrt{2}+\sqrt{3})$

d $(3\sqrt{2}-\sqrt{5})(5\sqrt{2}+2\sqrt{5})$

e $(\sqrt{7}+2\sqrt{11})(3\sqrt{7}+4\sqrt{11})$

f $(5\sqrt{3}-2\sqrt{2})(4\sqrt{3}-3\sqrt{2})$

g $(6+2\sqrt{10})(3\sqrt{10}-1)$

h $(\sqrt{7}-2\sqrt{5})(3\sqrt{5}+2\sqrt{7})$

4 Expand $(5+\sqrt{7})^2$. Select **A**, **B**, **C** or **D**.

EXAMPLE
32

A 12

B 32

C $32+10\sqrt{7}$

D $32+5\sqrt{7}$

5 Expand and simplify each expression.

a $(\sqrt{5}-\sqrt{3})^2$

b $(\sqrt{7}+\sqrt{2})^2$

c $(\sqrt{5}-2)^2$

d $(3+\sqrt{10})^2$

e $(5\sqrt{2}+3\sqrt{3})^2$

f $(5\sqrt{7}-2)^2$

g $(3\sqrt{2}+2\sqrt{5})^2$

h $(2\sqrt{5}+\sqrt{3})^2$

6 Expand and simplify each expression.

a $(\sqrt{3}-\sqrt{2})(\sqrt{3}+\sqrt{2})$

b $(5+\sqrt{3})(5-\sqrt{3})$

c $(6+2\sqrt{7})(6-2\sqrt{7})$

d $(\sqrt{5}-\sqrt{3})(\sqrt{5}+\sqrt{3})$

e $(\sqrt{11}-\sqrt{10})(\sqrt{11}+\sqrt{10})$

f $(5\sqrt{7}+3)(5\sqrt{7}-3)$

g $(3\sqrt{2}+\sqrt{5})(3\sqrt{2}-\sqrt{5})$

h $(4\sqrt{2}-5\sqrt{3})(4\sqrt{2}+5\sqrt{3})$

7 Expand and simplify $(5\sqrt{2}-4\sqrt{3})(5\sqrt{2}+4\sqrt{3})$. Select **A**, **B**, **C** or **D**.

A $25\sqrt{2}-16\sqrt{3}$

B $10\sqrt{2}+10\sqrt{6}$

C 2

D 26

8 Expand and simplify each expression.

a $(3\sqrt{7}-5)^2$

b $(5\sqrt{2}-4)(\sqrt{2}+5)$

c $(2\sqrt{7}+3\sqrt{5})(\sqrt{5}+\sqrt{7})$

d $(4\sqrt{3}+5)^2$

e $(4\sqrt{2}+\sqrt{3})(4\sqrt{2}-\sqrt{3})$

f $(3\sqrt{10}-\sqrt{2})^2$

☐ Foundation ○ Standard ○ Complex

INVESTIGATION

Making the denominator rational

1. What happens when we multiply the numerator and denominator of a fraction by the same number?

2. a Simplify $\frac{1}{\sqrt{2}} \times \frac{\sqrt{2}}{\sqrt{2}}$.

   b Mentally approximate the value of $\frac{\sqrt{2}}{2}$ given $\sqrt{2} \approx 1.4142$.

   c Check using a calculator that $\frac{1}{\sqrt{2}} = \frac{\sqrt{2}}{2}$. Why is this true?

3. a Is it true that $\frac{3}{\sqrt{7}} = \frac{3}{\sqrt{7}} \times \frac{\sqrt{7}}{\sqrt{7}}$? Why?

   b Simplify $\frac{3}{\sqrt{7}} \times \frac{\sqrt{7}}{\sqrt{7}}$. Compare your answer with those of other students.

   c Check using a calculator that $\frac{3}{\sqrt{7}} = \frac{3\sqrt{7}}{7}$.

4. a Explain why $\frac{3\sqrt{5}}{\sqrt{2}} = \frac{3\sqrt{5}}{\sqrt{2}} \times \frac{\sqrt{2}}{\sqrt{2}}$.

   b Show that $\frac{3\sqrt{5}}{\sqrt{2}} = \frac{3\sqrt{10}}{2}$.

4.14 Extension: Rationalising the denominator

If $\sqrt{2} \approx 1.4142$, what is the value of $\frac{3}{\sqrt{2}}$? Fractions containing surds in the denominator are difficult to work with. When approximating the value of $\frac{3}{\sqrt{2}}$, it is difficult to mentally divide by 1.4142. We can overcome this by making the denominator **rational** (that is, **not** a surd).

Numbers that have irrational denominators, such as $\frac{1}{\sqrt{5}}, \frac{3}{2\sqrt{7}}, \frac{\sqrt{3}}{\sqrt{2}}, \frac{5\sqrt{7}}{\sqrt{3}}$ can be rewritten with a rational denominator by multiplying both the numerator and denominator by the surd that appears in the denominator. This method is called **rationalising the denominator**.

Example 33

Video
Rationalising
the
denominator

Rationalise the denominator of each surd.

a $\frac{3}{\sqrt{2}}$ b $\frac{5}{4\sqrt{3}}$ c $\frac{8\sqrt{2}}{3\sqrt{5}}$ d $\frac{\sqrt{2}+1}{\sqrt{3}}$

SOLUTION

a $\frac{3}{\sqrt{2}} = \frac{3}{\sqrt{2}} \times \frac{\sqrt{2}}{\sqrt{2}}$ because $\frac{\sqrt{2}}{\sqrt{2}} = 1$

$= \frac{3\sqrt{2}}{2}$

We rationalise the denominator because it is easier to estimate $\dfrac{3}{\sqrt{2}}$ by approximating $\dfrac{3\sqrt{2}}{2}$ and mentally multiplying $\dfrac{3}{2}$ by 1.4142 than by dividing 3 by 1.4142.

EXTENSION

4.14

b $\dfrac{5}{4\sqrt{3}} = \dfrac{5}{4\sqrt{3}} \times \dfrac{\sqrt{3}}{\sqrt{3}}$

$= \dfrac{5\sqrt{3}}{4 \times 3}$

$= \dfrac{5\sqrt{3}}{12}$

c $\dfrac{8\sqrt{2}}{3\sqrt{5}} = \dfrac{8\sqrt{2}}{3\sqrt{5}} \times \dfrac{\sqrt{5}}{\sqrt{5}}$

$= \dfrac{8\sqrt{10}}{3 \times 5}$

$= \dfrac{8\sqrt{10}}{15}$

d $\dfrac{\sqrt{2}+1}{\sqrt{3}} = \dfrac{\sqrt{2}+1}{\sqrt{3}} \times \dfrac{\sqrt{3}}{\sqrt{3}}$

$= \dfrac{\sqrt{6}+\sqrt{3}}{3}$

EXERCISE (4.14) ANSWERS ON P. 613

Rationalising the denominator   (U) (F)

1. By rationalising the denominator, which surd is equivalent to $\dfrac{2}{\sqrt{6}}$?
   Select the correct answer **A**, **B**, **C** or **D**.

EXAMPLE
33

   A $2\sqrt{6}$ **B** $\dfrac{\sqrt{6}}{3}$ **C** $\dfrac{\sqrt{6}}{6}$ **D** $\dfrac{2\sqrt{6}}{3}$

2. Rationalise the denominator of each surd.

   a $\dfrac{1}{\sqrt{2}}$ **b** $\dfrac{1}{\sqrt{7}}$ **c** $\dfrac{1}{\sqrt{3}}$ **d** $\dfrac{3}{\sqrt{2}}$

   e $\dfrac{2}{\sqrt{7}}$ **f** $\dfrac{1}{3\sqrt{2}}$ **g** $\dfrac{1}{2\sqrt{3}}$ **h** $\dfrac{1}{4\sqrt{7}}$

   i $\dfrac{7}{3\sqrt{5}}$ **j** $\dfrac{\sqrt{2}}{3\sqrt{5}}$ **k** $\dfrac{3\sqrt{2}}{2\sqrt{6}}$ **l** $\dfrac{5\sqrt{3}}{4\sqrt{5}}$

3. Which surd is equivalent to $\dfrac{\sqrt{3}}{2\sqrt{5}}$? Select **A**, **B**, **C** or **D**.

   A $\dfrac{\sqrt{15}}{10}$ **B** $2\sqrt{15}$ **C** $\dfrac{\sqrt{15}}{3}$ **D** $\sqrt{5}$

4. Which surd is equivalent to $\dfrac{\sqrt{27}}{3\sqrt{18}}$? Select **A**, **B**, **C** or **D**.

   A $\dfrac{1}{2}$ **B** $\dfrac{\sqrt{2}}{2}$ **C** $\dfrac{\sqrt{5}}{6}$ **D** $\dfrac{\sqrt{6}}{6}$

5. Rationalise the denominator of each expression.

   a $\dfrac{\sqrt{2}-1}{\sqrt{2}}$ **b** $\dfrac{1-\sqrt{5}}{\sqrt{5}}$ **c** $\dfrac{5+\sqrt{3}}{2\sqrt{2}}$ **d** $\dfrac{\sqrt{2}-\sqrt{3}}{3\sqrt{6}}$

6. Simplify each expression, giving the answer with a rational denominator.

   a $\dfrac{1}{\sqrt{7}} + \dfrac{1}{\sqrt{2}}$ **b** $\dfrac{\sqrt{2}}{\sqrt{5}} + \dfrac{3}{\sqrt{3}}$ **c** $\dfrac{3}{2\sqrt{3}} - \dfrac{1}{\sqrt{2}}$

□ Foundation ○ Standard ○ Complex

1   Expand and simplify each expression.

    a $(x + 5)^3$ **b** $(y - 2)^3$ **c** $(a + b)^3$ **d** $(3d + 10)^3$

2   Use the given expansion to evaluate each square number without using a calculator.

    a $21^2 = (20 + 1)^2$ **b** $45^2 = (40 + 5)^2$

    c $29^2 = (30 - 1)^2$ **d** $59^2 = (60 - 1)^2$

    e $102^2 = (100 + 2)^2$ **f** $98^2 = 100 - 2)^2$

3   By expressing 31×29 as $(30 + 1)(30 - 1)$, evaluate 31×29 without using a calculator.

4   Use the method of question **3** to evaluate each expression.

    a 21×19 **b** 51×49 **c** 89×91 **d** 78×82

5   **a**   Is it true that $\dfrac{1}{3+\sqrt{2}} = \dfrac{1}{3+\sqrt{2}} \times \dfrac{3-\sqrt{2}}{3-\sqrt{2}}$? Explain.

    b   Simplify $\dfrac{1}{3+\sqrt{2}} \times \dfrac{3-\sqrt{2}}{3-\sqrt{2}}$. Is the denominator rational?

    c   Use a calculator to check that the value of your answer to part **b** is equal to the value of $\dfrac{1}{3+\sqrt{2}}$.

6   The largest cube that can fit inside a sphere must have its 8 vertices touching the surface of the sphere. Express the side length, s, of the cube in terms of the diameter, D, of the sphere.

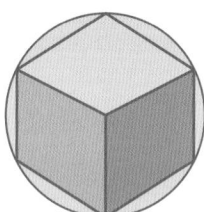

7   Squares are formed inside squares by joining the midpoints of the sides of the squares as shown. If $AB = 4$ cm, find the exact length of the side of the shaded square.

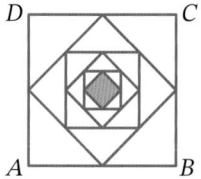

8   6 stormwater pipes, each 2 mm in diameter, are stacked as shown in the diagram. Find the exact height, h, of the stack.

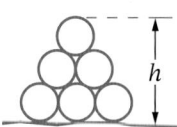

9   An equilateral triangle has an inscribed circle that contains another equilateral triangle inscribed in it. The difference between the areas of the triangles is 40 cm². Find the radius of the circle, leaving your answer as a surd.

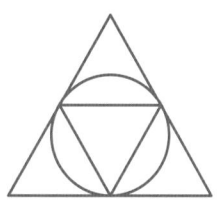

CHAPTER REVIEW

Language of maths

base	binomial product	coefficient	constant term
denominator	difference of 2 squares	exact value	expand
factorise	fractional	grouping in pairs	index law
indices	irrational number	perfect square	quadratic expression
rational number	rationalise	real number	reciprocal
root	surd	term	trinomial

Quiz
Language of maths 4

Worksheet
Algebra 6

Puzzles
Algebra crossword

Surds crossword

1 Explain the meaning of **quadratic** and **trinomial**. Give an example of a **quadratic trinomial**.

2 What is the difference between a **rational number** and a **real number**?

3 What is a **surd**?

4 What power is associated with the **reciprocal** of a term or number?

5 Copy and complete:

To factorise quadratic expressions of the form $x^2 + bx + c$, first find 2 numbers that have a
_____ of b and a _____ of c.

6 How do you **rationalise the denominator** of a surd expression?

Topic summary

- What was this topic about? What was the main theme?
- What content was new and what was revision for you?
- Write 3 index laws in both words and symbols
- Write 10 questions (with solutions) that could be used in a test for this chapter. Include some questions that you have found difficult to answer.
- List the sections of work in this chapter that you did not understand. Follow up this work.

Worksheet
Mind map:
Products, factors and surds

Print (or copy) and complete this mind map of the topic, adding detail to its branches and using pictures, symbols and colour where needed. Ask your teacher to check your work.

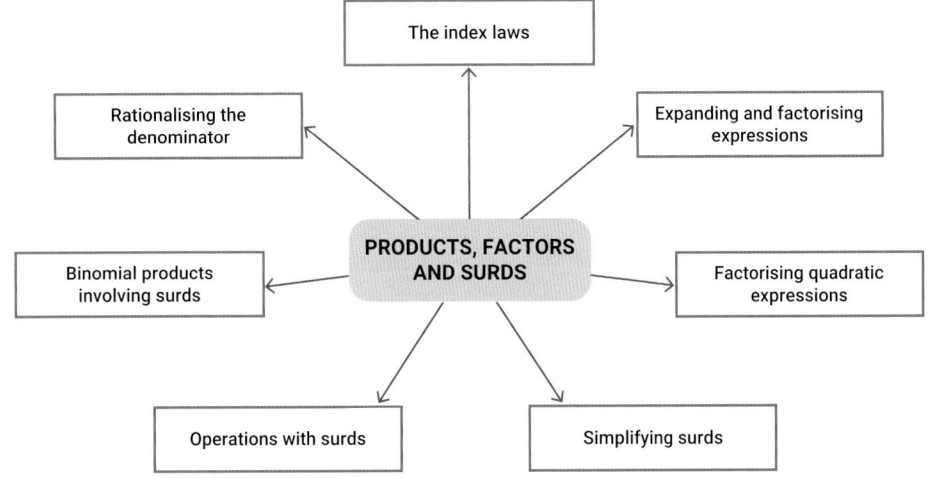

(4) TEST YOURSELF ANSWERS ON P. 613

4.01

1 Simplify each expression.

a $\left(\dfrac{2p}{3}\right)^0$

b $(4k)^{-1}$

c $\left(\dfrac{5y}{2}\right)^3$

4.01

2 Simplify each expression.

a $\left(\dfrac{1}{10}\right)^{-5}$

b $\left(\dfrac{3}{5}\right)^{-2}$

c $\left(\dfrac{4g}{7}\right)^{-3}$

d $\left(\dfrac{9}{2d}\right)^{-2}$

EXTENSION

e $(4m)^{-2}$

f $4m^{-2}$

g $\left(\dfrac{5b^8 y^6}{b^2 y^3}\right)^4$

h $(4t^4 u^5)^3 \times 8t^2 u$

4.02

3 Evaluate each expression.

a $400^{\frac{1}{2}}$

b $(-27)^{\frac{5}{3}}$

c $64^{-\frac{1}{2}}$

d $(-32)^{\frac{2}{5}}$

4.02

4 Simplify each expression.

a $\left(16a^4\right)^{\frac{3}{2}}$

b $\sqrt[4]{\left(81m^{12}\right)^5}$

c $\dfrac{1}{\left(\sqrt[3]{8p^6}\right)}$

d $\left(125x^3 y^6\right)^{-\frac{2}{3}}$

4.03

5 Expand and simplify each expression.

a $4fg(g - 6f) - 6f^2 g$

b $12(9 - n) - 5(2n + 3)$

c $x^2(6x + x^2) + 2x(3x^3 + x^2)$

d $3(7 - 2y) - 5y(7 - 2y)$

4.03

6 Factorise each expression.

a $15xy^2 - 30x^3 y^3$

b $6pt^2 + 12p^2 t - 48p^3$

c $32r^2 s^4 + 12r^4 s^3$

d $50x^4 y^3 - 75x^3 y^4$

e $-8p^3 q^3 + 48p^3 q^6$

f $n(n^2 + 6) - (n^2 + 6)$

4.04

7 Expand each binomial product.

a $(b + 3)(b + 10)$

b $(d + 8)(d - 7)$

c $(t - 6)(9 - t)$

d $(5x + 7)(4x - 3)$

e $(7y - 5)(7y + 5)$

f $(3p - 8)(7p - 2)$

EXTENSION

4.04

8 Expand each binomial product.

a $(n + 9)(n - 9)$

b $(3y + 2d)^2$

c $(4n - 11)(4n + 11)$

4.05

9 Factorise each expression.

a $3pu + 2qt + 2qu + 3pt$

b $4ab + 6bc - 6ad - 9dc$

c $b^2 - 100$

d $25 - 16y^2$

e $20x^2 - 125$

f $3r^3 - 27r$

4.06

10 Factorise each quadratic expression.

a $y^2 + 10y + 25$

b $x^2 - 21x + 20$

c $n^2 + 8n - 33$

d $a^2 - 11a + 28$

e $m^2 - 5m - 84$

f $p^2 + 3p - 54$

□ Foundation ○ Standard ○ Complex

11 Factorise each expression.

  a $3w^2 + 5w + 2$ **b** $2y^2 - 3y - 9$ **c** $60 - 5b - 5b^2$

  d $3p^2 + 10p - 8$ **e** $12x^2 - 46x + 14$ **f** $6n^2 - 13n + 6$

  g $40y^2 + 49y - 24$ **h** $48c^2 - 64c - 35$ **i** $10e^2 - 7e + 1$

12 Factorise each expression.

  a $5q^2 - 45$ **b** $20x^2 - 52x + 24$ **c** $c^3 - c^2 - c + 1$

  d $4 - 47k - 12k^2$ **e** $6m^2 + m - 40$ **f** $a^4 - a^2 + a^3 - a$

13 Is each number rational (R) or irrational (I)?

  a $\sqrt{8}$ **b** $\dfrac{22}{7}$ **c** $0.5\dot{7}$ **d** $3\sqrt{5}$

  e $\sqrt{81}$ **f** $\sqrt[3]{125}$ **g** $\sqrt[3]{-8}$ **h** $5+\sqrt{3}$

14 Simplify each surd.

  a $\sqrt{72}$ **b** $\sqrt{98}$ **c** $\sqrt{275}$ **d** $\sqrt{128}$

  e $3\sqrt{150}$ **f** $7\sqrt{28}$ **g** $4\sqrt{288}$ **h** $5\sqrt{45}$

15 Simplify each expression.

  a $\sqrt{200} + \sqrt{18}$ **b** $3\sqrt{5} + \sqrt{50} - 2\sqrt{125}$

  c $7\sqrt{32} - \sqrt{27} - 2\sqrt{98} + 4\sqrt{75}$ **d** $4\sqrt{45} - 3\sqrt{63} + 5\sqrt{80}$

  e $\sqrt{800} - 2\sqrt{243} + 3\sqrt{72} - 2\sqrt{27}$ **f** $7\sqrt{44} - 2\sqrt{99}$

16 Simplify each expression.

  a $\sqrt{5} \times \sqrt{11}$ **b** $\sqrt{72} \div \sqrt{12}$ **c** $\sqrt{98} \div \sqrt{7}$

  d $8\sqrt{42} \div 2\sqrt{7}$ **e** $\sqrt{125} \div 5\sqrt{5}$ **f** $\dfrac{\sqrt{75}}{3\sqrt{3}}$

  g $\dfrac{\sqrt{18} \times \sqrt{3}}{\sqrt{12}}$ **h** $\dfrac{\sqrt{6} \times \sqrt{24}}{\sqrt{27} \times 2\sqrt{3}}$ **i** $\dfrac{4\sqrt{90} \times 7\sqrt{8}}{5\sqrt{32} \times 6\sqrt{10}}$

17 Expand and simplify each expression.

  a $-3\sqrt{2}\left(2\sqrt{2} - 3\right)$ **b** $\sqrt{10}\left(1 - 5\sqrt{2}\right)$

  c $\left(3\sqrt{5} - 2\sqrt{7}\right)\left(3\sqrt{7} + \sqrt{5}\right)$ **d** $\left(\sqrt{7} - 4\right)^2$

  e $\left(5\sqrt{3} + \sqrt{2}\right)^2$ **f** $\left(3\sqrt{7} - 2\sqrt{5}\right)\left(3\sqrt{7} + 2\sqrt{5}\right)$

18 Rationalise the denominator of each surd.

  a $\dfrac{3}{\sqrt{2}}$ **b** $\dfrac{3}{4\sqrt{3}}$ **c** $\dfrac{5\sqrt{3}}{3\sqrt{2}}$ **d** $\dfrac{4+\sqrt{2}}{3\sqrt{2}}$

EXTENSION

4.07

4.08

4.09

4.10

4.11

4.12

4.13

4.14

CHAPTER 4 TEST YOURSELF

□ Foundation   ○ Standard   ○ Complex

5

STATISTICS

Comparing data

Is climate change affecting the amount of rainfall in different areas? What are the tourist numbers in different parts of Australia, and how much do they spend? How do we ensure accurate medical testing data to monitor the potential for pandemics such as COVID-19?

To answer these questions, sets of data need to be collected and then compared by looking at the shape of their displays or by analysing their measures of centre and spread.

Chapter outline

Proficiencies

5.01	Quartiles and interquartile range	U	F		
5.02	Boxplots	U	F	R	C
5.03	Parallel boxplots	U	F	R	C
5.04	Cumulative frequency and quartiles	U	F		
5.05	Cumulative frequency histograms and polygons	U	F		
5.06	Deciles and percentiles*	U	F	R	C
5.07	Standard deviation*	U	F	R	C
5.08	Comparing means and standard deviations*	U	F	R	C
5.09	Comparing data sets	U	F	R	C
5.10	Statistics in the media	U	F	R	C
5.11	Statistical investigations	U	F	PS	R	C
5.12	Scatterplots	U	F	R	C
5.13	Line of best fit	U	F	R	C
5.14	Association and two-way tables	U	F	R	C

* EXTENSION

U = Understanding   R = Reasoning
F = Fluency   C = Communicating
PS = Problem solving

Wordbank

association A measure of how two variables are statistically related to each other.

bivariate data Data that measures 2 variables, represented by an ordered pair of values that can be graphed on a scatterplot.

boxplot (or **box-and-whisker plot**) A graph that shows the quartiles of a set of data and the highest and lowest values; the box contains the middle 50% of values while the lines or 'whiskers' extend to the 2 extremes.

cumulative frequency A running total of all frequencies in a frequency distribution table.

five-number summary For a set of numerical data, the lowest value, lower quartile, median, upper quartile, highest value.

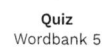

Quiz
Wordbank 5

(More next page)

Wordbank

interquartile range (IQR) The difference between the upper quartile and lower quartiles, IQR = $Q_3 - Q_1$, representing the middle 50% of values.

quartiles The values Q_1, Q_2, Q_3 that divide a set of data into quarters (4 equal parts).

scatterplot A graph consisting of dots on a number plane that represent bivariate data.

Videos (12):

5.01 Interquartile range 1 • Interquartile range 2

5.02 Box-and-whisker plots • Statistics

5.03 Double boxplots

5.04 Cumulative frequency and the median

5.07 Standard deviation on a Casio calculator

5.09 Comparing data sets • Back-to-back stem-and-leaf plots • Histogram vs boxplot

5.12 Scatterplots

5.13 Lines of best fit

Twig videos (3):

5.04 Cumulative frequency: You're fired

5.07 Freak waves

5.13, 5.14 Can eating fish prevent murder?

PhET interactive (1):

5.13 Least-squares regression

Quizzes (5):

- Wordbank 5
- SkillCheck 5
- Mental skills 5
- Language of maths 5
- Test yourself 5

Skillsheet (1):

SkillCheck Statistical measures

Worksheets (12):

5.01 Interquartile range

5.02 Five-number summaries

5.03 Box-and-whisker plots • Data 1

5.09 Comparing city temperatures • Comparing word lengths • Investigating young drivers

5.12 Scatterplots

5.13 Line of best fit • Trendlines • 2 mm grid paper

Mind map: Comparing data

Puzzles (4):

SkillCheck Statistical match-up

5.02 Mode, median and mean

5.12 Scatterplots matching game

Language of maths Data crossword

Technology (3):

5.02 Five-number summary

5.03 Parallel boxplots

5.13 Line of best fit

Spreadsheets (3):

5.02 Five-number summary

5.03 Parallel boxplots

5.13 Line of best fit

Presentation (1):

5.03 Analysing data

✴ **Nelson** MindTap

To access resources above, visit
cengage.com.au/nelsonmindtap

---

5 In this chapter you will:

✓ calculate quartiles and the interquartile range of a set of data

✓ calculate the five-number summary of a set of data and use it to construct a boxplot

✓ determine cumulative frequency of grouped data

✓ construct cumulative frequency histograms and polygons

✓ (EXTENSION) use cumulative frequency polygons to determine quartiles and percentiles

✓ (EXTENSION) use quartiles from cumulative frequency polygons to construct boxplots and compare spread of plots

✓ (EXTENSION) calculate the mean and standard deviation of a set of data and compare data sets

- ✓ construct histograms, dot plots, back-to-back stem-and-leaf plots and parallel boxplots to compare 2 or more sets of data
- ✓ compare shapes of boxplots, histograms and dot plots
- ✓ evaluate statistics presented in the media and identify biases in sampling, sources, graphs, interpretation, claims and conclusions
- ✓ analyse and evaluate media reports of statistical studies
- ✓ graph bivariate data on scatterplots to investigate patterns and relationships between independent and dependent variables, including strength and direction
- ✓ construct lines of best fit and use them to make predictions
- ✓ sort categorical data into two-way tables and calculate percentages
- ✓ use percentaged two-way tables to investigate the association between sets of categorical data

SkillCheck
ANSWERS ON P. 614

1   For each set of data, find:

    i   the range   **ii**   the mean (correct to one decimal place)

    iii   the median   **iv**   the mode.

  a   15, 13, 18, 14, 15, 18, 23, 14, 20, 16, 15

  b   8°C, 3°C, −5°C, 2°C, −4°C, 7°C, 3°C, 0°C

  c

Stem	Leaf
1	0 3 6
2	1 4 4 7 8
3	2 3 4 5 5 7 9
4	0 5 7 8
5	2 6 8

Key: 1|0 = 10

  d

Score	Frequency
0	2
1	5
2	8
3	4
4	3
5	1

2   A cricketer scored these numbers of runs in 10 innings.

34, 21, 78, 30, 26, 19, 41, 36, 16, 32

  a   Find:

    i   the median   **ii**   the mean   **iii**   the range.

  b   Which score is the outlier?

  c   **i**   Calculate the median, mean and range if the outlier is not included in the scores.

    ii   What effect does the outlier have on the mean, median and range?

Quiz
SkillCheck 5

Skillsheet
Statistical measures

Puzzle
Statistical match-up

5.01 Quartiles and interquartile range

Worksheet
Interquartile range

Quartiles

The **median**, being the middle value, divides a set of data into 2 equal parts (halves).

Quartiles are the values Q_1, Q_2 and Q_3 that divide the set of data into 4 equal parts (quarters).

Data values (in order)

lowest value	1st quartile	2nd quartile	3rd quartile	highest value
(or lower extreme)	(Q_1 or Q_L)	(Q_2 or median)	(Q_3 or Q_U)	(or upper extreme)

The **1st quartile** Q_1, also called the **lower quartile** Q_L, is the value that divides the lower 25% of values. $\frac{1}{4}$ of the values lie below Q_1.

The **2nd quartile** Q_2 is the value that divides the lower 50% of values, so it is also the **median**. $\frac{1}{2}$ of the values lie below Q_2.

The **3rd quartile** Q_3, also called the **upper quartile** Q_U, is the value that divides the lower 75% of values from the upper 25% of values. $\frac{3}{4}$ of the values lie below Q_3, $\frac{1}{4}$ of the values lie above it.

ⓘ Finding the quartiles of a data set

- Sort the values in order, find the median and call it Q_2.
- Find the median of the bottom half of the values and call it Q_1 (or Q_L).
- Find the median of the top half of values and call it Q_3 (or Q_U).

Example 1

Find the quartiles for each set of data.

a 9, 3, 8, 7, 6, 8, 4, 6, 2, 10, 9

b 15, 18, 7, 16, 23, 9, 15, 20, 16, 14, 13, 11, 19

c 65, 84, 75, 82, 97, 70, 68, 76, 93, 48, 79, 54, 80, 79, 82, 96, 63, 85, 72, 70

SOLUTION

a Arranging the 11 values in ascending order, we have:

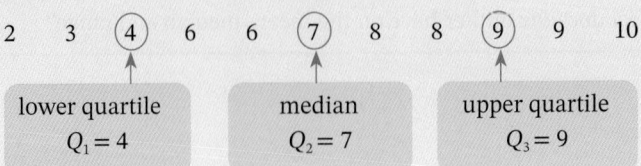

2   3   ④   6   6   ⑦   8   8   ⑨   9   10

lower quartile $Q_1 = 4$ median $Q_2 = 7$ upper quartile $Q_3 = 9$

Q_2 (median) = 7

Q_1 (lower quartile) = 4   The middle of the 5 values below 7.

Q_3 (upper quartile) = 9   The middle of the 5 values above 7.

b Arranging the 13 values in ascending order, we have:

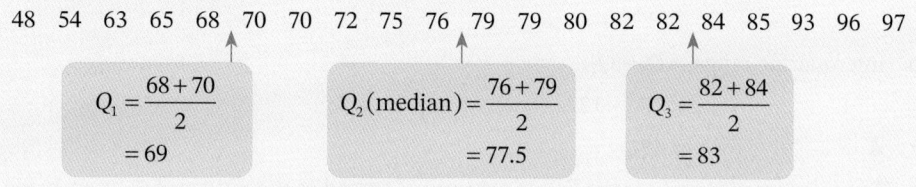

7   9   11   13   14   15   (15)   16   16   18   19   20   23

$$Q_1 = \frac{11+13}{2} = 12$$ $$Q_2 = 15$$ $$Q_3 = \frac{18+19}{2} = 18.5$$

c Arranging the 20 values in ascending order, we have:

48 54 63 65 68 70 70 72 75 76 79 79 80 82 82 84 85 93 96 97

$$Q_1 = \frac{68+70}{2} = 69$$ $$Q_2\,(\text{median}) = \frac{76+79}{2} = 77.5$$ $$Q_3 = \frac{82+84}{2} = 83$$

The interquartile range

The **range** is a **measure of spread** because it gives an indication of how widely the values are spread in a set of data. Another measure of spread is the interquartile range.

The **interquartile range** is the difference between the upper and lower quartiles and so it is the range of the middle 50% of the data.

Videos
Interquartile range 1

Interquartile range 2

ⓘ Interquartile range

Interquartile range (IQR) = upper quartile – lower quartile
$$= Q_3 - Q_1$$

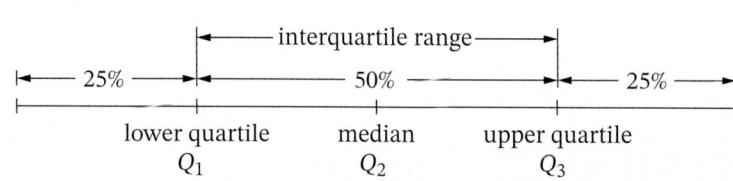

The interquartile range takes into account the middle 50% of values and ignores very low or very high values (**outliers**), so sometimes it is better to use than the range as a measure of spread.

Example 2

The number of runs scored by the Brisbane Heat Twenty20 cricket team per match during one season were:

76, 143, 127, 176, 142, 116, 137, 104, 161, 174, 149, 154, 180, 137, 175

a Find the range.

b Find the interquartile range.

c Which is the better measure of spread of the points scored by the team – the range or interquartile range?

First arrange the scores in order:

76   104   116   (127)   137   137   142   (143)   149   154   161   (174)   175   176   180

	lower quartile	median	upper quartile
	$Q_1 = 127$	$Q_2 = 143$	$Q_3 = 174$

a   range = 180 – 76   range = largest value – smallest value

= 104

b   interquartile range = $Q_3 - Q_1$

= 174 – 127

= 47

c   The interquartile range is the better measure of spread as the outlier of 76 is excluded. The score of 76 has affected the range, making it very big.

Example 3

Find the interquartile range of each data set.

a

```
              •
              •
              •
              •
        •     •     •
  •  •  •  •  •  •        •
 ┌──┬──┬──┬──┬──┬──┬──┬──→
  5  6  7  8  9 10 11 12
```

b

Stem	Leaf
1	2 7
2	0 3 4 4 5
3	1 2 2 4 6 8 8 9
4	0 1 3 7
5	1 2

Key: 1|2 = 12

a   There are 18 values, so the median is 'between' the 9th and 10th values, which are both 9s (see diagram).

$$\text{median} = Q_2 = \frac{9+9}{2} = 9$$

Q_1 is the median of the bottom half of 9 values (the 5th value). $Q_1 = 7$

Q_3 is the median of the top half of values (the 14th value). $Q_3 = 9$

$\therefore$ IQR = 9 – 7

= 2

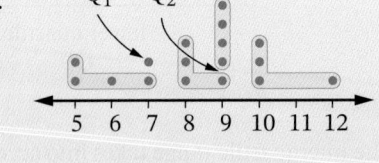

b   There are 21 values, so the median is the 11th value (see diagram).

$Q_2 = 34$

$$\text{lower quartile} = Q_1 = \frac{24+24}{2} = 24$$

$$\text{upper quartile} = Q_3 = \frac{40+41}{2} = 40.5$$

$\therefore$ IQR = 40.5 – 24

= 16.5

Stem	Leaf	
1	2 7	—Q_1 between 5th-6th values
2	0 3 4 4 5	
3	1 2 2 ④ 6 8 8 9	
4	0 1 3 7	—Q_2 11th value
5	1 2	—Q_3 between 16th-17th values

Quartiles and interquartile range   Ⓤ Ⓕ

1 Find the quartiles for each set of data.

EXAMPLE 1

   a   3, 7, 9, 5, 5, 6, 2, 8, 9, 7

   b   15, 19, 18, 12, 20, 34, 28, 18, 28, 20, 23, 25

   c   34, 45, 32, 38, 29, 40, 37, 33, 35, 30, 34, 35, 38, 37, 38, 31, 30, 34

2 Calculate the range and the interquartile range of each data set in question **1**.

EXAMPLE 2

3 Calculate the interquartile range for each set of data below.

   a   5, 6, 6, 7, 8, 9, 9, 10, 14, 14, 15, 16

   b   2, 0, 3, 5, 2, 1, 0, 6, 4, 3, 8, 4, 2

4 The monthly rainfall figures in mm for Adelaide in one particular year were:

31, 174, 288, 89, 15, 123, 26, 5, 8, 275, 38, 58

For this data, find:

   a   the range

   b   the interquartile range

5 Find the interquartile range for each set of data.

EXAMPLE 3

   a

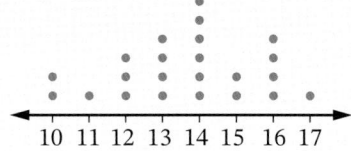

   b

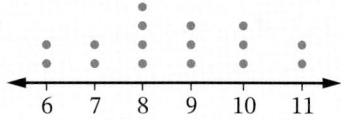

   c

Stem	Leaf
3	2 7
4	0 3 0 5
5	2 4 5 6 7 8 8
6	3 4 7
7	2

Key: 3|2 = 32

   d

Stem	Leaf
1	3 5 8 9
2	0 1 3 3 4 5 6
3	5 8 9 9
4	1 3
5	4

Key: 1|3 = 13

   e

Stem	Leaf
10	3 5 5 6 6
11	0 1 2
12	3 4 6 7 8
13	4 7
14	1

Key: 10|3 = 103

   f

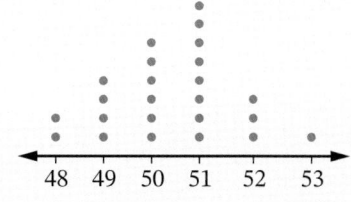

▷

☐ Foundation ◯ Standard ◇ Complex

6 The pulse rates for a group of students are as follows.

82, 81, 72, 58, 79, 77, 62, 66, 92, 78, 80, 67, 91, 75, 72, 68

a Find the range.

b Find the interquartile range.

c **i** List the values that lie between the lower and upper quartiles.

    ii What percentage of values lie between Q_1 and Q_3?

d What percentage of values lie above the lower quartile?

7 The number of points per game scored by a basketball team during one season were:

55, 35, 49, 53, 51, 55, 42, 48, 63, 43, 48, 48, 62

a Find:

    i the range   **ii** the interquartile range.

b Which is the better measure of spread?

c List the values that lie between Q_1 and Q_3. What percentage of the values is this?

5.02 Boxplots

A **boxplot** (or **box-and-whisker plot**) displays the quartiles of a set of data and the lowest and highest values (lower and upper extremes).

Videos
Box-and-whisker plots

Statistics

Worksheet
Five-number summaries

Puzzle
Mode, median and mean

Technology
Five-number summary

Spreadsheet
Five-number summary

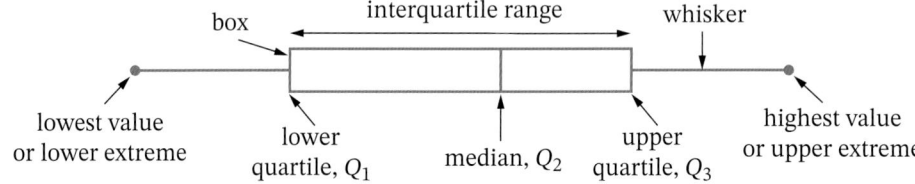

The 'box' represents the middle 50% of values and the interquartile range, while the 'whiskers' represent the lowest and highest 25% of values.

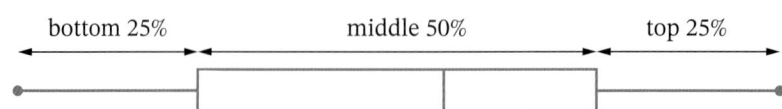

ⓘ Five-number summary

A boxplot gives a **five-number summary** of a data set, which includes:

- the lower extreme (or lowest value)
- the lower quartile, Q_1
- the median, Q_2
- the upper quartile, Q_3
- the upper extreme (or highest value).

Example 4

The number of hours per week Colette worked at Big Chicken in summer were:

5, 5, 4, 8, 10, 3, 12, 7, 7, 3, 8, 8, 15

a Find a five-number summary for this data.

b Represent this data on a boxplot.

iStock.com/YinYang

SOLUTION

a First arrange the values in order.

$$3 \quad 3 \quad 4 \quad \underset{\uparrow}{5} \quad 5 \quad 7 \quad ⑦ \quad 8 \quad 8 \quad 8 \quad \underset{\uparrow}{10} \quad 12 \quad 15$$

$$Q_1 \qquad\qquad \text{median } Q_2 \qquad\qquad Q_3$$

lowest value = 3

$Q_1 = \dfrac{4+5}{2} = 4.5$, $Q_3 = \dfrac{8+10}{2} = 9$

median = 7, highest value = 15

b

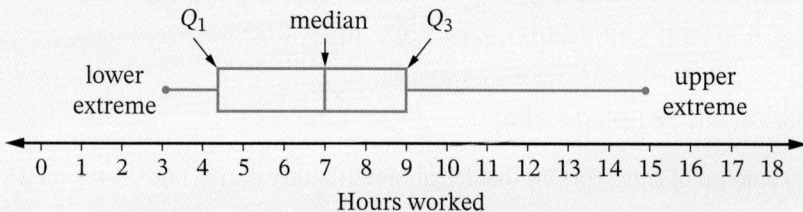

Example 5

The boxplot represents the results of 80 students in a science test.

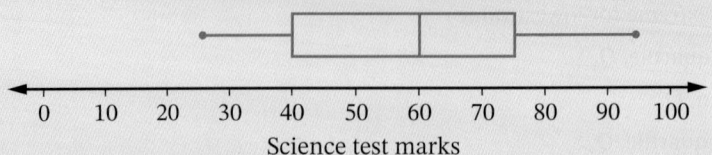

Science test marks

a   Find the range of the test results.

b   Find the median test value.

c   What is the interquartile range?

d   How many students had a test mark between:

   i   25 and 75?   ii   40 and 60?

e   What percentage of students scored more than 75?

SOLUTION

a   range = highest value – lowest value
       $= 95 - 25$
       $= 70$

b   median = 60

c   interquartile range = 75 – 40
       $= 35$

d   i   25 is the lowest value and 75 is Q_3,
       so $75\% \times 80 = 60$ students had a mark
       between 25 and 75.

   ii   40 is Q_1 and 60 is the median,
       so $25\% \times 80 = 20$ students had a mark
       between 40 and 60.

e   75 is Q_3, so $25\% \times 80 = 20$ students scored more than 75.

EXERCISE (5.02) ANSWERS ON P. 614

Boxplots   U F R C

1 The number of orders taken per hour at Bernoulli's Pizza on a weekend were:

3, 5, 1, 2, 4, 6, 8, 10, 7, 6, 12, 15, 10, 3, 5, 18, 5, 8, 9, 10

a   Find the five-number summary for this data.

b   Represent this data on a boxplot.

2 The daily amount of snow (in cm) that fell at Mount Buller during one ski season was:

2, 5, 5, 2, 5, 7, 1, 2, 2, 2, 2, 2, 12, 20, 12, 5, 40, 50, 10, 40, 13, 30, 5, 35, 2, 6

a   On how many days did it snow?

b   Find the five-number summary for this data.

c   Represent this data on a boxplot.

◻ Foundation   ○ Standard   ○ Complex

3 The monthly rainfall figures for Margaret River one year were:

98, 266, 149, 94, 15, 65, 19, 5, 24, 34, 67, 28

   a Find the range.

   b Find the five-number summary.

   c Represent the data on a boxplot.

5.02

4 This boxplot represents the number of hours worked in one week by the staff at a supermarket.

EXAMPLE
5

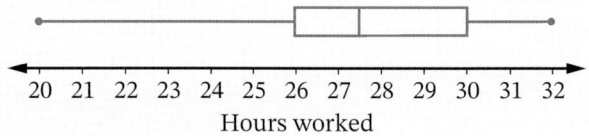

                                Hours worked

   a What is the median number of hours worked?

   b What is the lower quartile?

   c What is the upper quartile?

   d Find the interquartile range.

   e Estimate the percentage of staff who worked between 26 and 30 hours.

5 The ages of 16 people waiting at a bus stop are displayed in this boxplot.

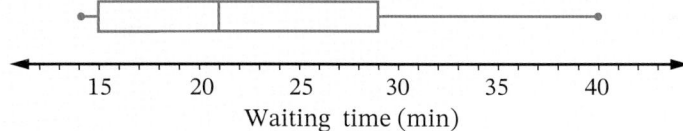

                           Waiting time (min)

   a What is the range?

   b What is the median age?

   c Find the interquartile range.

   d What percentage of people were aged from:

      i 21 to 29?   **ii** 15 to 40?

6 The boxplot shows the number of points per game scored by Ben in 28 basketball games during the season.

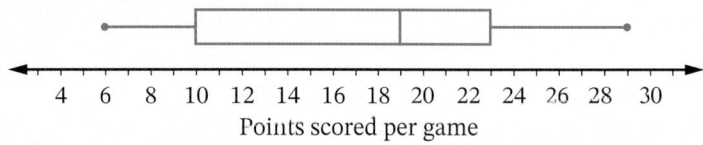

                           Points scored per game

   a What is the five-number summary for the boxplot?

   b Find the interquartile range.

   c In how many games did Ben score:

      i more than 19 points?   **ii** between 19 and 23 points?

      iii less than 10 points?   **iv** at least 10 points?

□ Foundation ○ Standard ○ Complex

▷

7 For each set of data, find the five-number summary and draw a boxplot.

a

Stem	Leaf
2	0 2 3 5
3	3 7
4	4 6 7 8 8 9 9
5	0 1 1 5 6
6	0 3 3 8 8
7	2 5 6
8	5 5 7 8

Key: 2|0 = 20

b

Stem	Leaf
3	0 7
4	2 6 6
5	1 2 5 9
6	0 4 7 7 9
7	2 3 5 6 8
8	3 4
9	5

Key: 3|0 = 30

c

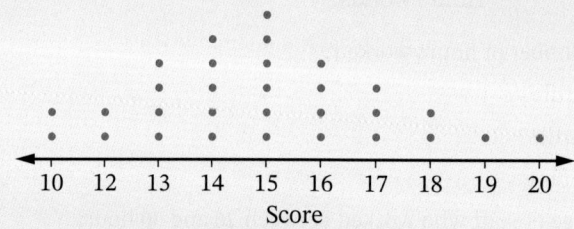

8 The results of a general knowledge quiz (out of 15) taken by Year 10 students are

(R)
(C)
displayed in the dot plot.

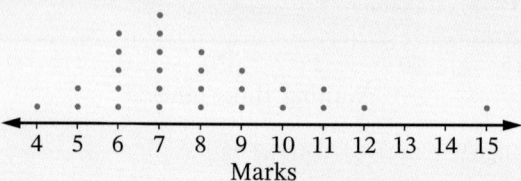

a Find the five-number summary for the dot plot and then draw a boxplot.

b Describe the shape of the dot plot and compare it to the shape of the boxplot.

c What is the outlier?

d Find the five-number summary for the data in the dot plot without the outlier and draw a boxplot.

e Compare the 2 boxplots. How are they:

i similar? **ii** different?

TECHNOLOGY

Boxplots

Use graphing software or a spreadsheet to draw boxplots.

1   Enter this set of data: 3, 3, 4, 4, 5, 6, 7, 7, 7, 8, 12

2   Choose appropriate settings for the scale on your boxplot.

3   Your boxplot should look similar to the one below.

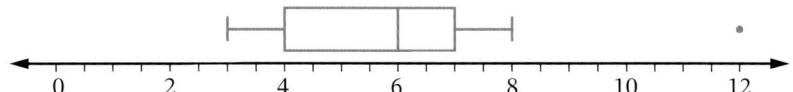

4   Write down the five-number summary for this data set.

5   Now enter the marks of an English exam completed by 2 classes, 10A and 10B, and create a boxplot for each class:

    10A: 21, 81, 33, 58, 67, 76, 64, 74, 56, 60, 54, 74, 49, 83, 66

    10B: 77, 63, 63, 35, 51, 42, 54, 55, 71, 43, 41, 41, 40, 76, 72

6   Complete the five-number summary for each class.

7   What is the IQR for each class?

8   Which class had the highest mark?

9   Which class had the lowest mark?

10 Which class performed better? Give reasons for your answer, including explanations using the five-number summaries you found in step **6**.

Parallel boxplots

Parallel box-and-whisker plots can be used to compare 2 or more sets of data. They are drawn on the same scale, but above each other.

Video
Double boxplots

Worksheets
Box-and-whisker plots

Data 1

Presentation
Analysing data

Example 6

Two sprinters run the following times (in seconds) over 100 metres.

Sam: 10.9, 10.5, 11.0, 9.9, 10.7, 10.5, 10.0, 11.2, 11.5, 10.3

Jesse: 11.0, 11.4, 10.1, 9.8, 10.8, 11.4, 10.7, 10.3, 11.1, 11.6

a   Find the five-number summary for each sprinter.

b   Draw parallel boxplots to display the data for both sprinters.

c   Find the interquartile range for each sprinter.

d   Find the range for each sprinter.

e   Which sprinter is more consistent? Justify your answer.

SOLUTION

a   Sam: 9.9   10.0   (10.3)   10.5   10.5   10.7   10.9   (11.0)   11.2   11.5

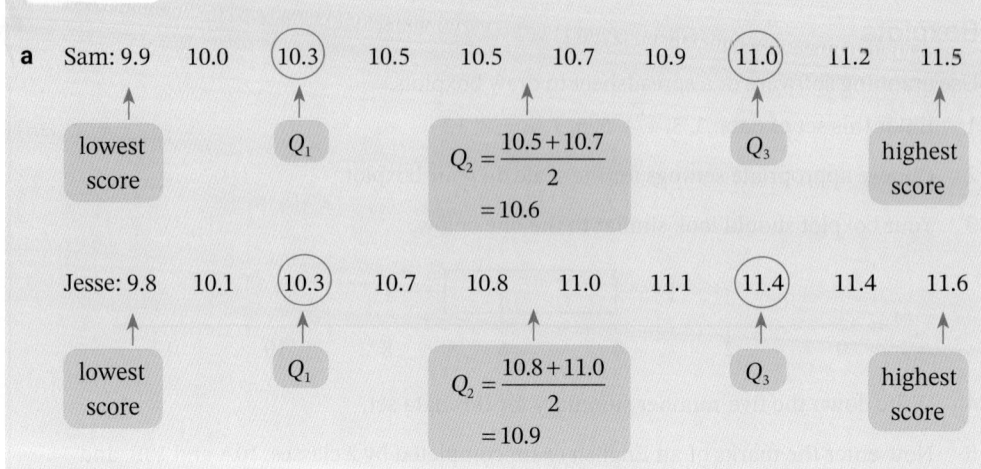

lowest score · Q_1 · $Q_2 = \dfrac{10.5+10.7}{2} = 10.6$ · Q_3 · highest score

Jesse: 9.8   10.1   (10.3)   10.7   10.8   11.0   11.1   (11.4)   11.4   11.6

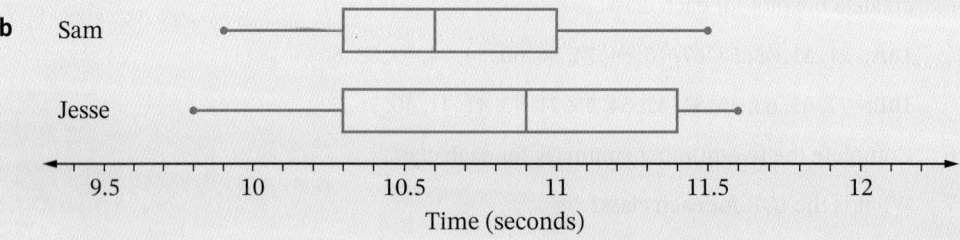

lowest score · Q_1 · $Q_2 = \dfrac{10.8+11.0}{2} = 10.9$ · Q_3 · highest score

b

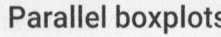

Sam

Jesse

Time (seconds)

c   interquartile range for Sam = 11.0 − 10.3 = 0.7 seconds

interquartile range for Jesse = 11.4 − 10.3 = 1.1 seconds

d   range for Sam = 11.5 − 9.9 = 1.6 seconds

range for Jesse = 11.6 − 9.8 = 1.8 seconds

e   Sam is the more consistent sprinter, since both the range and interquartile range of his times are lower than those of Jesse.

EXERCISE 5.03 ANSWERS ON P. 614

Parallel boxplots   U F R C

1 The parallel boxplots show the number of hours of sleep that Year 8 and Year 10 students usually have on a school night.

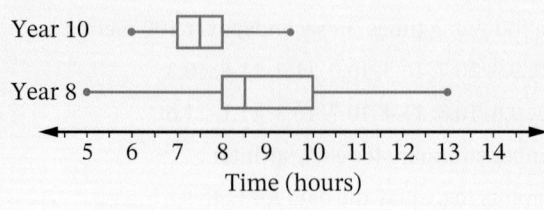

Year 10

Year 8

5 6 7 8 9 10 11 12 13 14
Time (hours)

a   For each Year group, find:

    i   the range   **ii**   the median   **iii**   the interquartile range.

b   What percentage of students usually had at most 8 hours of sleep on a school night in:

    i   Year 8?   **ii**   Year 10?

c   Forty students in both Year 8 and Year 10 were surveyed. How many students usually had at least 10 hours of sleep in:

    i   Year 8?   **ii**   Year 10?

2 The number of points scored per match by the Adelaide Thunderbirds and the NSW Swifts netball teams during a season are shown in the parallel boxplot.

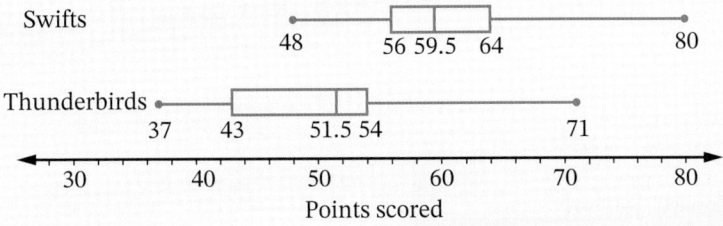

a   Find the range of points scored by:

    i   the NSW Swifts

    ii   the Adelaide Thunderbirds.

b   What is the median number of points scored for each team?

c   Find the interquartile range for each team.

d   Which team is more consistent?

e   Which team performed better? Give reasons.

Getty Images/Matt King

3 The boxplots show the test results of students from 2 different classes.

a   Find the range of marks for each class.

b   Find the median mark for each class.

c   Find the interquartile range for each class.

d   Which class is more consistent?

e   Find the percentage of students who scored 6 or more in 10K.

4 In a Year 10 class of 28 students, the marks for History and Geography tests were displayed using a double boxplot.

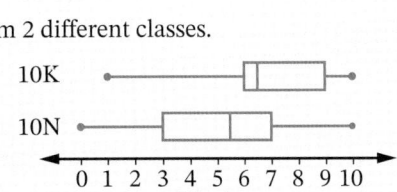

Which statement below could be true? Select the correct answer **A**, **B**, **C** or **D**.

A In Geography, more students scored between 60 and 75 than between 55 and 60.

B 14 students scored the same or more in History than the median mark in Geography.

C More students scored 60 or more in History than they did in Geography.

D The interquartile range for Geography is 5 less than the interquartile range for History.

5 The monthly mean maximum temperatures for the 4 eastern state capitals are shown in
the boxplots.

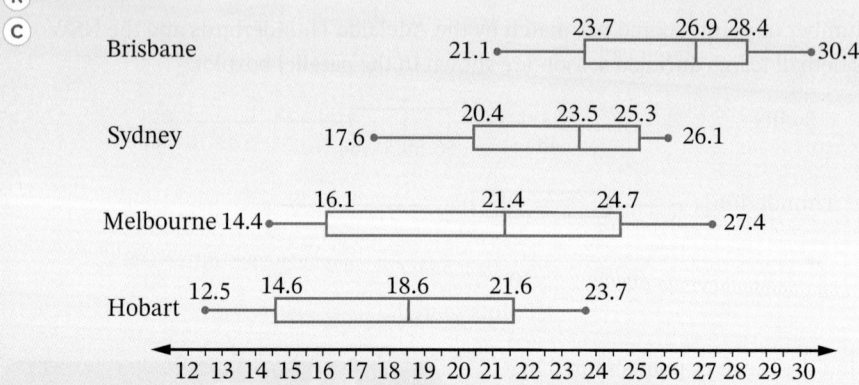

a Find the median, range and interquartile range for each city.

b Which capital city had the most spread in temperature?

c Which capital city had the highest mean monthly temperatures? Justify your answer.

d Which city is warmer – Sydney or Melbourne? Give reasons.

e Which city has consistent temperatures – Sydney or Melbourne? Give reasons.

6 The number of text messages received by a group of students in one hour are as follows.

Male: 2, 0, 3, 0, 1, 2, 5, 6, 2, 1, 3, 2, 3, 7, 4

Female: 4, 5, 6, 3, 7, 5, 8, 7,4, 2, 4, 5, 10, 4, 3

a Find the five-number summary for each gender.

b Draw parallel box-and-whisker plots to display the data.

c Find the interquartile range for each gender.

d Find the range for each gender.

e Compare the number of text messages that males and females receive. Are there any
significant differences between the spread of the 2 sets of data?

7 Students in a PE class had their heights measured (in cm).

Male: 174, 167, 164, 175, 189, 145, 165, 166, 165, 167, 171, 169

Female: 163, 155, 171, 162, 165, 183, 172, 175, 166, 163, 150, 186

a Find the five-number summary for each group and draw a parallel boxplot to display
the data.

b Find the range and interquartile range for each group.

c How does the spread of heights of male students compare with the spread of heights
of female students?

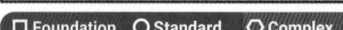

8 Students at a university were asked whether their frequency of exercise was high or low and then had their pulse taken.

(R) (C)

Low: 90, 78, 80, 84, 70, 66, 92, 80, 80, 77, 64, 88

High: 96, 71, 68, 56, 64, 60, 50, 76, 78, 49, 68, 74

    a Find the five-number summary for each group and then draw parallel boxplots to show the information.

    b Find the range and interquartile range for each group.

    c Compare the spread between the 2 groups. Are there significant differences between them?

    d Which group had the lower pulse rates?

9 The average maximum monthly temperatures (in °C) for Hobart and Darwin are shown.

(R) (C)

Hobart: 22.7, 22.3, 20.9, 18.2, 15.3, 13.0, 12.5, 13.5, 15.4, 17.4, 19.1, 20.8

Darwin: 31.8, 31.5, 32.0, 32.7, 32.1, 30.7, 30.6, 31.4, 32.6, 33.3, 33.3, 32.7

Source: Bureau of Meteorology

    a Find the five-number summary for each city and draw a parallel boxplot.

    b Find the range and interquartile range for each city.

    c Which city had more consistent average maximum monthly temperatures? Give reasons.

10 These boxplots show the numbers of points scored by 2 basketball players during the season.

(R) (C)

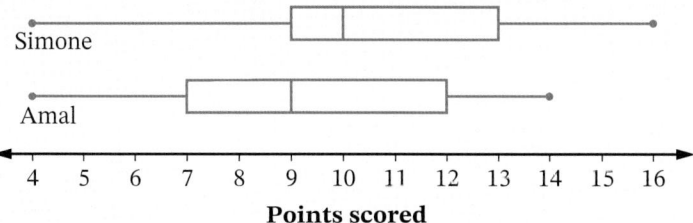

    a Which player has the most points scored for a single game?

    b What is the range of the points scored by each player?

    c By just looking at the range, which player would seem to be more consistent? Justify your answer.

    d Find the median score of each player.

    e Find the interquartile range for each player.

    f Which player is more consistent?

    g Estimate the percentage of games in which Simone scored 9 or 10 points.

    h Estimate the percentage of games in which Amal scored more than 12 points.

☐ Foundation   ○ Standard   ○ Complex

Videos
Cumulative
frequency
and the
median

Cumulative
frequency:
You're fired

The **cumulative frequency** of a data value is the sum of the frequencies of all data values less than or equal to that value.

Example 7

The marks of Year 10 students in a Maths quiz (out of 10) are shown in the frequency table.

Mark (x)	Frequency (f)
4	12
5	26
6	39
7	18
8	10
9	5

a How many Year 10 students were there?

b Copy the table and then add a column to the table to record the cumulative frequency. Complete the cumulative frequency for the table.

c How many students scored 5 or less?

d Use the cumulative frequency to find the median.

SOLUTION

a The sum of the Frequency column is 110.

There were 110 Year 10 students.

b The cumulative frequency column is a running total of the frequencies.

$12 + 26 = 38$

$38 + 39 = 77$, etc.

The last value in the cumulative frequency column should match the sum of the Frequency column (110).

Mark (x)	Frequency (f)	Cumulative frequency (cf)
4	12	12
5	26	38
6	39	77
7	18	95
8	10	105
9	5	110
	$\Sigma f = 110$	

c Using the cumulative frequency column, there were 38 students who scored 5 or less.

Σf is the sum of the frequency column; that is, the total number of values.

d There are 110 values (marks), so the 2 middle values are the 55th and 56th values. Using the cumulative frequency column, the 38th value is the last 5 and the 77th value is the last 6, so the 55th and 56th scores must both be 6s.

$$\text{median} = \frac{6+6}{2} = 6$$

Example 8

a Find the lower and upper quartiles of the data in Example 7 above and, hence, write the five-number summary for this set of data.

b Display the data in a boxplot.

> SOLUTION

a From the table in Example 7, there are 110 values (marks), so the 2 middle values are the 55th and 56th values, which are both 6s, so the median is 6.

The lower quartile is the middle of the lower half. There are 55 values in the lower half, so the middle value is the 28th value. Using the cumulative frequency column, the 28th value is 5 so $Q_1 = 5$.

The upper quartile is the middle of the upper half. This is the $55 + 28 = 83$rd value. Using the cumulative frequency column, the 83rd value is 7 so $Q_3 = 7$.

lowest value = 4, highest value = 9
The five-number summary is 4, 5, 6, 7, 9.

b

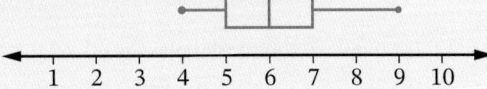

Class intervals for grouped data

A data set can sometimes have a large range depending on the variable being collected. For example, the heights of 28 students in a class could take on many different values making the interpretation and graphing quite complex. To overcome this problem, the heights of students could be grouped together into class intervals, which we have learned in Year 9.

When graphing grouped data on a frequency histogram or polygon, we use the centres of the class intervals on the horizontal axis.

Example 9

The percentage marks that 50 students scored for a History examination are shown.

60	56	86	34	67	70	14	59	72	89
37	75	48	64	72	61	53	48	57	68
19	34	96	66	84	90	71	66	37	26
48	29	78	63	59	54	68	74	81	69
45	63	67	74	68	54	44	38	57	65

a Sort this data into a frequency table using class intervals (0–9, 10–19, 20–29 ...), identify the class centres and complete a cumulative frequency column.

b Find the modal class and median class for this data set.

a The lowest mark is 19 and the highest is 90 so the class intervals should start with 10–19 and end at 90–99.

The half-way 'centre' value of the group 10–19 is $\frac{10+19}{2} = 14.5$. Do the same for the other intervals.

Class interval	Class centre	Frequency (f)	Cumulative frequency (cf)
10–19	14.5	2	2
20–29	24.5	2	4
30–39	34.5	5	9
40–49	44.5	5	14
50–59	54.5	8	22
60–69	64.5	14	36
70–79	74.5	8	44
80–89	84.5	4	48
90–99	94.5	2	50

b The interval with the highest frequency, 14, is 60–69. ∴ the modal class is 60–69.

There are 50 data values so the median class is the one that contains the 25th and 26th values. ∴ the median class is 60–69.

EXERCISE 5.04 ANSWERS ON P. 615

Cumulative frequency and quartiles Ⓤ Ⓕ

1 Copy and complete each frequency table, then use the cumulative frequency column to find the median.

a

Quiz score	Frequency (f)	Cumulative frequency (cf)
2	2	
3	1	
4	3	
5	4	
6	5	
7	8	
8	2	
9	2	
10	1	
	$\Sigma f =$	

b

Age	Frequency (f)	Cumulative frequency (cf)
12	13	
13	23	
14	19	
15	22	
16	15	
17	8	
	$\Sigma f =$	

c

Score	Frequency (f)	Cumulative frequency (cf)
93	15	
94	32	
95	28	
96	20	
97	18	
98	10	
99	2	
	$\Sigma f =$	

d

Number of siblings	Frequency (f)	Cumulative frequency (cf)
0	3	
1	9	
2	12	
3	5	
4	3	
5	2	
6	1	
	$\Sigma f =$	

e

Books read	Frequency (f)	Cumulative frequency (cf)
19	20	
20	18	
21	34	
22	24	
23	25	
24	18	
25	12	
26	9	
	$\Sigma f =$	

f

Number of pets	Frequency (f)	Cumulative frequency (cf)
0	13	
1	32	
2	8	
3	2	
4	1	
	$\Sigma f =$	

2 Determine the five-number summary for each data set in question **1** above.

EXAMPLE
8

3 A group of women were asked in a survey how many handbags they owned.

a How many women were surveyed?

b How many women owned 5 or fewer handbags?

c How many women owned 5 or more handbags?

d Display this data on a boxplot.

Number of handbags	Frequency (f)
2	1
3	1
4	4
5	3
6	5
7	7
8	8
9	6
10	5
	$\Sigma f =$

☐ Foundation ○ Standard ○ Complex

4 The finishing times of the competitors in a fun run are shown in this frequency table.

Time (mins)	12	13	14	15	16	17	18	19	20	21	22	23	24	25
Frequency	113	120	105	73	85	140	155	132	164	196	105	110	64	32

  a How many competitors were there?

  b How many competitors finished in 20 minutes or less?

  c Find the interquartile range.

  d Display this data on a boxplot.

5 Find the class centre for each class interval.

  a 5–13   **b** 11–20   **c** 55–60   **d** 24–35

EXAMPLE 9

6 The following results are the marks achieved by students in a Science exam.

71	65	95	70	52	33	87	72	69	76
52	73	62	47	56	63	73	53	41	48
47	68	58	87	68	71	76	70	60	67

  a Sort this data into a frequency table using class intervals (30–39, 40–49, 50–59 ...) and identify the class centres.

  b Add and complete a cumulative frequency column to the table.

  c What is the range of results for this test?

  d What is the median class?

7 The heights (in centimetres) of 50 students were measured.

139	163	142	155	173	138	174	168	155	147
147	181	177	164	168	176	184	180	171	163
163	147	158	150	146	159	170	163	166	154
168	152	158	164	175	163	177	170	150	156
183	174	163	157	159	162	172	167	178	161

  a Sort this data into a frequency table using class intervals (131–140, 141–150, 151–160 ...), identify the class centres and complete a cumulative frequency column.

  b Find the modal class and the median class for this data set.

8 The daily maximum temperature (in °C) in Yeppoon was recorded over a period of 30 days.

23.7	24.2	22.8	23.9	22.4	23.1	24.6	25.7	26.2	25.5
24.7	25.3	23.9	24.6	25.1	24.9	23.8	24.6	25.3	24.8
26.4	25.5	25.0	22.9	23.4	24.8	23.6	24.0	25.7	26.0

  a Sort this data into a frequency table using class intervals (22.0–22.4, 22.5–22.9, 23.0–23.4, 23.5–23.9 ...), identify the class centres and complete a cumulative frequency column.

  b What is the modal class for this data set?

☐ Foundation   ○ Standard   ○ Complex

9 This histogram shows the time taken, to the nearest hour, for hikers to complete a bushwalk. Complete a frequency table with a cumulative frequency column, then construct a boxplot to represent this data.

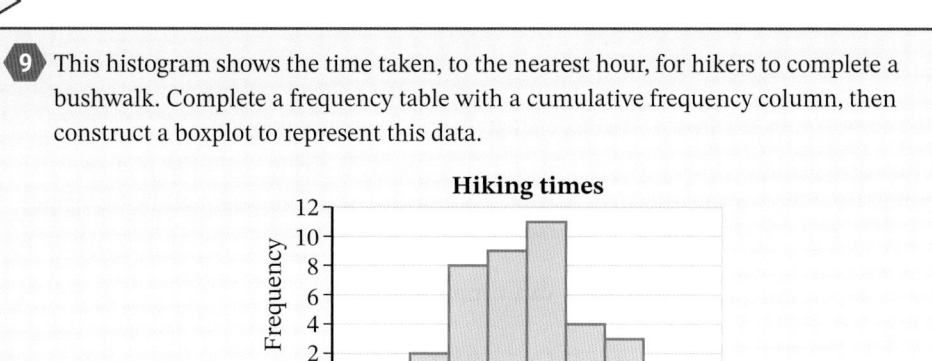

Cumulative frequency histograms and polygons

We learned about frequency histograms and polygons in Year 9.

A **frequency histogram** is a column graph of numerical data where the columns stand together without gaps between them.

A **frequency polygon** is a line graph that is constructed by joining the midpoints of the tops of the columns of a frequency histogram, starting and ending on the horizontal axis. It is called a 'polygon' because the graph and the horizontal axis together make a shape with straight sides.

Example 10

Construct a frequency histogram and a frequency polygon on the same set of axes for this data from Example 9.

Class interval	Class centre	Frequency (f)
10–19	14.5	2
20–29	24.5	2
30–39	34.5	5
40–49	44.5	5
50–59	54.5	8
60–69	64.5	14
70–79	74.5	8
80–89	84.5	4
90–99	94.5	2

□ Foundation ○ Standard ○ Complex

SOLUTION

Use the class centres to construct both a histogram and frequency polygon.

Note that each column of the histogram is centred on each class centre marked on the horizontal axis. There also needs to be a 'blank column' to the left and right of the histogram so that the polygon can be brought down to join the horizontal axis.

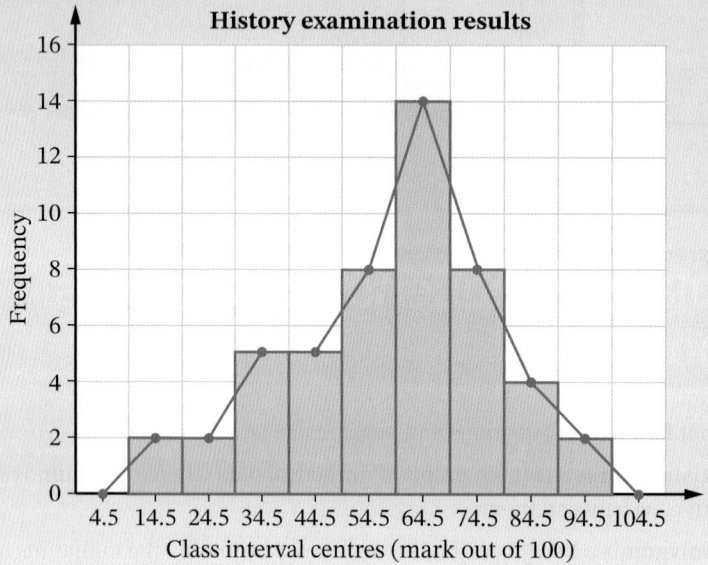

A **cumulative frequency histogram** and a **cumulative frequency polygon** is a special histogram and polygon of the cumulative frequency of a data set. However, with a **cumulative frequency polygon** (also called an **ogive** (pronounced 'oh-jive')), the line graph is drawn *inside* the columns of the histogram, joining their top right corners instead of their midpoints.

Example 11

The ages of the players in a junior soccer competition are shown in this frequency table.

Age	Frequency (f)
4	3
5	5
6	2
7	6
8	4
9	3
10	1

Construct a cumulative frequency histogram and polygon for this data.

SOLUTION

Age	Frequency (f)	Cumulative frequency (cf)
4	3	3
5	5	8
6	2	10
7	6	16
8	4	20
9	3	23
10	1	24

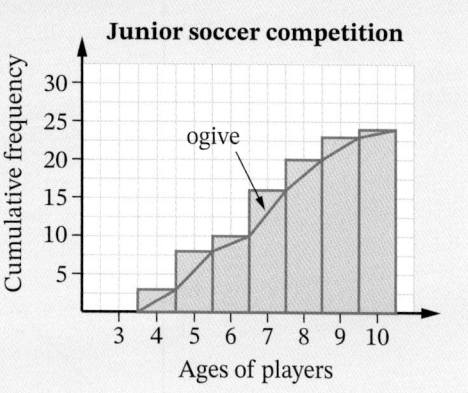

Junior soccer competition

Unlike frequency histograms and polygons, *cumulative frequency* histograms and polygons are graphs that are always increasing. Can you see why?

Example 12

Construct a cumulative frequency histogram and ogive for the data from Example 10.

Class interval	Class centre	Frequency (f)
10–19	14.5	2
20–29	24.5	2
30–39	34.5	5
40–49	44.5	5
50–59	54.5	8
60–69	64.5	14
70–79	74.5	8
80–89	84.5	4
90–99	94.5	2

SOLUTION

Class interval	Class centre (x)	Frequency (f)	Cumulative frequency (cf)
10–19	14.5	2	2
20–29	24.5	2	4
30–39	34.5	5	9
40–49	44.5	5	14
50–59	54.5	8	22
60–69	64.5	14	36
70–79	74.5	8	44
80–89	84.5	4	48
90–99	94.5	2	50
		$\Sigma f = 50$	

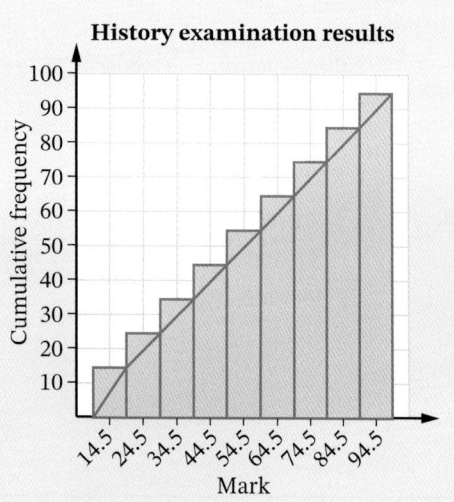

History examination results

This graph can also be displayed with the class intervals shown instead of the class centres.

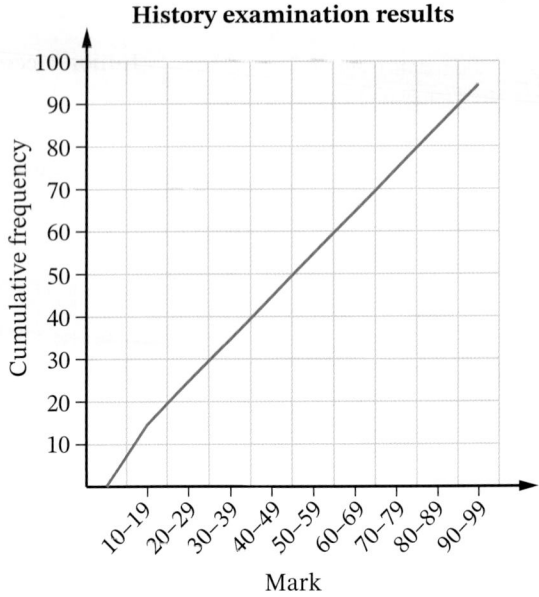

History examination results

EXERCISE 5.05 ANSWERS ON P. 617

Cumulative frequency histograms and polygons ⓤ ⓕ ⓡ ⓒ

EXAMPLE 10

1 Find the class centres for the class intervals of each frequency table, then construct a frequency histogram and a frequency polygon for each set of data.

a

Class interval	Frequency
6–10	3
11–15	7
16–20	13
20–25	12
26–30	5

b

Class interval	Frequency
15–24	6
25–34	9
35–44	22
45–54	18
55–64	20
65–74	14
75–84	11

c

Class interval	Frequency
31–45	4
46–60	7
61–75	12
76–90	9
91–105	15
106–120	13

d

Class interval	Frequency
10–13	6
14–17	4
18–21	9
22–25	2
26–29	4
30–33	6
34–37	11
38–41	8
42–45	4
46–49	6

☐ Foundation ○ Standard ○ Complex

2 Construct a cumulative frequency histogram and polygon for each set of data. You can refer to your answers to question **1** of Exercise 5.04 on pages 186–187.

EXAMPLE 11
5.05

a

Quiz score	Frequency (f)	Cumulative frequency (cf)
2	2	
3	1	
4	3	
5	4	
6	5	
7	8	
8	2	
9	2	
10	1	
Σf =		

b

Age	Frequency (f)	Cumulative frequency (cf)
12	13	
13	23	
14	19	
15	22	
16	15	
17	8	
Σf =		

c

Number of siblings	Frequency (f)	Cumulative frequency (cf)
0	3	
1	9	
2	12	
3	5	
4	3	
5	2	
6	1	
Σf =		

d

Number of pets	Frequency (f)	Cumulative frequency (cf)
0	13	
1	32	
2	8	
3	2	
4	1	
Σf =		

3 The heights of students in a Year 3 class were measured and grouped in this frequency table.

Construct a cumulative frequency histogram and polygon for this data set on the same set of axes.

Use the cumulative frequency polygon to estimate what the median height would be and explain your reasoning.

EXAMPLE 12

Height (cm)	Frequency
100–109	2
110 119	4
120–129	8
130–139	10
140–149	3
150–159	1

4 A fertiliser company is testing a new 'super' formula developed to help plants grow at a faster rate. The growth of seedlings over a two-week period is shown below:

Construct a cumulative frequency histogram and polygon for this data set on the same set of axes.

The average growth of seedlings over a two-week period with the use of this company's 'regular' fertiliser is 14 cm. Determine whether the company's 'super' formula is effective, providing evidence for your decision.

Growth (cm)	Frequency
5–9	2
10–14	5
15–19	9
20–24	3
25–29	8
30–34	10
35–39	6

☐ Foundation   ○ Standard   ○ Complex

5 This histogram shows the time taken, to the nearest hour, for hikers to complete a bushwalk. Construct a cumulative frequency polygon to represent this data set and then use it to estimate the interquartile range.

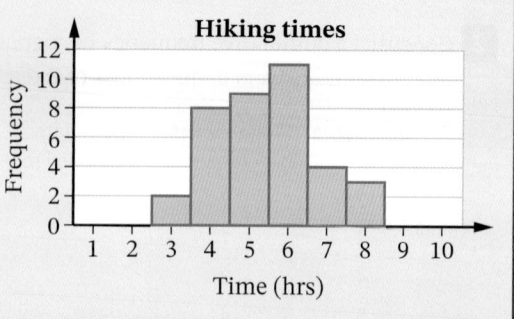

5.06 Extension: Deciles and percentiles

We already know that **quartiles** are the 3 values that divide a data set into 4 equal parts (quarters).

- Q_1 divides the lower 25% of values. $\frac{1}{4}$ of the values lie below Q_1.

- Q_2 divides the lower 50% of values, so it is also the **median**. $\frac{1}{2}$ of the values lie below Q_2.

- Q_3 divides the lower 75% of values. $\frac{1}{4}$ of the values lie below Q_3.

Deciles are the 9 values that divides a data set into 10 equal parts (tenths). For example:

- D_1 divides the lower 10% of values. $\frac{1}{10}$ of the values lie below D_1.

- D_4 divides the lower 40% of values. $\frac{4}{10}$ of the values lie below D_4.

- D_5 divides the lower 50% of values, so it is also the **median**. $\frac{1}{2}$ of the values lie below D_5.

- D_7 divides the lower 70% of values. $\frac{7}{10}$ of the values lie below D_7.

Quartiles and **deciles** are examples of **quantiles**, specific values in a sorted distribution that separate the data into equal-sized groups.

Another example of quantiles are **percentiles**, which are the 99 values that divides a data set into 100 equal parts (hundredths). For example:

- P_5 divides the lower 5% of values.

- P_{23} divides the lower 23% of values.

- P_{68} divides the lower 68% of values.

- P_{75} divides the lower 75% of values, so it is also the 3rd quartile Q_3.

$\frac{75}{100} = \frac{3}{4}$ of the values lie below P_{75}.

Special quantiles in a data set can be named in several different ways. For example, the quantile 0.5 can also be called the median, the 2nd quartile Q_2, the 5th decile D_5 or the 50th percentile P_{50}.

The values of a particular quantile can be estimated using a cumulative frequency polygon.

Example 13

A researcher collected data about the ages when a sample of dementia patients were diagnosed with the disease. The cumulative frequency polygon below illustrates the data.

a How many people first had dementia at age 65 years or younger?

b How many people first had dementia at age 80 years or older?

c Find the median.

d Find the 2nd decile, D_2.

e Find the 95th percentile, P_{95}.

f Find the interquartile range.

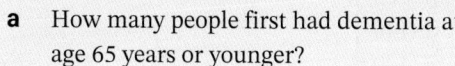

Age when dementia is diagnosed

SOLUTION

a According to the graph, when age = 65, the cumulative frequency is 40.

So, 40 people first had dementia at age 65 years or younger.

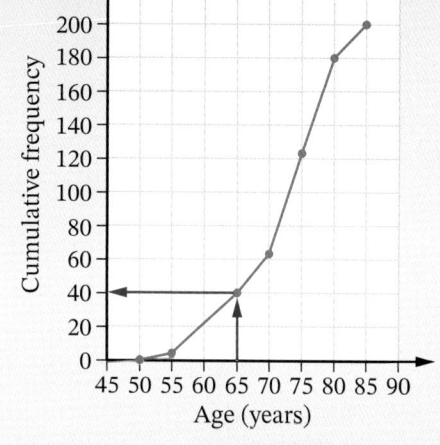

Age when dementia is diagnosed

b When age = 80, the cumulative frequency is 180.

There are 200 people overall because that is where the graph ends.

So, 200 – 180 = 20 people first had dementia at age 80 years or older.

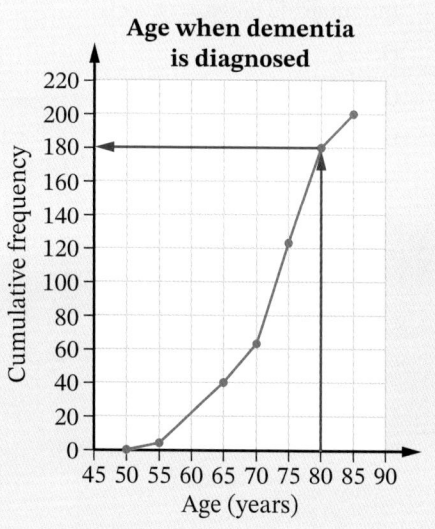

Age when dementia is diagnosed

c The median is the middle value, the 2nd quartile or the 50th percentile. The sample size is 200 so read from $\frac{1}{2} \times 200 = 100$ on the cumulative frequency axis.

median age = 73

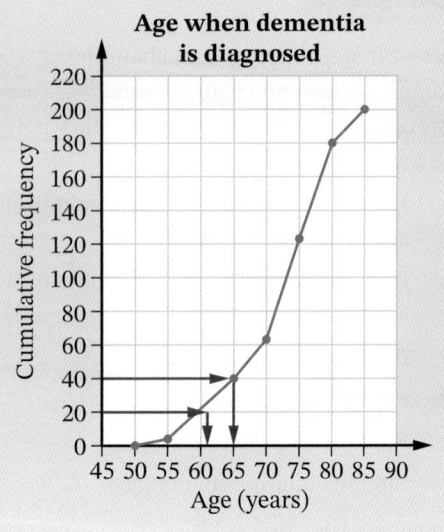

Age when dementia is diagnosed

d 1st decile, D_1:

$10\% \times 200 = 20$ on cumulative frequency axis.

1st decile, $D_1 = 61$

> This means 10% of the sample first had dementia at age 61 or before.

2nd decile, $D_2 = 65$

e 95th percentile, P_{95}:

$95\% \times 200 = 190$ on cumulative frequency axis.

$P_{95} = 83$

> This means 95% of the sample first had dementia at age 83 or before.

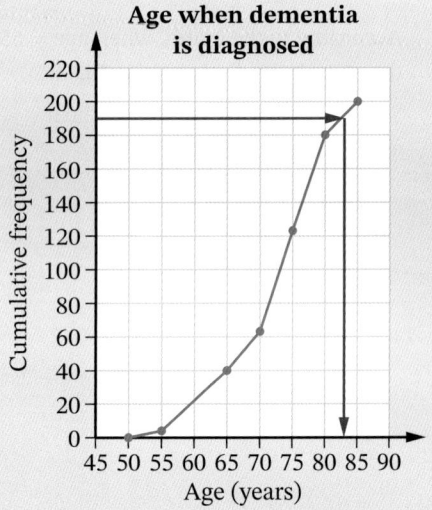

Age when dementia is diagnosed

f Interquartile range = $Q_3 - Q_1$

$Q_3 = 77$

(from $75\% \times 200 = 150$ on cf)

$Q_1 = 67$

(from $25\% \times 200 = 50$ on cf)

IQR = $77 - 67$

    = 10

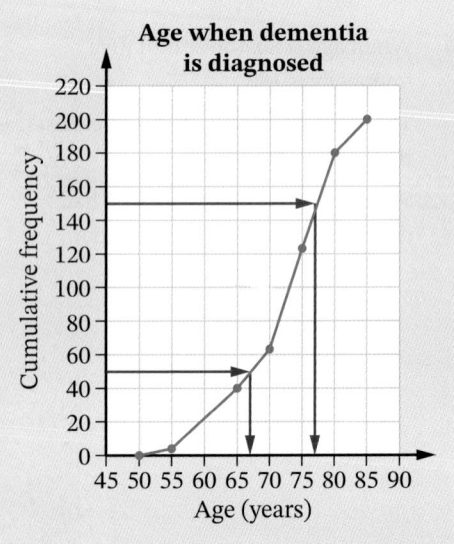

Age when dementia is diagnosed

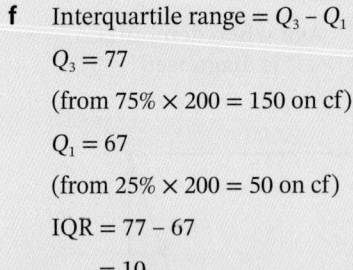

Deciles and percentiles U F R C

EXAMPLE
13

1 For each cumulative frequency polygon, find:

  i the median

  ii the interquartile range.

a

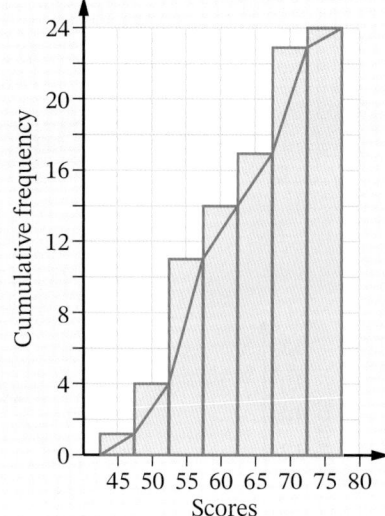

b

c

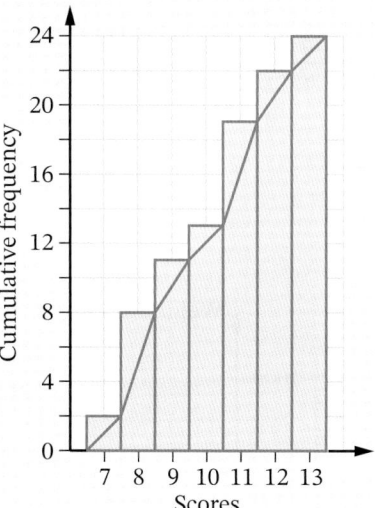

d

EXTENSION

2 Alisha counted the customers served by her coffee van each day.

a How many customers did Alisha serve in the first 10 days of her business?

b On which day did Alisha complete serving her first half of customers for the 10 days?

c On which day did she complete serving her first 90% of customers?

d On which day did she complete serving her first 36% of customers?

e What percentile does customer number 60 represent and on which day did they buy a coffee?

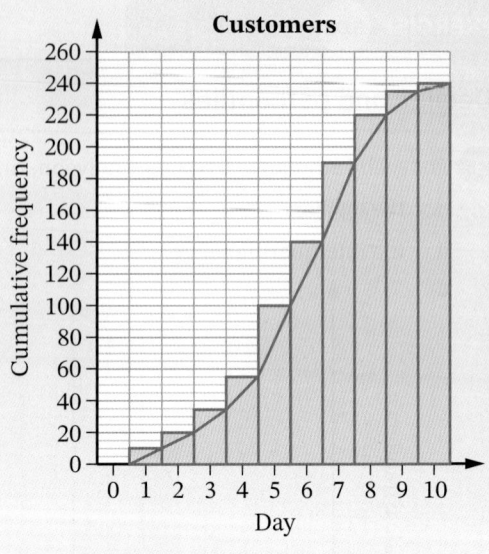

3 Mr Malone gave his class a 30-question multiple choice quiz.

a How many students are in the class?

b What was the range of results for the class?

c What was the interquartile range of results for the class?

d What was D_8, the 8th decile that cuts off the top 20% of results?

e What was P_{45}, the 45th percentile?

f What percentage of students scored a mark less than 27?

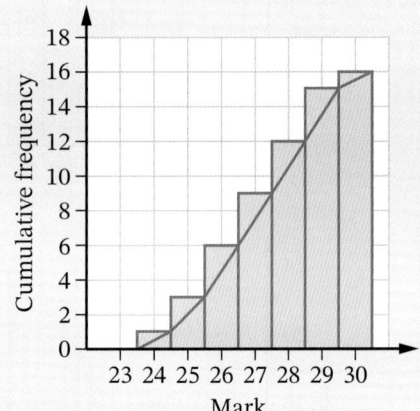

4 A potato chip company samples its product regularly to check that the packet weight is appropriate.

a How many packets weighed less than 60 g?

b What is the median weight for this sample?

c What weight is the 2nd decile D_2?

d What is the interquartile range?

e What is the 40th percentile?

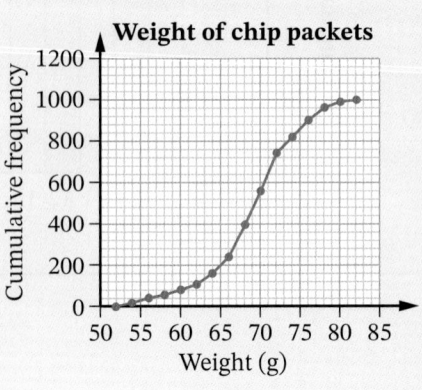

□ Foundation ○ Standard ○ Complex

EXTENSION   5.06

5 The weights of Year 10 students at Westlake High School were recorded and graphed on this ogive.

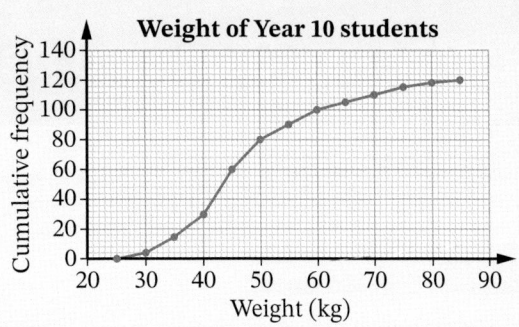

Weight of Year 10 students

a How many Year 10 students were weighed?

b What weight divides the lowest 70% of weights?

c What is the 90th percentile?

d The healthy weight range for a Year 10 student is from 40 kg to 67 kg.

What percentage of this sample is considered to be underweight and what percentage is overweight?

6 This ogive represents the test results for a Science class.

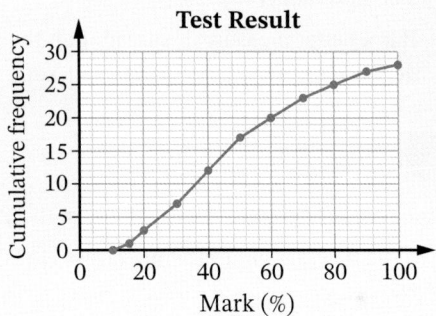

Test Result

a How many students are in the class?

b What is the median mark?

c What was the range of results for the middle 50% of students?

d What percentage of students scored a mark greater than 80?

e What is the 3rd decile?

f What mark divides the top 10% of students?

7 The heights of a sample of students were collected and graphed below.

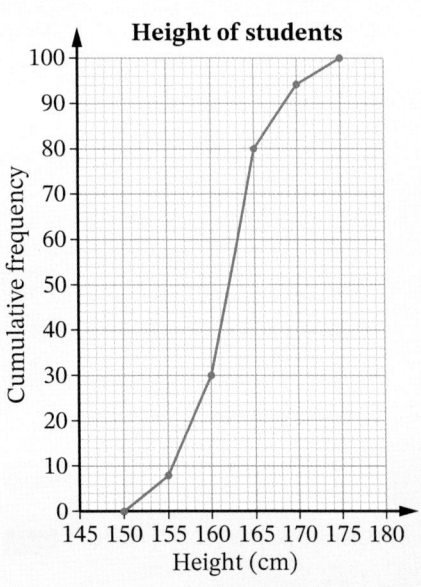

Height of students

a Find the median height.

b What is D_4?

c What is Q_1?

d What is P_{85}?

e What height divides the lower $\frac{1}{5}$ of students?

5.07 Extension: Standard deviation

The **standard deviation** is another measure of spread. Like the **mean**, it is calculated using all the values in a data set.

(i) Standard deviation

- The **standard deviation** of a set of data is an average of how different each value is from the mean.
- The symbol for standard deviation is σ or σ_n. ◄ σ is the lowercase Greek letter 'sigma'.
- Standard deviation has a complex formula so it is best calculated using the calculator's statistics mode.
- It is a better measure of spread than the range and interquartile range because its value depends on every value in the data set.

Example 14

Video
Standard deviation on a Casio calculator

Calculate, correct to 2 decimal places, the standard deviation of each set of data.

a The daily maximum temperature (in °C) in Campbelltown for 2 weeks in January.

45.0, 24.5, 24.8, 29.1, 35.0, 26.9, 31.8, 33.8, 32.9, 23.6, 22.1, 29.2, 27.1, 32.7

b The scores of Year 10 students in a Science quiz.

Score	2	3	4	5	6	7	8	9	10
Frequency	2	1	3	3	2	5	6	4	2

SOLUTION

Follow the instructions for the statistics mode (SD or STAT) on your calculator, as shown in the tables below.

a

Operation	Casio scientific	Sharp scientific
Start statistics mode.	MODE STAT 1-VAR	MODE STAT =
Clear the statistical memory	SHIFT 1 Edit, Del-A	2nd F DEL
Enter data	SHIFT 1 Data to get table 45.0 = 24.5 = , etc. to enter in column AC to leave table	45.0 M+ 24.5 M- , etc.
Calculate the standard deviation ($\sigma_x = 5.75$)	SHIFT 1 Var σ_x =	RCL σ_x
Return to normal (COMP) mode.	MODE COMP	MODE 0

$\sigma = 5.75$

9780170465595

b

Operation	Casio scientific	Sharp scientific
Start statistics mode.	**MODE** STAT 1-VAR	**MODE** STAT **=**
Clear the statistical memory	**SHIFT** 1 Edit, Del-A	**2nd F** **DEL**
Enter data	**SHIFT** 1 Data to get table 2 **=** 3 **=** , etc. To enter in x column 2 **=** 1 **=** , etc. in FREQ column **AC** to leave table	2 **2nd F** **STO** 2 **M+** 3 **2nd F** **STO** 1 **M-**
Calculate the standard deviation ($\sigma_x = 2.26$)	**SHIFT** 1 Var σ_x **=**	**RCL** σ_x
Return to normal (COMP) mode.	**MODE** COMP	**MODE** 0

$\sigma = 2.26$

EXERCISE 5.07 ANSWERS ON P. 618

Standard deviation

(U) (F) (R) (C)

Note: In this exercise, express all means and standard deviations to 2 decimal places.

EXAMPLE
14

1 Calculate the standard deviation of each set of data.

a   5, 4, 7, 8, 2, 9, 10

b   20, 23, 28, 24, 19, 25, 26, 24, 23

c

x	f
10	2
11	5
12	9
13	8
14	3
15	1

d

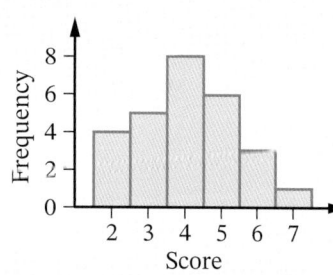

e

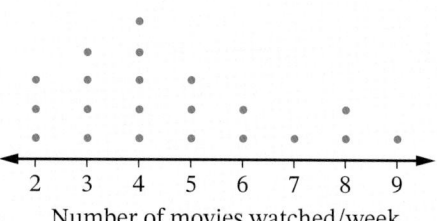

Number of movies watched/week

▷

☐ Foundation ○ Standard ◇ Complex

2 An English class of Year 10 students scored the following marks for their speeches:

12 15 14 16 16 12 11 18 7 10
15 14 13 13 18 10 12 12 14 13

a Which mark is the outlier?

b Find the standard deviation of the marks:

   i with the outlier   **ii** without the outlier

c What effect does removing the outlier have on the standard deviation?

3 For the 3 statistical distributions **A**, **B** and **C** shown, which one has:

R **a** the highest standard deviation?

b the lowest standard deviation?

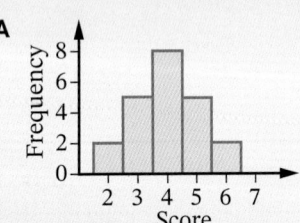 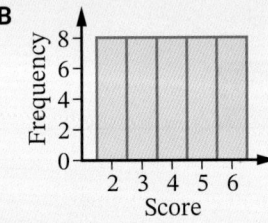 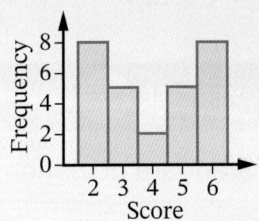

4 Find the standard deviation of each data set.

a

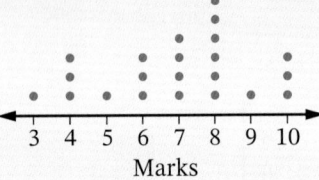

b

Stem	Leaf
2	0 2 7
3	5 5 6 8 9
4	1 2 4 5 6 6 7
5	0 3 4 5 9 9
6	1 5 5
7	6

Key: 3|5 = 35

5 The heights of girls in a Year 9 basketball team are:

R

151 161 171 175 176 157 175 163 164

a Calculate the mean and the standard deviation of heights of the basketball team.

b Divya joins the basketball team. What is her possible height if the standard deviation:

   i increases   **ii** decreases?

6 The training times (in seconds) of Harrison sprinting over 100 m were:

R

11.2 11.0 10.9 12.3 11.8 11.1 11.4 11.6 11.0

a Find the mean and standard deviation of his training times.

b What training time would Harrison have to do to:

   i increase the standard deviation?

   ii decrease the standard deviation?

☐ Foundation ○ Standard ○ Complex

7 Brooke's times (in seconds) for swimming 100 m were:

(R)

55.7   59.8   58.4   56.7   60.0   55.8   57.4   58.0

(C) An error was made in recording these times and 2 seconds needs to be added to each time.

Which of the following statements is true? Select the correct answer **A, B, C** or **D**.

A   The standard deviation will increase and the mean will stay the same.

B   The standard deviation will decrease and the mean will increase.

C   The standard deviation will stay the same and the mean will increase.

D   The standard deviation and the mean will both stay the same.

5.07

DID YOU KNOW?

The normal curve

Video
Freak
waves

If the heights of all the people in Australia were graphed on a frequency polygon, the graph would be a normal curve, a symmetrical bell-shaped curve that peaks in the middle.

The normal curve has the following features:

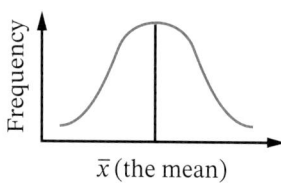

- The mean, median and mode are the same.

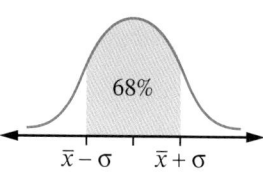

- About 68% of scores lie within one standard deviation of the mean.

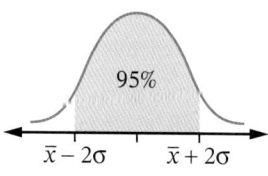

- About 95% lie within two standard deviations of the mean.

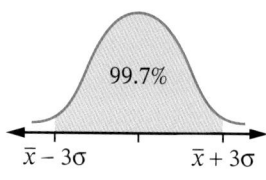

- About 99.7% lie within three standard deviations of the mean.

Measure and analyse the heights of the students at your school. Do the data follow a normal curve?

☐ Foundation   ○ Standard   ○ Complex

Chapter 5 | Comparing data   **235**

5.08 Extension: Comparing means and standard deviations

The mean and standard deviation can be used to compare different sets of data.

Example 15

The heights (in cm) of the girls and boys in a Year 10 PE class at Baramvale High were measured:

Girls: 163 155 171 162 165 158 172
166 163 150 160 181 160 156

Boys: 174 167 164 175 189 145 165 166
165 168 167 171 169 172 168

a Calculate, correct to 2 decimal places, the mean and standard deviation for:

  i the girls   ii the boys   iii the class.

b Which group has the greater spread of heights?

c Is there a significant difference between the heights of girls and boys?

SOLUTION

a i Girls: $\bar{x} = 163$ cm, $\sigma_n \approx 7.60$ ii Boys: $\bar{x} \approx 168.33$ cm, $\sigma_n \approx 8.64$

  iii Class: $\bar{x} \approx 165.76$ cm, $\sigma_n \approx 8.58$.

b The data for the boys in the class has the greater spread of heights as its standard deviation is higher.

c The mean height of boys was greater than that of the girls but the girls had the lower spread of heights.

Comparing measures of spread

The standard deviation is usually the most appropriate measure of spread as it uses all the values in the data set. The range is the easiest to calculate but its value only depends upon 2 values: the highest and the lowest.

If there are outliers in the data set, then the standard deviation and range will be affected by these extreme scores. In this case, the interquartile range is the better measure, because it is the range of the middle 50% of scores and so is not affected by outliers.

Example 16

a The ages of the children using a jumping castle and visiting a petting zoo are shown:

Jumping castle: 3 3 4 5 5 6 8 10 18

Petting zoo: 3 4 5 6 6 7 8 8 10

For each set of data, calculate

  i the range   ii the interquartile range

  iii the standard deviation (to 2 decimal places).

b Which is the best measure of spread for each set of data?

SOLUTION

a For the jumping castle:

    i range = 18 – 3

          = 15

    ii IQR = 9 – 3.5

          = 5.5

    iii $\sigma_n \approx 4.48$

For the petting zoo:

    i range = 10 – 3

          = 7

    ii IQR = 8 – 4.5

          = 3.5

    iii $\sigma_n \approx 2.05$

b The jumping castle data has an outlier, 18, which affects the range and standard deviation. The interquartile range is the best measure for this data set.

The petting zoo data do not have an outlier, so the standard deviation is the best measure for this data set.

EXERCISE 5.08 ANSWERS ON P. 618

Comparing means and standard deviations   U F R C

Note: In this exercise, express all means and standard deviations correct to 2 decimal places where necessary.

EXAMPLE
15

1 The pulse rates (in beats/minute) of a sample of men and women taken at a shopping centre are shown.

R
C **Men:**   68 72 75 73 81 77 69 68 79 83 65 59 60 72 70

  Women: 82 61 79 77 75 68 86 81 72 77 78 81 90 83 73

  a Find the mean and standard deviation of each group.

  b Is there a significant difference between the mean and standard deviation for men and women? Give reasons.

2 The reaction times (in seconds) for the dominant and non-dominant hands of a group of athletes were measured.

R
C **Dominant hand:**   0.41 0.29 0.35 0.42 0.42 0.43 0.39 0.61 0.38

                             0.34 0.75 0.34 0.38 0.47 0.34 0.32 0.29 0.30

  Non-dominant hand: 0.46 0.34 0.38 0.39 0.39 0.39 0.51 0.50 0.47

                             0.40 2.60 0.34 0.39 0.51 0.35 0.37 0.31 0.32

  a Find the mean and standard deviation for each data set.

  b Is there a significant difference between the results? Explain your answer.

  c **i** What are the outliers for the reaction time of the dominant hand?

      ii Find the mean and standard deviation without the outliers.

      iii What effect does removing the outliers have on the mean and standard deviation?

d Find the mean and standard deviation of the reaction time for the non-dominant hand without the outlier.

e On which group has the removal of outliers had the greater effect on the mean and standard deviation? Justify your answer.

3 The scores of 2 cricket teams were recorded on a back-to-back stem-and-leaf plot.

a Find the mean and standard deviation for each team.

b Which team was more consistent with its scores?

Western Tigers		Barrington City
5 2	7	
	8	3
7	9	0 8
8	10	7
	11	4 6
6	12	1 5
9 9 8 5	13	7
7 4	14	6
5	15	6 8

4 Vatha and Ana's times for running 100 m trials are shown.

Vatha: 13.0   13.5   14.2   13.7   13.2   14.7   13.5   14.3

Ana: 14.2   13.2   15.1   13.8   14.2   15.2   13.9   13.5

a Find the mean and standard deviation for each runner.

b Which runner is more consistent? Give reasons.

5 The dot plots show the test results of a class before and after using a tutorial website.

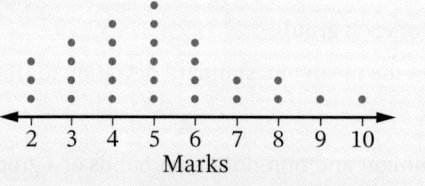
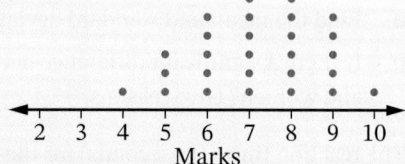

Which of the following is true?

A Both the mean and standard deviation increased.

B The mean increased and the standard deviation decreased.

C The mean decreased and the standard deviation increased.

D Both the mean and standard deviation decreased.

6 The marks obtained by students in Maths and Science exams are given below.

(R) (C)

Maths: 40 72 76 74 60 64 64 59 74 84 62 84 66 64

    71 68 78 63 57 55 73 80 67 86 57 87 62 52

Science: 42 54 61 72 76 54 65 80 39 74 82 54 57 63

    64 75 68 76 81 40 37 43 58 68 67 49 54 62

a For each subject, find:

  i the range   **ii** the interquartile range   **iii** the standard deviation.

b Find the mean for each subject.

c Determine in which subject the students performed better, giving reasons.

7 The points scored per match by the Roosters and the Dragons during a football

(R) (C) season were:

Roosters: 10 16 8 50 22 38 34 30 16 12 18 38 12 20 18

    36 40 28 42 28 56 22 22 24

Dragons: 10 6 17 25 19 13 10 18 14 32 0 14 14 16 10

    0 22 18 20 26 18 18 22 19

a For each team, find:

  i the range   **ii** the interquartile range

  iii the mean   **iv** the standard deviation.

b By comparing the means and the measures of spread, decide which was the better team.

Comparing data sets

5.09

Example 17

The back-to-back stem-and-leaf plot shows the results in Year 10 Maths and Science tests.

a Find the mean mark (correct to one decimal place) for each subject.

b Find the median for each subject.

c Find the range and interquartile range for each subject.

d For each subject:

  i describe the shape

  ii identify any outliers and **clusters**.

e In which subject did the students perform better? Justify your answer.

Maths		Science
5 2	3	6 8
8 6 3 0	4	4 6
8 7 7 4 1	5	1 5 9
8 8 7 6 6 3 2 0	6	0 2 8 9
6 5 4 2 1 1	7	2 3 4 4 5 8 8
6 4 3	8	0 0 2 4 5 6 7 8 9
6 0	9	0 4 4

Videos
Comparing data sets

Back-to-back stem-and-leaf plots

Worksheets
Comparing city temperatures

Comparing word lengths

Investigating young drivers

☐ Foundation ○ Standard ◇ Complex

SOLUTION

a Mean for Maths $= \dfrac{1919}{30}$

  $= 63.9666...$

  ≈ 64.0

Mean for Science $= \dfrac{2151}{30}$

  $= 71.7$

b Median for Maths $= \dfrac{66+66}{2} = 66$

Median for Science $= \dfrac{74+75}{2} = 74.5$

c Range for Maths $= 96 - 32 = 64$

  Interquartile range $= 74 - 54 = 20$

Range for Science $= 94 - 36 = 58$

  Interquartile range $= 85 - 60 = 25$

d **i** The results for Maths are symmetrical, while the results for Science are negatively skewed.

  ii No outliers. There is some clustering for the Maths results in the 60s and 70s, and in Science the clustering occurs in the 70s and 80s.

e The students have performed better in Science as the mean and median for it are greater than the mean and median for Maths. This can also be seen by the shape of the data on the stem-and-leaf plot.

Example 18

Video
Histogram vs boxplot

The number of text messages received per hour by a group of teenagers are displayed in the frequency histogram and the boxplot below.

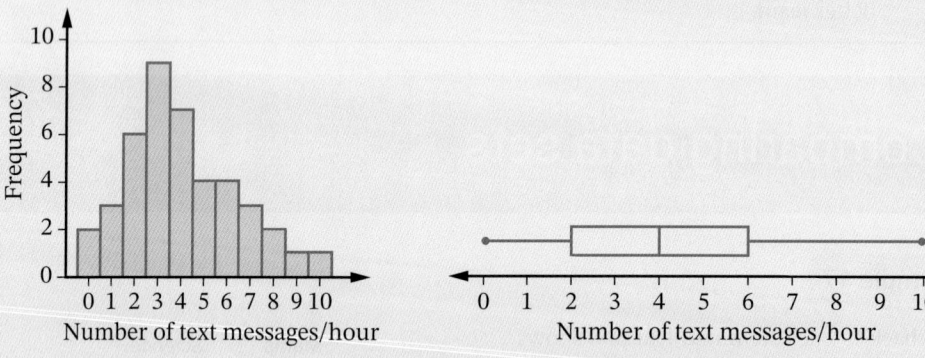

a How many teenagers received more than 6 text messages per hour?

b Find:

  i the mode

  ii the median

  iii the range

  iv the interquartile range.

c The shape of the distribution is positively skewed. How is this shown by:

  i the frequency histogram

  ii the boxplot?

d According to the boxplot, what percentage of teenagers received 2 or more text messages?

e What information is better seen on:

  i the frequency histogram

  ii the boxplot?

a number of teenagers receiving more than 6 text messages

$= 3 + 2 + 1 + 1$ using the frequency histogram

$= 7$

b **i** mode $= 3$ using the frequency histogram

    ii median $= 4$ using the boxplot

    iii range $= 10 - 0$ using the frequency histogram or boxplot

            $= 10$

    iv interquartile range $= 6 - 2$ using the boxplot

            $= 4$

c **i** The tail of the frequency histogram leans towards the higher values.

    ii The length of the boxplot to the right of the median (Q_2) is greater than its length to the left of the median.

d $Q_1 = 2$, so 75% of teenagers received 2 or more text messages per hour.

e **i** The mode and information regarding the number of text messages received by teenagers can be determined from the frequency histogram.

    ii The median, quartiles and interquartile range are easily determined from the boxplot.

EXERCISE **5.09**   ANSWERS ON P. 619

Comparing data sets   U F R C

1 The back-to-back stem-and-leaf plot shows the amount of cash (in dollars) carried by a sample of Year 11 students at Nelson Senior High.

R C

EXAMPLE 17

Boys		Girls
5 5 3	0	5 5 6 8 9
8 5 5 2 0	1	0 2 2 5 5 8 8 9
9 6 5 5 5 0 0	2	0 5 6 8 8 8
8 5 5 4 3 2 0 0	3	0 1 4 5 6
5 4 4 2 2 0	4	0 0 5 6
6 6 5 4 3	5	0 3 5
4 2 2	6	5 5 8
5	7	0 4

   a Find the mean amount of cash (correct to the nearest cent) carried by each group.

   b Find the median amount of cash carried by each group.

   c Find the range and interquartile range for each group.

   d For each group:

     i describe the shape   **ii** identify any outliers and clusters.

   e Who generally carries more cash – boys or girls? Justify your answer.

☐ Foundation   ○ Standard   ◇ Complex

2 The back-to-back histogram shows the number of goals scored by 2 football teams during a season.

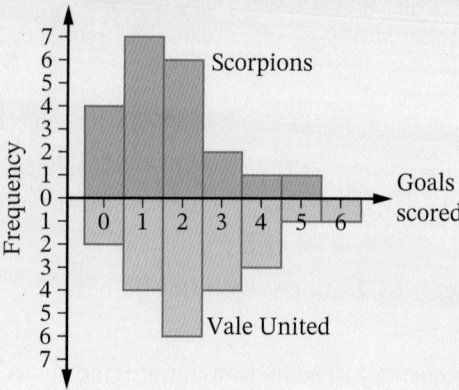

a How many games were played by each team?

b How many goals were scored by

   i the Scorpions

   ii Vale United?

c Find the mean number of goals scored by each team.

d What is the range for each team?

e Describe the shape of each team's results.

f Which team performed better? Give reasons.

3 The daily maximum temperatures for Sydney and Perth in February are shown.

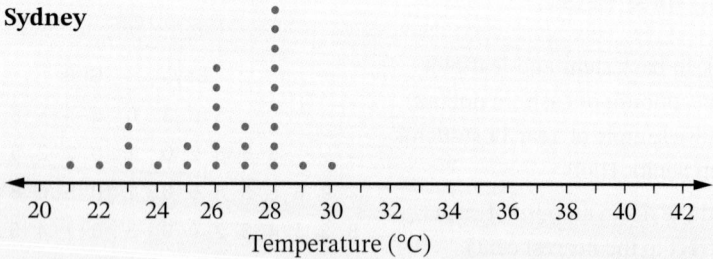

a Find the mean (to one decimal place), median and modal temperatures for each city.

b Find the range and interquartile range of temperatures for each city.

c Describe the shape of the temperatures for each city and identify any outliers or clusters.

d Compare the temperatures of Sydney and Perth. Comment on measures of central tendency (the mean, median and mode), and measures of spread (range and interquartile range).

□ Foundation ○ Standard ◯ Complex

4 The results for 2 quizzes taken by a Year 10 History class are shown.

Ⓡ
Ⓒ

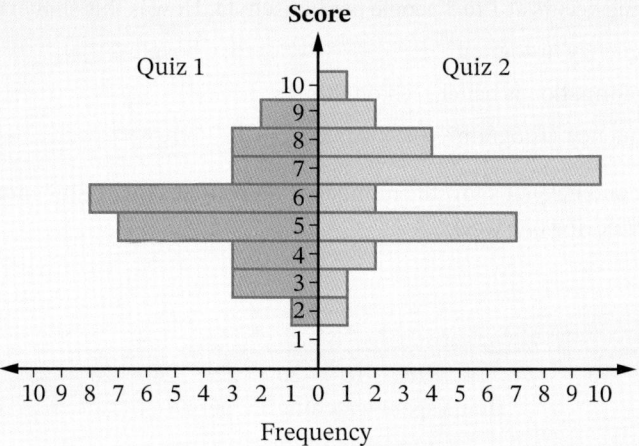

a How many students are in the Year 10 History class?

b Find the mean and mode for each quiz.

c Find the median for each quiz.

d For each quiz, find the:

  i range   **ii** interquartile range.

e Describe the distribution for each quiz, identifying any clusters and outliers.

f Are there significant differences between the results of the 2 quizzes?
Justify your answer.

5 A survey to determine the number of people per household was conducted in several
shopping centres. The results are shown in the frequency histogram and boxplot.

Ⓡ
Ⓒ

EXAMPLE
18

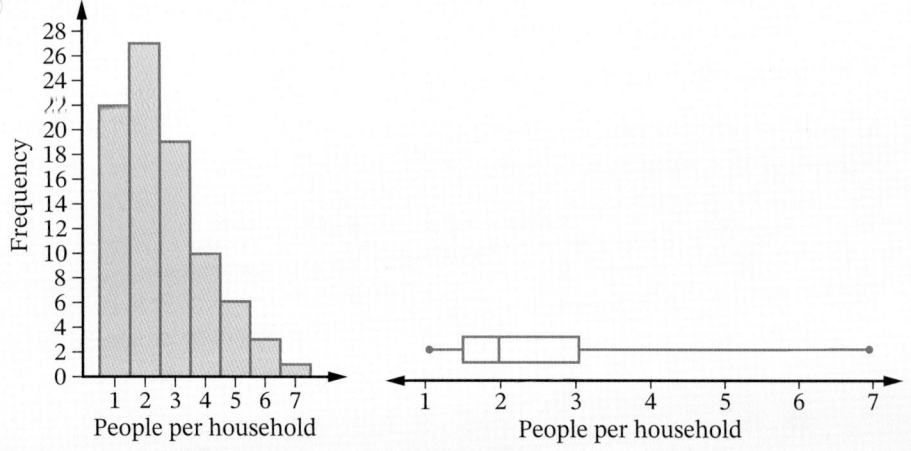

a How many households had 3 or more people?

b Find the:

  i mode   **ii** median

  iii range   **iv** interquartile range.

c Describe the shape of the distribution.

☐ Foundation ○ Standard ○ Complex

d According to the boxplot, what percentage of households had 2 or more people?

e Clustering occurs at 1 to 3 people per household. How is this shown on the:

   i frequency histogram?   **ii** boxplot?

f What information is better seen on the:

   i frequency histogram?   **ii** boxplot?

6 The dot plot and boxplot show the number of hours that Year 10 students spent watching TV during one week.

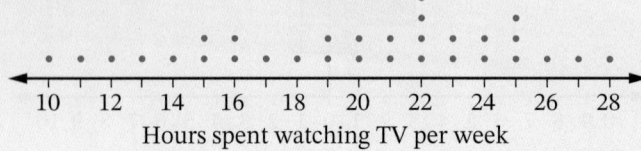

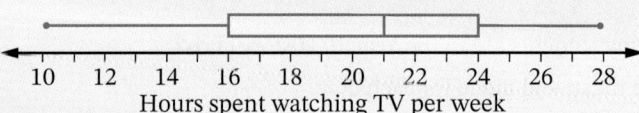

a How many students watched TV for:

   i fewer than 15 hours per week?   **ii** more than 20 hours per week?

b Find the:

   i mode   **ii** range   **iii** interquartile range.

c What is the shape of the distribution? How is this shown by the:

   i dot plot   **ii** boxplot?

d Which display of data, the dot plot or boxplot, is better for finding the:

   i mode   **ii** median

   iii number of students who watched TV for 25 hours

   iv interquartile range?

7 The speeds of cars were monitored along a main road in 2 different places. The results are shown in the back-to-back stem-and-leaf and parallel boxplots.

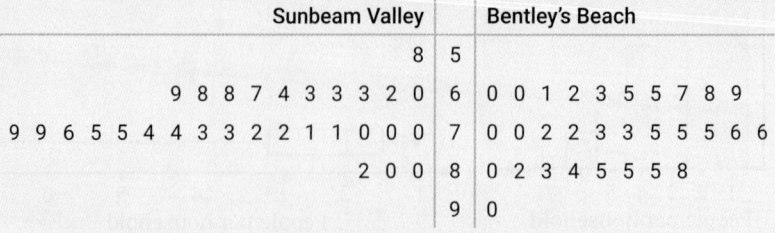

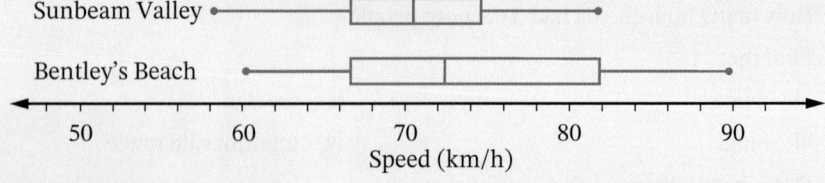

□ Foundation ○ Standard ◇ Complex

9780170465595

a   Find the range, median and interquartile range for each place.

    b   What is the shape of the distribution for each place?

    c   Are there any clusters or outliers in either place?

    d   According to the boxplot, what percentage of drivers in Bentley's Beach drive faster than all drivers in Sunbeam Valley?

    e   In which place do drivers generally drive faster? Give a possible reason for your answer.

8   Lamissa and Anneka shoot arrows at a target 50 m away during an archery contest.
(R)(C)   They scored 10 for a bullseye down to 1 for the outer ring. Their results are displayed in the back-to-back histogram and the parallel boxplots.

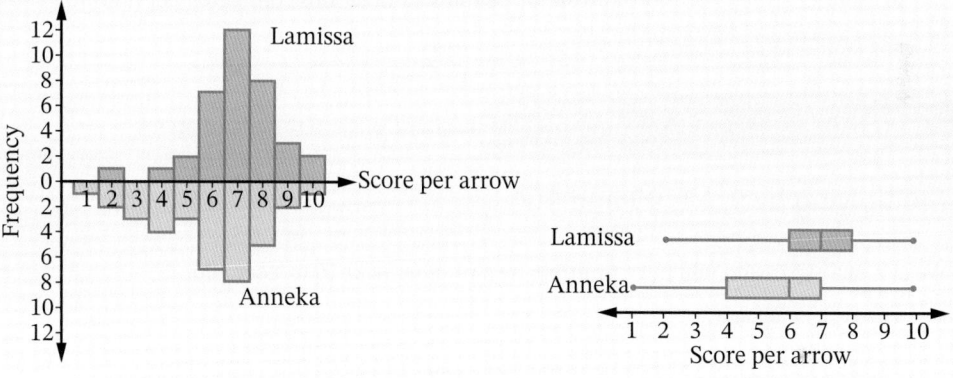

    a   How many arrows did Lamissa and Anneka shoot?

    b   Find the mode and median score per arrow for each contestant.

    c   Find the range and interquartile range for each contestant.

    d   Describe the shape of the distribution for each contestant.

    e   According to the boxplots, on what percentage of arrows shot was a score of 6 or less achieved by:

        i   Lamissa?   **ii**   Anneka?

    f   Who was the better archer during this contest? Justify your answer by referring to the measures of central tendency and spread.

9   The number of sit-ups per minute completed by men and women at the Full On Fitness
(R)(C)   Centre are displayed in the back-to-back stem-and-leaf plot and parallel boxplots.

Women		Men
8 7 5 4	1	0 6 7 9 9
9 9 9 8 8 7 4 4 3 3 1 0	2	0 2 3 4 4 5 5 7 7 8
7 6 5 5 5 4 3 2 1 0 0	3	0 2 4 5 6 6 7 7 8 8 8 8 9
7 5 4 3 2 0 0	4	1 3 4 6 6 6 6 7 7 9
2 1 0	5	0 1 3 4 7 7

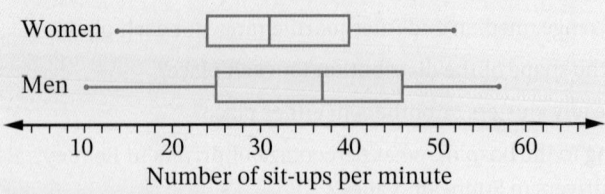

a   Why would a dot plot be an inappropriate way to display the data shown on the previous page?

b   What is the median number of sit-ups per minute completed by each group?

c   Find the range and interquartile range for each group.

d   Describe the shape of the distributions for each group.

e   Which group has more spread in the number of sit-ups completed per minute? Give reasons for your answer.

Quiz
Mental
skills 5

☆ **MENTAL SKILLS** (5) ANSWERS ON P. 620   **Maths without calculators**

Multiplying by 9, 11, 99 and 101

We can use expansion when we multiply by a number near 10 or near 100.

1   Study each example.

a $25 \times 11 = 25 \times (10 + 1)$
$= 25 \times 10 + 25 \times 1$
$= 250 + 25$
$= 275$

b $14 \times 9 = 14 \times (10 - 1)$
$= 14 \times 10 - 14 \times 1$
$= 140 - 14$
$= 126$

c $32 \times 12 = 32 \times (10 + 2)$
$= 32 \times 10 + 32 \times 2$
$= 320 + 64$
$= 384$

d $7 \times 99 = 7 \times (100 - 1)$
$= 7 \times 100 - 7 \times 1$
$= 700 - 7$
$= 693$

e $27 \times 101 = 27 \times (100 + 1)$
$= 27 \times 100 + 27 \times 1$
$= 2700 + 27$
$= 2727$

f $18 \times 8 = 18 \times (10 - 2)$
$= 18 \times 10 - 18 \times 2$
$= 180 - 36$
$= 144$

2   Now evaluate each product.

a 16×11
b 33×11
c 29×9
d 45×9

e 62×11
f 7×101
g 18×101
h 36×99

i 19×8
j 45×12
k 21×102
l 6×98

m 32×9
m 7×99
o 39×101
p 71×12

□ Foundation   ○ Standard   ○ Complex

Statistics in the media

We live in a world of 24-hour news, whether it is from internet, TV or newspapers, that often quote results from surveys. When survey data is used in the media we need to consider:

- where the news comes from and what samples the statistics are based on
- who supplied the information
- the number of samples and the sample size used
- the way in which the collected data has been presented.

Example 19

What concerns could be raised about the following claim?

'*The Daily Sun* newspaper reports that it has an average issue readership of 1.39 million and that its Travel section has a readership of 1.46 million.'

SOLUTION

The newspaper is reporting about its own readership, so it may be **biased**. It also states that its Travel section has a higher readership than its issue readership.

Example 20

The weights (in kg) of a large group of 18–20-year-olds attending university are:

57	58	62	84	64	74	57	55	56	90
68	63	49	66	63	65	60	60	46	70
85	60	70	41	73	75	67	63	70	85
51	49	75	77	87	54	60	75	58	68
55	65	66	57	85	75	56	60	62	75
74	58	51	62	50	55	71	57	58	100
72	58	103	64	52	55	80	96	45	87
81	80	48	54	65	54	59	50	78	60
74	70	64	59	72	78	104	63	102	95

a   How many students were in the group?

b   Randomly select 4 groups of 10 and for each sample calculate:

   i   the mean   ii   the median   iii   the interquartile range.

c   Use your results to estimate the mean, median and interquartile range of the population from your 4 samples.

d   Compare your estimates to the mean, median and interquartile range of the population.

a There were 90 students in the group.

b Randomly select 4 samples of 10 from the 'population'.

Sample 1:	90	63	75	48	74	85	51	96	60	78
Sample 2:	62	75	103	64	65	54	55	54	60	75
Sample 3:	68	70	57	52	78	74	60	63	58	87
Sample 4:	72	54	52	80	45	87	49	77	54	58

The statistics for each group are:

Sample 1: $\bar{x} = 72$ median = 74.5 interquartile range = 25

Sample 2: $\bar{x} = 66.7$ median = 63 interquartile range = 20

Sample 3: $\bar{x} = 66.7$ median = 65.5 interquartile range = 16

Sample 4: $\bar{x} = 62.8$ median = 56 interquartile range = 25

c Taking averages, population statistics estimates are:

$$\text{mean} = \bar{x} = \frac{72 + 66.7 + 66.7 + 62.8}{4} = 67.1 \qquad \text{(correct to 1 decimal place)}$$

$$\text{median} = \frac{74.5 + 63 + 65.5 + 56}{4} = 64.8 \qquad \text{(correct to 1 decimal place)}$$

$$\text{interquartile range} = \frac{25 + 20 + 16 + 25}{4} = 21.5$$

d The statistics for the population are:

mean, $\bar{x} = 66.9$ (correct to 1 decimal place)

median = 64

interquartile range = 18

The estimates for the mean, median and interquartile range compare very favourably with the population statistics.

EXERCISE 5.10 ANSWERS ON P. 620

Statistics in the media   U F R C

EXAMPLE 19

1 A TV network surveys 300 people in shopping centres between 9 am and 11 am to get feedback on its new game show.

   a How is this survey biased?

   b Suggest a better method for getting feedback about its game show.

2 A report about hot water systems recommended a heat pump system. The report stated that people in Queensland who had the heat pump hot water system saved 30% on their electricity bills. The company is using this information to advertise their product in NSW and Victoria. How might this information be unsuitable for people in NSW and Victoria? Give reasons.

□ Foundation ○ Standard ◇ Complex

3 Two reports on petrol prices over a 12-week period were written by 2 different companies. Each company used line graphs to show the price of petrol for the same period.

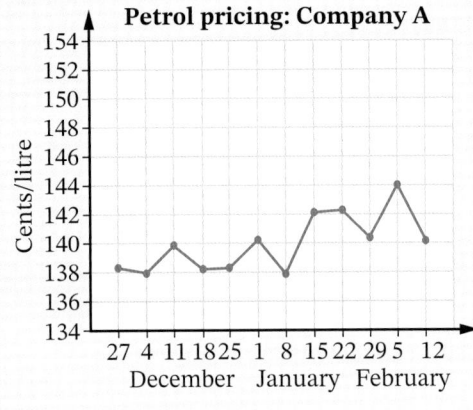

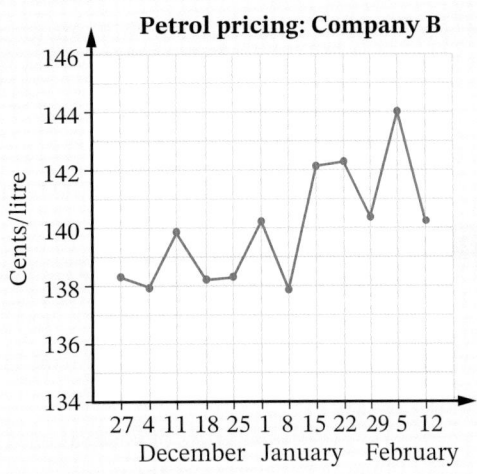

a What message is being suggested about petrol prices in the line graph presented by:

   i   Company A?   ii   Company B?

b How could both graphs be improved to give a true picture of changing petrol prices?

4 A report on the diesel fuel consumption of different cars was published in a motoring magazine, featuring this misleading graph.

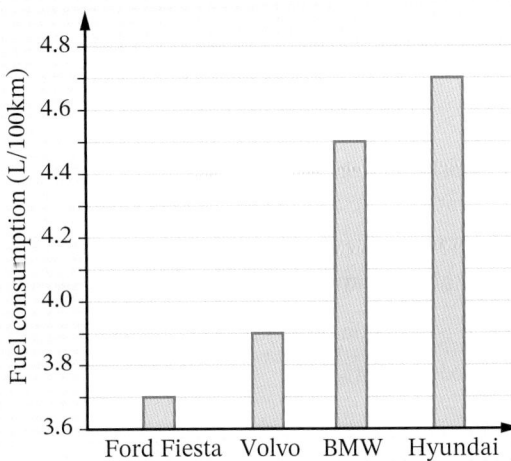

a What is the graph suggesting about the fuel consumption of the different cars?

b What is the difference in fuel consumption between the:

   i   Ford Fiesta and the Volvo?

   ii Ford Fiesta and the Hyundai?

   iii BMW and the Hyundai?

c How should the graph be redrawn so that it is not biased towards the Ford Fiesta and the Volvo?

5 A company sells a new app. After 3 months, they conduct a survey and customers are asked to rate the product as Excellent, Good or Satisfactory. Is the survey biased? Justify your answer.

6 A market research company working for a car manufacturer needs to determine the most popular car colours.

a Give an example of a biased question for this survey.

b What other information should the market research company use, apart from the survey, to determine the most popular car colour?

EXAMPLE 20

7 a Randomly select 4 samples of 10 weights from the population shown in Example 20, and for each sample calculate:

i the mean   **ii** the median   **iii** the interquartile range.

b Use your results to estimate the mean, median and interquartile range of the population from your 4 samples.

c How do the statistics of your samples compare to the mean, median and interquartile range of the population?

d How do the estimated statistics compare to the population statistics?

8 a Repeat the process of question **7** by taking 2 samples of size:

i 5   **ii** 15   **iii** 20

b Do the sample statistics become more accurate and move closer to the population statistics as sample size increases?

INVESTIGATION

Australian Bureau of Statistics

The *Australian Bureau of Statistics* (ABS) is the official organisation in charge of collecting data for government departments. The data collected covers many areas – from population, employment, weekly earnings, weight and obesity in adults, to health of children in Australia.

Visit the ABS website **www.abs.gov.au** to answer the following questions.

1 a What is the current population of Australia?

b What is the predicted population for:

   i 2027   **ii** 2030   **iii** 2040?

c What is Australia's rate of population increase?

2 Search for the Australian state populations according to the 2021 Census.

a What was the population in your state and its increase from 2016?

b Which state had the:

   i largest increase in population?

   ii smallest increase in population?

EXERCISE 5.11 ANSWERS ON P. 620

Statistical investigations

U F PS R C

1 This graph compares the number of passenger vehicles per 1000 people in Australia in 1955 and 2020.

a How many passenger vehicles per 1000 people were there in 1955?

b What was the percentage increase in the number of passenger vehicles per 1000 people between 1955 and 2020?

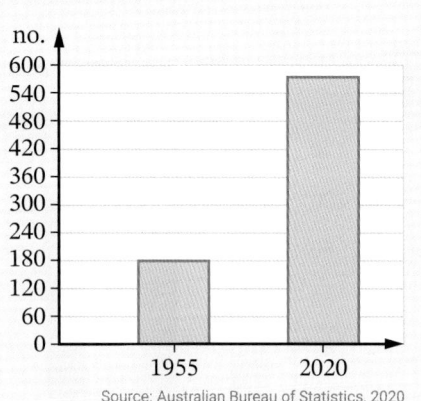

Source: Australian Bureau of Statistics, 2020

2 Visit the *Australian Bureau of Statistics* (*ABS*) website **www.abs.gov.au** and search for **Transport: Census**.

a What was the total number of vehicles registered last year?

b How many passenger vehicles were registered last year?

c What was the average annual growth rate over the last 5 years?

3 This graph compares the types of commuter transport used by Australians in 2016 and 2021.

C

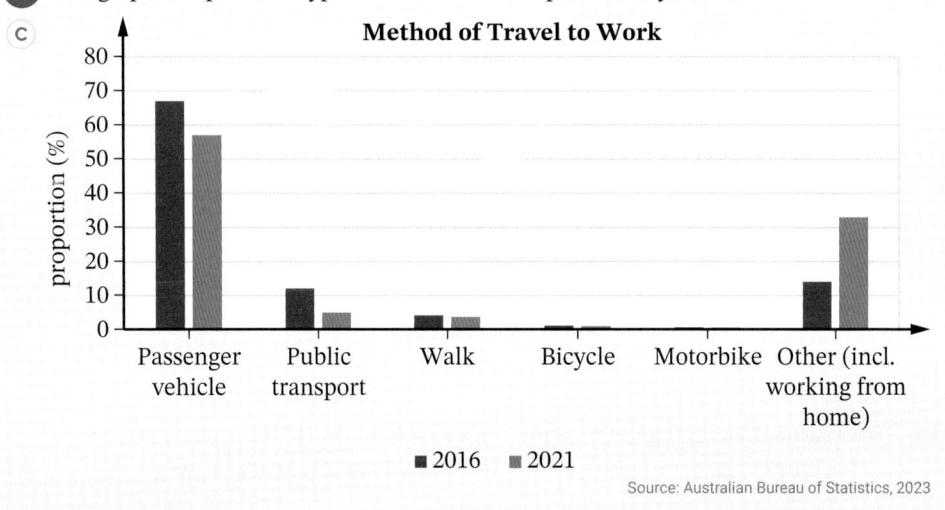

Source: Australian Bureau of Statistics, 2023

□ Foundation ○ Standard ○ Complex

a   What percentage of people used a passenger vehicle to get to work in 2016 and what change has occurred from 2016 to 2021?

b   What percentage of Australians used public transport in 2021? Perform an internet search to see whether this has changed in recent years.

c   Use the internet to find reasons for Australians choosing not to use public transport.

d   List 3 advantages for using public transport.

e   Use the internet to compare Australia's transport use with transport use in other countries (for example, Japan, India, France, UK and USA).

4   These graphs show the reasons Australians went on overnight trips in 2018.

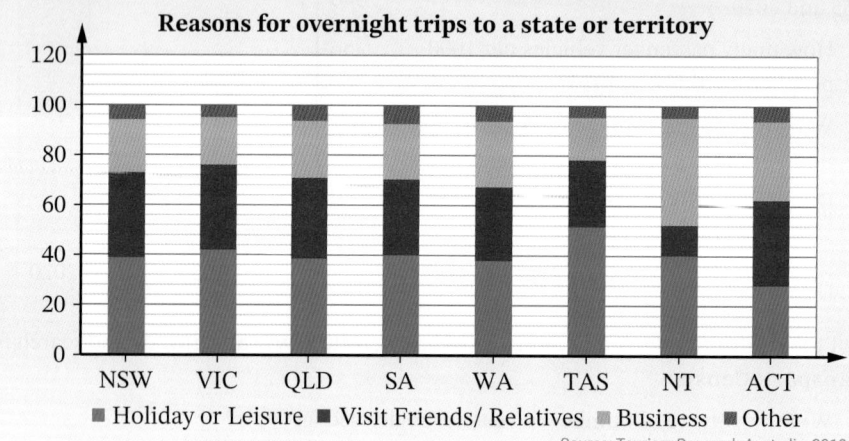

Reasons for overnight trips to a state or territory

■ Holiday or Leisure ■ Visit Friends/ Relatives ■ Business ■ Other

Source: Tourism Research Australia, 2018

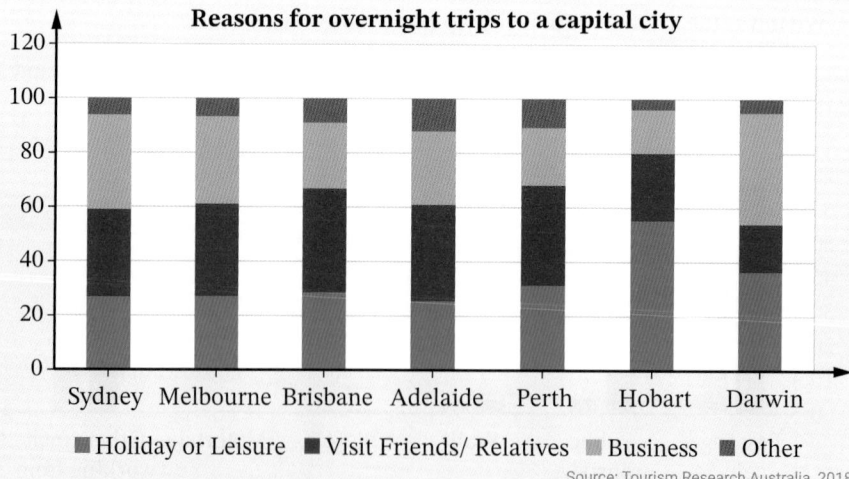

Reasons for overnight trips to a capital city

■ Holiday or Leisure ■ Visit Friends/ Relatives ■ Business ■ Other

Source: Tourism Research Australia, 2018

a   Which state/territory had the highest proportion of overnight trips for holiday or leisure?

b   What percentage of people visited South Australia for an overnight trip to see friends/relatives?

c Which capital city showed the highest percentage of business trips and which city had the lowest? Give possible reasons for your answer.

d The percentage of people taking business trips to Sydney and Melbourne is higher than the percentage of people taking business trips to Perth or Hobart. Give a possible reason for this.

e Which state/territory and which capital city had the lowest percentage of people visiting for holiday or leisure? Give a reason for each answer.

5 Summarise your answers to questions **1** to **3** in a brief report about passenger vehicle use in Australia. Using your results, indicate what action governments (Federal, State and local) should do in terms of building roads, accident research and consideration of the environment.

(R) (C)

6 'Life expectancy at birth is one of the most widely-used and internationally-recognised indicators of population health. High life expectancy at birth indicates low levels of infant mortality, a safe environment in which to live, a good health care system, sufficient food, and the adoption of preventative health measures.'

(PS) (R) (C)

(Australian Bureau of Statistics, 2011)

Investigate life expectancy trends in Australia, using ABS and life insurance websites. Investigate data such as:

- life expectancy graphs or tables at birth and for different ages
- comparison of life expectancy between Australia and other countries
- comparison of life expectancy between Australian states and territories
- infant mortality rates
- causes of death (such as cancer)
- life expectancy of Aboriginal and Torres Strait Islander Australians
- implications of higher life expectancy on health costs, disabilities associated with aging population, aged-care facilities, pensions.

7 Is Australia becoming a warmer continent? Investigate this by looking at data from the Australian Bureau of Statistics, **www.abs.gov.au**, and the Australian Bureau of Meteorology, **www.bom.gov.au**.

(PS) (R) (C)

8 Investigate tobacco and alcohol use by teenagers in Australia. Include tables and graphs in your report. Refer to the National Drug Strategy Household Survey (**www.nationaldrugstrategy.gov.au**) and search **alcohol and teenage statistics in Australia** on the internet.

(PS) (R) (C)

□ Foundation ○ Standard ○ Complex

5.12 Scatterplots

Worksheet
Scatterplots

Puzzle
Scatterplots matching game

Bivariate data is data that measures 2 variables, such as a person's height and arm span (distance between outstretched arms). Bivariate data is represented by an ordered pair of values that can be graphed on a **scatterplot** for analysis.

A **scatterplot** is a graph of points on a number plane. Each point represents the values of the 2 different variables and the resulting graph may show a pattern that may be linear or non-linear. If there is a pattern, then a relationship may exist between the 2 variables.

Example 21

The heights and arm spans of a group of students are shown in the table.

Height, H cm	162	182	153	145	172	163	150	142	183	145	192	171
Arm span, S cm	158	185	145	143	174	165	151	141	181	158	191	178

a Draw a scatterplot of the data.

b Describe the pattern of the plotted points.

c Describe the relationship between the students' heights and arm spans.

SOLUTION

a

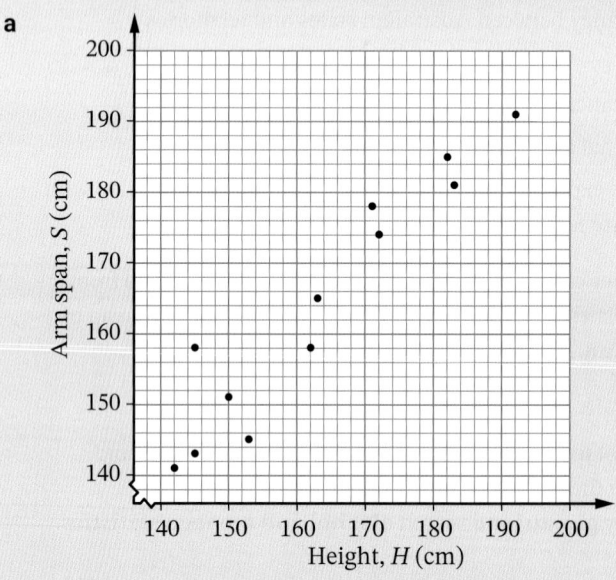

b The points form a linear pattern.

c As the heights of students increase, their arm spans tend to increase.

9780170465595

Strength and direction of linear relationships

The linear pattern will indicate the **strength** and **direction** of the relationship between the 2 variables. The strength of a relationship between 2 variables can be described as:

- **strong** if the points are close together
- **weak** if the points are more spread out
- **perfect** if all points lie on a straight line.

The direction of a relationship can be described as **positive** or **negative**:

x and y have a **positive relationship** if y increases as x increases.

x and y have a **negative relationship** if y decreases as x increases.

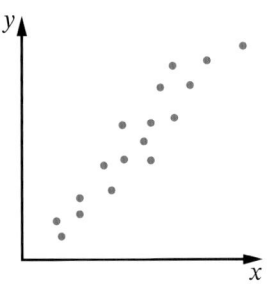

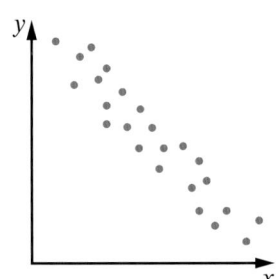

Example 22

Describe the strength and direction of the relationship shown in each scatterplot.

Video
Scatterplots

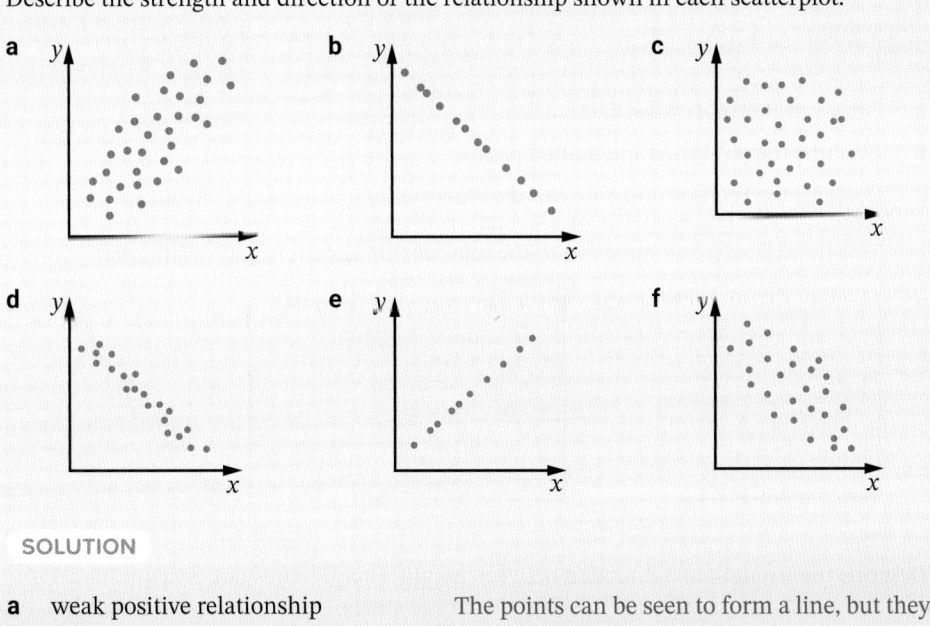

SOLUTION

a weak positive relationship — The points can be seen to form a line, but they are spread out.

b perfect negative relationship — The points lie on a decreasing straight line.

c no relationship — The points are very spread out with no pattern.

d	strong negative relationship	The points can be seen to form a decreasing line and they are close together.
e	perfect positive relationship	The points lie on an increasing straight line.
f	weak negative relationship	The points can be seen to form a decreasing line, but they are spread out.

Dependent and independent variables

If a variable y depends on the value of the variable x, y is called the **dependent variable** and x is called the **independent variable**. For example, stride length (the length of a person's walking step or pace) depends on the person's height, so stride length is the dependent variable and height is the independent variable. When graphing, the dependent variable is shown on the vertical (y-) axis while the independent variable is shown on the horizontal (x-) axis.

EXERCISE 5.12 ANSWERS ON P. 621

Scatterplots Ⓤ Ⓕ Ⓡ Ⓒ

EXAMPLE 21

1 The heights and handspans of a group of students are shown in the table.

Ⓒ

| Height, H cm | 168 | 175 | 175 | 156 | 160 | 173 | 171 | 180 | 185 | 175 | 182 | 180 |
| Handspan, S cm | 20.0 | 21.1 | 17.6 | 16.5 | 17.5 | 19.0 | 20.8 | 22.5 | 25.0 | 23.0 | 20.2 | 21.1 |

    a   Draw a scatterplot of the data.

    b   Describe the pattern of the plotted points.

    c   Describe the relationship between the students' heights and their hand spans.

EXAMPLE 22

2 Describe the strength and direction of the relationship shown in each scatterplot.

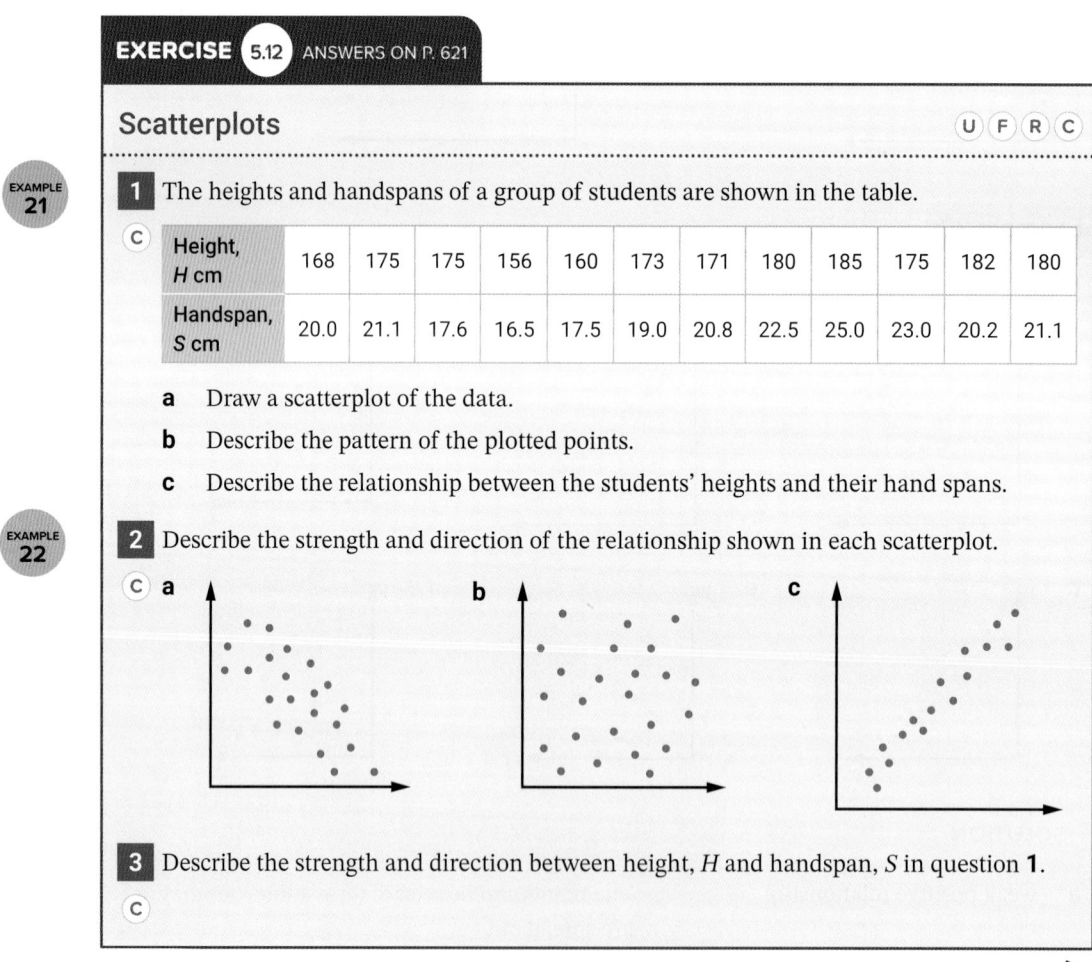

Ⓒ **a**   **b**   **c**

3 Describe the strength and direction between height, H and handspan, S in question **1**.

Ⓒ

☐ Foundation   ○ Standard   ○ Complex

4 The height and stride length measurements of some students are shown in the table.

Height, *H* cm	174	160	158	180	169	172	171	171	148	190	166	173
Stride length, *L* cm	72.2	64.0	66.4	74.7	70	71.5	70.9	71.2	61.4	78.9	68.0	71.9

    a Explain why stride length is the dependent variable.

    b Graph this data on a scatterplot.

    c Describe the pattern of the plotted points.

    d Describe the relationship between the students' heights and stride lengths.

    e Describe the strength and direction of the relationship.

    f Predict the stride length of a student who is 175 cm tall.

5 The table lists the points scored for and against each NRL team one season.

    a Graph this data on a scatterplot.

    b Is the pattern of the points linear?

    c Describe the strength and direction of the relationship between points scored for and points scored against.

Points scored for, *F*	Points scored against, *A*
568	369
579	361
559	438
497	403
597	445
545	536
445	441
481	447
405	438
506	551
449	477
448	488
462	626
497	609
409	575
431	674

6 Year 10 students were surveyed on the number of hours in a week they spent doing homework and the number of hours they spent on the computer.

Homework, *H*	2	15	12	5	4	2	4	15	14	5	2	5	20	4	2	11
Computer, *C*	25	30	18	35	6	30	20	22	6	40	8	3	20	30	5	8

    a Graph this data on a scatterplot.

    b Describe the strength and direction of the relationship between hours spent doing homework and hours spent on the computer.

☐ Foundation   ○ Standard   ◇ Complex

7 A survey was conducted to see whether there was a relationship between height and the age of students in a high school.

Age, A (years)	14	16	15	13	11	14	17	15	12	11	14	16	13	18
Height, H (cm)	162	174	182	162	132	173	187	160	154	145	165	171	151	181

a Graph this data on a scatterplot.

b Which variable could be considered as the dependent variable? Give reasons.

c Describe the strength and direction of the relationship between the age and height of students.

TECHNOLOGY

Scatterplot patterns

Investigate one of the following pairs of bivariate data for a group of students or people. You will need instruments (measuring tapes and/or trundle wheels) and stopwatches to help you collect your data.

- height vs arm span

- reaction time vs hours of sleep

- stride length vs 50 m sprint time

1 Enter your data into a spreadsheet. Graph it using **Scatter with Smooth Lines and Markers**.

2 Analyse your graph. What type of linear relationship does it show? Positive or negative? Strong or weak?

3 Write a brief summary describing the relationship between the 2 variables.

Alamy Stock Photo/Kim Karpeles

5.13 Line of best fit

Worksheets
Line of best fit

Trendlines

If 2 variables x and y show a strong linear relationship when graphed on a scatterplot, the linear relationship can be approximated by drawing a **line of best fit** through the points and finding its equation $y = mx + c$. This line can be done on paper but it is easier to graph it using technology such as a spreadsheet, dynamic geometry or graphing software.

□ Foundation   ○ Standard   ○ Complex

9780170465595

(i) Line of best fit

- It represents most or all the points as closely as possible.
- It goes through as many points as possible.
- It has roughly the same number of points above and below it.
- It is drawn so that the distances of points from the line are as small as possible.

Interactive
Least-
squares
regression

Technology
Line of
best fit

Spreadsheet
Line of
best fit

A line of best fit can be used to predict what might happen:

- between the points on the scatterplot, within the range of data (this is called **interpolation**, pronounced 'in-terp-o-lay-shun'), or
- beyond the points on the scatterplot, outside the range of data (this is called **extrapolation**, pronounced 'ex-trap-o-lay-shun').

Example 23

The arm span and right foot size of 12 Year 10 students were measured:

Arm span, S (cm)	177	179	162	182	181	171	161	176	175	190	168	165
Right foot size, F (cm)	25	26	24	28	27	25	23	25	24	30	24	24

Videos
Lines of
best fit

Can eating
fish prevent
murder?

a Graph the points on a scatterplot and construct a line of best fit.

b Find the equation of the line of best fit.

c Use the equation to estimate the foot size of a student with an arm span 173 cm.

d Use the graph to interpolate the foot size of a Year 10 student with an arm span of 185 cm.

e Use the graph to extrapolate the arm span of a Year 10 student who has a foot size of 22 cm.

SOLUTION

a

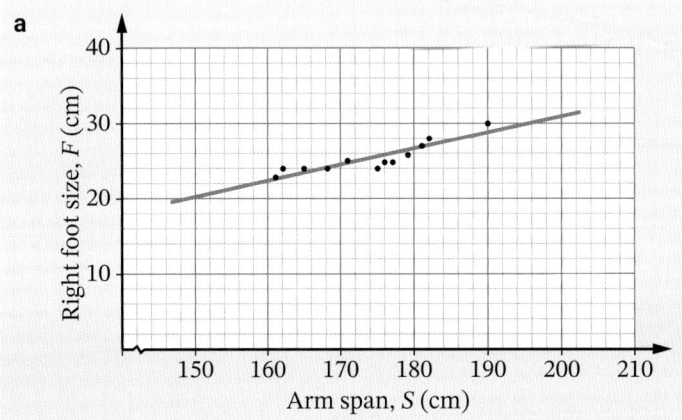

b Use the point–gradient formula $y - y_1 = m(x - x_1)$ to find the equation of the line.

$$m = \frac{y_2 - y_1}{x_2 - x_1}$$

$$= \frac{27 - 20}{181 - 150} \qquad \text{using 2 points on the line (150, 20) and (181, 27)}$$

$$= \frac{7}{31} \approx 0.226$$

$$y - 20 = 0.226(x - 150) \qquad \text{using the point (150, 20)}$$

$$= 0.226x - 33.9$$

$$y = 0.226x - 13.9$$

$$F = 0.226S - 13.9 \qquad \text{x and y are replaced by S and F respectively}$$

c When $S = 173$ cm,

$$F = 0.226 \times 173 - 13.9$$

$$= 25.198 \text{ cm}$$

A Year 10 student with an arm span of 173 cm would have a foot size of 25.198 cm.

d From the graph, a Year 10 student with an arm span of 185 cm would have a foot size of 28 cm.

> This is **interpolating** because we are reading from the graph **between** the given points.

e From the graph, a Year 10 student with a foot size of 22 cm would have an arm span of 158 cm.

> This is **extrapolating** because we are reading from the graph **outside** the given points.

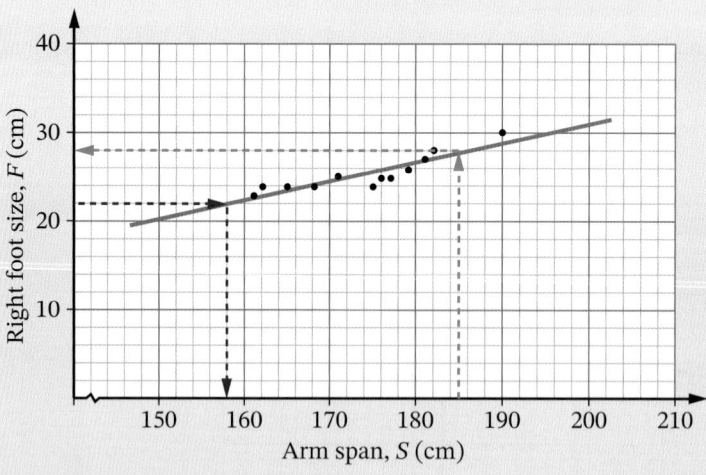

9780170465595

Line of best fit

U F R C

EXAMPLE
23

Worksheet
2 mm grid
paper

1 Forensic scientists can estimate people's heights from the lengths of their bones such
R as the tibia, femur, humerus and radius. This table gives the heights of females and the
lengths of their radius bones.

Length of radius, r (cm)	25.2	22	23	22.5	21.8	26.2	20.4	23.5	24.3	21.4
Height, H (cm)	173	158	165	161	158	179	152	167	169	156

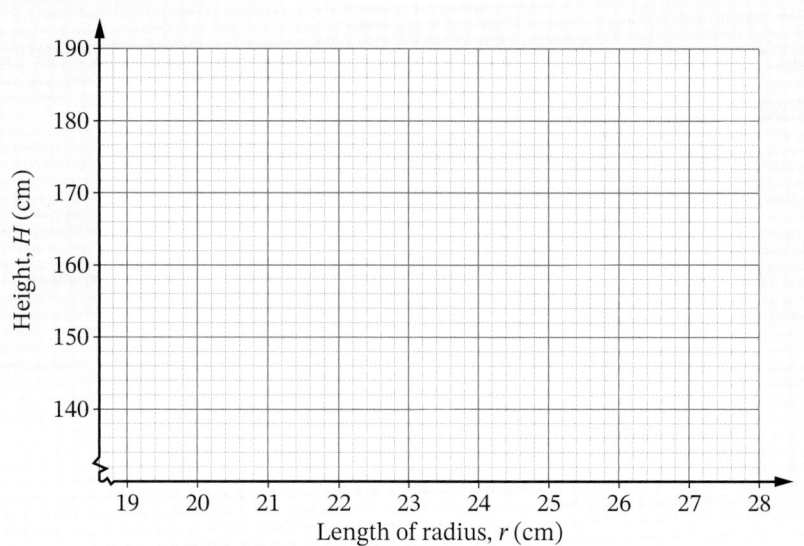

a Use graph paper with axes as shown to plot the points on a scatterplot and construct
a line of best fit.

b Find the equation of the line of best fit.

c Use your equation to find the height of a female whose radius is 25 cm long.

d If the radius is of length 27 cm, use the line of best fit to predict the height of
the female.

2 The heights and shoe size of a group of Year 11 students were measured and recorded in
the table.

Height, H (cm)	175	174	177	180	179	176	170	175	179	180	178	183	178	173	179	174
Shoe size, S	10.5	10	10	12	11	9.5	7.5	9	11.5	12.5	11	12.5	12	9.5	10.5	9

a Graph the points on a scatterplot and construct a line of best fit.

b Find the equation of the line of best fit.

c Use the equation to estimate the shoe size of a student whose height is 172 cm.

d Use the graph to interpolate the shoe size of a student who is 181 cm tall.

e Use the graph to extrapolate the shoe size of a student with height 185 cm.

☐ Foundation ○ Standard ○ Complex

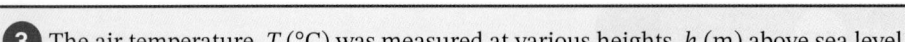

3 The air temperature, T (°C) was measured at various heights, h (m) above sea level.

Height, h (m)	0	500	1000	2000	2500	4000	5900	7500	10000
Temperature, T (°C)	20	14	8	3	−5	−13	−20	−35	−50

   a Graph the points on a scatterplot and construct a line of best fit.

   b Find the equation of the line of best fit.

   c Use the equation to estimate the temperature at a height of 1500 m.

   d Use the graph to find the height above sea level for a temperature of –10°C.

4 The results obtained by 18 Year 10 students in Maths and Science exams are shown.

Maths	59	52	72	85	75	45	65	64	62	58	78	90	40	70	50	45	82	50
Science	65	54	67	83	75	39	59	64	60	56	80	95	38	65	48	48	85	51

   a Graph the points on a scatterplot and construct a line of best fit.

   b Simone missed the Science test but obtained 80% in her Maths exam. Use the line of best fit to predict Simone's Science result.

   c If Mario obtained 96% in the Science exam, predict what result he might have achieved in the Maths exam.

5 Angelicki is measuring the amount by which a spring is stretched when different masses are hung from the spring for a Science experiment. Her results are shown.

Mass, M (g)	10	20	25	30	35	40	50
Spring stretch, S (cm)	5.9	11.2	12.3	14.8	17	22.4	25.2

   a Graph the points on a scatterplot and construct a line of best fit.

   b Use the line of best fit to predict the length the spring stretches for a mass of 45 g.

   c What mass would have to be attached to stretch the spring 28 cm?

   d Are there limitations to using the line of best fit to predict the length the spring is stretched by different masses?

6 The men's 100 m world record times for running are shown in the table.

Year	1964	1968	1983	1988	1991	1994	1996	1999	2005	2006	2007	2008	2009
Time (s)	10.06	9.95	9.93	9.92	9.86	9.85	9.84	9.79	9.77	9.76	9.74	9.69	9.58

   a Graph the points and construct a line of best fit.

   b Use the line of best fit to predict the time to run the 100 m in 2030.

   c What are the limitations of using the line of best fit to predict times to run 100 m?

☐ Foundation ○ Standard ◇ Complex

9780170465595

DID YOU KNOW?

Lightning Bolt

The current record of 9.58 seconds for running 100 metres is still held by Jamaica's Usain Bolt, who achieved this in 2009 at the World Championships in Berlin, Germany. In 2016, American sprinter Justin Gatlin achieved the time of 9.45 seconds on the Japanese television show Kasupe! but this record was disallowed. In the same year, at the Rio Olympics, Usain Bolt won the gold medal with a winning time of 9.81 seconds, Justin Gatlin won silver with 9.89 seconds, and Canadian Andre de Grasse won bronze with 9.91 seconds.

Find out why Justin Gatlin's record time was disallowed in 2016.

Shutterstock.com/Celso Pupo

TECHNOLOGY

Line of best fit

In this activity, we will use a spreadsheet to create a scatterplot and graph a line of best fit. The heights of men and the lengths of their femur bone are recorded in the table below.

Length of femur, f (cm)	40	42.9	44.2	46.1	46.8	47	48.4	50.3	51.2	57.2
Height, H (cm)	162	165	164	173	174	178	179	182	186	200

1   Enter the data from the table into a spreadsheet. Type **Length** of femur in cell A1 and **Height** in B1.

2   To graph a scatterplot, select all the values in cells B1 to K2, and under the **Insert** menu, select **Scatter and Scatter with Straight Lines and Markers**.

3   To draw the line of best fit, select one of the points on the scatterplot and right-click. Select **Add Trendline, Linear and Display Equation on chart**, then **Close**.

4   Check your answers to questions **1** to **3** from Exercise 5.13 using a spreadsheet.

Video
Can eating
fish prevent
murder?

Two-way tables are used to sort categorical data across 2 types of categorical variables. For example, this two-way table compares gender with handedness.

	Male	Female
Left-handed	14	18
Right-handed	86	65

Frequencies and relative frequencies for the categories are calculated to investigate any possible association between the two variables.

Example 24

A survey was conducted on the type of vehicle owned and the careers of 100 people.
Of those surveyed, 70 people were tradespeople and 52 owned a ute (utility vehicle).
Of the people in other careers, 16 owned other vehicles (not utes). Complete this two-way table and determine if there is an association between the categories.

	Tradespeople	Other careers	Total
Utes			
Other vehicles			
Total			

SOLUTION

Enter the information given in the question.

	Tradespeople	Other careers	Total
Utes	52		
Other vehicles		16	
Total	70		100

Use the totals to calculate the missing frequencies.

	Tradespeople	Other careers	Total
Utes	52	14	66
Other vehicles	18	16	34
Total	70	30	100

From the data, there seems to be a strong association between tradespeople and utes.

Compare the relative frequency of utes within the total group and utes within the tradespeople category.

Relative frequency of utes within the total group $= \dfrac{66}{100} = 0.66$

Relative frequency of utes within the tradespeople category $= \dfrac{52}{70} = 0.7428 \ldots$

The relative frequency of utes and tradespeople is higher, which suggests that there is an association between tradespeople and utes. Tradespeople are more likely to own a ute as a vehicle.

Association and two-way tables

U F R C

EXAMPLE 24

1 Data was collected on how students travelled to school and whether they attended high school or primary school. In a sample of 200 students, there were 96 high school students and 78 of them walked to school. There were 80 primary school students who did not walk to school.

R C

a Copy and complete this two-way table.

	High school	Primary school	Total
Walk			
Not walk			
Total			

b Calculate the relative frequency for students walking to school.

c For high school students only, what is the relative frequency of them walking to school?

d Determine the relative frequency for students not walking to school.

e For primary school children only, what is the relative frequency of them not walking to school?

f Determine if an association exists between the method of travelling to school and the category of school attended. Explain your reasoning.

2 A survey was conducted on 150 children to determine what sort of birthday party they would prefer: ten-pin bowling or ice-skating. There were 60 boys in the sample. Of the children surveyed, 25 girls preferred a bowling party and 80 children wanted an ice-skating party.

R C

a Copy and complete this two-way table.

	Boys	Girls	Total
Bowling			
Ice-skating			
Total			

b Determine the relative frequency for children selecting a bowling party.

c What is the relative frequency of selecting a bowling party if you are a girl?

d Determine the relative frequency for children selecting an ice-skating party.

e What is the relative frequency of selecting an ice-skating party if you are a boy?

f Determine if an association exists between gender and type of birthday party.

■ Foundation ○ Standard ○ Complex

3 Data was collected from 300 high school students on whether they could swim. Of the 120 senior students that participated, 45 could swim and 65 junior students could not swim. Determine if an association exists between being a senior student and being able to swim.

4 A survey was conducted in Year 10 Maths class to determine whether they studied for their weekly maths quiz and whether they passed the quiz. Of the 28 students in the class, 17 had studied. Of the students who did not study, 7 did not pass their quiz. 20 students in the class passed the quiz. Determine if an association exists between studying and passing the quiz.

5 Customers at an ice cream shop were classified on whether they liked sprinkles on their ice cream and whether they were adults or children. 160 people participated in the survey and 85 of them were adults. 25 adults liked sprinkles on their ice cream and 57 children liked sprinkles. Determine if an association exists between age and liking sprinkles on ice cream.

6 Data was collected on 500 people to determine whether there was an association between weight and diabetes. 300 of the participants were diabetic and 180 of them were overweight. Of the non-diabetics, 80 were in the normal weight range. Determine if an association exists between weight and being a diabetic.

7 A survey was conducted on 375 teenagers on their exercise and eating habits. Of those surveyed, 200 teenagers did regular exercise and 170 of them also ate healthy. 80 of the teenagers who said they did not do regular exercise also said they did not eat healthy. Determine if there is an association between eating healthy and exercise.

8 Data was collected on 400 domestic and international flights to determine whether they were arriving on time or late. Of the 300 domestic flights, 60 arrived late. 80 of the international flights were on time. Raeleigh believes that international flights are quite often late. Investigate Raeleigh's claim by determining if an association exists between flights being late and international flights.

9 A sample of 250 people was investigated to determine if there was an association between smoking and lung disease. Of the 250 participants in the sample, 150 had lung disease and 105 of these were smokers. 55 participants did not smoke and did not have lung disease. Does an association exist?

10 Data was collected on the effects of a new drug that was trialed on a small sample of elderly people to stop indigestion (in the stomach). Of the 24 participants in the sample, 15 had taken the drug and 8 of those had reported indigestion afterwards. There were 6 participants in this trial who had not taken the drug and did not have indigestion. Should the drug company release this drug for use to stop indigestion in elderly people?

INVESTIGATION

What is the association?

Design and carry out an investigation for one of the claims listed below.

- Boys are more likely to own a dog and girls are more likely to own a cat.
- People with blue eyes are more likely to have blonde hair and people with dark eyes are more likely to have dark hair.
- Girls prefer to watch action movies and boys prefer romance movies.
- Men prefer to drive large cars, whereas females prefer small to medium cars.
- Senior students are more likely to study 5 hours or more a week, whereas junior students are more likely to study fewer than 5 hours a week.
- Boys are more likely to play computer games in their free time, whereas girls are more likely to play sports.

Write a report that outlines the findings of your investigation. Your investigation will need to include the collection of data by appropriate methods (such as a survey or observation) and display of the data in a two-way table.

POWER PLUS ANSWERS ON P. 623

1   The strength and direction of the relationship between 2 variables can be measured by the correlation coefficient (r).

   a   Between which 2 values does the correlation coefficient lie?

   b   What is the strength and direction of the relationship if the correlation coefficient is zero?

   c   Write a possible value for the correlation coefficient for each relationship described.

      i   perfect positive   ii   weak negative   iii   strong negative.

2   Two variables may have a strong relationship, but this does not mean a change in one variable causes a change in the other. Which of the following pairs of variables have a causal relationship?

   a   height and weight of people

   b   the time it takes to walk to school and the distance from home to school

   c   the number of children per household and the number of mobile phones per household

   d   the age of people and their reaction time

   e   the price of petrol and the amount of petrol sold

   f   the interest rate of loans and the number of new home loans.

3   The following values are the test results on a History exam for a class of 20 students.

   13, 14, 16, 12, 14, 16, 18, 13, 15, 10, 9, 15, 13, 14, 13, 10, 8, 14, 16, 14

   a   Find the mean, median and mode.

   b   Find the range and interquartile range.

   c   An error was made in recording the values and 4 marks need to be added to each value. What effect will this have on the statistics calculated in parts **a** and **b**?

⑤ CHAPTER REVIEW

Language of maths

Quiz
Language
of maths 5

Puzzle
Data
crossword

association	bivariate data	boxplot	cluster
cumulative frequency	dependent variable	five-number summary	histogram
independent variable	interquartile range	line of best fit	mean
measure of central tendency	measure of spread	median	mode
outlier	quartile	polygon	range
scatterplot	strong	two-way table	weak

1 What is represented by the 'whiskers' on a boxplot?

2 What are the measures of central tendency and the measures of spread?

3 What are the 5 things found in a five-number summary?

4 What is a running total of the frequency called?

5 What type of graph is used to represent bivariate data?

6 What does association mean when analysing categorical data?

Topic summary

Worksheet
Mind map:
Comparing
data

Print (or copy) and complete this mind map of the topic, adding detail to its branches and using pictures, symbols and colour where needed. Ask your teacher to check your work.

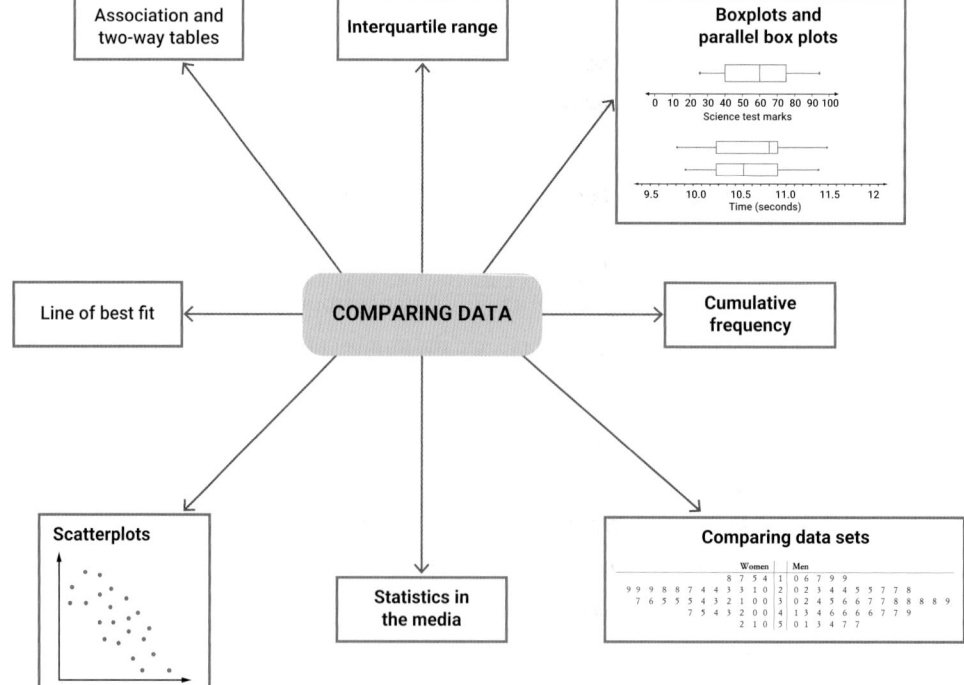

⑤ TEST YOURSELF ANSWERS ON P. 623

1 Find the interquartile range of each set of data.

a 5, 8, 8, 10, 12, 13, 14, 15, 18

b 24, 15, 23, 28, 20, 20, 18, 30, 21, 18

c

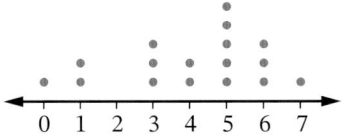

d

Stem	Leaf
3	0 1 2
4	3 5 8 8 9 9 9
5	4 5 6 6 8
6	0 1 3 7
7	2

Key: 3|0 = 30

5.01

Quiz
Test
yourself 5

2 The number of goals scored by the Under-18s Vale soccer team are:

2, 0, 0, 4, 2, 1, 1, 2, 3, 2, 3, 7, 4, 3, 1, 0, 4, 2

Draw a boxplot for the data.

5.02

3 The pulse rates of students were taken before and after exercising. The results were:

Before exercise: 78, 80, 66, 70, 56, 64, 68, 65, 50, 76, 80, 70, 70, 59

After exercise: 141, 140, 89, 95, 110, 126, 84, 82, 90, 88, 146, 98, 96, 92

a Find the five-number summary for the pulse rates before and after exercise.

b Construct parallel boxplots for the 2 sets of data.

c Find the range and interquartile range of the pulse rates:

  i before exercising

  ii after exercising.

d Compare the 2 sets of pulse rates. Are there significant differences between them? Justify your answer.

5.03

4 The ages of the students at a small regional high school are shown in this frequency table.

Score	12	13	14	15	16	17	18
Frequency	15	22	18	26	29	31	25

Use cumulative frequency to find the five number summary for this data set.

5.04

5 Data was collected on the stretch length of rubber bands before they snapped in a factory quality control room. The results are shown in this table.

a Construct a cumulative frequency histogram and polygon for this data set on the same set of axes.

b Use the cumulative frequency polygon to find the median stretch length.

Length (mm)	Frequency
15−19	30
20−24	34
25−29	42
30−34	58
35−39	67
40−44	41
45−49	28

5.05

☐ Foundation ◯ Standard ◯ Complex

6 A survey was conducted on the amount of pocket money students at a primary school received each month. The results of the survey were graphed on this cumulative frequency histogram and polygon.

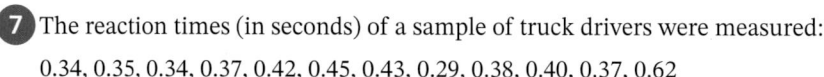

Monthly pocket money

a How many students received $50 or less a month?

b What is the median class?

c Estimate the first quartile, Q_1.

d Estimate the 75th percentile, P_{75}.

e Calculate the interquartile range.

7 The reaction times (in seconds) of a sample of truck drivers were measured:

0.34, 0.35, 0.34, 0.37, 0.42, 0.45, 0.43, 0.29, 0.38, 0.40, 0.37, 0.62

a Find, correct to 2 decimal places, the mean and standard deviation.

b Find the range and interquartile range.

c Which is the best measure of spread for this set of data? Justify your answer.

8 The Health exam results for a class of PE students are shown here.

Girls: 83, 78, 63, 84, 65, 51, 76, 69, 42, 84, 60, 64, 92, 73, 32

Boys: 65, 34, 75, 68, 56, 63, 79, 55, 68, 52, 49, 85, 64, 58, 54

a Find the mean and standard deviation of both groups.

b Which group performed better in the exam? Give reasons.

9 The speeds of cars (in km/h) were monitored between 1:00 and 1:30 pm on a main road. The results are shown in the stem-and-leaf plot and boxplot.

Stem	Leaf
7	0 3 7 9
8	0 2 2 3 5 6 8 8 9
9	0 0 1 3 5 5 7 8 9 9 9
10	0 0 4 4 6
11	0 1
12	6

Key: 11|0 = 110

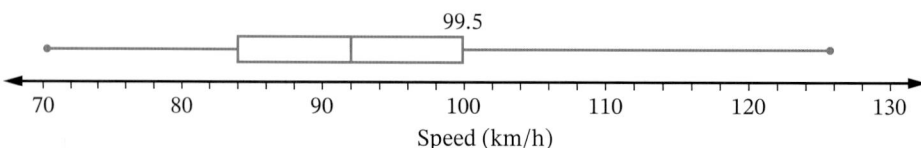

a Which display best indicates:

   i skewness?   **ii** clustering and outliers?

b Why would a dot plot be unsuitable for displaying the data?

c Find the:

   i median   **ii** interquartile range.

d What percentage of cars were travelling at a speed of at least 92 km/h?

10 An advertisement in a magazine states that a product is 75% fat-free.   (5.10)

a What impression is the advertisement trying to make about the product?

b What doesn't the advertisement say about the product?

11 Eleven boxes containing 60 oranges each were placed in cold storage for different periods.   (5.12)
After storage, the number of good oranges in each box was counted.

Weeks in storage (W)	2	5	12	8	14	6	5	9	10	3	11
Number of good oranges, (N)	58	50	33	40	28	50	52	38	35	55	33

a Which is the independent variable? Give reasons.

b Graph this data on a scatterplot.

c Describe the pattern of the plotted points.

d Describe the relationship between weeks in storage and the number of good oranges.

e Describe the strength and direction of the relationship between the variables W and N.

12 The heights and weights of 15 people were measured.   (5.13)

Height, H (cm)	152	160	179	180	185	174	165	150	145	142	155	153	175	155
Weight, W (kg)	50	65	72	77	81	77	65	57	48	53	61	67	72	56

a Graph the points on a scatter plot and construct a line of best fit.

b Find the equation of the line of best fit.

c Use the equation to estimate the weight of a student who is 170 cm tall.

d Use the graph to interpolate the weight of a student with height 163 cm.

e Use the graph to extrapolate the height of a student who weighs

   i 85 kg   **ii** 45 kg

13 A survey was conducted on 160 teenagers on whether they received pocket money from   (5.14)
their parents and whether they completed household jobs. 103 teenagers received pocket
money, and 76 of them completed household jobs. 35 of the teenagers who did not receive
pocket money did not also complete any household jobs. Determine whether there is an
association between a teenager completing household jobs and receiving pocket money.

☐ Foundation   ◯ Standard   ◯ Complex

6

ALGEBRA

Equations and logarithms

In 1962, when astronaut John Glenn was preparing to be the first American to orbit the Earth, he called upon mathematician Katherine Johnson (1918–2020) to check by hand the complex calculations being performed on NASA's new electronic computers. Johnson worked for NASA for 35 years and her story was told in the 2016 book and film *Hidden Figures*. During her career, she solved equations that guided the paths of spacecrafts and helped the United States send the first astronauts to the moon in 1969. Building on the ancient achievements of the Egyptians and Babylonians, Johnson opened the door to space travel and future space tourism.

stock.adobe.com/50photography

Chapter outline

Proficiencies

6.01	Linear equations	U	F			
6.02	Algebraic fractions*	U	F			
6.03	Equations with algebraic fractions*	U	F			
6.04	Quadratic equations $x^2 + bx + c = 0$	U	F		R	C
6.05	Simple cubic equations $ax^3 = c$*	U	F		R	C
6.06	Equation problems	U	F	PS	R	C
6.07	Equations and formulas	U	F		R	C
6.08	Changing the subject of a formula*	U	F		R	C
6.09	Graphing inequalities on a number line	U	F			C
6.10	Solving inequalities	U	F		R	C
6.11	Logarithms*	U	F		R	C
6.12	Logarithm laws*	U	F		R	
6.13	Exponential and logarithmic equations*	U	F	PS	R	

* EXTENSION

U = Understanding
F = Fluency
PS = Problem solving

R = Reasoning
C = Communicating

Wordbank

> 'is greater than'

< 'is less than'

cubic equation An equation involving a variable cubed (power of 3), such as $4x^3 = 500$

exponential equation An equation where the variable is a power, such as $3x = 243$

formula A rule written as an algebraic equation, using variables.

inequality A mathematical statement that 2 quantities are not equal, involving algebraic expressions and an inequality sign (>, ≥, <, or ≤).

logarithm The power of a number, to a given base. For example, log10 1000 = 3, meaning that the logarithm of 1000 to base 10 is 3, because $1000 = 10^3$

quadratic equation An equation involving a variable squared (power of 2), such as $3x^2 - 6 = 69$.

solution The answer to an equation, inequality or problem; the correct value(s) of the variable that makes an equation or inequality true.

Quiz
Wordbank 6

6 In this chapter you will:

✓ solve linear equations and problems involving equations

✓ (EXTENSION) solve linear equations involving algebraic fractions

✓ solve simple quadratic equations of the form $ax^2 = c$ and $x^2 + bx + c = 0$

✓ (EXTENSION) solve simple cubic equations of the form $ax^3 = c$

✓ use formulas to solve problems

✓ (EXTENSION) change the subject of a formula

✓ graph inequalities on a number line

✓ solve linear inequalities

✓ (EXTENSION) apply logarithms and the logarithm laws

✓ (EXTENSION) solve exponential and logarithmic equations

SkillCheck

ANSWERS ON P. 624

Quiz
SkillCheck 6

1 Simplify each expression.

a $\dfrac{a}{5} + \dfrac{3a}{4}$ **b** $\dfrac{7p}{2} - \dfrac{10p}{3}$ **c** $\dfrac{9h}{3} + \dfrac{4h}{2}$ **d** $\dfrac{5k}{2} - \dfrac{3k}{6}$

2 Factorise each expression.

a $k^2 + 5k + 4$ **b** $y^2 - 10y + 16$ **c** $m^2 - m - 56$

d $u^2 + 8u - 65$ **e** $w^2 - 10w + 21$ **f** $x^2 - 2x - 24$

Example 1

Solve each equation.

a $9x + 10 = 7x - 6$

b $5(p + 6) = 3p + 5$

SOLUTION

a
$$9x + 10 = 7x - 6$$
$$9x + 10 - 7x = 7x - 6 - 7x$$
$$2x + 10 = -6$$
$$2x + 10 - 10 = -6 - 10$$
$$2x = -16$$
$$\frac{2x}{2} = \frac{-16}{2}$$
$$x = -8$$

b Expand the LHS:
$$5(p + 6) = 3p + 5$$
$$5p + 30 = 3p + 5$$
$$5p + 30 - 3p = 3p + 5 - 3p$$
$$2p + 30 = 5$$
$$2p + 30 - 30 = 5 - 30$$
$$2p = -25$$
$$\frac{2p}{2} = \frac{-25}{2}$$
$$p = -12\frac{1}{2}$$

Videos
Equations with variables on both sides

Equations with brackets

Puzzles
Equations with unknowns on both sides

Equations

Equations order activity

Equations code puzzle

Example 2

Solve $4(y + 1) + 3(y - 5) = 8$.

SOLUTION

$$4(y + 1) + 3(y - 5) = 8$$
$$4y + 4 + 3y - 15 = 8$$
$$7y - 11 = 8$$
$$7y = 19$$
$$\frac{7y}{7} = \frac{19}{7}$$
$$y = 2\frac{5}{7}$$

Check:

LHS $= 4\left(2\frac{5}{7} + 1\right) + 3\left(2\frac{5}{7} - 5\right) = 8$

RHS $= 8$

LHS $=$ RHS

Linear equations   U F

EXAMPLE 1

1 Solve each equation.

a $\frac{k}{6} = 10$ b $w + 3 = -6$ c $5y - 1 = 9$

d $3a + 10 = 25$ e $2x + 6 = 22$ f $15a - 2 = 13$

g $12 - r = 18$ h $7w - 10 = 32$ i $9y - 6 = -24$

j $11 - 6a = -10$ k $7u = u + 32$ l $5a = a - 7$

2 Solve $6x - 3 = 27$. Select the correct answer **A**, **B**, **C** or **D**.

   A $x = 4$ **B** $x = 5$ **C** $x = 10$ **D** $x = 18$

3 Solve $10 - 2a = 20$. Select **A**, **B**, **C** or **D**.

   A $a = -15$ **B** $a = 8$ **C** $a = 32$ **D** $a = -5$

4 Solve each equation.

a $5y + 10 = 3y + 30$ b $8a + 20 = 4a + 10$ c $6y - 1 = 3y + 14$

d $12a + 30 = 5a + 9$ e $5y + 3 = 8y - 21$ f $14x - 20 = 8x - 14$

g $9y + 1 = 3y - 5$ h $15x - 15 = 8x - 85$ i $8m - 10 = 5 - 2m$

j $18 - 3y = 6 - 2y$ k $1 - 7a = 10 + 2a$ l $11 - 5x = 3x + 43$

5 Solve $4y = y - 15$. Select **A**, **B**, **C** or **D**.

   A $y = -3$ **B** $y = \frac{7}{4}$ **C** $y = -5$ **D** $y = 11$

6 Solve each equation.

a $3(x - 6) = 30$ b $5(m + 10) = 80$

c $2(5y + 3) = 46$ d $3(y + 2) = 5y - 10$

e $5(y + 4) = 3y + 6$ f $10(x - 3) = 5(x + 5)$

g $2(3m + 6) = 4(m - 1)$ h $5(2a + 7) = 5(4 - a)$

i $3(1 - 2y) = 18 - 3y$

7 Solve $2(y - 3) = 5 + 4y$. Select **A**, **B**, **C** or **D**.

   A $y = -9$ **B** $y = -5$ **C** $y = -\frac{11}{2}$ **D** $y = -\frac{1}{2}$

EXAMPLE 2

8 Solve each equation.

a $3(d + 3) + 4(d + 1) = 15$ b $3(y - 1) + 5(y + 4) = 10$

c $7(k + 1) + 2(k - 6) = 3$ d $5(g - 3) + 2(g - 2) = 4$

e $6(2h + 3) + 5(h - 3) = 9$ f $2(1 + p) + 3(4 + p) = 5$

☐ Foundation   ○ Standard   ◇ Complex

Extension: Algebraic fractions

Example 3

Simplify each expression.

a $\dfrac{a}{2}+\dfrac{a}{3}$

b $\dfrac{2x}{5}-\dfrac{x}{3}$

c $\dfrac{5}{y}+\dfrac{7}{2y}$

SOLUTION

a $\dfrac{a}{2}+\dfrac{a}{3}=\dfrac{3a}{6}+\dfrac{2a}{6}$

$\qquad =\dfrac{5a}{6}$

b $\dfrac{2x}{5}-\dfrac{x}{3}=\dfrac{6x}{15}-\dfrac{5x}{15}$

$\qquad =\dfrac{x}{15}$

c $\dfrac{5}{y}+\dfrac{7}{2y}=\dfrac{10}{2y}+\dfrac{7}{2y}$

$\qquad =\dfrac{17}{2y}$

Example 4

Simplify each expression.

a $\dfrac{6h+1}{8}+\dfrac{4h-7}{12}$

b $\dfrac{x}{3}-\dfrac{x+1}{5}$

SOLUTION

a $\dfrac{6h+1}{8}+\dfrac{4h-7}{12}=\dfrac{3(6h+1)}{24}+\dfrac{2(4h-7)}{24}$

$\qquad =\dfrac{18h+3}{24}+\dfrac{8h-14}{24}$

$\qquad =\dfrac{26h-11}{24}$

b $\dfrac{x}{3}-\dfrac{x+1}{5}=\dfrac{5x}{15}-\dfrac{3(x+1)}{15}$

$\qquad =\dfrac{5x}{15}-\dfrac{3x+3}{15}$

$\qquad =\dfrac{5x-3x-3}{15}$

$\qquad =\dfrac{2x-3}{15}$

Videos
Adding and subtracting algebraic fractions

Algebraic fractions

Puzzle
Algebraic fractions

Video
Algebraic fractions

EXTENSION

EXERCISE 6.02 ANSWERS ON P. 624

Algebraic fractions

(U) (F)

EXAMPLE **3**

1 Simplify each expression.

a $\dfrac{n}{2} - \dfrac{n}{7}$

b $\dfrac{3c}{2} + \dfrac{c}{5}$

c $\dfrac{4r}{7} + \dfrac{5r}{2}$

d $\dfrac{7y}{8} - \dfrac{5y}{3}$

e $\dfrac{4t}{3} + \dfrac{t}{9}$

f $\dfrac{5y}{16} + \dfrac{3y}{8}$

g $\dfrac{11t}{12} - \dfrac{5t}{9}$

h $\dfrac{3a}{10} + \dfrac{4a}{15}$

i $\dfrac{4}{k} + \dfrac{3a}{k}$

j $\dfrac{7d}{3y} - \dfrac{2d}{3y}$

k $\dfrac{12}{5x} - \dfrac{7}{5x}$

l $\dfrac{11p}{12} + \dfrac{3p}{12}$

m $\dfrac{5}{q} + \dfrac{3}{r}$

n $\dfrac{15}{4h} - \dfrac{2}{h}$

o $\dfrac{5}{3b} + \dfrac{3}{4b}$

p $\dfrac{9}{2n} - \dfrac{4}{3p}$

2 Simplify each expression.

a $\dfrac{w}{7} + \dfrac{n}{4}$

b $\dfrac{3x}{8} + \dfrac{5u}{7}$

c $\dfrac{2a}{15} - \dfrac{3h}{10}$

d $\dfrac{d}{16} - \dfrac{r}{24}$

e $\dfrac{4k}{5} - \dfrac{g}{9}$

f $\dfrac{5m}{12} + \dfrac{2r}{5}$

g $\dfrac{3h}{2} + \dfrac{4}{5}$

h $\dfrac{5u}{4} - \dfrac{3a}{7}$

i $\dfrac{a}{5} + \dfrac{c}{9}$

j $\dfrac{5q}{12} - \dfrac{11w}{18}$

k $\dfrac{5k}{8} + \dfrac{3}{11}$

l $\dfrac{4n}{9} + \dfrac{5n}{6}$

3 Simplify $\dfrac{5p}{6} - \dfrac{3p}{8}$. Select the correct answer **A**, **B**, **C** or **D**.

A $\dfrac{29p}{24}$

B $\dfrac{22p}{48}$

C $\dfrac{11p}{24}$

D $\dfrac{2p}{24}$

4 Simplify $\dfrac{1}{xw} + \dfrac{w}{xy}$. Select **A**, **B**, **C** or **D**.

A $\dfrac{y+w}{xyw}$

B $\dfrac{w^2+y}{xyw}$

C $\dfrac{y+w^2}{xy}$

D $\dfrac{y^2+w}{wx}$

EXAMPLE **4**

5 Simplify $\dfrac{4w-3}{5} - \dfrac{1+2w}{4}$. Select **A**, **B**, **C** or **D**.

A $\dfrac{6w-17}{20}$

B $\dfrac{6w-7}{20}$

C $\dfrac{26w-17}{20}$

D $\dfrac{26w-7}{10}$

6 Simplify each expression.

a $\dfrac{m+3}{5} + \dfrac{m-2}{4}$

b $\dfrac{3p}{5} + \dfrac{p+2}{3}$

c $\dfrac{y+3}{4} + \dfrac{2y-1}{3}$

d $\dfrac{x-1}{7} + \dfrac{x-2}{3}$

e $\dfrac{5h+6}{2} - \dfrac{2h+2}{9}$

f $\dfrac{k+3}{10} - \dfrac{2k-3}{7}$

☐ Foundation   ◯ Standard   ◇ Complex

9780170465595

Extension: Equations with algebraic fractions

For equations with more than one fraction, multiply both sides by a common multiple of the denominators to remove the fractions.

EXTENSION

Videos
Equations with algebraic fractions

Solving equations with fractions

Puzzles
Equations code puzzle

Equations order activity

Solving linear equations 1

Solving linear equations 2

Example 5

Solve each equation.

a $\dfrac{2m}{3} - \dfrac{m}{2} = 2$

b $\dfrac{2a+4}{5} = \dfrac{2}{3}$

SOLUTION

a $\dfrac{2m}{3} - \dfrac{m}{2} = 2$

$6\left(\dfrac{2m}{3} - \dfrac{m}{2}\right) = 6 \times 2$ Multiply both sides by 6, the LCM of 3 and 2

$6^2 \times \dfrac{2m}{3_1} - 6^3 \times \dfrac{m}{2_1} = 12$

$4m - 3m = 12$

$m = 12$ Check by substituting that this solution is correct.

Note: We can also solve this equation by simplifying the LHS first:

$\dfrac{4m}{6} - \dfrac{3m}{6} = 2$

$\dfrac{m}{6} = 2$

$m = 12$

However, the first method may be faster and easier because operations with fractions are not needed.

b $\dfrac{2a+4}{5} = \dfrac{2}{3}$

$\dfrac{2a+4}{5_1} \times 15^3 = \dfrac{2}{3_1} \times 15^5$ $6a = -2$

$3(2a+4) = 10$ $a = \dfrac{-2}{6}$

$6a + 12 = 10$ $a = -\dfrac{1}{3}$

Example 6

Solve $\dfrac{2n+1}{3} - \dfrac{3n-2}{2} = -5$.

SOLUTION

$$\dfrac{2n+1}{3} - \dfrac{3n-2}{2} = -5$$

$$\cancel{6}^{2}\left(\dfrac{2n+1}{\cancel{3}_{1}}\right) - \cancel{6}^{3}\left(\dfrac{3n-2}{\cancel{2}_{1}}\right) = 6\times(-5)$$

$$2(2n+1) - 3(3n-2) = -30$$

$$4n+2-9n+6 = -30$$

$$-5n+8 = -30$$

$$-5n = -38$$

$$n = \dfrac{-38}{-5}$$

$$= 7\dfrac{3}{5}$$

EXERCISE 6.03 ANSWERS ON P. 624

Equations with algebraic fractions Ⓤ Ⓕ

1 Solve each equation.

a $\dfrac{3y}{5} = 9$

b $\dfrac{2a}{9} = 2$

c $\dfrac{m}{2} + 5 = 6$

d $\dfrac{k}{5} - 2 = 11$

e $\dfrac{n+5}{3} = -10$

f $\dfrac{y-1}{4} = -2$

g $\dfrac{x+1}{4} + 2 = 10$

h $\dfrac{y-1}{5} - 6 = 3$

i $\dfrac{m+2}{5} - 1 = 3$

j $\dfrac{x-6}{5} + 7 = 0$

k $\dfrac{2(x+1)}{5} = 10$

l $\dfrac{3(m-2)}{4} = 6$

m $\dfrac{8(n+1)}{3} + 2 = 4$

n $\dfrac{5(1-n)}{2} - 1 = 3$

o $\dfrac{4(1+d)}{3} + 1 = 7\dfrac{1}{3}$

EXAMPLE 5

2 Solve each equation.

a $\dfrac{2k}{3} = \dfrac{5}{4}$

b $\dfrac{3w}{10} = \dfrac{2}{5}$

c $\dfrac{5x}{2} = -\dfrac{10}{3}$

d $\dfrac{x-1}{2} = \dfrac{x+1}{4}$

e $\dfrac{y+2}{5} = \dfrac{y-1}{2}$

f $\dfrac{a+5}{3} = \dfrac{a-1}{8}$

g $\dfrac{p+2}{5} = \dfrac{p-5}{2}$

h $\dfrac{2y-1}{5} = \dfrac{y+1}{4}$

i $\dfrac{3y+2}{3} = \dfrac{2y+1}{4}$

j $\dfrac{w}{5} + \dfrac{w}{2} = 7$

k $\dfrac{w}{2} - \dfrac{w}{5} = 15$

l $\dfrac{2w}{3} - \dfrac{w}{4} = 4$

m $\dfrac{3a}{2} + \dfrac{a}{3} = 1$

n $\dfrac{2y}{5} - \dfrac{y}{3} = 4$

o $\dfrac{a}{3} + \dfrac{3a}{4} = 2$

p $\dfrac{2m}{5} - \dfrac{m}{10} = 1$

q $\dfrac{4h}{3} + \dfrac{h}{5} = 3$

r $\dfrac{5y-2}{7} = \dfrac{3y+5}{3}$

▷

☐ Foundation ◯ Standard ◇ Complex

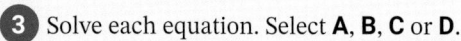

6.04

3 Solve each equation. Select **A**, **B**, **C** or **D**.

a $\dfrac{4m}{5} - \dfrac{m}{3} = 2$

   A $m = 10$ **B** $m = 12$ **C** $m = \dfrac{30}{7}$ **D** $m = \dfrac{4}{3}$

b $\dfrac{m+1}{2} = \dfrac{3+2m}{5}$

   A $m = 1$ **B** $m = 5$ **C** $m = \dfrac{5}{3}$ **D** $m = \dfrac{2}{3}$

4 Solve each equation.

EXAMPLE 6

a $\dfrac{x-1}{4} + \dfrac{2x}{7} = 0$

b $\dfrac{p+2}{3} + \dfrac{p+1}{4} = 10$

c $\dfrac{m+2}{3} + \dfrac{m+1}{4} = 12$

d $\dfrac{x-3}{5} + \dfrac{x-2}{2} = 6$

e $\dfrac{3x-10}{3} + \dfrac{x-2}{2} = 11$

f $\dfrac{3y+1}{4} - \dfrac{y+2}{3} = 4$

g $\dfrac{7+2a}{5} - \dfrac{a-1}{2} = 6$

h $\dfrac{6a-1}{4} - \dfrac{a+2}{3} = 8$

i $\dfrac{a-10}{5} - \dfrac{5-2a}{4} = \dfrac{1}{2}$

Quadratic equations $x^2 + bx + c = 0$

6.04

An equation in which the highest power of the variable is 2 is called a **quadratic equation**, for example, $x^2 = 5$, $3m^2 + 7 = 10$, $d^2 - d - 6 = 0$ and $4t^2 - 3t = 8$.

ⓘ The quadratic equation $x^2 = c$

The quadratic equation $x^2 = c$ (where c is a positive number) has 2 solutions:

$$x = \pm\sqrt{c}$$

(which means $x = \sqrt{c}$ and $x = -\sqrt{c}$).

Example 7

Solve each quadratic equation.

a $m^2 = 16$

b $3x^2 = 75$

c $4m^2 - 12 = 0$

Video
Simple quadratic equations

SOLUTION

a $m^2 = 16$

   $m = \pm\sqrt{16}$

   $= \pm 4$

b $3x^2 = 75$

   $x^2 = \dfrac{75}{3}$

   $x^2 = 25$

   $x = \pm\sqrt{25}$

   $= \pm 5$ Leave the answer as a surd (in exact form).

c $4m^2 - 12 = 0$

   $4m^2 - 12 + 12 = 0 + 12$

   $4m^2 = 12$

   $m^2 = \dfrac{12}{4}$

   $m^2 = 3$

   $m = \pm\sqrt{3}$

☐ Foundation ○ Standard ○ Complex

Example 8

Solve $7x^2 - 88 = 0$, writing the **solution** correct to one decimal place.

SOLUTION

$7x^2 - 88 = 0$

$7x^2 = 88$

$x^2 = \dfrac{88}{7}$

$x = \pm\sqrt{\dfrac{88}{7}}$

$x = \pm3.545\ 62...$

$\approx \pm 3.5$

ⓘ The quadratic equation $x^2 + bx + c = 0$

To solve quadratic equations of the form $x^2 + bx + c = 0$, factorise $x^2 + bx + c$ into binomial products.

Example 9

Video
Quadratic
equations
by
factorising

Solve $x^2 + 5x + 6 = 0$.

SOLUTION

$x^2 + 5x + 6 = 0$

$(x + 2)(x + 3) = 0$

The LHS has been factorised into 2 binomials, $(x + 2)$ and $(x + 3)$, whose product is 0.

If 2 numbers have a product of 0, then one of the numbers must be 0.

$\therefore x + 2 = 0$ or $x + 3 = 0$

$\therefore x = -2$ or $x = -3$

$\therefore$ the solution to $x^2 + 5x + 6 = 0$ is $x = -2$ or $x = -3$.

Check:

When $x = -2$,

$\text{LHS} = (-2)^2 + 5 \times (-2) + 6 = 0$

$\text{RHS} = 0$

$\text{LHS} = \text{RHS}$

When $x = -3$,

$\text{LHS} = (-3)^2 + 5 \times (-3) + 6 = 0$

$\text{RHS} = 0$

$\text{LHS} = \text{RHS}$

Example 10

Video
Quadratic equations by factorising

Solve each quadratic equation.

a $x^2 - x - 2 = 0$ **b** $u^2 + 3u - 28 = 0$

c $3m^2 = 6m$ **d** $w^2 - 10w + 25 = 0$

SOLUTION

a $x^2 - x - 2 = 0$

Find 2 numbers that have a sum of –1 and a product of –2.

They are –2 and 1.

$(x - 2)(x + 1) = 0$

$\therefore x - 2 = 0$ or $x + 1 = 0$

$\therefore x = 2$ or $x = -1$

$\therefore$ the solution to $x^2 - x - 2 = 0$ is $x = 2$ or $x = -1$.

Check:

When $x = 2$,   When $x = -1$,

LHS $= 2^2 - 2 - 2 = 0$ LHS $= (-1)^2 - (-1) - 2 = 0$

RHS $= 0$ RHS $= 0$

LHS = RHS   LHS = RHS

b $u^2 + 3u - 28 = 0$

Find 2 numbers that have a sum of 3 and a product of –28.

They are 7 and –4.

$(u + 7)(u - 4) = 0$

$\therefore u + 7 = 0$ or $u - 4 = 0$

$\therefore u = -7$ or $u = 4$

$\therefore$ the solution to $u^2 + 3u - 28 = 0$ is $u = -7$ or $u = 4$.

c $3m^2 = 6m$

$3m^2 - 6m = 0$

> You cannot divide both sides by m because if $m = 0$, then you are dividing by 0.

This requires a simpler factorisation as there are only 2 terms, both involving m.

$3m(m - 2) = 0$

$\therefore 3m = 0$ or $m - 2 = 0$

$\therefore m = 0$ or $m = 2$

$\therefore$ the solution to $3m^2 - 6m = 0$ is $m = 0$ or $m = 2$.

d $w^2 - 10w + 25 = 0$

Find 2 numbers that have a sum of –10 and a product of 25.

They are –5 and –5.

$(w - 5)(w - 5) = 0$

$\therefore w - 5 = 0$ or $w - 5 = 0$

$\therefore w = 5$ or $w = 5$

$\therefore$ the solution to $w^2 - 10w + 25 = 0$ is $w = 5$ (only one solution).

6.04

Note: Quadratic equations of the form $ax^2 + bx + c = 0$ will be met in Chapter 13: *Quadratic equations and the parabola*.

EXERCISE 6.04 ANSWERS ON P. 625

Quadratic equations $x^2 + bx + c = 0$

U F R C

1 Solve each quadratic equation, writing the solutions as surds if necessary.

a $m^2 = 144$	**b** $x^2 = 400$	**c** $y^2 = 35$	**d** $k^2 - 169 = 0$
e $y^2 - 1 = 0$	**f** $w^2 - 24 = 0$	**g** $x^2 + 10 = 14$	**h** $t^2 - 9 = 7$
i $\dfrac{a^2}{2} = 8$	**j** $4k^2 = 180$	**k** $3w^2 = 300$	**l** $d^2 + 60 = 204$
m $\dfrac{k^2}{2} = 7$	**n** $\dfrac{w^2}{10} = 2.5$	**o** $4x^2 = 1$	**p** $\dfrac{m^2}{4} = 10$
q $5y^2 = 5$	**r** $2p^2 + 3 = 21$	**s** $\dfrac{3k^2}{2} + 1 = 13$	**t** $\dfrac{y^2}{5} - 2 = 18$

2 Solve each equation, correct to one decimal place where necessary.

a $5m^2 - 20 = 0$	**b** $\dfrac{4a^2}{9} = 36$	**c** $m^2 = 28$
d $9m^2 - 2 = 32$	**e** $9k^2 + 10 = 13$	**f** $\dfrac{2x^2}{5} = 23$
g $\dfrac{k^2}{16} = 6$	**h** $\dfrac{3k^2}{10} = 27$	**i** $6y^2 = 0.726$
j $3a^2 + 11 = 267$	**k** $2y^2 - 14 = 63$	**l** $\dfrac{2w^2}{5} - 1 = 19$

3 Solve each quadratic equation. Select the correct answer **A**, **B**, **C** or **D**.

a $x^2 = 121$

   A $x = 12, -12$ **B** $x = 11, -11$ **C** $x = 10, 11$ **D** $x = 12, -11$

b $9m^2 - 1 = 35$

   A $m = 3, -3$ **B** $m = 2, -2$ **C** $m = 8, -8$ **D** $m = 9, -9$

4 Solve each equation.

a $x^2 + 3x + 2 = 0$	**b** $y^2 + 5y + 4 = 0$	**c** $y^2 + 16y + 48 = 0$
d $x^2 + x - 12 = 0$	**e** $x^2 + 2x - 3 = 0$	**f** $x^2 + 3x - 40 = 0$

5 Solve each equation.

a $x^2 - x - 30 = 0$	**b** $x^2 - 8x + 16 = 0$	**c** $x^2 - 5x - 66 = 0$
d $d^2 - 2d = 0$	**e** $x^2 - 3x - 10 = 0$	**f** $n^2 + 4n = 0$
g $k^2 - 7k = 0$	**h** $y^2 = 5y$	**i** $v^2 = 12v$

6 Explain why the quadratic equation $x^2 = -25$ has no solutions.

R C

7 State which of these quadratic equations have no solutions. Give reasons.

(R) (C)

a $x^2 = -9$ **b** $2k^2 + 5 = 9$ **c** $3m^2 + 8 = 4$

d $\dfrac{9w^2}{2} - 1 = 1$ **e** $4 + \dfrac{d^2}{3} = 8$ **f** $\dfrac{5a^2}{2} + 3 = 2$

8 Solve each quadratic equation. Select **A**, **B**, **C** or **D**.

a $x^2 + 4x - 60 = 0$

    A $x = -10, 6$ **B** $x = 12, -5$ **C** $x = 10, -6$ **D** $x = -12, 5$

b $q^2 + 3q = 0$

    A $q = 3, -3$ **B** $q = 6, -3$ **C** $q = 0, -3$ **D** $q = 0, 3$

Extension: Simple cubic equations $ax^3 = c$ 6.05

An equation in which the highest power of the variable is 3 is called a **cubic equation**, for example, $x^3 = 12$, $2m^3 + 1 = 25$, $d^3 - 14 = 4$ and $x^3 - 3x^2 + 5x + 4 = 0$.

EXTENSION

ⓘ The cubic equation $x^3 = c$

The cubic equation $x^3 = c$ has one solution:

$$x = \sqrt[3]{c} \ .$$

Example 11

Solve each cubic equation.

a $y^3 = 64$ **b** $p^3 = 50$ **c** $-2x^3 = 2000$

SOLUTION

a $y^3 = 64$

    $y = \sqrt[3]{64}$

    $= 4$

b $p^3 = 50$

    $p = \sqrt[3]{50}$

c $-2x^3 = 2000$

    $x^3 = \dfrac{2000}{-2}$

    $= -1000$

    $x = \sqrt[3]{-1000}$

    $= -10$

☐ Foundation   ◯ Standard   ◇ Complex

Example 12

Solve each cubic equation, writing the solution correct to one decimal place.

a $11x^3 - 102 = 0$

b $\dfrac{2y^3}{7} = -11$

SOLUTION

a $11x^3 - 102 = 0$

$11x^3 = 102$

$x^3 = \dfrac{102}{11}$

$= 9.272...$

$x = \sqrt[3]{9.272...}$

$= 2.1008...$

≈ 2.1

b $\dfrac{2y^3}{7} = -11$

$2y^3 = -11 \times 7$

$= -77$

$y^3 = \dfrac{-77}{2}$

$= -38.5$

$y = \sqrt[3]{-38.5}$

$= -3.3766...$

≈ -3.4

EXERCISE **6.05** ANSWERS ON P. 625

Simple cubic equations $ax^3 = c$

U F R C

1 Solve each cubic equation, writing the solution in exact form where necessary.

a $x^3 = 1$

b $m^3 = 125$

c $a^3 = 1331$

d $u^3 = -8$

e $y^3 = -729$

f $n^3 = 20$

g $h^3 = 11$

h $k^3 = -48$

i $5m^3 = -75$

j $7m^3 = 448$

k $-4x^3 = 81$

l $12x^3 = -480$

2 Solve each cubic equation, writing the solution correct to one decimal place.

a $w^3 - 16 = 0$

b $m^3 + 6 = 22$

c $5m^3 - 1080 = 0$

d $3t^3 - 10 = 87$

e $\dfrac{x^3}{3} = 9$

f $\dfrac{5x^3}{7} = -120$

g $\dfrac{3x^3}{4} = -10$

h $\dfrac{2x^3}{5} = 0.2048$

i $\dfrac{7a^3}{9} - 10 = 121$

j $a^3 - 0.064 = 0$

k $-\dfrac{7x^3}{9} = 10$

l $5t^3 + 46 = -370$

3 **a** Does a cubic equation of the form $ax^3 = c$ always have a solution?

R **b** When is the solution to $x^3 = c$ positive?

C **c** When is the solution to $x^3 = c$ negative?

d Can $x^3 = c$ have 2 solutions?

☐ Foundation ○ Standard ◇ Complex

Equation problems

6.06

Example 13

At a concert, an adult's ticket costs $5 more than twice the cost of a child's ticket. The total cost for 3 adults and 7 children is $327. Find the cost of a child's ticket and an adult's ticket.

SOLUTION

Let the cost of a child's ticket be $c.

∴ Cost of an adult's ticket = $(2c + 5)

$3(2c + 5) + 7c = 327$

$6c + 15 + 7c = 327$

$13c + 15 = 327$

$13c = 312$

$c = 24$

∴ Cost of an adult's ticket = 2 × $24 + 5

$= \$53$

∴ A child's ticket costs $24 and an adult's ticket costs $53.

Using a variable to represent an unknown quantity.

Forming an equation.

Solving the equation.

A child's ticket costs $24.

$(2c + 5)

Check: 3 × $53 + 7 × $24 = $327.

Example 14

Paris is 7 years older than Amy. 10 years from now, the sum of their ages will be 43. How old are they now?

SOLUTION

Let x = Amy's age now.

Then Paris' age now $= x + 7$.

Break the information into 'Now' and 'In 10 years' time':

	Now	In 10 years' time
Amy	x	$x + 10$
Paris	$x + 7$	$x + 7 + 10 = x + 17$

In 10 years' time:

sum of ages: $(x + 10) + (x + 17) = 43$

$2x + 27 = 43$

$2x = 16$

$x = 8$

Amy is 8 years old now.

Paris is $8 + 7 = 15$ years old now.

Check: In 10 years' time, the sum of their ages will be $18 + 25 = 43$.

Equation problems

U F PS R C

For each question, write an equation and solve it to answer the problem.

PS R C

1 The longer sides of an isosceles triangle are twice as long as the shorter side. The perimeter of the triangle is 90 mm. Find the lengths of the sides of the triangle.

2 At the football match, an adult's ticket costs $6 more than twice the cost of a child's ticket. The total cost for 3 adults and 5 children is $249. Find the cost of a child's ticket and an adult's ticket.

EXAMPLE 13

3 The length of a rectangle is 3 times as long as its width. The perimeter of the rectangle is 152 mm. Find its dimensions.

4 The length of a rectangle is 3 more than twice its width. Find the dimensions of the rectangle if its perimeter is 84 cm.

5 The sum of 3 **consecutive** integers is 186. Find the integers.

EXAMPLE 14

6 Vimal is 9 times the age of her son, Virendra. In 5 years, she will be 4 times the age of Virendra. How old are they now?

7 When 15 is subtracted from 3 times a certain number, the answer is 63. What is the number?

8 The product of 2 and a number is the same as 12 minus the number. Find the number.

9 The sum of the present ages of Vatha and Chris is 36. In 4 years' time, the sum of their ages will equal twice Vatha's present age. How old are they now?

10 Four consecutive integers have a sum of 858. Find the 4 integers.

11 The sum of 3 consecutive even numbers is 288. Find the numbers.

12 Manori's bag contained 10-cent and 20-cent coins. She had 202 coins, with a total value of $31.90. How many 20-cent coins did Manori have?

13 If 17 more than a number is 5 more than 3 times the number, what is the number?

14 The sum of Scott's age and his mother Kait's age is 45. In 5 years' time, 3 times Scott's age less 9 will be the same as Kait's age. Find the present ages of Scott and Kait.

15 One angle in a triangle is double the smallest angle, and the third angle in the triangle is 5 more than 4 times the smallest angle. Find the size of each angle in the triangle.

16 A large container of water is $\frac{7}{8}$ full. After 15 L has been taken out, the container is $\frac{2}{3}$ full. When full, how many litres does the container hold?

17 The total cost of a school camp for Year 10 students was $21 280. Each teacher paid $185 to attend and each student paid $165. There was one teacher for every 15 students. Find the numbers of teachers and students that attended the camp.

□ Foundation ○ Standard ○ Complex

Multiplying and dividing by 5, 15, 25 and 50

It is easier to multiply or divide a number by 10 than by 5. So, whenever we multiply or divide a number by 5, we can double the 5 (to make 10) and then adjust the first number.

1 Study each example.

a **To multiply by 5**, halve the number, then multiply by 10.

$$18 \times 5 = 18 \times \frac{1}{2} \times 10 \text{ (or } 9 \times 2 \times 10)$$

$$= 9 \times 10$$

$$= 90$$

b **To multiply by 50**, halve the number, then multiply by 100.

$$26 \times 50 = 26 \times \frac{1}{2} \times 100 \text{ (or } 13 \times 2 \times 100)$$

$$= 13 \times 100$$

$$= 1300$$

c **To multiply by 25**, quarter the number, then multiply by 100.

$$44 \times 25 = 44 \times \frac{1}{4} \times 100 \text{ (or } 11 \times 4 \times 25)$$

$$= 11 \times 100$$

$$= 1100$$

d **To multiply by 15**, halve the number, then multiply by 30.

$$8 \times 15 = 8 \times \frac{1}{2} \times 30 \text{ (or } 4 \times 2 \times 15)$$

$$= 4 \times 30$$

$$= 120$$

e **To divide by 5**, divide by 10 and double the answer. We do this because there are 2 lots of 5 in every 10.

$$140 \div 5 = 140 \div 10 \times 2$$

$$= 14 \times 2$$

$$= 28$$

f **To divide by 50**, divide by 100 and double the answer. This is because there are 2 lots of 50 in every 100.

$$400 \div 50 = 400 \div 100 \times 2$$

$$= 4 \times 2$$

$$= 8$$

▷

g **To divide by 25**, divide by 100 and multiply the answer by 4. This is because there are 4 lots of 25 in every 100.

$$600 \div 25 = 600 \div 100 \times 4$$
$$= 6 \times 4$$
$$= 24$$

h **To divide by 15**, divide by 30 and double the answer. This is because there are 2 lots of 15 in every 30.

$$240 \div 15 = 240 \div 30 \times 2$$
$$= 8 \times 2$$
$$= 16$$

2 Now evaluate each expression.

a 32×5	**b** 14×5	**c** 48×5	**d** 18×50
e 52×50	**f** 36×25	**g** 28×5	**h** 12×25
i 12×15	**j** 22×35	**k** $90 \div 5$	**l** $170 \div 5$
m $230 \div 5$	**n** $1300 \div 50$	**o** $900 \div 50$	**p** $300 \div 25$
q $1000 \div 25$	**r** $360 \div 45$	**s** $210 \div 15$	**t** $360 \div 15$

6.07 Equations and formulas

A **formula** is an equation that describes a relationship between variables. For example, the formula for the perimeter of a rectangle is $P = 2(l + w)$, where P is the perimeter, l is the rectangle's length and w is the rectangle's width. Because the formula is for the perimeter, P is called the **subject of the formula** and it is the variable on its own on the left-hand side of the '=' sign.

Example 15

Videos
Equations and formulas 2

Equations and formulas 1

Formulas and equations

Puzzle
Getting the right formula

The cost of a trip, C, in dollars, for a ride share company is $C = 5 + 2.4d$, where d is the distance travelled, in kilometres.

Shutterstock.com/Snapic_PhotoProduction

a Find the cost of a trip if the distance travelled is 15 km.

b Find the distance travelled if the cost of the trip was $78.20.

▷

SOLUTION

a When $d = 15$:

$C = 5 + 2.4 \times 15$

$\quad = 41$

The cost was $41.

b When $C = 78.20$:

$78.20 = 5 + 2.4d$

$73.20 = 2.4d$

$d = \dfrac{73.20}{2.4}$

$\quad = 30.5$

The distance travelled was 30.5 km.

Example 16

The surface area of a sphere is given by the formula $A = 4\pi r^2$, where r is the radius.

Find (correct to one decimal place):

a the surface area of a sphere with radius 2.8 cm

b the radius of a sphere with surface area 40 m².

Video
Equations and formulas 2

SOLUTION

a When $r = 2.8$:

$A = 4 \times \pi \times 2.8^2$

$\quad = 98.520...$

$\quad \approx 98.5$

The surface area of the sphere is 98.5 cm².

b When $A = 40$:

$40 = 4\pi r^2$

$4\pi r^2 = 40$

$r^2 = \dfrac{40}{4\pi}$

$\quad = 3.183...$

$r = \sqrt{3.183}$ $r > 0$ because the radius is positive.

$\quad = 1.784...$

$\quad \approx 1.8$

The radius of the sphere is 1.8 m.

Equations and formulas

U F R C

EXAMPLE
15

1 The formula for the perimeter of a rectangle is $P = 2(l + w)$.

R **a** Find the perimeter of a rectangle with length 10 cm and width 16 cm.

b Find the width of a rectangle whose perimeter is 58 m and length is 12 m.

2 A formula for converting speed expressed in m/s (metres/second) to a speed expressed in km/h is $k = 3.6M$, where M is the speed in m/s. Convert each speed to km/h.

R
C **a** 10 m/s **b** 24 m/s **c** 50 m/s

3 A car is travelling at a speed of 110 km/h on a freeway. Use the formula from question **2** to calculate how fast this is in m/s.

4 The formula for converting temperatures in °F to °C is $C = \frac{5}{9}(F - 32)$. Express each temperature in °C, correct to the nearest degree.

a 80°F **b** 32°F **c** 212°F **d** 102°F

5 The average of 2 numbers, m and n, is $A = \frac{m+n}{2}$. If 2 numbers have an average of 28 R and one of the numbers is 13, use the formula to find the other number.

EXAMPLE
16

6 Pythagoras' theorem is $c^2 = a^2 + b^2$, where c is the length of the hypotenuse in a right-angled triangle and a and b are the lengths of the other 2 sides. Find, correct to one decimal place where necessary:

a c, if $a = 5$ and $b = 10$ **b** a, if $c = 41$ and $b = 40$ **c** b, if $c = 20$ and $a = 10$.

7 The formula for the circumference of a circle is $C = 2\pi r$, where r is the radius. R Find, correct to one decimal place:

C **a** the circumference of a circle with radius 2.4 m

b the radius of a circle whose circumference is 200 cm.

8 The body mass index (BMI) of an adult is $B = \frac{M}{h^2}$, where M is the mass in kilograms and R h is the height in metres. Find, correct to one decimal place:

a the BMI of Radha who is 1.85 m tall and has a mass of 72 kg

b the mass of Dane with a BMI of 24, who is 2.1 m tall.

9 The volume of a sphere is $V = \frac{4}{3}\pi r^3$, where r is the radius. Find, correct to one R decimal place:

a the volume of a sphere with radius 3.2 cm

b the radius of a sphere with volume 500 m³.

□ Foundation ○ Standard ◇ Complex

10 The average speed in km/h of a car is given by the formula $S = \dfrac{D}{T}$, where D is the
(R) distance covered in kilometres and T is the time taken in hours. Find, correct to the
nearest whole number:

   a the average speed of a car that takes 4.5 hours to travel a distance of 420 km

   b the distance travelled, if a car maintains a speed of 87.2 km/h for 5 hours

   c the time taken, if a distance of 650 km is covered at a speed of 91 km/h.

11 The cost, C (in dollars), of a hire car is $C = 75 + 2.5d$, where d is the number of
(R) kilometres travelled. Calculate:

   a the cost of hiring a car to travel 350 km

   b the distance travelled, if the cost is $135.

12 The surface area of a closed cylinder is given by the formula $SA = 2\pi r^2 + 2\pi rh$.
(R) Calculate, correct to one decimal place:

   a the surface area of a cylinder with radius 2.1 m and height 3.5 m

   b the height of a cylinder with surface area 1255.38 cm² and radius 9 cm.

Extension: Changing the subject of a formula

6.08

Example 17

EXTENSION

Change the subject of the formula:

a $A = \dfrac{1}{2}bh$ to h **b** $v^2 = u^2 + 2as$ to s **c** $\dfrac{a+2}{a+10} = k$ to a

Video
Changing the
subject of a
formula

SOLUTION

a $A = \dfrac{1}{2}bh$

   $\dfrac{1}{2}bh = A$

   $bh = 2A$

   $h = \dfrac{2A}{b}$

b $v^2 = u^2 + 2as$

   $u^2 + 2as = v^2$

   $2as = v^2 - u^2$

   $s = \dfrac{v^2 - u^2}{2a}$

c $\dfrac{a+2}{a+10} = k$

   $a + 2 = k(a + 10)$

         $= ak + 10k$

   $a - ak = 10k - 2$

   $a(1 - k) = 10k - 2$

         $a = \dfrac{10k - 2}{1 - k}$

☐ Foundation   ○ Standard   ◇ Complex

EXERCISE 6.08 ANSWERS ON P. 625

Changing the subject of a formula Ⓤ Ⓕ Ⓡ Ⓒ

EXAMPLE 17

1 Make y the subject of each formula.

Ⓡ Ⓒ **a** $x + 2y = 5$ **b** $m + py = k$ **c** $P - ky = 8$ **d** $\dfrac{m}{3} = \dfrac{y}{5}$

e $D = K - My$ **f** $\dfrac{5+8y}{d} = 4$ **g** $\dfrac{ay-k}{2} = c$ **h** $\dfrac{y+3}{5} = \dfrac{4m}{3}$

i $xy^2 + 5 = w$ **j** $x = \sqrt{\dfrac{y}{k}}$ **k** $n = \dfrac{d}{5-y}$ **l** $T = \sqrt{\dfrac{y+k}{c}}$

2 Change the subject of each formula to the variable indicated in brackets.

Ⓡ Ⓒ **a** $a^2 + b^2 = c^2$ $[b]$ **b** $s = ut + \dfrac{1}{2}at^2$ $[a]$ **c** $v = u + at$ $[a]$

d $V = \dfrac{4}{3}\pi r^3$ $[r]$ **e** $A = \pi(R^2 - r^2)$ $[R]$ **f** $A = \pi r l + \pi r^2$ $[l]$

g $S = 180(n - 2)$ $[n]$ **h** $\dfrac{1}{x} + \dfrac{1}{r} = \dfrac{1}{s}$ $[r]$ **i** $x = \sqrt{b^2 - 4ac}$ $[b]$

j $x + y = 5 - 3x$ $[x]$ **k** $m = \dfrac{5A}{2A+n}$ $[A]$ **l** $S = \dfrac{a(p-1)}{p}$ $[p]$

m $X(a + b) = Y(a - b)$ $[a]$ **n** $\dfrac{5+x}{3x+a} = 2$ $[x]$ **o** $y = \dfrac{u+bx}{u+ab}$ $[b]$

6.09 Graphing inequalities on a number line

An **inequality** looks like an equation except that the equal sign ($=$) is replaced by an inequality symbol $>$, $\geq$, $<$ or $\leq$.

Worksheet
Graphing inequalities

ⓘ Inequality symbols

$>$ 'is greater than' $\geq$ 'is greater than or equal to'

$<$ 'is less than' $\leq$ 'is less than or equal to'

Inequality	In words	Meaning
$x > 3$	x is greater than 3	Values above 3
$x < 3$	x is less than 3	Values below 3
$x \geq 3$	x is greater than or equal to 3	Values above and including 3
$x \leq 3$	x is less than or equal to 3	Values below and including 3

Example 18

6.09

Video
Graphing
inequalities on
the number
line

Graph each inequality on a number line.

a $x \geq 1$ **b** $x < 5$ **c** $x > -3$

SOLUTION

a $x \geq 1$ means that x can be any number greater than 1 or equal to 1.

The filled circle at 1
means we include 1.

b $x < 5$ means that x can be any number less than 5, but not including 5.

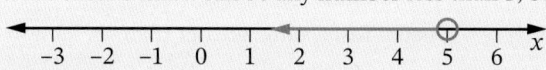

The open circle on
5 means that 5 is not
included.

c $x > -3$ means that x can be any number greater than -3, but not including -3.

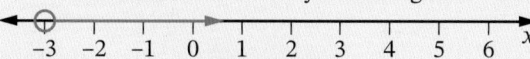

EXERCISE (6.09) ANSWERS ON P. 626

Graphing inequalities on a number line

(U) (F) (C)

EXAMPLE
18

1 Graph each inequality on a separate number line.

(C) **a** $x \geq 2$ **b** $x < -3$ **c** $x \leq 1$ **d** $x > 7$

     e $x \leq 4$ **f** $x > 0$ **g** $x \geq -2$ **h** $x < 10$

2 Write the inequality shown on each number line.

(C) **a** 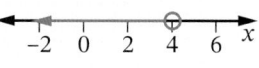   **b**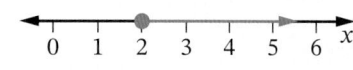

     c 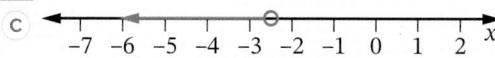   **d**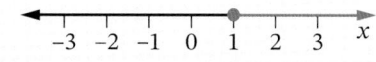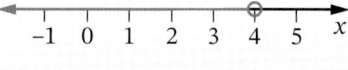

3 Which inequality is graphed below? Select the correct answer **A**, **B**, **C** or **D**.

(C)

     A $x > -2.5$ **B** $x < -2.5$ **C** $x < -3.5$ **D** $x > -3.5$

4 Write the inequality shown on each number line.

(C) **a**   **b**

     c   **d**

     e   **f**

     g   **h**

     i

☐ Foundation   ◯ Standard   ◇ Complex

6.10 Solving inequalities

Video
Solving
inequalities

Worksheet
Inequalities
review

Example 19

Solve $\frac{w+3}{2} > -1$ and graph its solution on a number line.

SOLUTION

$$\frac{w+3}{2} > -1$$

$$\frac{w+3}{2} \times 2 > -1 \times 2$$

$$w + 3 > -2$$

$$w + 3 - 3 > -2 - 3$$

$$w > -5$$

Check: Test a value greater than –5, let $w = -1$.

$$\text{LHS} = \frac{-1+3}{2} = 1$$

$$\text{RHS} = -1$$

$$1 > -1$$

$$\text{LHS} > \text{RHS}$$

(number line showing open circle at –5 with arrow to the right, marked w, points labelled $-6\ -5\ -4\ -3\ -2\ -1\ 0\ 1$)

ⓘ Solving inequalities

- Inequalities can be solved algebraically in the same way as equations, using inverse operations.
- However, when multiplying or dividing both sides of an inequality by a **negative** number, you must *reverse* the inequality sign.

Example 20

Solve each inequality.

a $\ 1 - 2x \geq -11$ **b** $\ 4 - r < 7$ **c** $\ \frac{a+5}{-3} > 4$

SOLUTION

a

$$1 - 2x \geq -11$$

$$1 - 2x - 1 \geq -11 - 1$$

$$-2x \geq -12$$

$$\frac{-2x}{-2} \leq \frac{-12}{-2}$$

$$x \leq 6$$

Dividing both sides by a negative number reverses the inequality sign.

Check: Test a value less than 6, let $x = 5$.

$$\text{LHS} = 1 - 2 \times 5 = -9$$

$$\text{RHS} = -11$$

$$-9 \geq -11$$

$$\text{LHS} \geq \text{RHS}$$

b

$$4 - r < 7$$

$$4 - r - 4 < 7 - 4$$

$$-r < 3$$

$$\frac{-r}{-1} > \frac{3}{-1}$$

$$r > -3$$

Check: Test a value greater than –3, let $r = 0$.

LHS $= 4 - 0 = 4$

RHS $= 7$

$4 < 7$

LHS < RHS

c $\quad \dfrac{a+5}{-3} > 4$

$$\frac{a+5}{-3} \times (-3) < 4 \times (-3)$$

$$a + 5 < -12$$

$$a + 5 - 5 < -12 - 5$$

$$a < -17$$

Check: Test a value less than –17, let $a = -20$.

LHS $= \dfrac{-20+5}{-3} = \dfrac{-15}{-3} = 5$

RHS $= 4$

$5 > 4$

LHS > RHS

EXERCISE 6.10 ANSWERS ON P. 626

Solving inequalities

(U) (F) (R) (C)

1 Solve each inequality and graph its solution on a number line.

EXAMPLE 19

(R) **a** $\quad x - 1 > 6$ **b** $\quad 3y \geq 12$ **c** $\quad m + 4 \leq 2$

(C) **d** $\quad \dfrac{x}{5} \geq -20$ **e** $\quad 12x < 60$ **f** $\quad 5y > -20$

    g $\quad 4a \geq 2$ **h** $\quad 3w \leq -30$ **i** $\quad 8a + 5 \geq 45$

    j $\quad 3a + 1 \leq 10$ **k** $\quad 6a + 4 \geq -2$ **l** $\quad 3w - 3 < -12$

    m $\quad 5a + 3 \leq -27$ **n** $\quad 5y + 1 \leq 16$ **o** $\quad 4a + 5 < 15$

2 Solve each inequality.

(R) **a** $\quad 3(x + 2) \geq 9$ **b** $\quad 5(m - 4) \leq 10$ **c** $\quad 2(y + 5) \leq -6$

    d $\quad 3(w - 2) > -6$ **e** $\quad 5(2w + 3) \leq 15$ **f** $\quad 4(2m - 5) \geq 8$

    g $\quad \dfrac{m + 5}{3} \geq 1$ **h** $\quad \dfrac{x - 1}{2} \leq 2$ **i** $\quad \dfrac{w - 2}{5} > -1$

    j $\quad \dfrac{2a + 1}{3} < 3$ **k** $\quad \dfrac{5a + 2}{4} \geq 8$ **l** $\quad \dfrac{2(m + 1)}{3} \leq 3$

    m $\quad \dfrac{5(m - 1)}{4} > 3$ **n** $\quad \dfrac{4(m - 2)}{3} \geq -6$ **o** $\quad 3 + \dfrac{x}{5} < 10$

3 Solve each inequality and graph its solution on a number line.

EXAMPLE 20

(R) **a** $\quad 5 - x \leq 2$ **b** $\quad 15 > 7 - y$ **c** $\quad 1 - k < 12$

(C) **d** $\quad 7 - m \geq 7$ **e** $\quad 2 - p > 8$ **f** $\quad -t + 6 \geq 10$

□ Foundation ○ Standard ◇ Complex

4 Solve each inequality.

a	$-2x < 6$	**b**	$\dfrac{k}{-3} \geq 4$	**c**	$-5t > 12$
d	$\dfrac{-x}{3} \leq -4$	**e**	$4 - 3w > 7$	**f**	$-4y + 3 \leq 11$
g	$3 - 2x \geq -5$	**h**	$8 - 5a < 3$	**i**	$-2d - 3 > 8$
j	$\dfrac{5+w}{-3} > 2$	**k**	$\dfrac{x-4}{-4} \geq 3$	**l**	$\dfrac{-p+2}{-3} < -2$

INVESTIGATION

Power tables

1 Copy and complete this table of powers of 2 from 0 to 20.

x	0	1	2	...	20
2^x					

2 Use the table to calculate 32×128. Explain the method you used.

3 Use the table to calculate:

    a 16×1024 **b** 128×2048

    c 256×64 **d** 4096×32

4 Use the table to calculate $262\,114 \div 8192$. Explain the method you used.

5 Use the table to calculate:

    a $16\,384 \div 512$ **b** $128 \div 8$

    c $8192 \div 1024$ **d** $1\,048\,576 \div 65\,536$

When powers are used this way in calculations, they may be called **logarithms.**

6.11 Extension: Logarithms

EXTENSION

Puzzles
Logarithms 1

Logarithms 2

The **logarithm** of a number is the power of the number, to a given positive base.

For example, the logarithm of 8 to the base 2 is 3, written **$\log_2 8 = 3$,** because $2^3 = 8$.

Example 21

Evaluate each expression.

a $\log_3 81$　　　　**b** $\log_4 16$　　　　**c** $\log_{10} 10\,000$

EXTENSION

6.11

Video
Logarithms

SOLUTION

a $\log_3 81$ means $3^? = 81$

Since $3^4 = 81$　　　3 to the power of
what equals 81?
then $\log_3 81 = 4$.

b $\log_4 16$ means $4^? = 16$

Since $4^2 = 16$　　　4 to the power of
what equals 16?
then $\log_4 16 = 2$.

c $\log_{10} 10\,000$ means $10^? = 10\,000$

Since $10^4 = 10\,000$

then $\log_{10} 10\,000 = 4$.

ⓘ Logarithms

If $y = a^x$, then $\log_a y = x$

where a is the base, $a > 0$, x is the power, and $y > 0$.

Since $a > 0$, $a^x > 0$ and $y > 0$.

Logarithms are only meaningful for positive numbers, y.

Example 22

Write each expression as a logarithm.

a　$243 = 3^5$　　　**b**　$0.01 = 10^{-2}$　　　**c**　$2 = 8^{\frac{1}{3}}$　　　**d**　$p = q^r$

SOLUTION

a　$243 = 3^5$

$\therefore \log_3 243 = 5$

b　$0.01 = 10^{-2}$

$\therefore \log_{10} 0.01 = -2$

c　$2 = 8^{\frac{1}{3}}$

$\therefore \log_8 2 = \dfrac{1}{3}$

d　$p = q^r$

$\therefore \log_q p = r$

Example 23

Rewrite $\log_n m = x$ in index form.

SOLUTION

$\log_n m = x$　　　　　　　　　n is the base, x is the power.

$\therefore m = n^x$

EXERCISE (6.11) ANSWERS ON P. 626

Logarithms

(U) (F) (R) (C)

EXAMPLE
21

1 Evaluate each expression.

(R) **a** $\log_5 25$ **b** $\log_2 8$ **c** $\log_7 49$ **d** $\log_2 16$

    e $\log_3 243$ **f** $\log_{10} 1000$ **g** $\log_5 125$ **h** $\log_6 36$

    i $\log_2 64$ **j** $\log_3 6561$ **k** $\log_{10} 1\,000\,000$ **l** $\log_8 512$

EXAMPLE
22

2 Write each expression in logarithmic form.

(R) **a** $5^2 = 25$ **b** $4^3 = 64$ **c** $10\,000 = 10^4$ **d** $25^{\frac{1}{2}} = 5$

(C) **e** $\dfrac{1}{16} = 2^{-4}$ **f** $3^{-2} = \dfrac{1}{9}$ **g** $8^{\frac{2}{3}} = 4$ **h** $0.01 = 10^{-2}$

    i $\sqrt{2} = 4^{\frac{1}{4}}$ **j** $16^{\frac{1}{2}} = 4$ **k** $9^{\frac{3}{2}} = 27$ **l** $\dfrac{1}{\sqrt{6}} = 6^{-\frac{1}{2}}$

EXAMPLE
23

3 Write each expression in index form.

(R) **a** $\log_5 125 = 3$ **b** $\log_{10} 10 = 1$ **c** $\log_{\sqrt{3}} 27 = 6$ **d** $\log_2 8\sqrt{2} = 3.5$

(C) **e** $\log_2 64 = 6$ **f** $\log_3\left(\dfrac{1}{81}\right) = -4$ **g** $\log_5\left(\dfrac{1}{125}\right) = -3$ **h** $\log_8 \sqrt{2} = \dfrac{1}{6}$

    i $\log_{100} 10 = \dfrac{1}{2}$ **j** $\log_5 5\sqrt{5} = \dfrac{3}{2}$ **k** $\log_8 2 = \dfrac{1}{3}$ **l** $\log_{100}\left(\dfrac{1}{100}\right) = -1$

4 Why can't you find the logarithm of a negative number or zero?

(R)

(C)

DID YOU KNOW?

The Richter scale

The size of an earthquake is measured using a scale developed by American seismologist and physicist Charles Richter in 1935. The scale uses base 10 logarithms, where each level is 10 times more powerful than the previous level. For example, a magnitude 4 earthquake is 10 times more powerful than a magnitude 3 earthquake. As the magnitude of the earthquake increases, the energy released also increases and so too the damage. A large lightning bolt releases as much energy as a magnitude 3 earthquake.

Magnitude	0	1	2	3	4	5	6	7	8
Damage	none	micro	minor	minor	light	moderate	strong	major	great

Earthquakes are rare in Australia. The most destructive earthquake occurred in Newcastle, NSW, in 1989, causing $4 billion in damage.

Research the strength of the Newcastle earthquake on the Richter scale.

☐ Foundation   ○ Standard   ◇ Complex

Extension: Logarithm laws

The index laws from Chapter 4, *Products, factors and surds*, are related to the logarithm laws.

ⓘ Logarithm of a product

The logarithm of a product of terms is equal to the sum of the logarithm of each term.

$$\log_a(xy) = \log_a x + \log_a y$$

For example, $\log_2(8 \times 4) = \log_2 8 + \log_2 4$.

This law corresponds to the index law $a^m \times a^n = a^{mn}$.

Proof:

Let $m = \log_a x$ and $n = \log_a y$.

$\therefore x = a^m$ and $y = a^n$

$xy = a^m \times a^n = a^{m+n}$

$xy = a^{m+n}$

$\therefore \log_a(xy) = m + n$

$= \log_a x + \log_a y$

ⓘ Logarithm of a quotient

The logarithm of a quotient of terms is equal to the difference between the logarithm of each term.

$$\log_a\left(\frac{x}{y}\right) = \log_a x - \log_a y$$

For example, $\log_3\left(\dfrac{243}{27}\right) = \log_3 243 - \log_3 27$

This law corresponds to the index law $a^m \div a^n = a^{m-n}$.

Proof:

Let $m = \log_a x$ and $n = \log_a y$.

$\therefore x = a^m$ and $y = a^n$

$\therefore \dfrac{x}{y} = \dfrac{a^m}{a^n} = a^{m-n}$

$\therefore \log_a\left(\dfrac{x}{y}\right) = m - n$

$= \log_a x - \log_a y$

ⓘ Logarithm of a power

The logarithm of a term raised to a power is equal to the power multiplied by the logarithm of the term.

$$\log_a x^n = n \log_a x$$

For example, $\log_4 8^2 = 2 \log_4 8$

This law corresponds to the index law $(a^m)^n = a^{mn}$.

Proof:

Let $m = \log_a x$ $\therefore \log_a x^n = mn$

$\therefore x = a^m$ $= (\log_a x) \times n$

$\therefore x^n = (a^m)^n$ $= n \log_a x$

$\qquad = a^{mn}$

ⓘ Properties of logarithms

$\log_a a^x = x$ $\log_a a = 1$, because $a^1 = a$

$\log_a 1 = 0$, because $a^0 = 1$ $\log_a = \left(\dfrac{1}{x}\right) - \log_a x$

Proof:

$\log_a\left(\dfrac{1}{x}\right) = \log x^{-1}$ Using the law $\log_a x^n = n \log_a x$

$\qquad = -\log_a x$

Example 24

Evaluate each expression.

a $\log_5 0.04$ **b** $\log_2 5 - \log_2 10$

c $2\log_3 6 - \log_3 4$ **d** $\log_5 10 + \log_5 2 - \log_5 4$

SOLUTION

a $\log_5 0.04 = \log_5\left(\dfrac{4}{100}\right)$ **b** $\log_2 5 - \log_2 10 = \log_2\left(\dfrac{5}{10}\right)$

$\qquad\qquad = \log_5\left(\dfrac{1}{25}\right)$ $= \log_2\left(\dfrac{1}{2}\right)$

$\qquad\qquad = \log_5\left(\dfrac{1}{5^2}\right)$ $= \log_2 2^{-1}$

$\qquad\qquad = \log_5 5^{-2}$ $= -1$ since $\log_a a^x = x$

$\qquad\qquad = -2$ since $\log_a a^x = x$

c $2\log_3 6 - \log_3 4 = \log_3 6^2 - \log_3 4$ **d** $\log_5 10 + \log_5 2 - \log_5 4 = \log_5(10 \times 2) - \log_5 4$

$\qquad\qquad = \log_3 36 - \log_3 4$ $= \log_5 20 - \log_5 4$

$\qquad\qquad = \log_3\left(\dfrac{36}{4}\right)$ $= \log_5\left(\dfrac{20}{4}\right)$

$\qquad\qquad = \log_3 9$ $= \log_5 5$

$\qquad\qquad = 2$ $= 1$

Example 25

Simplify each expression using the logarithm laws.

a $6 \log_a a + \log_a a^4 - \log_a a^9$ **b** $\log_2 x + \log_2 w - 2 \log_2 y$ **c** $\dfrac{\log_3 a^3}{5 \log_3 a}$

SOLUTION

a $6 \log_a a + \log_a a^4 - \log_a a^9 = 6 \times 1 + 4 - 9$

$$= 1$$

b $\log_2 x + \log_2 w - 2 \log_2 y = \log_2 (xw) - \log_2 y^2$

$$= \log_2 \left(\frac{xw}{y^2} \right)$$

c $\dfrac{\log_3 a^3}{5 \log_3 a} = \dfrac{3 \log_3 a}{5 \log_3 a}$

$$= \frac{3}{5}$$

Example 26

Given $\log_{10} 7 \approx 0.8451$, use logarithm laws to evaluate each expression.

a $\log_{10} 49$ **b** $\log_{10} 700$ **c** $\log_{10} (0.07)$

SOLUTION

a $\log_{10} 49 = \log_{10} 7^2$

$$= 2 \log_{10} 7$$

$$\approx 2 \times 0.8451$$

$$= 1.6902$$

b $\log_{10} 700 = \log_{10} (7 \times 100)$

$$= \log_{10} 7 + \log_{10} 100$$

$$\approx 0.8451 + 2$$

$$= 2.8451$$

c $\log_{10} (0.07) = \log_{10} \left(\dfrac{7}{100} \right)$

$$= \log_{10} 7 - \log_{10} 100$$

$$\approx 0.8451 - 2$$

$$= -1.1549$$

EXERCISE 6.12 ANSWERS ON P. 627

Logarithm laws

U F R

1 Evaluate each expression.

R **a** $\log_2 128$ **b** $\log_{10} 1000$ **c** $\log_8 64$

d $\log_5 \dfrac{1}{5}$ **e** $\log_2 \sqrt{2}$ **f** $\log_3 \dfrac{1}{9}$

g $\log_{10} 0.0001$ **h** $\log_2 \dfrac{1}{16}$ **i** $\log_8 2 + \log_8 4$

j $\log_4 32 - \log_4 2$ **k** $\log_{10} 4 + \log_{10} 25$ **l** $\log_5 200 - \log_5 8$

m $\log_2 18 - 2 \log_2 3$ **n** $3 \log_{10} 2 + \log_{10} 12.5$

EXAMPLE
24

☐ Foundation ○ Standard ◇ Complex

EXTENSION 6.12

2 Simplify each expression.

EXAMPLE 25

R **a** $\log_x 5 + \log_x 6$ **b** $\log_x 10 - \log_x 2$ **c** $3\log_x 2$

d $2\log_x 4 - \log_x 8$ **e** $\log_x 10 + \log_x 4$ **f** $\dfrac{1}{2}\log_x 100$

g $-\log_x 4$ **h** $\log_x 8 - (\log_x 10 + \log_x 4)$ **i** $\dfrac{1}{2}(\log_x 8 + \log_x 18)$

EXAMPLE 26

3 If $\log_{10} 4 = 0.6021$, evaluate each expression.

R **a** $\log_{10} 16$ **b** $\log_{10} 400$ **c** $\log_{10} 4000$ **d** $\log_{10} 2$

e $\log_{10} 0.4$ **f** $\log_{10} 160$ **g** $\log_{10} 2.5$ **h** $\log_{10} \sqrt{40}$

4 Evaluate each expression.

R **a** $\log_3 4 + \log_3 15 - \log_3 20$ **b** $\log_3 270 - (\log_3 2 + \log_3 5)$

c $\log_4 20 + (\log_4 32 - \log_4 10)$ **d** $2\log_{10} 25 - \log_{10} 6.25$

e $2\log_{10} 2 - (\log_{10} 5 + \log_{10} 8)$ **f** $\log_{100} 50 - \log_{100} 5$

g $2\log_5 10 + (\log_5 50 - \log_5 40)$ **h** $5\log_8 2 + \dfrac{1}{2}\log_8 4$

i $\dfrac{1}{2}\log_4 25 - 2\log_4 \sqrt{20}$ **j** $\dfrac{1}{3}\log_2 125 - 3\log_2 \sqrt[3]{80}$

5 Simplify each expression.

R **a** $\log_a a^2 + 3\log_a a$ **b** $\log_a (a^3)$ **c** $5\log_a a - \log_a a^4$

d $\dfrac{\log_a (x^7)}{\log_a x}$ **e** $\log_a y^3 - 3\log_a y$ **f** $\log_a \sqrt{x} - \log_a \dfrac{1}{x}$

6.13 Extension: Exponential and logarithmic equations

EXTENSION

Exponential equations are equations like $3^x = 243$, where the variable or unknown is a **power.**

Logarithms can be used to solve exponential equations rather than using a 'guess-and-check' method. The ■log■ key on your calculator calculates logarithms to the base 10, $\log_{10} x$.

Logarithms to the base 10 are called **common logarithms.**

Worksheet
Logarithms
review

Puzzle
Exponential
equations

⬜ Foundation ⭕ Standard ⭕ Complex

Example 27

Solve each exponential equation.

a $3^x = 243$

b $4^{m+1} = \dfrac{1}{8\sqrt{2}}$

SOLUTION

a $3^x = 243$ Taking $\log_{10}$ of both sides.

$\log_{10} 3^x = \log_{10} 243$

$x \log_{10} 3 = \log_{10} 243$

$x = \dfrac{\log_{10} 243}{\log_{10} 3} = 5$

On a calculator,

enter: [log] 243 [÷] [log] 3 [=]

Note: The [log] key means $\log_{10}$, and for convenience we will write log to mean $\log_{10}$.

b $\qquad 4^{m+1} = \dfrac{1}{8\sqrt{2}}$

$(m+1)\log 4 = -\log\left(8\sqrt{2}\right)$

$\log\left(4^{m+1}\right) = \log\left(\dfrac{1}{8\sqrt{2}}\right)$

$m+1 = \dfrac{-\log\left(8\sqrt{2}\right)}{\log 4}$

$(m+1)\log 4 = \log\left(\dfrac{1}{8\sqrt{2}}\right)$

$\qquad\qquad = -1.75$

$\qquad\qquad m = -2.75$

Example 28

Solve $5^x = 17$, writing the solution correct to 3 decimal places.

SOLUTION

$5^x = 17$

$\log 5^x = \log 17$

$x \log 5 = \log 17$

$x = \dfrac{\log 17}{\log 5}$

$= 1.7603...$

≈ 1.760

Logarithmic equations are equations like $\log_5 x = -3$, which can be solved by rewriting the equation in index form.

Example 29

Solve each logarithmic equation.

a $\log_5 x = -3$

b $\log_x 18 = 3$

SOLUTION

a $\log_5 x = -3$

$\therefore x = 5^{-3}$

$= \dfrac{1}{5^3}$

$= \dfrac{1}{125}$

b $\log_x 18 = 3$

$\therefore 18 = x^3$

$x = \sqrt[3]{18}$

$= 2.6207...$

≈ 2.62

EXERCISE 6.13 ANSWERS ON P. 627

Exponential and logarithmic equations

U F PS R

EXAMPLE
27

1 Solve each exponential equation.

R **a** $2^k = 512$ **b** $5^m = 78\,125$ **c** $3^d = 59\,049$

d $5^x = 25\sqrt{5}$ **e** $2^y = \dfrac{1}{16\sqrt{2}}$ **f** $4^a = 128$

g $3^{k+2} = 27\sqrt{3}$ **h** $6^{n-2} = \dfrac{1}{216\sqrt{6}}$ **i** $9^{1-d} = \dfrac{1}{27\sqrt{3}}$

EXAMPLE
28

2 Solve each exponential equation, writing the solution correct to 3 decimal places.

R **a** $7^x = 16$ **b** $5^x = 36$ **c** $11^x = 420$

d $2^x = 0.52$ **e** $3^x = 1.6$ **f** $4^x = \dfrac{2}{5}$

g $2^{x-2} = 47$ **h** $3^{x+4} = 72$ **i** $6^{x+3} = 29$

j $8^{5-x} = 4000$ **k** $5^y = 4.8$ **l** $7^{k+5} = 300$

3 Solve each exponential equation by expressing both sides to base 2.

R **a** $2^{x+2} = 16$ **b** $8^x = 32$ **c** $4^{x-1} = \sqrt{2}$

d $8^{1-x} = 16\sqrt{2}$ **e** $4^{2-x} = \dfrac{1}{8}$ **f** $8^{x+1} = \dfrac{1}{8\sqrt{2}}$

g $\left(\dfrac{1}{4}\right)^{1-x} = \sqrt{2}$ **h** $5\left(\dfrac{1}{2}\right)^x = 20$

4 Solve each logarithmic equation, expressing your answer correct to 3 decimal places where necessary.

EXAMPLE
29

R

a $\log_2 x = 3$ **b** $\log_{10} x = 3$ **c** $\log_5 x = -2$

d $\log_4 x = -3$ **e** $\log_{27} x = \dfrac{1}{3}$ **f** $\log_4 x = \dfrac{1}{2}$

g $\log_{10} x = -3$ **h** $\log_8 x = \dfrac{3}{2}$ **i** $\log_{10} x = -\dfrac{1}{2}$

j $\log_4 x = -\dfrac{3}{2}$ **k** $\log_4 x = 3\dfrac{1}{2}$ **l** $\log_{\sqrt{5}} x = -4$

m $\log_x 4 = 2$ **n** $\log_x 5 = -1$ **o** $\log_x \dfrac{1}{4} = 2$

p $\log_x 0.01 = 2$ **q** $\log_x 16 = 1$ **r** $\log_x 8 = 3$

s $\log_x 60 = 3$ **t** $\log_x 4.8 = \dfrac{1}{2}$

5 Use the compound interest formula $A = P(1 + r)^n$ to determine the number of years (to the nearest year) it will take an investment of \$1000 to grow to \$2000, if it earns compound interest at a rate of 6% p.a.

PS
R

☐ Foundation ◯ Standard ◯ Complex

6 Samaria invests $12 000 at 1% per month compound interest. How many whole months will it take for her investment to grow to $15 000?

(PS)
(R)

EXTENSION

7 A radioactive substance with a mass of 150 grams decays according to the equation

(PS)
(R)
$A = 150 \times \left(2^{-\frac{t}{20}}\right)$, where A (grams) is the amount remaining after t days.

Find, correct to the nearest whole number:

a the mass of substance remaining after 10 days

b the time taken for the substance to decay to half its original mass

c the time taken for the substance to decay to a mass of 20 g.

POWER PLUS ANSWERS ON P. 627

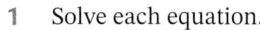

1 Solve each equation.

   a $\dfrac{3(1-y)}{5} = 4 - 2y$ **b** $\dfrac{50}{2y} = 10$ **c** $\dfrac{2m+5}{3} - 1 = m + 4$

2 If $y = \dfrac{ab+cd}{e}$, find d if $y = -12$, $a = -1$, $b = -8$, $c = 7$ and $e = 4$.

3 Rohan is 10 years older than Tarni. In 3 years' time, Rohan will be twice as old as Tarni. How old are Rohan and Tarni now?

4 One-third of a number added to one-sixth of a number is 18. What is the number?

5 Graph each inequality on a number line.

   a $1 \le x \le 4$ **b** $-2 \le x \le 3$ **c** $-12 < 4x \le 4$

6 The number of diagonals, D, in a polygon with n sides is $D = \dfrac{1}{2}n(n-3)$. Show that there is no polygon that has exactly 100 diagonals.

7 The 2 solutions of $x^2 - 8x - 11 = 0$ are in the form $x = p \pm q\sqrt{3}$, where p and q are integers. Find p and q.

8 Solve each logarithmic equation

   a $\log a + \log 3 = \log 21$ **b** $\log x - \log 4 = \log 5$

   c $\log 7 + \log m = \log (m + 12)$ **d** $\log (h + 7) - \log 3 = \log (h - 1)$

☐ Foundation   ○ Standard   ○ Complex

⑥ CHAPTER REVIEW

Language of maths

check	cubic equation	equation	expand
exponential equation	factorise	formula	greater than (>)
greater than or equal to (≥)	inequality	inverse operation	LHS
less than (<)	less than or equal to (≤)	logarithm	logarithmic equation
number line	quadratic equation	RHS	solution
solve	subject	substitute	variable

1 What type of equation has 2 as the highest power of x? Write an example of this type of equation.

2 Write $\log_7 a = -3$ in index form.

3 What is the difference between an equation and an inequality?

4 Why is it possible for a quadratic equation to have more than one solution?

5 When checking the solution to an equation, we need to show that 'LHS = RHS'. What does this mean?

6 What does '≤' mean? Provide an example with your explanation.

Topic summary

Print (or copy) and complete this mind map of the topic, adding detail to its branches and using pictures, symbols and colour where needed. Ask your teacher to check your work.

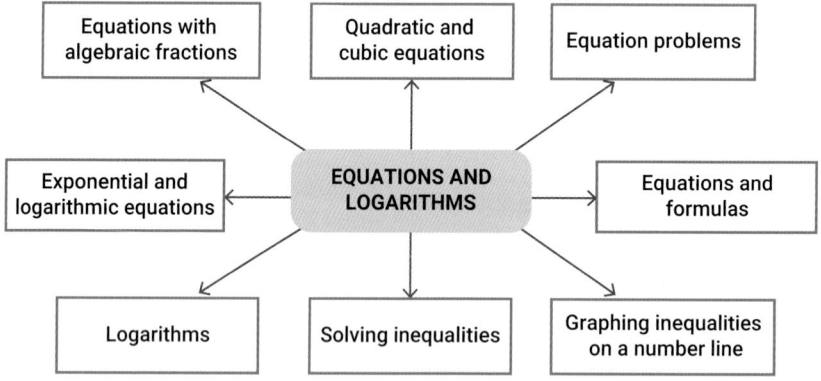

⑥ TEST YOURSELF ANSWERS ON P. 627

Quiz
Test
yourself 6

1 Solve each equation.

   a $3a + 10 = 43$ **b** $8y + 5 = 2y + 21$

   c $2a - 12 = 6a$ **d** $9 - 2y = 5 + 2y$

   e $3(m - 2) = 27$ **f** $2(2a + 1) = 3(a + 10)$

   g $5(h + 1) + 3(h - 2) = 12$ **h** $4(2y + 1) + 3(1 + 4y) = 20$

6.01

EXTENSION

2 Simplify each expression.

   a $\dfrac{r}{4} - \dfrac{3r}{5}$ **b** $\dfrac{5g}{3} + \dfrac{3g}{2}$ **c** $\dfrac{11x}{24} - \dfrac{2x}{3}$ **d** $\dfrac{3}{4} - \dfrac{2m}{7}$

   e $\dfrac{3k - 4}{5} + \dfrac{2k}{3}$ **f** $\dfrac{w + 1}{4} - \dfrac{w - 3}{9}$ **g** $\dfrac{2p + 5}{3} - \dfrac{7p}{12}$ **h** $\dfrac{5 + 2y}{11} + \dfrac{1 - y}{8}$

6.02

3 Solve each equation.

   a $\dfrac{3w + 2}{5} = 4$ **b** $\dfrac{h}{5} = \dfrac{7}{4}$ **c** $\dfrac{2a + 1}{2} = \dfrac{3a - 1}{4}$

   d $\dfrac{3m + 5}{6} = \dfrac{10 - m}{3}$ **e** $\dfrac{2s}{3} - \dfrac{s}{6} = 2$ **f** $\dfrac{x}{10} + \dfrac{x}{2} = 1$

   g $\dfrac{b - 1}{4} + \dfrac{b}{2} = 6$ **h** $\dfrac{y + 1}{3} + \dfrac{y - 1}{4} = \dfrac{1}{2}$ **i** $\dfrac{2n - 1}{4} - \dfrac{n - 4}{3} = \dfrac{4}{3}$

6.03

4 Solve each quadratic equation.

   a $y^2 = 4$ **b** $p^2 - 100 = 0$ **c** $4x^2 = 40$

   d $3m^2 - 3 = 0$ **e** $\dfrac{2w^2}{5} = 20$ **f** $x^2 + 8x + 7 = 0$

   g $h^2 - 8h - 9 = 0$ **h** $u^2 + 4u - 77 = 0$ **i** $k^2 + 5k = 0$

   j $m^2 - 2m = 0$ **k** $b^2 + 20b + 100 = 0$ **l** $w^2 = 9w$

6.04

EXTENSION

5 Solve each cubic equation, correct to one decimal place.

   a $u^3 - 7 = 0$ **b** $5m^3 - 125 = 0$ **c** $\dfrac{x^3}{2} = 1.5$

6.05

6 Grace is 3 years younger than her sister Jamiela. Twice the sum of their ages is 4 more than their father's age. If their father is 54, find the ages of Grace and Jamiela.

6.06

7 The braking distance (in metres) of a bicycle travelling at a speed of v metres/second is $d = \dfrac{v(v + 1)}{2}$. Calculate the braking distance when the speed of the bicycle is 15 m/s.

6.07

8 The volume of a pyramid is given by the formula $V = \dfrac{1}{3}Ah$, where A is the area of the base and h is the perpendicular height of the pyramid. Find:

   a   the volume of a pyramid with a base area of 48 mm² and a perpendicular height of 10 mm.

   b   the base area of a pyramid with a volume of 500 m³ and a perpendicular height of 5 m.

6.08

EXTENSION

9 Make a the subject of each formula.

   a $y = ax + b$ **b** $P = \sqrt{\dfrac{a}{m}}$ **c** $M(1 + a) = 1 - a$

6.08

□ Foundation   ○ Standard   ◇ Complex

10 Graph each inequality on a number line.

    a $x \geq 0$ **b** $x < 3$ **c** $x \leq -2$ **d** $x > -5$

 11 Solve each inequality.

    a $y - 6 \geq 10$ **b** $2y \leq -15$ **c** $3a + 10 > -5$

    d $10 - 6x < 28$ **e** $\dfrac{a+2}{-4} > \dfrac{7}{2}$ **f** $\dfrac{3-5x}{2} \geq 9$

EXTENSION

 12 Write each expression in index form.

    a $\log_6 216 = 3$ **b** $\log_2 \dfrac{1}{16} = -4$ **c** $\log_7 7\sqrt{7} = \dfrac{3}{2}$

 13 Evaluate each expression.

    a $\log_7 84 - \log_7 12$ **b** $\log_2 3 + \log_2 \dfrac{1}{3}$ **c** $2\log_3 9 + \log_3 2 - \log_3 6$

 14 If $\log_{10} 3 \approx 0.4771$, find the value of:

    a $\log_{10} 9$ **b** $\log_{10} 300$ **c** $\log_{10} \dfrac{10}{3}$ **d** $\log_{10} \sqrt{90}$

 15 Solve each exponential equation, correct to 3 decimal places.

    a $5^x = 11$ **b** $2^x = 0.52$ **c** $3^{x+4} = 105$ **d** $16^{2-x} = 5$

□ Foundation   ○ Standard   ◇ Complex

Practice set 2 ANSWERS ON P. 628

1 Solve each equation.

EXTENSION

a $\dfrac{3b+1}{4}=\dfrac{2b-1}{3}$ **b** $\dfrac{2x}{3}-\dfrac{x}{6}=5$ **c** $\dfrac{1}{5}(4-x)+\dfrac{1}{3}(x-7)=5$

6.02

2 Evaluate each expression.

a $64^{\frac{1}{3}}$ **b** $1024^{\frac{2}{5}}$ **c** $144^{-\frac{1}{2}}$ **d** $100^{-\frac{3}{2}}$

4.02

3 Expand each binomial product.

4.04

a $(x+7)^2$ **b** $(5m-2n)^2$ **c** $(3n-10)(3n+10)$

4 The maximum daily temperatures (°C) of Perth for the first 14 days in April were:

5.02

27.1 24.1 23.7 24.6 26.5 31.8 33.6 32.6 34.0 35.6 39.5 26.2 26.7 24.9

a Find the range and interquartile range for the temperatures.

b Find the five-number summary for the data.

c Draw a boxplot for the data.

d Identify any outliers.

5 Simplify each expression.

4.01

a $(3y)^{-2}$ **b** $3y^{-2}$ **c** $\left(\dfrac{4x^6 y^6}{x^3 y^2}\right)^3$

d $(2h^4 k^5)^3 \times 3h^2 k$ **e** $48v^5 w^8 \div (-4vw^2)^2$ **f** $\left(\dfrac{36a^4 b^2}{48ab^4}\right)^{-1}$

6 Describe the strength and direction of the relationship shown in each scatterplot.

5.12

a 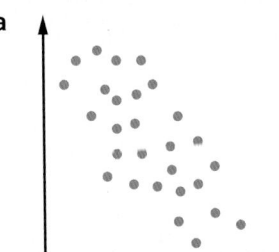 **b** 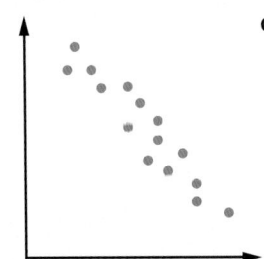 **c**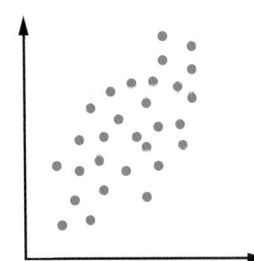

7 Solve each inequality.

6.10

a $21 + 4k < -7$ **b** $1 - 2y < 2(5 + 2y)$ **c** $\dfrac{2(4-x)}{3} \geq 1$

8 Simplify each expression.

EXTENSION

a $\sqrt{200}+\sqrt{18}$ **b** $7\sqrt{44}-6\sqrt{99}$ **c** $3\sqrt{6}+\sqrt{54}-2\sqrt{27}$ **d** $5\sqrt{72}-3\sqrt{45}+3\sqrt{50}$

4.11

9 Solve $5y^3 + 1000 = 0$, correct to one decimal place.

6.05

10 Rationalise the denominator of each surd.

a $\dfrac{1}{\sqrt{10}}$ **b** $\dfrac{5\sqrt{2}}{2\sqrt{3}}$ **c** $\dfrac{4+\sqrt{5}}{3\sqrt{5}}$ **d** $\dfrac{2\sqrt{6}-\sqrt{3}}{3\sqrt{3}}$

4.14

□ Foundation   ○ Standard   ◇ Complex

11 The speeds of cars (in km/h) were monitored during 2:30 to 4:00 p.m. in a school zone. The results are shown in the stem-and-leaf plot and boxplot below.

Stem	Leaf
2	0 3 7 9
3	0 2 2 3 5 6 8 8 9
4	0 0 1 3 5 5 7 8 9 9
5	1 1 4 4 6
6	0 1
7	6

Key: 2|0 = 20

Speed (km/h)

a Which plot gives the better indication of:

i skewness? **ii** clustering and outliers?

b Find the median. **c** Find the interquartile range.

 12 Solve each quadratic equation, correct to one decimal place where necessary.

a $p^2 - 144 = 0$ **b** $\dfrac{t^2}{4} = 25$ **c** $\dfrac{3w^2}{5} = 23$

EXTENSION

 13 Simplify and evaluate each expression.

a $\log_9 108 - \log_9 12$ **b** $\log_6 5 + \log_6 \dfrac{1}{5}$ **c** $3\log_5 10 - \log_5 8$

 14 Factorise each quadratic expression.

a $r^2 + 11r + 24$ **b** $y^2 - 31y + 30$ **c** $x^2 + 9x - 36$ **d** $t^2 - t - 72$

15 Ten boxes containing 60 apples each were placed in cold storage for different periods. After each period of storage, a box was withdrawn and the number of good apples was counted.

Weeks in storage (*W*)	2	3	5	6	7	8	9	10	12	14
Number of good apples (*N*)	56	53	48	48	50	39	36	30	34	26

a Which is the independent variable? Give reasons.

b Graph this data on a scatterplot.

c Describe the relationship between the weeks in storage and the number of good apples.

d Describe the strength and direction of the relationship between the variables *W* and *N*.

e Draw a line of best fit on your graph and use this to predict the number of good apples after 18 weeks of storage.

 16 Solve each quadratic equation.

a $x^2 + 8x + 7 = 0$ **b** $h^2 - 8h - 9 = 0$ **c** $u^2 + 4u - 77 = 0$ **d** $b^2 = 9b$

 17 Solve each problem using an equation.

a The sum of 3 consecutive numbers is 63. Find the 3 numbers.

b One angle in a triangle is double the size of the smallest angle, and the third angle in the triangle is 60° more than 3 times the size of the smallest angle. Find the size of each angle.

☐ Foundation ○ Standard ◇ Complex

18 Factorise each expression.

a $5n^2 + 7n + 2$ b $2a^2 - 7a - 15$ c $8x^2 + 14x - 15$

EXTENSION

4.07

6.09

19 Graph each inequality on a number line.

a $x \geq 0$ b $x < 4$ c $x \leq 1$ d $x > -6$

20 Solve each equation.

a $3\sqrt{3} = 9^x$ b $4^x = 120$, correct to 3 decimal places.

EXTENSION

6.13

4.13

21 Expand and simplify each expression.

a $\left(5\sqrt{10} - 4\sqrt{2}\right)\left(5\sqrt{10} + 4\sqrt{2}\right)$ b $\left(\sqrt{6} - 7\right)^2$ c $\left(2\sqrt{3} + 4\sqrt{5}\right)\left(3\sqrt{5} - \sqrt{3}\right)$

22 Data was collected on the weight loss of people who participated in a 12-week diet and exercise program. The results are shown in the table below.

5.05

Weight loss (kg)	Frequency
5–7	10
8–10	18
11–13	32
14–16	23
17–19	17

a Construct a cumulative frequency histogram and polygon for this data set on the same set of axes.

b Use the cumulative frequency polygon to estimate the median weight loss.

23 For the data set in question **22** above:

a estimate the first quartile b estimate the 75th percentile

c calculate the interquartile range.

5.06

5.08

24 The test results for 2 groups of students are shown.

Girls: 78, 73, 58, 79, 60, 46, 71, 64, 37, 79, 55, 59, 87, 68, 27

Boys: 70, 39, 80, 73, 61, 68, 84, 60, 73, 60, 54, 90, 69, 63, 59

a Find the mean and standard deviation of each group.

b Which group performed better in the exam? Give reasons.

25 Change the subject of each formula below to the variable indicated in brackets.

6.08

a $E = I^2 Rt$ $[\,I\,]$ b $\dfrac{c+n}{h} = k$ $[\,c\,]$ c $t = \sqrt{\dfrac{n}{3}}$ $[\,n\,]$

26 A survey was conducted on children at a childcare centre to determine whether they wanted to go to the movies or bowling as an excursion. Of the 60 children surveyed, 40 were girls, and 28 of the girls wanted to go to the movies. Sixteen of the boys wanted to go bowling. Determine whether there is an association between gender and type of activity.

5.14

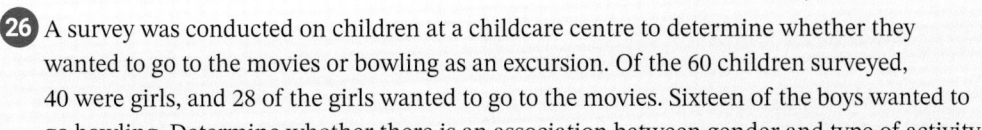

□ Foundation ○ Standard ○ Complex

7

ALGEBRA

Graphing curves

When an object is thrown upwards, its path is a curve called a parabola. The shape and length of the path will depend on the initial speed of the object and the angle at which it is thrown. Other examples of parabolas include car headlights and satellite dishes, which use mirrors or reflectors in the shape of a parabola.

Chapter outline

		Proficiencies			
7.01	Graphing quadratic functions $y = ax^2 + bx + c$	U F		R	C
7.02	Applying quadratic functions	U F PS		R	C
7.03	Direct proportion	U F PS		R	C
7.04	Inverse proportion*	U F PS		R	C
7.05	Graphing hyperbolas $y = \dfrac{k}{x}$ *	U F			
7.06	Graphing exponential functions $y = a^x$	U F		R	C
7.07	Exponential equations	U F		R	C
7.08	Exponential growth and decay	U F		R	C
7.09	Logarithmic scales	U F		R	C
7.10	Solving equations graphically	U F		R	C
7.11	Graphing circles $x^2 + y^2 = r^2$	U F		R	C
7.12	Identifying graphs	U F		R	C

* EXTENSION

U = Understanding
F = Fluency
PS = Problem solving

R = Reasoning
C = Communicating

Wordbank

asymptote A line that a curve gets very close to but never touches, for example, the x-axis is an asymptote of the exponential curve.

direct proportion A relationship between 2 variables of the form $y = kx$, where k is a constant; for example, if $y = 8.5x$, then y is directly proportional to x.

exponential function A function involving a variable as a power, such as $y = 3^x$, whose graph is an exponential curve.

exponential decay A rapid decrease of a quantity over time that follows the exponential function.

exponential growth A rapid increase of a quantity over time that follows the exponential function.

inverse proportion A relationship between 2 variables of the form $y = \dfrac{k}{x}$, where k is a constant; for example, if $y = \dfrac{50}{x}$, then y is inversely proportional to x.

parabola A U-shaped curve that is the graph of a quadratic equation.

quadratic equation An equation involving a variable squared (power of 2), such as $y = 3x^2 - 4x + 6$, whose graph is a curve called a parabola.

Quiz
Wordbank 7

7 **In this chapter you will:**

✓ graph parabolas of the form $y = ax^2 + bx + c$

✓ solve problems involving direct proportion

✓ (EXTENSION) solve problems involving inverse proportion

✓ (EXTENSION) graph hyperbolas of the form $y = \dfrac{k}{x}$

✓ graph exponential curves of the form $y = a^x$

✓ solve simple exponential equations

✓ solve problems involving exponential growth and decay

✓ interpret and use logarithmic scales

✓ solve equations graphically

✓ graph circles of the form $x^2 + y^2 = r^2$

✓ match graphs to their equations

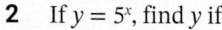

SkillCheck
ANSWERS ON P. 628

1 If $y = 2x^2 - 3x + 9$, find y if:

   a $x = 1$ **b** $x = 4$ **c** $x = 0$ **d** $x = -6$

2 If $y = 5^x$, find y if:

   a $x = 4$ **b** $x = 5$ **c** $x = 0$ **d** $x = -2$

3 If $y = \dfrac{8}{x}$, find y if:

   a $x = 2$ **b** $x = -16$ **c** $x = 5$ **d** $x = -2.5$

Quiz
SkillCheck 7

Graphing quadratic functions
$y = ax^2 + bx + c$

7.01

A function in which the highest power of the variable is 2 is called a **quadratic function**, for example, $y = 2x^2 - 5$, $y = x^2 + 7x + 12$ and $y = -5x^2$. The graph of a quadratic function is a smooth U-shaped curve called a **parabola**, which has a **vertex** (turning point) and an **axis of symmetry**.

A quadratic function has the general form $y = ax^2 + bx + c$, where a, b and c are constants.

Video
Quadratic functions

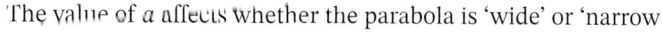

ⓘ The graph of $y = ax^2 + bx + c$

- If a is positive, the parabola is **concave up**.
- If a is negative, the parabola is **concave down**.
- The y-**intercept** is where $x = 0$, so it is the value of c.
- The x-**intercepts** are where $y = 0$.

The value of a affects whether the parabola is 'wide' or 'narrow'.

As the value of a increases, the parabola becomes 'narrower' and as the value of a decreases, the parabola 'widens'. If a is negative, then the parabola is concave down.

Interactive
Graphing quadratics

Worksheets
Graphing quadratic functions

Graphing quadratics

Graphing parabolas

Parabolas

Features of a parabola

Technology
Investigating parabolas 1

Spreadsheet
Investigating parabolas 1

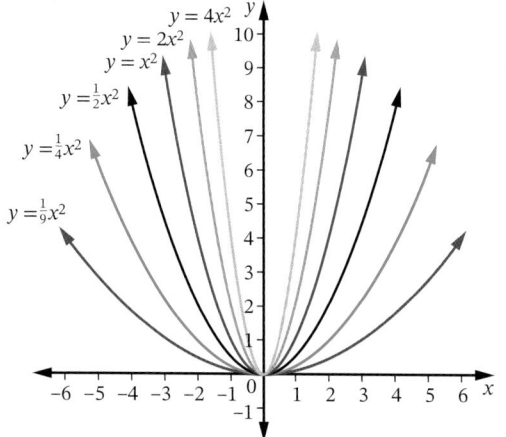

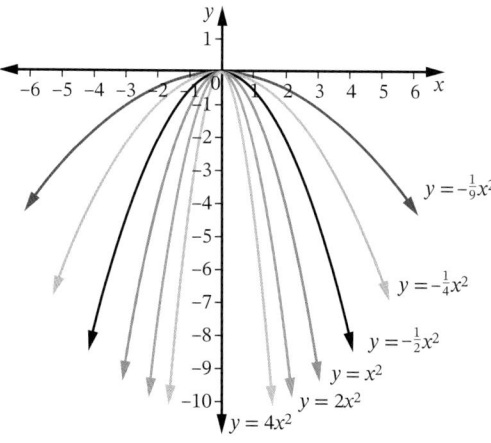

For the graph of $y = ax^2 + c$, where a and c are constants, the effect of c is to move the parabola up or down from the origin. Also, c is the y-intercept of the parabola.

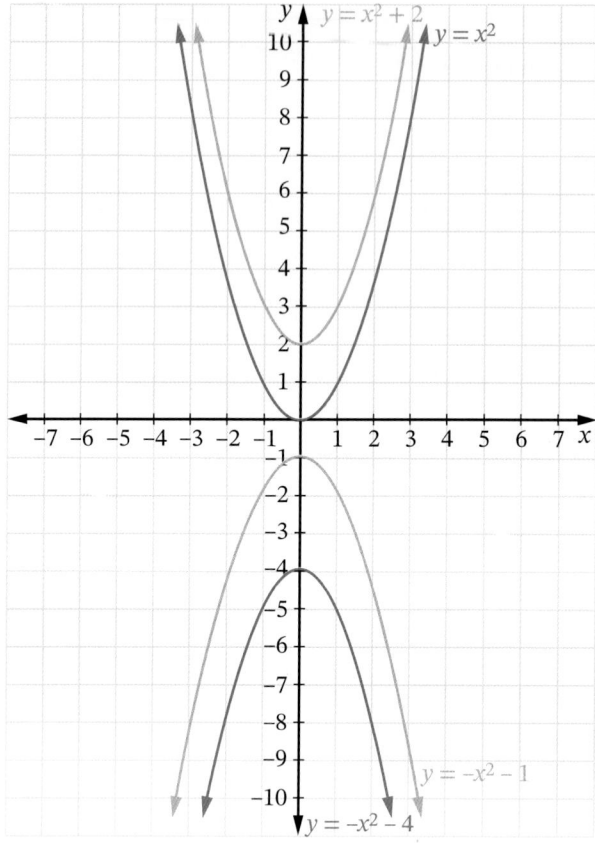

Example 1

For the graph of each quadratic function, state:

  i   whether the parabola is wider or narrower than the graph of $y = x^2$

  ii whether the parabola has moved up or down when compared to the graph of $y = x^2$

  iii the y-intercept.

a $y = 3x^2 - 1$ **b** $y = \frac{1}{3}x^2 + 2$

SOLUTION

a **i** The coefficient of x^2 is 3, while the coefficient of x^2 in $y = x^2$ is 1.

∴ the parabola will be narrower than $y = x^2$.

  ii The constant term is –1.

∴ the parabola has moved down.

 iii The y-intercept is –1.

Vertex at (0, –1).

b **i** The coefficient of x^2 is $\frac{1}{3}$.

∴ the parabola will be wider than $y = x^2$.

  ii The constant term is 2.

∴ the parabola has moved up.

 iii The y-intercept is 2.

Vertex at (0, 2).

Example 2

Graph each quadratic function and find the *x*- and *y*-intercepts of the parabola.

a $y = x^2 + 6x + 5$ **b** $y = -2x^2 + x + 10$

> **SOLUTION**

a **a** $y = x^2 + 6x + 5$

x	−6	−5	−4	−3	−2	−1	0	1
y	5	0	−3	−4	−3	0	5	12

You may need to extend your table of values to find the *x*-intercepts. A spreadsheet may also help.

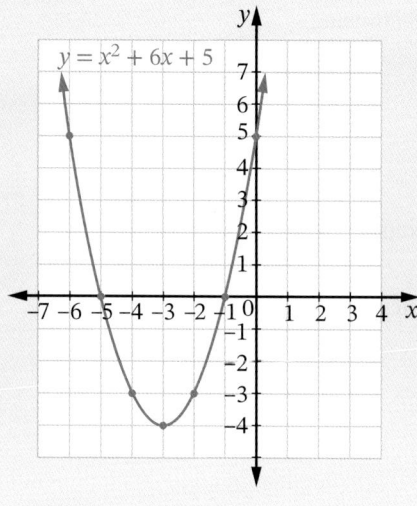

Note that this is the constant term, *c* = 5, in $y = x^2 + 6x + 5$.

The *x*-intercepts are −5 and −1. also, where $y = 0$

The *y*-intercept is 5. also, where $x = 0$

The vertex is at (−3, −4). from the graph or table

b $y = -2x^2 + x + 10$

x	−3	−2	−1	0	1	2	3
y	−11	0	7	10	9	4	−5

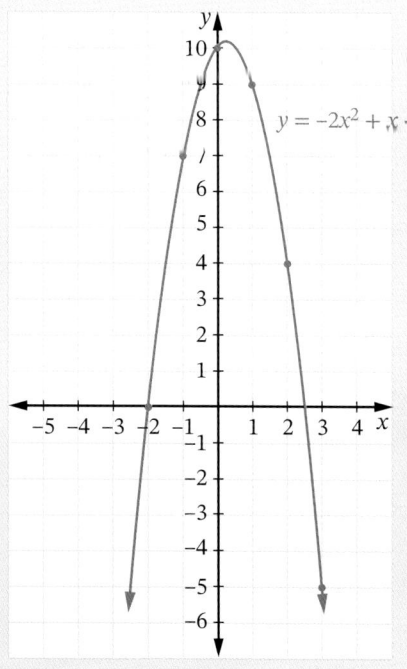

A concave down parabola because $a = -2 < 0$.

The *x*-intercepts are −2 and $2\frac{1}{2}$.

The *y*-intercept is 10.

Note that this is the constant term, *c* = 10, in $y = -2x^2 + x + 10$.

Example 3

a   Find the x-intercepts of the graph of $y = x^2 - 2x - 15$ by solving $y = 0$.

b   Find the y-intercept and vertex.

c   Graph $y = x^2 - 2x - 15$.

SOLUTION

a   Substitute $y = 0$ into the equation and solve:

$$0 = x^2 - 2x - 15$$
$$x^2 - 2x - 15 = 0$$
$$(x - 5)(x + 3) = 0 \qquad\qquad \text{factorising}$$
$$x - 5 = 0 \quad \text{or} \quad x + 3 = 0$$
$$x = 5 \quad \text{or} \quad x = -3$$

The x-intercepts are -3 and 5.

b   When $x = 0$, $y = 0^2 - 2(0) - 15 = -15$.

The y-intercept of $y = x^2 - 2x - 15$ is -15, the constant term, c, or the value of y when $x = 0$.

The x value of the vertex is halfway between the x-intercepts -3 and 5.

$$x = \frac{-3+5}{2} = 1$$

When $x = 1$, $y = 1^2 - 2(1) - 15 = -16$. The vertex is at $(1, -16)$.

c   Graphing the vertex and the intercepts:

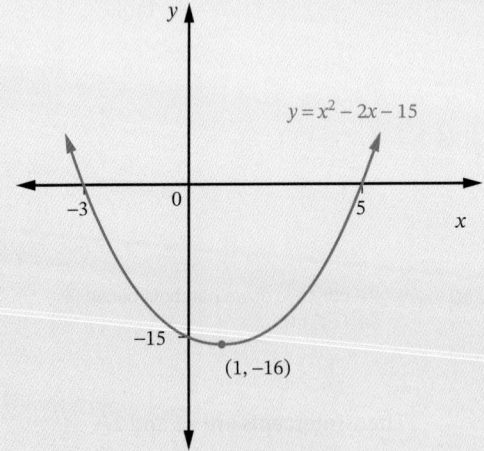

(i) The vertex of a parabola

The x value of the vertex of a parabola is halfway between the x-intercepts of the parabola. To find the y value of the vertex, substitute its x value into the quadratic function.

Graphing quadratic functions $y = ax^2 + bx + c$

U F R C

1 Which statement is false about this parabola? Select the correct answer **A**, **B**, **C** or **D**.

C

A Its axis of symmetry is the x-axis.

B It is concave down.

C Its vertex is at $(0, 1)$.

D It has a maximum value.

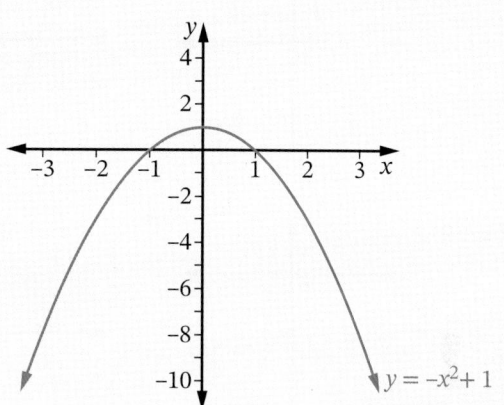

$y = -x^2 + 1$

2 Which diagram shows the graph of $y = x^2 - 2$? Select **A**, **B**, **C** or **D**.

R **A**

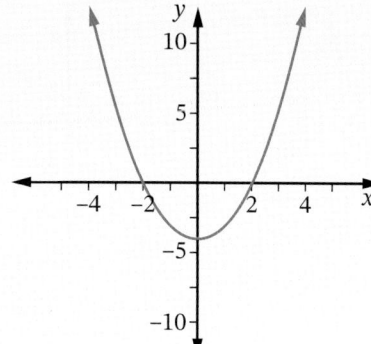

B

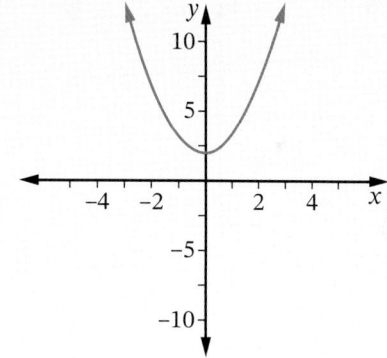

C

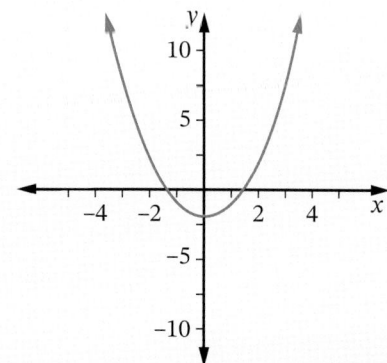

D

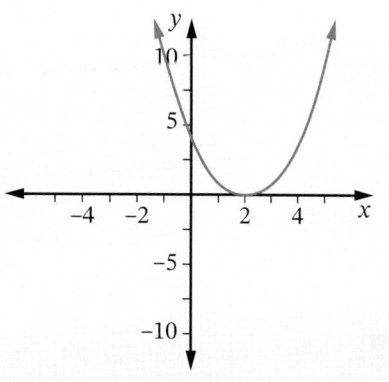

☐ Foundation ○ Standard ○ Complex

3 Match each graph with its correct quadratic equation (next page).

a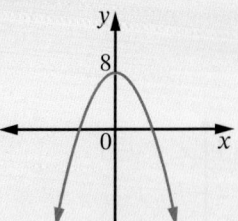

b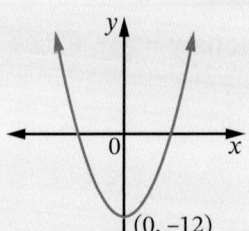

c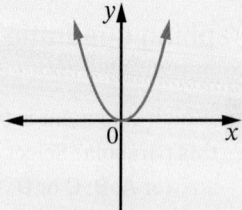

d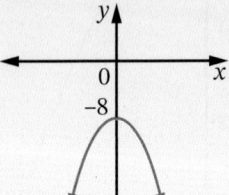

e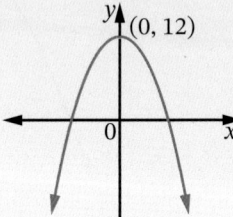

f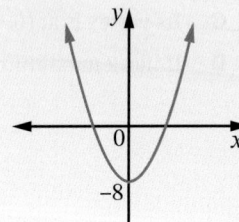

g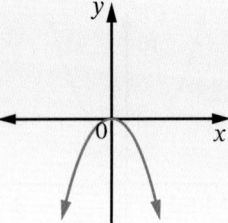

h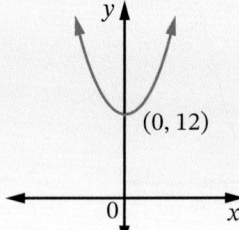

i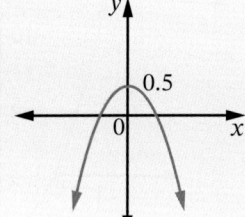

j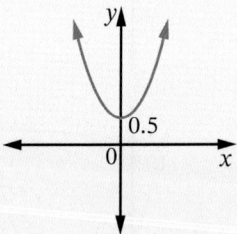

k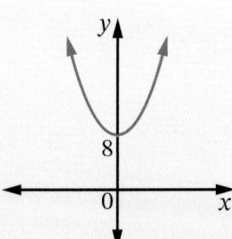

l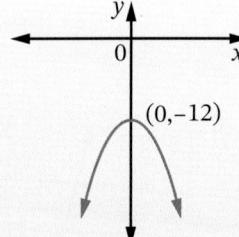

A $y = x^2$ **B** $y = -x^2$ **C** $y = x^2 - 8$ **D** $y = -12 - x^2$

E $y = \dfrac{1}{2} + x^2$ **F** $y = 8 - x^2$ **G** $y = 8 + x^2$ **H** $y = -x^2 + \dfrac{1}{2}$

I $y = x^2 - 12$ **J** $y = 12 - x^2$ **K** $y = -x^2 - 8$ **L** $y = x^2 + 12$

4 a Graph $y = -3x^2 + 2$ after copying and completing this table.

b Find the vertex.

c Write the equation of its axis of symmetry.

d Find its maximum value.

x	−2	−1	0	1	2
y					

☐ Foundation   ○ Standard   ○ Complex

5 Which statement is false about the graph of $y = 4x^2 - 1$? Select **A**, **B**, **C** or **D**.

(R) **A** Its axis of symmetry is $y = 0$.   **B** It is concave up.

(C) **C** The vertex is $(0, -1)$.   **D** It has a minimum value of -1.

6 For the graph of each given quadratic function, state:

EXAMPLE 1

(R)   **i** whether the parabola is wider or narrower than the graph of $y = x^2$

(C)   **ii** whether the parabola has moved up or down when compared to the graph of $y = x^2$

   iii the y-intercept.

   a $y = 2x^2 + 3$ **b** $y = \frac{1}{2}x^2 + 1$ **c** $y = 6x^2 - 5$ **d** $y = 0.2x^2 - 12$

7 Graph each quadratic function and find the x- and y-intercepts of the parabola.

EXAMPLE 2

(R) **a** $y = x^2 + 4x + 3$ **b** $y = 2x^2 + 7x + 3$

(C) **c** $y = -2x^2 + 3x + 9$ **d** $y = x^2 - 2x$

8 Find the y-intercept of the parabolas with equation:

   a $y = -3x^2 - 2x - 5$ **b** $y = 2x^2 + 6x + 3$ **c** $y = -5x^2 - 10x$

9 Which quadratic equation below represents a parabola with x-intercepts 2 and -5?

   A $y = x^2 + 7x - 10$ **B** $y = x^2 - 7x - 10$

   C $y = x^2 + 3x - 10$ **D** $y = x^2 - 3x - 10$

10 Find the x-intercepts of each quadratic function by solving $y = 0$, then find its y-intercept and vertex, then sketch its graph.

EXAMPLE 3

(R)
(C) **a** $y = x^2 - 4x$ **b** $y = 3x^2 + 6x$ **c** $y = -x^2 + 4x + 5$

   d $y = (x - 2)(2x - 5)$ **e** $y = -(x + 1)(3x + 2)$ **f** $y = x^2 + 6x + 8$

Applying quadratic functions

Real-world situations can be modelled using quadratic functions. Throwing a ball or shooting an arrow are referred to as 'projectile motion'. In these situations, the height of the object above the ground can be modelled by a quadratic function. The path of the object can also be described by a quadratic function, with the shape of a parabola.

Video
Applying quadratic functions

□ Foundation   ○ Standard   ◇ Complex

Example 4

Britney has 18 metres of fencing and wants to build a rectangular pig pen with the largest area possible. She sketches some possible pens using her 18 m of fencing.

$A = 14\ \text{m}^2$ 2 m

7 m

$A = 20\ \text{m}^2$ 4 m

5 m

$A = 19.25\ \text{m}^2$ 3.5 m

5.5 m

Let x and y be the length and width of the pen, in metres.

a Explain why $2x + 2y = 18$.

b Hence show that $y = 9 - x$.

c Hence show that the area of the pen, $A\ \text{m}^2$, is given by the function $A = -x^2 + 9x$.

d Find the largest possible area of the pen. What are the dimensions of the pen that give this maximum area?

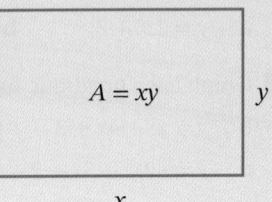

$A = xy$ y

x

SOLUTION

a perimeter of pen $= x + y + x + y = 18$

$$2x + 2y = 18$$

b $2y = 18 - 2x$ making y the subject

$y = \dfrac{18 - 2x}{2}$

$= 9 - x$

c $A = xy$

$= x(9 - x)$ substituting $y = 9 - x$

$= 9x - x^2$ expanding

$= -x^2 + 9x$

d Complete a table of values.

By graphing or reading from the table, the maximum value of A lies halfway between $x = 4$ and $x = 5$.

x	3	4	5	6	7
A	18	20	20	18	14

$x = \dfrac{4+5}{2} = 4.5$

When $x = 4.5$, $A = -4.5^2 + 9(4.5)$

$= 20.25$

The largest possible area is 20.25 m² when the pen is a square with length 4.5 m.

9780170465595

Applying quadratic functions   U F PS R C

The questions in this exercise may also be completed using graphing software.

1 A golf ball is hit into the air and its height, h metres, above the ground after time,
t seconds, is given by the quadratic function $h = -5t^2 + 24t$.

EXAMPLE
4

PS

R   **a** Find the height of the ball after 2 seconds.

C   **b** Show that the height of the ball after 1.8 and 3 seconds is the same. Why is this so?

   c After how many seconds does the ball reach its maximum height? How did you find this value?

   d Find the maximum height reached.

   e Why is this quadratic model not useful for values of t greater than 5?

2 Aayush has 18 m of wire fencing to border a new baby lamb enclosure. He wants to use
an existing brick wall as one side and sketches 3 possible enclosures.

PS

R

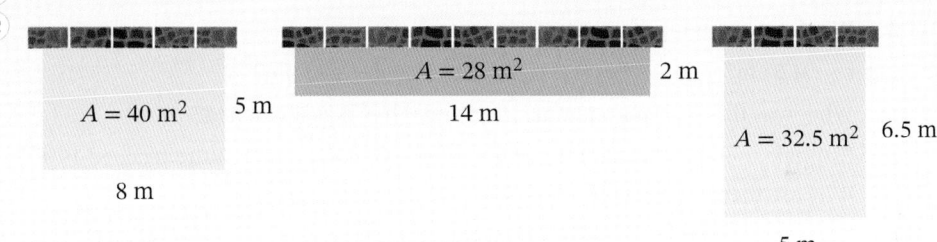

$A = 40$ m^2 5 m

8 m

$A = 28$ m^2 2 m

14 m

$A = 32.5$ m^2 6.5 m

5 m

   a If x m and y m are the length and width of the enclosure, explain why $x + 2y = 18$.

   b Hence show that $y = 9 - \dfrac{1}{2}x$.

   c Hence show that the area, A m^2, of the enclosure is $A = -\dfrac{1}{2}x^2 + 9x$.

   d Find the maximum area of the enclosure and the dimensions that give this area.

3 At an air show, the height (in metres) of a plane in a power dive is given by
$h = t^2 - 10t + 80$, where t is the time in seconds.

R

C   **a** Use a table of values to graph the function $h = t^2 - 10t + 80$ for values of t from 0 to 10.

   b What are the coordinates of the vertex?

   c What is the minimum value of h and what does this represent?

   d When is the lowest height of the plane reached?

   e What is the height of the plane at the start of the power dive?

☐ Foundation ◯ Standard ◯ Complex

4 A sky rocket is sent up into the air at a fireworks display. It reaches a maximum height, fizzles out and the leftover pieces fall back down to Earth. The quadratic function $d = 4.9t^2$ gives the distance, d metres, that a piece falls in t seconds.

   a Copy and complete this table of values.

t	0	1	2	3	4	5	6	7	8	9	10
d											

   b Graph this quadratic function.

   c How far does a piece fall in:

     i 3 seconds?   **ii** 30 seconds?

   d Find, correct to the nearest 0.1 second, how long it takes for a piece to fall:

     i 10 m?   **ii** 50 m?

5 The temperature, $T°C$, at a town n hours after 6 a.m. is given by the function

(PS)
(R)
(C)
$$T = -\frac{1}{6}n^2 + 2n + 14.$$

   a Graph this function for values of n from 0 to 15.

   b What was the temperature:

     i at 6 am?   **ii** at 2 pm?

   c What was the maximum temperature and when was it reached?

   d Estimate to the nearest half-hour the times when the temperature reached 19°C. Why are there 2 answers?

   e For how many hours (to the nearest whole number) was the temperature 19°C or higher?

   f This quadratic model is only accurate for values of n from 0 to 13. Why do you think the model does not hold for values of n above 13?

6 A stone is dropped from a cliff and its height (h metres) at any time (t seconds) is given by $h = 80 - 4.8t^2$.

(PS)
(R)
(C)

   a Draw a graph of the equation for values of t from 0 to 5.

   b What is the height of the cliff?

   c What is the height of the stone after 3 seconds?

   d When will the stone hit the ground?

   e How long after it is dropped is the stone 5 metres above the ground? Answer correct to 2 decimal places.

7 The fuel consumption of a car travelling at a speed of s km/h is modelled by the function $C = 0.01s^2 - s + 33$, where fuel consumption C is measured in L/100 km. Graph this function to determine the travelling speed at which fuel consumption is most economical (meaning it is at its lowest), and state the fuel consumption at this speed.

(PS)
(R)
(C)

8 The profit from selling tickets for the school musical depends on the price of each ticket. Using data from previous years, the profit made can be modelled by the function $p = -2t^2 + 100t + 50$, where p is the profit and t is the price of each ticket. Graph this function to determine the price that tickets should be sold at to obtain the maximum profit from the musical. Identify what profit can be made with this ticket price.

(PS)
(R)
(C)

□ Foundation   ○ Standard   ○ Complex

Direct proportion

Two variables are **directly proportional** to each other if one variable is a constant multiple of the other; when one variable changes, the other one changes by the same factor.

ⓘ Direct proportion

If y is directly proportional to x, then $y = kx$, where k is a constant (number) called the constant of proportionality or constant of variation.

- A direct linear relationship exists between x and y.
- If x increases (or decreases), y increases (or decreases).
- If x is doubled (or halved), y is doubled (or halved).
- Another way of saying 'y is directly proportional to x' is 'y varies directly with x'.
- The graph of direct proportion is a straight line going through $(0, 0)$ with gradient k.

Example 5

The distance (d) in metres travelled by a car is directly proportional to the number of rotations (r) of its tyres. After 540 rotations, 950 metres is travelled.

a What distance (correct to the nearest metre) will be travelled after 800 rotations?

b How many full rotations will be needed to cover 360 metres?

Videos
Direct proportion

Direct linear variation

SOLUTION

a d is directly proportional to r

$\therefore d = kr$ forming a proportion equation

To find k, substitute the information given for r and d.

When $r = 540$, $d = 950$:

$950 = k \times 540$ finding k

$k = \dfrac{950}{540}$ do not round k

$= 1.759...$

$\therefore d = 1.759... \, r$ rewriting the equation $d = kr$

When $r = 800$,   solving the problem

$d = 1.759... \times 800$

$= 1407.4074...$

≈ 1407 m

After 800 rotations, the distance travelled will be 1407 metres.

b   When $d = 360$,

$360 = 1.759... \times r$

solving the problem

rounding up for full rotations

$$r = \frac{360}{1.759...}$$

$= 204.661$

≈ 205 rotations

For a distance of 360 m, there will be approximately 205 rotations.

ⓘ Solving direct proportion problems

1   Identify the 2 variables (say x and y) and form a proportion equation, $y = kx$.

2   Substitute values for x and y to find k, the constant of proportionality.

3   Rewrite $y = kx$ using the value of k.

4   Substitute a value for x or y into $y = kx$ to solve the problem.

Example 6

M varies directly with n. If when $n = 6$, $M = 103.8$, find M when $n = 14.2$.

SOLUTION

$M = kn$

To find k, substitute $n = 6$ and $M = 103.8$.

$103.8 = k \times 6$

$$k = \frac{103.8}{6}$$

$= 17.3$

$\therefore M = 17.3n$

Substitute $n = 14.2$ to find M.

$M = 17.3 \times 14.2$

$= 245.66$

EXERCISE **7.03**   ANSWERS ON P. 631

Direct proportion

Ⓤ Ⓕ ⓅⓈ Ⓡ Ⓒ

1   Match each statement with its proportion equation (k is the constant of variation).

Ⓒ **a**   The distance, D, travelled is directly proportional to the time, T.

b   The wage, W, earned is directly proportional to the hours, h, worked.

c   The wedding cost, C, varies directly with the number of guests, n.

d   The interest, I, earned varies directly with the size of the deposit, D.

A $C = kn$ **B** $I = kD$ **C** $D = kT$ **D** $W = kh$

▷

☐ Foundation   ⭘ Standard   ◇ Complex

2 The distance, D, travelled by Connor, a marathon runner, varies directly with time, T.

(PS)
(R)
(C)

Time, T (min)	1	2	3
Distance, D (m)	190	380	570

a Find the constant of proportionality and write the equation for D.

b How far, in kilometres, will Connor run in:

    i 20 minutes?   **ii** 45 minutes?

c How long would it take Connor to run 12.35 kilometres? Answer in hours and minutes.

3 Mehta's earnings for working a shift at the local nursery are directly proportional to the number of hours she works. Yesterday, she earned $222.70 for working an 8.5-hour shift.

(PS)
(R)
(C)

a If Mehta's earnings are represented by E, and the number of hours worked is represented by h, find the constant of proportionality and write an equation for E.

b How much will she earn for working a 7-hour shift?

c How many hours did she work today if she earned $144.10 for the shift?

4 The amount of interest, I, earned for one year on an investment account varies directly with the size of the deposit, D.

(PS)
(R)
(C)

a If Caterina earns $16 interest on an investment of $425, find the variation equation for I, including the constant of variation.

b Hence, how much will she earn on an investment of $900?

c If she doubles the size of her investment in part **b**, how much will she earn in interest?

5 S varies directly with t. If when $t = 14$, $S = 106.4$, what is the value of S when $t = 0.3$? Select the correct answer **A**, **B**, **C** or **D**.

(R)
(C)

A 2.28   **B** 27.72   **C** 36.12   **D** 446.88

EXAMPLE 6

6 Find the linear formula for b in terms of a for this table of values.

a	4	8	12	16	20
b	10	20	30	40	50

7 The line graph shows that the cost of hamburgers purchased from the local takeaway store depends directly on the number of burgers purchased.

(PS)
(R)
(C)

a Copy this table and use the graph to complete it.

No. of burgers, h	1	2	3
Cost, c ($)			

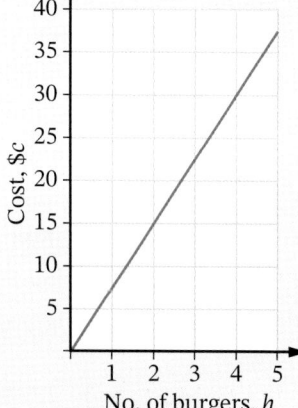

b Find the variation equation to represent the relationship between the cost (c) and the number of burgers (h).

c If Kendall buys 6 hamburgers, what is the total cost of the hamburgers?

d The total cost of one order of hamburgers is $82.50. How many hamburgers were ordered?

e Find the gradient of the line. How is it related to the constant of variation?

Foundation ☐   Standard ○   Complex ○

8 *K* varies directly with *L*. If *L* = 9.5 when *K* = 1045, what is the value of *K* when *L* = 1.65?
Select **A**, **B**, **C** or **D**.

A   0.015   **B**   93.7   **C**   181.5   **D**   1708.575

9 A linear relationship exists between the mass of a car (*m* kg) and its rate of fuel consumption (*F* L/100 km).

a   Find the variation equation for *F* if a 1000 kg car uses fuel at a rate of 6 L/100 km.

b   Find the fuel consumption of a 2500 kg car.

10 For an object that is cooling, the drop in temperature varies directly with time.
If the temperature drops 8°C in 5 minutes, how long would it take to drop 10°C?
Select **A**, **B**, **C** or **D**.

A   6.25 min   **B**   7 min   **C**   12 min   **D**   16 min

11 The weight of an astronaut on Mars is proportional to his weight on Earth.
A 72 kg astronaut weighs 27.4 kg on Mars.

a   Calculate how much a 60 kg astronaut weighs on Mars, correct to one decimal place.

b   If an astronaut weighs 32 kg on Mars, calculate his weight on Earth, correct to one decimal place.

7.04 Extension: Inverse proportion

EXTENSION

Videos
Inverse variation

The heartbeat formula

Worksheets
Direct and inverse proportion

Variation problems

Two variables are **inversely proportional** to each other if, when one variable increases, the other one decreases by the same factor.

The table below shows the different speeds of a car (*s* km/h), and the time it takes to travel 100 km (*t* min). As the speed increases, the time taken decreases.

Speed (*s* km/h)	50	60	80	100
Time (*t* min)	120	100	75	60

ⓘ Inverse proportion

If *y* is **inversely proportional** to *x*, then $y = \dfrac{k}{x}$, where *k* is a constant (number) called the **constant of proportionality** or **constant of variation**.

- If *x* increases, *y* decreases ('inverse' means 'opposite').
- If *x* decreases, *y* increases.
- If *x* is doubled, *y* is halved.
- If *x* is halved, *y* is doubled.
- Another way of saying '*y* is inversely proportional to *x*' is '*y* **varies inversely** with *x*'.

□ Foundation   ○ Standard   ◇ Complex

Example 7

The time (t) in minutes taken by a car to travel 100 km is inversely proportional to the speed (s km/h) of the car, as shown in the table. At 50 km/h, the time taken is 120 minutes.

Speed (s km/h)	50	60	80	100
Time (t min)	120	100	75	60

a Find the constant of proportionality and the inverse variation equation for t.

b How long did the car take to travel 100 km at:

   i 40 km/h   **ii** 110 km/h?

c Find the car's speed if it took 45 minutes to travel 100 km.

SOLUTION

a t is inversely proportional to s.

$\therefore t = \dfrac{k}{s}$ forming an inverse proportion equation

To find k, substitute the information given for s and t.

When $s = 50$, $t = 120$:   finding k, the constant of proportionality

$120 = \dfrac{k}{50}$

$\quad k = 120 \times 50$

$\qquad = 6000$

The constant of proportionality is 6000.

$\therefore t = \dfrac{6000}{s}$ rewriting the equation $t = \dfrac{k}{s}$

b **i** When $s = 40$, $t = \dfrac{6000}{40} = 150$ min

     At 40 km/h, the trip took 150 min (or 2 h 30 min).

   ii When $s = 110$,

     $t = \dfrac{6000}{110}$

     $\quad = 54.5454...$

     $\quad \approx 55$ min

     At 110 km/h, the trip took 55 minutes.

c When $t = 45$,

   $45 = \dfrac{6000}{s}$

   $45s = 6000$

     $s = \dfrac{6000}{45}$

     $\quad = 133\dfrac{1}{3}$ km/h

For a travel time of 45 minutes, the speed must be $133\dfrac{1}{3}$ km/h.

ⓘ Solving inverse proportion problems

1 Identify the 2 variables (say x and y) and form a proportion equation, $y = \dfrac{k}{x}$.

2 Substitute values for x and y to find k, the constant of proportionality.

3 Rewrite $y = \dfrac{k}{x}$ using the value of k.

4 Substitute a value for x or y into $y = \dfrac{k}{x}$ to solve the problem.

Example 8

The temperature, T (in degrees Celsius), of the air is inversely proportional to the height, h (in metres), above sea level. At 600 m above sea level, the temperature is 8°C.

a What is the temperature at 1000 m above sea level?

b Graph the relationship between temperature and height above sea level, for heights between 0 m and 5000 m.

SOLUTION

a T is inversely proportional to h.

$T = \dfrac{k}{h}$ forming a proportion equation

Substitute $h = 600$ and $T = 8$ to find k.

$8 = \dfrac{k}{600}$ finding k

$k = 8 \times 600$

$ = 4800$

$\therefore T = \dfrac{4800}{h}$ rewriting the equation $T = \dfrac{k}{h}$

When $h = 1000$,   solving the problem

$T = \dfrac{4800}{1000} = 4.8°C$

The temperature at a height of 1000 metres above sea level is 4.8°C.

b Draw a table of values for $T = \dfrac{4800}{h}$

h	1000	2000	3000	4000	5000
T	4.8	2.4	1.6	1.2	0.96

Note that as h increases, T decreases.

This graph is called a **hyperbola**.

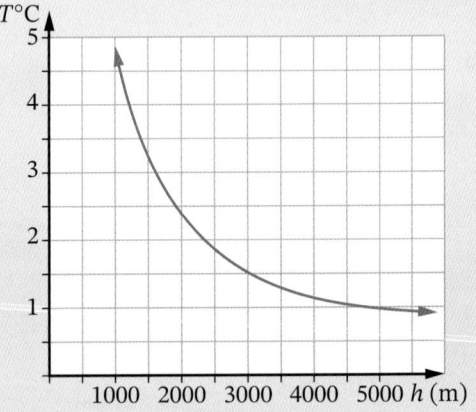

Example 9

EXTENSION

P varies inversely with q. If when $q = 4$, $P = 38$, find P when $q = 5$.

SOLUTION

$P = \dfrac{k}{q}$ forming a proportion equation

Substitute $q = 4$, $P = 38$

$38 = \dfrac{k}{4}$ finding k

$k = 38 \times 4 = 152$

$\therefore P = \dfrac{152}{q}$ rewriting the equation $P = \dfrac{k}{q}$

Substitute $q = 5$ to find P.   solving the problem

$P = \dfrac{152}{5} = 30.4$

EXERCISE 7.04   ANSWERS ON P. 631

Inverse proportion

(U) (F) (PS) (R) (C)

1   Match each statement with its inverse proportion equation
(C)   (k is the constant of variation).

    a   The travel time, T, varies inversely with the speed, S.

    b   The temperature, T, above sea level varies inversely with the altitude, h.

    c   The cost, C, per person of hiring a bus varies inversely as the number of people, n.

    d   The time, T, taken to move house varies inversely with the number of helpers, n.

    A $T = \dfrac{k}{n}$ **B** $T = \dfrac{k}{S}$ **C** $T = \dfrac{k}{h}$ **D** $C = \dfrac{k}{n}$

2   The time taken, T hours, to travel from Sydney to Melbourne varies inversely with the
(PS)   average speed, s km/h.

(R)
(C)   **a**   If it takes 11.5 hours at an average speed of 80 km/h, find the constant of
        proportionality and the variation equation for T.

    b   If the average speed is increased to 90 km/h, how long will the journey take?
        Answer in hours and minutes.

    c   Find the average speed needed to complete the trip in 10 hours.

EXAMPLE
7

▷

□ Foundation   ○ Standard   ○ Complex

EXAMPLE
8

3 The temperature, T (in degrees Celsius), of the air varies inversely with the height, h (in metres), above sea level. At 150 m above sea level, the temperature is 30°C.

a Find the constant of variation and write a variation equation for T.

b What is the temperature at:

   i 300 m above sea level   **ii** 2500 m above sea level?

c What is the height above sea level when the temperature is:

   i 8°C   **ii** 22.5°C?

d Graph the relationship between temperature and height above sea level. Use T on the vertical axis and h on the horizontal axis with $h = 0, 500, 1000, 1500 \dots 3000$.

4 The maximum number of diners, N, in Yen's restaurant varies inversely with the amount of floor space, S m², allocated to each diner. If 1.4 m² is allowed per diner, the restaurant can have 80 diners.

a Write a variation equation for N.

b How many diners could the restaurant contain if only 1.1 m² was allocated per person?

c How much space (correct to one decimal place) is allocated to each diner if the restaurant has a maximum capacity of 55 diners?

d During the COVID-19 pandemic of 2020, social distancing measures introduced to minimise the spread of the virus allocated 4 m² to each diner. How many diners could Yen's restaurant serve under this restriction?

5 The rate of vibration of a string varies inversely as its length. A string that is 8 cm long vibrates at 9375 Hz (hertz). What length of string will vibrate at 6250 Hz? Select the correct answer **A**, **B**, **C** or **D**.

  A 5 cm   **B** 7 cm   **C** 12 cm   **D** 73 cm

6 Which equation represents this table of values? Select **A**, **B**, **C** or **D**.

x	2	5	8	10
y	2.5	1	0.625	0.5

  A $y = \dfrac{10}{x}$ **B** $y = \dfrac{5}{x}$ **C** $y = \dfrac{2.5}{x}$ **D** $y = \dfrac{1}{x}$

EXAMPLE
9

7 K is inversely proportional to L. If $L = 2$ when $K = 7$, find K when $L = 15$.

8 Tavjot believes that at a train station, the number of people waiting on the platform is inversely proportional to the time until the next train arrives. According to his model, when there are 16 people waiting, the train will arrive in 2.5 minutes.

a When will the train arrive if there are 5 people waiting?

b How many people are waiting at the station 10 minutes before the train arrives?

□ Foundation   ○ Standard   ◇ Complex

9 Each graph shows an inverse relationship between a and b. Find each variation equation.

a

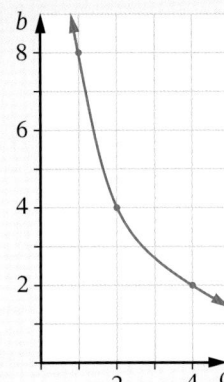

b

10 The frequency, F beats per second, that a bird beats its wings varies inversely as the length, L cm, of its wings. A bird with wings of length 14 cm beats them at a frequency of 8 beats per second.

a Find the variation equation for F in terms of L.

b Calculate, to the nearest whole number, the wingbeat frequency for wings of length 18 cm.

c A bird beats its wings with a frequency of 4.5 beats per second. What is the length of its wings, correct to the nearest centimetre?

11 For a certain equation, y varies inversely with x.

a Given $x = 0.2$ when $y = 10$, find y when $x = 32$.

b Find x when $y = 1.6$.

12 The amount of time it takes Supriya to move house is inversely proportional to the number of friends she has to help her. When she has 4 friends helping, the job takes $3\frac{3}{4}$ hours.

a How long will it take if Supriya has 6 friends helping?

b How many friends must she have to help her to move house in 3 hours?

INVESTIGATION

Graphing $y = \dfrac{1}{x}$

1 Copy and complete this table for $y = \dfrac{1}{x}$. Explain why no y value exists for $x = 0$.

x	−5	−4	−3	−2	−1	−0.5	−0.2	−0.1	0	0.1	0.2	0.5	1	2	3	4	5
y									−								

2 Hence graph $y = \dfrac{1}{x}$ on a number plane.

3 There are 2 parts or 'branches' to your graph. In which quadrants of the number plane are the branches?

□ Foundation ○ Standard ◇ Complex

EXTENSION

4   Use your graph to explain what happens to the y value as x becomes very large.

5   Explain what happens to the y value as x approaches 0.

6   The graph of $y = \dfrac{1}{x}$ has 2 axes of symmetry. Draw them on your graph.

7   Copy and complete the table from question **1** for $y = -\dfrac{1}{x}$.

8   Hence graph $y = -\dfrac{1}{x}$ on a number plane.

9   How does the graph of $y = -\dfrac{1}{x}$ compare with that of $y = \dfrac{1}{x}$?

TECHNOLOGY

Graphing $y = \dfrac{k}{x}$

1   Use graphing technology to graph each equation.

a $y = \dfrac{1}{x}$ b $y = \dfrac{2}{x}$ c $y = \dfrac{5}{x}$ d $y = \dfrac{10}{x}$

2   Compare the graphs from question **1**. What happens to the graph of
$y = \dfrac{k}{x}$ as k increases?

3   Graph $y = \dfrac{2}{x}$ and $y = \dfrac{-2}{x}$ and compare them.

4   Graph $y = \dfrac{4}{x}$ and use **Trace** to complete this table of values.

x	1	2	5	10	100	200	1000
y							

5   What happens to the y values when the x values become very large?

6   For $y = \dfrac{4}{x}$ use the **Trace** function to complete this table of values.

x	0.0001	0.01	0.1	0.5	1	5
y						

7   What happens to the y values when the x values become very small and close to 0?

7.05 Extension: Graphing hyperbolas $y = \dfrac{k}{x}$

EXTENSION

Worksheet
Graphing
hyperbolas

The graph of $y = \dfrac{k}{x}$, where k is a constant, is
a curve with 2 branches called a **hyperbola**
(pronounced 'hy-perb-o-la').

The graphs of $y = \dfrac{1}{x}$ and $y = -\dfrac{1}{x}$ are shown.

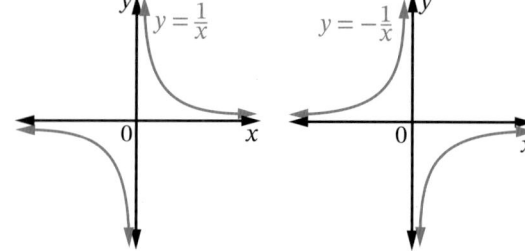

(i) The hyperbola $y = \dfrac{k}{x}$

- The hyperbola has 2 separate branches in different quadrants.
- If k is positive, the graph is in the 1st and 3rd quadrants.
- If k is negative, the graph is in the 2nd and 4th quadrants.
- The graph has 2 axes of symmetry: their equations are the straight lines $y = x$ and $y = -x$.
- The graph has rotational symmetry of $180°$ about $(0, 0)$.
- The higher the value of k, the further the hyperbola is from the x- and y-axes.
- As x becomes very large, y gets closer to 0.
- As x becomes closer to 0, y gets very large.
- The graph gets very close to the x- and y-axes but never crosses them. The x- and y-axes are called **asymptotes** because the graph approaches them but never touches them.

Example 10

Graph each hyperbola and mark the coordinates of one point on the curve.

a $y = \dfrac{2}{x}$ **b** $y = -\dfrac{3}{x}$

Video
Graphing
hyperbolas

SOLUTION

a Let $x = 2$.   choosing any value of x

$y = \dfrac{2}{2} = 1$

A point on the curve is $(2, 1)$.

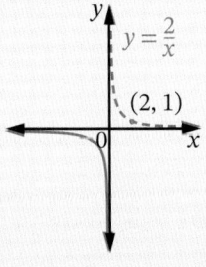

b Let $x = 3$.

$y = -\dfrac{3}{3} = -1$

A point on the curve is $(3, -1)$.

As $k = -3$ is negative, the hyperbola is in the 2nd and 4th quadrants.

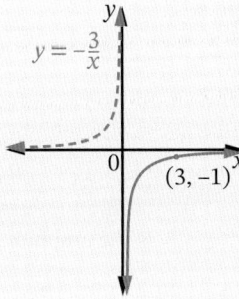

(i) The hyperbola $y = \dfrac{k}{x} + c$

The graph of $y = \dfrac{k}{x} + c$ is the hyperbola $y = \dfrac{k}{x}$ translated c units up (or down if c is negative).

ⓘ The hyperbola $y = \dfrac{k}{x-b}$

The graph of $y = \dfrac{k}{x-b}$ is the hyperbola $y = \dfrac{k}{x}$ translated b units to the right (or left if b is negative).

Example 11

Graph each hyperbola, find any intercepts and mark the coordinates of one point on the curve.

a $\quad y = \dfrac{2}{x} + 1$

b $\quad y = \dfrac{-3}{x-2}$

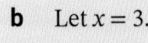 SOLUTION

a Let $x = 2$.   choosing any value of x

$y = \dfrac{2}{2} + 1 = 2$

A point on the curve is (2, 2).

The graph of $y = \dfrac{2}{x} + 1$ is the graph of

$y = \dfrac{2}{x}$ translated up 1 unit. This means

that the horizontal asymptote is now

at $y = 1$.

An x-intercept now occurs when $y = 0$.

$0 = \dfrac{2}{x} + 1$ multiplying both sides by x

$0 = 2 + x$

$x = -2$

The x-intercept is -2.

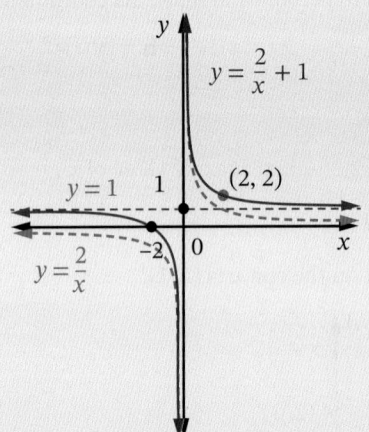

b Let $x = 3$.

$y = \dfrac{-3}{3-2} = -3$

A point on the curve is (3, –3).

The graph of $y = \dfrac{-3}{x-2}$ is the graph of

$y = \dfrac{-3}{x}$ translated right 2 units. This

means that the vertical asymptote is now

at $x = 2$.

A y-intercept now occurs when $x = 0$.

$y = \dfrac{-3}{0-2} = \dfrac{-3}{-2} = 1\dfrac{1}{2}$

The y-intercept is $1\dfrac{1}{2}$.

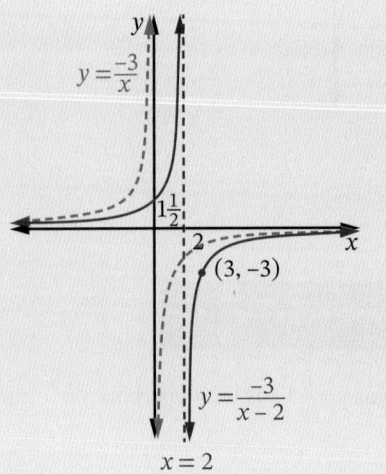

EXERCISE **7.05** ANSWERS ON P. 632

The hyperbola $y = \dfrac{k}{x}$

(U) (F) (R) (C)

EXAMPLE
10

1 a Copy and complete this table for $y = \dfrac{2}{x}$.

x	−3	−2	−1	0	1	2	3
y				−			

b Graph $y = \dfrac{2}{x}$, showing the coordinates of one point on the hyperbola.

c On your diagram, draw in the axes of symmetry for the hyperbola.

d What are the equations of these axes?

2 Graph each hyperbola and mark the coordinates of one point on the curve.

a $y = \dfrac{4}{x}$

b $y = -\dfrac{2}{x}$

c $y = \dfrac{3}{x}$

3 a The distance from Sydney to Melbourne is close to 1000 km. Using the equation $s = \dfrac{1000}{t}$, copy and complete the following table that relates time (t hours) and speed (s km/h) for the trip. Round your answers to the nearest km/h.

(R)
(C)

t	1	2	3	...	10
s					

b Hence graph the equation $s = \dfrac{1000}{t}$.

c Why are the values for t only positive numbers? Explain why t cannot be equal to 0.

d If the time is doubled, is the speed halved? Use the information from your graph to support your answer.

4 This curve is a hyperbola of the form $y = \dfrac{k}{x}$.

a Find the value of k,

b Hence state the equation of this hyperbola.

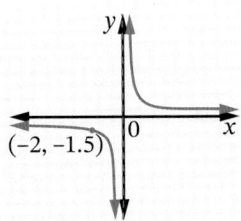

(−2, −1.5)

5 Graph each hyperbola and mark the coordinates of one point on the curve.

EXAMPLE
11

a $y = \dfrac{1}{x} + 2$

b $y = -\dfrac{2}{x} - 3$

c $y = \dfrac{2}{x-1}$

d $y = \dfrac{-3}{x+2}$

6 This curve is a hyperbola with equation $y = \dfrac{k}{x} + c$.

a Find the values of c and k.

b Hence state the equation of this hyperbola.

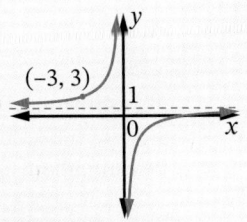

(−3, 3)

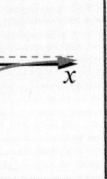

☐ Foundation ○ Standard ○ Complex

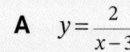

EXTENSION

7 Sarah and Amin want to buy a rectangular block of land that has an area of 800 m².
There are several blocks available with this area.

a Copy and complete this table that relates the length (L metres) and width (W metres) of the block of land.

L	10	20	30	...	100
W					

b What is the formula for W?

c Explain why the length or width cannot be equal to 0 metres.

d Graph the formula for W.

e What happens to the width as the length continues to increase? How is this shown on the graph?

f What happens to the width as the length approaches 0? How is this shown on the graph?

8 Which equation best represents this hyperbola? Select the correct answer **A**, **B**, **C** or **D**.

A $y=\dfrac{2}{x-3}$

B $y=\dfrac{-1}{x+3}$

C $y=\dfrac{2}{x}+3$

D $y=-\dfrac{1}{x}-3$

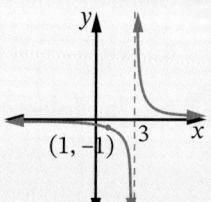

9 Find the asymptotes of the hyperbola with equation:

a $y=\dfrac{k}{x}$

b $y=\dfrac{k}{x}+c$

c $y=\dfrac{k}{x-b}$

d $y=\dfrac{k}{x-b}+c$

☆ **MENTAL SKILLS** (7) ANSWERS ON P. 633   **Maths without calculators**

Multiplying decimals

Quiz
Mental skills 7

1 Study each example.

a $3 \times 8 = 24$, so $3 \times 0.8 = 2.4$

       0 dp + 1 dp = 1 dp (dp = decimal places)

The number of decimal places in the answer is equal to the total number of decimal places in the question. Also, the answer sounds reasonable because, by estimation:

$3 \times 0.8 \approx 3 \times 1 = 3\ (2.4 \approx 3)$

b $6 \times 5 = 30$, so $0.6 \times 0.5 = 0.30 = 0.30$

       1 dp + 1 dp = 2 dp

By estimation, $0.6 \times 0.5 \approx 0.5 \times 0.5 = \dfrac{1}{2} \times \dfrac{1}{2} = \dfrac{1}{4} = 0.25\ (0.3 \approx 0.25)$.

c By estimation, $0.07 \times 0.3 \approx 0.07 \times \dfrac{1}{3} \approx 0.02\ (0.021 \approx 0.02)$.

□ Foundation   ○ Standard   ◇ Complex

2 Now evaluate each product.

   a 0.7×5 **b** 12×0.2 **c** 0.4×0.3 **d** $(0.6)^2$

   e 8×0.1 **f** 0.03×0.9 **g** 4×0.05 **h** 1.1×8

   i 0.3×0.8 **j** 0.2×0.06 **k** 9×0.2 **l** 0.07×0.4

3 Study each example.

   Given that $15 \times 23 = 345$, evaluate each product.

   a $1.5 \times 2.3 = 3.45$

        1 dp + 1 dp = 2 dp (*Estimate* $1.5 \times 2.3 \approx 2 \times 2 = 4$)

   b $150 \times 0.23 = 15 \times 10 \times 0.23 = 15 \times 0.23 \times 10 = 3.45 \times 10 = 34.5$

                     0 dp + 2 dp   = 2 dp

        (Estimate $150 \times 0.23 \approx 150 \times 0.2 = 150 \times \frac{1}{5} = 30$)

   c $0.15 \times 2300 = 0.15 \times 23 \times 100 = 3.45 \times 100 = 345$

              2 dp + 0 dp   = 2 dp

        (Estimate $0.15 \times 2300 \approx 0.2 \times 2300 = \frac{1}{5} \times 2300 = 460$)

4 Now given that $39 \times 17 = 663$, evaluate each product.

   a 3.9×17 **b** 39×170 **c** 39×0.17 **d** 0.39×1.7

   e 3.9×1.7 **f** 390×1.7 **g** 3.9×0.17 **h** 3.9×170

   i 3900×1.7 **j** 39×1.7 **k** 39×0.017 **l** 0.39×0.17

INVESTIGATION

Graphing $y = 2^x$

This activity can be completed using graphing technology.

1 Copy and complete this table of values for $y = 2^x$.

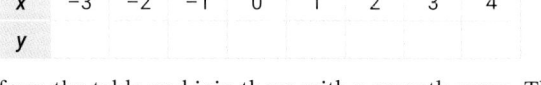

x	−3	−2	−1	0	1	2	3	4
y								

2 Graph the points from the table and join them with a smooth curve. The equation $y = 2^x$ is called an **exponential equation** and its graph is called an **exponential curve** (exponent means 'power').

3 Graph $y = 2^{-x}$ in a similar way.

4 Compare the graphs of $y = 2^x$ and $y = 2^{-x}$. Describe any similarities and differences.

5 The y-intercept of any graph with equation $y = a^x$ (where a is a positive constant) is always 1. Explain why.

6 The graph of $y = 2^x$ is increasing. Is the graph of $y = 2^{-x}$ increasing or decreasing? Give reasons.

7 Describe what happens to the graph of $y = 2^x$ when x approaches:

   a   a large positive number   **b**   a large negative number.

7.06 Graphing exponential functions $y = a^x$

Videos
The exponential curve

The emperor's chessboard

Worksheet
Graphing exponentials

An equation of the form $y = a^x$, where a is a positive constant and the variable x is a power, is called an **exponential function**, for example, $y = 5^x$, $y = 2^x$ and $y = 3^x$. The graph of an exponential function is called an **exponential curve**.

The table of values and graph of $y = 4^x$ is shown.

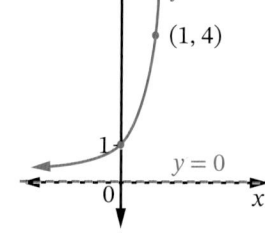

x	-2	-1	0	1	2	3	4
y	$\frac{1}{16}$	$\frac{1}{4}$	1	4	16	64	256

- The y-intercept of $y = a^x$ is always 1 since $a^0 = 1$.

- As x increases (to the right, in the positive direction), a^x becomes very large. Graphically, this means that the graph of $y = a^x$ increases sharply with a steep positive gradient.

- As x decreases (to the left, in the negative direction), a^x approaches 0. This means that the graph of $y = a^x$ flattens out and approaches the x-axis as x becomes a large negative number. The x-axis is an asymptote because the curve approaches it but never touches it.

- The exponential curve is always above the x-axis because the value of a^x is always positive.

Example 12

Sketch each exponential function and mark the *y*-intercept on each curve.

a $y = 2^x$ **b** $y = 3^{-x}$

SOLUTION

a
- The *y*-intercept of $y = 2^x$ is 1.
- When $x = 1$, $y = 2$, so $(1, 2)$ is a point on the curve.
- As *x* increases (to the right in the positive direction), 2^x becomes very large (steep positive gradient).
- As *x* decreases (to the left in the negative direction), 2^x approaches 0.
- The *x*-axis is an asymptote.

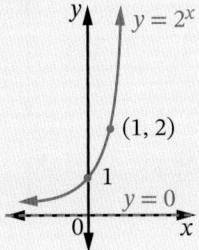

b
- The *y*-intercept of $y = 3^{-x}$ is 1.
- When $x = -1$, $y = 3$, so $(-1, 3)$ is a point on the curve.
- As *x* decreases (to the left in the negative direction), 3^{-x} becomes very large (steep negative gradient).
- As *x* increases (to the right in the positive direction), 3^{-x} approaches 0.
- The *x*-axis is an asymptote.

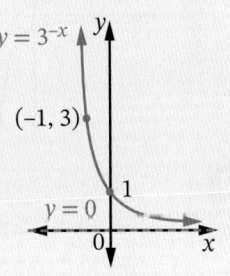

Note that the graph of $y = 3^{-x}$ (and of $y = a^{-x}$ in general) is decreasing, and is actually a reflection of $y = 3^x$ in the *y*-axis.

EXERCISE 7.06   ANSWERS ON P. 633

Graphing exponential functions $y = a^x$ U F R C

Some of this exercise may be completed using graphing technology.

1 a Graph each exponential function on the same axes.

  (R)   **i** $y = 2^x$ **ii** $y = 3^x$ **iii** $y = 5^x$

  (C) **b** What is the *y*-intercept of each curve?

     c Describe what happens to the graph of $y = a^x$ as *a* increases.

2 a Graph $y = 4^x$ and $y = 4^{-x}$ on the same axes.

     b Copy and complete:

       i The reflection of $y = 4^x$ in the *y*-axis is ...

       ii The reflection of $y = a^x$ in the *y*-axis is ...

EXAMPLE
12

☐ Foundation   ○ Standard   ○ Complex

3 Which graph represents $y = 2^{-x}$? Select the correct answer **A**, **B**, **C** or **D**.

(R)
(C)

A

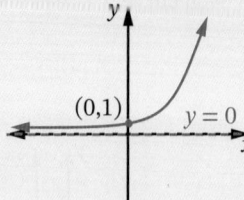

B

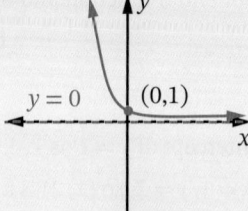

C

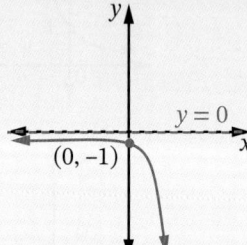

D

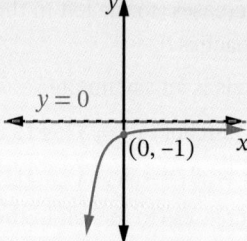

4 a Graph $y = 2^x$ and $y = -2^x$ on the same axes.

(R) **b** How are the 2 graphs related?

(C) **c** Copy and complete: The reflection of $y = a^x$ in the x-axis is ...

5 Graph $y = 3^x + 1$ and $y = 3^x - 1$ on the same axes and describe how they are related.

(R)
(C)

6 Sketch each exponential curve, showing the y-intercept.

    a $y = 2^x$ **b** $y = 3^{-x}$ **c** $y = -4^x$

    d $y = -2^{-x}$ **e** $y = 4^x + 1$ **f** $y = 4^x - 1$

7 Find an equation of the exponential function for this graph.

(R)
(C)

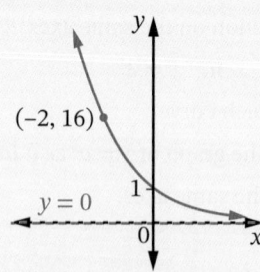

8 An exponential function is of the form $y = a^x$, where a is a positive constant.
Predict and investigate what happens when you try to graph:

(R)
(C)

    a $y = 1^x$ **b** $y = 0^x$ **c** $y = (-2)^x$

DID YOU KNOW?

Exponential growth

When an increase can be described using an exponential function, it is called exponential growth. Examples include the growth of a virus, population (people or animals) and compound interest investments.

Population growth is monitored in different countries through the fertility (birth) and mortality (death) rates as well as migration. The data collected for these figures can often be modelled as an exponential function.

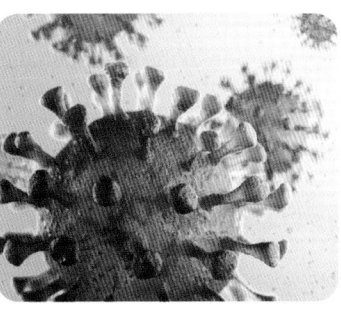

By modelling the changes in population, predictions of future changes in population can be simulated and towns and cities can prepare for possible expansion in the numbers of schools, hospitals, housing and other necessary infrastructure.

At what rate is the population of Australia growing?
What about the world's population?

Exponential equations   7.07

An **exponential equation** is an equation of the form $a^x = c$, where a and c are constants, a is positive and $a \neq 1$.

Example 13

Solve each exponential equation.

a $6^x = 216$ **b** $2^x = 128$ **c** $5^{x+2} = 625$ **d** $3^{2x-12} = \dfrac{1}{9}$

Video
Exponential
equations 1

SOLUTION

a $6^x = 216$

Find the power of 6 that equals 216.

$6^3 = 216$

$\therefore x = 3$ by guess-and-check on the calculator

b $2^x = 128$

Find the power of 2 that equals 128.

$2^7 = 128$

$\therefore x = 7$

c $5^{x+2} = 625$

Find the power of 5 that equals 625.

$5^4 = 625$

$\therefore x + 2 = 4$

$x = 2$

d $3^{2x-12} = \dfrac{1}{9}$

Find the power of 3 that equals $\dfrac{1}{9}$.

$3^{-2} = \dfrac{1}{9}$

$\therefore 2x - 12 = -2$

$2x = 10$

$x = 5$

If the RHS of the equation is not a whole-numbered power of the base on the LHS, we can either estimate or use a formula involving logarithms.

> ### ⓘ The solution of $a^x = c$
>
> The solution to the exponential equation $a^x = c$ is
> $$x = \frac{\log(c)}{\log(a)}$$

Example 14

Video
Exponential
equations 2

Solve each exponential equation.

a $7^x = 15$ **b** $16^{3x} = 8$ **c** $4^{x+1} = 12$

SOLUTION

a $7^x = 15$

Method 1: Guess-and-check

$7^{1.3} = 12.5495...$

$7^{1.4} = 15.2453...$

$\therefore x \approx 1.4$

Method 2: Formula

$x = \dfrac{\log(c)}{\log(a)}$

$= \dfrac{\log(15)}{\log(7)}$

$= 1.391\,66...$

≈ 1.39 Check the solution by substituting it back into the equation.

b $16^{3x} = 8$

Method 1: Guess-and-check

$16^{0.7} = 6.9644...$ This value is closer to 8.

$16^{0.8} = 9.1895...$

$\therefore 3x \approx 0.7$

$x \approx 2.3$

Method 2: Formula

$3x = \dfrac{\log(8)}{\log(16)}$

$= 0.75$

$x = \dfrac{0.75}{3}$

$x = 0.25$

c $4^{x+1} = 12$

Method 1: Guess-and-check

$4^{1.7} = 10.5560...$

$4^{1.8} = 12.1257...$

$\therefore x + 1 \approx 1.8$

$x \approx 0.8$

Method 2: Formula

$x + 1 = \dfrac{\log(12)}{\log(4)}$

$= 1.7924...$

$x = 0.7924...$

≈ 0.79

Exponential equations

(U) (F) (R) (C)

1 Write each number as a power of the base shown inside the brackets. For example, in part **a**, write 64 in the form 2^x where x is a number.

a   64   (2)   b   729   (9)   c   243   (3)   d   4096   (8)

e   256   (4)   f   49   (7)   g   625   (5)   h   216   (6)

2 Solve each exponential equation.

a $2^x = 2^4$ b $4^x = 4^{12}$ c $8^x = 8^3$ d $3^x = 3^7$

e $9^3 = 9^x$ f $5^x = 25$ g $12^x = 2\,985\,984$ h $7^x = 16\,807$

i $3^{x+2} = 3^6$ j $9^{x-5} = 9^{-8}$ k $2^{x+7} = 2^2$ l $7^{x-3} = 7^4$

m $4^{x+3} = 262\,144$ n $6^{x+12} = 60\,466\,176$ o $10^{x-8} = \dfrac{1}{1\,000\,000}$ p $15^{x+5} = \dfrac{1}{3375}$

EXAMPLE 13

3 Solve each exponential equation.

a $2^x = 1024$ b $10^{x+3} = 10\,000$ c $4^{2x} = 256$ d $5^{2x-2} = 625$

e $3^{3x+1} = 2187$ f $8^{2(x-3)} = 64$ g $6^{2(x+1)} = 1296$ h $9^{2(x-7)} = 81$

i $2^{x+3} = \dfrac{1}{8}$ j $4^{x-6} = \dfrac{1}{16}$ k $9^{x-1} = \dfrac{1}{81}$ l $3^{3(x+2)} = \dfrac{1}{729}$

m $8^{x-6} = \dfrac{1}{512}$ n $5^{2x} = \dfrac{1}{625}$ o $7^{x-9} = \dfrac{1}{49}$ p $6^{-\frac{x}{2}} = \dfrac{1}{216}$

EXTENSION

EXAMPLE 15

4 Solve each exponential equation, rounding the solution to 2 decimal places where appropriate.

a $4^x = 17$ b $9^x = 52$ c $8^{2x} = 26$ d $6^{x+2} = 125$

e $3^{4x-12} = 90$ f $7^{x+10} + 5 = 89$ g $11^{x-8} - 5 = 54$ h $20^{-6x-17} + 12 = 50$

5 An exponential equation is of the form $a^x = c$, where a is a positive constant and $a \neq 1$.
(R) Predict and investigate what happens when you try to solve:
(C) a $1^x - 10$ b $0^x = 4$ c $(-2)^x = 20$ d $(-2)^x = 64$

6 Harshita and Rhea had to solve the equation $4^{5x+2} = 8^{3x-1}$ in class. Harshita feels that
(R) she has done something wrong as her solution is different from Rhea's solution. Is she
(C) correct in thinking this? Clearly explain whose solution is incorrect and where they have made a mistake.

Harshita's solution	Rhea's solution
$4^{5x+2} = 8^{3x-1}$	$4^{5x+2} = 8^{3x-1}$
$2^{2(5x+2)} = 2^{3(3x-1)}$	$2^{2(5x+2)} = 2^{3(3x-1)}$
$2^{10x+4} = 2^{9x-3}$	$2^{10x+4} = 2^{9x-1}$
$10x + 4 = 9x - 3$	$10x + 4 = 9x - 1$
$10x - 9x = -3 - 4$	$10x - 9x = -1 - 4$
$x = -7$	$x = -5$

□ Foundation   ○ Standard   ◇ Complex

Exponential growth and decay

Real-world applications of exponential functions involve growth and decay. Population growth, compound interest, radioactive decay and depreciation are a few examples of exponential growth and decay.

Exponential growth occurs when an initial quantity increases by the same factor over equal time periods. In Chapter 3 *Interest and depreciation*, we learned about **compound interest**, an example of exponential growth, in which an investment increases by the same percentage (the interest rate) repeatedly. The compound interest formula is $A = P(1 + r)^n$, where A is the amount of the investment, P is the principal, r is the interest rate per compounding period, expressed as a decimal and n is the number of compounding periods. A more general formula for exponential growth is shown below.

ⓘ Exponential growth formula

$$y = b(1 + r)^x$$

where y is the **final amount**

b is the **initial amount**

r is the **growth rate** per period, expressed as a positive decimal

x is the number of **time periods**

This can also be written as

$$y = ba^x$$

where $a = 1 + r$ is called the **growth factor**.

Example 16

The population of MindTap Springs was 20 000 in the year 2021. If the annual rate of population growth is 1.5%, calculate the population in the year 2031.

SOLUTION

In the formula $y = b(1 + r)^x$,

$b = 20\,000$, $r = 1.5\% = 0.015$, $x = 10$ (years).

$y = b(1 + r)^x$

$\quad = 20\,000(1 + 0.015)^{10}$

$\quad = 20\,000(1.015)^{10}$

$\quad = 23\,210.8165$

$\quad \approx 23\,210$

The population of MindTap Springs in 2031 is approximately 23 210.

Identifying the values to substitute into the exponential growth formula.

If using the formula $y = ba^x$, then $a = 1 + 0.015 = 1.015$ is the growth factor.

Round down to the nearest whole number for population.

Exponential decay occurs when an initial quantity decreases by the same factor over equal time periods. In Chapter 3, *Interest and depreciation*, we learned about **depreciation**, an example of exponential decay, in which the value of an asset decreases by the same percentage (the depreciation rate) repeatedly. The depreciation formula is $A = P(1 - r)^n$, similar to the compound interest formula but with the '+' replaced by a '−'. A more general formula for exponential decay is shown below.

ⓘ Exponential decay formula

$$y = b(1 - r)^x$$

where r is the **decay rate** per period, expressed as a positive decimal

$\qquad x$ is the number of **time periods**

This can also be written as

$$y = ba^x$$

where $a = 1 - r$ is called the **decay factor**.

Example 17

Rinku buys a new car for $60 000. The value of the car depreciates by 12% each year. Determine the value of Rinku's car 5 years after it was purchased.

SOLUTION

In the formula $y = b(1 + r)^x$,

$b = 60\,000, r = 12\% = 0.12, x = 5$ (years).

Identifying the values to substitute into the exponential decay formula.

$y = b(1 + r)^x$

$\quad = 60\,000(1 - 0.12)^5$

$\quad = 60\,000(0.88)^5$

If using the formula $y = ba^x$, then $a = 1 - 0.12 = 0.88$ is the decay factor.

$\quad = 31\,663.915\,01$

Round down to the nearest whole dollar for depreciation.

$\quad \approx 31\,663$

The value of Rinku's car after 5 years is approximately $31 663.

Example 18

A bacterial colony is established with one cell at the start of a day and the colony then doubles every half-hour. Determine the number of bacterial cells in the colony after 6 hours.

SOLUTION

Colony doubles every half-hour, so we can use the formula $y = ba^x$ where $a = 2$.

$b = 1, x = 12$ (half-hours)

$y = ba^x$

$\quad = 1(2)^{12}$

$\quad = 4096$

There are 4096 bacterial cells in the colony after 6 hours.

Exponential growth and decay

(U) (F) (R) (C)

1 Determine if each function represents exponential growth or decay.

(R) **a** $y = 8000(1 - 0.25)^x$ **b** $y = 15(1 - 0.02)^x$ **c** $y = 100(1 + 0.15)^x$

(C) **d** $y = 2000 (1 + 0.075)^x$ **e** $y = 120\,000(0.915)^x$ **f** $y = 125(1.22)^x$

2 For each equation in question **1** above,

(R) **i** state the initial value

(C) **ii** determine the growth or decay rate, r.

3 The population of Nelson Valley was 135 000 in the year 2015. If the population grows at
(R) a rate of 1.2% every year, what is the estimated population in the year 2030?

4 Gajendra buys a new $75 000 photocopier for his business. The photocopier depreciates
(R) by 10% each year. What will be the value of Gajendra's photocopier in 4 years?

5 The temperature of a bowl of soup decreases by 7.5% each minute. If its original
(R) temperature was 95°C, determine the temperature of the soup in the bowl
after 15 minutes.

6 Kailash invests $20 000 into an account. The investment increases in value at a rate of
(R) 5.25% per annum. Determine the future value of Kailash's investment after a period
of 20 years.

7 A new virus has infected one person. It then triples the number of infected people every
(R) 2 hours. Determine the number of infected people at the end of one day.

8 There are 128 teams in a sporting competition. After each round, half of the teams are
(R) eliminated from the competition. How many teams will be remaining after 5 rounds?

9 Rabbits are known to breed at a rapid rate. A local rabbit population doubles every
(R) 4 weeks. If the rabbit population is currently 16 384, how many rabbits were in this
population one year ago?

10 The half-life of a medication is the amount of time for half of the drug taken to be
(R) eliminated from the body. The half-life of the drug Ibuprofen is represented by
the equation

$$R = I\left(\frac{1}{2}\right)^{\frac{t}{2}}$$

where R is the amount remaining in the body, I is the initial amount and t is the time in
hours. Ramesh takes Ibuprofen and after 6 hours there are 37.5 milligrams of the drug
remaining in his body. What initial dosage did Ramesh take?

☐ Foundation   ○ Standard   ○ Complex

Logarithmic scales

When graphing exponential functions, you may notice that the y values and the curve increase rapidly and soon becomes 'off the chart'.

That's because both the x- and y-axes use a **linear scale** where the values on the axes increase at a constant rate, such as intervals of 1. When graphing exponential growth, however, it often makes more sense to use a **logarithmic scale** on the y-axis, that is, to compress the y-axis so that the values on the axis increase by powers, for example, 1, 10, 100, 1000, 10 000 ... instead of 0, 1, 2, 3, 4. During the COVID-19 pandemic, graphs showing the rising number of cases used a logarithmic scale to allow the bigger values to be represented. Most 'log scales' use powers of 10 but it is possible to use other bases such as base 2.

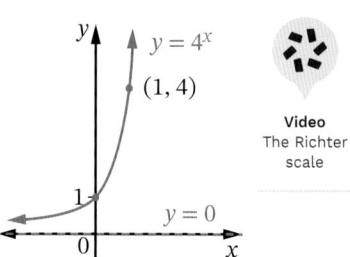

Video
The Richter scale

+10 +10 +10	×10 ×10 ×10
0 10 20 30 40 50	1 10 100 1000 10 000 100 000
Linear scale	**Logarithmic scale (base 10)**

The following 2 graphs show the same rise in COVID cases in Australia from January 2020 to September 2022 with a linear and logarithmic scale on the vertical axis.

Linear scale (1 unit = 2 000 000)

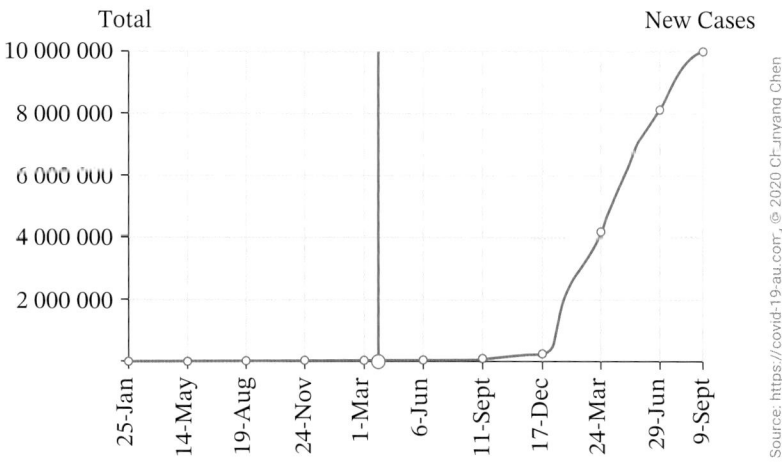

Source: https://covid-19-au.com, © 2020 CJunyang Chen

Logarithmic scale (1 unit = 10 times higher)

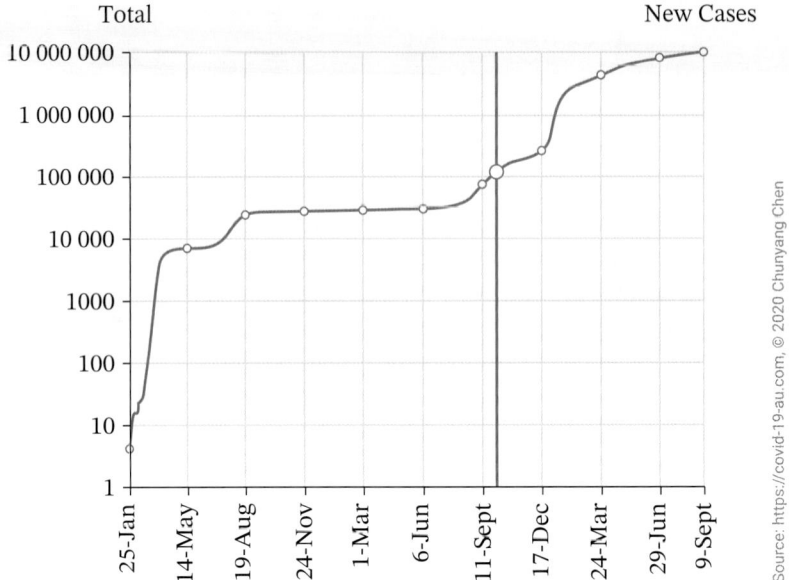

Total   New Cases

Source: https://covid-19-au.com, © 2020 Chunyang Chen

Notice that the logarithmic scale shows the initial rise in cases more prominently, whereas on the linear scale it looks like a 'flat line' at the start because of the scale. Where the curve flattens at the end indicates when the number of cases stops growing exponentially.

> If the exponential function $y = a^x$ was graphed with a logarithmic scale on the y-axis, then it would look like a straight line of $y = x + 1$.

A logarithmic scale can be written in different ways as shown on the following page. The most common way is to list the actual values of the powers of 10. Alternatively, we could write the values in power form (powers of 10) or logarithm form (just listing the power or index).

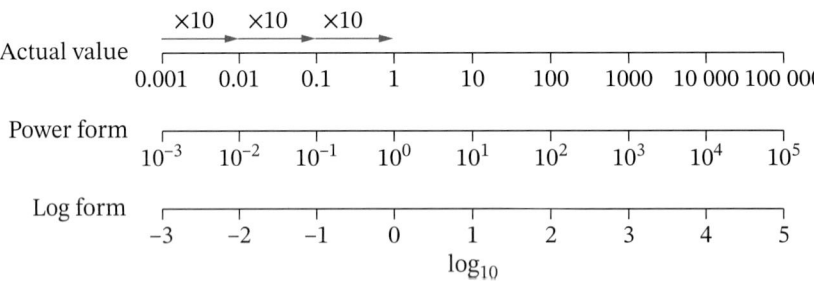

Example 19

Convert each actual value to logarithm form (power of 10), correct to 2 decimal places where necessary.

a 10 000   **b** 0.1   **c** 4550   **d** 0.0073

SOLUTION

a $10\,000 = 10^4$
So, $\log(10\,000) = 4$.

b $0.1 = \dfrac{1}{10} = 10^{-1}$
So, $\log(0.1) = -1$.

   9780170465595

c $\log(4550) = 3.6580...$ Use the **log** key on your calculator.   **d** $\log(0.0073) = -2.1366...$

≈ 3.66

≈ -2.14

Example 20

Convert each logarithm form value to an actual value, rounding where necessary.

a 2   **b** –6   **c** 5.12   **d** –3.27

SOLUTION

Logarithm form values are powers, so we need to evaluate them as powers of 10.

a actual value $= 10^2$

$= 100$

b actual value $= 10^{-6}$

$= 0.000\,006$

c actual value $= 10^{5.12}$

$= 131\,825.6739$

$\approx 131\,826$

d actual value $= 10^{-3.27}$

$= 0.000\,5370$

$\approx 0.000\,54$

Some real-world examples of the use of logarithmic scales:

- decibel scale for measuring loudness
- pH scale for measuring acidity levels
- Richter scale for measuring the magnitude of earthquakes

Example 21

The decibel (dB) scale is used to measure the loudness (or intensity) of sounds and is a logarithmic scale. The table shows the decibel rating and intensity for a number of different sounds.

Sound	Intensity (watts/m²)	Decibels
Whisper	10^{-10}	20
Music	10^{-8}	40
Loud conversation	10^{-6}	60
Heavy traffic	10^{-4}	80
Jet	10^{-2}	100
Thunder	10^{-1}	110

a Plot the sound intensity of heavy traffic and a whisper on a log scale in logarithm form.

b What is the difference between these sounds in decibels?

c So how many times louder is the sound of heavy traffic than the sound of a whisper?

SOLUTION

a List the powers of 10 on the logarithmic scale, then plot 10^{-10} and 10^{-4}.

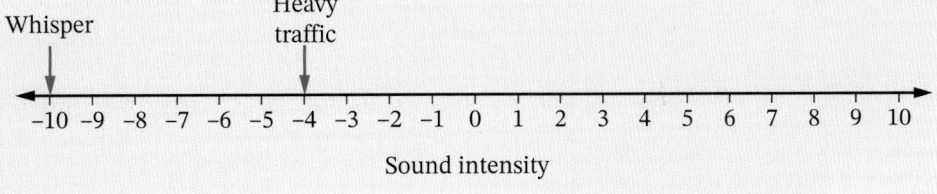

b Difference in decibels = 80 − 20

$$= 60$$

c Heavy traffic to whisper = $10^{-4} \div 10^{-10}$ (or by counting on the log scale above)

$$= 10^6$$

The sound of heavy traffic is 1 000 000 times more intense than a whisper.

Example 23

Video
Logarithmic
scales

The Richter scale for the strength of an earthquake is logarithmic.

Magnitude	Description
1	Very slight tremor, not felt by anyone.
2	Slight tremor, felt by a few people.
3	Minor earthquake, felt by some people.
4	Light shaking/rattling of objects, felt by most people, minimal damage.
5	Moderate shaking, felt by everyone, furniture moves, slight damage. Kalgoorlie, WA (2010), 5.2, Marble Bar, WA (2021), 5.3, Bowen-Townsville, QLD (2011), 5.4, Newcastle, NSW (1989), 5.6
6	Strong shaking, damage to buildings, felt hundreds of kilometres from epicentre. Collier Bay, WA (1997), 6.3, Tennant Creek, NT (1988), 6.7, highest in Australia, felt in Perth and Adelaide.
7	Major earthquake causing death and destruction, damage to most buildings within 250 km of epicentre, cracks in the ground, broken pipes underground.
8	Major damage to buildings, bridges and structures collapsed, felt across large regions. Peru (2001) and Indonesia (2007), 8.4; Chile (2010), 8.8.
9	Total destruction to all buildings, permanent damage to land, 1-in-10-to-50-year event. Indonesia (2004), 9.1, and Japan (2010), 9.1.

a How much stronger is an earthquake of magnitude 6 than an earthquake of magnitude 4?

b Correct to one decimal place, how much stronger was the earthquake in Japan (9.1) compared to Chile (8.8) in 2010?

SOLUTION

a Difference in magnitude = 6 − 4 = 2

But each unit on a logarithmic scale is 10 times more.

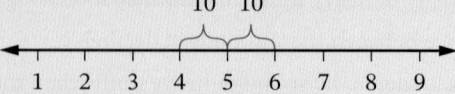

So, the difference is $10^2 = 100$.

An earthquake of magnitude 6 is 100 times stronger than an earthquake of magnitude 4.

b Difference in magnitude = 9.1 − 8.8 = 0.3.

So, the difference is $10^{0.3} = 1.995\,26... \approx 2.0$.

The earthquake in Japan was 2.0 times stronger than the earthquake in Chile.

EXERCISE 7.09 ANSWERS ON P. 635

Logarithmic scales

U F R C

1 Convert each value to logarithm form (power of 10), correct to 2 decimal places.

C **a** 8000 **b** 750 **c** 0.0035 **d** 0.000 07

2 Convert each logarithm form value to an actual value, rounding where necessary.

C **a** 6.3 **b** 3.47 **c** −2.5 **d** −4.18

3 Convert this scale from power form to log form.

C

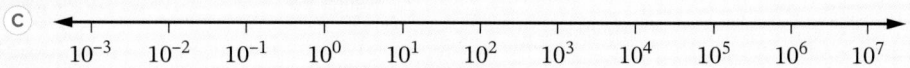

$$10^{-3} \quad 10^{-2} \quad 10^{-1} \quad 10^{0} \quad 10^{1} \quad 10^{2} \quad 10^{3} \quad 10^{4} \quad 10^{5} \quad 10^{6} \quad 10^{7}$$

4 Convert this scale from log form to actual values.

C

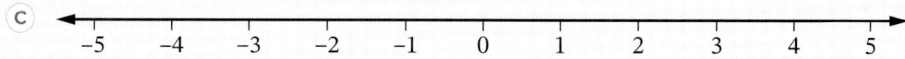

$$-5 \quad -4 \quad -3 \quad -2 \quad -1 \quad 0 \quad 1 \quad 2 \quad 3 \quad 4 \quad 5$$

5 This log scale shows the wavelength, in metres, of different types of
R electromagnetic radiation.
C

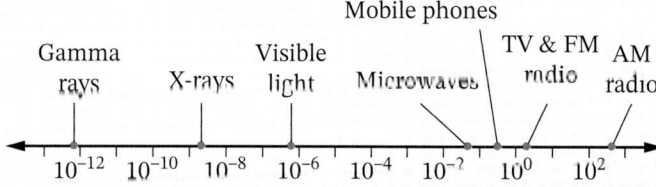

Mobile phones

Gamma rays   X-rays   Visible light   Microwaves   TV & FM radio   AM radio

$$10^{-12} \quad 10^{-10} \quad 10^{-8} \quad 10^{-6} \quad 10^{-4} \quad 10^{-2} \quad 10^{0} \quad 10^{2}$$

How many times bigger are the wavelengths of TV than the wavelengths of X-rays?

■ Foundation ○ Standard ○ Complex

EXAMPLE 21

6 This table shows the approximate diameters of the Sun and planets in our solar system.

(R)

(C) **a** Construct a log scale for plotting the diameters of the Sun and planets.

b Approximately how many times larger is the Sun compared to Mercury?

Planet	Diameter (km)
Sun	1 391 400
Mercury	4880
Venus	12 100
Earth	12 800
Mars	6800
Jupiter	143 000
Saturn	120 500
Uranus	51 100
Neptune	49 500

7 This table lists the masses of different animals.

(R) **a** Construct a log scale for plotting the

(C) masses of these animals.

b How many times larger is the blue whale compared to an ant?

Animal	Mass (kg)
Ant	0.000 005
Cockroach	0.000 12
Sugar glider	0.75
Rat	2
Wombat	35
Kangaroo	90
Horse	300
Dolphin	650
Giraffe	1900
Elephant	5400
Killer Whale	5990
Blue Whale	190 000

EXAMPLE 23

8 This table lists some of the earthquakes experienced in Australia and their strengths on the Richter scale.

(R)

(C)

Year	Location	Strength
1988	Tennant Creek, NT	6.7
1989	Newcastle, NSW	5.6
1997	Collier Bay, WA	6.3
2010	Kalgoorlie, WA	5.2
2011	Bowen-Townsville, QLD	5.4
2015	Coral Sea Fraser Coast, QLD	5.5
2021	Marble Bar, WA	5.3

Use the table to find the difference in magnitude (correct to one decimal place) between the earthquakes in:

a Newcastle and Kalgoorlie

b Collier Bay and Marble Bar

c Tennant Creek and Newcastle

d Bowen-Townsville and Coral Sea

e Collier Bay and Coral Sea

□ Foundation ○ Standard ○ Complex

9780170465595

9 The population of 2 countries are separated by 4.1 units on a log scale. What is the approximate ratio of their populations?

R
C

10 An average height of a human is approximately 175 cm and the diameter of a red blood cell is approximately 0.0008 cm. Determine the number of units which separate these two measurements on a log scale, correct to 2 decimal places.

R
C

11 The pH scale is a log scale that measures the acidity of substances. The scale is based on concentration of hydrogen ions in the substance. The lower the pH value, the more acidic the substance. How much more acidic is sauerkraut than milk?

R
C

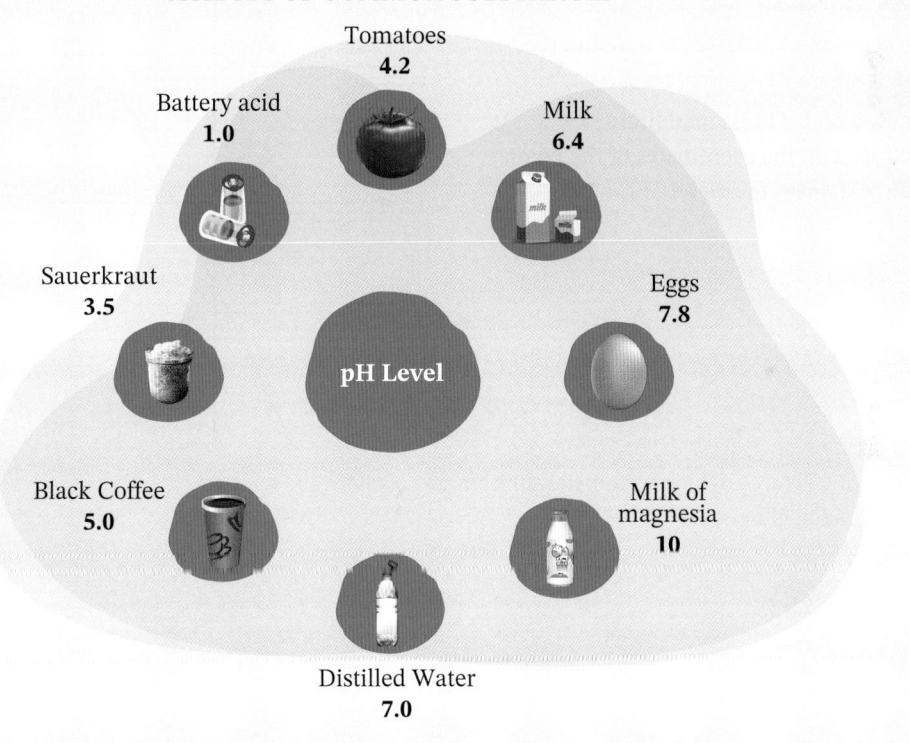

ACIDITY OF COMMON SUBSTANCES

Tomatoes
4.2

Battery acid
1.0

Milk
6.4

Sauerkraut
3.5

pH Level

Eggs
7.8

Black Coffee
5.0

Milk of magnesia
10

Distilled Water
7.0

☐ Foundation   ○ Standard   ◇ Complex

7.09

Solving equations graphically

In Chapter 6, *Equations and inequalities*, we solved equations **algebraically**. We can also solve an equation **graphically** by first graphing it on the number plane.

Example 24

Solve the equation $2x - 3 = 5$ graphically.

SOLUTION

Graph $y = 2x - 3$ (the LHS of the equation) on a number plane.

To solve $2x - 3 = 5$, we need to find the point whose y-coordinate is 5.

Draw a dotted horizontal line at $y = 5$ and read off the coordinates of the point where it meets the graph of $y = 2x - 3$.

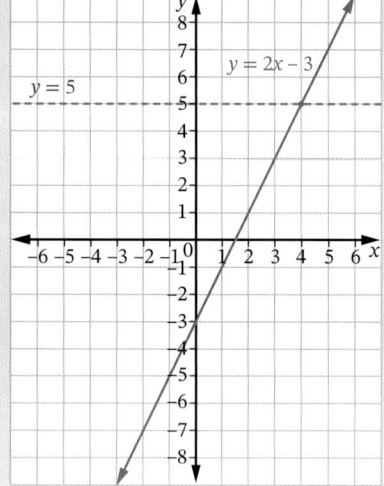

This point is $(4, 5)$, which means the solution to the equation is $x = 4$.

Check: $2 \times 4 - 3 = 5$

Example 25

Solve the equation $2x^2 + 3x + 3 = 5$ graphically.

SOLUTION

First simplify this quadratic equation before graphing.

$2x^2 + 3x + 3 = 5$

$2x^2 + 3x - 2 = 0$

Graph $y = 2x^2 + 3x - 2$ (the LHS) on a number plane.

To solve $2x^2 + 3x - 2 = 0$, we need to find the point(s) whose y-coordinate is 0.

These are the 2 x-intercepts of the parabola.

The solutions to the equation are $x = -2$ and $\frac{1}{2}$.

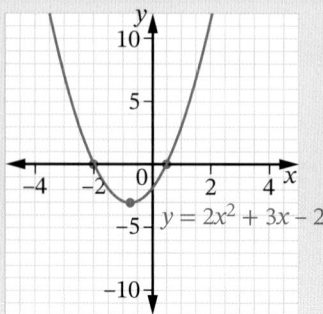

Check: $2(-2)2 + 3(-2) + 3 = 5$

$2\left(\frac{1}{2}\right)^2 + 3\left(\frac{1}{2}\right) + 3 = 5$

Solving equations graphically is best achieved using graphing technology such as dynamic geometry software or graphing websites. The TRACE and ZERO functions can be used to locate the specific points on the graph that solve the equation.

EXERCISE 7.10 ANSWERS ON P. 635

Solving equations graphically

U F R C

This exercise is best completed using graphing technology.

1 Use the graph in Example **24** on the previous page to solve each equation. Check your solutions.

   a $2x - 3 = 7$ **b** $2x - 3 = -4$ **c** $2x - 3 = -1$

EXAMPLE **24**

2 Graph $y = -2x - 1$ and use it to solve each equation graphically.

   a $-2x - 1 = -3$ **b** $-2x - 1 = 0$ **c** $-2x - 1 = 3$

3 Graph $y = \frac{1}{2}x + 3$ and use it to solve each equation graphically.

   a $\frac{1}{2}x + 3 = 5$ **b** $\frac{1}{2}x + 3 = 1$ **c** $\frac{1}{2}x + 3 = 2$

4 Solve each equation in question **3** algebraically.

5 Solve each quadratic equation graphically.

   a $x^2 - x - 20 = 0$ **b** $2x^2 - 6x + 5 = 1$ **c** $2x^2 + 5x + 4 = 7$ **d** $x^2 + 6x = -9$

EXAMPLE **25**

6 Solve each exponential equation graphically, correct to one decimal place.

   a $2^x = 3$ **b** $2^x = 5$ **c** $3^x = 10$ **d** $3^x = 6$

7 Solve each quadratic equation graphically.

   a $x^2 - 10$ **b** $2x^2 + 5 - 0$ **c** $-2x^2 - 4$ **d** $-3x^2 + 7 - 0$

8 For equations of the form $ax^2 + c = 0$ where a is negative, explain why it is necessary for
R c to be positive in order for there to be solutions to the equation.
C

9 For equations of the form $a^x + c = 0$, explain why there are no solutions if both a and c
R   are positive.
C

☐ Foundation   ○ Standard   ○ Complex

Graphing circles $x^2 + y^2 = r^2$

Technology
Curve
sketcher

Spreadsheet
Curve
sketcher

The equation of a circle on the number plane is unusual in that it involves x^2 and y^2 and is not in the form $y = \ldots$

Let O be the origin and $P(x, y)$ a point on a number plane so that the distance $OP = 2$.

If we plotted every possible position of P, we would have a circle centred at O with a radius of 2. We can use Pythagoras' theorem to find the equation of this circle by drawing a right-angled triangle where OP is the hypotenuse.

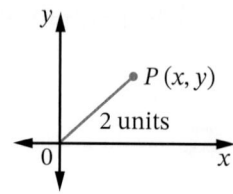

Since P has coordinates (x, y), the triangle must have a base length of x and a height of y, so by Pythagoras' theorem: $x^2 + y^2 = 2^2 = 4$.

$\therefore$ the equation of a circle with centre $(0, 0)$ and radius 2 is $x^2 + y^2 = 4$.

This can be generalised for a circle of any radius.

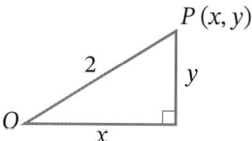

ⓘ The equation of a circle

The equation of a circle with centre $(0, 0)$ and radius r units is

$$x^2 + y^2 = r^2$$

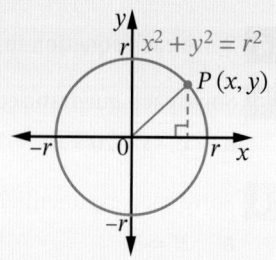

Example 26

Graph the circle $x^2 + y^2 = 9$.

SOLUTION

The centre is $(0, 0)$.

The radius is r, where $r^2 = 9$.

$r = \sqrt{9} = 3$

radius = 3 units

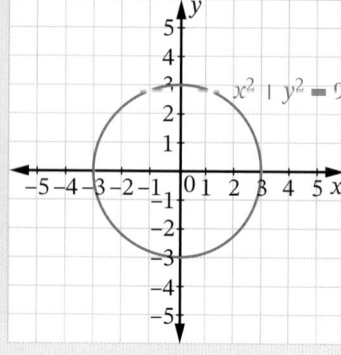

Example 27

Find the equation of a circle with centre $(0, 0)$ and diameter 14 units.

SOLUTION

radius $= \dfrac{1}{2} \times 14 = 7$ units

The equation of the circle is

$x^2 + y^2 = 7^2$

$x^2 + y^2 = 49$

EXERCISE 7.11 ANSWERS ON P. 636

Graphing circles $x^2 + y^2 = r^2$ (U) (F) (R)

Some of this exercise may be completed using graphing technology.

1 Find the centre and radius of the circle with equation:

a $x^2 + y^2 = 4$ **b** $x^2 + y^2 = 36$ **c** $x^2 + y^2 = 64$

d $x^2 + y^2 = 100$ **e** $x^2 + y^2 = 81$ **f** $x^2 + y^2 = 50$

EXAMPLE 26

2 What is the equation of this circle?
Select the correct answer **A**, **B**, **C** or **D**.

A $x^2 + y^2 = 2$

B $x^2 + y^2 = 4$

C $x^2 + y^2 = 8$

D $x^2 + y^2 = 16$

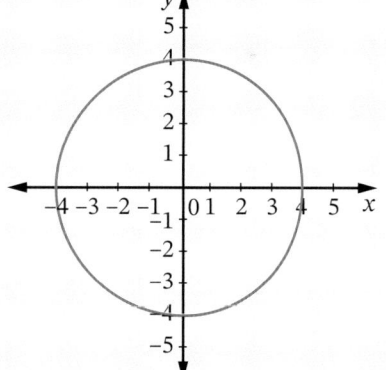

3 What is the equation of a circle with centre $(0, 0)$ and radius 3 units? Select **A**, **B**, **C** or **D**.

A $x^2 + y^2 = -9$ **B** $x^2 + y^2 = 3$ **C** $x^2 + y^2 = -3$ **D** $x^2 + y^2 = 9$

4 Find the equation of a circle with centre $(0, 0)$ and:

a radius 1   **b** diameter 6   **c** diameter 10   **d** radius $\dfrac{1}{3}$

EXAMPLE 27

5 Graph the circle with equation:

a $x^2 + y^2 = 16$ **b** $x^2 + y^2 = 121$ **c** $x^2 + y^2 = \dfrac{1}{4}$

6 Find the equation of a circle with centre $(0, 0)$ and radius 10 units. Select **A**, **B**, **C** or **D**.

A $x^2 + y^2 = 10$ **B** $2x^2 + 2y^2 = 20$ **C** $3x^2 + 3y^2 = 300$ **D** $4x^2 + 4y^2 = 14$

□ Foundation ○ Standard ○ Complex

>

7 **a** Show that the point $(8, 6)$ lies on the circle $x^2 + y^2 = 100$.

Ⓡ **b** Show that the point $(5, 9)$ does not lie on the circle $x^2 + y^2 = 100$.

c Does $(5, 9)$ lie inside or outside this circle?

8 Given the equation of the circle $x^2 + y^2 = 4$, substitute each of the following points into
Ⓡ the equation and determine whether the points are *inside*, *on* or *outside* the circle.

a $(0, 0)$ **b** $(2, 0)$ **c** $(3, 1)$ **d** $(1, 1)$ **e** $(-5, 2)$

7.12 Identifying graphs

Puzzle
Matching
graphs

ⓘ **Graphs**

Straight line: $y = mx + c$ or $ax + by + c = 0$

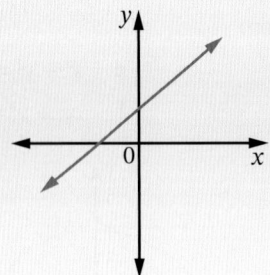

Parabola: $y = ax^2 + bx + c$

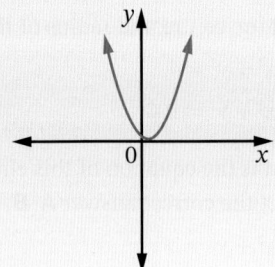

Exponential curve: $y = a^x$

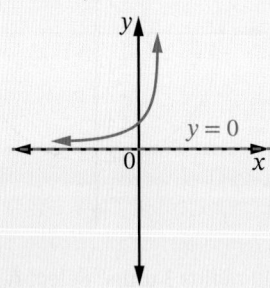

Circle: $x^2 + y^2 = r^2$

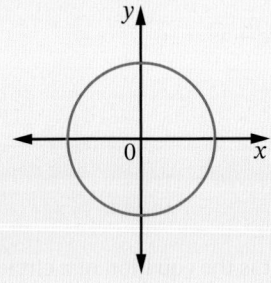

Example 28

State whether each equation represents a straight line, a parabola, an exponential curve
or a circle.

a $y = 3x^2 + 4x - 1$ **b** $y = 5x + 7$ **c** $y = -\dfrac{1}{2}x^2 - 10x + 3$

d $x^2 + y^2 = 4$ **e** $y = 3^x$

SOLUTION

a $y = 3x^2 + 4x - 1$ is a parabola because it is of the form $y = ax^2 + bx + c$.

b $y = 5x + 7$ is a straight line because it is of the form $y = mx + c$.

□ Foundation ○ Standard ○ Complex

c $y = -\frac{1}{2}x^2 - 10x + 3$ is a parabola because it is of the form $y = ax^2 + bx + c$.

d $x^2 + y^2 = 4$ is a circle because it is of the form $x^2 + y^2 = r^2$.

e $y = 3^x$ is an exponential curve because it is of the form $y = a^x$.

Example 29

Match each graph with its equation.

a
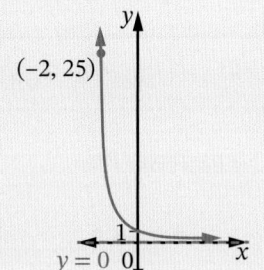

b
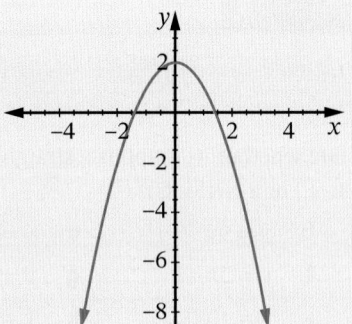

Video
Identifying graphs

c
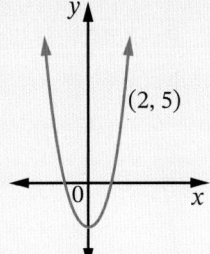

d
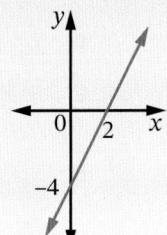

e
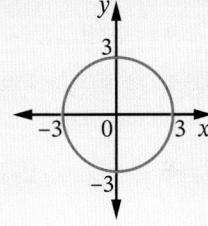

A $y = 2x - 4$

B $x^2 + y^2 = 9$

C $y = 2x^2 - 3$

D $y = 5^x$

E $y = -x^2 + 2$

SOLUTION

When matching graphs to equations, the coordinates of a point on the graph may need to be substituted into the equation to verify that the equation represents the graph.

a This is an exponential curve. The only possible match is **D**, $y = 5^{-x}$.

test point: $(-2, 25)$

LHS $= 25$

RHS $= 5^{-(-2)} = 5^2 = 25 =$ LHS

b This is a concave down parabola with a y-intercept of 2. The only possible match is **E**, $y = -x^2 + 2$.

c This is a concave up parabola that matches with **C**, $y = 2x^2 - 3$.

Test point: (2, 5)

LHS = 5

RHS = $2 \times 2^2 - 3 = 5$ = LHS

d This is a straight line with a y-intercept of -4 that matches with **A**, $y = 2x - 4$.

e This is a circle with centre (0, 0) and radius 3. The only possible match is **B**, $x^2 + y^2 = 9$.

EXERCISE (7.12) ANSWERS ON P. 636

Identifying graphs

(U) (F) (R) (C)

EXAMPLE
28

(R)
(C)

1 For each equation state whether its graph is a straight line (L), a parabola (P), an exponential curve (E) or a circle (C).

a $y = 9x^2 - 4x$	**b** $y = 9x$	**c** $y = 9^x$	**d** $y = 9$
e $x^2 + y^2 = 81$	**f** $y = 3x - 8$	**g** $y = 3x^2 + 5x - 8$	**h** $y = 2x + 5$
i $y = 6 - x^2$	**j** $y = 10^{-x}$	**k** $y = 7x^2 + 2x - 3$	**l** $x^2 + y^2 = 36$

EXAMPLE
29

(R)
(C)

2 Match each equation with its graph (more next page).

a $x = 4$	**b** $y = -\frac{1}{2}x + 1$	**c** $y = 1 - x^2$	**d** $y = 5$
e $y = 3x^2 - 1$	**f** $y = 3^x$	**g** $x^2 + y^2 = 9$	**h** $y = 3^{-x}$
i $y = 2x^2$	**j** $y = 9x^2 - 4$		

A

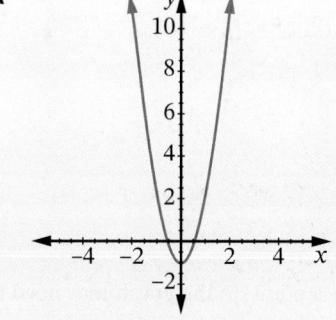

B

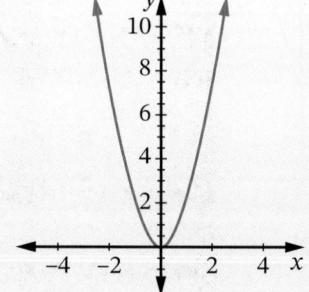

C

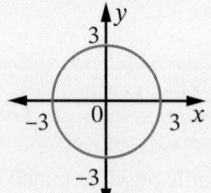

D

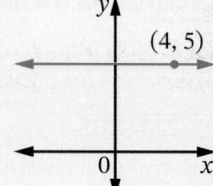

▷

E

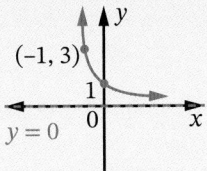

(−1, 3)

1

$y = 0$

0

x

y

F

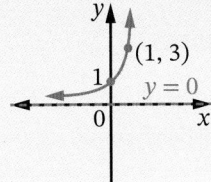

(1, 3)

1

$y = 0$

0

x

y

G

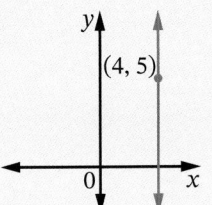

(4, 5)

0

x

y

H

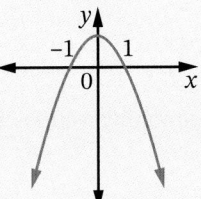

−1 1

0

x

y

I

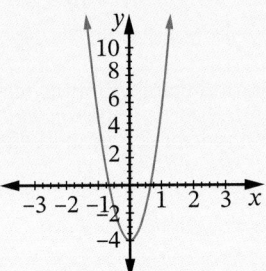

10
8
6
4
2
−3 −2 −1
−2
−4
1 2 3 x
y

J

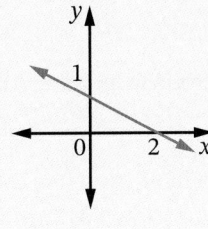

1

0 2 x

y

3 Sketch each equation, showing a point on the curve.

a $y = x^2 + 2x - 3$ b $y = 5^x$ c $y = -x^2 + 4$ d $x^2 + y^2 = 49$

e $y = \frac{1}{2}x^2$ f $y = -2x + 4$ g $x^2 + y^2 = 144$

4 Find the y-intercept of the graph of each equation.

a $y = 3^x$ b $y = 2x^2 + 3$ c $y = -7x^2 + 10x - 6$ d $y = 5^{-x}$

□ Foundation ○ Standard ○ Complex

7.12

Identifying graphs

1 Use graphing technology to graph each equation and classify it as either a straight line (L), a parabola (P) or an exponential curve (E).

a $y = 2x$

b $y = x^2 + 7x - 2$

c $y = x^2 + 1$

d $y = 2^x$

e $y = 2x^2 + 3$

f $y = 4 - 2x$

g $y = 3^x$

h $y = 2 - x$

i $y = 4 - x^2$

j $y = 5^{-x}$

2 Without using graphing technology, classify each equation.

a $y = 3x - 2$

b $y = x^2 + 3x$

c $y = 2^x + 1$

d $y = 3 + 4x - x^2$

e $y = 4x^2 - 1$

f $y = 3^x - 2$

g $y = 4^x - 1$

h $y = 3x^2 - 10x + 4$

i $y = 10 - 2x^2$

j $y = -2x^2$

3 Check your answers to question **2** by drawing each equation using graphing technology.

4 State briefly in words how you distinguish between each type of equation in question **2**.

5 Use graphing technology to find the x-intercepts and y-intercepts (if they exist) of the graphs in questions **1** and **3**. Provide approximate answers where necessary.

POWER PLUS ANSWERS ON P. 638

1 On the same set of axes, draw the graph of each equation.

a $y = x^2$

b $y = (x + 1)^2$

c $y = (x - 2)^2$

2 On the same set of axes, draw the graph of each equation.

a $y = -x^2$

b $y = -(x - 3)^2$

c $y = -(x + 2)^2$

3 For the graph of the parabola $y = (x + a)^2$, describe the effect on the graph of different values of a.

4 Sketch the graph of each equation and find the centre and radius of the graph.

a $y = \sqrt{16 - x^2}$

b $y = \sqrt{25 - x^2}$

c $y = -\sqrt{9 - x^2}$

5 Find the centre and radius of the circle with equation:

a $x^2 + y^2 = 5$

b $(x - 3)^2 + y^2 = 3$

c $(x + 4)^2 + (y - 2)^2 = \frac{1}{4}$

⑦ CHAPTER REVIEW

Language of maths

asymptote	axis	base	centre
circle	coefficient	concave down	concave up
constant	curve	decay	direct proportion
exponential	final	growth	initial
logarithmic scale	parabola	quadratic	radius
variable	vertex	x-intercept	y-intercept

Quiz
Language
of maths 7

Puzzle
Graphing
curves
crossword

1 What is the coefficient of x^2 in the quadratic function $y = 3x^2 + 7x - 10$?
2 What is the graph of a **quadratic function** called?
3 True or false: The exponential curve $y = 2^x$ passes through the point $(0, 0)$.
4 In the variation equation $y = kx$, which is the **constant of proportionality**?
5 Write down the equation of a parabola that is concave down and has a y-intercept of 3.
6 What is the asymptote of the exponential curve $y = a^x$?

Topic summary

- Which parts of this chapter were new to you?
- What is the difference between exponential growth and decay?
- Do you know the equations of a parabola, exponential curve and circle, and how to graph them?
- Explain how the graph of $y = 2x^2 + 3$ is different from the graph of $y = -2x^2 + 3$. How are they similar?

Worksheet
Mind map:
Graphing
curves

Print (or copy) and complete this mind map of the topic, adding detail to its branches and using pictures, symbols and colour where needed. Ask your teacher to check your work.

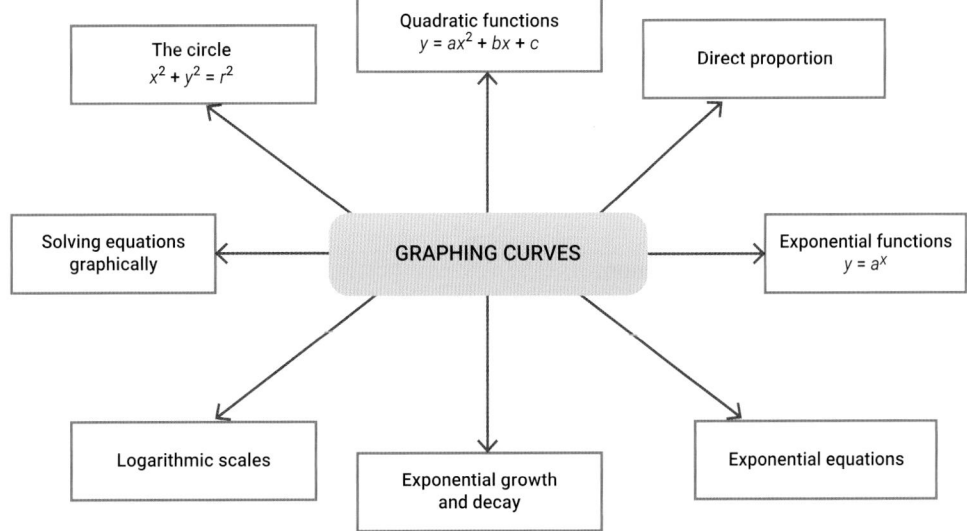

7.01

Quiz
Test
yourself 7

1 Match each graph to its correct equation.

a 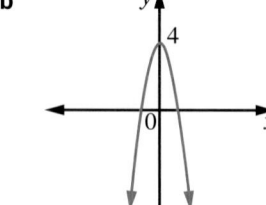 b 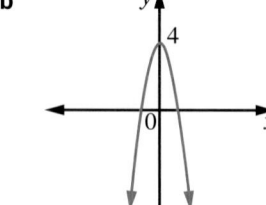 c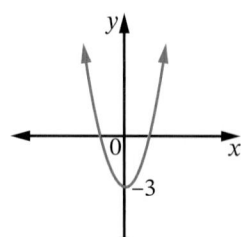

d 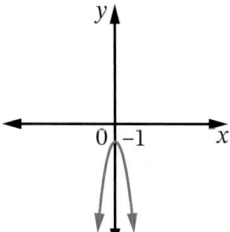 e 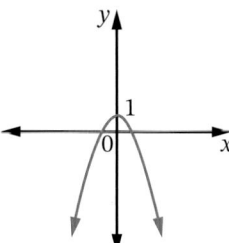 f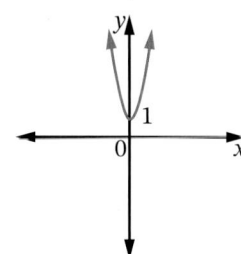

A $y = x^2 - 3$ **B** $y = 3x^2 + 1$ **C** $y = \frac{1}{2}x^2 - 3$

D $y = -x^2 + 1$ **E** $y = -4x^2 - 1$ **F** $y = 4 - 3x^2$

7.02

2 An arrow is shot into the air from a height of 1.5 m and its height can be modelled by the function $y = -5x^2 + 29x + 1.5$, where y is the height above the ground in metres and x is the time in seconds after its release. Graph the function for values of x from 0 to 6 and use it to determine:

   a   the total time the arrow is in the air (correct to one decimal place)

   b   the maximum height that it reaches (correct to the nearest metre).

7.03

3 H is directly proportional to t. If when $t = 12$, $H = 138$, find H when $t = 27$.

EXTENSION

4 The temperature, T (in degrees Celsius), of the air is inversely proportional to the height, h (in metres), above sea level. At 400 m above sea level, the temperature is 15°C. What is the temperature at 600 m above sea level?

7.04

7.05

5 Sketch the graph of $y = \frac{2}{x+1}$, showing the x- and y-intercepts and a point on the curve.

7.06

6 Graph each exponential function.

   a $y = 4^x$ **b** $y = 4^{-x}$ **c** $y = -4^x$ **d** $y = -4^{-x}$

7.07

7 Solve each exponential equation.

   a $3^x = 177\ 147$ **b** $7^{x+1} = 16\ 807$ **c** $3^{2x} = 13$

7.08

8 Pardeep consumes a drink that contains 150 mg of caffeine. The amount of caffeine in Pardeep's body decays by 12% each hour. How many milligrams of caffeine (correct to one decimal place) will remain in his body after 6 hours?

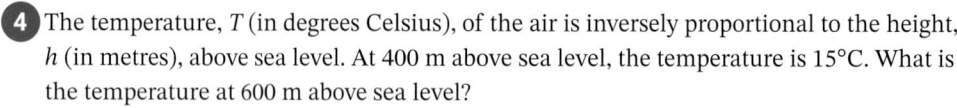
☐ Foundation ○ Standard ○ Complex

9 Raina bought a block of land for $85 000 in 1985. If the value of the land increased by 4.5% per year, what would the value of the land be in 2025, to the nearest hundred dollars?

10 In 1997, an earthquake in Collier Bay measured 6.3 on the logarithmic Richter scale. How many times stronger (to the nearest whole number) was this than the 2022 earthquake in Arthur River, which measured 4.7?

7.09

11 Solve the equation $-3x^2 + 12 = 0$ graphically and algebraically.

7.10

12 Find the centre and radius of each circle described below.

   a $x^2 + y^2 = 100$ **b** $x^2 + y^2 = 36$ **c** $x^2 + y^2 = 49$

7.11

13 What is the equation of the circle with centre $(0, 0)$ and radius 8 units?

7.11

14 Match each equation with its correct graph.

7.12

   a $y = \frac{1}{4}x^2$ **b** $y = 3^x$ **c** $y = -2x^2 - 1$

   d $x = -5$ **e** $y = -3x^2$ **f** $y = 2x^2 - 1$

   g $y = 3^{-x}$ **h** $x^2 + y^2 = 25$ **i** $y = x^2$

   j $y = x + 1$ **k** $y = -5$ **l** $y = -2 - 2x$

A

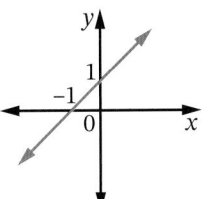

B

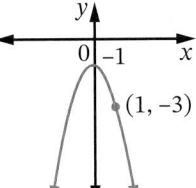

C

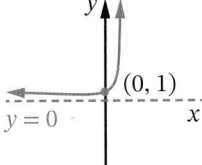

D

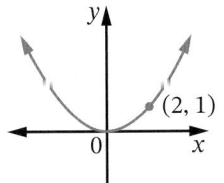

E

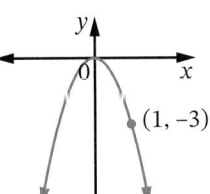

F

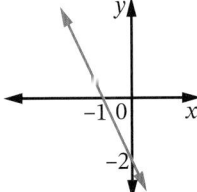

G

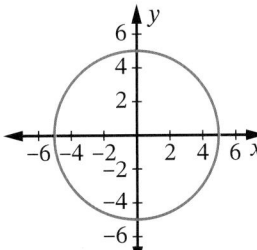

H

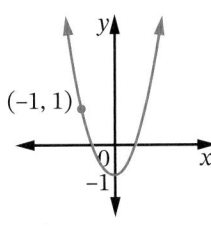

I

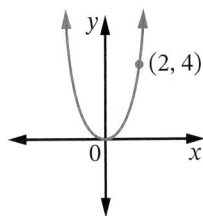

J

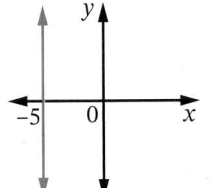

K

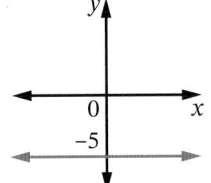

L

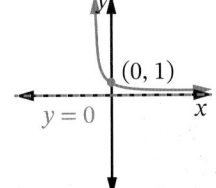

☐ Foundation ○ Standard ○ Complex

8

Trigonometry

Trigonometry is a branch of mathematics that uses the relationship between angles and sides of triangles. Trigonometry is applied in navigation to locate the position or bearing of a destination from a known location, and to calculate the distances between places that cannot be physically measured.

Trigonometry helps us to understand physical phenomena that are periodic or cyclic such as tidal movements, phases of the moon, average monthly temperatures and sound waves. It is also used in construction, engineering, physics and gaming.

stock.adobe.com/chungking

Chapter outline

		Proficiencies
8.01	Right-angled trigonometry	U F PS
8.02	Bearings	U F PS R C
8.03	Pythagoras' theorem and trigonometry in 3D	U F PS R C
8.04	Complementary relations and exact ratios*	U F R C
8.05	The trigonometric functions*	U F PS C
8.06	Trigonometric equations*	U F PS R C
8.07	The sine rule*	U F
8.08	The sine rule for angles*	U F
8.09	The cosine rule*	U F
8.10	The cosine rule for angles*	U F
8.11	The area of a triangle*	U F
8.12	Problems involving the sine and cosine rules*	U F PS R C

* EXTENSION

U = Understanding
F = Fluency
PS = Problem solving
R = Reasoning
C = Communicating

Wordbank

angle of depression The angle of looking down, measured from the horizontal.

angle of elevation The angle of looking up, measured from the horizontal.

bearing The angle used to show the direction of one location from a given point.

complementary angles 2 angles that add to 90°

cosine rule A rule that relates the 3 sides and one of the angles of any triangle: $c^2 = a^2 + b^2 - 2ab \cos C$

exact ratio The sine, cosine and tangent of the special angles 30°, 45° and 60°, which can be expressed as exact fractions or surds rather than decimal approximations

included angle The angle between 2 known sides

sine rule A rule that relates the sides of any triangle to the sine of their opposite angles: $\dfrac{a}{\sin A} = \dfrac{b}{\sin B} = \dfrac{c}{\sin C}$

Quiz
Wordbank 8

Videos (23):

SkillCheck Trigonometry • Trigonometry on a calculator • Rounding angle sizes

8.01 Finding an unknown side • Finding the hypotenuse • Finding an unknown angle • Trigonometry • Trigonometry 2 • Angles of elevation and depression • Angle of depression 1 • Angle of depression 2

8.02 Three-figure bearings • Bearings • Trigonometry 2 • True bearings • Problems involving bearings

8.04 The exact trigonometric ratios

8.06 Trigonometric equations

8.07 The sine rule

8.08 Obtuse angles using the sine rule • The sine rule

8.09 The cosine rule

8.10 The cosine rule for angles 2 • The cosine rule • The cosine rule for angles 1

8.11 The sine area formula

8.12 The sine and cosine rules

Quizzes (5):

- Wordbank 8
- SkillCheck 8
- Mental skills 8
- Language of maths 8
- Test yourself 8

Worksheets (17):

SkillCheck Trigonometric calculations

8.01 Trigonometry review • Trigonometry problems

8.02 A page of bearings • NSW map bearings • 16 points of the compass • Elevations and bearings

8.04 The exact ratios

8.05 Unit circle investigation

8.06 Trigonometric equations

8.07 Discovering the sine rule

8.08 Sine rule problems

8.10 Cosine rule problems

8.12 Finding an unknown side • Finding an unknown angle • The sine and cosine rules

Mind map: Trigonometry (Advanced)

Puzzles (11):

SkillCheck Trigonometry match-up • Trigonometry equations 1 • Trigonometry equations 2 • Finding an unknown angle

8.01 Solving triangles • Trigonometry squaresaw • Trigonometry: Finding angles

8.02 Bearings match-up

8.03 Pythagorean two-step problems

8.12 The sine and cosine rules

Language of maths Trigonometry crossword (Advanced)

Presentations (2):

8.01 Applications of triangles

8.03 2D and 3D applications of trigonometry

Technology (1):

8.05 Trigonometric graphs

Spreadsheet (1):

8.05 Trigonometric graphs

Nelson MindTap

To access resources above, visit
cengage.com.au/nelsonmindtap

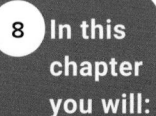

8 In this chapter you will:

✓ use trigonometry to solve problems involving right-angled triangles

✓ solve trigonometry problems involving angles of elevation and depression, and bearings

✓ use Pythagoras' theorem and trigonometry to solve three-dimensional problems

✓ (EXTENSION) learn the complementary relations and the exact trigonometric ratios for 30°, 45° and 60°

✓ (EXTENSION) use the unit circle to define and graph trigonometric functions

✓ (EXTENSION) solve trigonometric equations

✓ (EXTENSION) use the sine and cosine rules to find an unknown side or angle in any triangle

✓ (EXTENSION) use the formula $A = \frac{1}{2}ab \sin C$ to find the area of a triangle with side lengths a, b and included angle C

9780170465595

Videos
Trigonometry

Trigonometry on a calculator

Rounding angle sizes

Quiz
SkillCheck 8

Worksheet
Trigonometric calculations

SkillCheck

ANSWERS ON P. 639

1 Evaluate each expression correct to 4 decimal places.

    a $\cos 32°$ **b** $\sin 50.9°$ **c** $200 \tan 18°$

    d $\tan 8°45'$ **e** $14 \sin 87°40'$ **f** $\dfrac{13}{\cos 18°27'}$

2 Convert each angle to degrees and minutes, correct to the nearest minute.

    a $45.8°$ **b** $33.175°$ **c** $5.346°$

3 Find the size of angle A, correct to the nearest minute.

    a $\cos A = \dfrac{3}{7}$ **b** $\tan A = 2.7$ **c** $\sin A = 0.4716$

Right-angled trigonometry

8.01

Puzzles
Trigonometry match-up

Trigonometry equations 1

Trigonometry equations 2

Finding an unknown angle

Videos
Finding an unknown side

Finding the hypotenuse

Finding an unknown angle

Trigonometry

Trigonometry 2

Quiz
SkillCheck 8

Worksheets
Trigonometry review

Trigonometry problems

ⓘ The trigonometric ratios

Ratio	Abbreviation	Meaning
sine	sin	$\sin \theta = \dfrac{\text{opposite}}{\text{hypotenuse}}$
cosine	cos	$\cos \theta = \dfrac{\text{adjacent}}{\text{hypotenuse}}$
tangent	tan	$\tan \theta = \dfrac{\text{opposite}}{\text{adjacent}}$

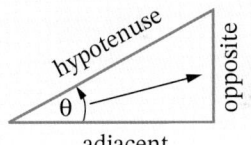

Example 1

Find the value of each variable, correct to one decimal place.

a
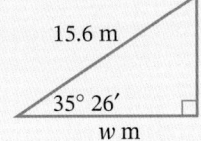

b
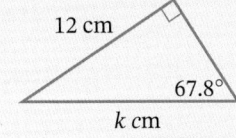

SOLUTION

a $\cos 35° 26' = \dfrac{w}{15.6}$

    $w = 15.6 \cos 35° 26'$

      $= 12.710...$

      ≈ 12.7 m

b $\sin 67.8° = \dfrac{12}{k}$

    $k = \dfrac{12}{\sin 67.8°}$

      $= 12.960...$

      ≈ 13.0 cm

Puzzles
Solving
triangles

Trigonometry
squaresaw

Trigonometry:
Finding angles

Presentation
Applications
of triangles

Example 2

Find the value of θ, correct to the nearest minute.

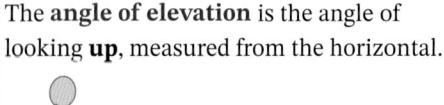

SOLUTION

$\tan\theta = \dfrac{35}{24}$

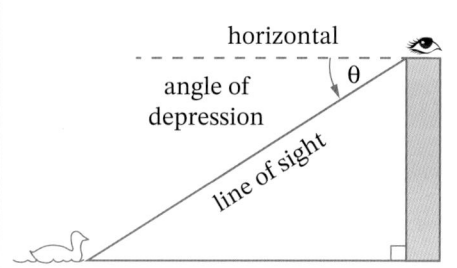

$\theta = 55.561...$

SHIFT tan 35 [÷] 24 =

$= 55° 33' 39.64''$

Press [°'"] or DMS

$\approx 55° 34'$

From the diagram, 55° 34' seems reasonable.

ⓘ Angles of elevation and depression

Video
Trigonometry 2

The **angle of elevation** is the angle of looking **up**, measured from the horizontal.	The **angle of depression** is the angle of looking **down**, measured from the horizontal.

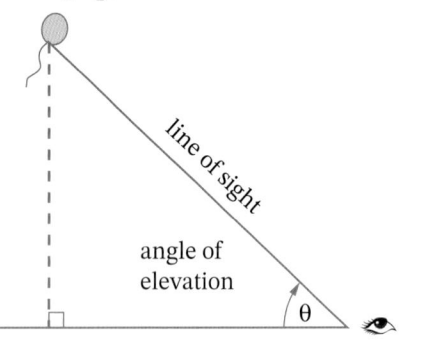

Problems involving angles of elevation and depression usually require the tan ratio in their solutions.

Example 3

Video
Angles of
elevation and
depression

The angle of elevation from a yacht to the top of a cliff is 18°. If the yacht is 190 m from the base of the cliff, find correct to one decimal place the height of the cliff.

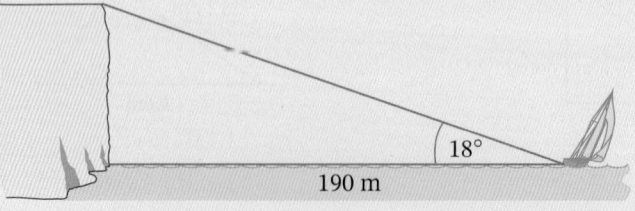

SOLUTION

Let the height be x metres.

$\tan 18° = \dfrac{x}{190}$

$\quad x = 190 \tan 18°$

$\qquad = 61.73474\ldots$

$\qquad \approx 61.7 \text{ m}$

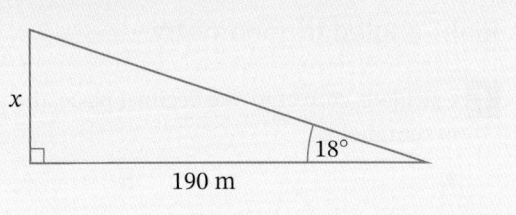

The height of the cliff is 61.7 m.

Example 4

The angle of depression of a boat from the top of a cliff is 8°. If the boat is 350 m from the base of the cliff, calculate the height of the cliff, correct to the nearest metre.

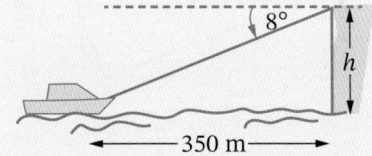

Videos
Angles of elevation and depression

Angle of depression 1

Angle of depression 2

SOLUTION

By alternate angles on parallel lines, the angle of elevation of the top of the cliff from the boat is also 8°.

$\tan 8° = \dfrac{h}{350}$

$\quad h = 350 \tan 8°$

$\qquad = 49.1892\ldots$

$\qquad \approx 49$

The height of the cliff is 49 metres.

Alternative method

The 3rd angle in the triangle (adjacent to the angle of depression) = $90° - 8° = 82°$.

$\tan 82° = \dfrac{350}{h}$

$\quad h = \dfrac{350}{\tan 82°} = 49.1892\ldots \approx 49$

Right-angled trigonometry

(U) (F) (PS)

1 Calculate, correct to one decimal place, the value of each variable. All measurements are in centimetres.

a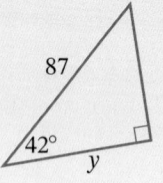

b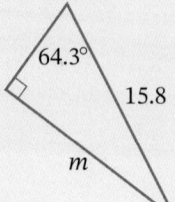

c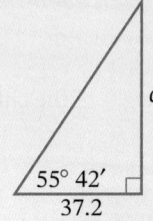

d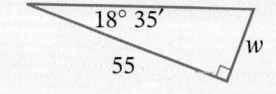

e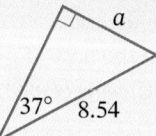

f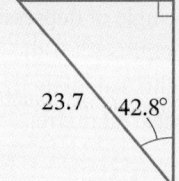

g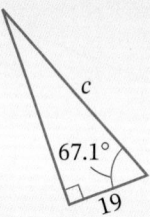

h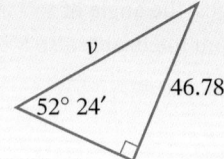

i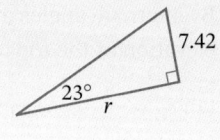

2 In △PQR, ∠P is a right angle, ∠Q = 46° 12′ and PR = 8.7 m. Find the length of QR. Select the correct answer **A**, **B**, **C** or **D**.

A 6.3 m   **B** 6.0 m   **C** 12.1 m   **D** 8.3 m

3 Find the value of θ, correct to the nearest minute.

a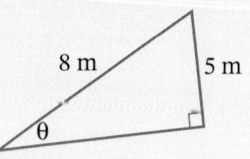

b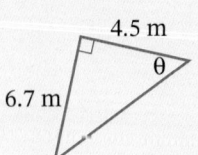

c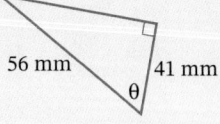

d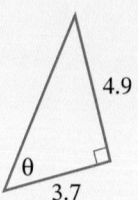

e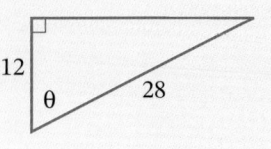

f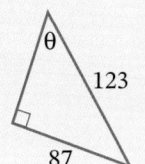

▷

☐ Foundation ○ Standard ○ Complex

4 A 6-metre ladder rests against a wall. The foot of the ladder is 1.8 m from the base of the wall. Find:

a the angle (to the nearest degree) that the ladder makes with the ground

b the distance (correct to one decimal place) that the ladder reaches up the wall.

5 A walking trail falls 11 m for every 125 m travelled along the trail. At what angle is the trail inclined to the horizontal? Select **A**, **B**, **C** or **D**.

A 5° **B** 8.5° **C** 7° **D** 5.4°

6 Calculate the take-off angle (to the nearest minute) of a passenger plane if its altitude after 30 seconds is 600 m and it has flown a distance of 2500 m.

7 A kite attached to a string is flying at a height of 75 m. If the string makes an angle of 49° with the vertical, what is the length of the string, correct to the nearest metre?

8 The entrance to a bank has a ramp for wheelchair access that is 3.6 m long. If the ramp is inclined at an angle of 10° to the ground, what is the height of the entrance (to the nearest cm)?

9 A section on a water slide has a vertical rise of 50 m and a horizontal run of 40 m.

a At what angle is the slide descending, correct to the nearest minute?

b What is the gradient of the section?

10 The training of a football team involves running up and down a sandhill 25 times. If the hill is 30 m high and inclined at an angle of 35° to the horizontal, how far does the team run during training? Answer correct to the nearest 0.1 km.

11 A roof has a pitch of 18° 26′. The height of the roof is 4.1 m. Calculate the overall width of the roof (correct to one decimal place).

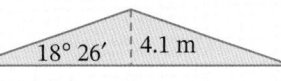

12 A glider is descending at an angle of 25° to the horizontal. The length of its flight path until it lands is 3.5 km. What was the altitude (to the nearest 0.1 km) of the glider?

13 A radio tower is supported by cables as shown. The cables make an angle of 75° with the ground and are fixed 3.2 m from the base of the tower. Calculate, correct to one decimal place:

a the length of each cable

b how far up the tower each cable is fastened.

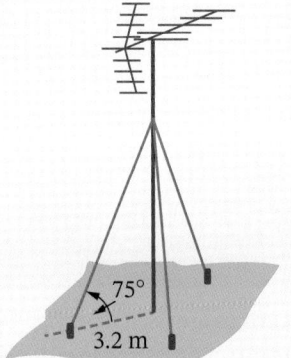

8.01

□ Foundation ○ Standard ◇ Complex

EXAMPLE 3

14 The angle of elevation of a hot air balloon at a height of 455 m is 33°. How far (to the nearest metre) has the balloon has drifted from its starting point?

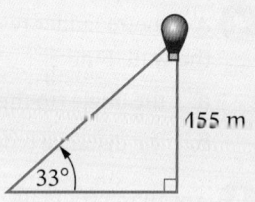

15 A 2.2 m flag on a golf course casts a shadow 1.1 m long. Find the angle of elevation of the sun (to the nearest degree).

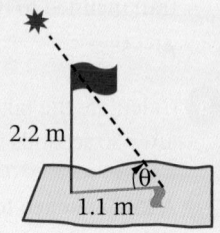

EXAMPLE 4

16 The angle of depression of Collingwood Beach from Point Perpendicular is 0° 21′ 29″. If the height of Point Perpendicular above sea level is 75 m, calculate the distance to the beach, correct to the nearest kilometre.

17 The angle of depression of a car from the top of a building is 41°. If the car is 110 m from the base of the building, find the height of the building (correct to one decimal place).

18 From a lookout, the angle of depression to the centre of a town is 5° 47′. The horizontal distance from the centre of town to the lookout is 1.72 km. If the elevation (height above sea level) of the town is 690 m, calculate the elevation of the lookout.

19 Emily is walking towards a 72 m tall building. The angle of elevation to the top of the building is first 22° and 5 minutes later, 68°. How far has Emily walked towards the building?

20 From the window of Joshua's apartment, the angles of elevation and depression to the top and bottom of another apartment building are 42° and 32° respectively. If the buildings are 85 m apart, how tall, correct to the nearest metre, is the building that Joshua is looking at?

8.02 Bearings

Bearings are used in navigation. A **bearing** is an angle measurement used to precisely describe the direction of one location from a given reference point.

☐ Foundation   ○ Standard   ◇ Complex

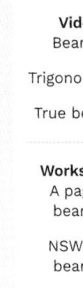
ⓘ Bearings

Three-figure bearings, also called **true bearings**, use angles from 000° to 360° to show the amount of turning measured **clockwise from north 000°**. Note that the angles are always written with 3 digits.

Compass bearings refer to the 16 points of a mariner's compass.

N = north   NE = northeast
E = east   SE = southeast
S = south   SW = southwest
W = west   NW = northwest
NNE = north-northeast   ENE = east-northeast
ESE = east-southeast   SSE = south-southeast
SSW = south-southwest   WSW = west-southwest
WNW = west-northwest   NNW = north-northwest

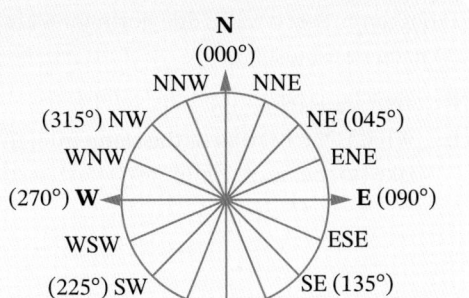

Videos
Bearings
Trigonometry 2
True bearings

Worksheets
A page of bearings
NSW map bearings
16 points of the compass
Elevations and bearings

Puzzle
Bearings match-up

Example 5

Write the three-figure bearing of each point from O.

a
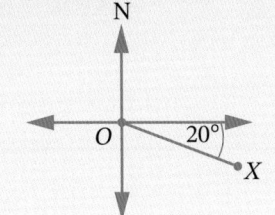

b
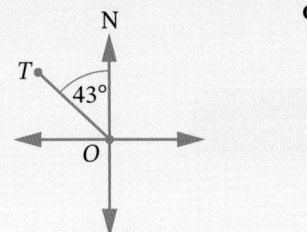

c
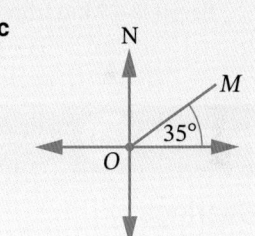

SOLUTION

a Bearing of X from O is $90° + 20° = 110°$.

b Bearing of T from O is $360° - 43° = 317°$.

c Bearing of M from O is $90° - 35° = 055°$.   must be written as a three-digit angle

Example 6

The bearing of Y from X is 130°.
What is the bearing of X from Y?

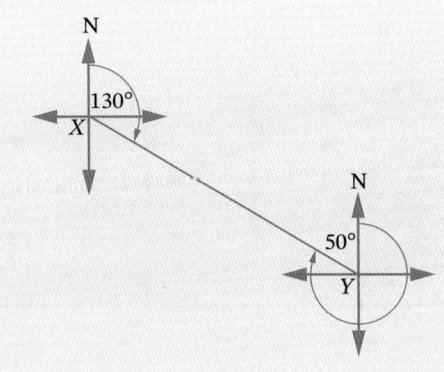

SOLUTION

Sketch the bearing of Y from X.

On the same diagram, draw a compass rose at Y and find $\angle NYX$.

$\angle NYX = 50°$ (co-interior angles, $NX \parallel NY$)

∴ bearing of X from $Y = 360° - 50° = 310°$

Video
Three-figure bearings

Example 7

Video
Problems involving bearings

From camp, Seerit walks due north for 6 km, then 3 km due west to a lake.

a How far is Seerit from the camp?

b What is the bearing of the camp from the lake (to the nearest minute)?

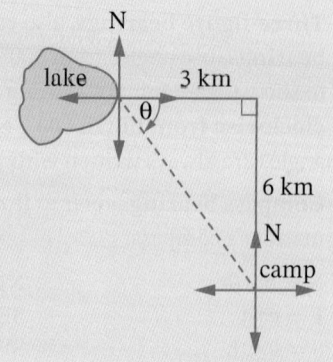

SOLUTION

a Let x = distance from camp.

$$x^2 = 6^2 + 3^2$$
$$= 45$$
$$x = \sqrt{45}$$
$$= 6.708...$$
$$\approx 6.7 \text{ km}$$

Seerit is 6.7 km from the camp.

b Note angle θ in the diagram.

$$\tan\theta = \frac{6}{3} = 2$$
$$\theta = 63.434...°$$
$$= 63°26'5.82''$$
$$\approx 63°26'$$

Bearing of camp from lake $= 90° + 63°26'$
$$= 153°26'$$

EXERCISE 8.02 ANSWERS ON P. 640

Bearings

U F PS R C

EXAMPLE 5

1 Write the three-figure bearing of each point from O.

C **a**

N
27° O
P

b

N
M 70°
O

c

N
40° F
O

d

N
O
25°
H

e

N
O
30°
T

f

N
O
40° W

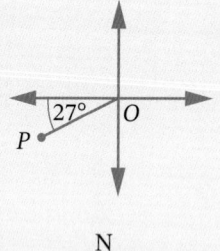

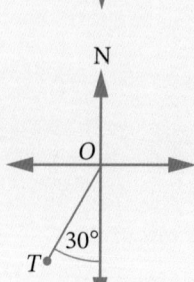

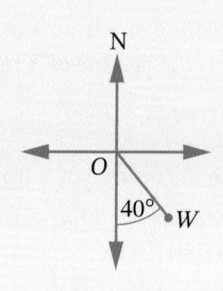

☐ Foundation ○ Standard ○ Complex

g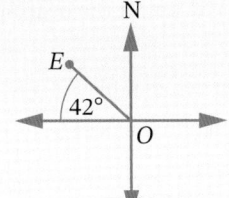

h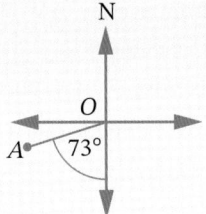

i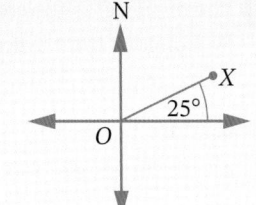

2 What is the bearing of each point from *O*?

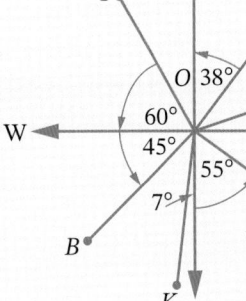

a N   **b** E

c S   **d** W

e *F*   **f** *Q*

g *T*   **h** *B*

i *H*   **j** *K*

3 Sketch each bearing on a compass rose.

a 220°   **b** 060°

c 260°   **d** 125°

e 350°   **f** 267°

g 171°   **h** 032°

4 a What is the compass direction halfway between northwest and north?

b What is the three-figure bearing of this compass direction?

5 Sketch *P* on a compass rose if *P* has a bearing of:

a 132° from *T*   **b** 260° from *M*   **c** 335° from *X*   **d** 010° from *K*.

EXAMPLE
6

6 If the bearing of *P* from *A* is 060°, what is the bearing of *A* from *P*?

7 The bearing of *T* from *Y* is 100°. What is the bearing of *Y* from *T*?

8 What is the (smallest) angle between:

a S and SW   **b** NE and SE   **c** E and NW

d NE and SSW   **e** E and SSW   **f** SW and WNW?

9 The compass bearing of *H* from *M* is WNW. Find the compass bearing of *M* from *H*.

10 Declan leaves Nyngan and drives 204 km to Bourke. The bearing of Bourke from Nyngan is 323°.

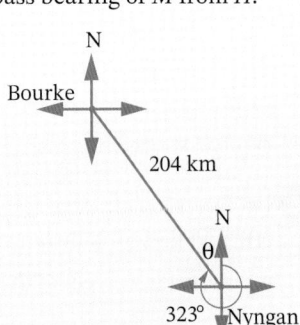

a Find the value of θ.

b How far north (to the nearest km) of Nyngan is Bourke?

c What is the bearing of Nyngan from Bourke?

11 The distance 'as the crow flies' from Sydney to Wollongong is 69 km. If the bearing of Wollongong from Sydney is 205°, calculate:

    a how far south Wollongong is from Sydney (correct to one decimal place)

    b how far east Sydney is from Wollongong (correct to one decimal place)

    c the bearing of Sydney from Wollongong.

EXAMPLE 7

12 Jana cycles 10 km due south, then 7 km due west.

    a How far (correct to one decimal place) is Jana from her starting point?

    b What is her three-figure bearing from the starting point, correct to the nearest degree?

    c What is the bearing of the starting point from Jana?

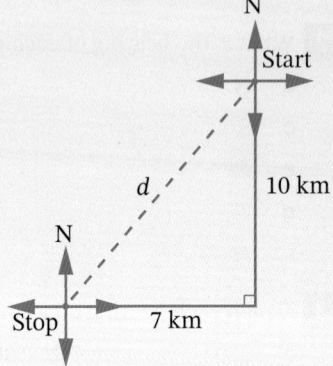

13 A hiking group walks from Sandy Flats to Black Ridge (a distance of 20.9 km) in the direction 078°. They then turn and hike due south to Rivers End, then due west back to Sandy Flats. How far have they hiked altogether (to the nearest 0.1 km)?

PS C

14 A plane takes off from Darwin at 10:15 am and flies on a bearing of 150° at 700 km/h.

PS   **a** How far (to the nearest km) due south of Darwin is the plane at 1:45 pm?

C   **b** What is the bearing (correct to the nearest degree) of Darwin from the plane?

15 A fishing trawler sails 30 km from port on a bearing of 120° until it reaches a submerged reef. How far (to the nearest km) is the port:

PS C   **a** north of the reef   **b** west of the reef?

16 Two racing pigeons are set free at the same time. The first bird flies on a course of 040° whereas the second bird flies on a course of 130°.

PS C   **a** The first bird flies 200 km until it is due north of the second bird. Find their distance apart, correct to 2 decimal places.

    b How far has the second bird flown? Give your answer correct to 2 decimal places.

17 Two horse riders start from the same stable. The rider of the black horse goes due west for 5.5 km and stops. The rider of the chestnut horse travels in a direction of 303° until he is due north of the black horse. How far did the rider of the chestnut horse travel? Answer correct to 2 significant figures.

PS C

18 Lai flies 1200 km on a *NE* compass bearing and then changes direction to a bearing of *NW* and flies for a distance of 450 km.

PS C   **a** How far, correct to the nearest km, is Lai from his starting point?

    b What is the bearing of the plane from its starting point, to the nearest minute?

□ Foundation ○ Standard ○ Complex

19 A fishing boat leaves Albany on a compass bearing of *ESE* and after 15 nautical miles,
changes direction to a bearing of *SSW* and travels a further 10 nautical miles.
Find the bearing of Albany from the boat's final position, correct to the nearest minute.

PS

C

☆ **MENTAL SKILLS** (8) ANSWERS ON P. 641 | **Maths without calculators**

Quiz
Mental
skills 8

Divisibility tests

A number is divisible by:	if:
2	its last digit is 2, 4, 6, 8 or 0
3	the sum of its digits is divisible by 3
4	its last two digits form a number divisible by 4
5	its last digit is 0 or 5
6	it is even and the sum of its digits is divisible by 3
9	the sum of its digits is divisible by 9
10	its last digit is 0

1 Study each example.

a Test whether 748 is divisible by 2, 3 or 4.

- Last digit is 8 (even), ∴ 748 is divisible by 2.

  Sum of digits $= 7 + 4 + 8 = 19$, which is not divisible by 3, ∴ 748 is not divisible by 3.

- 48 is divisible by 4, ∴ 748 is divisible by 4 ($748 ÷ 4 = 187$).

b Test whether 261 is divisible by 5 or 9.

- Last digit is 1, not 0 or 5, ∴ 261 is not divisible by 5.

- $2 + 6 + 1 = 9$, which is divisible by 9, ∴ 261 is divisible by 9 ($261 ÷ 9 = 29$).

c Test whether 570 is divisible by 4, 6 or 10.

- 70 is not divisible by 4, ∴ 570 is not divisible by 4.

- 570 is even and $5 + 7 + 0 = 12$, which is divisible by 3, ∴ 570 is divisible by 6 ($570 ÷ 6 = 95$).

- Last digit is 0, ∴ 570 is divisible by 10 ($570 ÷ 10 = 57$).

2 Test whether each number is divisible by 2, 3, 5 or 6.

a	250	**b**	189	**c**	78	**d**	465
e	1024	**f**	840	**g**	715	**h**	627

3 Test whether each number is divisible by 4, 9 or 10.

a	144	**b**	280	**c**	522	**d**	4170
e	936	**f**	726	**g**	342	**h**	5580

☐ Foundation ○ Standard ○ Complex

Puzzle
Pythagorean
two-step
problems

Pythagoras' theorem and trigonometry can be applied to problems in 3 dimensions.

Example 8

A wooden rectangular box has dimensions
18 cm × 8 cm × 4 cm.

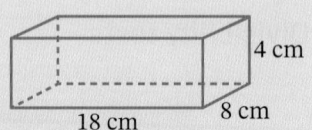

a Find, correct to one decimal place, the length of the longest pencil that can lie flat in the base of the box.

b Find, correct to one decimal place, the length of the longest diagonal of the box.

c Find, correct to the nearest degree, the angle that the longest diagonal makes with the base of the box.

SOLUTION

Label the box as shown. *HD* is the length of the longest
pencil that can lie flat in the base of the box, while
ED is the longest diagonal of the box.

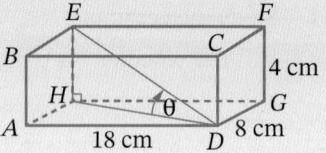

a Using the right-angled triangle *DAH*:

$$HD^2 = DA^2 + AH^2$$
$$= 18^2 + 8^2$$
$$= 388$$
$$HD = \sqrt{388}$$
$$= 19.6977...$$
$$\approx 19.7 \text{ cm}$$

The longest pencil that can lie flat
in the base of the box is 19.7 cm.

b $$ED^2 = HD^2 + HE^2$$
$$ED^2 = \left(\sqrt{388}\right)^2 + 4^2$$
$$= 404$$
$$ED = \sqrt{404}$$
$$= 20.0997...$$
$$\approx 20.1 \text{ cm}$$

The longest diagonal of the box is 20.1 cm.

c In the right-angled triangle *EHD*, θ is the
angle that the longest diagonal makes
with the base of the box.

$$\tan\theta = \frac{EH}{HD} = \frac{4}{\sqrt{388}}$$

$$\theta = 11.4789...°$$
$$\approx 11°$$

The longest diagonal makes an angle
of 11° with the base of the box.

or use sin or cos since *ED* is also known

Example 9

A 100 m flagpole is observed from 2 different locations. From point A, due south of the flagpole the angle of elevation of the top of the flagpole is 35°; from point B, due east of the flagpole the angle of elevation is 22°. Find the distance between A and B, correct to the nearest metre.

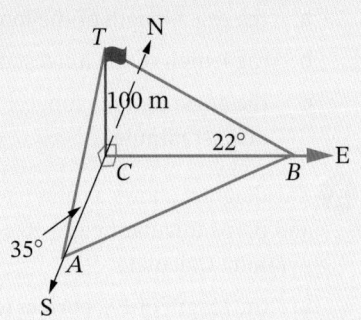

SOLUTION

There are 3 right-angled triangles in this diagram.

To find AB, we must first find AC and CB using trigonometry.

In $\triangle ACT$,

$\tan 35° = \dfrac{100}{AC}$

$AC = \dfrac{100}{\tan 35°}$

$= 142.8148...$ Do not round yet.

In $\triangle BCT$,

$\tan 22° = \dfrac{100}{CB}$

$CB = \dfrac{100}{\tan 22°}$

$\approx 247.5086...$

In $\triangle ABC$,

$AB^2 = AC^2 + CB^2$

$= (142.8148...)^2 + (247.5086...)^2$

$= 81\,656.6166...$

$AB = \sqrt{81656.6166...}$

$= 285.7562...$

≈ 286 m

From the diagram, 286 m seems to be a reasonable answer.

The distance between A and B is approximately 286 metres.

EXERCISE 8.03 ANSWERS ON P. 641

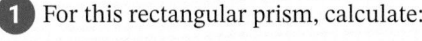

Pythagoras' theorem and trigonometry in 3D   U F PS R C

1 For this rectangular prism, calculate:

   a the length of AE in surd form

   b the length of AF, correct to one decimal place

   c the size of $\angle FAE$, correct to the nearest degree.

EXAMPLE 8

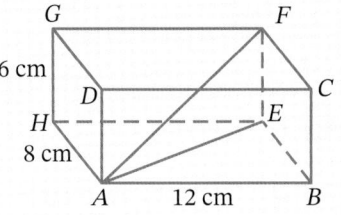

□ Foundation ○ Standard ○ Complex

2 Sketch a diagram of a cube of length 20 cm, then find:

  a the exact length of the longest diagonal on any face

  b the length of the longest diagonal of the cube, correct to 2 decimal places

  c the angle that the longest diagonal makes with the base, correct to the nearest minute.

3 The diagram shows a square pyramid with base length 8 cm
(R) and perpendicular height 20 cm. *PX* is the slant height of the pyramid. Calculate:

  a the length of *PX*, correct to 2 decimal places

  b the angle of inclination of *PX*, correct to the nearest degree.

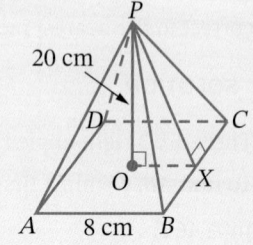

4 A cone has a base diameter of 2.8 m and a slant height of 2.5 m. Find the angle that the
(R) cone makes with the vertical at the top of the cone.

5 A fruit juice container is a square prism with dimensions 8 cm by 3 cm by 3 cm.

(R) **a** Find, correct to one decimal place, the length of the longest drinking straw that fits inside the container.

  b To the nearest degree, what angle does the longest straw make with the vertical?

6 From a point *X*, 37 m from the base of a tree, the angle of elevation is 55° while the angle
(PS) of elevation of the tree, from a point *Y* due east of the tree, is 25°. Find, correct to the
(R) nearest metre:

  a the height of the tree   **b** the distance of the tree from point *Y*.

EXAMPLE
9

7 From a point, *A*, at the base of a mountain, the mountain
(PS) peak, *P*, is due north and has an angle of elevation of 20°.
(R) From a point, *B*, 2 km due east of *A* on the same level, the mountain peak has a bearing of 320°.

  a What is the size of ∠*CBA*?

  b Calculate the height, *PC*, of the mountain correct to the nearest metre.

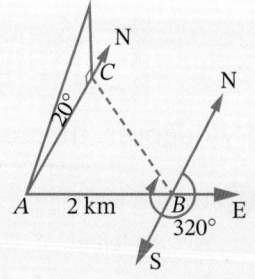

8 From the top of her 55-metre office building, Mehtaab observes
(PS) 2 cars parked at ground level. The angle of depression of the car
(R) due east of the building is 48° and the angle of depression of the car parked due south of the building is 33°.

Calculate, correct to the nearest metre, how far:

  a each car is from the building

  b the cars are apart.

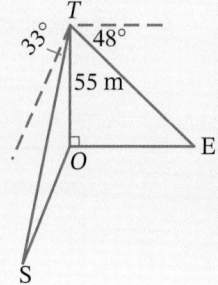

□ Foundation ○ Standard ○ Complex

9 A 15 m flagpole stands on level ground. From point *P*, due west of the flagpole the angle of elevation of the top of the pole is 38°. From point *Q*, due north of the flagpole, the flagpole has an angle of elevation of 25°. Find *PQ*, correct to one decimal place.

10 Hassan observes a transmission tower at an elevation angle of 12° and bearing 038°. Fatima stands 375 m due east of Hassan and observes the tower at a bearing of 308°.

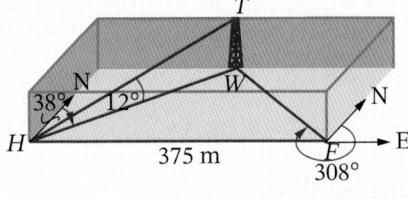

Presentation
2D and 3D applications of trigonometry

   a Find the sizes of the angles of △*FHW*.

   b Find the height of the tower *TW*, correct to one decimal place.

11 A plane flies 6 km due west of Keira Bay at a constant height of 800 m. Xander sees the plane from his house 1.6 km south of Keira Bay.

Find, correct to the nearest degree:

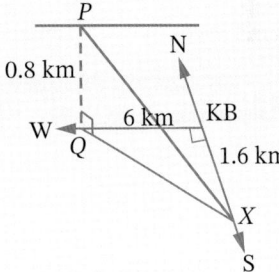

   a the bearing of the plane from Xander

   b the angle of elevation of the plane from Xander.

12 Sophia observes a plane due north at an angle of elevation of 40°. The plane is flying due east at an altitude of 4000 m and at a speed of 200 km/h. After 2 minutes, find:

   a the angle of elevation and the bearing of the plane from Sophia to the nearest degree

   b the distance from Sophia to the plane to the nearest metre.

13 From a lighthouse 95 m above sea level, a boat is observed on a compass bearing of SSE and at an angle of depression of 2°. Another boat is seen on a bearing of ENE and at angle of depression of 1.5°.

   a Calculate the distance (correct to one decimal place) between the boats.

   b What is the bearing of the first boat from the second boat? Give your answer to the nearest minute.

Extension: Complementary relations and exact ratios

Trigonometric ratios of complementary angles

In $\triangle ABC$, $\angle C = 90°$ so $\angle A + \angle B = 90°$ due to the angle sum of a triangle.

$\therefore A$ and B are complementary angles.

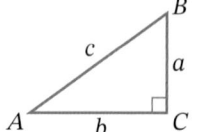

Now $\sin A = \dfrac{a}{c}$ and $\cos A = \dfrac{b}{c}$

But $\sin B = \dfrac{b}{c}$ and $\cos B = \dfrac{a}{c}$

$\therefore \sin A = \cos B$ and $\cos A = \sin B$

But $B = 90° - A$ (the complement of A)

$\therefore \sin A = \cos (90° - A)$ and $\cos A = \sin (90° - A)$

> ### ⓘ The sine and cosine ratios of complementary angles
>
> $$\sin A = \cos (90° - A)$$
> $$\cos A = \sin (90° - A)$$

Because of this complementary relationship, the sine and cosine ratios are called **complementary ratios**. That is why **co-sine** is named as the complement of **sine**.

Example 10

a If $\sin 35° = \cos \alpha$, find α.

b If $P + Q = 90°$ and $\sin Q = \dfrac{15}{17}$, find:

    i $\cos P$ **ii** $\cos Q$

SOLUTION

a $\sin 35° = \cos (90° - 35°)$ $\sin A = \cos (90 - A)$

           $= \cos 55°$

        $\alpha = 55°$ $35°$ and α are complementary angles

b **i**   Since $P + Q = 90°$

         $\cos P = \sin Q$ P and Q are complementary angles

           $= \dfrac{15}{17}$

   ii   Since $\sin Q = \dfrac{15}{17}$, draw a right-angled triangle to find $\cos Q$.

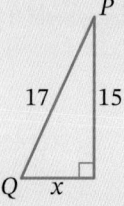

           $x^2 = 17^2 - 15^2 = 64$

           $x = \sqrt{64} = 8$

      $\therefore \cos Q = \dfrac{8}{17}$

Exact trigonometric ratios of 30°, 45° and 60°

EXTENSION 8.04

The value of most trigonometric ratios can only be approximated in decimal form. However, the trigonometric ratios of the special angles 30°, 45° and 60° can be written in exact (surd) form. These are called the **exact ratios**.

For 45°, consider an isosceles right-angled triangle with 2 equal sides 1 unit, 2 equal angles 45° and hypotenuse h units.

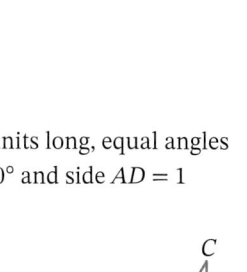

Worksheet
The exact ratios

By Pythagoras' theorem,

$h^2 = 1^2 + 1^2 = 2$

$h = \sqrt{2}$

$\therefore \sin 45° = \dfrac{1}{\sqrt{2}}, \cos 45° = \dfrac{1}{\sqrt{2}}, \tan 45° = \dfrac{1}{1} = 1$

For 30° and 60°, consider an equilateral triangle ABC with equal sides 2 units long, equal angles of 60° and an axis of symmetry CD. This means $\angle ACD = 30°$, $\angle ADC = 90°$ and side $AD = 1$ (half of 60°, 180° and 2 respectively).

By Pythagoras' theorem,

$CD^2 = 2^2 - 1^2 = 3$

$CD = \sqrt{3}$

$\therefore \sin 30° = \dfrac{1}{2}, \cos 30° = \dfrac{\sqrt{3}}{2}, \tan 30° = \dfrac{1}{\sqrt{3}}$

$\sin 60° = \dfrac{\sqrt{3}}{2}, \cos 60° = \dfrac{1}{2}, \tan 60° = \sqrt{3}$

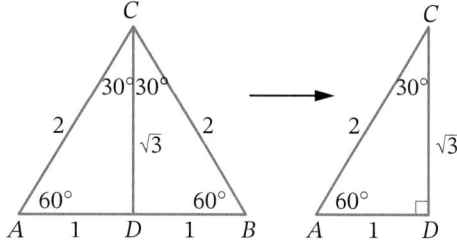

ⓘ The trigonometric ratios

	30°	45°	60°
sin	$\dfrac{1}{2}$	$\dfrac{1}{\sqrt{2}}$	$\dfrac{\sqrt{3}}{?}$
cos	$\dfrac{\sqrt{3}}{2}$	$\dfrac{1}{\sqrt{2}}$	$\dfrac{1}{2}$
tan	$\dfrac{1}{\sqrt{3}}$	$\dfrac{1}{\sqrt{2}}$	$\sqrt{3}$

Note that $\sin 30° = \cos 60°$, $\sin 60° = \cos 30°$, and $\sin 45° = \cos 45°$, because 30° and 60° are complementary angles and 45° is the complement of itself.

Learn the values in this table by looking for patterns in the exact values.

Example 11

Find the exact value of each variable.

a

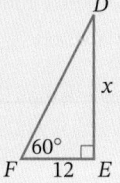

b

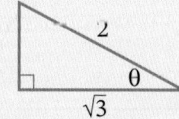

Video
The exact trigonometric ratios

SOLUTION

a $\tan 60° = \dfrac{x}{12}$

$x = 12 \tan 60°$

$= 12\sqrt{3} \qquad \tan 60° = \sqrt{3}$

b $\cos \theta = \dfrac{\sqrt{3}}{2}$

$\theta = 30°$

EXERCISE (8.04) ANSWERS ON P. 641

Complementary relations and exact ratios U F R

1 Find the value of each variable.

a $\sin 47° = \cos X$ **b** $\cos 74° = \sin Y$ **c** $\sin 2.55° = \cos P$

d $\cos 55.2° = \sin \theta$ **e** $\sin 38° \, 17' = \cos M$ **f** $\cos 65° \, 26' = \sin T$

g $\sin (A + 28°) = \cos 37°$ **h** $\cos (M - 35°) = \sin 67°$ **i** $\sin 49° = \cos (T + 12°)$

2 Simplify each expression.

a $\cos 22° - \sin 68°$ **b** $\dfrac{\sin 57°}{\cos 33°}$ **c** $\dfrac{\sin (90° - \theta)}{\cos \theta}$ **d** $\dfrac{\cos 28° + \sin 62°}{\sin 62°}$

3 If $\sin \alpha = \dfrac{5}{13}$ and $\alpha + \beta = 90°$, find $\cos \beta$, $\cos \alpha$ and $\sin \beta$.

(R)

4 Given $\cos E = \dfrac{40}{41}$, and E and F are complementary angles, find $\sin F$, $\sin E$ and $\cos F$.

(R)

5 If $X + Y = 90°$, find the exact values of $\cos Y$, $\sin Y$ and $\sin X$, given $\cos X = \dfrac{2}{3}$.

6 Find the exact values of $\cos \phi$, $\sin \phi$ and $\cos \theta$ if $\sin \theta = \dfrac{\sqrt{5}}{4}$ and $\theta = 90° - \phi$.

7 In each triangle, find the exact value of the variable.

a 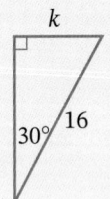 **b** 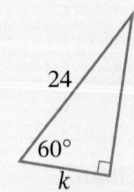 **c** 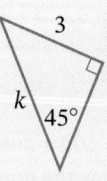 **d**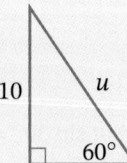

e 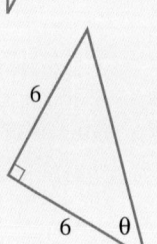 **f** 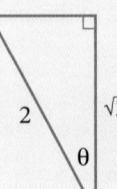 **g**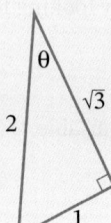

□ Foundation ○ Standard ○ Complex

8 Find the width of this river in exact form.

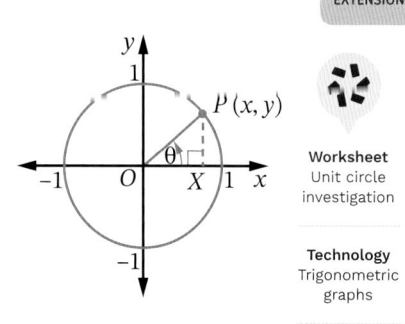

60°

35 m

9 Find the exact value of w in each diagram.

a

w

60° 15°

8 cm

b

w

30°

15°

5 cm

Extension: The trigonometric functions 8.05

Trigonometric ratios of any angle

The sine, cosine and tangent ratios can be extended to include angles that are over 90°, that is, obtuse and reflex angles. The trigonometric ratios for angles of any size can be best explained using a **unit circle**.

A unit circle is a circle of radius 1 drawn on a number plane, with the origin as the centre of the circle. Starting from the positive direction of the x-axis, angles can be measured around this circle in an anti-clockwise direction.

Let $P(x, y)$ be any point on the unit circle as shown and θ the angle that PO makes with the positive x-axis.

Let the vertical interval from P meet the x-axis at X to make the right-angled triangle OXP. Since P has coordinates (x, y), $OX = x$ and $XP = y$.

In $\triangle XOP$, $\cos \theta = \dfrac{OX}{OP}$ $OP = 1$ because it is the radius of the unit circle

$\qquad\qquad\quad = \dfrac{x}{1}$

$\therefore \cos \theta = x$ The x-coordinate of point P on the unit circle

Worksheet
Unit circle investigation

Technology
Trigonometric graphs

Spreadsheet
Trigonometric graphs

□ Foundation   ○ Standard   ○ Complex

Also, $\sin \theta = \dfrac{XP}{OP}$

$= \dfrac{y}{1}$

$\therefore \sin \theta = y$ The y-coordinate of the point P on a unit circle

and $\tan \theta = \dfrac{XP}{OX}$

$\therefore \tan \theta = \dfrac{y}{x}$

ⓘ Trigonometric ratios on the unit circle

If $P(x, y)$ is any point on the unit circle, and θ is the angle that
PO makes with the positive x-axis, then:

$$\sin \theta = y\text{-coordinate of } P$$

$$\cos \theta = x\text{-coordinate of } P$$

$$\tan \theta = \frac{y\text{-coordinate of } P}{x\text{-coordinate of } P}$$

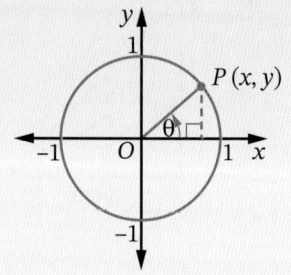

The x- and y-axes divide the number plane into 4 equal **quadrants**. Now we can investigate the
trigonometric ratios for all angles from $\theta = 0°$ to $360°$, by looking at $P(x, y)$ on the unit circle in
the 1st, 2nd, 3rd and 4th quadrants.

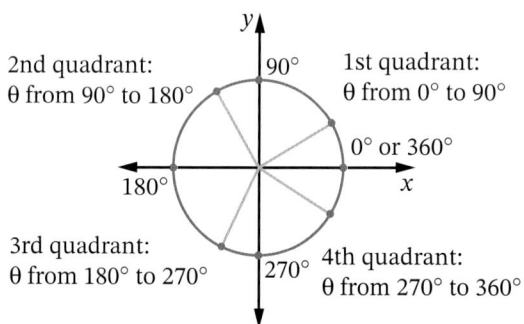

The unit circle can also be used to define the trigonometric ratios for
angles below $0°$ and above $360°$.

Negative angles (below $0°$) are measured in a clockwise direction
on the unit circle. In this diagram, M represents $-40°$ but it could
also represent $360° - 40° = 320°$.

Angles above 360° are measured on the unit circle by going around
the circle more than once. In the diagram, P represents $40°$, but it
could also represent $360° + 40° = 400°$.

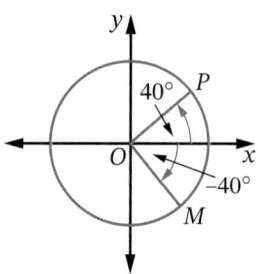

The tangent ratio

The tangent ratio can be expressed in terms of the sine and cosine ratios.

Since $\sin\theta = y$ and $\cos\theta = x$,

$$\frac{\sin\theta}{\cos\theta} = \frac{y}{x}$$

But $\tan\theta = \frac{y}{x}$ $\therefore \tan\theta = \frac{\sin\theta}{\cos\theta}$

ⓘ The tangent ratio

$$\tan\theta = \frac{\sin\theta}{\cos\theta}$$

Example 12

Given that $\sin\alpha = \frac{2}{\sqrt{13}}$ and $\cos\alpha = \frac{3}{\sqrt{13}}$, find $\tan\alpha$.

SOLUTION

$$\tan\alpha = \frac{\sin\alpha}{\cos\alpha}$$

$$= \frac{2}{\sqrt{13}} \div \frac{3}{\sqrt{13}}$$

$$= \frac{2}{3}$$

The sine curve

$\sin\theta = y$-coordinate of P (the height of P above the x-axis), so note its value as θ moves around the unit circle (in an anti-clockwise direction) from $0°$ to $360°$.

θ	0°	1st quadrant 0° to 90°	90°	2nd quadrant 90° to 180°	180°	3rd quadrant 180° to 270°	270°	4th quadrant 270° to 360°	360°
sin θ	0	from 0 to 1	1	from 1 to 0	0	from 0 to −1	−1	from −1 to 0	0

Note that the value of $\sin\theta$ always lies between 1 and −1.

The graph of $y = \sin\theta$ for θ from $0°$ to $360°$ is a 'wave curve' that repeats itself after $360°$.

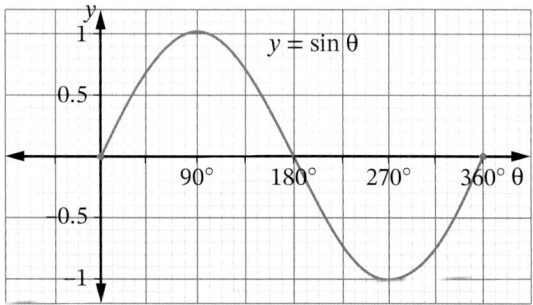

The cosine curve

cos θ = x-coordinate of P (the length of P from the y-axis), so note its value for θ from 0° to 360°.

θ	0°	1st quadrant 0° to 90°	90°	2nd quadrant 90° to 180°	180°	3rd quadrant 180° to 270°	270°	4th quadrant 270° to 360°	360°
cos θ	1	from 1 to 0	0	from 0 to -1	-1	from -1 to 0	0	from 0 to 1	1

Note that the value of cos θ always lies between 1 and −1.

The graph of $y = \cos θ$ for θ from 0° to 360° is another 'wave curve' that repeats itself after 360°.

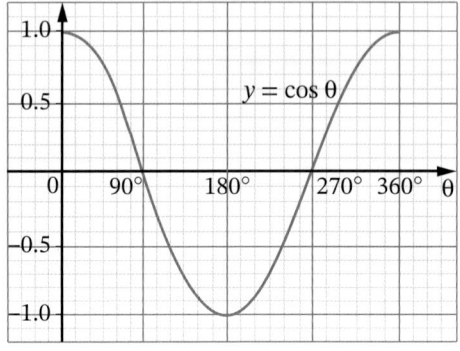

The tangent curve

$\tan θ = \dfrac{y\text{-coordinate of } P}{x\text{-coordinate of } P} = \dfrac{\sin θ}{\cos θ}$, so note its value for θ from 0° to 360°.

θ	0°	1st quadrant 0° to 90°	90°	2nd quadrant 90° to 180°	180°
tan θ	$\dfrac{0}{1} = 0$	$\dfrac{+}{+}$ = positive	$\dfrac{1}{0}$ = undefined	$\dfrac{+}{-}$ = negative	$\dfrac{0}{-1} = 0$

θ	3rd quadrant 180° to 270°	270°	4th quadrant 270° to 360°	360°
tan θ	$\dfrac{-}{-}$ = positive	$\dfrac{-1}{0}$ = undefined	$\dfrac{-}{+}$ = negative	$\dfrac{0}{1} = 0$

Note that the value of tan θ has no value at 90° and 270°.

The graph of $y = \tan θ$ for θ from 0° to 360° is a curve that repeats itself after 180°, with asymptotes at θ = 90° and 270°.

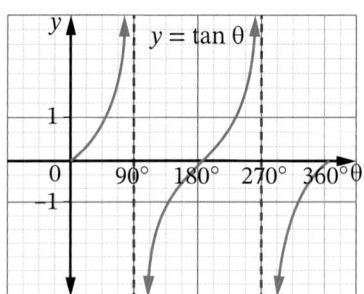

Trigonometric ratios of supplementary angles

For obtuse angles (between 90° and 180°, represented by the 2nd quadrant in the unit circle), we can use this diagram where Q is a reflection of P across the y-axis.

QO makes an angle of 180° − θ with the positive x-axis.

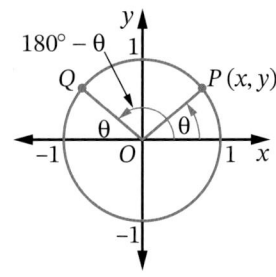

In the 2nd quadrant, Q has a negative x-coordinate and a positive y-coordinate, so if the coordinates of P are (x, y), then the coordinates of Q are $(-x, y)$.

$\therefore \cos(180° - \theta) = -x$

$\qquad = -\cos\theta$

$\therefore \sin(180° - \theta) = y$

$\qquad = \sin\theta$

$\therefore \tan(180° - \theta) = \dfrac{y}{-x}$

$\qquad = -\dfrac{y}{x}$

$\qquad = -\tan\theta$

ⓘ Supplementary relations

For obtuse angles (in the second quadrant), sine is positive while cosine and tangent are negative.

$$\sin(180° - A) = \sin A$$

The sine of an obtuse angle is equal to the **sine** of its supplement.

$$\cos(180° - A) = -\cos A$$

The cosine of an obtuse angle is equal to the **negative cosine** of its supplement.

$$\tan(180° - A) = -\tan A$$

The tangent of an obtuse angle is equal to the **negative tangent** of its supplement.

Example 13

If θ is acute, find θ if:

a $\tan 140° = -\tan\theta$ **b** $\sin 100° = \sin\theta$ **c** $\cos 120° = -\cos\theta$

SOLUTION

a $\theta = 180° - 140°$

$\qquad = 40°$

$\therefore \tan 140° = -\tan 40°$

b $\theta = 180° - 100°$

$\qquad = 80°$

$\therefore \sin 100° = \sin 80°$

c $\theta = 180° - 120°$

$\qquad = 60°$

$\therefore \cos 120° = -\cos 60°$

Example 14

Find the exact value of each expression.

a $\sin 120°$ **b** $\tan 135°$

SOLUTION

a $\sin 120° = \sin(180° - 120°)$

$\qquad = \sin 60°$

$\qquad = \dfrac{\sqrt{3}}{2}$

b $\tan 135° = -\tan(180° - 135°)$

$\qquad = -\tan 45°$

$\qquad = -1$

EXTENSION

EXERCISE 8.05 ANSWERS ON P. 641

The trigonometric functions

(U) (F) (R) (C)

EXAMPLE 12

1 a If $\sin A = \dfrac{60}{109}$ and $\cos A = \dfrac{91}{109}$, find $\tan A$

b If $\sin Y = 0.2$ and $\cos Y = 0.15$, find $\tan Y$

c If $\sin X = \dfrac{2}{\sqrt{13}}$ and $\cos X = \dfrac{3}{\sqrt{13}}$, find $\tan X$

d If $\cos Q = \dfrac{3}{7}$ and $\sin Q = \dfrac{\sqrt{40}}{7}$, find $\tan Q$

e If $\tan X = \dfrac{24}{7}$ and $\sin X = \dfrac{24}{25}$, find $\cos X$

f If $\tan X = \dfrac{2}{\sqrt{5}}$ and $\cos X = \dfrac{\sqrt{5}}{3}$, find $\sin X$

2 State whether each acute or obtuse angle is positive (P) or negative (N).

a $\sin 95°$ **b** $\cos 46°$ **c** $\tan 153°$ **d** $\cos 171°$

e $\sin 142°$ **f** $\tan 91°$ **g** $\tan 130°$ **h** $\cos 87°$

3 Evaluate, correct to 2 decimal places, each trigonometric expression.

a $\cos 153°$ **b** $\tan 349°$ **c** $\sin 230°$

d $\tan 173° 42'$ **e** $\cos 300.9°$ **f** $\sin 324.8°$

g $\sin 176° 54'$ **h** $\cos 245° 23'$ **i** $\tan (-38°)$

j $\sin (-61°)$ **k** $\tan 370°$ **l** $\cos 434°$

4 a Copy and complete this table of values for $y = \sin \theta$, evaluating y correct to 2 decimal places.

(R) (C)

θ	0°	30°	60°	...	360°
y	0	0.5	0.87	...	0

b Graph $y = \sin \theta$, either by using graphing technology or on paper using a scale of 1 cm = 30° on the θ-axis and a scale of 4 cm = 1 unit on the y-axis.

c Comment on the shape of the graph $y = \sin \theta$. What are the maximum and minimum values of the graph and when do they occur?

d Does the graph have an axis of symmetry? If so, what is it?

e Does the graph have rotational symmetry? If so, what is the centre of symmetry?

f For what range of values of θ is $\sin \theta$:

i positive   **ii** negative?

▷

☐ Foundation ○ Standard ◇ Complex

396 Nelson Maths 10 Advanced   9780170465595

5 **a** Copy and complete this table of values for $y = \cos \theta$, evaluating y correct to 2 decimal places.

R
C

θ	0°	30°	60°	...	360°
y	1	0.87	0.5	...	1

b Graph $y = \cos \theta$, either by using graphing technology or on paper.

c Comment on the shape of the graph $y = \cos \theta$. What are the maximum and minimum values of the graph and when do they occur?

d Does the graph have an axis of symmetry? If so, what is it?

e Does the graph have rotational symmetry? If so, what is the centre of symmetry?

f For what range of values of θ is cos θ:

   i positive   **ii** negative?

g Comment on the similarities and differences between the graphs of $y = \sin x$ and $y = \cos x$.

6 If θ is acute, find θ if:

EXAMPLE
13

   a $\cos 170° = -\cos \theta$ **b** $\sin 110° = \sin \theta$ **c** $\tan 130° = -\tan \theta$

   d $\tan 97° = -\tan \theta$ **e** $\cos 115° = -\cos \theta$ **f** $\sin 168° = \sin \theta$

7 Write each expression in terms of sin A, cos A or tan A, where A is acute.

   a $\cos 142°$ **b** $\sin 105°$ **c** $\cos 155°$ **d** $\tan 102°$

   e $\cos 172.7°$ **f** $\sin 115.5°$ **g** $\cos 139° \, 35'$ **h** $\tan 170.8°$

   i $\sin 120° \, 35'$ **j** $\tan 160° \, 10'$ **k** $\sin 95.5°$ **l** $\tan 139.5°$

8 Find the exact value of each expression.

EXAMPLE
14

   a $\sin 150°$ **b** $\tan 135°$ **c** $\sin 135°$ **d** $\cos 120°$

   e $\tan 150°$ **f** $\sin 120°$ **g** $\cos 150°$ **h** $\tan 120°$

   i $\sin 90°$ **j** $\cos 135°$

9 **a** Copy and complete this table of values for $y = \tan \theta$, evaluating y correct to 2 decimal places.

R
C

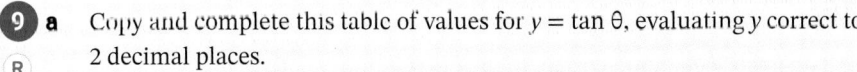

θ	0°	30°	60°	...	360°
y	0	0.58	1.73	...	0

b Graph $y = \tan \theta$, either by using graphing technology or on paper.

c Comment on the shape of the graph $y = \tan \theta$. When does it start to repeat itself?

d Does the graph have an axis of symmetry? If so, what is it?

e Does the graph have rotational symmetry? If so, what is the centre of symmetry?

f For what range of values of θ is tan θ:

   i positive?   **ii** negative?

☐ Foundation   ○ Standard   ○ Complex

Video
Trigonometric
equations

Worksheet
Trigonometric
equations

Example 15

Solve each trigonometric equation, giving all possible acute and obtuse solutions correct to the nearest degree.

a $\sin \theta = 0.7538$ **b** $\tan \theta = -2.5$

SOLUTION

a $\sin \theta = 0.7538$

$\qquad \theta = 48.9206...$ On a calculator: `SHIFT` `sin` 0.7538 `=`

$\qquad \approx 49°$ On some calculators, `2nd F` instead of `SHIFT`

But θ could be obtuse, because $\sin \theta$ is   (Check: $\sin 49° = \sin 131° = 0.7547...$)
also positive in the second quadrant.

$\theta \approx 180° - 49°$

$\quad = 131°$

$\therefore \theta \approx 49°$ or $131°$.

b $\tan \theta = -2.5$ On a calculator: `SHIFT` `tan` `(−)` 2.5 `=`

$\qquad \theta = -68.1985...$

$\qquad \approx -68°$

But θ is obtuse, because $\tan \theta$ is
negative in the second quadrant.

$\theta \approx 180° - 68°$ On a calculator: 180 `−` `Ans` `=`

$\quad = 112°$ (Check: $\tan 112° = -2.4750...$)

Example 16

Solve each trigonometric equation correct to the nearest minute, if x is obtuse.

a $\cos x = -0.09$ **b** $\sin x = 0.64$

SOLUTION   `SHIFT` `cos` automatically gives the obtuse angle
when you enter a negative value.

a $\cos x = -0.09$

$\quad x = 95.1636...$ On a calculator: `SHIFT` `cos` `(−)` 0.09 `=`

$\quad = 95° \, 9'48.99''$ On a calculator: `° ' ''` or `DMS`

$\quad \approx 95° \, 10'$

b $\sin x = 0.64$

    $x = 39.7918...$ On a calculator: **SHIFT** **sin** 0.64 **=**

   But x is obtuse, so:

   $x = 180 - 39.7918...$ 180 **−** **Ans** **=**

    $= 140.2081...$

    $= 140° \, 12' \, 29.45''$ **°,,,** or **DMS**

    $\approx 140° \, 12'$

EXERCISE **8.06** ANSWERS ON P. 642

Trigonometric equations   Ⓤ Ⓕ

1 Solve each trigonometric equation, giving all possible acute and obtuse solutions, correct to the nearest degree.

   a $\sin\theta = 0.84$ **b** $\tan\theta = -\dfrac{3}{4}$ **c** $\cos\theta = -0.342$

   d $\cos\theta = -\dfrac{7}{11}$ **e** $\sin\theta = 0.1164$ **f** $\tan\theta = -1$

   g $\tan\theta = -5.8671$ **h** $\sin\theta = \dfrac{3}{7}$ **i** $\cos\theta = -0.4$

   j $\sin\theta = \dfrac{3.8}{7}$ **k** $\cos\theta = -\dfrac{21}{80}$ **l** $\tan\theta = -\dfrac{15}{8}$

EXAMPLE **15**

2 Solve each trigonometric equation, correct to the nearest minute, if x is obtuse. Note: some equations have no solution.

   a $\sin A = \dfrac{4}{7}$ **b** $\sin A = 0.7438$ **c** $\sin A = 0.3514$

   d $\sin A = 0.108$ **e** $\sin A = \dfrac{5}{11}$ **f** $\sin A = 0.9$

   g $\cos x = 0.6$ **h** $\cos x = -0.6$ **i** $\tan x = 0.3$

   j $\tan x = -0.3$ **k** $\sin x = 0.8$ **l** $\sin x = \dfrac{3}{7}$

EXAMPLE **16**

3 Solve each trigonometric equation correct to the nearest degree, if A is between $0°$ and $180°$.

   a $\cos x = -\dfrac{8}{11}$ **b** $\tan x = -0.95$ **c** $\sin x = \dfrac{7}{8}$

   d $4\cos x = \sqrt{2}$ **e** $3\sin x = 2$ **f** $-4\tan x = 3$

   g $\tan x = 1$ **h** $\cos x = \dfrac{1}{2}$ **i** $\sin x = \dfrac{1}{\sqrt{2}}$

□ Foundation   ○ Standard   ◐ Complex

INVESTIGATION

Sides and opposite angles

This activity can also be done using dynamic geometry software.

1 Construct 3 triangles of different sizes.

2 Label the angles of each triangle A, B and C and the sides opposite them a, b and c respectively.

3 Measure the sides of each triangle correct to the nearest millimetre and the angles to the nearest degree. Copy the table below and record your results in it.

	Side a	Angle A	$\frac{a}{\sin A}$	Side b	Angle B	$\frac{b}{\sin B}$	Side c	Angle C	$\frac{c}{\sin C}$
Triangle 1									
Triangle 2									
Triangle 3									

4 Complete the table by calculating $\frac{a}{\sin A}$, $\frac{b}{\sin B}$ and $\frac{c}{\sin C}$ correct to 2 decimal places.

5 Compare the values of $\frac{a}{\sin A}$, $\frac{b}{\sin B}$ and $\frac{c}{\sin C}$ for each triangle. What do you notice?

8.07 Extension: The sine rule

Worksheet
Discovering the sine rule

The angles of a triangle are labelled with capital letters while the sides are labelled with lowercase letters. By convention, we use a to label the side opposite ∠A, b to label the side opposite ∠B, and so on.

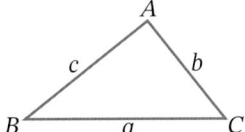

There is a relationship between each angle in a triangle and its opposite side. The longest side is always opposite the largest angle, the next smallest side is opposite the next smallest angle and so on. This relationship is called the **sine rule**.

ⓘ The sine rule

For any triangle ABC:

$$\frac{a}{\sin A} = \frac{b}{\sin B} = \frac{c}{\sin C}$$

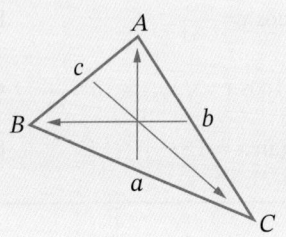

The ratios of the sides in a triangle to the sine of their opposite angles are equal.

The sine rule allows us to apply trigonometry to any triangle, not just right-angled triangles.

The sine rule is used in problems involving 2 sides of a triangle and the 2 angles opposite them.

Example 17

Find y, correct to one decimal place.

EXTENSION

8.07

Video
The sine
rule

SOLUTION

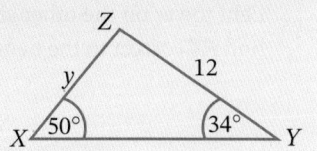

$$\frac{a}{\sin A} = \frac{b}{\sin B}$$

$$\frac{y}{\sin 34°} = \frac{12}{\sin 50°}$$ sides and opposite angles

$$y = \frac{12 \sin 34°}{\sin 50°}$$

$$= 8.7596...$$ From the diagram, an answer of 8.8 cm

$$\approx 8.8 \text{ cm}$$ looks reasonable.

EXERCISE (8.07) ANSWERS ON P. 642

The sine rule   U F PS R

1 Evaluate each expression, correct to one decimal place.

a $\dfrac{14.7 \sin 64°}{\sin 46°}$

b $\dfrac{34.5 \sin 33.4°}{\sin 115.7°}$

c $\dfrac{69 \sin 107° 33'}{\sin 38° 47'}$

2 Find the value of each variable, correct to 2 decimal places.

EXAMPLE
17

a
12.3
73°
35°
a

b
25°
123°
6
b

c
36°29'
c
106°27'
7.8

d
38°43'
4.5
43°18'
d

e
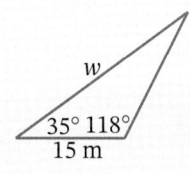
37.6°
e
62.1°
21.3

f
f
104.3°
9.7   20.8°

g
67°
k
72°
8.4 cm

h
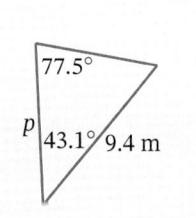
w
35° 118°
15 m

i
77.5°
p 43.1° 9.4 m

□ Foundation ○ Standard ◌ Complex

3 X and Y are 2 light towers 50 m apart on one side of a park. P is a
(PS) light tower on the other side of the park. If ∠Y = 59° and ∠P = 33°,
(R) find PX correct to the nearest metre.

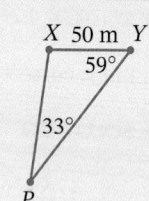

4 A golfer drives a ball 275 m at an angle
(PS) of 5° off centre. The ball lands at an
(R) angle of 107° from the hole. Calculate
the distance of the ball from the hole,
correct to the nearest metre.

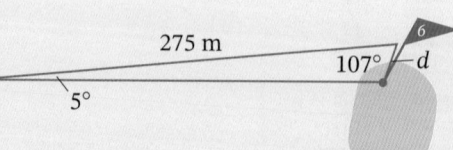

5 A 6 m television antenna is mounted on a roof pitched at an
(PS) angle of 23°. It is supported by 2 wires, PQ and PR, inclined
(R) at 55° to the horizontal.

   a Show that ∠PSR = 113°.

   b Calculate the length of the wire PR, correct to the
   nearest centimetre.

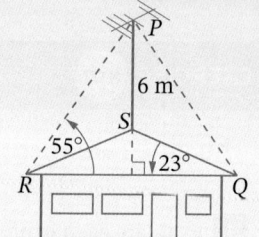

6 To avoid a swamp, Jesinta runs 70 m on a bearing of 050° to V.
(PS) She then turns and runs to W on a bearing of 120°.
(R) If W is directly east of U:

   a find ∠UVW

   b calculate UW, correct to one decimal place.

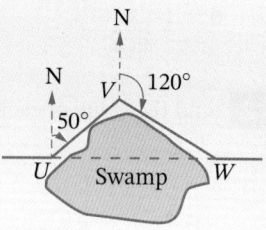

7 Two planes leave the airport at the same time. One flies
(PS) due south at 400 km/h and lands at a second airport after
(R) $1\frac{1}{2}$ hours. The other flies on a bearing of 130° and after

$1\frac{1}{2}$ hours is at a bearing of 075° from the second airport.

How far (to the nearest km) is the slower plane from the
second airport?

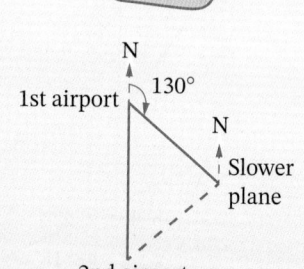

8 The angle of elevation of a tower from a point L is 62°.
(PS) From a point K, 50 m further from the tower, the angle of
(R) elevation is 47°.

   a Use the sine rule in △KTL to show that $TL = \frac{50\sin 47°}{\sin 15°}$.

   b Let the height of the tower be h. In the right-angled
   △LMT, show that $TL = \frac{h}{\sin 62°}$.

   c Hence show that $h = \frac{50\sin 47° \sin 62°}{\sin 15°}$.

   d Hence calculate the height of the tower, correct to
   one decimal place.

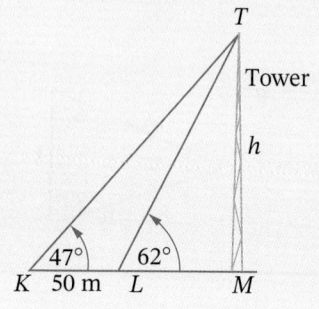

9 From the top of a cliff, the angles of depression of 2 boats at sea that are 0.5 km apart are 55° and 33°.

(PS)
(R) **a** Let the height of the cliff be h.

Show that $h = \dfrac{0.5\sin 33° \sin 55°}{\sin 22°}$.

b Hence calculate the height, to the nearest metre.

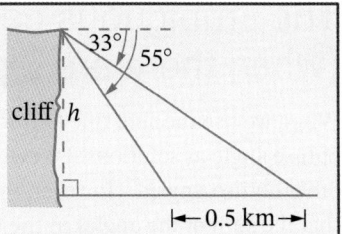

Extension: The sine rule for angles

8.08

Example 18

Video
Obtuse angles using the sine rule

Worksheets
Sine rule problems

Find angle Z, correct to the nearest degree.

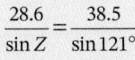 **SOLUTION**

$\dfrac{28.6}{\sin Z} = \dfrac{38.5}{\sin 121°}$

sides and opposite angles

$\dfrac{\sin Z}{28.6} = \dfrac{\sin 121°}{38.5}$

inverting both sides so that Z is in the numerator

$\sin Z = \dfrac{28.6 \sin 121°}{38.5}$

$= 0.636...$

$Z = 39.55...$

on a calculator: SHIFT sin Ans =

From the diagram, an answer of 40°

$\approx 40°$

looks reasonable.

Example 19

Find θ correct to the nearest minute if it is an obtuse angle.

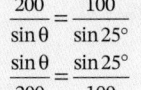 **SOLUTION**

$\dfrac{200}{\sin \theta} = \dfrac{100}{\sin 25°}$

$\dfrac{\sin \theta}{200} = \dfrac{\sin 25°}{100}$ $\theta = 57.697...$

$\sin \theta = \dfrac{200 \sin 25°}{100}$ But θ is obtuse, so: $\theta = 180 - 57.697... = 122.3027...$

$= 0.845...$ $= 122°18'9.77''$

$\approx 122°18'$

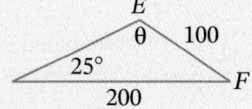

☐ Foundation ○ Standard ◇ Complex

The ambiguous case
(when there are 2 possible answers)

When we use the sine rule to find an angle, it is possible to find both an acute angle and an obtuse angle as solutions. Likewise, there could be 2 possible triangles: one acute-angled, the other obtuse-angled. However, the obtuse-angled triangle may not be possible. We need to check that the sum of the angles in the triangle is not greater than 180°.

Example 20

Video
The sine rule

a In $\triangle DEF$, $\angle D = 42°$, $d = 5$ cm and $f = 7$ cm. Find $\angle F$, correct to the nearest degree.

b In $\triangle LMN$, $\angle M = 130°$, $LN = 15$ cm and $LM = 7$ cm. Find $\angle N$, correct to the nearest degree.

SOLUTION

a Draw a rough diagram.

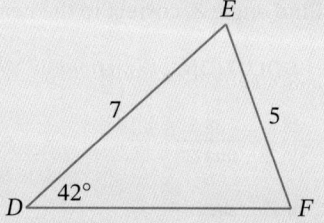

$$\frac{7}{\sin F} = \frac{5}{\sin 42°}$$

$$\frac{\sin F}{7} = \frac{\sin 42°}{5}$$

$$\sin F = \frac{7\sin 42°}{5}$$

$$= 0.93678...$$

$$F = 69.5181...$$

$$\approx 70°$$

But F could be obtuse.

$$F = 180° - 70°$$

$$= 110°$$

Checking the third angle of the obtuse-angled triangle:

$$\angle E = 180° - 42° - 110°$$

$$= 28°$$

∴ the obtuse-angled solution is possible.

∴ $\angle F = 70°$ or $110°$

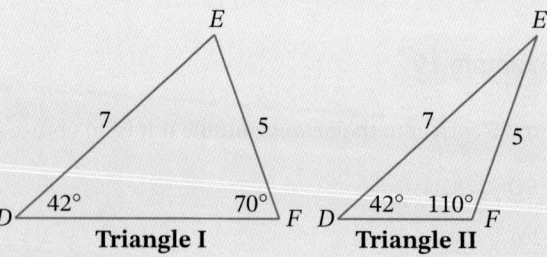

Triangle I **Triangle II**

b Draw a rough diagram.

$$\frac{\sin N}{7} = \frac{\sin 130°}{15}$$

$$\sin N = \frac{7\sin 130°}{15}$$

$$= 0.3574...$$

$$N = 20.9459...$$

$$\approx 21°$$

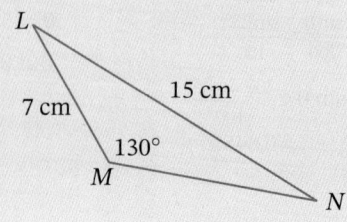

But N could be obtuse.

$N = 180° - 21°$

$\quad = 159°$

Checking the third angle of the obtuse-angled triangle:

$\angle L = 180° - 130° - 159°$

$\quad = -109°$ impossible

$\therefore$ the obtuse-angled solution is not possible.

$\therefore \angle N = 21°$

EXERCISE **8.08** ANSWERS ON P. 642

The sine rule for angles   (U) (F) (PS) (R) (C)

1 Find the acute angle X in each equation, correct to the nearest degree.

     a $\sin X = \dfrac{5.3 \sin 123°}{9.7}$ **b** $\sin X = \dfrac{39 \sin 85°29'}{64}$ **c** $\sin X = \dfrac{467 \sin 63.8°}{518}$

2 Find α in each triangle if α is acute, correct to the nearest 0.1 degree.

EXAMPLE 18

     a 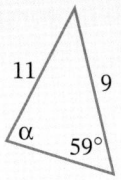   **b** 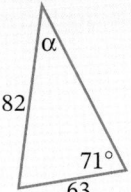   **c**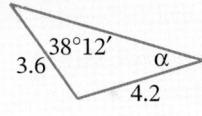

     d 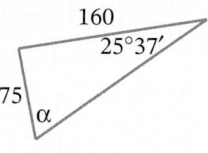   **e** 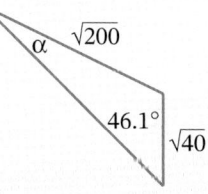   **f**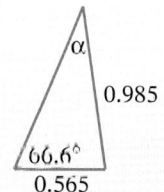

3 Find the size of $\angle A$ to the nearest minute if $\angle A$ is obtuse.

EXAMPLE 19

     a 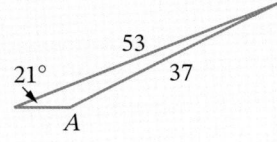   **b** 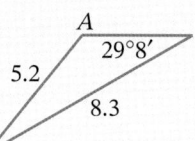   **c**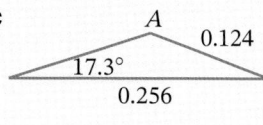

     d 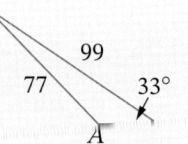   **e** 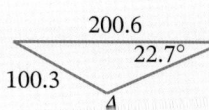   **f** 15°45'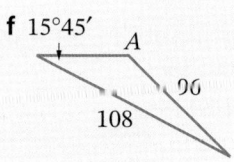

☐ Foundation   ○ Standard   ○ Complex

4 Find all possible angles for each triangle, correct to the nearest degree.

(R) a In $\triangle PQR$, $\angle P = 35°$, $p = 8$ cm, and $q = 10$ cm. Find $\angle Q$.

(C) b In $\triangle UVW$, $\angle W = 95°$, $w = 16$ cm, and $v = 10$ cm. Find $\angle V$.

c In $\triangle XYZ$, $\angle Y = 24°$, $y = 3.4$ km, and $z = 5.7$ km. Find $\angle Z$.

d In $\triangle DEF$, $\angle E = 37°$, $e = 107$ mm, and $d = 121$ mm. Find $\angle D$.

5 Find θ in each triangle correct to the nearest degree, given that θ is acute.

a

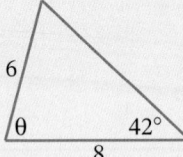

b

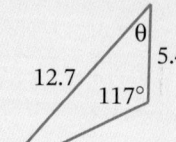

c

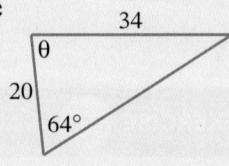

8.09 Extension: The cosine rule

The **cosine rule** is a relationship between the 3 sides of a triangle and one of its angles. It is an extension of Pythagoras' theorem that can be applied to any triangle, not just right-angled ones.

ⓘ The cosine rule

For any triangle ABC:

$$c^2 = a^2 + b^2 - 2ab \cos C$$

where c is the unknown side, C is the angle opposite c, and a and b are the other 2 sides.

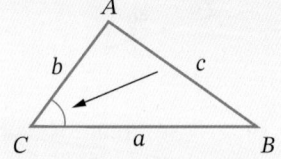

The cosine rule can be used in problems involving 3 sides of a triangle and one of the angles.

Example 21

Video
The cosine
rule

Find x, correct to 2 decimal places.

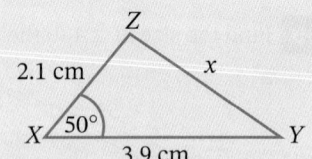

SOLUTION

$c^2 = a^2 + b^2 - 2ab \cos C$

$x^2 = 2.1^2 + 3.9^2 - 2 \times 2.1 \times 3.9 \cos 50°$ $50°$ is the angle opposite x.

$\quad = 9.091\,138...$

$x = \sqrt{9.091\,138...}$

$\quad = 3.015\,15...$

$\quad \approx 3.02$ cm

From the diagram, an answer of 3.02 cm looks reasonable.

☐ Foundation   ○ Standard   ◇ Complex

The cosine rule

(U) (F) (PS) (R) (C)

EXAMPLE
21

1 Solve each equation for x, correct to one decimal place, if x is positive.

a $\quad x^2 = 8^2 + 9^2 - 2 \times 8 \times 9 \times \cos 38°$

b $\quad x^2 = 11.3^2 + 9.7^2 - 2 \times 11.3 \times 9.7 \times \cos 76.9$

c $\quad x^2 = 17^2 + 20.1^2 - 2 \times 17 \times 20.1 \times \cos 149°45'$

2 Find, correct to 2 decimal places, the value of each variable.

a
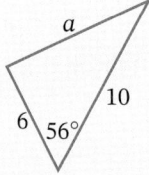

b
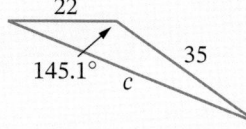

c
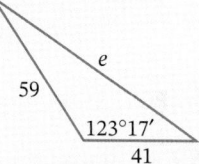

d
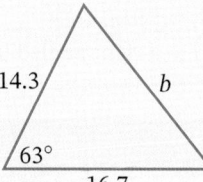

e
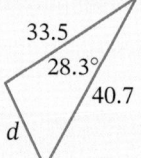

f
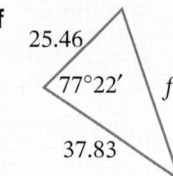

3 In a game of lawn bowls, Jayden is aiming to hit the jack (target ball) 8.4 m away. If he
(PS) bowls 2°15′ off centre and his bowl travels 7.9 m, how far is his bowl from the jack?
(R) Answer correct to one decimal place.

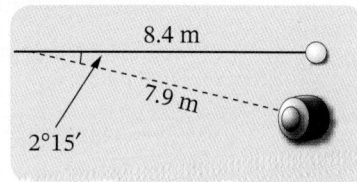

4 In a cricket match, the distance between the bowler and the batter was 20 m. During one
(PS) bowl, the batter hit the ball at an angle of 8° to the line of the pitch and the bowler ran
(R) and caught the ball after it had travelled 18 m. How far did the bowler run to catch the
ball? Select **A**, **B**, **C** or **D**.

A $\quad$ 1.1 m $\qquad$ B $\quad$ 2.0 m $\qquad$ C $\quad$ 3.3 m $\qquad$ D $\quad$ 4.0 m

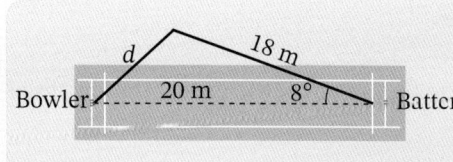

☐ Foundation ○ Standard ◇ Complex

5 A yacht sails from X to Y on a bearing of 130° for 4.2 km.
(PS) It then turns and travels to Z on a bearing of 025° for 2.9 km.
(R) **a**   Copy the diagram and mark the given information on it.
(C) **b**   Explain why $\angle XYZ = 75°$.
     c   Calculate the distance XZ, correct to one decimal place.

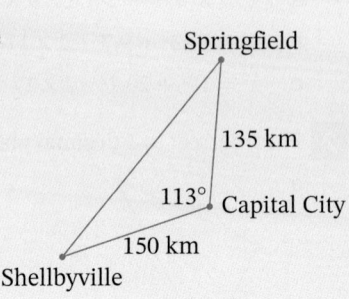

6 Three towns are joined by straight roads. What distance
(PS) (correct to the nearest kilometre) is saved by going
(R) directly from Springfield to Shellbyville instead of
(C) travelling via Capital City?

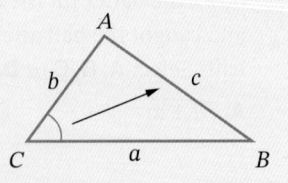

Springfield

135 km

113° Capital City

150 km

Shellbyville

7 **a**   What is the value of cos 90°?
    b   What does $c^2 = a^2 + b^2 - 2ab \cos C$ simplify to if $C = 90°$?
    c   Hence what happens to the cosine rule when it is applied to a right-angled triangle?

8.10 Extension: The cosine rule for angles

If we rewrite the cosine rule so that cos C is the subject, then we will have a formula for finding an unknown angle when the 3 sides of a triangle are known.

$c^2 = a^2 + b^2 - 2ab \cos C$

$c^2 + 2ab \cos C = a^2 + b^2$ adding $2ab$ cos C to both sides so that cos C appears on the LHS

$2ab \cos C = a^2 + b^2 - c^2$

$\therefore \cos C = \dfrac{a^2 + b^2 - c^2}{2ab}$

Worksheet
Cosine rule
problems

(i) The cosine rule for angles

For any triangle ABC:

$$\cos C = \frac{a^2 + b^2 - c^2}{2ab}$$

where C is the unknown angle, c is the side opposite C, and
a and b are the other 2 sides.

The cosine rule can be used to find an unknown angle if the lengths of the 3 sides are known.

□ Foundation   ○ Standard   ◇ Complex

Example 22

Find the size of the marked angle Y, correct to the nearest degree.

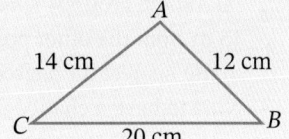

SOLUTION

$\cos C = \dfrac{a^2 + b^2 - c^2}{2ab}$

$\cos Y = \dfrac{7^2 + 8^2 - 9^2}{2 \times 7 \times 8}$ 9 m is opposite angle Y

$= \dfrac{32}{112}$

$Y = 73.398...$ From the diagram, an answer of 73°

$\approx 73°$ looks reasonable.

Video
The cosine
rule for
angles 2

Example 23

Calculate, correct to the nearest minute, the size of the
largest angle in this triangle.

SOLUTION

The largest angle is opposite the longest side, so it is $\angle A$.

$\cos A = \dfrac{14^2 + 12^2 - 20^2}{2 \times 14 \times 12}$ cos is negative so the angle will be obtuse

$= \dfrac{-60}{336}$

$A = 100.286\,56...$ From the diagram, an answer of 100°17′

$= 100°17'11.6''$ looks reasonable.

$\approx 100°17'$

Videos
The cosine
rule

The cosine
rule for
angles 1

EXERCISE 8.10 ANSWERS ON P. 642

The cosine rule for angles   U F PS R

1 Solve each equation for X, correct to the nearest degree.

a $\cos X = \dfrac{12^2 + 14^2 - 15^2}{2 \times 12 \times 14}$ b $\cos X = \dfrac{5.7^2 + 6.8^2 - 3.7^2}{2 \times 5.7 \times 6.8}$

c $\cos X = \dfrac{5^2 + 6^2 - 9^2}{2 \times 5 \times 6}$ d $\cos X = \dfrac{9.2^2 + 4.7^2 - 12.8^2}{2 \times 9.2 \times 4.7}$

☐ Foundation   ○ Standard   ◇ Complex

2 Find the size of α in each triangle, correct to the nearest degree.

a

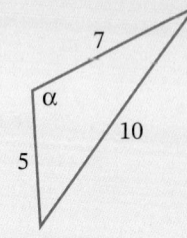

b

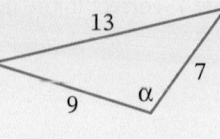

c

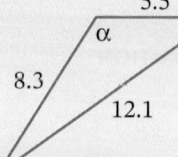

d

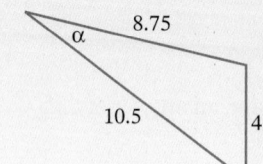

e

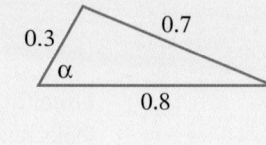

f

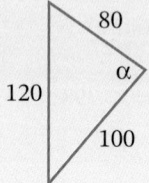

3 A soccer goal is 8 m wide. Nina shoots for goal (along the ground) when 20 m from one post and 15 m from the other post. Within what angle (correct to the nearest 0.1 degree) must the shot be made for Nina to have a chance of scoring a goal?

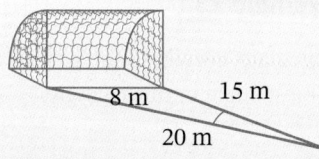

EXAMPLE
23

4 Two cars leave an intersection at the same time. Car *A* drives down the dirt road at 60 km/h and car *B* drives down the highway at 100 km/h. After 45 minutes they are 69 km apart. Find the angle between the 2 roads, correct to the nearest minute.

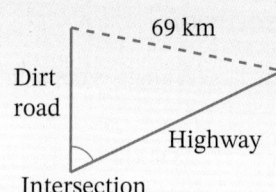

5 A triangle has sides of 21 m, 17 m and 10 m. Find the size of the largest angle, correct to the nearest degree.

8.11 ## Extension: The area of a triangle

We already know that the formula for the area of a triangle is $A = \frac{1}{2}bh$, but there is also a trigonometric formula if we know the lengths of 2 sides of the triangle and the size of the **included angle** between them.

> We've learned about **included angles** with the congruent and similar triangles tests.

□ Foundation   ○ Standard   ○ Complex

ⓘ The area of a triangle

$$A = \frac{1}{2}ab\sin C$$

where C is the included angle between sides a and b.

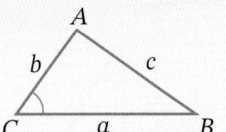

Example 24

Find, correct to one decimal place, the area of this triangle.

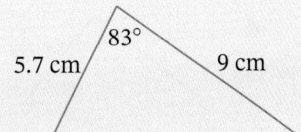

Video
The sine
area
formula

SOLUTION

$A = \frac{1}{2}ab\sin C$

$\quad = \frac{1}{2} \times 5.7 \times 9 \times \sin 83°$ 83° is the included angle between 5.7 cm and 9 cm.

$\quad = 25.458...$

$\quad \approx 25.5 \text{ cm}^2$

EXERCISE 8.11 ANSWERS ON P. 642

The area of a triangle

U F PS R

1 Find, correct to one decimal place, the area of each triangle.

EXAMPLE
24

PS **a**

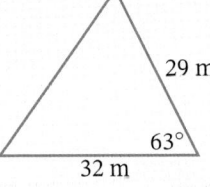

b 23.3 cm

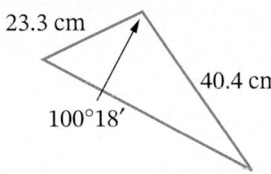

40.4 cm

100°18′

c 27 mm

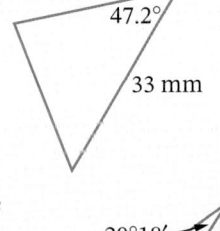

47.2°

33 mm

d 14 mm

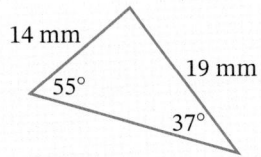

19 mm

55°

37°

e

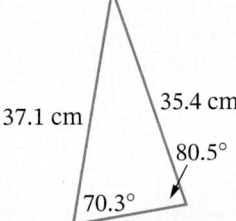

35.4 cm

37.1 cm

80.5°

70.3°

f

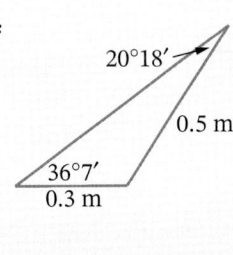

20°18′

0.5 m

36°7′

0.3 m

☐ Foundation   ○ Standard   ○ Complex

2 Calculate, correct to one decimal place, the area of each shape. All measurements are in metres.

a

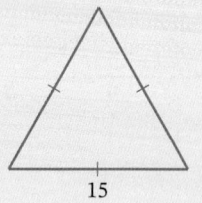

15

b

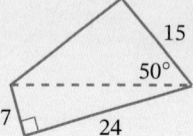

40

75°

12

c

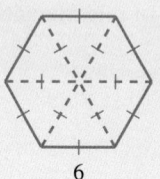

10   25

100°

d

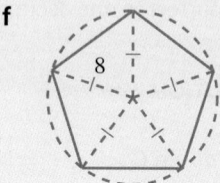

15

50°

7   24

e

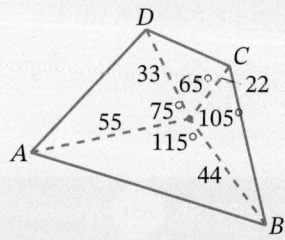

6

f

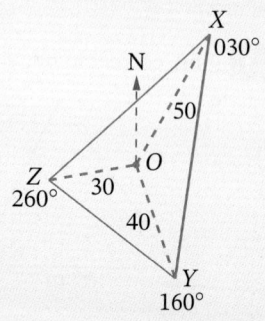

8

3 The diagram shows the results of a radial survey of a block of land. All distances are in metres.

a Use the cosine rule to find the lengths of *AB*, *BC*, *CD* and *AD* and, hence, find the perimeter of the block of land (to the nearest metre).

b Use the area formula to find the area of each triangle and, hence, calculate the area of the block of land (to the nearest m²).

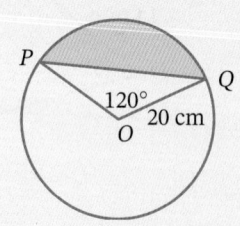

D

C

33   65°   22

55   75°   105°

115°

A   44

B

4 Poonam completed a radial survey as shown in the diagram. All measurements are in metres.

a Find the size of ∠*XOY*.

b Calculate, correct to 2 decimal places, the area of △*XOY*.

X
030°
N
50
O
Z   30
260°
40
Y
160°

5 *O* is the centre of a circle of radius 20 cm. Calculate, correct to one decimal place, the area of:

a sector *OPQ*

b triangle *OPQ*

c the shaded segment.

P
120°
Q
20 cm
O

6 A triangular prism has base edges of 8 cm, 10 cm and 15 cm, and a height of 20 cm.

PS

R **a** Calculate the size ∠PRQ, correct to nearest degree.

b Find the area of △PQR, correct to the nearest cm².

c Find the volume of the prism, correct to the nearest cm³.

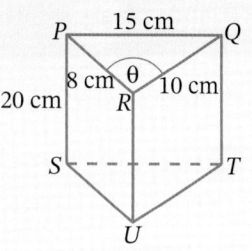

Extension: Problems involving the sine and cosine rules

ⓘ The sine and cosine rules

The sine rule is used for triangle problems involving 2 sides and the 2 angles opposite them.

$$\frac{a}{\sin A} = \frac{b}{\sin B} = \frac{c}{\sin C}$$

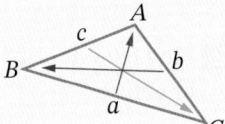

The cosine rule is used for triangle problems involving 3 sides and one angle.

$$c^2 = a^2 + b^2 - 2ab \cos C$$

$$\cos C = \frac{a^2 + b^2 - c^2}{2ab}$$

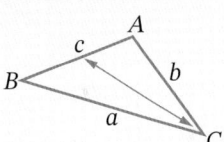

EXTENSION

Worksheets
Finding an unknown side

Finding an unknown angle

The sine and cosine rules

Puzzle
The sine and cosine rules

Video
The sine and cosine rules

Example 25

a Find the value of k, correct to one decimal place.

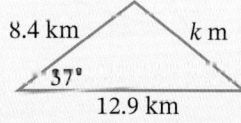

b Find the value of θ, correct to the nearest minute.

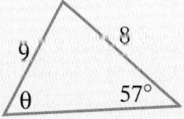

SOLUTION

a The problem involves 3 sides and one angle so use the cosine rule.

$k^2 = 8.4^2 + 12.9^2 - 2 \times 8.4 \times 12.9 \times \cos 37°$

$\quad = 63.889...$

$k = \sqrt{63.889...}$

$\quad = 7.993...$

$\quad ≈ 8.0$ m

b The problem involves 2 sides and the 2 angles opposite them, so use the sine rule.

$\dfrac{\sin \theta}{8} = \dfrac{\sin 57°}{9}$

$\sin \theta = \dfrac{8 \sin 57°}{9}$

$\quad = 0.7454...$

$\theta = 48.2007...$

$\quad = 48°12'2.77''$

$\quad ≈ 48°12'$

☐ Foundation ○ Standard ◇ Complex

EXERCISE (8.12) ANSWERS ON P. 642

Problems involving the sine and cosine rules (U) (F) (PS) (R) (C)

EXAMPLE
25

1 Find, correct to one decimal place, the value of each variable.

a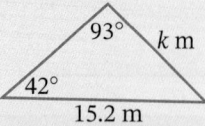

b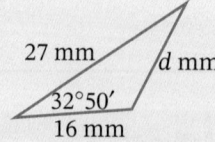

c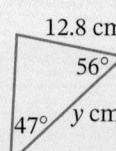

d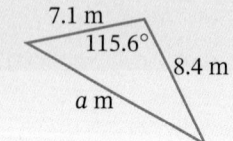

e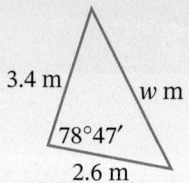

f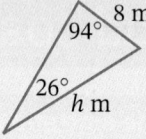

2 Find the value of θ to the nearest degree. Use the diagrams to note whether θ is acute or obtuse.

a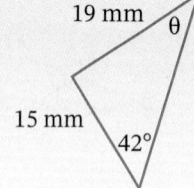

b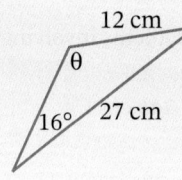

c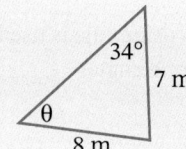

d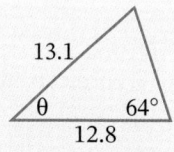

e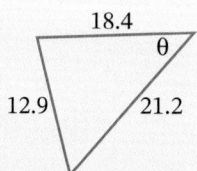

f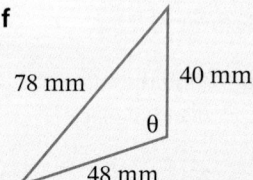

3 The angles of elevation of a building measured from 2 positions 80 m apart are 32° and 55°.

(PS)
(C) **a** Explain why ∠ATB = 23°.

b Find, correct to 2 decimal places, the length of BT.

c Hence find the height, h, of the building, correct to the nearest metre.

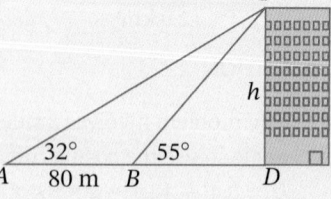

4 a What is the value of sin 90°?

(PS) **b** Find, correct to one decimal place, the value of d using:

(RC) **i** the sine rule

ii the sine ratio for right-angled triangles.

c What do you notice about your results? Give reasons.

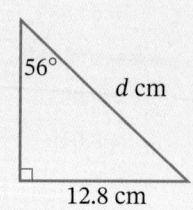

□ Foundation ○ Standard ○ Complex

EXTENSION

8.12

5 Mikayla needs to run around a cross-country course, as shown. What is the length of the course, correct to one decimal place?

(PS)
(R)

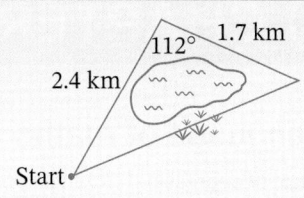

112° 1.7 km
2.4 km
Start

6 A plane flew on a bearing of 150° for 370 km. It then changed direction and flew another 285 km on a bearing of 235°. How far, correct to the nearest kilometre, is the plane from its starting point?

(PS)
(R)

POWER PLUS ANSWERS ON P. 642

1 For this diagram, find the exact value of:

a the length of AB

b the area of $\triangle ADB$

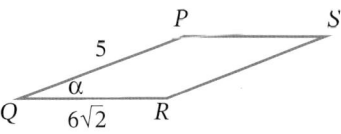

D
2 m
45°
30°
A   B   C

2 For θ between 0° and 180°, find θ if:

a $\sin \theta = \cos \theta$ b $\sin \theta = \sqrt{3} \cos \theta$ c $\sqrt{3} \sin \theta = \cos \theta$

d $\cos \theta = -\sqrt{3} \sin \theta$ e $\sin \theta = -\sqrt{3} \cos \theta$ f $\cos \theta = -\sin \theta$

g $\sin^2 \theta = \dfrac{3}{4}$ h $\tan^2 \theta = \dfrac{1}{3}$ i $\cos^2 \theta = \dfrac{1}{2}$

3 Show that:

a $\sin (180° - B) + \cos (90° - B) = 2 \sin B$

b $\dfrac{\sin (180° - B)}{\cos (180° - B)} = -\tan B$

c $\sin (180° - B) \cos (180° - B) \tan (180° - B) = \sin^2 B$

d $\dfrac{(\sin A)^2 + \sin A \cos A}{(\cos A)^2 + \sin A \cos A} = \tan A$

4 Express $\cos 45° + \sin 45°$ as a surd in simplest form.

5 The area of the parallelogram shown is 30 cm². Find 2 possible values for α, correct to the nearest degree.

P   S
5
α
Q 6√2 R

□ Foundation   ○ Standard   ○ Complex

⑧ CHAPTER REVIEW

Quiz
Language of
maths 8

Puzzle
Trigonometry
crossword

Language of maths

angle of depression	angle of elevation	bearing	compass bearing
complementary	cosine rule	degree (°)	denominator
exact ratio	horizontal	included angle	inverse ($^{-1}$)
minute (′)	obtuse	right-angled	second (″)
sine rule	supplementary	surd	tangent (tan)
theta (θ)	three-figure bearing	trigonometric ratio	vertical

1   What is an **angle of depression**?

2   What is an **exact ratio**? Give an example of one.

3   Describe the shape of the **sine curve**.

4   Copy and complete: A **bearing** is an _____ used to precisely describe the _____ of one location from a given reference point.

5   The word **minute** has an alternative pronunciation and meaning. What is its alternative meaning?

6   What does **inverse** mean and how is it used in trigonometry?

Worksheet
Mind map:
Trigonometry
(Advanced)

Topic summary

Print (or copy) and complete this mind map of the topic, adding detail to its branches and using pictures, symbols and colour where needed. Ask your teacher to check your work.

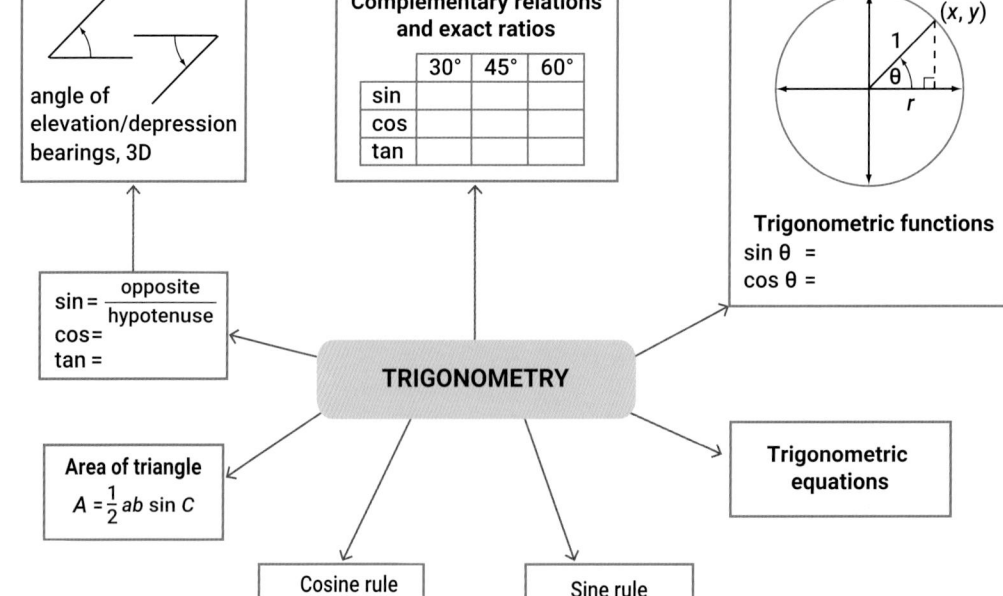

1 Find, correct to one decimal place, the value of each variable.

a
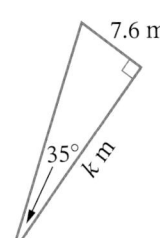
7.6 m
35°
k m

b
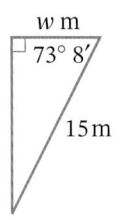
w m
73° 8'
15 m

c
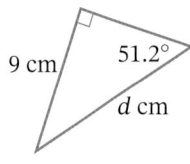
9 cm
51.2°
d cm

8.01

2 Find the value of θ, correct to the nearest minute.

8.01

a
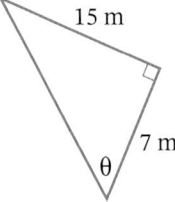
15 m
7 m
θ

b
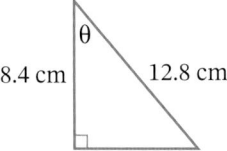
θ
8.4 cm
12.8 cm

c
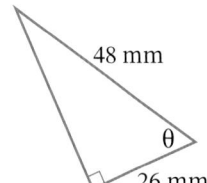
48 mm
θ
26 mm

3 Find the angle of depression (correct to the nearest degree) of a boat that is 100 m from the base of a 55 m cliff.

8.01

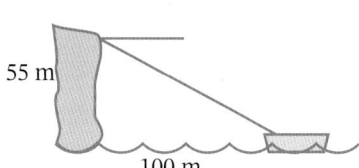
55 m
100 m

4 What is the bearing of:

a Canberra from Sydney

b Sydney from Canberra?

8.02

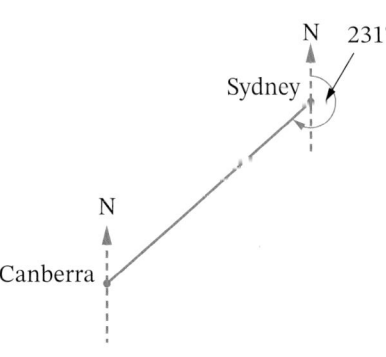

N 231°
Sydney
N
Canberra

5 Two planes leave an airport at the same time. The first travels on a bearing of 063° at 500 km/h. The second travels on a bearing of 153° at 400 km/h.

8.02

a How far apart are the planes after 2 hours (correct to the nearest km)?

b Calculate, correct to the nearest degree, the bearing of the first plane from the second plane.

☐ Foundation ○ Standard ○ Complex

CHAPTER 8 TEST YOURSELF

8.03　**6** Adhiraj sails from Perth on a compass bearing of SSW for 12 nautical miles and then changes direction to a bearing of WNW and sails a further 42 nautical miles.

   a　How far is he from Perth?

   b　What is the bearing of Adhiraj from Perth?

   c　On what three-figure bearing will he have to sail on his way directly back to Perth?

8.03　**7** A box in the shape of a square prism has a base of 10 cm by 10 cm and is 30 cm tall. Find, to the nearest whole number:

   a　the length of the longest diagonal of the box

   b　the angle that the longest diagonal makes with the base.

EXTENSION

8.04　**8** Find the exact value of x in each triangle.

a 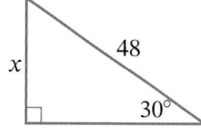　　**b** 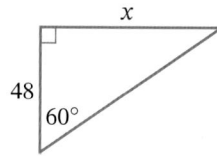　　**c**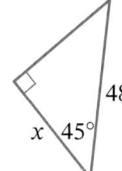

8.05　**9** Graph $y = \cos \theta$ for θ from $0°$ to $360°$.

8.06　**10** Find the acute angle α if:

   a　$\sin 123° = \sin \alpha$　　　**b**　$\tan 93° = -\tan \alpha$　　　**c**　$\cos 110° = -\cos \alpha$

8.07　**11** Solve each trigonometric equation, giving all possible acute and obtuse solutions correct to the nearest minute.

   a　$\cos x = -\dfrac{4}{5}$　　　**b**　$\tan x = \dfrac{15}{7}$　　　**c**　$\sin x = \dfrac{3}{14}$

8.07　**12** Find the value of each variable, correct to one decimal place.

a 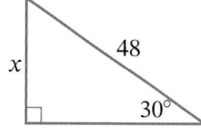　　**b** 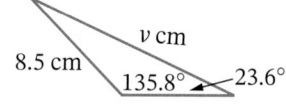　　**c**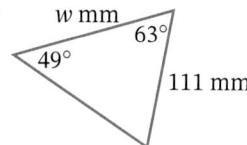

8.08　**13** Find the value of each variable, correct to the nearest minute.

a 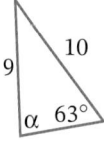　　**b** 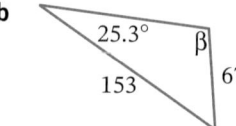　　**c**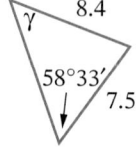

☐ Foundation　◯ Standard　◇ Complex

14 Find the value of each variable, correct to one decimal place.

EXTENSION

8.09

a

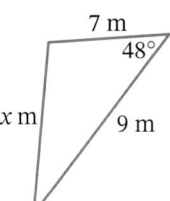

b

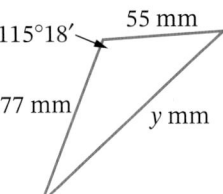

c

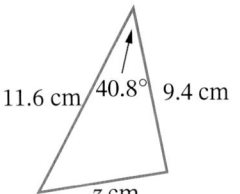

15 Find the size of each marked angle, correct to the nearest degree.

8.10

a

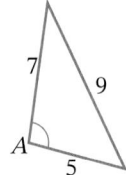

b

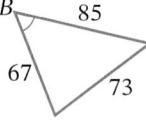

c

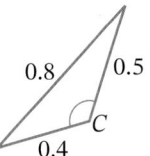

16 Find, correct to the nearest whole number, the area of each triangle.

8.11

a

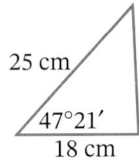

b

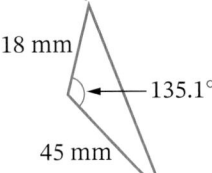

c

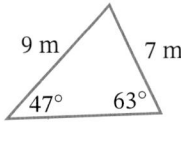

17 A parallelogram has sides of 12 cm and 6 cm and one interior angle of 65° 35′. Find the length of the longer diagonal, correct to one decimal place.

8.12

18 The distance AB is 65 m. Calculate the height of the flagpole, correct to one decimal place.

8.12

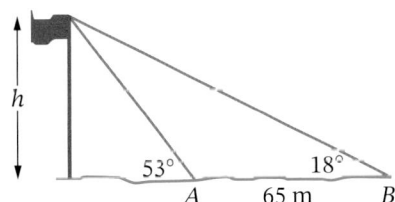

□ Foundation ○ Standard ○ Complex

9

SPACE

Networks

During the 18th century, in the Prussian town of Königsberg (now Kaliningrad, Russia), there were 7 bridges connecting 2 islands and the banks of the Pregel River (see map below). There was a tradition where people would walk through the town to try to cross each bridge only once and return to their starting position. No person was able to do it but no one could prove that it was impossible.

In 1736, the Swiss mathematician, Leonhard Euler, solved the problem by reducing the map to a network diagram, creating a new field of mathematics called graph theory. Euler proved that it was impossible to do the walk. Eventually, another bridge was built.

stock.adobe.com/unikyluckk

Chapter outline

		Proficiencies
9.01	Networks	U F R C
9.02	Polyhedra	U F R C
9.03	Traversable networks	U F PS R C
9.04	Spanning trees	U F R C
9.05	Shortest path	U F R C

U = Understanding   R = Reasoning
F = Fluency   C = Communicating
PS = Problem solving

Wordbank

edge A line that connects vertices (points) together in a network or polyhedron.

face Flat surface of a solid shape.

network An arrangement of edges (lines) that connect a set of vertices (points).

Quiz
Wordbank 9

polyhedron A solid shape with polygons as surfaces.

spanning tree Any smaller tree within a network that connects all vertices.

traversable A network which has a way of travelling over every edge of the network just once.

tree A connected network in which any 2 vertices are connected by only one path.

vertex (of a network) A point that represents an object that is connected to other objects by a system of links called edges (lines).

vertex (of a polyhedron) A corner of a polyhedron where edges meet.

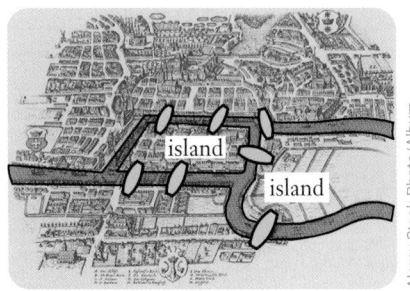

Alamy Stock Photo/Album

9 **In this chapter you will:**

✓ identify the faces, vertices and edges of a network
✓ identify the faces, vertices and edges of a polyhedron
✓ investigate the properties of polyhedra including the Platonic solids
✓ investigate Euler's rule for networks and polyhedra
✓ investigate how networks are used to represent real-life situations in which items are connected by links
✓ apply networks to solve problems involving travelling, connecting, spanning, minimising costs and time .

Quiz
SkillCheck 9

SkillCheck
ANSWERS ON P. 643

Copy and complete this table for each solid.

	Name of solid	Shape(s) of faces	Number of faces	Number of vertices (corners)	Number of edges (lines)
1					
2					
3					
4					
5					
6					
7					
8					
9					
10					
11					
12					

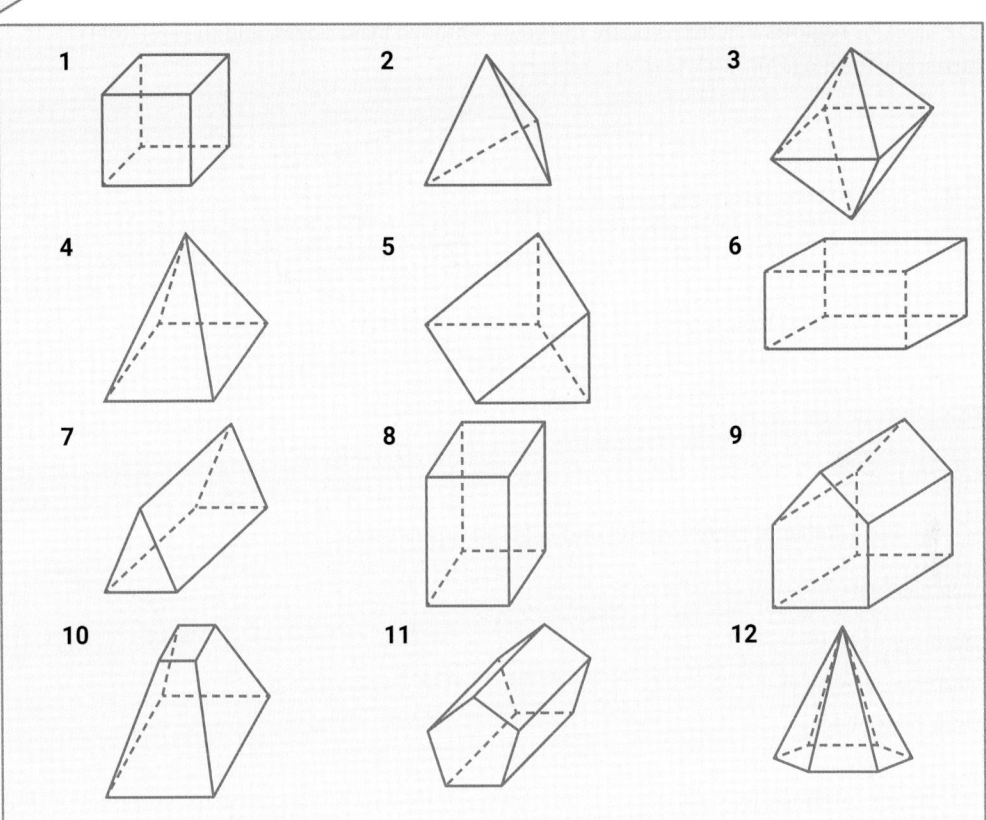

Networks

A **network** is a collection of points called **vertices** connected by lines called **edges**. It is a set of objects connected to each other in some way; for example, a computer network, the electrical wiring inside a building, roads connecting towns, and friendships between a large group of people (such as on social media). A **network** can be represented by a **network diagram**, an arrangement of lines showing how a group of people, objects or tasks interconnect. A network diagram is also called a **graph**, and if its edges don't cross each other (overlap), then it is called a **planar graph** (planar meaning 2D, flat, of a plane).

Video
Networks

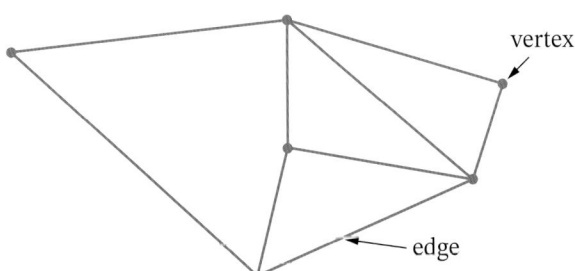

vertex

edge

The **faces** or **regions** of a network are the areas bounded by its edges, and the area that surrounds the diagram.

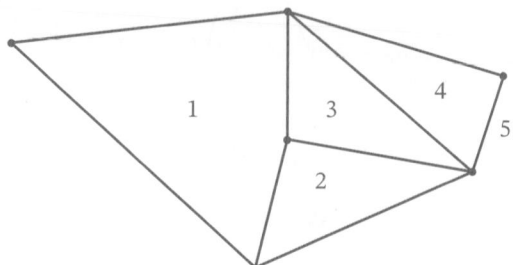

This network has 5 faces.

Example 1

Count the number of faces, vertices and edges in this network.

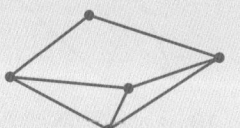

SOLUTION

number of faces = 3 + 1 = 4

number of vertices = 5

number of edges = 7

In 1758, the Swiss mathematician Leonhard Euler (pronounced 'oiler') discovered a relationship between the number of faces and vertices ($F + V$) and number of edges (E) for all networks that are planar graphs (no overlapping edges).

For the network in Example 1, $F + V = 4 + 5 = 9$ and $E = 7$.

For the network *before* Example 1, $F + V = 5 + 6 = 11$ and $E = 9$.

ⓘ Euler's formula for planar graphs

For a planar graph with F faces, V vertices and E edges, **Euler's formula** states:
$$F + V = E + 2$$

This formula can also be written as $V + F - E = 2$.

Example 2

Video
Euler's formula for planar graphs

Test Euler's formula on this network.

SOLUTION

faces $F = 7$, vertices $V = 7$, edges $E = 12$

$F + V = 7 + 7$

$\qquad = 14$

$E + 2 = 12 + 2$ So, $F + V = E + 2$.

$\qquad = 14$ Euler's formula holds.

Networks U F R C

R C Copy and complete this table according to the networks below to test Euler's formula on each network.

EXAMPLES 1, 2

	Number of faces, F	Number of vertices, V	$F + V$	Number of edges, E	$E + 2$
1					
2					
3					
4					
5					
6					
7					
8					
9					
10					

1

2

3

4

5

6

7

8

9

10

☐ Foundation ○ Standard ○ Complex

9.02 Polyhedra

Video
Polyhedra:
Platonic
solids

A **polyhedron** (plural: **polyhedra**) is a three-dimensional solid with flat faces made up of polygons. The plural of polyhedron is polyhedra or polyhedrons. A polyhedron also has faces, vertices (corners) and edges (lines around the faces).

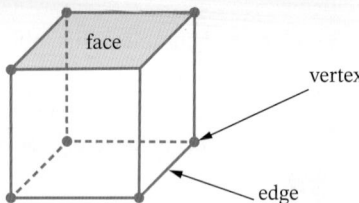

This cube has 6 faces, 8 vertices and 12 edges.

Prisms and pyramids are polyhedra. Each cross-section parallel to the base (including the base) of a prism or pyramid is a polygon. The side faces of a pyramid are all triangles.

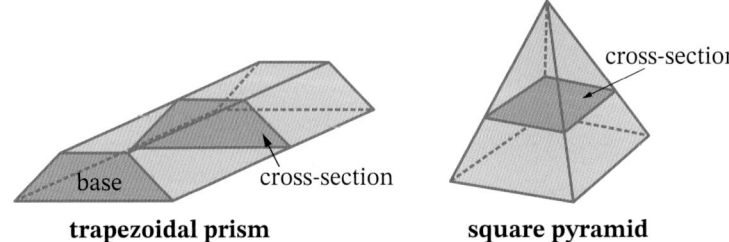

trapezoidal prism   **square pyramid**

A **regular polyhedron** or **Platonic solid** is a polyhedron whose faces are the same regular polygon. There are only 5 Platonic solids, each named by the number of faces.

 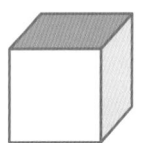 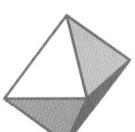 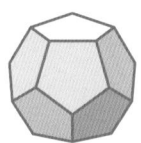 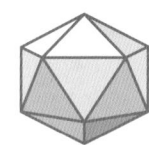

tetrahedron   **hexahedron**   **octahedron**   **dodecahedron**   **icosahedron**
                  (cube)

Platonic solid	Number of faces	Shape of each face
Regular tetrahedron (equilateral triangular pyramid)	tetra = 4	Equilateral triangle
Regular hexahedron (cube)	hexa = 6	Square
Regular octahedron	octa = 8	Equilateral triangle
Regular dodecahedron	dodeca = 12	Regular pentagon
Regular icosahedron	icosa = 20	Equilateral triangle

9780170465595

Platonic solids are used as dice, such as a 12-sided die or a 20-sided die.

iStock.com/Dincer AGIN

Euler's formula is also true for polyhedra because a polyhedron is a 3D representation of a network (planar graph).

ⓘ Euler's formula for polyhedra

For a polyhedron with F faces, V vertices and E edges:

$$F + V = E + 2$$

For a cube, faces $F = 6$, vertices $V = 8$, edges $E = 12$.

$F + V = 6 + 8$

$\quad = 14$

$E + 2 = 12 + 2$ So, $F + V = E + 2$.

$\quad = 14$ Euler's formula holds.

EXERCISE 9.02 ANSWERS ON P. 643

Polyhedra   U Γ R C

1 The nets of the Platonic solids are shown below and can also be downloaded as the worksheet 'Nets of Platonic solids'. Make a copy of each net (on cardboard for best results), cut them out and build the solids.

Worksheet
Nets of Platonic solids

Tetrahedron

5 cm   5 cm

5 cm

5 cm   5 cm   5 cm   5 cm

5 cm   5 cm

▷

☐ Foundation   ◯ Standard   ◇ Complex

Cube (hexahedron)

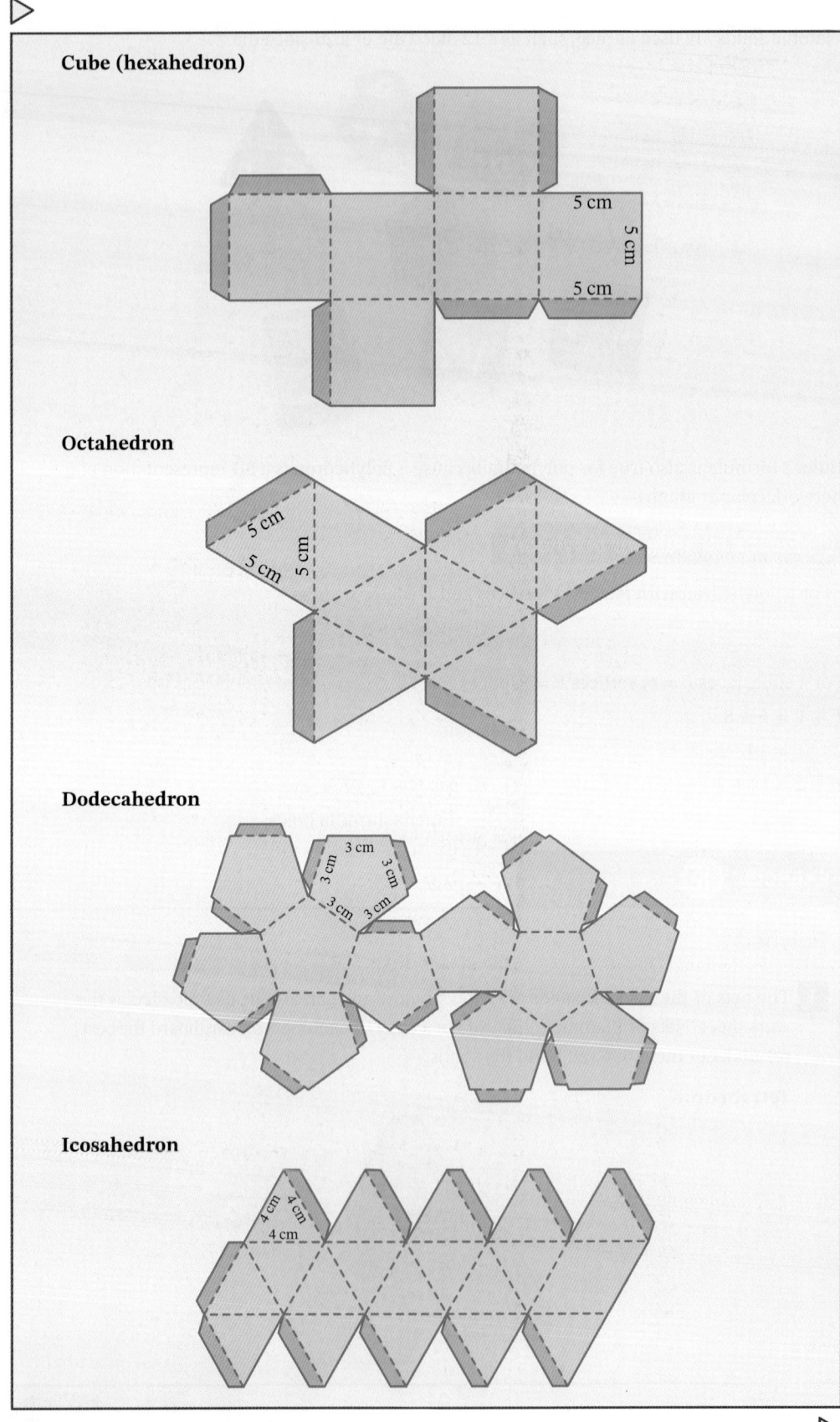

5 cm

5 cm

5 cm

Octahedron

5 cm

5 cm

5 cm

Dodecahedron

3 cm

3 cm

3 cm

3 cm

3 cm

Icosahedron

4 cm

4 cm

4 cm

2 Which Platonic solid:

(R) **a** has 12 faces? **b** is a pyramid?

(C) **c** has 12 edges? **d** has 12 vertices?

e is a prism? **f** has pentagonal faces?

g has a flattened 'soccer ball' pattern?

h is a composite shape of 2 square pyramids?

3 Copy and complete this table and check that Euler's formula is true.

(R)
(C)

Platonic solid	Number of faces (F)	Number of vertices (V)	F + V	Number of edges (E)	E + 2
Tetrahedron					
Cube					
Octahedron					
Dodecahedron					
Icosahedron					

4 Copy and complete this table and check that Euler's formula is true.

(R)
(C)

	Polyhedron	Number of faces (F)	Number of vertices (V)	F + V	Number of edges (E)
a	Triangular prism				
b	Hexagonal prism				
c	Square pyramid				
d	Pentagonal prism				
e	Trapezoidal prism				
f	Hexagonal pyramid				
g	Octagonal prism				
h	Truncated square pyramid				

a

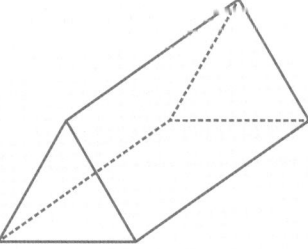

b

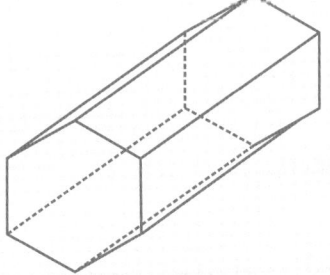

☐ Foundation ○ Standard ◇ Complex

c

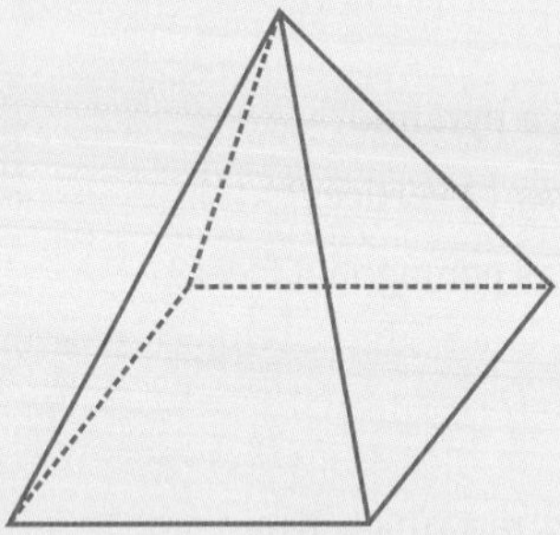

d

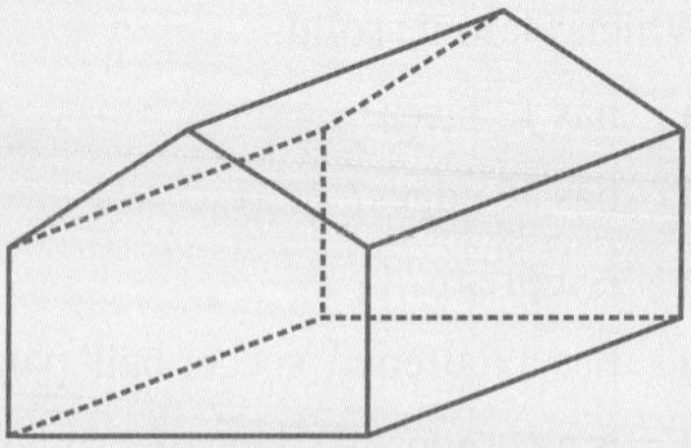

e

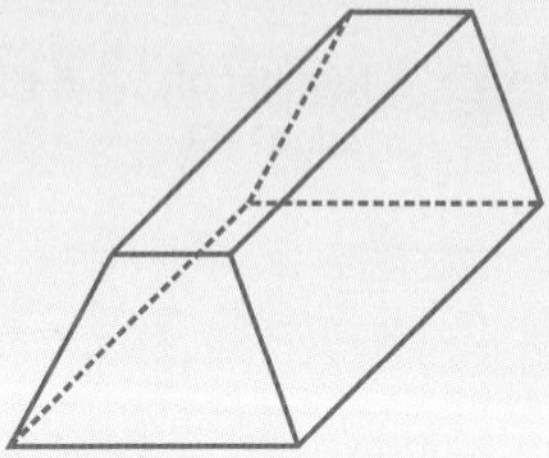

f

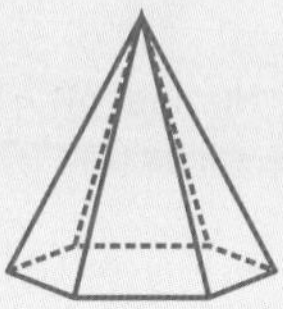

g

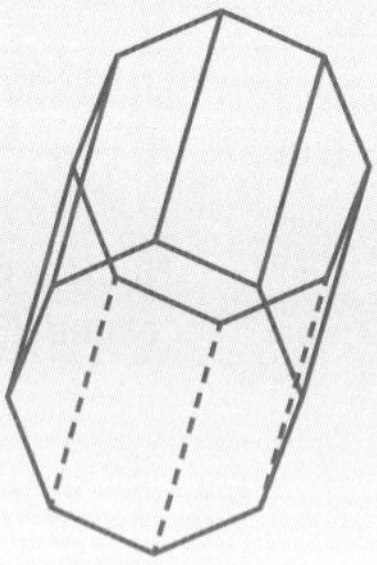

h

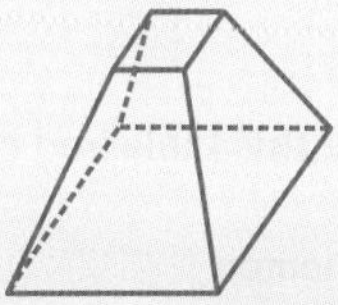

5 Draw a polyhedron that has 8 faces and 18 edges.

R C

DID YOU KNOW?

The Platonic solids

The Platonic solids were discovered by the Greeks in the 5th century BCE. However, ancient artefacts displaying pictures of these solids have been found in Europe, Egypt, Africa and South America. It was believed that these shapes had mystical properties. The Greek philosopher Plato (427–327 BC) claimed that these regular polyhedra were 'cosmic bodies' representing the elements.

- The tetrahedron stood for Fire.
- The hexahedron stood for Earth.
- The octahedron stood for Air.

- The icosahedron represented Water.
- The dodecahedron represented the ether or the Universe.

1 **Find out about how the Pythagoreans, Theaetetus and Plato described and explored the Platonic solids.**

2 **What did the mathematician Euclid and the astronomer Kepler discover about the Platonic solids?**

INVESTIGATION

Tracing over a network

Can you trace over every edge of the network without lifting your finger from the page?

You should be able to, but it will depend on where you started.

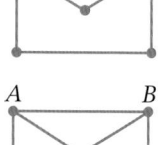

If you started at *A* or *B* then you are able to trace over every edge of the network.

To determine where to start, it can help to look at how many edges are connected at a vertex.

For example, for the network shown:

Vertex	Number of edges connected	Can I start here?	Where do I finish?
A	3	Yes	*B*
B	3	Yes	*A*
C	2	No	–
D	2	No	–
E	2	No	–

Consider whether the networks below can be traced without lifting the pencil. You may wish to create a similar table as the one above to show each vertex of the network.

1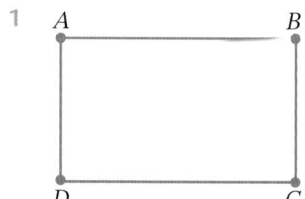

2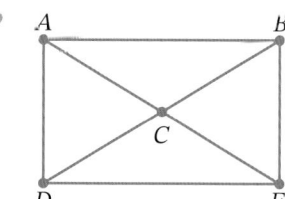

3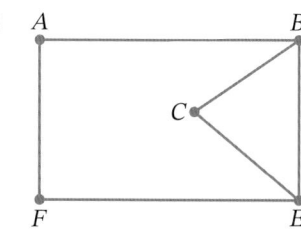

4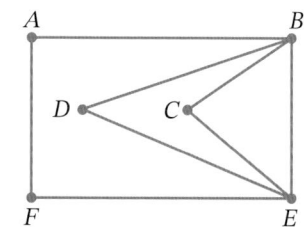

5

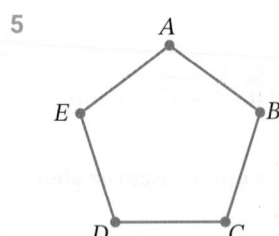

6

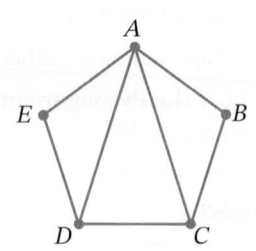

7

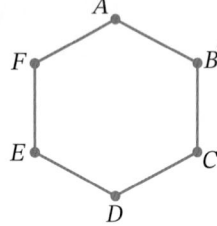

8

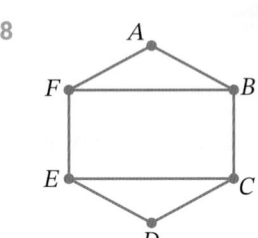

9

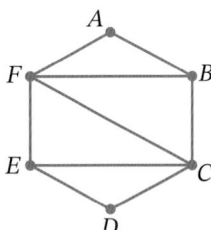

10

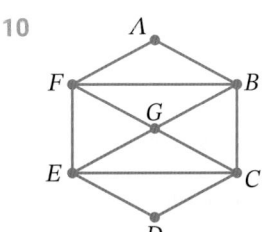

Write down anything that you have noticed about which networks can be traced.
How many vertices with odd edges do these networks have?

9.03 Traversable networks

The **degree** (or **order**) of a vertex is the number of
edges connected to it. The degree of each vertex in
this network is shown on the diagram.

An **even vertex** has an even number of edges
connected to it. An **odd vertex** has an odd number
of edges. This network has 4 even vertices and
2 odd vertices.

A network is **traversable** if there is a way of travelling
over every edge of the network just once. The network
shown is traversable.

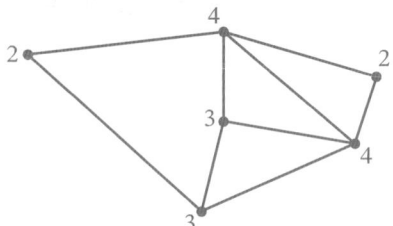

The 'Seven bridges of Königsberg' problem was described at the front of this chapter. The challenge was to cross all 7 bridges only once and returning to your starting position, but the Swiss mathematician Leonhard Euler proved that this was impossible. Euler drew the problem as a network diagram, representing the land as vertices and the bridges as edges.

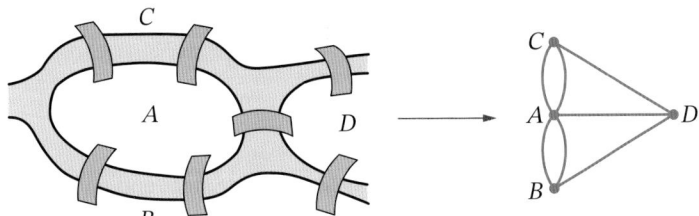

Euler discovered the following rule about traversable networks.

ⓘ Traversable networks

A network is traversable if it has exactly 2 odd vertices, or if all vertices are even.

This makes sense because the start vertex and finish vertex need at least one edge for going out and in respectively, and all the other vertices within the path (called an **Eulerian trail**) require 2 edges (or multiples of 2) for going in *and* out. If exactly 2 vertices are odd, then the path will start and finish at different vertices. If all vertices are even, then the path will start and end at the same vertex, completing an **Eulerian circuit**.

Example 3

Determine whether each network is traversable.

a

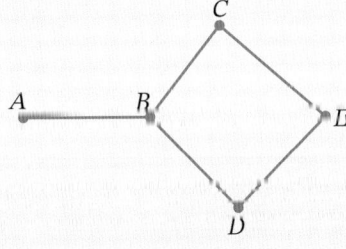

b

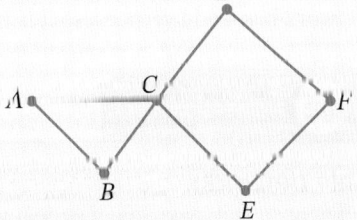

c

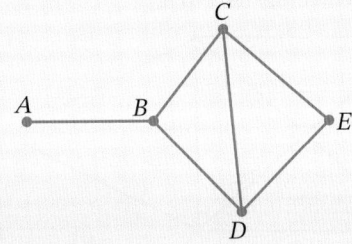

Video
Eulerian
trails

a

Vertex	Degree	Odd or even?	Start here?	Finish point
A	1	odd	yes	B
B	3	odd	yes	A
C	2	even	no	-
D	2	even	no	-
E	2	even	no	-

This network has 2 odd vertices so it is traversable. The start/end points are *A* or *B*.

b

Vertex	Degree	Odd or even?	Start here?	Finish point
A	2	even	yes	A
B	2	even	yes	B
C	4	even	yes	C
D	2	even	yes	D
E	2	even	yes	E
F	2	even	yes	F

This network has all even vertices so it is traversable. All points can be start/end points.

c

Vertex	Number of edges/odd or even	Odd or even?	Start here?	Finish point
A	1	odd	no	-
B	3	odd	no	-
C	3	odd	no	-
D	3	odd	no	-
E	2	even	no	-

This network has 4 odd vertices, so it is **not** traversable.

EXERCISE 9.03 ANSWERS ON P. 644

Traversable networks

U F R C

1 Copy each network and write down the degree of each vertex next to it.

a
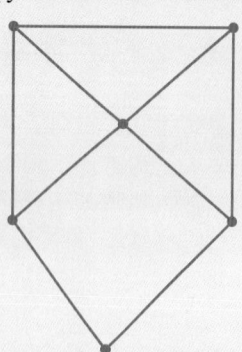

b
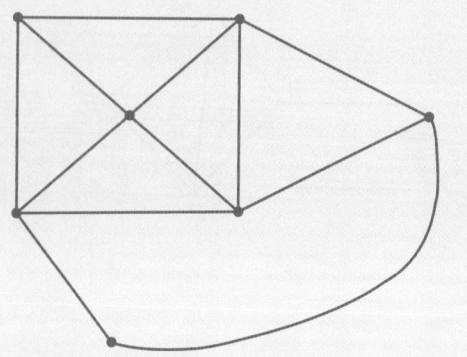

□ Foundation ○ Standard ◇ Complex

2 Copy each network and write odd or even next to each vertex based on its degree.

a
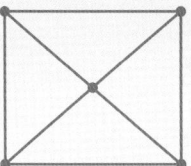

b
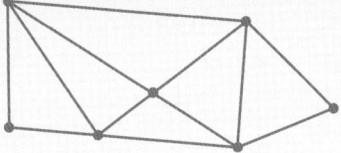

9.03

3 Copy and complete the table for each network in questions **1** and **2**.

Network	Traversable?	Number of odd vertices
1 a		
1 b		
2 a		
2 b		

4 In the ancient Prussian city of Königsberg there were 7 bridges crossing the river.

EXAMPLE
3

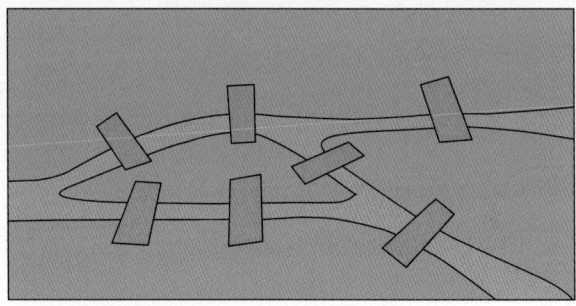

   a   Why was it impossible to cross every bridge only once?

   b   Copy the diagram above and add an 8th bridge to the network so that it is traversable.

5 Determine whether each network is traversable.

a
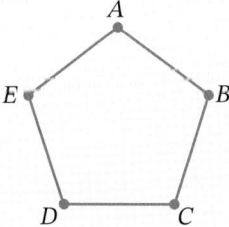

b
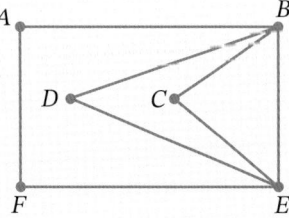

c
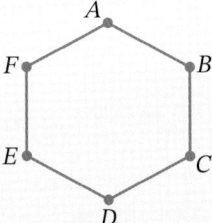

d
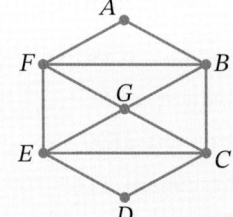

☐ Foundation   ◯ Standard   ◯ Complex

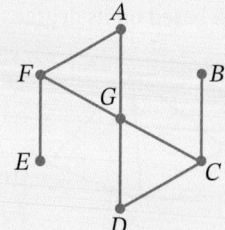

e

f

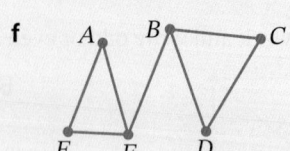

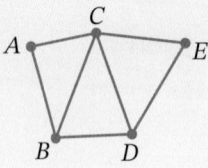

g

h

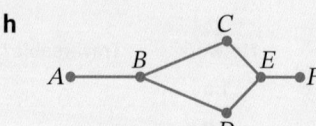

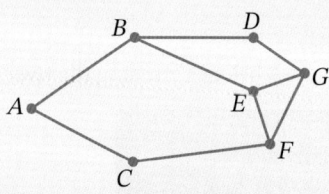

i

j

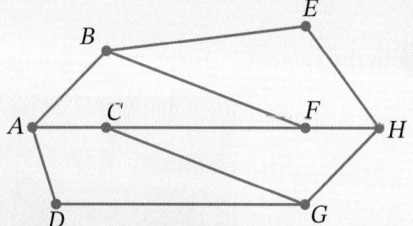

6 Draw a network that has 3 vertices, 8 edges and state how many faces it has.

7 Is the network you drew in question **7** traversable? If not, add edge(s) to make it traversable.

Quiz
Mental
skills 9

☆ **MENTAL SKILLS** (9) ANSWERS ON P. 645 **Maths without calculators**

The unitary method with percentages

1 Study each example.

a If 8% of a number is 24, what is the number?

8% of the number = 24

∴ 1% of the number = 24 ÷ 8 = 3

∴ 100% of the number = 3 × 100 = 300

The number is 300.   Check: 8% × 300 = 24

b If 15% of an amount is $90, what is the whole amount?

15% of the amount = $90

∴ 1% of the amount = $90 ÷ 15 = $6

∴ 100% of the amount = $6 × 100 = $600

The amount is $600.   Check: 15% × $600 = $90

☐ Foundation   ○ Standard   ○ Complex

2 Find the whole amount if:

a   5% of the amount is $35   b   11% of the amount is $88

c   20% of the amount is 80   d   6% of the amount is 42

e   90% of the amount is $270   f   15% of the amount is $60

g   40% of the amount is 100   h   120% of the amount of $360

i   25% of the amount is $75   j   8% of the amount is 40

Spanning trees

A **tree** is a network in which any 2 vertices are connected by only one path. This means that a tree is connected and has no cycles (enclosed faces).

These are trees.

These are not trees.

           Not connected.   Contains a cycle, so 2 vertices can be connected by different paths.

A **spanning tree** in a network is a tree in the network that connects all the vertices.
A network can have many different spanning trees

Example 4

Draw 4 different spanning trees for this network.

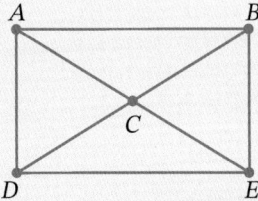

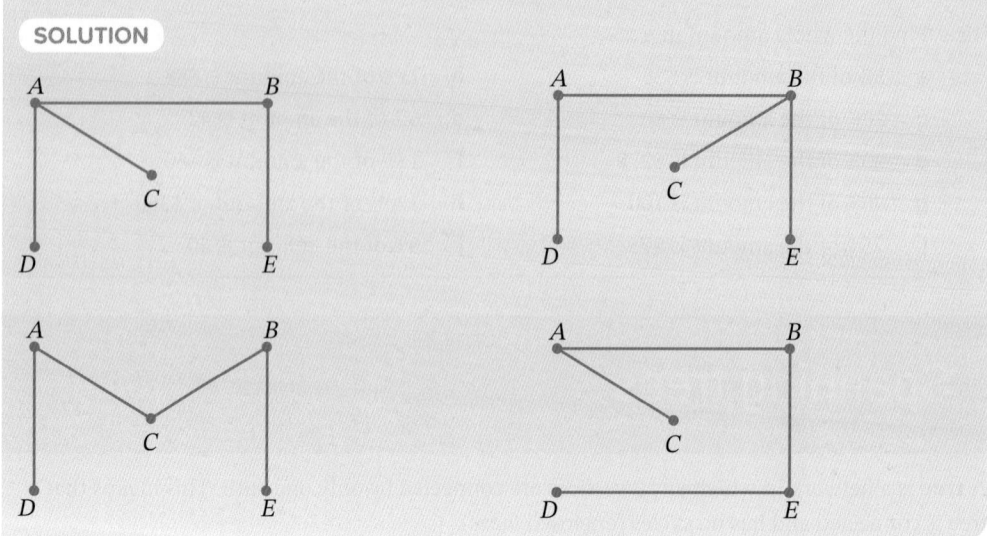

Networks can have numbers shown on their edges that might represent a distance between two vertices or the cost of providing a service between two vertices.

Example 5

This network diagram represents 8 computers that are to be connected with optical fibre cables. The numbers show the costs (in $100s) of the cables.

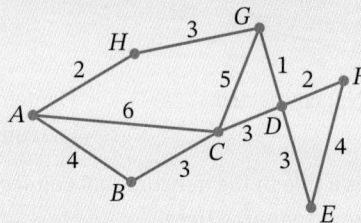

Draw 2 spanning trees for the network and determine the better option.

Two possible spanning trees (shown in red) are:

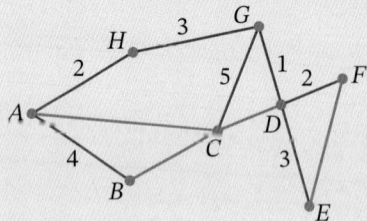 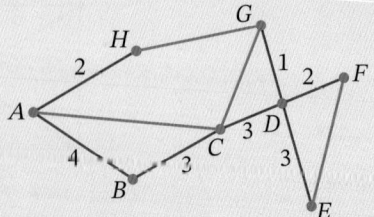

weight = 2 + 4 + 3 + 5 + 1 + 2 + 3

   = 20

cost = $2000

weight = 2 + 4 + 3 + 3 + 3 + 1 + 2

   = 18

cost = $1800

Lower cost, so this option is better.

Spanning trees

(U) (F) (R) (C)

1 For each network, state whether or not it is a tree. Give reasons if not.

a

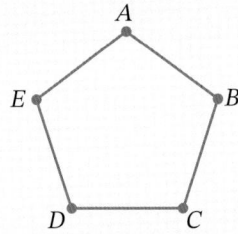

b

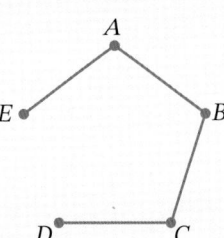

c

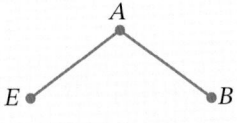

d

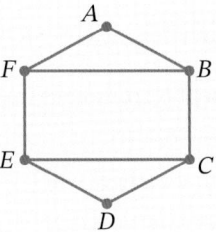

e

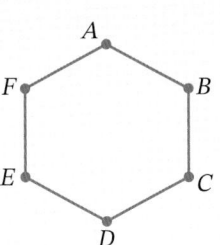

f

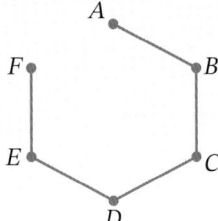

g

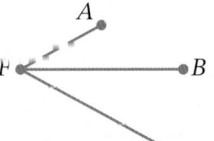

h

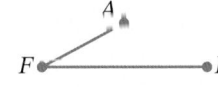

i

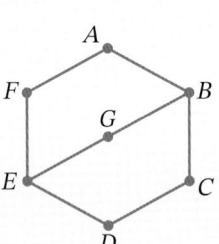

j

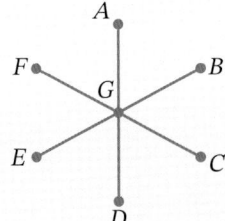

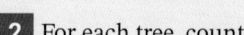

2 For each tree, count:

    i   the number of vertices   **ii**   the number of edges

a

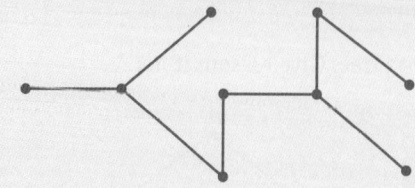

b

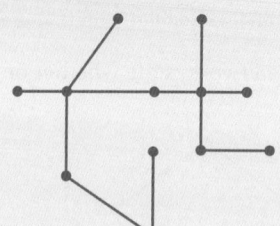

c

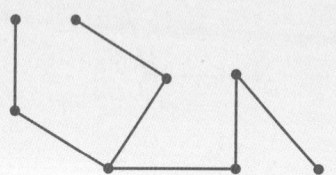

3 Which statement is true about trees? Select the correct answer **A**, **B**, **C** or **D**.

    A   The number of vertices is equal to the number of edges.

    B   A tree with n vertices will have $(n-1)$ edges.

    C   A tree with n vertices will have $(n+1)$ edges

    D   A tree with n vertices will have $2n$ edges.

4 Determine which of the following are spanning trees of the network shown.

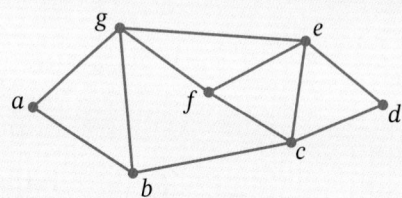

a

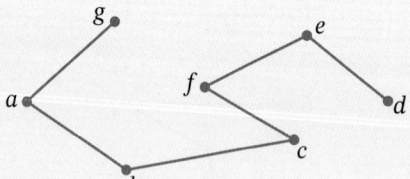

b

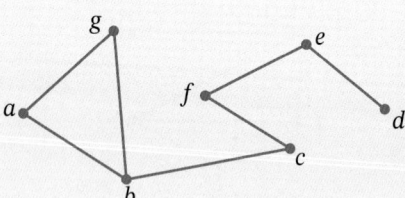

c

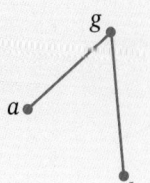

d

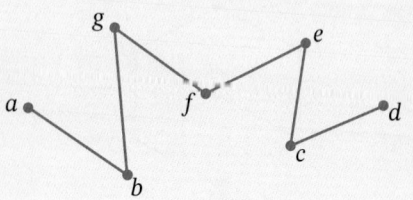

☐ Foundation ○ Standard ◇ Complex

e

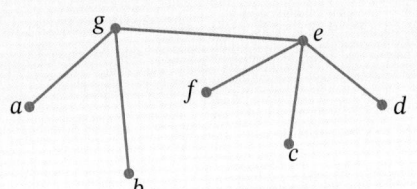

f

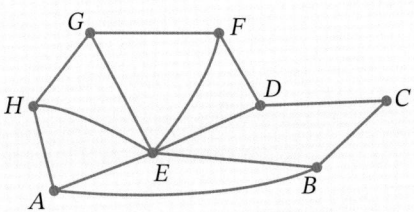

EXAMPLE 4

5 Draw 3 spanning trees for this network.

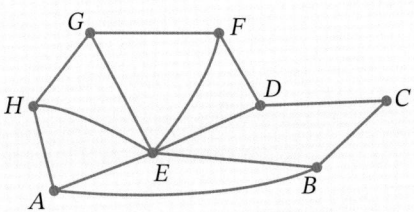

6 Draw a spanning tree for each network.

a

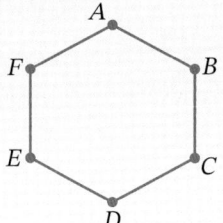

b

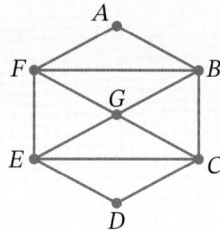

c

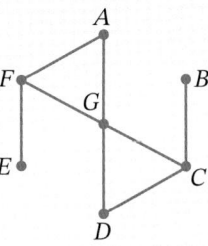

d

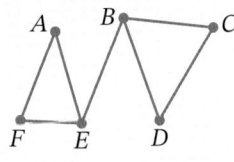

e

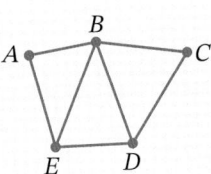

f

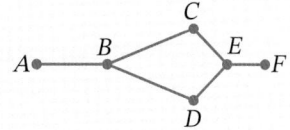

☐ Foundation ○ Standard ○ Complex

EXAMPLE 5

7 This network shows the cost of laying power cables from a mains power supply (*M*) to different areas of a caravan park.

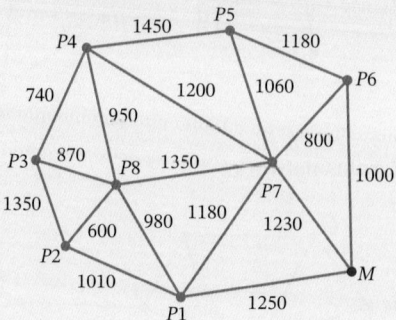

a Spanning trees for the network are shown below. Find the total cost of each tree.

i

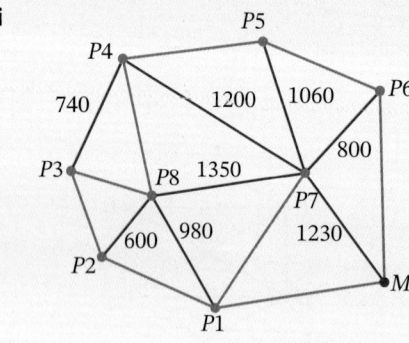

ii

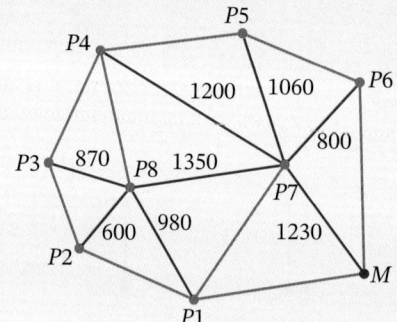

iii

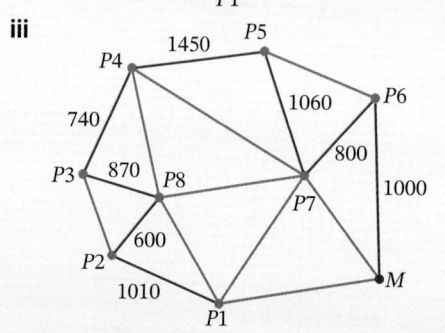

iv

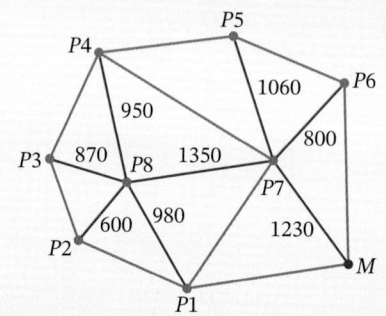

b Which spanning tree is the cheapest option?

8 This network shows the distances between different points in a large garden. Pipes need to be laid so the garden can be watered from a water tank at *T*.

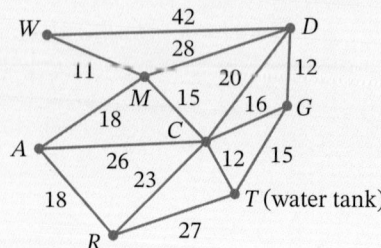

Draw the spanning tree that gives the minimum length of water pipe required to supply water to all parts of the garden.

☐ Foundation ○ Standard ○ Complex

9780170465595

9 This network shows distances between different branches of Laila's pizza store in kilometres.

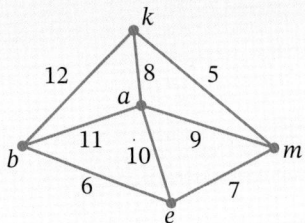

a List the edges of this network in increasing order.

b Use the list to draw the minimum spanning tree of this network.

c What is the weight (total distances) of the minimum spanning tree?

Shortest path

9.05

GPS navigation apps use networks to map out the shortest route between 2 locations, so that you can reach your destination as quickly as possible. On a network diagram of distances between vertices, the shortest path between 2 vertices can be found by looking at the network (by inspection) and using trial and error, or using more formal methods such as a table of vertices and backtracking that considering all possible pathways one vertex at a time.

Example 6

This network shows the travel time, in minutes, along the roads from Abhi's house to Owen's house. Find the shortest path.

Video
Shortest
path

SOLUTION

Method 1

Use a table to keep track of your options, starting with point A. This shows the quickest way to get to each vertex and shows the previous vertex you came from, so that it is easy to backtrack once you have the shortest time.

Vertex	Shortest path to vertex	From vertex
A		Starting point
B	7	A
C	17	B
D	15	B
E	20	C
F	22	E

□ Foundation ○ Standard ◇ Complex

B: Only one way to *B*, from *A*. 7 min.

C: Only one way to *C*, from *B*. $7 + 10 = 17$ min.

D: Only one way to *D*, from *B*. $7 + 8 = 15$ min.

E: 2 ways to *E*, from *C* or *D*. Choose *C*. $17 + 3 = 20$ min.

F: Only one way to *F*, from *E*. $20 + 2 = 22$ min.

To find the path, use the table to backtrack from *F* to *E*, from *E* to *C*, from *C* to *B* and then to *A*.

The shortest path is *A–B–C–E–F* (22 min).

Method 2

This is similar to the table method but using the network diagram instead.

Redraw the network with circles at each vertex.

B: Only one way to *B*, from *A*. 7 min.

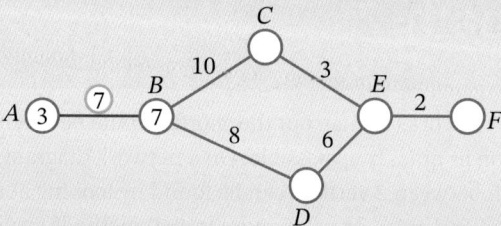

C: Only one way to *C*, from *B*. $7 + 10 = 17$ min.

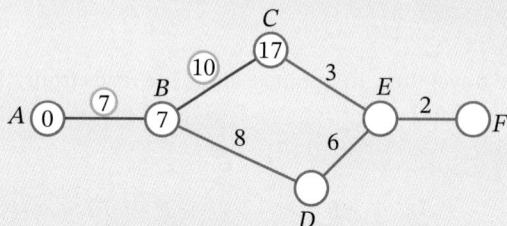

D: Only one way to *D*, from *B*. $7 + 8 = 15$ min.

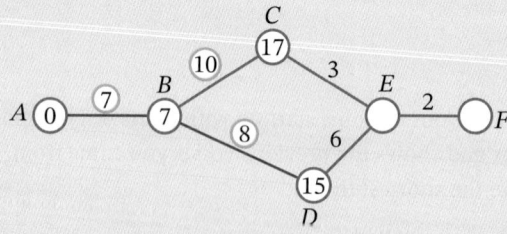

E: 2 ways to *E*, from *C* or *D*. Choose *C*. 17 + 3 = 20 min.

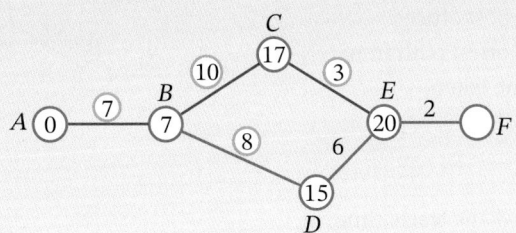

F: Only one way to *F*, from *E*. 20 + 2 = 22 min.

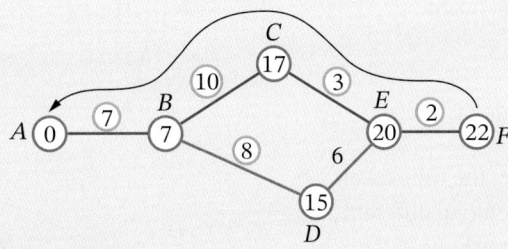

Backtrack along highlighted path to find the shortest path *A–B–C–E–F* (22 min).

EXERCISE 9.05 ANSWERS ON P. 645

Shortest path

U F R C

1 This network shows the travel times, in minutes, between train stations. Write down the shortest path from *A* to *E*, and the time taken.

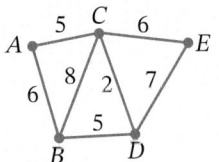

2 This network shows the travel times, in minutes, between small towns. Write down the shortest path from *A* to *F*, and the time taken.

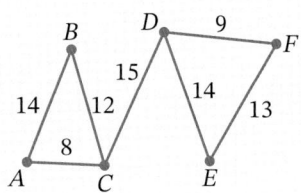

3 This network shows the distances, in kilometres, between large towns. Write down the shortest path from *A* to *G*, and the distance.

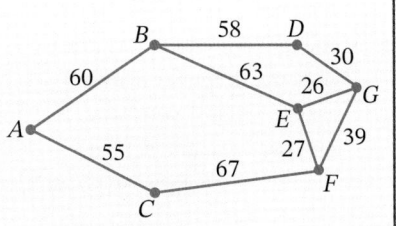

□ Foundation ○ Standard ○ Complex

4 This network shows the travel times, in minutes, between post offices. Write down the shortest path from *A* to *F*, and the time taken.

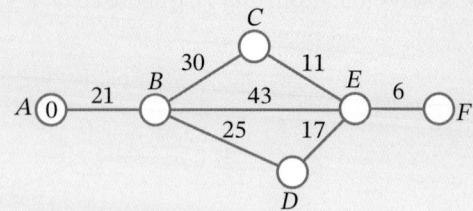

EXAMPLE 8

5 This network shows the travel time, in minutes, along the roads from *A* to *H*. Write down the shortest path from *A* to *G*, and the time taken.

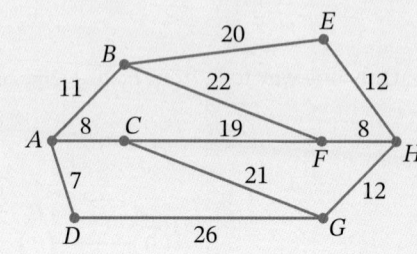

6 This network shows the time taken, in minutes, to walk along different trails in a national park. Find the shortest time taken to walk from the entry to the lake.

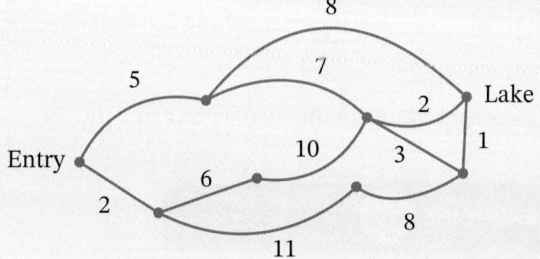

7 Georgia takes a bus between her house and her school. This diagram shows the different bus routes, and the travelling times between stops in minutes. What is the shortest possible time that a bus could take to go from Georgia's house to school?

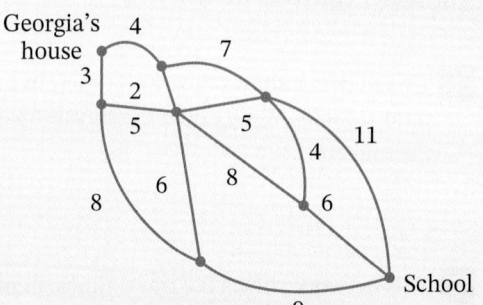

8 This network shows some nature trails and the time taken to walk along each path. Find the shortest distance from the statue to the lookout and determine how much longer it would take if you lost your way and used the longest path.

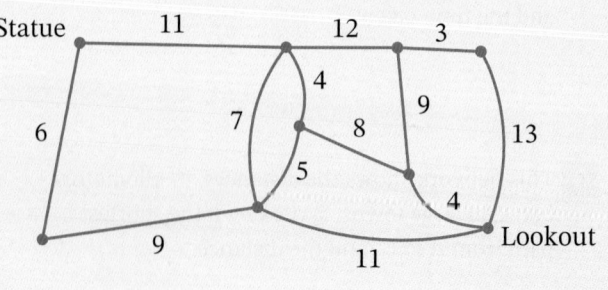

9 This network shows the cost of tickets for travelling by coach on different routes from Armadale to Walpole.

a Find the path that results in the lowest cost.

b Write down 2 reasons someone might pay a fare that is not the lowest to travel from Armadale to Walpole.

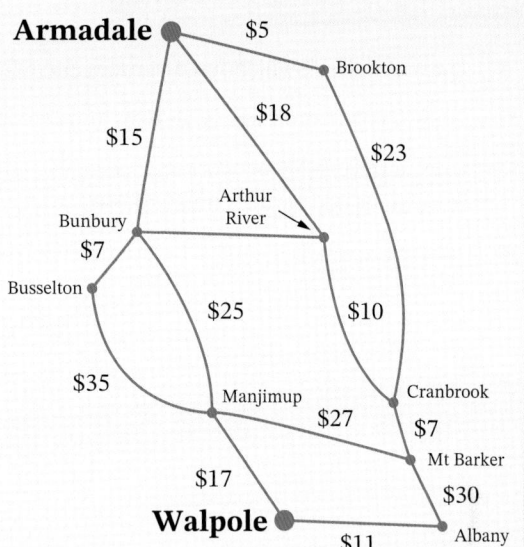

10 The top diagram shows the distances (in km) between suburbs, whereas the bottom diagram shows the driving times (in min) between the suburbs.

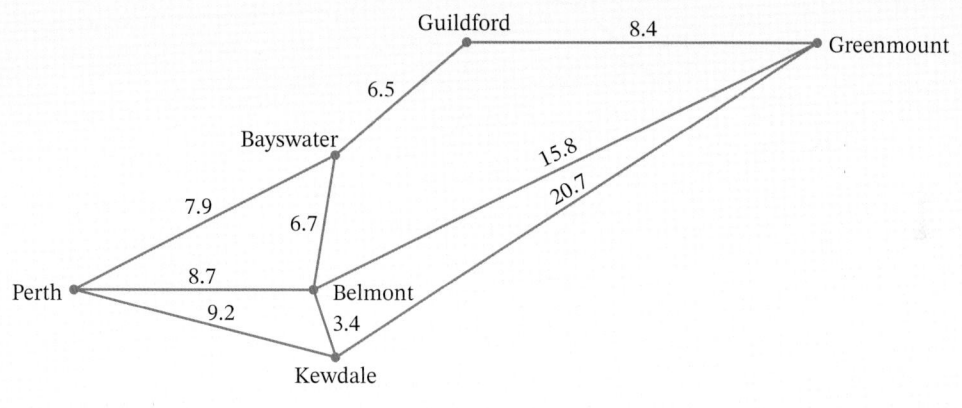

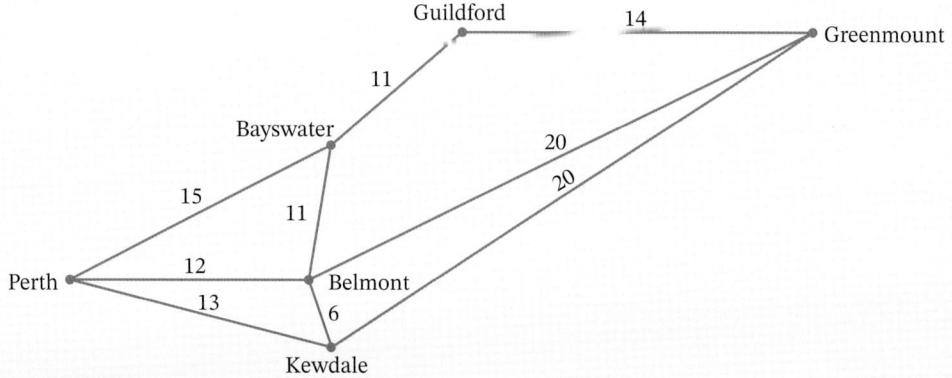

a Find the shortest distance from Perth to Greenmount

b Find the shortest driving time from Perth to Greenmount.

c When might you travel by the shortest time and why would the shortest distance be relevant?

1 Draw a network which has 5 vertices and 6 faces. How many edges must it have?

2 Draw a polyhedron with 9 vertices and 16 edges. How many faces must it have?

3 Draw a traversable network with 9 edges and 5 faces. How many vertices must it have? How many odd vertices must it have?

4 How many spanning trees are possible for this network. Draw them.

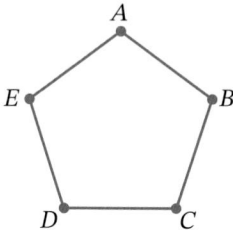

5 Determine the shortest path from A to every other vertex in this network.

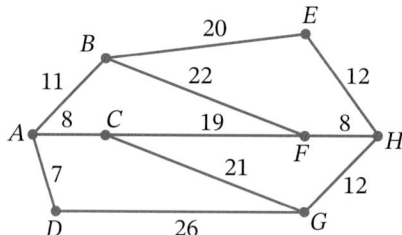

6 Add one path to this network in order to make it traversable.

⑨ CHAPTER REVIEW

Language of maths

degree	dodecahedron	edge	Euler's formula
even	face	graph	hexahedron
icosahedron	minimum	network	octahedron
odd	path	Platonic solid	polygon
polyhedra	polyhedron	shortest path	spanning tree
tetrahedron	traversable	tree	vertex

1 What is **Euler's formula**?

2 What is the more common name for a hexahedron?

3 Why can't a **tree** have a cycle?

4 How many odd vertices can a **traversable network** have? (2 answers)

5 Does a tree have more edges or vertices?

6 How many faces does a tree have?

Topic summary

Print (or copy) and complete this mind map of the topic, adding detail to its branches and using pictures, symbols and colour where needed. Ask your teacher to check your work.

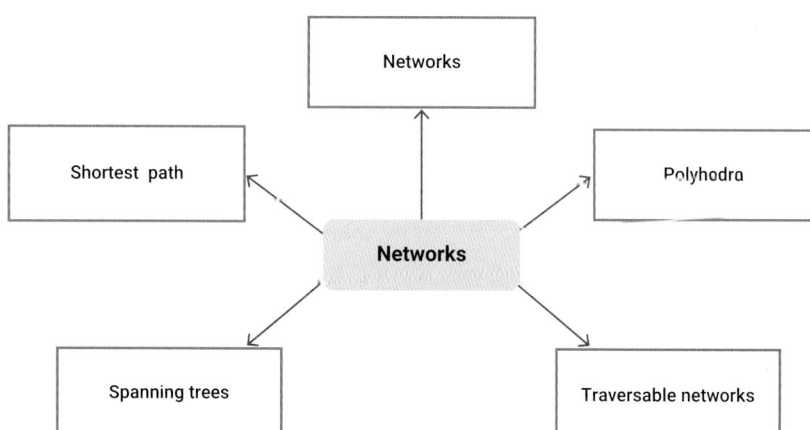

9.01

1 Count the number of faces, vertices and edges on this network and show that it follows Euler's formula $F + V = E + 2$.

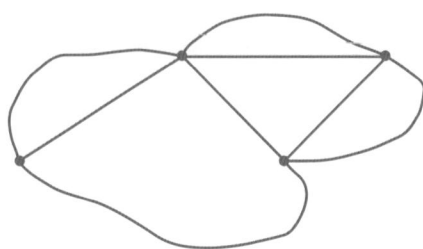

9.01

2 Find the degree of each vertex in this network.

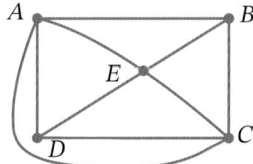

9.02

3 Count the number of faces, vertices and edges on this heptagonal prism and show that it follows Euler's formula $F + V = E + 2$.

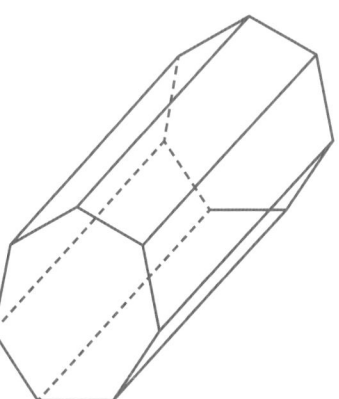

9.03

4 Find a path that shows that this network is traversable.

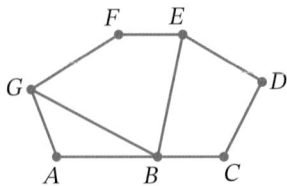

□ Foundation   ○ Standard   ○ Complex

5 Determine whether each network is traversable by counting how many odd vertices it has.

9.03

a

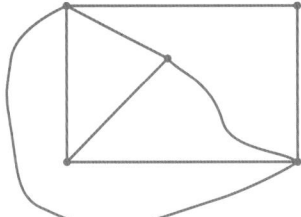

b

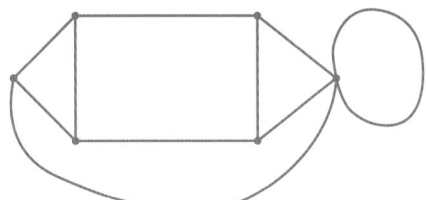

c

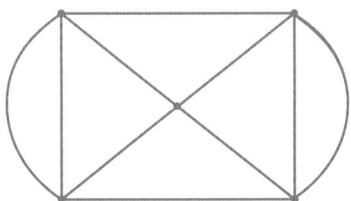

6 Draw 3 possible spanning trees for this network.

9.04

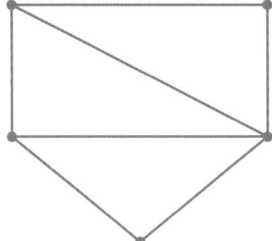

7 This diagram shows the distances in kilometres between suburbs in the inner city. Design a spanning tree for a light rail network that will connect all suburbs using the minimum amount of track.

9.04

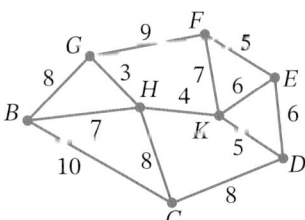

8 Find the shortest path through this network from Start to Finish.

9.05

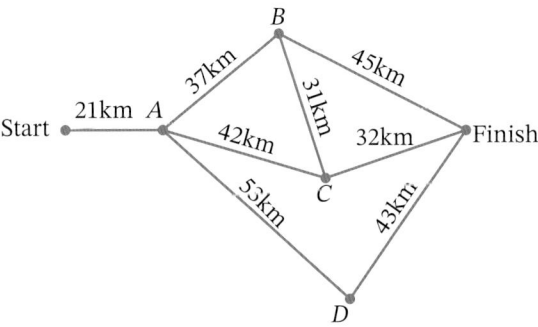

□ Foundation ○ Standard ○ Complex

1 If a network has 3 vertices and 5 faces, how many edges must it have? Explain your reasoning.

 2 *T* varies directly with *h*. If $T = 48$ when $h = 5$, find *T* when $h = 16.5$.

 3 Which of the following points lies on the circle with equation $x^2 + y^2 = 9$? Select the correct answer **A**, **B**, **C** or **D**.

    A   (0, 3)   **B**   (2, 2)   **C**   (4, 1)   **D**   (1.5, 2)

EXTENSION

 4 Find correct to one decimal place:

    a   the area of this triangle

    b   the value of *d*.

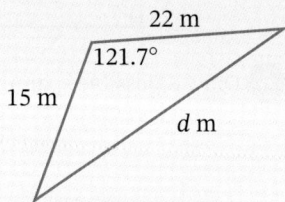

8.08 **5** Find θ, correct to the nearest minute.

    a 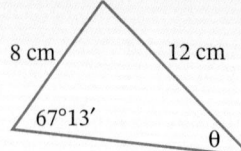   **b** 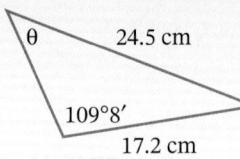   **c**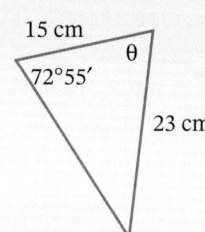

7.01 **6 a** Graph each quadratic equation, showing the vertex of each parabola.

    i $y = x^2 + 2x + 1$ **ii** $y = 4 - x^2$ **iii** $y = 3x^2 + 1$ **iv** $y = 3 - 2x^2$

9.01,
9.03   **b** State which graphs you have drawn in part **a**:

    i   are concave up   **ii**   are concave down   **iii**   have a turning point at (0, 1).

7 a Count the number of faces, vertices and edges of this network.

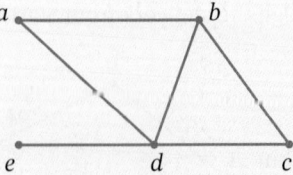

    b Copy the network and then draw a path that shows that this network is traversable.

    c Explain why this network is traversable.

 8 An octahedron has 8 triangular faces and 6 vertices. How many edges does it have? Explain your reasoning.

9 Calculate the value of each variable, correct to one decimal place.

a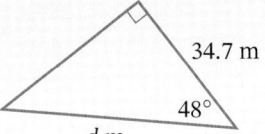

34.7 m

48°

d m

b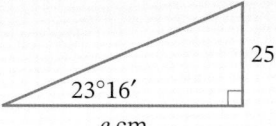

25 cm

23°16′

e cm

c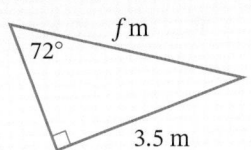

f m

72°

3.5 m

10 Find the exact value of each expression.

a cos 45°   **b** sin 60°   **c** tan 30°   **d** cos 30°

11 A kite is flying at the end of a string that is 85 m long. The string makes an angle of 57° with the ground. At what height is the kite flying? Answer correct to the nearest metre.

12 Which of these could be a graph of $y = 1 - 2x^2$? Select **A**, **B**, **C** or **D**.

A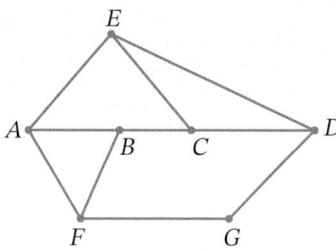

B

C

D

13 Which of the following is a spanning tree of this network? Select **A**, **B**, **C** or **D**.

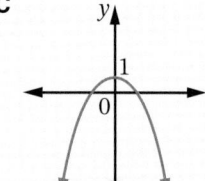

A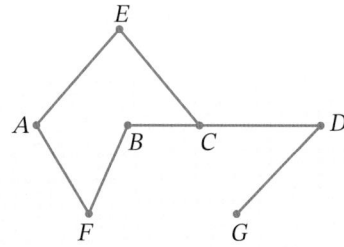

B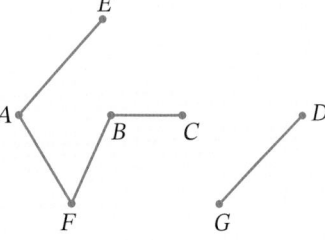

C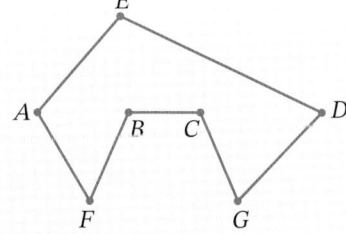

D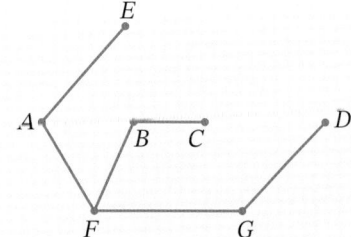

EXTENSION

□ Foundation ○ Standard ◇ Complex

8.01 **14** Find θ, correct to the nearest degree.

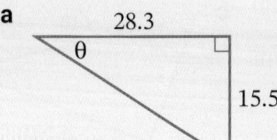

a 28.3 θ 15.5

b 12 θ 17

c 4.9 3.6 θ

8.01 **15** A 4 m ladder is placed against the side of a house. The foot of the ladder is 80 cm from the base of the house. Find the angle between the ladder and the ground, correct to the nearest degree.

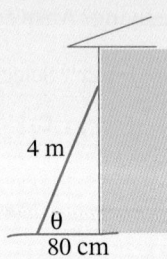

4 m

θ

80 cm

7.06 **16** The temperature of a mug of hot chocolate decreases exponentially by 4.5% each minute. If the initial temperature was 85°C, determine the temperature of the hot chocolate in the mug after 10 minutes.

9.03 **17** Copy the network and add one edge to make it traversable, then explain what has changed in order to make the network traversable.

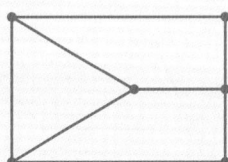

7.01 **18** A parabola has the equation $y = 4x^2 - 3$. Find the x-coordinates of the points on the parabola that have a y-coordinate of 13.

7.06 **19** Sketch each exponential curve, showing the y-intercept.

a $y = 10^x$ **b** $y = 2^x - 3$ **c** $y = 4^{-x}$ **d** $y = 5^x + 2$

20 Match each equation to its graph.

a $y = 2x^2 - 2$	**b** $x = -3$	**c** $y = 2^{-x}$	**d** $x + y = 1$
e $y = 2 - x^2$	**f** $x^2 + y^2 = 1$	**g** $y = 2x^2$	**h** $y = 3^x$
i $3x^2 + 3y^2 = 75$	**j** $y = x$	**k** $y = -3$	**l** $y = 4^x - 1$

A

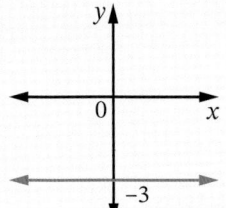

B

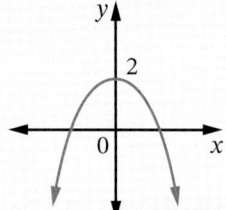

C

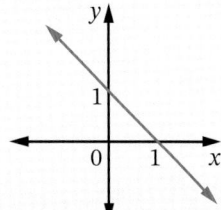

D

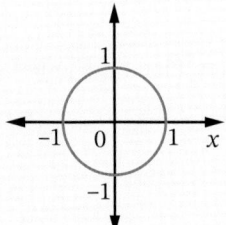

E

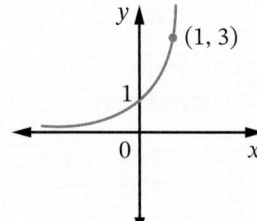

F

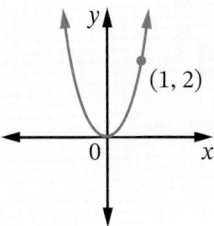

G

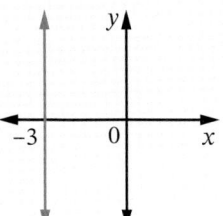

H

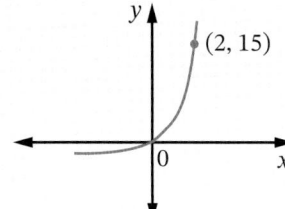

I

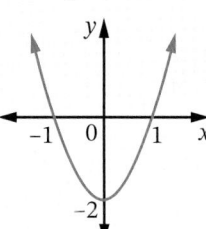

J

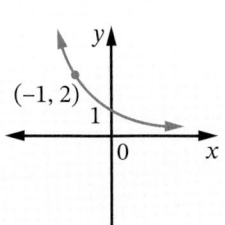

K

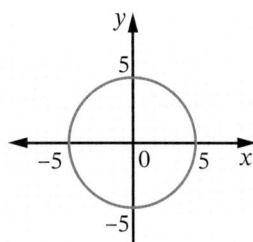

L

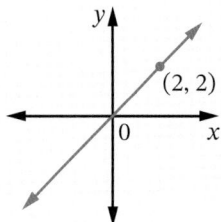

☐ Foundation ◯ Standard ◇ Complex

EXTENSION

8.03

21 A flagpole is at the corner of a rectangular courtyard in a school. The distance from A to the top of the flagpole is 62 metres.

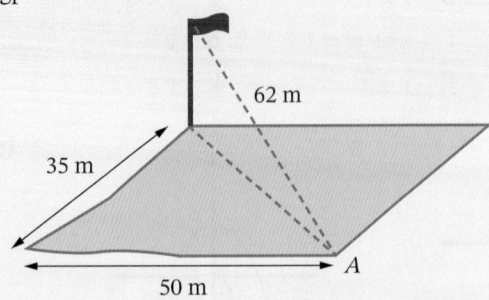

a Calculate, correct to one decimal place, the height of the flagpole.

b Calculate, correct to the nearest minute, the angle of elevation from A to the top of the flagpole.

9.05

22 This network shows the distances between suburbs in kilometres. Find the shortest path from R to N and the distance along this path.

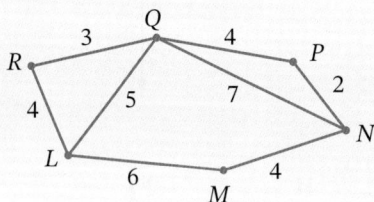

EXTENSION

8.10

23 Find α, correct to the nearest minute.

a

6.4 cm α 7.9 cm

11.5 cm

b

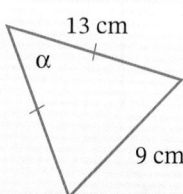

8.01

24 In $\triangle ABC$, $\angle C = 90°$, $AC = 56$ mm and $AB = 72$ mm. Find the size of $\angle B$, correct to the nearest minute.

8.02

25 A plane flies on a bearing of 294° from Canberra for a distance of 740 km.

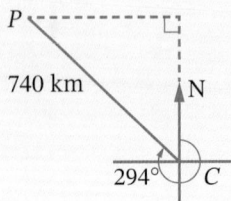

a How far north has the plane travelled (correct to the nearest kilometre)?

b What is the bearing of Canberra from the plane's position?

☐ Foundation   ○ Standard   ◐ Complex

26 R varies directly with M. If $R = 80$ when $M = 50$, what is the value of M when $R = 110$? Select **A**, **B**, **C** or **D**.

A   176   **B**   128   **C**   68.75   **D**   58.25

27 Lord Howe Island is 781 km from Sydney on a bearing of 073°. How far east of Sydney, to the nearest kilometre, is Lord Howe Island?

28 In $\triangle ABC$, $\angle A = 38°$, $a = 7$ cm and $c = 9$ cm. Find the possible values for the size of $\angle C$ (correct to the nearest degree).

29 This network shows the distances in metres between the office and cabins in a coastal holiday resort. Pathways are to be laid between the cabins and the office (*O*).

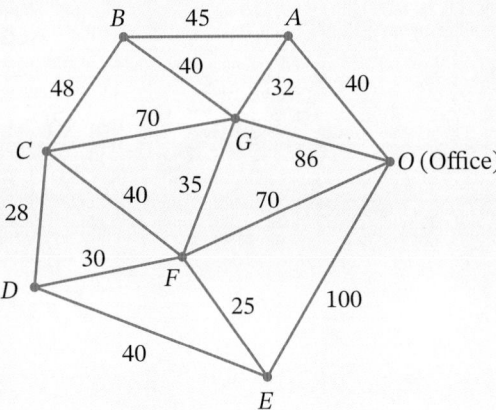

Find the spanning tree that connects all cabins and the office and minimises the total length of the pathways, and state this minimum total length.

10

ALGEBRA

Simultaneous equations

Many scientific, natural, economic and social phenomena can be modelled by equations. Often these models consist of more than one equation. For example, when manufacturing milk, equations can be written that describe relationships between quantity, cost and income. These equations can then be solved simultaneously to obtain information about pricing and the quantities that need to be produced and sold to make the most profit.

Chapter outline

		Proficiencies
10.01	Solving simultaneous equations graphically	U F R C
10.02	The elimination method	U F
10.03	The substitution method	U F
10.04	Problems involving simultaneous equations	U F PS R C

U = Understanding   **R** = Reasoning
F = Fluency   **C** = Communicating
PS = Problem solving

Wordbank

coefficient The numerical part of an algebraic term. For example, in $3x^2 + 7x - 1$ the coefficient of x is 7.

elimination method A method of solving simultaneous equations that involves combining them to eliminate one of the variables.

graphical method A method of solving simultaneous equations that involves graphing them on a number plane and identifying the point(s) of intersection.

simultaneous equations 2 (or more) equations that must be solved together so that the solution satisfies both equations. For example, $y = 2x + 1$ and $y = 3x$ are simultaneous equations that have a solution of $x = 1, y = 3$.

substitution method A method of solving simultaneous equations that involves substituting one equation into another equation.

Quiz
Wordbank 10

10 In this chapter you will:

✓ solve linear simultaneous equations graphically, including using graphing technology
✓ solve linear simultaneous equations algebraically using the elimination and substitution methods
✓ solve problems using linear simultaneous equations

Quiz
SkillCheck 10

SkillCheck
ANSWERS ON P. 647

1 Given the equation $y = 2x + 5$, find y when:

   a $x = 0$ **b** $x = 4$ **c** $x = \dfrac{1}{2}$ **d** $x = -3$

2 Given the equation $y = 4 - 3x$, find y when:

   a $x = 5$ **b** $x = 1$ **c** $x = -1$ **d** $x = -\dfrac{1}{2}$

3 By completing a table of values, graph each equation.

   a $y = x + 1$ **b** $y = 3x$ **c** $y = \dfrac{x}{2} - 1$

   d $y = 3 - x$ **e** $x + y = 4$ **f** $2x - y = 5$

4   Test whether the point $(-2, 3)$ lies on the line represented by each equation.

    a $y = 1 - x$ **b** $x + y = 3$ **c** $2x - y = 7$

    d $\frac{1}{2}x + y = 2$ **e** $y = 3x + 7$ **f** $2y = 3x$

5   **a**   Show that the point $(2, 5)$ lies on both the lines $y = 2x + 1$ and $x + y = 7$.

    b   At what point do these 2 lines intersect?

6   Use the y-intercept and the gradient to graph each equation.

    a $y = -2x + 3$ **b** $y = \frac{5}{2}x - 2$ **c** $y = -\frac{4}{3}x + 5$

INVESTIGATION

When 2 lines meet

1   Copy and complete the table of values for each equation.

    a $x + 2y = 0$

x	-2	-1	0	1	2
y					

    b $y = x + 4$

x	-2	-1	0	1	2
y					

2   Which coordinates satisfy both equations?

3   On the same set of axes, draw the graphs of $x + 2y = 0$ and $y = x + 4$.

4   **a**   Do the lines you drew in question **3** intersect?

    b   What are the coordinates of the point of intersection?

5   Repeat questions **1** to **4** for these pairs of equations.

    a $x - y = 5$ **b** $3x + y = 8$

        $2x + y = 1$ $x + 2y = 1$

6   Copy and complete.

    a   The coordinates of the p_____ of intersection between 2 lines satisfy both equations.

    b   The values of x and y that satisfy both equations are the coordinates of the _____.

10.01 Solving simultaneous equations graphically

Worksheets
Testing simultaneous equations

Intersection of lines

Technology
Solving simultaneous equations

Spreadsheet
Simultaneous equations solver

A linear equation such as $3x + 5 = 11$ is in one variable (x) and has only one solution ($x = 2$). However, a linear equation in **2** variables, such as $x + 3y = 5$, has more than one solution (for example, $x = 2, y = 1$, or $x = 5, y = 0$, and so on). The equation has an **infinite number** of solutions.

We will now look at solving 2 equations simultaneously to see if there is a solution that satisfies **both** equations. These are called **simultaneous equations**, which can be solved **graphically** or **algebraically**.

ⓘ Solving simultaneous equations graphically

- Linear simultaneous equations can be graphed as lines on the same number plane.
- If 2 lines are drawn, the lines will intersect (unless they are parallel).
- At the point of intersection, the x-coordinate and y-coordinate represent the solution to the simultaneous equations.

Example 1

On the same set of axes, graph $3x + y = 4$ and $x + y = -2$, then solve the equations simultaneously.

SOLUTION

Step 1

Construct tables of values.

$3x + y = 4$

x	0	1	2
y	4	1	-2

$x + y = -2$

x	0	1	2
y	-2	-3	-4

Step 2

Graph the equations.

The lines intersect at (3, –5).

∴ the solution of the simultaneous equations $3x + y = 4$ and $x + y = -2$ is $x = 3, y = -5$.

> Check that $x = 3, y = -5$ satisfies both equations.
> $3 \times 3 + (-5) = 9 - 5 = 4$ ✓
> $3 + (-5) = 3 - 5 = -2$ ✓

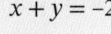
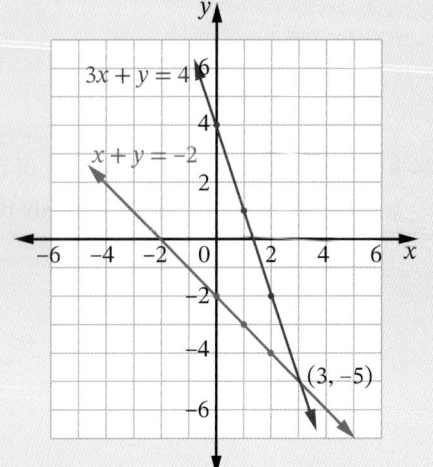

9780170465595

Solving simultaneous equations graphically   U F R C

1 Use the graph to write the solution to each pair
  C of simultaneous equations.

  a $x - y = 4$ and $2x + y = 5$

  b $2x + y = 5$ and $y = 2x - 3$

  c $x - y = 4$ and $y = 2x - 3$

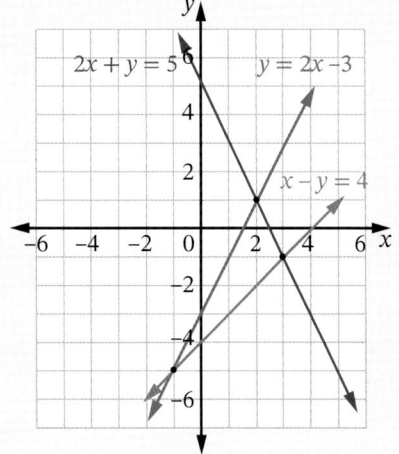

2 Graph each pair of equations on the same set of axes. Use the graph to determine the
solution to the pair of simultaneous equations.

  a $y = 2x$ and $y = 3 - x$ **b** $y = 2x + 1$ and $y = x - 4$

  c $x + y = 3$ and $4x + y = 6$ **d** $y = -x + 2$ and $y = 3x + 4$

  e $y = 2x - 5$ and $y = 5x + 1$ **f** $2x + y = 6$ and $y = 1 - x$

  g $y = 7 - x$ and $y = 3x + 5$ **h** $x + 2y = 7$ and $2x - y = 4$

  i $3x - 2y = 12$ and $x + 2y = 8$ **j** $y = x + 3$ and $2x - y = 2$

  k $5x - y = 5$ and $x + y = 4$ **l** $5x + 3y = 20$ and $y = x - 4$

EXAMPLE
1

3 a   On the same set of axes, draw the graphs of $y = 1 - 2x$ and $2x + y = 4$.

  R **b**   Why isn't there a solution to the equations $y = 1 - 2x$ and $2x + y = 4$ in part **a**?

  C

□ Foundation   ○ Standard   ◇ Complex

Solving simultaneous equations graphically

You can use graphing technology to solve simultaneous equations graphically.
Write each answer as coordinates in the form (x, y) representing the point of intersection.

1   Use the graphing software to graph these linear equations.

$y = -x + 1$

$y = x + 3$

2   Find the coordinates of the point of intersection of the lines.

3   Repeat the method used in questions **1** and **2** to solve each pair of
simultaneous equations.

a $y = 2$	**b** $y = -2x + 4$	**c** $y = 5x + 2$	**d** $y = -1$
$x = 3$	$y = x - 5$	$y = 3x - 1$	$x = 0$
e $y = -x - 8$	**f** $y = 2x + 6$	**g** $2x - y = 5$	**h** $3x + y = 4$
$y = -3x + 4$	$y = x + 9$	$x + y = 4$	$x + 2y = 3$

4   **a**   Use the graphing software to graph each pair of simultaneous equations.

   i $y = x + 4$ **ii** $y = -2x + 2$

   $y = x + 6$ $y = -2x$

   b   What do you notice about these 2 pairs of equations? Do they intersect?

5   Graph each set of equations and find their point of intersection.

   a $y = 3x, y = -x + 2$ and $x = 0.5$

   b $y = -4x + 1, y = -5x$ and $y = x + 6$

10.02 The elimination method

Using graphs to solve simultaneous equations can be time-consuming and inaccurate.

Algebraic methods provide a better way of solving things. There are 2 algebraic methods: the
elimination method and the **substitution method**.

In the elimination method, equations are added or subtracted to eliminate one of the variables.

Example 2

Solve the simultaneous equations $x + 3y = 7$ and $4x - 3y = 13$ using the elimination method.

SOLUTION

Label each equation.

$x + 3y = 7$ [1]

$4x - 3y = 13$ [2]

Since there is the same number of ys in each equation, and since they are opposite in sign ($3y$ and $-3y$), add equations [1] and [2] to eliminate the variable y.

$5x = 20$ [1] + [2]

$\dfrac{5x}{5} = \dfrac{20}{5}$

$\therefore x = 4$

Substitute $x = 4$ into equation [1] to find the y value.

$x + 3y = 7$

$4 + 3y = 7$

$4 + 3y - 4 = 7 - 4$

$3y = 3$

$\therefore y = 1$

$\therefore$ the solution is $x = 4$, $y = 1$.   Check that this solution works for both equations [1] and [2].

Example 3

Solve the simultaneous equations $2k + 3m = 9$ and $2k - 5m = 1$.

SOLUTION

Label each equation.

$2k + 3m = 9$ [1]

$2k - 5m = 1$ [2]

Since there is the same number of ks in each equation, and because they have the same sign ($2k$ and $2k$), subtract equation [2] from [1] to eliminate k.

$8m = 8$ [1] - [2]

$\dfrac{8m}{8} = \dfrac{8}{8}$

$\therefore m = 1$

Substitute $m = 1$ into equation [1] to find the value of k.

$2k + 3m = 9$

$2k + 3 \times 1 = 9$

$2k + 3 = 9$

$2k + 3 - 3 = 9 - 3$

$2k = 6$

$\dfrac{2k}{2} = \dfrac{6}{2}$

$\therefore k = 3$

$\therefore$ the solution is $m = 1$, $k = 3$.   Check that this solution works for both equations [1] and [2].

Example 4

Solve $3a + 4c = 8$ and $2a - 3c = 11$.

SOLUTION

Label each equation.

$3a + 4c = 8$ [1]

$2a - 3c = 11$ [2]

In this case, neither adding nor subtracting equations [1] and [2] will eliminate a variable. Let's choose to eliminate c. We need to make the **coefficient** of c the same in both equations ($12c$).

The **coefficient** of c is the number in front of the c in the equation.

$9a + 12c = 24$ [3]   multiplying both sides of [1] by 3

$8a - 12c = 44$ [4]   multiplying both sides of [2] by 4

      $17a = 68$ [3] + [4]

      $\therefore a = 4$

Substitute $a = 4$ in [1] to find c.

    $3a + 4c = 8$

$3 \times 4 + 4c = 8$

    $12 + 4c = 8$

        $4c = -4$

         $c = -1$

$\therefore$ the solution is $a = 4$, $c = -1$.

EXERCISE 10.02 ANSWERS ON P. 649

The elimination method

(U) (F)

EXAMPLE **2**

1 For each pair of simultaneous equations, eliminate one variable by adding the equations, then solve the equations.

a $4k + d = 5$ **b** $2x - w = 6$ **c** $3g + 5h = 4$
    $2k - d = 7$ $x + w = 9$ $2g - 5h = 6$

d $7p - 4n = -20$ **e** $4q + 3r = 8$ **f** $-5k - 3x = 8$
    $3p + 4n = 10$ $-q - 3r = 7$ $5k + 4x = -3$

g $-4c - 6e = -12$ **h** $-3y + 5k = 21$ **i** $a + 3f = 8$
    $4c - 10e = -4$ $3y + k = -3$ $-a + 4f = 6$

2 For each pair of simultaneous equations, eliminate one variable by subtracting the equations, then solve the equations.

EXAMPLE 3

a $5k + d = 16$
$3k + d = 4$

b $4a + 3c = 7$
$a + 3c = 4$

c $4h + 3y = 24$
$4h - y = 8$

d $3x + 5e = 16$
$3x - 2e = -5$

e $4q - 2w = -1$
$7q - 2w = 8$

f $6p + 5c = 39$
$4p + 5c = 31$

g $5y + 3m = 18$
$2y + 3m = 6$

h $3a + 2r = 8$
$a + 2r = 10$

i $-x + 5w = 8$
$-x + 3w = 4$

j $4y + 7g = 2$
$4y - 3g = 22$

k $2e - 3n = 14$
$5e - 3n = -1$

l $7k - 5h = 31$
$7k + 3h = 43$

3 Solve each pair of simultaneous equations.

a $3w + q = 6$
$2w - 3q = 15$

b $2x + m = 5$
$3x + 2m = 3$

c $2d + 3h = 25$
$d + 4h = -5$

d $-3g + 2n = 9$
$g + 5n = 14$

e $5m - h = 10$
$m - 3h = 2$

f $2y + 3e = -6$
$5y - 2e = 23$

g $3q - 2w = 11$
$2q - 5w = 22$

h $5a + 3d = 4$
$4a + 2d = 3$

i $-2p + 3k = 19$
$7p + 4k = 6$

j $5a + 2f = -14$
$2a - 3f = 2$

k $5r - 3c = 2$
$-3r + 2c = -14$

l $5y - 4x = 1$
$2y - 3x = 6$

m $3x + 4y = 20$
$2x - 5y = 21$

n $7g + 3h = 39$
$3g + 5h = 26$

o $5w - 3k = 25$
$3w - 7k = 28$

The substitution method

With the substitution method, **substitute** the x or y variables from one equation into the other equation.

Example 5

Solve the simultaneous equations $y = x + 4$ and $y = 3x - 2$.

SOLUTION

Label each equation.
$y = x + 4$ [1]
$y = 3x - 2$ [2]

Video Simultaneous equations 1

Puzzles Simultaneous equations order activity

Simultaneous equations by substitution

Use equation [1] to substitute for y in equation [2] and solve for x.

$$x + 4 = 3x - 2$$
$$x + 4 - 3x = 3x - 2 - 3x$$
$$-2x + 4 = -2$$
$$-2x + 4 - 4 = -2 - 4$$
$$-2x = -6$$
$$\frac{-2x}{-2} = \frac{-6}{-2}$$
$$x = 3$$

Now substitute $x = 3$ into equation [1] to find y.

$$y = x + 4$$
$$y = 3 + 4$$
$$= 7$$

$\therefore$ the solution is $x = 3$ and $y = 7$.

Example 6

Video
Simultaneous
equations 2

Solve the simultaneous equations $5x + 3y = 9$ and $y = 7 - 3x$.

SOLUTION

Label each equation.

$$5x + 3y = 9 \quad [1]$$
$$y = 7 - 3x \quad [2]$$

Since y is the subject in [2], substitute equation [2] into equation [1] to give an equation using x only.

$$5x + 3(7 - 3x) = 9$$
$$5x + 21 - 9x = 9$$
$$-4x = -12$$
$$\frac{-4x}{-4} = \frac{-12}{-4}$$
$$x = 3$$

Now substitute $x = 3$ into equation [2] to find y.

$$y = 7 - 3x$$
$$y = 7 - 3 \times 3$$
$$= -2$$

$\therefore$ the solution is $x = 3$ and $y = -2$.

9780170465595

The substitution method   (U)(F)

1 Use the substitution method to solve each pair of simultaneous equations.

EXAMPLE
5

a $y = 2x + 1$ and $y = x + 3$ b $y = 5 - 2x$ and $y = 3x + 2$

c $x = 3 + 2y$ and $x = 9 - y$ d $y = -x$ and $y = 3x - 8$

e $x = 1 - 4y$ and $x = 2y + 7$ f $x = 2y$ and $x = 6 - y$

2 Solve each pair of simultaneous equations.

EXAMPLE
6

a $y = 2x + 3$ and $3x - y = 6$ b $y = x - 2$ and $3x + y = 18$

c $y = 1 - 4x$ and $4x + 2y = 3$ d $x = 2y - 5$ and $4x - y = -13$

e $x = 3y - 4$ and $5x - 4y = 2$ f $x = 5 - 3y$ and $4y - x = 23$

g $2x - 5y = -1$ and $y = 10 - x$ h $6y - 2x = 9$ and $y = \frac{x+2}{2}$

i $x = \frac{9-y}{3}$ and $3x + 2y = 10$ j $y = 3x + 5$ and $4x - 3y = 1$

INVESTIGATION

Elimination or substitution method?

With 2 algebraic methods of solving simultaneous equations, often it is more efficient to use one method than the other.

1   Consider these pairs of simultaneous equations.

   a $x - 2y = 9$ [1]   b $4a + 3c = 18$ [1]   c $3a - 2y = -5$ [1]

     $3x + 2y = 11$ [2] $4a - 3c = -6$ [2] $2a + 5y = 3$ [2]

    i   Why might the **elimination method** be the more appropriate method to use with these equations?

    ii   What feature in the pairs of equations do you look for to decide if the elimination method is the best one to use?

    iii   Solve the 3 pairs of simultaneous equations using the elimination method.

2   Consider these pairs of simultaneous equations.

   a $m = 2p$ [1]   b $m = 4 - p$ [1]   c $p = 2m - 5$ [1]

     $m + p = 15$ [2] $4m - 3p = -6$ [2] $5m - 3p = 11$ [2]

    i   Why might the **substitution method** be the more appropriate method to use with these equations?

    ii   What feature in the pairs of equations do you look for to decide if the substitution method is the best one to use?

    iii   Solve the 3 pairs of simultaneous equations using the substitution method.

▷

☐ Foundation   ○ Standard   ○ Complex

3   Using whichever method is more efficient, solve each pair of simultaneous equations.

a $7c + 2y = 13$ [1]
    $3c + 2y = 1$ [2]

b $m = 5 - k$ [1]
    $2m - k = 4$ [2]

c $3x + 8y = 10$ [1]
    $x = 3 - 2y$ [2]

d $4h - 3w = 8$ [1]
    $4h + 7w = 12$ [2]

e $3d = q$ [1]
    $q + 4d = 14$ [2]

f $3h + 5r = 7$ [1]
    $2h - 3r = -8$ [2]

Break-even point

Manufacturers use simultaneous equations to make decisions about how many products they should make and sell. Linear equations can be formed to determine total revenue (the amount made from selling products) and total costs (the cost of making the products).

Total revenue = cost per item × number of items made.

Total costs include rent and production costs.

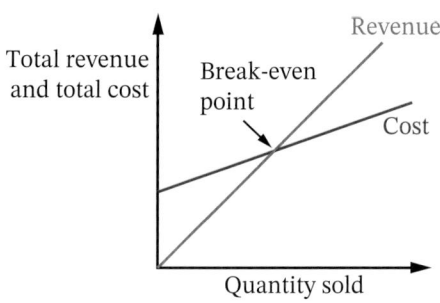

The equations can be graphed as shown. The point where the 2 lines intersect is called the **break-even point** and occurs when total revenue is equal to total cost.

A publisher receives $35 per book sold. There are fixed costs of $110 000 and production costs per book are $8.50.

a   **Determine the equations for total revenue and total costs.**

b   **Graph the equations to find the break-even point.**

c   **How many books must be sold before the publisher makes a profit?**

Sometimes, worded problems can be solved using simultaneous equations. In these situations, follow these steps:

1 Read the problem carefully.

2 Identify the variables to be used.

3 Use the variables to write simultaneous equations from the information given in the problem.

4 Solve the equations.

5 Solve the problem by answering in words.

Video
The chase

Worksheet
Simultaneous equations problems

Presentation
Simultaneous equations

Example 7

At an art show there were 520 guests. If there were 46 more women than men, how many women attended the show?

SOLUTION

Let the number of women attending be w.

Let the number of men attending be m.

$w + m = 520$ [1]	520 people altogether
$w = m + 46$ [2]	46 more women than men

Use equation [2] to substitute for w in equation [1].

$$m + 46 + m = 520$$
$$2m + 46 = 520$$
$$2m + 46 - 46 = 520 - 46$$
$$2m = 474$$
$$m = 237$$

Substitute $m = 237$ into equation [2] to find w.

$$w = 237 + 46$$
$$= 283$$

∴ there were 283 women who attended the art show.

Video
Simultaneous
equations
problems

Example 8

Masi and Amir spent $1582 on shrubs and trees to plant on their large block of land. Altogether they bought 73 plants. The shrubs cost $19 each, whereas the trees cost $32 each. How many of each plant did they buy?

SOLUTION

Let x be the number of shrubs.

Let y be the number of trees.

$\therefore x + y = 73$ [1]   73 plants altogether

and $19x + 32y = 1582$ [2] $19 per shrub plus $32 per tree equals $1582

Neither adding nor subtracting equations [1] and [2] will eliminate a variable. Let's choose to eliminate x.

We will need to make the coefficient of x the same in both equations ($19x$).

$19x + 32y = 1582$ [2]

$19x + 19y = 1387$ [3]   multiplying both sides of equation [1] by 19

$\qquad 13y = 195$ [2] – [3]

$\qquad\quad y = 15$

Substitute $y = 15$ in [1] to find the value of x.

$\quad x + y = 73$

$x + 15 = 73$

$\qquad x = 58$

So, Masi and Amir bought 58 shrubs and 15 trees.

EXERCISE 10.04 ANSWERS ON P. 650

Problems involving simultaneous equations   (U) (F) (PS) (R) (C)

EXAMPLE
7

1 At a school concert, there were 640 people in the audience. There were 70 more women
(R) than men. How many of the audience were men?
(C)

2 At a circus, there were twice as many children as there were adults in attendance.
(R) Altogether, 1020 attended the circus. How many were children?
(C)

3 Tickets to a concert cost $15 for children and $28 for adults. Altogether, 650 people attended the concert and ticket sales totalled $13 052. Let a stand for the number of adults and c stand for the number of children in the audience.

    a Explain why the equations $a + c = 650$ and $28a + 15c = 13\ 052$ correctly match the information.

    b Solve the equations simultaneously to find the number of children that attended the concert.

EXAMPLE 8
10.04

4 Ashleigh bought a total of 130 meat pies and sausage rolls for the canteen of the local football club. Each meat pie cost her $3 and the sausage rolls were $2 each. Altogether, Ashleigh spent $335. How many sausage rolls did she buy?

5 Tayyab is 3 times as old as Sejuti. The sum of their ages is 48. How old is Tayyab and how old is Sejuti?

6 The sum of the ages of Hayley and her mother is 70. The difference between their ages is 38 years. How old is Hayley?

7 A business bought a total of 60 ink cartridges. Some of them were black, costing $35 each. The others were colour, each costing $49. How many of each type did the business buy if the total cost of the ink cartridges was $2422?

8 The cost of going to the movies for 3 adults and 5 children is $142, whereas the cost for 5 adults and 8 children is $231.50. Find the cost for an adult and the cost for a child.

9 Raj's Pizzas sells supreme pizzas for $15.90 each and vegetarian pizzas for $13.50 each. If 45 pizzas were sold at lunchtime, totalling $684.30, how many of each pizza were sold?

10 Patrick bought 4 punnets of strawberries and 7 punnets of blueberries for $40.30. Eden bought 5 punnets of strawberries and 2 punnets of blueberries for $26.75. What was the cost of each punnet of strawberries and blueberries?

11 A money box contains only 20-cent coins and 50-cent coins. Altogether, there are 853 coins in the money box and they amount to $281. Let x be the number of 20c coins and y be the number of 50c coins.

    a Explain why the equations $x + y = 853$ and $20x + 50y = 28\ 100$ correctly match the information.

    b Solve the equations to determine the number of 20-cent and 50-cent coins in the money box.

□ Foundation   ○ Standard   ◇ Complex

12 The initial cost for producing bottles of fresh orange juice is $135 plus $1.20 for each bottle. The bottles of juice are sold for $3 each. C is the cost in dollars, R is the total sales in dollars and n is the number of bottles produced and/or sold.

PS
R
C

a Explain why the equations $C = 135 + 1.2n$ and $R = 3n$ correctly match the information.

b Copy and complete the tables of values below for both equations.

$C = 135 + 1.2n$

n	0	50	100
C			

$R = 3n$

n	0	50	100
R			

c Draw the graphs of both equations on the same axes for values of 0 to 100 for n on the horizontal axis and values of $0 to $300 on the vertical axis.

d For what value of n is total sales equal to total cost (the break-even point)?

Quiz
Mental
skills 10

☆ **MENTAL SKILLS** (10) ANSWERS ON P. 650 | **Maths without calculators**

Simplifying fractions and ratios

When simplifying a fraction or a ratio, look for a common factor to divide into both the numerator and the denominator, preferably the highest common factor (HCF).

1 Study each example.

a Simplify $\dfrac{27}{45}$

$$\dfrac{27^{9}}{45^{15}} = \dfrac{9}{15}$$ \qquad dividing numerator and denominator by 3

$$\dfrac{9^{3}}{15^{5}} = \dfrac{3}{5}$$ \qquad dividing numerator and denominator by 3 again

Note: This fraction could be simplified in one step if you divided by 9, the highest common factor (HCF) of 27 and 45.

b Simplify $\dfrac{160}{400}$

$$\dfrac{160^{16}}{400^{40}} = \dfrac{16}{40}$$ \qquad dividing numerator and denominator by 10

$$\dfrac{16^{2}}{40^{5}} = \dfrac{2}{5}$$ \qquad dividing numerator and denominator by 8

Note: This fraction could be simplified in one step if you divided by 80, the HCF of 160 and 400.

☐ Foundation ○ Standard ◇ Complex

c Simplify 24 : 36.

$24^4 : 36^6 = 4 : 6$ dividing both terms by 6

$4^2 : 6^3 = 2 : 3$ dividing both terms by 2

Note: This fraction could be simplified in one step if you divided by 12, the HCF of 24 and 36.

d Simplify 135 : 90.

$135^{27} : 90^{18} = 27 : 18$ dividing both terms by 5

$27^3 : 18^2 = 3 : 2$ dividing both terms by 9

e Calculate $\dfrac{3}{8} \times \dfrac{2}{15}$ in simplest form.

$\dfrac{3}{8^4} \times \dfrac{2^1}{15} = \dfrac{3}{4} \times \dfrac{1}{15}$ dividing 2 and 8 by 2

$\dfrac{3^1}{4} \times \dfrac{1}{15^5} = \dfrac{1}{20}$ dividing 3 and 15 by 3

f What fraction is 36 minutes of 1 hour?

$\dfrac{36}{1 \text{ hour}} = \dfrac{36 \text{ min}}{60 \text{ min}} = \dfrac{3}{5}$ dividing 36 and 60 by 12

2 Now simplify each fraction or ratio.

  a $\dfrac{10}{15}$ **b** $\dfrac{16}{20}$ **c** $\dfrac{30}{42}$ **d** $\dfrac{8}{16}$

  e $\dfrac{20}{80}$ **f** $\dfrac{6}{36}$ **g** $\dfrac{20}{24}$ **h** $\dfrac{12}{30}$

  i 20 : 36   **j** 25 : 45   **k** 18 : 40   **l** 28 : 35

  m 27 : 21   **n** 16 : 12   **o** $\dfrac{5}{6} \times \dfrac{18}{25}$ **p** $\dfrac{12}{50} \times \dfrac{10}{21}$

3 Express each as a simplified fraction.

  a 425 g of 1 kg   **b** 8 months of 1 year   **c** 64 cm of 1 m

  d 750 mL of 3 L   **e** 10 hours of 2 days   **f** 80c of $10

1   With simultaneous equations in 2 variables, we have 2 equations to solve.
    With simultaneous equations in 3 variables, we have 3 equations to solve.

    Step 1: Take 2 of the equations and eliminate one of the variables.

    Step 2: Take another 2 of the equations and eliminate the same variable.

    Step 3: Solve the 2 new simultaneous equations from Steps 1 and 2.

    Step 4: Use substitution to find the values of the other 2 variables.

    Use the above steps to solve the following sets of simultaneous equations.

    a $2x + y - 3w = -16$ **b** $3a - 2c + d = 5$ **c** $2m + 3n - p = 9$

    $x - y + 4w = 25$ $5a + 2c + d = 25$ $3m - 2n + 5p = 27$

    $3x - y + 2w = 19$ $4a + 3c - d = 10$ $4m + 3n + 2p = 13$

2   **a**   Show that the solutions to the simultaneous equations $ax + by = c$ and $dx + ey = f$
        are $x = \dfrac{ce - bf}{ae - bd}$ and $y = \dfrac{af - cd}{ae - bd}$.

    b   The solutions in part **a** do not work when $ae = bd$. Explain why.

    c   Solve the equations $3x - 2y = 11$ and $5x + y = 14$ by either the substitution or
        elimination method. Check that the results in part **a** give the same answer.

    d   Set up a spreadsheet to solve simultaneous equations of the form $ax + by = c$ and
        $dx + ey = f$ using the solutions $x = \dfrac{ce - bf}{ae - bd}$ and $y = \dfrac{af - cd}{ae - bd}$.

        Use your spreadsheet to solve each pair of simultaneous equations.

        i $3x + y = 4$ **ii** $3x - 5y = 4$ **iii** $15x + 6y = 17$

            $2x - y = 6$ $2x - 3y = 8$ $2x + 3y = 8$

⑩ CHAPTER REVIEW

Language of maths

algebraic	axes	coefficient	elimination method
graphical	linear	point of intersection	satisfy
simultaneous equations	solution	substitution method	variable

Quiz
Language of maths 10

Puzzle
Simultaneous equations crossword

1 How do you think **simultaneous equations** got their name?

2 What are the 2 algebraic methods for solving simultaneous equations?

3 Which algebraic method involves cancelling one of the variables?

4 What word means the answer to an equation or problem?

5 What does '**linear**' mean?

6 Which method of solving simultaneous equations involves finding the point of intersection of lines on a number plane?

Topic summary

Worksheet
Mind map: Simultaneous equations

• In your own words, write down the new things you have learnt about simultaneous equations.

• What parts of this topic did you like?

• What parts of the topic did you find difficult or not understand?

Print (or copy) and complete this mind map of the topic, adding detail to its branches and using pictures, symbols and colour where needed. Ask your teacher to check your work.

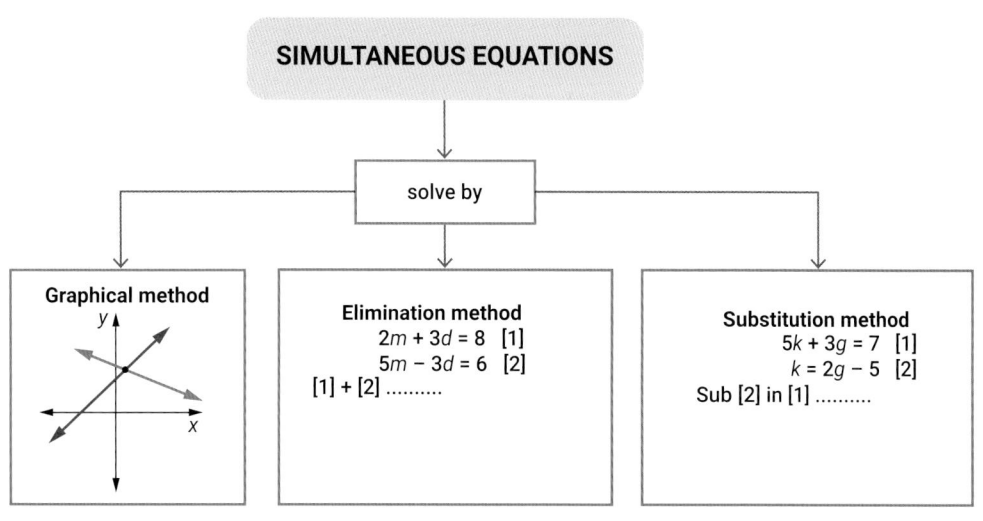

Quiz
Test
yourself 10

(10.01) **1** Use the graph to write the solution to each pair of simultaneous equations.

   a $x - y = 4$ and $2x + y = 2$

   b $2x + 5y = 8$ and $x - y = 4$

   c $2x + 5y = 8$ and $2x + y = 2$ (fractional answers)

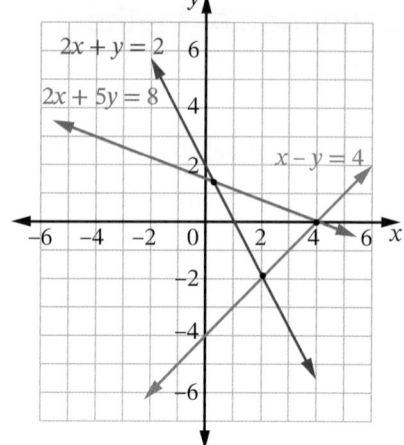

(10.01) **2** Graph each pair of simultaneous equations on the same set of axes. By finding their point of intersection, write the solution to each pair of equations.

  a $y = x + 2$ **b** $y = 3 - \dfrac{x}{2}$ **c** $y = 4 - 3x$

       $y = 6 + 2x$ $y = 2x - 7$ $y = x$

  d $y = 2x + 3$ **e** $x + y = 7$ **f** $y = 5 - 2x$

       $y = 9 - x$ $y = 2x + 1$ $y = -1 - x$

(10.02) **3** Use the elimination method to solve each pair of simultaneous equations.

  a $5m + 2c = 6$ **b** $2x + 3y = 5$ **c** $3a + 4d = 7$

       $3m + 2c = -4$ $5x - 3y = 9$ $3a + d = 4$

  d $4x - y = 9$ **e** $x - 4y = 3$ **f** $3d - 2w = 11$

       $x - y = -9$ $x + 2y = -9$ $2d - 5w = 44$

(10.03) **4** Use the substitution method to solve each pair of simultaneous equations.

  a $y = 7x - 3$ **b** $m = 4 - p$ **c** $h = 3t - 2$

       $y = x + 9$ $m = -2 + p$ $h = t + 6$

  d $a = 4 - 2c$ **e** $x + 2y = 3$ **f** $p = 4 - 2q$

       $a = 6c$ $y = 2 - x$ $p = 3q + 24$

□ Foundation ○ Standard ○ Complex

5 Solve each problem using simultaneous equations.

a In an audience of 2500, there were 700 more adults than children. Find the number of adults and the number of children that were in the audience.

b Rosanna bought 30 movie passes as raffle prizes at a school fete for a total cost of $322.50. Movie passes for children cost $8.25 each and the adult price was $14.50. How many of each did she buy?

c It costs 2 adults and 5 children $191 to go to a football game, whereas the cost for 3 adults and 2 children is $160. Find the cost of an adult ticket.

d At a cake stall, the student council sells 2 types of cakes: cheesecakes for $4 each and mud cakes for $3 each. Altogether, they sold 75 cakes for a total of $253. How many of each cake did they sell?

e In Year 10, there are 213 students. There are 27 more boys than girls. Find the number of boys and girls in Year 10.

CHAPTER 10 TEST YOURSELF

11

PROBABILITY

Probability

Probability theory, the study of chance, began in the 17th century when 2 great mathematicians, Blaise Pascal and Pierre de Fermat, wrote to each other to discuss mathematical problems arising from games of chance. Since then, probability has become an essential branch of mathematics that is used widely in fields such as weather forecasting, finance, insurance, politics and medical testing.

stock.adobe.com/Alberto

Chapter outline

		Proficiencies				
11.01 Relative frequency	U	F			R	C
11.02 Venn diagrams	U	F			R	C
11.03 Two-way tables	U	F			R	C
11.04 Tree diagrams	U	F	PS		R	C
11.05 Selecting with and without replacement	U	F	PS		R	C
11.06 Conditional probability	U	F	PS		R	C
11.07 Dependent and independent events	U	F	PS		R	C
11.08 Probability simulations	U	F			R	C
11.09 The multiplication principle of counting*	U	F	PS		R	C
11.10 Permutations*	U	F			R	
11.11 Combinations*	U	F	PS		R	

*EXTENSION

U = Understanding
F = Fluency
PS = Problem solving

R = Reasoning
C = Communicating

Wordbank

relative frequency The frequency of an event over repeated trials as a fraction of the total number of trials.

simulation A way of imitating or mimicking a probability experiment using technology or actual objects such as dice, coins, spinners and cards.

tree diagram A diagram of branches for listing all the possible outcomes of a multi-step chance experiment.

trial One go or run of a repeated probability experiment; for example, one roll of a die.

two-step experiment A chance experiment with 2 steps or stages, such as rolling a pair of dice.

two-way table A way of grouping items into 2 overlapping categories, such as height and the ability to drive a car.

Venn diagram A diagram of circles (usually overlapping) for grouping items into categories.

Quiz
Wordbank 11

11 **In this chapter you will:**

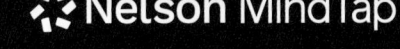

✓ calculate the probabilities and relative frequencies of events

✓ describe compound events using terminology such as 'and', exclusive 'or', inclusive 'or' and 'at least'

✓ use Venn diagrams and two-way tables to represent sample spaces and compound events to solve probability problems

✓ use tree diagrams and tables (arrays) to represent the sample space of two- and three-step chance experiments, with and without replacement, to solve probability problems

✓ solve problems involving conditional probability

✓ identify dependent and independent events, and use the product rule for independent events

✓ design and use probability simulations to model situations involving compound events and conditional probability

✓ (EXTENSION) use the multiplication principle to count the number of possible outcomes in multi-stage events

✓ (EXTENSION) understand and calculate permutations and combinations

1 If a die is rolled, which of the following is more likely? Select the correct answer **A**, **B**, **C** or **D**.

    A a number less than 3   **B** an even number

    C a number that is 3 or more   **D** a number that is a prime number

2 A bag contains five 10-cent coins, four 20-cent coins and three 50-cent coins. A coin is drawn at random from the bag.

    a How many outcomes are in the sample space?

    b Are the outcomes equally likely?

3 For this spinner, the red sector is twice as large as each of the other sectors.

Find the probability that when the spinner is spun, the arrow lands on:

    a red

    b purple or blue

    c not green.

4 A normal die is rolled. What is the probability of rolling:

    a a 7   **b** a number less than 7?

5 The probability of Danica hitting a bullseye when playing darts is 0.6. What is the probability of Danica not hitting the bullseye?

6 Aditi bought 10 tickets in a raffle in which 400 tickets were sold and there is only one prize. What is the probability that Aditi will win the prize? Select **A**, **B**, **C** or **D**.

    A $\frac{1}{400}$ **B** 2.5%   **C** 0.0025   **D** 0.975

7 The probability of cloudy skies tomorrow is 0.85. What is the probability of clear skies?

Quiz
SkillCheck 11

Worksheet
Probability
review

Relative frequency

11.01

Probability calculated using the formula:

$$P(\text{event}) = \frac{\text{number of favourable outcomes}}{\text{total number of outcomes}}$$

is more specifically called **theoretical probability**.

We can also determine probability based on the results of a **trial** that has been repeated many times, such as testing the effectiveness of 100 light globes, or rely on past statistics, such as weather patterns or the ages of drivers having car accidents. This type of probability is called **experimental probability** or **observed probability**, which is based on **relative frequency**, the number of times an **event** occurred as a fraction of the total frequency of **outcomes**.

Videos
Experimental
probability

Freak waves

Worksheet
Relative
frequencies

Interactive
Plinko
probability

Puzzle
Dice
probability

Technology
Long-run
proportion

Spreadsheet
Long-run
proportion

(i) Experimental probability

$$P(E) = \frac{\text{number of times the event happened}}{\text{total number of trials}}$$

$$\text{or } P(E) = \frac{\text{frequency of } E}{\text{total frequency}}$$

Expected frequency is the expected number of times an event will occur over repeated trials.

(i) Expected frequency

expected frequency = theoretical probability × number of trials.

Example 1

This spinner was spun 160 times and the results are shown.

Outcome	Frequency
Red	30
Blue	32
Yellow	50
Purple	48

a Calculate, as a decimal:

  i the experimental probability that the arrow stops on blue

  ii the theoretical probability that the arrow stops on blue.

b Are the experimental and theoretical probabilities similar?

c If the spinner is spun 500 times, calculate the expected frequency of the arrow stopping on purple based on the theoretical probability.

SOLUTION

a **i** Experimental probability:

$$P(\text{blue}) = \frac{32}{160}$$

$$= 0.2$$

ii Theoretical probability:

$$P(\text{blue}) = \frac{1}{6}$$

$$= 0.1666\ldots$$

$$\approx 0.17$$

b By comparing the decimals for the 2 answers, we see that the experimental and theoretical probabilities are similar.

c expected frequency of purple $= \frac{1}{3} \times 500$ probability × number of trials

$$= 166.6666\ldots$$

$$\approx 167$$

Example 2

James rolled a die 100 times and recorded the results in a table.

Outcome	Frequency
1	23
2	19
3	11
4	12
5	18
6	17

a Find the experimental probability of rolling:

   i an even number

   ii an even number or a number greater than 4

   iii an even number less than or equal to 4.

> 'Even number or a number greater than 4' is an example of a **compound event**.

b Calculate the probability of rolling a 2 or 3:

   i as an experimental probability

   ii as a theoretical probability.

c If the die is rolled 100 times, what is the expected frequency of rolling a 2 or a 3?

How does this compare with James' observed frequency?

SOLUTION

a **i**   rolls of even numbers $= 19 + 12 + 17$ frequencies for outcomes 2, 4, 6

$$= 48$$

experimental $P(\text{even}) = \dfrac{48}{100} = \dfrac{12}{25}$

   ii   rolls of even numbers or numbers   frequencies for outcomes 2, 4, 6, 5
greater than $4 = 19 + 12 + 17 + 18$

$$= 66$$

experimental $P(\text{even or} > 4) = \dfrac{66}{100} = \dfrac{33}{50}$

   iii   rolls of even numbers less than or   frequencies for 2 and 4
equal to $4 = 19 + 12$

$$= 31$$

experimental $P(\text{even and} \leq 4) = \dfrac{31}{100}$

b **i**   rolls of 2 or 3 $= 19 + 11$ frequencies for 2 and 3

$$= 30$$

experimental $P(2 \text{ or } 3) = \dfrac{30}{100} = \dfrac{3}{10}$

   ii   theoretical $P(2 \text{ or } 3) = \dfrac{2}{6} = \dfrac{1}{3}$

c   expected frequency of 2 or 3 $= \dfrac{1}{3} \times 100$ probability $\times$ number of trials

$$= 33.333\ldots$$

$$\approx 33$$

From the table, the observed frequency $= 19 + 11 = 30$, which is close to 33.

Relative frequency

(U) (F) (R) (C)

EXAMPLE
1

1 Aashima spun this spinner 200 times and recorded the results.

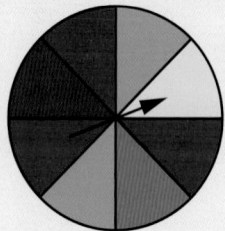

Event	Frequency
Red	85
Green	42
Blue	28
Yellow	15
Purple	30

a Calculate, as a decimal, the experimental probability that the arrow points to:

   i red   **ii** blue   **iii** green

b Calculate, as a decimal, the theoretical probability that the arrow points to:

   i red   **ii** blue   **iii** green

c Are the experimental and theoretical probabilities similar?

d For 200 spins, what is the expected frequency of red or purple based on the theoretical probability? How does this compare with the observed frequency?

2 A coin is tossed.

a What is the expected number of heads if the coin is tossed 100 times?

b Toss a coin 100 times. Copy this table and record your results in it.

Outcome	Frequency
Head	
Tail	

c Calculate, as a decimal:

   i the experimental probability of tossing a head

   ii the theoretical probability of tossing a tail.

d Are the experimental and theoretical probabilities similar?

EXAMPLE
2

3 A die was repeatedly rolled and the results are shown in the table.

a How many times was the die rolled?

b Find the experimental probability (as a decimal) of rolling:

   i an odd number   **ii** a number less than 4

   iii a 2 or a 3

   iv a number less than 4 or an even number.

c Find the theoretical probability (as a decimal) of rolling:

   i an odd number   **ii** a number less than 4

   iii a 2 or a 3   **iv** a number less than 4 or an even number.

d Compare the experimental probabilities to the theoretical probabilities.

Outcome	Frequency
1	95
2	119
3	108
4	87
5	78
6	113

▢ Foundation ◯ Standard ◯ Complex

▷

4 Tara spun this spinner 50 times and the results are shown.

R
C

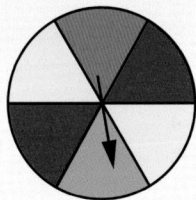

Event	Frequency
Red	15
Blue	6
Yellow	24
Green	5

a What is the experimental probability (as a decimal) of the arrow stopping on

    i red?   **ii** blue?   **iii** yellow?   **iv** green?

b What is the theoretical probability (as a decimal) of the arrow stopping on

    i red?   **ii** blue?   **iii** yellow?   **iv** green?

c Are the experimental and theoretical probabilities similar?

d What is the expected frequency of the arrow stopping on a colour that is not yellow? How does this compare with Tara's observed frequency?

5 Two dice are rolled and the sum of the numbers rolled was recorded in the frequency histogram.

a How many times were the dice rolled?

b Based on these results, what is the experimental probability of rolling a sum:

    i of 2?   **ii** of 7?

    iii of 10?   **iv** greater than 7?

    v less than 7?   **vi** of 7 or 8?

    vii that is even and greater than 6?

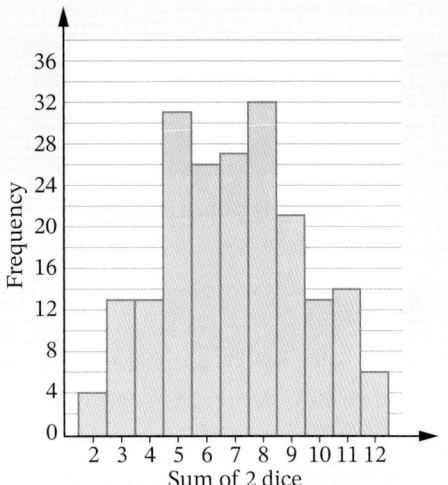

6 Children at a shopping mall were asked how they travelled to school.

R
C

a How many students were surveyed?

b Based on these results, find the probability that a student chosen at random will:

    i walk to school

    ii be driven to school

    iii catch a bus to school

    iv catch a train to school

    v ride a skateboard to school.

Mode of transport	Frequency
Walk	27
Bus	80
Car	62
Train	21
Bicycle	5
Skateboard	1
Other	4

c What mode of transport could 'Other' include?

d Survey 100 students at your school and make up a table showing the results. How do the results from your school compare with the results from the survey?

Foundation   Standard   Complex

7 A die is rolled 100 times.

a What is the probability of rolling a 6? (Express your answer as a fraction and as a decimal.)

b How many times would you expect a 6 to appear if the die was rolled 100 times?

c Roll a die 100 times and record your results in a table similar to the one shown.

d What is the relative frequency of rolling a 6? (Express your answer as a fraction and as a decimal.)

e How does the theoretical probability of rolling a 6 compare with the experimental probability?

Outcome	Tally	Frequency
1		
2		
3		
4		
5		
6		

8 'If there are 10 horses in a race, the probability of each horse winning is 1 in 10'. Explain why this statement is not true. Give at least 2 reasons.

11.02 Venn diagrams

A **Venn diagram** is a diagram of circles (usually overlapping) that is used to group items into categories.

Videos
Venn diagrams 1

Venn diagrams 2

Puzzle
Venn diagrams matching activity

Example 3

This Venn diagram shows the results of a survey on what type of movies – action (A), comedy (C) or drama (D) – students prefer to watch.

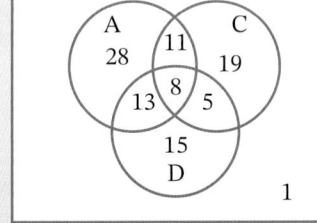

a How many students were surveyed?

b How many students preferred to watch 2 types of movies only?

c Calculate, as a decimal, the probability of selecting a student who prefers to watch:

   i action movies only   **ii** action or comedy movies, but not dramas

   iii action and drama movies   **iv** all types.

d A student is chosen from those who like action and comedy movies. What is the probability that they also like to watch drama movies?

e What is the probability of selecting a student who does not like watching any of the 3 movie types?

☐ Foundation   ○ Standard   ◇ Complex

SOLUTION

a Number of students $= 28 + 11 + 8 + 13 + 5 + 19 + 15 + 1$

$$= 100$$

b 29 students preferred 2 types of movies only. $11 + 13 + 5 = 29$

c **i** Students preferring action movies only $= 28$

the region of A that doesn't overlap C or D

$$P(\text{action only}) = \frac{28}{100} = 0.28$$

    ii Students preferring action or comedy only

the regions of A and C that don't overlap with D

$$= 28 + 19 + 11 = 58$$

$$P(\text{action or comedy only}) = \frac{58}{100} = 0.58$$

> 'Action or comedy only' is an example of a **compound event**.

    iii Students preferring action and drama $= 13 + 8 = 21$

the regions where A and D intersect

$$P(\text{action and drama}) = \frac{21}{100} = 0.21$$

    iv Students preferring all types $= 8$

the region where the 3 circles intersect

$$P(\text{all types}) = \frac{8}{100} = 0.08$$

d Students preferring action and comedy $= 11 + 8 = 19$

Students preferring action and comedy and drama $= 8$

$$P(\text{drama if preferring action and comedy}) = \frac{8}{19} \approx 0.42$$

e There is one student who doesn't prefer action, comedy or drama.

$$P(\text{not action, comedy or drama}) = \frac{1}{100} = 0.01$$

When we combine 2 or more simple events, we get a **compound event**. In the above example, 'action and drama' and 'all types' are compound events.

'And' vs 'or'

For 2 categories or events A and B, the compound event '**A and B**' means to have both of them occurring together. For example, 'to drive a car' **and** 'to ride a bus' means to do both things.

If A and B are **overlapping**, the compound event '**A or B**' means to have A or B or both. For example, 'to drive a car' or 'to ride a bus' means to drive a car only, or to ride a bus only, or to do both. In this case, 'A or B' actually **includes** 'A and B' so this is an example of an **inclusive** 'or'.

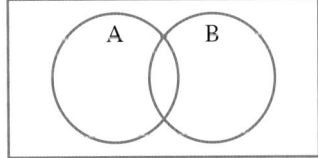

Overlapping events:
'A or B' means A or B or both

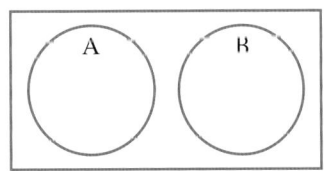

Mutually exclusive events:
'A or B' means A or B but not both

If A and B are **mutually exclusive**, this means that they are **not overlapping** and on a Venn diagram they appear as 2 separate circles. For mutually exclusive categories or events, the phrase '**A or B**' means to have A only or B only (but not both). For example, 'male' **or** 'female' means to be male or female, but not both. In this case, 'A or B' **excludes** 'A and B' so this is an example of an **exclusive** 'or'.

Example 4

A survey of 110 students at Hamper Valley College showed that 34 students study Art, 65 students study Chemistry, and 23 students study both Chemistry and Art.

a Represent this information on a Venn diagram.

b How many students study Art and Chemistry, but not both?

c What is the probability of randomly selecting a student from this group who takes:

  i Chemistry

  ii Art and Chemistry

  iii Art or Chemistry

  iv neither Art nor Chemistry?

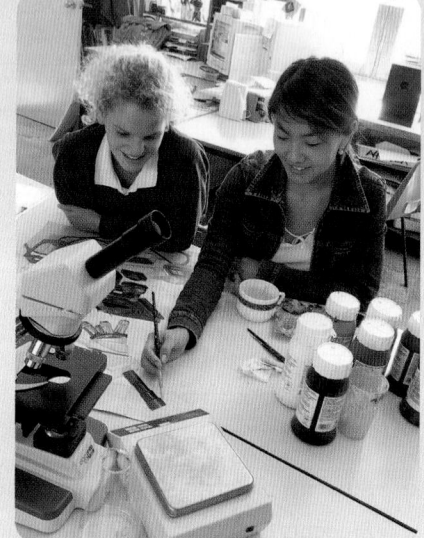

Alamy Stock Photo/Ian Shaw

SOLUTION

a S = students surveyed

  A = students doing Art

  C = students doing Chemistry

  There are 23 students who take both Art and Chemistry.

  ∴ students doing Art only = 34 − 23 = 11

  ∴ students doing Chemistry only = 65 − 23 = 42

  ∴ students who take neither Art nor Chemistry = 110 − 11 − 42 − 23 = 34

b Number of students studying Art and Chemistry only = 11 + 42 = 53

> 'Art and Chemistry only' is a compound event.

c **i** 65 students take Chemistry.

$$P(\text{Chemistry}) = \frac{65}{110} = \frac{13}{22}$$

  ii $P(\text{Art and Chemistry}) = \frac{23}{110}$

  iii Number of students who take Art or Chemistry = 11 + 23 + 42 = 76

$$P(\text{Art or Chemistry}) = \frac{76}{110} = \frac{38}{55}$$

  iv $P(\text{neither Art nor Chemistry}) = \frac{34}{110} = \frac{17}{55}$

Venn diagrams

Ⓤ Ⓕ Ⓡ Ⓒ

1 This Venn diagram shows the number of competitors who swam in freestyle (F) and butterfly (B) events at the school swimming carnival.

How many students swam in Freestyle or Butterfly, but not both? Select the correct answer **A, B, C** or **D**.

A 28   **B** 34   **C** 40   **D** 60

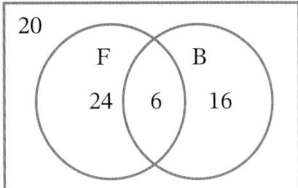

EXAMPLE **3**

2 50 people were asked whether they had breakfast (B) or lunch (L) today. The results are shown in the Venn diagram.

Ⓒ

  a What is the probability of selecting a person from this group who had:

    i breakfast?   **ii** lunch?

    iii breakfast but not lunch?

    iv breakfast and lunch?   **v** breakfast or lunch only?

  b Of the people who had lunch, find the probability that a person also had breakfast.

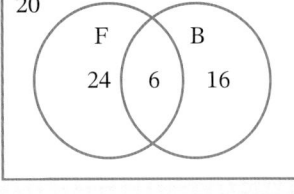

3 The Venn diagram shows the number of Year 10 students who play basketball (B), touch football (F) or tennis (T).

Ⓒ

  a How many students are in Year 10?

  b Find the probability of selecting a student who plays:

    i basketball only   **ii** tennis only

    iii touch football and tennis

    iv touch football or tennis

    v basketball but not touch football

    vi all 3 sports.

  c Of the students that play touch football, find the probability of selecting a student who also plays tennis.

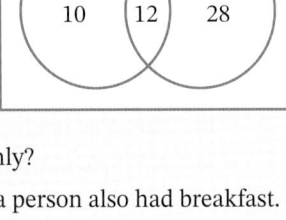

4 This Venn diagram shows the results of a survey asking people whether they watch TV or read (R) at home.

Ⓡ

  a How many people were surveyed?

  b Find the probability of selecting a person who watches TV only.

  c What is the probability of selecting a person who doesn't watch TV or read?

  d Of the people who read, find the probability that they also watch TV.

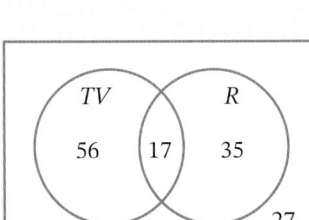

▷

Ⓛ Foundation   Ⓞ Standard   ◇ Complex

EXAMPLE
4

5 Of the 54 Year 10 Music students, 23 students sing (*S*), 43 students play a musical instrument (*P*) and 12 students sing and play a musical instrument.

(R)
(C)

a Show this information on a Venn diagram.

b Find the probability of selecting a Music student who:

   i sings or plays an instrument   **ii** sings only

   iii plays a musical instrument only

   iv sings or plays an instrument, but not both.

6 This Venn diagram shows the number of countries that won gold (G), silver (S) and bronze (B) medals at the Winter Olympic Games in Beijing, China in 2022.

(R)

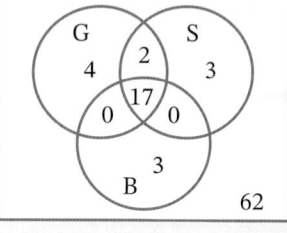

a How many countries competed at these games?

b What is the probability of randomly selecting a country that:

   i won only gold medals

   ii won gold, silver and bronze medals

   iii won gold or silver medals, but not bronze

   iv did not win a gold or silver medal?

c Of the countries that won medals, what is the probability of selecting a country that

   i won gold medals   **ii** won bronze, but no gold or silver?

7 At Riverside College, Year 10 students are asked what language they are studying. 64 students take French (*F*), 47 students take Japanese (*J*), 15 students take both French and Japanese, and 27 do not study a language.

(R)
(C)

a How many students are in Year 10?

b Show the information on a Venn diagram.

c How many students studied only one language?

d Find the probability of selecting a Year 10 student at random who studies:

   i French but not Japanese   **ii** Japanese but not French

   iii no languages   **iv** only one language.

8 People were surveyed on the day they preferred to shop: Monday to Friday (*MF*), Saturday (*SA*) or Sunday (*SU*). The results are shown in the Venn diagram.

(R)
(C)

a How many people were surveyed?

b What is the probability of selecting a person who prefers to shop on:

   i Monday to Friday   **ii** Saturday

   iii Sunday   **iv** on the weekend only

   v on Saturday or Sunday   **vi** any day (has no preference)?

c Find the probability of selecting a person who only prefers Saturday or Sunday, but not both.

d Is it necessary to include the rectangle in this Venn diagram? Give reasons.

□ Foundation   ○ Standard   ◇ Complex

9 This Venn diagram shows the number of countries that won gold, silver, bronze or no medals at the (postponed) 2021 Olympic Games in Tokyo, Japan.

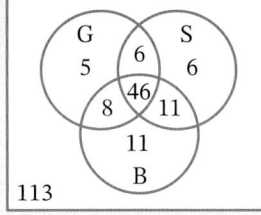

a Find the total number of countries that competed at these games.

b What is the probability of randomly selecting a country that:

   i won a silver medal only? **ii** won one medal only?

   iii won at least 2 medals? **iv** won at most one medal only?

c Out of the countries that won gold medals, find the probability of selecting a country that:

   i won gold and silver, but not bronze **ii** won gold, silver and bronze.

Two-way tables

A **two-way table** is another way of grouping items into overlapping categories, especially when there are many overlaps that cannot easily be represented by a Venn diagram.

Videos
Two-way tables 1

Two way tables 2

Worksheets
Two-way tables

Two-way probability tables

Puzzle
Combined events: Two-way tables

Example 5

Year 11 students at Southbank College were surveyed on whether they had part-time jobs.

	Part-time work	No part-time work
Male	43	27
Female	35	31

a How many students are in Year 11 at Southbank College?

b How many students had part-time work?

c How many male students were in Year 11?

d What is the probability of selecting a student at random that:

   i works part-time? **ii** is female and works part-time?

   iii is male and doesn't work? **iv** doesn't work?

e What is the probability of selecting a student working part-time given that:

   i the student is male? **ii** the student is female?

SOLUTION

a Number of Year 11 students = 43 + 27 + 35 + 31 = 136

b Students with part-time work = 43 + 35 = 78

c Male students in Year 11 = 43 + 27 = 70

□ Foundation ○ Standard ○ Complex

d **i** P(student works part-time) $= \frac{78}{136} = \frac{39}{68}$

    ii There are 35 female students who work part-time.

      P(female and part-time) $= \frac{35}{136}$

> 'Female and works part-time' is a compound event.

    iii There are 27 males who don't work.

      P(male and not working) $= \frac{27}{136}$

    iv Number of students not working $= 27 + 31 = 58$

      P(not working) $= \frac{58}{136} = \frac{29}{68}$

e **i** There are 70 male students and 43 of them work part-time.

    P(working part-time given that student is male) $= \frac{43}{70}$

    ii There are 66 female students and 35 of them work part-time.

    P(working part-time given that student is female) $= \frac{35}{66}$

EXERCISE 11.03 ANSWERS ON P. 652

Two-way tables

U F R C

EXAMPLE 5

1 (R)(C) People attending the *Staying Alive* Fitness Centre early on a Saturday morning either went swimming or did a workout in the gym. The numbers are shown in the table.

	Swimming	Gym
Male	32	53
Female	24	41

  a How many people went to the fitness centre?

  b Find the probability that a person selected at random:

    i was female and went swimming

    ii was male and did a workout in the gym   **iii** went swimming.

  c Find the percentage (to the nearest whole number) of females who did a workout in the gym.

2 (R)(C) Year 10 students at Nelson Secondary College were given a choice of 2 activities on a sports afternoon in wet weather: bowling or indoor soccer.

	Bowling	Indoor soccer
Boys	25	48
Girls	43	12

  a How many students are in Year 10?

  b How many students:

    i went bowling?   **ii** played indoor soccer?

  c What is the probability of randomly selecting a student who went bowling?

  d What is the probability of randomly selecting a girl who played indoor soccer?

□ Foundation ○ Standard ◇ Complex

3 The composition of the Legislative Assembly (the lower house) in the State Parliament is shown in the table.

R

	Liberal/Nationals	Labor	Greens/Other
Male	41	20	5
Female	11	14	6

The Liberal National coalition are in government and the others are in opposition.

a How many members of parliament (MPs) are there in the Legislative Assembly?

b Find the percentage probability of randomly selecting an MP who is:

   i female   **ii** male and in the Opposition   **iii** Greens/Other.

c What percentage probability of:

   i Government MPs are female?   **ii** Opposition MPs are female?

d Compare your answers to part **c** and comment on the differences between the 2 results.

4 People were asked to name their favourite takeaway food. The results are shown in the table.

R
C

	Pizza	Hamburger	Fish and Chips
Men	22	35	18
Women	43	26	6

a How many people were surveyed?

b Find the probability (as a decimal) that a person selected at random:

   i is male   **ii** is female and likes fish and chips

   iii likes pizza   **iv** is male and likes hamburgers.

c If a male is selected at random, what is the probability that his favourite takeaway food is pizza?

5 Year 7 students were asked about their favourite drink.

R
C

a How many students were in Year 7?

b What is the probability of randomly selecting a student that:

   i prefers water   **ii** is a boy and likes milk

   iii is a girl and likes soft drinks?

c What is the probability that if a girl is randomly selected, she prefers water?

	Boys	Girls
Water	21	35
Milk	11	12
Juice	15	17
Soft drink	31	18

6 A survey looked at whether people ate breakfast and whether they exercised regularly.

	Exercise	No exercise
Ate breakfast	72	27
Did not eat breakfast	38	63

a How many people were surveyed?

b What percentage of people exercised?

c Find the percentage probability of picking a person at random who:

  i eats breakfast

  ii does not exercise regularly

  iii eats breakfast and exercises regularly

  iv does not eat breakfast and does not exercise.

d Of the people who exercise regularly, what is the probability of picking someone who eats breakfast?

7 Students at Mt Badger College were asked to indicate their preference for dark or milk chocolate in a survey.

		Milk chocolate	
		Like	Dislike
Dark chocolate	Like	545	134
	Dislike	157	42

a How many students attended the college?

b What is the probability (correct to 3 decimal places) of selecting a student at random who:

  i likes dark chocolate? **ii** likes both milk chocolate and dark chocolate?

  iii likes dark chocolate, but dislikes milk chocolate?

  iv dislikes both dark and milk chocolate?

Tree diagrams

A **two-** or **three-step experiment** is a **chance experiment** that has 2 or 3 parts or stages, for example:

- rolling 2 or 3 dice
- drawing 2 or 3 prizes in a raffle
- observing the weather each day over a weekend or a long weekend
- throwing 2 or 3 coins together.

A **tree diagram** lists all the possible outcomes of each stage. Branches stretch out to show the possible pathways of outcomes at each step or stage. An outcomes column at the end of the diagram lists the **sample space**.

The sample space for two-step experiments can be displayed using lists, tables or tree diagrams, but the sample space for three-step experiments is best displayed using a tree diagram.

Video
Tables
and tree
diagrams

Worksheet
Tree
diagrams

Puzzle
Combined
events: Tree
diagrams

Example 6

A coin is tossed and a die is rolled.

a Use a table to display the sample space.

b Find the probability of rolling:

    i a tail and a 3   **ii** a head and an even number.

SOLUTION

a The sample space of a coin is a head (H) and a tail (T).

The sample space for a die is 1, 2, 3, 4, 5 and 6.

The sample space of tossing a coin and rolling a die is shown in the table below.

		Die					
		1	2	3	4	5	6
Coin	H	H1	H2	H3	H4	H5	H6
	T	T1	T2	T3	T4	T5	T6

Using a table ensures that all outcomes are counted.

b **i** There are 12 outcomes in the sample space.

$\therefore$ P(a tail and a 3) = P(T3) = $\frac{1}{12}$ 'Tail and 3' is a compound event.

    ii There are 3 outcomes that make up the event of a head and an even number: H2, H4, H6

$\therefore$ P(a head and an even number) = $\frac{3}{12} = \frac{1}{4}$

Videos
Tree
diagrams 3

Tree
diagrams 1

Tree
diagrams 2

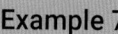

Example 7

Two coins are tossed.

a Use a tree diagram to list the sample space.

b Find the probability of tossing:

    i 2 heads   **ii** a head and a tail (in any order).

SOLUTION

a There are 2 outcomes for the first coin, followed by 2 outcomes for the second coin. There are $2 \times 2 = 4$ possible outcomes.

Using a tree diagram ensures that all outcomes are counted.

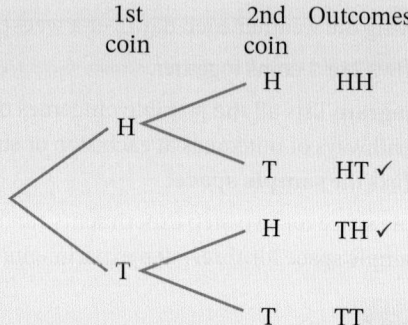

b **i** There is one outcome out of a possible 4 for 2 heads.

$$\therefore P(2 \text{ heads}) = \frac{1}{4}$$

    ii There are 2 outcomes for a head and a tail (✓ on the tree diagram).

$$\therefore P(\text{a head and a tail}) = \frac{2}{4} = \frac{1}{2}$$

EXERCISE (11.04) ANSWERS ON P. 653

Tree diagrams   Ⓤ Ⓕ ⓅⓈ Ⓡ Ⓒ

EXAMPLE
6

1 A boy and a girl are to be chosen from this shortlist to represent the school
Ⓡ at a conference:
Ⓒ **Boys:** Ben, Christian, Eugene, Kartik.

    Girls: Becky, Cassandra, Maryanne, Millie, Nancy, Pooja.

    a List all the possible pairs of a boy and a girl.

    b Find the probability of selecting:

        i Christian and Nancy

        ii a boy and a girl whose names begin with a B or a C

        iii a pair that includes Millie.

2 Two coins are tossed together.

(R) (C) **a** Copy and complete the table to find all the outcomes in the sample space.

b What is the probability of tossing:

i 2 tails? **ii** a head and a tail? **iii** at least one head?

		1st coin	
		H	T
2nd coin	H		
	T		

3 Two dice are rolled.

(PS) (R) **a** Copy and complete this table to list the sample space.

(C) **b** How many possible outcomes are there?

c Find the probability of rolling:

i two 6s

ii at least one 6

iii doubles

iv 2 even numbers **v** at least one 2

vi 2 numbers greater than 3 **vii** one odd and one even number

viii 2 numbers where the first number is greater than the second number.

		1st die					
		1	2	3	4	5	6
2nd die	1	1, 1	2, 1				
	2						
	3						
	4			3, 4			
	5						
	6						

4 Three coins are tossed.

(PS) (R) (C) **a** Copy and complete the tree diagram.

b How many outcomes are there in the sample space?

c Use the tree diagram to find:

i P(3 heads)

ii *P*(2 heads)

iii P(3 tails)

iv P(head, then tail and then head)

v P(2 heads or 3 heads)

d Find the probability of tossing:

i at least 1 tail **ii** at most 2 tails.

e If 3 coins are tossed 200 times, find the expected frequency of:

i tossing 2 heads **ii** tossing no tails.

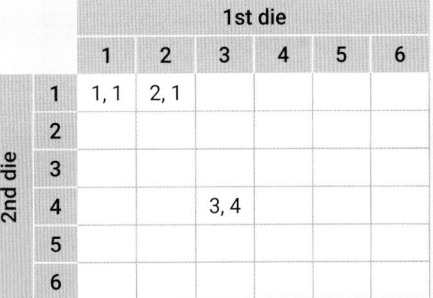

EXAMPLE 7

5 Use a tree diagram to display all possible outcomes when a coin and die are tossed together.

(R) (C)

□ Foundation ○ Standard ○ Complex

11.04

6 A 6-sided die and a 4-sided die (numbered 1, 2, 3 and 4) are rolled together.

(PS) **a** Construct a table to list the outcomes in the sample space.

(R) **b** How many outcomes are in the sample space?

(C) **c** Find the probability of rolling:

    i doubles   **ii** 2 even numbers

    iii one even and one odd number

    iv a pair of numbers that are both less than 4

    v a pair of numbers that are both greater than 4.

7 Two dice are rolled and the sum of the 2 numbers is calculated.

(PS)

(R) **a** Copy and complete this table to show all

(C) possible sums.

		1st die					
		1	2	3	4	5	6
2nd die	1	2					
	2						
	3				7		
	4						
	5						
	6					11	

  b Find the of probability of rolling a sum:

    i of 5   **ii** of 12

    iii of 7   **iv** that is even

    v less than 2   **vi** more than 7

    vii at least 7   **viii** between 4 and 8.

8 Four coins are tossed.

(PS) **a** Use a tree diagram to list the sample space.

(R) **b** Find the probability of tossing:

(C)

    i 4 heads   **ii** 1 head   **iii** 2 tails

    iv at least 1 tail   **v** 2 heads and then 2 tails   **vi** not more than 1 tail.

  c If 4 coins are tossed 1000 times, find the expected frequency of having:

    i 4 heads   **ii** 2 heads and 2 tails   **iii** at least one tail.

9 The weather on a long weekend will either be fine or raining on each day, with each outcome being equally likely.

(PS)

(R) **a** Draw a tree diagram to show the possible outcomes for Saturday, Sunday

(C) and Monday.

  b What is the probability that:

    i it rains on all 3 days   **ii** it is fine on 2 of the 3 days.

    iii it is fine on Saturday and Sunday, but rains on Monday

    iv it rains on at least one day of the long weekend?

□ Foundation   ○ Standard   ◇ Complex

Percentage increase and decrease

Quiz
Mental
skills 11

The fraction equivalents of commonly-used percentages can help us when we need to increase or decrease a number by a percentage.

Percentage	1%	5%	10%	$12\frac{1}{2}\%$	20%	25%	$33\frac{1}{3}\%$	50%
Fraction	$\frac{1}{100}$	$\frac{1}{20}$	$\frac{1}{10}$	$\frac{1}{8}$	$\frac{1}{5}$	$\frac{1}{4}$	$\frac{1}{3}$	$\frac{1}{2}$

1 Study each example.

a Increase 360 by 25%.

25% of $360 = \frac{1}{4} \times 360$

$= 360 \div 4 = 90$

$360 + 90 = 450$

b Increase $80 by 5%.   or   10% of $80 = $8

5% of $\$80 = \frac{1}{20} \times \$80$ $\therefore 5\%$ of $\$80 = \$8 \div 2$

$= \$80 \div 20$ $= \$4$

$= \$4$

$\$80 + \$4 = \$84$

2 Now increase:

a $340 by 20%   **b** 66 by 50%   **c** 150 by $33\frac{1}{3}\%$

d $400 by 1%   **e** 640 by 5%   **f** $72 by $12\frac{1}{2}\%$

g $470 by 10%   **h** 180 by 25%   **i** 420 by $33\frac{1}{3}\%$

j $80 by 5%   **k** $280 by 25%   **l** 70 by 20%

3 Study each example.

a Decrease $225 by $33\frac{1}{3}\%$.

$33\frac{1}{3}\%$ of $\$225 = \frac{1}{3} \times \$225$

$= \$225 \div 3$

$= \$75$

$\$225 - \$75 = \$150$

b Decrease $70 by 15%

10% of $\$70 = \frac{1}{10} \times \$70 = \$7$

$\therefore 5\%$ of $\$70 = \frac{1}{2} \times \$7 = \$3.50$

$\therefore 15\%$ of $\$70 = (10\% \times \$70) + (5\% \times \$70)$

$= \$7 + \$3.50$

$= \$10.50$

4 Now decrease:

a 440 by 25%   **b** $300 by 20%   **c** 2400 by $33\frac{1}{3}\%$

d $500 by 15%   **e** $250 by 10%   **f** $120 by 50%

g $72 by $12\frac{1}{2}\%$ **h** 80 by 5%   **i** $85 by 20%

j $3800 by 1%   **k** $440 by 15%   **l** $150 by $33\frac{1}{3}\%$

The birth month paradox

A **paradox** is a statement or proposition that seems impossible but is actually true.

1   Copy this table.

Group	Outcome (Y or N)
1	
2	
3	
4	
5	

2   Randomly select a group of 5 people and ask them what month they were born in. If 2 or more people have the same birth month, record a Y in the table for Group 1, otherwise write N.

3   Repeat this process 4 more times, recording your results in the table.

4   Combine your results with those of 6 other students so that you have the outcomes for 30 groups.

5   What fraction of the groups had repeated birth months?

6   Collect the results of another group of 6 students. What fraction of the groups had a repeated birth month?

7   The birth month paradox is that in any randomly selected group of 5 people, the probability that at least 2 people have the same birth month is greater than 0.5. Have your results shown this to be true?

8   Can you show the following?

a   For every 23 people selected at random, the probability that at least 2 people will share the same birthday is 50%.

b   If 30 people are selected at random, this probability is 70%.

c   If 50 people are selected at random, this probability is 97%

Selecting with and without replacement 11.05

In two- and three-step experiments where an item is selected repeatedly, the outcome of the second or third step may be affected by the outcome of the previous step. This depends on whether each selected item is **returned** to the set of items before the next item is selected. If it is, then this is called **selecting 'with replacement'**. If it isn't, then it is called **selecting 'without replacement'**.

Video
Selecting with and without replacement

Worksheet
Multi-step experiments

Example 8

Two cards are selected at random from a set of cards numbered 1 to 5, to form a 2-digit number.

a Make a list of all possible outcomes if the cards are drawn:

  i with replacement **ii** without replacement.

b If the first card is replaced before the second card is drawn, find the probability that the number formed is:

  i even **ii** greater than 30 **iii** divisible by 5.

c If the first card is not replaced, find the probability that the number formed is:

  i even **ii** odd **iii** less than 20

SOLUTION

a **i** The possible outcomes, **with replacement**, are:

		1st digit			
		1	2	3	4	5
2nd digit	1	11	21	31	41	51
	2	12	22	32	42	52
	3	13	23	33	43	53
	4	14	24	34	44	54
	5	15	25	35	45	55

There are $5 \times 5 = 25$ different outcomes possible.

ii The possible outcomes, **without replacement**, are:

		1st digit			
		1	2	3	4	5
2nd digit	1	-	21	31	41	51
	2	12	-	32	42	52
	3	13	23	-	43	53
	4	14	24	34	-	54
	5	15	25	35	45	-

There are fewer outcomes for 'without replacement' because numbers with repeated digits such as 11 and 44 are not allowed.

There are $5 \times 4 = 20$ different outcomes possible.

b **i** With replacement, there are 10 even numbers.

$$P(\text{even number}) = \frac{10}{25} = \frac{2}{5}$$

ii There are 15 numbers greater than 30.

$$P(\text{number} > 30) = \frac{15}{25} = \frac{3}{5}$$

iii There are 5 numbers divisible by 5.   15, 25, 35, 45 and 55

$$P(\text{number divisible by 5}) = \frac{5}{25} = \frac{1}{5}$$

c **i** Without replacement, there are 8 even numbers.

$$P(\text{even}) = \frac{8}{20} = \frac{2}{5}$$

ii There are 12 odd numbers.

$$P(\text{odd}) = \frac{12}{20} = \frac{3}{5}$$

iii There are 4 numbers less than 20.

$$P(\text{number} < 20) = \frac{4}{20} = \frac{1}{5}$$

Example 9

A bag contains 3 red badges and one blue badge. Three badges are drawn at random without replacement.

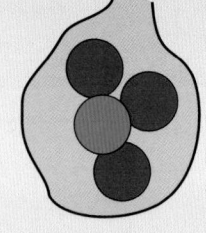

a Use a tree diagram to display all possible outcomes.

b Find the probability of drawing:

  i 2 red badges

  ii a red, blue and red in that order

  iii at least one red badge.

SOLUTION

a The tree diagram will have 4 branches for the first step or stage, followed by 3 branches for the second step, followed by 2 branches for the third step.

So, there are $4 \times 3 \times 2 = 24$ outcomes in the sample space.

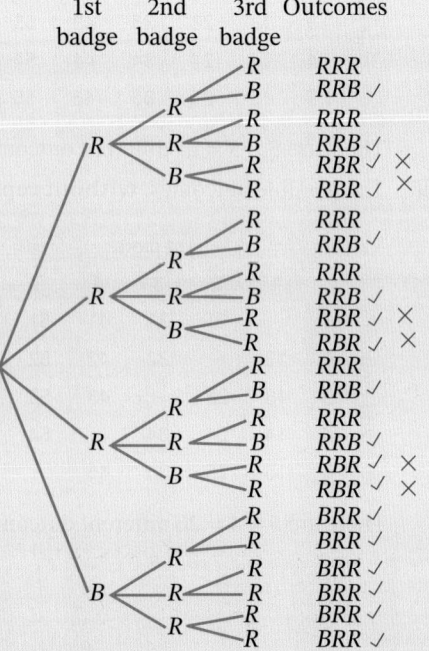

b **i** There are 18 outcomes with 2 red badges ($\checkmark$ on the tree diagram)

∴ P(2 red badges) $= \dfrac{18}{24} = \dfrac{3}{4}$

ii Red, blue, red (RBR) occurs 6 times ($\times$ on the tree diagram).

∴ P(red, blue, red) $= \dfrac{6}{24} = \dfrac{1}{4}$

iii All outcomes contain at least one red badge.

∴ P(at least one red badge) $= \dfrac{24}{24} = 1$

EXERCISE **11.05** ANSWERS ON P. 654

Selecting with and without replacement

(U) (F) (PS) (R) (C)

1 The positions of captain and vice-captain of a netball team are to be selected from Cate, Arushi, Lisa, Teresa, Wei-June and Rekha.
(R)
(C) **a** List the possible pairings of captain and vice-captain.

b What is the probability of Arushi being captain or vice-captain?

c What is the probability of Wei-June becoming vice-captain?

EXAMPLE 8

2 Two cards are drawn from a set of cards labelled A, B, C, D and E.
(PS) **a** Make a list of all possible outcomes if the cards are drawn:
(R)   **i** with replacement   **ii** without replacement.
(C) **b** If the first card is replaced before the second card is drawn, find the probability that:

i both letters are the same   **ii** both letters are vowels

iii one letter is a vowel and the other is a consonant.

▷

☐ Foundation ○ Standard ◇ Complex

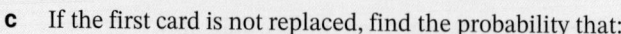

c If the first card is not replaced, find the probability that:

   i both letters are vowels

   ii one letter is a vowel and the other is a consonant

   iii the first letter is a B or a D   **iv** the last letter is not A.

3 When staying at a hotel, David and Sarah can select one item from each course of a breakfast menu.

1st course	2nd course
Cereal (C)	Bacon and eggs (B)
Fruit (F)	Ham and cheese croissants (H)
Yoghurt (Y)	Pancakes (P)
	Sausages and tomatoes (S)
	Toast and jam (T)

a Copy and complete the table to list all the different 2-course breakfasts available.

b If one of the combinations of breakfasts is chosen at random, what is the probability that it includes:

   i fruit?

   ii cereal but not bacon and eggs?

   iii fruit and croissants?

		2nd course				
		B	H	P	S	T
1st course	C					
	F					
	Y					

EXAMPLE 9

4 The numbers 3, 4, 6 and 7 are written on separate cards and placed in a bag. Three cards are drawn at random without replacement to form a 3-digit number.

a Copy and complete the tree diagram to show all 24 possible outcomes.

b Find the probability of forming a number:

   i that is even

   ii greater than 400

   iii between 400 and 700

   iv that is even and greater than 400.

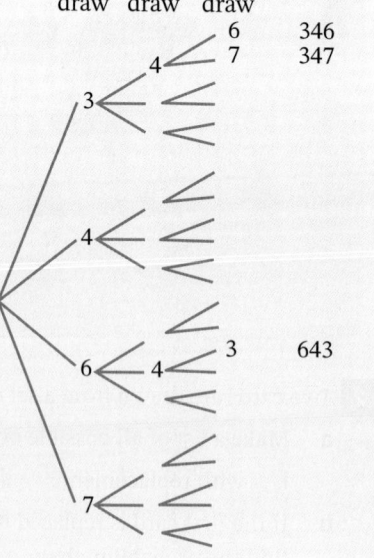

☐ Foundation   ○ Standard   ◇ Complex

5 The numbers 4, 5 and 9 are written on separate cards and placed in a bag. Three cards are drawn at random with replacement to form a 3-digit number.

(PS)

(R) **a** Use a tree diagram to show all 27 possible outcomes.

(C) **b** Find the probability of forming a number:

  i with all digits the same   **ii** that is odd

  iii less than 500   **iv** with all digits different.

6 A bag contains 2 red marbles, 1 green marble and 1 yellow marble. Three marbles are drawn from the bag at random without replacement.

(PS)

(R)

(C) **a** Copy and complete the tree diagram to list the sample space.

  b Find the probability of drawing:

   i 2 red marbles

   ii a red, green, and red marble in that order

   iii at least one red marble.

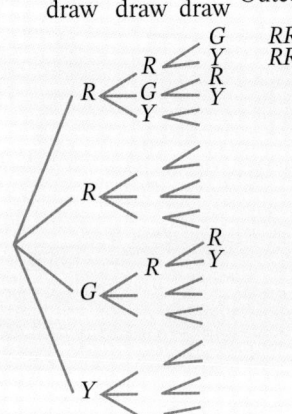

7 A family has 3 children.

(PS) **a** Use a tree diagram to list all possible outcomes in the sample space.

(R) **b** What is the probability that the family consists of:

(C)

  i 3 boys?   **ii** 3 girls?

  iii 2 girls and a boy?   **iv** a girl and then 2 boys?

8 Two ice-cream flavours are selected from vanilla, strawberry and chocolate.

(PS) **a** Draw a tree diagram to show the sample space if the flavours are selected:

(R) **i** with replacement (repetition allowed)   **ii** without replacement.

(C) **b** If the flavours are selected with replacement, find the probability of selecting:

  i 2 identical flavours   **ii** 2 different flavours

  iii no vanilla   **iv** at least one strawberry flavour.

  c If the flavours are selected without replacement, find the probability of selecting:

   i 2 identical flavours   **ii** 2 different flavours

   iii no vanilla   **iv** at least one strawberry flavour.

□ Foundation   ○ Standard   ○ Complex

11.06 Conditional probability

Videos
The card counter

The prisoner's dilemma

Bayesian robots

Worksheet
Conditional probability

Puzzle
Conditional probability: Two-way tables

In many practical situations, events are **dependent**. For example, the probability of a student arriving at school on time when catching a bus may be dependent on the amount of traffic.

Conditional probability is used to calculate probabilities for dependent events.

The **conditional probability** of an event *B given event A*, also written as $P(B|A)$, is the probability that event *B* occurs, given that event *A* has already occurred.

Example 10

A bag contains 3 red marbles and 2 yellow marbles. Two marbles are drawn at random from the bag without replacement. What is the probability that the second marble is yellow, given that the first marble was also yellow?

SOLUTION

If the first marble is yellow, then there are 3 red marbles and 1 yellow marble left in the bag.

∴ P(second marble yellow, given the first marble is yellow) $= \dfrac{1}{4}$

Example 11

Two dice are rolled and their total is calculated.

a Use a table to show all possible totals.

b Given that the total is 7, what is the probability that one of the dice shows a 3?

c Given that one of the dice shows a 4, what is the probability that the total is 10?

d Given that the total is 6, what is the probability of a double?

e Given that a double is rolled, what is the probability of:

   i a total of 12?   **ii** a total less than 10?

Video
Conditional probability

SOLUTION

a

		1st die				
		1	**2**	**3**	**4**	**5**	**6**
2nd die	**1**	2	3	4	5	6	7
	2	3	4	5	6	7	8
	3	4	5	6	7	8	9
	4	5	6	7	8	9	10
	5	6	7	8	9	10	11
	6	7	8	9	10	11	12

36 possible outcomes in the sample space.

b There are 6 outcomes that give a total of 7. $(1, 6), (2, 5), (3, 4), (4, 3), (5, 2), (6, 2)$

If one of the dice shows a 3, the possible outcomes are $(3, 4)$ and $(4, 3)$.

The conditional event 'total of 7' reduces the sample space from 36 to 6 outcomes.

P(one die is 3, given total is 7) $= \dfrac{2}{6} = \dfrac{1}{3}$

c There are 11 outcomes that have 4 showing on one die. $(4, 1), (4, 2), (4, 3), (4, 4), (4, 5), (4, 6),$ $(1, 4), (2, 4), (3, 4), (5, 4), (6, 4)$

Of these outcomes, only 2 have a total of 10. $(6, 4)$ and $(4, 6)$

P(total is 10, given one die is 4) $= \dfrac{2}{11}$

The conditional event 'one die is 4' reduces the sample space to 11 outcomes.

d There are 5 outcomes that give a total of 6. $(1, 5), (2, 4), (3, 3), (4, 2), (5, 1)$

There is only 1 double. $(3, 3)$

P(double | total is 6) $= \dfrac{1}{5}$

'|' means 'given that'; 'total of 6' reduces the sample space to 5 outcomes.

e **i** There are 6 doubles that can be rolled. $(1, 1), (2, 2), (3, 3), (4, 4), (5, 5), (6, 6)$

$(6, 6)$ is the only double with a total of 12.

The conditional event 'a double' reduces the sample space to 6 outcomes.

P(total is 12 | double) $= \dfrac{1}{6}$

 ii $(1, 1), (2, 2), (3, 3)$ and $(4, 4)$ are the doubles with a total less than 10.

P(total < 10 | double) $= \dfrac{4}{6} = \dfrac{2}{3}$

Conditional probability

EXAMPLE
10

1 A bag contains 4 yellow and 3 red marbles. 2 marbles are drawn from the bag
(R) without replacement.

    a   Given that the first marble was red, what is the probability that the second marble is also red?

    b   Given that the first marble was yellow, what is the probability that the second marble is red?

2 Ten remote-controlled cars are delivered to a toy store, 3 of which are defective.
(R) Two cars are randomly selected and tested. What is the probability that the second car
(C) tested is defective, given that the first car tested was defective and was not replaced?

3 In a physics class, there are 5 boys and 7 girls. Two students are randomly selected to
(R) help with an experiment. If the first student was a boy, what is the probability that:

    a   both students chosen were boys?   **b**   a boy and a girl were chosen?

4 In Kavya's pencil case, there are 3 red pens, 4 blue pens and 5 black pens. Kavya takes
(R) out 2 pens at random. Find:
(C) **a**   P(2nd pen red | 1st pen red)   **b**   P(2nd pen blue | 1st pen red)

    c   P(2nd pen black | 1st pen black)   **d**   P(2nd pen black | 1st pen blue)

5 A die is rolled and a number less than 4 is the result. What is the probability that the
number is even?

6 A coin is tossed and a die is rolled at the same time. Knowing that an even number has
(R) been rolled, what is the probability of the result being a head and a 4?
(C)

7 Two dice are rolled and the sum of the numbers is calculated.

(PS) **a** Draw up a table to show all possible sums.

(R) **b** Given that the sum is 9, find the probability that:
(C)   **i** one of the dice shows a 4
  ii one of the dice shows an even number.

c Knowing that one of the dice shows a 6, find the probability that the sum is 11.

d Given that one of the dice shows an even number, find the probability that:
  i the sum is even   **ii** the sum is 7.

e If the dice show a double, what is the probability of a sum of 4?

8 A drawer contains 5 different pairs of coloured socks: black, blue, red, brown and white.

(R) **a** Haylee randomly takes 2 socks from the drawer. Find:
(C)   **i** P(2nd sock blue | 1st sock blue)
  ii P(2nd sock not blue | 1st sock blue)

b Haylee selects a red sock and a blue sock. What is the probability that the third sock she selects will form a matching pair?

c What is the maximum number of socks that Haylee will need to take from the drawer before she has at least one matching pair of socks?

9 Lotto is a game of chance in which 6 balls are selected at random from a barrel containing balls numbered 1 to 45. What is the chance of Yuri winning Lotto with the 6th ball, given that he has the first 5 numbers?

(R)

10 Three cards are chosen at random from a normal deck of 52 cards. Given that the 3 cards are hearts, what is the probability that the 4th card is also a heart?

(R)

11 A card is drawn at random from a deck of 52 cards. What is P(Queen | heart card)?

(R) (C)

12 Two dice are rolled. What is P(2nd dice = 6 | 1st die = 6)?

(R) (C)

13 Two dice are rolled and the difference between the numbers is calculated.

(PS) **a** Copy and complete this table to show all possible outcomes.
(R)
(C)

		1st die				
	1	2	3	4	5	6
1						
2				3		
3						
4		1				
5						
6						

(2nd die)

$6 - 1 = 5$

The difference between these numbers is 5.

EXAMPLE 11

11.06

□ Foundation ○ Standard ○ Complex

Shutterstock.com/kirilldz

b What is the probability of rolling a difference:

    i of 0?   **ii** of 5?   **iii** greater than 3?

c Knowing that the difference is 4, what is the probability that one of the dice shows:

    i a 1?   **ii** a 3?

d If one of the dice shows a 4, find the probability that the difference is:

    i 0   **ii** 1

e Given that the difference is odd, find the probability that one of the dice shows:

    i a 3   **ii** an even number.

INVESTIGATION

Dependent or independent?

Work in pairs.

You will need: a coin, 3 blue pens and 2 red pens.

1 **a** **i** Toss a coin and record the outcome (head or tail).

    ii What is the probability of obtaining your outcome?

  b **i** Toss the coin a second time and record the outcome.

    ii What is the probability of obtaining the second outcome?

  c Is the outcome of the second toss affected by the outcome of the first toss? Is the probability of the second outcome independent or dependent on the first outcome? Justify your answer.

2 **a** Copy this table.

  b Put 3 blue pens and 2 red pens in a bag. Randomly draw a pen from the bag and record its colour.

With replacement	1st draw	2nd draw
Blue		
Red		
	40	40

  c Put back the pen you drew and shake the bag. Draw a pen again and record its colour.

  d Repeat the procedure from parts **a** and **b** 40 times and record the totals of each outcome in the table.

  e Use your results to find:

    i P(blue pen drawn first)   **ii** P(blue pen drawn second)

  f **i** Are your 2 results for part **e** the same?

    ii Would you expect the results to be the same? Give reasons.

  g Is the outcome of the second draw dependent on the outcome of the first draw?

□ Foundation   ○ Standard   ○ Complex

3 **a** Copy this table.

Without replacement	1st draw	2nd draw
Blue		
Red		
	40	40

b Again, place 3 blue pens and 2 red pens in a bag. Randomly draw a pen from the bag and record its colour.

c Do not return the pen, shake the bag and draw a second pen, recording its colour.

d Repeat the procedure from parts **a** and **b** 40 times and record the totals of each outcome in the table.

e Use your results to find:

   i P(blue pen drawn first)   **ii** P(blue pen drawn second)

f **i** Are your 2 results for part **e** the same?

   ii Would you expect your results to be the same? Give reasons.

g Is the outcome of the second draw dependent on the outcome of the first draw? Compare your results with those of other students in your class.

Dependent and independent events   11.07

Videos
The birthday paradox

The Monty Hall problem

Two events are **independent** if the outcome of one event **does not affect** the outcome of the other event. So, one event occurring does not change the probability of the other event. For example, if a coin and a die are tossed together, the 2 events are independent as the outcome on the coin does not affect the outcome on the die. Wearing blue socks and passing a driving test are also independent events.

Two events are **dependent** if the outcome of one event **does affect** the outcome of the other event. So, one event occurring changes the probability of the other event occurring. For example, when selecting 2 coloured pencils from a pencil case without replacement, the 2 events are dependent because the outcome of the second draw is affected by the outcome of the first draw. Raining on a school sports day and sport being cancelled are also dependent events.

Example 12

A coin and a die are tossed together.

a List the outcomes in the sample space.

b Find:

   i P(head on the coin)   **ii** P(even number on the die)

   iii P(head and even number)

c Is P(head and even number) = P(head) × P(even number)?

d Are the 2 events dependent or independent?

SOLUTION

a The outcomes are H1, H2, H3, H4, H5, H6, T1, T2, T3, T4, T5 and T6.

b **i** $P(\text{head}) = \dfrac{1}{2}$ **ii** $P(\text{even}) = \dfrac{3}{6} = \dfrac{1}{2}$

iii $P(\text{head and even}) = \dfrac{3}{12} = \dfrac{1}{4}$ H2, H4 and H6

c Yes, since $P(\text{head and even}) = \dfrac{1}{4}$ and $P(\text{head}) \times P(\text{even}) = \dfrac{1}{2} \times \dfrac{1}{2} = \dfrac{1}{4}$.

d The 2 events are independent since the outcome when tossing a coin does not affect the outcome when rolling a die.

ⓘ The product rule for independent events

Two events are **independent** if the outcome of one event does not affect the outcome of the other event. If A and B are 2 independent events, then

$$P(A \text{ and } B) = P(A) \times P(B).$$

Example 13

A bag contains 3 brown chocolates and 1 white chocolate. Two chocolates are drawn from the bag, without replacement.

a Find the probability of:

i selecting a brown chocolate with the first draw

ii selecting a brown chocolate with the second draw if the first chocolate was brown.

b Are selecting a brown chocolate with the first and second draws dependent or independent?

SOLUTION

a **i** $P(\text{brown on the first draw}) = \dfrac{3}{4}$

ii After drawing a brown chocolate, there are 3 chocolates left, of which 2 are brown.
∴ $P(\text{brown on the second draw}) = \dfrac{2}{3}$

b The bag contains 2 brown chocolates and 1 white chocolate for the second draw, so $P(\text{brown})$ decreases from $\dfrac{3}{4}$ to $\dfrac{2}{3}$. The second event is dependent on the first event.

EXERCISE 11.07 ANSWERS ON P. 656

Dependent and independent events

U F PS R C

1 State whether each pair of events are dependent or independent.

a Rolling 4 on a die and rolling an even number on another die

b Rolling 6 on a die and rolling 6 again on the same die

c Training hard at soccer and winning a soccer match

☐ Foundation ○ Standard ○ Complex

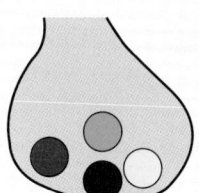

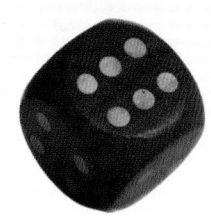

d Drawing a red ball from a bag containing red and blue balls, replacing it and then drawing a blue ball from the bag

e Electing a team captain from a group of players and then electing a vice-captain from the same group

f Tossing 2 coins and obtaining a head on the first coin and a head on the second coin

g Finding $20 on the street and getting a phone call from your parent

2 In Lotto, 6 balls are drawn without replacement. Are the events of drawing each of the balls dependent or independent events? Give reasons.

3 A coin is tossed 3 times and the result is heads each time.

a Are each of the 3 coin tosses dependent or independent events?

b The coin is tossed a 4th time. What is the probability of obtaining a head on the 4th toss?

4 A normal die is rolled and a marble is drawn from a bag containing a yellow marble, green marble, blue marble and red marble.

EXAMPLE **12**

a Find the probability of:

  i rolling a number less than 3 with the die

  ii drawing a green marble from the bag.

b List the outcomes for rolling the die and drawing a marble from the bag.

c What is the probability of rolling a number less than 3 and drawing a green marble?

d Is P(rolling a number less than 3) × P(drawing a green marble) = P(a number less than 3 and a green marble)?

e Are the events of rolling a number less than 3 and drawing a green marble dependent or independent?

5 A red die and a blue die are rolled.

a Find:

  i P(5 on the red die)   **ii** P(an even number on the blue die)

b Hence, find P(5 on the red die AND an even number on the blue die).

6 A bag contains 5 red balls and 4 yellow balls. Two balls are drawn at random without replacement.

EXAMPLE **13**

a What is the probability of drawing a red ball first?

b What is the probability of drawing a red ball on the second draw if the first ball was red?

c Are the 2 events dependent or independent? Give reasons.

☐ Foundation ○ Standard ○ Complex

Shutterstock.com/Andrejs83

11.07

9780170465595   Chapter 11 | Probability   **515**

7 A bag contains 5 yellow counters and 3 red counters. Two draws are made with no replacement. Find the probability of drawing:

a **i** a yellow counter on the first draw

    ii a yellow counter on the second draw after a yellow counter was drawn with the first draw

b **i** a red counter on the first draw

    ii a yellow counter on the second draw after a red counter was drawn on the first draw

c **i** a yellow counter on the first draw

    ii a red counter on the second draw after a yellow counter was drawn on the first draw

d **i** a red counter on the first draw

    ii a red counter on the second draw after a red counter was drawn on the first draw.

8 Three children in a family are all girls. What is the probability that the next child in this family will be a girl?

9 A pair of dice are rolled. Use the product rule to find the probability of rolling:

a a 6 on the first die and an odd number on the second die

b a 1 on both dice

c a prime number on the first die and a factor of 6 on the second die

d an even number on the first die and a number between 2 and 5 on the second die.

10 The probability that Natalie wins her tennis match is $\frac{13}{20}$. The chance that she will pass her Science exam is $\frac{4}{5}$. What is the probability that Natalie:

a wins her tennis match and passes her Science exam?

b loses her tennis match and passes her Science exam?

11 The probability that it will rain on Saturday is 0.6. The probability that it will rain on Sunday is 0.25. What is the probability that it will rain:

a on both Saturday and Sunday   **b** on Sunday only

c on neither Saturday nor Sunday?

12 A main road has 3 sets of traffic lights, each with a probability of 0.7 of being green. Use the product rule to find the probability of:

a green on the first 2 lights, red (or amber) on the 3rd light

b green on all 3 lights   **c** red (or amber) on all 3 lights

d only one of the 3 lights being green.

□ Foundation ○ Standard ○ Complex

Probability simulations

Spreadsheets, apps, cards, dice, spinners and coins can all be used to design a probability model to recreate random events. These models are called probability **simulations** and can be used to collect data to calculate experimental probabilities. It is possible to simulate chance experiments involving conditional probabilities or compound events. Simulations are used when it is impractical or impossible to run the actual chance experiment. Simulations can also be used to verify the theoretical probability of an event.

Example 14

How likely is it for a family of 2 children to have both children of the same gender; that is, either 2 boys or 2 girls? Design and conduct a probability simulation to determine a solution to this question.

SOLUTION

Each child can be modelled by flipping a coin as there are 2 outcomes to represent the 2 genders.

Flip 2 coins together for a 2-child family.

Let heads represent boys (B) and tails represent girls (G).

The 4 possible outcomes for a 2-child family are BB, BG, GB and GG.

Flip both coins and tally the outcomes. This can be done manually using actual coins or using an online coin-flipping simulator such as **flipacoin.fun**. With the simulator, select 'flip 2 coins' for '30 times' and then start the flip. Once you stop the simulation, scroll down the list of results to fill out the tally table on the following page.

Result	Tally	Frequency	Experimental probability
BB	⦀̸ II	7	$\dfrac{7}{30}$
BG	⦀̸ I	6	$\dfrac{6}{30}$
GB	⦀̸ IIII	9	$\dfrac{9}{30}$
GG	⦀̸ III	8	$\dfrac{8}{30}$
		Total 30	

P(same gender) = P(BB or GG)

$$= \frac{7}{30} + \frac{8}{30}$$

$$= \frac{15}{30}$$

$$= \frac{1}{2}$$

Probability simulations

U F PS R C

EXAMPLE
14

1 A prize has 6 different categories of prizes in it. These categories include toys, pens, lollies, chocolates, rubbers and stickers. A winner is allowed to select two random prizes out of the prize box. Design and conduct a probability experiment to determine the probability of selecting two toys of the same category.

2 A spinner for a game is broken into 5 equal sectors with 2 of the sectors being red. A contestant gets to spin it 3 times and they win a prize if they spin red twice or more. Design a probability experiment to determine the probability of winning a prize.

3 Two out of every 3 people who have a runny nose and fever have been infected by a virus. Design a probability experiment to predict the number of people infected by this virus from 1000 trials.

4 Three in every 4 adults have gym memberships and only 30% of these gym members are women. Design a probability simulation to model this situation and then conduct an experiment to investigate the claim.

5 Four out of every 6 children do not like eating lamb. 35% of the children who do not like eating lamb are boys. Design a probability simulation to model this situation and then conduct an experiment to investigate the claim.

6 Five out of every 7 people own a pet. Of these pet owners, 80% have a dog. Design a probability simulation to model this situation and then conduct an experiment to investigate the claim.

11.09 Extension: The multiplication principle of counting

EXTENSION

For compound events with multiple stages, it is sometimes impractical to list all the possible outcomes using a tree diagram or a table as the total number of possibilities may be too large. In these situations, the multiplication principle can be used to count the number of all possible outcomes.

ⓘ **The multiplication principle for counting outcomes of multi-stage events**

If A has a outcomes, B has b outcomes, C has c outcomes, and so on, then A, B, C. ... together have $a \times b \times c \times$ ... outcomes.

☐ Foundation   ◯ Standard   ◇ Complex

We can use boxed values to represent the sequence of operations as seen below:

Possible outcomes $= \boxed{a} \times \boxed{b} \times \boxed{c} \times \boxed{\times} \dots \boxed{\times}$

Example 15

A bike's combination lock is unlocked using a 4-digit code where each digit could be from 0 to 9. How many different codes are available for this lock?

SOLUTION

There are 10 possible numbers for each digit: 0, 1, 2, 3, 4, 5, 6, 7, 8, 9.

There are 4 digits required in the code.

Possible codes $= \boxed{10} \times \boxed{10} \times \boxed{10} \times \boxed{10}$

$= 10\,000$ possible combinations

Counting without replacement

It is important to notice when a probability situation involves non-replacement.
With multi-stage events without replacement, the number of possible outcomes remaining for each stage reduces.

Example 16

A 4-digit number is made using cards numbered 0 to 9, which means that once a card is used (without replacement), it cannot be used again. How many different numbers are possible?

SOLUTION

For the 1st digit in the number, there are 10 possible values.

For the 2nd digit in the number, there are 9 possible values (1 less because the 1st digit has been used).

For the 3rd digit in the number, there are 8 possible values.

For the last digit in the number, there are 7 possible values.

Possible numbers $= \boxed{10} \times \boxed{9} \times \boxed{8} \times \boxed{7}$

$= 5040$ possible combinations

Example 17

A fruit basket contains 4 nectarines and 5 apples. Nandini selects 2 pieces of fruit at random from the basket. Determine the probability of Nandini selecting:

a   2 nectarines

b   an apple and a nectarine

SOLUTION

a Number of fruit = 4 + 5

                   = 9

Count how many fruits.

    Possible outcomes = 9 × 8

                       = 72

Count how many possible pairings of fruit (from 9 fruit), without replacement.

    Number of pairings of 2 nectarines = 4 × 3

                                  = 12

Count how many possible pairings of 2 nectarines (from 4 nectarines).

    P(2 nectarines) = $\frac{12}{72} = \frac{1}{6}$

Calculate the probability.

b Number of different fruit

      pairings = NA or AN

Count how many possible pairings of 2 apples (A) and nectarines (N), that is, NA or AN.

           = 4 × 5 + 5 × 4

           = 20 + 20

           = 40

Calculate the probability.

    P(2 different fruit) = $\frac{40}{72} = \frac{5}{9}$

These answers can be checked using a tree diagram:

a P(2 nectarines) = $\frac{4}{9} \times \frac{3}{8} = \frac{1}{6}$.

b P(2 different fruit) = NA + AN

$$= \frac{4}{9} \times \frac{5}{8} + \frac{5}{9} \times \frac{4}{8}$$

$$= \frac{5}{9}$$

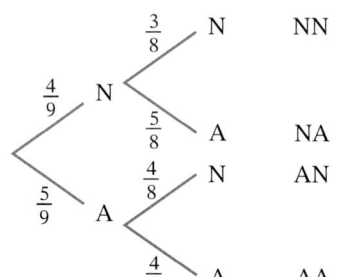

1st	2nd	Outcomes

EXERCISE (11.09) ANSWERS ON P. 656

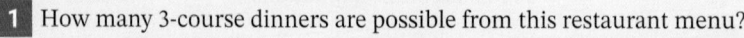

The multiplication principle of counting   U F PS R C

EXAMPLE 15

1 How many 3-course dinners are possible from this restaurant menu?

R

Entrée	Main course	Dessert
Spring rolls	Chicken and cashews	Deep fried ice-cream
Salt and pepper calamari	Mongolian lamb	Egg custard tarts
Prawn toast	Sweet and sour pork	Red bean balls
Money bags	Garlic prawns	Sweet tofu pudding
Steamed dim sum	Special fried rice	
	Combination noodles	

☐ Foundation   ○ Standard   ◇ Complex

2 In the game of Yahtzee, 5 dice are rolled together. How many different outcomes are possible?

3 A security gate is opened using a 6-character code where the first 4 characters are letters from A to G and the last 2 characters are digits from 0 to 9. One such code is AAGB87. How many different codes are possible? Select the correct answer **A**, **B**, **C** or **D**.

A 490 000 **B** 211 680 **C** 240 100 **D** 75 600

EXAMPLE
16

4 A 4-letter password is required to be made without repeating any letters. How many different passwords are possible?

5 Jay's ID code at work is made up of 2 letters followed by 3 digits followed by another 2 letters. None of the letters or digits can be repeated. How many different ID codes are possible?

6 The password for a computer starts with the letter P, then has 3 digits that do not repeat and ends with 2 letters other than P that do not repeat. How many possible passwords are there?

EXAMPLE
17

7 A box contains 10 charged batteries and 2 flat batteries. Lai takes 2 batteries out of the box at random.
  a Use the multiplication principle to determine the probability of Lai selecting 2 flat batteries.
  b Confirm your answer using a tree diagram.

8 Mrs Bhagwati's prize jar contains 5 lollies and 8 toys. Wei-June gets to take 2 prizes from the jar for winning a game during the lesson.
  a Determine the probability of Wei-June selecting two different types of prizes.
  b Confirm your answer using a tree diagram.

9 The senior student council at a high school is comprised of 8 year 10 students, 7 year 11 students and 10 year 12 students. Three students are selected at random to represent the school at an event at Parliament House.
  a Determine the probability of selecting one student from each year level.
  b Confirm your answer using a tree diagram.

10 In the late 1990s, telephone numbers in Australia changed from 7 digits to 8 digits.
  a Why do you think this happened?
  b How many extra phone numbers were possible by the addition of the extra digit?

11 On the drive to school, Max's mum passes through 4 sets of traffic lights. The probability of facing a red light on each traffic light is $\frac{2}{5}$. Determine the probability of Max's mum facing exactly 2 green lights.

Foundation Standard Complex

DID YOU KNOW?

Subsets of a set

A normal human instinct is to sort or classify things. Placing elements into different categories or sets allows you to organise your world and help you deal with large quantities of information. Let's take a look at some terminology associated to sets:

- **Set** – a collection of items
- **Elements** – the items in a set
- **Set notation** – a way of showing elements included in a set (symbolised by using these curly brackets { } called **braces**)
- **Universal set** - all elements being considered (symbolised by U)
- **Empty set** – a set that contains no element (identified by symbol $\varnothing$).

It is often necessary to break large sets down into smaller more manageable sets. These smaller sets are called **subsets**.

For example, if we had a universal set with 2 elements a and b, written '$U = \{a,b\}$', its subsets can be seen in this Venn diagram:

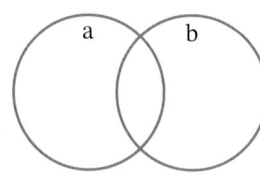

There are 2 circles and one overlapping region which make up 3 subsets of this set. There is another subset that is the empty set $\varnothing$. (The empty set is a subset of every set). Therefore, for set {a,b} above, there are 4 possible subsets - {$\varnothing$, {a}, {b}, {a,b}}.

It is possible to use a tree diagram to systematically list the number of subsets that a set may have.

This tree diagram is constructed to indicate whether each part of the set is included, and the outcomes list the subsets.

'a' included	'b' included	Outcomes
	Y	ab
Y	N	a
N	Y	b
	N	o

How many subsets does {a} have?

INVESTIGATION

Subsets of a set

There is a rule for finding the number of subsets that can be made from a set with *n* elements.

1   Construct a Venn diagram to show the subsets of set {a, b, c}.

2   List the subsets of set {a, b, c}.

3   Construct a tree diagram to show the possible subsets of:

   a   set {a, b, c}   b   set {a, b, c, d}

   c   set {a, b, c, d, e}   d   set {a, b, c, d., e, f}

4   Copy and complete this table using your answers from Question 3 (the first 3 rows have been completed).

Set	Number of elements (*n*)	List of subsets	Number of subsets
{} – Empty set	0	∅	1
{a}	1	{∅, {a}}	2
{a, b}	2	{∅, {a}, {b}, {a,b}}	4
{a, b, c}			
{a, b, c, d}			
{a, b, c, d, e}			
{a, b, c, d, e, f}			

5   Use the table to develop a general formula for the number of subsets that can be made from any given set with *n* elements.

Extension: Permutations   11.10

Factorial notation, *x*!

The multiplication principle of counting for multi-stage events without replacement involves multiplying descending whole numbers, such as $4 \times 3 \times 2$. There is a special shorthand for the product of whole numbers from *x* down to 1, called **factorial notation**, written *x*!.

For example, $6! = 6 \times 5 \times 4 \times 3 \times 2 \times 1$, read as '6 factorial'.

Your calculator has an $\boxed{X!}$ key that you can use to evaluate an answer. You may need to press the $\boxed{\text{SHIFT}}$ or $\boxed{\text{2nd F}}$ key to use it. Enter 6 $\boxed{X!}$ $\boxed{=}$ to show that $6! = 720$.

Worksheets
Factorial
notation

Ordered and
unordered
selections

Permutations

Permutation
calculations

ⓘ *n* factorial (*n*!)

If *n* is a positive integer, ***n*!** (read as '***n* factorial**'), is the product of all positive integers less than or equal to ***n***:

$$n! = n \times (n-1) \times (n-2) \times (n-3) \times \ldots \times 2 \times 1$$

Special case: $0! = 1$

Example 18

a Write $8 \times 7 \times 6 \times 5 \times 4 \times 3 \times 2 \times 1$ using factorial notation.

b Evaluate 9!.

SOLUTION

a $8 \times 7 \times 6 \times 5 \times 4 \times 3 \times 2 \times 1 = 8!$

b $9! = 362\,880$ Enter 9 [x!] [=].

Counting arrangements

Permutations are the different ways of arranging a set of objects when the order matters. They are arrangements or ordered selections.

Some situations will require careful consideration in determining whether the number of arrangements should be calculated with repetition or without. For situations without repetition, factorial notation can be used.

Example 19

a How many different 5-letter permutations can be made with the letters in the word MATHS?

b How many different permutations are possible for a number plate with 3 letters and 3 numbers?

SOLUTION

a Number of permutations $= 5 \times 4 \times 3 \times 2 \times 1$ 5 positions, 5 letters, no replacement/
$\qquad\qquad\qquad\qquad = 5!$ repetition (use factorial).
$\qquad\qquad\qquad\qquad = 120$

b Permutations $= 26 \times 26 \times 26 \times 10 \times 10 \times 10$ 3 positions, 26 letters, 3 positions,
$\qquad\qquad\quad = 26^3 \times 10^3$ 10 digits, repetition allowed.
$\qquad\qquad\quad = 17\,576\,000$

ⓘ Permutations formula

The number of permutations of n objects when taking r at a time is:

$$P = \frac{n!}{(n-r)!}$$

Example 20

A bag contains 8 letters of the alphabet. How many different 3-letter codes are possible?

SOLUTION

$n = 8, r = 3$

$P = \dfrac{n!}{(n-r)!}$

$ = \dfrac{8!}{(8-3)!}$

$ = \dfrac{8!}{5!}$

$ = 336$

> Your scientific calculator has a nP_r key.
> You might need to press **SHIFT** or **2nd F** first to use it.

Note also that $P = 8 \times 7 \times 6 = 336$ and that the formula works because

$$\dfrac{8!}{5!} = \dfrac{8 \times 7 \times 6 \times 5 \times 4 \times 3 \times 2 \times 1}{5 \times 4 \times 3 \times 2 \times 1} = 8 \times 7 \times 6.$$

Note that after cancelling out, there are r values (3, the number of places required) being multiplied together.

EXERCISE 11.10 ANSWERS ON P. 656

Permutations   U F R

1 Write each product using factorial notation.

   a $4 \times 3 \times 2 \times 1$ **b** $7 \times 6 \times 5 \times 4 \times 3 \times 2 \times 1$

   c $9 \times 8 \times 7 \times 6 \times 5 \times 4 \times 3 \times 2 \times 1$

   d $12 \times 11 \times 10 \times 9 \times 8 \times 7 \times 6 \times 5 \times 4 \times 3 \times 2 \times 1$

   e $3 \times 2 \times 1$ **f** $6 \times 5 \times 4 \times 3 \times 2 \times 1$

EXAMPLE 18

2 Evaluate each product.

   a 5!   **b** 10!   **c** 8!   **d** 3!   **e** 11!   **f** 7!

3 There are 4 seats in a car other than the driver's seat. Four friends, Nandini, Harshita, Rhea and Kavya, are going for a car ride. How many different ways can they be seated in the car if only one person can sit in one seat at a time?   (R)

EXAMPLE 19

4 How many permutations are possible for a 6-digit security access code?

5 In how many different ways can the letters of the word BERMUDA be arranged?

6 Billal rolls 9 dice and records the number rolled on each one in order. How many different permutations are possible?

☐ Foundation ◯ Standard ◯ Complex

▷

7 Nina bought 20 novels at a sale for her summer reading. She would like to read 7 of these
Ⓝ novels during her overseas trip, in a particular order. How many permutations of books
Ⓒ are possible for Nina to read?

8 45 people apply for a job at Rohan's Ribs. There are 5 different roles available to be filled
Ⓡ at the restaurant. How many different permutations of staffing are possible?

9 Two students are to be elected from a group of 10 Year 12 students to be school captain
Ⓡ and vice-captain, then 3 more students will be selected to be senior prefect, middle
prefect and junior prefect. Determine how many different leadership teams are possible.

10 There are 24 horses in a race. A trifecta is a bet on the first 3 horses in a race in the
Ⓡ correct order, while a superfecta is a bet on the first 6 horses in a race in the correct
order. Approximately how many times more superfecta permutations exist compared to
trifecta permutations?

11.11 Extension: Combinations

Combinations are the different ways of arranging a set of objects when the order doesn't
matter. They are unordered selections.

Suppose a men's doubles team needs to be selected for a table tennis competition from a
particular club that has 4 worthy candidates – Alan, Brad, Cafun and Dyson (A, B, C, D).
The list of possible teams is given by:

AB	BA	CA	DA
AC	BC	CB	DB
AD	BD	CD	DC

The number of selections could have been calculated using theory that there are 4 ways of
choosing the first member of the team and 3 ways of choosing the second member. Therefore,
there are $4 \times 3 = 12$ possible selections of a doubles team.

However, in a doubles team, there is **no order** for selection as the 2 members of the team could
'swap places' and the team would still be the same. For example, AB is the same as BA, CA is
the same as AC, and so on, as shown below:

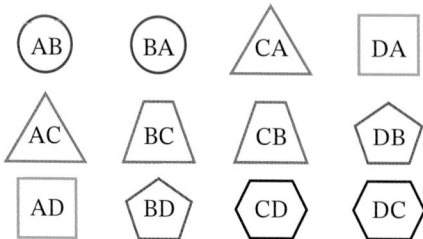

The number of possible doubles teams is therefore found by dividing 12 by 2! or 2.

9780170465595

$$\text{Number of combinations} = \frac{4 \times 3}{2 \times 1} \quad \begin{bmatrix} \text{No. arrangements of 2 players from 4 players} \\ \text{No. of ways 2 players can arrange themselves} \end{bmatrix}$$

$$= 6$$

The number of combinations of n objects when selecting r at a time is:

$$\frac{n \times (n-1) \times (n-2) \times \ldots}{r!} \quad \longleftarrow \; r \text{ terms}$$

For example, the number of combinations of 8 objects when taking 4 at a time is:

$$\frac{8 \times 7 \times 6 \times 5}{4 \times 3 \times 2 \times 1} \quad \longleftarrow \; 4 \text{ terms}$$

Notice that the product in the numerator, $8 \times 7 \times 6 \times 5$, is actually the number of permutations, P. So the number of combinations is $C = \dfrac{P}{r!}$.

But $P = \dfrac{n!}{(n-r)!}$, so

$$C = \frac{\dfrac{n!}{(n-r)!}}{r!}$$

$$= \frac{n!}{(n-r)!r!}$$

ⓘ Combinations formula

The number of combinations of n objects when selecting r at a time is:

$$C = \frac{n!}{(n-r)!r!}$$

Example 21

In the Lotto game of chance, 6 balls are randomly selected from a barrel of balls numbered 1 to 45. How many different combinations are possible in Lotto?

SOLUTION

There are 45 balls and 6 positions: $n = 45$, $r = 6$, therefore need 6 terms in numerator and denominator.

$$C = \frac{45 \times 44 \times 43 \times 42 \times 41 \times 40}{6 \times 5 \times 4 \times 3 \times 2 \times 1}$$

$$= \frac{45 \times 44 \times 43 \times 42 \times 41 \times 40}{6!}$$

$$= 8\,145\,060$$

or using the formula:

$$C = \frac{n!}{(n-r)!r!}$$

$$= \frac{45!}{(45-6)!6!}$$

Your scientific calculator has a ⁿCᵣ key.

$$= \frac{45!}{39!6!}$$

You might need to press SHIFT or 2nd F first to use it.

$$= 8\,145\,060$$

There are over 8 million different combinations of 6 numbers possible in Lotto.

Example 22

In the Powerball game, 7 balls are randomly selected from a main barrel of balls numbered 1 to 35, and then one Powerball is drawn from a Powerball barrel of balls numbered 1 to 20. This means a total of 8 balls are selected in the game. How many different combinations are possible in Powerball?

SOLUTION

Main barrel: $n = 35$ balls, $r = 7$ positions, 7 terms in numerator and denominator.

Powerball barrel: $n = 20$ balls, $r = 1$ position, 1 term in numerator and denominator.

Balls are selected from both barrels: must multiply the individual combinations.

$$C = \frac{35 \times 34 \times 33 \times 32 \times 31 \times 30 \times 29}{7!} \times \frac{20}{1!}$$

$$= 134\,490\,400$$

or using the formula:

$$C = \frac{35!}{(35-7)!7!} \times \frac{20!}{(20-1)!1!}$$

$$= \frac{35!}{28!7!} \times \frac{20!}{19!}$$

$$= 134\,490\,400$$

There are over 134 million combinations in Powerball.

Example 23

A committee of 6 people is to be formed from a group of 5 men and 4 women. How many committees would contain at least 4 men?

SOLUTION

'At least 4 men' means committee must have either 4 or 5 men.

Men: $n = 5$, $r = 4$ or 5 positions.

Women: $n = 4$, $r = 2$ or 1 positions.

> Can't be 6 men because there are only 5 men to choose from.

Committee combinations = (4 men AND 2 women) OR (5 men AND 1 woman)

$$C = \left(\frac{5 \times 4 \times 3 \times 2}{4!} \times \frac{4 \times 3}{2!} \right) + \left(\frac{5 \times 4 \times 3 \times 2 \times 1}{5!} \times \frac{4}{1!} \right)$$

> AND means ×, OR means +

$$= 30 + 4$$

$$= 34$$

or using the formula:

$$C = \left[\frac{5!}{(5-4)!4!} \times \frac{4!}{(4-2)!2!} \right] + \left[\frac{5!}{(5-5)!5!} \times \frac{4!}{(4-1)!1!} \right]$$

$$= \left[\frac{5!}{4!} \times \frac{4!}{2!2!} \right] + \left[\frac{5!}{0!5!} \times \frac{4!}{3!} \right]$$

$$= 30 + 4$$

$$= 34$$

There are 34 combinations of a committee that have at least 4 men.

EXERCISE 11.11   ANSWERS ON P. 657

Combinations   U F PS R

EXAMPLE
21

1 Abbie would like to study 2 languages at university. She can choose from Japanese, French, Italian and Danish.

   a Calculate the number of possible combinations for studying 2 languages.
   b Confirm your answer to part a by listing all possible language combinations.

2 Kartik has 2 spare movie tickets and would like to take 2 of his 5 friends – Armaan, Neel, Tiby, Will and Zain.

   a Calculate the number of possible combinations for selecting 2 friends.
   b Confirm your answer to part a by listing all possible friend pairs.

3 There are 5 members in a debating team - Ashton, Harry, Jeremi, Shazeb and Takumi. Only 3 of these members will speak during a debate.

   a Calculate the number of possible combinations for a speaking team of 3.
   b Confirm your answer to part a by listing all possible team combinations.

4 Laila buys 2 puppies from her local pet store. The store has 8 different breeds of puppies
   R for sale. How many possible combinations of puppies are there for Laila to possibly select?

5 Mr Shivin has 27 students in his Year 9 maths class. He has organised a game for
   R the lesson and students are required to play in groups of 3. How many different
      combinations of groups are possible in Mr Shivin's lesson?

6 Beno's Burgers has 15 employees. A team of 5 employees is rostered onto each
   R shift. How many different combinations of 5 employees are possible for each shift?
   C

EXAMPLE
22

7 In how many different ways can a team of 4 boys and 3 girls be formed from a group
   R consisting of 6 boys and 4 girls?
PS

8 A school offers 9 maths/science subjects and 15 English/humanities subjects to
   R Year 11 students. How many different ways can a student choose 3 maths/science
   PS subjects and 3 English/humanities subjects?

9 Juanita's bookshelf holds 6 mystery books and 7 science fiction books. She wishes to
   R read 2 mystery books and 3 science fiction books during the school holidays. How many
   PS combinations of books could she select?

10 Ramesh and Kailash have Yum Cha for lunch. There are 15 fried dishes and 20 steamed
   R dishes on the menu. They would like to eat 6 steamed dishes and 5 fried dishes.
   PS How many combinations of dishes could be selected?

11 Caleb is travelling to Asia and plans to join in 6 tours. There are 5 nature tours and
   R 7 food tours available. How many of his tour combinations would contain at least
   PS 3 nature tours?

EXAMPLE
23

12 A mixed cricket team of 12 must be chosen from a group of 15 men and 10 women.
   R How many possible team combinations would contain at least 8 women?
PS

☐ Foundation ○ Standard ○ Complex

1   Students at Nelson Secondary College were surveyed about which sport they like to watch and what type of movies they like to see.

	Horror/Drama	Fantasy	Comedy	Action
Football	23	34	30	48
Cricket	25	12	45	34
Tennis	8	12	32	17

a   How many students were surveyed?

b   If a student is selected at random, what is the probability that the student likes to watch:

    i   horror/drama movies   ii   comedy and football

    iii   tennis, but not fantasy   iv   action, but not cricket or tennis?

c   Given that a student likes to watch football, find the probability that the student also likes to watch action movies.

d   Of the students who like comedy, what is the probability that they also like to watch cricket?

2   A bag contains 3 red and 4 blue marbles. 2 marbles are taken out of the bag without replacement.

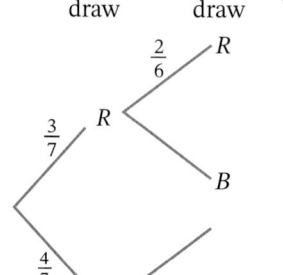

a   A probability tree is a tree diagram that has the probability of each step or stage listed on the branches. Copy and complete the probability tree shown to list all possible outcomes.

b   Use the probability tree diagram to find the probability of drawing:

    i   2 red marbles

    ii   2 blue marbles

    iii   a blue and a red marble

    iv   at least one blue marble.

3   a   Find:

    i $P(A)$ ii $P(B)$ iii $P(A \text{ and } B)$

    iv $P(A \mid B)$ v $P(B \mid A)$

    b   i   Find the value of $\dfrac{P(A \text{ and } B)}{P(B)}$.

        ii   Is $P(A \mid B) = \dfrac{P(A \text{ and } B)}{P(B)}$?

    c   Show, by calculation, that $P(B \mid A) = \dfrac{P(A \text{ and } B)}{P(A)}$.

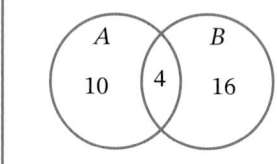

Language of maths

combination	compound event	conditional probability
dependent event	event	expected frequency
experimental probability	independent event	mutually exclusive
observed frequency	overlapping	permutation
random	relative frequency	sample space
simulation	table	theoretical probability
tree diagram	trial	two-step experiment
two-way table	Venn diagram	with/without replacement

Quiz
Language
of maths 11

Puzzle
Probability
crossword

1   What is the meaning of **expected frequency**?

2   What term from the above list is another name for **experimental probability**?

3   On a **Venn diagram**, what does the rectangle represent?

4   Give an example of **dependent events**.

5   When are **tree diagrams** used in probability?

6   For 2 events A and B, what is the difference between '**A or B**' and '**A and B**'?

Topic summary

Print (or copy) and complete this mind map of the topic, adding detail to its branches and using pictures, symbols and colour where needed. Ask your teacher to check your work.

Worksheet
Mind map:
Probability

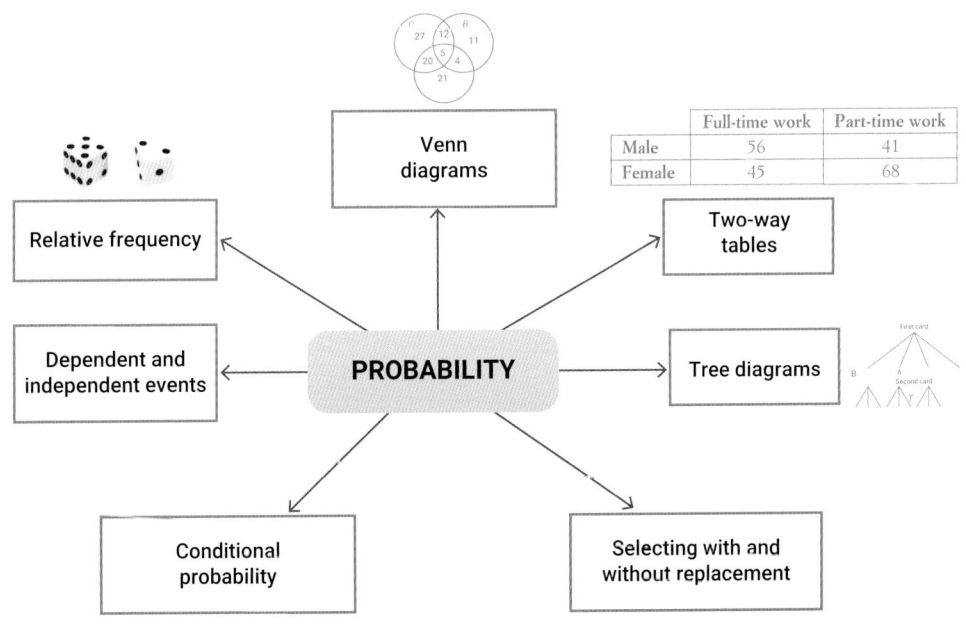

11.01

Quiz
Test
yourself 11

1 For the spinner shown, the red and blue sectors are twice as large as the other sectors. Rafiya spun the spinner 100 times and her results are shown in the table.

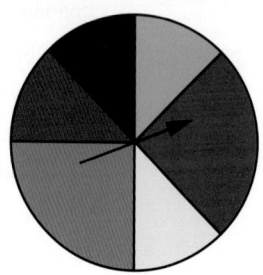

Outcome	Frequency
Red	22
Blue	29
Yellow	10
Purple	12
Black	13
Green	14

a What is the experimental probability (as a decimal) of the arrow stopping on:
 i red **ii** blue **iii** yellow **iv** green?

b What is the theoretical probability (as a decimal) of the arrow stopping on:
 i red **ii** blue **iii** yellow **iv** green?

c Are the experimental and theoretical probabilities similar?

d What is the experimental probability of the arrow stopping at purple or black?

e What is the expected frequency of a colour that is not purple or black? How does this compare with Rafiya's observed frequency?

11.01

2 Three coins are tossed 150 times and the number of heads at each trial is recorded in the table.

Number of heads	Frequency
0	20
1	53
2	64
3	13

a Find correct to 3 decimal places the relative frequency of tossing:
 i one head **ii** 2 heads
 iii 3 heads **iv** at least 2 heads.

b Find correct to 3 decimal places the experimental probability of:
 i at least one head **ii** 3 tails.

c Are the answers in part **b** the same or different? Explain why.

11.02

3 People at a beach were asked whether they prefer to read fiction (*F*) or non-fiction (*NF*) books. The results are shown in the Venn diagram.

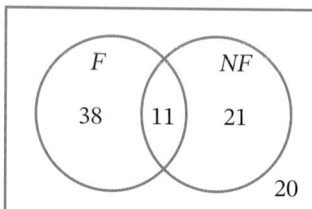

a How many people were surveyed?

b Find the probability of selecting a person from this group who only reads fiction books.

c What is the probability of selecting a person who doesn't read fiction or non-fiction books?

d Of the people who read fiction books, find the probability that they read non-fiction books.

□ Foundation ○ Standard ○ Complex

4 Of 20 people in an office, 6 have blue eyes (*B*), 8 have dark hair (*D*) and 3 have blue eyes and dark hair.

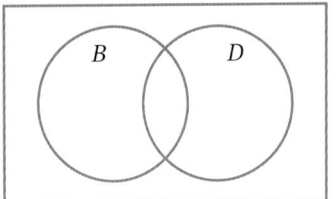

11.02

a Copy and complete the Venn diagram to show the given information.

b What is the probability of selecting a person at random from the office who has:

   i blue eyes only   **ii** dark hair

   iii blue eyes and dark hair   **iv** hair that is not dark?

c What is the probability of selecting a person at random who has neither blue eyes nor dark hair?

5 Students were asked what type of activities they would like to do on a camp.

11.03

	Hiking	Rock climbing	Kayaking
Boys	25	38	47
Girls	45	23	22

a How many students were surveyed?

b Find the probability (as a decimal) that a student selected at random:

   i likes rock climbing

   ii likes kayaking and is a girl

   iii is a girl who likes hiking

   iv is a boy who likes rock climbing or kayaking.

c If a boy is selected at random, what is the probability that his favourite activity is hiking?

d If a student who likes kayaking is chosen, what is the probability that the student is:

   i a boy   **ii** a girl?

6 A pair of dice are rolled and the sum of the 2 numbers is calculated. Find the probability of rolling a sum of 6. Select the correct answer **A**, **B**, **C** or **D**.

11.04

A $\frac{1}{5}$ **B** $\frac{1}{9}$ **C** $\frac{5}{6}$ **D** $\frac{5}{36}$

7 A pair of 4-sided dice (numbered 1, 2, 3 and 4) are rolled.

11.05

		1st die		
	1	2	3	4
2nd die 1				
2		2, 2		
3				
4			3, 4	

a Copy and complete this table.

b How many possible outcomes are there?

c Find the probability of rolling:

   i one odd and one even number

   ii 2 even numbers

   iii at least one 3   **iv** 2 numbers less than 3

   v a double   **vi** 2 numbers so that the first number is odd.

☐ Foundation ○ Standard ○ Complex

11.05 **8** Two marbles are drawn from a bag containing a red, a blue, a green, a yellow and a black marble.

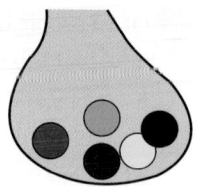

a Make up a list to show all the possible outcomes if the marbles are taken:

   i with replacement

   ii without replacement.

b If the first marble is replaced before the second marble is drawn, find the probability of drawing:

   i 2 red marbles   **ii** 2 marbles of the same colour

   iii a yellow and a black marble   **iv** at least one green marble.

c If the first marble is not replaced, find the probability of drawing:

   i a green marble and a yellow marble   **ii** no red marbles.

11.05 **9** The numbers 2, 4, and 7 are written on separate cards and placed in a bag. 3 cards are drawn at random to form a 3-digit number.

a Make up a tree diagram to list the sample space if the cards are drawn:

   i with replacement   **ii** without replacement.

b If the cards are drawn with replacement, find the probability of forming:

   i an even number   **ii** a number less than 400

   iii the numbers 222, 444 or 777   **iv** an odd number greater than 400.

c If the cards are drawn without replacement, find the probability of forming:

   i an odd number   **ii** a number greater than 400

   iii a number beginning with 7   **iv** a number divisible by 4.

11.06 **10** Two hair ties are drawn without replacement from a bag containing 3 purple and 2 red hair ties.

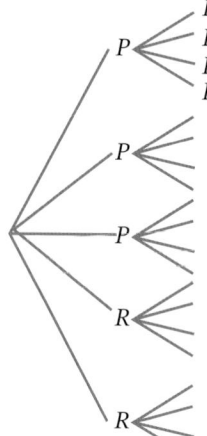

1st draw   2nd draw   Outcomes

a Copy and complete the tree diagram to show the sample space.

b Given that the first hair tie drawn is purple, what is the probability that the second hair tie will be:

   i red   **ii** purple?

c Given that the first hair tie drawn is red, find the probability that the second hair tie is:

   i red   **ii** purple.

d Given that the drawn hair ties are the same colour, what is the probability that they are:

   i both red   **ii** both purple?

☐ Foundation ◯ Standard ◇ Complex

11 The pair of 4-sided dice from question **8** are rolled and the sum of the numbers is calculated.

    a   Draw up a table to show all possible sums.

    b   Given that the sum is 5, find the probability that one of the dice shows:

        i   a 2   **ii**   an odd number.

    c   Find P(sum of 7 | one die is 4).

    d   Given that one of the dice shows an even number, find the probability that the sum:

        i   is even   **ii**   is 5.

    e   Find P(sum of 2 | dice show a double).

(11.06)

12 State whether the following pairs of events are dependent or independent.

    a   Tossing a tail from a coin and then a head from the same coin.

    b   Drawing a ticket in a raffle and winning a first prize and then drawing a second ticket and winning a second prize.

    c   Electing a president for a cricket club and then electing the vice-president of the cricket club.

    d   A family's first 3 children are girls and then the 4th child is also a girl.

    e   Rain in your town or city today and a car accident.

    f   The Roosters winning a football match and you winning Lotto.

(11.07)

13 At a particular movie screening, 6 out of every 10 viewers are children and 4 are adults. Two viewers are selected at random to receive free movie tickets. Design a probability experiment to determine the probability of 2 adults receiving the free movie tickets.

(11.08)

14 Evan has to choose his clothes to wear to a party. He has 8 tops, 6 pants and 5 pairs of shoes to choose from. How many outfits are possible for Evan to select?

EXTENSION

(11.09)

15 In how many different ways can the letters of the word DECAGON be arranged?

(11.10)

16 Five girls, Biel, Coco, Judy, Nandini and Sandy, enter a science competition. Only 2 of them will be chosen to present their project on the day.

    a   Calculate the number of possible combination pairs to present their projects.

    b   Confirm your answer to part **a** by listing all possible pairs.

(11.11)

☐ Foundation   ○ Standard   ○ Complex

12

SPACE, MEASUREMENT

Congruent and similar figures

The word 'geometry' comes from the Greek word *geometria*, which means 'earth measuring'. The principles and ideas of geometry are evident in many aspects of our lives. For example, geometry can be seen in the design of buildings, bridges, roads and transport networks.

stock.adobe.com/SERGEYMANSUROV

Chapter outline		Proficiencies				
12.01	Congruent triangle proofs	U	F		R	C
12.02	Tests for quadrilaterals	U	F	PS	R	C
12.03	Proving properties of triangles and quadrilaterals	U	F		R	C
12.04	Formal geometrical proofs*	U	F	PS	R	C
12.05	Similar figures	U	F		R	C
12.06	Scale diagrams, maps and plans	U	F			C
12.07	Finding sides in similar figures	U	F	PS	R	
12.08	Similar triangle proofs	U	F		R	C
12.09	Areas of similar figures	U	F		R	C
12.10	Surface areas and volumes of similar solids	U	F	PS	R	C

* EXTENSION

U = Understanding
F = Fluency
PS = Problem solving

R = Reasoning
C = Communicating

Wordbank

congruence test One of 4 tests for proving that triangles are congruent: SSS, SAS, AAS and RHS.

congruent Identical, exactly the same (symbol: ≡).

enlargement An increase in the size of a shape.

included angle The angle between 2 given sides of a shape.

scale factor The amount by which a shape has been enlarged or reduced, equal to $\dfrac{\text{image length}}{\text{original length}}$.

similar To have the same shape but not necessarily the same size, an enlargement or reduction (symbol: |||).

similarity test One of 4 tests for proving that triangles are similar: SSS, SAS, AA and RHS.

Quiz
Wordbank 12

Videos (11):

SkillCheck Geometry

12.01 Test for congruent triangles
• Congruent triangles proofs

12.02 Tests for quadrilaterals

12.03 Proving properties of a rectangle

12.06 Scale drawings

12.07 Finding an unknown side in similar figures

12.08 Tests for similar triangles • Similar triangle proofs

12.09 Areas of similar figures

12.10 Surface areas and volumes of similar solids

Twig videos (6):

12.06 Jai Singh (sundial) • Modelling the Spitfire • Queen Hatshepsut's ship • The history of the golden ratio • Fractals: The Koch snowflake

12.10 The incredible strength of ants

Quizzes (5):

• Wordbank 12
• SkillCheck 12
• Mental skills 12
• Language of maths 12
• Test yourself 12

Skillsheet (1):

12.07 Finding sides in similar triangles

Worksheets (14):

12.01 Congruent triangles proofs
• Congruent triangles • Congruent and similar triangle proofs

12.02 Quadrilaterals: True or false?

12.03 Quadrilaterals: True or false?
• Proving properties of quadrilaterals • Congruent and similar triangle proofs

12.05 A page of similar figures
• Enlargements and reductions
• Enlarging a logo

12.06 Problems involving scale drawings

12.07 Finding sides in similar figures

12.08 Congruent and similar triangle proofs
• Congruence and similarity review

12.09 Investigating paper sizes

12.10 Areas and volumes of similar figures

Mind map: Congruent and similar figures

Puzzles (5):

SkillCheck Finding angles

12.03, 12.04 Geometrical proofs order activity

12.05 Cartoon enlargement

12.07 Similar triangles

Language of maths Geometry crossword

Technology (2):

12.06 Converting map scales to ratios

12.09 Area of similar shapes

Spreadsheets (2):

12.06 Converting map scales to ratios

12.09 Area of similar shapes

Presentation (1):

12.03 Geometric problems and proofs

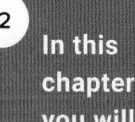 **Nelson MindTap**

To access resources above, visit
cengage.com.au/nelsonmindtap

12

In this chapter you will:

✓ write formal proofs for congruent triangles

✓ identify and use the definitions and tests for the special quadrilaterals

✓ investigate properties of special triangles and quadrilaterals using congruent triangles

✓ formulate proofs involving congruent triangles and angle properties

✓ write formal geometrical proofs using logical reasoning

✓ solve problems involving scale diagrams, scaled maps and building plans

✓ use scale factors to find unknown sides in similar figures

✓ identify and use the 4 tests for similar triangles

✓ write formal proofs for similar triangles

✓ investigate ratios of areas of similar figures

✓ investigate ratios of surface areas and volumes of similar solids

9780170465595

SkillCheck
ANSWERS ON P. 658

1 Find the value of each variable.

a
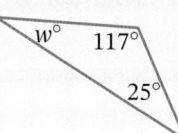

b
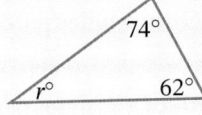

c
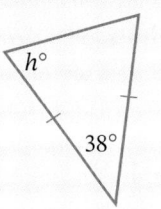

Video
Geometry

Quiz
SkillCheck 12

Puzzle
Finding
angles

d
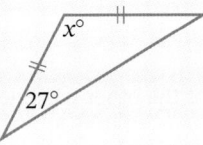

e
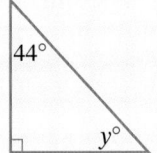

f
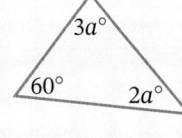

2 Match shapes that are congruent.

A    **B** 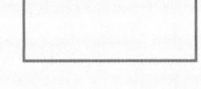   **C** 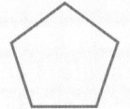   **D**

E 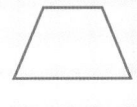   **F**    **G** 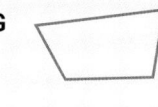   **H**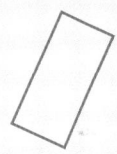

I 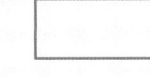   **J**    **K**    **L**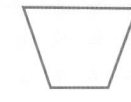

3 Find the value of p in each diagram.

a
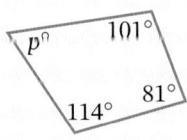

b
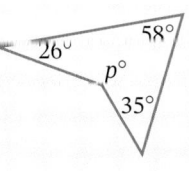

c
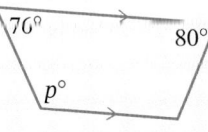

d
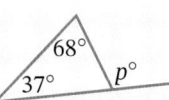

e
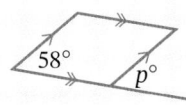

f
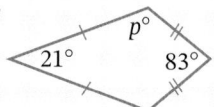

4 Triangles *MNP* and *WXY* are similar.
  a List all pairs of matching angles.
  b List all pairs of matching sides.

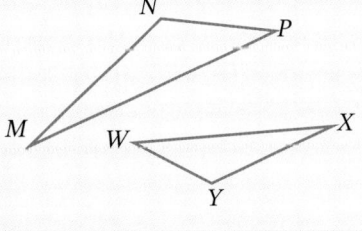

Videos
Test for
congruent
triangles

Congruent
triangles
proofs

Worksheets
Congruent
triangles
proofs

Congruent
triangles

Congruent
and similar
triangle
proofs

Two figures are **congruent** if they are identical in shape and size. For **congruent figures**, **matching sides** are equal and **matching angles** are equal.

There are 4 sets of conditions that can be used to determine if **2 triangles** are congruent. These are called the **tests for congruent triangles** or **congruence tests**.

ⓘ Congruence tests

There are 4 tests for congruent triangles: **SSS**, **SAS**, **AAS** or **RHS**.

Two triangles are congruent if:

- the 3 sides of one triangle are respectively equal to the 3 sides of the other triangle (**SSS** rule)

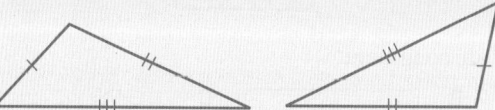

- 2 sides and the **included angle** of one triangle are respectively equal to 2 sides and the **included angle** of the other triangle (**SAS** rule)

- 2 angles and one side of one triangle are respectively equal to 2 angles and the matching side of the other triangle (**AAS** rule)

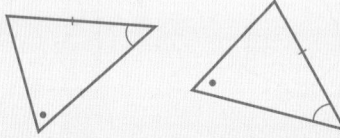

- they are right-angled and the hypotenuse and another side of one triangle are respectively equal to the hypotenuse and another side of the other triangle (**RHS** rule).

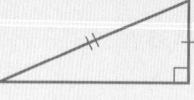 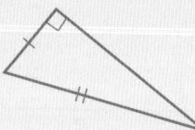

The congruence symbol ≡

The 2 triangles below are congruent, so we can write $\triangle ABC \equiv \triangle XYZ$.

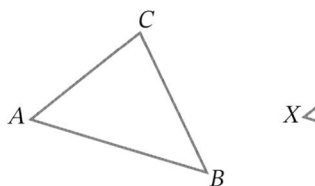

When using this notation, the vertices (angles) are written in matching order:

$\triangle ABC \equiv \triangle XYZ$ means $\angle A = \angle X$, $\angle B = \angle Y$, $\angle C = \angle Z$.

To formally prove that 2 triangles are congruent, we need to use one of the 4 tests.

Example 1

In the diagram, $PQ \parallel LM$, $QR \parallel MN$ and $QR = MN$.
Prove that $\triangle PQR \equiv \triangle LMN$.

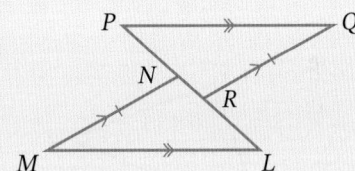

SOLUTION

In $\triangle PQR$ and $\triangle LMN$:   matching order of vertices

$QR = MN$ (given)   stating each part of the congruence test,

$\angle P = \angle L$ (alternate angles, $PQ \parallel LM$)   giving reasons

$\angle QRP = \angle MNL$ (alternate angles, $QR \parallel MN$)

$\therefore \triangle PQR \equiv \triangle LMN$ (AAS)   conclusion, stating the test used

---

EXERCISE (12.01) ANSWERS ON P. 659

Congruent triangle proofs   (U) (F) (R) (C)

1 For each set of triangles next page:

(R)   **i**   decide which 2 are congruent and state the congruence test used

(C)   **ii**   use the correct notation to write a congruency statement relating those 2 triangles.

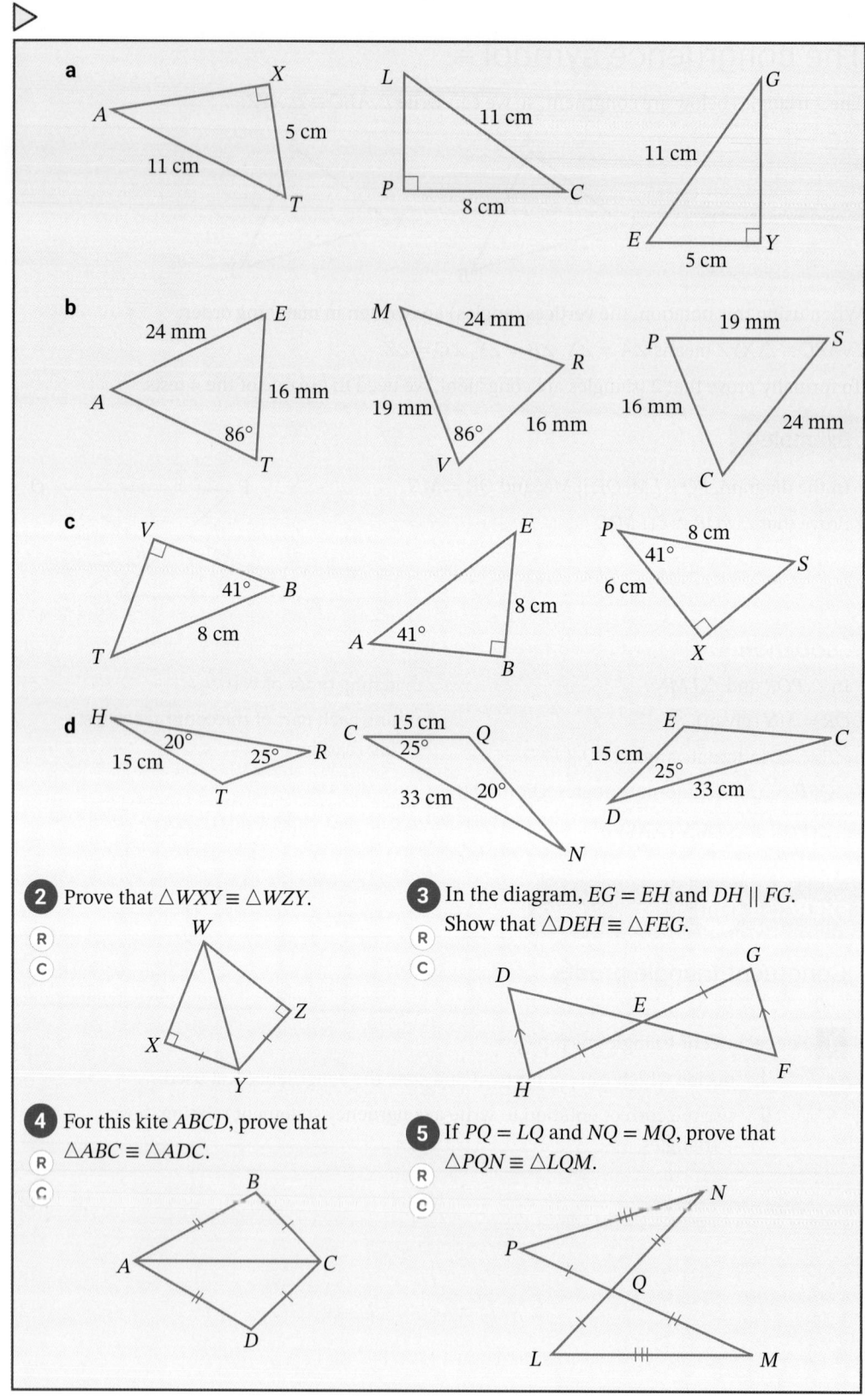

a

X

A

5 cm

11 cm

T

L

11 cm

P

8 cm

C

G

11 cm

E

5 cm

Y

b

E

24 mm

A

16 mm

86°

T

M

24 mm

R

19 mm

86°

16 mm

V

P

19 mm

S

16 mm

24 mm

C

c

V

41°

B

8 cm

T

E

8 cm

A

41°

B

P

8 cm

41°

6 cm

S

X

d

H

20°

15 cm

25°

R

T

C

15 cm

25°

Q

33 cm

20°

N

E

15 cm

25°

C

33 cm

D

EXAMPLE 1

2 Prove that $\triangle WXY \equiv \triangle WZY$.

R

C

W

Z

X

Y

3 In the diagram, $EG = EH$ and $DH \parallel FG$. Show that $\triangle DEH \equiv \triangle FEG$.

R

C

D

G

E

H

F

4 For this kite $ABCD$, prove that $\triangle ABC \equiv \triangle ADC$.

R

C

B

A

C

D

5 If $PQ = LQ$ and $NQ = MQ$, prove that $\triangle PQN \equiv \triangle LQM$.

R

C

N

P

Q

L

M

□ Foundation ○ Standard ◇ Complex

9780170465595

6 Prove that △WXY ≡ △YVW.

(R) (C)

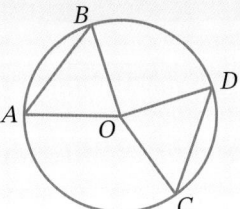

7 O is the centre of the circle and AB = CD.
Prove that △AOB ≡ △COD.

(R) (C)

8 Prove that △FNM ≡ △TMN.

(R) (C)

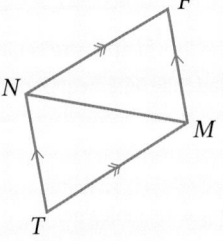

9 If ∠ABC = ∠DCB and AB = DC in the
diagram, prove that △ABC ≡ △DCB.

(R) (C)

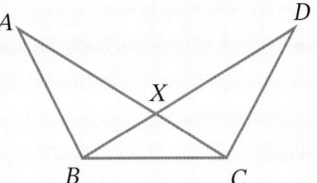

10 TS ∥ PL and K is the midpoint of TL.
Prove that △TSK ≡ △LPK.

(R) (C)

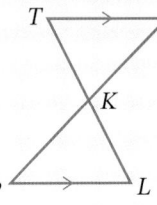

11 PW ∥ QT, RW ∥ QV and PQ = QR. Prove that
△PVQ ≡ △QTR.

(R) (C)

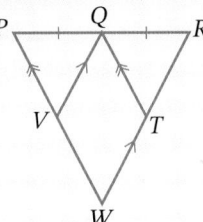

12 If ∠DEG = ∠EDF and GE = FD,
prove that △DEG ≡ △EDF.

(R) (C)

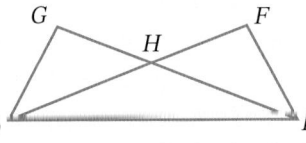

13 In △ABC, AB = AC and AD ⊥ BC. Prove that
△ABD ≡ △ACD and hence AD bisects ∠BAC.

(R) (C)

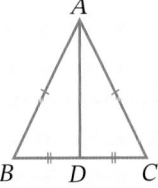

14 If CX ⊥ AB, BY ⊥ AC and XC = YB,
prove that △BCX ≡ △CBY.

(R) (C)

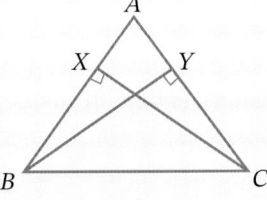

15 XW = XZ in this isosceles triangle and Y is the
midpoint of WZ. Prove that △WYX ≡ △ZYX.

(R) (C)

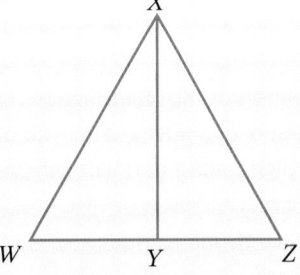

☐ Foundation ○ Standard ◎ Complex

Worksheet
Quadrilaterals:
True or false?

ⓘ The special quadrilaterals

Quadrilateral	Formal definition	Properties
Trapezium	A quadrilateral with at least one pair of opposite sides parallel.	None
Kite	A convex quadrilateral with 2 pairs of equal adjacent sides.	• One pair of opposite angles equal • Diagonals intersect at right angles
Parallelogram	A quadrilateral with both pairs of opposite sides parallel.	• Opposite sides equal • Opposite angles equal • Diagonals bisect each other
Rhombus	A parallelogram with 2 adjacent sides equal in length.	• All sides equal • Diagonals bisect each other at right angles • Diagonals bisect the angles of the rhombus
Rectangle	A parallelogram with one right angle.	• All angles are right angles • Diagonals are equal in length
Square	A rectangle with 2 adjacent sides equal in length.	• All sides equal • All angles are right angles • Diagonals are equal in length • Diagonals bisect each other at right angles • Diagonals bisect the angles of a square

Note that the definitions of the quadrilaterals give *minimum conditions*. For example, a rhombus is defined as 'a parallelogram with 2 adjacent sides equal in length'. However, opposite sides are equal in a parallelogram so that means the rhombus has *all* sides equal in length.

Some properties of the quadrilaterals can be used as minimum conditions to prove or test that a quadrilateral is a parallelogram, rectangle, square or rhombus. For example, if opposite angles are equal, then it *must* be a parallelogram.

9780170465595

ⓘ Tests for quadrilaterals

A quadrilateral is a **parallelogram** if one of these conditions is true:
- both pairs of opposite angles are equal, or
- both pairs of opposite sides are equal, or
- both pairs of opposite sides are parallel, or
- one pair of opposite sides are equal and parallel, or
- the diagonals bisect each other.

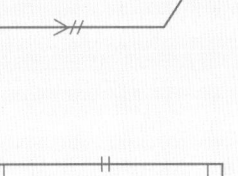

A quadrilateral is a **rectangle** if one of these conditions is true:
- all angles are 90°, or
- diagonals are equal and bisect each other.

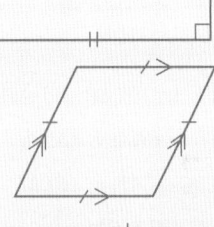

A quadrilateral is a **rhombus** if one of these conditions is true:
- all sides are equal, or
- diagonals bisect each other at right angles.

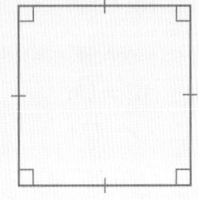

A quadrilateral is a **square** if one of these conditions is true:
- all sides are equal and one angle is 90°, or
- all angles are 90° and 2 adjacent sides are equal, or
- diagonals are equal and bisect each other at right angles.

Example 2

ABCD is a quadrilateral with BD as a diagonal.
Prove that if the opposite sides of ABCD are equal,
then it must be a parallelogram.

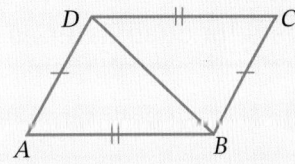

Video
Tests for
quadrilaterals

SOLUTION

In $\triangle ABD$ and $\triangle CDB$;

$AD = CB$	(opposite sides of ABCD are equal)
$AB = CD$	(opposite sides of ABCD are equal)
BD is common	
$\therefore \triangle ABD \equiv \triangle CDB$	(SSS)
$\therefore \angle ABD = \angle CDB$	(matching angles of congruent triangles)
$\therefore AB \parallel CD$	(alternate angles are equal)
Also, $\angle ADB = \angle CBD$	(matching angles of congruent triangles)
$\therefore AD \parallel CB$	(alternate angles are equal)
$\therefore ABCD$ is a parallelogram	(opposite sides are parallel)

Example 3

In the diagram, $KP \parallel BM$, $AP \parallel LM$ and $KP = BM$.

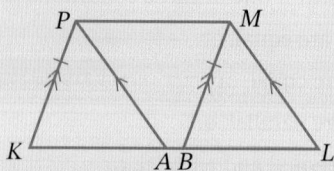

Prove that:

a $\triangle KAP \equiv \triangle BLM$

b $ALMP$ is a parallelogram

SOLUTION

a In $\triangle KAP$ and $\triangle BLM$:

$\angle PKA = \angle MBL$	(corresponding angles, $KP \parallel BM$)
$\angle KAP = \angle BLM$	(corresponding angles, $AP \parallel LM$)
$KP = BM$	(given)
$\therefore \triangle KAP \equiv \triangle BLM$	(AAS)

b

$AP = LM$	(matching sides of congruent triangles)
$AP \parallel LM$	(given)
$\therefore ALMP$ is a parallelogram	(one pair of opposite sides are parallel and equal)

EXERCISE 12.02 ANSWERS ON P. 659

Tests for quadrilaterals   U F PS R C

EXAMPLE 2

1 $LMNP$ is a quadrilateral in which $LM = NP$ and $LM \parallel NP$.

PS
R
C

Prove that if a pair of opposite sides in a quadrilateral are equal and parallel, then the quadrilateral must be a parallelogram.

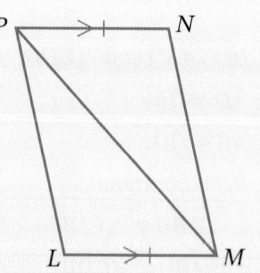

2 $DEGH$ is a quadrilateral whose diagonals DG and EH bisect each other. Prove that it must be a parallelogram.

PS
R
C

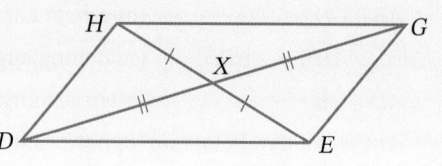

▷

☐ Foundation   ○ Standard   ○ Complex

3 *CDEF* is a quadrilateral whose diagonals *CE* and *DF* bisect each other at right angles. Prove that *CDEF* must be a rhombus.

PS
R
C

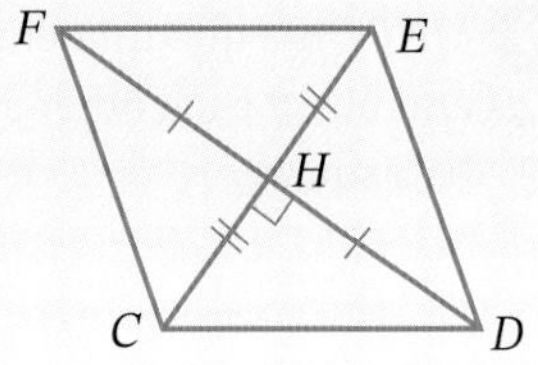

4 *ABCD* is a quadrilateral in which opposite angles are equal. Prove that *ABCD* must be a parallelogram.

PS
R
C

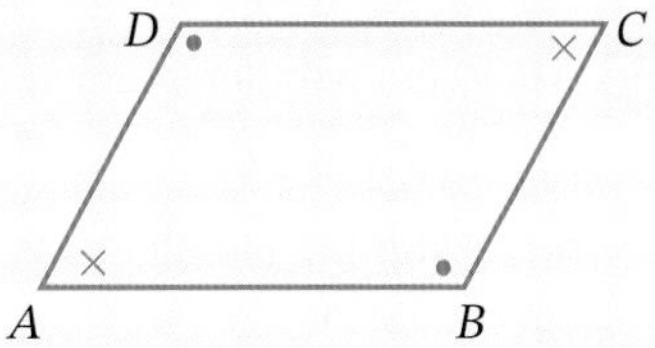

5 *VWXY* is a quadrilateral whose diagonals *VX* and *WY* are equal and bisect each other. Prove that it must be a rectangle.

PS
R
C

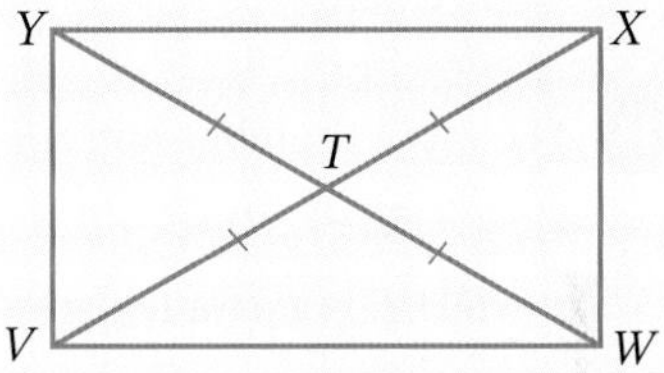

6 *BCDE* is a quadrilateral with all angles equal to 90°.

PS
R
C

Prove that its opposite sides are parallel as well and hence it must be a rectangle.

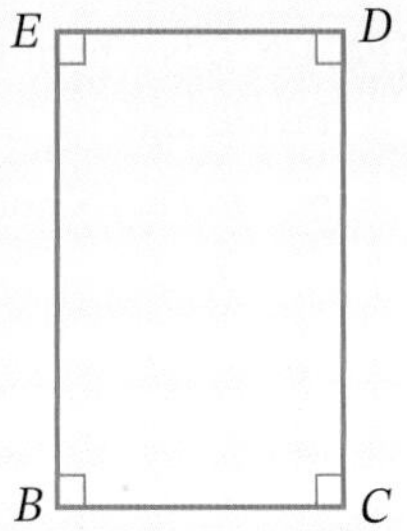

7 *TWME* is a quadrilateral with all sides equal and ∠*M* = 90°.

PS
R
C

Prove that the other angles are 90° as well and hence it must be a square.

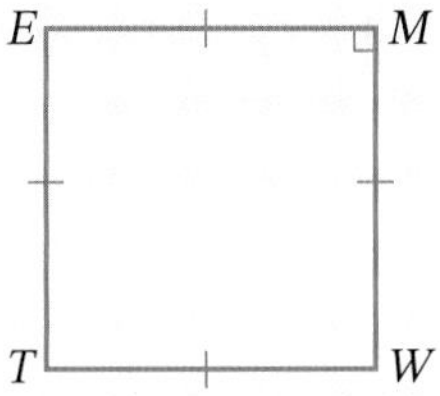

8 *GHKL* is a quadrilateral with all angles equal to 90° and *GH* = *GL*.

PS
R
C

Prove that all sides are equal as well and hence it must be a square.

12.02

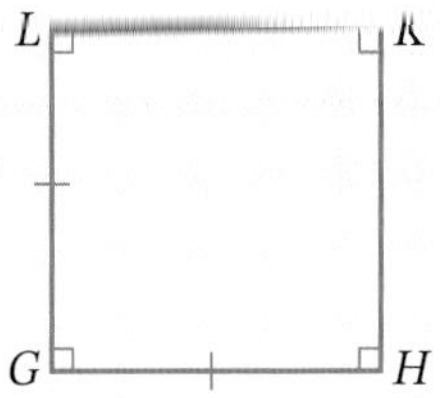

9 *MNPT* is a quadrilateral whose diagonals *MP* and *NT* are equal and bisect each other at right angles. Prove that *MNPT* must be a square.

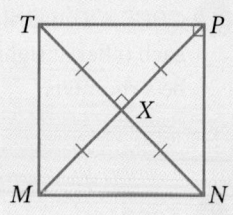

EXAMPLE 3

10 *ABCD* is a parallelogram and *BX* = *DY*. Prove that:

a △*ABX* ≡ △*CDY*

b *AXCY* is a parallelogram.

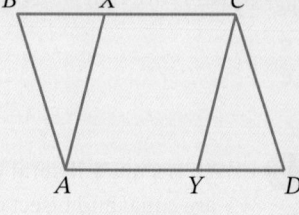

11 *AECD* is a rhombus and *AE* = *EB*. Prove that:

a △*CBE* ≡ △*DAE*

b *BCDE* is a parallelogram.

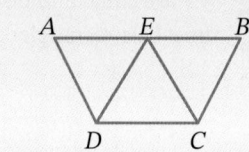

12 *ABCD* is a parallelogram and *AP* = *AS* = *CQ* = *CR*. Prove that:

a *RQ* = *PS* and *PQ* = *RS*

b *PQRS* is a parallelogram.

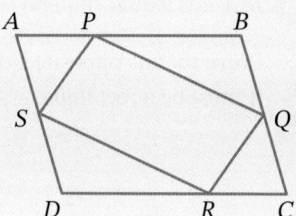

13 *AC* and *DB* are diameters of concentric circles with centre *O*. Prove that *ABCD* is a parallelogram.

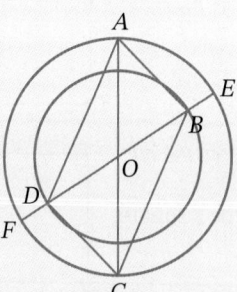

14 *PR* and *SQ* are diameters of concentric circles, centre *O* and *TU* ⊥ *SQ*. Prove that *PQRS* is a rhombus.

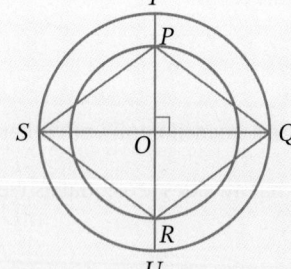

15 *DEFG* is a rectangle. *W*, *X*, *Y* and *Z* are the midpoints of the sides.
Prove that *WXYZ* is a rhombus.

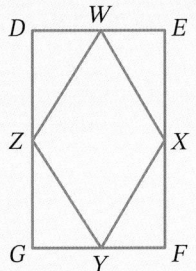

16 *ABCD* is a parallelogram. *P*, *Q*, *R* and *T* are the midpoints of the sides. Prove that *PQRT* is a parallelogram.

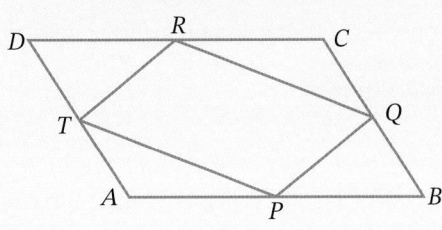

INVESTIGATION

Is a square a rhombus?

Using the definitions of the special quadrilaterals, we see that a parallelogram can also be classified as a trapezium since it has at least one pair of opposite sides parallel. This means that trapeziums are **inclusive** of parallelograms. The set of trapeziums includes all parallelograms, or put another way, a parallelogram is a special type of trapezium. Similarly, parallelograms are inclusive of rectangles and rectangles are inclusive of squares. This can be represented by a Venn diagram:

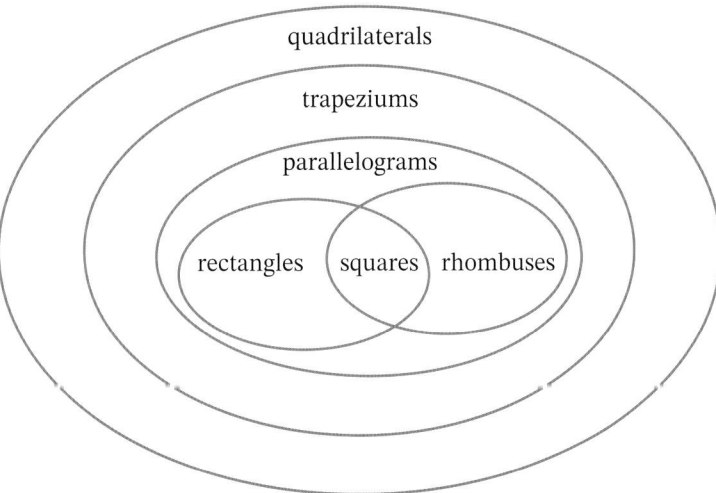

1   Why is a rectangle a special type of parallelogram but a parallelogram is not always a rectangle? How can you use the Venn diagram to explain this?

2   Where would you put **kites** on the Venn diagram?

☐ Foundation   ○ Standard   ○ Complex

Properties of triangles and quadrilaterals can be proved using the congruence tests.

Example 4

$\triangle ABC$ is an isosceles triangle with $AB = AC$. D is the midpoint of BC.

a Which congruence test can be used to prove that
$\triangle ABD \equiv \triangle ACD$?

b Explain why $\angle B = \angle C$.

c What geometrical result about isosceles triangles does this prove?

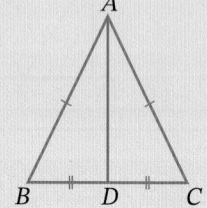

SOLUTION

a For $\triangle ABD$ and $\triangle ACD$:

$AB = AC$ (given)

AD is common.

$BD = CD$ (D is the midpoint of BC)

$\therefore$ the congruence test is SSS.

b $\angle B = \angle C$ because they are matching angles of congruent triangles.

c The angles opposite the equal sides of an isosceles triangle are equal.

Example 5

a If $LMNP$ is a rectangle, prove that $\triangle PNT \equiv \triangle MLT$.

b Prove that the diagonals of a rectangle bisect each other.

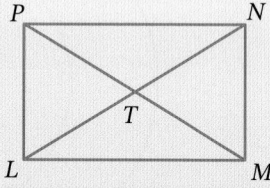

SOLUTION

a In $\triangle PNT$ and $\triangle MLT$:

$PN = ML$ (opposite sides of a rectangle)

$\angle PNT = \angle MLT$ (alternate angles, $PN \parallel ML$ for a rectangle)

$\angle PTN = \angle MTL$ (vertically opposite angles)

$\therefore \triangle PNT \equiv \triangle MLT$ (AAS)

b $PT = MT$ and $NT = LT$ (matching sides of congruent triangles)

$\therefore T$ is the midpoint of the diagonals LN and MP.

$\therefore$ the diagonals of a rectangle bisect each other.

Proving properties of triangles and quadrilaterals   U F R C

1 $\triangle ABC$ is an isosceles triangle, with $AB = AC$.

(R) D is the midpoint of BC.

(C) **a** Which congruence test can be used to prove that $\triangle ABD \equiv \triangle ACD$?

b Explain why $\angle ADB = \angle ADC$.

c Hence prove that $AD \perp BC$.

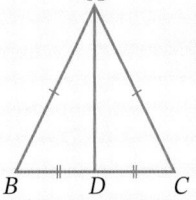

EXAMPLE 4

2 In the diagram, $\angle S = \angle T$ and $WP \perp ST$.

(R) **a** Which congruence test can be used to prove
(C)   that $\triangle SPW \equiv \triangle TPW$?

b Explain why $WS = WT$.

c What geometrical result about triangles does this prove?

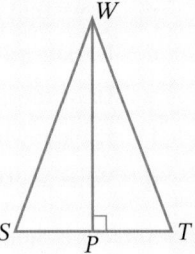

3 $\triangle ABC$ is an equilateral triangle ($AB = BC = AC$). X is the midpoint of BC.

(R)
(C)

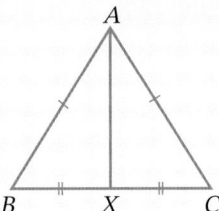 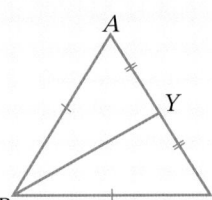

a Which congruence test can be used to prove that $\triangle ABX \equiv \triangle ACX$?

b Explain why $\angle B = \angle C$.

c In the second diagram, $\triangle ABC$ is redrawn so that Y is the midpoint of AC. Which congruence test can be used to prove that $\triangle BAY \equiv \triangle BCY$?

d Is $\angle A = \angle C$? Why?

e Calculate the sizes of the 3 angles of $\triangle ABC$.

f What geometrical property of equilateral triangles does this prove?

4 In $\triangle PMN$, $\angle M = \angle N$ and YP bisects $\angle MPN$.

(R) **a** Explain why $\angle MPY = \angle NPY$.

(C) **b** Which congruence test can be used to prove that $\triangle PMY \equiv \triangle PNY$?

c Explain why $MY = NY$.

d Is $\angle PYM = \angle PYN$? Why?

e Prove that $PY \perp MN$.

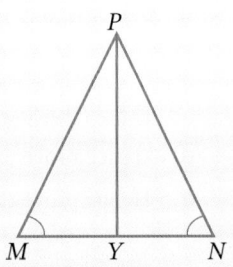

EXAMPLE 5

5 *ABCD* is a quadrilateral whose opposite sides are equal.

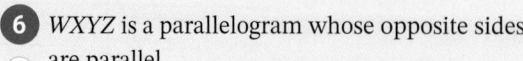

(R) a Prove that $\triangle ABC \equiv \triangle CDA$.

(C) b Explain why $\angle BAC = \angle DCA$ and $\angle BCA = \angle DAC$.

c Hence state why $AB \parallel CD$ and $AD \parallel CB$.

d What type of quadrilateral is *ABCD*?

6 *WXYZ* is a parallelogram whose opposite sides

(R) are parallel.

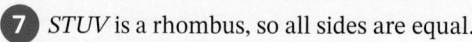

(C) a Copy the diagram.

b On your diagram, show 2 pairs of equal alternate angles.

c Prove that $\triangle WXZ \equiv \triangle YZX$.

d Explain why $\angle W = \angle Y$.

e Draw the other diagonal *WY* and prove that $\triangle WXY \equiv \triangle YZW$.

f Explain why $\angle WXY = \angle YZW$.

g What angle property of a parallelogram does this prove?

7 *STUV* is a rhombus, so all sides are equal.

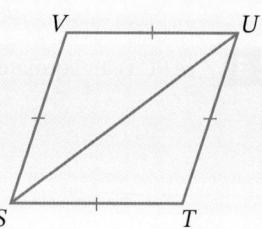

(R) a Prove that $\triangle VUS \equiv \triangle TUS$.

(C) b Prove that the diagonal *US* bisects $\angle VUT$ and $\angle VST$.

8 *ABCD* is a parallelogram with opposite sides parallel.

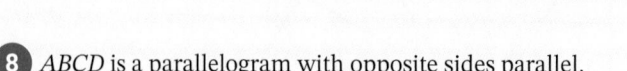

(R) a Prove that $\triangle ABD \equiv \triangle CDB$.

(C) b Explain why $AB = CD$ and $AD = CB$.

c What property of a parallelogram does this prove?

9 *BEGH* is a rhombus (a parallelogram with equal sides)

(R) whose diagonals *BG* and *EH* intersect at *L*.

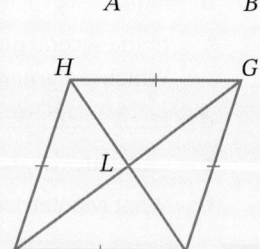

(C) a Prove that $\triangle BEL \equiv \triangle GHL$.

b Prove that the diagonals of a rhombus bisect each other.

c $\triangle BEH$ is isosceles, so which equation is true?
Select **A**, **B**, **C** or **D**.

   A $\angle BEH = \angle BHE$ **B** $\angle BLE = \angle BEH$

   C $\angle HBE = \angle BEH$ **D** $\angle BEH = \angle EBH$

d Hence prove that $\triangle BEL \equiv \triangle BHL$.

e Hence prove that the diagonals of a rhombus cross at right angles.

☐ Foundation   ○ Standard   ◇ Complex

10 *ABCD* is a kite, so pairs of adjacent sides are equal.

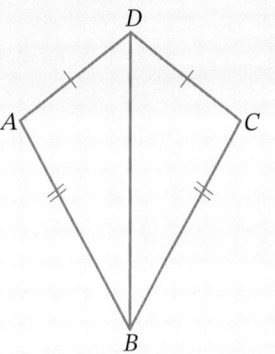

- (R) **a** Prove that $\triangle ABD \equiv \triangle CBD$.
- (C) **b** Prove that $\angle A = \angle C$.
- **c** Prove that diagonal *DB* bisects $\angle ADC$ and $\angle ABC$.
- **d** Copy the diagram and draw the other diagonal *AC*, intersecting *DB* at point *X*.
- **e** Prove that $\triangle DAX \equiv \triangle DCX$.
- **f** Prove that diagonal *DB* bisects diagonal *AC*.
- **g** Prove that $DB \perp AC$.

☆ **MENTAL SKILLS** ⑫ ANSWERS ON P. 660   **Maths without calculators**

Dividing a quantity in a given ratio

Quiz
Mental
skills 12

1   Study this example.

Divide $5600 between Alice and Peter in the ratio $5:3$.

Total number of parts $= 5 + 3 = 8$.

1 part $= \$5600 \div 8 = \$700$

Alice's share $= 5 \times \$700 = \$3500$

Peter's share $= 3 \times \$700 = \$2500 + \$2100 = \$5600$ (original amount)

2   Now divide each of these quantities in the given ratio.

- **a**   Divide $150 between Mark and Jenni in the ratio $2:1$.
- **b**   Divide $2100 between Simon and Sunil in the ratio $4:3$.
- **c**   Divide $720 between Lisa and Bree in the ratio $2:7$.
- **d**   Divide $2000 between William and Adriana in the ratio $1:3$.
- **e**   Divide $4500 between Anne and Pete in the ratio $3:2$.
- **f**   Divide $3000 between Sharanya and Asam in the ratio $3:7$.
- **g**   Divide $3600 between Cindy and Carmen in the ratio $5:1$.
- **h**   Divide $1600 between Nancy and John in the ratio $3:5$.
- **i**   Divide $990 between Carol and Louis in the ratio $5:4$.
- **j**   Divide $4000 between Yvette and Andre in the ratio $1:4$.
- **k**   Divide $4900 between Arden and Ivan in the ratio $3:4$.
- **l**   Divide $3200 between Tan and Mai in the ratio $5:3$.

□ Foundation   ○ Standard   ◐ Complex

12.04 Extension: Formal geometrical proofs

EXTENSION

General geometrical results can be proved by writing a geometrical argument, where reasons are given at each step of the argument. This is called **deductive geometry.**

Example 6

Puzzle
Geometrical
proofs order
activity

In the diagram, $AB \parallel CD$, $KL = DL$ and $\angle LDP = 115°$.

Find the value of w, giving reasons.

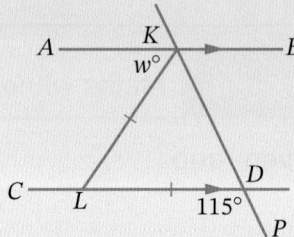

SOLUTION

$\angle KDL = 180° - 115°$	(angles on a straight line)
$\quad = 65°$	
$\therefore \angle LKD = 65°$	(equal angles of isosceles $\triangle KLD$)
$\angle AKD = 115°$	(corresponding angles, $AB \parallel CD$)
$\therefore w = 115° - 65°$	
$\quad = 50°$	

Example 7

In the diagram, $AC \parallel ED$, $AE \parallel BD$, $BE \parallel CD$ and $CB = CD$.

Prove that $\triangle ABE$ is an isosceles triangle.

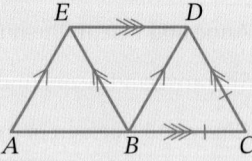

SOLUTION

$\angle EBD = \angle CDB$	(alternate angles, $BE \parallel CD$)
and $\angle EBD = \angle AEB$	(alternate angles, $AE \parallel BD$)
$\therefore \angle CDB = \angle AEB$	
But $\angle CDB = \angle CBD$	(equal angles of isosceles $\triangle CBD$)
and $\angle BAE = \angle CBD$	(corresponding angles, $AE \parallel BD$)
$\therefore \angle CDB = \angle BAE$	
$\therefore \angle AEB = \angle BAE$	
$\therefore \angle ABE$ is an isosceles triangle	(2 equal angles)

9780170465595

EXERCISE (12.04) ANSWERS ON P. 660

Formal geometrical proofs

(U)(F)(PS)(R)(C)

EXAMPLE
6

1 *KL = ML* and *MN = MP*.
Find *x*, giving reasons.

(PS)(R)(C)

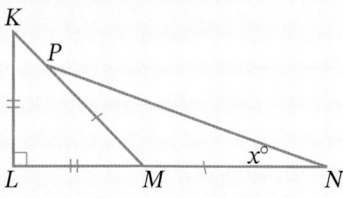

2 *CE* || *AB*, *CD = BD* and *AC = BC*.
Find *m*, giving reasons.

(PS)(R)(C)

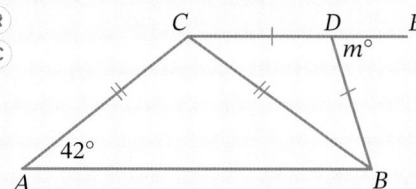

3 *NK* bisects ∠*HKL*. Find the size of
∠*NHK*, giving reasons.

(PS)(R)(C)

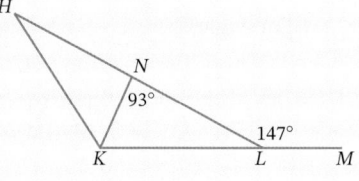

4 *BCDE* is a rhombus with the diagonals
intersecting at *G*. Find the value of *x*,
giving reasons for each step.

(PS)(R)(C)

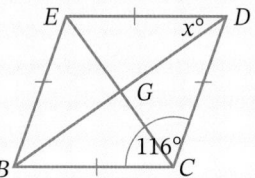

5 △*ABC* is an isosceles triangle where
AB = AC and *BC* || *ED*. Prove that
△*ADE* is an isosceles triangle.

(PS)(R)(C)

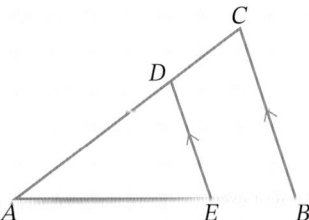

6 *PY* bisects ∠*XYW*, *PW* bisects
∠*TWY* and *YX* || *WT*. Prove that
∠*YPW* = 90°.

(PS)(R)(C)

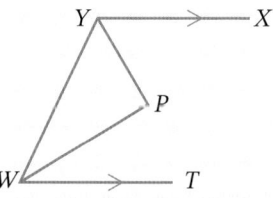

EXAMPLE
7

7 *TWXZ* is a parallelogram and
TZ = TY = UX.

(R)(C)

a Prove that △*TZY* ≡ △*XWU*.

b Hence prove that *TUXY* is a
parallelogram.

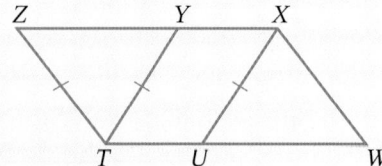

8 *MNPT* is a square. *W* and *Y* are the
midpoints of sides *TP* and *MT*.

(R)(C)

a Prove that △*MNY* ≡ △*MTW*.

b Prove that *MW* ⊥ *NY*.

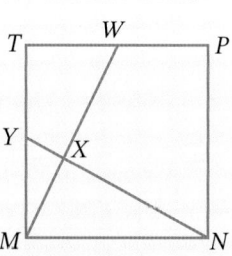

□ Foundation ○ Standard ◇ Complex

▷

9 *ABDE* is a parallelogram and *BC = BD*.
Prove that $\angle AED = 2\angle BCD$.

PS
R
C

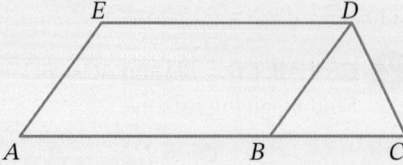

10 *A* and *B* are the centres of 2 circles
that intersect at *C* and *D*.

R
C

a Prove that $\triangle ADB \equiv \triangle ACB$.

b Hence prove that $\triangle DXB \equiv \triangle CXB$
and *DX = CX*.

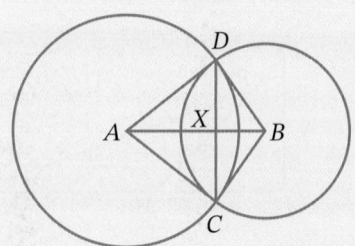

11 If *AC = BC* and *DC = EC*, prove that
AB || DE.

PS
R
C

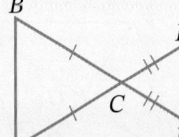

12 $\triangle UXY$ is an equilateral triangle and
WX = XU. Prove that $\angle WUY$ is a
right angle.

PS
R
C

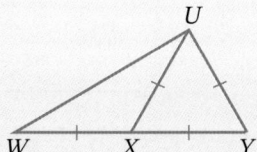

13 If *WY || PQ*, prove that the angle sum
of $\triangle PQT$ is 180°.

PS
R
C

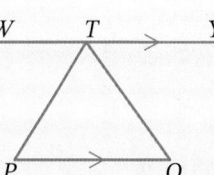

14 *CA* bisects $\angle FAB$ and *DA* bisects
$\angle HAB$. Prove that $\angle CAD = 90°$.

PS
R
C

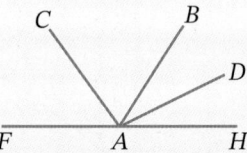

15 Prove that the exterior angle of a
triangle is equal to the sum of the
interior opposite angles (that is,
prove that $\angle CBD = \angle CAB + \angle BCA$).

PS
R
C

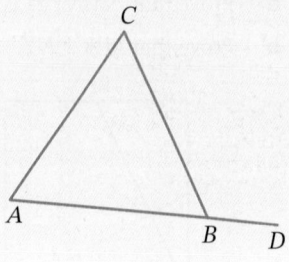

16 *AC* is the diameter of a semicircle
with centre *O*. *B* is a point on the
semicircle. Let $\angle ABO = x°$ and
$\angle CBO = y°$. Prove that $\angle ABC$ is a
right angle.

PS
R
C

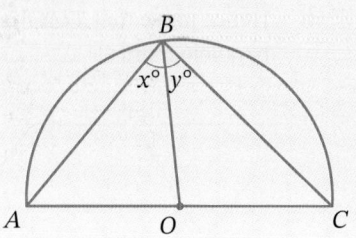

☐ Foundation ◯ Standard ◯ Complex

Properties of similar figures

We will use dynamic geometry software to look at the properties of similar figures.

1 Construct a 5-sided polygon as shown.

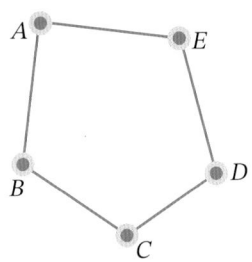

2 Show the lengths of the sides of the polygon as well.

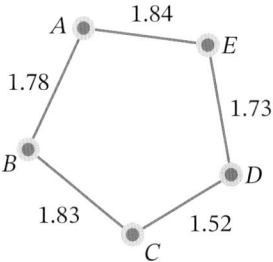

3 Enlarge the polygon by a scale factor of 2 to obtain the image *AFGHI* as shown.

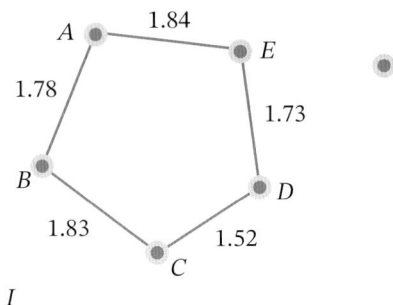

4 The lengths of the sides of the image are shown. Is the ratio of matching sides the same for all sides?

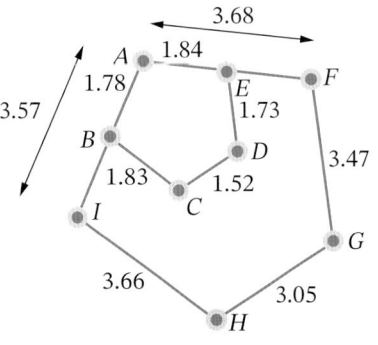

5 Measure the angles of the polygon and its image. An example is shown of some of the matching angles on the right. Are the matching angles equal?

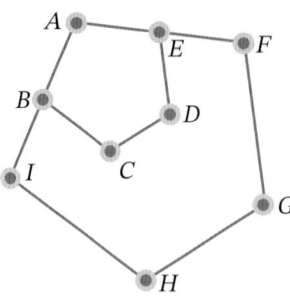 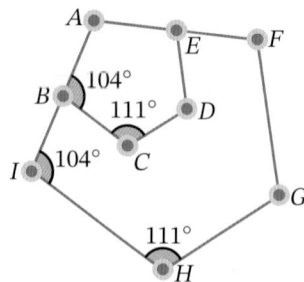

6 Repeat Steps **1** to **5** for:

a a triangle

b a quadrilateral.

7 For similar figures:

a are matching angles equal?

b are matching sides in the same ratio?

12.05 Similar figures

Worksheets
A page of similar figures

Enlargements and reductions

Enlarging a logo

Puzzle
Cartoon enlargement

Similar figures have the same shape, but are not necessarily the same size.

When a figure is enlarged or reduced, a **similar figure** is created. The original figure is called the **original**, while the enlarged or reduced figure is called the **image**.

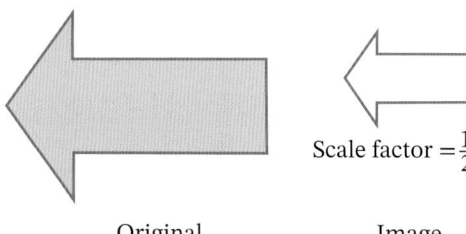

Scale factor $= \frac{1}{2}$

Original   Image

The **scale factor** describes by how much a figure has been enlarged or reduced.

> **ⓘ Scale factor**
>
> $$\text{Scale factor} = \frac{\text{image length}}{\text{original length}}$$
>
> • If the scale factor is greater than 1, then the image is an enlargement.
> • If the scale factor is between 0 and 1, then the image is a reduction.

Example 8

Find the scale factor for each pair of similar figures.

> In all questions, assume the left figure is the original and the right figure the image.

a

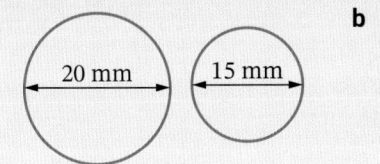

20 mm   15 mm

b

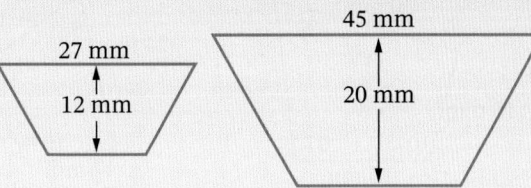

27 mm

12 mm

45 mm

20 mm

SOLUTION

a Scale factor $= \dfrac{15}{20}$ $\dfrac{\text{image length}}{\text{original length}}$

$= \dfrac{3}{4}$

b Scale factor $= \dfrac{45}{27}$ $\left(\text{or } \dfrac{20}{12}\right)$

$= \dfrac{5}{3}$

The symbol for 'is similar to' is '|||'. As with congruence notation, we must make sure that the vertices (angles) of similar figures are written in matching order.

ⓘ Properties of similar figures

- Matching angles are equal
- Matching sides are in the same ratio

Example 9

The 2 quadrilaterals *KLMN* and *PQRT* are similar.

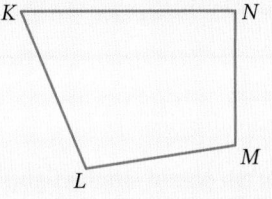

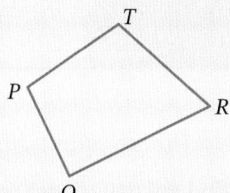

a List all pairs of matching sides and matching angles.

b Use the correct notation to write a similarity statement relating these 2 quadrilaterals.

SOLUTION

a By rotating the figure *KLMN*, its shape can be matched with *PQRT*.

The pairs of matching sides are:

KN and *QR*
MN and *PQ*
ML and *PT*
LK and *TR*.

The pairs of matching angles are:

∠*K* and ∠*R*
∠*N* and ∠*Q*
∠*M* and ∠*P*
∠*L* and ∠*T*.

b ∠*K* matches with ∠*R*, ∠*L* matches with ∠*T*, ∠*M* matches with ∠*P*, ∠*N* matches with ∠*Q*.

∴ *KLMN* ||| *RTPQ*   matching order of vertices

Example 10

Test whether each pair of figures are similar.

a

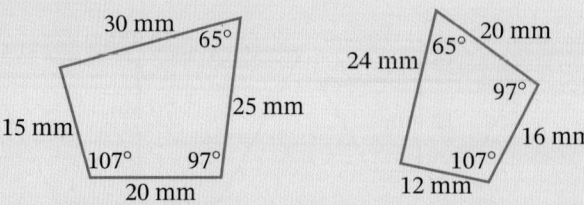

b

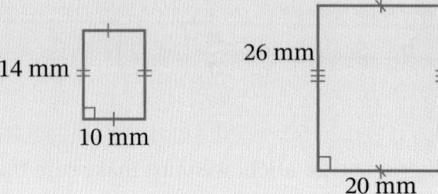

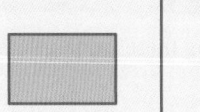

26 mm

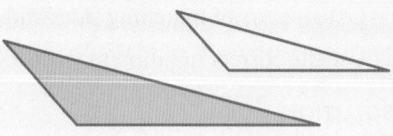

20 mm

SOLUTION

a For the 2 quadrilaterals, matching angles are equal and the ratios of matching sides are equal.

$$\frac{20}{16}=\frac{5}{4}, \frac{25}{20}=\frac{5}{4}, \frac{30}{24}=\frac{5}{4}, \frac{15}{12}=\frac{5}{4}$$

∴ the quadrilaterals are similar.

b For the 2 rectangles, matching angles are equal (90°), but the ratios of matching sides are not equal.

$$\frac{10}{20}=\frac{1}{2} \text{ but } \frac{14}{26}=\frac{7}{13}$$

∴ the rectangles are not similar.

EXERCISE 12.05 ANSWERS ON P. 660

Similar figures

(U)(F)(R)(C)

EXAMPLE 8

1 By measurement, find the scale factor for each pair of similar figures.

a
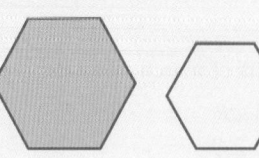

b
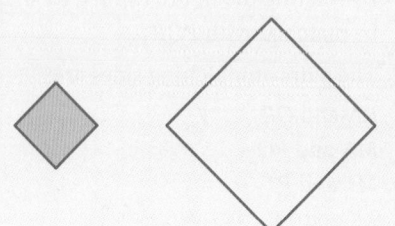

c

d

▷

□ Foundation ○ Standard ◇ Complex

560   Nelson Maths 10 Advanced

9780170465595

2 Copy each figure onto graph paper and draw its image using the given scale factor.

a Scale factor = 2

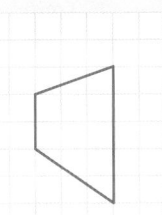

b Scale factor = 2.5

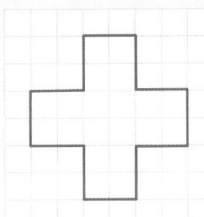

c Scale factor = $\frac{1}{2}$

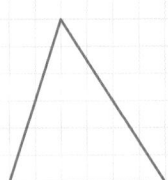

d Scale factor = $\frac{2}{3}$

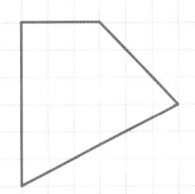

3 For each pair of similar figures:

EXAMPLE
9

    i list all pairs of matching angles

    ii list all pairs of matching sides

    iii use the correct notation to write a similarity statement relating them.

a

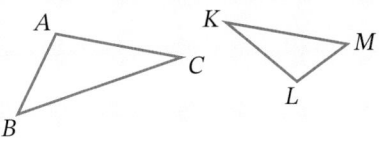

b

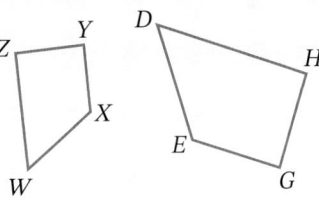

c

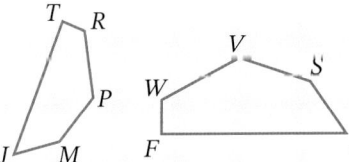

d

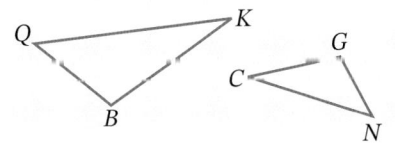

Foundation   Standard   Complex

EXAMPLE
10

4 Test whether each pair of figures are similar.

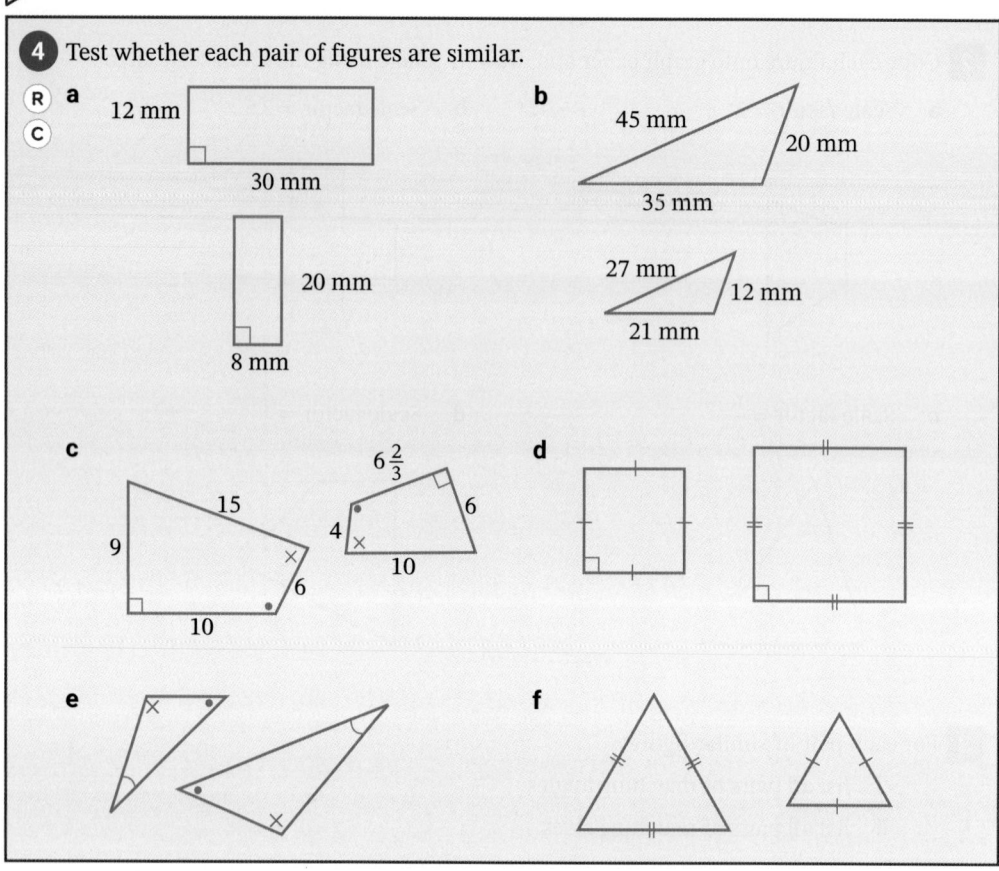

12.06 Scale diagrams, maps and plans

Videos
Scale
drawings

Jai Singh
(sundial)

Modelling the
Spitfire

Queen
Hatshepsut's
ship

The history
of the golden
ratio

Fractals:
The Koch
snowflake

Scale diagrams, maps and plans are all two-dimensional representations of things that can be found in real life, drawn in proportion or 'to scale'. A **scale diagram** accurately represents a larger or smaller object such that the lengths and distances on it are in the same ratio as the real lengths and distances. The scale factor used is called the **scale** of the diagram.

A **scaled map** is a representation of different places and the paths and roads that link them. A **plan** is a set of working drawings that define all construction specifications for a building, they are sometimes called **blueprints**.

A scale may be represented in different ways.

● 1 cm = 10 m or 1 cm to 10 m (a pair of corresponding measurements)

● 1 : 50 (a ratio)

● 0   1   2   3   4   5 km (a line drawn to scale)

☐ Foundation   ○ Standard   ○ Complex

The scale on a scale diagram is written as a ratio of **scaled length : real length**, where **scaled length** is the length on the diagram.

For example, a scale of 1 : 100 means that the real lengths are 100 times larger than the lengths on the diagram.

Example 11

A scale diagram of a rectangular block of land has been drawn. What scale has been used?

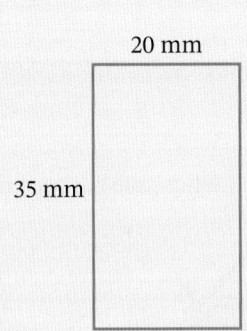

Shutterstock.com/jax10289

SOLUTION

By measurement, the length and width of the scale drawing are 35 mm and 20 mm.

Scale = 35 mm : 35 m (or 20 mm : 20 m)   scaled length : real length

   = 35 mm : 35 000 mm (or 20 mm : 20 000 m)   1 m = 1000 mm

   = 1 : 1000

Example 12

The scale on a map is 1 : 5 000 000. If the distance from Perth to Kalgoorlie on the map is 12 cm, calculate the actual distance from Perth to Kalgoorlie.

SOLUTION

Scaled distance = 12 cm

Actual distance = 12 × 5 000 000 cm

$\qquad$ = 60 000 000 cm

$\qquad$ = 600 000 m   1 m = 100 cm

$\qquad$ = 600 km   1 km = 1000 m

Example 13

A window on a house plan with scale 1 : 50 is 3 cm wide. What width (in millimetres) of window should be ordered for the house?

SOLUTION

scaled distance = 3 cm
actual distance = 3 × 50 cm
      = 150 cm
      = 1500 mm   1 cm = 10 mm

EXERCISE 12.06 ANSWERS ON P. 661

Scale diagrams, maps and plans   U F

EXAMPLE 11

1 The scale diagram on the left is of the alarm clock on the right. What scale has been used?

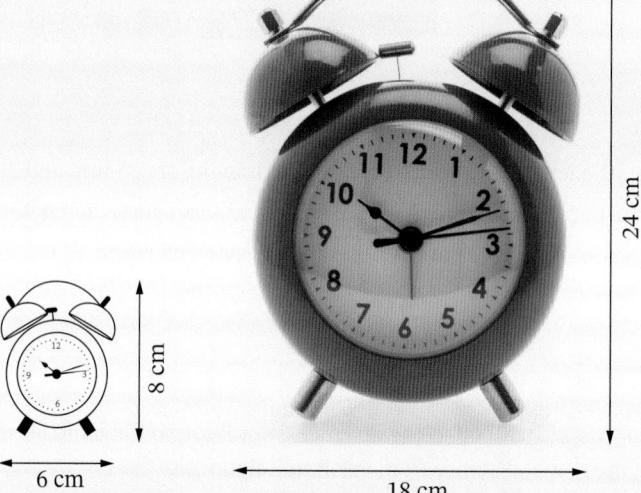

24 cm

8 cm

6 cm

18 cm

2 A scale diagram of a tidy bin has been drawn. What scale has been used?

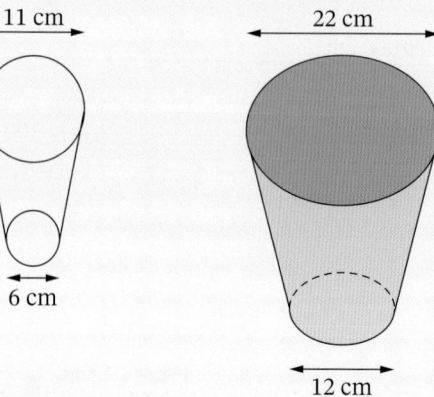

11 cm

22 cm

6 cm

12 cm

☐ Foundation   ○ Standard   ○ Complex

Freepik/lifeforstock

3 A scale diagram of a ladder has been drawn. What is the scale?

230 cm

11.5 cm

3 cm

60 cm

4 A scale diagram of a TV has been drawn. What is the scale?

20 inches

12 inches

21.6 inches

36 inches

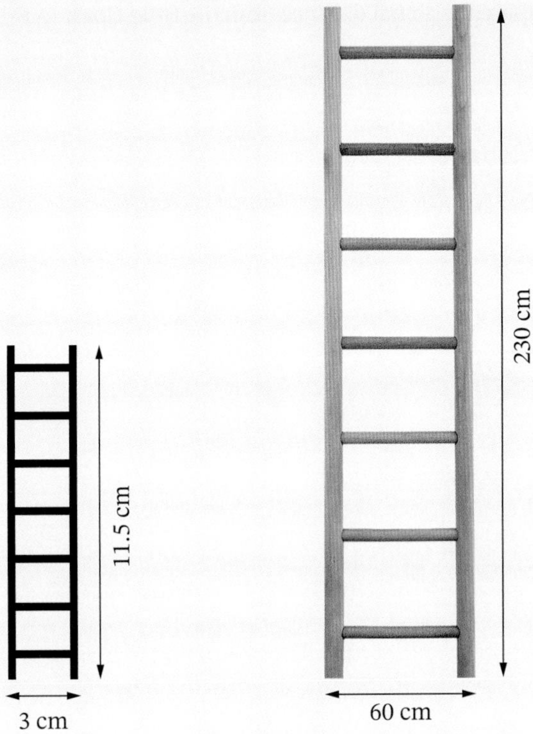

Shutterstock.com/Den Rozhnovsky

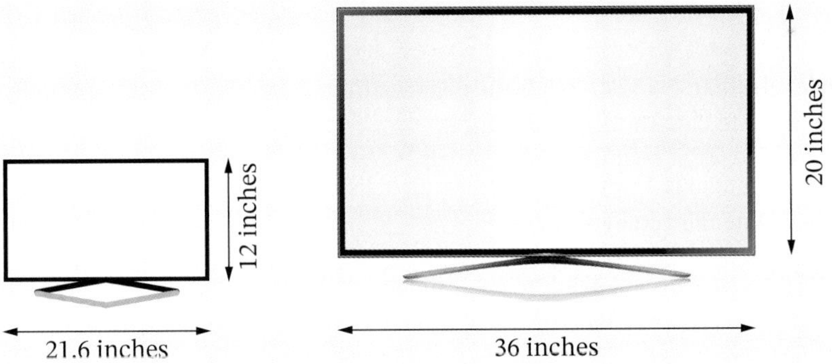

Shutterstock.com/Uranium

12.06

▷

EXAMPLE
12

5 The scale on a map is 1 : 500 000. If the distance from the Gold Coast to Brisbane on the map is 16 cm, calculate the actual distance from the Gold Coast to Brisbane.

Map data ©2023 Google

6 The scale on a map is 1 : 200 000. If the distance from Byron Bay to Mullumbimby is 9 cm on the map, calculate the actual distance.

7 The scale on a map is 1 : 5 000 000. If the scaled distance from Perth to Carnarvon is 18 cm, calculate the actual distance.

8 The scale on a treasure map is 1 : 5000. If the direct distance from the starting point to the treasure is 7 cm, calculate the direct distance from the starting point to the treasure.

EXAMPLE
13

9 The length of the house on a house plan is 14 cm. The scale for the plan is 1 : 50. What is the actual length of the house?

10 The width of a house on a plan with scale 1 : 50 is 11 cm. What is the actual width of the house?

11 The length and width of a bedroom on a house plan are 8 cm and 6 cm respectively. The scale of the plan is 1 : 50. What are the actual dimensions of the bedroom?

12 The blueprint for a warehouse represents a length of 10 m and width of 8 m for the building. The scale of the blueprint is 1 : 50. What is the scaled length and width of the building on the blueprint?

13 The scale of a map is 1 : 500. What length on the map would represent a real life distance of 40 metres?

□ Foundation ○ Standard ◇ Complex

Example 14

The 2 triangles are similar. Find the values of d and k.

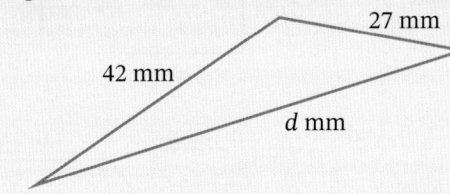
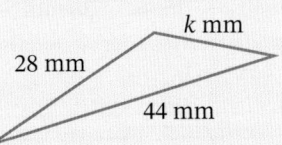

27 mm

42 mm

d mm

k mm

28 mm

44 mm

SOLUTION

Since the triangles are similar, the ratios of matching sides are equal.

$\dfrac{d}{44} = \dfrac{42}{28}$

$d = \dfrac{42}{28} \times 44$

$= 66$

$\dfrac{k}{27} = \dfrac{28}{42}$

$k = \dfrac{28}{42} \times 27$

$= 18$

Alternative method:

Scale factor $= \dfrac{28}{42} = \dfrac{2}{3}$

$d = 44 \div \dfrac{2}{3}$

$= 66$

$k = 27 \times \dfrac{2}{3}$

$= 18$

Video
Finding an unknown side in similar figures

Skillsheet
Finding sides in similar triangles

Worksheet
Finding sides in similar figures

Puzzle
Similar triangles

Example 15

$\triangle KLN \;|||\; \triangle PMN$. Find the value of y.

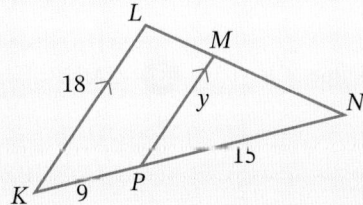

L

M

18

y

N

15

K   9   P

SOLUTION

$\dfrac{MP}{LK} = \dfrac{PN}{KN}$ ratios of matching sides are equal

$\dfrac{y}{18} = \dfrac{15}{24}$ $KN = 9 + 15 = 24$

$y = \dfrac{15}{24} \times 18$

$= 11\dfrac{1}{4}$

Finding sides in similar figures

U F PS R

EXAMPLE
14

1 Find the value of each variable in each pair of similar figures.

R **a**

16 mm w mm 20 mm
28 mm

b

15 cm 27 cm m cm 18 cm

c

p mm
25 mm 12 mm h mm
35 mm 15 mm

d

x mm 45 cm
12 mm 30 mm

e

8 cm
a cm 10 cm
w cm
6 cm 16 cm

f

q cm 20 cm
27 cm 15 cm
g cm 10 cm

g

20 mm 16 mm 16 mm 12 mm
× ×
y mm b mm

h

5 cm × 8 cm 11 cm 8 cm
t cm × u cm

EXAMPLE
15

2 △ABC ||| △ADE. Find the value of h.

R

A
7
D E
8
5
B h C

3 △MNP ||| △MWY. Find the value of x.

R

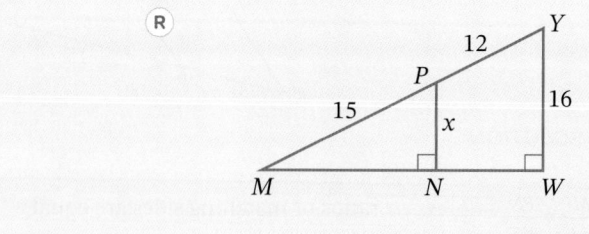

Y
12
P 16
15 x
M N W

□ Foundation ○ Standard ○ Complex

4 This photograph has been enlarged so that its length is 24 cm. If the dimensions of
the original photo were 15 cm × 10 cm, what is the width of the enlargement?

10 cm

15 cm

5 A building that is 40 m high casts a shadow 15 m long. At the same time, the shadow of
a tree is 4.5 m long. What is the height of the tree?

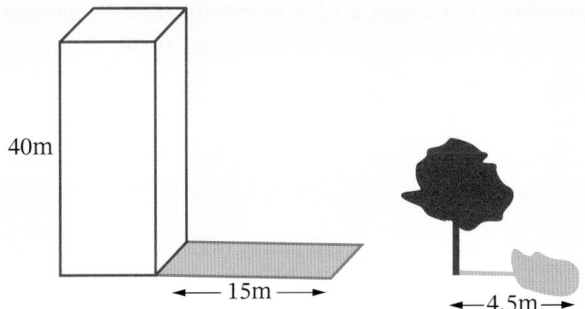

40m

15m

4.5m

6 △WXY ||| △WDE. What is the value of x?
Select the correct answer **A**, **B**, **C** or **D**.

A 4	**B** 6
C 8	**D** 10

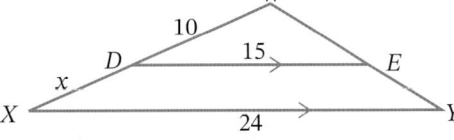

7 Katrina is 1.72 m tall and casts a shadow that is 2.5 m long. At the same time, a flagpole
casts a shadow that is 3.5 m long. How long is the flagpole?

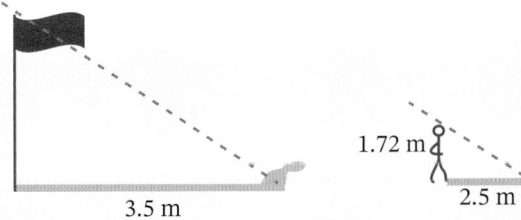

3.5 m

1.72 m

2.5 m

☐ Foundation   ○ Standard   ○ Complex

12.07

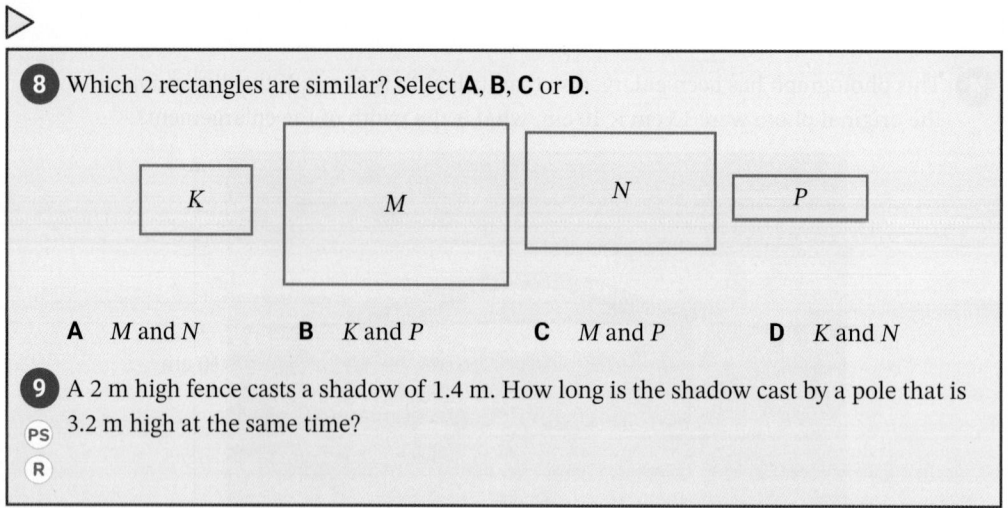

8 Which 2 rectangles are similar? Select **A**, **B**, **C** or **D**.

A M and N **B** K and P **C** M and P **D** K and N

9 A 2 m high fence casts a shadow of 1.4 m. How long is the shadow cast by a pole that is 3.2 m high at the same time?

12.08 Similar triangle proofs

There are 4 sets of conditions that can be used to determine if 2 triangles are similar. These are called the tests for similar triangles or **similarity tests**.

Worksheets
Congruent and similar triangle proofs

Congruence and similarity review

ⓘ Similarity tests

There are 4 tests for similar triangles: SSS, SAS, AA, RHS.

Two triangles are similar if:

- the 3 sides of one triangle are proportional to the 3 sides of the other triangle ('**SSS**')

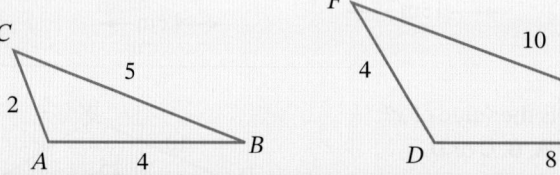

- 2 sides of one triangle are proportional to 2 sides of the other triangle, and the **included angles** are equal ('**SAS**')

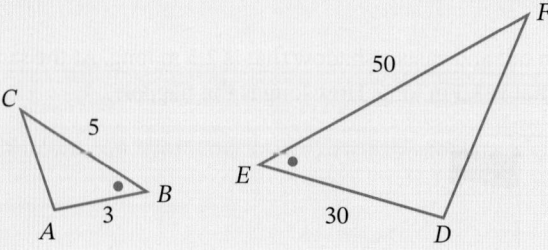

☐ Foundation ○ Standard ◇ Complex

9780170465595

- 2 angles of one triangle are equal to 2 angles of the other triangle ('**AA**' or '**equiangular**')

12.08

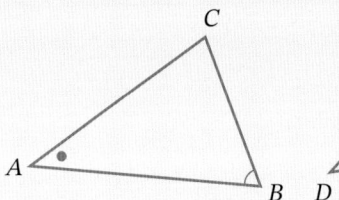

> **Equiangular** means 'equal angles'.

- they are right-angled and the hypotenuse and a second side of one triangle are proportional to the hypotenuse and a second side of the other triangle ('**RHS**').

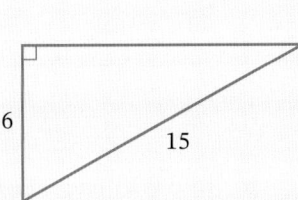

Example 16

Which test can be used to prove that each pair of triangles are similar?

a

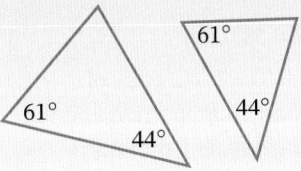

b

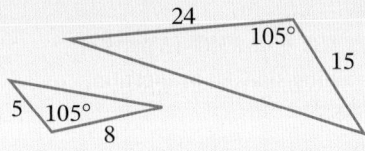

c

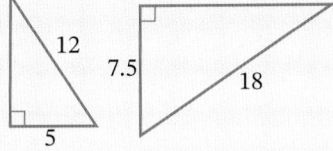

d

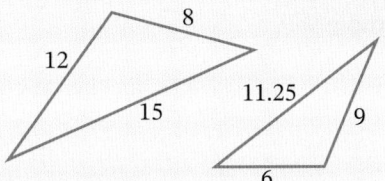

> **Video**
> Tests for similar triangles

SOLUTION

a   2 pairs of angles are equal, or equiangular ('AA').

b   2 pairs of matching sides are in the same ratio and the included angles in both triangles are equal ('SAS').

$$\frac{15}{5} = \frac{24}{8} = 3$$

c   Both have right angles, and the pairs of hypotenuses and second sides are in the same ratio ('RHS').

$$\frac{7.5}{5} = \frac{18}{12} = \frac{3}{2}$$

d   All 3 pairs of matching sides are in the same ratio ('SSS').

$$\frac{11.25}{15} = \frac{9}{12} = \frac{6}{8} = \frac{3}{4}$$

To formally prove that 2 triangles are similar, we use a specific format that involves applying one of the 4 similarity tests: 'SSS', 'SAS', 'AA', 'RHS'.

Example 17

Video
Similar triangle proofs

Prove that each pair of triangles are similar.

a

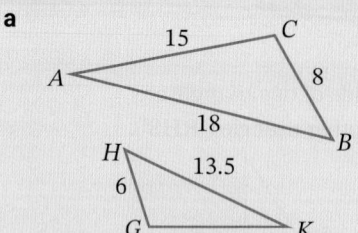

b

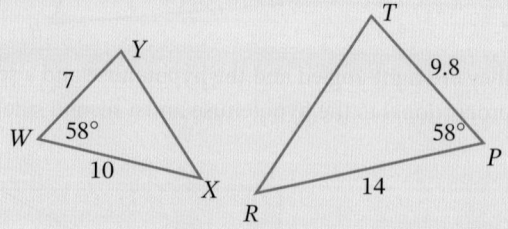

SOLUTION

a In $\triangle ABC$ and $\triangle KHG$:

$$\frac{AB}{KH} = \frac{18}{13.5} = \frac{4}{3}$$

$$\frac{AC}{KG} = \frac{15}{11.25} = \frac{4}{3} \quad \frac{BC}{HG} = \frac{8}{6} = \frac{4}{3}$$

$$\therefore \frac{AB}{KH} = \frac{AC}{KG} = \frac{BC}{HG}$$

$\therefore \triangle ABC \,|||\, \triangle KHG$ (3 pairs of matching sides in proportion, or 'SSS')

b In $\triangle WXY$ and $\triangle PRT$:

$$\frac{WX}{PR} = \frac{10}{14} = \frac{5}{7}$$

$$\frac{WY}{PT} = \frac{7}{9.8} = \frac{5}{7}$$

$$\therefore \frac{WX}{PR} = \frac{WY}{PT}$$

$$\angle W = \angle P = 58°$$

$\therefore \triangle WXY \,|||\, \triangle PRT$ (2 pairs of matching sides in proportion and the included angles equal, or 'SAS')

Example 18

Prove that $\triangle ABC \,|||\, \triangle EDC$ and hence find the value of m.

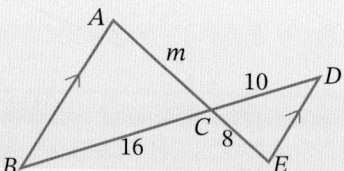

SOLUTION

In $\triangle ABC$ and $\triangle EDC$:

$\angle A = \angle E$ (alternate angles, $AB \parallel DE$)

$\angle B = \angle D$ (alternate angles, $AB \parallel DE$)

$\therefore \triangle ABC \,|||\, \triangle EDC$ (equiangular, or 'AA')

$$\therefore \frac{m}{8} = \frac{16}{10} \quad \text{(matching sides in similar triangles)}$$

$$m = \frac{16}{10} \times 8$$

$$= 12.8$$

Similar triangle proofs

(U) (F) (R) (C)

EXAMPLE
16

1 Which test can be used to prove that each pair of triangles are similar?

R
C

a

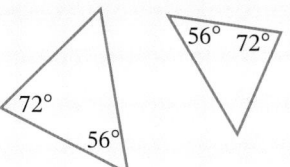

b

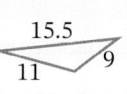

c

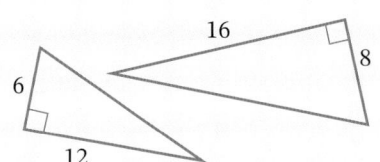

d

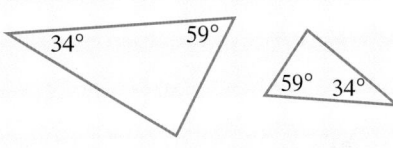

e

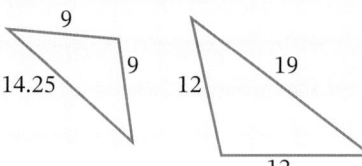

f

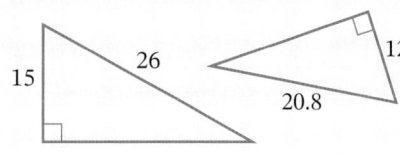

g

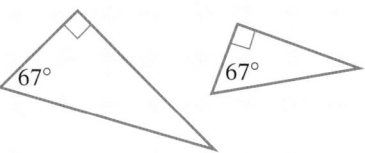

h

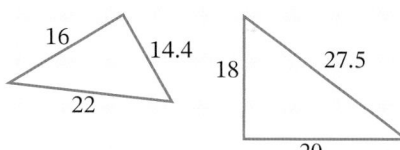

i

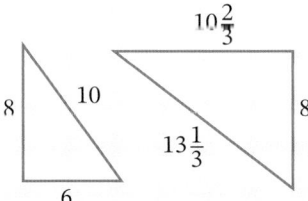

j

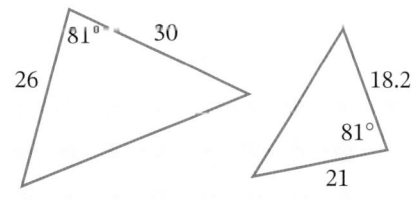

2 Use the correct notation to write a similarity statement relating each pair of
similar triangles.

R
C

a

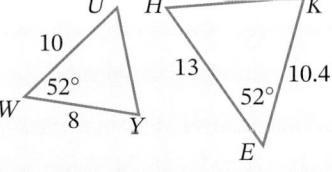

b

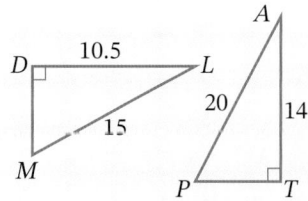

Foundation Standard Complex

c

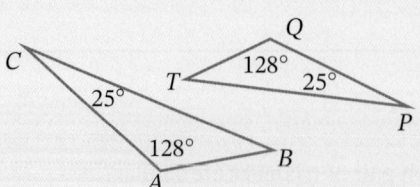

d

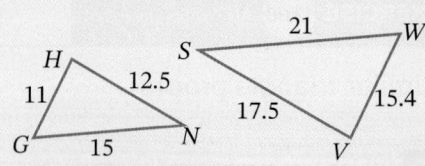

EXAMPLE 17

3 Prove that each pair of triangles are similar.

R **C**

a

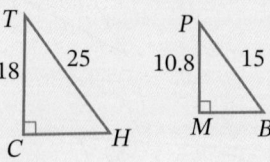

b

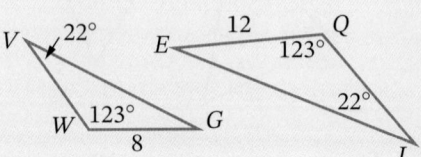

c

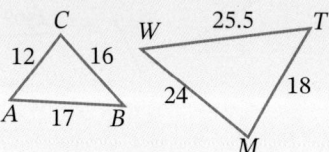

d

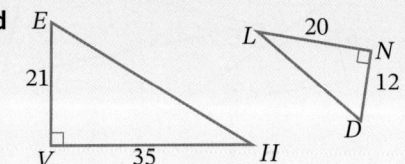

4 D and *F* are the midpoints of *AB* and *AC*. Prove that △*ADE* ||| △*ABC*.

R **C**

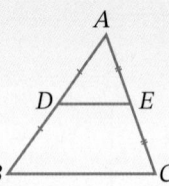

5 *AC* || *FD* and *BF* || *CE*. Prove that △*ABF* ||| △*FDE*.

R **C**

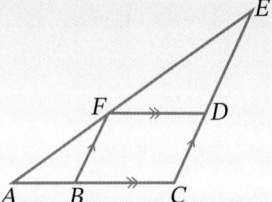

6 Prove that △*WXY* ||| △*TXW*.

R **C**

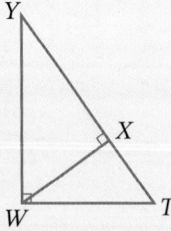

7 Prove that △*NDL* ||| △*NQR*.

R **C**

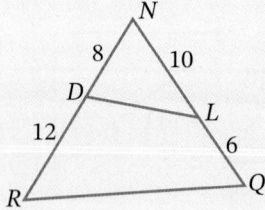

8 *HW* || *XY*. Prove that △*XWH* ||| △*XYW*.

R **C**

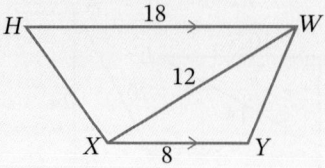

9 *NCKL* is a parallelogram. Prove that △*NML* ||| △*KLP*.

R **C**

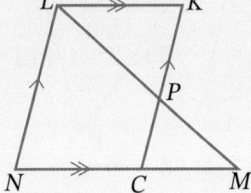

9780170465595

10 **a** Prove that △*FLN* ||| △*FDE*.

b Find the value of *d*.

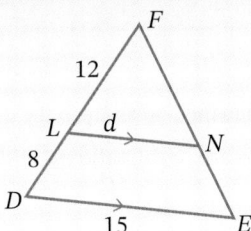

11 **a** Prove that △*ACE* ||| △*BCD*.

b Find the value of *y*.

EXAMPLE 18 12.08

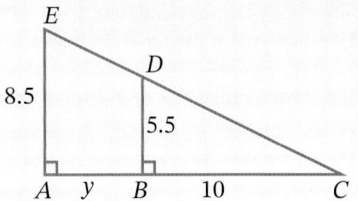

12 **a** Prove that △*YRT* ||| △*WUT*.

b Find the value of *g*.

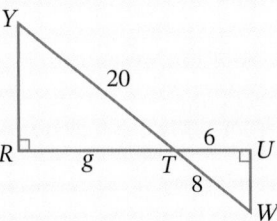

13 **a** Prove that △*NMP* ||| △*PCB*

b Find the value of *w*.

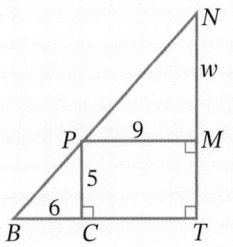

14 **a** Prove that △*TYN* ||| △*YNM*.

b Find the value of *h*.

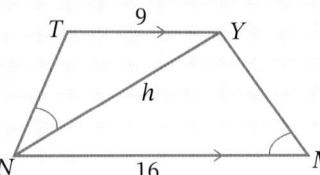

15 **a** Prove that △*BHU* ||| △*XBD*.

b Find the value of *y*.

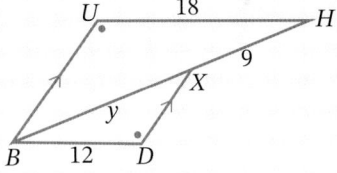

16 *GHLM* is a rectangle and *K* is the midpoint of *HL*.

a Prove that △*MXG* ||| *KXL*.

b Find the value of *x*.

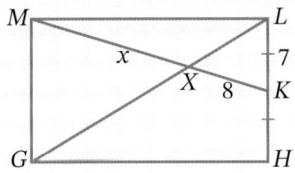

17 **a** Prove that △*CLW* ||| △*LTE*.

b If *WT* = 5 cm, *CE* = 15 cm and *EL* = 6 cm, find the length of *TL*.

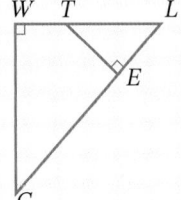

18 *PTUK* is a rectangle and *KB* ⊥ *PU*.

a Prove that △*PTU* ||| △*KBP*.

b If *BU* = 21 cm and *KP* = 10 cm, find the length of *PB*.

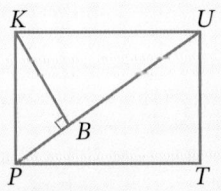

□ Foundation ○ Standard ○ Complex

Video
Areas of
similar
figures

Technology
Area of
similar
shapes

Spreadsheet
Area of
similar
shapes

Worksheet
Investigating
paper sizes

ⓘ Areas of similar figures

- If the matching sides of 2 similar figures are in the ratio $1:k$, then their areas are in the ratio $1:k^2$.
- If the matching sides are in the ratio $m:n$, then their areas are in the ratio $m^2:n^2$.

$$A_1 : A_2 = m^2 : n^2 \quad \text{or} \quad \frac{A_1}{A_2} = \frac{m^2}{n^2}$$

Example 19

What is the ratio of the areas of the similar rectangles shown?

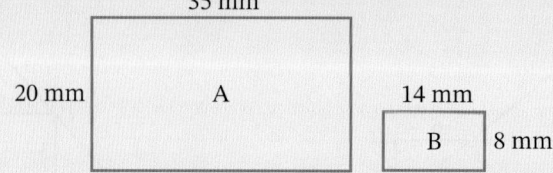

SOLUTION

ratio of matching sides (A to B) $= 35:14$ ratio of areas $= 5^2:2^2$

$= 5:2$ $= 25:4$

Example 20

Two similar pentagons have areas in the ratio $144:169$. Find the ratio of the lengths of their matching sides.

SOLUTION

ratio of areas $= m^2:n^2 = 144:169$

$\therefore$ ratio of sides $= m:n = \sqrt{144} : \sqrt{169} = 12:13$

Example 21

Two similar triangles have matching sides in the ratio $3:5$. If the area of the larger triangle is 225 cm^2, find the area of the smaller triangle.

SOLUTION

Let the area of the smaller figure be A.

ratio of matching sides $= 3:5$

ratio of areas $= 3^2:5^2 = 9:25$

$\therefore \dfrac{A}{225} = \dfrac{9}{25}$

$A = \dfrac{9}{25} \times 225 = 81$ cm^2

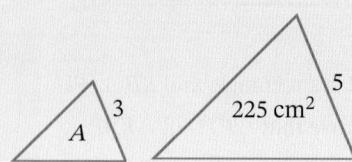

The area of the smaller triangle is 81 cm^2.

Areas of similar figures   U F R C

1 For each pair of similar figures, find the ratio of their areas.

EXAMPLE
19

a 3 cm   1 cm   **b**

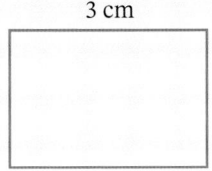

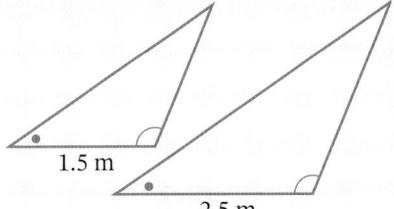

1.5 m

2.5 m

c   **d**

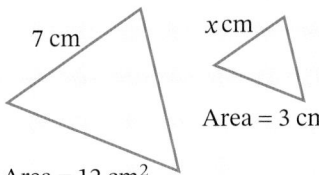

9 cm   5 cm

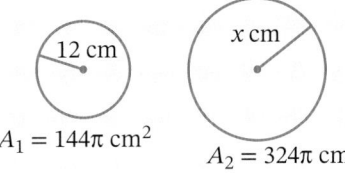

4 cm   6 cm

2 For each ratio of the areas of 2 similar figures, find the ratio of the lengths of their matching sides.

EXAMPLE
20

a 9:25   **b** 1:100   **c** 64:25   **d** 16:81

3 Find x for each pair of similar figures.

EXAMPLE
21

a

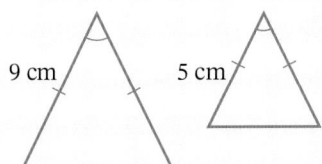

7 cm x cm

Area = 3 cm^2

Area = 12 cm^2

b

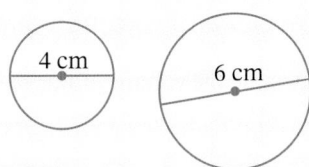

12 cm x cm

$A_1 = 144\pi$ cm^2

$A_2 = 324\pi$ cm^2

c

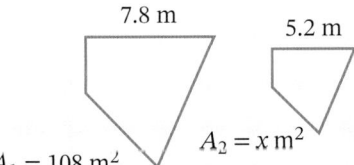

7.8 m   5.2 m

$A_2 = x$ m^2

$A_1 = 108$ m^2

d

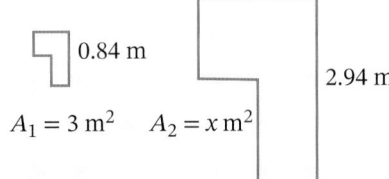

0.84 m

2.94 m

$A_1 = 3$ m^2 $A_2 = x$ m^2

4 Two circles have radii in the ratio 3:5. If the larger area is 150 cm^2, find the area of the
R smaller circle.

5 Two squares have sides in the ratio 7:4. If the area of the smaller square is 14.4 cm^2,
R find the area of the larger square.

6 Two similar triangles have areas in the ratio 4:9. If the length of the base of the smaller
R triangle is 5 cm, find the length of the base of the larger triangle.

7 Two similar rectangles have their areas in the ratio 36:121. If the width of the smaller
rectangle is 84 cm, find the width of the larger rectangle.

☐ Foundation ○ Standard ○ Complex

8 If the radius of a circle is doubled, how has its area changed?

Ⓡ Ⓒ

9 If the area of a square is divided by 9, how has its side length changed?

Ⓡ Ⓒ

10 If the sides of a triangle are increased by 2.5, how has its area changed?

Ⓡ Ⓒ

11 If the area of a trapezium is decreased by $\dfrac{1}{100}$, how have its sides changed?

Ⓡ Ⓒ

INVESTIGATION

Surface areas and volumes of similar solids

1 a Calculate the volume of this rectangular prism.

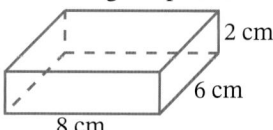

b Calculate the surface area of the rectangular prism.

c If the length, width and height are all doubled, what happens to:

  i the volume?　　　　**ii** the surface area?

d Copy and complete:

  If the length, width and height are all doubled, the volume is increased _____ times and the surface area is increased _____ times.

2 a Explain why these rectangular prisms are similar solids.

b What is the ratio of their matching sides?

c What is the ratio of their surface areas?

d What is the ratio of their volumes?

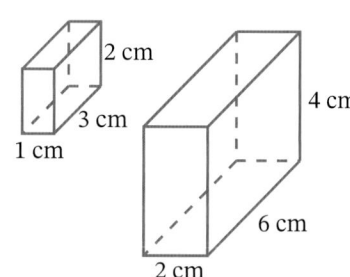

3   For the spheres A and B, find the ratio of:

   a   their radii

   b   their surface areas

   c   their volumes.

4   How is the ratio of surface areas of similar solids related to the ratio of matching sides?

5   How is the ratio of volumes of similar solids related to the ratio of their matching sides?

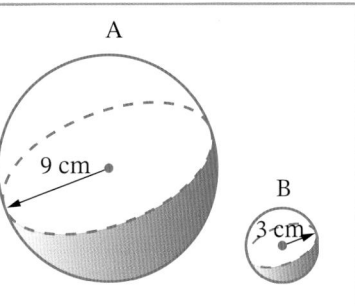

Surface areas and volumes of similar solids   12.10

ⓘ Surface areas and volumes of similar solids

- If the matching sides of 2 similar solids are in the ratio $1:k$, then their surface areas are in the ratio $1:k^2$ and their volumes are in the ratio $1:k^3$.

- If the matching sides are in the ratio $m:n$, then their surface areas are in the ratio $m^2:n^2$ and their volumes are in the ratio $m^3:n^3$.

$$\frac{SA_1}{SA_2} = \frac{m^2}{n^2} \quad \text{and} \quad \frac{V_1}{V_2} = \frac{m^3}{n^3}$$

Video
The incredible strength of ants

Worksheet
Areas and volumes of similar figures

Video
Surface areas and volumes of similar solids

Example 22

For these 2 similar triangular prisms, find the ratio of their:

a   surface areas

b   volumes

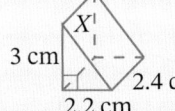

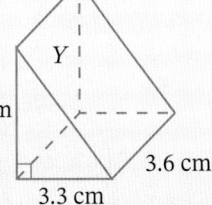

SOLUTION

a   ratio of sides (X to Y) = 3:4.5 (or 2.2:3.3 or 2.4:3.6)

                  = 2:3

    ratio of surface areas = $2^2:3^2$

                        = 4:9

b   ratio of volumes = $2^3:3^3$

                = 8:27

Example 23

Two similar cylinders have their surface areas in the ratio $25:36$. If the volume of the smaller cylinder is 250 cm³, find the volume of the larger solid.

SOLUTION

ratio of surface areas $= 25:36$

∴ ratio of matching sides $= \sqrt{25}:\sqrt{36}$

$\qquad = 5:6$

∴ ratio of volumes $= 5^3:6^3$

$\qquad = 125:216$

Let the volume of the larger cylinder be V.

$$\frac{V}{250} = \frac{216}{125}$$

$$V = \frac{216}{125} \times 250$$

$$= 432$$

∴ volume of the larger cylinder is 432 cm³.

EXERCISE 12.10 ANSWERS ON P. 662

Surface areas and volumes of similar solids

EXAMPLE 22

1 For each pair of similar solids, find the ratio of:

i the smaller surface area to larger surface area

ii the larger volume to the smaller volume.

a

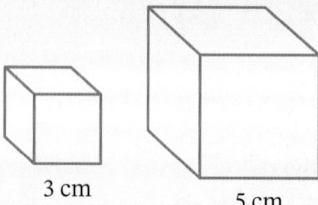

3 cm 5 cm

b

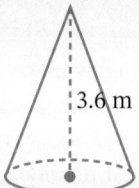

3.6 m

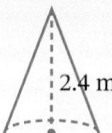

2.4 m

c

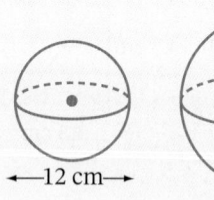

←12 cm→ ←15 cm→

d

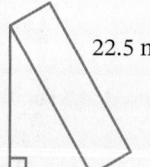

22.5 m

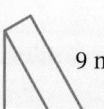

9 m

EXAMPLE 23

2 Two similar pyramids have surface areas of 81 cm² and 100 cm². Find the ratio of their:

a matching side lengths   **b** volumes.

3 Two similar prisms have volumes of 125 cm³ and 343 cm³. Find the ratio of their:

a matching sides   **b** surface areas.

4 Blocks of chocolate are sold in the shape of similar triangular prisms. The areas of the
(R) triangular faces of two prisms are 6400 mm² and 1600 mm². If the volume of the smaller prism is 9600 mm³, find the volume of the larger prism.

▷

☐ Foundation   ○ Standard   ○ Complex

5 Two drink cans have the shapes of similar cylinders. The larger can is 15 cm high and contains 350 mL of drink. If the smaller can is 9 cm high, how much drink does it contain?

6 A box of washing powder is 12 cm tall and contains 750 g of washing powder. A similar box is 18 cm tall. How much washing powder does it contain?

7 A large fish tank has a capacity of 624 L. A smaller similar fish tank has half the length, width and depth of the large tank. Find the capacity of the smaller tank.

8 A cylinder has its height and radius increased 1.5 times. By what factor has its:
a   surface area increased?   b   volume increased?

9 A balloon has a radius of 8 cm. By what factor is the volume decreased if the radius changes to 6 cm?

POWER PLUS ANSWERS ON P. 662

1   a   Explain why $\angle KMN = \angle KRP$.

    b   Prove that $\triangle KMN \equiv \triangle KRP$.

    c   Hence prove that $KN = KP$ and that $\triangle KNP$ is an isosceles triangle.

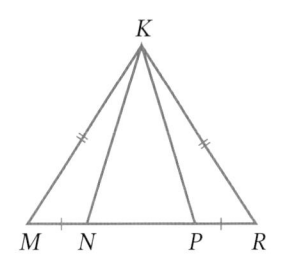

2   $\triangle JDC \,|||\, \triangle JLP$. Find the value of x.

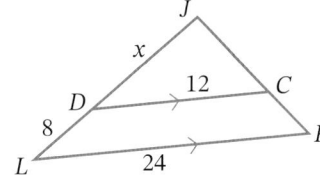

3   G and H are the midpoints of CD and CE respectively. Prove that:

    a $\triangle CGH \,|||\, \triangle CDE$

    b $GH \,||\, DE$

    c $GH = \dfrac{1}{2}DE$

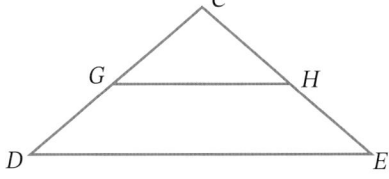

4   a   Which similarity test proves that $\triangle STY \,|||\, \triangle SVW$?

    b   Find the value of y.

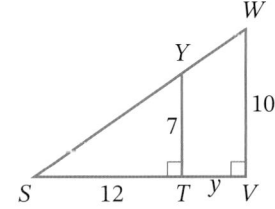

□ Foundation   ○ Standard   ○ Complex

(12) CHAPTER REVIEW

Quiz
Language of
maths 12

Puzzle
Geometry
crossword

Language of maths

AA	AAS	congruence test	congruent (≡)
enlargement	equiangular	hypotenuse	image
included angle	map	matching	original
plan	proof	proportional	reduction
RHS	SAS	scale factor	similar (|||)
similarity test	SSS	scaled length	scale diagram

1 Name the special quadrilateral that is a rectangle with 2 adjacent sides equal in length.

2 What is the symbol and meaning of 'is similar to'?

3 What happens to a figure that is changed by a scale factor of $\frac{1}{2}$?

4 What are the 4 tests for similar triangles?

5 What is the meaning of the 'A' in the SAS test for congruent triangles?

6 What does **equiangular** mean in the similarity tests?

Worksheet
Mind map:
Congruent
and similar
figures

Topic summary

Print (or copy) and complete this mind map of the topic, adding detail to its branches and using pictures, symbols and colour where needed. Ask your teacher to check your work.

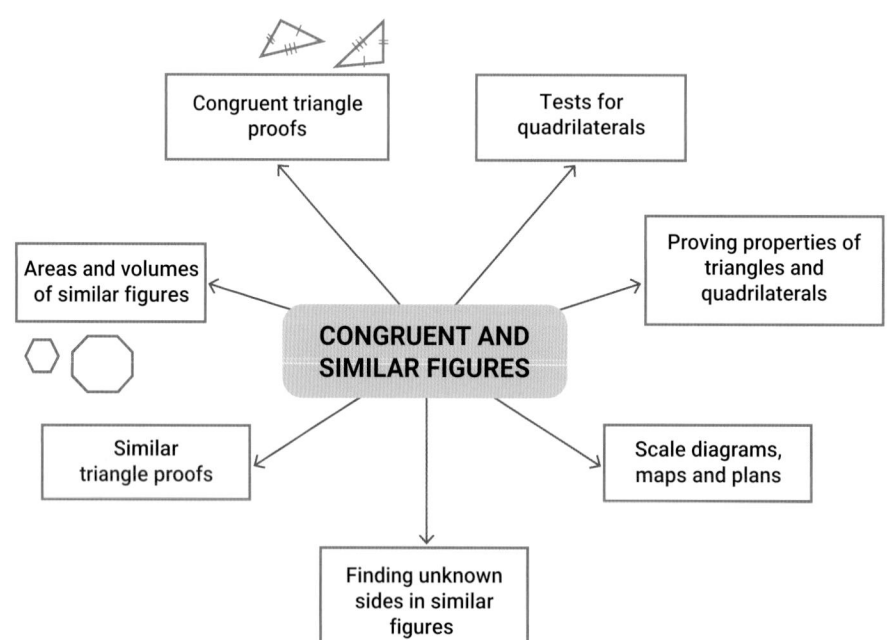

1 Which congruence test (SSS, SAS, AAS or RHS) can be used to prove that each pair of triangles are congruent?

a

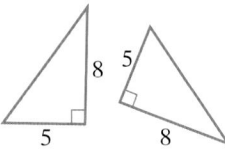

b

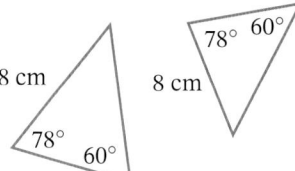

Quiz
Test
yourself 12

c

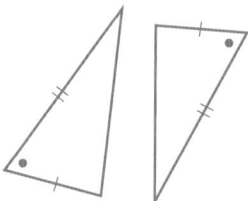

12.01

2 In △WXY, ∠W = ∠X and YZ ⊥ WX. Prove that △WZY ≡ △XZY.

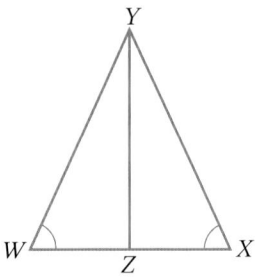

12.01

3 ABCD is a parallelogram and BC = BY = DX.

   a   Prove that △DAX ≡ △BCY.

   b   Hence, prove that BXDY is a parallelogram.

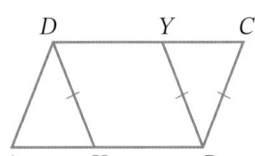

12.02

4 PNML is a rectangle.

   a   Which congruence test can be used to prove that △PML ≡ △NLM?

   b   Hence explain why PM = NL.

   c   What geometrical result about rectangles does this prove?

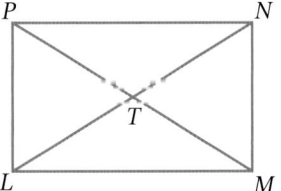

12.03

☐ Foundation ○ Standard ○ Complex

5 *PNMQ* is a square and *AM* = *BQ*. Prove that △*NPC* is isosceles.

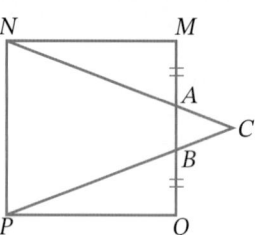

6 Test whether each pair of figures are similar.

a

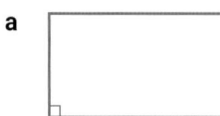

b

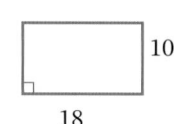

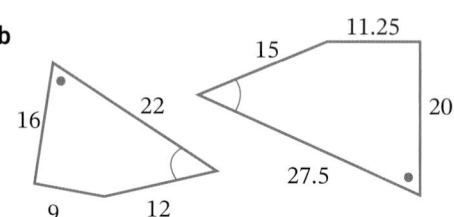

7 The scale on a map is 1 : 50 000. If the distance from Albany to Dog Rock is 2.4 cm on the map, calculate the actual distance from Albany to Dog Rock.

8 The width of a garage door is shown on a house plan with scale 1 : 50 as 10 cm. What is the actual width of the garage door? Is this likely to fit 2 cars side by side?

9 Find the value of the variable in each pair of similar figures.

a

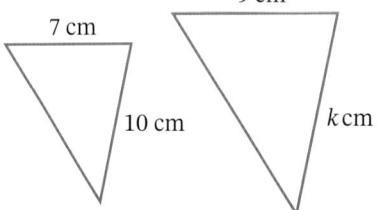

b

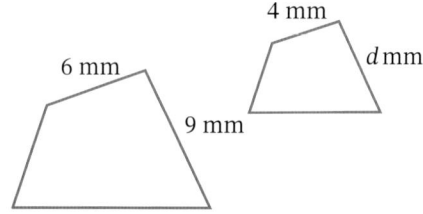

c

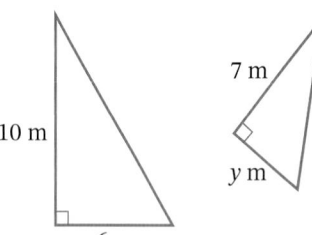

d

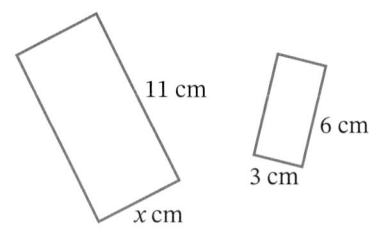

10 The top diagram is a scale diagram of the pencil below it. What is the scale?

12.4 cm

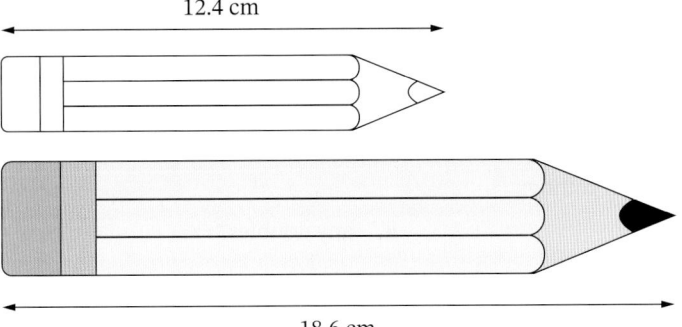

18.6 cm

11 If $\triangle ABE \;|||\; \triangle ACD$, find the value of d.

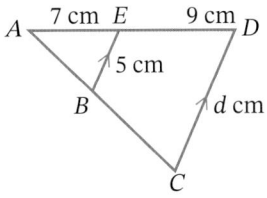

12 Which test can be used to prove that each pair of triangles are similar?

a

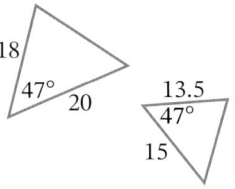

b

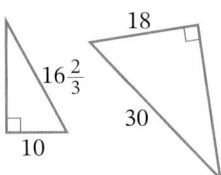

c

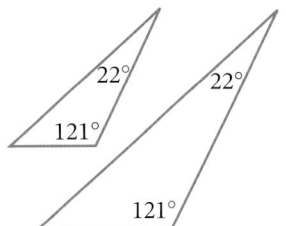

13 Prove that $\triangle ASB \;|||\; \triangle RST$ and, hence, find the values of x and y.

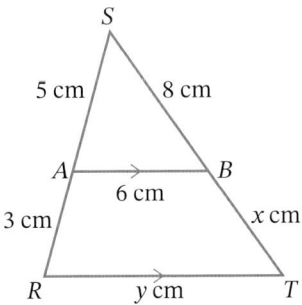

14 **a** Two circles have radii in the ratio $4:5$. If the smaller area is 150 cm², find the area of the larger circle.

    b The radius of a circle is increased by a factor of $2\frac{1}{2}$. By what factor has the area increased?

15 **a** Two similar prisms have their surface areas in the ratio $64:81$. If the volume of the smaller prism is 32 cm³, find the volume of the larger prism.

    b Two similar pyramids have volumes of 216 cm³ and 343 cm³. Find the ratio of their surface areas.

☐ Foundation ○ Standard ○ Complex

1 Two dice are rolled.

   a How many outcomes are possible?

   b What is the probability of rolling:

      i double 1s?   **ii** any doubles?

      iii 2 numbers both less than 4?

2 A die was rolled and the outcomes were recorded in this frequency histogram.

   a How many times was the die rolled?

   b Find the relative frequency of rolling:

      i a 1

      ii an even number

      iii a number less than 4

      iv at least a 3.

   c What is the theoretical probability of rolling a 6? How does this compare with the experimental probability of rolling a 6?

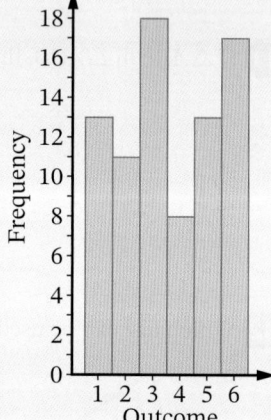

3 Of 160 Year 11 students at Westvale High, 54 take Biology (*B*), 75 take Chemistry (*C*) and 68 study Physics (*P*). Also, 55 students take both Chemistry and Physics, 20 are in Biology and Chemistry and 10 students take all three.

   a Copy and complete the Venn diagram to show this information.

   b Find the probability of selecting a student who:

      i only takes Physics

      ii does not do Biology, Chemistry or Physics

      iii does Chemistry and Physics but not Biology

      iv studies Chemistry or Biology

      v only does one Science subject.

   c Of the students who do Biology, what is the probability that a student also takes Physics?

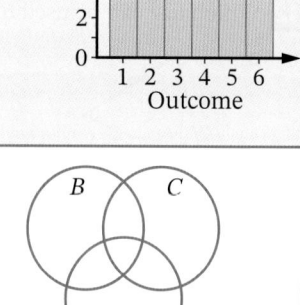

□ Foundation   ○ Standard   ○ Complex

4 This Venn diagram shows the results of a survey on whether people prefer to watch movies by streaming (*S*) or at the cinema (*C*).

11.02

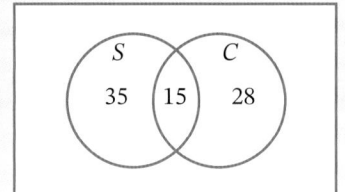

  a How many people were surveyed?

  b Find the probability of selecting a person from this survey who prefers to watch movies:

  i by streaming   **ii** only at the cinema.

  c What is the probability of selecting a person who likes to stream movies only?

5 Tracey spun this spinner twice, landing on red both times. Is the second outcome dependent or independent of the outcome of the first spin?

11.07

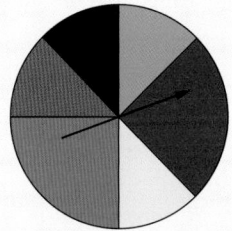

6 By measurement, calculate the scale factor for each pair of similar figures.

12.04

  a

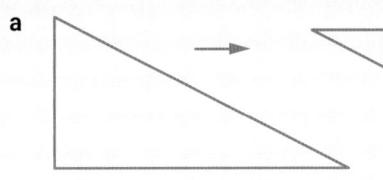

  b

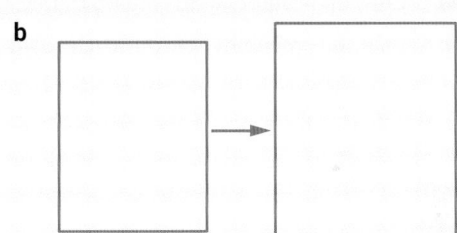

7 A bag contains 4 red, 5 black and 3 green marbles. Shweta selects a marble at random, records its colour and then returns the marble to the bag. Shweta does this process 150 times. The results are shown in the table.

11.05

Outcome	Frequency
Red	58
Black	65
Green	27

  a Find, correct to 2 decimal places, the relative frequency of selecting a marble that is:

  i red   **ii** black   **iii** green.

  b Find, correct to 2 decimal places, the theoretical probability of selecting a marble that is

  i red   **ii** black   **iii** green.

  c For which outcome are the experimental and theoretical probabilities most similar?

  d What is the expected frequency of selecting a red or green marble? How does this compare with the observed frequency?

□ Foundation   ○ Standard   ○ Complex

8 Prove that $\triangle ABC \equiv \triangle CDA$.

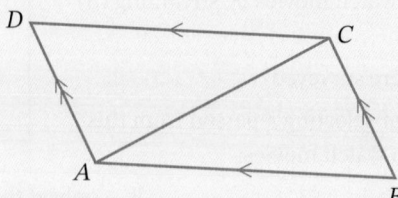

 9 Solve each pair of simultaneous equations graphically.

a $y = 2x - 3$ and $x + y = 6$ **b** $2x + y = 1$ and $y = 3x - 4$

10 A 6-sided die and a 4-sided die are rolled together and the product of the 2 numbers is calculated.

	1	2	3	4	5	6
1						
2						
3						
4						

a Copy and complete this table to show all possible products.

b Find the probability of rolling a product:

   i of 20   **ii** of 6   **iii** that is odd

   iv of at least 12   **v** less than 10   **vi** from 11 to 23.

 11 $LM = LN$ and P is the midpoint of MN. Prove that $\triangle LMP \equiv \triangle LNP$ and hence that $\angle LPM = \angle LPN = 90°$.

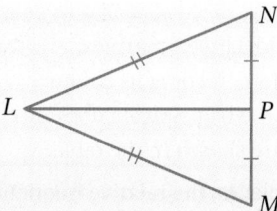

12 Shoppers at a mall were asked whether they had a pet dog or cat. The results are shown in the 2-way table.

	Cat	No cat
Dog	28	35
No dog	32	40

a How many shoppers were surveyed?

b Find the probability of randomly selecting a shopper from the survey who does not have a cat or dog.

c What is the probability of randomly selecting a shopper who:

   i has only a dog or cat (not both)   **ii** has a cat   **iii** does not have a dog?

☐ Foundation ○ Standard ◐ Complex

13 Find the value of the variable in each pair of similar figures.

12.06

a

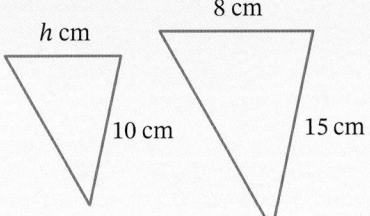

b

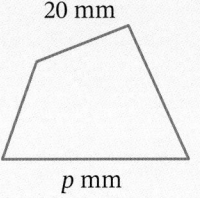

14 Three cards are drawn from a set of cards numbered 2, 3, 4 and 5, without replacement, to form a 3-digit number.

11.04

a Copy and complete the tree diagram to list all possible outcomes.

b Find the probability of forming:

   i an even number

   ii a number ending in 3

   iii a number greater than 400

   iv a number between 200 and 500

   v a number divisible by 5.

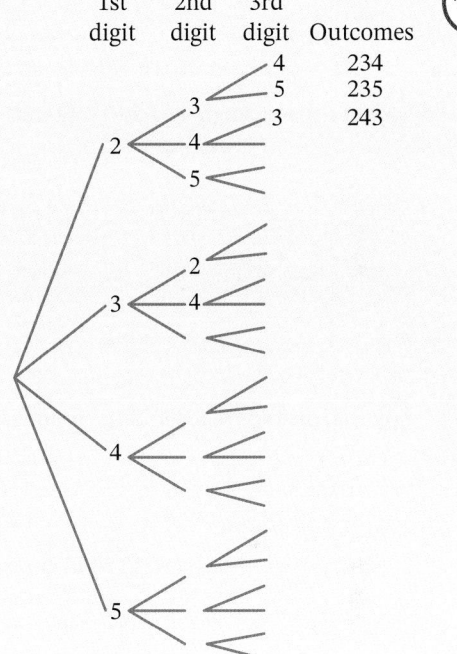

15 Tickets to the school play cost $20 for adults and $15 for children. Altogether, 395 people attended and ticket sales totalled $6700. Let A stand for the number of adults and C for the number of children that attended the school play.

10.04

a Write a pair of simultaneous equations to represent this situation.

b Solve the simultaneous equations to find the number of children who attended the play.

16 A bag contains 3 yellow and 2 red marbles. 2 marbles are drawn from the bag, without replacing the marble from the first draw.

11.07

a Find the probability of:

   i selecting a red marble with the first draw

   ii selecting a red marble with the second draw if the first marble was yellow.

b Are the 2 draws dependent or independent? Justify your answer.

c If the 2 draws are made with replacement of the marble after the first draw, are the draws dependent or independent? Justify your answer.

□ Foundation ○ Standard ○ Complex

10.02

17 Solve each pair of simultaneous equations using the elimination method.

a $3g - 2w = 8$

   $g - 2w = 4$

b $2y + 3f = 15$

   $5y - 2f = 9$

c $3a - 4c = 5$

   $5a - 3c = 1$

 12.06

18 If $\triangle ABC \;|||\; \triangle AED$, find the value of y (correct to one decimal place).

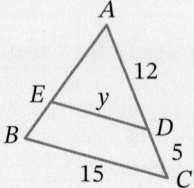

 12.04

19 *XYVW* is a rhombus and *TX* bisects $\angle VXY$. Prove that $\angle XTY = 3 \times \angle TXY$.

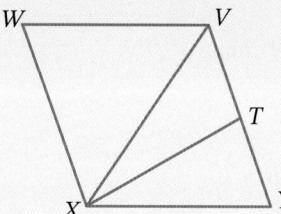

11.06

20 Two dice are rolled and the product of the 2 numbers is calculated.

		1st die					
		1	2	3	4	5	6
2nd die	1						
	2						
	3						
	4						
	5						
	6						

a   Copy and complete the table to show all possible outcomes.

b   Given that one of the numbers was 3, what is the probability of obtaining a product that is odd?

c   Given that one of the numbers is 4, what is the probability of obtaining a product:

   i   that is even?

   ii   that is odd?

d   Find P(an even product | the first number is odd)

e   Find P(an even product | an even number and an odd number are obtained).

21 *VWXY* is a rectangle with diagonals intersecting at *T*.

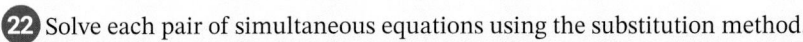

a   Since *YX* || *VW*, list the 2 pairs of equal alternate angles between them.

b   Why is *YX = VW*?

c   Which congruence test can now be used to prove that $\triangle YXT \equiv \triangle WVT$?

d   Explain why *YT = WT* and *XT = VT*.

e   Which property of a rectangle has been proved?

22 Solve each pair of simultaneous equations using the substitution method.

a $y = x + 3$
    $y = 5x - 7$

b $2w + p = 5$
    $p = 2w - 3$

c $3k - 2g = 8$
    $k = 4g + 1$

23 Two similar containers have volumes 600 cm³ and 2025 cm³ respectively. If the height of the larger container is 60 cm, what is the height of the smaller container?

24 A pentagon is increased by a scale factor of 3. By how much has its area of the shape increased?

25 *PQRT* is a quadrilateral in which *PQ = RT* and *PT = RQ*. Prove that:

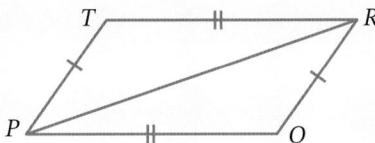

a $\triangle PRT \equiv \triangle RPQ$

b   *PQRT* is a parallelogram.

26 Two similar squares have sides in the ratio 3 : 5. If the smaller area is 360 cm², find the area of the larger square.

27 *ABCD* is a trapezium.

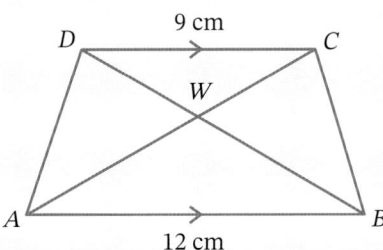

a   Prove that $\triangle CDW \,|||\, \triangle ABW$.

b   If *AC* = 11 cm, find the length of *CW*.

□ Foundation   ○ Standard   ○ Complex

General practice ANSWERS ON P. 664

 1 Anita is a real estate agent and is paid a commission of 2.5% on the value of apartments she sells. She also receives a weekly retainer of $1250. How much will Anita earn in a week if she sells an apartment for $578 000?

 2 Find the gradient, m, and y-intercept, c, of each linear equation.

    a $y = 3x - 4$ **b** $y = 5 - 2x$ **c** $4x + 3y - 9 = 0$

 3 Find the interquartile range for each set of data.

    a 4, 7, 8, 12, 5, 8, 10, 7, 13, 6, 9, 2   **b**

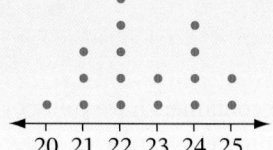

 4 Factorise each expression.

    a $8x^2 + 16x$ **b** $y^2 - 25$ **c** $a^2 + 6a + 8$ **d** $4p + 6 - 2p^2$

 5 Find the surface area of each solid, correct to the nearest mm². All measurements shown are in millimetres.

    a   **b**   **c**

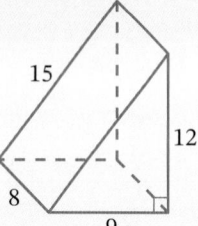 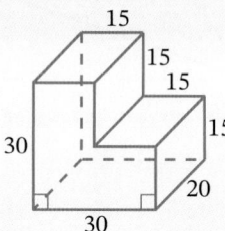 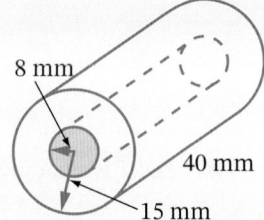

 6 Count the number of faces and vertices in this network and use Euler's formula to find the number of edges.

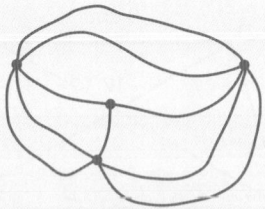

 7 Solve the simultaneous equations $y = 3x + 5$ and $y = 7 - x$.

 8 Simplify each expression, writing your answer with a positive index where necessary.

    a $7x^5 \times 8x^7$ **b** $4x^2 \div 16x^{-3}$ **c** $(3y)^{-2}$ **d** $m^{-6}n^3 \times mn^{-1} \div m^2n$

□ Foundation   ○ Standard   ○ Complex

9 Students in Year 10 at Nelson Secondary College were asked if they had studied Japanese.

CHAPTER 11

	Male	Female
Japanese	35	87
No Japanese	67	21

a How many students are in Year 10 at the school?

b What is the probability of selecting a Year 10 student at random who is:

i male and has studied Japanese? **ii** female or has studied Japanese?

c Find the probability, expressed as a percentage to the nearest whole number, of randomly selecting a male in Year 10 who has not studied Japanese.

d Given that a student is a Year 10 female, what is the probability that she has studied Japanese?

10 Find the value of the variable in each diagram, correct to one decimal place.

CHAPTER 8

a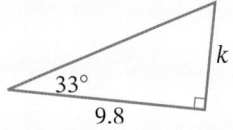
b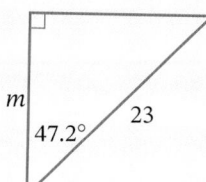
c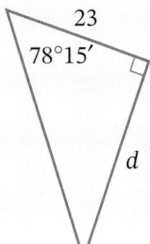

d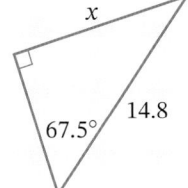
e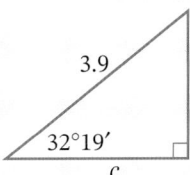
f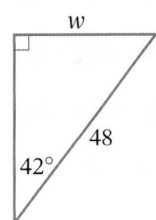

11 Calculate the volume of each solid, correct to the nearest cubic millimetre.

EXTENSION
CHAPTER 2

a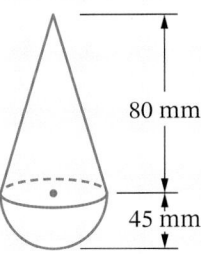
b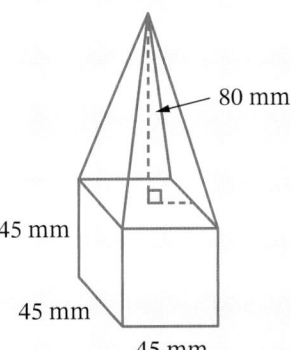

☐ Foundation ○ Standard ○ Complex

EXTENSION

CHAPTER
2

12 Find, correct to one decimal place, the surface area of each solid.

a

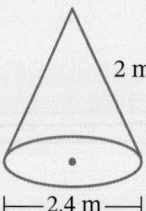

2 m

|—2.4 m—|

b

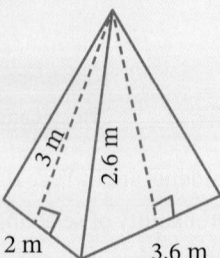

3 m

2.6 m

2 m   3.6 m

CHAPTER
5

13 Students were surveyed about the amount of time they typically spend on the internet over a weekend. The results for boys and girls are displayed in these parallel boxplots.

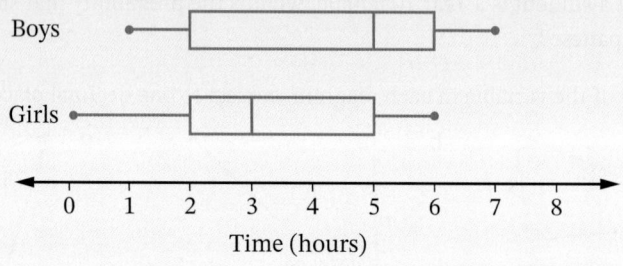

Boys

Girls

0   1   2   3   4   5   6   7   8

Time (hours)

a Calculate the interquartile range for the boys.

b What is the median amount of time spent on the internet by the girls surveyed?

c What percentage of girls usually spend fewer than 5 hours on the internet over the weekend?

CHAPTER
12

14 Prove that $\triangle ABC \equiv \triangle DEF$.

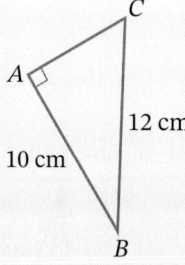

C

A

12 cm

10 cm

B

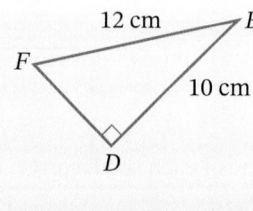

12 cm   E

F

10 cm

D

CHAPTER
6

15 Solve each inequality and graph its solution on a number line.

a $5y + 3 \geq -2$

b $\dfrac{2x+5}{2} < 4$

c $5 - 4x > 17$

☐ Foundation ○ Standard ◇ Complex

CHAPTER 1

16 For each line, find:

i the gradient **ii** the *y*-intercept **iii** the equation of the line.

a 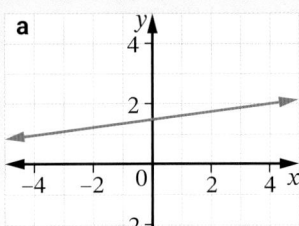 **b** 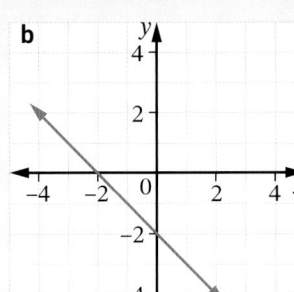 **c**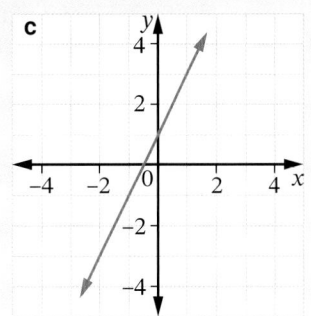

17 Solve each pair of simultaneous equations.

a $3x - y = 4$

$2x + y = 6$

b $2m - 3p = 5$

$5m - 2p = 7$

18 Is this network traversable?

19 Find the equation of this circle.

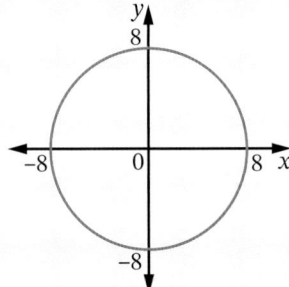

20 Calculate the simple interest on each investment.

a \$500 invested at 4% p.a. for 2 years **b** \$280 invested at 2.5% p.a. for 7 months

21 Find θ, correct to the nearest degree, if:

a $\sin\theta = \dfrac{3}{7}$ **b** $\tan\theta = 6$ **c** $\cos\theta = 0.816$

22 Calculate the final amount for each investment.

a \$800 invested at 4% p.a. for 4 years, compounded annually

b \$1260 invested at 8% p.a. for 3 years, compounded quarterly

☐ Foundation ○ Standard ○ Complex

23 For the interval joining each pair of points, find:

    i   the length of the interval, correct to one decimal place

    ii the midpoint of the interval   **iii** the gradient of the interval

  a $C(2, 1)$ and $D(6, 9)$ **b** $X(-7, -2)$ and $Y(5, 4)$

24 For each triangle, find θ:

    i   correct to the nearest degree   **ii** correct to the nearest minute

  a   **b**   **c**

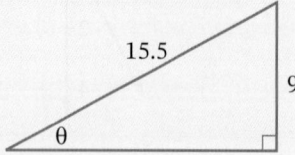
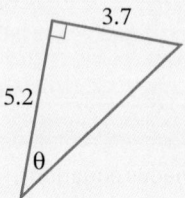
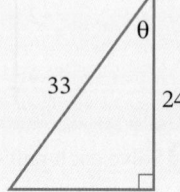

25 Graph each function on a number plane.

  a $y = x^2 - x + 6$ **b** $y = -x^2 + 3$ **c** $y = 3^x$

26 Find the value of each variable in this pair of similar figures.

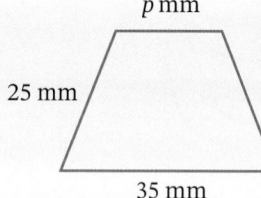

27 Fariba sailed due south for 40 km. Then she sailed due east for 40 km to a reef.

What is the bearing of the reef from Fariba's starting point? Select the correct answer **A**, **B**, **C** or **D**.

  A 225°   **B** 045°

  C 090°   **D** 135°

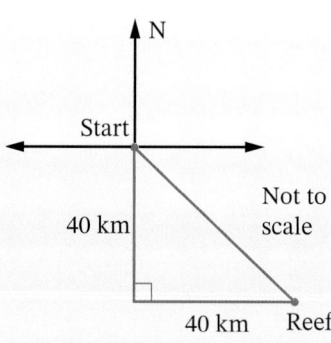

28 A computer depreciates by 25% each year. If the computer originally cost $4950, what will its value be in 5 years' time and by how much will it depreciate?

29 Find the five-number summary for this data and construct a box-and-whisker plot.

    2   4   8   5   5   10   12   7   7   8   8   13   3

30 The weather on a long weekend will either be fine or rainy each day, with each outcome being equally likely.

  a Draw a tree diagram to show the possible outcomes for Saturday, Sunday and Monday.

  b What is the probability that it is fine:

    i on all 3 days?   **ii** on exactly 2 of the days?   **iii** on at least one of the days?

☐ Foundation ○ Standard ◇ Complex

31 For an object that is cooling, the drop in temperature is directly proportional to the time. The temperature drops 5°C in 12 minutes. How long will it take to drop 8°C?

CHAPTER 7

32 Graph $y = 2x^2 - x - 15$ on a number plane, showing x- and y-intercepts.

CHAPTER 7

33 Simplify $3\sqrt{8} - \sqrt{32} + \sqrt{50}$.

EXTENSION

34 Rationalise the denominator of $\dfrac{3\sqrt{2}}{2\sqrt{5}}$.

CHAPTER 4

35 Find θ correct to the nearest minute.

CHAPTER 4

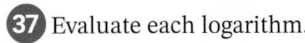

CHAPTER 8

36 Find d correct to one decimal place.

CHAPTER 8

37 Evaluate each logarithm.

a $\log_{10} 0.1$ b $\log_3 81$ c $\log_6 \sqrt{6}$

CHAPTER 6

38 Simplify and evaluate each expression.

a $\log_3 9 + \log_3 27$ b $\log_5 125 - \log_5 25$ c $\log_2 128 - 5\log_2 4$

CHAPTER 6

□ Foundation   ○ Standard   ○ Complex

Answers

Note: Answers to Chapters 13 to 16 online.

CHAPTER 1

SkillCheck

1 a $(6, 1)$ b $(-5, -4)$ c 6
   d 6   e $AC = BC = 4.5$ f isosceles
   g $\frac{1}{3}$ h $-\frac{2}{3}$

Exercise 1.01

1 B   2 C   3 A
4 a $\frac{1}{3}$ b -2 c $\frac{7}{3}$
5 a i 2.2   ii $(6, 2.5)$ iii $-\frac{1}{2}$
   b i 10.8   ii $(3.5, 3)$ iii $\frac{2}{3}$
   c i 7.1   ii $(-2.5, -0.5)$ iii -1
   d i 7.6   ii $(0.5, -7.5)$ iii $-\frac{3}{7}$
   e i 10.2   ii $(-6, -3)$ iii -5
   f i 5.7   ii $(5, 0)$ iii 1
6 a $\sqrt{89}$ b $\sqrt{194}$ c $\sqrt{82}$
7 $k: m = \frac{1}{5}$; $l: m = -\frac{1}{2}$
8 B
9 a

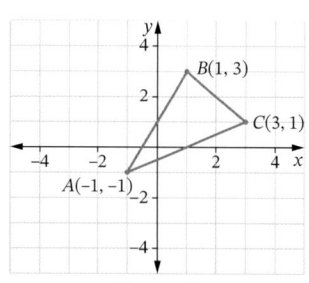

   b $AB = AC = \sqrt{20}$ or $2\sqrt{5}$, $BC = \sqrt{8}$ or $2\sqrt{2}$
   c $AB = AC = \sqrt{20}$ or $2\sqrt{5}$
   d isosceles
   e 11.8
10 a

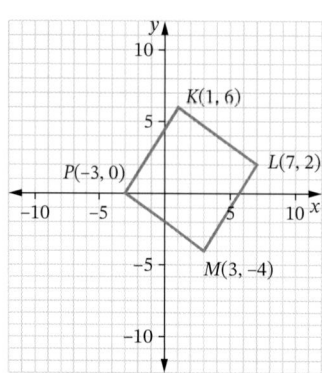

   b square   c $m_{KL} = -\frac{2}{3}$, $m_{PM} = -\frac{2}{3}$
   d $m_{KP} = \frac{3}{2}$, $m_{LM} = \frac{3}{2}$
   e The gradients are equal; they are parallel.
   f $KL = LM = PM = KP = \sqrt{52}$ or $2\sqrt{13}$
   g 28.8   h 52 square units
11 a $P(-2, 1)$, $Q(1, 3)$
   b $PQ = 3.6$, $AC = 7.2$; $AC = 2 \times PQ$
   c $m_{PQ} = \frac{2}{3}$, $m_{AC} = \frac{2}{3}$; the gradients are equal, therefore PQ and AC are parallel.
12 a 72°   b 27°   c 45°
   d 68°   e 117°   f 37°
   g 174°   h 146°
13 a 1.73   b -0.40 c 0.90
   d -14.30 e 0.14   f -1
   g -0.05 h 0

Exercise 1.02

1 a neither   b perpendicular   c parallel
   d neither   e parallel   f neither
2 a 4   b -2 c $\frac{1}{3}$ d -0.2
3 a -1 b $\frac{1}{6}$ c $\frac{2}{3}$ d $-\frac{2}{5}$
4 D   5 B   6 A
7 a $m_{AB} = -\frac{4}{3}$, $m_{CD} = -\frac{4}{3}$; $\therefore AB \parallel CD$
   b $m_{PQ} = \frac{3}{4}$, $m_{CD} = -\frac{4}{3}$; $\therefore PQ \perp CD$
8 a $\frac{1}{3}$ b -3

Exercise 1.03

Teacher to check graphs.
1 a i $\frac{1}{3}$ ii -1 b i -2.5 ii 5
   c i 4   ii 4   d i -1 ii -2
   e i 0   ii 0   f i -6 ii 3
2 a 2, 4   b -4, 2

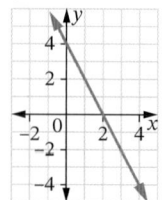   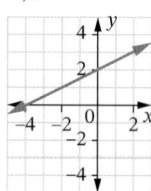

c −6, 6

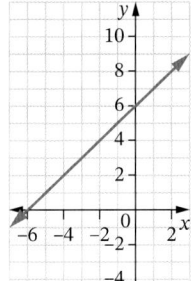

d 4, −6

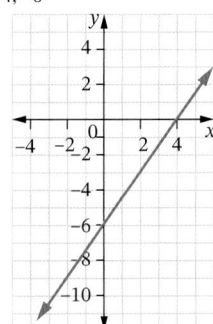

e 2.5, 2.5

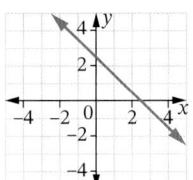

f 6, 3

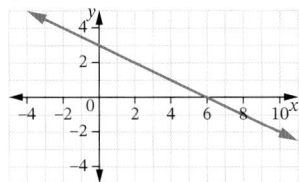

g −2, 4

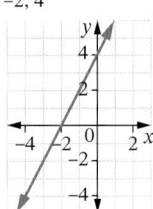

h 3, 5

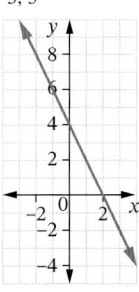

i 2, −6

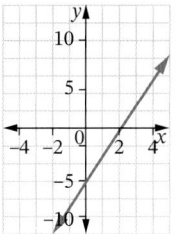

j 10, −4

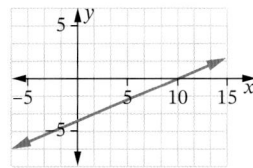

k 2, 4

l 2, −$\frac{1}{2}$

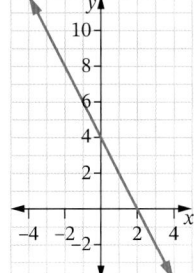
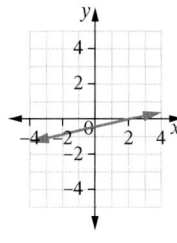

3 a no   **b** yes   **c** yes
   d yes   **e** no   **f** no

4 C

5 a $x = -4$ **b** $x = 1$ **c** $y = 5$ **d** $y = -3$

6 a

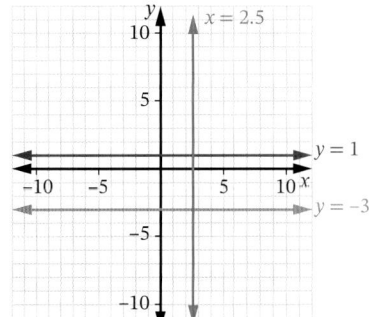

b

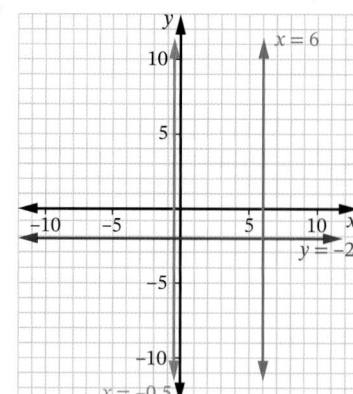

7 a $y = 2$ **b** $x = 4$ **c** $x = -1$ **d** $y = -2$

  e $y = 3$ **f** $x = -1$ **g** $y = 6$ **h** $x = -1$

8 A   **9** C   **10 a** x-axis **b** y-axis

Exercise 1.04

1 a $m = 3, c = -2$ **b** $m = -2, c = 7$

  c $m = 1, c = 4$ **d** $m = -1, c = 9$

  e $m = \frac{3}{4}, c = 6$ **f** $m = 1, c = 0$

  g $m = \frac{1}{2}, c = -11$ **h** $m = \frac{2}{3}, c = 6$

  i $m = -\frac{1}{3}, c = -8$ **j** $m = 2, c = -6$

  k $m = -3, c = 11$ **l** $m = 1, c = -\frac{7}{2}$

2 a $y = 2x + 1$ **b** $y = \frac{3}{4}x + 2$

  c $y = -7x + 5$ **d** $y = -\frac{2}{5}x + 3$

  e $y = -2x - 3$ **f** $y = -3x + \frac{1}{2}$

3 a $m = 2, c = 1$

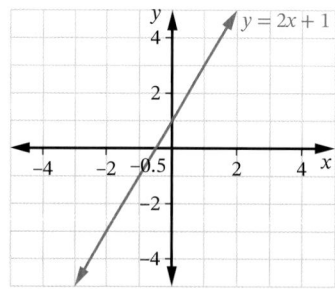

b $m = 3, c = -2$

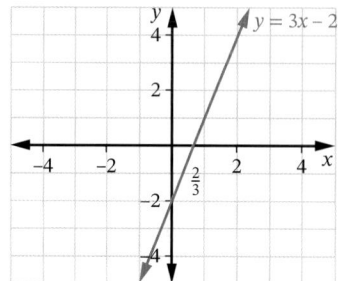

c $m = 2, c = 0$

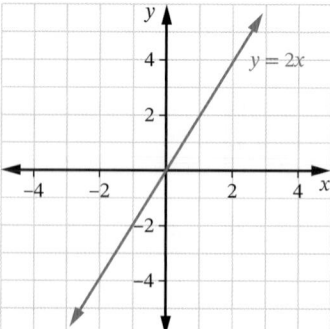

d $m = \frac{1}{2}, c = -1$

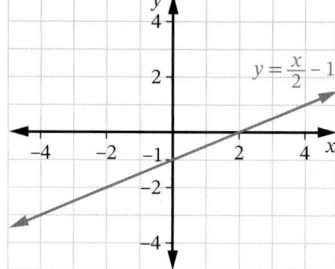

e $m = -2, c = 3$

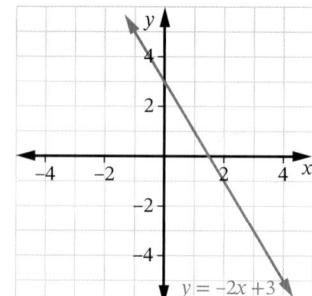

f $m = -\frac{3}{4}, c = 0$

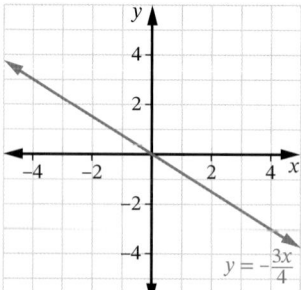

g $m = -\frac{5}{2}, c = 1$

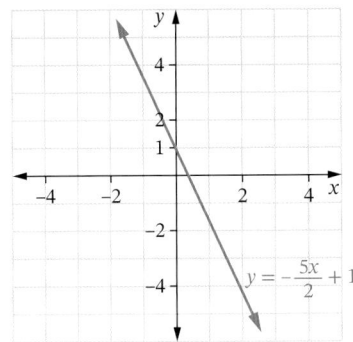

$y = -\frac{5x}{2} + 1$

h $m = \frac{3}{5}, c = -4$

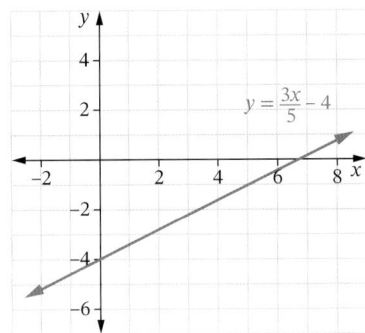

$y = \frac{3x}{5} - 4$

4 $y = 2x$

5 a C **b** B **c** D **d** A

6 a C **b** B, D **c** B
d C, D **e** A, B **f** D

7 a $y = 4x + 3, y = 4x - 6$
b $3x - y + 7 = 0, y = 3x - 2$

Mental skills 1

2 a 11 **b** 40 **c** 7 **d** 24
e 23 **f** 6 **g** 43 **h** 80
i 18 **j** 15 **k** 40 **l** 65
m 11 **n** 14 **o** 12 **p** 135

Exercise 1.05

1 a $x - y + 2 = 0$ **b** $3x - y - 1 = 0$
c $5x - y + 8 = 0$ **d** $x + 2y - 3 = 0$
e $x - 2y - 6 = 0$ **f** $8x - y + 2 = 0$
g $6x - y - 3 = 0$ **h** $x - 2y - 6 = 0$
i $3x - 5y + 10 = 0$

2 a $m = -2, c = 6$ **b** $m = 4, c = -5$
c $m = \frac{3}{2}, c = 2$ **d** $m = -2, c = 1$
e $m = -2, c = -5$ **f** $m = -\frac{4}{3}, c = 4$

3 B **4** B

5 a $4x - 12y + 3 = 0$ **b** $5x + 8y - 12 = 0$
c $15x - 20y - 8 = 0$ **d** $2x + 4y + 3 = 0$
e $15x - 10y + 4 = 0$ **f** $27x + 30y + 14 = 0$

Exercise 1.06

1 a $2x - y + 1 = 0$ **b** $x + y + 2 = 0$
c $4x - y - 20 = 0$ **d** $2x - 3y - 4 = 0$
e $x + 5y + 38 = 0$ **f** $3x + y - 4 = 0$
g $4x + y + 1 = 0$ **h** $3x - 4y + 10 = 0$
i $2x + y + 10 = 0$

2

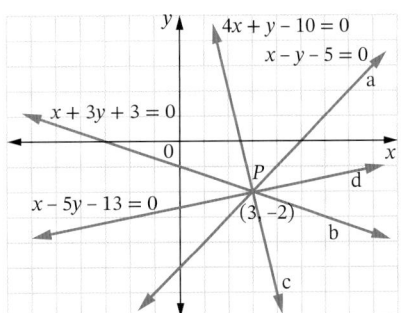

$4x + y - 10 = 0$
$x - y - 5 = 0$
a
$x + 3y + 3 = 0$
$x - 5y - 13 = 0$
P
$(3, -2)$
d
b
c

3 a $x - y - 4 = 0$ **b** $4x - 5y + 18 = 0$
c $5x - 6y + 23 = 0$ **d** $8x + 3y - 10 = 0$
e $3x + 2y - 6 = 0$ **f** $5x - 3y - 1 = 0$
g $6x + 11y + 38 = 0$ **h** $x + y - 3 = 0$
i $4x - 3y - 11 = 0$

4 $k: x + 2y - 7 = 0, l: 3x - y + 7 = 0$

5 $4x + y - 20 = 0$ **6** $5x - 7y + 42 = 0$
7 $2x - 3y + 18 = 0$ **8** $3x + 5y - 30 = 0$
9 a $2x - y + 1 = 0$ **b** same
10 a Proof: see worked solutions.
b $x - y - 4 = 0$ **c** same

Exercise 1.07

1 a $y = 2x + 5$ **b** $y = -\frac{3}{4}x + 3$ **c** $y = -3x + 6$
d $y = -x + 3$ **e** $y = \frac{1}{2}x + 3$ **f** $y = -3x - 3$

2 a $y = \frac{1}{2}x + 2$ **b** $y = x$ **c** $y = -\frac{1}{2}x + 5$
d $y = -\frac{1}{2}x + 3$ **e** $y = -3x - 3$ **f** $y = -x - 2$
g $y = 3x - 10$ **h** $y = \frac{2}{5}x + 2$ **i** $y = 2x - 3$

Exercise 1.08

1 a $y = 2x + 4$ **b** $y = 3x + 6$ **c** $y = -\frac{1}{2}x + \frac{11}{2}$
d $y = 2x - 12$ **e** $y = -5x - 13$ **f** $y = \frac{1}{2}x - 10$

2 a $y = -2x - 2$ **b** $y = \frac{1}{5}x - \frac{1}{5}$ **c** $y = -\frac{1}{3}x + \frac{4}{3}$
d $y = -3x - 3$ **e** $y = x + 6$ **f** $y = -\frac{1}{3}x + \frac{31}{3}$

3 **a** $m = 2$ **b** $M(0, 2)$

   c $-\frac{1}{2}$ **d** $y = -\frac{1}{2}x + 2$

4 **a** $y = \frac{1}{3}x + 1$ **b** -3 **c** $y = -3x + 11$

5 **a** $y = -\frac{4}{5}x + 8$ **b** $A(10, 0)$ **c** $\frac{5}{4}$

   d $y = \frac{5}{4}x - \frac{25}{2}$ **e** $(0, -12.5)$

Exercise 1.09

1 **a**

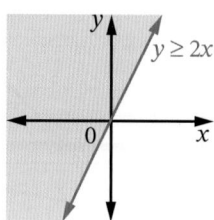

b

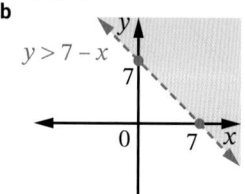

c

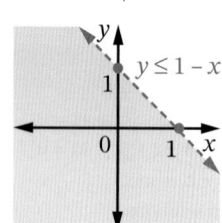

d

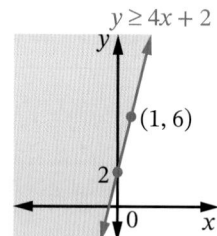

e

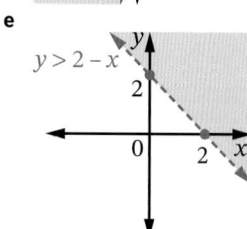

f

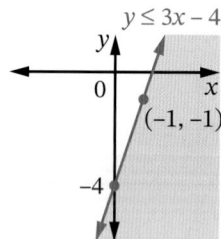

2 **a**

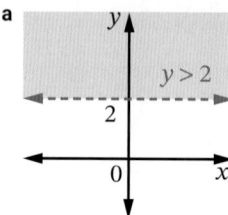

b

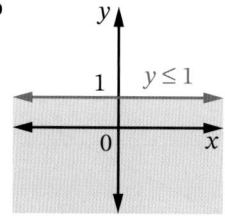

c

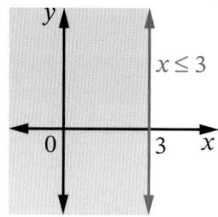

d

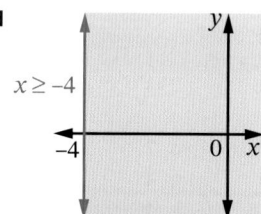

e

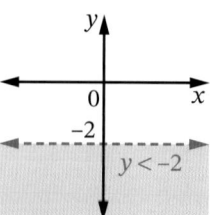

f

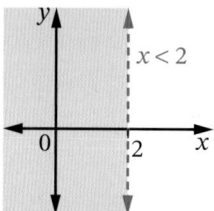

602   Nelson Maths 10 Advanced   9780170465595

3 B **4** A **5** C **6** D **7** B

8 a $y > x - 12$

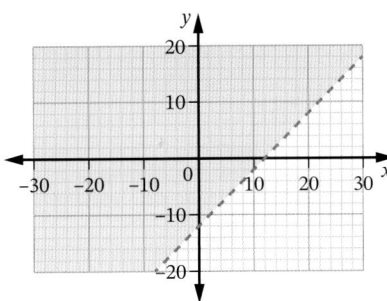

b $x - y \geq -5$

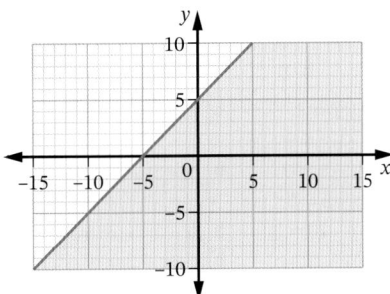

c $4 - y > x$

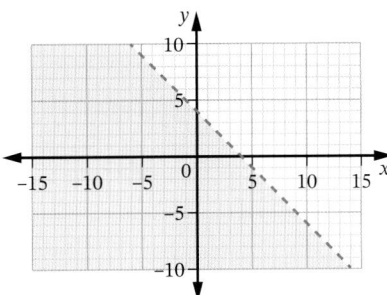

d $y \geq 2x - 5$

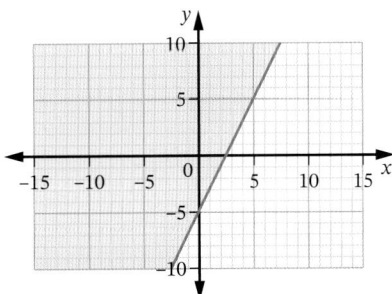

e $2y \leq -4x + 12$

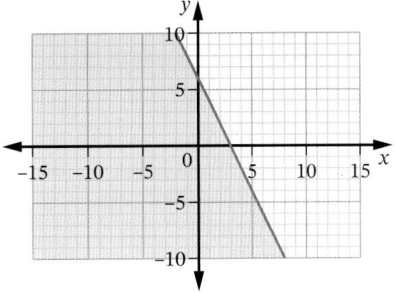

f $6x + 3y > 12$

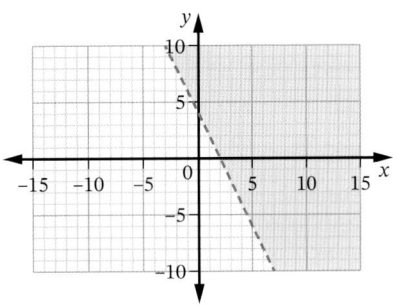

g $-2y \leq 6 - x$

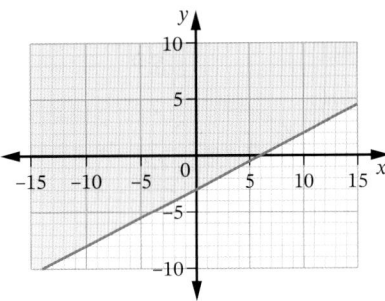

h $-24x - 8y > -48$

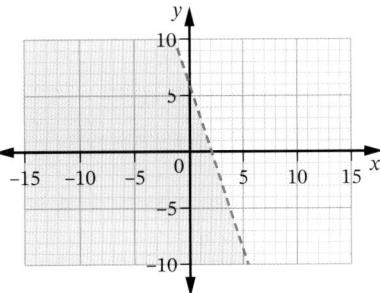

9 a $y > x - 3$ **b** $y \le x + 2$ **c** $y \ge 2x + 5$
d $y < -2x - 2$ **e** $y \ge -x + 3$ **f** $y < 2x$

10 a $30x + 15y \ge 6000$

b $2x + y \ge 400$ (or $y \ge -2x + 400$)

c

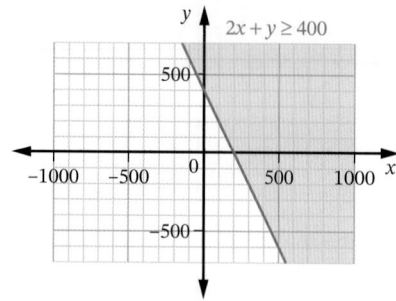

Ticket sales combinations include

Adult	0	200	20	40	80
Child	400	0	360	320	240

Other combinations possible.

11 $10x + 25y > 1600$ (or $2x + 5y > 320$), where x = number of regular scooters, y = number of electric scooters.

Sample of combinations below. Teacher to check other combinations.

Regular	160	145	100	50	10	0
Electric	0	6	24	44	60	64

Power plus

1 a $\dfrac{2}{3}$ **b** $y = \dfrac{2}{3}x - 2$ **c** $y = 4$

2 $k = 5$ **3** $B(2, -1)$ **4** $X(-2, 3)$

5 Teacher to check, see worked solutions.

6 a $-\dfrac{3}{2}$ **b** $3x + 2y + 2 = 0$ or $y = -\dfrac{3x}{2} - 1$

7 $(-3, 5)$ or $(7, 9)$ or $(1, 3)$

1 a $HJ = JK = KL = HL = \sqrt{58}$

b $m_{HJ} = \dfrac{3}{7}, m_{JK} = \dfrac{7}{3}, m_{KL} = \dfrac{3}{7}, m_{HL} = \dfrac{7}{3}$

c $HK = \sqrt{200}$ or $10\sqrt{2}$, $JL = \sqrt{32}$ or $4\sqrt{2}$

d rhombus

2 a $72°$ **b** $51°$ **c** $135°$ **d** $146°$

3 a $-\dfrac{1}{2}$ **b** 2

4 a

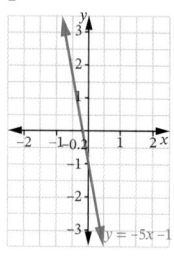

b

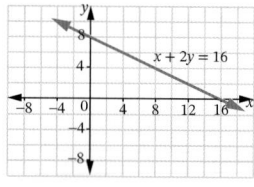

c

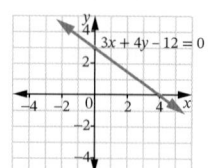

5 C

6 a $m = 2, c = -10$ **b** $m = 4, c = 3$

c $m = -\dfrac{3}{8}, c = \dfrac{1}{2}$

7 a C **b** B **c** A **d** D

8 a $m = 1, c = 2$ **b** $m = \dfrac{1}{4}, c = 1$

c $m = -3, c = 9$

9 a $3x - y + 5 = 0$ **b** $2x - 5y - 50 = 0$

c $x - 3y - 6 = 0$

10 a $3x + y - 20 = 0$ **b** $2x - 3y + 26 = 0$

11 a $3x - 5y - 20 = 0$ **b** $x + y + 3 = 0$

12 a $y = 2x + 3$ **b** $y = -\dfrac{1}{2}x - 4$

The product of their gradients, 2 and $-\dfrac{1}{2}$, is equal to –1, so they are perpendicular.

13 a $y = 3x - 6$ **b** $y = -2x$

14 $8x + 3y - 95 = 0$

15 a

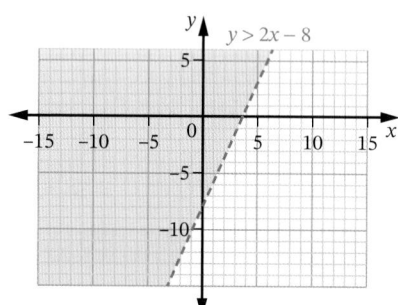

b

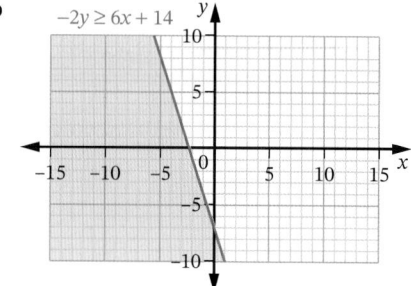

CHAPTER 2

SkillCheck

1 **a** 696 cm² **b** 336.96 cm² **c** 900 cm²
  d 814.2 cm² **e** 54.9 cm² **f** 1.14 cm²
2 **a** 35.3 cm² **b** 40.8 m² **c** 1.7 m²

Exercise 2.01

1 **a** 5 cm **b** 0.04 kg **c** 8 mL **d** 5 minutes
2 **a** 1 L (1000 mL) **b** 9 cm
  c 1 kg **d** 35°
3 **a** 13 mL, 0.013 **b** 0.2 cm, 0.022
  c 0.07 kg, 0.065 **d** 0.7°, 0.020
4 **a** volume of water **b** mass of the carrots
5 1.09% **6** 9.09%
7 percentage error of Lachlan's estimate = 3.33%
  percentage error of Aaria's estimate = 2%
  Aaria's estimate is more accurate.
8 percentage error of Kartik's estimate = 18.85%
  percentage error of Nandini's estimate = 12.71%
  Nandini's estimate is more accurate.
9 **a** **i** 1 mm **ii** 0.5 mm
  b **i** 1°C **ii** 0.5°C
  c **i** 1° **ii** 0.5°
  d **i** 5 km/h **ii** 2.5 km/h
  e **i** 250 g **ii** 125 g
  f **i** 10 mL **ii** 5 mL
  g **i** 1 kL **ii** 0.5 kL (500mL)
  h **i** $\frac{1}{4}$ tank **ii** $\frac{1}{8}$ tank
10 **a** 1 cm **b** 0.5 cm
  c 0.5 mm **d** 26.75 to 26.85 cm
11 1.25% **12** 0.75%
13 actual value = $21 202.78; Yes, the actual value of the painting is greater than $20 000.
14 Range is 7.3 to 8.7 inclusive. Based on this range it is not possible for a pencil in this batch to weigh 6.5 g as it is below the lower limit.

Exercise 2.02

1 **a** 7 **b** 7.4 **c** 7.45 **d** 7.4569
2 **a** 175 **b** 175.9
  c 175.95 **d** 175.956 98
3 **a** 7 **b** 7.5 **c** 7.46 **d** 7.4569
4 **a** 41.48 m, 107.5369 m²
  b 41.2 m, 106.09 m², 0.7%, 1.3%
  c 40 m, 100 m², 3.6%, 7.0%
5 **a** 50.131 95 cm² **b** 15.2352 cm
  c 50.16 cm², 15.2315 cm, 0.1%, 0.0%
  d 45.5 cm², 14.7648 cm, 9.2%, 3.2%
6 **a** 2400.1768 mm **b** 2398.96 mm, 0.1%
  c 380 mm, 2387.6104 mm, 0.5%
7 **a** $1998.05 **b** $1997.28, 0.0%
  c $2004.96, 0.3%
8 **a** $3800.52 **b** $3802.75, 0.1%
  c $4097.60, 7.8%

9 **a** 11.5 cm to 12.5 cm **b** 359.5 mL to 360.5 mL
  c 7.5 kg to 8.5 kg **d** 749.5 mm to 750.5 mm
  e 5.5 L to 6.5 L **f** 1249.5 g to 1250.5 g
  g 72.5 m to 73.5 m **h** 4.5 kL to 5.5 kL
  i 86.5 km to 87.5 km **j** 59.5 mg to 60.5 mg
10 **a** 144 cm² **b** 11.5 cm to 12.5 cm
  c 132.25 cm², 8.16% **d** 156.25 cm², 8.51%
11 **a** 18.8496 m **b** 2.5 m to 3.5 m
  c 15.7080 m, 16.67% **d** 21.9911 m, 16.67%
12 43.2%
13 **a** 56.5487 m³ **b** 56.52 m³, 0.1%
  c 29.4524 m³, 47.92% **d** 96.2113 m³, 70.14%
14 minimum cost = $4446 (with perimeter of 36 m fencing); maximum cost = $4940 (with perimeter of 40 m fencing)
15 **a** 180°C **b** 163°C **c** 9.4%

Exercise 2.03

1 **a** 897.5 m² **b** 127.5 cm² **c** 283 cm²
  d 486 cm² **e** 70.5 cm² **f** 364 cm²
  g 2093 m² **h** 287 cm² **i** 174.08 cm²
  j 252 cm² **k** 900 m² **l** 356.5 m²
2 **a** 1399.8 m² **b** 2.5 m² **c** 145.1 m²
  d 1.1 m² **e** 88.8 m² **f** 814.2 m²
  g 50.3 m² **h** 131.7 m² **i** 78.5 m²
  j 601.9 m² **k** 159.0 m² **l** 54.9 m²
3 **a** 35.3 cm² **b** 40.8 m² **c** 1.7 m²
4 **a** 2.25 m **b** 2226
5 D
6 **a** 1.50 m² **b** 72.8%
7 **a** 0.16 m² **b** 750 **c** $9514.80
8 **a** 7694 m² **b** 154 × $29.50 = $4543
9 **a** 414 m² **b** 240 m² **c** 58% **d** $2044.50

Exercise 2.04

1 **a** cube, 8.64 m² **b** triangular prism, 75.6 m²
  c trapezoidal prism, 295 m²
  d rectangular prism, 27.76 m²
2 **a** 282 m² **b** 298 cm² **c** 2720 mm²
  d 204 m² **e** 1288 mm² **f** 165 m²
3 A **4** **a** 80 m², $4400 **b** 171.4 m²
5 **a** 1036 cm² **b** 1020 mm² **c** 204 m²
  d 390 cm² **e** 672 cm² **f** 5672 mm²
6 B
7 **a** 60 336 cm² **b** need 7 m², cost = $175

Exercise 2.05

1 **a** 31.7 m² **b** 12 370.0 cm²
  c 805.8 cm² **d** 41.7 m²
2 **a** 35 m² **b** 3478 cm²
3 224π cm² **4** D
5 **a** 102π cm² **b** $\frac{165\pi}{16}$ or 10.3125π m²
  c $\frac{39\pi}{200}$ or 0.195π m² or 1950π cm²

6 a 1009 m²   **b** 3054 cm²   **c** 1355 cm²
   d 7 m²   **e** 905 cm²   **f** 39 m²
   g 17 m²   **h** 5 m²   **i** 1253 cm²
7 a 64.4 m²   **b** 8 L
8 a 27.3 m²   **b** 56.7 m²
   c cost = 28 × \$18.50 + 57 × \$21.75 = \$1757.75

Exercise 2.06

1 a 432 cm²   **b** 2150 cm²   **c** 173.2 cm²
2 a 275 m²   **b** 564 mm²   **c** 472 cm²
3 B
4 a 166.4 m²   **b** 3456 mm²   **c** 743.1 cm²
5 a 843 cm²   **b** 1592 cm²   **c** 3116 cm²
6 85 854 m²   **7** 1869 m²
8 a 1344 mm²   **b** 80 cm²   **c** 343.4 cm²
9 a 42 m   **b** $A = 735$ m²
   c 35 m   **d** 28 m

Exercise 2.07

1 a 101 cm²   **b** 628 cm²   **c** 2419 cm²
2 a 392.7 mm²   **b** 62.8 m²   **c** 192.4 cm²
3 a 1695.0 cm²   **b** 2.0 m²   **c** 614.3 cm²
4 a 90π m²   **b** 224π mm²   **c** 450π cm²
5 a 2827.4 mm²   **b** 380.1 m²   **c** 366.4 cm²
6 a 432π m²   **b** 192π cm²   **c** 768π mm²
7 B
8 a 314 m²   **b** 628 m²   **c** 628 m²   **d** 402 m²
9 a 5.11×10^8 km²   **b** 149 000 000 km²
   c 5.17%
10 5525 cm²
11 a 30.16 cm   **b** 4.80 cm
   c 8 cm   **d** 193.02 cm²
12 a 21.9 mm   **b** 25.2 mm   **c** 30.9 mm
13 a 6.9 cm   **b** 85.3 cm   **c** 85 cm

Exercise 2.08

1 a 446.96 cm²   **b** 49 270 cm²   **c** 864 cm²
   d 11 064 cm²   **e** 45 160 cm²   **f** 40 270.7 cm²
2 464 cm²
3 a 352 cm²   **b** 76 cm²
4 a 9721.7 cm²   **b** 14 031.4 cm²   **c** 14 778.1 cm²
   d 2858.8 cm²   **e** 2793.5 cm²   **f** 394.7 cm²
5 B
6 2953 cm²
7 a 26.14 m²   **b** 19 m²
8 1028.32 cm²   **9** A   **10** 19 858.0 cm²
11 a 857.7 cm²   **b** 412.3 cm²   **c** 1042.0 cm²
   d 5969.0 cm²   **e** 250.6 cm²   **f** 628.3 cm²
   g 282.7 cm²   **h** 652.9 cm²   **i** 501.6 cm²
   j 3769.9 cm²   **k** 1148.8 cm²   **l** 3017.7 cm²
   m 6615.4 cm²   **n** 3908.4 cm²   **o** 7940 cm²

Mental skills 2

2 a 8 hours 30 mins   **b** 5 hours 40 mins
   c 3 hours 25 mins   **d** 8 hours 15 mins
   e 11 hours 25 mins   **f** 1 hour 40 mins
   g 5 hours 10 mins   **h** 5 hours 45 mins
   i 7 hours 55 mins   **j** 7 hours 40 mins

Exercise 2.09

1 a 1399.6 m³   **b** 46.6 m³   **c** 56 160 cm³
   d 17 066 cm³   **e** 33 931.8 cm³   **f** 192.4 m³
   g 1.2 m³   **h** 21 756 cm³   **i** 208.8 m³
2 a 251.3 cm³   **b** 320 cm³   **c** 21.5%
3 350.4 m³   **4 a** 118 800 L   **b** 113 040 L
5 2 500 000 L   **6 a** 182.83 m³ **b** \$21.94 per day
7 1415.7 cm³
8 a 4825.49 cm³   **b** 5026.55 cm³   **c** 1989.38 cm³
   d 6375.00 cm³   **e** 5301.44 cm³   **f** 3084.96 cm³
   g 536.19 cm³   **h** 1884.96 cm³   **i** 167.33 cm³
   j 12 900 cm³   **k** 167.55 cm³   **l** 794.12 cm³

Exercise 2.10

1 a 149.3 cm³   **b** 240 cm³   **c** 120 cm³
   d 336 m³   **e** 1200 cm³   **f** 106.7 m³
2 a 33.75 m³   **b** 19 tonne
3 a i 24 cm   **ii** 3200 cm³   **iii** 3200 mL or 3.2 L
   b i 20 m   **ii** 19 200 m³   **iii** 19 200 kL
   c i 40 mm   **ii** 4320 mm³   **iii** 4.32 mL
   d i 60 mm   **ii** 28 160 mm³   **iii** 28.16 mL
   e i 7.7 m   **ii** 133.06 m³   **iii** 133.06 kL
   f i 84 cm   **ii** 564 480 cm³
   iii 564 480 mL or 564.48 L
4 a 2 592 100 m³   **b** 1.127 m³
5 27 m   **6** 76 mm   **7** 4.9 cm
8 a 209.4 m³   **b** 872.3 cm³   **c** 1272.3 mm³
   d 615.8 cm³   **e** 392.7 cm³   **f** 2544.7 mm³
9 a i 6.93 cm   **ii** 116.08 cm³   **iii** 116.08 mL
   b i 27.22 m   **ii** 13 796.95 m³   **iii** 13 796.95 kL
   c i 12.37 cm   **ii** 377.82 cm³   **iii** 377.82 mL
   d i 3.51 m   **ii** 2.35 m³   **iii** 2.35 kL
   e i 244.65 m   **ii** 296 162.05 m³   **iii** 296 162.05 kL
   f i 71.88 cm   **ii** 129 638.36 cm³ **iii** 129 638.36 mL
10 a 14 137.2 mm³ **b** 696.9 m³   **c** 659.6 cm³
   d 3619.1 m³   **e** 1072.3 cm³   **f** 8578.6 mm³
11 1.09×10^{12} km³   **12** 9.7 cm
13 8.8 m   **14** 5.23 m   **15** A
16 a 20 106.2 cm³   **b** 87.5%

Exercise 2.11

1 a 59 m³   **b** 59 kL
2 a 343 cm³   **b** 240 cm³   **c** 1152 cm³
   d 6100 cm³   **e** 6048 cm³   **f** 2500 cm³
3 a i 31 416 cm³   **ii** 31.416 L
   b i 616 cm³   **ii** 0.616 L
   c i 264 cm³   **ii** 0.264 L

4   28.27 kL

5   **a** 12 balls   **b** 60 balls   **c** 31 416 cm³   **d** 48%

6   **a** 1963 cm³   **b** 0.55 cm³/s

7   **a** 250 m³   **b** 210 kL   **c** $415.80

8   **a** 1696 m³   **b** 1018 t

Power plus

Teacher to check.

TEST YOURSELF 2

1   6.32% error

2   **a** 1256.6371 cm²   **b** 1256 cm², 0.1%

3   **a** 326.7 cm²   **b** 1318.2 cm²
c 151.7 m²   **d** 1039.1 cm²

4   **a** 1.08 m²   **b** 3150 mm²
c 5236 cm²   **d** 277.6 m²

5   **a** 17.4 m²   **b** 14 294.2 cm²
c 5871.2 cm²   **d** 4427.8 cm²

6   **a** 960 cm²   **b** 7776 cm²   **c** 1356 cm²

7   **a** 704 m²   **b** 4524 m²   **c** 2488 m²
d 452 m²   **e** 681 m²   **f** 5890 m²

8   **a** 3180 cm²   **b** 1268 cm²   **c** 395 cm²
d 3318 cm²   **e** 1728 cm²   **f** 3436 cm²

9   **a** 11 m³   **b** 36 816 m³
c 20 160 m³   **d** 10 016 m³

10   127.875 L   **11 a** 59.11 kL   **b** 1.44 m

12   **a** 322.67 m³   **b** 540 cm³   **c** 1568 mm³
d 1340.41 cm³   **e** 10 262.54 mm³ **f** 904.78 m³

13   **a** 360 498 mm³   **b** 145 125 mm³   **c** 455 cm³
d 229 m³   **e** 3054 cm³   **f** 18 096 m³

CHAPTER 3

SkillCheck

1   **a** 36   **b** 24   **c** 60

2   **a** 52   **b** 26   **c** 365   **d** 4
e 12   **f** 8 years and 4 months

3   **a** 1152   **b** 50   **c** 0.06

4   **a** $5962.59   **b** $33 433.46
c $18 481.63   **d** $64 937.10

Exercise 3.01

1   **a** $874   **b** $938.80   **c** $734.40

2   Juanita earns more per week by $27.48.

3   **a** $3461.86   **b** $6923.73   **c** $15 053.33

4   Job 1: $1104.64, Job 2: $1160; Job 2 by $55.36

5 $1107.40   **6** $851.18   **7** $780.86

8   A   **9** $13 312.50   **10** $1394.40

11 $2115   **12** 54   **13** $63.95

14   **a** $834   **b** $700   **c** $956.87   **d** $625.55

15   **a** $972.12   **b** $680.48   **c** $4568.96

Exercise 3.02

1   **a** $45 697   **b** $5318.53

2   **a** $144 719   **b** $38 613.03

3   **a** $90 904   **b** $20 010.80

4   C   **5** $18 555.91   **6** $49 976.10

7 $696.42   **8** $623.52

9   **a** $462   **b** $1699.10   **c** 25.4%

10   **a** $468   **b** $1732.65   **c** 24.5%

11   **a** $2296   **b** $468   **c** $1634.73

12   **a** $2304.91   **b** $470   **c** $1543.71

13   Gross weekly income = $825.30; Total deductions
= $374.10; Net weekly income = $451.20

Exercise 3.03

1   **a** $5040   **b** $1047.15   **c** $102.50
d $263.60   **e** $37.40   **f** $1192.32

2   **a** $87.50   **b** $5925.15   **c** $207 000
d $690   **e** $1404   **f** $723.04

3   A

4   **a** $11 200   **b** $1551.30
c $9392.50   **d** $10 695.31

5   **a** $1440   **b** $7440   **6** 4.5%

7   **a** $6400   **b** 5.82%

8   5.85% p.a.   **9** approx. 2 years

10   30 weeks   **11** 137 days   **12** C

13   31 months   **14** 2.6% p.a.

15   **a** $18.90   **b** $1063.90   **16** B

Exercise 3.04

1   **a** Check with your teacher.
Investment after 1st year = $24 150;
Investment after 2nd year = $25 357.50
b Compound interest = $2357.50

2   **a** $16 153.36   **b** $1153.36

3   **a** $38 459.48   **b** $4359.48

4   **a** $5408, $408   **b** $30 245.29, $2445.29
c $11 113.20, $1513.20   **d** $41 905.55, $2405.55
e $19 337.39, $937.39

5   **a** $4791.80   **b** $1642.38   **c** $308.93
d $3913.84   **e** $6834.42

Mental skills 3

2   **a** 18   **b** $126   **c** 39   **d** $30.30
e $7.50   **f** 10.8   **g** $27   **h** 60
i $240   **j** $3.30   **k** 900   **l** $52.50

4   **a** 10   **b** 166   **c** $50   **d** $22
e 37.5   **f** $5.80   **g** 135   **h** $22.60

6   **a** 500   **b** $20   **c** 4.5   **d** $6.25
e $81   **f** $35   **g** 16.5   **h** 74.5
i $195   **j** $425   **k** $31.50   **l** 290

0   **a** 100   **b** $1.50   **c** 7.5   **d** $32.50
e $67.50   **f** $31.25   **g** 38   **h** 170

Exercise 3.05

1 B

2 a i $9754.75   **ii** $3254.75
  b i $13 858.59   **ii** $3858.59
  c i $12 634.81   **ii** $394.81
  d i $43 949.46   **ii** $9349.46
  e i $8427.39   **ii** $427.39

3 D   **4** $1 301 018.83   **5** B   **6** A

7 a i $11 273.62   **ii** $1273.62
  b i $52 751.13   **ii** $17 251.13
  c i $9448.23   **ii** $548.23
  d i $48 063.26   **ii** $6063.26
  e i $17 829.56   **ii** $1329.56
  f i $4990.24   **ii** $90.24

8 C

9 a $600   **b** $615   **c** Tamsin by $15.

10 a D   **b** A   **c** C   **d** B

11 a $17 807.64   **b** $124 less

12 a i $5746.85   **ii** $5793.89
    iii $5817.79   **iv** $5833.87
  b Monthly, because it earns the most interest.

13 D

Exercise 3.06

1 $933.89

2 a $20 429.69   **b** $29 560.31

3 a i $659.66   **ii** 60.0%
  b i $17 406.69   **ii** 45.2%
  c i $5073.42   **ii** 60.0%
  d i $1024   **ii** 41.0%
  e i $14 020.37   **ii** 51.0%
  f i $1073.44   **ii** 37.0%
  g i $403.03   **ii** 46.3%
  h i $1782.95   **ii** 68.6%

4 a i 63%   **ii** 24.99%   **iii** 6.25%
  b By trial and error; in approx. 1.5 years

5 a i $10 000   **ii** $8000   **iii** $4096
  b 32.8%

6 a $17 969   **b** $7521

7 a $71 680   **b** $103 320
  c Approx. 5 years and 7 months
  d 13.4%

8 Yes, it will lose approximately 52% after 7 years.

9 a $1800   **b** 5 years   **c** $798.67
  d Yes, in the 30th year.   **e** no

Power plus

1 4 years and 61 days   **2** $4444.44

3 $12 838.71   **4** $63 367.50

5 $2276.87   **6** 790 000

7 a 18 years   **b** 18 years
  c No. The size of the interest rate and the number of compounding periods determine how quickly the principal takes to double in value.

TEST YOURSELF 3

1 $13 045.75   **2** $1349.18

3 a $879.45   **b** $1115.40

4 a $1052.51   **b** $736.76   **c** $4946.80

5 a $67 725   **b** $12 477.63

6 a $2400   **b** $245.31
  c $45.90   **d** $238.19

7 a $5360.85   **b** $360.85

8 $36 282.78   **9** $12 107.19

10 $291.98   **11** $13 145.47

12 a $487.50   **b** $4387.50   **c** $1908.56
  d $6296.06   **e** $174.89   **f** $6783.56

13 a $14 756   **b** $10 234   **c** 59.0%

PRACTICE SET 1

1 $2199.12

2 a 13.9   **b** $\left(-1\frac{1}{2},\ 3\right)$ **c** $-\frac{12}{7}$

3 a 616 m²   **b** 280.5 cm²   **c** 935 m²
  d 452.4 m²   **e** 1268.3 cm²   **f** 457.1 cm²

4 a $1505.94   **b** $1054.16   **c** $7077.92

5 a 117.5 m²   **b** 480 m²   **c** 324 m²

6 a $575   **b** $1164.38   **c** $1495

7 a $-\frac{4}{3}$ **b** $\frac{3}{4}$

8 a $71 904
  b $13 835 (rounded down to nearest whole dollar)

9

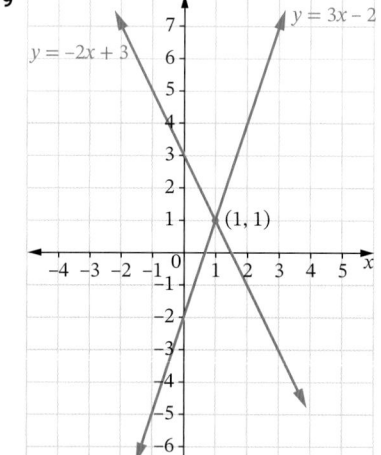

10 143°

11 a 9349.4 cm²   **b** 1979.2 cm²   **c** 279.4 cm²

12 $2x + 3y + 7 = 0$

13 B   **14** $5x + 4y - 7 = 0$

15 a

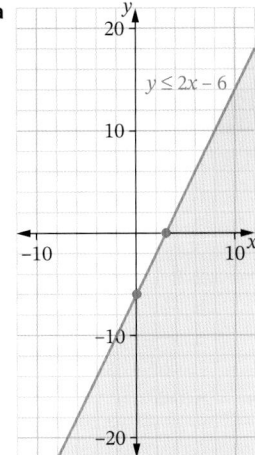

$y \le 2x - 6$

b

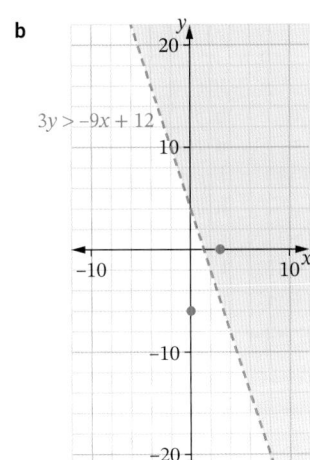

$3y > -9x + 12$

16 a 1352 m² **b** 22 m² **c** 2822 m²
17 a $52 042.84 **b** $52 142.72 **c** $52 165.50
18 $44 791.90
19 a $m = -3, c = 8$ **b** $m = 1, c = 7$
   c $m = -\frac{2}{3}, c = 1$
20 a $2x - y - 3 = 0$ **b** $2x - y - 5 = 0$
   c $3x - 4y + 24 = 0$
21 a 2269 cm² **b** 134.0 m² **c** 13 824 cm²
22 a 183 m² **b** 510 m² **c** 66 m²
23 a $y = 4x + 32$ **b** $y = 5x$
24 a $26 237.44 **b** $13 752.56 **c** 65.6%
25 C
26 $5x - 2y - 30 = 0$
27 a 6426 cm³ **b** 69 552 cm³ **c** 9896.0 cm³
28 a $34.70 **b** $5413.20
29 a 65 m³ **b** $137.15
30 A
31 a 50.2655 m² **b** 56.7450 m², 12.89%

SkillCheck

1 a g^9 **b** r^6 **c** d^{15} **d** k^2
   e h^{10} **f** m^4 **g** a **h** 1
   i $6e^7$ **j** $3n^4$ **k** $1000w^9$ **l** 25
   m v^5w^5 **n** $\frac{m^3}{n^3}$ **o** $\frac{1}{y}$ **p** $\frac{1}{p^2}$
2 81, 25, 100, 16, 64
3 a $m^2 + 10m + 21$ **b** $y^2 - 3y - 4$
   c $n^2 - 5n + 6$ **d** $6d^2 + 11d + 3$
   e $4 - 17p - 15p^2$ **f** $3a^2 + 17af + 10f^2$
   g $x^2 + 8x + 16$ **h** $y^2 - 6y + 9$
   i $4k^2 + 4k + 1$ **j** $a^2 - 25$
   k $t^2 - 49$ **l** $9m^2 - 16$

Exercise 4.01

1 a $24m^{14}$ **b** $\frac{6k^8}{5}$ **c** $-y^{10}$ **d** $9q^6$
   e $4a^6d$ **f** $21x^7y^{12}$ **g** $-5e^{10}g^4$ **h** $-3wy^7$
   i $64c^{21}$ **j** $-32p^5$ **k** $\frac{3k^2m}{2}$ **l** $54u^4v^3w^{10}$

2 a $l^{18}m^{30}$ **b** $\frac{n^3}{8}$ **c** $\frac{w^{20}}{m^{15}}$ **d** 1
   e $64k^2y^{10}$ **f** $81p^8q^{12}r^{16}$ **g** 4 **h** $-125d^9y^{15}$
   i $\frac{16b^4}{81d^4}$ **j** -9 **k** 12 **l** $-\frac{27k^{12}}{1000}$

3 a 1 **b** 5 **c** -64 **d** 64
   e 36 **f** 1 **g** $\frac{1}{8}$ **h** 5
   i 1 **j** 49 **k** 1 **l** 1
   m $\frac{1}{15}$ **n** $\frac{1}{16}$ **o** 2 **p** 25

4 D

5 a $\frac{1}{8}$ **b** $\frac{1}{1000000}$ **c** $\frac{1}{8}$ **d** $\frac{1}{36}$ **e** $\frac{1}{81}$

6 a $\frac{1}{5^4}$ **b** $\frac{1}{8^2}$ **c** $\frac{1}{w^6}$ **d** $\frac{1}{m^5}$
   e $\frac{4}{y^3}$ **f** $\frac{1}{a^2d^2}$ **g** $\frac{1}{32x^5}$ **h** $\frac{3m}{p^2}$
   i $\frac{10}{g^2h^3}$ **j** $\frac{1}{256u^4}$ **k** $\frac{2a^5}{q^2}$ **l** $\frac{4p^2}{x^3}$
   m $\frac{10c^3}{a^5}$ **n** $\frac{-1}{27r^{18}}$ **o** $\frac{3}{4q^2p}$ **p** $\frac{4}{125k^9}$

7 C

8 a $\frac{4d^2}{25}$ **b** $\frac{5}{y^2}$ **c** $\frac{1}{125m^3}$ **d** $\frac{x^2y^3}{w^2}$
   e $\frac{9}{16y^6}$ **f** $\frac{7k}{a}$ **g** $\frac{8}{9a^2b^4}$ **h** $\frac{5k^2}{6c}$

9 a 16 **b** $\frac{27}{125}$ **c** $\frac{81}{625}$ **d** $\frac{25}{169}$
   e $\frac{m^3}{64}$ **f** $\frac{49}{9a^2}$ **g** $-\frac{y^5}{32}$ **h** $\frac{25}{64q^4}$
   i $-\frac{w^9}{64}$ **j** $\frac{d^{10}}{k^4}$ **k** $-\frac{243d^{15}}{100000g^{20}}$ **l** $\frac{625}{2401h^{24}}$

10 a $5000x^{28}y^6$ **b** $256k^{44}m^4$ **c** $2r^8q^{-14} = \frac{2r^8}{q^{14}}$
   d $\frac{2}{9w^7m}$ **e** $\frac{256x^{16}}{a^4}$ **f** $\frac{4}{9g^4n^8}$
   g $-128p^{-3}h^{21} = \frac{-128h^{21}}{p^3}$ **h** $-8d^5n^4$
   i $-1000c^{21}e^{18}$

Exercise 4.02

1 **a** 8   **b** -3 **c** 25   **d** 10
  e 2   **f** -0.2 **g** 0.1   **h** -2
  i -2 **j** -9 **k** 2   **l** 5

2 **a** $\sqrt[3]{7}$ **b** $\sqrt{15}$ **c** $\sqrt[4]{d}$ **d** $\sqrt{y}$
  e $\sqrt[6]{4x}$ **f** $\sqrt{10m^3}$ **g** $\sqrt[10]{2a^7}$ **h** $\sqrt[3]{12m}$

3 C

4 **a** $80^{\frac{1}{3}}$ **b** $40^{\frac{1}{6}}$ **c** $20^{\frac{1}{2}}$ **d** $c^{\frac{1}{4}}$
  e $b^{\frac{1}{2}}$ **f** $(xy)^{\frac{1}{3}}$ **g** $(25w)^{\frac{1}{5}}$ **h** $(4y)^{\frac{1}{8}}$

5 **a** 8   **b** 3125   **c** $-\dfrac{1}{243}$ **d** 4
  e $-\dfrac{1}{8}$ **f** $\dfrac{1}{2}$ **g** 100 000   **h** $\dfrac{1}{30}$
  i 32   **j** $\dfrac{1}{2187}$ **k** $\dfrac{1}{1296}$ **l** $\dfrac{1}{9}$

6 B

7 **a** -6.30 **b** 6.08   **c** 0.14   **d** -2.02
  e 0.10   **f** 4.90   **g** 0.01   **h** 3.01

8 **a** $k^{\frac{3}{4}}$ **b** $m^{-\frac{1}{2}}$ **c** $x^{\frac{7}{3}}$ **d** $y^{\frac{3}{2}}$
  e $d^{-\frac{2}{5}}$ **f** $\left(2a^3\right)^{\frac{1}{2}}$ **g** $(4p)^{-\frac{1}{5}}$ **h** $(vw)^{-\frac{1}{4}}$

9 D

10 **a** $3125m^{20}$ **b** $4y^4$ **c** $64x^3w^9$ **d** $\dfrac{1}{243c^{10}}$
  e $\dfrac{1}{16k^{12}}$ **f** $\dfrac{1}{4p^6}$ **g** $\dfrac{1}{100n^2w^3}$ **h** $81x^8y^4$
  i $36p^{\frac{8}{3}}n^3$ **j** $\dfrac{1}{125y^6d^3}$ **k** 4   **l** $36a^4b^6$

Exercise 4.03

1 **a** $5d + 55$ **b** $-3r - 30$
  c $7x - 63y$ **d** $-4a + 20w$
  e $-2 + p^2$ **f** $-20e^3 - 30e$
  g $6y + 42y^2$ **h** $12x^2y^2 - 4xy$
  i $16rq^2 - 8r^2q$ **j** $12ab^2 - 21a^2b$
  k $-6h^2 + 18h^3$ **l** $-25x^3 - 20xy$
  m $-3 - 8a$ **n** $-6m^3 + 8m^2n$
  o $15g + 35g^3$ **p** $-5e + 12$

2 C

3 **a** yes   **b** no   **c** yes

4 **a** $3k^2 - 20k$ **b** $-23h + 7h^2$
  c $3w^3 - 15w$ **d** $49x^3 - 10x^4$
  e $2 + 21d$ **f** $12n - 26n^2$
  g $4y^2 - 6y + 5$ **h** $5 - 13a - 4a^2$
  i $16 + 50w$ **j** $20y^3 - 8y^2 + 8$
  k $-2v^2 - v - 6$ **l** $8 - 9a + a^2$
  m $10c^2 - 30c + 20$ **n** $2m^2 + 18m^3$
  o $20x + 26xy - 60y$

5 **a** $5(3y - 4)$ **b** $7(3 + 5w)$
  c $p(2 + p)$ **d** $10y(3 - 2y)$
  e $12d(3d + 2)$ **f** $7k(4k - 3)$
  g $(c - 5)(8 - c)$ **h** $(3 + 2m)(m + 7)$
  i $-q(q + 36)$ **j** $-4x(2 - 3x)$
  k $(3b + 5)(b - 2)$ **l** $-4cd(3d - 2)$
  m $-hn(n - h)$ **n** $-3g(5g + 6)$
  o $6q(8q - 9)$

6 B

7 **a** $4my(2my - 3)$ **b** $9bc(4ab + 3)$
  c $12mn(2m - 9n)$ **d** $5g(4dg - 7a)$
  e $8wy^2(5y + 3w)$ **f** $25gh(3g^2h - 5)$
  g $p(1 - 8p - 4p^2)$ or $-p(4p^2 + 8p - 1)$
  h $3mn(2n + 1 + 16m)$
  i $8pg(4p^2 + g - 1)$ **j** $3a^2(6a^3 - 4 + 5a^2)$
  k $7mh^2(4m^2 - 3)$ **l** $3w(5kp - 8p^2 - 3k)$

Exercise 4.04

1 D   **2** B

3 **a** $9b^2 - 24b + 16$ **b** $25a^2 + 60a + 36$
  c $10q^2 - 21q - 49$ **d** $5p^2 - 9p - 18$
  e $12d^2 - 29d - 11$ **f** $-8r^2 + 38r - 45$
  g $-14y^2 + 15y + 9$ **h** $64h^2 - 9$
  i $-49w^2 + 126w - 81$ **j** $16d^2 - 1$
  k $3f^2 - 2f - 1$ **l** $-36u^2 + 60u - 25$

4 B

5 **a** $16y$ **b** h^2 **c** m^2
  d $+ 22u$ **e** $+ 30k$ **f** $-48xw, 9w^2$

6 **a** $h^2 + 14h + 49$ **b** $p^2 - 10p + 25$
  c $w^2 - 12w + 36$ **d** $16 - 8c + c^2$
  e $121 + 22y + y^2$ **f** $d^2 - 2dw + w^2$
  g $100 - 20x + x^2$ **h** $d^2 + 2dq + q^2$
  i $25u^2 + 10u + 1$ **j** $9b^2 + 42b + 49$
  k $49e^2 - 154e + 121$ **l** $4 - 20h + 25h^2$
  m $64x^2 - 48xy + 9y^2$ **n** $36m^2 + 60mc + 25c^2$
  o $g^2 + 24gw + 144w^2$ **p** $4 + \dfrac{8}{a} + \dfrac{4}{a^2}$
  q $\dfrac{36}{m^2} - 12 + m^2$ **r** $\dfrac{9}{x^2} + 18 + 9x^2$

7 D

8 **a** $k^2 - 49$ **b** $x^2 - 64$ **c** $g^2 - 1$
  d $144 - w^2$ **e** $16 - d^2$ **f** $49b^2 - 25$
  g $9h^2 - 49$ **h** $100e^2 - 1$ **i** $121 - 16y^2$
  j $1 - 25p^2$ **k** $9a^2 - 49c^2$ **l** $81h^2 - 25m^2$
  m $\dfrac{16}{m^2} - m^2$ **n** $9g^2 - \dfrac{1}{g^2}$ **o** $\dfrac{16a^2}{9} - 4$

9 B

10 **a** $9t^2 - 6td + d^2$ **b** $49k^2 + 42k + 9$
  c $81 - 16g^2$ **d** $4a^2 - 25$
  e $a^2b^2 - 64$ **f** $20n^2 + 9pn - 20p^2$
  g $100x^2 - 140xy + 49y^2$ **h** $4 - 121h^2m^2$
  i $x^2y^2 - \dfrac{1}{y^2}$

11 **a** $2y + 1 + 8y^2$ **b** $12w + 70 - 2w^2$
  c $-3a^2 + 2ab$ **d** $-p^2 - 65p + 220$
  e $-12y$ **f** $4x^2 + 25$
  g $-m^2 + 8m + 4$ **h** $17 - 35d + 2d^2$

12 C

13 **a** $(3x - 10)(2x + 15)$ **b** $6x^2 + 25x - 150$
  c $-6x^2 - 25x + 750$

14 **a** $3k(k + 5) = 3k^2 + 15k$ cm²
  b length $= 3k - 8$, width $= k + 1$
  c $(3k - 8)(k + 1)$
  d $3k^2 - 5k - 8$
  e $20k + 8$

15 a length = $a + 3$, width = $b + 1$
  b area = $(a + 3)(b + 1)$
  c area = $ab + a + 3b + 3$
  d increase in area = $a + 3b + 3$

16 a $10d^2 + d - 21$ **b** $\frac{33}{2}k^2 + 2k - 6$

  c $\frac{3\pi(25a^2 + 40a + 16)}{4}$ or $\frac{75\pi a^2 + 120\pi a + 48\pi}{4}$

17 Proof: see worked solutions

Exercise 4.05

1 a $(3p + 2q)(x + y)$ **b** $(h + k)(2w - 3u)$
  c $(3k + 4g)(5m + 2n)$ **d** $(x - 2a)(4y + 7a)$
  e $(7a + 4)(2k - 5f)$ **f** $(d + y)(c - h)$
  g $4(m + t)(a + e)$ **h** $3(y + 4)(k - 2b)$
  i $(3c + 5w)(4a - 7m)$ **j** $(3k - 4e)(7h + 2p)$
  k $3(2y - 1)(5y - q)$ **l** $(4h + 3k)(8g - m)$
  m $(2g + 5h)(3n - 2c)$ **n** $(w - p)(p + 1)(p - 1)$
  o $(m + a)(d - 3 - x)$ **p** $(k + d)(x + y + e)$
2 a $(d + 4)(d - 4)$ **b** $(x + 5)(x - 5)$
  c $(y + 13)(y - 13)$ **d** $(p + 9)(p - 9)$
  e $(5 - h)(5 + h)$ **f** $(11 - a)(11 + a)$
  g $(2r + 3d)(2r - 3d)$ **h** $(5g + 2e)(5g - 2e)$
  i $(12 - 7m)(12 + 7m)$ **j** $(9y + 4k)(9y - 4k)$
  k $(1 + 2d)(1 - 2d)$ **l** $(m + 5n)(m - 5n)$
  m $(5q + 3b)(5q - 3b)$ **n** $(8b + u)(8b - u)$
  o $(12x + 1)(12x - 1)$ **p** $(6k + w)(6k - w)$
  q $(g + 4p)(g - 4p)$ **r** $(2e + 11d)(2e - 11d)$
  s $(mp - 5)(mp + 5)$ **t** $(a + qw)(a - qw)$
  u $\left(x+\frac{1}{4}\right)\left(x-\frac{1}{4}\right)$ **v** $\left(\frac{5}{3}+h\right)\left(\frac{5}{3}-h\right)$
  w $\left(\frac{5}{2}+3c\right)\left(\frac{5}{2}-3c\right)$ **x** $\left(4v-\frac{3}{2}\right)\left(4v+\frac{3}{2}\right)$
3 a $4(m + 2p)(m - 2p)$ **b** $3(y + 3)(y - 3)$
  c $w(w + 6)(w - 6)$ **d** $q(1 - 8q)(1 + 8q)$
  e $12(1 + 2u)(1 - 2u)$ **f** $r(h + r)(h - r)$
  g $5(5ab + 2v)(5ab - 2v)$
  h $3(x^2 + 3p)(x^2 - 3p)$
  i $6gp(3g + p)(3g - p)$ **j** $7c(2 - 3w)(2 + 3w)$
  k $36e^3(2e + 1)(2e - 1)$
  l $9\left(d-\frac{1}{2}\right)\left(d+\frac{1}{2}\right)$ or $\frac{9}{4}(2d-1)(2d+1)$
  m $25\left(2k-\frac{1}{2}\right)\left(2k+\frac{1}{2}\right)$ or $\frac{25}{4}(4k-1)(4k+1)$
  n $2(7a + w)(7a - w)$
  o $\left(c-\frac{4}{3}\right)\left(c+\frac{4}{3}\right)$ or $\frac{1}{9}(3c-4)(3c+4)$
  p $27m(2mn - 1)(2mn + 1)$
4 a $\left(\frac{1}{5}-x\right)\left(\frac{1}{5}+x\right)$ or $\frac{1}{25}(1-5x)(1+5x)$
  b $\left(\frac{d}{3}-\frac{w}{7}\right)\left(\frac{d}{3}+\frac{w}{7}\right)$ **c** $3\left(p-\frac{4}{p}\right)\left(p+\frac{4}{p}\right)$
  d $4\left(\frac{4b}{5}-\frac{y}{9}\right)\left(\frac{4b}{5}+\frac{y}{9}\right)$ **e** $(u - 2)(u + 2)(u^2 + 4)$
  f $(m - 2)(m + 8)$ **g** $x(x - 2y)$

h $2a(a - 3)(a + 3)(a^2 + 9)$ **i** $4px$
j $\frac{1}{9}\left(2c-\frac{e}{2}\right)\left(2c+\frac{e}{2}\right)$ **k** $(g + 2k)(3g - 2k)$
l $5w(w - 2)(w + 2)(w^2 + 4)$

Exercise 4.06

1 a $-3, 5$ **b** $-10, -4$ **c** $6, 7$ **d** $-3, 2$
  e $5, 9$ **f** $6, -4$ **g** $6, 9$ **h** $-4, 4$
  i $-2, 5$ **j** $-7, -5$
2 a $(q - 10)(q + 2)$ **b** $(h - 9)(h + 4)$
  c $(y + 11)(y - 4)$ **d** $(x - 9)(x + 7)$
  e $(u + 10)(u - 1)$ **f** $(e + 10)(e - 3)$
  g $(a - 11)(a + 10)$ **h** $(y + 9)(y - 3)$
  i $(m - 7)(m + 1)$ **j** $(c + 9)(c - 2)$
  k $(k + 9)(k - 6)$ **l** $(r - 11)(r + 2)$
  m $(p - 8)(p + 4)$ **n** $(u + 15)(u - 3)$
  o $(b - 8)(b + 2)$
3 a $(h - 1)^2$ **b** $(x + 5)(x + 10)$
  c $(r + 8)(r + 12)$ **d** $(a + 4)(a - 7)$
  e $(u + 5)(u - 12)$ **f** $(y - 9)^2$
  g $(v - 8)(v + 7)$ **h** $(w - 15)(w + 4)$
  i $(g + 6)(g - 3)$ **j** $(p + 6)(p + 8)$
  k $(e + 8)(e - 1)$ **l** $(x - 7)(x - 12)$

Mental skills 4

2 Exact answers shown
  a 331   **b** 157   **c** 1587   **d** 255
  e 421   **f** 203   **g** 413   **h** 734
  i 6723   **j** 15 744   **k** 276   **l** $72\frac{3}{7}$
4 Exact answers shown, or rounded to 4 decimal places.
  a 28.231   **b** 14.187   **c** 177.4967
  d 416.752   **e** 2.4156   **f** 5.0237
  g 3.6890   **h** 5.8065   **i** 23.9121

Exercise 4.07

1 a $2(k + 3)(k + 5)$ **b** $3(q + 5)(q - 6)$
  c $5(x - 4)(x - 7)$ **d** $6(y + 3)(y - 1)$
  e $n(n - 9)(n - 7)$
  f $-(a - 6)(a + 4)$ or $(6 - a)(a + 4)$
  g $-(p - 8)(p + 4)$ **h** $-x^2(x - 3)(x + 7)$
  i $-4(h - 5)(h - 1)$
2 a $(3d + 5)(2d + 3)$ **b** $(4m + 3)(2m + 1)$
  c $(2y + 5)(y + 1)$ **d** $(2w + 1)(w + 15)$
  e $(3k + 4)(2k + 5)$ **f** $(3u + 7)(u + 5)$
  g $(4x + 9)(x + 3)$ **h** $(5e + 4)(e + 7)$
  i $(3h + 1)(4h + 3)$
3 a $(4k - 3)(k - 2)$ **b** $(3w - 1)(2w - 5)$
  c $(5p - 3)(p - 4)$ **d** $(2g - 7)(3g - 7)$
  e $(3x - 2)(x - 10)$ **f** $(3m - 2)(7m - 4)$
  g $(5r - 2)(4r - 3)$ **h** $(2a + 1)(5a - 6)$
  i $(5u + 3)(4u - 7)$ **j** $(2p + 1)(p - 9)$
  k $(3y - 8)(2y + 5)$ **l** $(4b + 1)(3b - 5)$
  m $(6q + 5)(2q - 3)$ **n** $(4h - 3)(h + 4)$
  o $(5n - 2)(2n + 7)$

4 a $(4w-7)^2$ **b** $(11h+8)^2$ **c** $(3p-15)^2$

5 a $3(2m+5)(m-4)$ **b** $2x(4x-1)(x-2)$
c $-(5e-1)(e+6)$ **d** $-3(2w+7)(3w-2)$
e $-4(3k+1)(4k-1)$ **f** $-(5n-4)(3n+2)$
g $6(4d+3)(2d+5)$ **h** $-3(4h+1)(2h-3)$
i $-(7p-3)(4p+1)$

6 A

7 a $(7d-1)(4d-1)$ **b** $-2(5y+3)(2y-1)$
c $(10w-3)(3w+5)$ **d** $(4p+3)(p+5)$
e $-(2a-3)(5a-4)$ **f** $(9r+20)(r+1)$
g $(7k+3y)(4k+y)$ **h** $-3p(p-4)(p+6)$
i $-(6m-1)(3m+4)$ **j** $-2g(6g-1)(3g+5)$
k $(11u-3)(4u+1)$ **l** $(8h-3m)(4h+5m)$

Exercise 4.08

1 a $15(2y-1)(2y+1)$ **b** $(5m-2)(3m-7)$
c $(k-7)^2$ **d** $-(2a-3)(a-4)$
e $(3g+4c)(2y+3p)$ **f** $-(4x-3)(x+5)$
g $(8q-1)^2$ **h** $9(3r-2w)(3r+2w)$
i $(bn-p)(3n+2d)$ **j** $(3k+4)(2k+5)$
k $(6a+7)(7a+4)$ **l** $4(1-5h)(1+5h)$
m $(9c-7)(4c+9)$ **n** $-(7d-2)(5d+8)$
o $(5u+2)^2$ **p** $(3y+4)(x-2w)$
q $(b-1)^2(b+1)$ **r** $(7c-4h)(4c+h)$
s $(5n+7)(3n-8)$ **t** $ap(a-1)(a+1)$
u $2(8r-k)(r-9k)$

2 a $3(4c+5)(4c-5)$ **b** $2(q+4)(4q-5)$
c $-x^2(2x+5)(x-3)$ **d** $(9p+4r)(3p-4r)$
e $3(3w-7)(w+5)$ **f** $n^2(n-2)(n+2)$
g $y(y-1)^2(y+1)$ **h** $(12u+7)(3u+7)$
i $(11k-9)^2$ **j** $(c-3d)(3c-d)$
k $2(2y+3d)(5y+3)$ **l** $ah(h-6-h^2)$
m $9(2b+3)(b-3)$ **n** $8g(2-gy)(2+gy)$
o $-2(6e-1)(3e+4)$ **p** $3p(3q+1)(3q-1)$
q $-15h(h+2)(h-1)$ **r** $(w-1)(w^3-w-1)$
s $a^3(a-16)(a+16)$ **t** $(m-k)(m+k+9)$
u $5(3a-1)(2a+5)$

3 D

Exercise 4.09

1 C   **2** B

3 $\sqrt{32}, \sqrt{33}, \sqrt{4.9}, \sqrt{52}, \sqrt{200}$

4 a R **b** I **c** R **d** R
e R **f** R **g** R **h** R
i I **j** R **k** I **l** I

5 a $1\frac{4}{7}, \frac{\pi}{2}, \sqrt{2}$ **b** $2\frac{7}{9}, \sqrt[3]{20}, 2.\dot{6}$

6 a -1.8 **b** 0.7 **c** 0.4 **d** -3.5
e -2.5 **f** 2.6 **g** 1.6 **h** 1.9

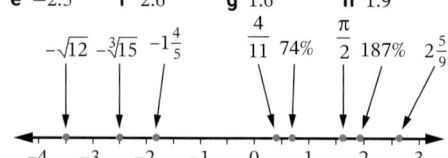

7 1.4

8 Teacher to check, $\sqrt{5} \approx 2.24, \sqrt{10} \approx 3.16, \sqrt{17} \approx 4.12$

Exercise 4.10

1 a 2 **b** 5 **c** 27 **d** 250
e 0.09 **f** 28 **g** 45 **h** 50

2 a $5\sqrt{2}$ **b** $3\sqrt{3}$ **c** $2\sqrt{6}$ **d** $3\sqrt{6}$
e $9\sqrt{3}$ **f** $3\sqrt{5}$ **g** $4\sqrt{3}$ **h** $10\sqrt{2}$
i $4\sqrt{6}$ **j** $3\sqrt{7}$ **k** $12\sqrt{2}$ **l** $6\sqrt{3}$
m $5\sqrt{3}$ **n** $7\sqrt{3}$ **o** $4\sqrt{2}$ **p** $11\sqrt{2}$
q $9\sqrt{2}$ **r** $7\sqrt{5}$ **s** $5\sqrt{5}$ **t** $16\sqrt{2}$

3 a $25\sqrt{2}$ **b** $6\sqrt{2}$ **c** $12\sqrt{3}$ **d** $56\sqrt{2}$
e $\sqrt{10}$ **f** $\sqrt{3}$ **g** $\frac{\sqrt{7}}{3}$ **h** $6\sqrt{6}$
i $18\sqrt{17}$ **j** $\frac{5\sqrt{5}}{2}$ **k** $3\sqrt{2}$ **l** $3\sqrt{3}$
m $40\sqrt{10}$ **n** $15\sqrt{3}$ **o** $14\sqrt{17}$ **p** $\frac{\sqrt{13}}{3}$

4 B   **5** B

6 a false **b** false **c** true
d true **e** true **f** false

Exercise 4.11

1 a $7\sqrt{7}$ **b** $-5\sqrt{2}$ **c** $6\sqrt{5}$ **d** $4\sqrt{5}$
e 0 **f** $\sqrt{10}$ **g** $8\sqrt{15}$ **h** $-\sqrt{6}$
i $2\sqrt{3}$ **j** $10\sqrt{5}$ **k** $6\sqrt{10}$ **l** $-5\sqrt{3}$

2 a $5\sqrt{5}-8$ **b** $13\sqrt{10}+3\sqrt{2}$ **c** $5\sqrt{2}-9\sqrt{3}$
d $7\sqrt{15}+8\sqrt{2}$ **e** $-2\sqrt{5}-3\sqrt{7}$ **f** $2\sqrt{6}-8\sqrt{3}$
g $13\sqrt{11}-\sqrt{3}$ **h** $11\sqrt{7}-6\sqrt{13}$ **i** $-6\sqrt{7}$
j $-3\sqrt{5}$

3 a D   **b** A

4 a $6\sqrt{2}$ **b** $3\sqrt{3}$ **c** $-2\sqrt{5}$
d $-\sqrt{7}$ **e** $5\sqrt{6}$ **f** $7\sqrt{5}$
g $-\sqrt{10}$ **h** $8\sqrt{11}$ **i** $6\sqrt{2}$
j $8\sqrt{3}$ **k** $3\sqrt{2}$ **l** $9\sqrt{2}$
m $11\sqrt{3}$ **n** $-\sqrt{5}$ **o** $-6\sqrt{3}$
p $30\sqrt{3}$ **q** $5\sqrt{7}$ **r** $41\sqrt{2}$
s $5\sqrt{6}$ **t** $29\sqrt{2}$ **u** $-15\sqrt{3}$
v 0 **w** $6\sqrt{2}+2\sqrt{3}$ **x** $12\sqrt{3}+3\sqrt{6}$
y $3\sqrt{2}-6\sqrt{5}$ **z** $4\sqrt{6}$

Exercise 4.12

1 a $\sqrt{14}$ **b** $-\sqrt{35}$ **c** $4\sqrt{3}$ **d** 6
e $-5\sqrt{2}$ **f** 45 **g** $15\sqrt{30}$ **h** $-10\sqrt{21}$
i 140 **j** $-30\sqrt{2}$ **k** 36 **l** $-60\sqrt{2}$
m -112 **n** $24\sqrt{6}$ **o** 80 **p** $90\sqrt{6}$
q -396 **r** $160\sqrt{5}$ **s** $216\sqrt{2}$ **t** $-96\sqrt{6}$
u $36\sqrt{5}$ **v** $-60\sqrt{10}$ **w** $252\sqrt{3}$ **x** 144

2 a $\sqrt{5}$ **b** $-\sqrt{3}$ **c** $3\sqrt{6}$
d $2\sqrt{2}$ **e** $-\frac{\sqrt{7}}{2}$ **f** 21
g 1 **h** 8 **i** $5\sqrt{3}$
j $5\sqrt{2}$ **k** $4\sqrt{3}$ **l** $2\sqrt{6}$
m $2\sqrt{14}$ **n** $-\frac{\sqrt{2}}{4}$ **o** 1
p 10 **q** 4 **r** $-21\sqrt{2}$
s 12 **t** 2 **u** $\frac{2}{3}$

3 a 6 **b** 7 **c** 6
d $15y$ **e** x **f** $a\sqrt{a}$
4 C **5** A
6 a 2 **b** $4\sqrt{6}$ **c** $\sqrt{30}$
d $\dfrac{2}{45}$ **e** $14\sqrt{3}$ **f** 2

Exercise 4.13

1 a $\sqrt{15}+\sqrt{10}$ **b** $2\sqrt{3}-\sqrt{6}$ **c** $\sqrt{6}+\sqrt{14}$
d $3\sqrt{10}-5$ **e** $6+6\sqrt{6}$ **f** $\sqrt{55}-4\sqrt{11}$
g $42-8\sqrt{7}$ **h** $5\sqrt{5}+75$ **i** $24+3\sqrt{6}$
2 C
3 a $10+\sqrt{10}-6\sqrt{5}-3\sqrt{2}$ **b** $7+2\sqrt{7}-\sqrt{21}-2\sqrt{3}$
c $28\sqrt{6}+21+8\sqrt{2}+2\sqrt{3}$ **d** $20+\sqrt{10}$
e $109+10\sqrt{77}$ **f** $72-23\sqrt{6}$
g $16\sqrt{10}+54$ **h** $-16-\sqrt{35}$
4 C
5 a $8-2\sqrt{15}$ **b** $9+2\sqrt{14}$ **c** $9-4\sqrt{5}$
d $19+6\sqrt{10}$ **e** $77+30\sqrt{6}$ **f** $179-20\sqrt{7}$
g $38+12\sqrt{10}$ **h** $23+4\sqrt{15}$
6 a 1 **b** 22 **c** 8 **d** 2
e 1 **f** 166 **g** 13 **h** -43
7 C
8 a $88-30\sqrt{7}$ **b** $21\sqrt{2}-10$ **c** $5\sqrt{35}+29$
d $73+40\sqrt{3}$ **e** 29 **f** $92-12\sqrt{5}$

Exercise 4.14

1 B
2 a $\dfrac{\sqrt{2}}{2}$ **b** $\dfrac{\sqrt{7}}{7}$ **c** $\dfrac{\sqrt{3}}{3}$ **d** $\dfrac{3\sqrt{2}}{2}$
e $\dfrac{2\sqrt{7}}{7}$ **f** $\dfrac{\sqrt{2}}{6}$ **g** $\dfrac{\sqrt{3}}{6}$ **h** $\dfrac{\sqrt{7}}{28}$
i $\dfrac{7\sqrt{5}}{15}$ **j** $\dfrac{\sqrt{10}}{15}$ **k** $\dfrac{\sqrt{3}}{2}$ **l** $\dfrac{\sqrt{15}}{4}$
3 A **4** D
5 a $\dfrac{2-\sqrt{2}}{2}$ **b** $\dfrac{\sqrt{5}-5}{5}$
c $\dfrac{5\sqrt{2}+\sqrt{6}}{4}$ **d** $\dfrac{2\sqrt{3}-3\sqrt{2}}{18}$
6 a $\dfrac{2\sqrt{7}+7\sqrt{2}}{14}$ **b** $\dfrac{\sqrt{10}+5\sqrt{3}}{5}$ **c** $\dfrac{\sqrt{3}-\sqrt{2}}{2}$

Power plus

1 a $x^3 + 15x^2 + 75x + 125$
b $y^3 - 6y^2 + 12y - 8$
c $a^3 + 3a^2b + 3ab^2 + b^3$
d $27d^3 + 270d^2 + 900d + 1000$
2 a 441 **b** 2025 **c** 841
d 3481 **e** 10 404 **f** 9604
3 899
4 a 399 **b** 2499 **c** 8099 **d** 6396
5 a Yes, because you are multiplying by 1
b $\dfrac{3-\sqrt{2}}{7}$, yes
6 $s=\dfrac{\sqrt{3}D}{3}$ **7** $\dfrac{\sqrt{2}}{2}$ cm
8 $(2+2\sqrt{3})$ mm **9** $\dfrac{4}{3}\sqrt{\dfrac{10\sqrt{3}}{3}}$ cm

TEST YOURSELF 4

1 a 1 **b** $\dfrac{1}{4k}$ **c** $\dfrac{125y^3}{8}$
2 a 100 000 **b** $\dfrac{25}{9}$ **c** $\dfrac{343}{64g^3}$ **d** $\dfrac{4d^2}{81}$
e $\dfrac{1}{16m^2}$ **f** $\dfrac{4}{m^2}$ **g** $625b^{24}y^{12}$ **h** $512t^{14}u^{16}$
3 a 20 **b** -243 **c** $\dfrac{1}{8}$ **d** 4
4 a $64a^6$ **b** $243m^{15}$ **c** $\dfrac{1}{2p^2}$ **d** $\dfrac{1}{25x^2y^4}$
5 a $4fg^2 - 30f^2g$ **b** $93 - 22n$
c $8x^3 + 7x^4$ **d** $10y^2 - 41y + 21$
6 a $15xy^2(1 - 2x^2y)$ **b** $6p(t^2 + 2pt - 8p^2)$
c $4r^2s^3(8s + 3r^2)$ **d** $25x^3y^3(2x - 3y)$
e $-8p^3q^3(1 - 6q^3)$ **f** $(n^2 + 6)(n - 1)$
7 a $b^2 + 13b + 30$ **b** $d^2 + d - 56$
c $15t - 54 - t^2$ **d** $20x^2 + 13x - 21$
e $49y^2 - 25$ **f** $21p^2 - 62p + 16$
8 a $n^2 - 81$ **b** $9y^2 + 12yd + 4d^2$
c $16n^2 - 121$
9 a $(t + u)(3p + 2q)$ **b** $(2a + 3c)(2b - 3d)$
c $(b + 10)(b - 10)$ **d** $(5 - 4y)(5 + 4y)$
e $5(2x + 5)(2x - 5)$ **f** $3r(r + 3)(r - 3)$
10 a $(y + 5)^2$ **b** $(x - 20)(x - 1)$
c $(n + 11)(n - 3)$ **d** $(a - 7)(a - 4)$
e $(m - 12)(m + 7)$ **f** $(p + 9)(p - 6)$
11 a $(3w + 2)(w + 1)$ **b** $(2y + 3)(y - 3)$
c $-5(b + 4)(b - 3)$ **d** $(3p - 2)(p + 4)$
e $2(3x - 1)(2x - 7)$ **f** $(3n - 2)(2n - 3)$
g $(8y - 3)(5y + 8)$ **h** $(4c - 7)(12c + 5)$
i $(5e - 1)(2e - 1)$
12 a $5(q - 3)(q + 3)$ **b** $4(5x - 3)(x - 2)$
c $(c - 1)^2(c + 1)$ **d** $-(12k - 1)(k + 4)$
e $(3m + 8)(2m - 5)$ **f** $a(a - 1)(a + 1)^2$
13 a I **b** R **c** R **d** I
e R **f** R **g** R **h** I
14 a $6\sqrt{2}$ **b** $7\sqrt{2}$ **c** $5\sqrt{11}$ **d** $8\sqrt{2}$
e $15\sqrt{6}$ **f** $14\sqrt{7}$ **g** $48\sqrt{2}$ **h** $15\sqrt{5}$
15 a $13\sqrt{2}$ **b** $5\sqrt{2}-7\sqrt{5}$ **c** $14\sqrt{2}+17\sqrt{3}$
d $32\sqrt{5}-9\sqrt{7}$ **e** $38\sqrt{2}-24\sqrt{3}$ **f** $8\sqrt{11}$
16 a $\sqrt{55}$ **b** $\sqrt{6}$ **c** $\sqrt{14}$
d $4\sqrt{6}$ **e** 1 **f** $\dfrac{5}{3}$
g $\dfrac{3}{\sqrt{2}}=\dfrac{3\sqrt{2}}{2}$ **h** $\dfrac{2}{3}$ **i** $\dfrac{7}{5}$
17 a $9\sqrt{2}-12$ **b** $\sqrt{10}-10\sqrt{5}$ **c** $7\sqrt{35}-27$
d $23-8\sqrt{7}$ **e** $77+10\sqrt{6}$ **f** 43
18 a $\dfrac{3\sqrt{2}}{2}$ **b** $\dfrac{\sqrt{3}}{4}$ **c** $\dfrac{5\sqrt{6}}{6}$ **d** $\dfrac{2\sqrt{2}+1}{3}$

CHAPTER 5

SkillCheck

1 **a i** 10 **ii** 16.5 **iii** 15 **iv** 15
  b i 13 **ii** 1.8 **iii** 2.5 **iv** 3
  c i 48 **ii** 34.3 **iii** 34.5 **iv** 24, 35
  d i 5 **ii** 2.2 **iii** 2 **iv** 2

2 **a i** 31 **ii** 33.3 **iii** 62
  b 78
  c i median = 30, mean = 28.3, range = 25
    ii The outlier has increased the median (by 1), the mean (by 5), and the range (by 37).

Exercise 5.01

1 **a** 5, 6.5, 8 **b** 18, 20, 26.5 **c** 32, 34.5, 38

2 **a** range = 7, IQR = 3
  b range = 22, IQR = 8.5
  c range = 16, IQR = 6

3 **a** 7.5 **b** 3

4 **a** 283 mm **b** 128 mm

5 **a** 3 **b** 2.5 **c** 17.5
  d 19 **e** 21.5 **f** 1.5

6 **a** 34 **b** 13
  c i 68, 72, 72, 75, 77, 78, 79, 80 **ii** 50%
  d 75%

7 **a i** 28 **ii** 9.5
  b The interquartile range, as it is not affected by the value of 35, which is an outlier.
  c 48, 48, 48, 49, 51, 53, 55; 54%

Exercise 5.02

1 **a** 1, 4.5, 6.5, 10, 18
  b
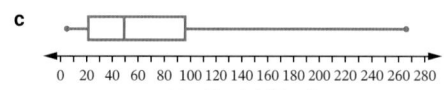
    Number of orders/h

2 **a** 26 **b** 1, 2, 5, 13, 50
  c
    Amount of snow (cm)

3 **a** 261 **b** 5, 21.5, 49.5, 96, 266
  c
    Monthly rainfall (mm)

4 **a** 27.5 h **b** 26 h **c** 30 h
  d 4 h **e** 50%

5 **a** 26 **b** 21 **c** 14
  d i 25% **ii** 75%

6 **a** 6, 10, 19, 23, 29 **b** 13
  c i 14 **ii** 7 **iii** 7 **iv** 21

7 **a** 20, 46, 51, 68, 88

b 30, 51, 65.5, 75, 95
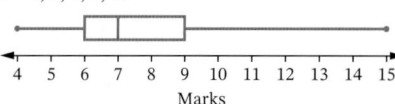

c 10, 13, 15, 16, 20

8 **a** 4, 6, 7, 9, 15
    Marks

  b Dot plot is positively skewed. The length of the boxplot from the median to the highest value is greater than the length from the median to the lowest value.

  c 15

  d 4, 6, 7, 9, 12
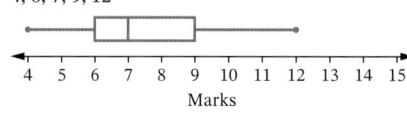
    Marks

  e i The box plots are the same up to Q_3.
    ii The whisker from Q_3 is reduced without the outlier.

Exercise 5.03

1 **a i** Year 10: 3.5; Year 8: 8
    ii Year 10: 7.5; Year 8: 8.5
    iii Year 10: 1; Year 8: 2
  b i 25% **ii** 75% **c i** 10 **ii** 0

2 **a i** 32 **ii** 34
  b Swifts: 59.5, Thunderbirds: 51.5
  c Swifts: 8, Thunderbirds: 11
  d The range for the Swifts is slightly smaller (32) and the IQR (8) for the Swifts is less than the IQR (11) for the Thunderbirds, indicating that the Swifts is more consistent in their performance.
  e The position of the Swifts boxplot shows that they scored more points in games, they have a higher median of 59.5 than the Thunderbirds who had a median of 51.5, so the Swifts performed better in the season.

3 **a** 10K: 9; 10N: 10 **b** 10K: 6.5; 10N: 5.5
  c 10K: 3; 10N: 4
  d 10K – lower range and IQR
  e 75%

4 C

5 **a** Brisbane: 26.9, 9.3, 4.7
    Sydney: 23.5, 8.5, 4.9
    Melbourne: 21.4, 13, 8.6
    Hobart: 18.6, 11.2, 7
  b Melbourne – it has the highest range and IQR.
  c Brisbane, more than half of the mean monthly temperatures are higher than most of the mean monthly temperatures of the other cities.

d Sydney's median temperature is significantly higher than Melbourne's, so Sydney is the warmer city.

e Sydney has the smaller range and IQR of mean monthly temperatures, so it has consistent temperatures.

6 a male: 0, 1, 2, 4, 7; female: 2, 4, 5, 7, 10

b

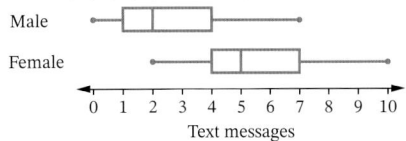

c male: 3; female: 3 **d** male: 7; female: 8

e Both are positively skewed, the interquartile range is the same, and the range of females is one more than that of the males. Females do receive more text messages, as the boxplot shows that 75% of females receive more messages than 75% of males.

7 a male: 145, 165, 167, 172.5, 189; female: 150, 162.5, 165.5, 173.5, 186

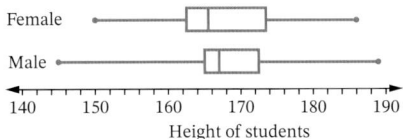

b male: range = 44   IQR = 7.5
female: range = 36   IQR = 11

c Male students have a greater range (44 compared to 36), but a smaller interquartile range (7.5 compared to 12).

8 a low: 64, 73.5, 80, 86, 92; high: 49, 58, 68, 75, 96

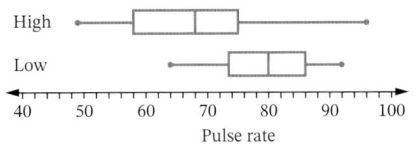

b i 28, 12.5   **ii** 47, 17

c The range and interquartile range of the High Frequency group are both greater than the Low Frequency group.

d the High Frequency group

9 a Hobart: 12.5, 14.4, 17.8, 20.85, 22.7; Darwin: 30.6, 31.45, 32.05, 32.7, 33.3

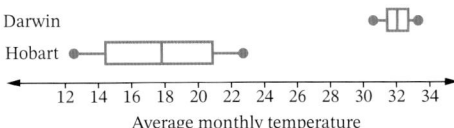

b Hobart: 10.2°, 6.45°   Darwin: 2.7°, 1.25°

c Darwin's average monthly temperatures were more consistent than Hobart's, since its range (2.7) was much smaller than Hobart's (10.2), whereas Hobart's IQR was much larger (6.5) than Darwin's (1.25).

10 a Simone   **b** Simone: 12; Amal: 10

c Amal, smaller range

d Simone: 10; Amal: 9

e Simone: 4; Amal: 5

f Not enough information given to make a valid decision. The interquartile range and range only differ by 1.

g 25%   **h** 25%

Exercise 5.04

1 a

Score	f	cf
2	2	2
3	1	3
4	3	6
5	4	10
6	5	15
7	8	23
8	2	25
9	2	27
10	1	28
	Σf =28	

median = 6

b

Age	f	cf
12	13	13
13	23	36
14	19	55
15	22	77
16	15	92
17	8	100
	Σf =100	

median = 14

c

Score	f	cf
93	15	15
94	32	47
95	28	75
96	20	95
97	18	113
98	10	123
99	2	125
	Σf =125	

median = 95

d

Siblings	f	cf
0	3	3
1	9	12
2	12	24
3	5	29
4	3	32
5	2	34
6	1	35
	$\Sigma f = 35$	

median = 2

e

Books	f	cf
19	20	20
20	18	38
21	34	72
22	24	96
23	25	121
24	18	139
25	12	151
26	9	160
	$\Sigma f = 160$	

median = 22

f

Pets	f	cf
0	13	13
1	32	45
2	8	53
3	2	55
4	1	56
	$\Sigma f = 56$	

median = 1

2 a 2, 5, 6, 7, 10   **b** 12, 13, 14, 15, 17
c 93, 94, 95, 96, 99   **d** 0, 1, 2, 3, 6
e 19, 21, 22, 23, 26   **f** 0, 1, 1, 1, 4

3 a 40   **b** 9   **c** 34
d

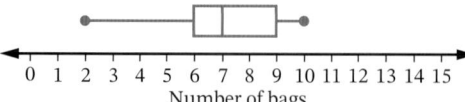

Number of bags

4 a 1594   **b** 1087   **c** 6
d

10 11 12 13 14 15 16 17 18 19 20 21 22 23 24 25 26 27 28 29 30
Time (minutes)

5 a 9   **b** 15.5   **c** 57.5   **d** 29.5
6 a, b

Class Interval	Class Centre	f	cf
30–39	34.5	1	1
40–49	44.5	4	5
50–59	54.5	5	10
60–69	64.5	8	18
70–79	74.5	9	27
80–89	84.5	2	29
90–99	94.5	1	30

c 62   **d** 60–69

7 a

Class Interval	Class Centre	Frequency	Cumulative frequency
131–140	135.5	2	2
141–150	145.5	7	9
151–160	155.5	10	19
161–170	165.5	17	36
171–180	175.5	11	47
181–190	185.5	3	50

b modal class: 161–170, median class: 161–170

8 a

Class Interval	Class Centre	f	cf
22.0–22.4	22.2	1	1
22.5–22.9	22.7	2	3
23.0–23.4	23.2	2	5
23.5–23.9	23.7	5	10
24.0–24.4	24.2	2	12
24.5–24.9	24.7	7	19
25.0–25.4	25.2	4	23
25.5–25.9	25.7	4	27
26.0–26.4	26.2	3	30
		$\Sigma f = 30$	

b modal class 24.5 – 24.9

9

Time (hours)	f	cf
3	2	2
4	8	10
5	9	19
6	11	30
7	4	34
8	3	37

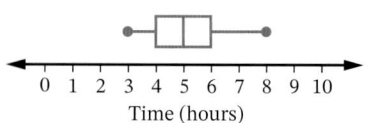

Time (hours)

Exercise 5.05

1 a

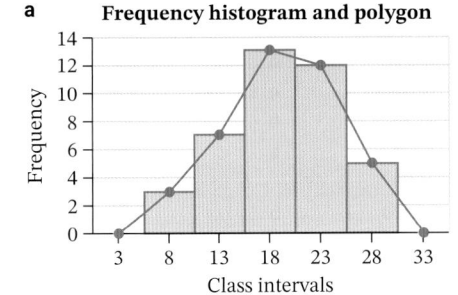

Frequency histogram and polygon

b

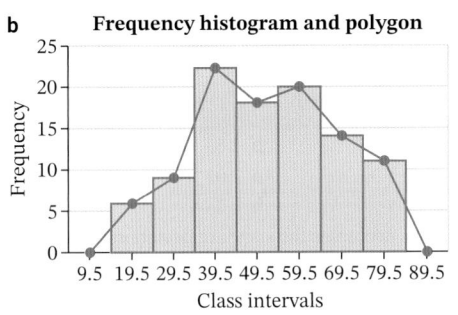

Frequency histogram and polygon

c

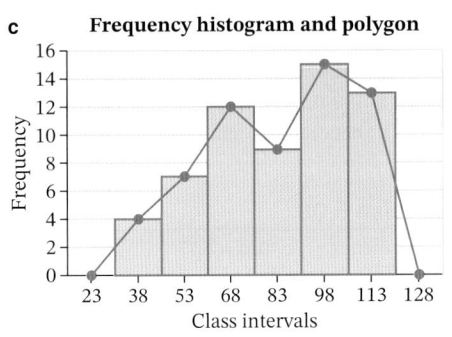

Frequency histogram and polygon

d

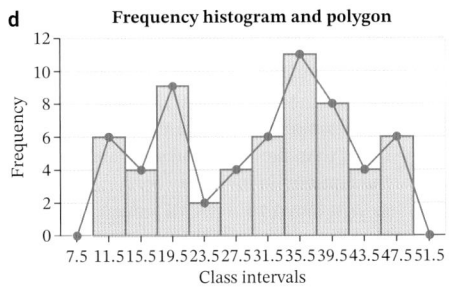

Frequency histogram and polygon

2 a

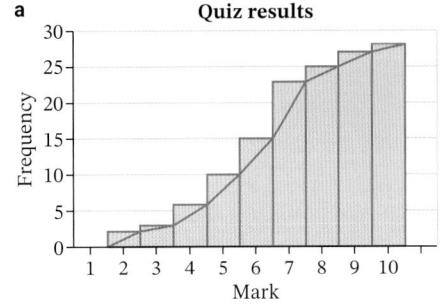

Quiz results

b

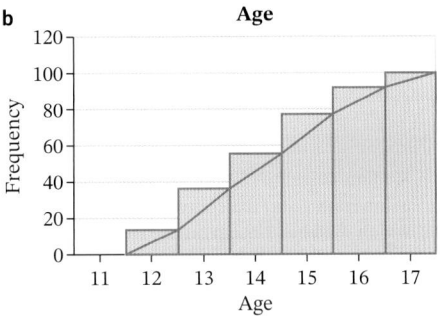

Age

c

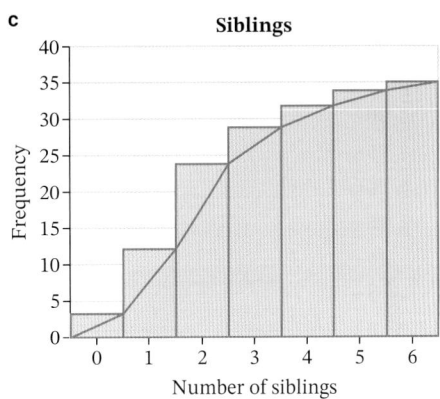

Siblings

d

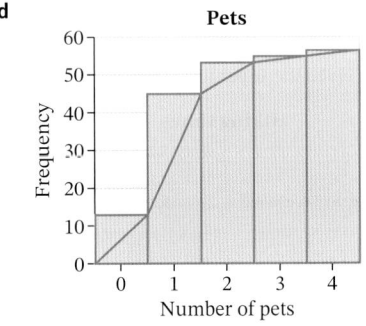

Pets

3

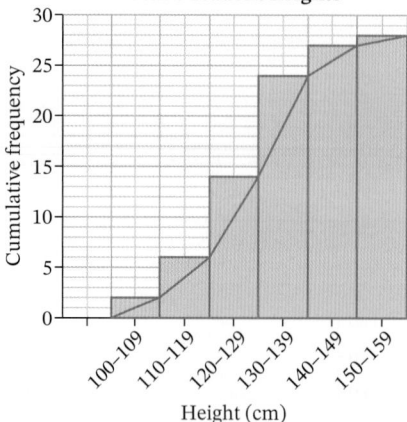

Year 3 student heights

Median height ≈ 129 cm. With 28 students, draw a line from 14 on the cumulative frequency axis, which matches 129 cm on the Height axis.

4

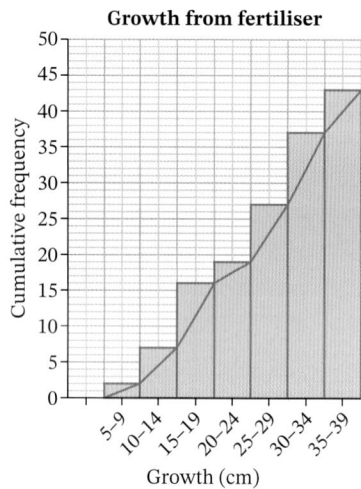

Growth from fertiliser

The super formula is effective as 36 out of 43 plants (about 84%) grew more than 14 cm after being given the super formula.

5

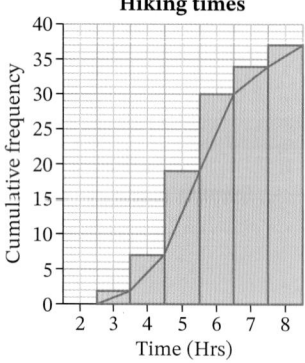

Hiking times

b interquartile range = 6 – 5 = 1

Exercise 5.06

1 a i 60   **ii** 15   **b i** 16   **ii** 3
   c i 10   **ii** 3   **d i** 24   **ii** 11

2 a 240   **b** day 6   **c** day 8
   d day 5   **e** 25th percentile, day 5

3 a 16   **b** 6   **c** 2.5
   d 29   **e** 27   **f** 43.75%

4 a 80   **b** 69 g   **c** 65 g   **d** 5 g   **e** 68 g

5 a 120   **b** 54 kg   **c** 68 kg
   d under: 25%, over: 10%

6 a 28   **b** 45   **c** 33%
   d 11%   **e** 32   **f** 81

7 a 162 cm   **b** 161 cm   **c** 159 cm
   d 167 cm   **e** 157.5 cm

Exercise 5.07

1 a 2.66   **b** 2.63   **c** 1.19
   d 1.33   **e** 2.01

2 a 7   **b i** 2.64   **ii** 2.28
   c decreases the standard deviation

3 a C   **b** A   **4**   **a** 1.99   **b** 13.43

5 a $\bar{x} = 165.89, \sigma = 8.37$
   b i less than 157 or greater than 175
     ii between 157 and 174

6 a $\bar{x} = 11.37, \sigma = 0.43$
   b i less than 10.9, greater than 11.8
     ii between 10.9 and 11.8

7 C

Exercise 5.08

1 a men: $\bar{x} = 71.40, \sigma = 6.77$
    women: $\bar{x} = 77.53, \sigma = 6.96$
   b Yes, the mean of women's pulse rates is much higher. The standard deviation for women is slightly higher.

2 a dominant hand: $\bar{x} = 0.40, \sigma = 0.11$; non-dominant hand: $\bar{x} = 0.52, \sigma = 0.51$
   b Yes, the mean reaction time and standard deviation of the dominant hand are much lower than the mean and standard deviation of the non-dominant hand.
   c i 0.61 and 0.75   **ii** $\bar{x} = 0.37, \sigma = 0.05$
     iii Removing the outliers has reduced the mean from 0.40 to 0.37 and more than halved the standard deviation.
   d $\bar{x} = 0.40, \sigma = 0.06$
   e The removal of the outlier from the non-dominant hand had the greater effect on the mean and standard deviation as the outlier of 2.60 was a more extreme value than the outliers for the dominant hand.

3 a Western Tigers: $\bar{x} = 122.92, \sigma = 26.98$; Barrington City: $\bar{x} = 120.92, \sigma = 23.62$
   b The Barrington City team is slightly more consistent as the standard deviation is 23.62 compared with 26.98 for the Western Tigers.

4 a Vatha: $\bar{x} = 13.76$, $\sigma = 0.55$; Ana: $\bar{x} = 14.14$, $\sigma = 0.66$

b Vatha is more consistent as the standard deviation for her times is significantly lower than the standard deviation for Ana's times.

5 B

6 a Maths: **i** range = 47   **ii** IQR = 14
                  iii $\sigma = 10.97$
    Science: **i** range = 45   **ii** IQR = 19
                  iii $\sigma = 13.16$

b Maths: $\bar{x} = 67.82$; Science: $\bar{x} = 61.25$

c The students performed better in Maths as the mean was 67.82 compared to 61.25 for Science. The marks for Maths were also more consistent as the IQR and standard deviation were both lower than those of Science.

7 a Roosters: **i** range = 48   **ii** IQR = 20
                     iii $\bar{x} = 26.67$ **iv** $\sigma = 12.55$
    Dragons: **i** range = 32   **ii** IQR = 8
                     iii $\bar{x} = 15.88$ **iv** $\sigma = 7.36$

b The range, IQR and the standard deviation for the Dragons are significantly lower than those of the Roosters, which show that the Dragons are more consistent in the number of points they scored per match.

However, the mean of the Roosters is significantly greater than the mean of the Dragons, which would indicate they are a better team as they were able to score many more points per match.

Exercise 5.09

1 a boys: $34.58, girls: $31.78

b boys: $33.50, girls: $28

c boys: range = 72, IQR = 25
    girls: range = 69, IQR = 30.5

d **i** Boys are approximately symmetric, girls are positively skewed.
   ii There are no outliers, clustering occurs for the boys in the 20–30s and for the girls in the 10–20s.

e Boys generally carry more cash – they have a higher mean than the girls and the shape of the data for girls is positively skewed.

2 a 21 games   **b i** 34   **ii** 51

c Scorpions: $\bar{x} = 1.6$ goals; Vale United: $\bar{x} = 2.4$

d Scorpions 5, Vale United 6

e Both teams' results are positively skewed. Clustering for Scorpions occurs at 1 and 2 and for Vale United it occurs at 2.

f Vale United performed better as its mean was 2.4 goals/game compared to Scorpions 1.6 goals/game.

3 a Sydney: $\bar{x} = 26.2$, median = 26.5, mode = 28
    Perth: $\bar{x} = 34.3$, median = 35, mode = 38

b Sydney: range = 9°, IQR = 3
    Perth: range = 16°, IQR = 8

c The temperatures for Sydney and Perth are both negatively skewed, there are no outliers. Sydney's temperatures are clustered from 26 to 28, while Perth's have no distinct cluster.

d Sydney's temperatures are lower than Perth's, as evidenced by the significantly lower mean, median and mode. The range and interquartile range for Perth are greater than the range and interquartile range for Sydney, indicating greater spread.

4 a 30

b Quiz 1: $\bar{x} = 5.6$, mode = 6; Quiz 2: $\bar{x} = 6.3$, mode = 7

c Quiz 1: 6; Quiz 2: 7

d Quiz 1:   **i** range = 7   **ii** IQR = 2
    Quiz 2:   **i** range = 8   **ii** IQR = 2

e Quiz 1: Results are symmetrical with clustering at 5–6, no outliers.
    Quiz 2: Results are bimodal with clustering at 5 and 7–8, no outliers.

f Scores for Quiz 2 are better than Quiz 1, as the mean of Quiz 2 is higher than the mean of Quiz 1. The spread for both quizzes are similar as there is only a difference of 1 between the ranges and the IQRs are equal.

5 a 39

b **i** mode = 2   **ii** median = 2
   iii range = 6   **iv** IQR = 1.5

c positively skewed, no outliers

d 50%

e **i** by the highest columns
   ii by the short length of the box when compared to the whole length of the boxplot

f **i** The shape of the distribution, the frequency for each household size and the mode. The mean can also be calculated from the histogram.
   ii The shape of the distribution, the median and the quartiles Q_1 and Q_2.

6 a **i** 5   **ii** 16

b **i** mode = 22   **ii** range = 18
   iii IQR = 24 − 16 = 8

c negatively skewed
   i The tail of the dot plot goes to the left.
   ii The length of the boxplot from the lowest value to the median is longer than from the median to the highest value.

d **i** dot plot   **ii** boxplot
   iii dot plot   **iv** boxplot

7 a Sunbeam Valley: range = 24, median = 71, IQR = 8
    Bentley's Beach: range = 30, median = 73, IQR = 15

b Sunbeam Valley: negatively skewed (slight)
    Bentley's Beach: positively skewed

c Sunbeam Valley's speeds are clustered in the 70s. There are no outliers in both.

d 25%

e Bentley's Beach – higher median. 25% of drivers drive faster than all drivers in Sunbeam Valley. This may be due to more main roads with higher speed limits.

8 a 36

b Lamissa: mode = 7, median = 7
Anneka: mode = 7, median = 6

c Lamissa: range = 8, IQR = 8 – 6 = 2
Anneka: range = 9, IQR = 7 – 4 = 3

d Lamissa's distribution of values is negatively skewed with clustering at 7. Anneke's distribution is negatively skewed with clustering at 6 and 7.

e i 25%   **ii** 50%

f Lamissa is the better archer. Her median score is higher than Anneke's. According to the boxplot, roughly 25% of Lamissa's scores are less than 6 compared to Anneke's 50%, and 50% of Lamissa's scores are equal to or better than 75% of Anneke's. Lamissa's range and IQR are also slightly smaller than Anneke's, which suggests she is the more consistent archer.

9 a The range (47) is too large.

b women: 31   men: 37

c women: range = 38, IQR = 40 – 24 = 16
men: range = 47, IQR = 46 – 25 = 21

d Distribution for women is positively skewed. Distribution for men is symmetrical.

e Men have the greater spread in the number of sit-ups completed, as the range and IQR are both greater than those for women.

Mental skills 5

2 a 176   **b** 363   **c** 261   **d** 405
e 682   **f** 707   **g** 1818   **h** 3564
i 152   **j** 540   **k** 2142   **l** 588
m 288   **n** 693   **o** 3939   **p** 852

Exercise 5.10

1 a Just surveying 300 people between 9 am and 11 am in shopping centres only targets a narrow group of people in certain areas.

b The sample needs to be more random and over a large area, not just in shopping centres. A telephone survey should produce more accurate feedback.

2 The report does not say what conditions are needed for the hot water system to work effectively. The temperature in Queensland is much warmer than in NSW and Victoria. Consequently, with the cooler climate in NSW and Victoria, especially in winter, the heat pump system may not provide the savings that people in Queensland obtain.

3 a i The price of petrol has shown little increase from December to February.

ii The price of petrol has shown marked rises and falls over the period from December to February.

b Both graphs could be improved by starting the vertical scale at 0 cents/litre and/or putting a slash at the bottom.

4 a That there is a marked difference between the fuel consumption of the different cars.

b i 0.2 L/100 km

ii 1 L/100 km

iii 0.2 L/100 km

c Begin the scale on the vertical axis with 0 and use a scale of 1 cm = 0.5 L/100 km instead of 1 cm = 0.2 L/100 km.

5 Yes, as there is no option for a customer to rate the app as unsatisfactory or poor.

6 a An example of a biased question could be: Which of these colours do you prefer – red, black, silver, blue?

b Apart from surveying people, they need to look at the sales figures of all cars. This will give information about the most popular car colour.

7, 8 Teacher to check

Exercise 5.11

1 a approx. 180   **b** approx. 220%

2 Teacher to check

3 a 67%, decreased by 10%   **b** 5%
c–e Teacher to check

4 a Tasmania   **b** 30%

c highest: Darwin – long distance to travel to, business travellers typically need to stay overnight
lowest: Hobart – more focused on local activities, tourism and agriculture

d Business activity is predominantly held in larger cities of Sydney and Melbourne, which are closer, whereas it is much further (in distance and time) to travel to Perth and Hobart.
ACT: travellers for business and government (work-related)

e Adelaide: compared to other capital cities not a major tourist destination, also less accessible

5, 6, 7, 8 Teacher to check

Exercise 5.12

1 a

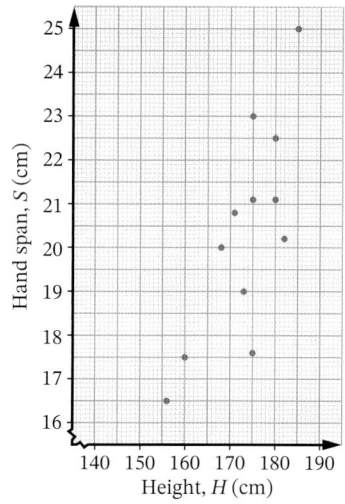

b linear

c As the heights of students increase, their hand spans tend to increase.

2 a weak negative relationship

b no relationship

c strong positive relationship

3 weak positive

4 a Stride length depends on a person's height; the taller the person is, the longer their legs are.

b

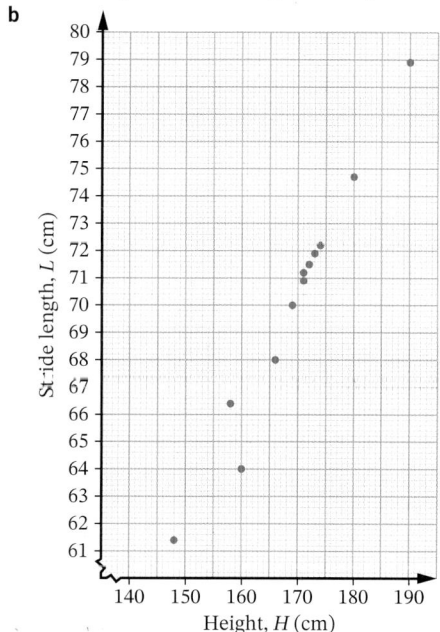

c linear

d Students' stride length tend to increase with height.

e strong positive relationship

f about 72.5–73 cm

5 a

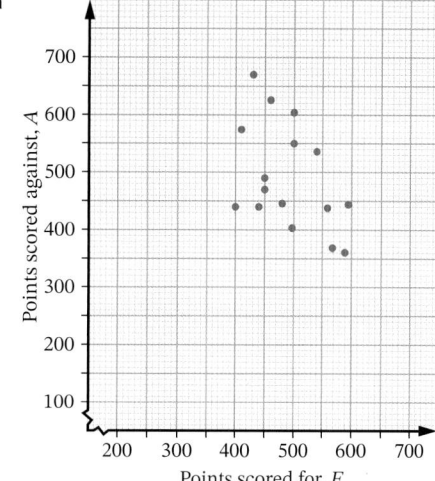

b yes   **c** weak negative relationship

6 a

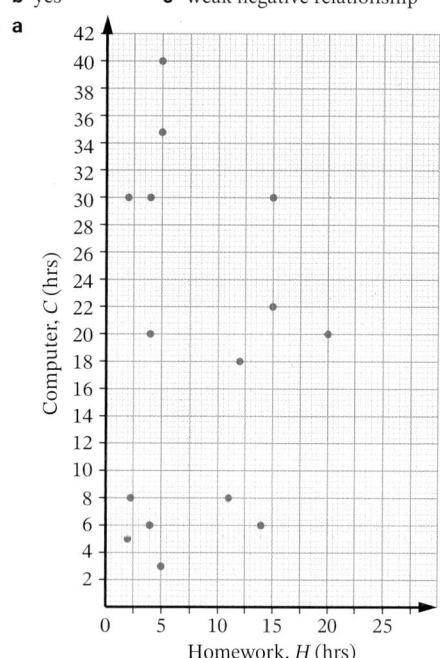

b no relationship

7 a

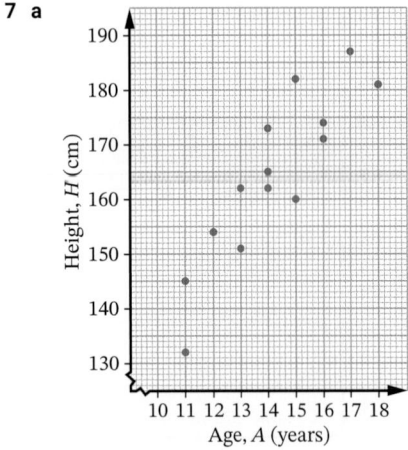

Age, A (years)

b Height, because its value depends on age (not the other way around).

c weak positive relationship

Exercise 5.13

Answers will vary as equations of lines will vary.

1 a

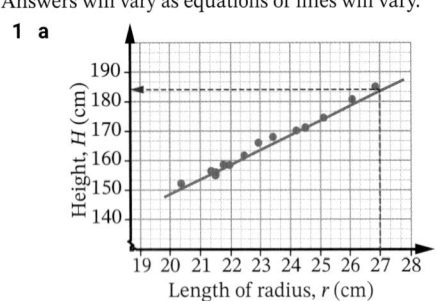

Length of radius, r (cm)

b $H = 5r + 48.5$ **c** 173.5 cm   **d** 184 cm

2 a

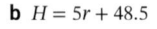
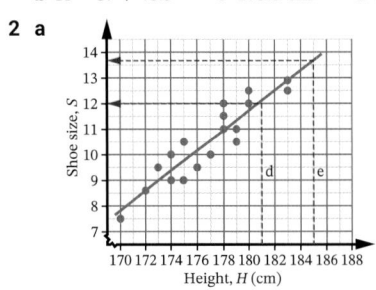

Height, H (cm)

b $S = 0.39H - 59$ **c** 8

d 12   **e** 13.5

3 a

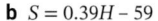
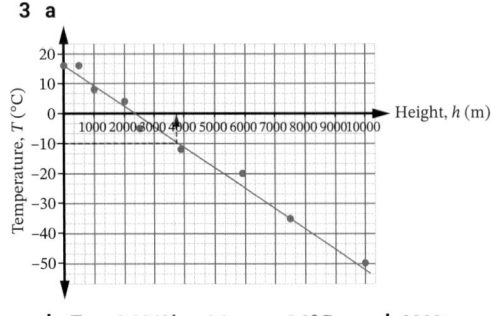

b $T = -0.0068h + 16$ **c** 5.8°C   **d** 3800 m

4 a

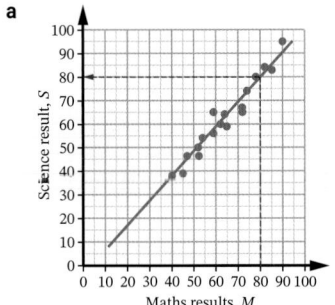

Maths results, M

b 80   **c** 95

5 a

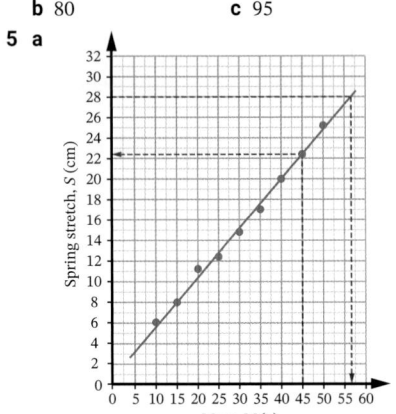

Mass, M (g)

b 22.4 cm   **c** 56 g

d Yes, because a spring has an elastic limit, which is the point at which a spring will not return to its original length as a result of the mass attached to the spring being too heavy.

6 a

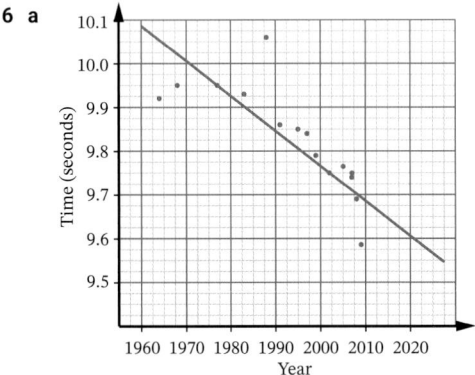

Year

b 9.53 s

c There is a limit to how fast a person can run.

Exercise 5.14

1 a

	High school	Primary school	Total
Walk	78	24	102
Not walk	18	80	98
Total	96	104	200

b 0.51   **c** 0.81   **d** 0.49   **e** 0.77

f If you are in high school you are more likely to walk (relative frequency = 0.81) and if you are in primary school you are more likely to travel by other means (relative frequency = 0.77). This suggests that there is an association between the method of travelling to school and the category of school attended.

2 a

	Boys	Girls	Total
Bowling	45	25	70
Ice-skating	15	65	80
Total	60	90	150

b 0.47   **c** 0.28

d 0.53   **e** 0.25

f Girls are less likely to select a ten-pin bowling party and boys are less likely to select an ice-skating party. Hence, this suggests that there is an association between gender and type of birthday party.

3 Relative frequency (RF) of swimming = 0.53; RF of swimming given senior student = 0.38. Senior students are less likely to be able to swim. Hence, this suggests that there is an association between being a senior student and being able to swim.

4 RF of pass = 0.71; RF of pass given study = 0.80. Students are more likely to pass if they study for the quiz. Hence, this suggests that there is an association between studying and passing the quiz.

5 RF of liking sprinkles = 0.51; RF of sprinkles given adult = 0.29; RF of sprinkles given child = 0.76. Children are more likely to like sprinkles. Hence, this suggests that there is an association between age and liking sprinkles on ice cream.

6 RF of diabetic = 0.6; RF of overweight = 0.6; RF of diabetic given overweight = 0.6. There is no association as all relative frequencies are the same.

7 RF of eating healthy = 0.71; RF of eating healthy given exercise − 0.85. People are more likely to eat healthy when they exercise. Hence, this suggests that there is an association between eating healthy and exercise.

8 RF of late flight = 0.20; RF of late given international flight = 0.20. No association as the relative frequency is the same.

9 RF of lung disease = 0.60; RF of lung disease given smoker = 0.70. People are more likely to have lung disease if they are a smoker. Hence, this suggests that there is an association.

10 RF of indigestion = 0.46; RF of indigestion given drug taken = 0.53. Association exists and relative frequency of indigestion after taking the drug is slightly higher. The company should conduct some more trials before releasing the drug.

Power plus

1 a −1 and 1

b There is no relationship between the variables.

c i 1   **ii** −0.4   **iii** −0.8

Other answers are possible, teacher to check.

---

2 b, d, f

3 a $\bar{x}$ = 13.35, median = 14, mode = 14

b range = 10, IQR = 15 − 12.5 = 2.5

c The mean, median, and mode will increase by 4, the range and the interquartile range remain unchanged.

TEST YOURSELF 5

1 a 6.5   **b** 6   **c** 2.5   **d** 12.5

2

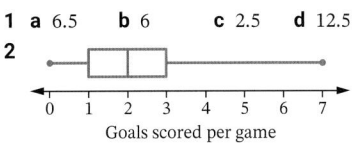

Goals scored per game

3 a Before: 50, 64, 69, 76, 80; After: 82, 89, 95.5, 126, 146

b

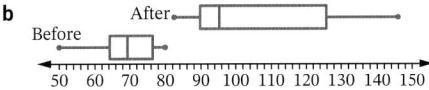

c i range = 30, IQR = 12

    ii range = 64, IQR = 37

d The pulse rates for after exercise are significantly higher. In fact, all the rates for after exercise are above all the rates for before exercise. The median pulse for after exercise is 95.5 compared to the median pulse of 69 for before exercise. The range and interquartile range are also greater for the after exercise pulse rate.

4 12, 14, 16, 17, 18

5 a

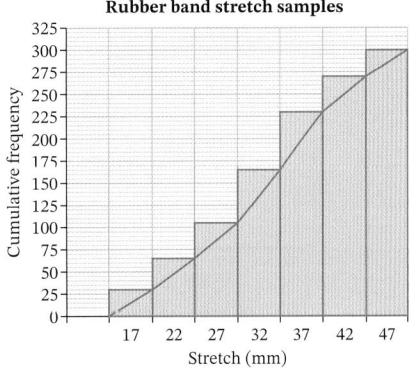

b approximately 33 mm

6 a 300   **b** 51–60   **c** 46   **d** 80   **e** 34

7 a $\bar{x}$ = 0.40, σ = 0.08

b range = 0.33, IQR = 0.08

c The interquartile range is the better measure as the standard deviation is affected by the outlier 0.62.

8 a Girls: $\bar{x}$ = 67.73, σ = 16.08

    Boys: x = 61.67, σ = 12.35

b The girls performed better than the boys as their mean mark was about 6 more than the mean mark of the boys. However, the boys' marks had less spread than the girls'.

9 a i both   **ii** stem-and-leaf plot

b The range (126 – 70 = 56) is too large.

c i median = 92

   ii IQR = 99.5 – 84 = 15.5

d 50%

10 a The product is healthy.

b There is no data given on the actual fat content in the product. This should also be stated in terms of a percentage of daily requirement of fat or mg of fat.

11 a Weeks in storage: this determines how many oranges stay good.

b

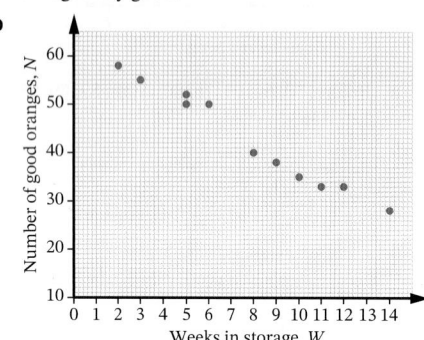

c linear

d The longer the oranges remain in storage, the fewer good oranges are in the box.

e strong negative correlation

12 a

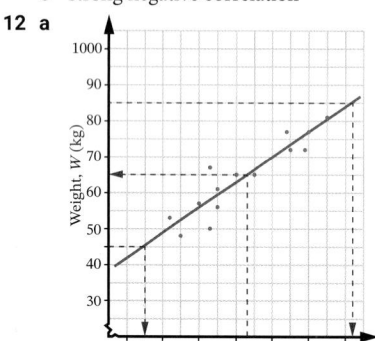

b $W = 0.7H - 49$ **c** 70 kg   **d** 65 kg

e i 192 cm   **ii** 135 cm

13 Relative frequency of doing chores = 0.61; Relative frequency of doing chores given pocket money = 0.76. Teenagers are slightly more likely to complete chores around the house if they receive pocket money. Hence this suggests there is an association between a teenager completing household jobs and receiving pocket money.

CHAPTER 6

SkillCheck

1 a $\frac{19a}{20}$ **b** $\frac{p}{6}$ **c** 5h   **d** 2k

2 a $(k + 4)(k + 1)$ **b** $(y - 8)(y - 2)$

   c $(m - 8)(m + 7)$ **d** $(u + 13)(u - 5)$

   e $(w - 7)(w - 3)$ **f** $(x - 6)(x + 4)$

Exercise 6.01

1 a $k = 60$ **b** $w = -9$ **c** $y = 2$

   d $a = 5$ **e** $x = 8$ **f** $a = 1$

   g $r = -6$ **h** $w = 6$ **i** $y = -2$

   j $a = 3\frac{1}{2}$ **k** $u = 5\frac{1}{3}$ **l** $a = -1\frac{3}{4}$

2 B   **3** D

4 a $y = 10$ **b** $a = -2\frac{1}{2}$ **c** $y = 5$

   d $a = -3$ **e** $y = 8$ **f** $x = 1$

   g $y = -1$ **h** $x = -10$ **i** $m = 1\frac{1}{2}$

   j $y = 12$ **k** $a = -1$ **l** $x = -4$

5 C

6 a $x = 16$ **b** $m = 6$ **c** $y = 4$

   d $y = 8$ **e** $y = -7$ **f** $x = 11$

   g $m = -8$ **h** $a = -1$ **i** $y = -5$

7 C

8 a $d = \frac{2}{7}$ **b** $y = -\frac{7}{8}$ **c** $k = \frac{8}{9}$

   d $g = 3\frac{2}{7}$ **e** $h = \frac{6}{17}$ **f** $p = -1\frac{4}{5}$

Exercise 6.02

1 a $\frac{5n}{14}$ **b** $\frac{17c}{10}$ **c** $\frac{43r}{14}$ **d** $\frac{-19y}{24}$

   e $\frac{13t}{9}$ **f** $\frac{-y}{16}$ **g** $\frac{13t}{36}$ **h** $\frac{17a}{30}$

   i $\frac{3a+4}{k}$ **j** $\frac{5d}{3y}$ **k** $\frac{1}{x}$ **l** $\frac{7p}{6}$

   m $\frac{5r+3q}{qr}$ **n** $\frac{7}{4h}$ **o** $\frac{29}{12b}$ **p** $\frac{27p-8n}{6np}$

2 a $\frac{4w+7n}{28}$ **b** $\frac{21x+40u}{56}$ **c** $\frac{4a-9h}{30}$ **d** $\frac{3d-2r}{48}$

   e $\frac{36k-5q}{45}$ **f** $\frac{25m+24r}{60}$ **g** $\frac{15h+8}{10}$ **h** $\frac{35u-12a}{28}$

   i $\frac{9a+5c}{45}$ **j** $\frac{15q-22w}{36}$ **k** $\frac{55k+24}{88}$ **l** $\frac{23n}{18}$

3 C   **4** B   **5** A

6 a $\frac{9m+2}{20}$ **b** $\frac{14p+10}{15}$ **c** $\frac{11y+5}{12}$ **d** $\frac{10x-17}{21}$

   e $\frac{41h+50}{18}$ **f** $\frac{-13k+51}{70}$ **g** $\frac{a-3}{6}$ **h** $\frac{32d-69}{42}$

   i $\frac{14y+49}{36}$ **j** $\frac{27-37w}{70}$ **k** $\frac{33-7e}{6}$ **l** $\frac{-23-34x}{44}$

Exercise 6.03

1 a $y = 15$ **b** $a = 9$ **c** $m = 2$

   d $k = 65$ **e** $n = -35$ **f** $y = -7$

   g $x = 31$ **h** $y = 46$ **i** $m = 18$

   j $x = -29$ **k** $x = 24$ **l** $m = 10$

   m $n = -\frac{1}{4}$ **n** $n = -\frac{3}{5}$ **o** $d = 3\frac{3}{4}$

2 **a** $k=1\frac{7}{8}$ **b** $w=1\frac{1}{3}$ **c** $x=-1\frac{1}{3}$

   d $x=3$ **e** $y=3$ **f** $a=-8\frac{3}{5}$

   g $p=9\frac{2}{3}$ **h** $y=3$ **i** $y=-\frac{5}{6}$

   j $w=10$ **k** $w=50$ **l** $w=9\frac{3}{5}$

   m $a=\frac{6}{11}$ **n** $y=60$ **o** $a=1\frac{11}{13}$

   p $m=3\frac{1}{3}$ **q** $h=1\frac{22}{23}$ **r** $y=-6\frac{5}{6}$

3 **a** C   **b** A

4 **a** $x=\frac{7}{15}$ **b** $p=15\frac{4}{7}$ **c** $x=19$

   d $x=10\frac{6}{7}$ **e** $x=10\frac{2}{9}$ **f** $y=10\frac{3}{5}$

   g $a=-41$ **h** $a=7\frac{9}{14}$ **i** $a=5\frac{5}{14}$

Exercise 6.04

1 **a** $m=\pm12$ **b** $x=\pm20$
   c $y=\pm\sqrt{35}$ **d** $k=\pm13$
   e $y=\pm1$ **f** $w=\pm\sqrt{24}$ $\left(\text{or } \pm2\sqrt{6}\right)$
   g $x=\pm2$ **h** $t=\pm4$
   i $a=\pm4$ **j** $k=\pm\sqrt{45}$ $\left(\text{or } \pm3\sqrt{5}\right)$
   k $w=\pm10$ **l** $d=\pm12$
   m $k=\pm\sqrt{14}$ **n** $w=\pm5$
   o $x=\pm\frac{1}{2}$ **p** $m=\pm\sqrt{40}$ $\left(\text{or } \pm2\sqrt{10}\right)$
   q $y=\pm1$ **r** $p=\pm3$
   s $k=\pm\sqrt{8}$ $\left(\text{or } \pm2\sqrt{2}\right)$ **t** $y=\pm10$

2 **a** $m=\pm2$ **b** $a=\pm9$ **c** $m\approx\pm5.3$
   d $m\approx\pm1.9$ **e** $k\approx\pm0.6$ **f** $x\approx\pm7.6$
   g $k\approx\pm9.8$ **h** $k\approx\pm9.5$ **i** $y\approx\pm0.3$
   j $a\approx\pm9.2$ **k** $y\approx\pm6.2$ **l** $w\approx\pm7.1$

3 **a** B   **b** B

4 **a** $x=-2,-1$ **b** $y=-4,-1$ **c** $y=-4,-12$
   d $x=-4,3$ **e** $x=-3,1$ **f** $x=-8,5$

5 **a** $x=6,-5$ **b** $x=4$ **c** $x=11,-6$
   d $d=0,2$ **e** $x=5,-2$ **f** $n=0,-4$
   g $k=0,7$ **h** $y=0,5$ **i** $v=0,12$

6 You cannot take the square root of a negative number.

7 **a, c, f:** cannot find the square root of a negative number.

8 **a** A   **b** C

Exercise 6.05

1 **a** $x=1$ **b** $m=5$ **c** $a=11$
   d $u=-2$ **e** $y=-9$ **f** $n=\sqrt[3]{20}$
   g $h=\sqrt[3]{11}$ **h** $k=\sqrt[3]{-48}$ **i** $m=\sqrt[3]{-15}$
   j $m=4$ **k** $x=\sqrt[3]{\frac{-81}{4}}$ **l** $x=\sqrt[3]{-40}$

2 **a** $w=2.5$ **b** $m=2.5$ **c** $m=6$
   d $t=3.2$ **e** $x=3$ **f** $x=-5.5$
   g $x=-2.4$ **h** $x=0.8$ **i** $a=5.5$
   j $a=0.4$ **k** $x=-2.3$ **l** $t=-4.4$

3 **a** yes   **b** when c is positive
   c when c is negative   **d** no

Exercise 6.06

1 18 mm, 36 mm, 36 mm   **2** Child: $21, adult: $48
3 57 mm, 19 mm
4 13 cm, 29 cm   **5** 61, 62, 63
6 Vimal is 27, Virendra is 3.   **7** 26   **8** 4
9 Vatha is 22, Chris is 14.
10 213, 214, 215, 216   **11** 94, 96, 98
12 117   **13** 6
14 Scott is 11, Kait is 34.   **15** 25°, 50°, 105°
16 72 L when full   **17** 8 teachers, 120 students

Mental skills 6

2 **a** 160   **b** 70   **c** 240   **d** 900
   e 2600   **f** 900   **g** 140   **h** 300
   i 180   **j** 770   **k** 18   **l** 34
   m 46   **n** 26   **o** 18   **p** 12
   q 40   **r** 8   **s** 14   **t** 24

Exercise 6.07

1 **a** 52 cm   **b** 17 m
2 **a** 36 km/h   **b** 86.4 km/h   **c** 180 km/h
3 30.5 km/h
4 **a** 27°C   **b** 0°C   **c** 100°C   **d** 39°C
5 43
6 **a** 11.2   **b** 9   **c** 17.3
7 **a** 15.1 m   **b** 31.8 cm
8 **a** 21.0   **b** 105.8 kg
9 **a** 137.3 cm³   **b** 4.9 m
10 **a** 93 km/h   **b** 436 km   **c** 7 h
11 **a** $950   **b** 24 km
12 **a** 73.9 m²   **b** $h=13.2$ cm

Exercise 6.08

1 **a** $y=\frac{5-x}{2}$ **b** $y=\frac{k-m}{p}$

   c $y=\frac{P-8}{k}$ **d** $y=\frac{5m}{3}$

   e $y=\frac{K-D}{M}$ **f** $y=\frac{4d-5}{8}$

   g $y=\frac{2c+k}{a}$ **h** $y=\frac{20m}{3}-3$ or $y=\frac{20m-9}{3}$

   i $y=\pm\sqrt{\frac{w-5}{x}}$ **j** $y=kx^2$

   k $y=\frac{5n-d}{n}$ or $y=5-\frac{d}{n}$

   l $y=cT^2-k$

2 **a** $b=\pm\sqrt{c^2-a^2}$ **b** $a=\frac{2(s-ut)}{t^2}$

   c $a=\frac{v-u}{t}$ **d** $r=\sqrt[3]{\frac{3V}{4\pi}}$

   e $R=\pm\sqrt{\frac{A+\pi r^2}{\pi}}$ **f** $l=\frac{A-\pi r^2}{\pi r}$

   g $n=\frac{S+360}{180}$ or $\frac{S}{180}+2$ **h** $r=\frac{sx}{x-s}$

   i $b=\pm\sqrt{x^2+4ac}$ **j** $x=\frac{5-y}{4}$

k $A = \dfrac{mn}{5-2m}$ 　　l $p = \dfrac{a}{a-S}$

m $a = \dfrac{b(X+Y)}{Y-X}$ 　　n $x = \dfrac{5-2a}{5}$ or $1-\dfrac{2a}{5}$

o $b = \dfrac{u(y-1)}{x-ay}$

Exercise 6.09

1 a

b

c

d

e

f

g

h

2 a $x<4$　b $x\ge2$　c $x>-6$　d $x\le1$

3 B

4 a $x\ge1$ 　　b $x<4$ 　　c $x>6$

d $x\le2$ 　　e $x>-6$ 　　f $x\le-1$

g $x\ge-4$ 　　h $x\ge25$ 　　i $x<0$

Exercise 6.10

1 a $x>7$

b $y\ge4$

c $m\le-2$

d $x\ge-100$

e $x<5$

f $y>-4$

g $a\ge\dfrac{1}{2}$

h $w\le-10$

i $a\ge5$

j $a\le3$

k $a\ge-1$

l $w<-3$

m $a\le-6$

n $y\le3$

o $a<2\dfrac{1}{2}$

2 a $x\ge1$ 　　b $m\le6$ 　　c $y\le-8$

d $w>0$ 　　e $w\le0$ 　　f $m\ge3\dfrac{1}{2}$

g $m\ge-2$ 　　h $x\le5$ 　　i $w>-3$

j $a<4$ 　　k $a\ge6$ 　　l $m\le3\dfrac{1}{2}$

m $m>3\dfrac{2}{5}$ 　　n $m\ge-2\dfrac{1}{2}$ 　　o $x<35$

3 a $x\ge3$

b $y>-8$

c $k>-11$

d $m\le0$

e $p<-6$

f $t\le-4$

4 a $x>-3$ 　　b $k\le-12$ 　　c $t<-2\dfrac{2}{5}$

d $x\ge12$ 　　e $w<-1$ 　　f $y\ge-2$

g $x\le4$ 　　h $a>1$ 　　i $d<-5\dfrac{1}{2}$

j $w<-11$ 　　k $x\le-8$ 　　l $p<-4$

Exercise 6.11

1 a 2 　b 3 　c 2 　d 4

e 5 　f 3 　g 3 　h 2

i 6 　j 8 　k 6 　l 3

2 a $\log_5 25 = 2$ 　　b $\log_4 64 = 3$

c $\log_{10} 10\,000 = 4$

d $\log_{25} 5 = \dfrac{1}{2}$ 　　e $\log_2 \dfrac{1}{16} = -4$ 　　f $\log_3 \dfrac{1}{9} = -2$

g $\log_8 4 = \dfrac{2}{3}$ 　　h $\log_{10} 0.01 = -2$ 　i $\log_4 \sqrt{2} = \dfrac{1}{4}$

j $\log_{16} 4 = \dfrac{1}{2}$ 　　k $\log_9 27 = \dfrac{3}{2}$ 　　l $\log_6 \dfrac{1}{\sqrt{6}} = -\dfrac{1}{2}$

3 a $125 = 5^3$ **b** $10 = 10^1$ **c** $27 = \sqrt{3}^6$

d $8\sqrt{2} = 2^{3.5}$ **e** $64 = 2^6$ **f** $\frac{1}{81} = 3^{-4}$

g $\frac{1}{125} = 5^{-3}$ **h** $\sqrt{2} = 8^{\frac{1}{6}}$ **i** $10 = 100^{\frac{1}{2}}$

j $5\sqrt{5} = 5^{\frac{3}{2}}$ **k** $2 = 8^{\frac{1}{3}}$ **l** $\frac{1}{100} = 100^{-1}$

4 Because a base raised to any power always gives a positive number.

Exercise 6.12

1 a 7 **b** 3 **c** 2 **d** −1 **e** $\frac{1}{2}$

f −2 **g** −4 **h** −4 **i** 1 **j** 2

k 2 **l** 2 **m** 1 **n** 2

2 a $\log_x 30$ **b** $\log_x 5$ **c** $\log_x 8$

d $\log_x 2$ **e** $\log_x 40$ **f** $\log_x 10$

g $\log_x \frac{1}{4}$ **h** $\log_x \frac{1}{5}$ **i** $\log_x 12$

3 a 1.2042 **b** 2.6021 **c** 3.6021 **d** 0.301 05

e −0.3979 **f** 2.2042 **g** 0.3979 **h** 0.801 05

4 a 1 **b** 3 **c** 3 **d** 2 **e** −1

f 0.5 **g** 3 **h** 2 **i** −1 **j** −4

5 a 5 **b** 3 **c** 1

d 7 **e** 0 **f** $\frac{3}{2}\log_a x$ or $\log_a\left(\sqrt{x}\right)^3$

Exercise 6.13

1 a $k = 9$ **b** $m = 7$ **c** $d = 10$

d $x = 2.5$ **e** $y = -4.5$ **f** $a = 3.5$

g $k = 1.5$ **h** $n = -1.5$ **i** $d = 2.75$

2 a $x = 1.425$ **b** $x = 2.227$ **c** $x = 2.519$

d $x = -0.943$ **e** $x = 0.428$ **f** $x = -0.661$

g $x = 7.555$ **h** $x = -0.107$ **i** $x = -1.121$

j $x = 1.011$ **k** $y = 0.975$ **l** $k = -2.069$

3 a $x = 2$ **b** $x = 1\frac{2}{3}$ **c** $x = 1\frac{1}{4}$ **d** $x = -\frac{1}{2}$

e $x = 3\frac{1}{2}$ **f** $x = -2\frac{1}{6}$ **g** $x = 1\frac{1}{4}$ **h** $x = -2$

4 a $x = 8$ **b** $x = 1000$ **c** $x = \frac{1}{25}$ **d** $x = \frac{1}{64}$

e $x = 3$ **f** $x = 2$ **g** $x = \frac{1}{1000}$ **h** $x = 22.627$

i $x = 0.316$ **j** $x = \frac{1}{8}$ **k** $x = 128$ **l** $x = \frac{1}{25}$

m $x = 2$ **n** $x = \frac{1}{5}$ **o** $x = \frac{1}{2}$ **p** $x = 0.1$

q $x = 16$ **r** $x = 2$ **s** $x = 3.915$ **t** $x = 23.04$

5 $11.89 \approx 12$ years **6** $22.43 \approx 23$ months

7 a $A = 106$ g **b** $t = 20$ days **c** $t = 58$ days

Power plus

1 a $v = 2\frac{3}{7}$ **b** $v = 2\frac{1}{2}$ **c** $m = -10$

2 $d = -8$

3 Rohan is 17, Tarni is 7.

4 The number is 36.

5 a

b

c

6 The solution to $D = \frac{1}{2}n(n-3) = 100$ is not a positive integer.

7 $p = 4, q = 3$

8 a $a = 7$ **b** $x = 20$ **c** $m = 2$ **d** $h = 5$

TEST YOURSELF 6

1 a $a = 11$ **b** $y = 2\frac{2}{3}$ **c** $a = -3$

d $y = 1$ **e** $m = 11$ **f** $a = 28$

g $h = 1\frac{5}{8}$ **h** $y = \frac{13}{20}$

2 a $-\frac{7r}{20}$ **b** $\frac{19g}{6}$ **c** $-\frac{5x}{24}$ **d** $\frac{21-8m}{28}$

e $\frac{19k-12}{15}$ **f** $\frac{5w+21}{36}$ **g** $\frac{p+20}{12}$ **h** $\frac{5y+51}{88}$

3 a $w = 6$ **b** $h = 8\frac{3}{4}$ **c** $a = -3$

d $m = 3$ **e** $s = 4$ **f** $x = 1\frac{2}{3}$

g $b = 8\frac{1}{3}$ **h** $y = \frac{5}{7}$ **i** $n = 1\frac{1}{2}$

4 a $y = \pm 2$ **b** $p = \pm 10$

c $x = \pm\sqrt{10}$ **d** $m = \pm 1$

e $w = \pm\sqrt{50}$ $\left(\text{or } \pm 5\sqrt{2}\right)$ **f** $x = -7, -1$

g $h = 9, -1$ **h** $u = 7, -11$ **i** $k = 0, -5$

j $m = 0, 2$ **k** $b = -10$ **l** $w = 0, 9$

5 a $u = 1.9$ **b** $m = 2.9$ **c** $x = 1.4$

6 Grace: 13, Jamiela: 16 **7** 120 m

8 a 160 mm^3 **b** 300 m^2

9 a $a = \frac{y-b}{x}$ **b** $a = mP^2$ **c** $a = \frac{1-M}{M+1}$

10 a $x \geq 0$

b $x < 3$

c $x \leq -2$

d $x > -5$

11 a $y \geq 16$ **b** $y \leq -7\frac{1}{2}$ **c** $a > -5$

d $x > -3$ **e** $a < -16$ **f** $x \leq -3$

12 a $6^3 = 216$ **b** $2^{-4} = \frac{1}{16}$ **c** $7^{\frac{3}{2}} = 7\sqrt{7}$

13 a 1 **b** 0 **c** 3

14 a 0.9542 **b** 2.4771 **c** 0.5229 **d** 0.9771

15 a $x = 1.490$ **b** $x = -0.943$

c $x = 0.236$ **d** $x = 1.420$

PRACTICE SET 2

1 a $b = -7$ **b** $x = 10$ **c** $x = 49$

2 a 4 **b** 16 **c** $\frac{1}{12}$ **d** $\frac{1}{1000}$

3 a $x^2 + 14x + 49$ **b** $25m^2 - 20mn + 4n^2$
   c $9n^2 - 100$

4 a range = 15.8, interquartile range = 8.7
   b 23.7, 24.9, 26.9, 33.6, 39.5
   c April's maximum temperature first
      fortnight 2020

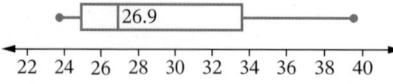

   d 39.5°C

5 a $\frac{1}{9y^2}$ **b** $\frac{3}{y^2}$ **c** $64x^9y^{12}$
   d $24h^{14}k^{16}$ **e** $3v^3w^4$ **f** $\frac{4b^2}{3a^3}$

6 a weak negative **b** strong negative
   c weak positive

7 a $k < -7$ **b** $y \geq -1\frac{1}{2}$ **c** $x \leq 2\frac{1}{2}$

8 a $13\sqrt{2}$ **b** $-4\sqrt{11}$
   c $6\sqrt{6} - 6\sqrt{3}$ **d** $45\sqrt{2} - 9\sqrt{5}$

9 $y = -5.8$

10 a $\frac{\sqrt{10}}{10}$ **b** $\frac{5\sqrt{6}}{6}$ **c** $\frac{4\sqrt{5}+5}{15}$ **d** $\frac{6\sqrt{2}-3}{9}$

11 a i stem-and-leaf plot **ii** stem-and-leaf plot
   b median = 41 **c** interquartile range = 18

12 a $p = \pm 12$ **b** $t = \pm 10$ **c** $w = \pm 6.2$

13 a 1 **b** 0 **c** 3

14 a $(r + 8)(r + 3)$ **b** $(y - 30)(y - 1)$
   c $(x + 12)(x - 3)$ **d** $(t - 9)(t + 8)$

15 a The independent variable is W, the weeks in stor-
      age. The number of weeks in storage is set first,
      after which the number of good apples is counted.
   b

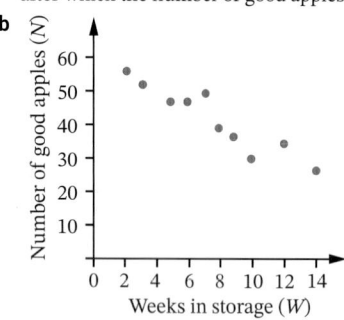

   c The number of good apples decreases the longer
      the apples are in storage.
   d There is a strong and negative relationship
      between the variables W and N.
   e around 20

16 a $x = -7, -1$ **b** $h = 9, -1$
   c $u = -11, 7$ **d** $b = 0, 9$

17 a 20, 21, 22 **b** 20, 40, 120

18 a $(5n+2)(n+1)$ **b** $(2a+3)(a-5)$ **c** $(4x-3)(2x+5)$

19 a

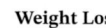

   b
   c
   d

20 a $x = \frac{3}{4}$ **b** $x \approx 3.453$

21 a 218 **b** $55 + 14\sqrt{6}$ **c** $2\sqrt{15} + 54$

22 a

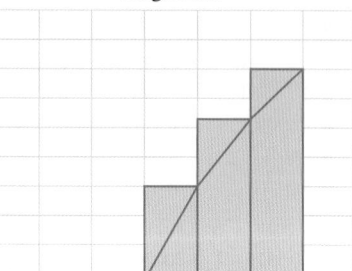

   b approximately 12 kg

23 a approximately 9.5 kg
   b approximately 18 kg **c** 8.5 kg

24 a Girls: $\bar{x} = 62.7$, $\sigma = 16.1$
      Boys: $\bar{x} = 66.9$, $\sigma = 12.2$
   b The boys performed better as their mean is
      higher. They are also more consistent as their
      standard deviation is lower.

25 a $I = \pm\sqrt{\dfrac{E}{Rt}}$ **b** $c = kh - n$ **c** $n = 3t^2$

26 Relative frequency of cinema = 0.53; Relative
   frequency of cinema given girl = 0.88. Relative
   frequency of bowling = 0.47; Relative frequency of
   bowling given boy = 0.57. Girls are more likely to
   select the cinema for the excursion. Hence, there is
   an association between gender and type of activity.

CHAPTER 7

SkillCheck

1 a 8 **b** 29 **c** 9 **d** 99

2 a 625 **b** 3125 **c** 1 **d** $\frac{1}{25}$

3 a 4 **b** $-\frac{1}{2}$ **c** $\frac{8}{5}$ **d** -3.2

Exercise 7.01

1 A   **2** C

3 a F **b** I **c** A **d** K
   e J **f** C **g** B **h** L
   i H **j** E **k** G **l** D

4 a −10, −1, 2, −1, −10

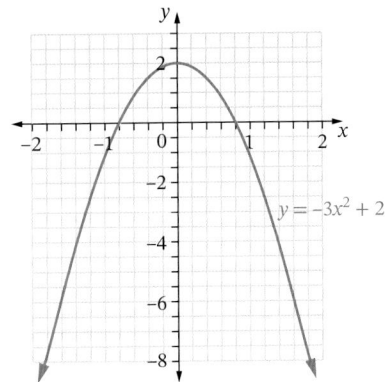

$y = -3x^2 + 2$

b (0, 2) **c** $x = 0$ **d** 2

5 A

6 a i narrower **ii** up **iii** 3
  b i wider **ii** up **iii** 1
  c i narrower **ii** down **iii** −5
  d i wider **ii** down **iii** −12

7 a x-intercepts −3 and −1, y-intercept 3

x	−3	−2	−1	0	1	2	3
y	0	−1	0	3	8	15	24

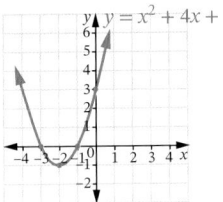

$y = x^2 + 4x + 3$

b x-intercepts −3 and $-\frac{1}{2}$, y-intercept 3

x	−3	−2	−1	0	1	2	3
y	0	−3	−2	3	12	25	42

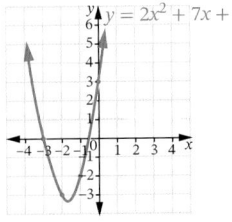

$y = 2x^2 + 7x + 3$

c x-intercepts $-1\frac{1}{2}$ and 3, y-intercept 9

x	−3	−2	−1	0	1	2	3
y	−18	−5	4	9	10	7	0

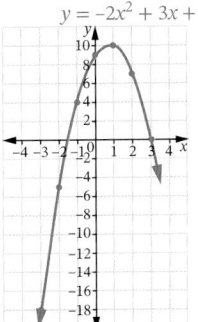

$y = -2x^2 + 3x + 9$

d x-intercepts 0 and 2, y-intercept 0

x	−3	−2	−1	0	1	2	3
y	15	8	3	0	−1	0	3

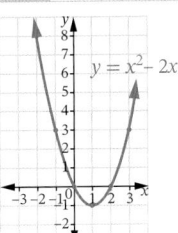

$y = x^2 - 2x$

8 a −5 **b** 3 **c** 0 **9** C

10 a

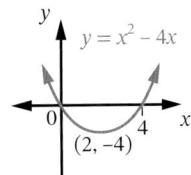

$y = x^2 - 4x$
(2, −4)

b

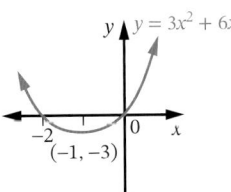

$y = 3x^2 + 6x$
(−1, −3)

c

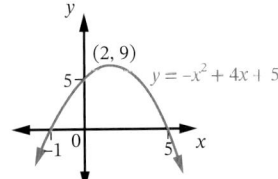

(2, 9)
$y = -x^2 + 4x + 5$

d

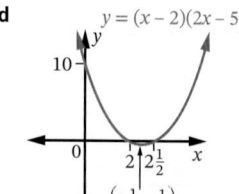

$y = (x - 2)(2x - 5)$

e

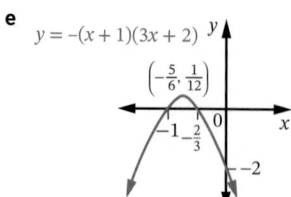

$y = -(x + 1)(3x + 2)$

f

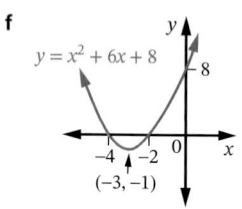

$y = x^2 + 6x + 8$

Exercise 7.02

1 **a** 28 m

b 27 m, going up at 1.8 s, then coming down at 3 s

c 2.4 s (halfway between 1.8 s and 3 s)

d 28.8 m

e h is negative and height cannot be negative. The ball has already returned to the ground after 5 seconds.

2 **a** Length of fencing $= x + y + y = x + 2y$, but amount of fencing wire = 18 m. So, $x + 2y = 18$.

b $2y = 18 - x$

$y = 9 - \frac{1}{2}x$

c $A = xy = x\left(9 - \frac{1}{2}x\right) = 9x - \frac{1}{2}x^2 = -\frac{1}{2}x^2 + 9x$

d 40.5 m², 9 m by 4.5 m

3 **a**

t	0	1	2	3	4	5	6	7	8	9	10
h	80	71	64	59	56	55	56	59	64	71	80

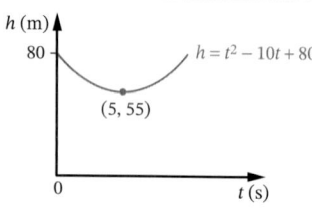

$h = t^2 - 10t + 80$

(5, 55)

b (5, 55)

c 55 m, the lowest height of the plane during the dive

d 5 s   **e** 80 m

4 **a**

t	0	1	2	3	4	5	6	7	8	9	10
d	0	4.9	19.6	44.1	78.4	122.5	176.4	240.1	313.6	396.9	490

b

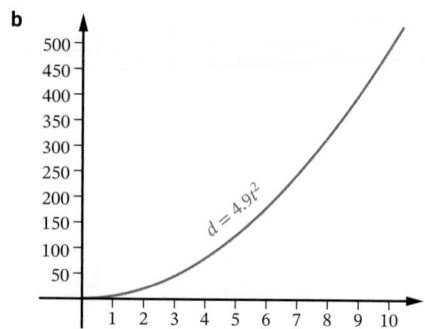

$d = 4.9t^2$

c **i** 44.1 m   **ii** 4410 m

d **i** 1.4 s   **ii** 3.2 s

5 **a**

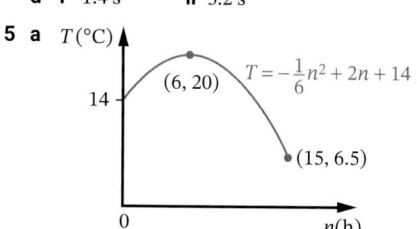

$T = -\frac{1}{6}n^2 + 2n + 14$

(6, 20)

(15, 6.5)

b **i** 14°C   **ii** $19\frac{1}{3}$°C

c 20°C at 12 noon

d 9:30 am and 2:30 pm; temperature rising at 9:30 am, temperature falling at 2:30 pm

e 5 hours

f Temperature will not continue to fall indefinitely after 13 hours but will eventually rise (and fall) again.

6 **a**

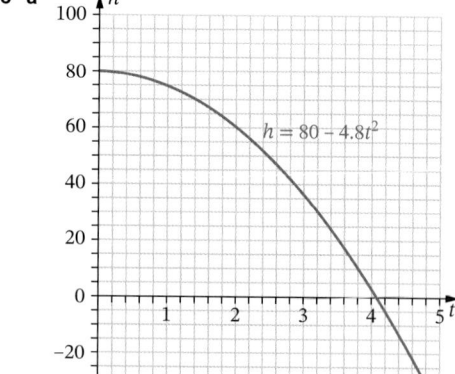

$h = 80 - 4.8t^2$

b 80 m   **c** 36.8 m   **d** 4.1 s   **e** 3.95 s

9780170465595

7 Fuel consumption is 8 L/100 when the car is travelling at 50 km/h.

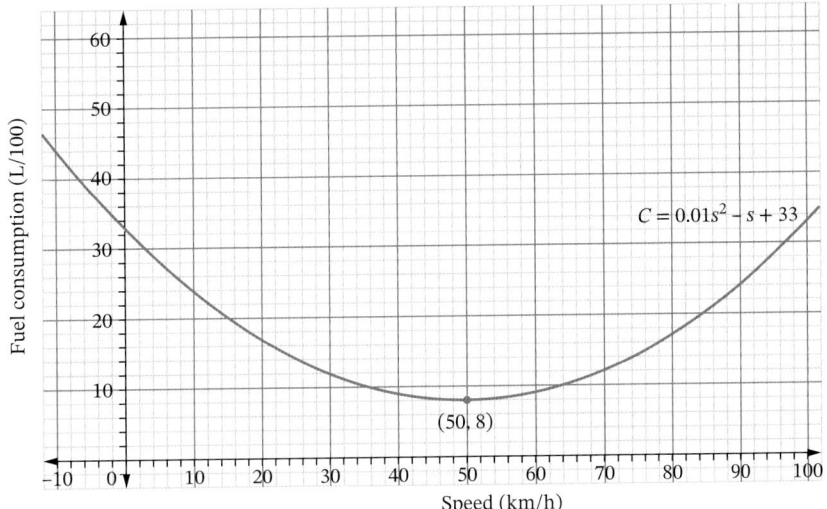

$$C = 0.01s^2 - s + 33$$

(50, 8)

Fuel consumption (L/100)

Speed (km/h)

8 Based on the function from previous years, ticket price of $25 will make the maximum profit $1300.

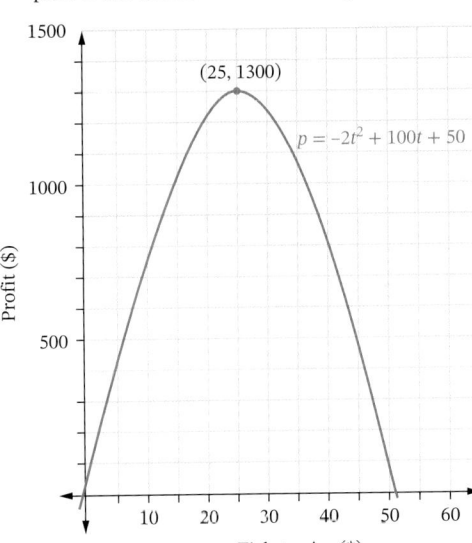

(25, 1300)

$$p = -2t^2 + 100t + 50$$

Profit ($)

Ticket price ($)

Exercise 7.03

1 a C   **b** D   **c** A   **d** B

2 a 190, $D = 190T$

  b i 3.8 km   **ii** 8.55 km   **c** 1 h 5 min

3 a 26.2, $E = 26.2h$ **b** $183.40   **c** 5.5 h

4 a $I = \frac{16D}{425}$ **b** $33.88   **c** $67.76

5 a A   **6** $b = 2.5a$

7 a 7.50, 15, 22.50 **b** $c - 7.5h$ **c** $45

  d 11   **e** 7.5. It is the same.   **8** C

9 a $F = 0.006\,m$ **b** 15 L/100 km

10 A   **11 a** 22.8 kg   **b** 84.1 kg

Exercise 7.04

1 a B   **b** C   **c** D   **d** A

2 a 920, $T = \frac{920}{s}$ **b** 10 h 13 min   **c** 92 km/h

3 a 4500, $T = \frac{4500}{h}$

  b i 15°C   **ii** 1.8°C   **c i** 562.5 m   **ii** 200 m

  d

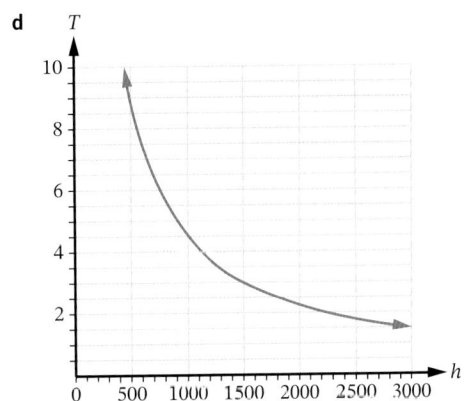

T

h

4 a $N = \frac{112}{S}$ **b** 101   **c** 2.0 m²   **d** 28

5 C   **6** B   **7** $\frac{14}{15}$

8 a 8 min   **b** 4 people

9 a $b = \frac{8}{a}$ **b** $b = \frac{100}{a}$

10 a $F = \frac{112}{L}$ **b** 6 beats/sec   **c** 25 cm

11 a $y = \frac{1}{16}$ **b** $x = 1\frac{1}{4}$

12 a 2.5 h   **b** 5 friends

1 a

x	−3	−2	−1	0	1	2	3
y	$-\frac{2}{3}$	−1	−2	–	2	1	$\frac{2}{3}$

b, c

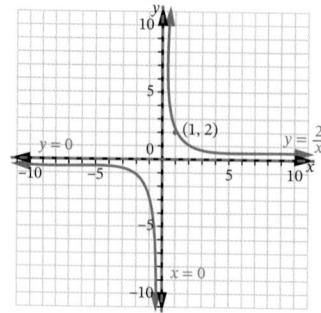

d $y = x$, $y = -x$

2 a

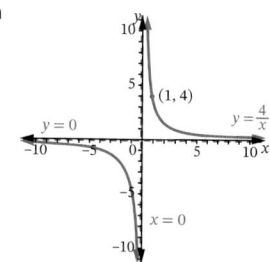

b

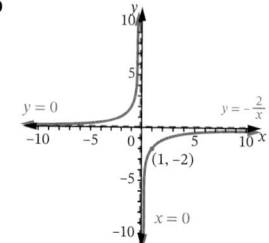

c

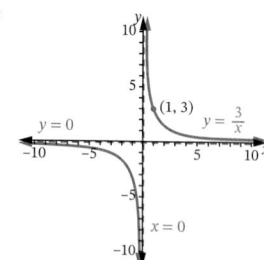

3 a

t	1	2	3	4	5	6	7	8	9	10
S	1000	500	333	250	200	167	143	125	111	100

b

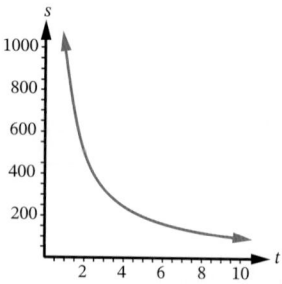

c The time taken is always positive and it is impossible to travel with zero time. Also, you cannot divide by zero.

d Yes, when $t = 2$ h, $s = 500$ km/h and when $t = 4$ h, $s = 250$ km/h.

4 a $k = 3$ **b** $y = \dfrac{3}{x}$

5 a

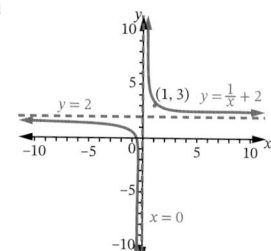

b

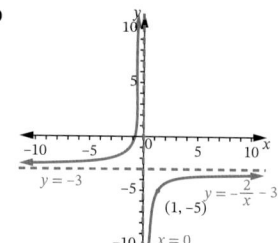

c

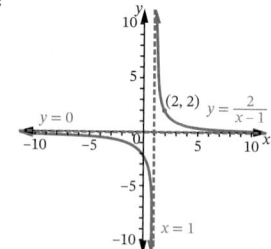

d

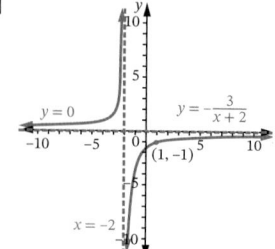

6 a $c = 1$, $k = -6$ **b** $y = -\dfrac{6}{x} + 1$

7 a

L	10	20	30	40	50	60	70	80	90	100
W	80	40	27	20	16	13	11	10	9	8

b $WL = 800$ or $W = \dfrac{800}{L}$

c If the length or width equals zero, the block of land doesn't exist.

d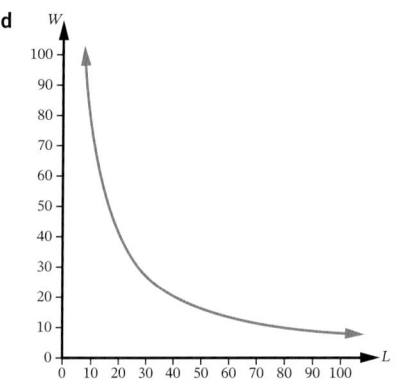

e As the length increases, the width decreases. The graph flattens out and gets closer to the horizontal axis, but never touches it (an asymptote).

f As the length decreases, the width increases. The graph is steeper and gets closer to the vertical axis, but never touches it (an asymptote).

8 A

9 a $x = 0, y = 0$ **b** $x = 0, y = c$

  c $x = b, y = 0$ **d** $x = b, y = c$

Mental skills 7

2 a 3.5   **b** 2.4   **c** 0.12   **d** 0.36

  e 0.8   **f** 0.027   **g** 0.2   **h** 8.8

  i 0.24   **j** 0.012   **k** 1.8   **l** 0.028

4 a 66.3   **b** 6630   **c** 6.63   **d** 0.663

  e 6.63   **f** 663   **g** 0.663   **h** 663

  i 6630   **j** 66.3   **k** 0.663   **l** 0.0663

Exercise 7.06

1 a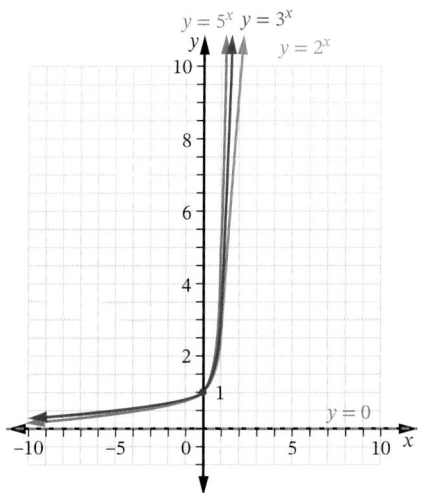

b 1

c becomes steeper in 1st quadrant

2 a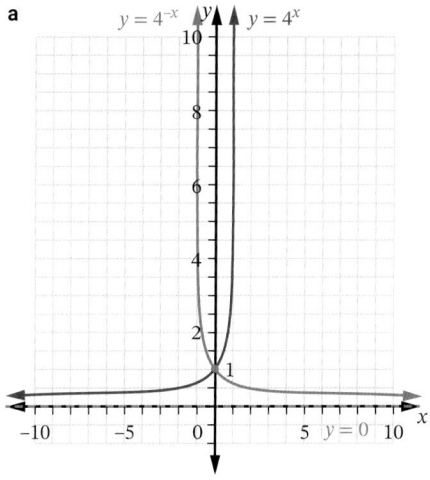

b i $y = 4^{-x}$ **ii** $y = a^{-x}$

3 B

4 a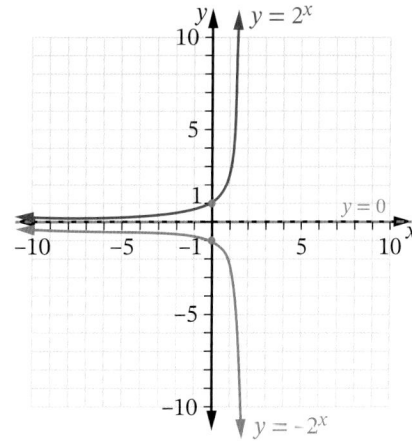

b One is the reflection of the other in the x-axis.

c $y = -a^x$

5 Same shape, shifted down 2 units.

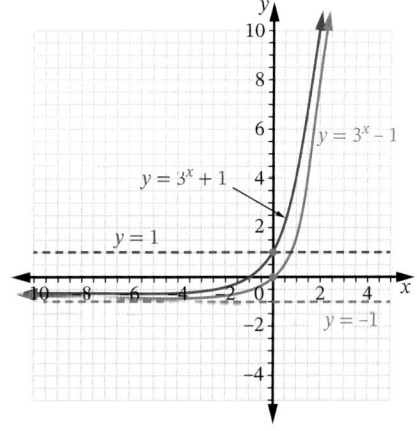

6 a

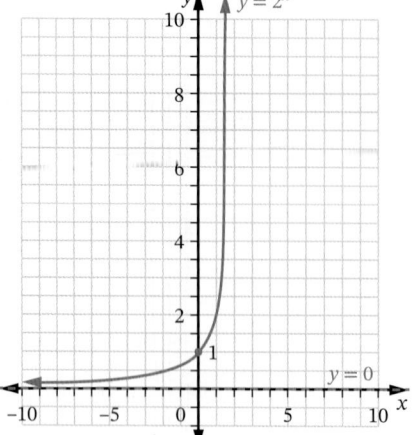

b

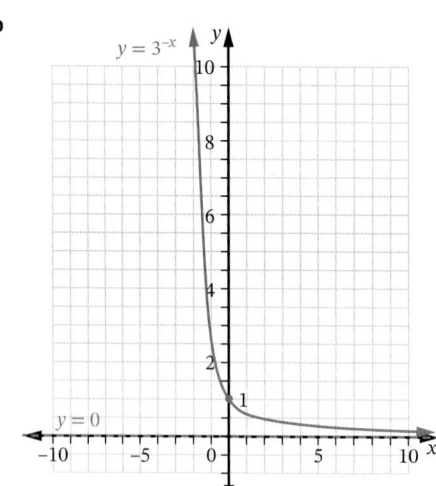

c

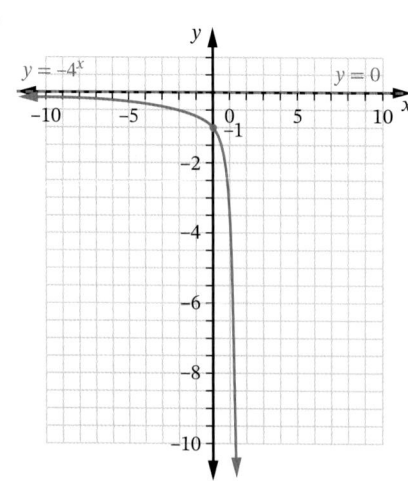

d

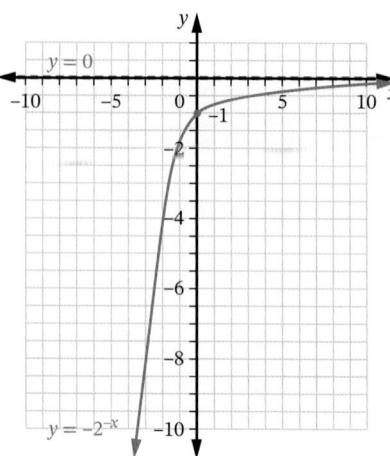

e

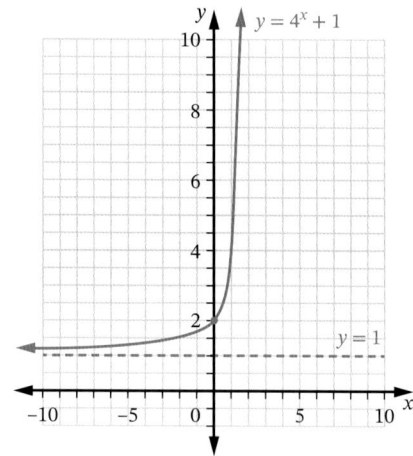

f

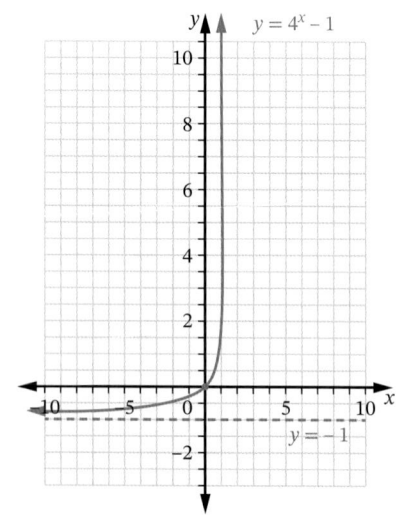

7 $y = 4^{-x}$

8 Teacher to check

Exercise 7.07

1 a 2^6 **b** 9^3 **c** 3^5 **d** 8^4
   e 4^4 **f** 7^2 **g** 5^4 **h** 6^3
2 a $x = 4$ **b** $x = 12$ **c** $x = 3$ **d** $x = 7$
   e $x = 3$ **f** $x = 2$ **g** $x = 6$ **h** $x = 5$
   i $x = 4$ **j** $x = -3$ **k** $x = -5$ **l** $x = 7$
   m $x = 6$ **n** $x = -2$ **o** $x = 2$ **p** $x = -8$
3 a $x = 10$ **b** $x = 1$ **c** $x = 2$ **d** $x = 3$
   e $x = 2$ **f** $x = 4$ **g** $x = 1$ **h** $x = 8$
   i $x = -6$ **j** $x = 4$ **k** $x = -1$ **l** $x = -4$
   m $x = 3$ **n** $x = -2$ **o** $x = 7$ **p** $x = 6$
4 a $x = 2.04$ **b** $x = 1.80$ **c** $x = 0.78$
   d $x = 0.69$ **e** $x = 4.02$ **f** $x = -7.72$
   g $x = 9.70$ **h** $x = -3.04$
5 a, b, c Teacher to check, no solution.
   d $x = 6$
6 Harshita's solution is correct. Rhea did not expand brackets correctly on the right-hand side of the equation. She should have multiplied 3 by (–1) to get –3 but she left the part of the solution as –1.

4
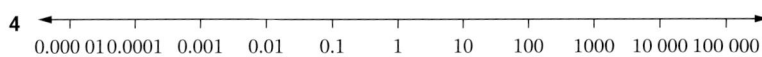
0.000 01 0.0001 0.001 0.01 0.1 1 10 100 1000 10 000 100 000

5 10^9 or 1 000 000 000 or one billion

6 a

Planet	Diameter (km)	Log (diameter)
Sun	1 391 400	6.1
Mercury	4880	3.7
Venus	12 100	4.1
Earth	12 800	4.1
Mars	6800	3.8
Jupiter	143 000	5.2
Saturn	120 500	5.1
Uranus	51 100	4.7
Neptune	49 500	4.7

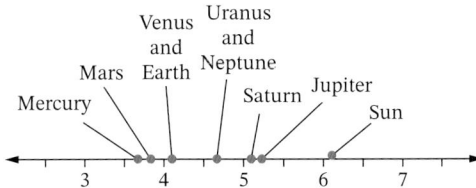

b 6.1 – 3.7 = 2.4. The Sun is approximately $10^{2.4} = 251$ times larger than Mercury using the log scale.

7 a

Animal	Mass (kg)	Log (mass)
Ant	0.000 005	–5.3
Cockroach	0.000 12	–3.9
Sugar glider	0.75	–0.1
Rat	2	0.3
Wombat	35	1.5
Kangaroo	100	2

Exercise 7.08

1 a decay **b** decay **c** growth
   d growth **e** decay **f** growth
2 a i 8000 **ii** 0.25 **b i** 15 **ii** 0.02
   c i 100 **ii** 0.15 **d i** 2000 **ii** 0.075
   e i 120 000 **ii** 0.085 **f i** 125 **ii** 0.22
3 161 451 **4** $49 207.50 **5** 29.5°C
6 $55 650.89 **7** 531 441 **8** 4 teams
9 2 rabbits in the initial population
10 300 mg

Exercise 7.09

1 a 3.9 **b** 2.88 **c** –2.46 **d** –4.15
2 a 1 995 262.32 **b** 2951.21
   c 0.0032 **d** 0.000 066

3
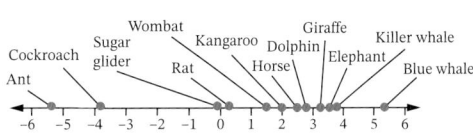

Animal	Mass (kg)	Log (mass)
Horse	300	2.5
Dolphin	650	2.8
Giraffe	1900	3.3
Elephant	5 400	3.7
Killer Whale	5 990	3.8
Blue Whale	190 000	5.3

b 5.3 – (–5.3) = 10.6
   A blue whale is approximately $10^{10.6} = 3.98 \times 10^{10}$ times larger than an ant using the log scale.
8 a 2.5 **b** 10 **c** 12.6 **d** 0.8 **e** 6.3
9 The larger country is approximately $10^{4.1} \approx 12\,589$ times larger than the smaller country.
10 5.34
11 Difference of pH 2.9, so $10^{2.9} \approx 794$ times more acidity.

Exercise 7.10

1 a $x = 5$ **b** $x = -\dfrac{1}{2}$ **c** $x = 1$
2 a $x = 1$ **b** $x = -\dfrac{1}{2}$ **c** $x = -2$
3, 4 a $x = 4$ **b** $x = -4$ **c** $x = -2$
5 a $x = -4, 5$ **b** $x = 1, 2$ **c** $x = -3, \dfrac{1}{2}$ **d** $x = -3$
6 a $x \approx 1.6$ **b** $x \approx 2.3$ **c** $x \approx 2.1$ **d** $x \approx 1.6$

7 a $x \approx \pm 3.2$ **b** no solution

   c no solution   **d** $x \approx \pm 1.5$

8 If a is negative, the parabola $y = ax^2 + c$ is a concave down curve. If c is also negative, then the vertex of the parabola is positioned under the x-axis and there will be no solutions to $ax^2 + c = 0$ as the parabola will not cross the x-axis.

9 If both a and c are positive, then the asymptote of the exponential curve $y = a^x + c$ will be above the x-axis, so there will be no solutions to $a^x + c = 0$ because the curve will not cross the x-axis.

Exercise 7.11

1 a centre $(0, 0)$, $r = 2$ **b** centre $(0, 0)$, $r = 6$

   c centre $(0, 0)$, $r = 8$ **d** centre $(0, 0)$, $r = 10$

   e centre $(0, 0)$, $r = 9$ **f** centre $(0, 0)$, $r = 5\sqrt{2}$

2 D   **3** D

4 a $x^2 + y^2 = 1$ **b** $x^2 + y^2 = 9$

   c $x^2 + y^2 = 25$ **d** $x^2 + y^2 = \dfrac{1}{9}$

5 a

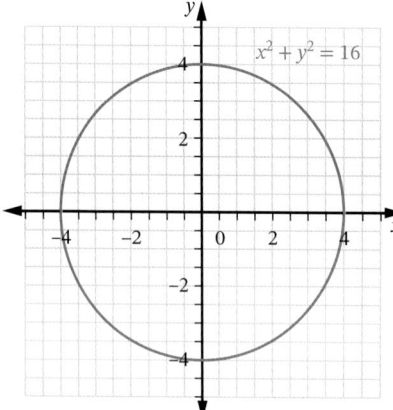

b

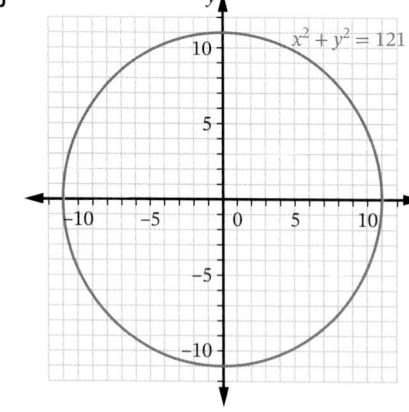

c

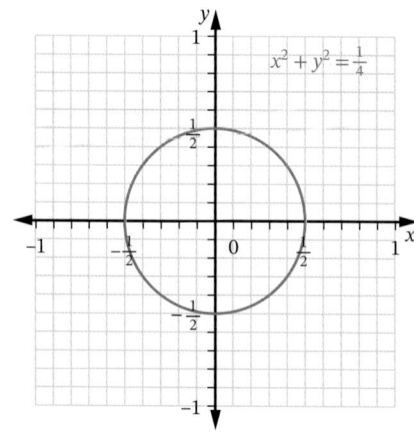

6 C

7 a, b Proof: see worked solutions

   c outside

8 a inside   **b** on   **c** outside

   d inside   **e** outside

Exercise 7.12

1 a P   **b** L   **c** E   **d** L

   e C   **f** L   **g** P   **h** L

   i P   **j** E   **k** P   **l** C

2 a G   **b** J   **c** H   **d** D   **e** A

   f F   **g** C   **h** E   **i** B   **j** I

3 a

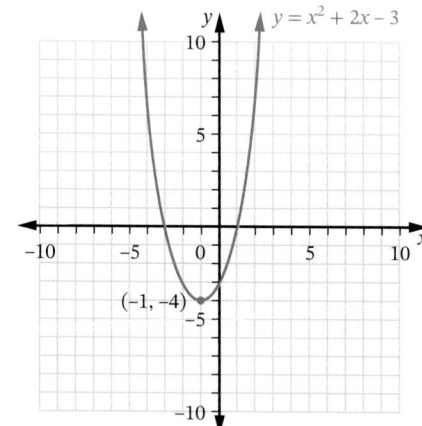

b

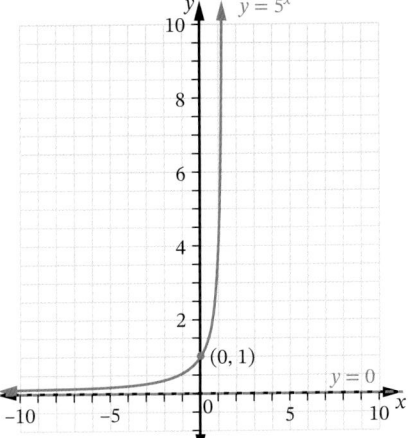

c

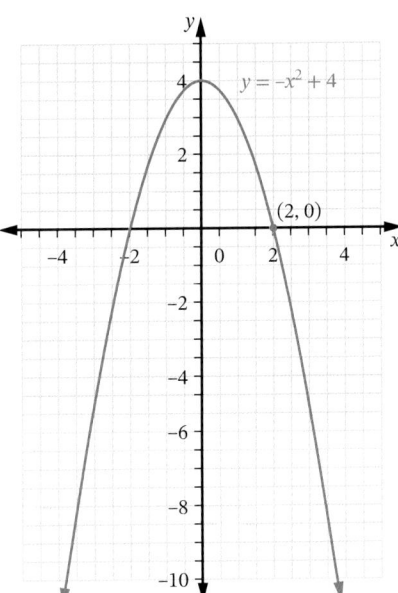

d

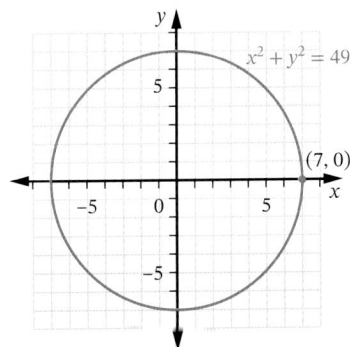

e

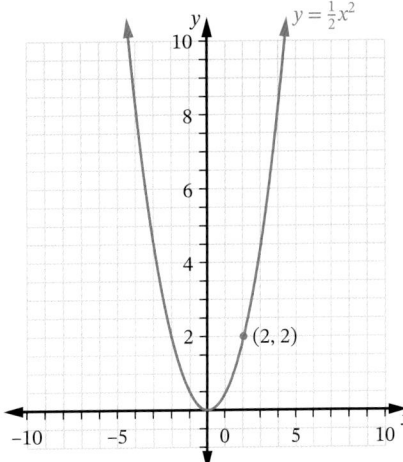

f

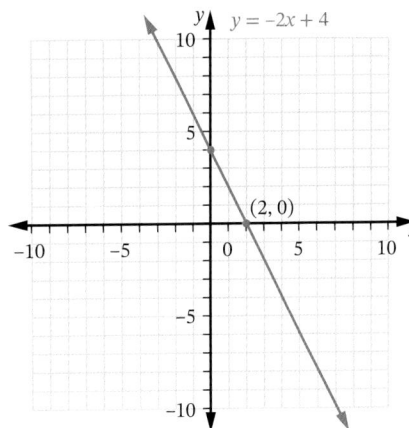

g

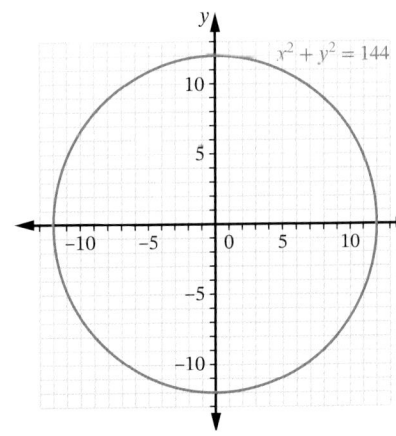

4 a 1   **b** 3   **c** −6   **d** 1

Power plus

1

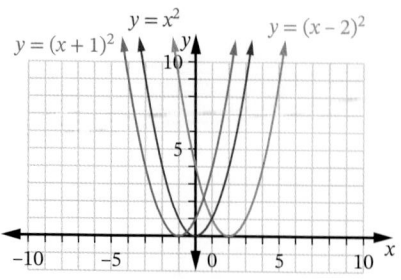

2

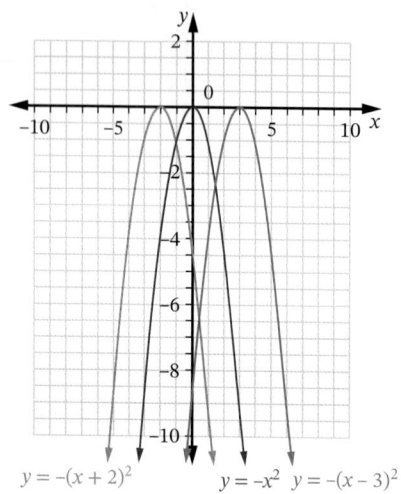

3 If a is positive, the parabola $y = x^2$ is shifted left a units.

If a is negative, the parabola $y = x^2$ is shifted right a units.

4 **a** centre $(0, 0)$ and $r = 4$

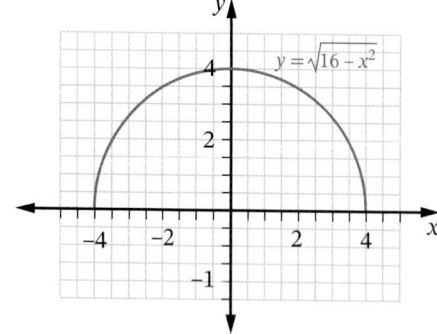

b centre $(0, 0)$ and $r = 5$

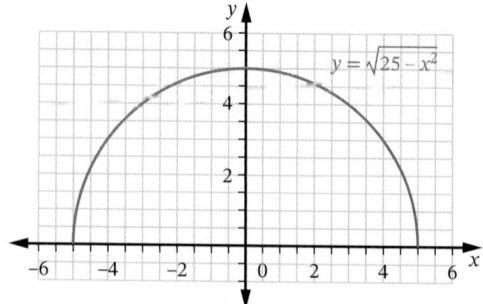

c centre $(0, 0)$ and $r = 3$

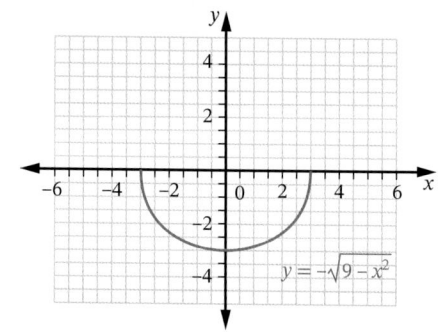

5 **a** centre $(0, 0)$, radius $\sqrt{5}$

b centre $(3, 0)$, radius $\sqrt{3}$

c centre $(-4, 2)$, radius $\dfrac{1}{2}$

TEST YOURSELF 7

1 **a** C   **b** F   **c** A

d E   **e** D   **f** B

2

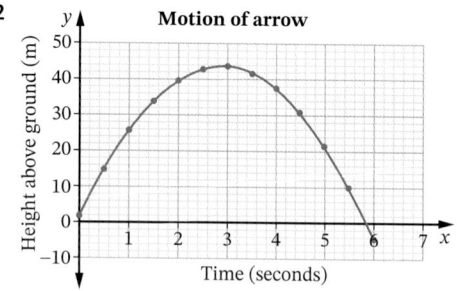

a 5.8 s   **b** 44 m

3 $H = 310.5$ **4** 10°C

5

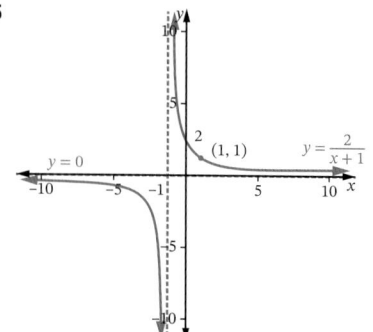

6 a

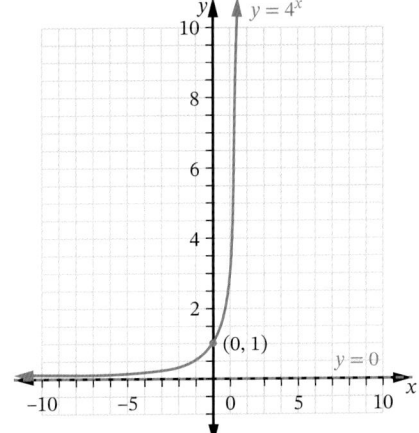

b

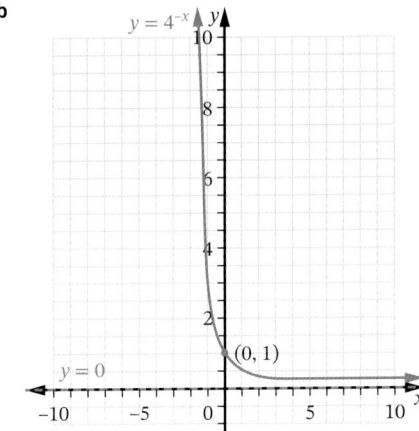

c

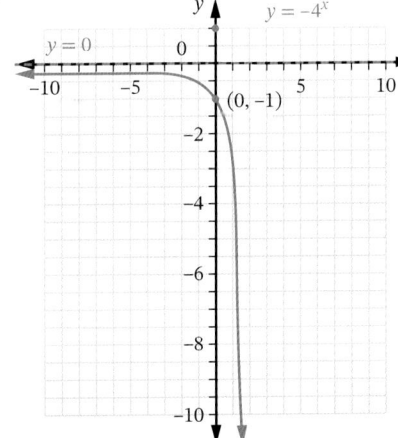

d

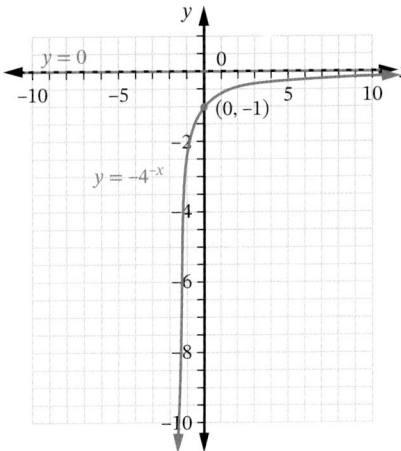

7 a $x = 11$ **b** $x = 4$ **c** $x \approx 1.17$

8 69.7 mg   **9** $494 400

10 40 times   **11** $x = \pm 2$

12 a centre $(0, 0)$, radius 10

   b centre $(0, 0)$, radius 6

   c centre $(0, 0)$, radius 7

13 $x^2 + y^2 = 64$

14 a D   **b** C   **c** B   **d** J

   e E   **f** H   **g** L   **h** G

   i I   **j** A   **k** K   **l** F

CHAPTER 8

SkillCheck

1 a 0.8480   **b** 0.7760   **c** 64.9839

   d 0.1539   **e** 13.9884   **f** 13.7044

2 a 45°48′   **b** 33°11′   **c** 5°21′

3 a 64°37′   **b** 69°41′   **c** 28°8′

Exercise 8.01

1 a 64.7 cm   **b** 14.2 cm   **c** 54.5 cm

   d 18.5 cm   **e** 5.1 cm   **f** 17.4 cm

   g 48.8 cm   **h** 59.0 cm   **i** 17.5 cm

2 C

3 a 38°41′   **b** 56°7′   **c** 42°56′

   d 52°57′   **e** 64°37′   **f** 45°1′

4 a 73°   **b** 5.7 m

5 A   **6** 13°53′

7 114 m   **8** 0.63 m or 63 cm

9 a 51°20′   **b** $\dfrac{5}{4}$

10 2.6 km   **11** 24.6 m   **12** 1.5 km

13 a 12.4 m   **b** 11.9 m

14 701 m   **15** 63°   **16** 12 km   **17** 95.6 m

18 864 m above sea level

19 149.1 m   **20** 129.6 m

Exercise 8.02

1 **a** 243° **b** 290° **c** 040°
   d 115° **e** 210° **f** 140°
   g 312° **h** 253° **i** 065°

2 **a** 000° **b** 090° **c** 180° **d** 270°
   e 038° **f** 125° **g** 330° **h** 225°
   i 072° **j** 187°

3 **a**

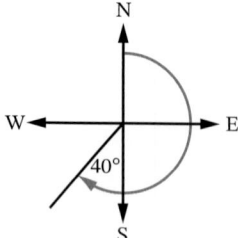

b

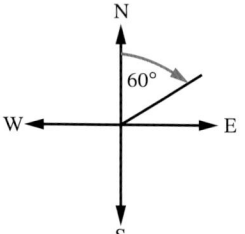

c

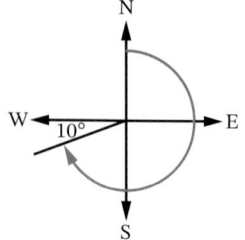

d

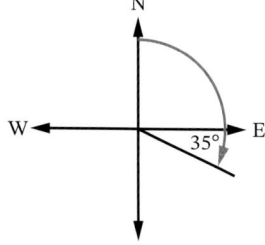

e

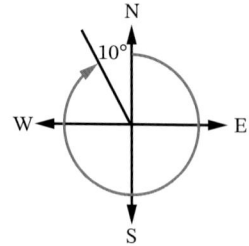

f

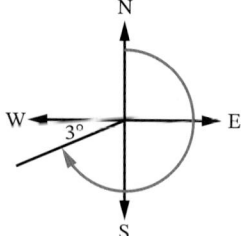

g

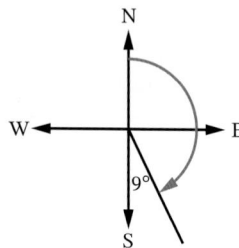

h

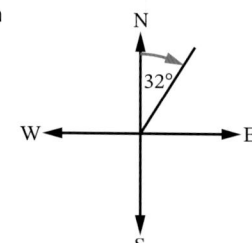

4 **a** NNW **b** 337.5°

5 **a**

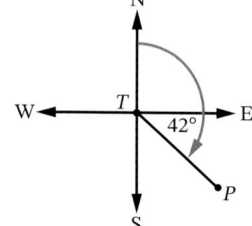

b

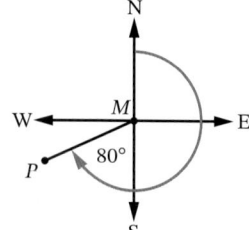

c

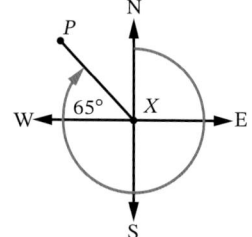

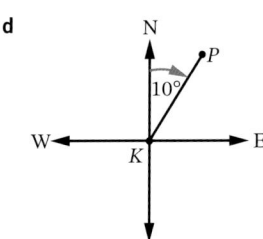

d

6 240° **7** 280°

8 a 45° **b** 90° **c** 135°
d 157.5° **e** 112.5° **f** 67.5°

9 ESE

10 a 37° **b** 163 km **c** 143°

11 a 62.5 km **b** 29.2 km **c** 025°

12 a 12.2 km **b** 215° **c** 035°

13 45.7 km

14 a 2122 km **b** 330°

15 a 15 km **b** 26 km

16 a 261.08 km **b** 167.82 km

17 6.6 km

18 a 1282 km **b** 024°27′

19 326°11′

Mental skills 8

2 a 2, 5 **b** 3 **c** 2, 3, 6 **d** 3, 5
e 2 **f** 2, 3, 5, 6 **g** 5 **h** 3

3 a 4, 9 **b** 4, 10
c 9 **d** 10
e 4, 9 **f** none of these
g 9 **h** 4, 9, 10

Exercise 8.03

1 a $4\sqrt{13}$ cm **b** 15.6 cm **c** 23°

2 a $\sqrt{800}$ cm or $20\sqrt{2}$ cm
b 34.64 cm **c** 35°16′

3 a 20.40 cm **b** 79° **4** 34°

5 a 9.1 cm **b** 28°

6 a 53 m **b** 113 m

7 a 50° **b** 868 m

8 a 85 m, 50 m **b** 99 m apart **9** 37.5 m

10 a $\angle WHF = 52°$, $\angle WFH = 38°$ and $\angle HWF = 90°$
b 49.1 m

11 a 285° **b** 7° **12 a** 26°, 054° **b** 9120 m

13 a 4.5 km **b** 210°38′

Exercise 8.04

1 a 43° **b** 16° **c** 87.45°
d 34.8° **e** 51° 43′ **f** 24° 34′
g 25° **h** 58° **i** 29°

2 a 0 **b** 1 **c** 1 **d** 2

3 $\cos\beta = \frac{5}{13}$, $\cos\alpha = \frac{12}{13}$, $\sin\beta = \frac{12}{13}$

4 $\sin F = \frac{40}{41}$, $\sin E = \frac{9}{41}$, $\cos F = \frac{9}{41}$

5 $\cos Y = \frac{\sqrt{5}}{3}$, $\sin Y = \frac{2}{3}$, $\sin X = \frac{\sqrt{5}}{3}$

6 $\cos\phi = \frac{\sqrt{5}}{4}$, $\sin\phi = \frac{\sqrt{11}}{4}$, $\cos\theta = \frac{\sqrt{11}}{4}$

7 a 8 **b** 12 **c** $3\sqrt{2}$
d $\frac{20}{\sqrt{3}}$ or $\frac{20\sqrt{3}}{3}$ **e** 45° **f** 30° **g** 30°

8 $35\sqrt{3}$ m

9 a $8\left(1 - \frac{1}{\sqrt{3}}\right)$ or $\frac{8(3-\sqrt{3})}{3}$ **b** $5(\sqrt{3}-1)$

Exercise 8.05

1 a $\tan A = \frac{60}{91}$ **b** $\tan Y = 1.\dot{3}$ **c** $\tan X = \frac{2}{3}$
d $\tan Q = \frac{\sqrt{40}}{3}$ $\left(\text{or } \frac{2\sqrt{10}}{3}\right)$ **e** $\cos X = \frac{7}{25}$
f $\sin X = \frac{2}{3}$

2 a P **b** P **c** N **d** N
e P **f** N **g** N **h** P

3 a −0.89 **b** −0.19 **c** −0.77 **d** −0.11
e 0.51 **f** −0.58 **g** 0.05 **h** −0.42
i −0.78 **j** −0.87 **k** 0.18 **l** 0.28

4 a, b Teacher to check.
c The graph has a wave shape that repeats itself after 360°.
Maximum $y = 1$ at $\theta = 90°$; Minimum $y = -1$ at $\theta = 270°$.
d No
e Yes, centre of symmetry at (180°, 0).
f **i** 0° < θ < 180° (1st and 2nd quadrants)
ii 180° < θ < 360° (3rd and 4th quadrants)

5 a, b Teacher to check.
c The graph has a wave shape that repeats itself after 360°.
Maximum $y = 1$ at $\theta = 0°$ and $\theta = 360°$;
Minimum $y = -1$ at $\theta = 180°$
d Yes, axis of symmetry θ = 180°
e No
f **i** 0° < θ < 90° and 270° < θ < 360° (1st and 4th quadrants)
ii 90° < θ < 270° (2nd and 3rd quadrants)
g Similarities: Both graphs have the same wave shapes that run between $y = -1$ and $y = 1$ and repeat themselves after 360°.
Differences: The graphs have different x- and θ-intercepts

6 a 10° **b** 70° **c** 50°
d 83° **e** 65° **f** 12°

7 a −cos 38° **b** sin 75° **c** −cos 25°
d −tan 78° **e** −cos 7.3° **f** sin 64.5°
g −cos 40°25′ **h** −tan 9.2° **i** sin 59°25′
j −tan 19°50′ **k** sin 84.5° **l** −tan 40.5°

8 a $\frac{1}{2}$ **b** −1 **c** $\frac{1}{\sqrt{2}}$ **d** $-\frac{1}{2}$ **e** $-\frac{1}{\sqrt{3}}$
f $\frac{\sqrt{3}}{2}$ **g** $-\frac{\sqrt{3}}{2}$ **h** $-\sqrt{3}$ **i** 1 **j** $-\frac{1}{\sqrt{2}}$

9 **a, b** Teacher to check.

  c The tan graph is broken into 3 sections and repeats itself after 180°. It has asymptotes at 90° and 270°.

  d No   **e** centre of symmetry at (180°, 0).

  f **i** $0° < \theta < 90°$ and $180° < \theta < 270°$ (1st and 3rd quadrants).

    ii $90° < \theta < 180°$ and $270° < \theta < 360°$ (2nd and 4th quadrants).

Exercise 8.06

1 **a** 57°, 123°   **b** 143°   **c** 110°
  d 130°   **e** 7°, 173°   **f** 135°
  g 100°   **h** 25°, 155°   **i** 114°
  j 33°, 147°   **k** 105°   **l** 118°

2 **a** 145° 9′   **b** 131° 57′   **c** 159° 26′
  d 173° 48′   **e** 152° 58′   **f** 115° 51′
  g no solution   **h** 126° 52′   **i** no solution
  j 163° 18′   **k** 126° 52′   **l** 154° 37′

3 **a** 137°   **b** 136°   **c** 61°, 119°
  d 69°   **e** 42°, 138°   **f** 143°
  g 45°   **h** 60°   **i** 45°, 135°

Exercise 8.07

1 **a** 18.4   **b** 21.1   **c** 105.0
2 **a** $a = 20.51$ **b** $b = 11.91$ **c** $c = 12.58$
  d $d = 4.10$ **e** $e = 30.85$ **f** $f = 3.55$
  g $k = 5.99$ cm   **h** $w = 29.17$ m   **i** $p = 8.29$ m
3 79 m   4 25 m
5 **a** Proof: *see worked solutions*   **b** 1042 cm
6 **a** 110°   **b** 131.6 m   7 561 km
8 **a–c** Proof: *see worked solutions*   **d** 124.7 m
9 **a** Proof: see worked solutions   **b** 595 m

Exercise 8.08

1 **a** 27°   **b** 37°   **c** 54°
2 **a** 44.5°   **b** 46.6°   **c** 32.0°
  d 67.3°   **e** 18.8°   **f** 31.8°
3 **a** 149°7′   **b** 129°0′   **c** 142°8′
  d 135°33′   **e** 129°29′   **f** 162°13′
4 **a** 46° or 134°   **b** 39°
  c 43° or 137°   **d** 43° or 137°
5 **a** 75°   **b** 41°   **c** 84°

Exercise 8.09

1 **a** 5.6   **b** 13.1   **c** 35.8
2 **a** $a = 8.30$ **b** $c = 54.52$ **c** $e = 88.41$
  d $b = 16.33$ **e** $d = 19.44$ **f** $f = 40.72$
3 0.6 m   4 C
5 **a** Teacher to check
  b $\angle XYN = 180° - 130° = 50°$ (co-interior angles on parallel lines)
    $\angle XYZ = 50° + 25° = 75°$
  c 4.4 km

6 47 km
7 **a** 0   **b** $c^2 = a^2 + b^2$
  c With cos 90° = 0, the cosine rule reverts to Pythagoras' theorem.

Exercise 8.10

1 **a** 70°   **b** 33°   **c** 109°   **d** 131°
2 **a** 112°   **b** 108°   **c** 121°
  d 23°   **e** 60°   **f** 83°
3 20.8°   4 64°40′   5 99°

Exercise 8.11

1 **a** 413.4 m²   **b** 463.1 cm²   **c** 326.9 mm²
  d 132.9 mm²   **e** 320.4 cm²   **f** 0.1 m²
2 **a** 97.4 m²   **b** 463.6 m²   **c** 246.2 m²
  d 227.6 m²   **e** 93.5 m²   **f** 152.2 m²
3 **a** 225 m   **b** 2770 m²
4 **a** 130°   **b** 766.04 m²
5 **a** 418.9 cm²   **b** 173.2 cm²   **c** 245.7 cm²
6 **a** 112°   **b** 37 cm²   **c** 740 cm³

Exercise 8.12

1 **a** 10.2   **b** 16.1   **c** 17.1
  d 13.1   **e** 3.9   **f** 18.2
2 **a** 32°   **b** 142°   **c** 29°
  d 55°   **e** 37°   **f** 125°
3 **a** $\angle ATB = 55° - 32°$ (exterior angle of a triangle)
  b 108.50 m   **c** 89 m
4 **a** 1
  b i 15.4   **ii** 15.4
  c The results are the same. The sine rule
    $\dfrac{d}{\sin 90°} = \dfrac{12.8}{\sin 56°}$ becomes $d = \dfrac{12.8}{\sin 56°}$
    (since sin 90° = 1), which is the same result when using the sine ratio.
5 7.5 km   6 486 km

Power plus

1 **a** $\sqrt{3} - 1$ **b** $\frac{1}{2}(\sqrt{3} - 1)$
2 **a** 45°   **b** 60°   **c** 30°
  d 150°   **e** 120°   **f** 135°
  g 60°, 120°   **h** 30°, 150°   **i** 45°, 135°
3 Proofs: see worked solutions.
4 $\sqrt{2}$ 5 45°, 135°

TEST YOURSELF 8

1 **a** 10.9 m   **b** 4.4 m   **c** 11.5 cm
2 **a** 64° 59′   **b** 48° 59′   **c** 57° 12′
3 29°   4 **a** 231°   **b** 051°
5 **a** 1281 km   **b** 024°
6 **a** 43.7 nautical miles
  b 276.6°   **c** 096.6°
7 **a** 33 cm   **b** 65°
8 **a** 24   **b** $48\sqrt{3}$ **c** $\dfrac{48}{\sqrt{2}} = 24\sqrt{2}$

9

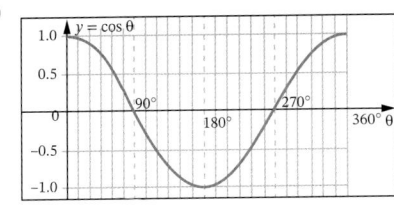

10 a 57° **b** 87° **c** 70°
11 a 143° 8' **b** 64° 59'
  c 12° 22', 167° 38'

12 a 0.4 **b** 14.8 **c** 136.4
13 a 81°54' or 98°6' **b** 77°24' or 102°36'
  c 49°37'
14 a 6.8 **b** 112.1 **c** 7.6
15 a 96° **b** 56° **c** 125°
16 a 165 cm² **b** 286 mm² **c** 30 m²
17 15.5 cm   **18** 28.0 m

CHAPTER 9

SkillCheck

	Name of solid	Shape(s) of faces	Number of faces	Number of vertices (corners)	Number of edges (lines)
1	Cube	Square	6	8	12
2	Triangular pyramid	Triangle	4	4	6
3	Octahedron	Triangle	8	6	12
4	Square pyramid	Triangle, square	5	5	8
5	Triangular prism	Triangle, rectangle	5	6	9
6	Rectangular prism	Rectangle	6	8	12
7	Triangular prism	Triangle, rectangle	5	6	9
8	Square prism (or rectangular prism)	Square, rectangle	6	8	12
9	Pentagonal prism	Pentagon, rectangle	7	10	15
10	Polyhedron (or truncated square pyramid)	Rectangle, trapezium	6	8	12
11	Pentagonal prism	Pentagon, rectangle	7	10	15
12	Hexagonal pyramid	Triangle, hexagon	7	7	12

Exercise 9.01

	Number of faces, F	Number of vertices, V	F + V	Number of edges, E	E + 2
1	4	6	10	8	10
2	2	6	8	6	8
3	5	7	12	10	12
4	5	6	11	9	11
5	7	7	14	12	14
6	7	7	14	12	14
7	8	8	16	14	16
8	9	8	17	15	17
9	3	7	10	8	10
10	6	7	13	11	13

Exercise 9.02

1

 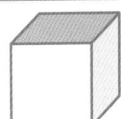 

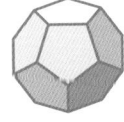 

2 a dodecahedron **b** tetrahedron
  c cube and octahedron
  d icosahedron **e** cube
  f dodecahedron **g** dodecahedron
  h octahedron

3

Platonic solid	Number of faces (F)	Number of vertices (V)	F + V	Number of edges (E)	E + 2
Tetrahedron	4	4	8	6	8
Cube	6	8	14	12	14
Octahedron	8	6	14	12	14
Dodecahedron	12	20	32	30	32
Icosahedron	20	12	32	30	32

4

	Polyhedron	Number of faces (F)	Number of vertices (V)	F + V	Number of edges (E)	E + 2
a	Triangular prism	5	6	11	9	11
b	Hexagonal prism	8	12	20	18	20
c	Square pyramid	5	5	10	8	10
d	Pentagonal prism	7	10	17	15	17
e	Trapezoidal prism	6	8	14	12	14
f	Hexagonal pyramid	7	7	14	12	14
g	Octagonal prism	10	16	26	24	26
h	Truncated square pyramid	6	8	14	12	14

5

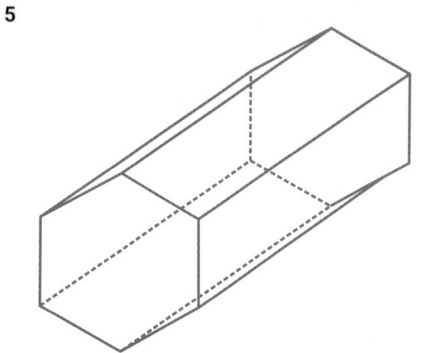

Answers may vary.

Exercise 9.03

1 a

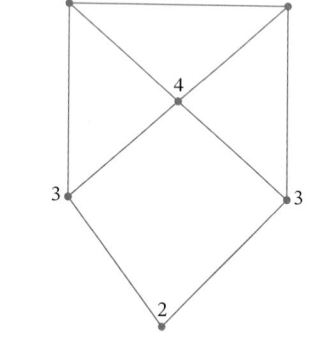

b

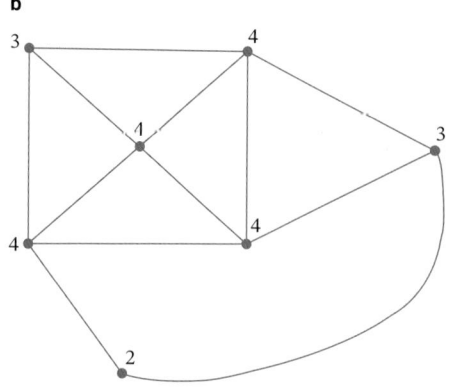

2 a

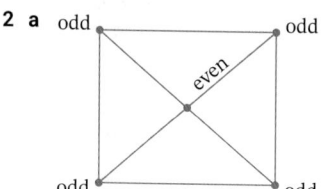

b

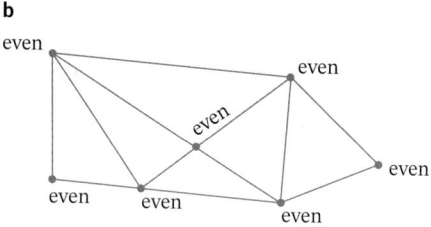

3

Network	Traversable?	Number of odd vertices
1 a	no	4
1 b	yes	2
2 a	no	4
2 b	yes	0

4

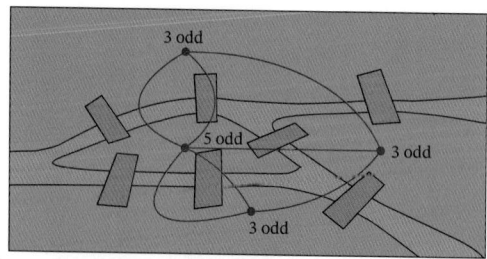

a If a network is drawn over the map of Königsberg there would be 4 odd vertices, not 0 or 2.

b Answers may vary. A new bridge between any 2 of the land regions will allow for every bridge to be crossed only once.

5 a yes   **b** yes   **c** yes
  d yes   **e** no
  f yes   **g** yes   **h** no
  i no   **j** no

6 Answers may vary, all must have 7 faces.

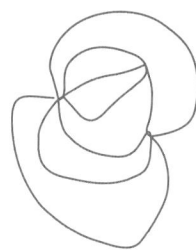

7 Answers may vary. For the above answer, it is not traversable so add an edge:

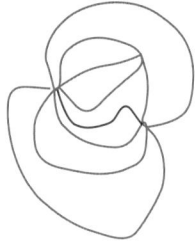

Mental skills 9

2 a $700   **b** $800   **c** 400
  d 700   **e** $300
  f $400   **g** 250   **h** $300
  i $300   **j** 500

Exercise 9.04

1 a no; contains a cycle **b** yes
  c no; not connected   **d** no; contains cycles
  e no; contains a cycle **f** yes
  g yes   **h** no; not connected
  i no; contains cycles **j** yes
2 a i 9 vertices   **ii** 8 edges
  b i 12 vertices   **ii** 11 edges
  c i 8 vertices   **ii** 7 edges
3 B   **4** a, d, e and f
5 Answers may vary, with 8 vertices and 7 edges.

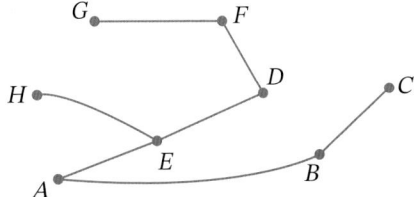

6 a The same network but with any one edge missing, so the tree has 6 vertices and 5 edges.
  b Answers may vary; must have 7 vertices and 6 edges
  c Answers may vary; must have 7 vertices and 6 edges
  d Many possible solutions; must have 6 vertices and 5 edges
  e Many possible solutions; must have 5 vertices and 4 edges
  f Many possible solutions; must have 6 vertices and 5 edges
7 a   **i** $7960   **ii** $8090   **iii** $7530   **iv** $7840
  b   **iii** is the best option.
8

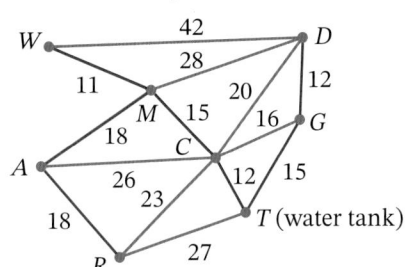

9 a

Edge	Weight
km	5
be	6
em	7
ak	8
am	9
ae	10
ab	11
bk	12

  b Edges in order: *km, be, em, ak*

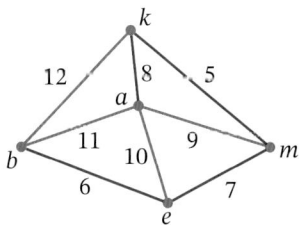

  c weight = 26 km

Exercise 9.05

1 *A-C-E*, 11 min   **2** *A-C-D-F*, 32 min
3 *A-B-D-G*, 148 km   **4** *A-B-C-E-F*, 68 min
5 *A-C-F-H*, 35 min   **6** 13 min
7 20 min

8 Shortest 26 min, longest 39 min. It would take 13 min longer if you lost your way and used the longest path.

9 a Either Armadale, Brookton, Cranbrook, Mt Barker then Albany or Armadale, Arthur River, Cranbrook, Mt Barker then Albany as both cost $65.

   b Answers may vary: The higher fare seems to be on a main road so could be a smoother, or shorter, or faster trip. The traveller could be meeting someone along the way that is getting on the bus at Bunbury. The traveller might want to travel along the coast as it is more scenic and are happy to pay more for that.

10 a 22.8 km   **b** 32 min

   c If you are trying to save car costs such as petrol you might travel the shortest route but if you are in a rush to get somewhere you might pick the quickest route.

Power plus

1 The network you draw must have 9 edges.

2 The polyhedron must have 9 faces.

3 The network must have 6 vertices. Either no vertices or 2 vertices must be odd.

4 5 possible spanning trees.

5 A to B 11 units A to C 8 units A to D 7 units
   A to E 31 units A to F 27 units A to G 29 units
   A to H 35 units

6 Draw one edge between any 2 vertices.

Test yourself 9

1 6 faces, 4 vertices and 8 edges

2 A 4, B 3, C 4, D 3, E 4

3 9 faces, 14 vertices and 21 edges

4 *GFEBGABCDE*

5 a Yes, it is traversable as it has 2 odd vertices.

   b No, it is not traversable as it has more than 2 odd vertices.

   c Yes, it is traversable as it has no odd vertices.

6 Answers may vary.

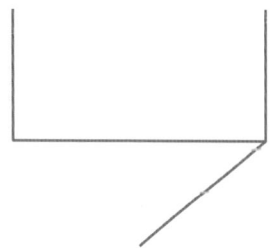

---

7 Other answers possible, but total amount of track must be 38.

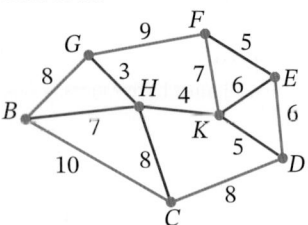

8 95 km

PRACTICE SET 3

1 a 6 edges, $F + V = 8$, $E + 2 = 8$, so $E = 6$.

2 $T = 158.4$ **3** A   **4 a** 140.4 m²   **b** 32.5

5 a 37°56′   **b** 41°33′   **c** 68°31′

6 a i

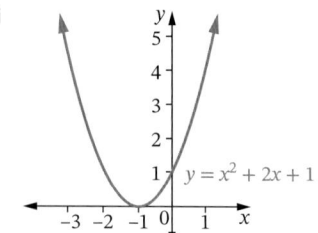

   ii

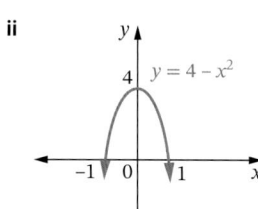

   iii

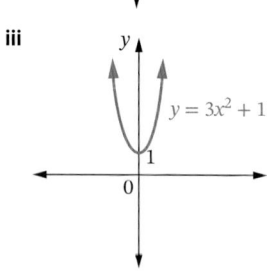

   iv

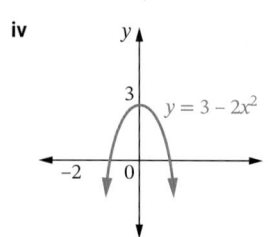

b **i** $y = x^2 + 2x + 1$, $y = 3x^2 + 1$
  ii $y = 4 - x^2$, $y = 3 - 2x^2$
  iii $y = 3x^2 + 1$

7 a $F = 3, V = 5, E = 6$
 b e–d–c–b–d–a–b (answers may vary, must start at or end at b or e)
 c The network has 2 odd vertices.

8 12 edges, $F + V = 8 + 6 = 14$, $E + 2 = 14$, so there must be 12 edges.

9 a $d = 51.9$ **b** $e = 58.1$ **c** $f = 3.7$

10 a $\dfrac{1}{\sqrt{2}}$ **b** $\dfrac{\sqrt{3}}{2}$ **c** $\dfrac{1}{\sqrt{3}}$ **d** $\dfrac{\sqrt{3}}{2}$

11 71 m   **12** C   **13** D

14 a 29°   **b** 45°   **c** 43°

15 78°   **16** 54°C

17
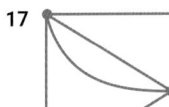

Anwers may vary. There were 4 odd vertices but adding an edge to join 2 of them made the network have 2 odd vertices.

18 (4, 13) and (–4, 13)

19 a
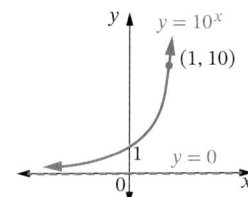

b
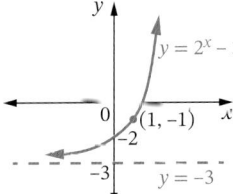

c
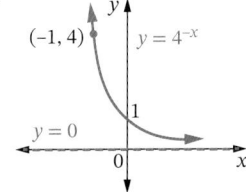

d
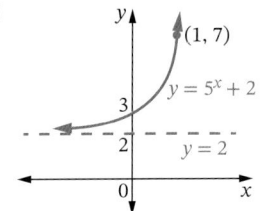

20 a I   **b** G   **c** J   **d** C
 e B   **f** D   **g** F   **h** E
 i K   **j** L   **k** A   **l** H

21 a 10.9 m   **b** 10° 8′   **22** *RQPN*, 9 km

23 a 106° 36′   **b** 40° 30′   **24** 51°3′

25 a 301 km   **b** 114°

26 C   **27** 747 km   **28** 52°, 128°

29
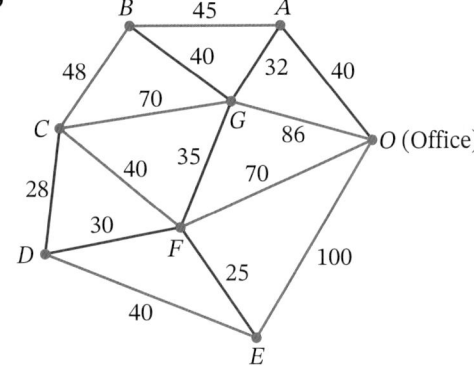

230 m

CHAPTER 10

SkillCheck

1 a 5   **b** 13   **c** 6   **d** –1

2 a –11   **b** 1   **c** 7   **d** $5\frac{1}{2}$

3 a
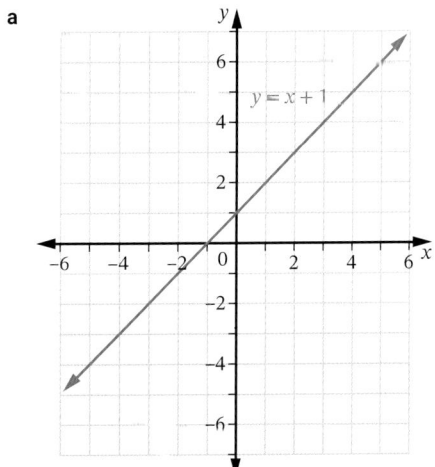

b

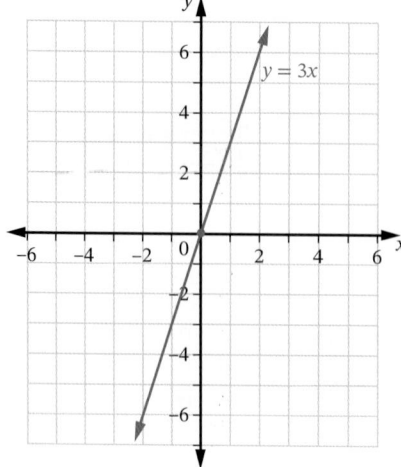

$y = 3x$

c

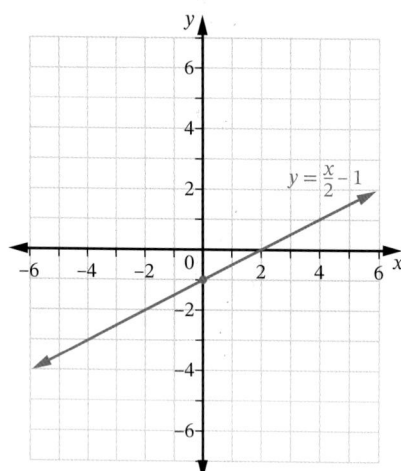

$y = \frac{x}{2} - 1$

d

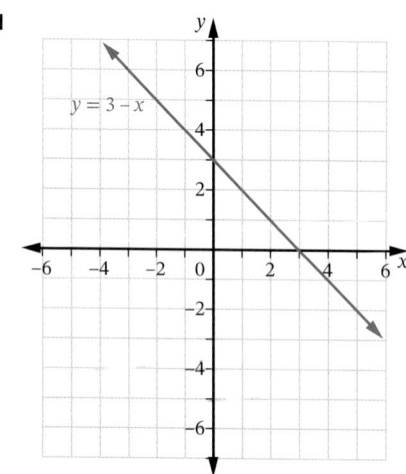

$y = 3 - x$

e

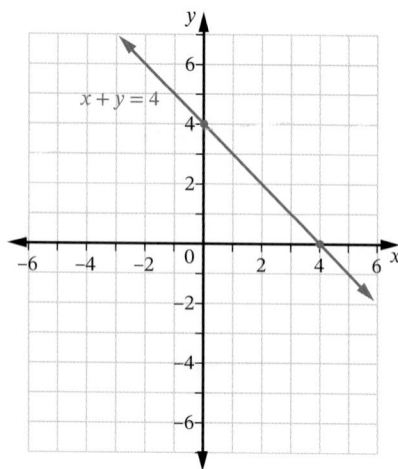

$x + y = 4$

f

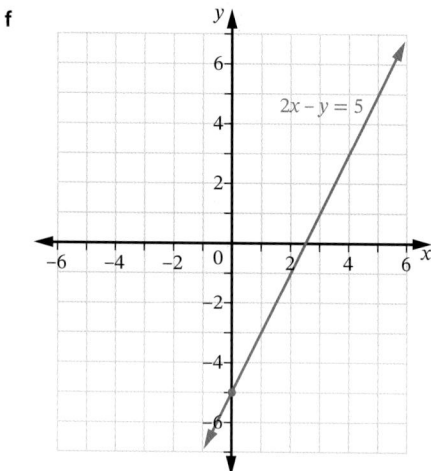

$2x - y = 5$

4 $(-2, 3)$ lies on **a, d**

5 a For $y = 2x + 1$, when $x = 2$, $y = 2 \times 2 + 1 = 5$
∴ $(2, 5)$ lies on $y = 2x + 1$
For $x + y = 7$, when $x = 2$, $y = 5$, $2 + 5 = 7$
∴ $(2, 5)$ lies on $x + y = 7$

b $(2, 5)$

6 a $m = -2, c = 3$

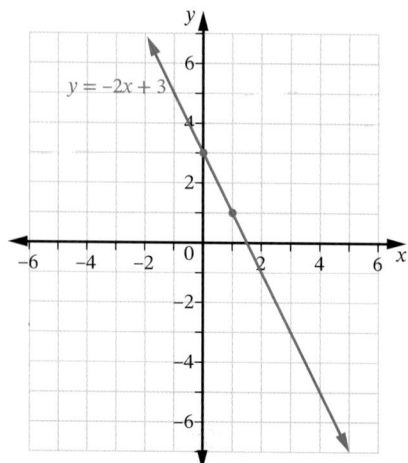

$y = -2x + 3$

b $m = \dfrac{5}{2}, c = -2$

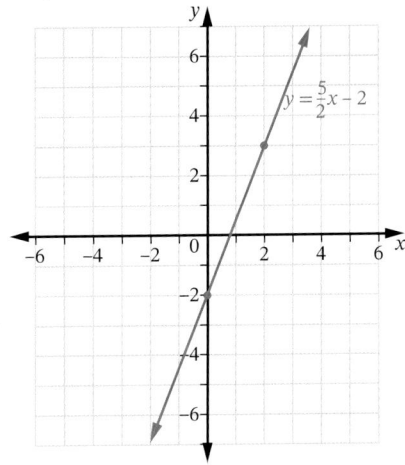

c $m = -\dfrac{4}{3}, c = 5$

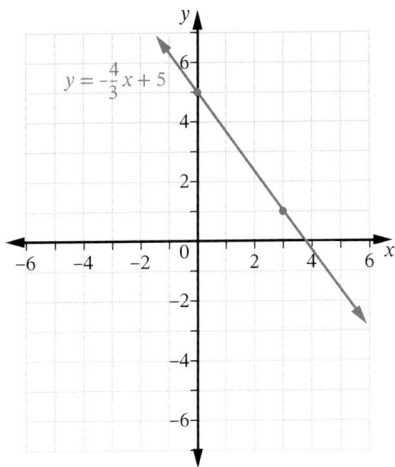

Exercise 10.01

1 a $x = 3, y = -1$ **b** $x = 2, y = 1$
   c $x = -1, y = -5$

2 a $x = 1, y = 2$ **b** $x = -5, y = -9$

   c $x = 1, y = 2$ **d** $x = -\dfrac{1}{2}, y = 2\dfrac{1}{2}$

   e $x = -2, y = -9$ **f** $x = 5, y = -4$

   g $x = \dfrac{1}{2}, y = 6\dfrac{1}{2}$ **h** $x = 3, y = 2$

   i $x = 5, y = 1\dfrac{1}{2}$ **j** $x = 5, y = 8$

   k $x = 1\dfrac{1}{2}, y = 2\dfrac{1}{2}$ **l** $x = 4, y = 0$

3 a

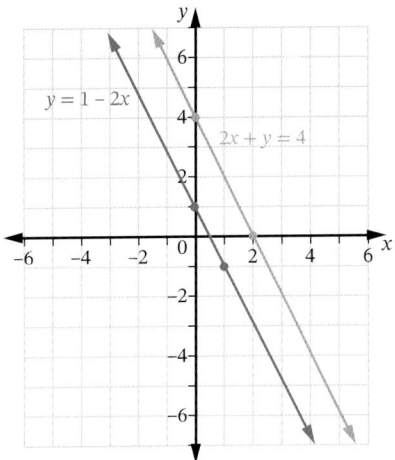

b The lines are parallel.

Exercise 10.02

1 a $d = -3, k = 2$ **b** $x = 5, w = 4$

   c $g = 2, h = -\dfrac{2}{5}$ **d** $n = 3\dfrac{1}{4}, p = -1$

   e $q = 5, r = -4$ **f** $k = -4\dfrac{3}{5}, x = 5$

   g $c = 1\dfrac{1}{2}, e = 1$ **h** $k = 3, y = -2$

   i $a = 2, f = 2$

2 a $d = -14, k = 6$ **b** $a = 1, c = 1$

   c $h = 3, y = 4$ **d** $e = 3, x = \dfrac{1}{3}$

   e $q = 3, w = 6\dfrac{1}{2}$ **f** $c = 3, p = 4$

   g $m = -\dfrac{2}{3}, y = 4$ **h** $a = -1, r = 5\dfrac{1}{2}$

   i $x = 2, w = 2$ **j** $g = -2, y = 4$

   k $e = -5, n = -8$ **l** $k = 5\dfrac{1}{2}, h = 1\dfrac{1}{2}$

3 a $q = -3, w = 3$ **b** $m = -9, x = 7$

   c $d = 23, h = -7$ **d** $g = -1, n = 3$

   e $h = 0, m = 2$ **f** $e = -4, y = 3$

   g $q = 1, w = -4$ **h** $a = \dfrac{1}{2}, d = \dfrac{1}{2}$

   i $k = 5, p = -2$ **j** $a = -2, f = -2$

   k $c = -64, r = -38$ **l** $x = -4, y = -3$

   m $x = 8, y = -1$ **n** $g = 4\dfrac{1}{2}, h = 2\dfrac{1}{2}$

   o $k = -2\dfrac{1}{2}, w = 3\dfrac{1}{2}$

Exercise 10.03

1 a $x = 2, y = 5$ **b** $x = \dfrac{3}{5}, y = 3\dfrac{4}{5}$ **c** $x = 7, y = 2$

   d $x = 2, y = -2$ **e** $x = 5, y = -1$ **f** $x = 4, y = 2$

2 a $x = 9, y = 21$ **b** $x = 5, y = 3$ **c** $x = -\dfrac{1}{4}, y = 2$

   d $x = -3, y = 1$ **e** $x = 2, y = 2$ **f** $x = -7, y = 4$

   g $x = 7, y = 3$ **h** $x = 5, y = 2\dfrac{1}{2}$ **i** $x = 2\dfrac{2}{3}, y = 1$

   j $x = -3\dfrac{1}{5}, y = -4\dfrac{3}{5}$

Exercise 10.04

1 285   **2** 680

3 a Teacher to check   **b** 396

4 55   **5** Tayyab 36, Sejuti 12

6 16   **7** black 37, colour 23

8 Children: $15.50, Adult: $21.50

9 Supreme: 32, Vegetarian: 13

10 Strawberries $3.95; Blueberries $3.50

11 a Teacher to check

     b 20-cent coins: 485, 50-cent coins: 368

12 a Teacher to check

     b

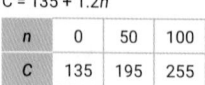

$C = 135 + 1.2n$

n	0	50	100
C	135	195	255

$R = 3n$

n	0	50	100
R	0	150	300

     c

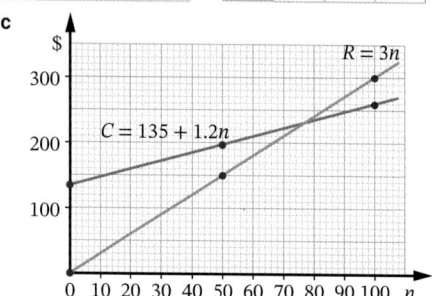

     d $n = 75$

Mental skills 10

2 a $\frac{2}{3}$ **b** $\frac{4}{5}$ **c** $\frac{5}{7}$ **d** $\frac{1}{2}$

   e $\frac{1}{4}$ **f** $\frac{1}{6}$ **g** $\frac{5}{6}$ **h** $\frac{2}{5}$

   i $5:9$ **j** $5:9$ **k** $9:20$ **l** $4:5$

   m $9:7$ **n** $4:3$ **o** $\frac{3}{5}$ **p** $\frac{4}{35}$

3 a $\frac{17}{40}$ **b** $\frac{2}{3}$ **c** $\frac{16}{25}$

   d $\frac{1}{4}$ **e** $\frac{5}{24}$ **f** $\frac{2}{25}$

Power plus

1 a $x = 1\frac{1}{2}, y = -5\frac{1}{2}, w = 4\frac{1}{2}$

   b $a = 1\frac{7}{13}, c = 4\frac{3}{13}, d = 8\frac{11}{13}$

   c $p = -11\frac{3}{13}, m = 18\frac{11}{13}, n = -13\frac{4}{13}$

2 a Teacher to check

   b $ae - bd = 0$ and a fraction cannot have denominator 0.

   c $x = 3, y = -1$

   d Teacher to check

     i $x = 2, y = -2$ **ii** $x = 28, y = 16$

     iii $x = \frac{1}{11}, y = 2\frac{20}{33}$

1 a $x = 2, y = -2$ **b** $x = 4, y = 0$ **c** $x = \frac{1}{4}, y = 1\frac{1}{2}$

2 a $x = -4, y = -2$

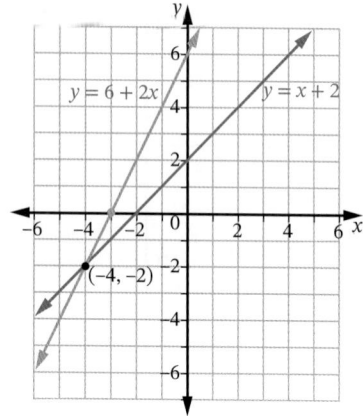

   b $x = 4, y = 1$

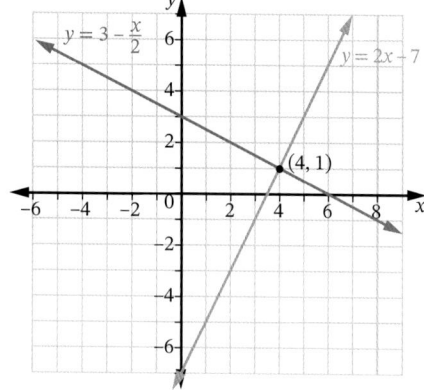

   c $x = 1, y = 1$

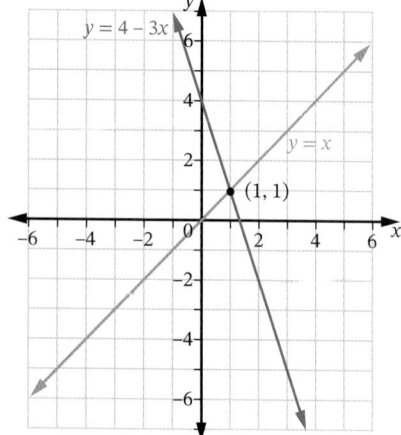

d $x = 2, y = 7$

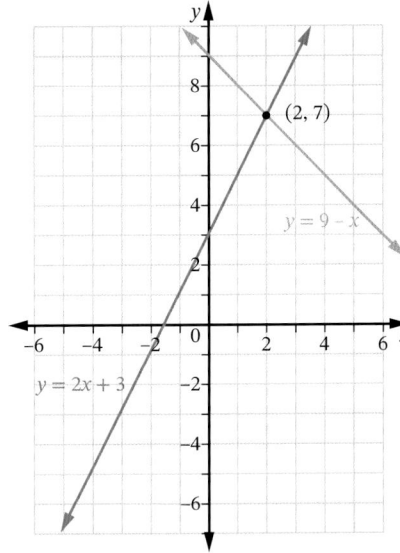

e $x = 2, y = 5$

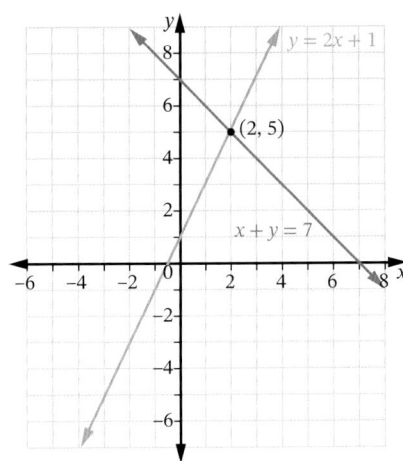

f $x = 6, y = -7$

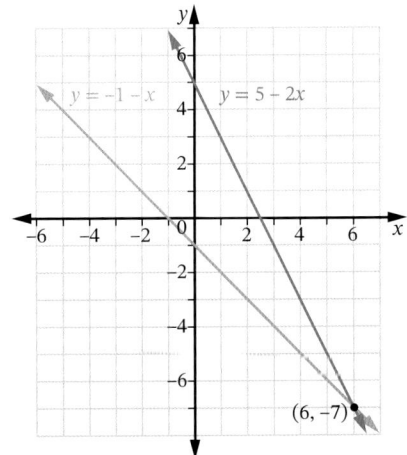

3 **a** $m = 5, c = -9\frac{1}{2}$ **b** $x = 2, y = \frac{1}{3}$

    c $a = 1, d = 1$ **d** $x = 6, y = 15$

    e $x = -5, y = -2$ **f** $d = -3, w = -10$

4 **a** $x = 2, y = 11$ **b** $m = 1, p = 3$

    c $h = 10, t = 4$ **d** $a = 3, c = \frac{1}{2}$

    e $x = 1, y = 1$ **f** $p = 12, q = -4$

5 **a** 1600 adults, 900 children

    b 18 children, 12 adults   **c** \$38

    d 28 cheesecakes, 47 mudcakes

    e 120 boys, 93 girls

CHAPTER 11

SkillCheck

1 C

2 **a** 3

    b no; P(10c coin) $= \frac{5}{12}$, P(20c coin) $= \frac{1}{3}$,

       P(50c coin) $= \frac{1}{4}$

3 **a** $\frac{1}{3}$ **b** $\frac{1}{3}$ **c** $\frac{5}{6}$

4 **a** 0   **b** 1

5 0.4   **6** B   **7** 0.15

Exercise 11.01

1 **a** **i** 0.425   **ii** 0.14   **iii** 0.21

    b **i** 0.375   **ii** 0.125   **iii** 0.25

    c yes

    d Expected frequency = 100. The observed frequency of red or purple is 115, which is more than the expected frequency.

2 **a** 50   **b** Teacher to check

    c **i** Teacher to check   **ii** $\frac{1}{2}$

    d Teacher to check

3 **a** 600

    b **i** $\frac{281}{600} \approx 0.468$ **ii** $\frac{322}{600} \approx 0.537$

       iii $\frac{227}{600} \approx 0.378$ **iv** $\frac{522}{600} = 0.87$

    c **i** 0.5   **ii** 0.5   **iii** 0.33   **iv** 0.83

    d The probabilities are similar.

4 **a** **i** $\frac{3}{10} = 0.3$ **ii** $\frac{3}{25} = 0.12$ **iii** $\frac{12}{25} = 0.48$ **iv** $\frac{1}{10} = 0.1$

    b **i** 0.33   **ii** 0.17   **iii** 0.33   **iv** 0.17

    c No, the experimental probability of yellow was higher and the experimental probability of green was lower.

    d Expected frequency of not yellow is 33. This is more than the observed frequency of 26.

5 a 200

  b i $\dfrac{4}{200}=0.02$ **ii** $\dfrac{27}{200}=0.135$

    iii $\dfrac{13}{200}=0.065$ **iv** $\dfrac{86}{200}=0.43$

    v $\dfrac{87}{200}=0.435$ **vi** $\dfrac{59}{200}=0.295$

    vii $\dfrac{51}{200}=0.255$

6 a 200

  b i $\dfrac{27}{200}=0.135$ **ii** $\dfrac{62}{200}=0.31$ **iii** $\dfrac{80}{200}=0.4$

    iv $\dfrac{21}{200}=0.105$ **v** $\dfrac{1}{200}=0.005$

  c Ferry, light rail (tram)

  d Teacher to check

7 a $\dfrac{1}{6}\approx0.17$ **b** 16 or 17 times

  c, d, e Teacher to check

8 Teacher to check; The probability of winning would be different for each horse, due to methods of training, strength of the horse and conditions of the racetrack, so it is not a simple probability of 1 in 10.

Exercise 11.02

1 C

2 a i $\dfrac{11}{25}$ **ii** $\dfrac{4}{5}$ **iii** $\dfrac{1}{5}$ **iv** $\dfrac{6}{25}$ **v** $\dfrac{19}{25}$

  b $\dfrac{3}{10}$

3 a 156

  b i $\dfrac{11}{52}$ **ii** $\dfrac{7}{52}$ **iii** $\dfrac{7}{78}$

    iv $\dfrac{22}{39}$ **v** $\dfrac{19}{78}$ **vi** $\dfrac{1}{26}$

  c $\dfrac{7}{31}$

4 a 135   **b** $\dfrac{56}{135}$ **c** $\dfrac{1}{5}$ **d** $\dfrac{17}{52}$

5 a

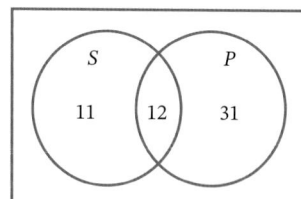

  b i 1   **ii** $\dfrac{11}{54}$ **iii** $\dfrac{31}{54}$ **iv** $\dfrac{7}{9}$

6 a 91

  b i 0   **ii** $\dfrac{17}{91}$ **iii** $\dfrac{5}{91}$ **iv** $\dfrac{5}{7}$

  c i $\dfrac{23}{29}$ **ii** $\dfrac{3}{29}$

7 a 123

  b

    F: 49   15   JA: 32   27

  c 81

  d i $\dfrac{49}{123}$ **ii** $\dfrac{32}{123}$ **iii** $\dfrac{9}{41}$ **iv** $\dfrac{27}{41}$

8 a 200

  b i $\dfrac{79}{200}$ **ii** $\dfrac{51}{100}$ **iii** $\dfrac{77}{200}$

    iv $\dfrac{121}{200}$ **v** $\dfrac{81}{100}$ **vi** $\dfrac{3}{50}$

  c $\dfrac{29}{40}$

  d No, because all the people surveyed indicated a day on which they preferred to shop.

9 a 206

  b i $\dfrac{3}{103}$ **ii** $\dfrac{11}{103}$ **iii** $\dfrac{71}{206}$ **iv** $\dfrac{62}{103}$

  c i $\dfrac{11}{65}$ **ii** $\dfrac{46}{65}$

Exercise 11.03

1 a 150

  b i $\dfrac{4}{25}$ **ii** $\dfrac{53}{150}$ **iii** $\dfrac{28}{75}$

  c 63%

2 a 128

  b i 68   **ii** 60

  c $\dfrac{17}{32}$ **d** $\dfrac{3}{32}$

3 a 97   **b i** 32.0% **ii** 25.8%   **iii** 11.3%

  c i 21.2%   **ii** 44.4%

  d The percentage of females in the opposition is just more than double that of females in the government.

4 a 150

  b i 0.5   **ii** 0.04   **iii** 0.43   **iv** 0.23

  c $\dfrac{22}{75}\approx0.293$

5 a 160

  b i $\dfrac{7}{20}=0.35$ **ii** $\dfrac{11}{160}\approx0.069$ **iii** $\dfrac{9}{80}\approx0.113$

  c $\dfrac{35}{82}\approx0.43$

6 a 200   **b** 55%

  c i 49.5%   **ii** 45%

    iii 36%   **iv** 31.5%

  d $\dfrac{72}{110}\approx65.5\%$

7 a 878

  b i $\dfrac{679}{878}=0.773$ **ii** $\dfrac{545}{878}=0.621$

    iii $\dfrac{67}{439}=0.153$ **iv** $\dfrac{21}{439}=0.048$

Exercise 11.04

1 a

	Girls					
		Be	Ca	Ma	Mi	N	P

Boys		Be	Ca	Ma	Mi	N	P
	Ben	Ben, Be	Ben, Ca	Ben, Ma	Ben, Mi	Ben, N	Ben, P
	C	C, Be	C, Ca	C, Ma	C, Mi	C, N	C, P
	E	E, Be	E, Ca	E, Ma	E, Mi	E, N	E, P
	K	K, Be	K, Ca	K, Ma	K, Mi	K, N	K, P

b i $\frac{1}{24}$ **ii** $\frac{1}{6}$ **iii** $\frac{1}{6}$

2 a

	H	T
H	HH	HT
T	TH	TT

b i $\frac{1}{4}$ **ii** $\frac{1}{2}$ **iii** $\frac{3}{4}$

3 a

		1st die					
		1	2	3	4	5	6
2nd die	1	1, 1	2, 1	3, 1	4, 1	5, 1	6, 1
	2	1, 2	2, 2	3, 2	4, 2	5, 2	6, 2
	3	1, 3	2, 3	3, 3	4, 3	5, 3	6, 3
	4	1, 4	2, 4	3, 4	4, 4	5, 4	6, 4
	5	1, 5	2, 5	3, 5	4, 5	5, 5	6, 5
	6	1, 6	2, 6	3, 6	4, 6	5, 6	6, 6

b 36

c i $\frac{1}{36}$ **ii** $\frac{11}{36}$ **iii** $\frac{1}{6}$ **iv** $\frac{1}{4}$

v $\frac{11}{36}$ **vi** $\frac{1}{4}$ **vii** $\frac{1}{2}$ **viii** $\frac{5}{12}$

4 a

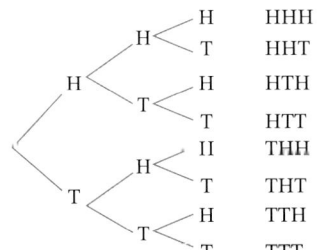

1st coin	2nd coin	3rd coin	Outcomes
		H	HHH
	H	T	HHT
H		H	HTH
	T	T	HTT
		H	THH
	H	T	THT
T		H	TTH
	T	T	TTT

b 8

c i $\frac{1}{8}$ **ii** $\frac{3}{8}$ **iii** $\frac{1}{8}$ **iv** $\frac{1}{8}$ **v** $\frac{1}{2}$

d i $\frac{7}{8}$ **ii** $\frac{7}{8}$ **e i** 75 **ii** 25

5 a

Coin	Die	Outcomes
	1	H 1
	2	H 2
	3	H 3
H	4	H 4
	5	H 5
	6	H 6
	1	T 1
	2	T 2
	3	T 3
T	4	T 4
	5	T 5
	6	T 6

6 a

		1st die					
		1	2	3	4	5	6
2nd die	1	1, 1	2, 1	3, 1	4, 1	5, 1	6, 1
	2	1, 2	2, 2	3, 2	4, 2	5, 2	6, 2
	3	1, 3	2, 3	3, 3	4, 3	5, 3	6, 3
	4	1, 4	2, 4	3, 4	4, 4	5, 4	6, 4

b 24

c i $\frac{1}{6}$ **ii** $\frac{1}{4}$ **iii** $\frac{1}{2}$ **iv** $\frac{3}{8}$ **v** 0

7 a

		1st die					
		1	2	3	4	5	6
2nd die	1	2	3	4	5	6	7
	2	3	4	5	6	7	8
	3	4	5	6	7	8	9
	4	5	6	7	8	9	10
	5	6	7	8	9	10	11
	6	7	8	9	10	11	12

b i $\frac{1}{9}$ **ii** $\frac{1}{36}$ **iii** $\frac{1}{6}$ **iv** $\frac{1}{2}$

v 0 **vi** $\frac{5}{12}$ **vii** $\frac{7}{12}$ **viii** $\frac{5}{12}$

8 a

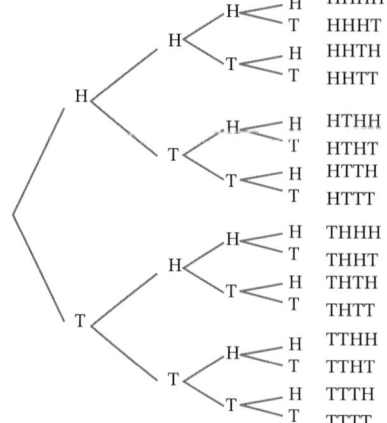

| | 1st coin | 2nd coin | 3rd coin | 4th coin | Outcomes |

(tree diagram with outcomes HHHH, HHHT, HHTH, HHTT, HTHH, HTHT, HTTH, HTTT, THHH, THHT, THTH, THTT, TTHH, TTHT, TTTH, TTTT)

b i $\frac{1}{16}$ **ii** $\frac{1}{4}$ **iii** $\frac{3}{8}$

iv $\frac{15}{16}$ **v** $\frac{1}{16}$ **vi** $\frac{5}{16}$

c i 63 **ii** 375 **iii** 938

9 a

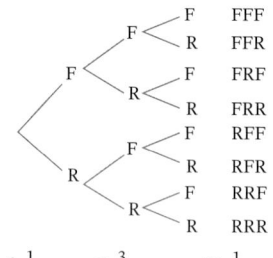

| | Sat | Sun | Mon | Outcomes |

(tree diagram with outcomes FFF, FFR, FRF, FRR, RFF, RFR, RRF, RRR)

b i $\frac{1}{8}$ **ii** $\frac{3}{8}$ **iii** $\frac{1}{8}$ **iv** $\frac{7}{8}$

Mental skills 11

2 a $408 **b** 99 **c** 200 **d** $404

   e 672 **f** $81 **g** $517 **h** 225

   i 560 **j** $84 **k** $350 **l** 84

4 a 330 **b** $240 **c** 1600 **d** $425

   e $225 **f** $60 **g** $63 **h** 76

   i $68 **j** $3762 **k** $374 **l** $100

Exercise 11.05

1 a C = Cate, A = Arushi, L = Lisa, T = Teresa,
W = Wei-June, R − Rekha

		Captain				
		C	A	L	T	W	R
Vice-captain	C	–	AC	LC	TC	WC	RC
	A	CA	–	LA	TA	WA	RA
	L	CL	AL	–	TL	WL	RL
	T	CT	AT	LT	–	WT	RT
	W	CW	AW	LW	TW	–	RW
	R	CR	AR	LR	TR	WR	–

30 possible pairings

b $\frac{1}{3}$ **c** $\frac{1}{6}$

---

2 a i

		2nd card			
		A	B	C	D	E
1st card	A	AA	AB	AC	AD	AE
	B	BA	BB	BC	BD	BE
	C	CA	CB	CC	CD	CE
	D	DA	DB	DC	DD	DE
	E	EA	EB	EC	ED	EE

ii

	A	B	C	D	E
A		AB	AC	AD	AE
B	BA		BC	BD	BE
C	CA	CB		CD	CE
D	DA	DB	DC		DE
E	EA	EB	EC	ED	

b i $\frac{1}{5}$ **ii** $\frac{4}{25}$ **iii** $\frac{12}{25}$

c i $\frac{1}{10}$ **ii** $\frac{3}{5}$ **iii** $\frac{2}{5}$ **iv** $\frac{4}{5}$

3 a

		2nd course			
		B	H	P	S	T
1st course	C	CB	CH	CP	CS	CT
	F	FB	FH	FP	FS	FT
	Y	YB	YH	YP	YS	YT

b i $\frac{1}{3}$ **ii** $\frac{4}{15}$ **iii** $\frac{1}{15}$

4 a

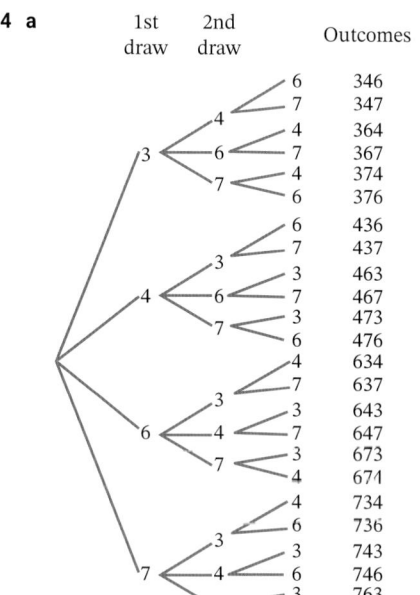

| 1st draw | 2nd draw | | Outcomes |

(tree diagram with outcomes 346, 347, 364, 367, 374, 376, 436, 437, 463, 467, 473, 476, 634, 637, 643, 647, 673, 674, 734, 736, 743, 746, 763, 764)

b i $\frac{1}{2}$ **ii** $\frac{3}{4}$ **iii** $\frac{1}{2}$ **iv** $\frac{1}{3}$

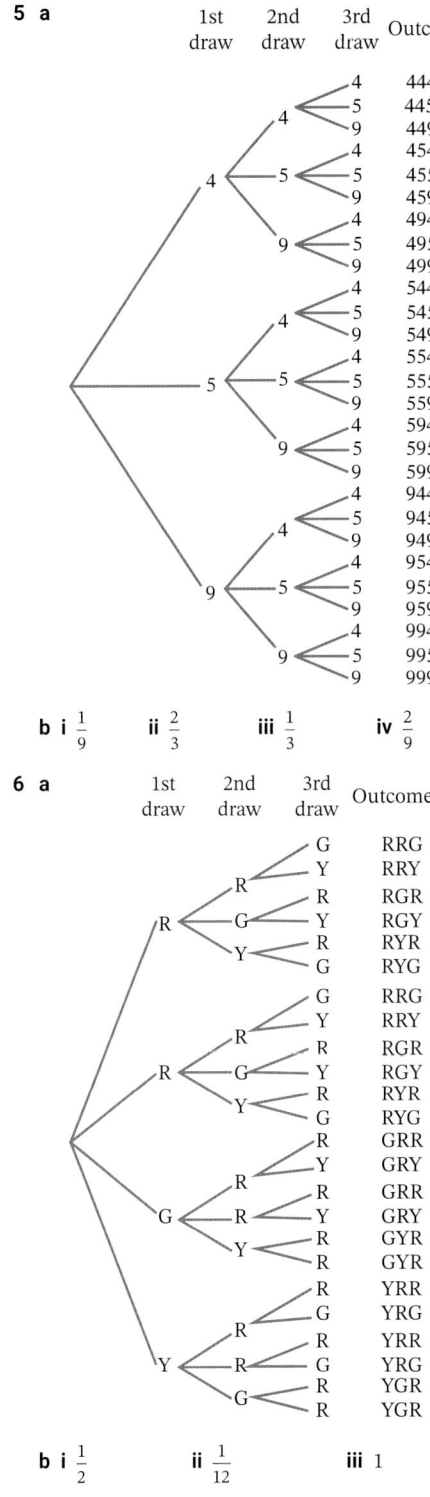

5 a

1st draw	2nd draw	3rd draw	Outcomes
4	4	4	444
		5	445
		9	449
	5	4	454
		5	455
		9	459
	9	4	494
		5	495
		9	499
5	4	4	544
		5	545
		9	549
	5	4	554
		5	555
		9	559
	9	4	594
		5	595
		9	599
9	4	4	944
		5	945
		9	949
	5	4	954
		5	955
		9	959
	9	4	994
		5	995
		9	999

b i $\frac{1}{9}$ **ii** $\frac{2}{3}$ **iii** $\frac{1}{3}$ **iv** $\frac{2}{9}$

6 a

1st draw	2nd draw	3rd draw	Outcomes
R	R	G	RRG
		Y	RRY
	G	R	RGR
		Y	RGY
	Y	R	RYR
		G	RYG
R	R	G	RRG
		Y	RRY
	G	R	RGR
		Y	RGY
	Y	R	RYR
		G	RYG
G	R	R	GRR
		Y	GRY
	R	R	GRR
		Y	GRY
	Y	R	GYR
		R	GYR
Y	R	R	YRR
		G	YRG
	R	R	YRR
		G	YRG
	G	R	YGR
		R	YGR

b i $\frac{1}{2}$ **ii** $\frac{1}{12}$ **iii** 1

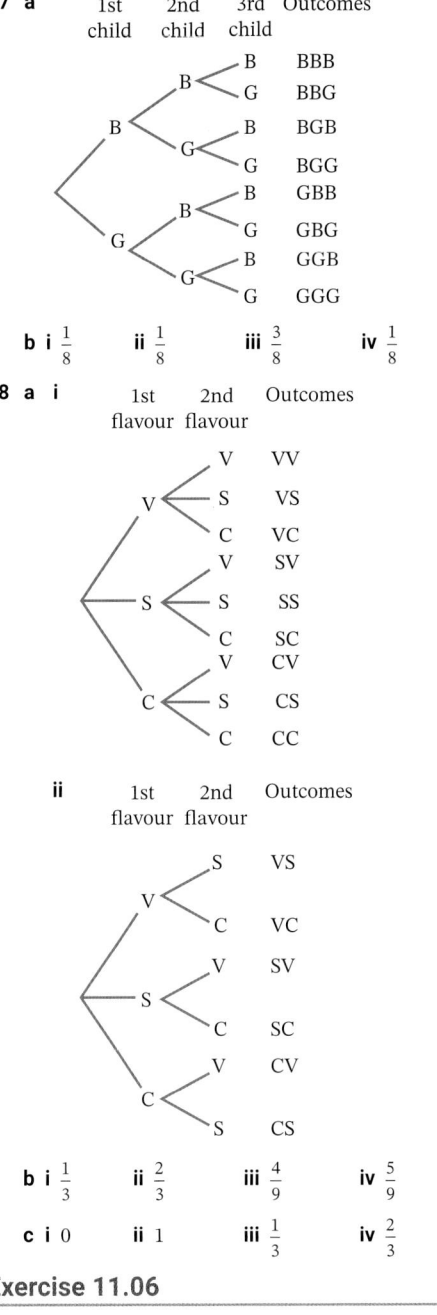

7 a

1st child	2nd child	3rd child	Outcomes
B	B	B	BBB
		G	BBG
	G	B	BGB
		G	BGG
G	B	B	GBB
		G	GBG
	G	B	GGB
		G	GGG

b i $\frac{1}{8}$ **ii** $\frac{1}{8}$ **iii** $\frac{3}{8}$ **iv** $\frac{1}{8}$

8 a i

1st flavour	2nd flavour	Outcomes
V	V	VV
	S	VS
	C	VC
S	V	SV
	S	SS
	C	SC
C	V	CV
	S	CS
	C	CC

ii

1st flavour	2nd flavour	Outcomes
V	S	VS
	C	VC
S	V	SV
	C	SC
C	V	CV
	S	CS

b i $\frac{1}{3}$ **ii** $\frac{2}{3}$ **iii** $\frac{4}{9}$ **iv** $\frac{5}{9}$

c i 0 **ii** 1 **iii** $\frac{1}{3}$ **iv** $\frac{2}{3}$

Exercise 11.06

1 a $\frac{2}{6} = \frac{1}{3}$ **b** $\frac{3}{6} = \frac{1}{2}$ **2** $\frac{2}{9}$

3 a $\frac{4}{11}$ **b** $\frac{7}{11}$

4 a $\frac{2}{11}$ **b** $\frac{4}{11}$ **c** $\frac{4}{11}$ **d** $\frac{5}{11}$

5 $\frac{1}{3}$ **6** $\frac{1}{6}$

7 a

		1st die					
		1	2	3	4	5	6
2nd die	1	2	3	4	5	6	7
	2	3	4	5	6	7	8
	3	4	5	6	7	8	9
	4	5	6	7	8	9	10
	5	6	7	8	9	10	11
	6	7	8	9	10	11	12

b i $\frac{1}{2}$ **ii** 1 **c** $\frac{2}{11}$

d i $\frac{9}{27} = \frac{1}{3}$ **ii** $\frac{6}{27} = \frac{2}{9}$ **e** $\frac{1}{6}$

8 a i $\frac{1}{9}$ **ii** $\frac{8}{9}$ **b** $\frac{2}{8} = \frac{1}{4}$ **c** 6

9 $\frac{1}{40}$ **10** $\frac{10}{49}$ **11** $\frac{1}{13}$ **12** $\frac{1}{6}$

13 a

		1st die					
		1	2	3	4	5	6
2nd die	1	0	1	2	3	4	5
	2	1	0	1	2	3	4
	3	2	1	0	1	2	3
	4	3	2	1	0	1	2
	5	4	3	2	1	0	1
	6	5	4	3	2	1	0

b i $\frac{1}{6}$ **ii** $\frac{1}{18}$ **iii** $\frac{1}{6}$

c i $\frac{1}{2}$ **ii** 0 **d i** $\frac{1}{11}$ **ii** $\frac{4}{11}$

e i $\frac{6}{18} = \frac{1}{3}$ **ii** 1

Exercise 11.07

1 a independent **b** independent **c** dependent
d independent **e** dependent **f** independent
g independent
2 Dependent, as the balls are not replaced when drawn.
3 a independent **b** $\frac{1}{2}$
4 a i $\frac{1}{3}$ **ii** $\frac{1}{4}$
b 1Y, 2Y, 3Y, 4Y, 5Y, 6Y, 1G, 2G, 3G, 4G, 5G, 6G, 1B, 2B, 3B, 4B, 5B, 6B, 1R, 2R, 3R, 4R, 5R, 6R,
c $\frac{1}{12}$ **d** yes, $\frac{1}{3} \times \frac{1}{4} = \frac{1}{12}$
e independent
5 a i $\frac{1}{6}$ **ii** $\frac{1}{2}$
b $\frac{1}{6} \times \frac{1}{2} = \frac{1}{12}$

6 a $\frac{5}{9}$ **b** $\frac{4}{8} = \frac{1}{2}$

c Dependent, as the first draw changes the contents of the bag.

7 a i $\frac{5}{8}$ **ii** $\frac{4}{7}$ **b i** $\frac{3}{8}$ **ii** $\frac{5}{7}$

c i $\frac{5}{8}$ **ii** $\frac{3}{7}$ **d i** $\frac{3}{8}$ **ii** $\frac{2}{7}$

8 $\frac{1}{2}$

9 a $\frac{1}{12}$ **b** $\frac{1}{36}$ **c** $\frac{1}{3}$ **d** $\frac{1}{6}$

10 a $\frac{13}{25}$ **b** $\frac{7}{25}$

11 a 0.15 **b** 0.1 **c** 0.3

12 a 0.147 **b** 0.343 **c** 0.027 **d** 0.189

Exercise 11.08

1 Teacher to check; probability should be around 0.17.
2 Teacher to check; probability should be around 0.35.
3 Teacher to check; expected frequency should be around 667.

4 a $\frac{2}{5}$ **b** Teacher to check

5 a 27.5% **b** Teacher to check

6 a 57% **b** Teacher to check

Exercise 11.09

1 120 **2** 7776 **3** C
4 358 800 **5** 258 336 000 **6** 432 000

7 a $\frac{2}{132} = \frac{1}{66}$ **b** Teacher to check

8 a $\frac{80}{156} = \frac{20}{39}$ **b** Teacher to check

9 a $\frac{560}{13800} = \frac{14}{345}$ **b** Teacher to check

10 a To increase the number of phone numbers available for use due to population increase and the uptake of home phone lines.
b Another 90 000 000 phone numbers were potentially possible

11 $\frac{2304}{10000} = \frac{144}{625}$

Exercise 11.10

1 a 4! **b** 7! **c** 9!
d 12! **e** 3! **f** 6!
2 a 120 **b** 3 628 800 **c** 40 320
d 6 **e** 39 916 800 **f** 5040
3 24 **4** 1 000 000 **5** 5040
6 10 077 696 **7** 390 700 800 **8** 146 611 080
9 30 240 **10** 7980

Exercise 11.11

1 a 6   **b** JF, JI, JD, FI, FD, ID

2 a 10

   b AN, AT, AW, AZ, NT, NW, NZ, TW, TZ, WZ

3 a 10

   b AHJ, AHS, AHT, AJS, AJT, AST, HJS, HJT, HST, SJT

4 28   **5** 2925   **6** 3003

7 60   **8** 38 220   **9** 525

10 116 396 280   **11** 462   **12** 66080

Power plus

1 a 320

   b i $\frac{7}{40} = 0.175$ **ii** $\frac{3}{32} \approx 0.094$

    iii $\frac{57}{320} \approx 0.178$ **iv** $\frac{3}{20} = 0.15$

   c $\frac{16}{45}$ **d** $\frac{45}{107}$

2 a

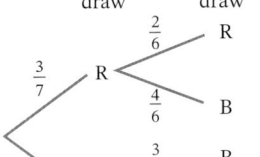

	1st draw	2nd draw	Outcomes

With tree diagram: $\frac{3}{7}$ R; $\frac{4}{7}$ B; $\frac{2}{6}$ R → RR, $\frac{4}{6}$ B → RB, $\frac{3}{6}$ R → BR, $\frac{3}{6}$ B → BB

   b i $\frac{1}{7}$ **ii** $\frac{2}{7}$ **iii** $\frac{4}{7}$ **iv** $\frac{6}{7}$

3 a i $\frac{14}{30} = \frac{7}{15}$ **ii** $\frac{20}{30} = \frac{2}{3}$ **iii** $\frac{4}{30} = \frac{2}{15}$

    iv $\frac{4}{20} = \frac{1}{5}$ **v** $\frac{4}{14} = \frac{2}{7}$

   b i $\frac{\frac{2}{15}}{\frac{2}{3}} = \frac{1}{5}$ **ii** yes

   c $P(B|A) = \frac{2}{7}, \frac{P(A \text{ and } B)}{P(A)} = \frac{\frac{2}{15}}{\frac{7}{15}} = \frac{2}{7}$

TEST YOURSELF 11

1 a i 0.22   **ii** 0.29   **iii** 0.1   **iv** 0.14

   b i 0.25   **ii** 0.25   **iii** 0.125   **iv** 0.125

   c yes   **d** 0.25

   e The expected number of times the arrow stops at a colour that is not purple or black is 75, which is the same as the observed number of times.

2 a i 0.353   **ii** 0.427   **iii** 0.087   **iv** 0.513

   b i 0.867   **ii** 0.133

   c Different – at least one head occurring excludes 0 heads occurring, which is the same as 3 tails occurring. The events are complementary.

3 a 90   **b** $\frac{19}{45}$ **c** $\frac{2}{9}$ **d** $\frac{11}{49}$

4 a

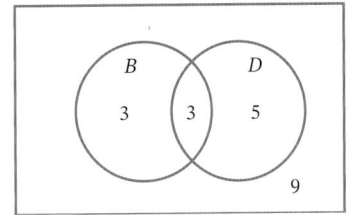

Venn diagram: B and D overlapping. B = 3, intersection = 3, D = 5, outside = 9

   b i $\frac{3}{20}$ **ii** $\frac{2}{5}$ **iii** $\frac{3}{20}$ **iv** $\frac{3}{5}$

   c $\frac{9}{20}$

5 a 200

   b i 0.305   **ii** 0.11   **iii** 0.225   **iv** 0.425

   c $\frac{25}{110} \approx 0.227$ **d i** $\frac{47}{69} \approx 0.681$ **ii** $\frac{22}{69} \approx 0.319$

6 D

7 a

		1st die		
	1	**2**	**3**	**4**
1	1, 1	2, 1	3, 1	4, 1
2	1, 2	2, 2	3, 2	4, 2
3	1, 3	2, 3	3, 3	4, 3
4	1, 4	2, 4	3, 4	4, 4

(2nd die on left axis)

   b 16

   c i $\frac{1}{2}$ **ii** $\frac{1}{4}$ **iii** $\frac{7}{16}$

    iv $\frac{1}{4}$ **v** $\frac{1}{4}$ **vi** $\frac{1}{2}$

8 a i RR, RB, RG, RY, RBla, BR, BB, BG, BY, BBla, GR, GB, GG, GY, GBla, YR, YB, YG, YY, YBla, BlaR, BlaB, BlaG, BlaY, BlaBla

    ii RB, RG, RY, RBla, BR, BG, BY, BBla, GR, GB, GY, GBla, YR, YB, YG, YBla, BlaR, BlaB, BlaG, BlaY

   b i $\frac{1}{25}$ **ii** $\frac{1}{5}$ **iii** $\frac{2}{25}$ **iv** $\frac{9}{25}$

   c i $\frac{1}{10}$ **ii** $\frac{3}{5}$

9 a i

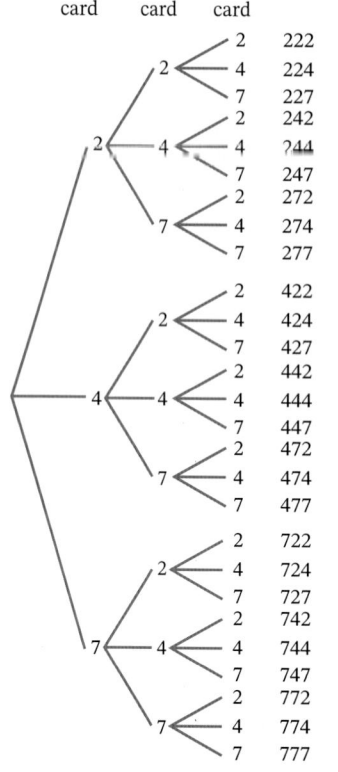

1st card	2nd card	3rd card	Outcomes
2	2	2	222
		4	224
		7	227
	4	2	242
		4	244
		7	247
	7	2	272
		4	274
		7	277
4	2	2	422
		4	424
		7	427
	4	2	442
		4	444
		7	447
	7	2	472
		4	474
		7	477
7	2	2	722
		4	724
		7	727
	4	2	742
		4	744
		7	747
	7	2	772
		4	774
		7	777

ii

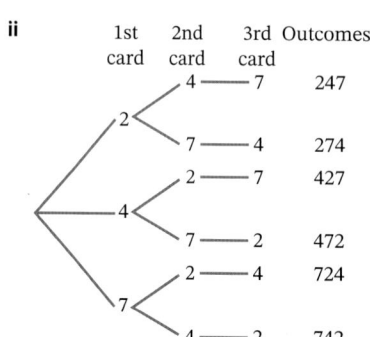

1st card	2nd card	3rd card	Outcomes
2	4	7	247
	7	4	274
4	2	7	427
	7	2	472
7	2	4	724
	4	2	742

b i $\frac{2}{3}$ **ii** $\frac{1}{3}$ **iii** $\frac{1}{9}$ **iv** $\frac{2}{9}$

c i $\frac{1}{3}$ **ii** $\frac{2}{3}$ **iii** $\frac{1}{3}$ **iv** $\frac{1}{3}$

10 a

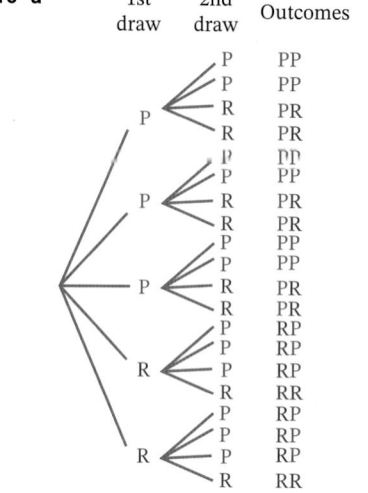

1st draw	2nd draw	Outcomes
P	P	PP
	P	PP
	R	PR
	R	PR
	P	PP
	P	PP
	R	PR
	R	PR
	P	PP
	P	PP
	R	PR
	R	PR
R	P	RP
	P	RP
	P	RP
	R	RR
	P	RP
	P	RP
	P	RP
	R	RR

b i $\frac{1}{2}$ **ii** $\frac{1}{2}$ **c i** $\frac{1}{4}$ **ii** $\frac{3}{4}$

d i $\frac{1}{4}$ **ii** $\frac{3}{4}$

11 a

		1st die			
		1	**2**	**3**	**4**
2nd die	**1**	2	3	4	5
	2	3	4	5	6
	3	4	5	6	7
	4	5	6	7	8

b i $\frac{1}{2}$ **ii** 1 **c** $\frac{2}{7}$

d i $\frac{1}{3}$ **ii** $\frac{1}{3}$ **e** $\frac{1}{4}$

12 a independent **b** dependent **c** dependent
d independent **e** dependent **f** independent
13 Teacher to check; probability should be around 0.36.

14 240
15 5040
16 a 10 **b** BC, BJ, BN, BS, CJ, CN, CS, JN, JS, NS

CHAPTER 12

SkillCheck

1 a $w = 38$ **b** $r = 44$ **c** $h = 71$
 d $x = 126$ **e** $y = 46$ **f** $a = 24$
2 A and G, C and J, D and F, H and I
3 a $p = 64$ **b** $p = 241$ **c** $p = 104$
 d $p = 105$ **e** $p = 58$ **f** $p = 128$
4 a $\angle M$ and $\angle X$, $\angle N$ and $\angle Y$, $\angle P$ and $\angle W$
 b MN and XY, NP and YW, MP and XW

Exercise 12.01

1 a $\triangle AXT \equiv \triangle GYE$ (RHS)

b $\triangle MVR \equiv \triangle SPC$ (SSS)

c $\triangle BTV \equiv \triangle PSX$ (AAS)

d $\triangle CNQ \equiv \triangle DCE$ (SAS)

2 In $\triangle WXY$ and $\triangle WZY$

$\angle X = \angle Z = 90°$ (given)

$XY = ZY$ (given)

WY is common.

$\therefore \triangle WXY \equiv \triangle WZY$ (RHS)

3 In $\triangle DEH$ and $\triangle FEG$

$\angle D = \angle F$ (alternate angles, $HD \parallel GF$)

$\angle H = \angle G$ (alternate angles, $HD \parallel GF$)

$EH = EG$ (given)

$\therefore \triangle DEH \equiv \triangle FEG$ (AAS)

4 In $\triangle ABC$ and $\triangle ADC$

$BC = DC$ (given)

$AB = AD$ (given)

AC is common.

$\therefore \triangle ABC \equiv \triangle ADC$ (SSS)

5–15 Proofs: see worked solutions

Exercise 12.02

1 In $\triangle LMP$ and $\triangle NPM$

$LM = NP$ (given)

PM is common

$\angle LMP = \angle NPM$ (alternate angles, $LM \parallel NP$)

$\therefore \triangle LMP \equiv \triangle NPM$ (SAS)

$\angle LPM = \angle NMP$ (matching angles of congruent triangles)

$\therefore LP \parallel NM$ (alternate angles are equal)

$\therefore LMNP$ is a parallelogram (opposite sides are parallel).

2 In $\triangle DXH$ and $\triangle GXE$

$\angle DXH = \angle GXE$ (vertically opposite angles)

$HX = EX$ (given)

$DX = GX$ (given)

$\therefore \triangle DXH \equiv \triangle GXE$ (SAS)

$\angle HDX = \angle EGX$ (matching angles of congruent triangles)

$\therefore HD \parallel EG$ (alternate angles are equal)

Similarly, $\angle GHX = \angle DEX$ (matching angles of congruent triangles HXG and EXD)

$\therefore HG \parallel ED$ (alternate angles are equal)

$\therefore DEGH$ is a parallelogram (opposite sides are parallel).

3 $\triangle FHC \equiv \triangle FHE \equiv \triangle DHE \equiv \triangle DHC$ (SAS)

$\therefore FC = FE = DE = DC$ (matching sides of congruent triangles)

Also, $\angle CFH = \angle EDH$ and $\angle CDH = \angle EFH$ (matching angles of congruent triangles)

$\therefore CDEF$ is a rhombus (opposite sides are parallel and all sides are equal).

4 $\angle A = \angle C$ and $\angle B = \angle D$

Now $\angle A + \angle C + \angle B + \angle D = 360°$ (angle sum of a quadrilateral)

$\therefore 2\angle A + 2\angle B = 360°$ ($\angle C = \angle A$, $\angle D = \angle B$)

$\therefore \angle A + \angle B = 180°$

$\therefore AD \parallel BC$ (co-interior angles are supplementary)

Also, from $\angle A + \angle C + \angle B + \angle D = 360°$ (angle sum of a quadrilateral)

$\therefore 2\angle A + 2\angle D = 360°$ ($\angle C = \angle A$, $\angle B = \angle D$)

$\therefore \angle A + \angle D = 180°$

$\therefore AB \parallel DC$ (co-interior angles are supplementary)

$\therefore ABCD$ is a parallelogram (opposite sides are parallel).

5–16 See worked solutions for proofs for remaining questions.

Exercise 12.03

1 a SSS

b $\angle ADB = \angle ADC$ (matching angles of congruent triangles)

c $\angle ADB + \angle ADC = 180°$ (angles on a line)

$\therefore \angle ADB = \angle ADC = 90°$

$\therefore AD \perp BC$

2 a AAS

b $WS = WT$ (matching sides of congruent triangles)

c A triangle with 2 equal angles is isosceles (has 2 equal sides) and the equal sides are the sides opposite the equal angles.

3 a $\triangle ABX \equiv \triangle ACX$ (SSS)

b $\angle B = \angle C$ (matching angles of congruent triangles)

c $\triangle BAY \equiv \triangle BCY$ (SSS)

d $\angle A = \angle C$ (matching angles of congruent triangles)

e Since $\angle B = \angle C$, $\angle A = \angle C$,

$\angle A = \angle B = \angle C$

$\angle A + \angle B + \angle C = 180°$ (angle sum of a triangle)

$\therefore \angle A = \angle B = \angle C = 60°$

f Each angle in an equilateral triangle is 60°.

4 a $\angle MPY = \angle NPY$ (PY bisects $\angle MPN$)

b $\triangle PMY \equiv \triangle PNY$ (AAS)

c $MY = NY$ (matching sides of congruent triangles)

d $\angle PYM = \angle PYN$ (matching angles of congruent triangles)

e $\angle PYM + \angle PYN = 180°$ (angles on a straight line)

$\therefore \angle PYM = \angle PYN = 90°$

$\therefore PY \perp MN$

5 a Proof: see worked solutions

b $\angle BAC = \angle DCA$ (matching angles of congruent triangles)

$\angle BCA = \angle DAC$ (matching angles of congruent triangles)

c $\therefore AB \parallel CD$ and $AD \parallel BC$ (alternate angles are equal)

d $ABCD$ is a parallelogram since opposite sides are parallel.

6 b

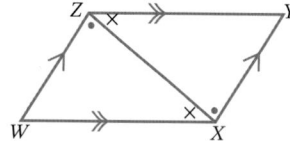

c Proof: see worked solutions

d $\angle W = \angle Y$ (matching angles of congruent triangles)

e Proof: see worked solutions

f $\angle WXY = \angle YZW$ (matching angles of congruent triangles)

g Opposite angles of a parallelogram are equal.

7 a Proof: see worked solutions

b $\angle VUS = \angle TUS$ (matching angles of congruent triangles)

$\angle VSU = \angle TSU$ (matching angles of congruent triangles)

∴ VS bisects $\angle VUT$ and $\angle VST$.

8 a Proof: see worked solutions

b $AD = CB$ (matching sides of congruent triangles)

$AB = CD$ (matching sides of congruent triangles)

c ∴ opposite sides of a parallelogram are equal.

9 a Proof: see worked solutions

b $BL = GL$ (matching sides of congruent triangles)

$EL = HL$ (matching sides of congruent triangles)

∴ diagonals of a rhombus bisect each other.

c A

d Proof: see worked solutions

e $\angle BLE = \angle BLH$ (matching angles of congruent triangles)

and $\angle BLE + \angle BLH = 180°$ (angles on a straight line)

∴ $\angle BLE = \angle BLH = 90°$

∴ the diagonals of a rhombus are at right angles.

10 a Proof: see worked solutions

b $\angle A = \angle C$ (matching angles of congruent triangles)

c $\angle ADB = \angle CDB$ (matching angles of congruent triangles)

$\angle ABD = \angle CBD$ (matching angles of congruent triangles)

∴ DB bisects $\angle ADB$ and $\angle ABC$.

d

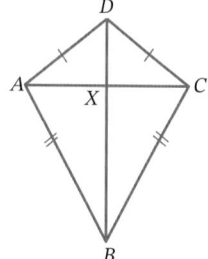

e Proof: see worked solutions

f $AX = CX$ (matching sides of congruent triangles)

∴ X is the midpoint of AC so diagonal DB bisects diagonal AC.

g $\angle AXD = \angle CXD$ (matching angles of congruent triangles)

and $\angle AXD + \angle CXD = 180°$ (angles on a straight line)

∴ $\angle AXD = \angle CXD = 90°$

∴ $DX \perp AC$

∴ $BD \perp AC$

Mental skills 12

2 a $100, $50   **b** $1200, $900   **c** $160, $560

d $500, $1500   **e** $2700, $1800   **f** $900, $2100

g $3000, $600   **h** $600, $1000   **i** $550, $440

j $800, $3200   **k** $2100, $2800   **l** $2000, $1200

Exercise 12.04

See worked solutions for full proofs.

Exercise 12.05

1 a 2   **b** $\dfrac{2}{3}$ **c** $\dfrac{4}{5}$ **d** $2\dfrac{1}{2}$

2 a

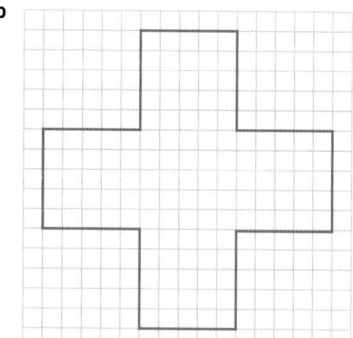

b

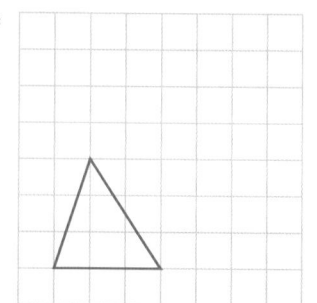

c

d

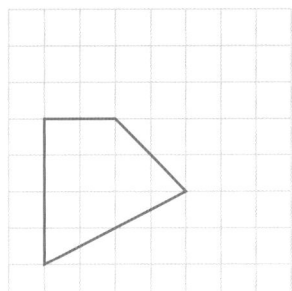

3 a i ∠A and ∠L, ∠B and ∠M, ∠C and ∠K.
   ii AC and LK, AB and LM, BC and MK.
   iii △ABC ||| △LMK

b i ∠W and ∠D, ∠X and ∠E, ∠Y and ∠G, ∠Z and ∠H.
   ii WX and DE, XY and EG, YZ and GH, WZ and DH.
   iii WXYZ ||| DEGH

c i ∠T and ∠F, ∠R and ∠W, ∠P and ∠V, ∠M and ∠S, ∠J and ∠K.
   ii TR and FW, RP and WV, PM and VS, MJ and SK, TJ and FK.
   iii TRPMJ ||| FWVSK

d i ∠Q and ∠N, ∠K and ∠C, ∠B and ∠G.
   ii QB and NG, BK and GC, KQ and CN.
   iii △QKB ||| △NCG

4 a yes, $\frac{8}{12} = \frac{20}{30} = \frac{2}{3}$ **b** yes, $\frac{12}{20} = \frac{27}{45} = \frac{21}{35} = \frac{3}{5}$

c yes, $\frac{4}{6} = \frac{6}{9} = \frac{6\frac{2}{3}}{10} = \frac{10}{15} = \frac{2}{3}$

d yes, all squares are similar.
e yes, matching angles are equal.
f yes, all equilateral triangles are similar.

Exercise 12.06

1 1 : 3   **2** 1 : 2   **3** 1 : 20
4 3 : 5   **5** 80 km   **6** 18 km
7 900 km   **8** 350 m   **9** 7 m
10 5.5 m   **11** length = 4 m, width = 3 m
12 length = 20 cm, width = 16 cm   **13** 8 cm

Exercise 12.07

1 a w = 22.4   **b** m = 10
   c p = 20, h = 21   **d** x = 18
   e a = 12.8, w = 7.5   **f** $g = 11\frac{1}{9}$, q = 18
   g $y = 26\frac{2}{3}$, $b = 9\frac{3}{5}$ or 9.6
   h $u = 12\frac{4}{5}$ or 12.8, $t = 6\frac{7}{8}$ or 6.875
2 $h = 13\frac{5}{7}$ **3** $x = 8\frac{8}{9}$
4 w = 16 cm   **5** 12 m   **6** B
7 h = 2.408 m   **8** D   **9** 2.24 m

Exercise 12.08

1 a 2 pairs of angles are equal (AA).
   b All 3 pairs of matching sides are in the same ratio, $\frac{9}{18} = \frac{11}{22} = \frac{15.5}{31} = \frac{1}{2}$ (SSS).
   c 2 pairs of matching sides are in the same ratio $\frac{6}{8} = \frac{12}{16} = \frac{3}{4}$ and the included angles are equal (SAS).
   d 2 pairs of angles are equal (AA).
   e All 3 pairs of matching sides are in the same ratio $\frac{9}{12} = \frac{9}{12} = \frac{14.25}{19} = \frac{3}{4}$ (SSS).
   f In both right-angled triangles, the pairs of hypotenuses and second sides are in the same ratio $\frac{12}{15} = \frac{20.8}{26} = \frac{4}{5}$ (RHS).
   g 2 pairs of angles are equal (AA).
   h All 3 pairs of matching sides are in the same ratio $\frac{18}{14.4} = \frac{27.5}{22} = \frac{20}{16} = \frac{5}{4}$ (SSS).
   i All 2 pairs of matching sides are in the same ratio $\frac{6}{8} = \frac{8}{10\frac{2}{3}} = \frac{10}{13\frac{1}{3}} = \frac{3}{4}$ (SSS).
   j 2 pairs of matching sides are in the same ratio $\frac{26}{18.2} = \frac{30}{21} = \frac{10}{7}$, and the included angles are equal (SAS).

2 a △UWY ||| △HEK (SAS)
   b △DML ||| △TPA (RHS)
   c △ABC ||| △QTP (AA)
   d △GHN ||| △WVS (SSS)

3 a In △CHT and △MBP:
   ∠C = ∠M = 90° (given)
   $\frac{HT}{BP} = \frac{25}{15} = 1\frac{2}{3}$
   $\frac{CT}{MP} = \frac{18}{10.8} = 1\frac{2}{3}$
   $\therefore \frac{HT}{BP} = \frac{CT}{MP} = 1\frac{2}{3}$
   △CHT ||| △MBP (both right triangles, hypotenuse and one pair of matching sides in proportion, or 'RHS')

b In △GVW and △LQE:
   ∠V = ∠L = 22° (given)
   ∠W = ∠Q = 123° (given)
   △GVW ||| △LQE (two pairs of matching angles are equal, or 'AA')

c In △ABC and △TWM:
   $\frac{TW}{AB} = \frac{25.5}{17} = 1\frac{1}{2}$
   $\frac{WM}{BC} = \frac{24}{16} = 1\frac{1}{2}$
   $\frac{CA}{MT} = \frac{18}{12} = 1\frac{1}{2}$
   $\therefore \frac{TW}{AB} = \frac{WM}{BC} = \frac{CA}{MT} = 1\frac{1}{2}$

$\triangle ABC \,|||\, \triangle TWM$ (3 pairs of matching sides in proportion, or 'SSS')

d In $\triangle EHV$ and $\triangle DNL$:

$\angle V = \angle N = 90°$ (given)

$\dfrac{EV}{DN} = \dfrac{21}{12} = 1\dfrac{3}{4}$

$\dfrac{VH}{NL} = \dfrac{35}{20} = 1\dfrac{3}{4}$

$\therefore \dfrac{EV}{DN} = \dfrac{VH}{NL} = 1\dfrac{3}{4}$

$\triangle EHV \,|||\, \triangle DNL$ (both right triangles, hypotenuse and one pair of matching sides in proportion, or 'RHS')

For questions 4 – 18, see worked solutions for complete proofs.

4 In $\triangle ADE$ and $\triangle ABC$

(D is the midpoint of AB)

(E is the midpoint of AC)

A is common

5 $AFB = FED$ (corresponding angles, $BF \parallel CE$)

$ABF = ACE$ (corresponding angles, $BF \parallel CE$)

$ACE = FDE$ (corresponding angles, $AC \parallel FD$)

$\therefore ABF \,|||\, FDE$

6 $WXY = TXW = 90°$ (given)

$YWX = 90° - WYX$ (angle sum of $\triangle WXY$)

$XTW = 90° - WXY$ (angle sum of $\triangle WTY$)

$= YWX$

7 N is common

8 $HWX = YXW$ (alternate angles, $HW \parallel YX$)

9 $NML = KLP$ (alternate angles, $NM \parallel LK$)

$LNM = PKL$ (opposite angles of a parallelogram)

10 a $FLN = FDE$ (corresponding angles, $LN \parallel DE$)

F is common

b $d = 9$

11 a $EAC = DBC = 90°$ (given)

C is common

b $y = 5\dfrac{5}{11}$

12 a $YRT = WUT = 90°$ (given)

$YTR = WTU$ (vertically opposite angles)

b $g = 15$

13 a $NMP = PCB = 90°$ (given)

$MNP = CPB$ (corresponding angles, $TN \parallel CP$)

b $w = 7.5$

14 a $TYN = MNY$ (alternate angles, $TY \parallel MN$)

$TNY = YMN$ (given)

b $h = 12$

15 a $BUH = XBD$ (given)

$UBH = DXB$ (alternate angles, $BU \parallel DX$)

b $y = 18$

16 a $GMX = LKX$ (alternate angles, $MG \parallel LH$)

$MGX = KLX$ (alternate angles, $MG \parallel LH$)

b $x = 16$

17 a $CWL = TEL = 90°$ (given)

L is common

b $TL = 9$ cm

18 a $PUT = KPB$ (alternate angles, $PK \parallel TU$)

$PTU = KBP = 90°$ (given)

b $PB = 4$ cm

Exercise 12.09

1 a $9:1$ **b** $9:25$ **c** $81:25$ **d** $4:9$

2 a $3:5$ **b** $1:10$ **c** $8:5$ **d** $4:9$

3 a 3.5 **b** 18 **c** 48 **d** 36.75

4 54 cm² **5** 44.1 cm² **6** 7.5 cm **7** 154 cm

8 The area is quadrupled ($\times 4$).

9 The sides are decreased by a factor of 3.

10 The area has increased by a factor of 6.25.

11 The sides have decreased by a factor of $\dfrac{1}{10}$.

Exercise 12.10

1 a i $9:25$ **ii** $125:27$

b i $4:9$ **ii** $27:8$

c i $16:25$ **ii** $125:64$ **d i** $4:25$ **ii** $125:8$

2 a $9:10$ **b** $729:1000$

3 a $5:7$ **b** $25:49$

4 $76\,800$ mm³ **5** 75.6 mL

6 2531.25 g or 2.531 kg **7** 78 L

8 a 2.25 **b** 3.375

9 There has been a $\dfrac{27}{64}$ decrease in the volume.

Power plus

1 a Angles opposite equal sides of isosceles $\triangle KMR$ are equal.

b Proof: see worked solutions

c $KN = KP$ (matching sides of congruent triangles)

$\therefore \triangle KNP$ is isosceles (2 sides equal)

2 $x = 8$

3 Proofs: see worked solutions

4 a 2 pairs of angles are equal (AA).

b $y = 5\dfrac{1}{7}$

TEST YOURSELF 12

1 a SAS **b** AAS **c** SAS

2 Proofs: see worked solutions

3 a, b Proofs: see worked solutions

4 a $\triangle PML \equiv \triangle NLM$ (SAS)

b $PM = NL$ (matching sides of congruent triangles)

c The diagonals of a rectangle are equal.

5 Prove $\triangle NMA \equiv \triangle PQB$ (SAS).

$\therefore \angle CAB = \angle CBA$

$\therefore AC = BC$ (sides opposite the equal angles in isosceles $\triangle CBA$)

Also, $NA = PB$ (matching sides of congruent triangles)

$\therefore NC = NA + AC = PB + BC = PC$

6 a yes, $\dfrac{18}{27} = \dfrac{10}{15} = \dfrac{2}{3}$

b yes, $\left(\dfrac{9}{11.25} = \dfrac{12}{15} = \dfrac{22}{27.5} = \dfrac{16}{20} = \dfrac{4}{5}\right)$

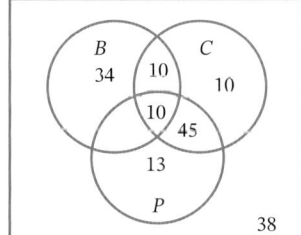

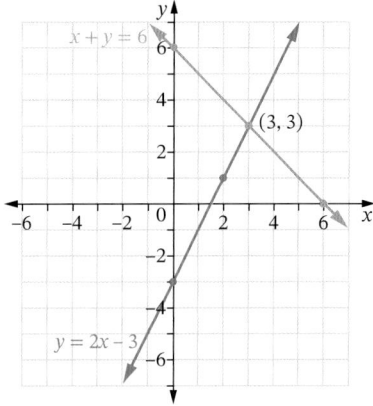

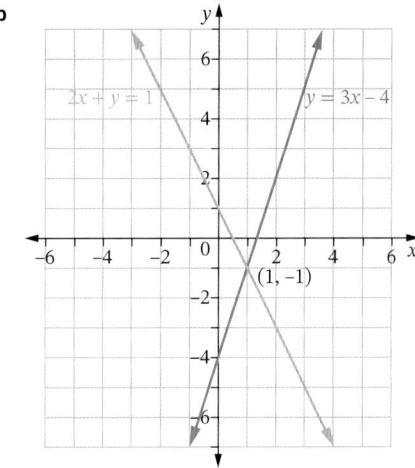

7 1.2 km

8 5 m, it will be close to wide enough but it may be difficult to get out of the cars

9 a $k = 12\frac{6}{7}$ **b** $d = 6$

c $y = 4\frac{1}{5}$ or 4.2 **d** $x = 5\frac{1}{2}$ or 5.5

10 2 : 3 **11** $d = 11\frac{3}{7}$

12 a 2 pairs of matching sides are in the same ratio $\frac{18}{13.5} = \frac{20}{15} = \frac{4}{3}$ and the included angles are equal (SAS).

b In both right-angled triangles, the pairs of hypotenuses and second sides are in the same ratio $\frac{16\frac{2}{3}}{30} = \frac{10}{18} = \frac{5}{9}$ (RHS)

c 2 pairs of angles are equal (AA).

13 For $\triangle ASB$ and $\triangle RST$

$\angle SBA = \angle STR$ (corresponding angles)

$\angle SAB = \angle SRT$ (corresponding angles)

$\triangle ASB \,|||\, \triangle RST$ (AA)

$x = 4.8, y = 9.6$

14 a 234.4 cm² **b** 6.25

15 a 45.5625 cm³ **b** 36 : 49

PRACTICE SET 4

1 a 36 **b i** $\frac{1}{36}$ **ii** $\frac{1}{6}$ **iii** $\frac{1}{4}$

2 a 80

b i $\frac{13}{80}$ **ii** $\frac{36}{80} = \frac{9}{20}$ **iii** $\frac{42}{80} = \frac{21}{40}$ **iv** $\frac{56}{80} = \frac{7}{10}$

c $\frac{1}{6} = 0.1\dot{6}$, which is lower than the experimental probability of $\frac{17}{80} = 0.2125$

3 a

b i $\frac{13}{160}$ **ii** $\frac{19}{80}$ **iii** $\frac{9}{32}$

iv $\frac{109}{160}$ **v** $\frac{57}{160}$

c $\frac{5}{27}$

4 a 78

b i $\frac{25}{39}$ **ii** $\frac{14}{39}$

c $\frac{35}{78}$

5 independent

6 a $\frac{1}{4}$ or 0.25 **b** $\frac{5}{4}$ or 1.25

7 a i 0.39 **ii** 0.43 **iii** 0.18

b i 0.33 **ii** 0.42 **iii** 0.25

c drawing a black marble

d 88, which is close to the observed frequency of 85

8 Proofs: see worked solutions

9 a

$x = 3, y = 3$

b

$x = 1, y = -1$

10 a

	1	2	3	4	5	6
1	1	2	3	4	5	6
2	2	4	6	8	10	12
3	3	6	9	12	15	18
4	4	8	12	16	20	24

b i $\frac{1}{24}$ **ii** $\frac{1}{8}$ **iii** $\frac{1}{4}$

iv $\frac{1}{3}$ **v** $\frac{5}{8}$ **vi** $\frac{7}{24}$

11 Proofs: see worked solutions

12 a 135 **b** $\frac{40}{135} = \frac{8}{27}$

c i $\frac{67}{135}$ **ii** $\frac{60}{135} = \frac{4}{9}$ **iii** $\frac{72}{135} = \frac{8}{15}$

13 a $h = 5\frac{1}{3}$ **b** $p = 35$

14 a

Outcomes

- 2 → 3 → 4 (234), 5 (235); 4 → 3 (243), 5 (245); 5 → 3 (253), 4 (254)
- 3 → 2 → 4 (324), 5 (325); 4 → 2 (342), 5 (345); 5 → 2 (352), 4 (354)
- 4 → 2 → 3 (423), 5 (425); 3 → 2 (432), 5 (435); 5 → 2 (452), 3 (453)
- 5 → 2 → 3 (523), 4 (524); 3 → 2 (532), 4 (534); 4 → 2 (542), 3 (543)

b i $\frac{1}{2}$ **ii** $\frac{1}{4}$ **iii** $\frac{1}{2}$ **iv** $\frac{3}{4}$ **v** $\frac{1}{4}$

15 a $A + C = 395, 20A + 15C = 6700$
b 240 children

16 a i $\frac{2}{5}$ **ii** $\frac{1}{2}$
b Dependent, as the sample space has reduced from 5 to 4.
c Independent, as the number of marbles in the bag remains the same.

17 a $g = 2, w = -1$ **b** $f = 3, y = 3$
c $a = -1, c = -2$

18 10.6

19 Proof: see worked solutions.

20 a

	1	2	3	4	5	6
1	1	2	3	4	5	6
2	2	4	6	8	10	12
3	3	6	9	12	15	18
4	4	8	12	16	20	24
5	5	10	15	20	25	30
6	6	12	18	24	30	36

b $\frac{5}{11}$

c i 1 **ii** 0 **d** $\frac{1}{2}$ **e** 1

21 a $\angle YXV = \angle WVX, \angle XYW = \angle VWY$
b Opposite sides of a rectangle are equal.
c AAS
d Matching sides of congruent triangles are equal.
e The diagonals of a rectangle bisect each other.

22 a $x = 2\frac{1}{2}, y = 5\frac{1}{2}$ **b** $w = 2, p = 1$
c $g = \frac{1}{2}, k = 3$

23 40 cm **24** 9
25 Proofs: see worked solutions. **26** 1000 cm²
27 a $\angle ABW = \angle CDW$ (alternate angles, $AB \parallel CD$)
  $\angle BAW = \angle DCW$ (alternate angles, $AB \parallel CD$)
b $CW = 4\frac{5}{7}$

GENERAL PRACTICE

1 $15 700
2 a $m = 3, c = -4$ **b** $m = -2, c = 5$
c $m = -\frac{4}{3}, c = 3$
3 a 4 **b** 2.5
4 a $8x(x + 2)$ **b** $(y + 5)(y - 5)$
c $(a + 4)(a + 2)$ **d** $-2(p + 1)(p - 3)$
5 a 396 mm² **b** 3750 mm² **c** 6792 mm²
6 $F = 7, V = 4, F + V = 11, E + 2 = 11$, so there are 9 edges.
7 $x = \frac{1}{2}, y = 6\frac{1}{2}$
8 a $56x^{12}$ **b** $\frac{x^5}{4}$ **c** $\frac{1}{9y^2}$ **d** $\frac{n}{m^7}$
9 a 210 **b i** $\frac{1}{6}$ **ii** $\frac{143}{210}$
c 32% **d** $\frac{29}{36}$
10 a 6.4 **b** 15.6 **c** 110.6
d 13.7 **e** 3.3 **f** 32.1
11 a 360 498 mm³ **b** 145 125 mm³
12 a 12.1 m² **b** 22.6 m²
13 a 4 **b** 3 h **c** 75%
14 Proofs: see worked solutions
15 a $y \geq -1$

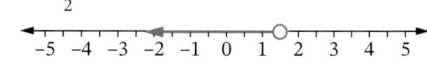

b $x < 1\frac{1}{2}$

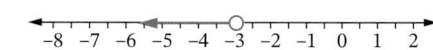

c $x < -3$

16 a i $\frac{1}{8}$ **ii** $\frac{3}{2}$ **iii** $y = \frac{x}{8} + \frac{3}{2}$
b i -1 **ii** -2 **iii** $y = -x - 2$
c i 2 **ii** 1 **iii** $y = 2x + 1$
17 a $x = 2, y = 2$ **b** $m = 1, p = -1$
18 Yes, as it has no odd vertices.
19 $x^2 + y^2 = 64$ **20 a** $40 **b** $4.08
21 a 25° **b** 81° **c** 35°
22 a $935.89 **b** $1597.98
23 a i 8.9 **ii** (4, 5) **iii** 2
b i 13.4 **ii** (-1, 1) **iii** $\frac{1}{2}$
24 a i 35° **ii** 35° 30′
b i 35° **ii** 35° 26′
c i 43° **ii** 43° 21′

24 a

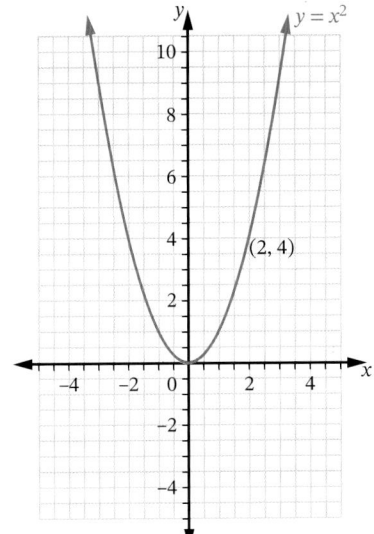

b

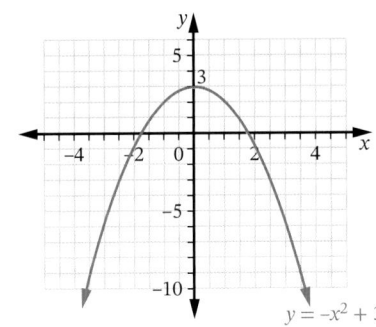

$y = -x^2 + 3$

c

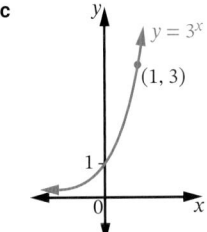

26 $h = 21, p = 20$ **27** D

28 $1174.66, $3775.34

29 2, 4.5, 7, 9, 13

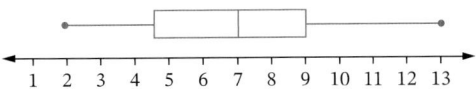

30 a   F = fine, R = rain

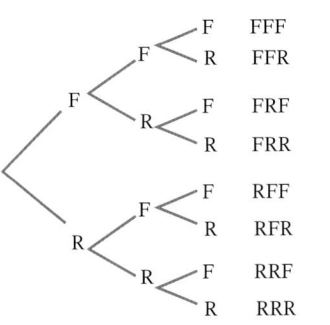

b i $\frac{1}{8}$ **ii** $\frac{3}{8}$ **iii** $\frac{7}{8}$

31 19.2 min

32 x-intercepts at $-2\frac{1}{2}$ and 3, y-intercept at -15

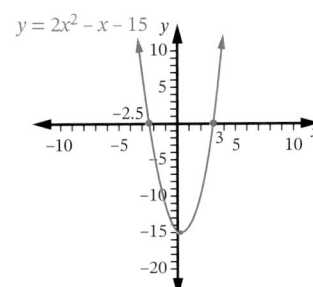

33 $7\sqrt{2}$ **34** $\frac{3\sqrt{10}}{10}$

35 $\theta = 141° 15'$

36 $d = 19.1$

37 a -1 **b** 4   **c** $\frac{1}{2}$

38 a 5   **b** 1   **c** -3

Note: Answers to Chapters 13 to 16 online.

Glossary and index

absolute error The difference between a measured value and its actual value. (p. 51)

adjacent side In a right-angled triangle, the side 'next to' the given angle, leading to the right angle. (p. 373)

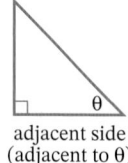

adjacent side
(adjacent to θ)

allowable (tax) deduction A part of a person's yearly income that is not taxed, such as work-related expenses or donations to charities. All deductions are subtracted from yearly income to determine **taxable income**. (p. 121)

angle of depression The angle of looking down, measured from the horizontal. (p. 374)

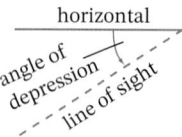

angle of elevation The angle of looking up, measured from the horizontal. (p. 374)

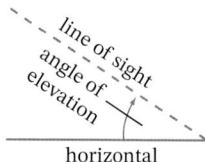

angle of inclination The angle that a line makes with the *x*-axis in the positive direction. (p. 9)

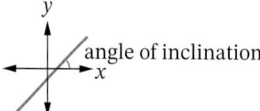

annual leave loading (or **holiday loading**) Extra payment to a worker during annual leave based on 17.5% of 4 weeks' pay. (p. 116)

annulus A ring shape between 2 different-sized circles with the same centre. (p. 62)

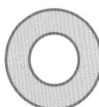

asymptote A line that a curve gets very close to but never touches; for example, the *x* axis is an asymptote of the exponential curve $y = 4^x$. (p. 337)

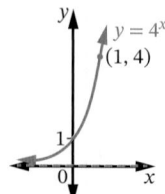

average *See* **mean**.

base (in index notation) When a number is raised to a power, the number raised is the base. In the expression 3^5, the 3 is the base.

bearing The angle used to show the direction of one location from a given point. *See also* **compass bearing** and **three-figure bearing**. (p. 378)

bias In statistics, something that causes a sample to not truly represent the population. (p. 247)

bisect To cut in half.

bimodal distribution A statistical distribution that has 2 peaks.

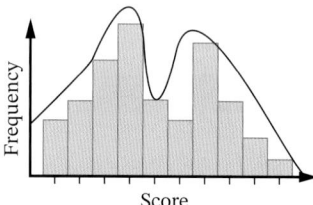

binomial expression An algebraic expression with 2 terms; for example, $x + 9$, $2y - 12$. (p. 162)

bivariate data Data that measures 2 variables, such as a person's height and arm span, represented by an ordered pair of values that can be graphed on a **scatterplot** for analysis. (p. 254)

boxplot (or **box-and-whisker plot**) A graph that shows the quartiles of a set of data and the highest and lowest values; the 'box' contains the middle 50% of values and the 'whiskers' extend to the 2 extremes. (p. 206)

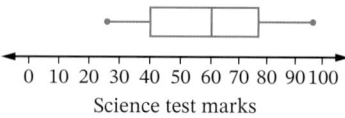

Science test marks

C

capacity The amount of material (usually liquid) that a container can hold, measured in millilitres (mL), litres (L), kilolitres (kL) and megalitres (ML). (p. 90) *See also* **volume**.

chance experiment An activity or process that involves chance; for example, rolling a die or tossing a coin. (p. 497)

chord An interval joining 2 points on a circle. (p. C4).

cluster A group of data values that are bunched or close together. (p. 239)

coefficient The number in front of a variable in an algebraic term. For example, the coefficient of x in $2x - 5$ is 2. (pp. 168, 466)

combination An unordered selection of objects from a group of objects. (p. 526) See also **permutation**.

commission Pay earned by salespeople and agents, calculated as a percentage of the value of items sold or income made. (p. 116)

compass bearing A bearing that refers to one of the 16 points of a mariner's compass; for example, north-northwest (NNW). (p. 379) *See also* **bearing** and **three-figure bearing**.

compass rose A cross-shaped diagram that shows the direction of north. (p. 379) *See also* **compass bearing**.

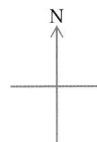

composite shape A shape made up of 2 or more basic shapes. (p. 61)

compound event A chance event that is a combination of 2 or more simple events, for example, 'female or left-handed'. (p. 489)

compound interest Interest that is calculated as a percentage of the original principal and the accumulated interest. (p. 129) *See also* **simple interest**.

conditional probability The probability that an event occurs given that another event occurs. (p. 508)

cone A solid shape with a circular base and curved surface that has an apex. (p. 74)

congruence test One of 4 tests for proving that 2 triangles are congruent: SSS, SAS, AAS and RHS. (p. 540)

congruent Identical, exactly the same. The symbol '≡' means 'is congruent to' or 'is identical to'. (p. 540)

congruent figures Identical figures, having the same shape and size. (p. 540)

consecutive numbers Any series of integers that follow each other in order; for example, 8, 9 and 10. (p. 288)

constant term The term in an algebraic expression that is a number only, with no variable. For example, the constant term in $x^2 - 4x + 6$ is 6. (pp. 18, P4)

cosine A ratio in a right-angled triangle:
$$\cos \theta = \frac{\text{side adjacent to } \theta}{\text{hypotenuse}}$$
where θ is an angle. (p. 373)

See also **sine** and **tangent**.

cosine rule A rule that relates the 3 sides and one of the angles of any triangle: $c^2 = a^2 + b^2 - 2ab \cos C$. (p. 406)

cross-section A 'slice' of a solid cut across it rather than along it.

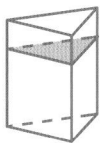

cubic curve The graph of a cubic equation such as $y = \frac{1}{2}x^3 + 1$. (p. P14)

cubic equation An equation in which the highest power of the variable is 3, that is, a variable cubed, for example, $x^3 = 12$. (p. 285)

cumulative frequency A progressive or running total of frequencies, the sum of frequencies of a particular data value and all values below it. (p. 216)

D

decile The values $D_1, D_2 \ldots D_9$ that divide a set of data into 10 equal parts. D_5 is the **median**. (p. 226) *See also* **percentile**, **quartile**.

degree (of a vertex) The number of edges connected to a vertex in a network diagram. (p. 432)

dependent event An event whose outcome (and probability) depends upon the outcome of another event; for example, the colour of the second marble drawn from a bag depends on the colour of the first marble drawn. (p. 513)

dependent variable A variable that depends on another variable for its value. For example, if y depends on x, then the dependent variable is y and the **independent variable** is x. (pp. 256, F4)

depreciation The decrease in the value of items over time due to ageing or use. (p. 138)

difference of 2 squares An algebraic expression of the form $a^2 - b^2$, that can be factorised into $(a + b)(a - b)$. For example, $x^2 - 25 = (x + 5)(x - 5)$. (p. 162)

direct proportion (or **direct variation**) A relationship between 2 variables of the form $y = kx$, where k is a constant called the **constant of proportionality**. For example, if $y = 8.5x$, then y is directly proportional to x. (p. 327)

dot plot A graph that uses dots above a number line to show the frequencies of data values.

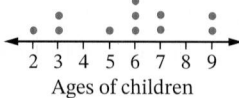
Ages of children

double time Overtime pay that is calculated at 2 times (double) the normal pay rate. (p. 115)

edges A line joining 2 vertices, which represents a connection, in a network diagram. (p. 423)

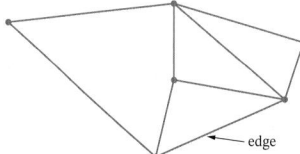
edge

elimination method A method of solving simultaneous equations that involves combining them to eliminate one of the variables. (p. 464)

equation A mathematical statement that 2 quantities are equal. For example, $8 + 2 = 10$ or $3b - 7 = 5$. (p. 18)

equiangular All angles equal. (p. 571)

equilateral triangle A triangle with all 3 sides equal (and all angles 60°).

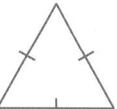

Euler's formula A formula that describes the relationship between the number of vertices (V), faces (F) and edges (E) on a solid shape or network. $V + F = E + 2$ (p. 424)

event In probability, a result involving one or more outcomes. For example, when rolling a die, the event 'rolling an even number' contains the 3 outcomes {2, 4, 6}. (p. 483)

exact ratio The sine, cosine and tangent of the special angles 30°, 45° and 60°, which can be expressed as exact fractions or surds rather than decimal approximations. (p. 389)

expected frequency The expected number of times an event will occur over repeated trials, calculated by multiplying the probability of the event by the number of trials. (p. 484)

experimental probability An estimate of theoretical probability; the **relative frequency** of an event in repeated trials of an experiment, found using

the formula $P(E) = \dfrac{\text{frequency of } E}{\text{total frequency}}$ (p. 483)

exponential curve The graph of an exponential function $y = a^x$. (p. 342) *See* **asymptote** for a diagram.

exponential decay A decrease in which a quantity decreases by the same (multiplication) factor over time, such as halving, according to the exponential function $y = b(1 - r)^x$ or $y = ba^x$, where r is positive. (p. 349). *See also* **exponential growth**.

exponential equation An equation of the form $a^x = c$, where a and c are constants, a is positive and $a \neq 1$. (p. 304)

exponential function A function of the form $y = a^x$, where a is a positive constant and the variable x is a power, for example, $y = 4^x$. (pp. 342, F14)

exponential growth An increase in which a quantity increases by the same (multiplication) factor over time, such as doubling, according to the exponential function $y = b(1 + r)^x$ or $y = ba^x$, where r is positive. (p. 348). *See also* **exponential decay**.

extrapolation Making judgements or predictions about a relationship shown by a scatterplot outside the range of data, outside the points. (p. 259). *See also* **interpolation**.

face An area bound by edges in a **network**. Also called a region. The network diagram below has 5 faces, which includes the outer region of the network. (p. 424)

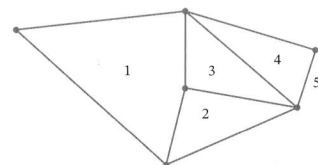

factor or **divisor** (of a number) A value that divides evenly into a given number. For example, the factors of 15 are 1, 3, 5 and 15. (p. 168)

factor theorem The rule that if $(x - a)$ is a factor of the polynomial $P(x)$, then $P(a) = 0$. (p. P11)

five-number summary For a set of numerical data, the lowest value, lower quartile, median, upper quartile, highest value; used to draw a **boxplot**. (p. 207)

flat rate interest *See* **simple interest**.

formula (plural: **formulas** or **formulae**) A rule written as an algebraic equation, using variables.

The formula for the area of a triangle is $A = \dfrac{1}{2}bh$. (p. 290)

fraction A number written in the form $\dfrac{a}{b}$, where a and b are integers and $b \neq 0$.

frequency The number of times an event occurs in repeated trials of a probability experiment, or the number of times a value appears in a set of data.

frequency histogram A column graph (see below) that shows the frequencies of numerical data. There are no spaces between the columns, and the graph looks like a row of office buildings. (p. 221)

frequency polygon A line graph that shows the frequencies of numerical data. It can be made by joining the midpoints of the tops of the columns of a histogram. The graph looks like a mountain. (p. 221)

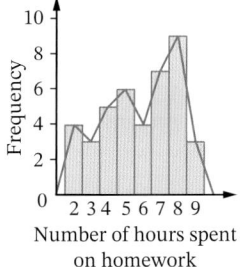

Number of hours spent
on homework

frequency (distribution) table A table listing the frequency of each value in a set of data, with columns for Score (x), Frequency (f) and sometimes Tally and fx.

function A rule or relationship between 2 variables where, for each value of the independent variable (input value), x, there is only one value of the dependent variable (output value), y. (p. F4)

function notation A way of writing a function using the form $y = f(x)$. (p. F7)

general form (of a linear equation) The equation of a straight line $ax + by + c = 0$, where a, b and c are integers and a is positive. (p. 27)

gradient The steepness of a line or interval, measured by the fraction $\dfrac{\text{rise}}{\text{run}}$. (p. 5)

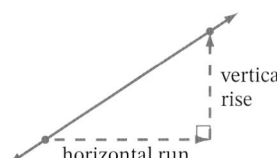

gradient–intercept form (of a linear equation) The equation of a straight line $y = mx + c$, where m is the **gradient** and c is the y-intercept. (p. 22)

gross pay Pay received before tax and other deductions are taken out. (p. 122)

hemisphere Half a **sphere**. (p. 79)

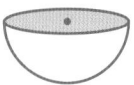

highest common factor (HCF) or **greatest common divisor (GCD)** The largest factor shared by 2 or more numbers or algebraic terms. For example, the HCF of 36 and 8 is 4 and the HCF of $6xy$ and $12y^2$ is $6y$.

horizontal Going across, sideways, flat. (p. 5)

horizontal

hyperbola The graph of $y = \dfrac{k}{x}$, where k is a constant, a curve with 2 branches. (p. 336)

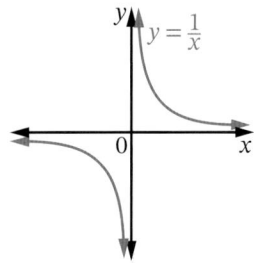

hypotenuse The longest side of a right-angled triangle, opposite the right angle. (p. 373)

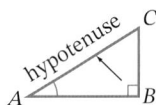

image A transformed shape after it has been enlarged or reduced. (p. 558)

included angle The angle between 2 given sides of a shape. For example, the included angle for sides AC and CB in this triangle is $\angle C$. (p. 410)

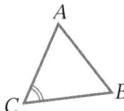

income tax A tax paid to the government based on the size of a person's income. (p. 121)

independent event An event whose outcome (and probability) does not depend upon the outcome of another event; for example, the number rolled on the second die does not depend on the number rolled on the first die. (p. 513)

independent variable A variable whose value does not depend on another variable. For example, if y depends on x, then the **dependent variable** is y and the independent variable is x. (pp. 256, F4)

index (Plural: **indices**, pronounced 'in-da-sees') *See* **power**. (p. 154)

index law An algebraic rule for simplifying expressions involving powers of the same base, for example, $a^m \times a^n = a^{m+n}$. (p. 154)

inequality A mathematical statement that 2 quantities are not equal, involving algebraic expressions and an inequality sign ($>$, $\geq$, $<$, or $\leq$), for example, $-3 > -10$ or $2x - 7 \leq 15$. (pp. 39, 294)

interpolation Making judgements or predictions about a relationship shown by a scatterplot within the range of data, between the points. (p. 259). *See also* **extrapolation**.

interquartile range (IQR) The difference between the upper quartile and lower quartiles, IQR $= Q_3 - Q_1$, representing the middle 50% of values. (p. 203)

interval A section of a line with a definite length, such as AB shown.

inverse function The reverse of a function $f(x)$, written $f^{-1}(x)$, which 'undoes' the original function, found by interchanging the dependent and independent variables (x and y). (p. F11)

inverse proportion (or **inverse variation**)
A relationship between 2 variables of the form $y = \dfrac{k}{x}$, where k is a constant; for example, if $y = \dfrac{50}{x}$, then y is inversely proportional to x. (p. 330)

irrational number A number such as π or $\sqrt{2}$ that cannot be expressed as a fraction (rational number). In decimal form, its digits run endlessly without repeating. *See also* **rational number** and **real number**. (p. 177)

isosceles triangle A triangle with 2 equal sides (and 2 equal angles opposite those sides).

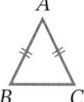

kite A quadrilateral with 2 pairs of equal adjacent sides. (p. 544)

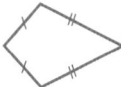

LHS The left-hand side (of an equation). (p. 19)

line of best fit A straight line drawn through the points on a scatterplot that best describes the bivariate data. (p. 258)

linear equation An equation involving a variable that is not raised to a power, such as $2x + 9 = 17$. (p. 18)

linear function A function whose graph is a straight line. (p. 18)

logarithm The power of a number, to a given base. For example, $\log_{10} 1000 - 3$, meaning that the logarithm of 1000 to base 10 is 3, because $1000 = 10^3$. (p. 298)

logarithmic equation An equation involving a logarithm such as $\log_5 x = -3$, which can be solved by rewriting the equation in index form. (p. 305)

logarithmic function A function of the form $y = \log_a x$, whose inverse is the exponential function. (p. F14)

logarithmic scale A scale whose values increase by powers, for example, 1, 10, 100, 1000 ... (powers of 10) instead of 0, 1, 2, 3 ... (linear scale). (p. 351)

mean The average of a set of data, represented by $\bar{x}$, calculated by dividing the sum of the values by the number of values. (p. 232)

measure of central tendency An average, middle or typical value of a set of data. The 3 measures of central tendency are the **mean**, **median** and **mode**. (p. 242)

measure of spread A statistical value that describes how the values in a data set are spread, for example, **range** or **interquartile range**. (p. 203)

median The middle value when the values of a data set are arranged in order. If the number of values is even, then the median is the average of the 2 middle values. (p. 202)

midpoint The point in the middle of an interval or halfway between 2 given points. (p. 5)

minute (symbol') A measure of angle size. $\dfrac{1}{60}$ of a degree. $1° = 60'$.

mode The most common or frequent value(s) in a set of data. (p. 235)

monic polynomial A polynomial that has a **leading coefficient** of 1, for example, $P(x) = x^4 - 7x^2 + x + 8$. (p. P4)

mutually exclusive events Events or categories that have no items in common. (p. 490)

negatively skewed *See* **skewed distribution**.

net pay Pay received after deductions from gross pay; 'take-home' pay. (p. 122)

network A system of interconnected people, objects or tasks. (p. 423)

network diagram A visual representation of a network with vertices connected by edges, representing the interconnections between a set of people, objects or tasks. (p. 423)

opposite side   In a right-angled triangle, the side directly facing the given angle. (p. 373)

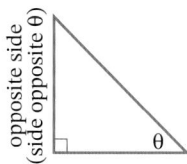

outcome   In probability, the result of a situation or experiment. For example, when rolling a die, one possible outcome is rolling a 4. (p. 483)

outlier   An extreme data value that is much different from the other values in a set. (p. 203)

overtime   Time worked beyond normal working hours, such as at night or on weekends, at a higher rate of pay. (p. 115)

parabola   A U-shaped curve that is the graph of a quadratic function such as $y = x^2$. (p. 317)

parallel lines   Lines that point in the same direction and do not intersect.

$AB \parallel CD$ means 'AB is parallel to CD'. (p. 13)

parallelogram   A quadrilateral in which the opposite sides are parallel. (p. 544)

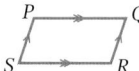

PAYG (Pay As You Go) tax   Income tax deducted from your pay each payday by your employer. (p. 122)

perimeter   The distance around the outside of a shape. The sum of the lengths of its sides.

per annum (p.a)   Per year. (p. 125)

percentage error   The absolute error as a percentage of the actual value. (p. 51) *See also* **absolute error**, **relative error**.

percentile   The values $P_1, P_2, P_3 \ldots P_{99}$ that divide a set of data into 100 equal parts. The 50th percentile is the **median**. (p. 226). *See also* **decile**, **quartile**.

perfect square   A square number or an algebraic expression that represents one; for example, 64, $(x + 9)^2$, $(a - b)^2$. (p. 162)

permutation   An ordered arrangement of objects from a group of objects. (p. 524) *See also* **combination**.

perpendicular lines   Lines that intersect to form a right angle. $AB \perp CD$ means 'AB is perpendicular to CD'. (p. 14)

piecework   Earnings based on the number of items processed, made or delivered, paid at a rate per item rather than on the number of hours worked. (p. 116)

Platonic solid   A polyhedron with faces that are the same regular polygon. (p. 426)

point-gradient form of a linear equation   The equation of a line with gradient m and that passes through the point (x_1, y_1), which is $y - y_1 = m(x - x_1)$. (p. 30)

polyhedron (plural: **polyhedra** or **polyhedrons**)   A three-dimensional solid with flat faces that are polygons. (p. 426)

polynomial   An algebraic expression involving powers of x that are positive integers. For example $P(x) = 8x^3 + 4x - 7$. (p. P4)

positively skewed   *See* **skewed distribution**.

power (or **index**)   The number of times a base is multiplied by itself. In 2^5, the power is 5. Also called the *exponent*.

principal   An amount of money invested or borrowed, on which interest is calculated. (p. 125)

prism   A solid shape with identical cross-sections and straight sides. (p. 66)

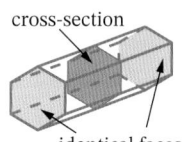

probability   The chance of an event occurring, measured as a fraction, decimal or percentage between 0 and 1. (p. 483)

product   The result of a multiplication. The product of 7 and 3 is 21. (p. 14)

pronumeral   Another name for variable.

pyramid   A solid with a polygon for a base and triangular faces that meet at a point called an **apex**. (p. 74)

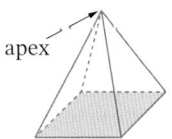

Pythagoras' theorem   The relationship $c^2 = a^2 + b^2$ for a right-angled triangle, where c is the length of the hypotenuse and a and b are the lengths of the other 2 shorter sides.

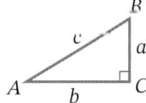

quadrant (of a circle)   A sector that is a quarter of a circle, containing a right angle. (p. 62)

quadratic expression   An algebraic expression in which the highest power of the variable is 2; for example, $x^2 - 5x + 7$, $x^2 - 15$, $2x^2 - 3x + 9$ and $-4x^2 + 7x$. (p. 168)

quadratic equation   An equation in which the highest power of the variable is 2, that is, a variable squared; for example, $3x^2 - 6 = 69$. (pp. 281, Q4)

quadratic formula   The formula for solving quadratic equations of the form $ax^2 + bx + c = 0$, which is $x = \dfrac{-b \pm \sqrt{b^2 - 4ac}}{2a}$. (p. Q10)

quadratic function   A function in which the highest power of the variable is 2, for example, $y = 3x^2 - 6$, whose graph is a **parabola**. (p. 317)

quadratic trinomial. *See* **trinomial**. (p. 168)

quadrilateral   Any polygon with 4 sides.

quadrilateral test   A property of a quadrilateral that proves that it is a particular type of quadrilateral, for example, if opposite angles are equal, then it *must* be a parallelogram. (p. 544)

quarterly   Occurring regularly 4 times a year, that is, every 3 months. (p. 135)

quartile   The values Q_1, Q_2, Q_3 that divide a set of data into 4 equal parts. The 1st quartile Q_1 is the lower quartile, the 2nd quartile Q_2 is the **median**, the 3rd quartile Q_3 is the upper quartile. (p. 202)

random   In probability, describing a situation where every possible outcome has an equal chance, or is equally likely.

range   In a set of data, the difference between the highest and lowest values. (p. 203)

rational number   A number that can be written as a fraction in the form $\dfrac{a}{b}$, where a and b are integers and $b \neq 0$. (p. 177) *See also* **irrational number** and **real number.**

rationalise the denominator   To simplify a fraction involving a surd by making its denominator rational (that is, not a surd). (p. 192)

real number   A rational or irrational number, that can be ordered on a number line. (p. 178)

reciprocal   The product of any number and its reciprocal is 1. The reciprocal of any number is found by first writing the number as a fraction and then swapping the numerator with the denominator. The reciprocal of 5 is $\dfrac{1}{5}$ and the reciprocal of $\dfrac{2}{3}$ is $\dfrac{3}{2}$.

rectangle   A quadrilateral with 4 right angles. (p. 544)

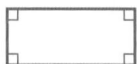

relative error   The absolute error as a fraction of the actual value. (p. 51) *See also* **absolute error, percentage error.**

relative frequency   The number of times an event or data value occurred, written as a fraction of the total number of events or data values. (p. 483) *See also* **experimental probability**.

remainder theorem   The rule that if a polynomial $P(x)$ is divided by the linear expression $(x - a)$ then the remainder is $P(a)$. (p. P10)

retainer   A fixed amount paid to a salesperson before commission is added. (p. 116)

rhombus   A quadrilateral with 4 equal sides. (p. 544)

RHS   The right-hand side (of an equation). (p. 19) *See also* **similarity test**.

rise   Short for 'vertical rise', this is the change in vertical position between 2 points on a line or interval, the number of units 'going up', used with the **run** to calculate the gradient of a line or interval. (p. 5) *See also* **gradient**.

rounding error   The error or inaccuracy in a measured or calculated answer caused by rounding values too early or severely in a measurement or partial answer. (p. 56)

run   Short for 'horizontal run', this is the change in horizontal position between 2 points on a line or interval, the number of units 'going right', used with the **rise** to calculate the gradient of a line or interval. (p. 5) *See also* **gradient**.

salary   A fixed yearly amount of money that is paid weekly, fortnightly or monthly, not dependent on the number of hours worked. (p. 115)

sample   In statistics, a group of people or items selected from a population for study.

sample space   In a probability situation, the set of all possible outcomes. (p. 497)

scale diagram   A diagram that represents a larger or smaller object where lengths and distances on it are in the same ratio as the real lengths and distances. (p. 562)

scale factor   The amount by which a shape has been enlarged or reduced, equal to $\dfrac{\text{image length}}{\text{original length}}$. (p. 558)

scatterplot   A graph of points on a number plane. Each point represents the values of the 2 different variables and the resulting graph may show a pattern. (p. 254)

secant   A line that intersects a curve at 2 points. *See also* **tangent.** (p. C4)

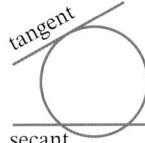

second (″)   A measure of angle size. $\frac{1}{60}$ of a minute. $1' = 60''$.

sector   A region of a circle cut off by 2 radii. (pp. 62, C4)

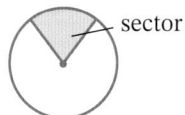

shape of a distribution   The way the data in a frequency distribution is spread, can be **symmetrical**, positively **skewed** or negatively **skewed**.

significant figures   The meaningful digits in a number that show its level of accuracy, the first non-zero digits; for example, 31 487 000 has 5 significant figures.

similar   To have the same shape but not necessarily the same size, an enlargement or reduction. The symbol '|||' means 'is similar to'. (p. 558)

similarity test   One of 4 tests for proving that 2 triangles are similar. (p. 570)

simple interest   Also known as flat rate interest. Interest that is calculated as a percentage of the original principal. (p. 125) *See also* **compound interest.**

simulation   A way of imitating or mimicking a probability experiment using technology or actual objects such as dice, coins, spinners and cards. (p. 517)

simultaneous equations   Two (or more) equations that must be solved together so that the solution satisfies both equations. For example, $y = 2x + 1$ and $y = 3x$ are simultaneous equations that have a solution of $x = 1, y = 3$. (p. 462)

sine   A ratio in a right-angled triangle:

$$\sin\theta = \frac{\text{side opposite to }\theta}{\text{hypotenuse}}$$

where θ is an angle. (p. 373)

See also **cosine** and **tangent.**

sine rule   A rule that relates the sides of any triangle to the sine of their opposite angles: $\frac{a}{\sin A} = \frac{b}{\sin B} = \frac{c}{\sin C}$. (p. 400)

skewed distribution   A distribution in which most of the values are clustered at one end, creating a 'tail' at the other end. The tail determines whether the skew is positive or negative. *See also* **symmetrical distribution.**

Negatively skewed   Positively skewed

slant height   The height of a pyramid or cone from its **apex** (top) to its base along a side face rather than its perpendicular height. (p. 74)

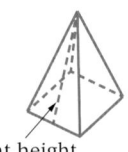

slant height

solution   The answer to an equation, inequality or problem, the correct value(s) of the variable that makes an equation or inequality true. (p. 282)

spanning tree   A tree in a network that connects all the vertices. (p. 437)

sphere   A ball shape, a solid that is completely round. (p. 79)

square   A quadrilateral with 4 equal sides and 4 right angles. (p. 544)

standard deviation (σ)   A measure of spread that depends on every value in the data set and their mean. (p. 232)

stem-and-leaf plot   A 'number graph' that lists all the data values, in groups. Each value is split into a 'stem' and a 'leaf'. This stem-and-leaf plot shows 12 test scores, from 42 to 82.

Stem	Leaf
4	2 5
5	0 2 8
6	6 7
7	3 5 7 7
8	2

Key: 5|8 stands for 58

subject of a formula   The variable for which a formula is written, the variable on the left-hand side of a formula. The subject of the formula $A = \frac{1}{2}bh$ is A. (p. 290)

substitution method   A method of solving simultaneous equations that involves substituting one equation into another equation. (p. 464)

surd   A square root (or other root) whose exact value cannot be found because it is **irrational**, such as $\sqrt{10}$ or $\sqrt[3]{7}$. (p. 177)

surface area   The total area of all the faces of a solid shape. (p. 66)

symmetrical distribution   A distribution in which all values are distributed equally on both sides of the centre, its shape having line symmetry. *See also* **skewed distribution**.

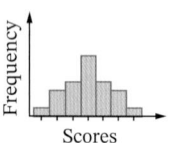

tangent   A ratio in a right-angled triangle:

$$\tan \theta = \frac{\text{side opposite to } \theta}{\text{side adjacent to } \theta}$$

where θ is an angle. (p. 373)

See also **sine** and **cosine**.

tangent   A line that touches a curve at one point but does not cross it. *See also* **secant** for diagram. (pp. C4, C19)

tax deduction   *See* **allowable deduction**.

taxable income   The part of a person's income that is taxed, equal to yearly income minus allowable deductions. (p. 121)

term (of an expression)   A part of an algebraic expression. For example, $b^2 + 6b - 9$ has 3 terms: b^2, $6b$ and -9. (p. 27)

test for a quadrilateral   *See* **quadrilateral test**. (p. 544)

theoretical probability   Probability calculated using the formula: $P(E) = \frac{\text{number of favourable outcomes}}{\text{total number of outcomes}}$ (p. 483)

three-figure bearing (or **true bearing**)   A bearing that uses 3 digit angles from 000° to 360° to show the amount of turning measured clockwise from north. (p. 379) *See also* **bearing** or **compass bearing**.

three-step experiment (or **three-stage experiment**)   A chance experiment with 3 steps or stages, such as tossing 3 coins together. (p. 497)

time-and-a-half   Overtime pay that is calculated at 1.5 times the normal pay rate. (p. 115)

trapezium   A quadrilateral with one pair of opposite sides parallel. (p. 544)

traversable   Describes a network that has a route that travels over every edge exactly once. (p. 432)

tree   A network in which any 2 vertices are connected by only one path. (p. 437)

tree diagram   A diagram of branches for listing all of the possible outcomes of a multi-step chance experiment. (p. 497)

trial   One go or run of a repeated probability experiment; for example, one roll of a die. (p. 483)

trigonometric ratio   The ratio of 2 sides in a right-angled triangle; for example, sine is the ratio of the opposite side to the hypotenuse. (p. 373)

trinomial   An algebraic expression with 3 terms, for example, $3x + 2y - 5$. In a **quadratic trinomial** such as $x^2 + 4x + 6$, the highest power of the variable is 2. (p. 168). *See also* **binomial** and **quadratic expression**.

two-step experiment (or **two-stage experiment**)   A chance experiment with 2 steps or stages, such as rolling a pair of dice. (p. 497)

two-way table   A table that shows the number of items belonging to overlapping categories. (p. 493)

	Can swim	Cannot swim
Boys	13	2
Girls	9	3

variable   A symbol, usually a letter of the alphabet, that stands for a number. Also called a **pronumeral** or **unknown**. (p. 168)

variation   *See* **direct proportion**.

Venn diagram   A diagram of circles (usually overlapping) for grouping items into categories. (p. 488)

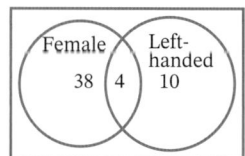

vertex (plural: **vertices**)   A corner of a shape, angle or curve.

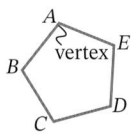

vertex   A point on a network diagram that represents a person, object or task. (p. 423)

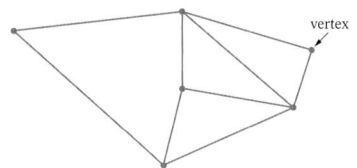

vertex

vertical   Going up and down, at a right angle to the horizontal. (p. 5)

volume   The amount of space taken up by a solid object, measured in cubic units.

wage   An amount of money paid to people for work, calculated on the number of hours worked. (p. 115)

x-axis   The horizontal axis of a number plane (running across).

x-intercept   The x value at which a graph cuts the x-axis. (p. 18)

y-axis   The vertical axis of a number plane (running up and down).

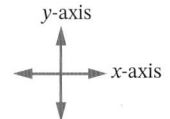

y-axis

x-axis

y-intercept   The y value at which a line cuts the y-axis. (p. 18)